Spon's Mechanical and Electrical Services Price Book

2006

Spon's Mechanical and Electrical Services Price Book

Edited by

DAVIS LANGDON MOTT GREEN WALL
Engineering Services

2006

Thirty-seventh edition

Taylor & Francis
Taylor & Francis Group

LONDON AND NEW YORK

First edition 1968
Thirty-seventh edition published 2006
by Taylor & Francis
2 Park Square, Milton Park, Abingdon, Oxon OX14 4RN

Simultaneously published in the USA and Canada
by Taylor & Francis
270 Madison Avenue, New York, NY 10016

Taylor & Francis is an imprint of the Taylor & Francis Group

Printed and bound in Great Britain by
TJ International Ltd, Padstow, Cornwall

Publisher's note
This book has been produced from camera-ready copy supplied by the authors.

British Library Cataloguing in Publication Data
A catalogue record for this book is available from the British Library

ISBN 0-415-37039-6
ISSN 0305-4543

Contents

Preface	vii
Special Acknowledgements	ix
Acknowledgements	xi

PART ONE: APPROXIMATE ESTIMATING

Directions	3
Cost Indices	4
RIBA Stage A Feasibility Costs	6
RIBA Stage C Elemental Rates	11
All-in-Rates	19
Elemental Costs	35

PART TWO: MATERIAL COSTS/MEASURED WORK PRICES

Mechanical Installations

Directions	63
R : Disposal Systems	
R10 : Rainwater Pipework/Gutters	69
R11 : Above Ground Drainage	88
S : Piped Supply Systems	
S10 : Cold Water	111
S11 : Hot Water	164
S32 : Natural Gas	168
S41 : Fuel Oil Storage/Distribution	172
S60 : Fire Hose Reels	174
S61 : Dry Risers	175
S63 : Sprinklers	176
S65 : Fire Hydrants	181
T : Mechanical/Cooling/Heating Systems	
T10 : Gas/Oil Fired Boilers	183
T13 : Packaged Steam Generators	196
T31 : Low Temperature Hot Water Heating	197
T33 : Steam Heating	284
T42 : Local Heating Units	288
T60 : Central Refrigeration Plant	289
T61 : Chilled Water	297
T70 : Local Cooling Units	302
U : Ventilation/Air Conditioning Systems	
U10 : General Ventilation	304
U14 : Ductwork: Fire Rated	391
U30 : Low Velocity Air Conditioning	412
U31 : VAV Air Conditioning	415
U41 : Fan Coil Air Conditioning	416
U70 : Air Curtains	420

Electrical Installations

    Directions   423

    V : Electrical Supply/Power/Lighting Systems
    V10 : Electrical Generation Plant   427
    V11 : HV Supply   429
    V20 : LV Distribution   434
    V21 : General Lighting   504
    V22 : General LV Power   513
    V32 : Uninterruptible Power Supply   520
    V40 : Emergency Lighting   522

    W : Communications/Security/Control
    W10 : Telecommunications   527
    W20 : Radio/Television   529
    W23 : Clocks   531
    W30 : Data Transmission   532
    W40 : Access Control   539
    W41 : Security Detection and Alarm   540
    W50 : Fire Detection and Alarm   541
    W51 : Earthing and Bonding   544
    W52 : Lightning Protection   545
    W60 : Central Control/Building Management   549

PART THREE: RATES OF WAGES

Mechanical Installations

    Rates of Wages   552

Electrical Installations

    Rates of Wages   559

PART FOUR: DAYWORK

Heating and Ventilating Industry   566
Electrical Industry   569
Building Industry Plant Hire Costs   572

Tables and Memoranda   585

Index   609

Preface

The Thirty Seventh edition of *Spon's Mechanical and Electrical Services Price Book* continues to cover the widest range and depth of services, reflecting the many alternative systems and products that are commonly used in the industry as well as current industry trends.

In terms of current pricing levels, the continuing boom in the Chinese economy and it's consumption of raw materials has led to sharp increases in the price of steel and copper. Both steel and copper tube manufacturers are reporting monthly increases in prices, and whilst these have been incorporated at the time of going to press, readers are advised to check the currency of such prices before using them. Likewise, the sustained high cost of crude oil will impact on products that are oil based i.e. UPVC as well as transport costs. However, as last year, the picture is less clear concerning manufacturer's and suppliers of plant and equipment utilising steel and copper, with some increasing costs and lead times due to the increasing demand, whilst others stating that they remain largely unaffected, at least for the present. Again, prices are current at the time of going to press, but readers are advised to check the currency of such prices before using them.

Before referring to prices or other information in the book, readers are advised to study the `Directions' which precede each section of the Materials Costs/Measured Work Prices. As before, no allowance has been made in any of the sections for Value Added Tax.

The order of the book reflects the order of the estimating process, from broad outline costs through to detailed unit rate items.

The approximate estimating section has been thoroughly reviewed to provide up to date key data in terms of square metre rates, all-in-rates for key elements and selected specialist activities and elemental analyses on a comprehensive range of building types.

The prime purpose of the Materials Costs/Measured Work Prices part is to provide industry average prices for mechanical and electrical services, giving a reasonably accurate indication of their likely cost. Supplementary information is included which will enable readers to make adjustments to suit their own requirements. It cannot be emphasised too strongly that it is not intended that these prices should be used in the preparation of an actual tender without adjustment for the circumstances of the particular project in terms of productivity, locality, project size and current market conditions. Adjustments should be made to standard rates for time, location, local conditions, site constraints and any other factor likely to affect the costs of a specific scheme. Readers are referred to the build up of the gang rates, where allowances are included for supervision, labour related insurances, and where the percentage allowances for overhead, profit and preliminaries are defined.

Readers are reminded of the service available on the Spon's website detailing significant changes to the published information. www.pricebooks.co.uk

As with previous editions the Editors invite the views of readers, critical or otherwise, which might usefully be considered when preparing future editions of this work.

While every effort is made to ensure the accuracy of the information given in this publication, neither the Editors nor Publishers in any way accept liability for loss of any kind resulting from the use made by any person of such information.

In conclusion, the Editors record their appreciation of the indispensable assistance received from the many individuals and organisations in compiling this book.

DAVIS LANGDON MOTT GREEN WALL
Engineering Services
MidCity Place
71 High Holborn
London WC1V 6QS

Telephone: 0207 061 7777
Facsimile: 0207 061 7009

e-mail: spons@mottgreenwall.co.uk

Special Acknowledgements

The Editors wish to record their appreciation of the special assistance given by the following organisations in the compilation of this edition.

T. Clarke plc

Electrical Engineers & Contractors
Stanhope House
116-118 Walworth Road
London SE17 1JY
Tel: 020 7358 5000
Fax: 020 7701 6265
e-mail: info@tclarke.co.uk
www.tclarke.co.uk

 **HARGREAVES**

DUCTWORK SPECIALISTS

Lord Street, Bury, Lancashire. BL9 0RG
Tel: 0161 764 5082 • Fax: 0161 762 2336
E-Mail: sales@senior-hargreaves.co.uk

AXIMA

Axima Building Services
Westmead, Farnborough
Bournemouth, Hants GU14 7LP
Tel: 01252 525500
Fax: 01252 378988
www.axima.eu.com

HOTCHKISS

Hampden Park Industrial Estate
Eastbourne
East Sussex
BN22 9AX
Tel : 01323 501234
Fax : 01323 508752
E-Mail : info@Hotchkiss.co.uk
www.Hotchkiss.co.uk

comunica

Comunica plc
The Hallmarks
146 Field End Road
Eastcote
Pinner
Middlesex
HA5 1RJ

Tel: 020 8429 9696
Fax: 020 8429 4982
Email: enquiries@comunicaplc.co.uk
www.comunicaplc.co.uk

Abbey

ABBEY THERMAL INSULATION LTD.
23-24, Riverside House,
Lower Southend Road, Wickford, Essex SS11 8BB
Telephone: 01268 572116- Facsimile: 01268 572117
E-mail: general@abbeythermal.com

J. & M. Insulations Limited.

For all aspects of Thermal Insulation & Fire Protection

257a Banbury Road,
Summertown, Oxford, OX2 7HN
Telephone: 01865 310220
Fax: 01865 512419
E-mail: jandminsualation@fsbdial.co.uk
www.jandminsulations.co.uk

Spon's International Construction Costs Handbook

This practical series of five easy-to-use Handbooks gathers together all the essential overseas price information you need. The Hand-books provide data on a country and regional basis about economic trends and construction indicators, basic data about labour and materials' costs, unit rates (in local currency), approximate estimates for building types and plenty of contact information.

Spon's African Construction Costs Handbook 2nd Edition
Countries covered: Algeria, Cameroon, Chad, Cote d'Ivoire, Gabon, The Gambia, Ghana, Kenya, Liberia, Nigeria, Senegal, South Africa, Zambia
2005: 234x156: 368 pp Hb: 0-415-36314-4: £170.00

Spon's Latin American Construction Costs Handbook
Countries covered: Argentina, Brazil, Chile, Colombia, Ecuador, French Guiana, Guyana, Mexico, Paraguay, Peru, Suriname, Uruguay, Venezuela
2000: 234x156: 332 pp Hb: 0-415-23437-9: £85.00

Spon's Middle East Construction Costs Handbook 2nd Edition
Countries covered: Bahrain, Eqypt, Iran, Jordan, Kuwait, Lebanon, Oman, Quatar, Saudi Arabia, Syria, Turkey, UAE
2005: 234x156: 384 pp Hb: 0-415-36315-2: £170.00

Spon's European Construction Costs Handbook 3rd Edition
Countries covered: Austria, Belgium, Cyprus, Czek Republic, Finland, France, Greece, Germany, Italy, Ireland, Netherlands, Portugal, Poland, Slovak Republic, Spain, Turkey
2000: 234x156: 332 pp Hb: 0-419-25460-9: £170.00

Spon's Asia Pacific Construction Costs Handbook 3rd Edition
Countries covered: Australia, Brunei Darassalem, China, Hong Kong, India, Japan, New Zealand, Indonesia, Malaysia, Philippines, Singapore, South Korea, Sri Lanka, Taiwan, Thailand, Vietnam
2000: 234x156: 332 pp Hb: 0-419-25470-6: £170.00

To Order: Tel: +44 (0) 1264 343071 Fax: +44 (0) 1264 343005, or
Post: Taylor and Francis Customer Services, Thomson Publishing Services, Cheriton House, Andover, Hants, SP10 5BE, UK Email: book.orders@tandf.co.uk

For a complete listing of all our titles visit:
www.sponpress.com

Taylor & Francis
Taylor & Francis Group plc

Acknowledgements

The editors wish to record their appreciation of the assistance given by many individuals and organisations in the compilation of this edition.

Manufacturers, Distributors and Sub-Contractors who have contributed this year include:-

A C Plastics Industries Ltd
Armstrong Road
Daneshill East
Basingstoke RG24 8NU
GRP Water Storage Tanks
Tel: 01256 329334
Fax: 01256 817862
www.acplastiques.com

Alfa Laval Limited
Unit 1, 6 Wellheads Road
Farburn Industrial Estate
Dyce
Aberdeen AB21 7HG
Heat Exchangers
Tel : 01224 424300
Fax : 01224 725213
www.alfalaval.com

Aquilar Limited
Dial Post Court
Horsham Road
Rusper
West Sussex RH12 4QX
Leak Detection
Tel : 08707 940310
Fax : 08707 940320
www.aquilar.co.uk

Arrow Electronics
Edinburgh Way
Harlow
Essex CM20 2DF
Cables
Tel : 01279 441144
Fax : 01279 455704
www.arrowne.com

Axima Building Services
80 Paul Street
London EC2A 4UD
Above Ground Drainage
Tel : (020) 7729 7634
Fax : (020) 7729 9756
www.axima-uk.com

Balmoral Tanks
Balmoral Park
Loirston
Aberdeen AB12 3GY
GRP Water Storage Tanks
Tel: 01224 859000
Fax: 01224 859123
www.balmoral-group.com

Braithwaite Engineers Ltd
Neptune Works
Uskway
Newport
South Wales NP9 2UY
Sectional Steel Water Storage Tanks
Tel: 01633 262141
Fax: 01633 250631
www.braithwaite.co.uk

Brights of London Ltd
Westgate Business Park
Westgate Carr Road
Pickering
N Yorks YO18 8LX
Clock Systems
Tel: (020) 8786 8466
Fax: (020) 8786 8477
www.brightsoflondon.co.uk

Broadcrown Limited
Alliance Works
Airfield Industrial Estate
Hixon
Staffs ST18 0PF
Generators
Tel: 01889 272200
Fax: 01889 272220
www.broadcrown.co.uk

Caradon Stelrad Ideal Boilers
PO Box 103
National Avenue
Kingston-upon-Hall
North Humberside HU5 4JN
Boilers/Heating Products
Tel: 08708 400030
Fax: 08708 400059
www.rycroft.com

Carrier Air Conditioning
United Technologies House
Guildford Road
Leatherhead
Surrey KT22 9UT
Chilled Water Plant
Tel: 0870 6001100
Fax: 01372 220221
www.carrier.uk.com

Chloride Power Protection
Unit C, George Curl Way
Southampton SO18 2RY
Static UPS Systems
Tel: 023 8061 0311
Fax: 023 8061 0852
www.chloridepower.com

Communica
Chatteris Airfield
Near March
Cambridgeshire PE15 0EA
Telephone Cables
Tel : 01354 742340
www.communicaplc.co.uk

Danfoss Flowmetering Ltd
Magflo House
Ebley Road
Stonehouse
Glos GL10 2LU
Energy Meters
Tel: 01453 828891
Fax: 01453 853860
www.danfoss-randall.co.uk

Dewey Waters Limited
Cox's Green
Wrington
Bristol BS40 5QS
Tanks
Tel : 01934 862601
Fax : 01934 862604
www.deweywaters.co.uk

Diffusion
Benson Environmental Limited
47 Central Avenue
West Molesey
Surrey KT8 2QZ
Fan Coil Units
Tel: (020) 8783 0033
Fax: (020) 8783 0140
www.diffusionenv.com

Dunham-Bush Limited
8 Downley Road
Havant
Hampshire PO9 2JD
Convectors and Heaters
Tel : 02392 477700
Fax : 02392 450396
www.dunham-bush.com

E&I Engineering Ltd
14 Springtown Road
Springtown Industrial Estate
Londonderry BT48 0LY
Low Voltage Switchgear
Tel: 01504 266404
Fax: 01504 371766
www.e-i-eng.com

EMS Radio Fire & Security Systems
Limited
Technology House
Sea Street
Herne Bay
Kent CT6 8JZ
Security
Tel : 01227 369570
Fax : 01227 369679
www.emsgroup.co.uk

Engineering Appliances Ltd
Unit 11
Sunbury Cross Ind Est
Brooklands Close
Sunbury On Thames TW16 7DX
**Expansion Joints, Air and Dirt
Separators**
Tel: 01932 788888
Fax: 01932 761263
e-mail:
info@engineering-appliances.co.uk
www.engineeringappliances.com

FCS Ductwork Limited
3rd Floor
Thomas Telford House
1 Heron Quay
Canary Wharf
London E14 5JD
Fire Rated Ductwork
Tel: (020) 7987 7692
Fax: (020) 7537 5627
www.fcsgroup.co.uk

Flakt Woods Limited
Tufnell Way
Colchester CO4 5AR
Air Handling Units
Tel : 01206 544122
Fax : 01206 574434

Furse and Company Limited
Wilford Road
Nottingham NG2 1EB
Lightning Protection
Tel: 0115 863471
Fax: 0115 9860071
www.tnb.com

Hall Fire Protection Limited
186 Moorside Road
Swinton
Manchester M27 9HA
Fire Protection Equipment
Tel : 0161 793 4822
Fax : 0161 794 4950
www.hallfire.co.uk

Halton
5 Waterside Business Park
Witham
Essex CM8 3YQ
Chilled Beams
Tel : 01376 503040
Fax : 01376 503060
www.haltongroup.com

Hattersley, Newman, Hender Ltd
Burscough Road
Ormskirk
Lancashire L39 2XG
Valves
Tel: 01695 577199
Fax: 01695 578775
e-mail: uksales@hattersley-valves.co.uk
www.hattersley.com

Honeywell CS Limited
Honeywell House
Anchor Boulevard
Crossways Business Park
Dartford
Kent DA2 6QH
Control Components
Tel : 01322 484800
Fax : 01322 484898
www.honeywell.com

Hoval Limited
Northgate
Newark
Notts NG24 1JN
Boilers
Tel : 01636 672711
Fax : 01636 673532
www.hoval.co.uk

HRS Hevac Ltd
10-12 Caxton Way
Watford Business Park
Watford
Herts WD18 8JY
Heat Exchangers
Tel: 01923 232335
Fax: 01923 230266
www.hrshevac.co.uk

Hudevad
Bridge House
Bridge Street
Walton on Thames
Radiators
Tel: 01932 247835
Fax: 01932 247694
www.hudevad.co.uk

Hydrotec (UK) Limited
Hydrotec House
5 Mannor Courtyard
Hughenden Avenue
High Wycombe HP13 5RE
Chemical Treatment
Tel : 01494 796040
Fax : 01494 796049
www.hydrotec.com

IAC
IEC House
Moorside Road
Winchester
Hampshire SO23 7US
Attenuators
Tel : 01962 873000
Fax : 01962 873102
www.industrialacoustics.com

K and W Fabrications Ltd
High Street
Handcross
Haywards Heath
West Sussex RH17 6BZ
Plastic Ductwork
Tel: 01444 401144
Fax: 01444 401188

Kampmann
Benson Environmental Limited
47 Central Avenue
West Molesey
Surrey KT8 2QZ
Trench Heating
Tel: (020) 8783 0033
Fax: (020) 8783 0140
www.diffusionenv.com

Kiddie Fire Protection Services
Enterprise House
Jasmine Grove
London SE20 8JW
Fire Protection Equipment
Tel : (020) 8659 7235
Fax : (020) 8659 7237
www.kfp.co.uk

Metcraft Ltd
Harwood Industrial Estate
Littlehampton
West Sussex BN17 7BB
Oil Storage Tanks
Tel: 01903 714226
Fax: 01903 723206
www.metcraft.co.uk

Osma Underfloor Heating
18 Apple Lane
Sowton Trade City
Exeter
Devon EX2 5GL
Underfloor Heating
Tel : 01392 444122
Fax : 01392 444135
www.osmaufh.co.uk

Pullen Pumps Limited
158 Beddington Lane
Croydon CR9 4PT
Pumps, Booster Sets
Tel: (020) 8684 9521
Fax: (020) 8689 8892
www.pullenpumps.co.uk

Rycroft
Duncombe Road
Bradford BD8 9TB
Storage Cylinders
Tel : 01274 490911
Fax : 01274 498580
www.rycroft.com

SF Limited
Pottington Business Park
Barnstaple
Devon EX31 1LZ
Flues
Tel : 01271 326633
Fax : 01271 334303

Simmtronic Limited
Waterside
Charlton Mead Lane
Hoddesdon
Hertfordshire EN11 0QR
Lighting Controls
Tel : 01992 456869
Fax : 01992 445132
www.simmtronic.com

Socomec Limited
Knowl Piece
Wilbury Way
Hitchin
Hertfordshire SG4 0TY
Automatic Transfer Switches
Tel : 01462 440033
Fax : 01462 431143
www.socomec.com

Spirax-Sarco Ltd
Charlton House
Cheltenham
Gloucestershire GL53 8ER
Traps and Valves
Tel: 01242 521361
Fax: 01242 573342
www.spiraxsarco.com

Tyco Limited
Unit 6 West Point Enterprize Park
Clarence Avenue
Trafford Park
Manchester M17 1QS
Fire Protection
Tel: 0161 875 0400
Fax: 0161 875 0491
www.tyco.com

Utile Engineering Company Ltd
Irthlingborough
Northants NN9 5UG
Gas Boosters
Tel: 01933 650216
Fax: 01933 652738
www.utileengineering.com

Vokes Ltd
Henley Park
Guildford
Surrey GU3 2AF
Air Filters
Tel: 01483 569971
Fax: 01483 235384
e-mail: vokes@btvinc.com
www.vokes.com

Waterloo Air Management
Mills Road
Aylesford
Kent ME20 7NB
Grilles & Diffusers
Tel: 01622 717861
Fax: 01622 710648
www.waterloo.co.uk

Whitecroft Lighting Limited
Burlington Street
Ashton-under-Lyne
Lancashire OL7 0AX
Lighting & Luminaires
Tel: 0870 5087087
Fax: 0870 5084210
www.whitecroftlighting.com

Woods of Colchester
Tufnell Way
Colchester
Essex CO4 5AR
Air Distribution, Fans, Anti-vibration mountings
Tel: 01206 544122
Fax: 01206 574434

PART ONE

Approximate Estimating

Directions, *page 3*
Cost Indices, *page 4*
RIBA Stage A Feasibility Costs, *page 6*
RIBA Stage C Elemental Rates, *page 11*
All-In-Rates, *page 19*
Elemental Costs, *page 35*

DIRECTIONS

The prices shown in this section of the book are average prices on a fixed price basis for typical buildings for completion during the second quarter of 2005. Unless otherwise noted, they exclude external services and professional fees.

The information in this section has been arranged to follow more closely the order in which estimates may be developed, in accordance with the RIBA stages of work;

a) Cost Indices and Regional Variations – These provide information regarding the adjustments to be made to estimates taking into account current pricing levels for different locations in the UK.

b) Feasibility Costs – These provide a range of data (based on a rate per square metre) for all-in engineering costs, excluding lifts, associated with a wide variety of building types. These would typically be used at work stage A/B (feasibility) of a project.

c) Elemental Rates – The outline costs for offices have been developed further to provide rates for the alternative solutions for each of the services elements. These would typically be used at work stage C, outline proposal.

   Where applicable, costs have been identified as Shell and Core and Fit Out to reflect projects where the choice of procurement has dictated that the project is divided into two distinctive contractual parts.

   Such detail would typically be required at work stage D, detailed proposals.

d) All-in-Rates – These are provided for a number of items and complete parts of a system i.e. boiler plant, ductwork, pipework, electrical switchgear and small power distribution, together with lifts and escalators. Refer to the relevant section for further guidance notes.

e) Elemental Costs – These are provided for a diverse range of building types; offices, laboratory, shopping mall, airport terminal building, supermarket, performing arts centre, sports hall, luxury hotel, hospital and secondary school. Also included is a separate analysis of a building management system for an office block. In each case, a full analysis of engineering services costs is given to show the division between all elements and their relative costs to the total building area. A regional variation factor has been applied to bring these analyses to a common London base.

Prices should be applied to the total floor area of all storeys of the building under consideration. The area should be measured between the external walls without deduction for internal walls and staircases/lift shafts i.e. G.I.A (Gross Internal Area).

Although prices are reviewed in the light of recent tenders it has only been possible to provide a range of prices for each building type. This should serve to emphasise that these can only be average prices for typical requirements and that such prices can vary widely depending on variations in size, location, phasing, specification, site conditions, procurement route, programme, market conditions and net to gross area efficiencies. Rates per square metre should not therefore be used indiscriminately and each case needs to be assessed on its own merits.

The prices do not include for incidental builder's work nor for profit and attendance by a Main Contractor where the work is executed as a sub-contract: they do however include for preliminaries, profit and overheads for the services contractor. Capital contributions to statutory authorities and public undertakings and the cost of work carried out by them have been excluded.

Where services works are procured indirectly, i.e. ductwork via a mechanical Sub Contractor, the reader should make due allowance for the addition of a further level of profit etc.

COST INDICES

The following tables reflect the major changes in cost to contractors but do not necessarily reflect changes in tender levels. In addition to changes in labour and materials costs, tenders are affected by other factors such as the degree of competition in the particular industry, the area where the work is to be carried out, the availability of labour and the prevailing economic conditions. This has meant in recent years that, when there has been an abundance of work, tender levels have tended to increase at a greater rate than can be accounted for solely by increases in basic labour and material costs and, conversely, when there is a shortage of work this has tended to result in keener tenders. Allowances for these factors are impossible to assess on a general basis and can only be based on experience and knowledge of the particular circumstances.

In compiling the tables the cost of labour has been calculated on the basis of a notional gang as set out elsewhere in the book. The proportion of labour to materials has been assumed as follows:
Mechanical Services - 30:70, Electrical Services - 50:50, (1976 = 100)

Mechanical Services

Year	First Quarter	Second Quarter	Third Quarter	Fourth Quarter
1997	361	356	358	363
1998	365	363	368	373
1999	368	363	370	384
2000	384	386	388	400
2001	401	401	405	411
2002	411	411	410	442
2003	443	446	447	456
2004	458	464	467	482
2005	P 486	F 488	F 490	F 503
2006	F 506	F 508	F 509	F 522

Electrical Services

Year	First Quarter	Second Quarter	Third Quarter	Fourth Quarter
1997	411	411	411	411
1998	410	423	422	422
1999	433	432	431	446
2000	458	464	465	468
2001	485	484	484	487
2002	508	508	508	513
2003	530	533	533	541
2004	571	574	576	589
2005	P 607	F 608	F 609	F 618
2006	F 634	F 633	F 636	F 645

(P = Provisional)
(F = Forecast)

COST INDICES

Regional Variations

Prices throughout this Book apply to work in the London area (see Directions at the beginning of the Mechanical Installations and Electrical Installations sections). However, prices for mechanical and electrical services installations will of course vary from region to region, largely as a result of differing labour costs but also depending on the degree of accessibility, urbanisation and local market conditions.

The following table of regional factors is intended to provide readers with indicative adjustments that may be made to the prices in the Book for locations outside of London. The figures are of necessity averages for regions and further adjustments should be considered for city centre or very isolated locations, or other known local factors.

Greater London	1.00	Yorkshire & Humberside	0.97
South East	1.00	North West	0.97
South West	0.99	North East	0.97
East Midlands	0.97	Scotland	0.98
West Midlands	0.96	Wales	0.99
East Anglia	0.99	Northern Ireland	0.96

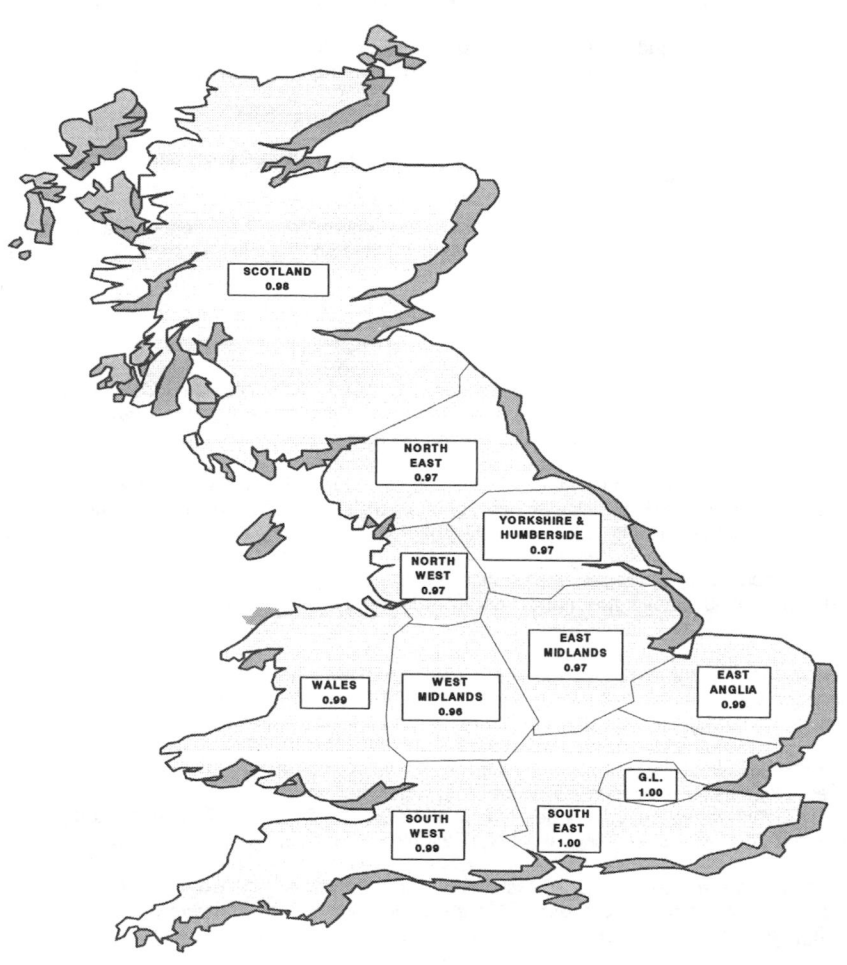

RIBA STAGE A FEASIBILITY COSTS

TYPICAL SQUARE METRE RATES FOR ENGINEERING SERVICES

The following examples indicate the range of rates within each building type for engineering services, excluding lifts, external services and professional fees. Based on gross internal floor area (GIFA).

Industrial Buildings   £/m²

Factories

Owner occupation: Includes for rainwater, soil/waste, LTHW heating via HL radiant heaters, BMS, LV installations, lighting, fire alarms, security, earthing...   114

Owner occupation: Includes for rainwater, soil/waste, sprinklers, LTHW heating via HL radiant heaters, local air conditioning, BMS, HV/LV installations, lighting, fire alarms, security, earthing...   170

Warehouses

High bay for owner occupation: Includes for rainwater, soil/waste, LTHW heating via HL gas fired heaters, BMS, HV/LV installations, lighting, fire alarms, security, earthing...   93

High bay for owner occupation: Includes for rainwater, soil/waste, sprinklers, LTHW heating via HL radiant heaters, local air conditioning, BMS, HV/LV installations, lighting, fire alarms, security, earthing   185

Distribution Centres

High bay for letting: Includes for rainwater, soil/waste, LTHW heating via HL gas fired heaters, BMS, HV/LV installations, lighting, fire alarms, security, earthing...   113

High bay for owner occupation: Includes for rainwater, soil/waste, sprinklers, LTHW heating via HL radiant heaters, local air conditioning, BMS, HV/LV installations, lighting, fire alarms, security...   216

Office Buildings

Offices for letting

Cat A non air conditioned; Includes for rainwater, soil/waste, cold water, hot water via local electrical heaters, LTHW heating via radiator heaters, toilet extract, BMS, LV installations, lighting, small power (landlords), fire alarms, earthing, security wireways, IT wireways   175

Cat A non air conditioned; Includes for rainwater, soil/waste, cold water, hot water, LTHW heating via perimeter heaters, toilet extract, BMS, LV installations, lighting, small power (landlords), fire alarms, earthing, security wireways, IT wireways   186

Cat A air conditioned; Includes for rainwater, soil/waste, VRV 3 pipe heat pumps , toilet extract, BMS, LV installations, lighting, small power (landlords), fire alarms, earthing, security wireways, IT wireways   370

Cat A air conditioned; Includes for rainwater, soil/waste, cold water, hot water via local electrical heaters, LTHW heating via perimeter heaters, 2 pipe FCU , toilet extract, BMS, LV installations, lighting, small power (landlords), fire alarms, earthing, security wireways, IT wireways   390

Offices for owner occupation

Non air conditioned; Includes for rainwater, soil/waste, cold water, hot water via local electrical heaters, dry risers, LTHW heating via radiator heaters, toilet extract, BMS, LV installations, lighting, small power (landlords), fire alarms, earthing, security, IT wireways...   217

Non air conditioned; Includes for rainwater, soil/waste, cold water, hot water, dry risers, LTHW heating via perimeter heaters, toilet extract, BMS, LV installations, lighting, small power (landlords), fire alarms, earthing, security, IT wireways   230

RIBA STAGE A FEASIBILITY COSTS

TYPICAL SQUARE METRE RATES FOR ENGINEERING SERVICES *continued*

Office Buildings *continued*

Offices for owner occupation *continued*   £/m²

Air conditioned; Includes for rainwater, soil/waste, cold water, hot water via local electrical heaters, dry risers, LTHW heating via perimeter heating, 2 pipe fcu air conditioning, toilet extract, kitchen extract, BMS, LV installations, life safety standby generators, lighting, small power, fire alarms, earthing, security, IT wireways   415

Air conditioned; Includes for rainwater, soil/waste, cold water, hot water via local electrical heaters sprinklers/dry risers, LTHW heating via perimeter heaters, VAV air conditioning, Comm room cooling, kitchen/toilet extract, car park extract, BMS, LV installations, standby generators, lighting, small power, fire alarms L1/P1, earthing, security, IT wireways   445

Health and Welfare Facilities

District general hospitals
Natural ventilation Includes for rainwater, soil/waste, cold water, hot water, dry risers, medical gases, LTHW heating via perimeter heating, toilet extract, kitchen extract, BMS, LV installations, standby generation, lighting, small power, fire alarms, earthing/lightning protection, nurse call systems, security, IT wireways.   405

Natural ventilation Includes for rainwater, soil/waste, cold water, hot water, dry risers, LTHW heating via perimeter heaters, localised VAV air conditioning, kitchen/toilet extract, BMS, LV installations, standby generation, lighting, small power, fire alarms, earthing/lightning protection, nurse call systems, security, IT wireways   573

Private hospitals
Air conditioned; Includes for rainwater, soil/waste, cold water, hot water, dry risers, medical gases, LTHW heating, 2 pipe fcu air conditioning, toilet extract, kitchen extract, BMS, LV installations, standby generation, lighting, small power, fire alarms, earthing, nurse call systems, nurse call system, security, IT wireways   600

Air conditioned; Includes for rainwater, soil/waste, cold water, hot water, dry risers, medical gases, LTHW heating , 4 pipe air conditioning, kitchen/toilet extract, BMS, LV installations, standby generation, lighting, small power, fire alarms, earthing, nurse call system, security, IT wireways..   620

Day care unit
Natural ventilation; Includes for rainwater, soil/waste, cold water, hot water via local electrical heaters, medical gases, LTHW heating, toilet extract, kitchen extract, BMS, LV installations, lighting, small power, fire alarms , earthing, security, IT wireways.   430

Comfort cooled; Includes for rainwater, soil/waste, cold water, hot water, medical gases, LTHW heating, DX air conditioning, kitchen/toilet extract, BMS, LV installations, lighting, small power, fire alarms, earthing, security, IT wireways   450

Entertainment and Recreation Buildings

Non Performing
Natural Ventilation; Includes for rainwater, soil/waste, cold water, central hot water, dry risers, LTHW heating, toilet extract, kitchen extract, BMS, LV installations, lighting, small power, fire alarms, earthing, security, IT wireways.   313

Comfort cooled; Includes for rainwater, soil/waste, cold water, hot water via local electrical heaters sprinklers/dry risers, LTHW heating , DX air conditioning, kitchen/toilet extract, BMS, LV installations, lighting, small power, fire alarms, earthing, security, IT wireways   501

RIBA STAGE A FEASIBILITY COSTS

TYPICAL SQUARE METRE RATES FOR ENGINEERING SERVICES *continued*

Entertainment and Recreation Buildings *continued*　　　　　　　　　　　£/m²

Performing Arts
Natural Ventilation; Includes for rainwater, soil/waste, cold water, central hot water, sprinklers/dry risers, LTHW heating, toilet extract, kitchen extract, BMS, LV installations, lighting, small power, fire alarms, earthing, security, IT wireways ....　450

Comfort Cooled; Includes for rainwater, soil/waste, cold water, central hot water, sprinklers/dry risers, LTHW heating, DX air conditioning, kitchen/toilet extract, BMS, LV installations, lighting, small power, fire alarms, earthing, security, IT wireways...　601

Sports Halls
Natural ventilation; Includes for rainwater, soil/waste, cold water, hot water gas fired heaters, LTHW heating, toilet extract, BMS, LV installations, lighting, small power, fire alarms, earthing, security.....　165

Comfort Cooled; Includes for rainwater, soil/waste, cold water, hot water via LTHW heat exchangers, LTHW heating, air conditioning via AHU's, toilet extract, BMS, LV installations, lighting, small power, fire alarms, earthing, security. ....　280

Multi Purpose Leisure Centre
Natural ventilation; Includes for rainwater, soil/waste, cold water, hot water gas fired heaters, LTHW heating, toilet extract, BMS, LV installations, lighting, small power, fire alarms, earthing, security, IT wireways ....　280

Comfort cooled; Includes for rainwater, soil/waste, cold water, hot water LTHW heat exchangers, LTHW heating, air conditioning via AHU, pool hall supply/extract, kitchen/toilet extract, BMS, LV installations, lighting, small power, fire alarms, earthing, security, IT wireways　385

Retail Buildings

Open Arcade
Natural ventilation; Includes for rainwater, soil/waste, cold water, hot water, sprinklers/dry risers, LTHW heating, toilet extract, smoke extract, BMS, LV installations, life safety standby generators, lighting, small power, fire alarms, public address, earthing/lightning protection, security, IT wireways　210

Enclosed Shopping Mall
Air conditioned; Includes for rainwater, soil/waste, cold water, hot water, sprinklers/dry risers, LTHW heating, air conditioning via AHU's, toilet extract, smoke extract, BMS, LV installations, life safety standby generators, lighting, small power, fire alarms, public address, earthing/lightning protection, CCTV/security, IT wireways people counting systems..　490

Department Stores
Air conditioned; Includes for rainwater, soil/waste, cold water, hot water, sprinklers/dry risers, LTHW heating, air conditioning via AHU's, toilet extract, smoke extract, BMS, LV installations, life safety standby generators, lighting, small power, fire alarms, public address, earthing, lightning protection, CCTV/security, IT wireways people counting systems...　350

Air conditioned; Includes for rainwater, soil/waste, cold water, hot water, sprinklers/dry risers, LTHW heating, air conditioning via AHU's, restaurant services, toilet extract, smoke extract, BMS, LV installations, life safety standby generators, lighting, small power, fire alarms, public address, earthing, lightning protection, CCTV/security, IT wireways...　400

RIBA STAGE A FEASIBILITY COSTS

TYPICAL SQUARE METRE RATES FOR ENGINEERING SERVICES *continued*

Retail Buildings *continued*   £/m²

Supermarkets

Comfort cooled; Includes for rainwater, soil/waste, cold water, hot water, sprinklers, LTHW heating, 2 pipe fcu air conditioning, toilet extract, BMS, LV installations, lighting, small power, fire alarms, earthing, lightning protection, security, IT wireways, refrigeration...   406

Air conditioned; Includes for rainwater, soil/waste, cold water, hot water, sprinklers, LTHW heating, air conditioning via AHU's, toilet extract, BMS, LV installations, lighting, small power, fire alarms, earthing, lightning protection, security, IT wireways, refrigeration...   566

Educational Buildings

Secondary Schools

Natural Ventilation; Includes for rainwater, soil/waste, cold water, central hot water, LTHW heating, toilet extract, BMS, LV installations, lighting, small power, fire alarms, earthing, security, IT wireways

                                                                          280

Natural vent with comfort cooling to selected areas (BB93 compliant); Includes for rainwater, soil/waste, cold water, central hot water, LTHW heating, DX air conditioning, general supply/extract, toilet extract, BMS, LV installations, lighting, small power, fire alarms, earthing, security, IT wireways   340

Scientific Buildings

Educational Research

Comfort cooled; Includes for rainwater, soil/waste, cold water, central hot water, dry risers, compressed air, medical gases, LTHW heating, 4 pipe fcu air conditioning, toilet extract, fume, BMS, LV installations, lighting, small power, fire alarms, earthing, lightning protection, security, IT wireways   700

Air conditioned; Includes for rainwater, soil/waste, laboratory waste, cold water, central hot water, specialist water, dry risers, compressed air, medical gases, steam, LTHW heating, 4 pipe FCU air conditioning, Comm room cooling, toilet extract, fume extract, BMS, LV installations, UPS, standby generators, lighting, small power, fire alarms, earthing, lightning protection, security, IT wireways   1200

Commercial Research

Air conditioned; Includes for rainwater, soil/waste, laboratory waste, cold water, central hot water, specialist water, dry risers, compressed air, medical gases, steam, LTHW heating, 4 pipe FCU air conditioning, Comm room cooling, toilet extract, fume extract, BMS, LV installations, UPS, standby generators, lighting, small power, fire alarms, earthing, lightning protection, security, IT wireways   1200

Air conditioned; Includes for rainwater, soil/waste, laboratory waste, cold water, central hot water, specialist water, dry risers, compressed air, medical gases, steam, LTHW heating, VAV air conditioning, toilet extract, fume extract, cold rooms, BMS, LV installations, UPS   1800

Comfort cooled throughout (sealed façade) to comply with BB93 including rainwater, soil/waste, cold water, central hot water, dry risers, compressed air, medical gases, LTHW heating, 4 pipe fcu air conditioning, toilet extract, fume, BMS, LV installations, lighting, small power, fire alarms, earthing, lightning protection, security IT wireways...   380

Approximate Estimating

RIBA STAGE A FEASIBILITY COSTS

TYPICAL SQUARE METRE RATES FOR ENGINEERING SERVICES *continued*

£/m²

Hotels

1 to 3 Star; Includes for rainwater, soil/waste, cold water, hot water, dry risers, 3 pipe VRV air conditioning, toilet extract, kitchen extract, BMS, LV installations, lighting, small power, fire alarms, earthing, lightning protection security, IT wireways   550

4 to 5 Star; Includes for rainwater, soil/waste, cold water, hot water, sprinklers, dry risers, 4 pipe fcu air conditioning, kitchen extract, toilet extract, BMS, LV installations, life safety standby generators, lighting, small power, fire alarms, earthing, security, IT wireways   750

Airport Buildings

Air conditioned; Includes for rainwater, soil/waste, cold water, hot water via local electrical heaters, dry risers, LTHW heating via perimeter heating, 2 pipe fcu air conditioning, toilet extract, kitchen extract, BMS, LV installations, lighting, small power, fire alarms, earthing, lightning protection, security, IT wireways   590

Air conditioned; Includes for rainwater, soil/waste, cold water, hot water via local electrical heaters sprinklers, dry risers, LTHW heating via perimeter heaters, VAV air conditioning, Comm room cooling, kitchen extract, toilet extract, car park extract, BMS, LV installations, lighting, small power, fire alarms, earthing, lightning protection, security, IT wireways   726

RIBA STAGE C ELEMENTAL RATES

ELEMENTAL RATES FOR ALTERNATIVE ENGINEERING SERVICES SOLUTIONS

The following examples of building types indicate the range of rates for alternative design solutions for each of the engineering services elements based on gross area for the Shell and Core and net area for the Fit Out. Fit Out is assumed to be to Cat A standard.

Consideration should be made for size of building, which may affect the economies of scale of rates i.e. the bigger the building the lower the rates

OFFICES MECHANICAL SERVICES	Shell & Core £/m² G.I.A.	Fit Out £/m² N.I.A.
Sanitaryware		
Building up to 3,000 m²	4 to 12	-
Building over 3,000 m² (low rise)	7 to 10	-
Disposal installation		
Building up to 3,000 m²	15 to 25	-
Building over 3,000 m²	10 to 15	-
Water installation		
Building up to 3,000 m²	5 to 10	-
Building over 3,000 m²	10 to 15	-
LPHW Heating Installation; including gas installations		
Building up to 3,000 m²	12 to 18	32 to 67
Building over 3,000 m²	10 to 15	30 to 37
Air Conditioning; including ventilation		
Comfort Cooling;		
2 pipe fan coil for building up to 3,000 m²	50 to 65	63 to 69
2 pipe fan coil for building over 3,000 m²	45 to 70	62 to 54
2 pipe variable refrigerant volume for building up to 3,000 m²	35 to 45	58 to 68
Full air conditioning;		
4 Pipe fan coil for building up to 3,000 m²	75 to 90	95 to 110
4 Pipe fan coil for building over 3,000 m²	65 to 80	80 to 90
3 pipe variable refrigerant volume for building up to 3,000 m²	60 to 70	70 to 80
Variable air volume for building over 3,000m²	90 to 100	60 to 75
Fan assisted variable air volume for building over 3,000m²	65 to 80	90 to 100
Ventilated (active) chilled beams for building over 3,000m²	65 to 80	95 to 110
Chilled beam exposed multi-service raft for building over 3,000m²	65 to 80	150 to 175
Concealed passive chilled beams for building over 3,000m	65 to 80	80 to 90
Chilled ceiling for building over 3,000m²	65 to 80	150 to 175
Chilled ceiling/perimeter chilled beam for building over 3,000m²	65 to 80	80 to 110
Displacement for building over 3,000m²	75 to 90	40 to 50

RIBA STAGE C ELEMENTAL RATES

ELEMENTAL RATES FOR ALTERNATIVE ENGINEERING SERVICES SOLUTIONS *continued*

OFFICES **MECHANICAL SERVICES**	Shell & Core £/m² G.I.A.	Fit Out £/m² N.I.A.
Ventilation systems		
Building up to 3,000 m²	25 to 30	-
Building over 3,000 m²	15 to 20	-
Fire Protection		
Dry risers	10 to 20	-
Sprinkler installation	10 to 15	10 to 18
BMS Controls: including MCC panels and control cabling		
Full air conditioning, fan coil/chilled ceiling.................................	15 to 20	10 to 15
Full air conditioning, variable air volume.................................	15 to 20	6 to 15
Full air conditioning, chilled beam.................................	15 to 20	10 to 15

RIBA STAGE C ELEMENTAL RATES

ELEMENTAL RATES FOR ALTERNATIVE ENGINEERING SERVICES SOLUTIONS *continued*

OFFICES ELECTRICAL SERVICES	Shell & Core £/m² G.I.A.	Fit Out £/m² N.I.A.
LV Installations		
Standby generators (life safety only)		
Buildings up to 3,000m²...	16 to 25	-
Buildings over 3,000m²...	10 to 15	-
LV distribution		
Buildings up to 3,000m²...	15 to 20	-
Buildings over 3,000m²...	20 to 25	-
Lighting Installations (including lighting controls and luminaries)		
Buildings up to 3,000m²...	10 to 15	40 to 60
Buildings over 3,000m²...	7 to 12	40 to 60
Small Power		
Buildings up to 3,000m²...	10 to 15	-
Buildings over 3,000m²...	8 to 12	-
Protective Installations		
Earthing		
Buildings up to 3,000m²...	2 to 3	1 to 2
Buildings over 3,000m²...	2 to 3	1 to 2
Lightning Protection		
Buildings up to 3,000m²...	3 to 4	-
Buildings over 3,000m²...	2 to 3	-
Communication Installations		
Fire Alarms (single stage)		
Buildings up to 3,000m²...	6 to 10	8 to 10
Buildings over 3,000m²...	6 to 8	8 to 10
Fire Alarms (phased evacuation)		
Buildings over 3,000m²...	10 to 12	10 to 15
IT (Wireways only)		
Buildings up to 3,000m²...	2 to 3	-
Buildings over 3,000m²...	2 to 3	-

RIBA STAGE C ELEMENTAL RATES

ELEMENTAL RATES FOR ALTERNATIVE ENGINEERING SERVICES SOLUTIONS *continued*

	Shell & Core £/m² G.I.A.	Fit Out £/m² N.I.A.
OFFICES **ELECTRICAL SERVICES** *continued*		
Security		
Buildings up to 3,000m²...	10 to 12	-
Buildings over 3,000m²...	8 to 10	-
Electrical Installations for Mechanical Plant		
Buildings up to 3,000m²...	5 to 8	-
Buildings over 3,000m²...	3 to 5	-

RIBA STAGE C ELEMENTAL RATES

ELEMENTAL RATES FOR ALTERNATIVE ENGINEERING SERVICES SOLUTIONS *continued*

HOTELS MECHANICAL SERVICES	Shell & Core £/m² G.I.A.	Fit Out £/m² N.I.A.
Sanitaryware and above ground disposal installation		
2 to 3 Star...	20 to 30	25 to 30
4 to 5 Star...	20 to 30	35 to 40
Water installation		
2 to 3 Star...	28 to 38	-
4 to 5 Star...	40 to 50	-
LPHW Heating Installation; including gas installations		
2 to 3 Star...	30 to 45	-
4 to 5 Star...	30 to 45	10 to 20
Air Conditioning; including ventilation		
2 to 3 Star – 4 pipe Fan coil...	200 to 240	-
4 to 5 Star – 4 pipe Fan coil...	200 to 240	-
2 to 3 Star - 3 pipe variable refrigerant volume	130 to 150	-
4 to 5 Star - 3 pipe variable refrigerant volume	130 to 150	-
Fire Protection		
2 to 3 Star - Dry risers...	8 to 12	-
4 to 5 Star - Dry risers...	8 to 12	-
2 to 3 Star - Sprinkler installation......................................	5 to 10	-
4 to 5 Star - Sprinkler installation......................................	5 to 10	-
BMS Controls: including MCC panels and control cabling		
2 to 3 Star...	10 to 12	10 to 15
4 to 5 Star...	20 to 30	15 to 25

HOTELS ELECTRICAL SERVICES	Shell & Core £/m²	Fit Out £/m²
LV Installations		
Standby generators (life safety only)		
2 to 3 Star...	10 to 20	-
4 to 5 Star...	10 to 20	-
LV distribution		
2 to 3 Star...	25 to 35	-
4 to 5 Star...	35 to 45	-

RIBA STAGE C ELEMENTAL RATES

ELEMENTAL RATES FOR ALTERNATIVE ENGINEERING SERVICES SOLUTIONS *continued*

HOTELS ELECTRICAL SERVICES *continued*	Shell & Core £/m² G.I.A.	Fit Out £/m² N.I.A.
Lighting Installations		
2 to 3 Star............	15 to 25	30 to 50
4 to 5 Star............	15 to 25	60 to 80
Small Power		
2 to 3 Star............	5 to 10	-
4 to 5 Star............	10 to 15	-
Protective Installations		
Earthing		
2 to 3 Star............	1 to 2	-
4 to 5 Star............	1 to 2	-
Lightning Protection		
2 to 3 Star............	1 to 2	-
4 to 5 Star............	1 to 2	-
Communication Installations		
Fire Alarms		
2 to 3 Star............	10 to 15	5 to10
4 to 5 Star............	10 to 15	5 to 10
IT		
2 to 3 Star............	10 to 20	-
4 to 5 Star............	10 to 20	-
Security		
2 to 3 Star............	15 to25	-
4 to 5 Star............	15 to25	-
Electrical Installations for Mechanical Plant		
2 to 3 Star............	5 to 8	-
4 to 5 Star............	5 to 8	-

RIBA STAGE C ELEMENTAL RATES

ELEMENTAL RATES FOR ALTERNATIVE ENGINEERING SERVICES SOLUTIONS *continued*

RESIDENTIAL MECHANICAL & ELECTRICAL SERVICES	Shell & Core £/m² G.I.A.	Fit Out £/m² N.I.A.
Sanitaryware and above ground disposal installation		
Housing Association	14 to 16	35 to 45
Shared Ownership	14 to 18	35 to 50
Private	15 to 20	50 to 80
Water installation		
Housing Association	11 to 14	35 to 40
Shared Ownership	11 to 14	40 to 45
Private	12 to 16	45 to 50
LPHW Heating Installation		
Housing Association	2 to 5	40 to 45
Shared Ownership	2 to 6	45 to 50
Private	-	45 to 55
Comfort cooling; including ventilation		
Private – 3 pipe variable refrigerant volume/split system	-	140 to 170
Ventilation (to façade)		
Housing Association	2 to 10	20 to 25
Shared Ownership	2 to 10	20 to 25
Private	2 to 10	20 to 30
Gas Installations		
Housing Association	2 to 5	5 to 7
Shared Ownership	2 to 5	5 to 7
Private	2 to 5	11 to 15
Electrical Installations		
Housing Association	30 to 40	30 to 40
Shared Ownership	35 to 45	40 to 50
Private	35 to 50	55 to 80
Protective Installations		
Housing Association	3 to 7	-
Shared Ownership	3 to 7	-
Private	5 to 15	-
Communication Installations		
Housing Association	15 to 20	15 to 20
Shared Ownership	20 to 25	20 to 25
Private	20 to 30	25 to 40

RIBA STAGE C ELEMENTAL RATES

ELEMENTAL RATES FOR ALTERNATIVE ENGINEERING SERVICES SOLUTIONS *continued*

RESIDENTIAL **MECHANICAL & ELECTRICAL SERVICES** *continued*	Shell & Core £/m² G.I.A.	Fit Out £/m² N.I.A.
Specialist Installations (no BMS)		
Housing Association..	2 to 5	5 to 7
Shared Ownership..	2 to 5	5 to 10
Private..	2 to 5	5 to 10

ALL-IN-RATES

ALL-IN-RATES FOR PRICING MECHANICAL APPROXIMATE QUANTITIES

	Cost per Point £
ABOVE GROUND DRAINAGE	
Soil and Waste	300 - 350
WATER INSTALLATIONS	
Cold Water	250 - 300
Hot Water	300 - 350

	Cost Per kW £
HEAT SOURCE	
Gas fired boilers including gas train and controls	16 - 21
Gas fired boilers including gas train, controls, flue, plantroom pipework, valves and insulation, pumps and pressurisation unit	62 - 118

SPACE HEATING AND AIR TREATMENT

	Cost per kW £
CHILLED WATER	
Air cooled R134a refrigerant chiller including control panel, anti vibration mountings	120 - 140
Air cooled R134a refrigerant chiller including control panel, antivibration mountings, plantroom pipework, valves, insulation, pumps and pressurisation units	160 - 220
Water cooled R134a refrigerant chiller including control panel, anti vibration mountings	60 - 80
Water cooled R134a refrigerant chiller including control panel, antivibration mountings, plantroom pipework, valves, insulation, pumps and pressurisation units	90 - 190
Absorption steam medium chiller including control panel, antivibration mountings, plantroom pipework, valves, insulation, pumps and pressurisation units	170 - 270

	Cost per kW (heat rejection) £
HEAT REJECTION	
Open circuit, forced draft cooling tower	8 - 12
Closed circuit, forced draft cooling tower	25 - 33
Dry Air	30 – 45

ALL-IN-RATES

ALL-IN-RATES FOR PRICING MECHANICAL APPROXIMATE QUANTITIES *continued*

SPACE HEATING AND AIR TREATMENT *continued*

	Cost per kPa £
PUMPS	
Pumps including flexible connections, antivibration mountings	10 - 50
Pumps including flexible connections, antivibration mountings, plantroom pipework, valves, insulation and accessories	30 - 110

DUCTWORK

The rates below allow for ductwork and for all other labour and material in fabrication, fittings, supports and jointing to equipment, stop and capped ends, elbows, bends, diminishing and transition pieces, regular and reducing couplings, volume control dampers, branch diffuser and 'snap on' grille connections, ties, 'Ys', crossover spigots, etc., turning vanes, regulating dampers, access doors and openings, handholes, test holes and covers, blanking plates, flanges, stiffeners, tie rods and all supports and brackets fixed to structure.

	Per m² of duct £
Rectangular galvanised mild steel ductwork as HVCA DW 144 up to 1000mm longest side	35 – 40
Rectangular galvanised mild steel ductwork as HVCA DW 144 up to 2500mm longest side	40 – 50
Rectangular galvanised mild steel ductwork as HVCA DW 144 3000mm longest side and above	55 – 60
Circular galvanised mild steel ductwork as HVCA DW 144	40 – 50
Flat oval galvanised mild steel ductwork as HVCA DW 144 up to 545mm wide	40 – 45
Flat oval galvanised mild steel ductwork as HVCA DW 144 up to 880mm wide	45 – 50
Flat oval galvanised mild steel ductwork as HVCA DW 144 up to 1785mm wide	55 – 60

PACKAGED AIR HANDLING UNITS	Cost per m³/s £
Air handling unit including LPHW pre-heater coil, pre-filter panel, LPHW heater coils, chilled water coil, filter panels, inverter drive, motorised volume control dampers, sound attenuation, flexible connections to ductwork and all anti-vibration mountings.	3,500 – 6,000

EXTRACT FANS

Extract fan including inverter drive, sound attenuation, flexible connections to ductwork and all anti-vibration mountings	1,000 – 2,000

ALL-IN-RATES

ALL-IN-RATES FOR PRICING MECHANICAL APPROXIMATE QUANTITIES *continued*

PROTECTIVE INSTALLATIONS

SPRINKLER INSTALLATION   £

Recommended maximum area coverage per sprinkler head:
  Extra light hazard, 21 m² of floor area
  Ordinary hazard, 12 m² of floor area
  Extra high hazard, 9 m² of floor area

Sprinkler equipment installation, pipework, valve sets, booster pumps and water storage   50,000 - 75,000

Price per sprinkler head; including pipework, valves and supports   160

PROTECTIVE INSTALLATIONS

HOSE REELS AND DRY RISERS

Wall mounted concealed hose reel with 36 metre hose including approximately 15 metres of pipework and isolating valve:

Price per hose reel...   1,200

100mm dry riser main including 2 way breeching valve and box,, 65mm landing valve, complete with padlock and leather strap and automatic air vent and drain valve.

Price per landing...   1,400

COMMUNICATIONS INSTALLATIONS

SECURITY

ACCESS CONTROL SYSTEMS

Door Mounted access control unit inclusive of door furniture, lock plus software. Including up to 50 meters of cable and termination. Including documentation testing and commissioning

Internal single leaf door...	960
Internal double door	1,120
External single leaf door	1,015
External Double leaf door...	1,175
Management control PC with printer software and commissioning up to 1000 users...	7,250

CCTV INSTALLATIONS

CCTV Equipment inclusive of 50 m of cable including testing and commissioning

Internal camera with Bracket	705
Internal camera with Housing...	765
Internal PTZ camera with Bracket...	1,110
External fixed camera with housing...	815
External PTZ camera dome...	1,800
External PTZ camera dome with power...	2,370

ALL-IN-RATES

ALL-IN-RATES FOR PRICING MECHANICAL APPROXIMATE QUANTITIES *continued*

IT INSTALLATIONS　　　　　　　　　　　　　　　　　　　　　£

DATA CABLING

Complete channel link including, patch leads, cable, panels, containment where required, testing and documentation (excludes cabinets and / or frames).

Krone Cat 5e outlets...	53.00
Avaya Cat 5e outlets...	53.00
Krone Cat 6 outlets...	65.00
Avaya Cat 6 outlets...	65.00

PIPEWORK *(excludes insulation, valves and ancillaries etc)*

Hot and Cold Water

Light gauge copper tube to BS 2871 part 1 table X with joints as described including allowance for waste, fittings and supports assuming average runs with capillary joints up to 54mm and bronze welded thereafter

Cost per metre
£

Horizontal Distribution	
15mm	13.14
22mm	16.39
28mm	19.11
35mm	27.81
42mm	34.15
54mm	44.79
67mm	71.64
Risers	
15mm	12.01
22mm	15.02
28mm	17.37
35mm	24.66
42mm	29.44
54mm	38.37
67mm	56.83
Toilet Areas etc	
15mm	42.88
22mm	50.36
28mm	59.85
35mm	91.06

ALL-IN-RATES

ALL-IN-RATES FOR PRICING MECHANICAL APPROXIMATE QUANTITIES *continued*

PIPEWORK *continued*

LTHW and Chilled Water
Distribution heating pipework *(excludes insulation, valves and ancillaries etc)*

Black heavy weight mild steel tube to BS1387 with joints in the running length, allowance for waste, fittings and supports assuming average runs

	Cost per metre	
	LTHW £	*Chilled Water* £
Horizontal Distribution – Basements etc		
15mm	37.09	-
20mm	46.98	50.90
25mm	52.29	55.62
32mm	63.47	66.41
40mm	73.17	76.23
50mm	85.81	88.93
65mm	89.42	92.28
80mm	105.02	108.35
100mm	115.20	118.33
125mm	128.65	131.98
150mm	164.93	168.47
200mm	219.90	223.86
Risers		
15mm	22.40	-
20mm	26.22	30.14
25mm	30.71	34.04
32mm	37.50	40.44
40mm	42.49	45.55
50mm	46.20	48.91
65mm	56.84	59.70
80mm	66.13	69.46
100mm	92.38	95.51
125mm	117.60	120.93
150mm	137.57	141.11
200mm	183.43	187.39
On Floor Distribution		
15mm	29.90	-
20mm	35.24	39.16
25mm	40.21	43.54
32mm	48.97	51.91
40mm	56.32	59.38
50mm	70.92	73.63
65mm	-	-
80mm	-	-
100mm	-	-
125mm	-	-
150mm	-	-
200mm	-	-

Approximate Estimating

ALL-IN-RATES

ALL-IN-RATES FOR PRICING MECHANICAL APPROXIMATE QUANTITIES *continued*

PIPEWORK *continued*

LTHW and Chilled Water
Distribution heating pipework *(excludes insulation, valves and ancillaries etc)*

Black heavy weight mild steel tube to BS1387 with joints in the running length, allowance for waste, fittings and supports assuming average runs

	Cost per metre	
	LTHW £	Chilled Water £
Plantroom Areas etc		
15mm	56.07	-
20mm	67.75	71.67
25mm	78.65	81.98
32mm	60.46	63.40
40mm	69.57	72.63
50mm	86.05	88.76
65mm	94.98	97.84
80mm	96.65	99.98
100mm	127.20	130.33
125mm	135.67	139.00
150mm	186.68	190.22
200mm	257.39	261.35

Rates reflect typical fittings to linear pipework ratio, hence some rates appear lower than preceding ones

ALL-IN-RATES

ALL-IN-RATES FOR PRICING ELECTRICAL APPROXIMATE QUANTITIES *continued*

HV/LV INSTALLATIONS

The cost of HV/LV equipment will vary according to the electricity suppliers requirements, the duty required and the actual location of the site. For estimating purposes the items indicated below are typical of the equipment required in a HV substation incorporated into a building.

RING MAIN UNIT	*Cost per Unit* £
Ring Main Unit , 11kv including electrical terminations	7,500 - 12,500
TRANSFORMERS	*Cost per KVA* £
Oil filled transformers, 11kv to 415v including electrical terminations	11
Cast Resin transformers, 11kv to 415v including electrical terminations... ...	13
HV SWITCHGEAR	*Cost per Section* £
Cubicle section HV switchpanel, Form 4 type 6 including air circuit breakers, meters and electrical terminations...	10,000 - 15,000
LV SWITCHGEAR	*Cost per Isolator* £
LV switchpanel, Form 3 including all isolators, fuses, meters and electrical terminations...	1,500 - 2,500
LV switchpanel, Form 4 type 5 including all isolators, fuses, meters and electrical terminations...	2,500 - 3,500
EXTERNAL PACKAGED SUB-STATION	£
Extra over cost for prefabricated packaged sub station housing excludes base and protective security fencing	20,000 – 25,000
STANDBY GENERATING SETS	*Cost per KVA* £
Diesel powered including control panel, flue, oil day tank and attenuation	
Approximate installed cost, LV	160 - 210
Approximate installed cost, HV	180 - 230
UNINTERRUPTIBLE POWER SUPPLY	*Cost per KVA* £
Rotary UPS including control panel, automatic bypass, DC isolator and batteries for 30 minutes standby (excludes distribution)	
Approximate installed cost (range 100KVA to 1000KVA)	250 - 350
Static UPS including control panel, automatic bypass, DC isolator and batteries for 30 minutes standby (excludes distribution)	
Approximate installed cost (range 100KVA to 1000KVA)...	200 - 300

Approximate Estimating

ALL-IN-RATES

ALL-IN-RATES FOR PRICING ELECTRICAL APPROXIMATE QUANTITIES *continued*

SMALL POWER

Approximate prices for wiring of power points of length not exceeding 20m, including accessories, wireways but excluding distribution boards.

	Per Point £
13 amp Accessories	
Wired in PVC insulated twin and earth cable in ring main circuit	
Domestic properties	55.00
Commercial properties	75.00
Industrial properties	75.00
Wired in PVC insulated twin and earth cable in radial circuit	
Domestic properties	70.00
Commercial properties	90.00
Industrial property	90.00
Wired in LSF insulated single cable in ring main circuit	
Commercial properties	80.00
Industrial property	80.00
Wired in LSF insulated single cable in radial circuit	
Commercial properties	100.00
Industrial property	100.00
45 amp wired in PVC insulated twin and earth cable	
Domestic properties	100.00

Low voltage power circuits

Three phase four wire radial circuit feeding an individual load, wired in LSF insulated single cable including wireways, isolator, *not exceeding 10 metres; in commercial properties.*

Cable size mm²	£
1.5	175.00
2.5	190.00
4	205.00
6	220.00
10	255.00
16	280.00

Three phase four core radial circuit feeding an individual load item, wired in LSF/SWA/XLPE insulated cable including terminations, isolator; clipped to surface, *not exceeding 10 metres in commercial properties.*

Cable size mm²	£
1.5	133.00
2.5	148.00
4	168.00
6	180.00
10	276.00
16	357.00

ALL-IN-RATES

ALL-IN-RATES FOR PRICING ELECTRICAL APPROXIMATE QUANTITIES *continued*

LIGHTING

Approximate prices for wiring of lighting points including rose, wireways but excluding distribution boards, luminaires and switches.

	Per Point £
Final Circuits	
Wired in PVC insulated twin and earth cable	
Domestic properties...	40.00
Commercial properties	50.00
Industrial properties	50.00
Wired in LSF insulated single cable	
Commercial properties	65.00
Industrial property	65.00

ELECTRICAL WORKS IN CONNECTION WITH MECHANICAL SERVICES

The cost of electrical connections to mechanical services equipment will vary depending on the type of building and complexity of the equipment. Therefore a rate of £ 5.00 per m² of gross floor area should be a useful guide to allow for power wiring, isolators and associated wireways.

FIRE ALARMS

Cost per point for two core MICC insulated wired system including all terminations, supports and wireways.

	Per Point £
Call point	235.00
Smoke detector	206.00
Smoke/heat detector	235.00
Heat detector	227.00
Heat detector and sounder	199.00
Input/output/relay units	276.00
Alarm sounder	223.00
Alarm sounder/beacon	260.00
Speakers/voice sounders	261.00
Speakers/voice sounders (weatherproof)	302.00
Beacon/strobe	205.00
Beacon/strobe (weatherproof)	302.00
Door release units	300.00
Beam detector	804.00

ALL-IN-RATES

ALL-IN-RATES FOR PRICING ELECTRICAL APPROXIMATE QUANTITIES *continued*

FIRE ALARMS *continued*

Cost per point for wireless system

	Per Point £
Call point	179.00
Smoke detector	178.00
Smoke/heat detector	214.00
Heat detector	187.00
Heat detector and sounder	376.00
Input/output/relay units	344.00
Alarm sounder	340.00
Alarm sounder/beacon	389.00
Speakers/voice sounders	353.00
Speakers/voice sounders (weatherproof)	427.00
Beacon/strobe	364.00
Beacon/strobe (weatherproof)	361.00
Door release units	334.00
Beam detector	950.00

For costs for zone control panel, battery chargers and batteries, see 'Prices for Measured Work' section.

EXTERNAL LIGHTING

Estate road lighting
Post type road lighting lantern 70 watt CDM-T 3000k complete with 5m high column with hinged lockable door, control gear and cut-out including 2.5 mm two core butyl cable internal wiring, interconnections and earthing fed by 16 mm^2 four core XLPE/SWA /LSF cable and terminations. Approximate installed price *per metre road length* (based on 300 metres run) including time switch but excluding builder's work in connection

   Columns erected at 30 m intervals ... ... £40.00 per m of road

Bollard lighting
Bollard lighting fitting 26 watt TC-D 3500k including control gear, all internal wiring, interconnections, earthing and 25 metres of 2.5 mm^2 three core XLPE/SWA/LSF cable

   Approximate installed price excluding builder's work in connection ... ... £850.00 *each*

Outdoor flood lighting
Wall mounted outdoor flood light fitting complete with tungsten halogen lamp, mounting bracket, wire guard and all internal wiring; fixed to brickwork or concrete and connected.

   Installed price 500 watt ... ... £80.00 - £ 140.00
   Installed price 1000 watt £110.00- £160.00

Pedestal mounted outdoor floor light fitting complete with1000 watt MBF/U lamp, mounting bracket, control gear, contained in weatherproof steel box, all internal wiring, interconnections and earthing; fixed to brickwork or concrete and connected

   Approximate installed price excluding builder's work in connection ... ... £970.00 *each*

ALL-IN-RATES FOR PRICING SPECIALIST APPROXIMATE QUANTITIES *continued*

LIFT INSTALLATIONS

The cost of lift installations will vary depending upon a variety of circumstances. The following prices assume a car height of 2.2 metres, manufacturers standard car finish, brushed stainless steel 2 panel centre opening doors to BSEN81 part 1 & 2 and Lift Regulations 1997.

Passenger Lifts – Machine Above	8 Person £	10 Person £	13 Person £	17 Person £	21 Person £	26 Person £
Electrically operated AC drive serving 2 levels with directional collective controls and a speed of 1.0 m/s	51,479	55,683	58,528	66,046	74,890	85,925
As above serving 4 levels and a speed of 1.0m/s	59,928	64,056	67,328	75,698	85,523	97,805
As above serving 6 levels and a speed of 1.0m/s	68,194	72,407	75,944	85,167	95,942	109,413
As above serving 8 levels and a speed of 1.0m/s	76,460	80,760	84,560	94,636	106,361	121,019
As above serving 10 levels and a speed of 1.0m/s	84,725	89,110	93,175	104,105	116,780	132,626
As above serving 12 levels and a speed of 1.0m/s	92,990	97,463	101,792	113,574	127,199	144,233
As above serving 14 levels and a speed of 1.0m/s	102,903	84,461	112,055	124,689	138,534	155,839
Add to above for:						
Increase speed from 1.0 to 1.6 m/s	3,655	3,465	3,702	3,692	3,692	3,692
Increase speed from 1.6m/s to 2.0m/s	775	775	1,030	1,030	1,300	1,300
Increase speed from 2.0m/s to 2.5m/s	1,800	1,800	2,200	2,200	2,590	2,590
Enhanced finish to car – Centre mirror, flat ceiling, carpet	2,486	2,716	2,642	3,100	3,604	4,235

Approximate Estimating

ALL-IN-RATES

ALL-IN-RATES FOR PRICING SPECIALIST APPROXIMATE QUANTITIES *continued*

LIFT INSTALLATIONS *continued*

Passenger Lifts Machine Room Above (cont'd)	8 Person £	10 Person £	13 Person £	16 Person £	21 Person £	26 Person £
Bottom motor room	6,450	6,450	6,450	7,750	7,750	8,000
Fire fighting control	5,150	5,150	5,150	5,150	5,150	5,150
Glass back	2,200	2,550	3,050	3,700	3,700	3,700
Glass doors	17,700	17,700	19,422	20,000	20,000	20,000
Painting to entire pit	1,907	1,907	1,907	1,907	1,907	1,907
Dual seal shaft	3,736	3,736	3,736	4,488	4,488	4,488
Dust sealing machine room	720	720	1,200	1,200	1,200	1,200
Intercom to reception desk and security room	338	338	338	338	338	338
Heating, cooling and ventilation to machine room	750	750	750	750	750	750
Shaft lighting / small power	3,580	3,580	3,580	3,580	3,580	3,580
Motor room lighting / small power	1,200	1,200	1,350	1,480	1,480	1,480
Lifting beams	1,224	1,224	1,224	1,224	1,224	1,224
10mm Equipotential bonding of all entrance metalwork	810	810	810	810	810	810
Shaft secondary steelwork	5,425	5,550	5,800	5,930	5,930	5,930
Independent insurance inspection	1,748	1,748	1,748	1,748	1,748	1,748
12 Month warranty service	1,691	1,691	1,691	1,691	1,691	1,691

ALL-IN-RATES

ALL-IN-RATES FOR PRICING SPECIALIST APPROXIMATE QUANTITIES *continued*

LIFT INSTALLATIONS *continued*

Passenger Lifts – Machine roomless	8 Person £	10 Person £	13 Person £	17 Person £	21 Person £	26 Person £
Electrically operated AC drive serving 2 levels with directional collective controls and a speed of 1.0 m/s	46,506	51,001	54,389	65,932	72,071	79,575
As above serving 4 levels and a speed of 1.0m/s	54,382	58,437	62,583	74,742	81,184	89,648
As above serving 6 levels and a speed of 1.0m/s	62,285	66,377	70,669	83,442	90,153	99,538
As above serving 8 levels and a speed of 1.0m/s	70,152	74,351	78,788	92,176	99,168	109,428
As above serving 10 levels and a speed of 1.0m/s	78,062	82,366	86,948	100,953	108,237	119,321
As above serving 12 levels and a speed of 1.0m/s	86,021	90,432	95,159	109,670	117,374	127,210
As above serving 14 levels and a speed of 1.0m/s	96,355	98,377	104,768	119,774	128,682	141,229

Add to above for:

	8 Person £	10 Person £	13 Person £	17 Person £	21 Person £	26 Person £
Increase speed from 1.0 to 1.6 m/s	2,669	2,399	2,585	3,871	4,423	5,680
Enhanced finish to car – Centre mirror, flat ceiling, carpet	2,487	2,451	2,642	2,933	3,882	4,439
Fire fighting control	6,425	6,425	6,425	-	-	-
Painting to entire pit	712	712	712	712	712	712
Dual seal shaft	660	667	692	836	886	886
Shaft lighting / small power	3,580	3,580	3,580	-	-	-

Approximate Estimating

ALL-IN-RATES

ALL-IN-RATES FOR PRICING SPECIALIST APPROXIMATE QUANTITIES *continued*

LIFT INSTALLATIONS *continued*

Passenger Lifts Machine Roomless (cont'd)	8 Person £	10 Person £	13 Person £	17 Person £	21 Person £	26 Person £
Add to above for:						
Intercom to reception desk and security room	338	338	338	338	338	338
Heating, cooling and ventilation to machine room	750	750	750	750	750	750
Lifting beams	800	800	800	1,117	1,175	1,175
10mm Equipotential bonding of all entrance metalwork	384	384	384	384	384	384
Shaft secondary steelwork	5,150	5,150	5,150	-	-	-
Independent insurance inspection	1,748	1,748	1,748	1,748	1,748	1,748
12 Month warranty service	741	768	778	801	823	823

Goods Lifts Machine Room Above	2000 kg £	2250 kg £	2500 kg £	3000 kg £
Electrically operated two speed serving 2 levels to take 1000 kg load, prime coated internal finish and a speed of 1.0 m/s	85,925	94,941	96,129	104,129
As above serving 4 levels and a speed of 1.0m/s	97,805	107,203	108,390	122,337
A As above serving 6 levels and a speed of 1.0m/s	109,412	119,214	120,377	134,572
As above serving 8 levels and a speed of 1.0m/s	121,019	131,178	132,365	149,793
As above serving 10 levels and a speed of 1.0m/s	132,626	143,168	144,353	165,014
As above serving 12 levels and a speed of 1.0m/s	144,233	155,152	156,340	180,234
As above serving 14 levels and a speed of 1.0m/s	155,839	167,140	168,327	195,456

ALL-IN-RATES

ALL-IN-RATES FOR PRICING SPECIALIST APPROXIMATE QUANTITIES *continued*

LIFT INSTALLATIONS *continued*

Goods Lifts Machine Room Above (cont'd)	2000 kg £	2250 kg £	2500 kg £	3000 kg £
Add to above for:				
Increased speed of travel from 1.0 to 1.6 metres per second	1,200	-	-	-
Enhanced finish to car – Centre mirror, flat ceiling, carpet	3,240	3,240	3,240	-
Bottom motor room	7,750	-	-	-
Painting to entire pit	583	1,233	1,233	1,233
Dual seal shaft	5,240	5,240	5,240	-
Intercom to reception desk and security room	338	338	338	338
Heating, cooling and ventilation to machine room	750	750	750	750
Lifting beams	1,117	1,117	1,117	1,117
10mm Equipotential bonding of all entrance metalwork	666	810	810	810
Independent insurance inspection	2,222	2,222	2,222	2,222
12 Month warranty service	610	1,116	1,116	-

Goods Lifts Machine Roomless	2000 kg £	2250 kg £	2500 kg £
Electrically operated two speed serving 2 levels to take 1000 kg load, prime coated internal finish and a speed of 1.0 m/s	77,658	83,061	88,470
As above serving 4 levels and a speed of 1.0m/s	87,731	93,320	98,910
A As above serving 6 levels and a speed of 1.0m/s	97,621	97,621	109,350
As above serving 8 levels and a speed of 1.0m/s	107,512	113,651	119,790
As above serving 10 levels and a speed of 1.0m/s	117,404	123,818	130,232
As above serving 12 levels and a speed of 1.0m/s	127,293	133,983	140,671

ALL-IN-RATES

ALL-IN-RATES FOR PRICING SPECIALIST APPROXIMATE QUANTITIES *continued*

LIFT INSTALLATIONS *continued*

Goods Lifts **Machine Roomless (cont'd)** As above serving 14 levels and a speed of 1.0m/s	**2000 kg** £ 139,313	**2250 kg** £ 145,213	**2500 kg** £ 151,111
Add to above for:			
Increased speed of travel from 1.0 to 1.6 metres per second	4,430	7,500	-
Add to above for:			
Enhanced finish to car – Centre mirror, flat ceiling, carpet	3,654	5,000	7,501
Add to above for:			
Painting to entire pit	712	-	840
Dual seal shaft	655	-	-
Intercom to reception desk and security room	338	-	-
Heating, cooling and ventilation to machine room	375	750	750
Lifting beams	1,078	1,000	1,000
10mm Equipotential bonding of all entrance metalwork	384	-	-
Independent insurance inspection	1,748	1,748	1,748
12 Month warranty service	610	610	610

ESCALATOR INSTALLATIONS

30Ø Pitch escalator with a rise of 3 to 6 metres with standard balustrades ... ... 1000mm step width	£ 86,500

Add to above for:

Balustrade Lighting	£ 8,000
Skirting Lighting	£ 8,650
Emergency stop button pedestals	£ 2,710
Truss cladding - Stainless steel...	£ 24,700
Truss cladding - Spray painted steel	£ 19,750

ELEMENTAL COSTS

Note : A regional variation factor has been applied to bring the following analyses to a common London base.

AIRPORT TERMINAL BUILDING

New build airport terminal building, located in the South East, handling both domestic and international flights with a gross internal floor area of 25,000m².

Cost Summary

El. Ref.	Element	Total Cost £	Cost/m² £
5A	Sanitaryware	64,956.00	2.59
5C	Disposal Installations		
	Rainwater	116,750.00	4.67
	Soil and waste	127,114.00	5.08
5D	Water Installations		
	Hot and cold water services	343,000.00	13.72
5E	Heat Source	Included in 5F	
5F	Space Heating and Air Treatment		
	LTHW Heating system	953,355.00	38.13
	Chilled water system	699,127.00	27.96
	Supply and extract air conditioning system...	3,673,592.00	146.94
	Allowance for services to communications rooms	63,557.00	2.54
	Ventilation to baggage handling...	425,000.00	17.00
5G	Ventilating Services		
	Mechanical ventilation to baggage handling and plantrooms	423,289.00	16.93
	Toilet extract ventilation	158,893.00	6.35
	Smoke extract installation	139,191.00	5.56
5H	Electrical Installation		
	HV/LV Switchgear	1,271,140.00	50.84
	Standby generator	444,899.00	17.79
	Mains and sub mains installation	476,678.00	19.06
	Small power installation...	317,785.00	12.71
	Lighting and luminaires...	2,029,692.00	81.18
	Emergency lighting installation...	174,782.00	6.99
	Power to mechanical services	69,892.00	2.79
5I	Gas Installation	25,423.00	1.01
5K	Protective Installations		
	Lightning protection	63,557.00	2.54
	Earthing and bonding	59,068.00	2.36
	Sprinkler installation	461,423.00	18.45
	Dry riser and hosereel installations	127,037.00	5.08
	Fire suppression installation to communications room	19,067.00	0.76
	Carried forward	12,303,692.00	492.03

Approximate Estimating

ELEMENTAL COSTS

AIRPORT TERMINAL BUILDING *continued*

El. Ref.	Element	Total Cost £	Cost/m² £
	Brought forward	12,303,692.00	492.03
5L	Communications Installations		
	Fire and smoke detection and alarm system	425,000.00	17.00
	Voice/public address system	317,702.00	12.70
	Intruder detection	158,895.00	6.35
	Security, CCTV and access control	1,315,000.00	52.60
	Wireways for telephones, data and structured cable	158,191.00	6.32
	Structured cable installation	572,012.00	22.88
	Flight information display system	682,500.00	27.30
5M	Special Installations		
	BMS Installation	953,327.00	38.13
	Summary total	15,886,119.00	675.31

ELEMENTAL COSTS

SHOPPING MALL (TENANTS FIT OUT EXCLUDED)

Natural ventilation shopping mall with two storey retail and below ground car park, with approximately 360,000m², situated in a town centre in South East England

Cost Summary

El. Ref.	Element	Total Cost £	Cost/m² £
5C	Disposal Installations		
	Rainwater	710,000.00	1.97
	Soil, waste and vent...	1,190,000.00	3.31
	Sanitary appliances	490,000.00	1.36
5D	Water Installations		
	Potable water installation	2,030,000.00	5.64
	Non potable water...	590,000.00	1.64
	Hot water installation	275,000.00	0.76
5E	Heat Source	Included	
5F	Space Heating and Air Treatment		
	Air conditioning to Management Suite	590,000.00	1.64
	Air conditioning to comms room and LWC	350,000.00	0.97
	Underfloor heating	130,000.00	0.36
	Overdoor heaters at entrances	150,000.00	0.42
	LTHW Installation	580,000.00	1.61
5G	Ventilation Services		
	General supply and extract ventilation...	3,030,000.00	8.42
	Staircase pressure/smoke relief damper...	245,000.00	0.68
	Car park ventilation	4,700,000.00	13.06
5H	Electrical Installation		
	LV Installation	4,305,000.00	11.96
	Mechanical services power supplies	525,000.00	1.46
	General lighting	8,375,000.00	23.26
	External lighting	2,475,000.000	6.88
	Small power	1,245,000.00	3.46
	Specialist containment	4,250,000.00	11.81
	Trace heating power supplies	26,000.00	0.07
	Earthing and bonding	1,130,000.00	3.14
5I	Gas Installation		
	Gas supplies to boilers	40,000.00	0.11
5K	Protective Installations		
	Lightning protection	160,000.00	0.44
	Sprinklers	4,100,000.00	11.39
5L	Communications Installations		
	Fire detection public address and voice alarms	5,000,000.00	13.89
	CCTV Installation	2,800,000.00	7.78
	IT/Data cabling Installation	2,675,000.00	7.43
	Carried forward	52,166,000.00	144.92

Approximate Estimating

ELEMENTAL COSTS

SHOPPING MALL (TENANTS FIT OUT EXCLUDED) *continued*

El. Ref.	Element	Total Cost £	Cost/m² £
	Brought forward	52,166,000.00	144.92
5M	Special Installations		
	Electrical and gas infrastructure...	5,500,000.00	15.28
	Car park ancillaries	2,000,000.00	5.56
	BMS/Controls	5,000,000.00	13.89
	Pedestrian counting	500,000.00	1.39
	Summary total	65,166,000.00	181.04

ELEMENTAL COSTS

OFFICE BUILDING

Speculative 14 storey office in Central London for single tenant occupancy with a gross floor area of 27,490m², 4 pipe fan coil system, with roof mounted air cooled chillers, gas fired boilers.

Category 'A' fit out nett area of 19,186m².

Cost Summary

El. Ref.	Element	Total Cost £	Cost/m² £
	SHELL AND CORE		
5A	Sanitaryware	166,040.00	6.04
5C	Disposal Installations		
	Rainwater/Soil and Waste	244,111.00	8.88
	Condensate...	25,841.00	0.94
5D	Water Installations		
	Hot and cold water services	253,458.00	9.22
5E	Heat Source	Included in 5F	
5F	Space Heating and Air Treatment		
	LTHW Heating...	307,338.00	11.18
	Chilled water...	639,967.00	23.28
	Ductwork	1,594,420.00	58.00
5G	Ventilating Services		
	Toilet extract ventilation	71,474.00	2.60
	Kitchen extract...	219,645.00	7.99
	Miscellaneous ventilation systems	164,940.00	6.00
5H	Electrical Installation		
	Generator	70,100.00	2.55
	HV/LV supply/distribution...	1,085,855.00	39.50
	General lighting...	551,175.00	20.05
	General power	75,598.00	2.75
	Electrical services for mechanical equipment...	100,339.00	3.65
5I	Gas Installation...	43,984.00	1.60
5K	Protection		
	Dry risers	45,084.00	1.64
	Sprinklers...	332,629.00	12.10
	Earthing and bonding	30,239.00	1.10
	Lightning protection	45,633.00	1.66
5L	Communication Installation		
	Fire/Voice alarms...	268,028.00	9.75
	Voice and data (wireways)	43,434.00	1.58
	Security (wireways)	27,490.00	1.00
	Disabled alarms...	28,865.00	1.05
	Carried forward	5,613,736.00	204.21

ELEMENTAL COSTS

OFFICE BUILDING *continued*

El. Ref.	Element	Total Cost £	Cost/m² £
	Brought forward	5,613,736.00	204.21
5M	Special Installation Building management systems	443,139.00	16.12
	Summary total (based on gross floor area).....................	6,878,826.00	250.33

El. Ref.	Element	Total Cost £	Cost/m² £
	CATEGORY 'A' FIT OUT		
5C	Disposal Installations Condensate..	98,232.00	5.12

5F	Space Heating and Air Treatment
	   LTHW Heating ....
	   Chilled water ....
	   Ductwork..
		402,906.00
		546,801.00
		1,390,985.00
			21.00
			28.50
			72.50

5H	Electrical Installation
	   Lighting installation...
	   Electrical services in connection...........................
	   Tenant distribution board ....
		1,079,596.00
		47,965.00
		59,477.00
			56.27
			2.50
			3.10

5K	Protection Sprinkler installation...	345,348.00	18.00
5L	Communication Installation Fire/Voice alarms..	148,895.00	7.50
5M	Special Installations Building management system..................................	264,000.000	13.76
	Summary total (based on nett area)............................	4,379,205.00	228.251

ELEMENTAL COSTS

BUSINESS PARK

New build office in South East within the M25 part of a speculative business park consisting of two 3 storey existing buildings and 1 new build, fitted out to Category A specification. Four pipe FCU system, external remote chiller, BMS controlled with all three buildings linked with an area of 7,500m² gross and nett area of 6,000m².

Cost Summary

El. Ref.	Element	Total Cost £	Cost/m² £
	SHELL AND CORE		
5A	Sanitaryware	32,250.00	4.30
5C	Disposal Installations		
	Rainwater	19,125.00	2.55
	Soil and waste	49,275.00	6.57
5D	Water Installations		
	Cold water services	32,250.00	4.70
	Hot water services	9,000.00	1.20
5E	Heat Source	Included in 5F	
5F	Space Heating and Air Treatment		
	LTHW Heating; plantroom and risers	179,625.00	23.95
	Chilled water; plantroom and risers	231,225.00	30.83
5G	Ventilating Services		
	Toilet and miscellaneous ventilation	27,300.00	3.64
5H	Electrical Installation		
	LV supply/distribution	113,850.00	15.18
	General lighting	129,525.00	17.27
	General power	27,000.00	3.60
5I	Gas Installation	6,000.00	0.80
5K	Protective Installation		
	Earthing and bonding	7,500.00	1.00
	Lightning protection	7,500.00	1.00
5L	Communication Installation		
	Fire alarms	48,225.00	6.43
	Security (wireways)	8,073.00	1.08
	Data and voice (wireways)	7,969.00	1.06
5M	Special Installation		
	Building management systems	127,500.00	17.00
	Electrical services in connection	4,658.00	0.62
	Summary total (based on gross floor area)	1,070,350.00	142.71

ELEMENTAL COSTS

BUSINESS PARK *continued*

El. Ref.	Element	Total Cost £	Cost/m² £
	CATEGORY 'A' FIT OUT		
5C	Disposal Installation		
	FCU Condensate	30,161.00	5.03
5F	Space Heating and Air Treatment		
	LTHW Heating	101,364.00	16.89
	Chilled water	123,890.00	20.65
	Supply and extract ductwork	397,750.00	66.29
5H	Electrical Installation		
	Distribution boards	14,963.00	2.49
	General lighting	230,832.00	38.47
5K	Protective Installation		
	Earthing and bonding	3,084.00	0.51
5L	Communication Installation		
	Fire alarms	25,578.00	4.26
5M	Special Installations		
	Building management systems	58,590.00	9.77
	Electrical services in connection	15,120.00	2.52
	Summary total (Based on nett area)	1,001,332.00	166.88

ELEMENTAL COSTS

PERFORMING ARTS CENTRE

Performing Arts centre with a gross floor area of 8,203m², upon which this cost analysis is based.

The development comprises of dance studios and theatre auditorium. The theatre has all the necessary stage lighting, machinery and equipment required in a modern professional theatre (excluded from rates).

Cost Summary

El. Ref.	Element	Total Cost £	Cost/m² £
5A	Sanitaryware...	72,988.00	8.89
5C	Disposal Installations		
	Soil and Waste	36,494.00	4.44
5D	Water Installations		
	Cold water services	61,188.00	7.45
	Hot water services	57,783.00	7.04
5E	Heat Source..	102,183.00	12.45
5F	Space Heating and Air Treatment		
	Heating with cooling	589,985.00	71.92
5G	Ventilating Services		
	Extract systems...	799,977.00	97.52
5H	Electrical Installation		
	LV supply/distribution	305,332.00	37.22
	General lighting	680,003.00	82.89
	Small power	178,820.00	21.79
5I	Gas Installation...	23,356.00	2.84
5K	Protection		
	Lighting protection...	7,299.00	0.88
5L	Communication Installation		
	Fire alarms and detection	145,976.00	17.79
	Voice and Data...	178,821.00	21.79
	Security..	164,222.00	20.01
5M	Special Installation		
	Building management systems...............................	267,622.00	32.62
	Theatre systems...	127,728.00	15.57
	Summary total	3,799,777.00	463.11

Approximate Estimating

ELEMENTAL COSTS

SPORTS HALL

Single storey sports hall, located in the South East, with a gross internal area of 1,200m² (40m x 30m).

Cost Summary

El. Ref.	Element	Total Cost £	Cost/m² £
5A	Sanitaryware..	11,522.00	9.60
5C	Disposal Installations		
	Rainwater	3,841.00	3.20
	Soil and waste	6,726.00	5.60
5D	Water Installations		
	Hot and cold water services	16,004.00	13.33
5E	Heat Source		
	Boiler, flues, pumps and controls	12,803.00	10.66
5F	Space Heating and Air Treatment		
	Warm air heating to sports hall area	15,363.00	12.80
	Radiator heating to ancillary areas	24,199.00	20.16
5G	Ventilating Services		
	Ventilation to changing, fitness and sports hall areas	15,495.00	12.91
5H	Electrical Installations		
	Main switchgear and sub-mains	13,297.00	11.08
	Small power	11,522.00	9.60
	Lighting and luminaries to sports hall areas	19,203.00	16.00
	Lighting and luminaries to ancillary areas	22,814.00	19.01
5I	Gas Installation	Included in 5E	
5K	Protective Installations		
	Lightning protection	3,841.00	3.20
5L	Communications Installations		
	Fire, smoke detection and alarm system, intruder detection ..	12,291.00	10.24
	CCTV Installation	14,902.00	12.41
	Public address and music systems	7,638.00	6.36
	Wireways for telephone and data	3,071.00	2.55
	Summary total	214,532.00	178.71

ELEMENTAL COSTS

LUXURY HOTEL

225 Bedroom, five star hotel, situated in Central London, with a gross internal floor area of 21,000m².

The development comprises a ten storey building with large suites on each guest floor, together with banqueting, meeting rooms and leisure facilities.

Cost Summary

El. Ref.	Element	Total Cost £	Cost/m² £
5A	Sanitaryware...	741,720.00	35.32
5C	Disposal Installations Rainwater, soil and waste	379,260.00	18.06
5D	Water Installations Hot and cold water services	715,470.00	34.67
5E	Heat Source Condensing boiler and pumps etc	175,980.00	8.38
5F	Space Heating and Air Treatment Air conditioning system; chillers, pumps, air handling units, ductwork, fan coil units etc; to guest rooms, public areas, meeting and banquet rooms	4,121,460.00	196.26
5G	Ventilating Services General toilet extract and ventilation to kitchens and bathrooms etc	279,510.00	13.31
5H	Electrical Installation HV/LV Installation, standby power, lighting, emergency lighting and small power to guest floors and public areas including earthing and lightning protection	2,844,660.00	135.46
5I	Gas Installation	43,890.00	2.09
5K	Protective Installations Dry risers and sprinkler installation	568,890.00	27.09
5L	Communications Installations Fire, smoke detection and alarm system	401,520.00	19.12
	Background music, AV wireways, disabled persons alarms and induction loops	158,340.00	7.54
	CCTV and security installation	106,260.00	5.06
	Telecommunications, data and T.V. wiring including tray and ladder racks	380,940.00	18.14
5M	Special Installations Building Management System	443,520.00	21.12
	Summary total	11,361,420.00	541.02

ELEMENTAL COSTS

STADIUM – NEW STAND

A three storey stand within an existing stadium, located in Greater London, with gross internal area of 4,500m² and incorporating 4,000 spectator seats

Cost Summary

El. Ref.	Element	Total Cost £	Cost/m² £
5A	Sanitaryware..	66,860.00	14.86
5C	Disposal Installations		
	Rainwater	8,380.00	1.86
	Above ground drainage	21,310.00	4.74
5D	Water Installations		
	Hot and cold water	103,420.00	22.98
5E	Heat Source	Included in 5F	
5F	Space Heating and Air Treatment		
	Server room cooling	4,540.00	1.01
	LTHW heating	194,510.00	43.22
5G	Ventilating Services		
	Ventilation	226,720.00	50.38
5H	Electrical Installation		
	HV/LV Supply	53,100.00	11.80
	LV Distribution	139,170.00	30.93
	General lighting	215,390.00	47.86
	Small power..	44,950.00	9.99
	Earthing and bonding	8,820.00	1.96
	Power supply to mechanical equipment	1,560.00	0.35
	Pitch lighting...	77,670.00	17.26
5I	Gas Installation	33,580.00	7.46
5K	Protective Installations		
	Lightning protection	2,000.00	0.44
5L	Communications Installations		
	Wireways for data, TV, telecom and PA	23,420.00	5.20
	Fire alarms	84,050.00	18.68
	Disabled/refuse alarm	26,220.00	5.83
5M	Special Installations		
	Plunge pools	68,850.00	15.30
	BMS/Controls..	91,010.00	20.22
	Demolitions and diversions	20,060.00	4.46
	Summary total	1,515,590.00	336.80

Cost per seat	£ 378.90

ELEMENTAL COSTS

PRIVATE HOSPITAL

New build project building. The works consist of a new 80 bed hospital of approximately 15,000m², eight storey with a plant room.

All heat is provided from existing steam boiler plant, medical gases are also served from existing plant. The project includes the provision of additional standby electrical generation to serve the wider site requirements.

This hospital has six operating theatres, ITU/HDU department, pathology facilities, diagnostic imaging, out patient facilities and physiotherapy.

Cost Summary

El. Ref.	Element	Total Cost £	Cost/m² £
5A	Sanitaryware	256,950.00	17.13
5C	Disposal Installations		
	Rainwater	30,300.00	2.02
	Soil and waste	284,000.00	18.94
	Specialist drainage (above ground)	18,000.00	1.20
5D	Water Installations		
	Hot and cold water services	660,150.00	44.01
5E	Heat Source	Included in 5F	
5F	Space Heating and Air Treatment		
	LPHW Heating	498,900.00	33.26
	Chilled Water	465,600.00	31.04
	Steam and condensate	284,550.00	18.97
5G	Ventilating Services		
	Ventilation, comfort cooling and air conditioning	1,702.050.00	113.47
5H	Electrical Installation		
	HV Distribution	24,900.00	1.66
	LV supply/distribution	344,550.00	22.97
	Standby Power	387,150.00	25.81
	UPS	289,500.00	19.30
	General lighting	505,800.00	33.72
	General power	496,650.00	33.11
	Emergency lighting	144,300.00	9.62
	Theatre lighting	187,950.00	12.53
	Specialist lighting	175,500.00	11.70
	External lighting	27,750.00	1.85
	Electrical supplies for mechanical equipment	154,650.00	10.31
5I	Gas Installation	34,200.00	2.28
	Oil Installations	74,100.00	4.94
5K	Protection		
	Dry risers	16,650.00	1.11
	Lightning Protection	3,450.00	0.23
	Carried forward	7,067,600.00	471.18

ELEMENTAL COSTS

PRIVATE HOSPITAL *continued*

El. Ref.	Element	Total Cost £	Cost/m² £
	Brought forward	7,067,600.00	471.18
5L	Communication Installation		
	Fire alarms and detection	261,750.00	17.45
	Voice and Data	165,900.00	11.06
	Security and CCTV	48,900.00	3.26
	Nurse call and cardiac alarm system	241,500.00	16.10
	Personnel paging	62,100.00	4.14
	Hospital radio (entertainment)	31,950.00	2.13
5M	Special Installation		
	Building management systems	559,350.00	37.29
	Pneumatic tube conveying system	39,600.00	2.64
	Group 1 Equipment	533,850.00	35.59
	Summary total (based on gross floor area)................	9,012,500.00	600.84

ELEMENTAL COSTS

SCHOOL

New build secondary school (Academy) located in Southern England, with a gross internal floor area of 10,000m².

The building comprises a three storey teaching block, including provision for music, drama, catering, sports hall, science laboratories, food technology, workshops and reception/admin (BB93 compliant).

Cost Summary

El. Ref.	Element	Total Cost £	Cost/m² £
5A	Sanitaryware		
	Toilet cores and changing facilities only	70,000.00	7.00
5C	Disposal Installations		
	Rainwater installations	30,000.00	3.00
	Soil and waste	100,000.00	10.00
5D	Water Installations		
	Potable hot and cold water services	120,000.00	12.00
	Non potable hot and cold water services to labs and art rooms	30,000.00	3.00
5E	Heat Source	120,000.00	12.00
5F	Space Heating and Air Treatment		
	LTHW Heating system (primary)	300,000.00	30.00
	LTHW Heating system (secondary)	70,000.00	7.00
	DX Cooling system to ICT server rooms	30,000.00	3.00
	Mechanical supply and extract ventilation including DX type cooling to Music, Drama, Kitchen/Dining and Sports Hall	400,000.00	40.00
5G	Ventilating Services		
	Toilet extract systems	30,000.00	3.00
	Changing area extract systems	30,000.00	3.00
	Extract ventilation from design/food technology and science labs	40,000.00	4.00
5H	Electrical Installation		
	Mains and sub-mains distribution	250,000.00	25.00
	Lighting and luminaries; including emergency fittings	600,000.00	60.00
	Small power installation	325,000.00	32.50
	Earthing and bonding	10,000.00	1.00
5I	Gas Installation	35,000.00	3.50
5K	Protective Installations		
	Lightning protection	30,000.00	3.00
5L	Communications Installations		
	Containment for telephone, IT data, AV and security systems .	20,000.00	2.00
	Fire, smoke detection and alarm system	130,000.00	13.00
	Security installations including CCTV, access control and intruder alarm	150,000.00	15.00
	Disabled toilet, refuge and induction loop systems	30,000.00	3.00
5M	Special Installations		
	Building Management system – To plant	190,000.00	19.00
	Building Management system – To opening vents/windows ...	60,000.00	6.00
	Excludes : Lifts, BWIC, IT Cabling		
	Summary total	3,200,000.00	320.00

Approximate Estimating

ELEMENTAL COSTS

RESIDENTIAL DEVELOPMENT

A ten storey, sixty apartment residential development, with a gross internal floor area of 5,000m², situated in a town centre in South East England. The development does not include a car park and is based on 85% efficiency.

The specification includes individual LTHW systems to each apartment, electric heating to the landlords areas, central cold water system, local controls, ventilation to the façade of the building, combination boilers and hot water, video entry and satellite TV and LV downlighters to kitchens and bathrooms.

Costs exclude utility and lift costs.

Cost Summary

El. Ref.	Element	Total Cost £	Cost/m² £
5A	Sanitaryware	66,500.00	13.30
5C	Disposal Installations	Included in 5F	
5D	Water Installations	85,000.00	17.00
5E	Heat Source	Included in 5F	
5F	Space Heating and Air Treatment	19,500.00	3.90
5G	Ventilating Services	51,000.00	10.20
5H	Electrical Installation	147,500.00	29.50
5I	Gas Installation	27,500.00	5.50
5K	Protective Installations	22,00.00	4.40
5L	Communications Installations	108,000.00	21.60
5M	Special Installations	19,500.00	3.90
	Summary total (based on gross floor area)	546,500.00	109.30

ELEMENTAL COSTS

RESIDENTIAL DEVELOPMENT *continued*

El. Ref.	Element	Total Cost £	Cost/m² £
	FIT OUT – PRIVATE		
5A	Sanitaryware	317,000.00	63.40
5C	Disposal Installations	Included in 5A	
5D	Water Installations	166,000.00	33.20
5F	Space Heating and Air Treatment	271,000.00	54.20
5G	Ventilating Services	110,500.00	22.10
5H	Electrical Installation	229,000.00	45.80
5I	Gas Installation	53,800.00	10.76
5K	Protective Installations	-	-
5L	Communications Installations Fire alarms	161,500.00	32.30
5M	Special Installations	22,000.00	4.40
	Summary total (based on gross floor area)	1,330,800.00	266.16

Approximate Estimating

ELEMENTAL COSTS

RESIDENTIAL DEVELOPMENT *continued*

El. Ref.	Element	Total Cost £	Cost/m² £
	FIT OUT – AFFORDABLE		
5A	Sanitaryware	183,600.00	36.72
5C	Disposal Installations	Included in 5A	
5D	Water Installations	231,500.00	46.30
5F	Space Heating and Air Treatment	86,500.00	17.30
5G	Ventilating Services	113,000.00	27.60
5H	Electrical Installation	156,000.00	31.20
5I	Gas Installation	27,000.00	5.40
5K	Protective Installations	-	-
5L	Communications Installations	70,000.00	14.00
5M	Special Installations	21,000.00	4.20
	Summary total (based on gross floor area)	888,600.00	182.72

ELEMENTAL COSTS

SUPERMARKET

Supermarket located in the South East with a total gross floor area of 4,000m², including a sales area of 2,350m². The building is on one level and incorporates a main sales, coffee shop, bakery, offices and amenities areas and warehouse.

Cost Summary

El. Ref.	Element	Total Cost £	Cost/m² £
5A	Sanitaryware	6,396.00	1.59
5C	Disposal Installations		
	Soil and Waste	10,341.00	2.58
5D	Water Installations		
	Hot and Cold water services	57,124.00	14.28
5E	Heat Source...	72,698.00	18.17
5F	Space Heating and Air Treatment		
	Heating with ventilation with supplemental cooling via DX units	137,768.00	34.44
5G	Ventilating Services		
	Supply and extract system	45,753.00	11.43
5H	Electrical Installation		
	Generator	13,203.00	3.30
	Panels / Boards...	41,951.00	10.48
	LV supply/distribution	120,942.00	30.23
	General lighting	96,926.00	24.23
	Emergency lighting	24,360.00	6.09
	Small power	72,909.00	18.22
5I	Gas Installation		
	Gas mains services to plantroom	13,858.00	3.46
5K	Protection		
	Sprinklers	106,391.00	26.59
	Lightning protection...	3,186.00	0.79
5L	Communication Installation		
	Fire alarms, detection and public address	25,204.00	6.30
	CCTV	20,473.00	5.11
	Intruder alarm, detection and store security	45,714.00	11.42
5M	Special Installations		
	BMS Installation	44,774.00	11.19
	Refrigeration		
	Installation	106,201.00	26.55
	Plant	109,087.00	27.27
	Cold Store	40,302.00	10.07
	Cabinets	299,047.00	74.76
	Summary total	1,513,978.00	371.55

Approximate Estimating

ELEMENTAL COSTS

DISTRIBUTION CENTRE

Distribution centre located in London with a total gross floor area of 75,000m², including a refrigerated cold box of 17,500m².

The building is on one level and incorporates a office area, vehicle recovery unit, gate house and plantrooms

Cost Summary

El. Ref.	Element	Total Cost £	Cost/m² £
5C	Disposal Installations		
	Soil and Waste	149,080.00	1.98
	Rainwater...	481,449.00	6.41
5D	Water Installations		
	Hot and Cold water services	128,866.00	1.71
5F	Space Heating and Air Treatment		
	Heating with ventilation to offices, displacement system to		
	main warehouse...	1,661,653.00	22.15
5G	Ventilating Services		
	Smoke extract system...	371,928.00	4.95
5H	Electrical Installation		
	Generator	1,127,576.00	15.03
	Main HV installation...	1,302,375.00	17.36
	MV distribution...	806,882.00	10.75
	Lighting installation...	740,320.00	9.87
	Small power installation...	907,828.00	12.10
5I	Gas Installation		
	Gas mains services to plantroom	41,397.00	0.55
5K	Protection		
	Sprinklers including racking protection...	3,295,392.00	43.93
	Lightning protection...	8,141.00	0.10
5L	Communication Installation		
	Fire alarms, detection and public address	839,091.00	11.18
	CCTV	538,693.00	7.18
5M	Special Installations		
	BMS Installation	419,347.00	5.59
	Refrigeration		
	Installation	2,678,883.00	35.71
	Summary total	14,760,860.00	206.45

ELEMENTAL COSTS

LONDON UNDERGROUND STATION (ABOVE GROUND)

New London Underground tube station. The station building is above ground and 943m². The provision of communications systems, ticket machines, gates and barriers are provided under the PFI/PPI contracts and are excluded from this model. All network wide services to the station are also excluded and will be provided on the same basis. All incoming services, with the exception of a dedicated substation, are excluded. Lifts are normally bespoke to LUL standards and are also excluded

Cost Summary

El. Ref.	Element	Total Cost £	Cost/m² £
5A	Sanitaryware	22,491.00	23.85
5C	Disposal Installations		
	Rainwater	6,635.00	7.04
	Soil and waste	10,616.00	11.26
5D	Water Installations		
	Hot and Cold water services	22,001.00	23.33
5E	Heat Source	Included in 5F	
5F	Space Heating and Air Treatment		
	LTHW Heating system	23,185.00	24.59
	Comfort cooling to ticket office and BoH areas	29,761.00	31.56
5G	Ventilating Services		
	Ventilation to staff accommodation and BoH areas	19,593.00	20.78
	Toilet extract installation	5,314.00	5.64
	Ventilation to mechanical and electrical plantrooms	9,212.00	9.77
5H	Electrical Installation		
	Incoming service and distribution system including new utility substation mains LV switchgear, submains supplies from switchboards within integrated containment system	278,108.00	294.92
	Earthing and bonding	3,747.00	3.97
	Electromagnetic Compatibility.............................	6,622.00	7.02
	Lighting system to all areas	82,843.00	87.85
	Emergency lighting to all areas	32,923.00	34.91
	Small power to BoH and public areas	23,957.00	25.41
	High security and essential supplies	13,243.00	14.04
	Power to mechanical systems, lifts, security and station equipment	23,176.00	24.58
5I	Gas Installation	12,600.00	13.36
5K	Protective Installations		
	Hosereels	7,787.00	8.26
	Lightning protection...	3,671.00	3.89
	Carried forward	637,485.00	676.03

Approximate Estimating

ELEMENTAL COSTS

LONDON UNDERGROUND STATION (ABOVE GROUND) *continued*

El. Ref.	Element	Total Cost £	Cost/m² £
	Brought forward	637,485.00	676.03
5L	Communication Installation		
	Fire, smoke detection and alarm system	55,148.00	58.48
	Public address	17,216.00	18.26
	Customer information system including all screens, associated cabling and control links incorporating the Passenger Help points and induction loops	67,540.00	71.62
	Telecommunications, data and TV wiring including tray and ladder racks	19,865.00	21.07
	CCTV installation	97,338.00	103.22
	Intruder alarm system...	13,243.00	14.06
	Access control system	19,865.00	21.07
5M	Special Installations		
	Building Management System	37,800.00	40.08
	Summary total	965,500.00	1,023.89

ELEMENTAL COSTS

LONDON STATION PLATFORMS (ABOVE GROUND)

Provision of new above ground station platforms

Cost Summary

El. Ref.	Element	Total Cost £
5A	Sanitaryware	N/A
5C	Disposal Installations	
	Rainwater	3,276.00
5D	Water Installations	
	Hot and Cold water services	N/A
5E	Heat Source	N/A
5F	Space Heating and Air Treatment	N/A
5G	Ventilating Services	N/A
5H	Electrical Installation	
	LV Switchgear and distribution (included in station costs)	N/A
	Earthing and bonding	1,326.00
	Electromagnetic Compatibility	1,326.00
	Lighting system to all areas including all luminaires, lamps, wiring, switching and control gear...	214,092.00
	Emergency lighting to all areas	5,303.00
	Small power to all operational areas of customer information system and security system including all switching and containment...	12,262.00
5I	Gas Installation	N/A
5K	Protective Installations	
	Hosereels	15,226.00
	Lightning protection...	5,538.00
5L	Communications Installation	
	Fire, smoke detection and alarm system	8,660.00
	Public address system	20,242.00
	CCTV Installation	98,114.00
	Access control system	12,264.00
	Customer information system including all screens, associated cabling and control links and incorporating the Passenger Help points and induction loops	29,013.00
	Drivers information system including all screens, associated cabling and containment	13,495.00
	Telecommunications, data and TV wiring including tray and ladder racks (by PFI/PPP Contractor)	N/A
5M	Special Installations	
	Building Management System (included in station costs)	N/A
	Summary total	473,137.00

Approximate Estimating

ELEMENTAL COSTS

BUILDING MANAGEMENT INSTALLATIONS

New office with a gross area of 10,000 m^2 and a nett lettable area of 7,200 m^2. Building comprises of 4 floors, basement and roof plantroom. System comprises monitoring and control of the mechanical services via direct digital control (DDC) outstations via a central operators terminal.

Whilst the shell and core installation is constant, we have identified three options for the Category A fit out.

Cost Summary

El. Ref.	Element	Total Cost £	Cost/Point £
	Shell and Core – 440 Points		
1.0	**Central Equipment** Operator Station Software Printers Laptop PC Modems, multiplexers etc...	11,445.00	26.01
2.0	**Field Equipment** Network devices Valves/Actuators Sensing/Interfacing devices...	35,470.00	80.61
3.0	**Cabling – Power/Control** Power – from MCC to equipment Control – from MCC/Outstations to equipment Cable ways...	91,572.00	208.12
4.0	**Motor Control Centres** Motor control centres including control equipment Field mount inverter drives...	57,249.00	130.11
5.0	**Programming** Central facility software Network devices software Graphics...	25,738.00	58.50
6.0	**On site testing and Commissioning** Operating stations & Equipment Software and graphics Power cabling Control cabling – point to point MCC's & inverters...	19,277.00	43.81
7.0	**On site testing and Commissioning** Operating stations & Equipment Software and graphics MCC's & inverters...	4,015.00	9.13
	Total for Shell and Core...	244,766.00	556.29

ELEMENTAL COSTS

BUILDING MANAGEMENT INSTALLATIONS *continued*

El. Ref.	Element	Total Cost £	Cost/Point £
	Category A Fit Out		
	Option 1 – 189 nr 4 pipe fan coil – 756 points		
1.0	**Field Equipment** Network devices Valves/actuators Sensing devices...	48,216.00	63.78
2.0	**Cabling** Power – from local isolator to DDC controller Control – from DDC controller to field equipment...	27,243.00	36.04
3.0	**Programming** Software – central facility Software – network devices Graphics...	15,081.00	19.95
4.0	**On site testing and commissioning** Equipment Programming/graphics Power and control cabling...	15,706.00	20.78
	Total Option 1 – four pipe fan coil...	106,246.00	140.55
	Category A Fit Out		
	Option 2 – 189 nr 2 pipe fan coil with electric heating – 756 points		
1.0	**Field Equipment** Network devices Valves/actuators/thyristors Sensing devices...	61,838.00	81.80
2.0	**Cabling** Power – from local isolator to DDC controller Control – from DDC controller to field equipment...	28,526.00	37.73
3.0	**Programming** Software – central facility Software – network devices Graphics...	15,081.00	19.95
4.0	**On site testing and commissioning** Equipment Programming/graphics Power and control cabling...	15,706.00	20.78
	Total Option 2 – 2 pipe fan coil with electric heating...	121,151.00	160.26

ELEMENTAL COSTS

BUILDING MANAGEMENT INSTALLATIONS *continued*

El. Ref.	Element	Total Cost £	Cost/Point £
	Category A Fit Out		
	Option 3 – 180 Nr Chilled Beams with perimeter heating – 567 points		
1.0	**Field Equipment** Network devices Valves/actuators Sensing devices...	43,676.00	77.03
2.0	**Cabling** Power – from local isolator to DDC controller Control – from DDC controller to field equipment...	28,973.00	51.10
3.0	**Programming** Software – central facility Software – network devices Graphics...	15,081.00	26.60
4.0	**On site testing and commissioning** Equipment Programming/graphics Power and control cabling...	16,120.00	28.42
	Total Option 3 – Chilled beams with perimeter heating.......	103,850.00	183.15
	Combined Shell & Core and Fit Out		
1.0	**Option 1 – 4 pipe fan coil – 1196 points** Shell and core Category A Fit out	351,022.00	293.50
2.0	**Option 2 – 2 pipe fan coil with electrical heating – 1196 points** Shell and core Category A Fit out	365,929.00	305.96
3.0	**Option 3 – Chilled beams with perimeter heating – 1007 points** Shell and core Category A Fit out	348,624.00	281.49

DAVIS LANGDON

Maximising value and reducing risk for clients investing in infrastructure, construction and property

managed
solutions

Project Management | Cost Management | Management Consulting | Legal Support | Specification Consulting | Engineering Services | Property Tax & Finance

DAVIS LANGDON

EUROPE & MIDDLE EAST
office locations

ENGLAND

DAVIS LANGDON

LONDON
Mid City Place
71 High Holborn
London WC1V 6QS
Tel: (020) 7061 7000
Fax: (020) 7061 7061
Email: neill.morrison@davislangdon.com

BIRMINGHAM
75-77 Colmore Row
Birmingham
B3 2HD
Tel: (0121) 710 1100
Fax: (0121) 710 1399
Email: david.daly@davislangdon.com

BRISTOL
St Lawrence House
29/31 Broad Street
Bristol BS1 2HF
Tel: (0117) 927 7832
Fax: (0117) 925 1350
Email: alan.francis@davislangdon.com

CAMBRIDGE
36 Storey's Way
Cambridge
CB3 0DT
Tel: (01223) 351 258
Fax: (01223) 321 002
Email: laurence.brett@davislangdon.com

LEEDS
No 4 The Embankment
Victoria Wharf
Sovereign Street
Leeds LS1 4BA
Tel: (0113) 243 2481
Fax: (0113) 242 4601
Email: duncan.sissons@davislangdon.com

LIVERPOOL
Cunard Building
Water Street
Liverpool L3 1JR
Tel: (0151) 236 1992
Fax: (0151) 227 5401
Email: andrew.stevenson@davislangdon.com

MAIDSTONE
11 Tower View
Kings Hill
West Malling
Kent ME19 4UY
Tel: (01732) 840 429
Fax: (01732) 842 305
Email: nick.leggett@davislangdon.com

MANCHESTER
Cloister House
Riverside
New Bailey Street
Manchester M3 5AG
Tel: (0161) 819 7600
Fax: (0161) 819 1818
Email: paul.stanion@davislangdon.com

MILTON KEYNES
Everest House
Rockingham Drive
Linford Wood
Milton Keynes
MK14 6LY
Tel: (01908) 304 700
Fax: (01908) 660 059
Email: kevin.sims@davislangdon.com

NORWICH
63 Thorpe Road
Norwich NR1 1UD
Tel: (01603) 628 194
Fax: (01603) 615 928
Email: michael.ladbrook@davislangdon.com

OXFORD
Avalon House
Marcham Road
Abingdon
Oxford OX14 1TZ
Tel: (01235) 555 025
Fax: (01235) 554 909
Email: paul.coomber@davislangdon.com

PETERBOROUGH
Clarence House
Minerva Business Park
Lynchwood
Peterborough PE2 6FT
Tel: (01733) 362 000
Fax: (01733) 230 875
Email: stuart.bremner@davislangdon.com

PLYMOUTH
1 Ensign House
Parkway Court
Longbridge Road
Plymouth PL6 8LR
Tel: (01752) 827 444
Fax: (01752) 221 219
Email: gareth.steventon@davislangdon.com

SOUTHAMPTON
Brunswick House
Brunswick Place
Southampton SO15 2AP
Tel: (023) 8033 3438
Fax: (023) 8022 6099
Email: chris.tremellen@davislangdon.com /
peter.boote@davislangdon.com

**DAVIS LANGDON
LEGAL SUPPORT**
Mid City Place
71 High Holborn
London WC1V 6QS
Tel: (020) 7061 7000
Fax: (020) 7061 7061
Email: mark.hackett@davislangdon.com

**DAVIS LANGDON
CONSULTANCY**
Mid City Place
71 High Holborn
London WC1V 6QS
Tel: (020) 7061 7007
Fax: (020) 7061 7005
Email: john.connaughton@davislangdon.com

**DAVIS LANGDON
SCHUMANN SMITH**
Southgate House
St Georges Way
Stevenage
Hertfordshire SG1 1HG
Tel: (01438) 742 642
Fax: (01438) 742 632
Email: nick.schumann@schumannsmith.com

**DAVIS LANGDON
MOTT GREEN & WALL**
Mid City Place
71 High Holborn
London WC1V 6QS
Tel: (020) 7061 7777
Fax: (020) 7061 7009
Email: general@mottgreenwall.co.uk

**DAVIS LANGDON
CROSHER & JAMES**
Mid City Place
71 High Holborn
London WC1V 6QS
Tel: (020) 7061 7077
Fax: (020) 7061 7078
Email: tony.llewellyn@crosherjames.com

BIRMINGHAM
102 New Street
Birmingham B2 4HQ
Tel: (0121) 632 3600
Fax: (0121) 632 3601
Email: clive.searle@crosherjames.com

CARDIFF
4 Piershead Street
Capital Waterside
Cardiff
CF10 4QP
Tel: (029) 2049 7497
Fax: (029) 2049 7111
Email: michael.murraym@crosherjames.com

EDINBURGH
39 Melville Street
Edinburgh
EH3 7JF
Tel: (0131) 220 4225
Fax: (0131) 220 4226
Email: ian.mcfarlane@crosherjames.com

GLASGOW
Monteith House
11 George Square
Glasgow
G2 1DY
Tel: (0141) 248 0333
Fax: (0141) 248 0313
Email: fraserk@nbwcrosherjames.com

MANCHESTER
Cloister House
Riverside
New Bailey Street
Manchester M3 5AG
Tel: (0161) 819 7600
Fax: (0161) 819 1818
Email: sharmas@nbwcrosherjames.com

SOUTHAMPTON
Brunswick House
Brunswick Place
Southampton SO15 2AP
Tel: (023) 8068 2800
Fax: (023) 8033 6360
Email: reesd@nbwcrosherjames.com

SCOTLAND

DAVIS LANGDON

GLASGOW
Monteith House
11 George Square
Glasgow G2 1DY
Tel: (0141) 248 0300
Fax: (0141) 248 0303
Email:
sam.mackenzie@davislangdon.com

EDINBURGH
39 Melville Street
Edinburgh
EH3 7JF
Tel: (0131) 240 1350
Fax: (0131) 240 1399
Email: erland.rendall@davislangdon.com

WALES

CARDIFF
4 Pierhead Street
Capital Waterside
Cardiff CF10 4QP
Tel: (029) 2049 7497
Fax: (029) 2049 7111
Email: paul.edwards@davislangdon.com

IRELAND

DAVIS LANGDON PKS

DUBLIN
24 Lower Hatch Street
Dublin 2
Ireland
Tel: (00 353 1) 676 3671
Fax: (00 353 1) 676 3672
Email: mwebb@dlpks.ie

GALWAY
Heritage Hall
Kirwan's Lane
Galway, Ireland
Tel: (00 353 91) 530 199
Fax: (00 353 91) 530 198
Email: joregan@dlpks.ie

LIMERICK
8 The Crescent
Limerick
Ireland
Tel: (00 353 61) 318 870
Fax: (00 353 61) 318 871
Email: cbarry@dlpks.ie

SPAIN

DAVIS LANGDON EDETCO

BARCELONA
C/Muntaner, 479, 12°
Barcelona 08021
Spain
Tel: (00 34 93) 418 6899
Fax: (00 34 93) 211 0003
Email: fmonells@barcelona.edetco.com

GIRONA
C/Salt 10
Girona 17005
Spain
Tel: (00 34 97) 223 8000
Fax: (00 34 97) 224 2661
Email: girona@girona.edetco.com

FRANCE

DAVIS LANGDON
5 Rue St Germain l'Auxerrois
75001 Paris
France
Tel: (00 33 1) 5340 9480
Fax: (00 33 1) 5340 9481
Email: andrew.richardson@dleparis.com

POLAND

DAVIS LANGDON
Warsaw Trade Tower
ul. Chlodna 51, 26th Floor
00-867 Warsaw, Poland
Tel: (00 48 22) 455 39 00
Fax: (00 48 22) 455 39 01
Email: warsaw@davislangdon-polska.pl

RUSSIA

DAVIS LANGDON
Office 5
Myasnitskaya
Moscow, 101000
Russia
Tel: (00 7 095) 933 7810
Fax: (00 7 095) 933 7811
Email: stephen.thomas@davislangdon.com

MIDDLE EAST

DAVIS LANGDON
PO Box 13-5422-Shouran
Beirut
Lebanon
Tel: (00 9611) 780 111
Fax: (00 9611) 809 045
Email: DLL.MI@cyberia.net.lb

ARABIAN GULF

DAVIS LANGDON

BAHRAIN
3rd Floor Building 256
Road No 3605
Area No 336
PO Box 640, Manama
State of Bahrain
Arabian Gulf
Tel: (00 973) 1782 7567
Fax: (00 973) 1772 8257
Email: david.galbraith@davislangdon-bahrain.com

UNITED ARAB EMIRATES
PO Box 7856
Office 410
Oud Metha Office Building
Dubai, UAE
Tel: (00 9714) 32 42 919
Fax: (00 9714) 32 42 838
Email: neil.taylor@davislangdon-dubai.com

QATAR
PO Box 3206, Doha
State of Qatar
Tel: (00 974) 4580 150
Fax: (00 974) 4697 905
Email: david.craig@davislangdon-qatar.com

EGYPT
35 Misr Helwan Road
Maadi 11431
Cairo
Egypt
Tel: (00 20 2) 526 2319
Fax: (00 20 2) 527 1338
Email: dlegypt@link.net

Specialist Service Lines
Project Management | Cost Management | Management Consulting | Legal Support | Specification Consulting | Engineering Services | Property Tax & Finance

Specialist Sectors
Arts | Commercial Offices | Distribution | Education | Food Processing | Health | Heritage | Hotels & Leisure | Industrial | Infrastructure | Public Buildings | Regeneration | Residential | Retail | Sports | Transportation

Davis Langdon LLP is a member firm of Davis Langdon & Seah International, with offices throughout Europe and the Middle East, Asia, Australasia, Africa and the USA

PART TWO

Material Costs/
Measured Work Prices

Mechanical Installations

R : Disposal Systems
R10 : Rainwater Pipework/Gutters   69
R11 : Above Ground Drainage   88

S : Piped Supply Systems
S10 : Cold Water   111
S11 : Hot Water   164
S32 : Natural Gas   168
S41 : Fuel Oil Storage/Distribution   172
S60 : Fire Hose Reels   174
S61 : Dry Risers   175
S63 : Sprinklers   176
S65 : Fire Hydrants   181

T : Mechanical/Cooling/Heating Systems
T10 : Gas/Oil Fired Boilers   183
T13 : Packaged Steam Generators   196
T31 : Low Temperature Hot Water Heating   197
T33 : Steam Heating   284
T42 : Local Heating Units   288
T60 : Central Refrigeration Plant   289
T61 : Chilled Water   297
T70 : Local Cooling Units   302

U : Ventilation/Air Conditioning Systems
U10 : General Ventilation   304
U14 : Ductwork; Fire Rated   391
U30 : Low Velocity Air Conditioning   412
U31 : VAV Air Conditioning   415
U41 : Fan Coil Air Conditioning   416
U70 : Air Curtains   420

Electrical Installations

V : Electrical Supply/Power/Lighting Systems
V10 : Electrical Generation Plant   427
V11 : HV Supply   429
V20 : LV Distribution   434
V21 : General Lighting   504
V22 : General LV Power   513
V32 : Uninterruptible Power Supply   520
V40 : Emergency Lighting   522

W : Communications/Security/Control
W10 : Telecommunications   527
W20 : Radio/Television   529
W23 : Clocks   531
W30 : Data Transmission   532
W40 : Access Control   539
W41 : Security Detection and Alarm   540
W50 : Fire Detection and Alarm   541
W51 : Earthing and Bonding   544
W52 : Lightning Protection   545
W60 : Central Control/Building Management   549

Mechanical Installations

Material Costs/Measured Work Prices

DIRECTIONS

The following explanations are given for each of the column headings and letter codes.

Unit	Prices for each unit are given as singular (i.e. 1 metre, 1 nr) unless stated otherwise
Net price	Industry tender prices, plus nominal allowance for fixings, waste and applicable trade discounts.
Material cost	Net price plus percentage allowance for overheads, profit and preliminaries.
Labour norms	In man-hours for each operation.
Labour cost	Labour constant multiplied by the appropriate all-in man-hour cost based on gang rate. (See also relevant Rates of Wages Section) plus percentage allowance for overheads, profit and preliminaries
Measured work Price (total rate)	Material cost plus Labour cost.

MATERIAL COSTS

The Material Costs given are based at Third Quarter 2005 but exclude any charges in respect of VAT.

MEASURED WORK PRICES

These prices are intended to apply to new work in the London area. The prices are for reasonable quantities of work and the user should make suitable adjustments if the quantities are especially small or especially large. Adjustments may also be required for locality (e.g. outside London – refer to cost indices in approximate estimating section for details of adjustment factors) and for the market conditions (e.g. volume of work secured or being tendered) at the time of use.

MECHANICAL INSTALLATIONS

The labour rate has been based on average gang rates per man hour effective from 9 January 2006 including allowances for all other emoluments and expenses. To this rate has been added 7.5% and 12.5% to cover preliminary items, site and head office overheads together with 5% for profit, resulting in an inclusive rate of £22.67 per man hour. The rate has been calculated on a working year of 2,016 hours; a detailed build-up of the rate is given at the end of these directions.

DUCTWORK INSTALLATIONS

The labour rate has been based on an average gang rate per man hour effective from 3 October 2005. To this rate has been added 12.50% plus 25% to cover shop, site and head office overheads and preliminary items together with 10% for profit, resulting in an inclusive rate of £28.20 per man hour. The rate has been calculated on a working year of 2,016 hours; a detailed build-up of the rate is given at the end of these directions.

In calculating the 'Measured Work Prices' the following assumptions have been made:
- (a) That the work is carried out as a sub-contract under the Standard Form of Building Contract.
- (b) That, unless otherwise stated, the work is being carried out in open areas at a height which would not require more than simple scaffolding.
- (c) That the building in which the work is being carried out is no more than six storey's high.

Where these assumptions are not valid, as for example where work is carried out in ducts and similar confined spaces or in multi-storey structures when additional time is needed to get to and from upper floors, then an appropriate adjustment must be made to the prices. Such adjustment will normally be to the labour element only.

Note : The rates do not include for any uplift applied i.e. if the ductwork package is procured via the Mechanical Sub Contractor

DIRECTIONS

LABOUR RATE - MECHANICAL

The annual cost of notional twelve man gang

		FOREMAN	SENIOR CRAFTSMAN (+2 Welding skill)	SENIOR CRAFTSMAN	CRAFTSMAN	INSTALLER	MATE (Over 18)	SUB TOTALS
		1 NR	1 NR	2 NR	4 NR	2 NR	2 NR	
Hourly Rate from 3 October 2005		13.20	11.35	10.90	10.00	9.07	7.64	
Working hours per annum per man		1,702.40	1,702.40	1,702.40	1,702.40	1,702.40	1,702.40	
x Hourly rate x nr of men = £ per annum		22,471.68	19,322.24	37,112.32	68,096.00	30,881.54	26,012.67	203,896.45
Overtime Rate		18.60	16.00	15.37	14.10	12.79	10.77	
Overtime hours per annum per man		313.60	313.60	313.60	313.60	313.60	313.60	
x Hourly rate x nr of men = £ per annum		5,832.96	5,017.60	9,640.06	17,687.04	8,021.88	6,754.94	52,954.50
Total		28,304.64	24,339.84	46,752.38	85,783.04	38,903.42	32,767.62	256,850.94
Incentive schemes	5.00%	1,415.23	1,216.99	2,337.62	4,289.15	1,945.17	1,638.38	12,842.55
Daily Travel Time Allowance (15-20 miles each way)		2.19	2.19	2.19	2.19	2.19	1.88	
Days per annum per man		224.00	224.00	224.00	224.00	224.00	224.00	
x nr of men = £ per annum		490.56	490.56	981.12	1,962.24	981.12	842.24	5,747.84
Daily Travel Fare (10-20 miles each way)		6.00	6.00	6.00	6.00	6.00	6.00	
Days per annum per man		224.00	224.00	224.00	224.00	224.00	224.00	
x nr of men = £ per annum		1,344.00	1,344.00	2,688.00	5,376.00	2,688.00	2,688.00	16,128.00
Employers Contributions to EasyBuild Stakeholder Pension (Death and accident cover is provided free):								
Number of weeks		52	52	52	52	52	52	
Total weekly £ contribution each		3.50	3.50	3.50	3.50	3.50	3.50	
£ Contributions/annum		182.00	182.00	364.00	728.00	364.00	364.00	2,184.00
National Insurance Contributions:								
Wkly gross pay (subject to NI) each		31,554.43	27,391.39	52,759.12	97,410.43	44,517.72	37,936.24	
% of NI Contributions		12.8	12.8	12.8	12.8	12.8	12.8	
£ Contributions/annum		3318.07	2785.20	5311.38	9584.95	4256.48	3414.05	28,670.12

DIRECTIONS

Holiday Credit and Welfare Contributions:								
Number of weeks		52	52	52	52	52	52	
Total weekly £ contribution each		68.61	59.86	57.68	53.33	48.88	42.03	
x nr of men = £ contributions/annum		3,567.72	3,112.72	5,998.72	11,092.64	5,083.52	4,371.12	33,226.44
Holiday Top-up Funding including overtime		12.20	10.40	10.01	9.23	8.37	7.05	
Cost		634.40	540.80	1,041.04	1,919.84	870.48	733.20	5,739.76
						SUB-TOTAL		361,389.65
			TRAINING (INCLUDING ANY TRADE REGISTRATIONS) – SAY				1.00%	3,613.90
			SEVERANCE PAY AND SUNDRY COSTS – SAY				1.50%	5,475.05
			EMPLOYER'S LIABILITY AND THIRD PARTY INSURANCE – SAY				2.00%	7,409.57
			ANNUAL COST OF NOTIONAL GANG					377,888.18
	MEN ACTUALLY WORKING = 10.5		THEREFORE ANNUAL COST PER PRODUCTIVE MAN					35,989.35
AVERAGE NR OF HOURS WORKED PER MAN = 2016			THEREFORE ALL IN MAN HOUR					17.85
			PRELIMINARY ITEMS - SAY				7.50%	1.34
			SITE AND HEAD OFFICE OVERHEADS - SAY				12.50%	2.40
			PROFIT - SAY				5.00%	1.08
			THEREFORE INCLUSIVE MAN HOUR					22.67

Notes:

(1)   The following assumptions have been made in the above calculations:-
(a)   The working week of 38 hours i.e. the normal working week as defined by the National Agreement.
(b)   The actual hours worked are five days of 9 hours each.
(c)   A working year of 2016 hours.
(d)   Five days in the year are lost through sickness or similar reason.
(2)   The incentive scheme addition of 5% is intended to reflect bonus schemes typically in use.
(3)   National insurance contributions are those effective from 6 April 2005.
(4)   Weekly Holiday Credit/Welfare Stamp values are those effective from 3 October 2005.
(5)   Rates are based from 3 October 2005.
(6)   Fares (Waterloo to New Malden) effective at June 2005.
(7)   Easybuild Stakeholder Pension Contributions effective from 4 August 2003.
(8)   Does not include for major project status.
(9)   Caution should be applied when utilising the labour rate and the 'all-in' rate it applies to, as the size and complexity of the project will reflect in the gang size.

DIRECTIONS

LABOUR RATE - DUCTWORK

The annual cost of notional eight man gang

		FOREMAN 1 NR	SENIOR CRAFTSMAN 1 NR	CRAFTSMAN 4 NR	INSTALLER 2 NR	SUB TOTALS
Hourly Rate from 3 October 2005		13.20	10.90	10.00	9.07	
Working hours per annum per man		1,702.40	1,702.40	1,702.40	1,702.40	
x Hourly rate x nr of men = £ per annum		22,471.68	18,556.16	68,096.00	30,881.54	140,005.38
Overtime Rate		18.60	15.37	14.10	12.79	
Overtime hours per annum per man		313.60	313.60	313.60	313.60	
x hourly rate x nr of men = £ per		5,832.96	4,820.03	17,687.04	8,021.88	36,361.92
Total		28,304.64	23,376.19	85.783.04	38,903.42	176,367.30
Incentive schemes	5.00%	1,415.23	1,168.81	4,289.15	1,945.17	8,818.36
Daily Travel Time Allowance (15-20 miles each way)		6.00	6.00	6.00	6.00	
Days per annum per man		224	224	224	224	
x nr of men = £ per annum		1,344.00	1,344.00	5,376.00	2,688.00	10,752.00
Daily Travel Fare (10-20 miles each		10.00	10.00	10.00	10.0	
Days per annum per man		224	224	224	224	
x nr of men = £ per annum		2,240.00	2,240.00	8,960.00	4.480.00	17,920.00
Employers Contributions to						
EasyBuild Stakeholder Pension (Death cover is provided free)						
Number of weeks		52	52	52	52	
Total weekly £ contribution each		3.50	3.50	3.50	3.50	
£ Contributions/annum		182.00	182.00	728.00	364.00	1,456.00
National Insurance Contributions:						
Weekly gross pay (subject to NI) each		33,303.87	28,129.00	104,408.19	48,016.60	
% of NI Contributions		12.8	12.8	12.8	12.8	
£ Contributions/annum		3,542.00	2,879.62	10,480.66	4,704.33	21,606.61
Holiday Credit and Welfare contributions:						
Number of weeks		52	52	52	52	
Total weekly £ contribution each		68.61	57.68	53.33	48.88	
x nr of men = £ Contributions/annum		3,567.72	2,999.36	11,092.64	5,083.52	22,743.24

DIRECTIONS

Holiday Top-up Funding including overtime		12.20	10.01	9.23	8.37	
Cost		634.40	520.52	1,919.84	870.48	3,945.24

SUB-TOTAL			263,608.75
TRAINING (INCLUDING ANY TRADE REGISTRATIONS) - SAY	1.00%		2,636.09
SEVERANCE PAY AND SUNDRY COSTS - SAY	1.50%		3,993.67
EMPLOYER'S LIABILITY AND THIRD PARTY INSURANCE - SAY	2.00%		5,404.77
ANNUAL COST OF NOTIONAL GANG			275,643.28
MEN ACTUALLY WORKING = 7.5 THEREFORE ANNUAL COST PER PRODUCTIVE MAN			36,572.44
AVERAGE NR OF HOURS WORKED PER MAN = 2016 THEREFORE ALL IN MAN HOUR			18.23
PRELIMINARY ITEMS - SAY	12.50%		2.28
SITE AND HEAD OFFICE OVERHEADS - SAY	25.00%		5.13
PROFIT - SAY	10.00%		2.56
THEREFORE INCLUSIVE MAN HOUR			28.20

Notes:

(1)   The following assumptions have been made in the above calculations:-
    (a)   The working week of 38 hours i.e. the normal working week as defined by the National Agreement.
    (b)   The actual hours worked are five days of 9 hours each.
    (c)   A working year of 2016 hours.
    (d)   Five days in the year are lost through sickness or similar reason.
(2)   The incentive scheme addition of 5% is intended to reflect bonus schemes typically in use.
(3)   National insurance contributions are those effective from 6 April 2005.
(4)   Weekly Holiday Credit/Welfare Stamp values are those effective from 6 October 2003.
(5)   Rates are based from 3 October 2005.
(6)   Fares (New Malden to Waterloo is £6.00 plus £4.00 Zone 1 Return) current at June 2005.
(7)   Easybuild Stakeholder Pension Contributions effective from 4 August 2003.
(8)   Does not include for major project status.
(9)   Caution should be applied when utilising the labour rate and the 'all-in' rate it applies to, as the size and complexity of the project will reflect in the gang size.

2nd Edition
Spon's Irish Construction Price Book

Franklin + Andrews

This new edition of *Spon's Irish Construction Price Book*, edited by Franklin + Andrews, is the only complete and up-to-date source of cost data for this important market.

• All the materials costs, labour rates, labour constants and cost per square metre are based on current conditions in Ireland

• Structured according to the new Agreed Rules of Measurement (second edition)

• 30 pages of Approximate Estimating Rates for quick pricing

This price book is an essential aid to profitable contracting for all those operating in Ireland's booming construction industry.

Franklin + Andrews, Construction Economists, have offices in 100 countries and in-depth experience and expertise in all sectors of the construction industry.

April 2004: 246x174 mm: 448 pages
HB: 0-415-34409-3: £125.00

To Order: Tel: +44 (0) 1264 343071 Fax: +44 (0) 1264 343005, or
Post: Taylor and Francis Customer Services, Thomson Publishing Services, Cheriton House, Andover, Hants, SP10 5BE, UK Email: book.orders@tandf.co.uk

For a complete listing of all our titles visit:
www.sponpress.com

Taylor & Francis
Taylor & Francis Group plc

Spon's Estimating Costs Guide to Finishings
Painting and Decorating, Plastering and Tiling

Bryan Spain

Especially written for contractors and small businesses carrying out small works, Spon's Estimating Costs Guide to Finishings contains accurate information on thousands of rates, each broken down to labour, material overheads and profit.

This is the first book to include typical project costs for painting and wallpapering, plasterwork, floor and wall tiles, rendering, and external work.

More than just a price book, it gives easy-to-read, professional advice on setting up and running a business including help on producing estimates faster, and keeping estimates accurate and competitive.

Suitable for any size firm from one-man-band to established business, this book contains valuable commercial and cost information that contractors can't afford to be without.

March 2005: 216x138 mm: 288 pages
PB: 0-415-34411-5: £24.99

To Order: Tel: +44 (0) 1264 343071 Fax: +44 (0) 1264 343005, or
Post: Taylor and Francis Customer Services, Thomson Publishing Services, Cheriton House, Andover, Hants, SP10 5BE, UK Email: book.orders@tandf.co.uk

For a complete listing of all our titles visit :
www.sponpress.com

Taylor & Francis
Taylor & Francis Group plc

R:DISPOSAL SYSTEMS

Item	Net Price £	Material £	Labour hours	Labour £	Unit	Total rate £
R10: RAINWATER PIPEWORK/GUTTERS						
PVC-U gutters: push fit joints; fixed with brackets to backgrounds; BS 4576, BS EN 607						
Half round gutter						
75mm	0.93	1.19	0.69	15.65	m	**16.84**
110 mm	1.77	2.27	0.64	14.51	m	**16.78**
150mm	2.79	3.57	0.82	18.60	m	**22.17**
Extra over fittings half round PVC-U gutter						
Union						
75mm	0.94	1.20	0.19	4.31	nr	**5.51**
112mm	2.02	2.59	0.24	5.44	nr	**8.03**
150mm	2.86	3.85	0.28	6.35	nr	**10.20**
Rainwater pipe outlets						
Running: 75 x 53mm dia	2.02	2.59	0.12	2.72	nr	**5.31**
Running: 100 x 68mm dia	2.50	3.20	0.12	2.72	nr	**5.92**
Running: 150 x 110mm dia	5.11	6.54	0.12	2.72	nr	**9.27**
Stop end: 100 x 68mm dia	2.42	3.10	0.12	2.72	nr	**5.82**
Internal stop ends: short						
75mm	0.91	2.08	0.09	2.04	nr	**4.12**
100mm	1.10	2.27	0.09	2.04	nr	**4.31**
150mm	1.88	2.41	0.09	2.04	nr	**4.45**
External stop ends: short						
75mm	2.74	3.51	0.09	2.04	nr	**5.55**
100mm	1.10	4.61	0.09	2.04	nr	**6.65**
150mm	1.88	2.41	0.09	2.04	nr	**4.45**
Angles						
75mm; 45 °	2.39	3.06	0.20	4.54	nr	**7.60**
75mm; 90 °	2.39	3.06	0.20	4.54	nr	**7.60**
100mm; 90 °	2.47	3.32	0.20	4.54	nr	**7.86**
100mm; 120 °	2.74	3.51	0.20	4.54	nr	**8.05**
100mm; 135 °	2.74	3.51	0.20	4.54	nr	**8.05**
100mm; Prefabricated to special angle	11.48	14.70	0.23	5.22	nr	**19.92**
100mm; Prefabricated to raked angle	11.93	15.28	0.23	5.22	nr	**20.50**
150mm; 90 °	4.68	5.99	0.20	4.54	nr	**10.53**
Gutter adaptors						
100mm; Stainless steel clip	1.34	1.72	0.16	3.63	nr	**5.34**
100mm; Cast iron spigot	3.62	4.64	0.23	5.22	nr	**9.85**
100mm; Cast iron socket	3.62	4.64	0.23	5.22	nr	**9.85**
100mm; Cast iron "ogee" spigot	3.66	4.69	0.23	5.22	nr	**9.90**
100mm; Cast iron "ogee" socket	3.66	4.69	0.23	5.22	nr	**9.90**
100mm; Half round to Square PVC-U	6.80	8.71	0.23	5.22	nr	**13.93**
100mm; Gutter overshoot guard	7.79	9.98	0.58	13.15	nr	**23.13**
Brackets: including fixing to backgrounds						
75mm; Fascia	0.57	0.73	0.15	3.40	nr	**4.13**
100mm; Jointing	1.34	1.72	0.16	3.63	nr	**5.34**
100mm; Support	0.61	0.78	0.16	3.63	nr	**4.41**
150mm; Fascia	0.95	1.22	0.16	3.63	nr	**4.85**

R:DISPOSAL SYSTEMS

Item	Net Price £	Material £	Labour hours	Labour £	Unit	Total rate £
R10: RAINWATER PIPEWORK/GUTTERS (cont'd)						
PVC-U gutters: push fit joints (cont'd)						
Fittings; half round gutter (cont'd)						
Bracket supports: including fixing to backgrounds						
Side rafter	2.36	3.02	0.16	3.63	nr	**6.65**
Top rafter	2.36	3.02	0.16	3.63	nr	**6.65**
Rise and fall	2.28	2.92	0.16	3.63	nr	**6.55**
Square gutter						
120mm	1.97	2.52	0.82	18.60	m	**21.12**
Extra over fittings square PVC-U gutter						
Rainwater pipe outlets						
Running: 62mm square	2.72	3.48	0.12	2.72	nr	**6.21**
Stop end: 62mm square	2.35	3.01	0.12	2.72	nr	**5.73**
Stop ends: short						
External	1.36	1.74	0.09	2.04	nr	**3.78**
Angles						
90 °	2.77	3.73	0.20	4.54	nr	**8.26**
120 °	10.05	13.52	0.20	4.54	nr	**18.05**
135 °	2.77	3.73	0.20	4.54	nr	**8.26**
Prefabricated to special angle	11.77	15.07	0.23	5.22	nr	**20.29**
Prefabricated to raked angle	12.07	15.46	0.23	5.22	nr	**20.68**
Gutter adaptors						
Cast iron	6.28	8.04	0.23	5.22	nr	**13.26**
Half round asbestos	6.28	8.04	0.23	5.22	nr	**13.26**
Brackets: including fixing to backgrounds						
Jointing	1.67	2.14	0.16	3.63	nr	**5.77**
Support	0.73	0.94	0.16	3.63	nr	**4.56**
Bracket support: including fixing to backgrounds						
Side rafter	2.82	3.61	0.16	3.63	nr	**7.24**
Top rafter	2.82	3.61	0.16	3.63	nr	**7.24**
Rise and fall	3.97	5.08	0.16	3.63	nr	**8.71**
High capacity square gutter						
137mm	4.88	6.25	0.82	18.60	m	**24.85**
Extra over fittings high capacity square UPV-C						
Rainwater pipe outlets						
Running: 75mm square	7.81	10.00	0.12	2.72	nr	**12.72**
Running: 82mm dia	7.81	10.00	0.12	2.72	nr	**12.72**
Running: 110mm dia	6.84	8.76	0.12	2.72	nr	**11.48**
Screwed outlet adaptor						
75mm square pipe	4.14	5.30	0.23	5.22	nr	**10.52**

R:DISPOSAL SYSTEMS

Item	Net Price £	Material £	Labour hours	Labour £	Unit	Total rate £
Stop ends: short						
External	2.74	3.51	0.09	2.04	nr	**5.55**
Angles						
90 °	7.28	9.79	0.20	4.54	nr	**14.33**
135 °	14.17	19.06	0.20	4.54	nr	**23.59**
Prefabricated to special angle	16.49	21.12	0.23	5.22	nr	**26.34**
Prefabricated to raked internal angle	28.67	36.72	0.23	5.22	nr	**41.94**
Prefabricated to raked external angle	28.67	36.72	0.23	5.22	nr	**41.94**
Brackets: including fixing to backgrounds						
Jointing	4.47	6.01	0.16	3.63	nr	**9.64**
Support	1.89	2.54	0.16	3.63	nr	**6.17**
Overslung	1.78	2.39	0.16	3.63	nr	**6.02**
Bracket supports: including fixing to backgrounds						
Side rafter	2.82	3.61	0.16	3.63	nr	**7.24**
Top rafter	2.82	3.61	0.16	3.63	nr	**7.24**
Rise and fall	3.97	5.08	0.16	3.63	nr	**8.71**
Deep eliptical gutter						
137mm	2.34	3.00	0.82	18.60	m	**21.59**
Extra over fittings deep eliptical PVC-U gutter						
Rainwater pipe outlets						
Running: 68mm dia	2.63	3.54	0.12	2.72	nr	**6.26**
Running: 82mm dia	2.63	3.37	0.12	2.72	nr	**6.09**
Stop end: 68mm dia	2.78	3.56	0.12	2.72	nr	**6.28**
Stop ends: short						
External	1.33	1.70	0.09	2.04	nr	**3.74**
Angles						
90 °	2.90	3.90	0.20	4.54	nr	**8.44**
135 °	2.90	3.90	0.20	4.54	nr	**8.44**
Prefabricated to special angle	8.13	10.93	0.23	5.22	nr	**16.15**
Gutter adaptors						
Stainless steel clip	1.93	2.47	0.16	3.63	nr	**6.10**
Marley deepflow	2.47	3.16	0.23	5.22	nr	**8.38**
Brackets: including fixing to backgrounds						
Jointing	0.73	0.98	0.16	3.63	nr	**4.61**
Support	2.60	3.50	0.16	3.63	nr	**7.13**
Bracket support: including fixing to backgrounds						
Side rafter	2.11	2.84	0.16	3.63	nr	**6.47**
Top rafter	2.11	2.84	0.16	3.63	nr	**6.47**
Rise and fall	3.16	4.25	0.16	3.63	nr	**7.88**
Ogee profile gutter						
122mm	2.71	3.47	0.82	18.60	m	**22.07**

R:DISPOSAL SYSTEMS

Item	Net Price £	Material £	Labour hours	Labour £	Unit	Total rate £
R10: RAINWATER PIPEWORK/GUTTERS (cont'd)						
PVC-U gutters: push fit joints (cont'd)						
Extra over fittings Ogee profile PVC-U gutter						
Rainwater pipe outlets						
Running: 68mm dia	2.87	3.68	0.12	2.72	nr	**6.40**
Stop ends: short						
Internal/External: left or right hand	1.49	1.91	0.09	2.04	nr	**3.95**
Angles						
90 °: internal or external	3.18	4.07	0.20	4.54	nr	**8.61**
135 °: internal or external	3.18	4.07	0.20	4.54	nr	**8.61**
Brackets: including fixing to backgrounds						
Jointing	2.09	2.68	0.16	3.63	nr	**6.31**
Support	0.88	1.13	0.16	3.63	nr	**4.76**
Overslung	0.88	1.13	0.16	3.63	nr	**4.76**
PVC-U rainwater pipe: dry push fit joints; fixed with brackets to backgrounds; BS 4576/ BS EN 607						
Pipe: circular						
53mm	2.76	3.54	0.61	13.83	m	**17.37**
68mm	2.92	3.74	0.61	13.83	m	**17.57**
Extra over fittings circular pipework PVC-U						
Pipe coupler: PVC-U to PVC-U						
68mm	1.09	1.40	0.12	2.72	nr	**4.12**
Pipe coupler: PVC-U to Cast Iron						
68mm: to 3" cast iron	2.35	3.01	0.17	3.86	nr	**6.87**
68mm: to 3.3/4" cast iron	10.28	13.17	0.17	3.86	nr	**17.02**
Access pipe: single socket						
68mm	6.61	8.47	0.15	3.40	nr	**11.87**
Bend: short radius						
53mm: 67.5 °	1.50	1.92	0.20	4.54	nr	**6.46**
68mm: 92.5 °	1.85	2.37	0.20	4.54	nr	**6.91**
68mm: 112.5 °	1.55	1.99	0.20	4.54	nr	**6.52**
Bend: long radius						
68mm: 112 °	1.84	2.36	0.20	4.54	nr	**6.89**
Branch						
68mm: 92 °	8.35	11.23	0.23	5.22	nr	**16.45**
68mm: 112 °	8.35	11.23	0.23	5.22	nr	**16.45**
Double branch						
68mm: 112 °	18.81	24.09	0.24	5.44	nr	**29.53**

R:DISPOSAL SYSTEMS

Item	Net Price £	Material £	Labour hours	Labour £	Unit	Total rate £
Shoe						
53mm	1.50	1.92	0.12	2.72	nr	**4.64**
68mm	1.26	1.61	0.12	2.72	nr	**4.34**
Rainwater head: including fixing to backgrounds						
68mm	6.69	8.57	0.29	6.58	nr	**15.15**
Pipe clip: including fixing to backgrounds						
68mm	0.88	1.13	0.16	3.63	nr	**4.76**
Pipe clip adjustable: including fixing to backgrounds						
53mm	0.87	1.11	0.16	3.63	nr	**4.74**
68mm	1.85	2.37	0.16	3.63	nr	**6.00**
Pipe clip drive in: including fixing to backgrounds						
68mm	2.08	2.66	0.16	3.63	nr	**6.29**
Pipe: square						
62mm	2.35	3.01	0.45	10.21	m	**13.22**
75mm	3.67	4.70	0.45	10.21	m	**14.91**
Extra over fittings square pipework PVC-U						
Pipe coupler: PVC-U to PVC-U						
62mm	1.47	1.88	0.20	4.54	nr	**6.42**
75mm	1.89	2.42	0.20	4.54	nr	**6.96**
Square to circular adaptor: single socket						
62mm to 68mm	2.24	2.87	0.20	4.54	nr	**7.40**
Square to circular adaptor: single socket						
75mm to 62mm	2.82	3.61	0.20	4.54	nr	**8.15**
Access pipe						
62mm	9.08	11.63	0.16	3.63	nr	**15.26**
75mm	11.40	14.60	0.16	3.63	nr	**18.23**
Bends						
62mm: 92.5 °	1.94	2.48	0.20	4.54	nr	**7.02**
62mm: 112.5 °	1.65	2.11	0.20	4.54	nr	**6.65**
75mm: 112.5 °	3.76	4.82	0.20	4.54	nr	**9.35**
Bends: prefabricated special angle						
62mm	9.02	11.55	0.23	5.22	nr	**16.77**
75mm	12.57	16.10	0.23	5.22	nr	**21.32**
Offset						
62mm	2.95	3.78	0.20	4.54	nr	**8.31**
75mm	8.24	10.55	0.20	4.54	nr	**15.09**
Offset: prefabricated special angle						
62mm	9.05	11.59	0.23	5.22	nr	**16.81**
Shoe						
62mm	1.55	1.99	0.12	2.72	nr	**4.71**
75mm	1.96	2.51	0.12	2.72	nr	**5.23**

R:DISPOSAL SYSTEMS

Item	Net Price £	Material £	Labour hours	Labour £	Unit	Total rate £
R10: RAINWATER PIPEWORK/GUTTERS (cont'd)						
PVC-U rainwater pipe; dry push fit joints (cont'd)						
Fittings; square pipework PVC-U (cont'd)						
Branch						
62mm	4.68	5.99	0.23	5.22	nr	**11.21**
75mm	12.26	15.70	0.23	5.22	nr	**20.92**
Double branch						
62mm	16.69	21.38	0.24	5.44	nr	**26.82**
Rainwater head						
62mm	6.01	7.70	0.29	6.58	nr	**14.27**
75mm	21.87	28.01	3.45	78.20	nr	**106.21**
Pipe clip: including fixing to backgrounds						
62mm	0.82	1.05	0.16	3.63	nr	**4.68**
75mm	1.59	2.04	0.16	3.63	nr	**5.67**
Pipe clip adjustable: including fixing to backgrounds						
62mm	2.42	3.10	0.16	3.63	nr	**6.73**
PVC-U rainwater pipe: solvent welded joints; fixed with brackets to backgrounds; BS 4576/ BS EN 607						
Pipe: circular						
82mm	6.74	8.63	0.35	7.94	m	**16.57**
Extra over fittings circular pipework PVC-U						
Pipe coupler: PVC-U to PVC-U						
82mm	2.39	3.06	0.21	4.76	nr	**7.82**
Access pipe						
82mm	14.40	18.44	0.23	5.22	nr	**23.66**
Bend						
82mm: 92, 112.5 and 135 °	5.92	7.58	0.29	6.58	nr	**14.16**
Shoe						
82mm	5.61	7.19	0.29	6.58	nr	**13.76**
110mm	7.05	9.03	0.32	7.26	nr	**16.29**
Branch						
82mm: 92, 112.5 and 135 °	8.99	11.51	0.35	7.94	nr	**19.45**
Rainwater head						
82mm	11.83	15.15	0.58	13.15	nr	**28.31**
110mm	10.80	13.83	0.58	13.15	nr	**26.99**

R:DISPOSAL SYSTEMS

Item	Net Price £	Material £	Labour hours	Labour £	Unit	Total rate £
Pipe clip: galvanised; including fixing to backgrounds						
82mm	1.88	2.41	0.58	13.15	nr	**15.56**
Pipe clip: galvanised plastic coated; including fixing to backgrounds						
82mm	2.58	3.30	0.58	13.15	nr	**16.46**
Pipe clip: PVC-U including fixing to backgrounds						
82mm	1.41	1.81	0.58	13.15	nr	**14.96**
Pipe clip: PVC-U adjustable: including fixing to backgrounds						
82mm	2.55	3.27	0.58	13.15	nr	**16.42**
Roof outlets: 178 dia; Flat						
50mm	11.14	14.27	1.15	26.08	nr	**40.35**
82mm	11.14	14.27	1.15	26.08	nr	**40.35**
Roof outlets: 178mm dia; Domed						
50mm	11.14	14.27	1.15	26.08	nr	**40.35**
82mm	14.14	18.11	1.15	26.08	nr	**44.19**
Roof outlets: 406mm dia; Flat						
82mm	21.75	27.86	1.15	26.08	nr	**53.94**
110mm	21.75	27.86	1.15	26.08	nr	**53.94**
Roof outlets: 406mm dia; Domed						
82mm	21.75	27.86	1.15	26.08	nr	**53.94**
110mm	21.75	27.86	1.15	26.08	nr	**53.94**
Roof outlets: 406mm dia; Inverted						
82mm	47.81	61.23	1.15	26.08	nr	**87.31**
110mm	47.81	61.23	1.15	26.08	nr	**87.31**
Roof outlets: 406mm dia; Vent Pipe						
82mm	31.43	40.26	1.15	26.08	nr	**66.34**
110mm	31.43	40.26	1.15	26.08	nr	**66.34**
Balcony outlets: screed						
82mm	18.51	23.71	1.15	26.08	nr	**49.79**
Balcony outlets:asphalt						
82mm	18.52	23.72	1.15	26.08	nr	**49.80**
Adaptors						
82mm x 62mm square pipe	1.38	1.77	0.21	4.76	nr	**6.53**
82mm x 68mm circular pipe	1.49	1.91	0.21	4.76	nr	**6.67**

R:DISPOSAL SYSTEMS

Item	Net Price £	Material £	Labour hours	Labour £	Unit	Total rate £
R10: RAINWATER PIPEWORK/GUTTERS (cont'd)						
For 110mm diameter pipework and fittings see R11: Above Ground Drainage						
Cast iron gutters: mastic and bolted joints; BS 460; fixed with brackets to backgrounds						
Half round gutter						
100 mm	13.99	17.92	0.85	19.28	m	**37.19**
115 mm	14.52	18.60	0.97	22.00	m	**40.60**
125 mm	16.75	21.45	0.97	22.00	m	**43.45**
150 mm	28.00	35.86	1.12	25.40	m	**61.26**
Extra over fittings half round gutter cast iron BS 460						
Union						
100 mm	3.47	4.44	0.39	8.84	nr	**13.29**
115 mm	4.22	5.40	0.48	10.89	nr	**16.29**
125 mm	4.87	6.24	0.48	10.89	nr	**17.12**
150 mm	5.48	7.02	0.55	12.47	nr	**19.49**
Stop end; internal						
100 mm	1.77	2.27	0.12	2.72	nr	**4.99**
115 mm	2.28	2.92	0.15	3.40	nr	**6.32**
125 mm	2.28	2.92	0.15	3.40	nr	**6.32**
150 mm	3.04	3.89	0.20	4.54	nr	**8.43**
Stop end; external						
100 mm	1.77	2.27	0.12	2.72	nr	**4.99**
115 mm	2.28	2.92	0.15	3.40	nr	**6.32**
125 mm	2.28	2.92	0.15	3.40	nr	**6.32**
150 mm	3.04	3.89	0.20	4.54	nr	**8.43**
90 ° angle; single socket						
100 mm	5.25	6.72	0.39	8.84	nr	**15.57**
115 mm	5.25	6.72	0.43	9.75	nr	**16.48**
125 mm	6.36	8.15	0.43	9.75	nr	**17.90**
150 mm	11.62	14.88	0.50	11.34	nr	**26.22**
90 ° angle; double socket						
100 mm	6.35	8.13	0.39	8.84	nr	**16.98**
115 mm	6.74	8.63	0.43	9.75	nr	**18.38**
125 mm	8.73	11.18	0.43	9.75	nr	**20.93**
135 ° angle; single socket						
100 mm	4.87	6.24	0.39	8.84	nr	**15.08**
115 mm	5.39	6.90	0.43	9.75	nr	**16.66**
125 mm	7.96	10.20	0.43	9.75	nr	**19.95**
150 mm	10.65	13.64	0.50	11.34	nr	**24.98**

R:DISPOSAL SYSTEMS

Item	Net Price £	Material £	Labour hours	Labour £	Unit	Total rate £
Running outlet						
65 mm outlet						
100 mm	5.10	6.53	0.39	8.84	nr	**15.38**
115 mm	5.57	7.13	0.43	9.75	nr	**16.89**
125 mm	6.36	8.15	0.43	9.75	nr	**17.90**
75 mm outlet						
100 mm	5.10	6.53	0.39	8.84	nr	**15.38**
115 mm	5.57	7.13	0.43	9.75	nr	**16.89**
125 mm	6.36	8.15	0.43	9.75	nr	**17.90**
150 mm	10.82	13.86	0.50	11.34	nr	**25.20**
100 mm outlet						
150 mm	11.00	11.00	0.50	11.34	nr	**22.34**
Stop end outlet; socket						
65 mm outlet						
100 mm	4.07	5.21	0.39	8.84	nr	**14.06**
115 mm	4.47	5.73	0.43	9.75	nr	**15.48**
75 mm outlet						
125 mm	5.66	7.25	0.43	9.75	nr	**17.00**
150 mm	10.82	13.86	0.50	11.34	nr	**25.20**
100mm outlet						
150 mm	10.82	13.86	0.50	11.34	nr	**25.20**
Stop end outlet; spigot						
65 mm outlet						
100 mm	4.07	5.21	0.39	8.84	nr	**14.06**
115 mm	4.47	5.73	0.43	9.75	nr	**15.48**
75 mm outlet						
125 mm	5.66	7.25	0.43	9.75	nr	**17.00**
150 mm	10.82	13.86	0.50	11.34	nr	**25.20**
100mm outlet						
150 mm	10.82	13.86	0.50	11.34	nr	**25.20**
Brackets; fixed to backgrounds						
Fascia						
100 mm	1.42	1.82	0.16	3.63	nr	**5.45**
115 mm	1.42	1.82	0.16	3.63	nr	**5.45**
125 mm	1.42	1.82	0.16	3.63	nr	**5.45**
150 mm	1.80	2.31	0.16	3.63	nr	**5.93**
Rise and fall						
100 mm	2.12	2.72	0.39	8.84	nr	**11.56**
115 mm	2.12	2.72	0.39	8.84	nr	**11.56**
125 mm	2.53	3.24	0.39	8.84	nr	**12.09**
150 mm	2.97	3.80	0.39	8.84	nr	**12.65**
Top rafter						
100 mm	1.36	1.74	0.16	3.63	nr	**5.37**
115 mm	1.36	1.74	0.16	3.63	nr	**5.37**
125 mm	1.40	1.79	0.16	3.63	nr	**5.42**
150 mm	2.12	2.72	0.16	3.63	nr	**6.34**

R:DISPOSAL SYSTEMS

Item	Net Price £	Material £	Labour hours	Labour £	Unit	Total rate £
R10: RAINWATER PIPEWORK/GUTTERS (cont'd)						
Cast iron gutters: mastic joints (cont'd)						
Fittings; half round cast iron gutter (cont'd)						
Brackets; fixed to background (cont'd)						
Side rafter						
100 mm	1.36	1.74	0.16	3.63	nr	**5.37**
115 mm	1.36	1.74	0.16	3.63	nr	**5.37**
125 mm	1.40	1.79	0.16	3.63	nr	**5.42**
150 mm	2.12	2.72	0.16	3.63	nr	**6.34**
Half round; 3 mm thick double beaded gutter						
100 mm	6.74	8.63	0.85	19.28	m	**27.91**
115 mm	7.18	9.20	0.85	19.28	m	**28.47**
125 mm	8.22	10.53	0.97	22.00	m	**32.53**
Extra over fittings Half Round 3mm thick Gutter BS 460						
Union						
100 mm	3.46	4.43	0.38	8.62	nr	**13.05**
115 mm	4.19	5.37	0.38	8.62	nr	**13.98**
125 mm	4.81	6.16	0.43	9.75	nr	**15.91**
Stop end; internal						
100 mm	1.58	2.02	0.12	2.72	nr	**4.75**
115 mm	2.25	2.88	0.12	2.72	nr	**5.60**
125 mm	2.29	2.93	0.15	3.40	nr	**6.33**
Stop end; external						
100 mm	1.58	2.02	0.12	2.72	nr	**4.75**
115 mm	2.25	2.88	0.12	2.72	nr	**5.60**
125 mm	2.29	2.93	0.15	3.40	nr	**6.33**
90 ° angle; single socket						
100 mm	5.35	6.85	0.38	8.62	nr	**15.47**
115 mm	5.52	7.07	0.38	8.62	nr	**15.69**
125 mm	6.72	8.61	0.43	9.75	nr	**18.36**
135 ° angle; single socket						
100 mm	5.35	6.85	0.38	8.62	nr	**15.47**
115 mm	5.52	7.07	0.38	8.62	nr	**15.69**
125 mm	6.72	8.61	0.43	9.75	nr	**18.36**
Running outlet						
65 mm outlet						
100 mm	5.35	6.85	0.38	8.62	nr	**15.47**
115 mm	5.41	6.93	0.38	8.62	nr	**15.55**
125 mm	6.58	8.43	0.43	9.75	nr	**18.18**
75 mm outlet						
115 mm	5.52	7.07	0.38	8.62	nr	**15.69**
125 mm	6.58	8.43	0.43	9.75	nr	**18.18**

R:DISPOSAL SYSTEMS

Item	Net Price £	Material £	Labour hours	Labour £	Unit	Total rate £
Stop end outlet; socket						
65 mm outlet						
100 mm	4.14	5.30	0.38	8.62	nr	**13.92**
115 mm	5.04	6.46	0.38	8.62	nr	**15.07**
125 mm	5.64	5.64	0.43	9.75	nr	**15.39**
75 mm outlet						
125 mm	5.64	7.22	0.43	9.75	nr	**16.98**
Stop end outlet; spigot						
65 mm outlet						
100 mm	4.14	5.30	0.38	8.62	nr	**13.92**
115 mm	5.04	6.46	0.38	8.62	nr	**15.07**
125 mm	5.64	7.22	0.43	9.75	nr	**16.98**
Brackets; fixed to backgrounds						
Fascia						
100 mm	3.20	4.10	0.16	3.63	nr	**7.73**
115 mm	3.20	4.10	0.16	3.63	nr	**7.73**
125 mm	4.08	5.23	0.16	3.63	nr	**8.85**
Deep half round gutter						
100 x 75 mm	11.47	14.69	0.85	19.28	m	**33.97**
125 x 75 mm	14.85	19.02	0.97	22.00	m	**41.02**
Extra over fittings Deep Half Round Gutter BS 460						
Union						
100 x 75 mm	5.67	7.26	0.38	8.62	nr	**15.88**
125 x 75 mm	6.12	7.84	0.43	9.75	nr	**17.59**
Stop end; internal						
100 x 75 mm	4.97	6.37	0.12	2.72	nr	**9.09**
125 x 75 mm	6.12	7.84	0.15	3.40	nr	**11.24**
Stop end; external						
100 x 75 mm	4.97	6.37	0.12	2.72	nr	**9.09**
125 x 75 mm	6.12	7.84	0.15	3.40	nr	**11.24**
90 ° angle; single socket						
100 x 75 mm	14.43	18.48	0.38	8.62	nr	**27.10**
125 x 75 mm	18.32	23.46	0.43	9.75	nr	**33.22**
135 ° angle; single socket						
100 x 75 mm	14.43	18.48	0.38	8.62	nr	**27.10**
125 x 75 mm	18.32	23.46	0.43	9.75	nr	**33.22**
Running outlet						
65 mm outlet						
100 x 75 mm	14.43	18.48	0.38	8.62	nr	**27.10**
125 x 75 mm	18.32	23.46	0.43	9.75	nr	**33.22**
75 mm outlet						
100 x 75 mm	14.43	18.48	0.38	8.62	nr	**27.10**
125 x 75 mm	18.32	23.46	0.43	9.75	nr	**33.22**

R:DISPOSAL SYSTEMS

Item	Net Price £	Material £	Labour hours	Labour £	Unit	Total rate £
R10: RAINWATER PIPEWORK/GUTTERS (cont'd)						
Cast iron gutters: mastic joints (cont'd)						
Fittings; deep half round gutter (cont'd)						
Stop end outlet; socket						
65 mm outlet						
100 x 75 mm	9.67	12.39	0.38	8.62	nr	**21.00**
75 mm outlet						
100 x 75 mm	9.67	12.39	0.38	8.62	nr	**21.00**
125 x 75 mm	12.36	15.83	0.43	9.75	nr	**25.58**
Stop end outlet; spigot						
65 mm outlet						
100 x 75 mm	9.67	12.39	0.38	8.62	nr	**21.00**
75 mm outlet						
100 x 75 mm	9.67	12.39	0.38	8.62	nr	**21.00**
125 x 75 mm	12.36	15.83	0.43	9.75	nr	**25.58**
Brackets; fixed to backgrounds						
Fascia						
100 x 75 mm	4.97	6.37	0.16	3.63	nr	**9.99**
125 x 75 mm	12.36	15.83	0.16	3.63	nr	**19.46**
Ogee gutter						
100 mm	7.79	9.98	0.85	19.28	m	**29.25**
115 mm	8.57	10.98	0.97	22.00	m	**32.97**
125 mm	8.99	11.51	0.97	22.00	m	**33.51**
Extra over fittings Ogee Cast Iron Gutter BS 460						
Union						
100 mm	3.32	4.25	0.38	8.62	nr	**12.87**
115 mm	3.47	4.44	0.43	9.75	nr	**14.20**
125 mm	4.35	5.57	0.43	9.75	nr	**15.32**
Stop end; internal						
100 mm	1.63	2.09	0.12	2.72	nr	**4.81**
115 mm	2.15	2.75	0.15	3.40	nr	**6.16**
125 mm	2.15	2.75	0.15	3.40	nr	**6.16**
Stop end; external						
100 mm	1.63	2.09	0.12	2.72	nr	**4.81**
115 mm	2.15	2.75	0.15	3.40	nr	**6.16**
125 mm	2.15	2.75	0.15	3.40	nr	**6.16**
90 ° angle; internal						
100 mm	5.48	7.02	0.38	8.62	nr	**15.64**
115 mm	5.93	7.60	0.43	9.75	nr	**17.35**
125 mm	6.47	8.29	0.43	9.75	nr	**18.04**

R:DISPOSAL SYSTEMS

Item	Net Price £	Material £	Labour hours	Labour £	Unit	Total rate £
90 ° angle; external						
100 mm	5.48	7.02	0.38	8.62	nr	**15.64**
115 mm	5.93	7.60	0.43	9.75	nr	**17.35**
125 mm	6.47	8.29	0.43	9.75	nr	**18.04**
135 ° angle; internal						
100 mm	5.57	7.13	0.38	8.62	nr	**15.75**
115 mm	6.05	7.75	0.43	9.75	nr	**17.50**
125 mm	6.60	8.45	0.43	9.75	nr	**18.20**
135 ° angle; external						
100 mm	5.48	7.02	0.38	8.62	nr	**15.64**
115 mm	5.93	7.60	0.43	9.75	nr	**17.35**
125 mm	6.60	8.45	0.43	9.75	nr	**18.20**
Running outlet						
65 mm outlet						
100 mm	5.57	7.13	0.38	8.62	nr	**15.75**
115 mm	5.93	7.60	0.43	9.75	nr	**17.35**
125 mm	6.47	8.29	0.43	9.75	nr	**18.04**
75 mm outlet						
125 mm	6.47	8.29	0.43	9.75	nr	**18.04**
Stop end outlet; socket						
65 mm outlet						
100 mm	4.25	5.44	0.38	8.62	nr	**14.06**
115 mm	4.25	5.44	0.43	9.75	nr	**15.20**
125 mm	5.04	6.46	0.43	9.75	nr	**16.21**
75 mm outlet						
125 mm	5.04	6.46	0.43	9.75	nr	**16.21**
Stop end outlet; spigot						
65 mm outlet						
100 mm	4.25	5.44	0.38	8.62	nr	**14.06**
115 mm	4.25	5.44	0.43	9.75	nr	**15.20**
125 mm	5.04	6.46	0.43	9.75	nr	**16.21**
75 mm outlet						
125 mm	5.04	6.46	0.43	9.75	nr	**16.21**
Brackets; fixed to backgrounds						
Fascia						
100 mm	1.64	2.10	0.16	3.63	nr	**5.73**
115 mm	1.60	2.05	0.16	3.63	nr	**5.68**
125 mm	1.82	2.33	0.16	3.63	nr	**5.96**
Notts Ogee Gutter						
115 mm	14.63	18.74	0.85	19.28	m	**38.01**
Extra over fittings Notts Ogee Cast Iron Gutter BS 460						
Union						
115 mm	13.57	17.38	0.38	8.62	nr	**26.00**
Stop end; internal						
115 mm	4.85	6.21	0.16	3.63	nr	**9.84**

R:DISPOSAL SYSTEMS

Item	Net Price £	Material £	Labour hours	Labour £	Unit	Total rate £
R10: RAINWATER PIPEWORK/GUTTERS (cont'd)						
Cast iron gutters: mastic joints (cont'd)						
Fittings; Notts Ogee cast iron gutter (cont'd)						
Stop end; external						
115 mm	4.85	6.21	0.16	3.63	nr	**9.84**
90 ° angle; internal						
115 mm	13.56	17.37	0.43	9.75	nr	**27.12**
90 ° angle; external						
115 mm	13.56	17.37	0.43	9.75	nr	**27.12**
135 ° angle; internal						
115 mm	13.56	17.37	0.43	9.75	nr	**27.12**
135 ° angle; external						
115 mm	13.56	17.37	0.43	9.75	nr	**27.12**
Running outlet						
65 mm outlet						
115 mm	16.28	20.85	0.43	9.75	nr	**30.60**
75 mm outlet						
115 mm	13.60	17.42	0.43	9.75	nr	**27.17**
Stop end outlet; socket						
65 mm outlet						
115 mm	10.74	13.76	0.43	9.75	nr	**23.51**
Stop end outlet; spigot						
65 mm outlet						
115 mm	12.91	16.54	0.43	9.75	nr	**26.29**
Brackets; fixed to backgrounds						
Fascia						
115 mm	4.85	6.21	0.16	3.63	nr	**9.84**
No 46 moulded Gutter						
100 x 75 mm	13.39	17.15	0.85	19.28	m	**36.43**
125 x 100 mm	19.27	24.68	0.97	22.00	m	**46.68**
Extra over fittings						
Union						
100 x 75 mm	5.57	7.13	0.38	8.62	nr	**15.75**
125 x 100 mm	6.57	8.41	0.43	9.75	nr	**18.17**
Stop end; internal						
100 x 75 mm	5.07	6.49	0.12	2.72	nr	**9.22**
125 x 100 mm	6.57	8.41	0.15	3.40	nr	**11.82**
Stop end; external						
100 x 75 mm	5.07	6.49	0.12	2.72	nr	**9.22**
125 x 100 mm	6.57	8.41	0.15	3.40	nr	**11.82**

R:DISPOSAL SYSTEMS

Item	Net Price £	Material £	Labour hours	Labour £	Unit	Total rate £
90 ° angle; internal						
100 x 75 mm	13.30	17.03	0.38	8.62	nr	**25.65**
125 x 100 mm	19.11	24.48	0.43	9.75	nr	**34.23**
90 ° angle; external						
100 x 75 mm	13.30	17.03	0.38	8.62	nr	**25.65**
125 x 100 mm	19.11	24.48	0.43	9.75	nr	**34.23**
135 ° angle; internal						
100 x 75 mm	13.30	17.03	0.38	8.62	nr	**25.65**
125 x 100 mm	19.11	24.48	0.43	9.75	nr	**34.23**
135 ° angle; external						
100 x 75 mm	13.30	17.03	0.38	8.62	nr	**25.65**
125 x 100 mm	19.11	24.48	0.43	9.75	nr	**34.23**
Running outlet						
65 mm outlet						
100 x 75 mm	13.30	17.03	0.38	8.62	nr	**25.65**
125 x 100 mm	19.11	24.48	0.43	9.75	nr	**34.23**
75 mm outlet						
100 x 75 mm	13.30	17.03	0.38	8.62	nr	**25.65**
125 x 100 mm	19.11	24.48	0.43	9.75	nr	**34.23**
100 mm outlet						
100 x 75 mm	13.30	17.03	0.38	8.62	nr	**25.65**
125 x 100 mm	19.11	24.48	0.43	9.75	nr	**34.23**
100 x 75 mm outlet						
125 x 100 mm	19.11	24.48	0.43	9.75	nr	**34.23**
Stop end outlet; socket						
65 mm outlet						
100 x 75 mm	10.55	13.51	0.38	8.62	nr	**22.13**
75 mm outlet						
125 x 100 mm	13.02	16.68	0.43	9.75	nr	**26.43**
Stop end outlet; spigot						
65 mm outlet						
100 x 75 mm	10.55	13.51	0.38	8.62	nr	**22.13**
75 mm outlet						
125 x 100 mm	13.02	16.68	0.43	9.75	nr	**26.43**
Brackets; fixed to backgrounds						
Fascia						
100 x 75 mm	2.69	3.45	0.16	3.63	nr	**7.07**
125 x 100 mm	2.69	3.45	0.16	3.63	nr	**7.07**
Box gutter						
100 x 75 mm	20.71	26.53	0.85	19.28	m	**45.80**
Extra over fittings Box Cast Iron Gutter BS 460						
Union						
100 x 75 mm	3.77	4.83	0.38	8.62	nr	**13.45**

R:DISPOSAL SYSTEMS

Item	Net Price £	Material £	Labour hours	Labour £	Unit	Total rate £
R10: RAINWATER PIPEWORK/GUTTERS (cont'd)						
Cast iron gutters: mastic joints (cont'd)						
Fittings; box cast iron gutter (cont'd)						
Stop end; external						
100 x 75 mm	2.92	3.74	0.12	2.72	nr	**6.46**
90 ° angle						
100 x 75 mm	10.03	12.85	0.38	8.62	nr	**21.46**
135 ° angle						
100 x 75 mm	10.03	12.85	0.38	8.62	nr	**21.46**
Running outlet						
65 mm outlet						
100 x 75 mm	10.04	12.86	0.38	8.62	nr	**21.48**
75 mm outlet						
100 x 75 mm	10.04	12.86	0.38	8.62	nr	**21.48**
100 x 75 mm outlet						
100 x 75 mm	10.04	12.86	0.38	8.62	nr	**21.48**
Brackets; fixed to backgrounds						
Fascia						
100 x 75 mm	2.96	3.79	0.16	3.63	nr	**7.42**
Cast iron rainwater pipe; dry joints; BS 460; fixed to backgrounds						
Circular						
Plain sockets						
65mm	12.85	16.46	0.69	15.65	m	**32.11**
75 mm	12.85	16.46	0.69	15.65	m	**32.11**
100 mm	17.55	22.48	0.69	15.65	m	**38.13**
Eared sockets						
65mm	13.74	17.60	0.62	14.06	m	**31.66**
75 mm	13.74	17.60	0.62	14.06	m	**31.66**
100 mm	18.43	23.61	0.62	14.06	m	**37.67**
Extra over fittings Circular Cast Iron Pipework BS 460						
Loose sockets						
Plain socket						
65mm	10.11	12.95	0.23	5.22	nr	**18.16**
75 mm	10.11	12.95	0.23	5.22	nr	**18.16**
100 mm	13.47	17.25	0.23	5.22	nr	**22.47**
Eared socket						
65mm	13.74	17.60	0.29	6.58	nr	**24.17**
75 mm	13.74	17.60	0.29	6.58	nr	**24.17**
100 mm	18.43	23.61	0.29	6.58	nr	**30.18**

R:DISPOSAL SYSTEMS

Item	Net Price £	Material £	Labour hours	Labour £	Unit	Total rate £
Shoe; front projection						
Plain socket						
65mm	13.74	17.60	0.23	5.22	nr	**22.81**
75 mm	13.74	17.60	0.23	5.22	nr	**22.81**
100 mm	18.43	23.61	0.23	5.22	nr	**28.82**
Eared socket						
65mm	10.11	12.95	0.29	6.58	nr	**19.53**
75 mm	10.11	12.95	0.29	6.58	nr	**19.53**
100 mm	13.47	17.25	0.29	6.58	nr	**23.83**
Access Pipe						
65mm	18.60	23.82	0.23	5.22	nr	**29.04**
75 mm	19.53	25.01	0.23	5.22	nr	**30.23**
100 mm	34.12	43.70	0.23	5.22	nr	**48.92**
100 mm; eared	38.49	49.30	0.29	6.58	nr	**55.87**
Bends; any °						
65mm	7.30	9.35	0.23	5.22	nr	**14.57**
75 mm	8.87	11.36	0.23	5.22	nr	**16.58**
100 mm	19.39	24.83	0.23	5.22	nr	**30.05**
Branch						
92.5 °s						
65mm	14.09	18.05	0.29	6.58	nr	**24.62**
75 mm	15.53	19.89	0.29	6.58	nr	**26.47**
100 mm	18.45	23.63	0.29	6.58	nr	**30.21**
112.5 °s						
65mm	11.29	14.46	0.29	6.58	nr	**21.04**
75 mm	12.44	15.93	0.29	6.58	nr	**22.51**
135 °s						
65mm	14.09	18.05	0.29	6.58	nr	**24.62**
75 mm	15.53	19.89	0.29	6.58	nr	**26.47**
Offsets						
75 to 150 mm projection						
65mm	11.18	14.32	0.25	5.67	nr	**19.99**
75 mm	11.18	14.32	0.25	5.67	nr	**19.99**
100 mm	21.09	27.01	0.25	5.67	nr	**32.68**
225 mm projection						
65mm	13.02	16.68	0.25	5.67	nr	**22.35**
75 mm	13.02	16.68	0.25	5.67	nr	**22.35**
100 mm	25.54	32.71	0.25	5.67	nr	**38.38**
305 mm projection						
65mm	15.24	19.52	0.25	5.67	nr	**25.19**
75 mm	16.00	20.49	0.25	5.67	nr	**26.16**
100 mm	25.54	32.71	0.25	5.67	nr	**38.38**
380 mm projection						
65mm	30.42	38.96	0.25	5.67	nr	**44.63**
75 mm	30.42	38.96	0.25	5.67	nr	**44.63**
100 mm	42.52	54.46	0.25	5.67	nr	**60.13**

R:DISPOSAL SYSTEMS

Item	Net Price £	Material £	Labour hours	Labour £	Unit	Total rate £
R10: RAINWATER PIPEWORK/GUTTERS (cont'd)						
Cast iron rainwater pipes: dry joints (cont'd)						
Fittings; circular cast iron pipework (cont'd)						
Offsets (cont'd)						
455 mm projection						
65mm	35.60	45.60	0.25	5.67	nr	**51.27**
75 mm	35.60	45.60	0.25	5.67	nr	**51.27**
100 mm	50.46	64.63	0.25	5.67	nr	**70.30**
Bracket; fixed to backgrounds						
65mm	4.41	5.65	0.29	6.58	nr	**12.23**
75 mm	4.44	5.69	0.29	6.58	nr	**12.26**
100 mm	4.50	5.76	0.29	6.58	nr	**12.34**
Wall spacer plate; eared pipework						
65mm	2.91	3.73	0.16	3.63	nr	**7.36**
75 mm	2.97	3.80	0.16	3.63	nr	**7.43**
100 mm	3.02	3.87	0.16	3.63	nr	**7.50**
Rectangular						
Plain socket						
100 x 75 mm	51.81	66.36	1.04	23.59	m	**89.94**
Eared Socket						
100 x 75 mm	52.75	67.56	1.16	26.31	m	**93.87**
Extra over fittings Rectangular Cast Iron Pipework BS 460						
Loose socket						
100 x 75 mm; plain	13.53	17.33	0.23	5.22	nr	**22.55**
100 x 75 mm; eared	22.40	28.69	0.29	6.58	nr	**35.27**
Shoe; front						
100 x 75 mm; plain	13.52	17.32	0.23	5.22	nr	**22.53**
100 x 75 mm; eared	22.40	28.69	0.29	6.58	nr	**35.27**
Shoe; side						
100 x 75 mm; plain	33.66	43.11	0.23	5.22	nr	**48.33**
100 x 75 mm; eared	42.56	54.51	0.29	6.58	nr	**61.09**
Bends; side; any °						
100 x 75 mm; plain	31.96	40.93	0.25	5.67	nr	**46.60**
100 x 75 mm; 135 °; plain	31.86	40.81	0.25	5.67	nr	**46.48**
Bends; side; any °						
100 x 75 mm; eared	35.79	45.84	0.25	5.67	nr	**51.51**
Bends; front; any °						
100 x 75 mm; plain	31.96	40.93	0.25	5.67	nr	**46.60**
100 x 75 mm; eared	35.79	45.84	0.25	5.67	nr	**51.51**

R:DISPOSAL SYSTEMS

Item	Net Price £	Material £	Labour hours	Labour £	Unit	Total rate £
Offset; side;						
Plain socket						
75mm projection	44.34	56.79	0.25	5.67	nr	**62.46**
115mm projection	46.12	59.07	0.25	5.67	nr	**64.74**
225mm projection	57.43	73.56	0.25	5.67	nr	**79.23**
305mm projection	66.21	84.80	0.25	5.67	nr	**90.47**
Offset; front						
Plain socket						
75mm projection	44.34	56.79	0.25	5.67	nr	**62.46**
150mm projection	56.93	72.92	0.25	5.67	nr	**78.59**
225mm projection	57.45	73.58	0.25	5.67	nr	**79.25**
305mm projection	66.21	84.80	0.25	5.67	nr	**90.47**
Eared socket						
75mm projection	42.34	54.23	0.25	5.67	nr	**59.90**
150mm projection	45.64	58.46	0.25	5.67	nr	**64.12**
225mm projection	59.91	76.73	0.25	5.67	nr	**82.40**
305mm projection	64.04	82.02	0.25	5.67	nr	**87.69**
Offset; plinth						
115mm projection; plain	34.82	44.60	0.25	5.67	nr	**50.27**
115mm projection; eared	43.98	56.33	0.25	5.67	nr	**62.00**
Bracket; fixed to backgrounds						
100 x 75mm; build in holdabat	19.51	24.99	0.35	7.94	nr	**32.93**
100 x 75mm; trefoil earband	15.26	19.54	0.29	6.58	nr	**26.12**
100 x 75mm; plain earband	14.75	18.89	0.29	6.58	nr	**25.47**
Rainwater heads						
Flat hopper						
210 x 160 x 185 mm; 65 mm outlet	9.32	11.94	0.40	9.07	nr	**21.01**
210 x 160 x 185 mm; 75 mm outlet	10.59	13.56	0.40	9.07	nr	**22.63**
250 x 215 x 215 mm; 100 mm outlet	23.46	30.05	0.40	9.07	nr	**39.12**
Flat rectangular						
225 x 125 x 125 mm; 65 mm outlet	16.29	20.86	0.40	9.07	nr	**29.94**
225 x 125 x 125 mm; 75 mm outlet	16.29	20.86	0.40	9.07	nr	**29.94**
280 x 150 x 130 mm; 100 mm outlet	22.49	28.81	0.40	9.07	nr	**37.88**
Rectangular						
250 x 180 x 175mm; 75 mm outlet	23.38	29.94	0.40	9.07	nr	**39.02**
250 x 180 x 175mm; 100 mm outlet	21.06	26.97	0.40	9.07	nr	**36.04**
300 x 250 x 200mm; 65 mm outlet	41.54	53.20	0.40	9.07	nr	**62.28**
300 x 250 x 200mm; 75 mm outlet	41.52	53.18	0.40	9.07	nr	**62.25**
300 x 250 x 200mm; 100 mm outlet	41.52	53.18	0.40	9.07	nr	**62.25**
300 x 250 x 200mm; 100 x 75 mm outlet	41.52	53.18	0.40	9.07	nr	**62.25**
Castellated rectangular						
250 x 180 x 175mm; 65 mm outlet	41.52	53.18	0.40	9.07	nr	**62.25**

R:DISPOSAL SYSTEMS

Item	Net Price £	Material £	Labour hours	Labour £	Unit	Total rate £
R11: ABOVE GROUND DRAINAGE						
Pricing note: ° angles are only indicated where material prices differ						
PVC-U overflow pipe; solvent welded joints; fixed with clips to backgrounds						
Pipe						
19mm	0.90	1.15	0.21	4.76	m	**5.92**
Extra over fittings overflow pipework PVC-U						
Straight coupler						
19mm	0.72	0.92	0.17	3.86	nr	**4.78**
Bend						
19mm: 91.25 °	0.85	1.09	0.17	3.86	nr	**4.94**
19mm: 135 °	0.85	1.09	0.17	3.86	nr	**4.94**
Tee						
19mm	0.91	1.17	0.18	4.08	nr	**5.25**
Reverse nut connector						
19mm	0.36	0.46	0.15	3.40	nr	**3.86**
BSP adaptor: solvent welded socket to threaded socket						
19mm x 3/4"	1.08	1.38	0.14	3.18	nr	**4.56**
Straight tank connector						
19mm	1.08	1.38	0.21	4.76	nr	**6.15**
32mm	1.97	2.52	0.28	6.35	nr	**8.87**
40mm	2.14	2.74	0.30	6.80	nr	**9.54**
Bent tank connector						
19mm	1.27	1.63	0.21	4.76	nr	**6.39**
Tundish						
19mm	16.64	21.31	0.38	8.62	nr	**29.93**
Pipe clip: including fixing to backgrounds						
19mm	0.30	0.38	0.18	4.08	nr	**4.47**
MuPVC waste pipe; solvent welded joints; fixed with clips to backgrounds; BS 5255						
Pipe						
32mm	1.43	1.83	0.23	5.22	m	**7.05**
40mm	1.78	2.28	0.23	5.22	m	**7.50**
50mm	2.75	3.52	0.26	5.90	m	**9.42**

R:DISPOSAL SYSTEMS

Item	Net Price £	Material £	Labour hours	Labour £	Unit	Total rate £
Extra over fittings waste pipework MuPVC						
Screwed access plug						
32mm	1.10	1.41	0.18	4.08	nr	**5.49**
40mm	1.18	1.51	0.18	4.08	nr	**5.59**
50mm	1.89	2.42	0.25	5.67	nr	**8.09**
Straight coupling						
32mm	0.75	0.96	0.27	6.12	nr	**7.08**
40mm	0.87	1.11	0.27	6.12	nr	**7.24**
50mm	1.33	1.70	0.27	6.12	nr	**7.83**
Expansion coupling						
32mm	1.27	1.63	0.27	6.12	nr	**7.75**
40mm	1.53	1.96	0.27	6.12	nr	**8.08**
50mm	2.07	2.65	0.27	6.12	nr	**8.77**
MuPVC to copper coupling						
32mm	1.10	1.41	0.27	6.12	nr	**7.53**
40mm	1.29	1.65	0.27	6.12	nr	**7.78**
50mm	1.85	2.37	0.27	6.12	nr	**8.49**
Spigot and socket coupling						
32mm	1.27	1.63	0.27	6.12	nr	**7.75**
40mm	1.53	1.96	0.27	6.12	nr	**8.08**
50mm	2.07	2.65	0.27	6.12	nr	**8.77**
Union						
32mm	2.97	3.80	0.28	6.35	nr	**10.15**
40mm	3.88	4.97	0.28	6.35	nr	**11.32**
50mm	6.05	7.75	0.28	6.35	nr	**14.10**
Reducer: socket						
32 x 19mm	0.98	1.26	0.27	6.12	nr	**7.38**
40 x 32mm	0.75	0.96	0.27	6.12	nr	**7.08**
50 x 32mm	1.32	1.69	0.27	6.12	nr	**7.81**
50 x 40mm	1.41	1.81	0.27	6.12	nr	**7.93**
Reducer: level invert						
40 x 32mm	1.25	1.60	0.27	6.12	nr	**7.72**
50 x 32mm	1.72	2.20	0.27	6.12	nr	**8.33**
50 x 40mm	1.64	2.10	0.27	6.12	nr	**8.22**
Swept bend						
32mm	1.14	1.46	0.27	6.12	nr	**7.58**
32mm: 165 °	1.37	1.75	0.27	6.12	nr	**7.88**
40mm	1.26	1.61	0.27	6.12	nr	**7.74**
40mm: 165 °	1.78	2.28	0.27	6.12	nr	**8.40**
50mm	2.08	2.66	0.30	6.80	nr	**9.47**
50mm: 165 °	2.31	2.96	0.30	6.80	nr	**9.76**
Knuckle bend						
32mm	1.10	1.41	0.27	6.12	nr	**7.53**
40mm	1.20	1.54	0.27	6.12	nr	**7.66**

R:DISPOSAL SYSTEMS

Item	Net Price £	Material £	Labour hours	Labour £	Unit	Total rate £
R11: ABOVE GROUND DRAINAGE (cont'd)						
MuPVC waste pipe; solvent welded (cont'd)						
Fittings; waste pipework MuPVC (cont'd)						
Spigot and socket bend						
32mm	1.29	1.65	0.27	6.12	nr	7.78
32mm: 150 °	1.25	1.60	0.27	6.12	nr	7.72
40mm	1.43	1.83	0.27	6.12	nr	7.95
50mm	3.32	4.25	0.30	6.80	nr	11.06
Swept tee						
32mm: 91.25 °	1.59	2.04	0.31	7.03	nr	9.07
32mm: 135 °	1.89	2.42	0.31	7.03	nr	9.45
40mm: 91.25 °	2.00	2.56	0.31	7.03	nr	9.59
40mm: 135 °	2.36	3.02	0.31	7.03	nr	10.05
50mm	3.60	4.61	0.31	7.03	nr	11.64
Swept cross						
40mm: 91.25 °	5.55	7.11	0.31	7.03	nr	14.14
50mm: 91.25 °	6.39	8.18	0.43	9.75	nr	17.94
50mm: 135 °	13.65	17.48	0.31	7.03	nr	24.51
Male iron adaptor						
32mm	1.25	1.60	0.28	6.35	nr	7.95
40mm	1.46	1.87	0.28	6.35	nr	8.22
Female iron adaptor						
32mm	1.25	1.60	0.28	6.35	nr	7.95
40mm	1.46	1.87	0.28	6.35	nr	8.22
50mm	2.07	2.65	0.31	7.03	nr	9.68
Reverse nut adaptor						
32mm	1.65	2.11	0.20	4.54	nr	6.65
40mm	1.65	2.11	0.20	4.54	nr	6.65
Automatic air admittance valve						
32mm	8.97	11.49	0.27	6.12	nr	17.61
40mm	8.97	11.49	0.28	6.35	nr	17.84
50mm	8.97	11.49	0.31	7.03	nr	18.52
MuPVC to metal adpator: including heat shrunk joint to metal						
50mm	3.88	4.97	0.38	8.62	nr	13.59
Caulking bush: including joint to metal						
32mm	1.72	2.20	0.31	7.03	nr	9.23
40mm	1.72	2.20	0.31	7.03	nr	9.23
50mm	1.72	2.20	0.32	7.26	nr	9.46
Weathering apron						
50mm	1.44	1.84	0.65	14.74	nr	16.59
Vent Cowl						
50mm	1.48	1.90	0.19	4.31	nr	6.20

R:DISPOSAL SYSTEMS

Item	Net Price £	Material £	Labour hours	Labour £	Unit	Total rate £
Pipe clip: including fixing to backgrounds						
32mm	0.28	0.36	0.13	2.95	nr	**3.31**
40mm	0.35	0.45	0.13	2.95	nr	**3.40**
50mm	0.60	0.77	0.13	2.95	nr	**3.72**
Pipe clip: expansion: including fixing to backgrounds						
32mm	0.31	0.40	0.13	2.95	nr	**3.35**
40mm	0.36	0.46	0.13	2.95	nr	**3.41**
50mm	0.83	1.06	0.13	2.95	nr	**4.01**
Pipe clip: metal; including fixing to backgrounds						
32mm	1.06	1.36	0.13	2.95	nr	**4.31**
40mm	1.25	1.60	0.13	2.95	nr	**4.55**
50mm	1.57	2.01	0.13	2.95	nr	**4.96**
ABS waste pipe; solvent welded joints; fixed with clips to backgrounds; BS 5255						
Pipe						
32mm	1.10	1.41	0.23	5.22	m	**6.62**
40mm	1.35	1.73	0.23	5.22	m	**6.95**
50mm	1.92	2.46	0.26	5.90	m	**8.36**
Extra over fittings waste pipework ABS						
Screwed access plug						
32mm	0.55	0.70	0.18	4.08	nr	**4.79**
40mm	0.55	0.70	0.18	4.08	nr	**4.79**
50mm	1.20	1.54	0.25	5.67	nr	**7.21**
Straight coupling						
32mm	0.55	0.70	0.27	6.12	nr	**6.83**
40mm	0.55	0.70	0.27	6.12	nr	**6.83**
50mm	1.20	1.54	0.27	6.12	nr	**7.66**
Expansion coupling						
32mm	1.20	1.54	0.27	6.12	nr	**7.66**
40mm	1.20	1.54	0.27	6.12	nr	**7.66**
50mm	2.33	2.98	0.27	6.12	nr	**9.11**
ABS to Copper coupling						
32mm	1.20	1.54	0.27	6.12	nr	**7.66**
40mm	1.20	1.54	0.27	6.12	nr	**7.66**
50mm	2.33	2.98	0.27	6.12	nr	**9.11**
Reducer: socket						
40 x 32mm	0.55	0.70	0.27	6.12	nr	**6.83**
50 x 32mm	0.55	0.70	0.27	6.12	nr	**6.83**
50 x 40mm	1.20	1.54	0.27	6.12	nr	**7.66**
Swept bend						
32mm	0.55	0.70	0.27	6.12	nr	**6.83**
40mm	0.55	0.70	0.27	6.12	nr	**6.83**
50mm	1.20	1.54	0.30	6.80	nr	**8.34**
Knuckle bend						
32mm	0.55	0.70	0.27	6.12	nr	**6.83**
40mm	0.55	0.70	0.27	6.12	nr	**6.83**

R:DISPOSAL SYSTEMS

Item	Net Price £	Material £	Labour hours	Labour £	Unit	Total rate £
R11: ABOVE GROUND DRAINAGE (cont'd)						
ABS waste pipe; solvent welded (cont'd)						
Fittings; waste pipework ABS (cont'd)						
Swept tee						
32mm	0.55	0.70	0.31	7.03	nr	**7.73**
40mm	0.55	0.70	0.31	7.03	nr	**7.73**
50mm	1.20	1.54	0.31	7.03	nr	**8.57**
Swept cross						
40mm	3.00	3.84	0.23	5.22	nr	**9.06**
50mm	3.48	4.46	0.43	9.75	nr	**14.21**
Male iron adaptor						
32mm	1.25	1.60	0.28	6.35	nr	**7.95**
40mm	1.46	1.87	0.28	6.35	nr	**8.22**
Female iron adapator						
32mm	1.25	1.60	0.28	6.35	nr	**7.95**
40mm	1.46	1.87	0.28	6.35	nr	**8.22**
50mm	1.95	2.50	0.31	7.03	nr	**9.53**
Tank connectors						
32mm	1.97	2.52	0.29	6.58	nr	**9.10**
40mm	2.14	2.74	0.29	6.58	nr	**9.32**
Caulking bush: including joint to pipework						
50mm	1.82	2.33	0.50	11.34	nr	**13.67**
Pipe clip: including fixing to backgrounds						
32mm	0.28	0.36	0.17	3.86	nr	**4.21**
40mm	0.35	0.45	0.17	3.86	nr	**4.30**
50mm	0.60	0.77	0.17	3.86	nr	**4.62**
Pipe clip: expansion: including fixing to backgrounds						
32mm	0.31	0.40	0.17	3.86	nr	**4.25**
40mm	0.36	0.46	0.17	3.86	nr	**4.32**
50mm	0.83	1.06	0.17	3.86	nr	**4.92**
Pipe clip: metal; including fixing to backgrounds						
32mm	1.06	1.36	0.17	3.86	nr	**5.21**
40mm	1.25	1.60	0.17	3.86	nr	**5.46**
50mm	1.57	2.01	0.17	3.86	nr	**5.87**
Polypropylene waste pipe; push fit joints; fixed with clips to backgrounds; BS 5254						
Pipe						
32mm	0.73	0.94	0.21	4.76	m	**5.70**
40mm	0.95	1.22	0.21	4.76	m	**5.98**
50mm	1.62	2.07	0.38	8.62	m	**10.69**

R:DISPOSAL SYSTEMS

Item	Net Price £	Material £	Labour hours	Labour £	Unit	Total rate £
Extra over fittings waste pipework polypropylene						
Screwed access plug						
32mm	0.57	0.73	0.16	3.63	nr	**4.36**
40mm	0.57	0.73	0.16	3.63	nr	**4.36**
50mm	0.95	1.22	0.20	4.54	nr	**5.76**
Straight coupling						
32mm	0.57	0.73	0.19	4.31	nr	**5.04**
40mm	0.57	0.73	0.19	4.31	nr	**5.04**
50mm	0.94	1.20	0.20	4.54	nr	**5.74**
Universal waste pipe coupler						
32mm dia.	1.37	1.75	0.20	4.54	nr	**6.29**
40mm dia.	1.41	1.81	0.20	4.54	nr	**6.34**
Reducer						
40 x 32mm	0.57	0.73	0.19	4.31	nr	**5.04**
50 x 32mm	0.57	0.73	0.19	4.31	nr	**5.04**
50 x 40mm	0.94	1.20	0.20	4.54	nr	**5.74**
Swept bend						
32mm	0.57	0.73	0.19	4.31	nr	**5.04**
40mm	0.57	0.73	0.19	4.31	nr	**5.04**
50mm	0.94	1.20	0.20	4.54	nr	**5.74**
Knuckle bend						
32mm	0.57	0.73	0.19	4.31	nr	**5.04**
40mm	0.57	0.73	0.19	4.31	nr	**5.04**
50mm	0.94	1.20	0.20	4.54	nr	**5.74**
Spigot and socket bend						
32mm	0.57	0.73	0.19	4.31	nr	**5.04**
40mm	0.57	0.73	0.19	4.31	nr	**5.04**
Swept tee						
32mm	0.57	0.73	0.22	4.99	nr	**5.72**
40mm	0.57	0.73	0.22	4.99	nr	**5.72**
50mm	0.94	1.20	0.23	5.22	nr	**6.42**
Male iron adaptor						
32mm	1.06	1.36	0.13	2.95	nr	**4.31**
40mm	1.20	1.54	0.19	4.31	nr	**5.85**
50mm	1.30	1.67	0.15	3.40	nr	**5.07**
Tank connector						
32mm	0.57	0.73	0.24	5.44	nr	**6.17**
40mm	0.57	0.73	0.24	5.44	nr	**6.17**
50mm	0.94	1.20	0.35	7.94	nr	**9.14**
Pipe clip: saddle; including fixing to backgrounds						
32mm	0.24	0.31	0.17	3.86	nr	**4.16**
40mm	0.24	0.31	0.17	3.86	nr	**4.16**
Pipe clip: including fixing to backgrounds						
50mm	0.49	0.63	0.17	3.86	nr	**4.48**

R:DISPOSAL SYSTEMS

Item	Net Price £	Material £	Labour hours	Labour £	Unit	Total rate £
R11: ABOVE GROUND DRAINAGE (cont'd)						
Polypropylene waste pipe; push fit joints (cont'd)						
Polypropylene traps; including fixing to appliance and connection to pipework; BS 3943						
Tubular P trap; 75mm seal						
32mm dia.	2.74	3.51	0.20	4.54	nr	**8.05**
40mm dia.	3.16	4.05	0.20	4.54	nr	**8.58**
Tubular S trap; 75mm seal						
32mm dia.	3.46	4.43	0.20	4.54	nr	**8.97**
40mm dia.	4.03	5.16	0.20	4.54	nr	**9.70**
Running tubular P trap; 75mm seal						
32mm dia.	4.17	5.34	0.20	4.54	nr	**9.88**
40mm dia.	4.57	5.85	0.20	4.54	nr	**10.39**
Running tubular S trap; 75mm seal						
32mm dia.	5.01	6.42	0.20	4.54	nr	**10.95**
40mm dia.	5.40	6.92	0.20	4.54	nr	**11.45**
Spigot and socket bend; converter from P to S Trap						
32mm	1.11	1.42	0.20	4.54	nr	**5.96**
40mm	1.19	1.52	0.21	4.76	nr	**6.29**
Bottle P trap; 75mm seal						
32mm dia.	3.05	3.91	0.20	4.54	nr	**8.44**
40mm dia.	3.63	4.65	0.20	4.54	nr	**9.19**
Bottle S trap; 75mm seal						
32mm dia.	3.66	4.69	0.20	4.54	nr	**9.22**
40mm dia.	4.43	5.67	0.25	5.67	nr	**11.34**
Bottle P trap; resealing; 75mm seal						
32mm dia.	3.79	4.85	0.20	4.54	nr	**9.39**
40mm dia.	4.42	5.66	0.25	5.67	nr	**11.33**
Bottle S trap; resealing; 75mm seal						
32mm dia.	4.45	5.70	0.20	4.54	nr	**10.24**
40mm dia.	5.15	6.60	0.25	5.67	nr	**12.27**
Bath trap, low level; 38mm seal						
40mm dia.	3.79	4.85	0.25	5.67	nr	**10.52**
Bath trap, low level; 38mm seal complete with overflow hose						
40mm dia.	5.83	7.47	0.25	5.67	nr	**13.14**
Bath trap; 75mm seal complete with overlow hose						
40mm dia.	5.81	7.44	0.25	5.67	nr	**13.11**
Bath trap; 75mm seal complete with overflow hose and overflow outlet						
40mm dia.	9.88	12.65	0.20	4.54	nr	**17.19**

R:DISPOSAL SYSTEMS

Item	Net Price £	Material £	Labour hours	Labour £	Unit	Total rate £
Bath trap; 75mm seal complete with overflow hose, overflow outlet and ABS chrome waste						
40mm dia.	13.13	16.82	0.20	4.54	nr	**21.35**
Washing machine trap; 75mm seal including stand pipe						
40mm dia.	6.91	8.85	0.25	5.67	nr	**14.52**
Washing machine standpipe						
40mm dia.	4.13	5.29	0.25	5.67	nr	**10.96**
Plastic unslotted chrome plated basin/sink waste including plug						
32mm	5.30	6.79	0.34	7.71	nr	**14.50**
40mm	7.08	9.07	0.34	7.71	nr	**16.78**
Plastic slotted chrome plated basin/sink waste including plug						
32mm	4.45	5.70	0.34	7.71	nr	**13.41**
40mm	7.25	9.29	0.34	7.71	nr	**17.00**
Bath overflow outlet; plastic; white						
42mm	3.65	4.67	0.37	8.39	nr	**13.07**
Bath overlow outlet; plastic; chrome plated						
42mm	4.08	5.23	0.37	8.39	nr	**13.62**
Combined cistern and bath overflow outlet; plastic; white						
42mm	7.08	9.07	0.39	8.84	nr	**17.91**
Combined cistern and bath overlow outlet; plastic; chrome plated						
42mm	7.69	9.85	0.39	8.84	nr	**18.69**
Cistern overflow outlet; plastic; white						
42mm	4.55	5.83	0.15	3.40	nr	**9.23**
Cistern overlow outlet; plastic; chrome plated						
42mm	5.14	6.58	0.15	3.40	nr	**9.99**
PVC-U soil and waste pipe; solvent welded joints; fixed with clips to backgrounds; BS 4514/ BS EN 607						
Pipe						
82mm	5.61	7.19	0.35	7.94	m	**15.12**
110mm	5.60	7.17	0.41	9.30	m	**16.47**
160mm	15.72	20.13	0.51	11.57	m	**31.70**
Extra over fittings solvent welded pipework PVC-U						
Straight coupling						
82mm	2.39	3.06	0.21	4.76	nr	**7.82**
110mm	2.97	3.80	0.22	4.99	nr	**8.79**
160mm	8.49	10.87	0.24	5.44	nr	**16.32**

R:DISPOSAL SYSTEMS

Item	Net Price £	Material £	Labour hours	Labour £	Unit	Total rate £
R11: ABOVE GROUND DRAINAGE (cont'd)						
PVC-U soil and waste pipe; solvent welded joints (cont'd)						
Fittings solvent welded pipework PVC-U (cont'd)						
Expansion coupling						
82mm	1.54	1.97	0.21	4.76	nr	6.73
110mm	1.50	1.92	0.22	4.99	nr	6.91
160mm	3.96	5.07	0.24	5.44	nr	10.51
Slip coupling; double ring socket						
82mm	7.32	9.38	0.21	4.76	nr	14.14
110mm	9.15	11.72	0.22	4.99	nr	16.71
160mm	23.33	29.88	0.24	5.44	nr	35.32
Puddle flanges						
110mm	72.55	92.92	0.45	10.21	nr	103.13
160mm	122.48	156.87	0.55	12.47	nr	169.34
Socket reducer						
82 to 50mm	3.61	4.62	0.18	4.08	nr	8.71
110 to 50mm	4.48	5.74	0.18	4.08	nr	9.82
110 to 82mm	4.61	5.90	0.22	4.99	nr	10.89
160 to 110mm	9.30	11.91	0.26	5.90	nr	17.81
Socket plugs						
82mm	3.20	4.10	0.15	3.40	nr	7.50
110mm	3.46	4.43	0.20	4.54	nr	8.97
160mm	7.80	9.99	0.27	6.12	nr	16.11
Access door; including cutting into pipe						
82mm	7.85	10.05	0.28	6.35	nr	16.40
110mm	7.85	10.05	0.34	7.71	nr	17.76
160mm	14.01	17.94	0.46	10.43	nr	28.38
Screwed access cap						
82mm	5.57	7.13	0.15	3.40	nr	10.54
110mm	6.57	8.41	0.20	4.54	nr	12.95
160mm	12.32	15.78	0.27	6.12	nr	21.90
Access pipe: spigot and socket						
110mm	9.68	12.40	0.22	4.99	nr	17.39
Access pipe: double socket						
110mm	9.68	12.40	0.22	4.99	nr	17.39
Swept bend						
82mm	5.92	7.58	0.29	6.58	nr	14.16
110mm	6.91	8.85	0.32	7.26	nr	16.11
160mm	17.15	21.97	0.49	11.11	nr	33.08
Bend; special angle						
82mm	12.24	15.68	0.29	6.58	nr	22.25
110mm	14.59	18.69	0.32	7.26	nr	25.94
160mm	24.68	31.61	0.49	11.11	nr	42.72

R:DISPOSAL SYSTEMS

Item	Net Price £	Material £	Labour hours	Labour £	Unit	Total rate £
Spigot and socket bend						
82mm	5.92	7.58	0.26	5.90	nr	**13.48**
110mm	6.91	8.85	0.32	7.26	nr	**16.11**
110mm: 135 °	7.52	9.63	0.32	7.26	nr	**16.89**
160mm: 135 °	16.60	21.26	0.44	9.98	nr	**31.24**
Variable bend: single socket						
110mm	12.89	16.51	0.33	7.48	nr	**23.99**
Variable bend: double socket						
110mm	12.89	16.51	0.33	7.48	nr	**23.99**
Access bend						
110mm	19.09	24.45	0.33	7.48	nr	**31.93**
Single branch: two bosses						
82mm	8.25	10.57	0.35	7.94	nr	**18.50**
82mm: 104 °	8.25	10.57	0.35	7.94	nr	**18.50**
110mm	8.25	10.57	0.42	9.52	nr	**20.09**
110mm: 135 °	9.52	12.19	0.42	9.52	nr	**21.72**
160mm	19.32	24.74	0.50	11.34	nr	**36.08**
160mm: 135 °	36.84	47.18	0.50	11.34	nr	**58.52**
Single branch; four bosses						
110mm	11.88	15.22	0.42	9.52	nr	**24.74**
Single access branch						
82mm	36.86	47.21	0.35	7.94	nr	**55.15**
110mm	15.59	19.97	0.42	9.52	nr	**29.49**
Unequal single branch						
160 x 160 x 110mm	21.81	27.93	0.50	11.34	nr	**39.27**
160 x 160 x 110mm: 135 °	23.45	30.03	0.50	11.34	nr	**41.37**
Double branch						
110mm	22.49	28.81	0.42	9.52	nr	**38.33**
110mm: 135 °	23.51	30.11	0.42	9.52	nr	**39.64**
Corner branch						
110mm	39.68	50.82	0.42	9.52	nr	**60.35**
Unequal double branch						
160 x 160 x 110mm	40.59	51.99	0.50	11.34	nr	**63.33**
Single boss pipe; single socket						
110 x 110 x 32mm	5.99	7.67	0.24	5.44	nr	**13.11**
110 x 110 x 40mm	5.99	7.67	0.24	5.44	nr	**13.11**
110 x 110 x 50mm	5.70	7.30	0.24	5.44	nr	**12.74**
Single boss pipe; triple socket						
110 x 110 x 40mm	4.03	5.16	0.24	5.44	nr	**10.60**

R:DISPOSAL SYSTEMS

Item	Net Price £	Material £	Labour hours	Labour £	Unit	Total rate £
R11: ABOVE GROUND DRAINAGE (cont'd)						
PVC-U soil and waste pipe; solvent welded joints (cont'd)						
Fittings; solvent welded pipework PVC-U (cont'd)						
Waste boss; including cutting into pipe						
82 to 32mm	3.25	4.16	0.29	6.58	nr	**10.74**
82 to 40mm	3.25	4.16	0.29	6.58	nr	**10.74**
110 to 32mm	3.25	4.16	0.29	6.58	nr	**10.74**
110 to 40mm	3.25	4.16	0.29	6.58	nr	**10.74**
110 to 50mm	3.38	4.33	0.29	6.58	nr	**10.91**
160 to 32mm	4.59	5.88	0.30	6.80	nr	**12.68**
160 to 40mm	4.59	5.88	0.35	7.94	nr	**13.82**
160 to 50mm	4.59	5.88	0.40	9.07	nr	**14.95**
Self locking waste boss; including cutting into pipe						
110 to 32mm	4.33	5.55	0.30	6.80	nr	**12.35**
110 to 40mm	4.53	5.80	0.30	6.80	nr	**12.61**
110 to 50mm	5.13	6.57	0.30	6.80	nr	**13.37**
Adaptor saddle; including cutting to pipe						
82 to 32mm	2.00	2.56	0.29	6.58	nr	**9.14**
110 to 40mm	2.48	3.18	0.29	6.58	nr	**9.75**
160 to 50mm	4.45	5.70	0.29	6.58	nr	**12.28**
Branch boss adaptor						
32mm	1.33	1.70	0.26	5.90	nr	**7.60**
40 mm	1.33	1.70	0.26	5.90	nr	**7.60**
50 mm	1.87	2.40	0.26	5.90	nr	**8.29**
Branch boss adaptor bend						
32mm	1.96	2.51	0.26	5.90	nr	**8.41**
40 mm	2.33	2.98	0.26	5.90	nr	**8.88**
50 mm	2.33	2.98	0.26	5.90	nr	**8.88**
Automatic air admittance valve						
82 to 110mm	20.78	26.61	0.19	4.31	nr	**30.92**
PVC-U to metal adpator: including heat shrunk joint to metal						
110mm	5.63	7.21	0.57	12.93	nr	**20.14**
Caulking bush: including joint to pipework						
82mm	5.54	7.10	0.46	10.43	nr	**17.53**
110mm	5.54	7.10	0.46	10.43	nr	**17.53**
Vent cowl						
82mm	1.71	2.19	0.13	2.95	nr	**5.14**
110mm	1.72	2.20	0.13	2.95	nr	**5.15**
160mm	4.42	5.66	0.13	2.95	nr	**8.61**
Weathering apron; to lead slates						
82mm	1.71	2.19	1.15	26.08	nr	**28.27**
110mm	1.95	2.50	1.15	26.08	nr	**28.58**
160mm	5.76	7.38	1.15	26.08	nr	**33.46**

R:DISPOSAL SYSTEMS

Item	Net Price £	Material £	Labour hours	Labour £	Unit	Total rate £
Weathering apron; to asphalt						
82mm	7.03	9.00	1.10	24.95	nr	**33.95**
110mm	7.03	9.00	1.10	24.95	nr	**33.95**
Weathering slate; flat; 406 x 406mm						
82mm	19.71	25.24	1.04	23.59	nr	**48.83**
110mm	19.71	25.24	1.04	23.59	nr	**48.83**
Weathering slate; flat; 457 x 457mm						
82mm	20.20	25.87	1.04	23.59	nr	**49.46**
110mm	20.20	25.87	1.04	23.59	nr	**49.46**
Weathering slate; angled; 610 x 610mm						
82mm	27.29	34.95	1.04	23.59	nr	**58.54**
110mm	27.29	34.95	1.04	23.59	nr	**58.54**
Galvanised steel pipe clip: including fixing to backgrounds						
82mm	1.88	2.41	0.18	4.08	nr	**6.49**
110mm	1.95	2.50	0.18	4.08	nr	**6.58**
160mm	4.61	5.90	0.18	4.08	nr	**9.99**
Plastic coated steel pipe clip: including fixing to backgrounds						
82mm	2.58	3.30	0.18	4.08	nr	**7.39**
110mm	2.58	3.30	0.18	4.08	nr	**7.39**
160mm	4.45	5.70	0.18	4.08	nr	**9.78**
Plastic pipe clip: including fixing to backgrounds						
82mm	1.41	1.81	0.18	4.08	nr	**5.89**
110mm	1.41	1.81	0.18	4.08	nr	**5.89**
Plastic coated steel pipe clip: adjustable; including fixing to backgrounds						
82mm	2.55	3.27	0.20	4.54	nr	**7.80**
110mm	2.62	3.36	0.20	4.54	nr	**7.89**
Galvanised steel pipe clip: drive in; including fixing to backgrounds						
110mm	3.99	5.11	0.22	4.99	nr	**10.10**
PVC-U soil and waste pipe; ring seal joints; fixed with clips to backgrounds; BS 4514/BS EN 607						
Pipe						
82mm dia.	6.31	8.08	0.35	7.94	m	**16.02**
110mm dia.	6.01	7.70	0.41	9.30	m	**17.00**
160mm dia.	15.91	20.38	0.51	11.57	m	**31.94**
Extra over fittings ring seal pipework PVC-U						
Straight coupling						
82mm	3.32	4.25	0.21	4.76	nr	**9.01**
110mm	3.54	4.53	0.22	4.99	nr	**9.52**
160mm	7.73	9.90	0.24	5.44	nr	**15.34**

R:DISPOSAL SYSTEMS

Item	Net Price £	Material £	Labour hours	Labour £	Unit	Total rate £
R11: ABOVE GROUND DRAINAGE (cont'd)						
PVC-U soil and waste pipe; ring seal joints (cont'd)						
Fittings; ring seal pipework PVC-U (cont'd)						
Straight coupling; double socket						
82mm	3.32	4.25	0.21	4.76	nr	9.01
110mm	5.99	7.67	0.22	4.99	nr	12.66
160mm	12.33	15.79	0.24	5.44	nr	21.23
Reducer; socket						
82 to 50mm	5.16	6.61	0.15	3.40	nr	10.01
110 to 50mm	3.42	4.39	0.15	3.40	nr	7.79
110 to 82mm	3.46	4.43	0.19	4.31	nr	8.74
160 to 110	7.03	9.00	0.31	7.03	nr	16.03
Access Cap						
82mm	6.20	7.94	0.15	3.40	nr	11.34
110mm	6.56	8.40	0.17	3.86	nr	12.26
Access Cap; pressure plug						
160mm	17.83	22.84	0.33	7.48	nr	30.32
Access pipe						
82mm	12.19	15.61	0.22	4.99	nr	20.60
110mm	11.91	15.25	0.22	4.99	nr	20.24
160mm	26.96	34.53	0.24	5.44	nr	39.97
Bend						
82mm	6.86	8.79	0.29	6.58	nr	15.36
82mm; adjustable radius	11.49	14.72	0.29	6.58	nr	21.29
110mm	8.16	10.45	0.32	7.26	nr	17.71
110mm; adjustable radius	10.97	14.05	0.32	7.26	nr	21.31
160mm	21.99	28.16	0.49	11.11	nr	39.28
160mm; adjustable radius	23.15	29.65	0.49	11.11	nr	40.76
Bend; spigot and socket						
110mm	7.93	10.16	0.32	7.26	nr	17.41
Bend; offset						
82mm	6.86	8.79	0.21	4.76	nr	13.55
110mm	7.29	9.34	0.32	7.26	nr	16.59
160mm	22.56	28.89	-	-	nr	28.89
Bend; access						
110mm	17.02	21.80	0.33	7.48	nr	29.28
Single branch						
82mm	10.05	12.87	0.35	7.94	nr	20.81
110mm	12.94	16.57	0.42	9.52	nr	26.10
110mm; 45 °	12.94	16.57	0.31	7.03	nr	23.60
160mm	26.19	33.54	0.50	11.34	nr	44.88
Single branch; access						
82mm	17.11	21.91	0.35	7.94	nr	29.85
110mm	23.65	30.29	0.42	9.52	nr	39.82

R:DISPOSAL SYSTEMS

Item	Net Price £	Material £	Labour hours	Labour £	Unit	Total rate £
Unequal single branch						
160 x 160 x 110mm	26.43	33.85	0.50	11.34	nr	**45.19**
160 x 160 x 110mm; 45 °	20.09	25.73	0.50	11.34	nr	**37.07**
Double branch; 4 bosses						
110mm	19.51	24.99	0.49	11.11	nr	**36.10**
Corner branch; 2 bosses						
110mm	46.14	59.10	0.49	11.11	nr	**70.21**
Multibranch; 4 bosses						
110mm	33.91	43.43	0.52	11.79	nr	**55.22**
Boss Branch						
110 x 32mm	2.66	3.41	0.34	7.71	nr	**11.12**
110 x 40mm	2.66	3.41	0.34	7.71	nr	**11.12**
Strap on boss						
110 x 32mm	3.26	4.18	0.30	6.80	nr	**10.98**
110 x 40mm	3.26	4.18	0.30	6.80	nr	**10.98**
110 x 50mm	3.26	4.18	0.30	6.80	nr	**10.98**
Patch boss						
82 x 32mm	2.61	3.34	0.31	7.03	nr	**10.37**
82 x 40mm	2.68	3.43	0.31	7.03	nr	**10.46**
82 x 50mm	2.84	3.64	0.31	7.03	nr	**10.67**
Boss Pipe; collar 4 boss						
110mm	11.37	14.56	0.35	7.94	nr	**22.50**
Boss adaptor; rubber; push fit						
32mm	1.42	1.82	0.26	5.90	nr	**7.72**
40 mm	1.42	1.82	0.26	5.90	nr	**7.72**
50 mm	1.94	2.48	0.26	5.90	nr	**8.38**
WC connector; cap and seal; solvent socket						
110mm	2.96	3.79	0.23	5.22	nr	**9.01**
110mm; 90 °	8.80	11.27	0.27	6.12	nr	**17.39**
Vent terminal						
82mm	1.89	2.42	0.13	2.95	nr	**5.37**
110mm	2.00	2.56	0.13	2.95	nr	**5.51**
160mm	5.53	7.08	0.13	2.95	nr	**10.03**
Weathering slate; inclined; 610 x 610mm						
82mm	21.35	27.34	1.04	23.59	nr	**50.93**
110mm	21.35	27.34	1.04	23.59	nr	**50.93**
Weathering slate; inclined; 450 x 450mm						
82mm	13.43	17.20	1.04	23.59	nr	**40.79**
110mm	13.43	17.20	1.04	23.59	nr	**40.79**
Weathering slate; flat; 400 x 400mm						
82mm	13.18	16.88	1.04	23.59	nr	**40.47**
110mm	13.18	16.88	1.04	23.59	nr	**40.47**
Air admittance valve						
82mm	33.22	42.55	0.19	4.31	nr	**46.86**
110mm	34.10	43.67	0.19	4.31	nr	**47.98**

R:DISPOSAL SYSTEMS

Item	Net Price £	Material £	Labour hours	Labour £	Unit	Total rate £
R11: ABOVE GROUND DRAINAGE (cont'd)						
Cast iron pipe; nitrile rubber gasket joint with continuity clip BS 416/6087; fixed to backgrounds						
Pipe						
50 mm	12.78	16.37	0.25	5.67	m	**22.04**
75 mm	13.94	17.85	0.45	10.21	m	**28.06**
100 mm	16.54	21.18	0.60	13.61	m	**34.80**
150 mm	33.69	43.15	0.70	15.88	m	**59.03**
Extra over fittings nitrile gasket cast iron pipework BS 416/6087						
Standard coupling						
50 mm	4.85	6.21	0.50	11.34	nr	**17.55**
75 mm	5.35	6.85	0.60	13.61	nr	**20.46**
100 mm	6.98	8.94	0.67	15.20	nr	**24.14**
150 mm	13.96	17.88	0.83	18.84	nr	**36.72**
Conversion coupling						
65 x 75 mm	5.66	7.25	0.60	13.61	nr	**20.86**
70 x 75 mm	5.66	7.25	0.60	13.61	nr	**20.86**
90 x 100 mm	7.32	9.38	0.67	15.20	nr	**24.57**
Access pipe; round door						
50 mm	20.53	26.29	0.41	9.30	nr	**35.59**
75 mm	20.53	26.29	0.46	10.43	nr	**36.73**
100 mm	-	-	0.67	15.22	nr	**15.22**
150 mm	35.92	46.01	0.83	18.84	nr	**64.84**
Access pipe; square door						
100 mm	42.55	54.50	0.67	15.22	nr	**69.72**
150 mm	65.13	83.42	0.83	18.84	nr	**102.25**
Taper reducer						
75 mm	11.21	14.36	0.60	13.61	nr	**27.97**
100 mm	14.91	19.10	0.67	15.20	nr	**34.30**
150 mm	29.03	37.18	0.83	18.84	nr	**56.02**
Blank cap						
50 mm	2.96	3.79	0.24	5.44	nr	**9.23**
75 mm	3.49	4.47	0.26	5.90	nr	**10.37**
100 mm	3.59	4.60	0.32	7.26	nr	**11.86**
150 mm	5.39	6.90	0.40	9.07	nr	**15.97**
Blank cap; 50 mm screwed tapping						
75 mm	7.29	9.34	0.26	5.90	nr	**15.23**
100 mm	7.83	10.03	0.32	7.26	nr	**17.29**
150 mm	9.41	12.05	0.40	9.07	nr	**21.12**
Universal connector						
50 x 56/48/40 mm	4.44	5.69	0.33	7.48	nr	**13.17**
Change piece; BS416						
100 mm	9.42	12.07	0.47	10.66	nr	**22.72**

R:DISPOSAL SYSTEMS

Item	Net Price £	Material £	Labour hours	Labour £	Unit	Total rate £
WC connector						
100 mm	13.10	16.78	0.49	11.11	nr	**27.89**
Boss pipe; 2 " BSPT socket						
50 mm	17.68	22.64	0.58	13.15	nr	**35.80**
75 mm	17.68	22.64	0.65	14.74	nr	**37.39**
100 mm	21.12	27.05	0.79	17.92	nr	**44.97**
150 mm	34.44	44.11	0.86	19.50	nr	**63.61**
Boss pipe; 2 " BSPT socket; 135 °						
100 mm	25.95	33.24	0.79	17.92	nr	**51.15**
Boss pipe; 2 x 2 " BSPT socket; opposed						
75 mm	23.88	30.59	0.65	14.74	nr	**45.33**
100 mm	27.31	34.98	0.79	17.92	nr	**52.89**
Boss pipe; 2 x 2 " BSPT socket; in line						
100 mm	27.58	35.32	0.79	17.92	nr	**53.24**
Boss pipe; 2 x 2 " BSPT socket; 90 °						
100 mm	27.31	34.98	0.79	17.92	nr	**52.89**
Bend; short radius						
50 mm	8.54	10.94	0.50	11.34	nr	**22.28**
75 mm	8.54	10.94	0.60	13.61	nr	**24.55**
100 mm	11.82	15.14	0.67	15.20	nr	**30.34**
100 mm; 11 °	10.19	13.05	0.67	15.20	nr	**28.25**
100 mm; 67 °	11.82	15.14	0.67	15.20	nr	**30.34**
150 mm	21.12	27.05	0.83	18.84	nr	**45.89**
Access bend; short radius						
50 mm	21.04	26.95	0.50	11.34	nr	**38.29**
75 mm	21.07	26.99	0.60	13.61	nr	**40.60**
100 mm	25.00	32.02	0.67	15.20	nr	**47.22**
100 mm; 45 °	25.00	32.02	0.67	15.20	nr	**47.22**
150 mm	35.51	45.48	0.83	18.84	nr	**64.32**
150 mm; 45 °	35.51	45.48	0.83	18.84	nr	**64.32**
Long radius bend						
75 mm	16.12	20.65	0.60	13.61	nr	**34.26**
100 mm	19.14	24.51	0.67	15.20	nr	**39.71**
100 mm; 5 °	11.82	15.14	0.67	15.20	nr	**30.34**
150 mm	41.73	53.45	0.83	18.84	nr	**72.28**
150 mm; 22.5 °	34.64	44.37	0.83	18.84	nr	**63.20**
Access bend; long radius						
75 mm	28.61	36.64	0.60	13.61	nr	**50.25**
100 mm	32.33	41.41	0.67	15.20	nr	**56.61**
150 mm	56.86	72.83	0.83	18.84	nr	**91.66**
Long tail bend						
100 x 250 mm long	15.27	19.56	0.70	15.88	nr	**35.44**
100 x 815 mm long	40.78	52.23	0.70	15.88	nr	**68.11**
Offset						
75 mm projection						
75 mm	8.44	10.81	0.53	12.02	nr	**22.83**
100 mm	12.40	15.88	0.66	14.97	nr	**30.85**

R:DISPOSAL SYSTEMS

Item	Net Price £	Material £	Labour hours	Labour £	Unit	Total rate £
R11: ABOVE GROUND DRAINAGE (cont'd)						
Cast iron pipe; nitrile rubber gasket joint (cont'd)						
Fittings; nitrile gasket cast iron pipework (cont'd)						
Offset (cont'd)						
115 mm projection						
75 mm	10.52	13.47	0.53	12.02	nr	25.49
100 mm	14.82	18.98	0.66	14.97	nr	33.95
150 mm projection						
75 mm	10.52	13.47	0.53	12.02	nr	25.49
100 mm	14.82	18.98	0.66	14.97	nr	33.95
225 mm projection						
100 mm	16.98	21.75	0.66	14.97	nr	36.72
300 mm projection						
100 mm	19.14	24.51	0.66	14.97	nr	39.48
Branch; equal and unequal						
50 mm	12.84	16.45	0.78	17.69	nr	34.13
75 mm	12.84	16.45	0.85	19.28	nr	35.73
100 mm	18.27	23.40	1.00	22.68	nr	46.08
150 mm	45.29	58.01	1.20	27.23	nr	85.23
150 x 100 mm; 87.5 °	34.66	44.39	1.21	27.33	nr	71.72
150 x 100 mm; 45 °	48.07	61.57	1.21	27.33	nr	88.90
Branch; 2" BSPT screwed socket						
100 mm	25.41	32.54	1.00	22.68	nr	55.22
Branch; long tail						
100 x 915 mm long	48.31	61.88	1.00	22.68	nr	84.55
Access branch; equal and unequal						
50 mm	25.35	32.47	0.78	17.69	nr	50.16
75 mm	25.35	32.47	0.85	19.28	nr	51.75
100 mm	31.45	40.28	1.02	23.14	nr	63.42
150 mm	60.41	77.37	1.20	27.23	nr	104.60
150 x 100 mm; 87.5 °	49.04	62.81	1.20	27.23	nr	90.04
150 x 100 mm; 45 °	61.03	78.17	1.20	27.23	nr	105.39
Parallel branch						
100 mm	19.14	24.51	1.00	22.68	nr	47.19
Double branch						
75 mm	21.59	27.65	0.95	21.54	nr	49.20
100 mm	22.59	28.93	1.30	29.49	nr	58.42
150 x 100 mm	63.64	81.51	1.56	35.38	nr	116.89
Double access branch						
100 mm	35.78	45.83	1.43	32.44	nr	78.27
Corner branch						
100 mm	30.38	38.91	1.30	29.49	nr	68.40

R:DISPOSAL SYSTEMS

Item	Net Price £	Material £	Labour hours	Labour £	Unit	Total rate £
Puddle flange; grey epoxy coated						
100 mm	21.68	27.77	1.00	22.68	nr	**50.45**
WC connector						
100 mm	13.10	16.78	0.66	14.97	nr	**31.75**
Roof vent connector; asphalt						
75 mm	26.67	34.16	0.90	20.41	nr	**54.57**
100 mm	20.41	26.14	0.97	22.00	nr	**48.14**
P trap						
100 mm	18.54	23.75	1.00	22.68	nr	**46.42**
P trap with access						
50 mm	28.99	37.13	0.77	17.46	nr	**54.59**
75 mm	28.99	37.13	0.90	20.41	nr	**57.54**
100 mm	32.13	41.15	1.16	26.31	nr	**67.46**
150 mm	56.11	71.87	1.77	40.14	nr	**112.01**
Bellmouth gully inlet						
100 mm	27.42	35.12	1.08	24.49	nr	**59.61**
Balcony gully inlet						
100 mm	58.05	74.35	1.08	24.49	nr	**98.84**
Roof outlet						
Flat grate						
75 mm	59.09	75.68	0.83	18.82	nr	**94.51**
100 mm	68.06	87.17	1.08	24.49	nr	**111.66**
Dome grate						
75 mm	60.52	77.51	0.83	18.82	nr	**96.34**
100 mm	59.46	76.16	1.08	24.49	nr	**100.65**
Top Hat						
100 mm	104.19	133.45	1.08	24.49	nr	**157.94**
Brackets; fixed to backgrounds						
50 mm	3.25	4.16	0.15	3.40	nr	**7.56**
75 mm	3.25	4.16	0.18	4.08	nr	**8.24**
100 mm	3.65	4.67	0.18	4.08	nr	**8.76**
150 mm	6.92	8.86	0.20	4.54	nr	**13.40**
Cast iron pipe; EPDM rubber gasket joint with continuity clip; BS EN877; fixed to backgrounds						
Pipe						
50 mm	10.31	13.60	0.25	5.67	m	**19.27**
70 mm	11.46	15.12	0.45	10.21	m	**25.32**
100 mm	13.38	17.65	0.60	13.61	m	**31.26**
125 mm	22.02	29.05	0.65	14.74	m	**43.79**
150 mm	26.23	34.60	0.70	15.87	m	**50.48**
200 mm	56.88	75.04	1.14	25.85	m	**100.89**
250 mm	59.53	78.53	1.25	28.35	m	**106.88**
300 mm	72.22	95.27	1.53	34.70	m	**129.97**

R:DISPOSAL SYSTEMS

Item	Net Price £	Material £	Labour hours	Labour £	Unit	Total rate £
R11: ABOVE GROUND DRAINAGE (cont'd)						
Cast iron pipe; EPDM rubber gasket joint (cont'd)						
Extra over fittings EPDM rubber jointed cast iron pipework BS EN 877						
Coupling						
50 mm	3.12	4.00	0.50	11.34	nr	15.34
70 mm	3.44	4.41	0.60	13.61	nr	18.02
100 mm	4.49	5.75	0.67	15.20	nr	20.95
125 mm	5.57	7.13	0.75	17.02	nr	24.15
150mm	8.98	11.50	0.83	18.84	nr	30.34
200 mm	20.08	25.72	1.21	27.44	nr	53.16
250 mm	27.23	34.88	1.33	30.16	nr	65.04
300 mm	31.50	40.34	1.63	36.97	nr	77.31
Push fit joint						
Plain socket						
50 mm	7.86	10.07	0.25	5.67	nr	15.74
70 mm	7.86	10.07	0.25	5.67	nr	15.74
100 mm	9.03	11.57	0.25	5.67	nr	17.24
Eared socket						
50 mm	8.11	10.39	0.25	5.67	nr	16.06
70 mm	8.11	10.39	0.25	5.67	nr	16.06
100 mm	9.81	12.56	0.25	5.67	nr	18.23
Slip socket						
50 mm	10.18	13.04	0.25	5.67	nr	18.71
70 mm	10.18	13.04	0.25	5.67	nr	18.71
100 mm	11.88	15.22	0.25	5.67	nr	20.89
Stack support pipe						
70 mm	11.62	14.88	0.74	16.78	nr	31.66
100 mm	12.91	16.54	0.88	19.96	nr	36.49
125 mm	14.33	18.35	1.00	22.68	nr	41.03
150 mm	30.45	39.00	1.19	26.99	nr	65.99
200 mm	30.15	38.62	1.31	29.71	nr	68.32
Access pipe; round door						
50 mm	14.42	18.47	0.54	12.25	nr	30.72
70 mm	15.27	19.56	0.64	14.51	nr	34.07
100 mm	16.78	21.49	0.60	13.61	nr	35.10
150 mm	30.37	38.90	0.83	18.82	nr	57.72
Access pipe; square door						
100 mm	32.47	41.59	0.60	13.61	nr	55.19
125 mm	33.78	43.27	0.67	15.19	nr	58.46
150 mm	50.81	65.08	0.71	16.10	nr	81.18
200 mm	100.94	129.28	1.21	27.44	nr	156.72
250 mm	158.81	203.40	1.31	29.71	nr	233.11
300 mm	198.10	253.72	1.43	32.43	nr	286.15

R:DISPOSAL SYSTEMS

Item	Net Price £	Material £	Labour hours	Labour £	Unit	Total rate £
Taper reducer						
70 mm	8.33	10.67	0.51	11.57	nr	**22.24**
100 mm	9.80	12.55	0.58	13.15	nr	**25.71**
125 mm	9.85	12.62	0.64	14.51	nr	**27.13**
150 mm	18.80	24.08	0.67	15.19	nr	**39.27**
200 mm	30.53	39.10	1.15	26.08	nr	**65.18**
250 mm	63.08	80.79	1.25	28.35	nr	**109.14**
300 mm	86.72	111.07	1.37	31.07	nr	**142.14**
Blank cap						
50 mm	2.18	2.79	0.24	5.44	nr	**8.23**
70 mm	3.30	4.23	0.26	5.90	nr	**10.12**
100 mm	2.69	3.45	0.32	7.26	nr	**10.70**
125 mm	3.78	4.84	0.35	7.94	nr	**12.78**
150 mm	3.87	4.96	0.40	9.07	nr	**14.03**
200 mm	17.10	21.90	0.60	13.61	nr	**35.51**
250 mm	34.92	44.73	0.65	14.74	nr	**59.47**
300 mm	44.49	56.98	0.72	16.33	nr	**73.31**
Blank cap; 50 mm screwed tapping						
70 mm	5.13	6.57	0.26	5.90	nr	**12.47**
100 mm	5.54	7.10	0.32	7.26	nr	**14.35**
150 mm	6.66	8.53	0.40	9.07	nr	**17.60**
Universal connector; EPDM rubber						
50 x 56/48/40 mm	4.44	5.69	0.30	6.80	nr	**12.49**
Blank end; push fit						
100 x 38/32 mm	4.44	5.69	0.39	8.84	nr	**14.53**
Boss pipe; 2 " BSPT socket						
50 mm	12.21	15.64	0.54	12.25	nr	**27.88**
75 mm	12.21	15.64	0.64	14.51	nr	**30.15**
100 mm	14.91	19.10	0.78	17.69	nr	**36.79**
150 mm	24.33	31.16	1.09	24.72	nr	**55.88**
Boss pipe; 2 x 2 " BSPT socket; opposed						
100 mm	19.27	24.68	0.78	17.69	nr	**42.37**
Boss pipe; 2 x 2 " BSPT socket; 90 °						
100 mm	19.27	24.68	0.78	17.69	nr	**42.37**
Manifold connector						
100 mm	29.74	38.09	0.78	17.69	nr	**55.78**
Bend; short radius						
50mm	5.41	6.93	0.50	11.34	nr	**18.27**
70mm	6.10	7.81	0.60	13.61	nr	**21.42**
100mm	7.22	9.25	0.67	15.20	nr	**24.45**
125 mm	12.79	16.38	0.78	17.69	nr	**34.07**
150mm	12.97	16.61	0.83	18.84	nr	**35.45**
200 mm; 45 °	35.58	45.57	1.21	27.44	nr	**73.01**
250 mm; 45 °	75.30	96.44	1.31	29.71	nr	**126.15**
300 mm; 45 °	105.92	135.66	1.43	32.43	nr	**168.09**
Access bend; short radius						
70 mm	11.82	15.14	0.64	14.51	nr	**29.65**
100mm	17.26	22.11	0.78	17.69	nr	**39.80**
150mm	26.83	34.36	0.83	18.84	nr	**53.20**

R:DISPOSAL SYSTEMS

Item	Net Price £	Material £	Labour hours	Labour £	Unit	Total rate £
R11: ABOVE GROUND DRAINAGE (cont'd)						
Cast iron pipe; EPDM rubber gasket joint (cont'd)						
Fittings; EPDM rubber jointed (cont'd)						
Bend; long radius bend						
100mm	17.10	21.90	0.67	15.20	nr	37.10
100 mm; 22 °	13.51	17.30	0.78	17.69	nr	34.99
150mm	49.72	63.68	0.83	18.84	nr	82.52
Access bend; long radius						
100mm	22.33	28.60	0.67	15.20	nr	43.80
Bend ; long tail						
100 mm	12.65	16.20	0.78	17.69	nr	33.89
Bend ; long tail double						
70 mm	19.60	25.10	0.64	14.51	nr	39.62
100 mm	21.62	27.69	0.78	17.69	nr	45.38
Bend; air pipe						
100 mm	23.18	29.69	0.78	17.69	nr	47.38
Offset						
75 mm projection						
100 mm	11.10	14.22	0.78	17.69	nr	31.91
130 mm projection						
50 mm	9.18	11.76	0.54	12.25	nr	24.00
70 mm	13.93	17.84	0.64	14.51	nr	32.36
100 mm	18.30	23.44	0.78	17.69	nr	41.13
125 mm	23.19	29.70	0.78	17.69	nr	47.39
Branch; equal and unequal						
50 mm	8.69	11.13	0.78	17.69	nr	28.82
70 mm	9.18	11.76	0.85	19.28	nr	31.04
100 mm	12.58	16.11	1.00	22.68	nr	38.79
125 mm	25.23	32.31	1.16	26.31	nr	58.62
150 mm	31.33	40.13	1.37	31.07	nr	71.20
200 mm	75.93	97.25	1.51	34.24	nr	131.49
250 mm	169.03	216.49	1.63	36.97	nr	253.46
300mm	315.17	403.67	1.77	40.14	nr	443.81
Branch; radius; equal and unequal						
70 mm	11.19	14.33	0.79	17.92	nr	32.25
100 mm	12.91	16.54	0.96	21.77	nr	38.31
125 mm	35.06	44.90	1.16	26.31	nr	71.21
150 mm	38.96	49.90	1.37	31.07	nr	80.97
200 mm	102.13	130.81	1.51	34.24	nr	165.05
Branch; long tail						
100 mm	41.05	52.58	0.96	21.77	nr	74.35
Access branch; radius; equal and unequal						
70 mm	16.39	20.99	0.79	17.92	nr	38.91
100 mm	22.22	28.46	0.96	21.77	nr	50.23
150 mm	47.03	60.24	1.20	27.23	nr	87.46

R:DISPOSAL SYSTEMS

Item	Net Price £	Material £	Labour hours	Labour £	Unit	Total rate £
Double branch; equal and unequal						
100mm	16.80	21.52	1.30	29.49	nr	**51.01**
100 mm; 69 °	18.49	23.68	1.30	29.49	nr	**53.17**
150 mm	51.72	66.24	1.37	31.07	nr	**97.31**
200 mm	90.72	116.19	1.51	34.24	nr	**150.44**
Double branch; radius; equal and unequal						
100 mm	15.98	20.47	1.30	29.49	nr	**49.96**
150 mm	55.93	71.63	1.37	31.07	nr	**102.70**
200 mm	100.00	128.08	1.51	34.24	nr	**162.32**
Corner branch						
100 mm	30.62	39.22	1.30	29.49	nr	**68.71**
Corner branch; long tail						
100 mm	48.24	61.79	1.30	29.49	nr	**91.28**
Roof vent connector; asphalt						
100 mm	20.34	26.05	0.78	17.69	nr	**43.74**
Roof vent connector; felt						
100 mm	49.72	63.68	0.78	17.69	nr	**81.37**
Movement connector						
100 mm	25.83	33.08	0.78	17.69	nr	**50.77**
150 mm	47.83	61.26	0.78	17.69	nr	**78.95**
Expansion plugs						
70 mm	10.52	13.47	0.32	7.26	nr	**20.73**
100 mm	11.36	14.55	0.39	8.84	nr	**23.39**
150 mm	16.97	21.73	0.55	12.47	nr	**34.21**
P trap						
100mm dia.	13.41	17.18	1.00	22.68	nr	**39.85**
P trap with access						
50 mm	20.46	26.20	0.54	12.25	nr	**38.45**
70 mm	20.46	26.20	0.64	14.51	nr	**40.72**
100mm	22.15	28.37	1.00	22.68	nr	**51.05**
150 mm	39.62	50.74	1.09	24.72	nr	**75.46**
Branch trap						
100 mm	49.34	63.19	1.17	26.53	nr	**89.73**
Balcony gully inlet						
100 mm	20.48	26.23	1.00	22.68	nr	**48.91**
Roof outlet						
Flat grate						
70 mm	59.09	75.68	1.00	22.68	nr	**98.36**
100 mm	68.06	87.17	1.00	22.68	nr	**109.85**
Dome grate						
70 mm	60.52	77.51	1.00	22.68	nr	**100.19**
100 mm	-	95.02	1.00	22.68	nr	**117.70**
Top Hat						
100 mm	104.19	133.45	1.00	22.68	nr	**156.12**

R:DISPOSAL SYSTEMS

Item	Net Price £	Material £	Labour hours	Labour £	Unit	Total rate £
R11: ABOVE GROUND DRAINAGE (cont'd)						
Floor drains; for cast iron pipework BS 416 and BS EN877						
Adjustable clamp plate body						
100 mm; 165mm nickel bronze grate and frame	43.55	55.78	0.50	11.34	nr	**67.12**
100 mm; 165mm nickel bronze rodding eye	51.18	65.55	0.50	11.34	nr	**76.89**
100 mm; 150 x 150mm nickel bronze grate and frame	46.32	59.33	0.50	11.34	nr	**70.67**
100 mm; 150 x 150 nickel bronze rodding eye	53.56	68.60	0.50	11.34	nr	**79.94**
Deck plate body						
100 mm; 165mm nickel bronze grate and frame	43.55	55.78	0.50	11.34	nr	**67.12**
100 mm; 165mm nickel bronze rodding eye	51.18	65.55	0.50	11.34	nr	**76.89**
100 mm; 150 x 150mm nickel bronze grate and frame	46.32	59.33	0.50	11.34	nr	**70.67**
100 mm; 150 x 150mm nickel bronze rodding eye	53.56	68.60	0.50	11.34	nr	**79.94**
Extra for						
100 mm; Srewed extension piece	13.75	17.61	0.30	6.80	nr	**24.41**
100 mm; Grating extension piece; screwed or spigot	13.75	17.61	0.30	6.80	nr	**24.41**
100 mm; Brewary trap	524.28	671.49	2.00	45.36	nr	**716.85**
Brackets; fixed to backgrounds						
Ductile iron						
50mm	2.94	3.77	0.10	2.27	nr	**6.03**
70 mm	2.94	3.77	0.10	2.27	nr	**6.03**
100 mm	3.22	4.12	0.15	3.40	nr	**7.53**
150 mm	6.10	7.81	0.20	4.54	nr	**12.35**
200 mm	23.24	29.77	0.25	5.67	nr	**35.44**
Mild steel; vertical						
125 mm	5.71	7.31	0.15	3.40	nr	**10.72**
Mild steel; stand off						
250 mm	12.43	15.92	0.25	5.67	nr	**21.59**
300 mm	13.68	17.52	0.25	5.67	nr	**23.19**
Stack support; rubber seal						
70 mm	6.79	8.70	0.74	16.78	nr	**25.48**
100 mm	9.00	11.53	0.88	19.96	nr	**31.48**
125 mm	9.98	12.78	1.00	22.68	nr	**35.46**
150 mm	13.53	17.33	1.19	26.99	nr	**44.32**
200 mm	27.67	35.44	1.31	29.71	nr	**65.15**
Wall spacer plate; cast iron (eared sockets)						
50 mm	2.48	3.18	0.10	2.27	nr	**5.44**
70 mm	2.48	3.18	0.10	2.27	nr	**5.44**
100 mm	2.48	3.18	0.10	2.27	nr	**5.44**

The Presentation and Settlement of Contractors' Claims
Second Edition

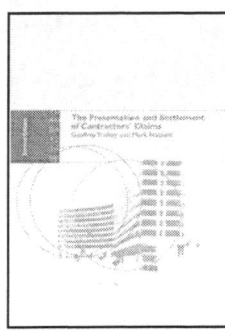

Geoffrey Trickey and Mark Hackett

Contractual disputes, often involving large sums of money, occur with increasing frequency in the construction industry. This book presents - in non-legal language - sound professional advice from a recognized expert in the field on the practical aspects of claims. This edition has been brought right up to date by taking into account legal decisions promulgated over the last 17 years, as well as reflecting the effect of current inflation on claims.

This new, fully updated edition of this practical guide is based on the 1998 JCT contract. The title contains numerous worked examples to support the advice offered, relating it to practitioners' experiences.

Contents: General. Introduction. 1998 edition of the Joint Contracts Tribunal standard form of building contract. Extensions of time. Variations and disruption. Ascertaining the loss or expense. Nominated sub-contractors and suppliers. Determination of the employment of the contractor. Comparison between the various editions of the JCT standard form of building contract. The JCT family of forms. The control of claims. A worked example of the ascertainment of direct loss and/or expense. Index.

November 2000: 234x156 mm: 512 pp.
5 line illustrations
HB: 0-419-20500-4: £85.00

To Order: Tel: +44 (0) 1264 343071 Fax: +44 (0) 1264 343005, or
Post: Taylor and Francis Customer Services, Thomson Publishing Services, Cheriton House, Andover, Hants, SP10 5BE, UK Email: book.orders@tandf.co.uk

For a complete listing of all our titles visit:
www.sponpress.com

Taylor & Francis
Taylor & Francis Group plc

Understanding JCT Standard Building Contracts
7th Edition

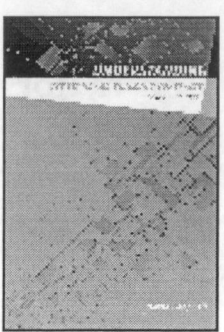

David Chappell

This latest edition of David Chappell's bestselling guide provides an expanded presentation of the Joint Contract Tribunal (JCT) standard contracts, the most common forms of building contract. The JCT Contract With Contractor's Design (WCD 98), also known as 'the design and build form', is now covered alongside the other three major forms of contract in the JCT series: JCT 98, IFC 98 and MW 98.

David Chappell has updated the book in line with amendments to the contracts and recent case law. He avoids legal jargon but writes with authority and precision, in a style which won, for the fifth edition of the book, the first prize in the Best Textbook category of the 1999 Chartered Institute of Building Literary Awards.

Architects, quantity surveyors and contractors should find this a straightforward and practical reference tool arranged by topic.

March 2003: 234x156 mm: 160 pp.
PB: 0-415-30631-0: £18.99

To Order: Tel: +44 (0) 1264 343071 Fax: +44 (0) 1264 343005, or
Post: Taylor and Francis Customer Services, Thomson Publishing Services, Cheriton House, Andover, Hants, SP10 5BE, UK Email: book.orders@tandf.co.uk

For a complete listing of all our titles visit:
www.sponpress.com

Taylor & Francis
Taylor & Francis Group plc

S:PIPED SUPPLY SYSTEMS

Item	Net Price £	Material £	Labour hours	Labour £	Unit	Total rate £
S10 : COLD WATER						
Y10 - PIPELINES						
MEDIUM DENSITY POLYETHYLENE - BLUE						
Pipes for water distribution; laid underground; electrofusion joints in the running length; BS 6572						
Coiled service pipe						
20mm dia.	0.22	0.29	0.37	8.39	m	8.68
25mm dia.	0.27	0.36	0.41	9.30	m	9.65
32mm dia.	0.47	0.62	0.47	10.66	m	11.28
50mm dia.	1.13	1.49	0.53	12.02	m	13.51
63mm dia.	1.79	2.36	0.60	13.61	m	15.97
Mains service pipe						
90mm dia.	4.86	6.41	0.90	20.41	m	26.82
110mm dia	8.21	10.52	1.10	24.95	m	35.46
125mm dia.	9.23	12.18	1.20	27.23	m	39.40
160mm dia	16.55	21.20	1.48	33.56	m	54.76
180mm dia	18.64	24.59	1.50	34.05	m	58.64
225mm dia	33.87	43.38	1.77	40.14	m	83.52
250mm dia.	37.58	49.58	1.75	39.72	m	89.29
315mm dia	55.28	70.80	1.90	43.09	m	113.89
Extra over fittings; MDPE blue; electrofusion joints						
Coupler						
20mm dia	3.61	4.62	0.36	8.16	nr	12.79
25mm dia	3.97	5.08	0.40	9.07	nr	14.16
32mm dia	4.28	5.48	0.44	9.98	nr	15.46
40mm dia	4.43	5.67	0.48	10.89	nr	16.56
50mm dia	4.57	5.85	0.52	11.79	nr	17.65
63mm dia.	4.82	6.17	0.58	13.15	nr	19.33
90mm dia.	7.11	9.11	0.67	15.19	nr	24.30
110mm dia	10.29	13.18	0.74	16.78	nr	29.96
125mm dia.	12.91	16.54	0.83	18.82	nr	35.36
160mm dia	19.32	24.74	1.00	22.68	nr	47.42
180mm dia.	23.98	30.71	1.25	28.35	nr	59.06
225mm dia	41.90	53.67	1.35	30.62	nr	84.28
250mm dia.	56.18	71.95	1.50	34.02	nr	105.97
315mm dia	72.97	93.46	1.80	40.82	nr	134.28
Extra over fittings; MDPE blue; butt fused joints						
Cap						
25mm dia	7.59	9.72	0.20	4.54	nr	14.26
32mm dia	7.91	10.13	0.22	4.99	nr	15.12
40mm dia	8.28	10.60	0.24	5.44	nr	16.05
50mm dia	8.35	10.69	0.26	5.90	nr	16.59
63mm dia.	8.45	10.82	0.32	7.26	nr	18.08
90mm dia.	13.69	17.53	0.37	8.39	nr	25.92

S:PIPED SUPPLY SYSTEMS

Item	Net Price £	Material £	Labour hours	Labour £	Unit	Total rate £
S10 : COLD WATER (cont'd)						
Y10 – PIPELINES (cont'd)						
MEDIUM DENSITY POLYETHYLENE – BLUE (cont'd)						
Fittings; butt fused joints (cont'd)						
Cap (cont'd)						
110mm dia	19.39	24.83	0.40	9.07	nr	**33.91**
125mm dia.	22.29	28.55	0.46	10.43	nr	**38.98**
160mm dia	30.10	38.55	0.50	11.34	nr	**49.89**
180mm dia.	42.80	54.82	0.60	13.61	nr	**68.42**
225mm dia	56.36	72.19	0.68	15.42	nr	**87.61**
250mm dia	75.22	96.34	0.75	17.01	nr	**113.35**
315mm dia	92.65	118.67	0.90	20.41	nr	**139.08**
Reducer						
63 x 32mm dia	8.32	10.66	0.54	12.25	nr	**22.90**
63 x 50mm dia	9.11	11.67	0.60	13.61	nr	**25.28**
90 x 63mm dia.	9.93	12.72	0.67	15.19	nr	**27.91**
110 x 90mm dia	14.98	19.19	0.74	16.78	nr	**35.97**
125 x 90mm dia.	19.91	25.50	0.83	18.82	nr	**44.32**
125 x 110mm dia	25.15	32.21	1.00	22.68	nr	**54.89**
160 x 110mm dia	29.98	38.40	1.10	24.95	nr	**63.34**
180 x 125mm dia.	36.52	46.77	1.25	28.35	nr	**75.12**
225 x 160mm dia	51.01	65.33	1.40	31.75	nr	**97.08**
250 x 180mm dia	73.39	94.00	1.80	40.82	nr	**134.82**
315 x 250mm dia	90.76	116.24	2.40	54.43	nr	**170.67**
Bend; 45 °						
50mm dia	10.42	13.35	0.50	11.34	nr	**24.69**
63mm dia.	12.42	15.91	0.58	13.15	nr	**29.06**
90mm dia.	17.45	22.35	0.67	15.19	nr	**37.54**
110mm dia	26.24	33.61	0.74	16.78	nr	**50.39**
125mm dia.	30.37	38.90	0.83	18.82	nr	**57.72**
160mm dia	46.62	59.71	1.00	22.68	nr	**82.39**
180mm dia.	66.77	85.52	1.25	28.35	nr	**113.87**
225mm dia	100.33	128.50	1.40	31.75	nr	**160.25**
250mm dia	131.06	167.86	1.80	40.82	nr	**208.68**
315mm dia	184.63	236.47	2.40	54.43	nr	**290.90**
Bend; 90 °						
50mm dia	10.42	13.35	0.50	11.34	nr	**24.69**
63mm dia.	12.42	15.91	0.58	13.15	nr	**29.06**
90mm dia.	19.18	24.57	0.67	15.19	nr	**39.76**
110mm dia	26.67	34.16	0.74	16.78	nr	**50.94**
125mm dia.	31.38	40.19	0.83	18.82	nr	**59.01**
160mm dia	49.12	62.91	1.00	22.68	nr	**85.59**
180mm dia.	71.19	91.18	1.25	28.35	nr	**119.53**
225mm dia	101.64	130.18	1.40	31.75	nr	**161.93**
250mm dia	132.81	170.10	1.80	40.82	nr	**210.92**
315mm dia	188.50	241.43	2.40	54.43	nr	**295.86**

S:PIPED SUPPLY SYSTEMS

Item	Net Price £	Material £	Labour hours	Labour £	Unit	Total rate £
Equal tee						
50mm dia	10.44	13.37	0.70	15.87	nr	**29.25**
63mm dia.	12.19	15.61	0.75	17.01	nr	**32.62**
90mm dia.	22.24	28.48	0.87	19.73	nr	**48.22**
110mm dia	34.54	44.24	1.00	22.68	nr	**66.92**
125mm dia.	42.56	54.51	1.08	24.49	nr	**79.00**
160mm dia	51.94	66.52	1.35	30.62	nr	**97.14**
180mm dia.	72.16	92.42	1.63	36.97	nr	**129.39**
225mm dia	84.66	108.43	1.90	43.09	nr	**151.52**
250mm dia	115.67	148.15	2.70	61.23	nr	**209.38**
315mm dia	151.55	194.10	3.60	81.64	nr	**275.75**
Extra over plastic fittings, compression joints						
Straight connector						
20mm dia.	2.12	2.72	0.38	8.62	nr	**11.34**
25mm dia.	2.44	3.13	0.45	10.21	nr	**13.33**
32mm dia.	4.82	6.17	0.50	11.34	nr	**17.51**
50mm dia.	11.41	14.61	0.68	15.43	nr	**30.04**
63mm dia.	17.44	22.34	0.85	19.28	nr	**41.62**
Reducing connector						
25mm dia.	3.55	4.55	0.38	8.62	nr	**13.17**
32mm dia.	5.96	7.63	0.45	10.21	nr	**17.84**
50mm dia.	13.69	17.53	0.50	11.34	nr	**28.87**
63mm dia.	20.01	25.63	0.62	14.07	nr	**39.70**
Straight connector; polyethylene to MI						
20mm dia.	1.76	2.25	0.31	7.03	nr	**9.29**
25mm dia.	2.23	2.86	0.35	7.94	nr	**10.79**
32mm dia.	3.28	4.20	0.40	9.07	nr	**13.27**
50mm dia.	8.11	10.39	0.55	12.48	nr	**22.86**
63mm dia.	11.25	14.41	0.65	14.75	nr	**29.15**
Straight connector; polyethylene to FI						
20mm dia.	2.31	2.96	0.31	7.03	nr	**9.99**
25mm dia.	2.53	3.24	0.35	7.94	nr	**11.18**
32mm dia.	3.11	3.98	0.40	9.07	nr	**13.05**
50mm dia.	9.46	12.12	0.55	12.48	nr	**24.59**
63mm dia.	13.09	16.77	0.75	17.01	nr	**33.78**
Elbow						
20mm dia.	2.53	3.24	0.38	8.62	nr	**11.86**
25mm dia.	3.72	4.76	0.45	10.21	nr	**14.97**
32mm dia.	5.41	6.93	0.50	11.34	nr	**18.27**
50mm dia.	12.61	16.15	0.68	15.43	nr	**31.58**
63mm dia.	17.13	21.94	0.80	18.14	nr	**40.08**
Elbow; polyethylene to MI						
25mm dia.	3.11	3.98	0.35	7.94	nr	**11.92**
Elbow; polyethylene to FI						
20mm dia.	2.29	2.93	0.31	7.03	nr	**9.97**
25mm dia.	3.11	3.98	0.35	7.94	nr	**11.92**
32mm dia.	4.62	5.92	0.42	9.52	nr	**15.44**
50mm dia.	10.95	14.02	0.50	11.34	nr	**25.36**
63mm dia.	14.30	18.32	0.55	12.48	nr	**30.79**

S:PIPED SUPPLY SYSTEMS

Item	Net Price £	Material £	Labour hours	Labour £	Unit	Total rate £
S10 : COLD WATER (cont'd)						
Y10 – PIPELINES (cont'd)						
MEDIUM DENSITY POLYETHYLENE – BLUE (cont'd)						
Fittings; plastic; compression joints (cont'd)						
Tank coupling						
25mm dia.	8.11	10.39	0.42	9.52	nr	**19.91**
Equal tee						
20mm dia.	3.70	4.74	0.53	12.02	nr	**16.76**
25mm dia.	5.61	7.19	0.55	12.48	nr	**19.66**
32mm dia.	7.15	9.16	0.64	14.52	nr	**23.68**
50mm dia.	16.68	21.36	0.75	17.01	nr	**38.38**
63mm dia.	24.92	31.92	0.87	19.74	nr	**51.65**
Equal tee; FI branch						
20mm dia.	3.31	4.24	0.45	10.21	nr	**14.44**
25mm dia.	5.16	6.61	0.50	11.34	nr	**17.95**
32mm dia.	6.58	8.43	0.60	13.61	nr	**22.04**
50mm dia.	22.81	29.21	0.68	15.43	nr	**44.64**
63mm dia.	25.42	32.56	0.81	18.38	nr	**50.94**
Equal tee; MI branch						
25mm dia.	5.91	7.57	0.50	11.34	nr	**18.91**
ABS PIPEWORK						
Pipes; solvent welded joints in the running length						
Class C (9 bar pressure)						
1" dia.	1.86	2.38	0.30	6.80	m	**9.19**
1 1/4" dia.	3.13	4.01	0.33	7.48	m	**11.49**
1 1/2" dia.	3.98	5.10	0.36	8.16	m	**13.26**
2" dia.	5.36	6.87	0.39	8.84	m	**15.71**
2 1/2" dia.	9.44	12.09	0.40	9.07	m	**21.16**
3" dia.	11.06	14.17	0.46	10.43	m	**24.60**
4" dia.	18.22	23.34	0.53	12.02	m	**35.36**
6" dia.	36.02	46.13	0.76	17.24	m	**63.37**
8" dia.	61.86	79.23	0.97	22.00	m	**101.23**
Class E (15 bar pressure)						
1/2" dia.	1.42	1.82	0.24	5.44	m	**7.26**
3/4" dia.	2.19	2.80	0.27	6.12	m	**8.93**
1" dia.	2.89	3.70	0.30	6.80	m	**10.50**
1 1/4" dia.	4.31	5.52	0.33	7.48	m	**13.00**
1 1/2" dia.	5.68	7.27	0.36	8.16	m	**15.44**
2" dia.	7.12	9.12	0.39	8.84	m	**17.96**
3" dia.	14.31	18.33	0.49	11.11	m	**29.44**
4" dia.	23.01	29.47	0.57	12.93	m	**42.40**

S:PIPED SUPPLY SYSTEMS

Item	Net Price £	Material £	Labour hours	Labour £	Unit	Total rate £
Extra over fittings; solvent welded joints						
Cap						
1/2" dia.	0.61	0.78	0.16	3.63	nr	4.41
3/4" dia.	0.70	0.90	0.19	4.31	nr	5.21
1" dia.	0.81	1.04	0.22	4.99	nr	6.03
1 1/4" dia.	1.35	1.73	0.25	5.67	nr	7.40
1 1/2" dia.	2.08	2.66	0.28	6.35	nr	9.01
2" dia.	2.64	3.38	0.31	7.03	nr	10.41
3" dia.	7.92	10.14	0.36	8.16	nr	18.31
4" dia.	12.11	15.51	0.44	9.98	nr	25.49
Elbow 90 °						
1/2" dia.	0.85	1.09	0.29	6.58	nr	7.67
3/4" dia.	1.02	1.31	0.34	7.71	nr	9.02
1" dia.	1.42	1.82	0.40	9.07	nr	10.89
1 1/4" dia.	2.41	3.09	0.45	10.21	nr	13.29
1 1/2" dia.	3.13	4.01	0.51	11.57	nr	15.57
2" dia.	4.76	6.10	0.56	12.70	nr	18.80
3" dia.	13.66	17.50	0.65	14.74	nr	32.24
4" dia.	20.41	26.14	0.80	18.14	nr	44.28
6" dia.	82.12	105.18	1.21	27.44	nr	132.62
8" dia.	125.35	160.55	1.45	32.88	nr	193.43
Elbow 45 °						
1/2" dia.	1.64	2.10	0.29	6.58	nr	8.68
3/4" dia.	1.66	2.13	0.34	7.71	nr	9.84
1" dia.	2.08	2.66	0.40	9.07	nr	11.74
1 1/4" dia.	3.05	3.91	0.45	10.21	nr	14.11
1 1/2" dia.	3.78	4.84	0.51	11.57	nr	16.41
2" dia.	5.25	6.72	0.56	12.70	nr	19.42
3" dia.	12.36	15.83	0.65	14.74	nr	30.57
4" dia.	25.61	32.80	0.80	18.14	nr	50.94
6" dia.	53.09	68.00	1.21	27.44	nr	95.44
8" dia.	114.25	146.33	1.45	32.88	nr	179.21
Reducing bush						
3/4" x 1/2" dia.	0.63	0.81	0.42	9.52	nr	10.33
1" x 1/2" dia.	0.81	1.04	0.45	10.21	nr	11.24
1" x 3/4" dia.	0.81	1.04	0.45	10.21	nr	11.24
1 1/4" x 1" dia.	1.09	1.40	0.48	10.89	nr	12.28
1 1/2" x 3/4" dia.	1.42	1.82	0.51	11.57	nr	13.38
1 1/2" x 1" dia.	1.42	1.82	0.51	11.57	nr	13.38
1 1/2" x 1 1/4" dia.	1.42	1.82	0.51	11.57	nr	13.38
2" x 1" dia.	1.86	2.38	0.56	12.70	nr	15.08
2" x 1 1/4" dia.	1.86	2.38	0.56	12.70	nr	15.08
2" x 1 1/2" dia.	1.86	2.38	0.56	12.70	nr	15.08
3" x 1 1/2" dia.	5.25	6.72	0.65	14.74	nr	21.47
3" x 2" dia.	5.25	6.72	0.65	14.74	nr	21.47
4" x 3" dia.	7.23	9.26	0.80	18.14	nr	27.40
6" x 4" dia.	22.28	28.54	1.21	27.44	nr	55.98
Union						
1/2" dia.	3.38	4.33	0.34	7.71	nr	12.04
3/4" dia.	3.65	4.67	0.39	8.84	nr	13.52
1" dia.	4.91	6.29	0.43	9.75	nr	16.04
1 1/4" dia.	6.02	7.71	0.50	11.34	nr	19.05
1 1/2" dia.	8.30	10.63	0.57	12.93	nr	23.56
2" dia.	10.82	13.86	0.62	14.06	nr	27.92

S:PIPED SUPPLY SYSTEMS

Item	Net Price £	Material £	Labour hours	Labour £	Unit	Total rate £
S10 : COLD WATER (cont'd)						
Y10 – PIPELINES (cont'd)						
ABS PIPEWORK (cont'd)						
Fittings; solvent welded joints (cont'd)						
Sockets						
1/2" dia.	0.63	0.81	0.34	7.71	nr	**8.52**
3/4" dia.	0.70	0.90	0.39	8.84	nr	**9.74**
1" dia.	0.81	1.04	0.43	9.75	nr	**10.79**
1 1/4" dia.	1.42	1.82	0.50	11.34	nr	**13.16**
1 1/2" dia.	1.71	2.19	0.57	12.93	nr	**15.12**
2" dia.	2.41	3.09	0.62	14.06	nr	**17.15**
3" dia.	9.68	12.40	0.70	15.87	nr	**28.27**
4" dia.	13.74	17.60	0.70	15.87	nr	**33.47**
6" dia.	34.31	43.94	1.26	28.57	nr	**72.52**
8" dia.	68.53	87.77	1.55	35.15	nr	**122.92**
Barrel nipple						
1/2" dia.	1.18	1.51	0.34	7.71	nr	**9.22**
3/4" dia.	1.54	1.97	0.39	8.84	nr	**10.82**
1" dia.	1.99	2.55	0.43	9.75	nr	**12.30**
1 1/4" dia.	2.76	3.54	0.50	11.34	nr	**14.87**
1 1/2" dia.	3.25	4.16	0.57	12.93	nr	**17.09**
2" dia.	3.94	5.05	0.62	14.06	nr	**19.11**
3" dia.	10.49	13.44	0.70	15.87	nr	**29.31**
Tee, 90°						
1/2" dia.	0.97	1.24	0.41	9.30	nr	**10.54**
3/4" dia.	1.35	1.73	0.47	10.66	nr	**12.39**
1" dia.	1.86	2.38	0.55	12.47	nr	**14.86**
1 1/4" dia.	2.69	3.45	0.64	14.51	nr	**17.96**
1 1/2" dia.	3.94	5.05	0.71	16.10	nr	**21.15**
2" dia.	6.02	7.71	0.78	17.69	nr	**25.40**
3" dia.	17.57	22.50	0.91	20.64	nr	**43.14**
4" dia.	25.78	33.02	1.12	25.40	nr	**58.42**
6" dia.	90.10	115.40	1.69	38.33	nr	**153.73**
8" dia.	140.48	179.93	2.03	46.04	nr	**225.96**
Full face flange						
1/2" dia.	10.04	12.86	0.10	2.27	nr	**15.13**
3/4" dia.	10.26	13.14	0.13	2.95	nr	**16.09**
1" dia.	11.02	14.11	0.15	3.40	nr	**17.52**
1 1/4" dia.	14.80	18.96	0.18	4.08	nr	**23.04**
1 1/2" dia.	17.04	21.82	0.21	4.76	nr	**26.59**
2" dia.	21.55	27.60	0.29	6.58	nr	**34.18**
3" dia.	39.23	50.25	0.37	8.39	nr	**58.64**
4" dia.	50.48	64.65	0.41	9.30	nr	**73.95**

S:PIPED SUPPLY SYSTEMS

Item	Net Price £	Material £	Labour hours	Labour £	Unit	Total rate £
PVC-U PIPEWORK						
Pipes; solvent welded joints in the running length						
Class C (9 bar pressure)						
2" dia.	5.94	7.61	0.41	9.30	m	**16.91**
3" dia.	11.38	14.58	0.47	10.66	m	**25.23**
4" dia.	20.20	25.87	0.50	11.34	m	**37.21**
6" dia.	43.71	55.98	1.76	39.91	m	**95.90**
Class D (12 bar pressure)						
1 1/4" dia.	3.46	4.43	0.41	9.30	m	**13.73**
1 1/2" dia.	4.76	6.10	0.42	9.52	m	**15.62**
2" dia.	7.38	9.45	0.45	10.21	m	**19.66**
3" dia.	15.80	20.24	0.48	10.89	m	**31.12**
4" dia.	26.46	33.89	0.53	12.02	m	**45.91**
6" dia.	49.09	62.87	0.58	13.15	m	**76.03**
Class E (15 bar pressure)						
1/2" dia.	1.69	2.16	0.38	8.62	m	**10.78**
3/4" dia.	2.42	3.10	0.40	9.07	m	**12.17**
1" dia.	2.82	3.61	0.41	9.30	m	**12.91**
1 1/4" dia.	4.14	5.30	0.41	9.30	m	**14.60**
1 1/2" dia.	5.38	6.89	0.42	9.52	m	**16.42**
2" dia.	8.41	10.77	0.45	10.21	m	**20.98**
3" dia.	18.20	23.31	0.47	10.66	m	**33.97**
4" dia.	29.88	38.27	0.50	11.34	m	**49.61**
6" dia.	64.72	82.89	0.53	12.02	m	**94.91**
Class 7						
1/2" dia.	3.00	3.84	0.32	7.26	m	**11.10**
3/4" dia.	4.19	5.37	0.33	7.48	m	**12.85**
1" dia.	6.40	8.20	0.40	9.07	m	**17.27**
1 1/4" dia.	8.80	11.27	0.40	9.07	m	**20.34**
1 1/2" dia.	10.89	13.95	0.41	9.30	m	**23.25**
2" dia.	18.10	23.18	0.43	9.75	m	**32.93**
Extra over fittings; solvent welded joints						
End cap						
1/2" dia.	0.57	0.73	0.17	3.86	nr	**4.59**
3/4" dia.	0.68	0.87	0.19	4.31	nr	**5.18**
1" dia.	0.76	0.97	0.22	4.99	nr	**5.96**
1 1/4" dia.	1.18	1.51	0.25	5.67	nr	**7.18**
1 1/2" dia.	1.99	2.55	0.28	6.35	nr	**8.90**
2" dia.	2.44	3.13	0.31	7.03	nr	**10.16**
3" dia.	7.48	9.58	0.36	8.16	nr	**17.74**
4" dia.	11.54	14.78	0.44	9.98	nr	**24.76**
6" dia.	27.89	35.72	0.67	15.19	nr	**50.92**

S:PIPED SUPPLY SYSTEMS

Item	Net Price £	Material £	Labour hours	Labour £	Unit	Total rate £
S10 : COLD WATER (cont'd)						
Y10 – PIPELINES (cont'd)						
PVC-U PIPEWORK (cont'd)						
Fittings; solvent welded joints (cont'd)						
Socket						
1/2" dia.	0.61	0.78	0.31	7.03	nr	**7.81**
3/4" dia.	0.68	0.87	0.35	7.94	nr	**8.81**
1" dia.	0.79	1.01	0.42	9.52	nr	**10.54**
1 1/4" dia.	1.42	1.82	0.45	10.21	nr	**12.02**
1 1/2" dia.	1.66	2.13	0.51	11.57	nr	**13.69**
2" dia.	2.36	3.02	0.56	12.70	nr	**15.72**
3" dia.	9.03	11.57	0.65	14.74	nr	**26.31**
4" dia.	13.09	16.77	0.80	18.14	nr	**34.91**
6" dia.	32.85	42.07	1.21	27.44	nr	**69.51**
Reducing socket						
3/4 x 1/2" dia.	0.72	0.92	0.31	7.03	nr	**7.95**
1 x 3/4" dia.	0.89	1.14	0.35	7.94	nr	**9.08**
1 1/4 x 1" dia.	1.71	2.19	0.42	9.52	nr	**11.72**
1 1/2 x 1 1/4" dia.	1.91	2.45	0.45	10.21	nr	**12.65**
2 x 1 1/2" dia.	2.89	3.70	0.51	11.57	nr	**15.27**
3 x 2" dia.	8.79	11.26	0.56	12.70	nr	**23.96**
4 x 3" dia.	13.01	16.66	0.65	14.74	nr	**31.40**
6 x 4" dia.	47.41	60.72	0.80	18.14	nr	**78.87**
8 x 6" dia.	73.43	94.05	1.21	27.44	nr	**121.49**
Elbow, 90°						
1/2" dia.	0.81	1.04	0.31	7.03	nr	**8.07**
3/4" dia.	0.97	1.24	0.35	7.94	nr	**9.18**
1" dia.	1.35	1.73	0.42	9.52	nr	**11.25**
1 1/4" dia.	2.36	3.02	0.45	10.21	nr	**13.23**
1 1/2" dia.	3.05	3.91	0.45	10.21	nr	**14.11**
2" dia.	4.51	5.78	0.56	12.70	nr	**18.48**
3" dia.	13.01	16.66	0.65	14.74	nr	**31.40**
4" dia.	19.60	25.10	0.80	18.14	nr	**43.25**
6" dia.	77.57	99.35	1.21	27.44	nr	**126.79**
Elbow 45°						
1/2" dia.	1.54	1.97	0.31	7.03	nr	**9.00**
3/4" dia.	1.64	2.10	0.35	7.94	nr	**10.04**
1" dia.	1.99	2.55	0.45	10.21	nr	**12.75**
1 1/4" dia.	2.85	3.65	0.45	10.21	nr	**13.86**
1 1/2" dia.	3.59	4.60	0.51	11.57	nr	**16.16**
2" dia.	5.04	6.46	0.56	12.70	nr	**19.16**
3" dia.	11.87	15.20	0.65	14.74	nr	**29.94**
4" dia.	24.39	31.24	0.80	18.14	nr	**49.38**
6" dia.	50.33	64.46	1.21	27.44	nr	**91.90**
Bend 90° (long radius)						
3" dia.	38.01	48.68	0.65	14.74	nr	**63.42**
4" dia.	73.26	93.83	0.80	18.14	nr	**111.97**
6" dia.	161.00	206.21	1.21	27.44	nr	**233.65**

S:PIPED SUPPLY SYSTEMS

Item	Net Price £	Material £	Labour hours	Labour £	Unit	Total rate £
Bend 45° (long radius)						
1 1/2" dia.	8.61	11.03	0.51	11.57	nr	**22.59**
2" dia.	14.07	18.02	0.56	12.70	nr	**30.72**
3" dia.	30.08	38.53	0.65	14.74	nr	**53.27**
4" dia.	58.54	74.98	0.80	18.14	nr	**93.12**
Socket union						
1/2" dia.	3.13	4.01	0.34	7.71	nr	**11.72**
3/4" dia.	3.59	4.60	0.39	8.84	nr	**13.44**
1" dia.	4.64	5.94	0.45	10.21	nr	**16.15**
1 1/4" dia.	5.78	7.40	0.50	11.34	nr	**18.74**
1 1/2" dia.	7.92	10.14	0.57	12.93	nr	**23.07**
2" dia.	10.24	13.12	0.62	14.06	nr	**27.18**
3" dia.	38.14	48.85	0.70	15.87	nr	**64.72**
4" dia.	51.63	66.13	0.89	20.18	nr	**86.31**
Saddle plain						
2" x 1 1/4" dia.	8.05	10.31	0.42	9.52	nr	**19.84**
3" x 1 1/2" dia.	11.30	14.47	0.48	10.89	nr	**25.36**
4" x 2" dia.	12.74	16.32	0.68	15.42	nr	**31.74**
6" x 2" dia.	14.95	19.15	0.91	20.64	nr	**39.79**
Straight tank connector						
1/2" dia.	2.07	2.65	0.13	2.95	nr	**5.60**
3/4" dia.	2.34	3.00	0.14	3.18	nr	**6.17**
1" dia.	4.99	6.39	0.14	3.18	nr	**9.57**
1 1/4" dia.	12.68	16.24	0.16	3.63	nr	**19.87**
1 1/2" dia.	13.91	17.82	0.18	4.08	nr	**21.90**
2" dia.	16.67	21.35	0.24	5.44	nr	**26.79**
3" dia.	17.08	21.88	0.29	6.58	nr	**28.45**
Equal tee						
1/2" dia.	0.94	1.20	0.44	9.98	nr	**11.18**
3/4" dia.	1.18	1.51	0.48	10.89	nr	**12.40**
1" dia.	1.79	2.29	0.54	12.25	nr	**14.54**
1 1/4" dia.	2.53	3.24	0.70	15.87	nr	**19.12**
1 1/2" dia.	3.65	4.67	0.74	16.78	nr	**21.46**
2" dia.	5.78	7.40	0.80	18.14	nr	**25.55**
3" dia.	16.75	21.45	1.04	23.59	nr	**45.04**
4" dia.	24.56	31.46	1.28	29.03	nr	**60.48**
6" dia.	85.54	109.56	1.93	43.77	nr	**153.33**
PVC - C						
Pipes; solvent welded in the running length						
Pipe; 3m long; PN25						
16 x 2.0mm	1.56	2.00	0.20	4.54	m	**6.53**
20 x 2.3mm	2.38	3.05	0.20	4.54	m	**7.58**
25 x 2.8mm	3.09	3.96	0.20	4.54	m	**8.49**
32 x 3.6mm	4.35	5.57	0.20	4.54	m	**10.11**
Pipe; 5m long; PN25						
40 x 4.5mm	5.52	7.07	0.20	4.54	m	**11.61**
50 x 5.6mm	8.36	10.71	0.20	4.54	m	**15.24**
63 x 7.0mm	12.81	16.41	0.20	4.54	m	**20.94**

S:PIPED SUPPLY SYSTEMS

Item	Net Price £	Material £	Labour hours	Labour £	Unit	Total rate £
S10 : COLD WATER (cont'd)						
Y10 – PIPELINES (cont'd)						
PVC-C PIPEWORK (cont'd)						
Extra over fittings; solvent welded joints						
Straight coupling; PN25						
16mm	0.25	0.32	0.20	4.54	nr	4.86
20mm	0.35	0.45	0.20	4.54	nr	4.98
25mm	0.44	0.56	0.20	4.54	nr	5.10
32mm	1.38	1.77	0.20	4.54	nr	6.30
40mm	1.77	2.27	0.20	4.54	nr	6.80
50mm	2.37	3.04	0.20	4.54	nr	7.57
63mm	4.17	5.34	0.20	4.54	nr	9.88
Elbow; 90°; PN25						
16mm	0.41	0.53	0.20	4.54	nr	5.06
20mm	0.63	0.81	0.20	4.54	nr	5.34
25mm	0.79	1.01	0.20	4.54	nr	5.55
32mm	1.64	2.10	0.20	4.54	nr	6.64
40mm	2.53	3.24	0.20	4.54	nr	7.78
50mm	3.51	4.50	0.20	4.54	nr	9.03
63mm	5.99	7.67	0.20	4.54	nr	12.21
Elbow; 45°; PN25						
20mm	0.63	0.81	0.20	4.54	nr	5.34
25mm	0.79	1.01	0.20	4.54	nr	5.55
32mm	1.64	2.10	0.20	4.54	nr	6.64
40mm	2.53	3.24	0.20	4.54	nr	7.78
50mm	3.51	4.50	0.20	4.54	nr	9.03
63mm	5.99	7.67	0.20	4.54	nr	12.21
Reducer fitting; single stage reduction						
20/16mm	0.45	0.58	0.20	4.54	nr	5.11
25/20mm	0.54	0.69	0.20	4.54	nr	5.23
32/25mm	1.08	1.38	0.20	4.54	nr	5.92
40/32mm	1.43	1.83	0.20	4.54	nr	6.37
50/40mm	1.64	2.10	0.20	4.54	nr	6.64
63/50mm	2.49	3.19	0.20	4.54	nr	7.72
Equal tee; 90°; PN25						
16mm	0.69	0.88	0.20	4.54	nr	5.42
20mm	0.94	1.20	0.20	4.54	nr	5.74
25mm	1.20	1.54	0.20	4.54	nr	6.07
32mm	1.96	2.51	0.20	4.54	nr	7.05
40mm	3.38	4.33	0.20	4.54	nr	8.86
50mm	5.05	6.47	0.20	4.54	nr	11.00
63mm	8.54	10.94	0.20	4.54	nr	15.47
Cap; PN25						
20mm	0.47	0.60	0.20	4.54	nr	5.14
25mm	0.63	0.81	0.20	4.54	nr	5.34
32mm	0.92	1.18	0.20	4.54	nr	5.71
40mm	1.27	1.63	0.20	4.54	nr	6.16
50mm	1.77	2.27	0.20	4.54	nr	6.80
63mm	2.81	3.60	0.20	4.54	nr	8.13

S:PIPED SUPPLY SYSTEMS

Item	Net Price £	Material £	Labour hours	Labour £	Unit	Total rate £
SCREWED STEEL PIPEWORK						
Galvanised steel pipes; screwed and socketed joints; BS 1387: 1985						
Galvanised; medium						
8mm dia.	2.23	2.86	0.51	11.57	m	**14.42**
10mm dia.	2.24	2.87	0.51	11.57	m	**14.44**
15mm dia.	2.02	2.59	0.52	11.79	m	**14.38**
20mm dia.	2.27	2.91	0.55	12.47	m	**15.38**
25mm dia.	3.18	4.07	0.60	13.61	m	**17.68**
32mm dia.	3.94	5.05	0.67	15.19	m	**20.24**
40mm dia.	4.57	5.85	0.75	17.01	m	**22.86**
50mm dia.	6.42	8.22	0.85	19.28	m	**27.50**
65mm dia.	8.70	11.14	0.93	21.09	m	**32.23**
80mm dia.	11.27	14.43	1.07	24.27	m	**38.70**
100mm dia.	15.93	20.40	1.46	33.11	m	**53.51**
125mm dia.	25.34	32.46	1.72	39.01	m	**71.46**
150mm dia.	29.43	37.69	1.96	44.45	m	**82.14**
Galvanised; heavy						
15mm dia.	2.39	3.06	0.52	11.79	m	**14.85**
20mm dia.	2.71	3.47	0.55	12.47	m	**15.94**
25mm dia.	3.86	4.94	0.60	13.61	m	**18.55**
32mm dia.	4.79	6.14	0.67	15.19	m	**21.33**
40mm dia.	5.59	7.16	0.75	17.01	m	**24.17**
50mm dia.	7.74	9.91	0.85	19.28	m	**29.19**
65mm dia.	10.52	13.47	0.93	21.09	m	**34.56**
80mm dia.	13.36	17.11	1.07	24.27	m	**41.38**
100mm dia.	18.62	23.85	1.46	33.11	m	**56.96**
125mm dia.	26.98	34.56	1.72	39.01	m	**73.56**
150mm dia.	31.55	40.41	1.96	44.45	m	**84.86**
Extra over steel flanges, screwed and drilled; metric; BS 4504						
Screwed flanges; PN6						
15mm dia.	9.67	12.39	0.35	7.94	nr	**20.32**
20mm dia.	10.01	12.82	0.47	10.66	nr	**23.48**
25mm dia.	10.11	12.95	0.53	12.02	nr	**24.97**
32mm dia.	10.15	13.00	0.62	14.06	nr	**27.06**
40mm dia.	10.15	13.00	0.70	15.87	nr	**28.87**
50mm dia.	10.96	14.04	0.84	19.05	nr	**33.09**
65mm dia.	14.96	19.16	1.03	23.36	nr	**42.52**
80mm dia.	18.11	23.20	1.23	27.89	nr	**51.09**
100mm dia.	21.71	27.81	1.41	31.98	nr	**59.78**
125mm dia.	45.84	58.71	1.77	40.14	nr	**98.85**
150mm dia.	45.84	58.71	2.21	50.12	nr	**108.83**

S:PIPED SUPPLY SYSTEMS

Item	Net Price £	Material £	Labour hours	Labour £	Unit	Total rate £
S10 : COLD WATER (cont'd)						
Y10 – PIPELINES (cont'd)						
SCREWED STEEL PIPEWORK (cont'd)						
Steel flanges; screwed and drilled (cont'd)						
Screwed flanges; PN16						
15mm dia.	13.11	16.79	0.35	7.94	nr	**24.73**
20mm dia.	13.13	16.82	0.47	10.66	nr	**27.48**
25mm dia.	13.23	16.94	0.53	12.02	nr	**28.96**
32mm dia.	14.03	17.97	0.62	14.06	nr	**32.03**
40mm dia.	14.03	17.97	0.70	15.87	nr	**33.84**
50mm dia.	14.82	18.98	0.84	19.05	nr	**38.03**
65mm dia.	18.53	23.73	1.03	23.36	nr	**47.09**
80mm dia.	21.88	28.02	1.23	27.89	nr	**55.92**
100mm dia.	26.25	33.62	1.41	31.98	nr	**65.60**
125mm dia.	47.63	61.00	1.77	40.14	nr	**101.14**
150mm dia.	41.83	53.58	2.21	50.12	nr	**103.69**
Extra over steel flanges, screwed and drilled; imperial; BS 10						
Screwed flanges; table E						
1/2" dia.	13.52	17.32	0.35	7.94	nr	**25.25**
3/4" dia.	13.86	17.75	0.47	10.66	nr	**28.41**
1" dia.	13.96	17.88	0.53	12.02	nr	**29.90**
1 1/4" dia.	14.00	17.93	0.62	14.06	nr	**31.99**
1 1/2" dia.	14.00	17.93	0.70	15.87	nr	**33.81**
2" dia.	14.21	18.20	0.84	19.05	nr	**37.25**
2 1/2" dia.	16.89	21.63	1.03	23.36	nr	**44.99**
3" dia.	19.77	25.32	1.23	27.89	nr	**53.22**
4" dia.	26.50	33.94	1.41	31.98	nr	**65.92**
5" dia.	54.59	69.92	1.77	40.14	nr	**110.06**
Extra over steel flange connections						
Bolted connection between pair of flanges; including gasket, bolts, nuts and washers						
50mm dia.	27.68	35.45	0.53	12.02	nr	**47.47**
65mm dia.	34.87	44.66	0.53	12.02	nr	**56.68**
80mm dia.	40.06	51.31	0.53	12.02	nr	**63.33**
100mm dia.	47.86	61.30	0.53	12.02	nr	**73.32**
125mm dia.	90.17	115.49	0.61	13.83	nr	**129.32**
150mm dia.	75.85	97.15	0.90	20.41	nr	**117.56**

S:PIPED SUPPLY SYSTEMS

Item	Net Price £	Material £	Labour hours	Labour £	Unit	Total rate £
Extra over heavy steel tubular fittings; BS 1387						
Long screw connection with socket and backnut						
15mm dia.	2.50	3.20	0.63	14.29	nr	17.49
20mm dia.	3.43	4.39	0.84	19.05	nr	23.44
25mm dia.	4.49	5.75	0.95	21.54	nr	27.30
32mm dia.	5.87	7.52	1.11	25.17	nr	32.69
40mm dia.	7.15	9.16	1.28	29.03	nr	38.19
50mm dia.	10.51	13.46	1.53	34.70	nr	48.16
65mm dia.	23.87	30.57	1.87	42.41	nr	72.98
80mm dia.	30.96	39.65	2.21	50.12	nr	89.77
100mm dia.	47.00	60.20	3.05	69.17	nr	129.37
Running nipple						
15mm dia.	0.71	0.91	0.50	11.34	nr	12.25
20mm dia.	0.88	1.13	0.68	15.42	nr	16.55
25mm dia.	0.95	1.22	0.77	17.46	nr	18.68
32mm dia.	1.53	1.96	0.90	20.41	nr	22.37
40mm dia.	2.06	2.64	1.03	23.36	nr	26.00
50mm dia.	3.14	4.02	1.23	27.89	nr	31.92
65mm dia.	6.75	8.65	1.50	34.02	nr	42.66
80mm dia.	10.52	13.47	1.78	40.37	nr	53.84
100mm dia.	16.48	21.11	2.38	53.97	nr	75.08
Barrel nipple						
15mm dia.	0.57	0.73	0.50	11.34	nr	12.07
20mm dia.	0.74	0.95	0.68	15.42	nr	16.37
25mm dia.	0.96	1.23	0.77	17.46	nr	18.69
32mm dia.	1.59	2.04	0.90	20.41	nr	22.45
40mm dia.	1.78	2.28	1.03	23.36	nr	25.64
50mm dia.	2.53	3.24	1.23	27.89	nr	31.13
65mm dia.	5.43	6.95	1.50	34.02	nr	40.97
80mm dia.	7.56	9.68	1.78	40.37	nr	50.05
100mm dia.	13.68	17.52	2.38	53.97	nr	71.50
125mm dia.	25.42	32.56	2.87	65.09	nr	97.64
150mm dia.	40.03	51.27	3.39	76.88	nr	128.15
Close taper nipple						
15mm dia.	0.84	1.08	0.50	11.34	nr	12.42
20mm dia.	1.09	1.40	0.68	15.42	nr	16.82
25mm dia.	1.43	1.83	0.77	17.46	nr	19.29
32mm dia.	2.13	2.73	0.90	20.41	nr	23.14
40mm dia.	2.64	3.38	1.03	23.36	nr	26.74
50mm dia.	4.06	5.20	1.23	27.89	nr	33.09
65mm dia.	6.40	8.20	1.50	34.02	nr	42.21
80mm dia.	10.49	13.44	1.78	40.37	nr	53.80
100mm dia.	19.95	25.55	2.38	53.97	nr	79.53

S:PIPED SUPPLY SYSTEMS

Item	Net Price £	Material £	Labour hours	Labour £	Unit	Total rate £
S10 : COLD WATER (cont'd)						
Y10 – PIPELINES (cont'd)						
SCREWED STEEL PIPEWORK (cont'd)						
Heavy steel tubular fittings (cont'd)						
90° bend with socket						
15mm dia.	2.28	2.92	0.64	14.51	nr	17.43
20mm dia.	3.06	3.92	0.85	19.28	nr	23.20
25mm dia.	4.70	6.02	0.97	22.00	nr	28.02
32mm dia.	6.75	8.65	1.12	25.40	nr	34.05
40mm dia.	8.24	10.55	1.29	29.26	nr	39.81
50mm dia.	12.82	16.42	1.55	35.15	nr	51.57
65mm dia.	25.87	33.13	1.89	42.86	nr	76.00
80mm dia.	38.47	49.27	2.24	50.80	nr	100.07
100mm dia.	68.16	87.30	3.09	70.08	nr	157.37
125mm dia.	175.00	224.14	3.92	88.90	nr	313.04
150mm dia.	250.00	320.20	4.74	107.50	nr	427.69
Extra over heavy steel fittings; BS 1740						
Plug						
15mm dia.	1.23	1.58	0.28	6.35	nr	7.93
20mm dia.	1.50	1.92	0.38	8.62	nr	10.54
25mm dia.	1.88	2.41	0.44	9.98	nr	12.39
32mm dia.	2.91	3.73	0.51	11.57	nr	15.29
40mm dia.	3.20	4.10	0.59	13.38	nr	17.48
50mm dia.	4.42	5.66	0.70	15.87	nr	21.54
65mm dia.	13.08	16.75	0.85	19.28	nr	36.03
80mm dia.	24.21	31.01	1.00	22.68	nr	53.69
100mm dia.	48.00	61.48	1.44	32.66	nr	94.13
Socket						
15mm dia.	0.60	0.77	0.64	14.51	nr	15.28
20mm dia.	0.69	0.88	0.85	19.28	nr	20.16
25mm dia.	0.90	1.15	0.97	22.00	nr	23.15
32mm dia.	1.32	1.69	1.12	25.40	nr	27.09
40mm dia.	1.69	2.16	1.29	29.26	nr	31.42
50mm dia.	2.54	3.25	1.55	35.15	nr	38.40
65mm dia.	4.35	5.57	1.89	42.86	nr	48.43
80mm dia.	6.08	7.79	2.24	50.80	nr	58.59
100mm dia.	11.60	14.86	3.09	70.08	nr	84.93
150mm dia.	57.31	73.40	4.74	107.50	nr	180.90
Elbow, female/female						
15mm dia.	4.75	6.08	0.64	14.51	nr	20.60
20mm dia.	5.79	7.42	0.85	19.28	nr	26.69
25mm dia.	7.87	10.08	0.97	22.00	nr	32.08
32mm dia.	15.71	20.12	1.12	25.40	nr	45.52
40mm dia.	15.71	20.12	1.29	29.26	nr	49.38
50mm dia.	20.28	25.97	1.55	35.15	nr	61.13
65mm dia.	51.62	66.11	1.89	42.86	nr	108.98
80mm dia.	67.17	86.03	2.24	50.80	nr	136.83
100mm dia.	126.74	162.33	3.09	70.08	nr	232.40

S:PIPED SUPPLY SYSTEMS

Item	Net Price £	Material £	Labour hours	Labour £	Unit	Total rate £
Equal tee						
15mm dia.	5.35	6.85	0.91	20.64	nr	**27.49**
20mm dia.	6.59	8.44	1.22	27.67	nr	**36.11**
25mm dia.	10.61	13.59	1.40	31.75	nr	**45.34**
32mm dia.	19.34	24.77	1.62	36.74	nr	**61.51**
40mm dia.	19.34	24.77	1.86	42.18	nr	**66.95**
50mm dia.	28.29	36.23	2.21	50.12	nr	**86.35**
65mm dia.	99.54	127.49	2.72	61.69	nr	**189.18**
80mm dia.	108.00	138.33	3.21	72.80	nr	**211.12**
100mm dia.	173.84	222.65	4.44	100.69	nr	**323.34**
Extra over malleable iron fittings; BS 143						
Cap						
15mm dia.	0.53	0.68	0.32	7.26	nr	**7.94**
20mm dia.	0.61	0.78	0.43	9.75	nr	**10.53**
25mm dia.	0.81	1.04	0.49	11.11	nr	**12.15**
32mm dia.	1.25	1.60	0.58	13.15	nr	**14.75**
40mm dia.	1.59	2.04	0.66	14.97	nr	**17.00**
50mm dia.	2.97	3.80	0.78	17.69	nr	**21.49**
65mm dia.	5.10	6.53	0.96	21.77	nr	**28.30**
80mm dia.	5.77	7.39	1.13	25.63	nr	**33.02**
100mm dia.	12.64	16.19	1.70	38.55	nr	**54.74**
Plain plug, hollow						
15mm dia.	0.41	0.53	0.28	6.35	nr	**6.88**
20mm dia.	0.52	0.67	0.38	8.62	nr	**9.28**
25mm dia.	0.64	0.82	0.44	9.98	nr	**10.80**
32mm dia.	0.99	1.27	0.51	11.57	nr	**12.83**
40mm dia.	1.53	1.96	0.59	13.38	nr	**15.34**
50mm dia.	2.15	2.75	0.70	15.87	nr	**18.63**
65mm dia.	3.75	4.80	0.85	19.28	nr	**24.08**
80mm dia.	5.61	7.19	1.00	22.68	nr	**29.86**
100mm dia.	10.33	13.23	1.44	32.66	nr	**45.89**
Plain plug, solid						
15mm dia.	1.14	1.46	0.29	6.58	nr	**8.04**
20mm dia.	1.23	1.58	0.38	8.62	nr	**10.19**
25mm dia.	1.62	2.07	0.44	9.98	nr	**12.05**
32mm dia.	2.24	2.87	0.51	11.57	nr	**14.44**
40mm dia.	3.02	3.87	0.59	13.38	nr	**17.25**
50mm dia.	3.96	5.07	0.70	15.87	nr	**20.95**
65mm dia.	4.38	5.61	0.85	19.28	nr	**24.89**
Elbow, male/female						
15mm dia.	0.60	0.77	0.64	14.51	nr	**15.28**
20mm dia.	0.80	1.02	0.85	19.28	nr	**20.30**
25mm dia.	1.34	1.72	0.97	22.00	nr	**23.71**
32mm dia.	2.72	3.48	1.12	25.40	nr	**28.88**
40mm dia.	3.76	4.82	1.29	29.26	nr	**34.07**
50mm dia.	4.84	6.20	1.55	35.15	nr	**41.35**
65mm dia.	10.79	13.82	1.89	42.86	nr	**56.68**
80mm dia.	14.75	18.89	2.24	50.80	nr	**69.69**
100mm dia.	25.79	33.03	3.09	70.08	nr	**103.11**

S:PIPED SUPPLY SYSTEMS

Item	Net Price £	Material £	Labour hours	Labour £	Unit	Total rate £
S10 : COLD WATER (cont'd)						
Y10 – PIPELINES (cont'd)						
SCREWED STEEL PIPEWORK (cont'd)						
Malleable iron fittings (cont'd)						
Elbow						
15mm dia.	0.53	0.68	0.64	14.51	nr	15.19
20mm dia.	0.73	0.94	0.85	19.28	nr	20.21
25mm dia.	1.13	1.45	0.97	22.00	nr	23.45
32mm dia.	2.13	2.73	1.12	25.40	nr	28.13
40mm dia.	3.19	4.09	1.29	29.26	nr	33.34
50mm dia.	3.73	4.78	1.55	35.15	nr	39.93
65mm dia.	8.33	10.67	1.89	42.86	nr	53.53
80mm dia.	12.24	15.68	2.24	50.80	nr	66.48
100mm dia.	21.02	26.92	3.09	70.08	nr	97.00
125mm dia.	50.57	64.77	4.44	100.69	nr	165.46
150mm dia.	94.14	120.57	5.79	131.31	nr	251.88
45 ° elbow						
15mm dia.	1.38	1.77	0.64	14.51	nr	16.28
20mm dia.	1.70	2.18	0.85	19.28	nr	21.45
25mm dia.	2.34	3.00	0.97	22.00	nr	25.00
32mm dia.	4.91	6.29	1.12	25.40	nr	31.69
40mm dia.	5.77	7.39	1.29	29.26	nr	36.65
50mm dia.	7.92	10.14	1.55	35.15	nr	45.30
65mm dia.	11.13	14.26	1.89	42.86	nr	57.12
80mm dia.	16.73	21.43	2.24	50.80	nr	72.23
100mm dia.	32.32	41.40	3.09	70.08	nr	111.47
150mm dia.	86.51	110.80	5.79	131.31	nr	242.11
Bend, male/female						
15mm dia.	1.06	1.36	0.64	14.51	nr	15.87
20mm dia.	1.74	2.23	0.85	19.28	nr	21.51
25mm dia.	2.44	3.13	0.97	22.00	nr	25.12
32mm dia.	3.71	4.75	1.12	25.40	nr	30.15
40mm dia.	5.43	6.95	1.29	29.26	nr	36.21
50mm dia.	10.21	13.08	1.55	35.15	nr	48.23
65mm dia.	15.63	20.02	1.89	42.86	nr	62.88
80mm dia.	21.20	27.15	2.24	50.80	nr	77.95
100mm dia.	52.51	67.25	3.09	70.08	nr	137.33
Bend, male						
15mm dia.	2.42	3.10	0.64	14.51	nr	17.61
20mm dia.	2.71	3.47	0.85	19.28	nr	22.75
25mm dia.	3.99	5.11	0.97	22.00	nr	27.11
32mm dia.	7.93	10.16	1.12	25.40	nr	35.56
40mm dia.	11.12	14.24	1.29	29.26	nr	43.50
50mm dia.	14.87	19.05	1.55	35.15	nr	54.20

S:PIPED SUPPLY SYSTEMS

Item	Net Price £	Material £	Labour hours	Labour £	Unit	Total rate £
Bend, female						
15mm dia.	1.08	1.38	0.64	14.51	nr	**15.90**
20mm dia.	1.55	1.99	0.85	19.28	nr	**21.26**
25mm dia.	2.17	2.78	0.97	22.00	nr	**24.78**
32mm dia.	3.80	4.87	1.12	25.40	nr	**30.27**
40mm dia.	4.53	5.80	1.29	29.26	nr	**35.06**
50mm dia.	7.14	9.14	1.55	35.15	nr	**44.30**
65mm dia.	15.63	20.02	1.89	42.86	nr	**62.88**
80mm dia.	23.18	29.69	2.24	50.80	nr	**80.49**
100mm dia.	48.63	62.28	3.09	70.08	nr	**132.36**
125mm dia.	129.72	166.14	4.44	100.69	nr	**266.84**
150mm dia.	189.88	243.20	5.79	131.31	nr	**374.50**
Return bend						
15mm dia.	4.26	5.46	0.64	14.51	nr	**19.97**
20mm dia.	6.88	8.81	0.85	19.28	nr	**28.09**
25mm dia.	8.59	11.00	0.97	22.00	nr	**33.00**
32mm dia.	12.20	15.63	1.12	25.40	nr	**41.03**
40mm dia.	14.54	18.62	1.29	29.26	nr	**47.88**
50mm dia.	22.18	28.41	1.55	35.15	nr	**63.56**
Equal socket, parallel thread						
15mm dia.	0.57	0.73	0.64	14.51	nr	**15.24**
20mm dia.	0.68	0.87	0.85	19.28	nr	**20.15**
25mm dia.	0.91	1.17	0.97	22.00	nr	**23.16**
32mm dia.	1.69	2.16	1.12	25.40	nr	**27.56**
40mm dia.	2.41	3.09	1.29	29.26	nr	**32.34**
50mm dia.	3.46	4.43	1.55	35.15	nr	**39.58**
65mm dia.	6.07	7.77	1.89	42.86	nr	**50.64**
80mm dia.	8.34	10.68	2.24	50.80	nr	**61.48**
100mm dia.	14.16	18.14	3.09	70.08	nr	**88.21**
Concentric reducing socket						
20 x 15mm dia.	0.83	1.06	0.76	17.24	nr	**18.30**
25 x 15mm dia.	1.08	1.38	0.86	19.50	nr	**20.89**
25 x 20mm dia.	1.02	1.31	0.86	19.50	nr	**20.81**
32 x 25mm dia.	1.77	2.27	1.01	22.91	nr	**25.17**
40 x 25mm dia.	2.33	2.98	1.16	26.31	nr	**29.29**
40 x 32mm dia.	2.59	3.32	1.16	26.31	nr	**29.62**
50 x 25mm dia.	4.48	5.74	1.38	31.30	nr	**37.03**
50 x 40mm dia.	3.62	4.64	1.38	31.30	nr	**35.93**
65 x 50mm dia.	6.32	8.09	1.69	38.33	nr	**46.42**
80 x 50mm dia.	7.88	10.09	2.00	45.36	nr	**55.45**
100 x 50mm dia.	15.72	20.13	2.75	62.37	nr	**82.50**
100 x 80mm dia.	14.58	18.67	2.75	62.37	nr	**81.04**
150 x 100mm dia.	38.48	49.28	4.10	92.98	nr	**142.27**
Eccentric reducing socket						
20 x 15mm dia.	1.65	2.11	0.76	17.24	nr	**19.35**
25 x 15mm dia.	4.71	6.03	0.86	19.50	nr	**25.54**
25 x 20mm dia.	5.34	6.84	0.86	19.50	nr	**26.34**
32 x 25mm dia.	6.20	7.94	1.01	22.91	nr	**30.85**
40 x 25mm dia.	7.11	9.11	1.16	26.31	nr	**35.41**
40 x 32mm dia.	3.84	4.92	1.16	26.31	nr	**31.23**
50 x 25mm dia.	4.61	5.90	1.38	31.30	nr	**37.20**
50 x 40mm dia.	4.61	5.90	1.38	31.30	nr	**37.20**
65 x 50mm dia.	7.88	10.09	1.69	38.33	nr	**48.42**
80 x 50mm dia.	12.81	16.41	2.00	45.36	nr	**61.76**

S:PIPED SUPPLY SYSTEMS

Item	Net Price £	Material £	Labour hours	Labour £	Unit	Total rate £
S10 : COLD WATER (cont'd)						
Y10 – PIPELINES (cont'd)						
SCREWED STEEL PIPEWORK (cont'd)						
Malleable iron fittings (cont'd)						
Hexagon bush						
20 x 15mm dia.	0.47	0.60	0.37	8.39	nr	**8.99**
25 x 15mm dia.	0.64	0.82	0.43	9.75	nr	**10.57**
25 x 20mm dia.	0.60	0.77	0.43	9.75	nr	**10.52**
32 x 25mm dia.	0.73	0.94	0.51	11.57	nr	**12.50**
40 x 25mm dia.	1.09	1.40	0.58	13.15	nr	**14.55**
40 x 32mm dia.	1.15	1.47	0.58	13.15	nr	**14.63**
50 x 25mm dia.	2.30	2.95	0.71	16.10	nr	**19.05**
50 x 40mm dia.	2.15	2.75	0.71	16.10	nr	**18.86**
65 x 50mm dia.	3.95	5.06	0.84	19.05	nr	**24.11**
80 x 50mm dia.	5.97	7.65	1.00	22.68	nr	**30.32**
100 x 50mm dia.	13.82	17.70	1.52	34.47	nr	**52.17**
100 x 80mm dia.	11.50	14.73	1.52	34.47	nr	**49.20**
150 x 100mm dia.	36.41	46.63	2.48	56.24	nr	**102.88**
Hexagon nipple						
15mm dia.	0.50	0.64	0.28	6.35	nr	**6.99**
20mm dia.	0.57	0.73	0.38	8.62	nr	**9.35**
25mm dia.	0.80	1.02	0.44	9.98	nr	**11.00**
32mm dia.	1.53	1.96	0.51	11.57	nr	**13.53**
40mm dia.	1.77	2.27	0.59	13.38	nr	**15.65**
50mm dia.	3.22	4.12	0.70	15.87	nr	**20.00**
65mm dia.	5.39	6.90	0.85	19.28	nr	**26.18**
80mm dia.	7.46	9.55	1.00	22.68	nr	**32.23**
100mm dia.	13.23	16.94	1.44	32.66	nr	**49.60**
150mm dia.	37.42	47.93	2.32	52.61	nr	**100.54**
Union, male/female						
15mm dia.	4.96	6.35	0.64	14.51	nr	**20.87**
20mm dia.	6.70	8.58	0.85	19.28	nr	**27.86**
25mm dia.	8.47	10.85	0.97	22.00	nr	**32.85**
32mm dia.	11.94	15.29	1.12	25.40	nr	**40.69**
40mm dia.	14.20	18.19	1.29	29.26	nr	**47.44**
50mm dia.	18.98	24.31	1.55	35.15	nr	**59.46**
65mm dia.	33.58	43.01	1.89	42.86	nr	**85.87**
Union, female						
15mm dia.	5.01	6.42	0.64	14.51	nr	**20.93**
20mm dia.	5.95	7.62	0.85	19.28	nr	**26.90**
25mm dia.	7.32	9.38	0.97	22.00	nr	**31.37**
32mm dia.	11.03	14.13	1.12	25.40	nr	**39.53**
40mm dia.	13.34	17.09	1.29	29.26	nr	**46.34**
50mm dia.	15.76	20.19	1.55	35.15	nr	**55.34**
65mm dia.	35.35	45.28	1.89	42.86	nr	**88.14**
80mm dia.	57.74	73.95	2.24	50.80	nr	**124.75**
100mm dia.	101.67	130.22	3.09	70.08	nr	**200.29**
Union elbow, male/female						
15mm dia.	2.92	3.74	0.64	14.51	nr	**18.25**
20mm dia.	3.66	4.69	0.85	19.28	nr	**23.96**
25mm dia.	5.14	6.58	0.97	22.00	nr	**28.58**

S:PIPED SUPPLY SYSTEMS

Item	Net Price £	Material £	Labour hours	Labour £	Unit	Total rate £
Twin elbow						
15mm dia.	3.22	4.12	0.91	20.64	nr	**24.76**
20mm dia.	3.56	4.56	1.22	27.67	nr	**32.23**
25mm dia.	5.76	7.38	1.39	31.52	nr	**38.90**
32mm dia.	10.38	13.29	1.62	36.74	nr	**50.03**
40mm dia.	13.15	16.84	1.86	42.18	nr	**59.02**
50mm dia.	16.89	21.63	2.21	50.12	nr	**71.75**
65mm dia.	27.30	34.97	2.72	61.69	nr	**96.65**
80mm dia.	46.52	59.58	3.21	72.80	nr	**132.38**
Equal tee						
15mm dia.	0.73	0.94	0.91	20.64	nr	**21.57**
20mm dia.	1.07	1.37	1.22	27.67	nr	**29.04**
25mm dia.	1.54	1.97	1.39	31.52	nr	**33.50**
32mm dia.	2.92	3.74	1.62	36.74	nr	**40.48**
40mm dia.	3.99	5.11	1.86	42.18	nr	**47.29**
50mm dia.	5.75	7.36	2.21	50.12	nr	**57.48**
65mm dia.	13.48	17.27	2.72	61.69	nr	**78.95**
80mm dia.	15.72	20.13	3.21	72.80	nr	**92.93**
100mm dia.	28.49	36.49	4.44	100.69	nr	**137.18**
125mm dia.	69.87	89.49	5.38	122.01	nr	**211.50**
150mm dia.	111.33	142.59	6.31	143.10	nr	**285.69**
Tee reducing on branch						
20 x 15mm dia.	1.09	1.40	1.22	27.67	nr	**29.06**
25 x 15mm dia.	1.49	1.91	1.39	31.52	nr	**33.43**
25 x 20mm dia.	1.70	2.18	1.39	31.52	nr	**33.70**
32 x 25mm dia.	2.97	3.80	1.62	36.74	nr	**40.54**
40 x 25mm dia.	3.76	4.82	1.86	42.18	nr	**47.00**
40 x 32mm dia.	5.51	7.06	1.86	42.18	nr	**49.24**
50 x 25mm dia.	4.99	6.39	2.21	50.12	nr	**56.51**
50 x 40mm dia.	7.76	9.94	2.21	50.12	nr	**60.06**
65 x 50mm dia.	11.97	15.33	2.72	61.69	nr	**77.02**
80 x 50mm dia.	16.18	20.72	3.21	72.80	nr	**93.52**
100 x 50mm dia.	23.60	30.23	4.44	100.69	nr	**130.92**
100 x 80mm dia.	36.41	46.63	4.44	100.69	nr	**147.33**
150 x 100mm dia.	82.00	105.02	6.31	143.10	nr	**248.13**
Equal pitcher tee						
15mm dia.	2.54	3.25	0.91	20.64	nr	**23.89**
20mm dia.	3.14	4.02	1.22	27.67	nr	**31.69**
25mm dia.	4.71	6.03	1.39	31.52	nr	**37.56**
32mm dia.	6.55	8.39	1.62	36.74	nr	**45.13**
40mm dia.	10.13	12.97	1.86	42.18	nr	**55.16**
50mm dia.	14.22	18.21	2.21	50.12	nr	**68.33**
65mm dia.	20.23	25.91	2.72	61.69	nr	**87.60**
80mm dia.	27.81	35.62	3.21	72.80	nr	**108.42**
100mm dia.	62.58	80.15	4.44	100.69	nr	**180.84**
Cross						
15mm dia.	2.11	2.70	1.00	22.68	nr	**25.38**
20mm dia.	3.31	4.24	1.33	30.16	nr	**34.40**
25mm dia.	4.20	5.38	1.51	34.24	nr	**39.62**
32mm dia.	5.60	7.17	1.77	40.14	nr	**47.31**
40mm dia.	7.54	9.66	2.02	45.81	nr	**55.47**
50mm dia.	11.72	15.01	2.42	54.88	nr	**69.89**
65mm dia.	16.73	21.43	2.97	67.35	nr	**88.78**
80mm dia.	22.25	28.50	3.50	79.37	nr	**107.87**
100mm dia.	40.45	51.81	4.84	109.76	nr	**161.57**

S:PIPED SUPPLY SYSTEMS

Item	Net Price £	Material £	Labour hours	Labour £	Unit	Total rate £
S10 : COLD WATER (cont'd)						
Y10 – PIPELINES (cont'd)						
COPPER PIPEWORK						
Microbore copper pipe; capillary or compression joints in the running length; BS 2871						
Table W						
6mm dia.	0.81	1.04	0.40	9.07	m	**10.11**
8mm dia.	0.97	1.24	0.40	9.07	m	**10.31**
10mm dia.	1.07	1.37	0.41	9.30	m	**10.67**
Table W; plastic coated gas and cold water service pipe for corrosive environments						
6mm dia.	1.05	1.41	0.44	9.98	m	**11.39**
8mm dia.	1.19	1.52	0.44	9.98	m	**11.50**
10mm dia.	1.48	1.90	0.48	10.89	m	**12.78**
Microbore accessories						
Manifold connectors; side entry one way flow, 22mm body						
4 x 8mm connections	8.22	10.53	0.59	13.38	nr	**23.91**
6 x 8mm connections	9.78	12.53	0.87	19.74	nr	**32.26**
2 x 10mm connections	5.37	6.88	0.33	7.48	nr	**14.36**
4 x 10mm connections	8.59	11.00	0.65	14.74	nr	**25.74**
Manifold connectors; linear flow, 22mm body						
4 x 8mm connections	7.07	9.06	0.59	13.38	nr	**22.44**
4 x 10mm connections	9.11	11.67	0.65	14.74	nr	**26.41**
Manifold connectors; linear flow, 28mm body						
6 x 8mm connections	10.15	13.00	0.87	19.74	nr	**32.74**
Copper pipe; capillary or compression joints in the running length; BS 2871						
Table X						
12mm dia.	0.68	0.87	0.39	8.84	m	**9.72**
15mm dia.	0.90	1.15	0.40	9.07	m	**10.22**
22mm dia.	1.76	2.25	0.47	10.66	m	**12.91**
28mm dia.	2.29	2.93	0.51	11.57	m	**14.50**
35mm dia.	5.35	6.85	0.58	13.15	m	**20.01**
42mm dia.	6.76	8.66	0.66	14.97	m	**23.63**
54mm dia.	9.09	11.64	0.72	16.33	m	**27.97**
67mm dia.	15.65	20.04	0.75	17.01	m	**37.05**
76mm dia.	22.60	28.95	0.76	17.24	m	**46.18**
108mm dia.	34.30	43.93	0.78	17.69	m	**61.62**
133mm dia.	43.50	55.71	1.05	23.81	m	**79.53**
159mm dia.	63.71	81.60	1.15	26.08	m	**107.68**

S:PIPED SUPPLY SYSTEMS

Item	Net Price £	Material £	Labour hours	Labour £	Unit	Total rate £
Table Y						
12mm dia.	5.06	6.48	0.41	9.30	m	**15.78**
15mm dia.	8.33	10.67	0.43	9.75	m	**20.42**
22mm dia.	14.33	18.35	0.50	11.34	m	**29.69**
28mm dia.	17.96	23.00	0.54	12.25	m	**35.25**
35mm dia.	20.41	26.14	0.62	14.06	m	**40.20**
42mm dia.	24.49	31.37	0.71	16.10	m	**47.47**
54mm dia.	41.35	52.96	0.78	17.69	m	**70.65**
67mm dia.	55.54	71.14	0.82	18.60	m	**89.73**
76mm dia.	62.25	79.73	0.60	13.61	m	**93.34**
108mm dia.	114.46	146.60	0.88	19.96	m	**166.56**
Table X; plastic coated gas and cold water service pipe for corrosive environments						
15mm dia.	2.15	2.75	0.59	13.38	m	**16.13**
22mm dia.	4.13	5.29	0.68	15.43	m	**20.72**
28mm dia.	5.14	6.58	0.74	16.79	m	**23.37**
35mm dia.	10.39	13.31	0.85	19.28	m	**32.59**
42mm dia.	12.27	15.72	0.96	21.78	m	**37.50**
54mm dia.	15.06	19.29	1.06	24.04	m	**43.33**
Table Y; plastic coated gas and cold water service pipe for corrosive environments						
15mm dia.	3.64	4.66	0.61	13.83	m	**18.50**
22mm dia.	6.36	8.15	0.69	15.65	m	**23.79**
28mm dia.	8.11	10.39	0.76	17.24	m	**27.62**
35mm dia.	12.48	15.98	0.87	19.73	m	**35.71**
42mm dia.	14.66	18.78	0.99	22.45	m	**41.23**
54mm dia.	23.27	29.80	1.09	24.72	m	**54.52**
Table X; profiled plastic coated central heating and hot water service pipe for heat loss reduction						
15mm dia.	2.27	2.91	0.59	13.38	m	**16.29**
22mm dia.	4.34	5.56	0.68	15.43	m	**20.99**
28mm dia.	5.40	6.92	0.74	16.79	m	**23.70**
35mm dia.	10.72	13.73	0.85	19.28	m	**33.01**
42mm dia.	12.60	16.14	0.96	21.78	m	**37.92**
54mm dia.	15.41	19.74	1.06	24.04	m	**43.78**
Table Y; profiled plastic coated central heating and hot water service pipe for heat loss reduction						
12mm dia.	2.34	3.00	0.61	13.83	m	**16.83**
15mm dia.	3.83	4.91	0.61	13.83	m	**18.74**
22mm dia.	6.67	8.54	0.69	15.65	m	**24.19**
Extra over copper pipes; capillary fittings; BS 864						
Stop end						
15mm dia.	0.67	0.86	0.13	2.95	nr	**3.81**
22mm dia.	1.27	1.63	0.14	3.18	nr	**4.80**
28mm dia.	2.27	2.91	0.17	3.86	nr	**6.76**
35mm dia.	5.00	6.40	0.19	4.31	nr	**10.71**
42mm dia.	8.61	11.03	0.22	4.99	nr	**16.02**
54mm dia.	12.01	15.38	0.23	5.22	nr	**20.60**

S:PIPED SUPPLY SYSTEMS

Item	Net Price £	Material £	Labour hours	Labour £	Unit	Total rate £
S10 : COLD WATER (cont'd)						
Y10 – PIPELINES (cont'd)						
COPPER PIPEWORK (cont'd)						
Copper pipes; capillary fittings (cont'd)						
Straight coupling; copper to copper						
6mm dia.	0.58	0.74	0.23	5.22	nr	**5.96**
8mm dia.	0.59	0.76	0.23	5.22	nr	**5.97**
10mm dia.	0.30	0.38	0.23	5.22	nr	**5.60**
15mm dia.	0.09	0.12	0.23	5.22	nr	**5.33**
22mm dia.	0.25	0.32	0.26	5.90	nr	**6.22**
28mm dia.	0.63	0.81	0.30	6.80	nr	**7.61**
35mm dia.	2.04	2.61	0.34	7.71	nr	**10.32**
42mm dia.	3.41	4.37	0.38	8.62	nr	**12.99**
54mm dia.	6.28	8.04	0.42	9.52	nr	**17.57**
67mm dia.	18.69	23.94	0.53	12.02	nr	**35.96**
Adaptor coupling; imperial to metric						
1/2" x 15mm dia.	1.47	1.88	0.27	6.12	nr	**8.01**
3/4" x 22mm dia.	1.29	1.65	0.31	7.03	nr	**8.68**
1" x 28mm dia.	2.55	3.27	0.36	8.16	nr	**11.43**
1 1/4" x 35mm dia.	4.26	5.46	0.41	9.30	nr	**14.75**
1 1/2" x 42mm dia.	5.41	6.93	0.46	10.43	nr	**17.36**
Reducing coupling						
15 x 10mm dia.	1.26	1.61	0.23	5.22	nr	**6.83**
22 x 10mm dia.	1.83	2.34	0.26	5.90	nr	**8.24**
22 x 15mm dia.	1.23	1.58	0.27	6.12	nr	**7.70**
28 x 15mm dia.	2.81	3.60	0.28	6.35	nr	**9.95**
28 x 22mm dia.	1.72	2.20	0.30	6.80	nr	**9.01**
35 x 28mm dia.	4.05	5.19	0.34	7.71	nr	**12.90**
42 x 35mm dia.	5.95	7.62	0.38	8.62	nr	**16.24**
54 x 35mm dia.	10.43	13.36	0.42	9.52	nr	**22.88**
54 x 42mm dia.	11.37	14.56	0.42	9.52	nr	**24.09**
Straight female connector						
15mm x 1/2" dia.	1.55	1.99	0.27	6.12	nr	**8.11**
22mm x 3/4" dia.	2.24	2.87	0.31	7.03	nr	**9.90**
28mm x 1" dia.	4.22	5.40	0.36	8.16	nr	**13.57**
35mm x 1 1/4" dia.	7.31	9.36	0.41	9.30	nr	**18.66**
42mm x 1 1/2" dia.	9.49	12.15	0.46	10.43	nr	**22.59**
54mm x 2" dia.	15.05	19.28	0.52	11.79	nr	**31.07**
Straight male connector						
15mm x 1/2" dia.	1.32	1.69	0.27	6.12	nr	**7.81**
22mm x 3/4" dia.	2.34	3.00	0.31	7.03	nr	**10.03**
28mm x 1" dia.	3.79	4.85	0.36	8.16	nr	**13.02**
35mm x 1 1/4" dia.	6.67	8.54	0.41	9.30	nr	**17.84**
42mm x 1 1/2" dia.	8.58	10.99	0.46	10.43	nr	**21.42**
54mm x 2" dia.	13.03	16.69	0.52	11.79	nr	**28.48**
67mm x 2 1/2" dia.	20.81	26.65	0.63	14.29	nr	**40.94**
Female reducing connector						
15mm x 3/4" dia.	3.56	4.56	0.27	6.12	nr	**10.68**

S:PIPED SUPPLY SYSTEMS

Item	Net Price £	Material £	Labour hours	Labour £	Unit	Total rate £
Male reducing connector						
15mm x 3/4" dia.	3.43	4.39	0.27	6.12	nr	**10.52**
22mm x 1" dia.	5.22	6.69	0.31	7.03	nr	**13.72**
Flanged connector						
28mm dia.	24.54	31.43	0.36	8.16	nr	**39.59**
35mm dia.	31.06	39.78	0.41	9.30	nr	**49.08**
42mm dia.	37.13	47.56	0.46	10.43	nr	**57.99**
54mm dia.	56.12	71.88	0.52	11.79	nr	**83.67**
67mm dia.	69.30	88.76	0.61	13.83	nr	**102.59**
Tank connector						
15mm x 1/2" dia.	3.29	4.21	0.25	5.67	nr	**9.88**
22mm x 3/4" dia.	5.01	6.42	0.28	6.35	nr	**12.77**
28mm x 1" dia.	6.59	8.44	0.32	7.26	nr	**15.70**
35mm x 1 1/4" dia.	8.44	10.81	0.37	8.39	nr	**19.20**
42mm x 1 1/2" dia.	11.07	14.18	0.43	9.75	nr	**23.93**
54mm x 2" dia.	16.91	21.66	0.46	10.43	nr	**32.09**
Tank connector with long thread						
15mm x 1/2" dia.	4.26	5.46	0.30	6.80	nr	**12.26**
22mm x 3/4" dia.	6.07	7.77	0.33	7.48	nr	**15.26**
28mm x 1" dia.	7.49	9.59	0.39	8.84	nr	**18.44**
Reducer						
15 x 10mm dia.	0.42	0.54	0.23	5.22	nr	**5.75**
22 x 15mm dia.	0.42	0.54	0.26	5.90	nr	**6.43**
28 x 15mm dia.	1.39	1.78	0.28	6.35	nr	**8.13**
28 x 22mm dia.	1.06	1.36	0.30	6.80	nr	**8.16**
35 x 22mm dia.	3.93	5.03	0.34	7.71	nr	**12.74**
42 x 22mm dia.	7.10	9.09	0.36	8.16	nr	**17.26**
42 x 35mm dia.	5.50	7.04	0.38	8.62	nr	**15.66**
54 x 35mm dia.	11.53	14.77	0.40	9.07	nr	**23.84**
54 x 42mm dia.	9.95	12.74	0.42	9.52	nr	**22.27**
67 x 54mm dia.	13.52	17.32	0.53	12.02	nr	**29.34**
Adaptor; copper to female iron						
15mm x 1/2" dia.	2.66	3.41	0.27	6.12	nr	**9.53**
22mm x 3/4" dia.	4.06	5.20	0.31	7.03	nr	**12.23**
28mm x 1" dia.	5.72	7.33	0.36	8.16	nr	**15.49**
35mm x 1 1/4" dia.	10.35	13.26	0.41	9.30	nr	**22.55**
42mm x 1 1/2" dia.	13.03	16.69	0.46	10.43	nr	**27.12**
54mm x 2" dia.	15.68	20.08	0.52	11.79	nr	**31.88**
Adaptor; copper to male iron						
15mm x 1/2" dia.	2.72	3.48	0.27	6.12	nr	**9.61**
22mm x 3/4" dia.	3.47	4.44	0.31	7.03	nr	**11.47**
28mm x 1" dia.	5.80	7.43	0.36	8.16	nr	**15.59**
35mm x 1 1/4" dia.	8.45	10.82	0.41	9.30	nr	**20.12**
42mm x 1 1/2" dia.	11.67	14.95	0.46	10.43	nr	**25.38**
54mm x 2" dia.	15.68	20.08	0.52	11.79	nr	**31.88**
Union coupling						
15mm dia.	3.67	4.70	0.41	9.30	nr	**14.00**
22mm dia.	5.89	7.54	0.45	10.21	nr	**17.75**
28mm dia.	8.59	11.00	0.51	11.57	nr	**22.57**
35mm dia.	11.26	14.42	0.64	14.51	nr	**28.94**
42mm dia.	16.46	21.08	0.68	15.42	nr	**36.50**
54mm dia.	31.32	40.11	0.78	17.69	nr	**57.80**
67mm dia.	53.03	67.92	0.96	21.77	nr	**89.69**

S:PIPED SUPPLY SYSTEMS

Item	Net Price £	Material £	Labour hours	Labour £	Unit	Total rate £
S10 : COLD WATER (cont'd)						
Y10 – PIPELINES (cont'd)						
COPPER PIPEWORK (cont'd)						
Copper pipes; capillary fittings (cont'd)						
Elbow						
15mm dia.	0.17	0.22	0.23	5.22	nr	**5.43**
22mm dia.	0.43	0.55	0.26	5.90	nr	**6.45**
28mm dia.	1.01	1.29	0.31	7.03	nr	**8.32**
35mm dia.	4.38	5.61	0.35	7.94	nr	**13.55**
42mm dia.	7.23	9.26	0.41	9.30	nr	**18.56**
54mm dia.	14.93	19.12	0.44	9.98	nr	**29.10**
67mm dia.	38.76	49.64	0.54	12.25	nr	**61.89**
Backplate elbow						
15mm dia.	2.76	3.54	0.51	11.57	nr	**15.10**
22mm dia.	5.93	7.60	0.54	12.25	nr	**19.84**
Overflow bend						
22mm dia.	8.36	10.71	0.26	5.90	nr	**16.60**
Return bend						
15mm dia.	4.14	5.30	0.23	5.22	nr	**10.52**
22mm dia.	8.13	10.41	0.26	5.90	nr	**16.31**
28mm dia.	10.38	13.29	0.31	7.03	nr	**20.32**
Obtuse elbow						
15mm dia.	0.53	0.68	0.23	5.22	nr	**5.89**
22mm dia.	1.10	1.41	0.26	5.90	nr	**7.31**
28mm dia.	2.12	2.72	0.31	7.03	nr	**9.75**
35mm dia.	6.60	8.45	0.36	8.16	nr	**16.62**
42mm dia.	11.75	15.05	0.41	9.30	nr	**24.35**
54mm dia.	21.26	27.23	0.44	9.98	nr	**37.21**
67mm dia.	38.57	49.40	0.54	12.25	nr	**61.65**
Straight tap connector						
15mm x 1/2" dia.	0.82	1.05	0.13	2.95	nr	**4.00**
22mm x 3/4" dia.	1.05	1.34	0.14	3.18	nr	**4.52**
Bent tap connector						
15mm x 1/2" dia.	1.05	1.34	0.13	2.95	nr	**4.29**
22mm x 3/4" dia.	3.22	4.12	0.14	3.18	nr	**7.30**
Bent male union connector						
15mm x 1/2" dia.	5.38	6.89	0.41	9.30	nr	**16.19**
22mm x 3/4" dia.	7.00	8.97	0.45	10.21	nr	**19.17**
28mm x 1" dia.	10.00	12.81	0.51	11.57	nr	**24.37**
35mm x 1 1/4" dia.	16.31	20.89	0.64	14.51	nr	**35.40**
42mm x 1 1/2" dia.	26.54	33.99	0.68	15.42	nr	**49.41**
54mm x 2" dia.	41.91	53.68	0.78	17.69	nr	**71.37**

S:PIPED SUPPLY SYSTEMS

Item	Net Price £	Material £	Labour hours	Labour £	Unit	Total rate £
Bent female union connector						
15mm dia.	5.38	6.89	0.41	9.30	nr	**16.19**
22mm x 3/4" dia.	7.00	8.97	0.45	10.21	nr	**19.17**
28mm x 1" dia.	10.00	12.81	0.51	11.57	nr	**24.37**
35mm x 1 1/4" dia.	16.31	20.89	0.64	14.51	nr	**35.40**
42mm x 1 1/2" dia.	26.54	33.99	0.68	15.42	nr	**49.41**
54mm x 2" dia.	41.91	53.68	0.78	17.69	nr	**71.37**
Straight union adaptor						
15mm x 3/4" dia.	2.30	2.95	0.41	9.30	nr	**12.24**
22mm x 1" dia.	3.26	4.18	0.45	10.21	nr	**14.38**
28mm x 1 1/4" dia.	5.27	6.75	0.51	11.57	nr	**18.32**
35mm x 1 1/2" dia.	8.13	10.41	0.64	14.51	nr	**24.93**
42mm x 2" dia.	10.26	13.14	0.68	15.42	nr	**28.56**
54mm x 2 1/2" dia.	15.85	20.30	0.78	17.69	nr	**37.99**
Straight male union connector						
15mm x 1/2" dia.	4.58	5.87	0.41	9.30	nr	**15.16**
22mm x 3/4" dia.	5.95	7.62	0.45	10.21	nr	**17.83**
28mm x 1" dia.	8.85	11.34	0.51	11.57	nr	**22.90**
35mm x 1 1/4" dia.	12.76	16.34	0.64	14.51	nr	**30.86**
42mm x 1 1/2" dia.	20.05	25.68	0.68	15.42	nr	**41.10**
54mm x 2" dia.	28.81	36.90	0.78	17.69	nr	**54.59**
Straight female union connector						
15mm x 1/2" dia.	4.58	5.87	0.41	9.30	nr	**15.16**
22mm x 3/4" dia.	5.95	7.62	0.45	10.21	nr	**17.83**
28mm x 1" dia.	8.85	11.34	0.51	11.57	nr	**22.90**
35mm x 1 1/4" dia.	12.76	16.34	0.64	14.51	nr	**30.86**
42mm x 1 1/2" dia.	20.05	25.68	0.68	15.42	nr	**41.10**
54mm x 2" dia.	28.81	36.90	0.78	17.69	nr	**54.59**
Male nipple						
3/4 x 1/2" dia.	2.27	2.91	0.28	6.35	nr	**9.26**
1 x 3/4" dia.	2.62	3.36	0.32	7.26	nr	**10.61**
1 1/4 x 1" dia.	3.58	4.59	0.37	8.39	nr	**12.98**
1 1/2 x 1 1/4" dia.	5.29	6.78	0.42	9.52	nr	**16.30**
2 x 1 1/2" dia.	10.84	13.88	0.46	10.43	nr	**24.32**
2 1/2 x 2" dia.	14.48	18.55	0.56	12.70	nr	**31.25**
Female nipple						
3/4 x 1/2" dia.	2.27	2.91	0.28	6.35	nr	**9.26**
1 x 3/4" dia.	2.62	3.36	0.32	7.26	nr	**10.61**
1 1/4 x 1" dia.	3.58	4.59	0.37	8.39	nr	**12.98**
1 1/2 x 1 1/4" dia.	5.29	6.78	0.42	9.52	nr	**16.30**
2 x 1 1/2" dia.	10.84	13.88	0.46	10.43	nr	**24.32**
2 1/2 x 2" dia.	14.48	18.55	0.56	12.70	nr	**31.25**
Equal tee						
10mm dia.	1.15	1.47	0.25	5.67	nr	**7.14**
15mm dia.	0.32	0.41	0.36	8.16	nr	**8.57**
22mm dia.	1.01	1.29	0.39	8.84	nr	**10.14**
28mm dia.	2.79	3.57	0.43	9.75	nr	**13.33**
35mm dia.	7.13	9.13	0.57	12.93	nr	**22.06**
42mm dia.	11.43	14.64	0.60	13.61	nr	**28.25**
54mm dia.	23.05	29.52	0.65	14.74	nr	**44.26**
67mm dia.	50.18	64.27	0.78	17.69	nr	**81.96**

S:PIPED SUPPLY SYSTEMS

Item	Net Price £	Material £	Labour hours	Labour £	Unit	Total rate £
S10 : COLD WATER (cont'd)						
Y10 – PIPELINES (cont'd)						
COPPER PIPEWORK (cont'd)						
Copper pipes; capillary fittings (cont'd)						
Female tee, reducing branch FI						
15 x 15mm x 1/4" dia.	3.44	4.41	0.36	8.16	nr	12.57
22 x 22mm x 1/2" dia.	2.40	3.07	0.39	8.84	nr	11.92
28 x 28mm x 3/4" dia.	8.27	10.59	0.43	9.75	nr	20.34
35 x 35mm x 3/4" dia.	11.93	15.28	0.47	10.66	nr	25.94
42 x 42mm x 1/2" dia.	14.33	18.35	0.60	13.61	nr	31.96
Backplate tee						
15 x 15mm x 1/2" dia.	6.53	8.36	0.62	14.06	nr	22.42
Heater tee						
1/2 x 1/2" x 15mm dia.	5.87	7.52	0.36	8.16	nr	15.68
Union heater tee						
1/2 x 1/2" x 15mm dia.	7.51	9.62	0.36	8.16	nr	17.78
Sweep tee - equal						
15mm dia.	4.67	5.98	0.36	8.16	nr	14.15
22mm dia.	6.01	7.70	0.39	8.84	nr	16.54
28mm dia.	10.10	12.94	0.43	9.75	nr	22.69
35mm dia.	14.33	18.35	0.57	12.93	nr	31.28
42mm dia.	21.24	27.20	0.60	13.61	nr	40.81
54mm dia.	23.53	30.14	0.65	14.74	nr	44.88
67mm dia.	40.95	52.45	0.78	17.69	nr	70.14
Sweep tee - reducing						
22 x 22 x 15mm dia.	5.03	6.44	0.39	8.84	nr	15.29
28 x 28 x 22mm dia.	8.54	10.94	0.43	9.75	nr	20.69
35 x 35 x 22mm dia.	14.33	18.35	0.57	12.93	nr	31.28
Sweep tee - double						
15mm dia.	5.27	6.75	0.36	8.16	nr	14.91
22mm dia.	7.18	9.20	0.39	8.84	nr	18.04
28mm dia.	10.91	13.97	0.43	9.75	nr	23.73
Cross						
15mm dia.	6.98	8.94	0.48	10.89	nr	19.83
22mm dia.	7.80	9.99	0.53	12.02	nr	22.01
28mm dia.	11.19	14.33	0.61	13.83	nr	28.17
Extra over copper pipes; high duty capillary fittings; BS 864						
Stop end						
15mm dia.	3.45	4.42	0.16	3.63	nr	8.05

S:PIPED SUPPLY SYSTEMS

Item	Net Price £	Material £	Labour hours	Labour £	Unit	Total rate £
Straight coupling; copper to copper						
15mm dia.	1.58	2.02	0.27	6.12	nr	**8.15**
22mm dia.	2.52	3.23	0.32	7.26	nr	**10.48**
28mm dia.	3.58	4.59	0.37	8.39	nr	**12.98**
35mm dia.	6.31	8.08	0.43	9.75	nr	**17.83**
42mm dia.	6.90	8.84	0.50	11.34	nr	**20.18**
54mm dia.	10.15	13.00	0.54	12.25	nr	**25.25**
Reducing coupling						
15 x 12mm dia.	2.97	3.80	0.27	6.12	nr	**9.93**
22 x 15mm dia.	3.45	4.42	0.32	7.26	nr	**11.68**
28 x 22mm dia.	4.75	6.08	0.37	8.39	nr	**14.47**
Straight female connector						
15mm x 1/2" dia.	3.88	4.97	0.32	7.26	nr	**12.23**
22mm x 3/4" dia.	4.38	5.61	0.36	8.16	nr	**13.77**
28mm x 1" dia.	6.46	8.27	0.42	9.52	nr	**17.80**
Straight male connector						
15mm x 1/2" dia.	3.78	4.84	0.32	7.26	nr	**12.10**
22mm x 3/4" dia.	4.38	5.61	0.36	8.16	nr	**13.77**
28mm x 1" dia.	6.46	8.27	0.42	9.52	nr	**17.80**
42mm x 1 1/2" dia.	12.60	16.14	0.53	12.02	nr	**28.16**
54mm x 2" dia.	20.47	26.22	0.62	14.06	nr	**40.28**
Reducer						
15 x 12mm dia.	1.96	2.51	0.27	6.12	nr	**8.63**
22 x 15mm dia.	1.91	2.45	0.32	7.26	nr	**9.70**
28 x 22mm dia.	3.45	4.42	0.37	8.39	nr	**12.81**
35 x 28mm dia.	4.38	5.61	0.43	9.75	nr	**15.36**
42 x 35mm dia.	5.64	7.22	0.50	11.34	nr	**18.56**
54 x 42mm dia.	9.10	11.66	0.39	8.84	nr	**20.50**
Straight union adaptor						
15mm x 3/4" dia.	3.15	4.03	0.27	6.12	nr	**10.16**
22mm x 1" dia.	4.27	5.47	0.32	7.26	nr	**12.73**
28mm x 1 1/4" dia.	5.64	7.22	0.37	8.39	nr	**15.61**
35mm x 1 1/2" dia.	10.22	13.09	0.43	9.75	nr	**22.84**
42mm x 2" dia.	12.94	16.57	0.50	11.34	nr	**27.91**
Bent union adaptor						
15mm x 3/4" dia.	8.20	10.50	0.27	6.12	nr	**16.63**
22mm x 1" dia.	11.06	14.17	0.32	7.26	nr	**21.42**
28mm x 1 1/4" dia.	14.89	19.07	0.37	8.39	nr	**27.46**
Adaptor; male copper to FI						
15mm x 1/2" dia.	5.85	7.49	0.27	6.12	nr	**13.62**
22mm x 3/4" dia.	5.96	7.63	0.32	7.26	nr	**14.89**
Union coupling						
15mm dia.	7.11	9.11	0.54	12.25	nr	**21.35**
22mm dia.	9.10	11.66	0.60	13.61	nr	**25.26**
28mm dia.	12.62	16.16	0.68	15.42	nr	**31.58**
35mm dia.	22.04	28.23	0.83	18.82	nr	**47.05**
42mm dia.	25.95	33.24	0.89	20.18	nr	**53.42**

S:PIPED SUPPLY SYSTEMS

Item	Net Price £	Material £	Labour hours	Labour £	Unit	Total rate £
S10 : COLD WATER (cont'd)						
Y10 – PIPELINES (cont'd)						
COPPER PIPEWORK (cont'd)						
Copper pipes; high duty capillary fittings (cont'd)						
Elbow						
15mm dia.	4.57	5.85	0.27	6.12	nr	11.98
22mm dia.	4.88	6.25	0.32	7.26	nr	13.51
28mm dia.	7.26	9.30	0.37	8.39	nr	17.69
35mm dia.	11.35	14.54	0.43	9.75	nr	24.29
42mm dia.	14.15	18.12	0.50	11.34	nr	29.46
54mm dia.	24.60	31.51	0.52	11.79	nr	43.30
Return bend						
28mm dia.	14.89	19.07	0.37	8.39	nr	27.46
35mm dia.	17.30	22.16	0.43	9.75	nr	31.91
Bent male union connector						
15mm x 1/2" dia.	10.60	13.58	0.54	12.25	nr	25.82
22mm x 3/4" dia.	14.29	18.30	0.60	13.61	nr	31.91
28mm x 1" dia.	25.95	33.24	0.68	15.42	nr	48.66
Composite flange						
35mm dia.	31.54	40.40	0.38	8.62	nr	49.02
42mm dia.	36.31	46.51	0.41	9.30	nr	55.80
54mm dia.	50.92	65.22	0.43	9.75	nr	74.97
Equal tee						
15mm dia.	5.25	6.72	0.44	9.98	nr	16.70
22mm dia.	6.61	8.47	0.47	10.66	nr	19.12
28mm dia.	8.71	11.16	0.53	12.02	nr	23.18
35mm dia.	14.89	19.07	0.70	15.87	nr	34.95
42mm dia.	18.96	24.28	0.84	19.05	nr	43.33
54mm dia.	29.86	38.24	0.79	17.92	nr	56.16
Reducing tee						
15 x 12mm dia.	8.53	10.92	0.44	9.98	nr	20.90
22 x 15mm dia.	10.10	12.94	0.47	10.66	nr	23.60
28 x 22mm dia.	14.41	18.46	0.53	12.02	nr	30.48
35 x 28mm dia.	22.82	29.23	0.73	16.56	nr	45.79
42 x 28mm dia.	29.15	37.33	0.84	19.05	nr	56.38
54 x 28mm dia.	46.14	59.09	1.01	22.91	nr	82.00
Extra over copper pipes; compression fittings; BS 864						
Stop end						
15mm dia.	1.14	1.46	0.10	2.27	nr	3.73
22mm dia.	1.65	2.11	0.29	6.58	nr	8.69
28mm dia.	3.13	4.01	0.15	3.40	nr	7.41
Straight connector; copper to copper						
15mm dia.	0.53	0.68	0.18	4.08	nr	4.76
22mm dia.	0.92	1.18	0.21	4.76	nr	5.94
28mm dia.	2.82	3.61	0.24	5.44	nr	9.05

S:PIPED SUPPLY SYSTEMS

Item	Net Price £	Material £	Labour hours	Labour £	Unit	Total rate £
Straight connector; copper to imperial copper						
22mm dia.	2.65	3.39	0.21	4.76	nr	8.16
Male coupling; copper to MI (BSP)						
15mm dia.	0.49	0.63	0.19	4.31	nr	4.94
22mm dia.	0.78	1.00	0.23	5.22	nr	6.22
28mm dia.	1.67	2.14	0.26	5.90	nr	8.04
Male coupling with long thread and backnut						
15mm dia.	2.94	3.77	0.19	4.31	nr	8.07
22mm dia.	3.72	4.76	0.23	5.22	nr	9.98
Female coupling; copper to FI (BSP)						
15mm dia.	0.60	0.77	0.19	4.31	nr	5.08
22mm dia.	0.86	1.10	0.23	5.22	nr	6.32
28mm dia.	2.33	2.98	0.27	6.12	nr	9.11
Elbow						
15mm dia.	0.65	0.83	0.18	4.08	nr	4.91
22mm dia.	1.10	1.41	0.21	4.76	nr	6.17
28mm dia.	3.45	4.42	0.24	5.44	nr	9.86
Male elbow; copper to FI (BSP)						
15mm x 1/2" dia.	1.15	1.47	0.19	4.31	nr	5.78
22mm x 3/4" dia.	1.48	1.90	0.23	5.22	nr	7.11
28mm x 1" dia.	3.61	4.62	0.27	6.12	nr	10.75
Female elbow; copper to FI (BSP)						
15mm x 1/2" dia.	1.77	2.27	0.19	4.31	nr	6.58
22mm x 3/4" dia.	2.55	3.27	0.23	5.22	nr	8.48
28mm x 1" dia.	4.49	5.75	0.27	6.12	nr	11.87
Backplate elbow						
15mm x 1/2" dia.	2.55	3.27	0.50	11.34	nr	14.61
Tank coupling; long thread						
22mm dia.	4.52	5.79	0.46	10.43	nr	16.22
Tee equal						
15mm dia.	0.92	1.18	0.28	6.35	nr	7.53
22mm dia.	1.54	1.97	0.30	6.80	nr	8.78
28mm dia.	6.50	8.33	0.34	7.71	nr	16.04
Tee reducing						
22mm dia.	3.68	4.71	0.30	6.80	nr	11.52
Backplate tee						
15mm dia.	4.84	6.20	0.62	14.06	nr	20.26
Extra over fittings; silver brazed welded joints						
Reducer						
76 x 67mm dia	20.04	25.67	1.40	31.75	nr	57.42
108 x 76mm dia	30.94	39.63	1.80	40.82	nr	80.45
133 x 108mm dia	46.61	59.70	2.20	49.89	nr	109.59
159 x 133mm dia	61.91	79.29	2.60	58.96	nr	138.26

S:PIPED SUPPLY SYSTEMS

Item	Net Price £	Material £	Labour hours	Labour £	Unit	Total rate £
S10 : COLD WATER (cont'd)						
Y10 – PIPELINES (cont'd)						
COPPER PIPEWORK (cont'd)						
Fittings; silver brazed welded joints (cont'd)						
90° elbow						
76mm dia	66.10	84.66	1.60	36.29	nr	**120.95**
108mm dia	126.19	161.62	2.00	45.36	nr	**206.98**
133mm dia	250.37	320.67	2.40	54.43	nr	**375.10**
159mm dia	313.50	401.53	2.80	63.50	nr	**465.03**
45° elbow						
76mm dia	60.10	76.98	1.60	36.29	nr	**113.26**
108mm dia	106.17	135.98	2.00	45.36	nr	**181.34**
133mm dia	214.34	274.52	2.40	54.43	nr	**328.95**
159mm dia	280.43	359.17	2.80	63.50	nr	**422.67**
Equal tee						
76mm dia	58.27	74.63	2.40	54.43	nr	**129.06**
108mm dia	105.61	135.26	3.00	68.04	nr	**203.30**
133mm dia	262.21	335.84	3.60	81.64	nr	**417.48**
159mm dia	291.36	373.17	4.20	95.25	nr	**468.42**
Extra over copper pipes; dezincification resistant compression fittings; BS 864						
Stop end						
15mm dia.	1.14	1.46	0.10	2.27	nr	**3.73**
22mm dia.	1.65	2.11	0.13	2.95	nr	**5.06**
28mm dia.	3.43	4.39	0.15	3.40	nr	**7.79**
35mm dia.	5.28	6.76	0.18	4.08	nr	**10.84**
42mm dia.	8.80	11.27	0.20	4.54	nr	**15.81**
Straight coupling; copper to copper						
15mm dia.	0.91	1.17	0.18	4.08	nr	**5.25**
22mm dia.	1.49	1.91	0.21	4.76	nr	**6.67**
28mm dia.	3.28	4.20	0.24	5.44	nr	**9.64**
35mm dia.	6.82	8.74	0.29	6.58	nr	**15.31**
42mm dia.	8.96	11.48	0.33	7.48	nr	**18.96**
54mm dia.	13.41	17.18	0.38	8.62	nr	**25.79**
Straight swivel connector; copper to imperial copper						
22mm dia.	3.19	4.09	0.20	4.54	nr	**8.62**
Male coupling; copper to MI (BSP)						
15mm x 1/2" dia.	0.81	1.04	0.19	4.31	nr	**5.35**
22mm x 3/4" dia.	1.24	1.59	0.23	5.22	nr	**6.80**
28mm x 1" dia.	2.33	2.98	0.26	5.90	nr	**8.88**
35mm x 1 1/4" dia.	5.18	6.63	0.32	7.26	nr	**13.89**
42mm x 1 1/2" dia.	7.77	9.95	0.37	8.39	nr	**18.34**
54mm x 2" dia.	11.48	14.70	0.57	12.93	nr	**27.63**
Male coupling with long thread and backnuts						
22mm dia.	4.49	5.75	0.23	5.22	nr	**10.97**
28mm dia.	4.98	6.38	0.24	5.44	nr	**11.82**

S:PIPED SUPPLY SYSTEMS

Item	Net Price £	Material £	Labour hours	Labour £	Unit	Total rate £
Female coupling; copper to FI (BSP)						
15mm x 1/2" dia.	0.98	1.26	0.19	4.31	nr	**5.56**
22mm x 3/4" dia.	1.43	1.83	0.23	5.22	nr	**7.05**
28mm x 1" dia.	3.01	3.86	0.27	6.12	nr	**9.98**
35mm x 1 1/4" dia.	6.22	7.97	0.32	7.26	nr	**15.22**
42mm x 1 1/2" dia.	8.37	10.72	0.37	8.39	nr	**19.11**
54mm x 2" dia.	12.28	15.73	0.42	9.52	nr	**25.25**
Elbow						
15mm dia.	1.10	1.41	0.18	4.08	nr	**5.49**
22mm dia.	1.75	2.24	0.21	4.76	nr	**7.00**
28mm dia.	4.24	5.43	0.24	5.44	nr	**10.87**
35mm dia.	9.20	11.78	0.29	6.58	nr	**18.36**
42mm dia.	12.47	15.97	0.33	7.48	nr	**23.46**
54mm dia.	21.45	27.47	0.38	8.62	nr	**36.09**
Male elbow; copper to MI (BSP)						
15mm x 1/2" dia.	1.85	2.37	0.19	4.31	nr	**6.68**
22mm x 3/4" dia.	2.07	2.65	0.23	5.22	nr	**7.87**
28mm x 1" dia.	3.88	4.97	0.27	6.12	nr	**11.09**
Female elbow; copper to FI (BSP)						
15mm x 1/2" dia.	1.98	2.54	0.19	4.31	nr	**6.84**
22mm x 3/4" dia.	2.86	3.66	0.23	5.22	nr	**8.88**
28mm x 1" dia.	4.33	5.55	0.27	6.12	nr	**11.67**
Backplate elbow						
15mm x 1/2" dia.	2.89	3.70	0.50	11.34	nr	**15.04**
Straight tap connector						
15mm dia.	1.69	2.16	0.13	2.95	nr	**5.11**
22mm dia.	3.56	4.56	0.15	3.40	nr	**7.96**
Tank coupling						
15mm dia.	2.32	2.97	0.19	4.31	nr	**7.28**
22mm dia.	2.57	3.29	0.23	5.22	nr	**8.51**
28mm dia.	5.28	6.76	0.27	6.12	nr	**12.89**
35mm dia.	9.14	11.71	0.32	7.26	nr	**18.96**
42mm dia.	14.86	19.03	0.37	8.39	nr	**27.42**
54mm dia.	19.14	24.51	0.31	7.03	nr	**31.54**
Reducing set; internal						
22mm dia.	1.06	1.36	0.23	5.22	nr	**6.57**
Tee equal						
15mm dia.	1.54	1.97	0.28	6.35	nr	**8.32**
22mm dia.	2.56	3.28	0.30	6.80	nr	**10.08**
28mm dia.	6.76	8.66	0.34	7.71	nr	**16.37**
35mm dia.	11.98	15.34	0.43	9.75	nr	**25.10**
42mm dia.	18.82	24.10	0.46	10.43	nr	**34.54**
54mm dia.	30.23	38.72	0.54	12.25	nr	**50.96**
Tee reducing						
22mm dia.	3.96	5.07	0.30	6.80	nr	**11.88**
28mm dia.	6.53	8.36	0.34	7.71	nr	**16.07**
35mm dia.	11.70	14.99	0.43	9.75	nr	**24.74**
42mm dia.	18.08	23.16	0.46	10.43	nr	**33.59**
54mm dia.	30.23	38.72	0.54	12.25	nr	**50.96**

S:PIPED SUPPLY SYSTEMS

Item	Net Price £	Material £	Labour hours	Labour £	Unit	Total rate £
S10 : COLD WATER (cont'd)						
Y10 – PIPELINES (cont'd)						
COPPER PIPEWORK (cont'd)						
Extra over copper pipes; bronze one piece brazing flanges; metric						
Bronze flange; PN6						
15mm dia.	13.44	17.21	0.27	6.12	nr	23.34
22mm dia.	15.84	20.29	0.32	7.26	nr	27.54
28mm dia.	18.15	23.25	0.36	8.16	nr	31.41
35mm dia.	25.96	33.25	0.47	10.66	nr	43.91
42mm dia.	31.41	40.23	0.54	12.25	nr	52.48
54mm dia.	44.23	56.65	0.63	14.29	nr	70.94
67mm dia.	50.98	65.29	0.77	17.46	nr	82.76
76mm dia.	59.13	75.73	0.93	21.09	nr	96.82
108mm dia.	79.20	101.44	1.14	25.85	nr	127.29
133mm dia.	95.66	122.52	1.41	31.98	nr	154.50
159mm dia.	136.19	174.43	1.74	39.46	nr	213.89
Bronze flange; PN10						
15mm dia.	17.34	22.21	0.27	6.12	nr	28.33
22mm dia.	20.10	25.74	0.32	7.26	nr	33.00
28mm dia.	20.31	26.01	0.38	8.62	nr	34.63
35mm dia.	28.17	36.08	0.47	10.66	nr	46.74
42mm dia.	33.31	42.66	0.54	12.25	nr	54.91
54mm dia.	46.90	60.07	0.63	14.29	nr	74.36
67mm dia.	50.98	65.29	0.77	17.46	nr	82.76
76mm dia.	65.37	83.73	0.93	21.09	nr	104.82
108mm dia.	96.07	123.05	1.14	25.85	nr	148.90
133mm dia.	110.21	141.16	1.41	31.98	nr	173.13
159mm dia.	168.65	216.01	1.74	39.46	nr	255.47
Bronze flange; PN16						
15mm dia.	17.34	22.21	0.27	6.12	nr	28.33
22mm dia.	20.10	25.74	0.32	7.26	nr	33.00
28mm dia.	20.92	26.79	0.38	8.62	nr	35.41
35mm dia.	28.17	36.08	0.47	10.66	nr	46.74
42mm dia.	33.31	42.66	0.54	12.25	nr	54.91
54mm dia.	49.45	63.34	0.63	14.29	nr	77.62
67mm dia.	60.05	76.91	0.77	17.46	nr	94.37
76mm dia.	77.13	98.79	0.93	21.09	nr	119.88
108mm dia.	99.07	126.89	1.14	25.85	nr	152.74
133mm dia.	161.49	206.83	1.41	31.98	nr	238.81
159mm dia.	202.56	259.44	1.74	39.46	nr	298.90

S:PIPED SUPPLY SYSTEMS

Item	Net Price £	Material £	Labour hours	Labour £	Unit	Total rate £
Extra Over copper pipes; bronze blank flanges; metric						
Bronze blank flange; PN6						
15mm dia.	11.28	14.45	0.27	6.12	nr	**20.57**
22mm dia.	14.39	18.43	0.27	6.12	nr	**24.55**
28mm dia.	14.79	18.94	0.27	6.12	nr	**25.07**
35mm dia.	24.20	31.00	0.32	7.26	nr	**38.25**
42mm dia.	32.65	41.82	0.32	7.26	nr	**49.07**
54mm dia.	35.44	45.39	0.34	7.71	nr	**53.10**
67mm dia.	44.29	56.73	0.36	8.16	nr	**64.89**
76mm dia.	57.06	73.08	0.37	8.39	nr	**81.47**
108mm dia.	90.66	116.12	0.41	9.30	nr	**125.41**
133mm dia.	106.95	136.98	0.58	13.15	nr	**150.13**
159mm dia.	134.75	172.59	0.61	13.83	nr	**186.42**
Bronze blank flange; PN10						
15mm dia.	13.64	17.47	0.27	6.12	nr	**23.59**
22mm dia.	17.65	22.61	0.27	6.12	nr	**28.73**
28mm dia.	19.54	25.03	0.27	6.12	nr	**31.15**
35mm dia.	24.20	31.00	0.32	7.26	nr	**38.25**
42mm dia.	45.36	58.10	0.32	7.26	nr	**65.35**
54mm dia.	51.71	66.23	0.34	7.71	nr	**73.94**
67mm dia.	55.48	71.06	0.46	10.43	nr	**81.49**
76mm dia.	71.28	91.29	0.47	10.66	nr	**101.95**
108mm dia.	108.86	139.43	0.51	11.57	nr	**150.99**
133mm dia.	114.93	147.20	0.58	13.15	nr	**160.35**
159mm dia.	210.19	269.21	0.71	16.10	nr	**285.31**
Bronze blank flange; PN16						
15mm dia.	13.64	17.47	0.27	6.12	nr	**23.59**
22mm dia.	17.92	22.95	0.27	6.12	nr	**29.08**
28mm dia.	19.54	25.03	0.27	6.12	nr	**31.15**
35mm dia.	24.20	31.00	0.32	7.26	nr	**38.25**
42mm dia.	45.36	58.10	0.32	7.26	nr	**65.35**
54mm dia.	51.71	66.23	0.34	7.71	nr	**73.94**
67mm dia.	80.42	103.00	0.46	10.43	nr	**113.43**
76mm dia.	95.25	122.00	0.47	10.66	nr	**132.65**
108mm dia.	121.08	155.08	0.51	11.57	nr	**166.64**
133mm dia.	198.71	254.51	0.58	13.15	nr	**267.66**
159mm dia.	254.35	325.77	0.71	16.10	nr	**341.87**
Extra Over copper pipes; bronze screwed flanges; metric						
Bronze screwed flange; 6 BSP						
15mm dia.	12.03	15.41	0.35	7.94	nr	**23.35**
22mm dia.	13.81	17.69	0.47	10.66	nr	**28.35**
28mm dia.	14.46	18.52	0.52	11.79	nr	**30.31**
35mm dia.	19.94	25.54	0.62	14.06	nr	**39.60**
42mm dia.	23.62	30.25	0.70	15.87	nr	**46.13**
54mm dia.	31.71	40.61	0.84	19.05	nr	**59.66**
67mm dia.	39.58	50.69	1.03	23.36	nr	**74.05**
76mm dia.	48.72	62.40	1.22	27.67	nr	**90.07**
108mm dia.	76.08	97.44	1.41	31.98	nr	**129.42**
133mm dia.	89.82	115.04	1.75	39.69	nr	**154.73**
159mm dia.	115.66	148.14	2.21	50.12	nr	**198.26**

S:PIPED SUPPLY SYSTEMS

Item	Net Price £	Material £	Labour hours	Labour £	Unit	Total rate £
S10 : COLD WATER (cont'd)						
Y10 – PIPELINES (cont'd)						
COPPER PIPEWORK (cont'd)						
Copper pipes; bronze screwed flanges (cont'd)						
Bronze screwed flange; 10 BSP						
15mm dia.	14.41	18.46	0.35	7.94	nr	26.39
22mm dia.	16.68	21.36	0.47	10.66	nr	32.02
28mm dia.	18.43	23.61	0.52	11.79	nr	35.40
35mm dia.	26.66	34.15	0.62	14.06	nr	48.21
42mm dia.	32.19	41.23	0.70	15.87	nr	57.10
54mm dia.	45.30	58.02	0.84	19.05	nr	77.07
67mm dia.	52.94	67.81	1.03	23.36	nr	91.16
76mm dia.	60.89	77.99	1.22	27.67	nr	105.65
108mm dia.	80.64	103.28	1.41	31.98	nr	135.26
133mm dia.	97.24	124.54	1.75	39.69	nr	164.23
159mm dia.	171.45	219.59	2.21	50.12	nr	269.71
Bronze screwed flange; 16 BSP						
15mm dia.	14.41	18.46	0.35	7.94	nr	26.39
22mm dia.	16.68	21.36	0.47	10.66	nr	32.02
28mm dia.	18.43	23.61	0.52	11.79	nr	35.40
35mm dia.	26.66	34.15	0.62	14.06	nr	48.21
42mm dia.	32.19	41.23	0.70	15.87	nr	57.10
54mm dia.	45.30	58.02	0.84	19.05	nr	77.07
67mm dia.	61.96	79.36	1.03	23.36	nr	102.72
76mm dia.	79.07	101.27	1.22	27.67	nr	128.94
108mm dia.	100.97	129.32	1.41	31.98	nr	161.30
133mm dia.	164.21	210.32	1.75	39.69	nr	250.01
159mm dia.	205.06	262.64	2.21	50.12	nr	312.76
Extra over copper pipes; labour						
Made bend						
15mm dia.	-	-	0.26	5.90	nr	5.90
22mm dia.	-	-	0.28	6.35	nr	6.35
28mm dia.	-	-	0.31	7.03	nr	7.03
35mm dia.	-	-	0.42	9.52	nr	9.52
42mm dia.	-	-	0.51	11.57	nr	11.57
54mm dia.	-	-	0.58	13.15	nr	13.15
67mm dia.	-	-	0.69	15.65	nr	15.65
76mm dia.	-	-	0.80	18.14	nr	18.14
Bronze butt weld						
15mm dia.	-	-	0.25	5.67	nr	5.67
22mm dia.	-	-	0.31	7.03	nr	7.03
28mm dia.	-	-	0.37	8.39	nr	8.39
35mm dia.	-	-	0.49	11.11	nr	11.11
42mm dia.	-	-	0.58	13.15	nr	13.15
54mm dia.	-	-	0.72	16.33	nr	16.33
67mm dia.	-	-	0.88	19.96	nr	19.96
76mm dia.	-	-	1.08	24.49	nr	24.49
108mm dia.	-	-	1.37	31.07	nr	31.07
133mm dia.	-	-	1.73	39.23	nr	39.23
159mm dia.	-	-	2.03	46.04	nr	46.04

S:PIPED SUPPLY SYSTEMS

Item	Net Price £	Material £	Labour hours	Labour £	Unit	Total rate £
PRESSFIT (copper fittings)						
Mechanical pressfit joints; butyl rubber O ring						
Coupler						
15mm dia	0.60	0.77	0.36	8.16	nr	**8.93**
22mm dia	0.93	1.19	0.36	8.16	nr	**9.36**
28mm dia	1.86	2.38	0.44	9.98	nr	**12.36**
35mm dia	2.36	3.02	0.44	9.98	nr	**13.00**
42mm dia	4.23	5.42	0.52	11.79	nr	**17.21**
54mm dia	5.41	6.93	0.60	13.61	nr	**20.54**
Stop end						
22mm dia	1.46	1.87	0.18	4.08	nr	**5.95**
28mm dia	2.30	2.95	0.22	4.99	nr	**7.94**
35mm dia	3.96	5.07	0.22	4.99	nr	**10.06**
42mm dia	5.96	7.63	0.26	5.90	nr	**13.53**
54mm dia	7.18	9.20	0.30	6.80	nr	**16.00**
Reducer						
22 x 15mm dia	0.69	0.88	0.36	8.16	nr	**9.05**
28 x 15mm dia	1.78	2.28	0.40	9.07	nr	**11.35**
28 x 22mm dia	1.85	2.37	0.40	9.07	nr	**11.44**
35 x 22mm dia	2.21	2.83	0.40	9.07	nr	**11.90**
35 x 28mm dia	2.44	3.13	0.44	9.98	nr	**13.10**
42 x 22mm dia	3.82	4.89	0.44	9.98	nr	**14.87**
42 x 28mm dia	3.64	4.66	0.48	10.89	nr	**15.55**
42 x 35mm dia	3.64	4.66	0.48	10.89	nr	**15.55**
54 x 35mm dia	4.92	6.30	0.52	11.79	nr	**18.09**
54 x 42mm dia	4.92	6.30	0.56	12.70	nr	**19.00**
90° elbow						
15mm dia	1.10	1.41	0.36	8.16	nr	**9.57**
22mm dia	1.44	1.84	0.36	8.16	nr	**10.01**
28mm dia	1.98	2.54	0.44	9.98	nr	**12.51**
35mm dia	4.94	6.33	0.44	9.98	nr	**16.31**
42mm dia	7.91	10.13	0.52	11.79	nr	**21.92**
54mm dia	9.46	12.12	0.60	13.61	nr	**25.72**
45° elbow						
15mm dia	0.77	0.99	0.36	8.16	nr	**9.15**
22mm dia	1.06	1.36	0.36	8.16	nr	**9.52**
28mm dia	3.20	4.10	0.44	9.98	nr	**14.08**
35mm dia	4.56	5.84	0.44	9.98	nr	**15.82**
42mm dia	7.60	9.73	0.52	11.79	nr	**21.53**
54mm dia	10.80	13.83	0.60	13.61	nr	**27.44**
Equal tee						
15mm dia	1.03	1.32	0.54	12.25	nr	**13.57**
22mm dia	1.86	2.38	0.54	12.25	nr	**14.63**
28mm dia	3.26	4.18	0.66	14.97	nr	**19.14**
35mm dia	5.64	7.22	0.66	14.97	nr	**22.19**
42mm dia	11.13	14.26	0.78	17.69	nr	**31.94**
54mm dia	13.89	17.79	0.90	20.41	nr	**38.20**

S:PIPED SUPPLY SYSTEMS

Item	Net Price £	Material £	Labour hours	Labour £	Unit	Total rate £
S10 : COLD WATER (cont'd)						
Y10 – PIPELINES (cont'd)						
PRESSFIT (cont'd)						
Mechanical pressfit joints (cont'd)						
Reducing tee						
22 x 15mm dia	1.52	1.95	0.54	12.25	nr	**14.19**
28 x 15mm dia	6.24	7.99	0.62	14.06	nr	**22.05**
28 x 22mm dia	3.84	4.92	0.62	14.06	nr	**18.98**
35 x 22mm dia	5.01	6.42	0.62	14.06	nr	**20.48**
35 x 28mm dia	5.58	7.15	0.62	14.06	nr	**21.21**
42 x 28mm dia	10.10	12.94	0.70	15.87	nr	**28.81**
42 x 35mm dia	10.10	12.94	0.70	15.87	nr	**28.81**
54 x 35mm dia	17.06	21.85	0.82	18.60	nr	**40.45**
54 x 42mm dia	17.06	21.85	0.82	18.60	nr	**40.45**
Male iron connector; BSP thread						
15mm dia	2.17	2.78	0.18	4.08	nr	**6.86**
22mm dia	3.12	4.00	0.18	4.08	nr	**8.08**
28mm dia	4.18	5.35	0.22	4.99	nr	**10.34**
35mm dia	7.56	9.68	0.22	4.99	nr	**14.67**
42mm dia	10.13	12.97	0.26	5.90	nr	**18.87**
54mm dia	19.55	25.04	0.30	6.80	nr	**31.84**
90° elbow; male iron BSP thread						
15mm dia	3.41	4.37	0.36	8.16	nr	**12.53**
22mm dia	5.33	6.83	0.36	8.16	nr	**14.99**
28mm dia	8.18	10.48	0.44	9.98	nr	**20.46**
35mm dia	10.63	13.61	0.44	9.98	nr	**23.59**
42mm dia	13.86	17.75	0.52	11.79	nr	**29.54**
54mm dia	20.27	25.96	0.60	13.61	nr	**39.57**
Female iron connector; BSP thread						
15mm dia	2.41	3.09	0.18	4.08	nr	**7.17**
22mm dia	3.17	4.06	0.18	4.08	nr	**8.14**
28mm dia	4.28	5.48	0.22	4.99	nr	**10.47**
35mm dia	8.37	10.72	0.22	4.99	nr	**15.71**
42mm dia	11.95	15.31	0.26	5.90	nr	**21.20**
54mm dia	20.50	26.26	0.30	6.80	nr	**33.06**
90° elbow; female iron BSP thread						
15mm dia	2.88	3.69	0.36	8.16	nr	**11.85**
22mm dia	4.23	5.42	0.36	8.16	nr	**13.58**
28mm dia	7.00	8.97	0.44	9.98	nr	**18.94**
35mm dia	9.03	11.57	0.44	9.98	nr	**21.54**
42mm dia	12.30	15.75	0.52	11.79	nr	**27.55**
54mm dia	18.09	23.17	0.60	13.61	nr	**36.78**

S:PIPED SUPPLY SYSTEMS

Item	Net Price £	Material £	Labour hours	Labour £	Unit	Total rate £
STAINLESS STEEL PIPEWORK						
Stainless steel pipes; capillary or compression joints; BS 4127						
Grade 304; satin finish						
15mm dia.	1.80	2.31	0.41	9.30	m	**11.60**
22mm dia.	2.53	3.24	0.51	11.57	m	**14.81**
28mm dia.	3.45	4.42	0.58	13.15	m	**17.57**
35mm dia.	5.21	6.67	0.65	14.75	m	**21.42**
42mm dia.	6.62	8.48	0.71	16.11	m	**24.59**
54mm dia.	9.21	11.80	0.80	18.14	m	**29.94**
Grade 316 satin finish						
15mm dia.	3.83	4.91	0.61	13.84	m	**18.74**
22mm dia.	4.51	5.78	0.76	17.25	m	**23.02**
28mm dia.	6.92	8.86	0.87	19.74	m	**28.60**
35mm dia.	7.31	9.36	0.98	22.23	m	**31.60**
42mm dia.	8.41	10.77	1.06	24.05	m	**34.82**
54mm dia.	10.58	13.55	1.16	26.31	m	**39.86**
Extra over stainless steel pipes; capillary fittings						
Straight coupling						
15mm dia.	1.13	1.45	0.25	5.67	nr	**7.12**
22mm dia.	1.50	1.92	0.28	6.35	nr	**8.27**
28mm dia.	2.81	3.60	0.33	7.48	nr	**11.08**
35mm dia.	3.97	5.08	0.37	8.39	nr	**13.48**
42mm dia.	4.57	5.85	0.42	9.52	nr	**15.38**
54mm dia.	6.89	8.82	0.45	10.21	nr	**19.03**
45° bend						
15mm dia.	3.14	4.02	0.25	5.67	nr	**9.69**
22mm dia.	4.66	5.97	0.30	6.73	nr	**12.69**
28mm dia.	6.74	8.63	0.33	7.48	nr	**16.12**
35mm dia.	9.31	11.92	0.37	8.39	nr	**20.32**
42mm dia.	12.37	15.84	0.42	9.52	nr	**25.37**
54mm dia.	17.36	22.23	0.45	10.21	nr	**32.44**
90° bend						
15mm dia.	4.01	5.14	0.28	6.35	nr	**11.49**
22mm dia.	4.91	6.29	0.28	6.35	nr	**12.64**
28mm dia.	6.83	8.75	0.33	7.48	nr	**16.23**
35mm dia.	10.39	13.31	0.37	8.39	nr	**21.70**
42mm dia.	14.30	18.32	0.42	9.52	nr	**27.84**
54mm dia.	19.39	24.83	0.45	10.21	nr	**35.04**
Reducer						
22 x 15mm dia.	5.25	6.72	0.28	6.35	nr	**13.07**
28 x 22mm dia.	6.00	7.68	0.33	7.48	nr	**15.17**
35 x 28mm dia.	6.75	8.65	0.37	8.39	nr	**17.04**
42 x 35mm dia.	7.59	9.72	0.42	9.52	nr	**19.25**
54 x 42mm dia.	22.51	28.83	0.48	10.90	nr	**39.73**
Tap connector						
15mm dia.	10.89	13.95	0.13	2.95	nr	**16.90**
22mm dia.	14.39	18.43	0.14	3.18	nr	**21.61**
28mm dia.	19.97	25.58	0.17	3.86	nr	**29.43**

S:PIPED SUPPLY SYSTEMS

Item	Net Price £	Material £	Labour hours	Labour £	Unit	Total rate £
S10 : COLD WATER (cont'd)						
Y10 – PIPELINES (cont'd)						
STAINLESS STEEL PIPEWORK (cont'd)						
Stainless steel pipes; capillary fittings (cont'd)						
Tank connector						
15mm dia.	14.07	18.02	0.13	2.95	nr	**20.97**
22mm dia.	20.93	26.81	0.13	2.95	nr	**29.76**
28mm dia	27.60	35.35	0.15	3.40	nr	**38.76**
35mm dia.	25.77	33.01	0.18	4.08	nr	**37.09**
42mm dia.	37.26	47.72	0.21	4.76	nr	**52.48**
54mm dia.	49.22	63.04	0.24	5.44	nr	**68.48**
Tee equal						
15mm dia.	5.29	6.78	0.37	8.39	nr	**15.17**
22mm dia.	6.58	8.43	0.40	9.07	nr	**17.50**
28mm dia.	7.95	10.18	0.45	10.21	nr	**20.39**
35mm dia.	14.49	18.56	0.59	13.39	nr	**31.95**
42mm dia.	17.87	22.89	0.62	14.07	nr	**36.96**
54mm dia.	36.11	46.25	0.67	15.20	nr	**61.45**
Unequal tee						
22 x 15mm dia.	8.13	10.41	0.37	8.39	nr	**18.81**
28 x 15mm dia.	9.16	11.73	0.45	10.21	nr	**21.94**
28 x 22mm dia.	9.16	11.73	0.45	10.21	nr	**21.94**
35 x 22mm dia.	16.00	20.49	0.59	13.39	nr	**33.88**
35 x 28mm dia.	16.00	20.49	0.59	13.39	nr	**33.88**
42 x 28mm dia.	19.67	25.19	0.62	14.07	nr	**39.26**
42 x 35mm dia.	19.67	25.19	0.62	14.07	nr	**39.26**
54 x 35mm dia.	40.73	52.17	0.67	15.20	nr	**67.37**
54 x 42mm dia.	40.73	52.17	0.67	15.20	nr	**67.37**
Union, conical seat						
15mm dia.	18.03	23.09	0.25	5.67	nr	**28.76**
22mm dia.	28.40	36.37	0.28	6.35	nr	**42.72**
28mm dia.	36.71	47.02	0.33	7.48	nr	**54.50**
35mm dia.	48.20	61.73	0.37	8.39	nr	**70.13**
42mm dia.	60.79	77.86	0.42	9.52	nr	**87.38**
54mm dia.	80.42	103.00	0.45	10.21	nr	**113.21**
Union, flat seat						
15mm dia.	18.83	24.12	0.25	5.67	nr	**29.79**
22mm dia.	29.33	37.57	0.28	6.35	nr	**43.92**
28mm dia.	37.91	48.55	0.33	7.48	nr	**56.04**
35mm dia.	49.52	63.42	0.37	8.39	nr	**71.82**
42mm dia.	62.39	79.91	0.42	9.52	nr	**89.43**
54mm dia.	83.67	107.16	0.45	10.21	nr	**117.37**

S:PIPED SUPPLY SYSTEMS

Item	Net Price £	Material £	Labour hours	Labour £	Unit	Total rate £
Extra over stainless steel pipes; compression fittings						
Straight coupling						
15mm dia.	11.39	14.59	0.18	4.08	nr	**18.67**
22mm dia.	21.70	27.79	0.22	4.99	nr	**32.78**
28mm dia.	29.21	37.41	0.25	5.67	nr	**43.08**
35mm dia.	45.10	57.76	0.30	6.80	nr	**64.57**
42mm dia.	52.64	67.42	0.40	9.07	nr	**76.49**
90° bend						
15mm dia.	14.36	18.39	0.18	4.08	nr	**22.47**
22mm dia.	28.52	36.53	0.22	4.99	nr	**41.52**
28mm dia.	38.90	49.82	0.25	5.67	nr	**55.49**
35mm dia.	78.77	100.89	0.33	7.48	nr	**108.37**
42mm dia.	115.11	147.43	0.35	7.94	nr	**155.37**
Reducer						
22 x 15mm dia.	20.67	26.47	0.28	6.35	nr	**32.82**
28 x 22mm dia.	28.31	36.26	0.28	6.35	nr	**42.61**
35 x 28mm dia.	41.36	52.97	0.30	6.80	nr	**59.78**
42 x 35mm dia.	55.03	70.48	0.37	8.39	nr	**78.88**
Stud coupling						
15mm dia.	11.84	15.16	0.42	9.52	nr	**24.69**
22mm dia.	20.03	25.65	0.25	5.67	nr	**31.32**
28mm dia.	27.80	35.61	0.25	5.67	nr	**41.28**
35mm dia.	44.53	57.03	0.37	8.39	nr	**65.43**
42mm dia.	52.64	67.42	0.42	9.52	nr	**76.95**
Equal tee						
15mm dia.	20.22	25.90	0.37	8.39	nr	**34.29**
22mm dia.	41.77	53.50	0.40	9.07	nr	**62.57**
28mm dia.	57.13	73.17	0.45	10.21	nr	**83.38**
35mm dia.	113.60	145.50	0.59	13.39	nr	**158.88**
42mm dia.	157.52	201.75	0.62	14.07	nr	**215.82**
Running tee						
15mm dia.	24.89	31.88	0.37	8.39	nr	**40.27**
22mm dia.	44.84	57.43	0.40	9.07	nr	**66.50**
28mm dia.	75.92	97.24	0.59	13.39	nr	**110.62**
PRESSFIT (stainless steel)						
Pressfit jointing system; butyl rubber O ring mechanical joint						
Pipework						
15mm dia	2.60	3.33	0.46	10.43	m	**13.76**
22mm dia	4.17	5.34	0.48	10.89	m	**16.23**
28mm dia	5.15	6.60	0.52	11.79	m	**18.39**
35mm dia	7.56	9.68	0.56	12.70	m	**22.38**
42mm dia	9.31	11.92	0.58	13.15	m	**25.08**
54mm dia	11.82	15.14	0.66	14.97	m	**30.11**

S:PIPED SUPPLY SYSTEMS

Item	Net Price £	Material £	Labour hours	Labour £	Unit	Total rate £
S10 : COLD WATER (cont'd)						
Y10 – PIPELINES (cont'd)						
PRESSFIT (stainless steel) (cont'd)						
Pressfit jointing system; butyl rubber (cont'd)						
Coupling						
15mm dia	2.11	2.70	0.36	8.16	nr	10.87
22mm dia	3.01	3.86	0.36	8.16	nr	12.02
28mm dia	3.73	4.78	0.44	9.98	nr	14.76
35mm dia	5.10	6.53	0.44	9.98	nr	16.51
42mm dia	6.13	7.85	0.52	11.79	nr	19.64
54mm dia	6.13	7.85	0.60	13.61	nr	21.46
Stop end						
22mm dia	2.34	3.00	0.18	4.08	nr	7.08
28mm dia	3.31	4.24	0.22	4.99	nr	9.23
35mm dia	3.83	4.91	0.22	4.99	nr	9.89
42mm dia	5.38	6.89	0.26	5.90	nr	12.79
54mm dia	6.23	7.98	0.30	6.80	nr	14.78
Reducer						
22 x 15mm dia	2.52	3.23	0.36	8.16	nr	11.39
28 x 15mm dia	2.86	3.66	0.40	9.07	nr	12.73
28 x 22mm dia	2.95	3.78	0.40	9.07	nr	12.85
35 x 22mm dia	3.61	4.62	0.40	9.07	nr	13.70
35 x 28mm dia	4.47	5.73	0.44	9.98	nr	15.70
42 x 35mm dia	4.72	6.05	0.48	10.89	nr	16.93
54 x 42mm dia	5.39	6.90	0.56	12.70	nr	19.60
90° bend						
15mm dia	3.03	3.88	0.36	8.16	nr	12.04
22mm dia	4.23	5.42	0.36	8.16	nr	13.58
28mm dia	5.34	6.84	0.44	9.98	nr	16.82
35mm dia	8.41	10.77	0.44	9.98	nr	20.75
42mm dia	14.04	17.98	0.52	11.79	nr	29.78
54mm dia	19.39	24.83	0.60	13.61	nr	38.44
45° bend						
15mm dia	4.12	5.28	0.36	8.16	nr	13.44
22mm dia	5.11	6.54	0.36	8.16	nr	14.71
28mm dia	5.95	7.62	0.44	9.98	nr	17.60
35mm dia	6.99	8.95	0.44	9.98	nr	18.93
42mm dia	11.23	14.38	0.52	11.79	nr	26.18
54mm dia	14.59	18.69	0.60	13.61	nr	32.29
Equal tee						
15mm dia	4.97	6.37	0.54	12.25	nr	18.61
22mm dia	6.09	7.80	0.54	12.25	nr	20.05
28mm dia	7.12	9.12	0.66	14.97	nr	24.09
35mm dia	9.02	11.55	0.66	14.97	nr	26.52
42mm dia	12.81	16.41	0.78	17.69	nr	34.10
54mm dia	15.32	19.62	0.90	20.41	nr	40.03

S:PIPED SUPPLY SYSTEMS

Item	Net Price £	Material £	Labour hours	Labour £	Unit	Total rate £
Reducing tee						
22 x 15mm dia	5.22	6.69	0.54	12.25	nr	**18.93**
28 x 15mm dia	6.32	8.09	0.62	14.06	nr	**22.16**
28 x 22mm dia	6.83	8.75	0.62	14.06	nr	**22.81**
35 x 22mm dia	8.12	10.40	0.62	14.06	nr	**24.46**
35 x 28mm dia	8.47	10.85	0.62	14.06	nr	**24.91**
42 x 28mm dia	12.03	15.41	0.70	15.87	nr	**31.28**
42 x 35mm dia	12.39	15.87	0.70	15.87	nr	**31.74**
54 x 35mm dia	14.00	17.93	0.82	18.60	nr	**36.53**
54 x 42mm dia	14.40	18.44	0.82	18.60	nr	**37.04**
FIXINGS						
For copper pipes						
Saddle band						
6mm dia.	0.07	0.09	0.11	2.49	nr	**2.58**
8mm dia.	0.07	0.09	0.12	2.72	nr	**2.81**
10mm dia.	0.07	0.09	0.12	2.72	nr	**2.81**
12mm dia.	0.07	0.09	0.12	2.72	nr	**2.81**
15mm dia.	0.08	0.10	0.13	2.95	nr	**3.05**
22mm dia.	0.08	0.10	0.13	2.95	nr	**3.05**
28mm dia.	0.09	0.12	0.16	3.63	nr	**3.74**
35mm dia.	0.14	0.18	0.18	4.08	nr	**4.26**
42mm dia.	0.29	0.37	0.21	4.76	nr	**5.13**
54mm dia.	0.39	0.50	0.21	4.76	nr	**5.26**
Single spacing clip						
15mm dia.	0.09	0.12	0.14	3.18	nr	**3.29**
22mm dia.	0.09	0.12	0.15	3.40	nr	**3.52**
28mm dia.	0.21	0.27	0.17	3.86	nr	**4.12**
Two piece spacing clip						
8mm dia. Bottom	0.07	0.09	0.11	2.49	nr	**2.58**
8mm dia. Top	0.07	0.09	0.11	2.49	nr	**2.58**
12mm dia. Bottom	0.07	0.09	0.13	2.95	nr	**3.04**
12mm dia. Top	0.07	0.09	0.13	2.95	nr	**3.04**
15mm dia. Bottom	0.08	0.10	0.13	2.95	nr	**3.05**
15mm dia. Top	0.08	0.10	0.13	2.95	nr	**3.05**
22mm dia. Bottom	0.08	0.10	0.14	3.18	nr	**3.28**
22mm dia. Top	0.08	0.10	0.14	3.18	nr	**3.28**
28mm dia. Bottom	0.08	0.10	0.16	3.63	nr	**3.73**
28mm dia. Top	0.14	0.18	0.16	3.63	nr	**3.81**
35mm dia. Bottom	0.09	0.12	0.21	4.76	nr	**4.88**
35mm dia. Top	0.21	0.27	0.21	4.76	nr	**5.03**
Single pipe bracket						
15mm dia.	0.96	1.23	0.14	3.18	nr	**4.40**
22mm dia.	1.10	1.41	0.14	3.18	nr	**4.58**
28mm dia.	1.32	1.69	0.17	3.86	nr	**5.55**

S:PIPED SUPPLY SYSTEMS

Item	Net Price £	Material £	Labour hours	Labour £	Unit	Total rate £
S10 : COLD WATER (cont'd)						
Y10 – PIPELINES (cont'd)						
FIXINGS (cont'd)						
For copper pipes (cont'd)						
Single pipe ring						
15mm dia.	1.72	2.20	0.26	5.90	nr	**8.10**
22mm dia.	1.83	2.34	0.26	5.90	nr	**8.24**
28mm dia.	2.18	2.79	0.31	7.03	nr	**9.82**
35mm dia.	2.35	3.01	0.32	7.26	nr	**10.27**
42mm dia.	2.54	3.25	0.32	7.26	nr	**10.51**
54mm dia.	3.07	3.93	0.34	7.71	nr	**11.64**
67mm dia.	7.16	9.17	0.35	7.94	nr	**17.11**
76mm dia.	9.05	11.59	0.42	9.52	nr	**21.12**
108mm dia.	14.01	17.94	0.42	9.52	nr	**27.47**
Double pipe ring						
15mm dia.	1.95	2.50	0.26	5.90	nr	**8.39**
22mm dia.	2.08	2.66	0.26	5.90	nr	**8.56**
28mm dia.	2.78	3.56	0.31	7.03	nr	**10.59**
35mm dia.	2.89	3.70	0.32	7.26	nr	**10.96**
42mm dia.	3.15	4.03	0.32	7.26	nr	**11.29**
54mm dia.	3.78	4.84	0.34	7.71	nr	**12.55**
67mm dia.	8.08	10.35	0.35	7.94	nr	**18.29**
76mm dia.	10.07	12.90	0.42	9.52	nr	**22.42**
108mm dia.	17.46	22.36	0.42	9.52	nr	**31.89**
Wall bracket						
15mm dia.	2.45	3.14	0.05	1.13	nr	**4.27**
22mm dia.	2.89	3.70	0.05	1.13	nr	**4.84**
28mm dia.	3.52	4.51	0.05	1.13	nr	**5.64**
35mm dia.	4.52	5.79	0.05	1.13	nr	**6.92**
42mm dia.	5.98	7.66	0.05	1.13	nr	**8.79**
54mm dia.	7.55	9.67	0.05	1.13	nr	**10.80**
Hospital bracket						
15mm dia.	2.08	2.66	0.26	5.90	nr	**8.56**
22mm dia.	2.19	2.80	0.26	5.90	nr	**8.70**
28mm dia.	2.67	3.42	0.31	7.03	nr	**10.45**
35mm dia.	2.89	3.70	0.32	7.26	nr	**10.96**
42mm dia.	4.05	5.19	0.32	7.26	nr	**12.44**
54mm dia.	5.50	7.04	0.34	7.71	nr	**14.76**
Screw on backplate, female						
15mm dia.	0.96	1.23	0.26	5.90	nr	**7.13**
22mm dia.	0.96	1.23	0.26	5.90	nr	**7.13**
28mm dia.	1.32	1.69	0.31	7.03	nr	**8.72**
35mm dia.	1.40	1.79	0.32	7.26	nr	**9.05**
42mm dia.	2.21	2.83	0.32	7.26	nr	**10.09**
54mm dia.	2.42	3.10	0.34	7.71	nr	**10.81**
67mm dia.	2.42	3.10	0.35	7.94	nr	**11.04**
76mm dia.	3.74	4.79	0.42	9.52	nr	**14.32**
108mm dia.	3.74	4.79	0.42	9.52	nr	**14.32**

S:PIPED SUPPLY SYSTEMS

Item	Net Price £	Material £	Labour hours	Labour £	Unit	Total rate £
Screw on backplate, male						
15mm dia.	0.90	1.15	0.26	5.90	nr	7.05
22mm dia.	0.90	1.15	0.26	5.90	nr	7.05
28mm dia.	1.23	1.58	0.31	7.03	nr	8.61
35mm dia.	1.32	1.69	0.32	7.26	nr	8.95
42mm dia.	2.03	2.60	0.32	7.26	nr	9.86
54mm dia.	2.35	3.01	0.34	7.71	nr	10.72
67mm dia.	2.35	3.01	0.35	7.94	nr	10.95
76mm dia.	3.74	4.79	0.42	9.52	nr	14.32
108mm dia.	3.74	4.79	0.42	9.52	nr	14.32
Pipe joist clips, single						
15mm dia.	0.42	0.54	0.08	1.81	nr	2.35
22mm dia.	0.42	0.54	0.08	1.81	nr	2.35
Pipe joist clips, double						
15mm dia.	0.59	0.76	0.08	1.81	nr	2.57
22mm dia.	0.59	0.76	0.08	1.81	nr	2.57

S:PIPED SUPPLY SYSTEMS

Item	Net Price £	Material £	Labour hours	Labour £	Unit	Total rate £
S10 : COLD WATER (cont'd)						
Y11 - PIPELINE ANCILLARIES						
VALVES						
Regulators						
Gunmetal; self-acting two port thermostat; single seat; screwed; normally closed; with adjustable or fixed bleed device						
25mm dia.	257.38	329.64	1.46	33.11	nr	362.76
32mm dia.	264.81	339.17	1.45	32.88	nr	372.05
40mm dia.	283.04	362.51	1.55	35.16	nr	397.67
50mm dia.	340.73	436.40	1.68	38.10	nr	474.50
Self acting temperature regulator for storage calorifier; integral sensing element and pocket; screwed ends						
15mm dia.	282.66	362.03	1.32	29.94	nr	391.96
25mm dia.	310.26	397.38	1.52	34.47	nr	431.85
32mm dia.	400.67	513.18	1.79	40.59	nr	553.77
40mm dia.	490.14	627.76	1.99	45.13	nr	672.89
50mm dia.	572.94	733.81	2.26	51.25	nr	785.06
Self acting temperature regulator for storage calorifier; integral sensing element and pocket; flanged ends; bolted connection						
15mm dia.	414.95	531.46	0.61	13.83	nr	545.30
25mm dia.	474.91	608.26	0.72	16.33	nr	624.59
32mm dia.	598.63	766.72	0.94	21.32	nr	788.04
40mm dia.	709.03	908.12	1.03	23.36	nr	931.48
50mm dia.	823.24	1054.39	1.18	26.76	nr	1081.16
Chrome plated thermostatic mixing valves including non-return valves and inlet swivel connections with strainers; copper compression fittings						
15mm dia.	104.69	134.08	0.69	15.65	nr	149.73
Chrome plated thermostatic mixing valves including non-return valves and inlet swivel connections with angle pattern combined isolating valves and strainers; copper compression fittings						
15mm dia.	109.92	140.79	0.69	15.65	nr	156.43
Gunmetal thermostatic mixing valves including non-return valves and inlet swivel connections with strainers; copper compression fittings						
15mm dia.	95.04	121.73	0.69	15.65	nr	137.38
Gunmetal thermostatic mixing valves including non-return valves and inlet swivel connections with angle pattern combined isolating valves and strainers; copper compression fittings						
15mm dia.	99.93	127.99	0.69	15.65	nr	143.64

S:PIPED SUPPLY SYSTEMS

Item	Net Price £	Material £	Labour hours	Labour £	Unit	Total rate £
Ball float valves						
Bronze, equilibrium; copper float; working pressure cold services up to 16 bar; flanged ends; BS 4504 Table 16/21; bolted connections						
25mm dia.	236.86	303.36	1.04	23.59	nr	326.95
32mm dia.	328.60	420.86	1.22	27.67	nr	448.53
40mm dia.	453.44	580.76	1.38	31.30	nr	612.06
50mm dia.	730.55	935.68	1.66	37.65	nr	973.33
65mm dia.	764.15	978.72	1.93	43.77	nr	1022.49
80mm dia.	944.68	1209.94	2.16	48.99	nr	1258.92
Heavy, equilibrium; with long tail and backnut; copper float; screwed for iron						
25mm dia.	132.81	170.11	1.58	35.83	nr	205.94
32mm dia.	206.37	264.31	1.78	40.37	nr	304.68
40mm dia.	224.11	287.04	1.90	43.09	nr	330.13
50mm dia.	366.80	469.80	2.65	60.10	nr	529.89
Brass, ball valve; BS 1212; copper float; screwed						
15mm dia.	7.55	9.67	0.25	5.67	nr	15.34
22mm dia	12.73	16.31	0.29	6.58	nr	22.89
28mm dia	47.95	61.41	0.35	7.94	nr	69.35
Gate valves						
DZR copper alloy wedge non-rising stem; capillary joint to copper						
15mm dia.	8.47	10.85	0.84	19.05	nr	29.90
22mm dia.	10.40	13.32	1.01	22.91	nr	36.23
28mm dia.	14.06	18.01	1.19	26.99	nr	45.00
35mm dia.	25.23	32.31	1.38	31.30	nr	63.61
42mm dia.	42.86	54.89	1.62	36.74	nr	91.63
54mm dia.	60.05	76.91	1.94	44.00	nr	120.91
Cocks; capillary joints to copper						
Stopcock; brass head with gun metal body						
15mm dia.	2.47	3.16	0.45	10.21	nr	13.37
22mm dia.	4.77	6.11	0.46	10.43	nr	16.54
28mm dia.	13.56	17.36	0.54	12.25	nr	29.61
Lockshield stop cocks; brass head with gun metal body						
15mm dia.	6.46	8.27	0.45	10.21	nr	18.47
22mm dia.	9.28	11.89	0.46	10.43	nr	22.32
28mm dia.	16.44	21.05	0.54	12.25	nr	33.30
DZR stopcock; brass head with gun metal body						
15mm dia.	6.41	8.22	0.45	10.21	nr	18.42
22mm dia.	11.11	14.23	0.46	10.43	nr	24.66
28mm dia.	18.52	23.71	0.54	12.25	nr	35.96
Gunmetal stopcock						
35mm dia.	29.04	37.20	0.69	15.65	nr	52.85
42mm dia.	38.56	49.39	0.71	16.10	nr	65.49
54mm dia.	57.60	73.78	0.81	18.37	nr	92.15

S:PIPED SUPPLY SYSTEMS

Item	Net Price £	Material £	Labour hours	Labour £	Unit	Total rate £
S10 : COLD WATER (cont'd)						
Y11 - PIPELINE ANCILLARIES						
VALVES						
Cocks; capillary joints (cont'd)						
Double union stopcock						
15mm dia.	12.15	15.56	0.60	13.61	nr	**29.17**
22mm dia.	14.94	19.14	0.60	13.61	nr	**32.75**
28mm dia.	27.64	35.40	0.69	15.65	nr	**51.04**
Double union DZR stopcock						
15mm dia.	13.43	17.20	0.60	13.61	nr	**30.81**
22mm dia.	16.52	21.15	0.61	13.83	nr	**34.99**
28mm dia.	30.54	39.12	0.69	15.65	nr	**54.77**
Double union gun metal stopcock						
35mm dia.	50.88	65.17	0.63	14.29	nr	**79.46**
42mm dia.	69.83	89.43	0.67	15.19	nr	**104.63**
54mm dia.	109.85	140.70	0.85	19.28	nr	**159.97**
Double union stopcock with easy clean cover						
15mm dia.	14.35	18.38	0.60	13.61	nr	**31.99**
22mm dia.	17.91	22.94	0.61	13.83	nr	**36.78**
28mm dia.	33.31	42.66	0.69	15.65	nr	**58.31**
Combined stopcock and drain						
15mm dia.	14.15	18.13	0.67	15.19	nr	**33.32**
22mm dia.	17.38	22.26	0.68	15.42	nr	**37.68**
Combined DZR stopcock and drain						
15mm dia.	18.70	23.95	0.67	15.19	nr	**39.15**
Gate valve						
DZR copper alloy wedge non-rising stem; compression joint to copper						
15mm dia.	8.47	10.85	0.84	19.05	nr	**29.90**
22mm dia.	10.40	13.32	1.01	22.91	nr	**36.23**
28mm dia.	14.06	18.01	1.19	26.99	nr	**45.00**
35mm dia.	25.23	32.31	1.38	31.30	nr	**63.61**
42mm dia.	42.86	54.89	1.62	36.74	nr	**91.63**
54mm dia.	60.05	76.91	1.94	44.00	nr	**120.91**
Cocks; compression joints to copper						
Stopcock; brass head gun metal body						
15mm dia.	3.10	3.97	0.42	9.52	nr	**13.49**
22mm dia.	5.44	6.97	0.42	9.52	nr	**16.49**
28mm dia.	14.19	18.17	0.45	10.21	nr	**28.37**
Lockshield stopcock; brass head gun metal body						
15mm dia.	6.73	8.62	0.42	9.52	nr	**18.15**
22mm dia.	9.49	12.16	0.42	9.52	nr	**21.68**
28mm dia.	20.14	25.79	0.45	10.21	nr	**36.00**

S:PIPED SUPPLY SYSTEMS

Item	Net Price £	Material £	Labour hours	Labour £	Unit	Total rate £
DZR Stopcock						
15mm dia.	7.45	9.55	0.38	8.62	nr	**18.16**
22mm dia.	12.24	15.68	0.39	8.84	nr	**24.52**
28mm dia.	20.26	25.94	0.40	9.07	nr	**35.02**
35mm dia.	39.19	50.19	0.52	11.79	nr	**61.99**
42mm dia.	55.58	71.19	0.54	12.25	nr	**83.44**
54mm dia.	75.82	97.11	0.63	14.29	nr	**111.40**
DZR Lockshield stopcock						
15mm dia.	9.14	11.70	0.38	8.62	nr	**20.32**
22mm dia.	14.32	18.34	0.39	8.84	nr	**27.19**
Combined stop/draincock						
15mm dia.	11.45	14.66	0.22	4.99	nr	**19.65**
22mm dia.	14.77	18.92	0.45	10.21	nr	**29.13**
DZR Combined stop/draincock						
15mm dia.	14.34	18.37	0.41	9.30	nr	**27.67**
22mm dia.	19.66	25.18	0.42	9.52	nr	**34.70**
Stopcock to polyethylene						
15mm dia.	7.29	9.33	0.38	8.62	nr	**17.95**
20mm dia.	11.32	14.50	0.39	8.84	nr	**23.34**
25mm dia.	13.87	17.77	0.40	9.07	nr	**26.84**
Draw off coupling						
15mm dia.	4.49	5.76	0.38	8.62	nr	**14.37**
DZR Draw off coupling						
15mm dia.	6.20	7.93	0.38	8.62	nr	**16.55**
22mm dia.	7.17	9.19	0.39	8.84	nr	**18.03**
Draw off elbow						
15mm dia.	4.60	5.89	0.38	8.62	nr	**14.51**
22mm dia.	5.27	6.75	0.39	8.84	nr	**15.60**
Lockshield drain cock						
15mm dia.	3.91	5.00	0.41	9.30	nr	**14.30**
Check valves						
DZR copper alloy and bronze, WRC approved cartridge double check valve; BS 6282; working pressure cold services up to 10 bar at 65°C; screwed ends						
32mm dia.	51.37	65.79	1.38	31.30	nr	**97.09**
40mm dia.	63.33	81.11	1.62	36.74	nr	**117.85**
50mm dia.	90.01	115.28	1.94	44.00	nr	**159.27**

S:PIPED SUPPLY SYSTEMS

Item	Net Price £	Material £	Labour hours	Labour £	Unit	Total rate £
S10 : COLD WATER (cont'd)						
Y20 - PUMPS						
Packaged cold water pressure booster set; fully automatic; 3 phase supply; includes fixing in position; electrical work elsewhere.						
Pressure booster set						
0.75 l/s at 30m head	2710.96	3472.17	9.38	212.72	nr	**3684.89**
1.5 l/s at 30m head	3219.27	4123.21	9.38	212.72	nr	**4335.93**
3 l/s at 30m head	3933.31	5037.74	10.38	235.40	nr	**5273.15**
6 l/s at 30m head	8883.24	11377.57	10.38	235.40	nr	**11612.97**
12 l/s at 30m head	11097.99	14214.19	12.38	280.76	nr	**14494.95**
0.75 l/s at 50m head	3086.14	3952.70	9.38	212.72	nr	**4165.42**
1.5 l/s at 50m head	3933.31	5037.74	9.38	212.72	nr	**5250.47**
3 l/s at 50m head	4344.80	5564.78	10.38	235.40	nr	**5800.18**
6 l/s at 50m head	9921.63	12707.52	10.38	235.40	nr	**12942.93**
12 l/s at 50m head	12187.22	15609.27	12.38	280.76	nr	**15890.03**
0.75 l/s at 70m head	3376.60	4324.72	9.38	212.72	nr	**4537.44**
1.5 l/s at 70m head	4342.38	5561.68	9.38	212.72	nr	**5774.40**
3 l/s at 70m head	4623.16	5921.30	10.38	235.40	nr	**6156.70**
6 l/s at 70m head	10831.74	13873.18	10.38	235.40	nr	**14108.59**
12 l/s at 70m head	13167.52	16864.83	12.38	280.76	nr	**17145.59**
Automatic sump pump for clear and drainage water; single stage centrifugal pump, presure tight electric motor; single phase supply; includes fixing in position; electrical work elsewhere						
Single pump						
1 l/s at 2.68m total head	136.01	174.20	3.50	79.37	nr	**253.58**
1 l/s at 4.68m total head	149.71	191.75	3.50	79.37	nr	**271.12**
1 l/s at 6.68m total head	197.66	253.16	3.50	79.37	nr	**332.53**
2 l/s at 4.38m total head	197.66	253.16	4.00	90.71	nr	**343.87**
2 l/s at 6.38m total head	197.66	253.16	4.00	90.71	nr	**343.87**
2 l/s at 8.38m total head	254.41	325.85	4.00	90.71	nr	**416.56**
3 l/s at 3.7m total head	197.66	253.16	4.50	102.05	nr	**355.21**
3 l/s at 5.7m total head	254.41	325.85	4.50	102.05	nr	**427.90**
4 l/s at 2.9m total head	197.66	253.16	5.00	113.39	nr	**366.55**
4 l/s at 4.9m total head	254.41	325.85	5.00	113.39	nr	**439.24**
4 l/s at 6.9m total head	705.50	903.60	5.00	113.39	nr	**1016.99**
Extra for high level alarm box with single float switch, local alarm and volt free contacts for remote alarm.	207.03	265.16	-	-	nr	**265.16**
Duty/standby pump unit						
1 l/s at 2.68m total head	258.32	330.86	5.00	113.39	nr	**444.25**
1 l/s at 4.68m total head	283.77	363.44	5.00	113.39	nr	**476.84**
1 l/s at 6.68m total head	383.57	491.28	5.00	113.39	nr	**604.67**
2 l/s at 4.38m total head	383.57	491.28	5.50	124.73	nr	**616.01**
2 l/s at 6.38m total head	383.57	491.28	5.50	124.73	nr	**616.01**
2 l/s at 8.38m total head	491.21	629.13	5.50	124.73	nr	**753.86**
3 l/s at 3.7m total head	383.57	491.28	6.00	136.07	nr	**627.35**
3 l/s at 5.7m total head	491.21	629.13	6.00	136.07	nr	**765.20**

S:PIPED SUPPLY SYSTEMS

Item	Net Price £	Material £	Labour hours	Labour £	Unit	Total rate £
4 l/s at 2.9m total head	383.57	491.28	6.50	147.41	nr	**638.68**
4 l/s at 4.9m total head	491.21	629.13	6.50	147.41	nr	**776.54**
4 /s at 6.9m total head	1305.32	1671.84	7.00	158.75	nr	**1830.59**
Extra for 4nr float switches to give pump on, off and high level alarm	216.30	277.03	-	-	nr	**277.03**
Extra for dual pump control panel, internal wall mounted IP54, including volt free contacts	1030.00	1319.21	4.00	90.71	nr	**1409.93**
Y21 - TANKS						
Cisterns; fibreglass; complete with ball valve, fixing plate and fitted covers						
Rectangular						
70 litres capacity	152.00	217.50	1.33	30.16	nr	**247.67**
110 litres capacity	158.00	226.09	1.40	31.75	nr	**257.84**
170 litres capacity	167.00	238.97	1.61	36.51	nr	**275.48**
280 litres capacity	272.00	389.22	1.61	36.51	nr	**425.73**
420 litres capacity	285.00	407.82	1.99	45.13	nr	**452.95**
710 litres capacity	470.00	672.55	3.31	75.07	nr	**747.61**
840 litres capacity	571.00	817.07	3.60	81.64	nr	**898.72**
1590 litres capacity	799.00	1143.33	13.32	302.08	nr	**1445.41**
2275 litres capacity	999.00	1429.52	20.18	457.65	nr	**1887.17**
3365 litres capacity	1244.00	1780.10	24.50	555.62	nr	**2335.73**
4545 litres capacity	1489.00	2130.69	29.91	678.31	nr	**2809.00**
Cisterns; polypropylene; complete with ball valve, fixing plate and cover; includes placing in position						
Rectangular						
18 litres capacity	7.42	9.42	1.00	22.68	nr	**32.10**
68 litres capacity	20.35	25.85	1.00	22.68	nr	**48.53**
91 litres capacity	20.76	26.36	1.00	22.68	nr	**49.03**
114 litres capacity	27.58	35.02	1.00	22.68	nr	**57.70**
182 litres capacity	49.31	62.62	1.00	22.68	nr	**85.30**
227 litres capacity	49.70	63.12	1.00	22.68	nr	**85.79**
Circular						
114 litres capacity	23.18	29.43	1.00	22.68	nr	**52.11**
227 litres capacity	35.16	44.65	1.00	22.68	nr	**67.33**
318 litres capacity	94.38	119.85	1.00	22.68	nr	**142.53**
455 litres capacity	107.26	136.21	1.00	22.68	nr	**158.88**

S:PIPED SUPPLY SYSTEMS

Item	Net Price £	Material £	Labour hours	Labour £	Unit	Total rate £
S10 : COLD WATER (cont'd)						
Y21 – TANKS (cont'd)						
Steel sectional water storage tank; hot pressed steel tank to BS 1564 TYPE 1; 5mm plate; pre-insulated and complete with all connections and fittings to comply with BSEN 13280; 2001 and WRAS water supply (water fittings) regulations 1999; externally flanged base and sides; cost of erection (on prepared base) is included within the net price, labour cost allows for offloading and positioning materials						
Note - Prices are based on the most economical tank size for each volume, and the cost will vary with differing tank dimensions, for the same volume						
Volume, size						
4,900 litres, 3.66m x 1.22m x 1,22m (h)	4343.90	5427.70	6.00	136.07	nr	**5563.77**
20,300 litres, 3.66m x 2.4m x 2.4m (h)	-	11561.87	12.00	272.14	nr	**11834.01**
52,000 litres, 6.1m x 3.6m x 2.4m (h)	-	20615.38	19.00	430.89	nr	**21046.27**
94,000 litres, 7.3m x 3.6m x 3.6m (h)	-	31014.46	28.00	635.00	nr	**31649.46**
140,000 litres, 9.7m x 6.1m x 2.44m (h)	32417.00	40505.04	28.00	635.00	nr	**41140.04**
GRP sectional water storage tank; pre-insulated and complete with all connections and fittings to comply with BSEN 13280; 2001 and WRAS water supply (water fittings) regulations 1999; externally flanged base and sides; cost of erection (on prepared base) is included within the net price, labour cost allows for offloading and positioning materials						
Note - Prices are based on the most economical tank size for each volume, and the cost will vary with differing tank dimensions, for the same volume						
Volume, size	-	-	-	-	nr	-
4,500 litres, 3m x 1m x 1.5m (h)	3224.10	4028.51	5.00	113.39	nr	**4141.90**
10,000 litres, 2.5m x 2m x 2m (h)	4285.60	5354.86	7.00	158.75	nr	**5513.61**
20,000 litres, 4m x 2.5m x 2m (h)	6164.40	7702.42	10.00	226.78	nr	**7929.20**
30,000 litres 5m x 3m x 2m (h)	7692.30	9611.53	12.00	272.14	nr	**9883.67**
40,000 litres, 5m x 4m x 2m (h)	9013.40	11262.24	12.00	272.14	nr	**11534.38**
50,000 litres, 5m x 4m x 2.5m (h)	11112.20	13884.69	14.00	317.50	nr	**14202.19**
60,000 litres, 6m x 4m x 2.5m (h)	12802.90	15997.22	16.00	362.85	nr	**16360.08**
70,000 litres, 7m x 4m x 2.5m (h)	14186.70	17726.28	16.00	362.85	nr	**18089.14**
80,000 litres, 8m x 4m x 2.5m (h)	16124.90	20148.06	16.00	362.85	nr	**20510.92**
90,000 litres, 6m x 5m x 3m (h)	16432.90	20532.91	16.00	362.85	nr	**20895.76**
105,000 litres, 7m x 5m x 3m (h)	18164.30	22696.29	24.00	544.28	nr	**23240.57**
120,000 litres, 8m x 5m x 3m (h)	19166.40	23948.42	24.00	544.28	nr	**24492.70**
135,000 litres, 9m x 6m x 2.5m (h)	22091.30	27603.08	24.00	544.28	nr	**28147.36**
144,000 litres, 8m x 6m x 3m (h)	21332.30	26654.71	24.00	544.28	nr	**27198.99**

S:PIPED SUPPLY SYSTEMS

Item	Net Price £	Material £	Labour hours	Labour £	Unit	Total rate £
Y25 - CLEANING AND CHEMICAL TREATMENT						
Electromagnetic water conditioner, complete with control box; maximum inlet pressure 16 bar; electrical work elsewhere						
Connection size, nominal flow rate at 50mbar						
20mm dia, 0.3l/s	1290.00	1652.22	1.25	28.35	nr	1680.57
25mm dia, 0.6l/s	1825.00	2337.44	1.45	32.88	nr	2370.33
32mm dia, 1.2l/s	2650.00	3394.09	1.55	35.15	nr	3429.25
40mm dia, 1.7l/s	3225.00	4130.55	1.65	37.42	nr	4167.97
50mm dia, 3.4l/s	4325.00	5539.42	1.75	39.69	nr	5579.10
65mm dia, 5.2l/s	4790.00	6134.98	1.90	43.09	nr	6178.07
100mm dia, 30.5l/s	15690.00	20095.60	3.00	68.04	nr	20163.63
Ultraviolet water sterillising unit, complete with control unit; UV lamp housed in quartz tube; unit complete with UV intensity sensor, flushing and discharge valve and facilities for remote alarm; electrical work elsewhere						
Maximum flow rate (at 250J/m2 exposure), connection size						
0.82l/s, 40mm dia	2930.00	3752.71	1.98	44.90	nr	3797.62
1.28l/s, 40mm dia	3780.00	4841.39	1.98	44.90	nr	4886.29
2.00l/s, 40mm dia	4220.00	5404.93	1.98	44.90	nr	5449.84
4.14l/s, 50mm dia	6800.00	8709.37	2.10	47.62	nr	8757.00
1.28l/s, 40mm dia	5750.00	7364.54	1.98	44.90	nr	7409.45
2.00l/s, 40mm dia	9415.00	12058.64	1.98	44.90	nr	12103.54
4.14l/s, 50mm dia	12190.00	15612.83	2.10	47.62	nr	15660.45
7.4l/s, 80mm dia	15175.00	19435.99	3.60	81.64	nr	19517.63
16.8l/s 100mm dia	17305.00	22164.07	3.60	81.64	nr	22245.71
32.3l/s 100mm dia	21950.00	28113.34	3.60	81.64	nr	28194.98
Base exchange water softener complete with resin tank, brine tank and consumption data monitoring facilities Capacities of softeners are based on 300ppm hardness and quoted in m³ of softened water produced. Design flow rates are recommended for continuous use						
Simplex configuration Design flow rate, min-max softenend water produced						
1l/s, 5.8m³-11.2m³	1480.00	1895.57	8.00	181.43	nr	2077.00
1.3l/s, 11.7m³-21.4m³	2060.00	2638.43	8.00	181.43	nr	2819.85
1.3l/s, 15.5m³-28.5m³	2360.00	3022.66	10.00	226.78	nr	3249.45
1.6l/s, 23.3m³-42.7m³	3025.00	3874.39	10.00	226.78	nr	4101.17
1.6l/s, 38.8m³-71.2m³	3420.00	4380.30	12.00	272.14	nr	4652.44
1.9l/s, 11.7m³-21.4m³	3420.00	4380.30	12.00	272.14	nr	4652.44
3.2l/s, 19.4m³-35.6m³	3710.00	4751.73	12.00	272.14	nr	5023.87
4.4l/s, 31m³-57m³	4390.00	5622.67	15.00	340.18	nr	5962.84
5.1l/s, 46.6m³-85.4m³	6590.00	8440.41	15.00	340.18	nr	8780.58
5.1l/s, 77.7m³-142.4m³	8080.00	10348.78	18.00	408.21	nr	10756.99

S:PIPED SUPPLY SYSTEMS

Item	Net Price £	Material £	Labour hours	Labour £	Unit	Total rate £
S10 : COLD WATER (cont'd)						
Y25 - CLEANING AND CHEMICAL TREATMENT (cont'd)						
Base exchange water softener (cont'd)						
Duplex configuration						
Design flow rate, min-max softenend water produced						
2l/s, 5.8m³-22.4m³	2430.00	3112.32	12.00	272.14	nr	**3384.46**
2.6l/s, 11.7m³-42.8m³	3370.00	4316.26	12.00	272.14	nr	**4588.40**
2.6l/s, 15.5m³-57m³	3540.00	4534.00	15.00	340.18	nr	**4874.17**
3.2l/s, 23.3m³-85.4m³	4630.00	5930.06	15.00	340.18	nr	**6270.23**
3.2l/s, 38.8m³-142.4m³	5570.00	7134.00	18.00	408.21	nr	**7542.21**
3.8l/s, 11.7m³-42.8m³	6020.00	7710.36	18.00	408.21	nr	**8118.57**
6.4l/s, 19.4m³-71.2m³	6490.00	8312.33	18.00	408.21	nr	**8720.54**
8.8l/s, 31.1m³-114m³	7470.00	9567.50	23.00	521.60	nr	**10089.10**
10.2l/s, 46.6m³-170.8m³	12090.00	15484.75	23.00	521.60	nr	**16006.35**
10.2l/s, 77.7m³-284.8m³	15040.00	19263.08	27.00	612.32	nr	**19875.40**
Triplex configuration						
Design flow rate, min-max softenend water produced						
3l/s, 5.8m³-33.6m³	3355.00	4297.05	15.00	340.18	nr	**4637.23**
3.9l/s, 11.7m³-64.2m³	4880.00	6250.26	15.00	340.18	nr	**6590.43**
3.9l/s, 15.5m³-85.5m³	5170.00	6621.68	18.00	408.21	nr	**7029.90**
4.8l/s, 23.3m³-128.1m³	6820.00	8734.99	18.00	408.21	nr	**9143.20**
4.8l/s, 38.8m³-213.6m³	7880.00	10092.63	22.00	498.92	nr	**10591.55**
5.7l/s, 11.7m³-64.2m³	8860.00	11347.80	22.00	498.92	nr	**11846.72**
9.6l/s, 19.4m³-106.8m³	9630.00	12334.01	22.00	498.92	nr	**12832.93**
13.2l/s, 31.1m³-171.0m³	11090.00	14203.96	27.00	612.32	nr	**14816.28**
15.3l/s, 46.6m³-256.2m³	18020.00	23079.84	27.00	612.32	nr	**23692.15**
15.3l/s, 77.7m³-427.2m³	22590.00	28933.05	32.00	725.71	nr	**29658.75**
Y50 -THERMAL INSULATION						
Flexible closed cell walled insulation; Class 1/Class O; adhesive joints; including around fittings						
6mm wall thickness						
15mm diameter	0.66	0.85	0.15	3.40	m	**4.25**
22mm diameter	0.78	1.00	0.15	3.40	m	**4.40**
28mm diameter	0.99	1.27	0.15	3.40	m	**4.67**
9mm wall thickness						
15mm diameter	0.70	0.90	0.15	3.40	m	**4.30**
22mm diameter	0.85	1.09	0.15	3.40	m	**4.49**
28mm diameter	0.93	1.19	0.15	3.40	m	**4.60**
35mm diameter	1.08	1.39	0.15	3.40	m	**4.79**
42mm diameter	1.26	1.61	0.15	3.40	m	**5.01**
54mm diameter	1.81	2.32	0.15	3.40	m	**5.72**

S:PIPED SUPPLY SYSTEMS

Item	Net Price £	Material £	Labour hours	Labour £	Unit	Total rate £
13mm wall thickness						
15mm diameter	0.91	1.17	0.15	3.40	m	**4.57**
22mm diameter	1.11	1.42	0.15	3.40	m	**4.82**
28mm diameter	1.35	1.73	0.15	3.40	m	**5.13**
35mm diameter	1.46	1.87	0.15	3.40	m	**5.28**
42mm diameter	1.74	2.23	0.15	3.40	m	**5.63**
54mm diameter	2.16	2.76	0.15	3.40	m	**6.17**
67mm diameter	3.41	4.36	0.15	3.40	m	**7.77**
76mm diameter	3.95	5.06	0.15	3.40	m	**8.46**
108mm diameter	5.78	7.41	0.15	3.40	m	**10.81**
19mm wall thickness						
15mm diameter	1.52	1.95	0.15	3.40	m	**5.35**
22mm diameter	1.85	2.37	0.15	3.40	m	**5.77**
28mm diameter	2.54	3.26	0.15	3.40	m	**6.66**
35mm diameter	2.96	3.79	0.15	3.40	m	**7.19**
42mm diameter	3.51	4.49	0.15	3.40	m	**7.89**
54mm diameter	4.46	5.71	0.15	3.40	m	**9.11**
67mm diameter	5.33	6.83	0.15	3.40	m	**10.23**
76mm diameter	6.14	7.86	0.22	4.99	m	**12.85**
108mm diameter	9.04	11.58	0.22	4.99	m	**16.57**
25mm wall thickness						
15mm diameter	3.02	3.87	0.15	3.40	m	**7.27**
22mm diameter	3.33	4.27	0.15	3.40	m	**7.67**
28mm diameter	3.78	4.84	0.15	3.40	m	**8.24**
35mm diameter	4.20	5.38	0.15	3.40	m	**8.78**
42mm diameter	4.47	5.73	0.15	3.40	m	**9.13**
54mm diameter	5.28	6.76	0.15	3.40	m	**10.17**
67mm diameter	6.44	8.25	0.15	3.40	m	**11.65**
76mm diameter	7.48	9.58	0.22	4.99	m	**14.57**
32mm wall thickness						
15mm diameter	3.82	4.90	0.15	3.40	m	**8.30**
22mm diameter	4.20	5.38	0.15	3.40	m	**8.78**
28mm diameter	4.88	6.25	0.15	3.40	m	**9.65**
35mm diameter	4.95	6.34	0.15	3.40	m	**9.74**
42mm diameter	5.75	7.37	0.15	3.40	m	**10.77**
54mm diameter	7.25	9.28	0.15	3.40	m	**12.68**
76mm diameter	10.84	13.89	0.22	4.99	m	**18.88**

For mineral fibre insulation rates see section T31 - Low Temperature Hot Water Heating

S:PIPED SUPPLY SYSTEMS

Item	Net Price £	Material £	Labour hours	Labour £	Unit	Total rate £
S11 - HOT WATER						
Y10 - PIPELINES						
For pipework prices refer to section S10 - Cold Water						
Y11 - PIPELINE ANCILLARIES						
For prices for ancillaries refer to section S10 - Cold Water						
Y23 - STORAGE CYLINDERS/CALORIFIERS CYLINDERS						
Insulated copper storage cylinders; BS 699; includes placing in position						
Grade 3 (maximum 10m working head)						
BS size 6; 115 litres capacity; 400mm dia.; 1050mm high	90.40	115.78	1.50	34.05	nr	**149.84**
BS size 7; 120 litres capacity; 450mm dia.; 900mm high	106.89	136.90	2.00	45.36	nr	**182.26**
BS size 8; 144 litres capacity; 450mm dia.; 1050mm high	113.62	145.52	2.80	63.52	nr	**209.05**
Grade 4 (maximum 6m working head)						
BS size 2; 96 litres capacity; 400mm dia.; 900mm high	69.99	89.64	1.50	34.05	nr	**123.69**
BS size 7; 120 litres capacity; 450mm dia.; 900mm high	84.59	108.34	1.50	34.05	nr	**142.39**
BS size 8; 144 litres capacity; 450mm dia.; 1050mm high	87.81	112.47	1.50	34.05	nr	**146.52**
BS size 9; 166 litres capacity; 450mm dia.; 1200mm high	128.39	164.44	1.50	34.05	nr	**198.49**
Storage cylinders; brazed copper construction; to BS 699; screwed bosses; includes placing in position						
Tested to 2.2 bar, 15m maximum head						
144 litres	397.93	509.66	3.00	68.10	nr	**577.77**
160 litres	449.84	576.15	3.00	68.10	nr	**644.25**
200 litres	463.68	593.88	3.76	85.26	nr	**679.13**
255 litres	527.69	675.86	3.76	85.26	nr	**761.12**
290 litres	712.81	912.96	3.76	85.26	nr	**998.22**
370 litres	816.63	1045.93	4.50	102.15	nr	**1148.09**
450 litres	1112.41	1424.76	5.00	113.39	nr	**1538.16**
Tested to 2.55 bar, 17m maximum head						
550 litres	1204.52	1542.74	5.00	113.39	nr	**1656.13**
700 litres	1408.20	1803.61	6.02	136.62	nr	**1940.23**
800 litres	1628.76	2086.10	6.54	148.22	nr	**2234.32**
900 litres	1762.48	2257.37	8.00	181.43	nr	**2438.79**
1000 litres	1859.91	2382.15	8.00	181.43	nr	**2563.58**
1250 litres	2037.03	2609.01	13.16	298.40	nr	**2907.41**
1500 litres	3099.83	3970.23	15.15	343.61	nr	**4313.84**
2000 litres	3720.06	4764.62	17.24	391.01	nr	**5155.62**
3000 litres	5225.42	6692.67	24.39	553.13	nr	**7245.80**

S:PIPED SUPPLY SYSTEMS

Item	Net Price £	Material £	Labour hours	Labour £	Unit	Total rate £
Indirect cylinders; copper; bolted top; up to 5 tappings for connections; BS 1586; includes placing in position						
Grade 3, tested to 1.45 bar, 10m maximum head						
74 litres capacity	181.26	232.16	1.50	34.05	nr	**266.21**
96 litres capacity	184.55	236.37	1.50	34.05	nr	**270.42**
114 litres capacity	189.49	242.70	1.50	34.05	nr	**276.75**
117 litres capacity	196.67	251.89	2.00	45.36	nr	**297.25**
140 litres capacity	202.66	259.56	2.50	56.70	nr	**316.26**
162 litres capacity	283.41	362.99	3.00	68.10	nr	**431.09**
190 litres capacity	309.78	396.76	3.51	79.57	nr	**476.34**
245 litres capacity	362.51	464.30	3.80	86.23	nr	**550.53**
280 litres capacity	642.62	823.06	4.00	90.71	nr	**913.77**
360 litres capacity	695.35	890.60	4.50	102.15	nr	**992.75**
440 litres capacity	807.40	1034.11	4.50	102.15	nr	**1136.26**
Grade 2, tested to 2.2 bar, 15m maximum head						
117 litres capacity	261.98	335.54	2.00	45.36	nr	**380.90**
140 litres capacity	285.07	365.11	2.50	56.70	nr	**421.81**
162 litres capacity	326.25	417.86	2.80	63.52	nr	**481.38**
190 litres capacity	379.00	485.42	3.00	68.10	nr	**553.52**
245 litres capacity	458.09	586.72	4.00	90.71	nr	**677.43**
280 litres capacity	731.60	937.03	4.00	90.71	nr	**1027.74**
360 litres capacity	807.40	1034.11	4.50	102.15	nr	**1136.26**
440 litres capacity	955.69	1224.04	4.50	102.15	nr	**1326.19**
Grade 1, tested 3.65 bar, 25m maximum head						
190 litres capacity	563.54	721.78	3.00	68.10	nr	**789.88**
245 litres capacity	640.96	820.94	3.00	68.10	nr	**889.04**
280 litres capacity	906.27	1160.74	4.00	90.71	nr	**1251.46**
360 litres capacity	1146.85	1468.87	4.50	102.15	nr	**1571.03**
440 litres capacity	1392.34	1783.30	4.50	102.15	nr	**1885.45**
Indirect cylinders, including manhole; BS 853						
Grade 3, tested to 1.5 bar, 10m maximum head						
550 litres capacity	1172.02	1501.11	5.21	118.12	nr	**1619.23**
700 litres capacity	1297.60	1661.95	6.02	136.62	nr	**1798.57**
800 litres capacity	1506.89	1930.01	6.54	148.22	nr	**2078.23**
1000 litres capacity	1883.62	2412.52	7.04	159.71	nr	**2572.23**
1500 litres capacity	2176.62	2787.79	10.00	226.78	nr	**3014.58**
2000 litres capacity	3013.79	3860.03	16.13	365.78	nr	**4225.81**
Grade 2, tested to 2.55 bar, 15m maximum head						
550 litres capacity	1299.40	1664.26	5.21	118.12	nr	**1782.37**
700 litres capacity	1626.29	2082.94	6.02	136.62	nr	**2219.55**
800 litres capacity	1716.18	2198.07	6.54	148.22	nr	**2346.29**
1000 litres capacity	2124.80	2721.42	7.04	159.71	nr	**2881.13**
1500 litres capacity	2615.14	3349.45	10.00	226.78	nr	**3576.23**
2000 litres capacity	3268.93	4186.81	16.13	365.78	nr	**4552.59**
Grade 1, tested to 4 bar, 25m maximum head						
550 litres capacity	1511.87	1936.39	5.21	118.12	nr	**2054.50**
700 litres capacity	1716.18	2198.07	6.02	136.62	nr	**2334.68**
800 litres capacity	1838.77	2355.08	6.54	148.22	nr	**2503.30**
1000 litres capacity	2451.70	3140.11	7.04	159.71	nr	**3299.82**
1500 litres capacity	2942.02	3768.11	10.00	226.78	nr	**3994.89**
2000 litres capacity	3595.81	4605.48	16.13	365.78	nr	**4971.26**

S:PIPED SUPPLY SYSTEMS

Item	Net Price £	Material £	Labour hours	Labour £	Unit	Total rate £
S11 - HOT WATER (cont'd)						
Y23 - STORAGE CYLINDERS/CALORIFIERS CYLINDERS (cont'd)						
Storage calorifiers; copper; heater battery capable of raising temperature of contents from 10°C to 65°C in one hour; static head not exceeding 1.35 bar; BS 853; includes fixing in position on cradles or legs						
Horizontal; primary LPHW at 82°C/71°C						
400 litres capacity	1754.05	2246.57	7.04	159.71	nr	2406.28
1000 litres capacity	2806.48	3594.51	8.00	181.43	nr	3775.94
2000 litres capacity	5612.99	7189.06	14.08	319.41	nr	7508.48
3000 litres capacity	6928.52	8873.98	25.00	566.96	nr	9440.94
4000 litres capacity	8419.46	10783.56	40.00	907.14	nr	11690.70
4500 litres capacity	9488.36	12152.60	50.00	1133.92	nr	13286.52
Vertical; primary LPHW at 82°C/71°C						
400 litres capacity	1718.98	2201.65	7.04	159.71	nr	2361.36
1000 litres capacity	2762.66	3538.39	8.00	181.43	nr	3719.81
2000 litres capacity	5262.17	6739.73	14.08	319.41	nr	7059.15
3000 litres capacity	6577.72	8424.68	25.00	566.96	nr	8991.64
4000 litres capacity	8068.65	10334.25	40.00	907.14	nr	11241.38
4500 litres capacity	9121.09	11682.20	50.00	1133.92	nr	12816.12
Storage calorifiers; galvanised mild steel; heater battery capable of raising temperature of contents from 10°C to 65°C in one hour; static head not exceeding 1.35 bar; BS 853; includes fixing in position on cradles or legs						
Horizontal; primary LPHW at 82°C/71°C						
400 litres capacity	1754.05	2246.57	7.04	159.71	nr	2406.28
1000 litres capacity	2806.48	3594.51	8.00	181.43	nr	3775.94
2000 litres capacity	5612.99	7189.06	14.08	319.41	nr	7508.48
3000 litres capacity	6928.52	8873.98	25.00	566.96	nr	9440.94
4000 litres capacity	8419.46	10783.56	40.00	907.14	nr	11690.70
4500 litres capacity	9488.36	12152.60	50.00	1133.92	nr	13286.52
Vertical; primary LPHW at 82°C/71°C						
400 litres capacity	1718.98	2201.65	7.04	159.71	nr	2361.36
1000 litres capacity	2762.66	3538.39	8.00	181.43	nr	3719.81
2000 litres capacity	5262.17	6739.73	14.08	319.41	nr	7059.15
3000 litres capacity	6577.72	8424.68	25.00	566.96	nr	8991.64
4000 litres capacity	8068.65	10334.25	40.00	907.14	nr	11241.38
4500 litres capacity	9121.09	11682.20	50.00	1133.92	nr	12816.12

S:PIPED SUPPLY SYSTEMS

Item	Net Price £	Material £	Labour hours	Labour £	Unit	Total rate £
Indirect cylinders; mild steel, welded throughout, galvanised; with bolted connections; includes placing in position						
3.2mm plate						
136 litres capacity	647.80	829.70	2.50	56.70	nr	**886.39**
159 litres capacity	697.64	893.53	2.80	63.52	nr	**957.05**
182 litres capacity	857.12	1097.79	3.00	68.10	nr	**1165.89**
227 litres capacity	1056.43	1353.07	3.00	68.10	nr	**1421.17**
273 litres capacity	1232.32	1578.34	4.00	90.71	nr	**1669.06**
364 litres capacity	1435.15	1838.13	4.50	102.15	nr	**1940.28**
455 litres capacity	1482.33	1898.55	5.00	113.39	nr	**2011.95**
683 litres capacity	2398.86	3072.44	6.02	136.62	nr	**3209.05**
910 litres capacity	2786.09	3568.40	7.04	159.71	nr	**3728.10**
Y50 - INSULATION						
Refer to sections S10 - Cold Water and T31 - Low Temperature Hot Water Heating for details						

S:PIPED SUPPLY SYSTEMS

Item	Net Price £	Material £	Labour hours	Labour £	Unit	Total rate £
S32 : NATURAL GAS						
Y10 - PIPELINES						
MEDIUM DENSITY POLYETHELENE - YELLOW						
Pipe; laid underground; electrofusion joints in the running length; BS 6572; BGT PL2 standards						
Coiled service pipe						
20mm dia.	0.42	0.55	0.37	8.39	m	8.95
25mm dia.	0.55	0.73	0.41	9.30	m	10.02
32mm dia.	0.88	1.16	0.47	10.66	m	11.82
63mm dia.	3.37	4.45	0.60	13.61	m	18.05
90mm dia.	7.95	10.49	0.90	20.41	m	30.90
Mains service pipe						
63mm dia.	4.02	5.15	0.60	13.61	m	18.76
90mm dia.	5.38	6.89	0.90	20.41	m	27.30
125mm dia.	10.29	13.18	1.20	27.21	m	40.39
180mm dia.	20.96	26.85	1.50	34.02	m	60.86
250mm dia.	20.25	25.94	1.75	39.69	m	65.62
Extra over fittings, electrofusion joints						
Straight connector						
32mm dia.	2.81	3.60	0.47	10.66	nr	14.26
63mm dia.	5.26	6.74	0.58	13.15	nr	19.89
90mm dia.	8.33	10.67	0.67	15.19	nr	25.86
125mm dia.	14.15	18.12	0.83	18.82	nr	36.95
180mm dia.	27.07	34.67	1.25	28.35	nr	63.02
Reducing connector						
90 x 63mm dia.	11.42	14.63	0.67	15.19	nr	29.82
125 x 90mm dia.	22.94	29.38	0.83	18.82	nr	48.20
180 x 125mm dia.	42.04	53.84	1.25	28.35	nr	82.19
Bend; 45°						
90mm dia.	18.90	24.21	0.67	15.19	nr	39.40
125mm dia.	32.91	42.15	0.83	18.82	nr	60.97
180mm dia.	72.36	92.68	1.25	28.35	nr	121.03
Bend; 90°						
63mm dia.	13.67	17.51	0.58	13.15	nr	30.66
90mm dia.	20.77	26.60	0.67	15.19	nr	41.80
125mm dia.	33.99	43.53	0.83	18.82	nr	62.36
180mm dia.	77.17	98.84	1.25	28.35	nr	127.19
Extra over malleable iron fittings, compression joints						
Straight connector						
20mm dia.	7.63	9.77	0.38	8.62	nr	18.39
25mm dia.	8.33	10.67	0.45	10.21	nr	20.87
32mm dia.	9.34	11.96	0.50	11.34	nr	23.30
63mm dia.	18.77	24.04	0.85	19.28	nr	43.32

S:PIPED SUPPLY SYSTEMS

Item	Net Price £	Material £	Labour hours	Labour £	Unit	Total rate £
Straight connector; polyethylene to MI						
20mm dia.	6.43	8.24	0.31	7.03	nr	**15.27**
25mm dia.	7.01	8.98	0.35	7.94	nr	**16.92**
32mm dia.	7.84	10.04	0.40	9.07	nr	**19.11**
63mm dia.	13.13	16.82	0.65	14.75	nr	**31.56**
Straight connector; polyethylene to FI						
20mm dia.	6.26	8.02	0.31	7.03	nr	**15.05**
25mm dia.	6.83	8.75	0.35	7.94	nr	**16.69**
32mm dia.	7.63	9.77	0.40	9.07	nr	**18.84**
63mm dia.	12.79	16.38	0.75	17.01	nr	**33.39**
Elbow						
20mm dia.	9.84	12.60	0.38	8.62	nr	**21.22**
25mm dia.	10.74	13.76	0.45	10.21	nr	**23.96**
32mm dia.	12.03	15.41	0.50	11.34	nr	**26.75**
63mm dia.	24.17	30.96	0.80	18.14	nr	**49.10**
Equal tee						
20mm dia.	11.45	14.67	0.53	12.02	nr	**26.69**
25mm dia.	13.33	17.07	0.55	12.48	nr	**29.55**
32mm dia.	16.82	21.54	0.64	14.52	nr	**36.06**

SCREWED STEEL

For prices for steel pipework refer to section T31 - Low Temperature Hot Water Heating

PIPE IN PIPE

Note - for pipe in pipe, a sleeve size two pipe sizes bigger than actual pipe size has been allowed. All rates refer to actual pipe size.

Black steel pipes –
Screwed and socketed joints; BS 1387: 1985 upto 50mm pipe size.
Butt welded joints; BS 1387: 1985 65mm pipe size and above.

Item	Net Price £	Material £	Labour hours	Labour £	Unit	Total rate £
Pipe						
25mm	7.80	9.99	1.73	39.23	m	**49.22**
32mm	10.21	13.08	1.95	44.22	m	**57.30**
40mm	11.69	14.97	2.16	48.99	m	**63.96**
50mm	15.23	19.51	2.44	55.34	m	**74.84**
65mm	19.90	25.49	2.95	66.90	m	**92.39**
80mm	25.80	33.04	3.42	77.56	m	**110.60**
100mm	32.31	41.38	4.00	90.71	m	**132.10**

S:PIPED SUPPLY SYSTEMS

Item	Net Price £	Material £	Labour hours	Labour £	Unit	Total rate £
S32 : NATURAL GAS (cont'd)						
Y10 – PIPELINES (cont'd)						
PIPE IN PIPE (cont'd)						
Extra over black steel pipes -						
Screwed pipework; black malleable iron						
fittings; BS 143.						
Welded pipework; butt welded steel fittings;						
BS 1965						
Bend, 90 °						
25mm	4.29	5.49	2.91	65.99	m	71.49
32mm	6.56	8.40	3.45	78.24	m	86.64
40mm	7.18	9.20	5.34	121.10	m	130.30
50mm	8.64	11.07	6.53	148.09	m	159.16
65mm	10.63	13.61	8.84	200.48	m	214.09
80mm	17.09	21.89	10.73	243.34	m	265.23
100mm	23.66	30.30	12.76	289.38	m	319.68
Bend, 45 °						
25mm	5.28	6.76	2.91	65.99	m	72.76
32mm	8.14	10.43	3.45	78.24	m	88.67
40mm	8.26	10.58	5.34	121.10	m	131.68
50mm	9.53	12.21	6.53	148.09	m	160.30
65mm	10.70	13.70	8.84	200.48	m	214.18
80mm	17.81	22.81	10.73	243.34	m	266.15
100mm	22.85	29.27	12.76	289.38	m	318.64
Equal tee						
25mm	9.02	11.55	4.18	94.80	m	106.35
32mm	12.80	16.39	4.94	112.03	m	128.43
40mm	26.18	33.53	7.28	165.10	m	198.63
50mm	29.36	37.60	8.48	192.31	m	229.92
65mm	46.06	58.99	11.47	260.12	m	319.11
80mm	80.43	103.01	14.23	322.71	m	425.73
100mm	91.50	117.19	17.92	406.40	m	523.59
GAS BOOSTERS						
Complete skid mounted gas booster set,						
including AV mounts, flexible						
connections, low pressure switch,control						
panel and NRV (for run/standby unit); 3						
phase supply; in accordance with						
IGE/UP/2; includes delivery, offloading						
and positioning						
Single unit						
Flow, pressure range						
0-200 m³/hour, 0.1-2.6 kPa	1119.30	1433.59	10.00	226.78	nr	1660.37
0-200 m³/hour, 0.1-4.0 kPa	1277.15	1635.76	10.00	226.78	nr	1862.54
0-200 m³/hour, 0.1-7 kPa	1486.25	1903.57	10.00	226.78	nr	2130.36
0-200 m³/hour, 0.1-9.5 kPa	1547.75	1982.34	10.00	226.78	nr	2209.13
0-200 m³/hour 0.1-11.0 kPa	1729.18	2214.72	10.00	226.78	nr	2441.50
0-400 m³/hour, 0.1-4.0 kPa	1410.40	1806.43	10.00	226.78	nr	2033.21
0-1000 m³/hour, 0.1-7.4 kPa	1953.65	2502.22	10.00	226.78	nr	2729.00

S:PIPED SUPPLY SYSTEMS

Item	Net Price £	Material £	Labour hours	Labour £	Unit	Total rate £
50-1000 m³/hour, 0.1-16.0 kPa	3650.03	4674.92	20.00	453.57	nr	**5128.49**
50-1000 m³/hour, 0.1-24.5 kPa	4126.65	5285.37	20.00	453.57	nr	**5738.94**
50-1000 m³/hour, 0.1-31.0 kPa	4693.48	6011.36	20.00	453.57	nr	**6464.93**
50-1000 m³/hour, 0.1-41.0 kPa	5180.35	6634.94	20.00	453.57	nr	**7088.51**
50-1000 m³/hour, 0.1-51.0 kPa	5375.10	6884.37	20.00	453.57	nr	**7337.94**
100-1800 m³/hour, 3.5-23.5 kPa	5515.53	7064.24	20.00	453.57	nr	**7517.80**
100-1800 m³/hour, 4.5-27.0 kPa	5949.10	7619.55	20.00	453.57	nr	**8073.12**
100-1800 m³/hour, 6.0-32.5 kPa	6588.70	8438.74	20.00	453.57	nr	**8892.31**
100-1800 m³/hour, 7.2-39.0 kPa	7579.88	9708.23	20.00	453.57	nr	**10161.80**
100-1800 m³/hour, 9.0-42.0 kPa	7967.33	10204.48	20.00	453.57	nr	**10658.04**
Run/Standby unit						
Flow, pressure range						
0-200 m³/hour, 0.1-2.6 kPa	6392.93	8188.00	16.00	362.85	nr	**8550.86**
0-200 m³/hour, 0.1-4.0 kPa	6549.75	8388.85	16.00	362.85	nr	**8751.71**
0-200 m³/hour, 0.1-7 kPa	6701.45	8583.15	16.00	362.85	nr	**8946.00**
0-200 m³/hour, 0.1-9.5 kPa	6867.50	8795.83	16.00	362.85	nr	**9158.68**
0-200 m³/hour 0.1-11.0 kPa	6981.28	8941.55	16.00	362.85	nr	**9304.41**
0-400 m³/hour, 0.1-4.0 kPa	7698.78	9860.52	16.00	362.85	nr	**10223.37**
0-1000 m³/hour, 0.1-7.4 kPa	9813.35	12568.84	25.00	566.96	nr	**13135.80**
50-1000 m³/hour, 0.1-16.0 kPa	13450.05	17226.69	25.00	566.96	nr	**17793.65**
50-1000 m³/hour, 0.1-24.5 kPa	15205.88	19475.54	25.00	566.96	nr	**20042.50**
50-1000 m³/hour, 0.1-31.0 kPa	16957.60	21719.12	25.00	566.96	nr	**22286.08**
50-1000 m³/hour, 0.1-41.0 kPa	18714.45	23969.28	25.00	566.96	nr	**24536.24**
50-1000 m³/hour, 0.1-51.0 kPa	19418.63	24871.19	25.00	566.96	nr	**25438.15**
100-1800 m³/hour, 3.5-23.5 kPa	16512.75	21149.37	25.00	566.96	nr	**21716.33**
100-1800 m³/hour, 4.5-27.0 kPa	17810.40	22811.38	25.00	566.96	nr	**23378.34**
100-1800 m³/hour, 6.0-32.5 kPa	18683.70	23929.90	25.00	566.96	nr	**24496.86**
100-1800 m³/hour, 7.2-39.0 kPa	22691.45	29062.98	25.00	566.96	nr	**29629.94**
100-1800 m³/hour, 9.0-42.0 kPa	23851.75	30549.08	25.00	566.96	nr	**31116.04**

S:PIPED SUPPLY SYSTEMS

Item	Net Price £	Material £	Labour hours	Labour £	Unit	Total rate £
S41 : FUEL OIL STORAGE/DISTRIBUTION						
Y10 - PIPELINES						
For pipework prices refer to Section T31 - Low Temperature Hot Water Heating						
Y21 - TANKS						
Fuel storage tanks; mild steel; with all necessary screwed bosses; oil resistant joint rings; includes placing in position						
Rectangular						
1360 litres (300 gallon) capacity; 2mm plate	274.24	351.25	12.03	272.82	nr	**624.07**
2730 litres (600 gallon) capacity; 2.5mm plate	366.45	469.35	18.60	421.82	nr	**891.17**
4550 litres (1000 gallon) capacity; 3mm plate	768.30	984.02	25.00	566.96	nr	**1550.98**
Fuel storage tanks; 5mm plate mild steel to BS 799 type J; complete with raised neck manhole with bolted cover, screwed connections, vent and fill connections, drain valve, gauge and overfill alarm; includes placing in position; excludes pumps and control panel						
Nominal capacity, size						
5,600 litres, 2.5m x 1.5m x 1.5m high	1799.75	2305.10	20.00	453.57	nr	**2758.67**
Extra for bund unit (internal use)	1035.00	1325.62	30.00	680.35	nr	**2005.97**
Extra for external use with bund (watertight)	655.50	839.56	2.00	45.36	nr	**884.91**
10,200 litres, 3.05m x 1.83m x 1.83m high	2236.75	2864.81	30.00	680.35	nr	**3545.16**
Extra for bund unit (internal use)	1506.50	1929.51	40.00	907.14	nr	**2836.65**
Extra for external use with bund (watertight)	805.00	1031.04	2.00	45.36	nr	**1076.39**
15,000 litres, 3.75m x 2m x 2m high	2829.00	3623.35	40.00	907.14	nr	**4530.49**
Extra for bund unit (internal use)	2024.00	2592.32	55.00	1247.31	nr	**3839.63**
Extra for external use with bund (watertight)	943.00	1207.79	2.00	45.36	nr	**1253.14**
20,000 litres, 4m x 2.5m x 2m high	3731.75	4779.59	50.00	1133.92	nr	**5913.51**
Extra for bund unit (internal use)	2455.25	3144.66	65.00	1474.10	nr	**4618.76**
Extra for external use with bund (watertight)	1115.50	1428.72	2.00	45.36	nr	**1474.08**
Extra for BMS output (all tank sizes)	391.00	500.79	-	-	nr	**500.79**
Fuel storage tanks; plastic; with all necessary screwed bosses; oil resistant joint rings; includes placing in position						
Cylindrical; horizontal						
1250 litres (285 gallon) capacity	222.53	285.01	3.73	84.59	nr	**369.60**
1350 litres (300 gallon) capacity	204.45	261.85	4.30	97.52	nr	**359.37**
2500 litres (550 gallon) capacity	350.11	448.41	4.88	110.67	nr	**559.08**
Cylindrical; vertical						
1365 litres (300 gallon) capacity	139.96	179.25	3.73	84.59	nr	**263.85**
2600 litres (570 gallon) capacity	212.99	272.80	4.88	110.67	nr	**383.47**
3635 litres (800 gallon) capacity	332.06	425.30	4.88	110.67	nr	**535.97**
5455 litres (1200 gallon) capacity	483.74	619.57	5.95	134.94	nr	**754.51**

S:PIPED SUPPLY SYSTEMS

Item	Net Price £	Material £	Labour hours	Labour £	Unit	Total rate £
Bunded tanks						
1135 litres (250 gallon) capacity	448.64	574.61	4.30	97.52	nr	**672.13**
1590 litres (350 gallon) capacity	533.73	683.59	4.88	110.67	nr	**794.26**
2500 litres (550 gallon) capacity	634.40	812.53	5.95	134.94	nr	**947.47**
5000 litres (1100 gallon) capacity	1280.16	1639.61	6.53	148.09	nr	**1787.70**

S:PIPED SUPPLY SYSTEMS

Item	Net Price £	Material £	Labour hours	Labour £	Unit	Total rate £
S60 : FIRE HOSE REELS						
Y10 - PIPELINES						
For pipework prices refer to section S10 - Cold water						
Y11 - PIPELINE ANCILLARIES						
For prices for ancillaries refer to section S10 - Cold water						
Hose reels; automatic; connection to 25mm screwed joint; reel with 30.5 metres, 19mm rubber hose; suitable for working pressure up to 7 bar						
Reels						
Non-swing pattern	156.59	195.36	3.75	86.83	nr	**282.19**
Recessed non-swing pattern	200.81	250.53	3.75	86.83	nr	**337.36**
Swinging pattern	209.11	260.88	3.75	86.83	nr	**347.71**
Recessed swinging pattern	215.72	269.13	3.75	86.83	nr	**355.97**
Hose reels; manual; connection to 25mm screwed joint; reel with 30.5 metres, 19mm rubber hose; suitable for working pressure up to 7 bar						
Reels						
Non-swing pattern	157.71	196.76	3.25	75.25	nr	**272.01**
Recessed non-swing pattern	185.12	230.95	3.25	75.25	nr	**306.20**
Swinging pattern	199.76	249.22	3.25	75.25	nr	**324.48**
Recessed swinging pattern	206.96	258.20	3.25	75.25	nr	**333.45**

S:PIPED SUPPLY SYSTEMS

Item	Net Price £	Material £	Labour hours	Labour £	Unit	Total rate £
S61 : DRY RISERS						
Y10 - PIPELINES						
For pipework prices refer to section S10 - Cold water						
Y11 - PIPELINE ANCILLARIES VALVES (BS 5041, parts 2 and 3)						
Bronze/gunmetal inlet breeching for pumping in with 65mm dia. instantaneous male coupling; with cap, chain and 25mm drain valve						
Double inlet with back pressure valve, flanged to steel	141.86	176.98	1.75	40.52	nr	**217.50**
Quadruple inlet with back pressure valve, flanged to steel	317.63	396.27	1.75	40.52	nr	**436.79**
Bronze/gunmetal gate type outlet valve with 65mm dia. instantaneous female coupling; cap and chain; wheel head secured by padlock and leather strap						
Flanged to BS 4504 PN6 (bolted connection to counter flanges measured separately)	113.77	141.94	1.75	40.52	nr	**182.46**
Bronze/gunmetal landing type outlet valve, with 65mm dia. instantaneous female coupling; cap and chain; wheelhead secured by padlock and leather strap; bolted connections to counter flanges measured separately						
Horizontal, flanged to BS 4504 PN6	123.90	154.58	1.50	34.73	nr	**189.31**
Oblique, flanged to BS 4504 PN6	123.90	154.58	1.50	34.73	nr	**189.31**
Air valve, screwed joints to steel						
25mm dia.	24.62	30.72	0.55	12.74	nr	**43.45**
INLET BOXES (BS 5041, part 5)						
Steel dry riser inlet box with hinged wire glazed door suitably lettered (fixing by others)						
610 x 460 x 325mm; double inlet	151.80	189.39	3.00	69.47	nr	**258.86**
610 x 610 x 356mm; quadruple inlet	283.32	353.46	3.00	69.47	nr	**422.93**
OUTLET BOXES (BS 5041, part 5)						
Steel dry riser outlet box with hinged wire glazed door suitably lettered (fixing by others)						
610 x 460 x 325; single outlet	148.24	184.95	3.00	69.47	nr	**254.41**

S:PIPED SUPPLY SYSTEMS

Item	Net Price £	Material £	Labour hours	Labour £	Unit	Total rate £
S63 : SPRINKLERS						
Y10 - PIPELINES						
Prefabricated black steel pipework; screwed joints, including all couplings, unions and the like to BS 1387:1985; includes fixing to backgrounds						
Medium weight						
25mm dia	0.47	0.59	0.47	10.88	m	**11.47**
32mm dia	0.53	0.66	0.53	12.27	m	**12.93**
40mm dia	0.58	0.72	0.58	13.43	m	**14.15**
50mm dia	0.63	0.79	0.63	14.59	m	**15.37**
Extra over fittings						
Plug						
25mm dia	0.40	0.50	0.40	9.26	nr	**9.76**
32mm dia	0.44	0.55	0.44	10.19	nr	**10.74**
40mm dia	0.48	0.60	0.48	11.11	nr	**11.71**
50mm dia	0.56	0.70	0.56	12.97	nr	**13.67**
Reducer						
32mm dia	0.48	0.60	0.48	11.11	nr	**11.71**
40mm dia	0.55	0.69	0.55	12.74	nr	**13.42**
50mm dia	0.60	0.75	0.60	13.89	nr	**14.64**
Elbow; any degree						
25mm dia	0.44	0.55	0.44	10.19	nr	**10.74**
32mm dia	0.53	0.66	0.53	12.27	nr	**12.93**
40mm dia	0.60	0.75	0.60	13.89	nr	**14.64**
50mm dia	0.65	0.81	0.65	15.05	nr	**15.86**
Tee						
25mm dia	0.51	0.64	0.51	11.81	nr	**12.45**
32mm dia	0.54	0.67	0.54	12.50	nr	**13.18**
40mm dia	0.65	0.81	0.65	15.05	nr	**15.86**
50mm dia	0.78	0.97	0.78	18.06	nr	**19.03**
Cross tee						
25mm dia	1.16	1.45	1.16	26.86	nr	**28.31**
32mm dia	1.40	1.75	1.40	32.42	nr	**34.16**
40mm dia	1.60	2.00	1.60	37.05	nr	**39.04**
50mm dia	1.68	2.10	1.68	38.90	nr	**41.00**
Prefabricated black steel pipework; welded joints, including all couplings, unions and the like to BS 1387:1985; fixing to backgrounds						
Medium weight						
65mm dia	0.65	0.81	0.65	15.05	m	**15.86**
80mm dia	0.70	0.87	0.70	16.21	m	**17.08**
100mm dia	0.85	1.06	0.85	19.68	m	**20.74**
150mm dia	1.15	1.43	1.15	26.63	m	**28.06**

S:PIPED SUPPLY SYSTEMS

Item	Net Price £	Material £	Labour hours	Labour £	Unit	Total rate £
Extra over fittings						
Reducer						
65mm dia	2.70	3.37	2.70	62.52	nr	**65.89**
80mm dia	2.86	3.57	2.86	66.22	nr	**69.79**
100mm dia	3.22	4.02	3.22	74.56	nr	**78.58**
150mm dia	4.20	5.24	4.20	97.25	nr	**102.49**
Elbow; any °						
65mm dia	3.06	3.82	3.06	70.86	nr	**74.67**
80mm dia	3.40	4.24	3.40	78.73	nr	**82.97**
100mm dia	3.70	4.62	3.70	85.67	nr	**90.29**
150mm dia	5.20	6.49	5.20	120.41	nr	**126.90**
Branch bend						
65mm dia	3.60	4.49	3.60	83.36	nr	**87.85**
80mm dia	3.80	4.74	3.80	87.99	nr	**92.73**
100mm dia	5.10	6.36	5.10	118.09	nr	**124.45**
150mm dia	7.50	9.36	7.50	173.66	nr	**183.02**
Prefabricated black steel pipe; victaulic joints; including all couplings and the like to BS 1387: 1985; fixing to backgrounds						
Medium weight						
65mm dia	0.70	0.87	0.70	16.21	m	**17.08**
80mm dia	0.78	0.97	0.78	18.06	m	**19.03**
100mm dia	0.93	1.16	0.93	21.53	m	**22.69**
150mm dia	1.25	1.56	1.25	28.94	m	**30.50**
Extra over fittings						
Coupling						
65mm dia	0.26	0.32	0.26	6.02	nr	**6.34**
80mm dia	0.26	0.32	0.26	6.02	nr	**6.34**
100mm dia	0.32	0.40	0.32	7.41	nr	**7.81**
150mm dia	0.35	0.44	0.35	8.10	nr	**8.54**
Reducer						
65mm dia	0.48	0.60	0.48	11.11	nr	**11.71**
80mm dia	0.43	0.54	0.43	9.96	nr	**10.49**
100mm dia	0.46	0.57	0.46	10.65	nr	**11.23**
150mm dia	0.45	0.56	0.45	10.42	nr	**10.98**
Elbow; any °						
65mm dia	0.56	0.70	0.56	12.97	nr	**13.67**
80mm dia	0.63	0.79	0.63	14.59	nr	**15.37**
100mm dia	0.71	0.89	0.71	16.44	nr	**17.33**
150mm dia	0.80	1.00	0.80	18.52	nr	**19.52**
Equal tee						
65mm dia	0.74	0.92	0.74	17.13	nr	**18.06**
80mm dia	0.83	1.04	0.83	19.22	nr	**20.25**
100mm dia	0.94	1.17	0.94	21.77	nr	**22.94**
150mm dia	1.05	1.31	1.05	24.31	nr	**25.62**

S:PIPED SUPPLY SYSTEMS

Item	Net Price £	Material £	Labour hours	Labour £	Unit	Total rate £
S63 : SPRINKLERS (cont'd)						
Y11 - PIPELINE ANCILLARIES						
SPRINKLER HEADS						
Sprinkler heads; brass body; frangible glass bulb; manufactured to standard operating temperature of 57-141°C; quick response; RTI<50						
Conventional pattern; 15mm dia.	2.95	3.68	0.15	3.47	nr	**7.15**
Sidewall pattern; 15mm dia.	4.34	5.41	0.15	3.47	nr	**8.88**
Conventional pattern; 15mm dia.; satin chrome plated	3.47	4.32	0.15	3.47	nr	**7.80**
Sidewall pattern; 15mm dia.; satin chrome plated	4.50	5.62	0.15	3.47	nr	**9.09**
Fully concealed; fusible link; 15mm dia	10.83	13.51	0.15	3.47	nr	**16.98**
VALVES						
Wet system alarm valves; including internal non-return valve; working pressure up to 12.5 bar; BS4504 PN16 flanged ends; bolted connections						
100mm dia.	937.13	1169.15	25.00	578.88	nr	**1748.03**
150mm dia.	1144.72	1428.15	25.00	578.88	nr	**2007.03**
Wet system by-pass alarm valves; including internal non-return valve; working pressure up to 12.5 bar; BS4504 PN16 flanged ends; bolted connections						
100mm dia.	1651.89	2060.89	25.00	578.88	nr	**2639.77**
150mm dia.	2088.56	2605.67	25.00	578.88	nr	**3184.55**
Alternate system wet/dry alarm station; including butterfly valve, wet alarm valve, dry pipe differential pressure valve and pressure gauges; working pressure up to 10.5 bar; BS4505 PN16 flanged ends; bolted connections						
100mm dia.	2047.27	2554.16	40.00	926.21	nr	**3480.37**
150mm dia.	2385.69	2976.38	40.00	926.21	nr	**3902.59**
Alternate system wet/dry alarm station; including electrically operated butterfly valve, water supply accelerator set, wet alarm valve, dry pipe differential pressure valve and pressure gauges; working pressure up to 10.5 bar; BS4505 PN16 flanged ends; bolted connections						
100mm dia.	2333.64	2911.43	45.00	1041.99	nr	**3953.42**
150mm dia.	2675.44	3337.86	45.00	1041.99	nr	**4379.85**
ALARM/GONGS						
Water operated motor alarm and gong; stainless steel and aluminum body and gong; screwed connections						
Connection to sprinkler system and drain pipework	285.65	356.38	6.00	138.93	nr	**495.31**

S:PIPED SUPPLY SYSTEMS

Item	Net Price £	Material £	Labour hours	Labour £	Unit	Total rate £
Y21 - WATER TANKS						
Note - Prices are based on the most economical tank size for each volume, and the cost will vary with differing tank dimensions, for the same volume						
Steel sectional sprinkler tank; ordinary hazard, life safety classification; two compartment tank, complete with all fittings and accessories to comply with LPCB type A requirements; cost of erection (on prepared supports) is included within net price, labour cost allows for offloading and positioning of materials						
Volume, size						
70m³, 6.1m x 4.88m x 2.44m (h)	21178.70	26462.79	24.00	544.28	nr	**27007.07**
105m³, 7.3m x 6.1m x 2.44m (h)	24852.00	31052.57	28.00	635.00	nr	**31687.57**
168m³, 9.76m x 4.88mx 3.66m (h)	30705.30	38366.27	28.00	635.00	nr	**39001.27**
211m³, 9.76m x 6.1m x 3.66m (h)	33899.00	42356.80	32.00	725.71	nr	**43082.51**
Steel sectional sprinkler tank; ordinary hazard, property protection classification; single compartment tank, complete with all fittings and accessories to comply with LPCB type A requirements; cost of erection (on prepared supports) is included within net price, labour cost allows for offloading and positioning of materials						
Volume, size						
70m³, 6.1m x 4.88m x 2.44m (h)	14933.00	18658.78	24.00	544.28	nr	**19203.07**
105m³, 7.3m x 6.1m x 2.44m (h)	18448.25	23051.09	28.00	635.00	nr	**23686.08**
168m³, 9.76m x 4.88m x 3.66m (h)	23838.30	29785.96	28.00	635.00	nr	**30420.95**
211m³, 9.76m x 6.1m x 3.66m (h)	26748.60	33422.38	32.00	725.71	nr	**34148.08**
GRP sectional sprinkler tank; ordinary hazard, life safety classification; two compartment tank, complete with all fittings and accessories to comply with LPCB type A requirements; cost of erection (on prepared supports) is included within net price, labour cost allows for offloading and positioning of materials						
Volume, size						
55m³, 6m x 4m x 3m (h)	22681.00	28339.91	14.00	317.50	nr	**28657.41**
70m³, 6m x 5m x 3m (h)	25359.00	31686.07	16.00	362.85	nr	**32048.92**
80m³, 8m x 4m x 3m (h)	26281.00	32838.11	16.00	362.85	nr	**33200.96**
105m³, 10m x 4m x 3m (h)	29739.00	37158.88	24.00	544.28	nr	**37703.16**
125m³, 10m x 5m x 3m (h)	33539.00	41906.98	24.00	544.28	nr	**42451.26**
140m³, 8m x 7m x 3m (h)	35984.00	44962.01	24.00	544.28	nr	**45506.29**
135m³, 9m x 6m x 3m (h)	34928.00	43642.54	24.00	544.28	nr	**44186.82**
160m³, 13m x 5m x 3m (h)	39507.00	49364.00	24.00	544.28	nr	**49908.28**
185m³, 12m x 6m x 3m (h)	41791.00	52217.85	24.00	544.28	nr	**52762.14**

S:PIPED SUPPLY SYSTEMS

Item	Net Price £	Material £	Labour hours	Labour £	Unit	Total rate £
S63 : SPRINKLERS (cont'd)						
Y21 - WATER TANKS (cont'd)						
GRP sectional sprinkler tank; ordinary hazard, property protection classification; single compartment tank, complete with all fittings and accessories to comply with LPCB type A requirements; cost of erection (on prepared supports) is within net price, labour cost allows for offloading and positioning of materials						
Volume, size						
55m³, 6m x 4m x 3m (h)	17449.00	21802.53	14.00	317.50	nr	**22120.02**
70m³, 6m x 5m x 3m (h)	19713.00	24631.39	16.00	362.85	nr	**24994.25**
80m³, 8m x 4m x 3m (h)	21041.00	26290.73	16.00	362.85	nr	**26653.58**
105m³, 10m x 4m x 3m (h)	24650.00	30800.18	24.00	544.28	nr	**31344.46**
125m³, 10m x 5m x 3m (h)	27874.00	34828.56	24.00	544.28	nr	**35372.84**
140m³, 8m x 7m x 3m (h)	29505.00	36866.50	24.00	544.28	nr	**37410.78**
135m³, 9m x 6m x 3m (h)	28856.00	36055.57	24.00	544.28	nr	**36599.85**
160m³, 13m x 5m x 3m (h)	33989.00	42469.26	24.00	544.28	nr	**43013.54**
185m³, 12m x 6m x 3m (h)	35706.00	44614.65	24.00	544.28	nr	**45158.93**

S:PIPED SUPPLY SYSTEMS

Item	Net Price £	Material £	Labour hours	Labour £	Unit	Total rate £
S65 : FIRE HYDRANTS						
EXTINGUISHERS						
Fire extinguishers; hand held; BS 5423; placed in position						
Water type; cartridge operated; for Class A fires						
Water type, 9 litres capacity; 55gm CO2 cartridge; Class A fires (fire rating 13A)	65.85	82.15	1.00	23.16	nr	**105.31**
Foam type, 9 litres capacity; 75gm CO2 cartridge; Class A & B fires (fire rating 13A:183B)	78.10	97.44	1.00	23.16	nr	**120.59**
Dry powder type; cartridge operated; for Class A, B & C fires and electrical equipment fires						
Dry powder type, 1kg capacity; 12gm CO2 cartridge; Class A, B & C fires (fire rating 5A:34B)	27.85	34.75	1.00	23.16	nr	**57.90**
Dry powder type, 2kg capacity; 28gm CO2 cartridge; Class A, B & C fires (fire rating 13A:55B)	37.50	46.78	1.00	23.16	nr	**69.94**
Dry powder type, 4kg capacity; 90gm CO2 cartridge; Class A, B & C fires (fire rating 21A:183B)	66.80	83.34	1.00	23.16	nr	**106.49**
Dry powder type, 9kg capacity; 190gm CO2 cartridge; Class A, B & C fires (fire rating 43A:233B)	89.50	111.66	1.00	23.16	nr	**134.81**
Dry powder type; stored pressure type; for Class A, B & C fires and electrical equipment fires						
Dry powder type, 1kg capacity; Class A, B & C fires (fire rating 5A:34B)	25.65	32.00	1.00	23.16	nr	**55.16**
Dry powder type, 2kg capacity; Class A, B & C fires (fire rating 13A:55B)	30.45	37.99	1.00	23.16	nr	**61.14**
Dry powder type, 4kg capacity; Class A, B & C fires (fire rating 21A:183B)	56.88	70.96	1.00	23.16	nr	**94.12**
Dry powder type, 9kg capacity; Class A, B & C fires (fire rating 43A:233B)	73.70	91.95	1.00	23.16	nr	**115.10**
Carbon dioxide type; for Class B fires and electrical equipment fires						
CO2 type with hose and horn, 2kg capacity, Class B fires (fire rating 34B)	70.45	87.89	1.00	23.16	nr	**111.05**
CO2 type with hose and horn, 5kg capacity, Class B fires (fire rating 55B)	110.40	137.73	1.00	23.16	nr	**160.89**
Glass fibre blanket, in GRP container						
1100 x 1100mm	22.35	27.88	0.50	11.58	nr	**39.46**
1200 x 1200mm	24.50	30.57	0.50	11.58	nr	**42.14**
1800 x 1200mm	32.68	40.77	0.50	11.58	nr	**52.35**

S:PIPED SUPPLY SYSTEMS

Item	Net Price £	Material £	Labour hours	Labour £	Unit	Total rate £
S65 : FIRE HYDRANTS (cont'd)						
HYDRANTS						
Fire hydrants; bolted connections						
Underground hydrants, complete with frost plug to BS 750						
sluice valve pattern type 1	183.88	229.41	4.50	104.20	nr	**333.61**
screw down pattern type 2	133.56	166.63	4.50	104.20	nr	**270.83**
Stand pipe for underground hydrant; screwed base; light alloy						
Single outlet	105.75	131.93	1.00	23.16	nr	**155.09**
Double outlet	154.74	193.05	1.00	23.16	nr	**216.21**
64mm diameter bronze/gunmetal outlet valves						
Oblique flanged landing valve	115.75	144.41	1.00	23.16	nr	**167.56**
Oblique screwed landing valve	115.75	144.41	1.00	23.16	nr	**167.56**
Cast iron surface box; fixing by others						
400 x 200 x 100mm	101.35	126.44	1.00	23.16	nr	**149.60**
500 x 200 x 150mm	136.56	170.37	1.00	23.16	nr	**193.53**
Frost Plug	24.60	30.69	0.25	5.79	nr	**36.48**

The Construction Sector in the Asian Economies

Michael Anson, Y. H. Chiang and John Raftery

A collection of essential data on 11 Asian economies, outlining new trends and highlighting increasing differences between developed and developing countries. Features a detailed analysis of the state of the construction industry and its economic effects in Australia, China Mainland, China Hong Kong, India, Indonesia, Japan, South Korea, Philippines, Singapore, Sri Lanka and Vietnam.

Foreword 1. Regional Overview 2. Australia 3. China Mainland 4. China Hong Kong 5. India 6. Indonesia 7. Japan 8. Singapore 9. South Korea 10. Sri Lanka 11. Vietnam.

November 2004: 246x174 mm: 512 pages
HB: 0-415-28613-1: £85.00

To Order: Tel: +44 (0) 1264 343071 Fax: +44 (0) 1264 343005, or
Post: Taylor and Francis Customer Services, Thomson Publishing Services, Cheriton House, Andover, Hants, SP10 5BE, UK Email: book.orders@tandf.co.uk

For a complete listing of all our titles visit:
www.sponpress.com

Taylor & Francis
Taylor & Francis Group plc

4th Edition
Design of Electrical Services for Buildings

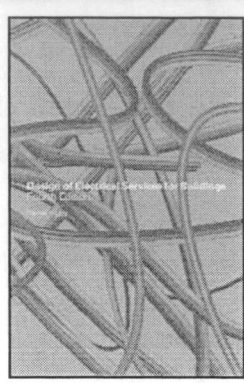

B Rigby

Electrical services are a vital component in any building, so it is necessary for construction professionals to understand the basic principle of services design. *The Design of Electrical Services for Buildings* aims to provide a basic grounding for students and graduates in the field. It covers methods of wiring, schemes of distribution and protection for lighting and power installations. Systems such as alarms and standby supplies are also covered. Each method is described in detail and examples of calculations are given.

For this fourth edition, the coverage of wiring and electrical regulations have been brought fully up-to-date, and the practical information has been revised.

December 2004: 234x156mm: 352 pages
120 line figures, 55 b+w photos, 25 tables
HB: 0-415-31082-2: £60.00
PB: 0-415-31083-0: £29.99

To Order: Tel: +44 (0) 1264 343071 Fax: +44 (0) 1264 343005, or
Post: Taylor and Francis Customer Services, Thomson Publishing Services, Cheriton House, Andover, Hants, SP10 5BE, UK Email: book.orders@tandf.co.uk

For a complete listing of all our titles visit :
www.sponpress.com

Taylor & Francis
Taylor & Francis Group plc

T:MECHANICAL/COOLING/HEATING SYSTEMS

Item	Net Price £	Material £	Labour hours	Labour £	Unit	Total rate £
T10 : GAS/OIL FIRED BOILERS						
DOMESTIC						
Domestic water boilers; stove enamelled casing; electric controls; placing in position; assembling and connecting; electrical work elsewhere						
Gas fired; floor standing; connected to conventional flue						
9 to 12 kW	419.17	536.87	8.59	194.81	nr	**731.68**
12 to 15 kW	440.97	564.80	8.59	194.81	nr	**759.60**
15 to 18 kW	469.69	601.57	8.88	201.38	nr	**802.96**
18 to 21 kW	469.69	601.57	9.92	224.97	nr	**826.54**
21 to 23 kW	604.93	774.79	10.66	241.75	nr	**1016.54**
23 to 29 kW	784.59	1004.89	11.81	267.83	nr	**1272.72**
29 to 37 kW	927.98	1188.54	11.81	267.83	nr	**1456.38**
37 to 41 kW	965.05	1236.03	12.68	287.56	nr	**1523.59**
Gas fired; wall hung; connected to conventional flue						
9 to 12 kW	368.42	471.86	8.59	194.81	nr	**666.67**
12 to 15 kW	475.64	609.20	8.59	194.81	nr	**804.01**
13 to 18 kW	603.64	773.14	8.59	194.81	nr	**967.95**
Gas fired; floor standing; connected to balanced flue						
9 to 12 kW	523.63	670.66	9.16	207.73	nr	**878.39**
12 to 15 kW	544.81	697.79	10.95	248.33	nr	**946.11**
15 to 18 kW	586.44	751.11	11.98	271.69	nr	**1022.79**
18 to 21 kW	691.06	885.10	12.78	289.83	nr	**1174.93**
21 to 23 kW	797.05	1020.86	12.78	289.83	nr	**1310.69**
23 to 29 kW	1015.93	1301.19	15.45	350.38	nr	**1651.57**
29 to 37 kW	1953.03	2501.42	17.65	400.27	nr	**2901.69**
Gas fired; wall hung; connected to balanced flue						
6 to 9 kW	395.35	506.36	9.16	207.73	nr	**714.09**
9 to 12 kW	452.42	579.46	9.16	207.73	nr	**787.19**
12 to 15kW	512.30	656.15	9.45	214.31	nr	**870.46**
15 to 18kW	614.27	786.75	9.74	220.89	nr	**1007.63**
18 to 22kW	652.03	835.11	9.74	220.89	nr	**1056.00**
Gas fired; wall hung; connected to fan flue (including flue kit)						
6 to 9kW	452.18	579.14	9.16	207.73	nr	**786.88**
9 to 12kW	503.91	645.40	9.16	207.73	nr	**853.13**
12 to 15kW	547.01	700.60	10.95	248.33	nr	**948.93**
15 to 18kW	589.22	754.66	11.98	271.69	nr	**1026.35**
18 to 23kW	767.72	983.29	12.78	289.83	nr	**1273.12**
23 to 29kW	994.18	1273.33	15.45	350.38	nr	**1623.71**
29 to 35kW	1220.57	1563.29	17.65	400.27	nr	**1963.57**
Oil fired; floor standing; connected to conventional flue						
12 to 15	820.43	1050.80	10.38	235.40	nr	**1286.20**
15 to 19	855.84	1096.15	12.20	276.68	nr	**1372.83**
21 to 25	976.75	1251.01	14.30	324.30	nr	**1575.31**
26 to 32	1070.88	1371.57	15.80	358.32	nr	**1729.89**
35 to 50	1209.06	1548.55	20.46	464.00	nr	**2012.55**

T:MECHANICAL/COOLING/HEATING SYSTEMS

Item	Net Price £	Material £	Labour hours	Labour £	Unit	Total rate £
T10 : GAS/OIL FIRED BOILERS (cont'd)						
DOMESTIC (cont'd)						
Domestic water boilers; stove enamelled (cont'd)						
Fire place mounted natural gas fire and back boiler; cast iron water boiler; electric control box; fire output 3kW with wood surround						
10.50kW	229.03	293.34	8.88	201.38	nr	494.73
FORCED DRAFT						
Commercial cast iron sectional floor standing boilers; pressure jet burner; including controls, enamelled jacket, insulation, assembly and commissioning; electrical work elsewhere						
Gas fired (on/off type), connected to conventional flue						
16-26 kW; 3 sections; 125mm dia. flue	1582.90	2027.37	8.00	181.43	nr	2208.79
26-33 kW; 4 sections; 125mm dia. flue	1687.66	2161.53	8.00	181.43	nr	2342.96
33-40 kW; 5 sections; 125mm dia. flue	1908.80	2444.77	8.00	181.43	nr	2626.19
35-50 kW; 3 sections; 153mm dia. flue	2095.02	2683.28	8.00	181.43	nr	2864.71
50-65 kW; 4 sections; 153mm dia. flue	2257.97	2891.98	8.00	181.43	nr	3073.41
65-80 kW; 5 sections; 153mm dia. flue	2455.83	3145.40	8.00	181.43	nr	3326.83
80-100 kW; 6 sections; 180mm dia. flue	2853.88	3655.22	8.00	181.43	nr	3836.65
100-120 kW; 7 sections; 180mm dia. flue	3608.09	4621.21	8.00	181.43	nr	4802.63
105-140 kW; 5 sections; 180mm dia. flue	4190.04	5366.56	8.00	181.43	nr	5547.99
140-180 kW; 6 sections; 180mm dia. flue	4771.99	6111.92	8.00	181.43	nr	6293.34
180-230 kW; 7 sections; 200mm dia. flue	5353.94	6857.27	8.00	181.43	nr	7038.70
230-280 kW; 8 sections; 200mm dia. flue	5703.11	7304.49	8.00	181.43	nr	7485.91
280-330 kW; 9 sections; 200mm dia. flue	6401.45	8198.91	8.00	181.43	nr	8380.34
Gas fired (high/low type), connected to conventional flue						
105-140 kW; 5 sections; 180mm dia. flue	5004.77	6410.06	8.00	181.43	nr	6591.49
140-180 kW; 6 sections; 180mm dia. flue	5377.22	6887.09	8.00	181.43	nr	7068.51
180-230 kW; 7 sections; 200mm dia. flue	6098.84	7811.33	8.00	181.43	nr	7992.76
230-280 kW; 8 sections; 200mm dia. flue	6517.84	8347.98	8.00	181.43	nr	8529.41
280-330 kW; 9 sections; 200mm dia. flue	6983.40	8944.27	8.00	181.43	nr	9125.70
300-390 kW; 8 sections; 250mm dia. flue	8380.08	10733.12	12.00	272.14	nr	11005.26
390-450 kW; 9 sections; 250mm dia. flue	9229.73	11821.34	12.00	272.14	nr	12093.48
450-540 kW; 10 sections; 250mm dia. flue	10125.93	12969.19	12.00	272.14	nr	13241.33
540-600 kW; 11 sections; 300mm dia. flue	10358.71	13267.33	12.00	272.14	nr	13539.47
600-670 kW; 12 sections; 300mm dia. flue	12889.94	16509.30	12.00	272.14	nr	16781.44
670-720 kW; 13 sections; 300mm dia. flue	13122.72	16807.44	12.00	272.14	nr	17079.58
720-780 kW; 14 sections; 300mm dia. flue	13297.30	17031.05	12.00	272.14	nr	17303.19
754-812 kW; 14 sections; 400mm dia. flue	13413.69	17180.12	12.00	272.14	nr	17452.26
812-870 kW; 15 sections; 400mm dia. flue	16905.39	21652.25	12.00	272.14	nr	21924.40
870-928 kW; 16 sections; 400mm dia. flue	18302.07	23441.11	12.00	272.14	nr	23713.25
928-986 kW; 17 sections; 400mm dia. flue	18767.63	24037.39	12.00	272.14	nr	24309.53
986-1044 kW; 18 sections; 400mm dia. flue	19582.36	25080.89	12.00	272.14	nr	25353.03

T:MECHANICAL/COOLING/HEATING SYSTEMS

Item	Net Price £	Material £	Labour hours	Labour £	Unit	Total rate £
1044-1102 kW; 19 sections; 400mm dia. flue	20047.92	25677.18	12.00	272.14	nr	**25949.32**
1102-1160 kW; 20 sections; 400mm dia. flue	20560.04	26333.09	12.00	272.14	nr	**26605.23**
1160-1218 kW; 21 sections; exceeding 400mm dia. flue	21677.38	27764.17	12.00	272.14	nr	**28036.31**
1218-1276 kW; 22 sections; exceeding 400mm dia. flue	22804.72	29208.05	12.00	272.14	nr	**29480.19**
1276-1334 kW; 23 sections; exceeding 400mm dia. flue	23607.81	30236.64	12.00	272.14	nr	**30508.78**
1334-1392 kW; 24 sections; exceeding 400mm dia. flue	24655.32	31578.28	12.00	272.14	nr	**31850.42**
1392-1450 kW; 25 sections; exceeding 400mm dia. flue	25353.66	32472.71	12.00	272.14	nr	**32744.85**
Oil fired (on/off type), connected to conventional flue						
16-26 kW; 3 sections; 125mm dia. flue	1163.90	1490.71	8.00	181.43	nr	**1672.14**
26-33 kW; 4 sections; 125mm dia. flue	1280.29	1639.78	8.00	181.43	nr	**1821.21**
33-40 kW; 5 sections; 125mm dia. flue	1396.68	1788.85	8.00	181.43	nr	**1970.28**
35-50 kW; 3 sections; 153mm dia. flue	1641.10	2101.90	8.00	181.43	nr	**2283.33**
50-65 kW; 4 sections; 153mm dia. flue	1722.57	2206.25	8.00	181.43	nr	**2387.68**
65-80 kW; 5 sections; 153mm dia. flue	1792.41	2295.70	8.00	181.43	nr	**2477.12**
80-100 kW; 6 sections; 180mm dia. flue	2676.97	3428.64	8.00	181.43	nr	**3610.06**
100-120 kW; 7 sections; 180mm dia. flue	3026.14	3875.85	8.00	181.43	nr	**4057.28**
105-140 kW; 5 sections; 180mm dia. flue	3491.70	4472.13	8.00	181.43	nr	**4653.56**
140-180 kW; 6 sections; 180mm dia. flue	3957.26	5068.42	8.00	181.43	nr	**5249.85**
180-230 kW; 7 sections; 200mm dia. flue	4888.38	6260.99	8.00	181.43	nr	**6442.42**
230-280 kW; 8 sections; 200mm dia. flue	5353.94	6857.27	8.00	181.43	nr	**7038.70**
280-330 kW; 9 sections; 200mm dia. flue	5935.89	7602.63	8.00	181.43	nr	**7784.06**
Oil fired (high/low type), connected to conventional flue						
105-140 kW; 5 sections; 180mm dia. flue	2805.00	3592.61	8.00	181.43	nr	**3774.04**
140-180 kW; 6 sections; 180mm dia. flue	3026.14	3875.85	8.00	181.43	nr	**4057.28**
180-230 kW; 7 sections; 200mm dia. flue	3375.31	4323.06	8.00	181.43	nr	**4504.49**
230-280 kW; 8 sections; 200mm dia. flue	3980.54	5098.23	8.00	181.43	nr	**5279.66**
280-330 kW; 9 sections; 200mm dia. flue	6285.06	8049.84	8.00	181.43	nr	**8231.27**
300-390 kW; 8 sections; 250mm dia. flue	6983.40	8944.27	12.00	272.14	nr	**9216.41**
390-450 kW; 9 sections; 250mm dia. flue	7507.16	9615.09	12.00	272.14	nr	**9887.23**
450-540 kW; 10 sections; 250mm dia. flue	8496.47	10882.19	12.00	272.14	nr	**11154.33**
540-600 kW; 11 sections; 300mm dia. flue	8927.11	11433.76	12.00	272.14	nr	**11705.90**
600-670 kW; 12 sections; 300mm dia. flue	9543.98	12223.83	12.00	272.14	nr	**12495.97**
670-720 kW; 13 sections; 300mm dia. flue	10824.27	13863.62	12.00	272.14	nr	**14135.76**
720-780 kW; 14 sections; 300mm dia. flue	10998.85	14087.22	12.00	272.14	nr	**14359.36**
754-812 kW; 14 sections; 400mm dia. flue	11150.16	14281.02	12.00	272.14	nr	**14553.16**
812-870 kW; 15 sections; 400mm dia. flue	14897.92	19081.11	12.00	272.14	nr	**19353.25**
870-928 kW; 16 sections; 400mm dia. flue	15468.23	19811.56	12.00	272.14	nr	**20083.70**
928-986 kW; 17 sections; 400mm dia. flue	16003.63	20497.28	12.00	272.14	nr	**20769.42**
986-1044 kW; 18 sections; 400mm dia. flue	16643.77	21317.17	12.00	272.14	nr	**21589.32**
1044-1102 kW; 19 sections; 400mm dia. flue	17458.50	22360.67	12.00	272.14	nr	**22632.81**
1102-1160 kW; 20 sections; 400 mm dia. flue	18436.18	23612.87	12.00	272.14	nr	**23885.01**
1160-1218 kW; 21 sections; exceeding 400mm dia. flue	19460.41	24924.70	12.00	272.14	nr	**25196.84**
1218-1276 kW; 22 sections; exceeding 400mm dia. flue	20426.44	26161.99	12.00	272.14	nr	**26434.13**
1276-1334 kW; 23 sections; exceeding 400mm dia. flue	21148.06	27086.23	12.00	272.14	nr	**27358.37**
1334-1392 kW; 24 sections; exceeding 400mm dia. flue	22387.62	28673.84	12.00	272.14	nr	**28945.98**
1392-1450 kW; 25 sections; exceeding 400mm dia. flue	23208.17	29724.79	12.00	272.14	nr	**29996.93**

T:MECHANICAL/COOLING/HEATING SYSTEMS

Item	Net Price £	Material £	Labour hours	Labour £	Unit	Total rate £
T10 : GAS/OIL FIRED BOILERS (cont'd)						
FORCED DRAFT (cont'd)						
Commercial steel shell floor standing boilers; pressure jet burner; including controls, enamelled jacket, insulation, placing in position and commissioning; electrical work elsewhere						
Gas fired (on/off type), connected to conventional flue						
130-190kW	4173.09	5344.85	8.00	181.43	nr	5526.28
200-250kW	4726.79	6054.03	8.00	181.43	nr	6235.45
280-360kW	5661.30	7250.94	8.00	181.43	nr	7432.36
375-500kW	6899.78	8837.17	8.00	181.43	nr	9018.60
Gas fired (high/low type), connected to conventional flue						
130-190kW	5082.74	6509.92	8.00	181.43	nr	6691.35
200-250kW	5428.52	6952.79	8.00	181.43	nr	7134.22
280-360kW	6488.46	8310.35	8.00	181.43	nr	8491.78
375-500kW	7238.78	9271.36	8.00	181.43	nr	9452.78
580-730kW	9137.18	11702.81	10.00	226.78	nr	11929.59
655-820kW	9323.63	11941.61	10.00	226.78	nr	12168.40
830-1040kW	9356.40	11983.58	12.00	272.14	nr	12255.72
1070-1400kW	12374.63	15849.30	12.00	272.14	nr	16121.44
1420-1850kW	15409.81	19736.73	12.00	272.14	nr	20008.87
1850-2350kW	17502.57	22417.12	14.00	317.50	nr	22734.61
2300-3000kW	20651.88	26450.72	14.00	317.50	nr	26768.22
2800-3500kW	26783.26	34303.73	14.00	317.50	nr	34621.23
Oil fired (on/off type), connected to conventional flue						
130-190kW	3820.53	4893.30	8.00	181.43	nr	5074.72
200-250kW	4171.96	5343.40	8.00	181.43	nr	5524.83
Oil fired (high/low type), connected to conventional flue						
130-190kW	4158.40	5326.04	8.00	181.43	nr	5507.46
200-250kW	4509.83	5776.15	8.00	181.43	nr	5957.57
280-360kW	5199.13	6658.99	8.00	181.43	nr	6840.42
375-500kW	6216.13	7961.56	8.00	181.43	nr	8142.98
580-730kW	6914.47	8855.98	10.00	226.78	nr	9082.77
655-820kW	7099.79	9093.34	10.00	226.78	nr	9320.12
830-1040kW	8213.97	10520.37	12.00	272.14	nr	10792.51
1070-1400kW	10036.66	12854.85	12.00	272.14	nr	13126.99
1420-1850kW	12153.15	15565.63	12.00	272.14	nr	15837.77
1850-2350kW	15563.49	19933.56	14.00	317.50	nr	20251.06
2300-3000kW	18179.44	23284.05	14.00	317.50	nr	23601.54
2800-3500kW	24310.82	31137.06	14.00	317.50	nr	31454.55

T:MECHANICAL/COOLING/HEATING SYSTEMS

Item	Net Price £	Material £	Labour hours	Labour £	Unit	Total rate £
ATMOSPHERIC						
Commercial cast iron sectional floor standing boilers; atmospheric; including controls, enamelled jacket, insulation, assembly and commissioning; electrical work elsewhere						
Gas (on/off type), connected to conventional flue						
30-40kW	1486.29	1903.63	8.00	181.43	nr	**2085.05**
40-50kW	1629.48	2087.02	8.00	181.43	nr	**2268.45**
50-60kW	1731.60	2217.82	8.00	181.43	nr	**2399.24**
60-70kW	1890.33	2421.12	8.00	181.43	nr	**2602.54**
70-80kW	2003.55	2566.13	8.00	181.43	nr	**2747.55**
80-90kW	2340.99	2998.32	8.00	181.43	nr	**3179.74**
90-100kW	2435.34	3119.16	8.00	181.43	nr	**3300.59**
100-110kW	2580.75	3305.40	8.00	181.43	nr	**3486.83**
110-120kW	2729.49	3495.90	8.00	181.43	nr	**3677.33**
Gas (high/low type), connected to conventional flue						
30-40kW	1687.20	2160.95	8.00	181.43	nr	**2342.38**
40-50kW	1789.32	2291.74	8.00	181.43	nr	**2473.17**
50-60kW	1923.63	2463.77	8.00	181.43	nr	**2645.19**
60-70kW	2097.90	2686.97	8.00	181.43	nr	**2868.40**
70-80kW	2221.11	2844.78	8.00	181.43	nr	**3026.20**
80-90kW	2468.64	3161.81	8.00	181.43	nr	**3343.24**
90-100kW	2602.95	3333.83	8.00	181.43	nr	**3515.26**
100-110kW	2756.13	3530.02	8.00	181.43	nr	**3711.45**
110-120kW	2928.18	3750.38	8.00	181.43	nr	**3931.81**
120-140kW	4392.27	5625.58	8.00	181.43	nr	**5807.00**
140-160kW	4503.27	5767.74	8.00	181.43	nr	**5949.17**
160-180kW	4579.86	5865.84	8.00	181.43	nr	**6047.27**
180-200kW	5008.32	6414.61	8.00	181.43	nr	**6596.03**
200-220kW	5224.77	6691.83	10.00	226.78	nr	**6918.62**
220-260kW	5677.65	7271.88	10.00	226.78	nr	**7498.66**
260-300kW	6191.58	7930.11	10.00	226.78	nr	**8156.90**
300-340kW	6603.39	8457.56	12.00	272.14	nr	**8729.70**
CONDENSING						
Commercial condensing cast aluminium boilers; including controls, enamelled jacket; placing in position; electrical work elsewhere						
Wall hung, fully modulating, connected to conventional flue						
13-45kW	1538.46	1970.44	11.00	249.46	nr	**2219.91**
45-60kW	1892.55	2423.96	11.00	249.46	nr	**2673.42**
60-80kW	2147.85	2750.94	11.00	249.46	nr	**3000.41**
Floor standing, fully modulating, connected to conventional flue						
40-50kW	2019.30	2586.30	8.00	181.43	nr	**2767.73**
50-70kW	2575.80	3299.06	8.00	181.43	nr	**3480.49**
70-94kW	3291.30	4215.46	8.00	181.43	nr	**4396.89**
94-116kW	3858.40	4941.80	8.00	181.43	nr	**5123.23**

T:MECHANICAL/COOLING/HEATING SYSTEMS

Item	Net Price £	Material £	Labour hours	Labour £	Unit	Total rate £
T10 : GAS/OIL FIRED BOILERS (cont'd)						
FLUE SYSTEMS						
Flues; suitable for domestic, medium sized industrial and commercial oil and gas appliances; stainless steel, twin wall, insulated; for use internally or externally						
Straight length; 120mm long; including one locking band						
127mm dia.	32.70	41.88	0.49	11.11	nr	**53.00**
152mm dia.	36.65	46.94	0.51	11.57	nr	**58.50**
175mm dia.	42.54	54.49	0.54	12.25	nr	**66.74**
203mm dia.	48.41	62.00	0.58	13.15	nr	**75.16**
254mm dia.	57.25	73.32	0.70	15.87	nr	**89.19**
304mm dia.	71.71	91.85	0.74	16.78	nr	**108.63**
355mm dia.	102.69	131.53	0.80	18.14	nr	**149.67**
Straight length; 300mm long; including one locking band						
127mm dia.	50.45	64.62	0.52	11.79	nr	**76.41**
152mm dia.	57.04	73.06	0.52	11.79	nr	**84.85**
178mm dia.	65.54	83.94	0.55	12.47	nr	**96.42**
203mm dia.	74.17	95.00	0.64	14.51	nr	**109.51**
254mm dia.	82.25	105.35	0.79	17.92	nr	**123.26**
304mm dia.	98.68	126.39	0.86	19.50	nr	**145.90**
355mm dia.	108.28	138.68	0.94	21.32	nr	**160.00**
400mm dia.	115.87	148.41	1.03	23.36	nr	**171.76**
450mm dia.	132.54	169.75	1.03	23.36	nr	**193.11**
500mm dia.	142.15	182.07	1.10	24.95	nr	**207.02**
550mm dia.	156.88	200.93	1.10	24.95	nr	**225.87**
600mm dia.	173.10	221.71	1.10	24.95	nr	**246.66**
Straight length; 500mm long; including one locking band						
127mm dia.	59.30	75.95	0.55	12.47	nr	**88.43**
152mm dia.	66.11	84.67	0.55	12.47	nr	**97.14**
178mm dia.	74.46	95.36	0.63	14.29	nr	**109.65**
203mm dia.	87.03	111.47	0.63	14.29	nr	**125.76**
254mm dia.	101.08	129.46	0.86	19.50	nr	**148.96**
304mm dia.	121.10	155.11	0.95	21.54	nr	**176.65**
355mm dia.	136.00	174.18	1.03	23.36	nr	**197.54**
400mm dia.	148.50	190.20	1.12	25.40	nr	**215.60**
450mm dia.	171.50	219.66	1.12	25.40	nr	**245.06**
500mm dia.	184.79	236.68	1.19	26.99	nr	**263.66**
550mm dia.	203.69	260.89	1.19	26.99	nr	**287.88**
600mm dia.	211.00	270.25	1.19	26.99	nr	**297.24**
Straight length; 1000mm long; including one locking band						
127mm dia.	106.01	135.77	0.62	14.06	nr	**149.83**
152mm dia.	118.14	151.31	0.68	15.42	nr	**166.74**
178mm dia.	132.93	170.26	0.74	16.78	nr	**187.04**
203mm dia.	156.57	200.54	0.80	18.14	nr	**218.68**
254mm dia.	177.44	227.27	0.87	19.73	nr	**247.00**
304mm dia.	204.82	262.34	1.06	24.04	nr	**286.38**
355mm dia.	235.04	301.04	1.16	26.31	nr	**327.34**

T:MECHANICAL/COOLING/HEATING SYSTEMS

Item	Net Price £	Material £	Labour hours	Labour £	Unit	Total rate £
400mm dia.	251.71	322.38	1.26	28.57	nr	**350.96**
450mm dia.	265.60	340.17	1.26	28.57	nr	**368.75**
500mm dia.	288.22	369.15	1.33	30.16	nr	**399.31**
550mm dia.	316.99	405.99	1.33	30.16	nr	**436.16**
600mm dia.	333.01	426.52	1.33	30.16	nr	**456.68**
Adjustable length; boiler removal; internal use only; including one locking band						
127mm dia.	48.59	62.23	0.52	11.79	nr	**74.03**
152mm dia.	54.92	70.34	0.55	12.47	nr	**82.81**
178mm dia.	62.22	79.69	0.59	13.38	nr	**93.07**
203mm dia.	71.36	91.40	0.64	14.51	nr	**105.91**
254mm dia.	105.81	135.52	0.79	17.92	nr	**153.44**
304mm dia.	126.73	162.31	0.86	19.50	nr	**181.82**
355mm dia.	142.12	182.03	0.99	22.45	nr	**204.48**
400mm dia.	248.69	318.52	0.91	20.64	nr	**339.16**
450mm dia.	266.21	340.95	0.91	20.64	nr	**361.59**
500mm dia.	290.34	371.87	0.99	22.45	nr	**394.32**
550mm dia.	316.74	405.68	0.99	22.45	nr	**428.13**
600mm dia.	331.58	424.68	0.99	22.45	nr	**447.13**
Inspection length; 500mm long; including one locking band						
127mm dia.	124.90	159.97	0.55	12.47	nr	**172.44**
152mm dia.	129.33	165.64	0.55	12.47	nr	**178.12**
178mm dia.	136.21	174.46	0.63	14.29	nr	**188.74**
203mm dia.	144.24	184.75	0.63	14.29	nr	**199.03**
254mm dia.	186.50	238.86	0.86	19.50	nr	**258.36**
304mm dia.	202.12	258.88	0.95	21.54	nr	**280.42**
355mm dia.	228.21	292.30	1.03	23.36	nr	**315.65**
400mm dia.	366.15	468.97	1.12	25.40	nr	**494.37**
450mm dia.	376.11	481.72	1.12	25.40	nr	**507.12**
500mm dia.	412.70	528.58	1.19	26.99	nr	**555.57**
550mm dia.	431.56	552.74	1.19	26.99	nr	**579.72**
600mm dia.	438.89	562.13	1.19	26.99	nr	**589.12**
Adapters						
127mm dia.	10.44	13.37	0.49	11.11	nr	**24.49**
152mm dia.	11.42	14.63	0.51	11.57	nr	**26.20**
178mm dia.	12.22	15.65	0.54	12.25	nr	**27.89**
203mm dia.	13.91	17.82	0.58	13.15	nr	**30.97**
254mm dia.	15.31	19.61	0.70	15.87	nr	**35.49**
304mm dia.	19.10	24.46	0.74	16.78	nr	**41.24**
355mm dia.	23.20	29.71	0.80	18.14	nr	**47.86**
400mm dia.	26.01	33.32	0.89	20.18	nr	**53.50**
450mm dia.	27.79	35.59	0.89	20.18	nr	**55.77**
500mm dia.	29.49	37.77	0.96	21.77	nr	**59.55**
550mm dia.	34.30	43.93	0.96	21.77	nr	**65.70**
600mm dia.	41.21	52.78	0.96	21.77	nr	**74.55**

T:MECHANICAL/COOLING/HEATING SYSTEMS

Item	Net Price £	Material £	Labour hours	Labour £	Unit	Total rate £
T10 : GAS/OIL FIRED BOILERS (cont'd)						
Fittings for flue system						
90° insulated tee; including two locking bands						
127mm dia.; including locking plug	121.43	155.53	1.89	42.86	nr	198.39
152mm dia.; including locking plug	140.15	179.51	2.04	46.26	nr	225.77
178mm dia.; including locking plug	153.17	196.18	2.39	54.20	nr	250.38
203mm dia.; including locking plug	179.35	229.71	2.56	58.06	nr	287.77
254mm dia.; including locking plug	181.43	232.38	2.95	66.90	nr	299.28
304mm dia.; including locking plug	225.94	289.39	3.41	77.33	nr	366.72
355mm dia.; including locking plug	288.05	368.93	3.77	85.50	nr	454.43
400mm dia.	379.57	486.15	4.25	96.38	nr	582.53
450mm dia.	395.61	506.70	4.76	107.95	nr	614.65
500mm dia.	447.67	573.37	5.12	116.11	nr	689.49
550mm dia.	481.21	616.33	5.61	127.23	nr	743.56
600mm dia.	500.70	641.30	5.98	135.62	nr	776.91
135° insulated tee; including two locking bands						
127mm dia.; including locking plug	157.49	201.71	1.89	42.86	nr	244.57
152mm dia ; including locking plug	170.28	218.09	2.04	46.26	nr	264.36
178mm dia.; including locking plug	186.18	238.46	2.39	54.20	nr	292.66
203mm dia.; including locking plug	236.28	302.63	2.56	58.06	nr	360.69
254mm dia.; including locking plug	268.48	343.86	2.95	66.90	nr	410.76
304mm dia.; including locking plug	202.28	259.08	3.41	77.33	nr	336.41
355mm dia.; including locking plug	398.03	509.79	3.77	85.50	nr	595.29
400mm dia.	523.96	671.08	4.25	96.38	nr	767.46
450mm dia.	567.20	726.47	4.76	107.95	nr	834.42
500mm dia.	660.80	846.35	5.12	116.11	nr	962.46
550mm dia.	677.98	868.35	5.61	127.23	nr	995.57
600mm dia.	715.53	916.44	5.98	135.62	nr	1052.06
Wall sleeve; for 135° tee through wall						
127mm dia.	16.13	20.65	1.89	42.86	nr	63.52
152mm dia.	21.63	27.70	2.04	46.26	nr	73.97
178mm dia.	22.66	29.02	2.39	54.20	nr	83.22
203mm dia.	25.47	32.62	2.56	58.06	nr	90.68
254mm dia.	28.42	36.40	2.95	66.90	nr	103.30
304mm dia.	33.12	42.42	3.41	77.33	nr	119.75
355mm dia.	36.79	47.12	3.77	85.50	nr	132.62
15° insulated elbow; including two locking bands						
127mm dia.	84.28	107.94	1.57	35.61	nr	143.54
152mm dia.	93.65	119.95	1.79	40.59	nr	160.55
178mm dia.	100.16	128.29	2.05	46.49	nr	174.78
203mm dia.	106.19	136.00	2.33	52.84	nr	188.84
254mm dia.	109.36	140.07	2.45	55.56	nr	195.63
304mm dia.	138.27	177.09	3.43	77.79	nr	254.88
355mm dia.	184.97	236.91	4.71	106.82	nr	343.72
30° insulated elbow; including two locking bands						
127mm dia.	84.28	107.94	1.44	32.66	nr	140.60
152mm dia.	93.65	119.95	1.62	36.74	nr	156.69
178mm dia.	100.16	128.29	1.89	42.86	nr	171.15
203mm dia.	106.19	136.00	2.17	49.21	nr	185.21
254mm dia.	109.36	140.07	2.16	48.99	nr	189.05
304mm dia.	138.27	177.09	2.74	62.14	nr	239.23
355mm dia.	184.62	236.46	3.17	71.89	nr	308.35

T:MECHANICAL/COOLING/HEATING SYSTEMS

Item	Net Price £	Material £	Labour hours	Labour £	Unit	Total rate £
400mm dia.	184.97	236.91	3.53	80.05	nr	**316.96**
450mm dia.	214.37	274.57	3.88	87.99	nr	**362.56**
500mm dia.	224.75	287.85	4.24	96.16	nr	**384.01**
550mm dia.	241.20	308.92	4.61	104.55	nr	**413.47**
600mm dia.	263.01	336.86	4.96	112.48	nr	**449.34**
45° insulated elbow; including two locking bands						
127mm dia.	84.28	107.94	1.44	32.66	nr	**140.60**
152mm dia.	93.65	119.95	1.51	34.24	nr	**154.20**
178mm dia.	100.16	128.29	1.58	35.83	nr	**164.12**
203mm dia.	106.19	136.00	1.66	37.65	nr	**173.65**
254mm dia.	109.36	140.07	1.72	39.01	nr	**179.08**
304mm dia.	138.27	177.09	1.80	40.82	nr	**217.91**
355mm dia.	184.97	236.91	1.94	44.00	nr	**280.90**
400mm dia.	235.88	302.11	2.01	45.58	nr	**347.69**
450mm dia.	247.07	316.45	2.09	47.40	nr	**363.85**
500mm dia.	265.03	339.45	2.16	48.99	nr	**388.43**
550mm dia.	289.05	370.22	2.23	50.57	nr	**420.79**
600mm dia.	296.38	379.60	2.30	52.16	nr	**431.76**
Flue supports						
Wall support, galvanised; including plate and brackets						
127mm dia.	51.29	65.70	2.24	50.80	nr	**116.50**
152mm dia.	56.40	72.23	2.44	55.34	nr	**127.57**
178mm dia.	62.26	79.74	2.52	57.15	nr	**136.89**
203mm dia.	64.82	83.02	2.77	62.82	nr	**145.84**
254mm dia.	77.31	99.02	2.98	67.58	nr	**166.60**
304mm dia.	87.42	111.96	3.46	78.47	nr	**190.43**
355mm dia.	117.01	149.86	4.08	92.53	nr	**242.39**
400mm dia.; including 300mm support length and collar	300.55	384.95	4.80	108.86	nr	**493.80**
450mm dia.; including 300mm support length and collar	320.44	410.42	5.62	127.45	nr	**537.87**
500mm dia.; including 300mm support length and collar	350.08	448.37	6.24	141.51	nr	**589.89**
550mm dia.; including 300mm support length and collar	383.01	490.55	6.97	158.07	nr	**648.62**
600mm dia.; including 300mm support length and collar	404.33	517.86	7.49	169.86	nr	**687.72**
Ceiling/floor support						
127mm dia.	15.87	20.33	1.86	42.18	nr	**62.51**
152mm dia.	17.66	22.61	2.14	48.53	nr	**71.14**
178mm dia.	21.13	27.06	1.93	43.77	nr	**70.83**
203mm dia.	31.82	40.76	2.74	62.14	nr	**102.90**
254mm dia.	36.30	46.49	3.21	72.80	nr	**119.29**
304mm dia.	41.49	53.14	3.68	83.46	nr	**136.60**
355mm dia.	49.44	63.33	4.28	97.06	nr	**160.39**
400mm dia.	250.90	321.35	4.86	110.22	nr	**431.57**
450mm dia.	264.14	338.31	5.46	123.82	nr	**462.14**
500mm dia.	278.84	357.13	6.04	136.98	nr	**494.11**
550mm dia.	305.25	390.96	6.65	150.81	nr	**541.77**
600mm dia.	310.46	397.64	7.24	164.19	nr	**561.83**

T:MECHANICAL/COOLING/HEATING SYSTEMS

Item	Net Price £	Material £	Labour hours	Labour £	Unit	Total rate £
T10 : GAS/OIL FIRED BOILERS (cont'd)						
Flue supports (cont'd)						
Ceiling/floor firestop spacer						
127mm dia.	3.09	3.96	0.66	14.97	nr	18.93
152mm dia.	3.44	4.41	0.69	15.65	nr	20.06
178mm dia.	3.88	4.97	0.70	15.87	nr	20.85
203mm dia.	4.61	5.90	0.87	19.73	nr	25.63
254mm dia.	4.75	6.09	0.91	20.64	nr	26.72
304mm dia.	5.72	7.33	0.95	21.54	nr	28.87
355mm dia.	10.42	13.34	0.99	22.45	nr	35.79
Wall band; internal or external use						
127mm dia.	18.70	23.95	1.03	23.36	nr	47.31
152mm dia.	19.53	25.01	1.07	24.27	nr	49.27
178mm dia.	20.30	25.99	1.11	25.17	nr	51.17
203mm dia.	21.43	27.44	1.18	26.76	nr	54.21
254mm dia.	22.30	28.56	1.30	29.48	nr	58.04
304mm dia.	24.09	30.85	1.45	32.88	nr	63.74
355mm dia.	25.64	32.84	1.65	37.42	nr	70.26
400mm dia.	31.79	40.72	1.85	41.96	nr	82.67
450mm dia.	33.88	43.39	2.39	54.20	nr	97.59
500mm dia.	40.72	52.16	2.25	51.03	nr	103.18
550mm dia.	42.66	54.64	2.45	55.56	nr	110.20
600mm dia.	45.09	57.75	2.66	60.32	nr	118.07
Flashings and terminals						
Insulated top stub; including one locking band						
127mm dia.	46.07	59.00	1.49	33.79	nr	92.79
152mm dia.	52.09	66.71	1.90	43.09	nr	109.80
178mm dia.	56.08	71.82	1.92	43.54	nr	115.37
203mm dia.	59.68	76.43	2.20	49.89	nr	126.32
254mm dia.	63.36	81.15	2.49	56.47	nr	137.62
304mm dia.	86.61	110.93	2.79	63.27	nr	174.21
355mm dia.	114.35	146.45	3.19	72.34	nr	218.80
400mm dia.	110.25	141.21	3.59	81.42	nr	222.63
450mm dia.	119.78	153.41	3.97	90.03	nr	243.44
500mm dia.	138.56	177.46	4.38	99.33	nr	276.79
550mm dia.	144.98	185.69	4.78	108.40	nr	294.09
600mm dia.	150.05	192.18	5.17	117.25	nr	309.43
Rain cap; including one locking band						
127mm dia.	24.62	31.53	1.49	33.79	nr	65.32
152mm dia.	25.73	32.95	1.54	34.92	nr	67.88
178mm dia.	28.34	36.29	1.72	39.01	nr	75.30
203mm dia.	33.89	43.41	2.00	45.36	nr	88.76
254mm dia.	44.56	57.07	2.49	56.47	nr	113.54
304mm dia.	60.07	76.94	2.80	63.50	nr	140.44
355mm dia.	80.49	103.09	3.19	72.34	nr	175.43
400mm dia.	80.29	102.83	3.45	78.24	nr	181.07
450mm dia.	87.32	111.84	3.97	90.03	nr	201.87
500mm dia.	94.42	120.94	4.38	99.33	nr	220.27
550mm dia.	101.32	129.77	4.78	108.40	nr	238.17
600mm dia.	108.32	138.73	5.17	117.25	nr	255.98

T:MECHANICAL/COOLING/HEATING SYSTEMS

Item	Net Price £	Material £	Labour hours	Labour £	Unit	Total rate £
Round top; including one locking band						
127mm dia	47.08	60.30	1.49	33.79	nr	**94.09**
152mm dia	51.34	65.75	1.65	37.42	nr	**103.17**
178mm dia	58.53	74.97	1.92	43.54	nr	**118.51**
203mm dia	68.88	88.22	2.20	49.89	nr	**138.12**
254mm dia	81.43	104.30	2.49	56.47	nr	**160.77**
304mm dia	106.95	136.98	2.80	63.50	nr	**200.48**
355mm dia	142.69	182.76	3.19	72.34	nr	**255.10**
Coping cap; including one locking band						
127mm dia.	26.37	33.77	1.49	33.79	nr	**67.56**
152mm dia.	27.62	35.38	1.65	37.42	nr	**72.80**
178mm dia.	30.39	38.93	1.92	43.54	nr	**82.47**
203mm dia.	36.47	46.70	2.20	49.89	nr	**96.60**
254mm dia.	44.56	57.07	2.49	56.47	nr	**113.54**
304mm dia.	60.07	76.94	2.79	63.27	nr	**140.21**
355mm dia.	80.49	103.09	3.19	72.34	nr	**175.43**
Storm collar						
127mm dia.	5.01	6.41	0.52	11.79	nr	**18.20**
152mm dia.	5.35	6.85	0.55	12.47	nr	**19.32**
178mm dia.	5.93	7.59	0.57	12.93	nr	**20.52**
203mm dia.	6.20	7.95	0.66	14.97	nr	**22.91**
254mm dia.	7.78	9.96	0.66	14.97	nr	**24.93**
304mm dia.	8.11	10.38	0.72	16.33	nr	**26.71**
355mm dia.	8.66	11.09	0.77	17.46	nr	**28.55**
400mm dia.	22.97	29.42	0.82	18.60	nr	**48.01**
450mm dia.	25.28	32.38	0.87	19.73	nr	**52.11**
500mm dia.	27.57	35.31	0.92	20.86	nr	**56.17**
550mm dia.	29.87	38.25	0.98	22.22	nr	**60.48**
600mm dia.	32.16	41.20	1.03	23.36	nr	**64.55**
Flat flashing; including storm collar and sealant						
127mm dia.	28.07	35.95	1.49	33.79	nr	**69.75**
152mm dia.	29.01	37.15	1.65	37.42	nr	**74.57**
178mm dia.	30.44	38.98	1.92	43.54	nr	**82.53**
203mm dia.	33.33	42.69	2.20	49.89	nr	**92.58**
254mm dia.	45.55	58.34	2.49	56.47	nr	**114.81**
304mm dia.	54.43	69.71	2.80	63.50	nr	**133.21**
355mm dia.	85.77	109.85	3.20	72.57	nr	**182.42**
400mm dia.	119.65	153.24	3.59	81.42	nr	**234.66**
450mm dia.	137.45	176.04	3.97	90.03	nr	**266.07**
500mm dia.	148.91	190.72	4.38	99.33	nr	**290.05**
550mm dia.	158.10	202.50	4.78	108.40	nr	**310.90**
600mm dia.	163.81	209.81	5.17	117.25	nr	**327.06**
5°-30° rigid adjustable flashing; including storm collar and sealant						
127mm dia.	47.82	61.24	1.49	33.79	nr	**95.03**
152mm dia.	50.38	64.53	1.65	37.42	nr	**101.95**
178mm dia.	53.58	68.63	1.92	43.54	nr	**112.17**
203mm dia.	56.33	72.15	2.20	49.89	nr	**122.04**
254mm dia.	59.30	75.95	2.49	56.47	nr	**132.42**
304mm dia.	73.39	94.00	2.80	63.50	nr	**157.50**
355mm dia.	83.47	106.91	3.19	72.34	nr	**179.25**
400mm dia.	269.09	344.65	3.59	81.42	nr	**426.07**
450mm dia.	314.04	402.22	3.97	90.03	nr	**492.25**
500mm dia.	335.26	429.40	4.38	99.33	nr	**528.73**
550mm dia.	350.82	449.33	4.77	108.18	nr	**557.51**
600mm dia.	381.70	488.88	5.17	117.25	nr	**606.12**

T:MECHANICAL/COOLING/HEATING SYSTEMS

Item	Net Price £	Material £	Labour hours	Labour £	Unit	Total rate £
T10 : GAS/OIL FIRED BOILERS (cont'd)						
Domestic and small commercial; twin walled gas vent system suitable for gas fired appliances; domestic gas boilers; small commercial boilers with internal or external flues						
152mm long						
100mm dia.	5.11	6.54	0.52	11.79	nr	**18.33**
125mm dia.	6.28	8.05	0.52	11.79	nr	**19.84**
150mm dia.	6.80	8.71	0.52	11.79	nr	**20.51**
305mm long						
100mm dia.	7.75	9.93	0.52	11.79	nr	**21.72**
125mm dia.	9.10	11.65	0.52	11.79	nr	**23.44**
150mm dia.	10.78	13.81	0.52	11.79	nr	**25.60**
457mm long						
100mm dia.	8.58	10.99	0.55	12.47	nr	**23.46**
125mm dia.	9.64	12.35	0.55	12.47	nr	**24.82**
150mm dia.	11.93	15.28	0.55	12.47	nr	**27.76**
914mm long						
100mm dia.	15.32	19.63	0.62	14.06	nr	**33.69**
125mm dia.	17.85	22.87	0.62	14.06	nr	**36.93**
150mm dia.	20.48	26.22	0.62	14.06	nr	**40.29**
1524mm long						
100mm dia.	22.14	28.35	0.82	18.60	nr	**46.95**
125mm dia.	27.23	34.88	0.84	19.05	nr	**53.93**
150mm dia.	29.24	37.46	0.84	19.05	nr	**56.51**
Adjustable length 305mm long						
100mm dia.	9.81	12.56	0.56	12.70	nr	**25.26**
125mm dia.	11.02	14.11	0.56	12.70	nr	**26.81**
150mm dia.	13.89	17.79	0.56	12.70	nr	**30.49**
Adjustable length 457mm long						
100mm dia.	13.22	16.93	0.56	12.70	nr	**29.63**
125mm dia.	16.03	20.54	0.56	12.70	nr	**33.24**
150mm dia.	17.84	22.85	0.56	12.70	nr	**35.55**
Adjustable elbow 0°-90°						
100mm dia.	11.19	14.33	0.48	10.89	nr	**25.21**
125mm dia.	13.22	16.93	0.48	10.89	nr	**27.82**
150mm dia.	16.57	21.22	0.48	10.89	nr	**32.10**
Draughthood connector						
100mm dia.	3.46	4.43	0.48	10.89	nr	**15.31**
125mm dia.	3.89	4.98	0.48	10.89	nr	**15.86**
150mm dia.	4.23	5.41	0.48	10.89	nr	**16.30**
Adaptor						
100mm dia.	8.37	10.72	0.48	10.89	nr	**21.61**
125mm dia.	8.55	10.96	0.48	10.89	nr	**21.84**
150mm dia.	8.73	11.19	0.48	10.89	nr	**22.07**

T:MECHANICAL/COOLING/HEATING SYSTEMS

Item	Net Price £	Material £	Labour hours	Labour £	Unit	Total rate £
Support plate						
100mm dia.	6.05	7.74	0.48	10.89	nr	**18.63**
125mm dia.	6.43	8.24	0.48	10.89	nr	**19.12**
150mm dia.	6.88	8.81	0.48	10.89	nr	**19.70**
Wall band						
100mm dia.	5.46	6.99	0.48	10.89	nr	**17.88**
125mm dia.	5.82	7.45	0.48	10.89	nr	**18.34**
150mm dia.	7.38	9.45	0.48	10.89	nr	**20.34**
Firestop						
100mm dia.	2.37	3.04	0.48	10.89	nr	**13.92**
125mm dia.	2.37	3.04	0.48	10.89	nr	**13.92**
150mm dia.	2.71	3.47	0.48	10.89	nr	**14.36**
Flat flashing						
125mm dia.	16.10	20.62	0.55	12.47	nr	**33.10**
150mm dia.	22.41	28.70	0.55	12.47	nr	**41.17**
Adjustable flashing 5°-30°						
100mm dia.	41.98	53.77	0.55	12.47	nr	**66.24**
125mm dia.	65.54	83.94	0.55	12.47	nr	**96.42**
Storm collar						
100mm dia.	3.34	4.28	0.55	12.47	nr	**16.76**
125mm dia.	3.42	4.39	0.55	12.47	nr	**16.86**
150mm dia.	3.51	4.50	0.55	12.47	nr	**16.97**
Gas vent terminal						
100mm dia.	12.77	16.35	0.55	12.47	nr	**28.83**
125mm dia.	14.03	17.98	0.55	12.47	nr	**30.45**
150mm dia.	18.00	23.06	0.55	12.47	nr	**35.53**
Twin wall galvanised steel flue box, 125mm dia.; fitted for gas fire, where no chimney exists						
Free standing	81.17	103.96	2.15	48.76	nr	**152.72**
Recess	81.17	103.96	2.15	48.76	nr	**152.72**
Back boiler	59.80	76.59	2.40	54.43	nr	**131.02**

T:MECHANICAL/COOLING/HEATING SYSTEMS

Item	Net Price £	Material £	Labour hours	Labour £	Unit	Total rate £
T13 : PACKAGED STEAM GENERATORS						
Packaged steam boilers; boiler mountings centrifugal water feed pump; insulation; and sheet steel wrap around casing; plastic coated						
Gas fired						
293 kW rating	14874.33	19050.90	86.45	1960.55	nr	**21011.44**
1465 kW rating	31726.58	40635.08	148.22	3361.39	nr	**43996.47**
2930 kW rating	45560.50	58353.44	207.50	4705.77	nr	**63059.21**
Oil fired						
293 kW rating	13490.94	17279.06	86.45	1960.55	nr	**19239.61**
1465 kW rating	29348.51	37589.28	148.22	3361.39	nr	**40950.67**
2930 kW rating	44417.21	56889.11	207.50	4705.77	nr	**61594.88**

T:MECHANICAL/COOLING/HEATING SYSTEMS

Item	Net Price £	Material £	Labour hours	Labour £	Unit	Total rate £
T31 : LOW TEMPERATURE HOT WATER HEATING						
Y10 - PIPELINES						
SCREWED STEEL						
Black steel pipes; screwed and socketed joints; BS 1387: 1985						
Varnished; medium						
8mm dia	1.37	1.75	0.51	11.57	m	**13.32**
10mm dia	1.37	1.75	0.51	11.57	m	**13.32**
15mm dia	1.47	1.88	0.52	11.79	m	**13.68**
20mm dia	1.73	2.22	0.55	12.47	m	**14.69**
25mm dia	2.48	3.18	0.60	13.61	m	**16.78**
32mm dia	3.07	3.93	0.67	15.19	m	**19.13**
40mm dia	3.56	4.56	0.75	17.01	m	**21.57**
50mm dia	5.01	6.42	0.85	19.28	m	**25.69**
65mm dia	6.81	8.72	0.93	21.09	m	**29.81**
80mm dia	8.84	11.32	1.07	24.27	m	**35.59**
100mm dia	12.53	16.05	1.46	33.11	m	**49.16**
125mm dia	19.98	25.59	1.72	39.01	m	**64.60**
150mm dia	23.20	29.71	1.96	44.45	m	**74.16**
Varnished; heavy						
15mm dia	1.75	2.24	0.52	11.79	m	**14.03**
20mm dia	2.07	2.65	0.55	12.47	m	**15.12**
25mm dia	3.03	3.88	0.60	13.61	m	**17.49**
32mm dia	3.76	4.82	0.67	15.19	m	**20.01**
40mm dia	4.38	5.61	0.75	17.01	m	**22.62**
50mm dia	6.08	7.79	0.85	19.28	m	**27.06**
65mm dia	8.27	10.59	0.93	21.09	m	**31.68**
80mm dia	10.53	13.49	1.07	24.27	m	**37.75**
100mm dia	14.69	18.81	1.46	33.11	m	**51.93**
125mm dia	21.30	27.28	1.72	39.01	m	**66.29**
150mm dia	24.91	31.90	1.96	44.45	m	**76.35**
Extra over black steel screwed pipes; black steel flanges, screwed and drilled; metric; BS 4504						
Screwed flanges; PN6						
15mm dia	4.52	5.79	0.35	7.94	nr	**13.73**
20mm dia	4.52	5.79	0.47	10.66	nr	**16.45**
25mm dia	4.52	5.79	0.53	12.02	nr	**17.81**
32mm dia	4.52	5.79	0.62	14.06	nr	**19.85**
40mm dia	4.52	5.79	0.70	15.87	nr	**21.66**
50mm dia	4.82	6.17	0.84	19.05	nr	**25.22**
65mm dia	6.70	8.58	1.03	23.36	nr	**31.94**
80mm dia	7.86	10.07	1.23	27.89	nr	**37.96**
100mm dia	9.36	11.99	1.41	31.98	nr	**43.96**
125mm dia	20.54	26.31	1.77	40.14	nr	**66.45**
150mm dia	20.54	26.31	2.21	50.12	nr	**76.43**

T:MECHANICAL/COOLING/HEATING SYSTEMS

Item	Net Price £	Material £	Labour hours	Labour £	Unit	Total rate £
T31 : LOW TEMPERATURE HOT WATER HEATING (cont'd)						
Y10 - PIPELINES (cont'd)						
SCREWED STEEL (cont'd)						
Extra over black steel screwed pipes; black steel flanges, screwed and drilled; metric; BS 4504 (cont'd)						
Screwed flanges; PN16						
15mm dia	6.14	7.86	0.35	7.94	nr	15.80
20mm dia	6.14	7.86	0.47	10.66	nr	18.52
25mm dia	6.14	7.86	0.53	12.02	nr	19.88
32mm dia	6.14	7.86	0.62	14.06	nr	21.92
40mm dia	6.14	7.86	0.70	15.87	nr	23.74
50mm dia	6.43	8.24	0.84	19.05	nr	27.29
65mm dia	8.17	10.46	1.03	23.36	nr	33.82
80mm dia	9.09	11.64	1.23	27.89	nr	39.54
100mm dia	10.80	13.83	1.41	31.98	nr	45.81
125mm dia	21.27	27.24	1.77	40.14	nr	67.38
150mm dia	21.27	27.24	2.21	50.12	nr	77.36
Extra over black steel screwed pipes; black steel flanges, screwed and drilled; imperial; BS 10						
Screwed flanges; Table E						
1/2" dia	6.44	8.25	0.35	7.94	nr	16.19
3/4" dia	6.44	8.25	0.47	10.66	nr	18.91
1" dia	6.44	8.25	0.53	12.02	nr	20.27
1 1/4" dia	6.44	8.25	0.62	14.06	nr	22.31
1 1/2" dia	6.44	8.25	0.70	15.87	nr	24.12
2" dia	6.44	8.25	0.84	19.05	nr	27.30
2 1/2" dia	7.67	9.82	1.03	23.36	nr	33.18
3" dia	8.69	11.13	1.23	27.89	nr	39.02
4" dia	23.50	30.10	1.41	31.98	nr	62.08
5" dia	24.91	31.90	1.77	40.14	nr	72.05
6" dia	49.82	63.81	2.21	50.12	nr	113.93
Extra over black steel screwed pipes; black steel flange connections						
Bolted connection between pair of flanges; including gasket, bolts, nuts and washers						
50mm dia	14.82	18.98	0.53	12.02	nr	31.00
65mm dia	18.53	23.73	0.53	12.02	nr	35.75
80mm dia	21.88	28.02	0.53	12.02	nr	40.04
100mm dia	26.24	33.61	0.61	13.83	nr	47.44
125mm dia	47.63	61.00	0.61	13.83	nr	74.84
150mm dia	50.35	64.49	0.90	20.41	nr	84.90

T:MECHANICAL/COOLING/HEATING SYSTEMS

Item	Net Price £	Material £	Labour hours	Labour £	Unit	Total rate £
Extra over black steel screwed pipes; black heavy steel tubular fittings; BS 1387						
Long screw connection with socket and backnut						
15mm dia	2.47	3.16	0.63	14.29	nr	**17.45**
20mm dia	3.10	3.97	0.84	19.05	nr	**23.02**
25mm dia	4.07	5.21	0.95	21.54	nr	**26.76**
32mm dia	5.34	6.84	1.11	25.17	nr	**32.01**
40mm dia	6.52	8.35	1.28	29.03	nr	**37.38**
50mm dia	9.56	12.24	1.53	34.70	nr	**46.94**
65mm dia	21.82	27.95	1.87	42.41	nr	**70.36**
80mm dia	30.00	38.42	2.21	50.12	nr	**88.54**
100mm dia	48.48	62.09	3.05	69.17	nr	**131.26**
Running nipple						
15mm dia	0.63	0.81	0.50	11.34	nr	**12.15**
20mm dia	0.79	1.01	0.68	15.42	nr	**16.43**
25mm dia	0.97	1.24	0.77	17.46	nr	**18.70**
32mm dia	1.37	1.75	0.90	20.41	nr	**22.17**
40mm dia	1.84	2.36	1.03	23.36	nr	**25.72**
50mm dia	2.81	3.60	1.23	27.89	nr	**31.49**
65mm dia	6.04	7.74	1.50	34.02	nr	**41.75**
80mm dia	9.41	12.05	1.78	40.37	nr	**52.42**
100mm dia	14.74	18.88	2.38	53.97	nr	**72.85**
Barrel nipple						
15mm dia	0.44	0.56	0.50	11.34	nr	**11.90**
20mm dia	0.58	0.74	0.68	15.42	nr	**16.16**
25mm dia	0.75	0.96	0.77	17.46	nr	**18.42**
32mm dia	1.12	1.43	0.90	20.41	nr	**21.85**
40mm dia	1.38	1.77	1.03	23.36	nr	**25.13**
50mm dia	1.97	2.52	1.23	27.89	nr	**30.42**
65mm dia	4.22	5.40	1.50	34.02	nr	**39.42**
80mm dia	5.88	7.53	1.78	40.37	nr	**47.90**
100mm dia	10.64	13.63	2.38	53.97	nr	**67.60**
125mm dia	19.77	25.32	2.87	65.09	nr	**90.41**
150mm dia	31.14	39.88	3.39	76.88	nr	**116.76**
Close taper nipple						
15mm dia	0.75	0.96	0.50	11.34	nr	**12.30**
20mm dia	0.97	1.24	0.68	15.42	nr	**16.66**
25mm dia	1.27	1.63	0.77	17.46	nr	**19.09**
32mm dia	1.91	2.45	0.90	20.41	nr	**22.86**
40mm dia	2.37	3.04	1.03	23.36	nr	**26.39**
50mm dia	3.63	4.65	1.23	27.89	nr	**32.54**
65mm dia	7.04	9.02	1.50	34.02	nr	**43.03**
80mm dia	8.69	11.13	1.78	40.37	nr	**51.50**
100mm dia	17.84	22.85	2.38	53.97	nr	**76.82**
125mm dia	22.51	28.83	2.87	65.09	nr	**93.92**
150mm dia	31.54	40.40	3.39	76.88	nr	**117.28**

T:MECHANICAL/COOLING/HEATING SYSTEMS

Item	Net Price £	Material £	Labour hours	Labour £	Unit	Total rate £
T31 : LOW TEMPERATURE HOT WATER HEATING (cont'd)						
Y10 - PIPELINES (cont'd)						
SCREWED STEEL (cont'd)						
Extra over black steel screwed pipes; black heavy steel tubular fittings; BS 1387 (cont'd)						
90° bend with socket						
15mm dia	1.99	2.55	0.64	14.51	nr	**17.06**
20mm dia	2.76	3.54	0.85	19.28	nr	**22.81**
25mm dia	4.23	5.42	0.97	22.00	nr	**27.42**
32mm dia	6.07	7.77	1.12	25.40	nr	**33.17**
40mm dia	7.43	9.52	1.29	29.26	nr	**38.77**
50mm dia	11.55	14.79	1.55	35.15	nr	**49.94**
65mm dia	22.60	28.95	1.89	42.86	nr	**71.81**
80mm dia	33.50	42.91	2.24	50.80	nr	**93.71**
100mm dia	49.47	63.36	3.09	70.08	nr	**133.44**
125mm dia	173.04	221.63	3.39	76.88	nr	**298.51**
Extra over black steel screwed pipes; black heavy steel fittings; BS 1740						
Plug						
15mm dia	0.51	0.65	0.30	6.80	nr	**7.46**
20mm dia	0.72	0.92	0.40	9.07	nr	**9.99**
25mm dia	1.38	1.77	0.45	10.21	nr	**11.97**
32mm dia	1.99	2.55	0.53	12.02	nr	**14.57**
40mm dia	2.36	3.02	0.61	13.83	nr	**16.86**
50mm dia	3.35	4.29	0.72	16.33	nr	**20.62**
65mm dia	8.04	10.30	0.88	19.96	nr	**30.25**
80mm dia	16.49	21.12	1.04	23.59	nr	**44.71**
100mm dia	28.84	36.94	1.53	34.70	nr	**71.64**
150mm dia	192.98	247.17	2.73	61.91	nr	**309.08**
Socket						
15mm dia	0.43	0.55	0.64	14.51	nr	**15.06**
20mm dia	0.50	0.64	0.85	19.28	nr	**19.92**
25mm dia	0.67	0.86	0.97	22.00	nr	**22.86**
32mm dia	1.01	1.29	1.12	25.40	nr	**26.69**
40mm dia	1.16	1.49	1.29	29.26	nr	**30.74**
50mm dia	1.80	2.31	1.55	35.15	nr	**37.46**
65mm dia	3.55	4.55	1.89	42.86	nr	**47.41**
80mm dia	4.60	5.89	2.24	50.80	nr	**56.69**
100mm dia	8.67	11.10	3.09	70.08	nr	**81.18**
125mm dia	19.35	24.78	3.92	88.90	nr	**113.68**
150mm dia	27.70	35.48	4.74	107.50	nr	**142.97**
Cone seat unions						
15mm dia	5.56	7.12	0.64	14.51	nr	**21.64**
20mm dia	7.56	9.68	0.85	19.28	nr	**28.96**
25mm dia	10.29	13.18	0.97	22.00	nr	**35.18**
32mm dia	20.58	26.36	1.12	25.40	nr	**51.76**
40mm dia	25.13	32.19	1.29	29.26	nr	**61.44**
50mm dia	36.98	47.36	1.55	35.15	nr	**82.52**

T:MECHANICAL/COOLING/HEATING SYSTEMS

Item	Net Price £	Material £	Labour hours	Labour £	Unit	Total rate £
Elbow, male/female						
15mm dia	3.47	4.44	0.64	14.51	nr	**18.96**
20mm dia	4.42	5.66	0.85	19.28	nr	**24.94**
25mm dia	7.17	9.18	0.97	22.00	nr	**31.18**
32mm dia	13.90	17.80	1.12	25.40	nr	**43.20**
40mm dia	14.26	18.26	1.29	29.26	nr	**47.52**
50mm dia	24.89	31.88	1.55	35.15	nr	**67.03**
Elbow, female/female						
15mm dia	2.66	3.41	0.64	14.51	nr	**17.92**
20mm dia	3.47	4.44	0.85	19.28	nr	**23.72**
25mm dia	4.71	6.03	0.97	22.00	nr	**28.03**
32mm dia	8.76	11.22	1.12	25.40	nr	**36.62**
40mm dia	10.45	13.38	1.29	29.26	nr	**42.64**
50mm dia	17.02	21.80	1.55	35.15	nr	**56.95**
65mm dia	41.83	53.58	1.89	42.86	nr	**96.44**
80mm dia	49.87	63.87	2.24	50.80	nr	**114.67**
100mm dia	86.42	110.69	3.09	70.08	nr	**180.76**
Equal tee						
15mm dia	3.30	4.23	0.91	20.64	nr	**24.86**
20mm dia	3.84	4.92	1.22	27.67	nr	**32.59**
25mm dia	5.66	7.25	1.40	31.75	nr	**39.00**
32mm dia	11.69	14.97	1.62	36.74	nr	**51.71**
40mm dia	12.73	16.30	1.86	42.18	nr	**58.49**
50mm dia	20.70	26.51	2.21	50.12	nr	**76.63**
65mm dia	50.04	64.09	2.72	61.69	nr	**125.78**
80mm dia	53.70	68.78	3.21	72.80	nr	**141.58**
100mm dia	86.43	110.70	4.44	100.69	nr	**211.39**
Extra over black steel screwed pipes; black malleable iron fittings; BS 143						
Cap						
15mm dia	0.38	0.49	0.32	7.26	nr	**7.74**
20mm dia	0.43	0.55	0.43	9.75	nr	**10.30**
25mm dia	0.54	0.69	0.49	11.11	nr	**11.80**
32mm dia	0.87	1.11	0.58	13.15	nr	**14.27**
40mm dia	1.03	1.32	0.66	14.97	nr	**16.29**
50mm dia	2.17	2.78	0.78	17.69	nr	**20.47**
65mm dia	3.61	4.62	0.96	21.77	nr	**26.40**
80mm dia	4.08	5.23	1.13	25.63	nr	**30.85**
100mm dia	8.94	11.45	1.70	38.55	nr	**50.00**
Plain plug, hollow						
15mm dia	0.26	0.33	0.28	6.35	nr	**6.68**
20mm dia	0.34	0.44	0.38	8.62	nr	**9.05**
25mm dia	0.46	0.59	0.44	9.98	nr	**10.57**
32mm dia	0.59	0.76	0.51	11.57	nr	**12.32**
40mm dia	1.11	1.42	0.59	13.38	nr	**14.80**
50mm dia	1.56	2.00	0.70	15.87	nr	**17.87**
65mm dia	2.54	3.25	0.85	19.28	nr	**22.53**
80mm dia	3.96	5.07	1.00	22.68	nr	**27.75**
100mm dia	7.30	9.35	1.44	32.66	nr	**42.01**
125mm dia	17.44	22.34	1.98	44.90	nr	**67.24**
150mm dia	20.92	26.79	2.53	57.38	nr	**84.17**

T:MECHANICAL/COOLING/HEATING SYSTEMS

Item	Net Price £	Material £	Labour hours	Labour £	Unit	Total rate £
T31 : LOW TEMPERATURE HOT WATER HEATING (cont'd)						
Y10 - PIPELINES (cont'd)						
SCREWED STEEL (cont'd)						
Extra over black steel screwed pipes; black malleable iron fittings; BS 143 (cont'd)						
Plain plug, solid						
15mm dia	0.82	1.05	0.28	6.35	nr	7.40
20mm dia	0.79	1.01	0.38	8.62	nr	9.63
25mm dia	1.17	1.50	0.44	9.98	nr	11.48
32mm dia	1.56	2.00	0.51	11.57	nr	13.56
40mm dia	2.20	2.82	0.59	13.38	nr	16.20
50mm dia	2.90	3.71	0.70	15.87	nr	19.59
65mm dia	3.30	4.23	0.85	19.28	nr	23.50
Elbow, male/female						
15mm dia	0.43	0.55	0.64	14.51	nr	15.06
20mm dia	0.58	0.74	0.85	19.28	nr	20.02
25mm dia	0.96	1.23	0.97	22.00	nr	23.23
32mm dia	1.64	2.10	1.12	25.40	nr	27.50
40mm dia	2.74	3.51	1.29	29.26	nr	32.76
50mm dia	3.53	4.52	1.55	35.15	nr	39.67
65mm dia	7.63	9.77	1.89	42.86	nr	52.63
80mm dia	10.42	13.35	2.24	50.80	nr	64.15
100mm dia	18.22	23.34	3.09	70.08	nr	93.41
Elbow						
15mm dia	0.39	0.50	0.64	14.51	nr	15.01
20mm dia	0.53	0.68	0.85	19.28	nr	19.96
25mm dia	0.82	1.05	0.97	22.00	nr	23.05
32mm dia	1.39	1.78	1.12	25.40	nr	27.18
40mm dia	2.33	2.98	1.29	29.26	nr	32.24
50mm dia	2.73	3.50	1.55	35.15	nr	38.65
65mm dia	5.89	7.54	1.89	42.86	nr	50.41
80mm dia	8.65	11.08	2.24	50.80	nr	61.88
100mm dia	16.68	21.36	3.09	70.08	nr	91.44
125mm dia	35.74	45.78	4.44	100.69	nr	146.47
150mm dia	66.54	85.22	5.79	131.31	nr	216.53
45° elbow						
15mm dia	0.92	1.18	0.64	14.51	nr	15.69
20mm dia	1.14	1.46	0.85	19.28	nr	20.74
25mm dia	1.69	2.16	0.97	22.00	nr	24.16
32mm dia	3.20	4.10	1.12	25.40	nr	29.50
40mm dia	3.92	5.02	1.29	29.26	nr	34.28
50mm dia	5.38	6.89	1.55	35.15	nr	42.04
65mm dia	7.87	10.08	1.89	42.86	nr	52.94
80mm dia	11.82	15.14	2.24	50.80	nr	65.94
100mm dia	22.84	29.25	3.09	70.08	nr	99.33
150mm dia	63.80	81.71	5.79	131.31	nr	213.02

T:MECHANICAL/COOLING/HEATING SYSTEMS

Item	Net Price £	Material £	Labour hours	Labour £	Unit	Total rate £
Bend, male/female						
15mm dia	0.76	0.97	0.64	14.51	nr	**15.49**
20mm dia	1.10	1.41	0.85	19.28	nr	**20.69**
25mm dia	1.64	2.10	0.97	22.00	nr	**24.10**
32mm dia	2.41	3.09	1.12	25.40	nr	**28.49**
40mm dia	3.80	4.87	1.29	29.26	nr	**34.12**
50mm dia	6.64	8.50	1.55	35.15	nr	**43.66**
65mm dia	11.05	14.15	1.89	42.86	nr	**57.01**
80mm dia	14.98	19.19	2.24	50.80	nr	**69.99**
100mm dia	37.11	47.53	3.09	70.08	nr	**117.61**
Bend, male						
15mm dia	1.75	2.24	0.64	14.51	nr	**16.76**
20mm dia	1.96	2.51	0.85	19.28	nr	**21.79**
25mm dia	2.87	3.68	0.97	22.00	nr	**25.67**
32mm dia	5.79	7.42	1.12	25.40	nr	**32.82**
40mm dia	8.11	10.39	1.29	29.26	nr	**39.64**
50mm dia	10.85	13.90	1.55	35.15	nr	**49.05**
Bend, female						
15mm dia	0.70	0.90	0.64	14.51	nr	**15.41**
20mm dia	0.99	1.27	0.85	19.28	nr	**20.54**
25mm dia	1.40	1.79	0.97	22.00	nr	**23.79**
32mm dia	2.45	3.14	1.12	25.40	nr	**28.54**
40mm dia	3.27	4.19	1.29	29.26	nr	**33.44**
50mm dia	4.61	5.90	1.55	35.15	nr	**41.06**
65mm dia	9.84	12.60	1.89	42.86	nr	**55.47**
80mm dia	15.68	20.08	2.24	50.80	nr	**70.88**
100mm dia	34.37	44.02	3.09	70.08	nr	**114.10**
125mm dia	91.68	117.42	4.44	100.69	nr	**218.11**
150mm dia	140.04	179.36	5.79	131.31	nr	**310.67**
Return bend						
15mm dia	3.52	4.51	0.64	14.51	nr	**19.02**
20mm dia	5.69	7.29	0.85	19.28	nr	**26.56**
25mm dia	7.10	9.09	0.97	22.00	nr	**31.09**
32mm dia	10.19	13.05	1.12	25.40	nr	**38.45**
40mm dia	12.14	15.55	1.29	29.26	nr	**44.80**
50mm dia	18.52	23.72	1.55	35.15	nr	**58.87**
Equal socket, parallel thread						
15mm dia	0.41	0.53	0.64	14.51	nr	**15.04**
20mm dia	0.49	0.63	0.85	19.28	nr	**19.90**
25mm dia	0.65	0.83	0.97	22.00	nr	**22.83**
32mm dia	1.15	1.47	1.12	25.40	nr	**26.87**
40mm dia	1.69	2.16	1.29	29.26	nr	**31.42**
50mm dia	2.53	3.24	1.55	35.15	nr	**38.39**
65mm dia	4.29	5.49	1.89	42.86	nr	**48.36**
80mm dia	5.90	7.56	2.24	50.80	nr	**58.36**
100mm dia	10.01	12.82	3.09	70.08	nr	**82.90**

T:MECHANICAL/COOLING/HEATING SYSTEMS

Item	Net Price £	Material £	Labour hours	Labour £	Unit	Total rate £
T31 : LOW TEMPERATURE HOT WATER HEATING (cont'd)						
Y10 - PIPELINES (cont'd)						
SCREWED STEEL (cont'd)						
Extra over black steel screwed pipes; black malleable iron fittings; BS 143 (cont'd)						
Concentric reducing socket						
20 x 15mm dia	0.59	0.76	0.76	17.24	nr	**17.99**
25 x 15mm dia	0.70	0.90	0.85	19.28	nr	**20.17**
25 x 20mm dia	0.74	0.95	0.86	19.50	nr	**20.45**
32 x 25mm dia	1.29	1.65	1.01	22.91	nr	**24.56**
40 x 25mm dia	1.62	2.07	1.16	26.31	nr	**28.38**
40 x 32mm dia	1.68	2.15	1.16	26.31	nr	**28.46**
50 x 25mm dia	3.14	4.02	1.38	31.30	nr	**35.32**
50 x 40mm dia	2.35	3.01	1.38	31.30	nr	**34.31**
65 x 50mm dia	4.28	5.48	1.69	38.33	nr	**43.81**
80 x 50mm dia	5.57	7.13	2.00	45.36	nr	**52.49**
100 x 50mm dia	11.11	14.23	2.75	62.37	nr	**76.60**
100 x 80mm dia	10.31	13.20	2.75	62.37	nr	**75.57**
150 x 100mm dia	27.19	34.82	4.10	92.98	nr	**127.81**
Eccentric reducing socket						
20 x 15mm dia	1.05	1.34	0.73	16.56	nr	**17.90**
25 x 15mm dia	3.03	3.88	0.85	19.28	nr	**23.16**
25 x 20mm dia	3.44	4.41	0.85	19.28	nr	**23.68**
32 x 25mm dia	4.03	5.16	1.01	22.91	nr	**28.07**
40 x 25mm dia	4.97	6.37	1.16	26.31	nr	**32.67**
40 x 32mm dia	2.49	3.19	1.16	26.31	nr	**29.50**
50 x 25mm dia	3.22	4.12	1.38	31.30	nr	**35.42**
50 x 40mm dia	3.00	3.84	1.38	31.30	nr	**35.14**
65 x 50mm dia	5.57	7.13	1.69	38.33	nr	**45.46**
80 x 50mm dia	9.05	11.59	2.00	45.36	nr	**56.95**
Hexagon bush						
20 x 15mm dia	0.34	0.44	0.37	8.39	nr	**8.83**
25 x 15mm dia	0.41	0.53	0.43	9.75	nr	**10.28**
25 x 20mm dia	0.43	0.55	0.43	9.75	nr	**10.30**
32 x 25mm dia	0.52	0.67	0.51	11.57	nr	**12.23**
40 x 25mm dia	0.81	1.04	0.58	13.15	nr	**14.19**
40 x 32mm dia	0.75	0.96	0.58	13.15	nr	**14.11**
50 x 25mm dia	1.68	2.15	0.71	16.10	nr	**18.25**
50 x 40mm dia	1.56	2.00	0.71	16.10	nr	**18.10**
65 x 50mm dia	2.60	3.33	0.85	19.28	nr	**22.61**
80 x 50mm dia	4.22	5.40	1.00	22.68	nr	**28.08**
100 x 50mm dia	9.77	12.51	1.52	34.47	nr	**46.98**
100 x 80mm dia	8.13	10.41	1.52	34.47	nr	**44.88**
150 x 100mm dia	25.73	32.95	2.57	58.28	nr	**91.24**
Hexagon nipple						
15mm dia	0.36	0.46	0.28	6.35	nr	**6.81**
20mm dia	0.41	0.53	0.38	8.62	nr	**9.14**
25mm dia	0.58	0.74	0.44	9.98	nr	**10.72**
32mm dia	1.11	1.42	0.51	11.57	nr	**12.99**
40mm dia	1.29	1.65	0.59	13.38	nr	**15.03**
50mm dia	2.33	2.98	0.70	15.87	nr	**18.86**

T:MECHANICAL/COOLING/HEATING SYSTEMS

Item	Net Price £	Material £	Labour hours	Labour £	Unit	Total rate £
65mm dia	3.81	4.88	0.85	19.28	nr	24.16
80mm dia	5.51	7.06	1.00	22.68	nr	29.74
100mm dia	9.35	11.98	1.44	32.66	nr	44.63
150mm dia	27.59	35.34	2.32	52.61	nr	87.95
Union, male/female						
15mm dia	4.10	5.25	0.64	14.51	nr	19.77
20mm dia	5.54	7.10	0.85	19.28	nr	26.37
25mm dia	7.01	8.98	0.97	22.00	nr	30.98
32mm dia	9.97	12.77	1.12	25.40	nr	38.17
40mm dia	11.86	15.19	1.29	29.26	nr	44.45
50mm dia	15.85	20.30	1.55	35.15	nr	55.45
65mm dia	23.29	29.83	1.89	42.86	nr	72.69
80mm dia	28.50	36.50	2.24	50.80	nr	87.30
Union, female						
15mm dia	4.11	5.26	0.64	14.51	nr	19.78
20mm dia	4.53	5.80	0.85	19.28	nr	25.08
25mm dia	5.99	7.67	0.97	22.00	nr	29.67
32mm dia	8.49	10.87	1.12	25.40	nr	36.27
40mm dia	10.27	13.15	1.29	29.26	nr	42.41
50mm dia	13.04	16.70	1.55	35.15	nr	51.85
65mm dia	28.59	36.62	1.89	42.86	nr	79.48
80mm dia	46.70	59.81	2.24	50.80	nr	110.61
100mm dia	91.49	117.18	3.09	70.08	nr	187.26
Union elbow, male/female						
15mm dia	7.04	9.02	0.55	12.47	nr	21.49
20mm dia	9.48	12.14	0.85	19.28	nr	31.42
25mm dia	11.44	14.65	0.97	22.00	nr	36.65
Twin elbow						
15mm dia	2.22	2.84	0.91	20.64	nr	23.48
20mm dia	2.46	3.15	1.22	27.67	nr	30.82
25mm dia	3.98	5.10	1.39	31.52	nr	36.62
32mm dia	7.58	9.71	1.62	36.74	nr	46.45
40mm dia	9.60	12.30	1.86	42.18	nr	54.48
50mm dia	12.33	15.79	2.21	50.12	nr	65.91
65mm dia	19.30	24.72	2.72	61.69	nr	86.40
80mm dia	32.88	42.11	3.21	72.80	nr	114.91
Equal tee						
15mm dia	0.53	0.68	0.91	20.64	nr	21.32
20mm dia	0.77	0.99	1.22	27.67	nr	28.65
25mm dia	1.11	1.42	1.39	31.52	nr	32.94
32mm dia	1.88	2.41	1.62	36.74	nr	39.15
40mm dia	2.89	3.70	1.86	42.18	nr	45.88
50mm dia	4.16	5.33	2.21	50.12	nr	55.45
65mm dia	9.12	11.68	2.72	61.69	nr	73.37
80mm dia	11.11	14.23	3.21	72.80	nr	87.03
100mm dia	20.13	25.78	4.44	100.69	nr	126.47
125mm dia	51.53	66.00	5.38	122.01	nr	188.01
150mm dia	82.11	105.17	6.31	143.10	nr	248.27

T:MECHANICAL/COOLING/HEATING SYSTEMS

Item	Net Price £	Material £	Labour hours	Labour £	Unit	Total rate £
T31 : LOW TEMPERATURE HOT WATER HEATING (cont'd)						
Y10 - PIPELINES (cont'd)						
SCREWED STEEL (cont'd)						
Extra over black steel screwed pipes; black malleable iron fittings; BS 143 (cont'd)						
Tee reducing on branch						
20 x 15mm dia	0.70	0.90	1.22	27.67	nr	**28.56**
25 x 15mm dia	0.96	1.23	1.39	31.52	nr	**32.75**
25 x 20mm dia	1.15	1.47	1.39	31.52	nr	**33.00**
32 x 25mm dia	1.85	2.37	1.62	36.74	nr	**39.11**
40 x 25mm dia	2.45	3.14	1.86	42.18	nr	**45.32**
40 x 32mm dia	3.20	4.10	1.86	42.18	nr	**46.28**
50 x 25mm dia	3.64	4.66	2.21	50.12	nr	**54.78**
50 x 40mm dia	5.42	6.94	2.21	50.12	nr	**57.06**
65 x 50mm dia	8.46	10.84	2.72	61.69	nr	**72.52**
80 x 50mm dia	11.44	14.65	3.21	72.80	nr	**87.45**
100 x 50mm dia	16.68	21.36	4.44	100.69	nr	**122.06**
100 x 80mm dia	25.73	32.95	4.44	100.69	nr	**133.65**
150 x 100mm dia	60.48	77.46	6.31	143.10	nr	**220.56**
Equal pitcher tee						
15mm dia	1.62	2.07	0.91	20.64	nr	**22.71**
20mm dia	2.02	2.59	1.22	27.67	nr	**30.25**
25mm dia	3.03	3.88	1.39	31.52	nr	**35.40**
32mm dia	4.26	5.46	1.62	36.74	nr	**42.20**
40mm dia	6.58	8.43	1.86	42.18	nr	**50.61**
50mm dia	9.25	11.85	2.21	50.12	nr	**61.97**
65mm dia	14.30	18.32	2.72	61.69	nr	**80.00**
80mm dia	19.66	25.18	3.21	72.80	nr	**97.98**
100mm dia	44.23	56.65	4.44	100.69	nr	**157.34**
Cross						
15mm dia	1.59	2.04	1.00	22.68	nr	**24.71**
20mm dia	2.39	3.06	1.33	30.16	nr	**33.22**
25mm dia	3.03	3.88	1.51	34.24	nr	**38.13**
32mm dia	4.09	5.24	1.77	40.14	nr	**45.38**
40mm dia	5.27	6.75	2.02	45.81	nr	**52.56**
50mm dia	8.55	10.95	2.42	54.88	nr	**65.83**
65mm dia	11.82	15.14	2.97	67.35	nr	**82.49**
80mm dia	15.73	20.15	3.50	79.37	nr	**99.52**
100mm dia	28.59	36.62	4.84	109.76	nr	**146.38**

T:MECHANICAL/COOLING/HEATING SYSTEMS

Item	Net Price £	Material £	Labour hours	Labour £	Unit	Total rate £
PRESS FIT						
Press fit jointing system; operating temperature -20°C to +120°C; operating pressure 16 bar ; butyl rubber 'O' ring mechanical joint						
Carbon steel						
Pipework						
15mm dia	1.00	1.28	0.46	10.43	m	**11.71**
22mm dia	1.61	2.06	0.48	10.89	m	**12.95**
28mm dia	2.25	2.88	0.52	11.79	m	**14.67**
35mm dia	2.91	3.73	0.56	12.70	m	**16.43**
42mm dia	3.99	5.11	0.58	13.15	m	**18.26**
54mm dia	5.17	6.62	0.66	14.97	m	**21.59**
Extra over for Carbon Steel pressfit fittings						
Coupling						
15mm dia	0.76	0.97	0.36	8.16	nr	**9.14**
22mm dia	0.92	1.18	0.36	8.16	nr	**9.34**
28mm dia	1.17	1.50	0.44	9.98	nr	**11.48**
35mm dia	1.95	2.50	0.44	9.98	nr	**12.48**
42mm dia	2.62	3.36	0.52	11.79	nr	**15.15**
54mm dia	3.09	3.96	0.60	13.61	nr	**17.56**
Reducer						
22 x 15mm dia	0.70	0.90	0.36	8.16	nr	**9.06**
28 x 15mm dia	0.92	1.18	0.40	9.07	nr	**10.25**
28 x 22mm dia	0.97	1.24	0.40	9.07	nr	**10.31**
35 x 22mm dia	1.08	1.38	0.40	9.07	nr	**10.45**
35 x 28mm dia	1.16	1.49	0.44	9.98	nr	**11.46**
42 x 35mm dia	2.50	3.20	0.48	10.89	nr	**14.09**
54 x 22mm dia	7.24	9.27	0.48	10.89	nr	**20.16**
54 x 28mm dia	7.29	9.34	0.52	11.79	nr	**21.13**
54 x 42mm dia	7.67	9.82	0.56	12.70	nr	**22.52**
90° bend						
15mm dia	1.10	1.41	0.36	8.16	nr	**9.57**
22mm dia	1.44	1.84	0.36	8.16	nr	**10.01**
28mm dia	1.98	2.54	0.44	9.98	nr	**12.51**
35mm dia	4.94	6.33	0.44	9.98	nr	**16.31**
42mm dia	7.91	10.13	0.52	11.79	nr	**21.92**
54mm dia	9.46	12.12	0.60	13.61	nr	**25.72**
45° bend						
15mm dia	1.31	1.68	0.36	8.16	nr	**9.84**
22mm dia	1.46	1.87	0.36	8.16	nr	**10.03**
28mm dia	2.00	2.56	0.44	9.98	nr	**12.54**
35mm dia	3.91	5.01	0.44	9.98	nr	**14.99**
42mm dia	4.92	6.30	0.52	11.79	nr	**18.09**
54mm dia	5.55	7.11	0.60	13.61	nr	**20.72**

T:MECHANICAL/COOLING/HEATING SYSTEMS

Item	Net Price £	Material £	Labour hours	Labour £	Unit	Total rate £
T31 : LOW TEMPERATURE HOT WATER HEATING (cont'd)						
Y10 - PIPELINES (cont'd)						
PRESS FIT (cont'd)						
Carbon Steel press fit fittings (cont'd)						
Equal tee						
15mm dia	2.11	2.70	0.54	12.25	nr	14.95
22mm dia	2.43	3.11	0.54	12.25	nr	15.36
28mm dia	3.27	4.19	0.66	14.97	nr	19.16
35mm dia	5.08	6.51	0.66	14.97	nr	21.47
42mm dia	7.51	9.62	0.78	17.69	nr	27.31
54mm dia	9.01	11.54	0.90	20.41	nr	31.95
Reducing tee						
22 x 15mm dia	2.40	3.07	0.54	12.25	nr	15.32
28 x 15mm dia	3.24	4.15	0.62	14.06	nr	18.21
28 x 22mm dia	3.51	4.50	0.62	14.06	nr	18.56
35 x 15mm dia	4.75	6.08	0.62	14.06	nr	20.14
35 x 22mm dia	5.12	6.56	0.62	14.06	nr	20.62
35 x 28mm dia	5.20	6.66	0.62	14.06	nr	20.72
42 x 22mm dia	6.86	8.79	0.70	15.87	nr	24.66
42 x 28mm dia	7.11	9.11	0.70	15.87	nr	24.98
42 x 35mm dia	6.95	8.90	0.70	15.87	nr	24.78
54 x 22mm dia	8.18	10.48	0.82	18.60	nr	29.07
54 x 28mm dia	8.33	10.67	0.82	18.60	nr	29.27
54 x 35mm dia	8.58	10.99	0.82	18.60	nr	29.59
54 x 42mm dia	9.00	11.53	0.82	18.60	nr	30.12
MECHANICAL GROOVED						
Mechanical grooved jointing system; working temperature not exceeding 82°C BS 5750; pipework complete with grooved joints; painted finish						
Grooved Joints						
65 mm	7.27	9.31	0.58	13.15	m	22.46
80 mm	7.80	9.99	0.68	15.42	m	25.41
100 mm	10.22	13.09	0.79	17.92	m	31.01
125 mm	14.31	18.33	1.02	23.13	m	41.46
150mm	17.99	23.04	1.15	26.08	m	49.12
Extra over mechanical grooved system fittings						
Couplings						
65mm	9.44	12.09	0.41	9.30	nr	21.39
80mm	9.79	12.54	0.41	9.30	nr	21.84
100mm	12.19	15.61	0.66	14.97	nr	30.58
125mm	19.58	25.08	0.68	15.42	nr	40.50
150mm	26.71	34.21	0.80	18.14	nr	52.35

T:MECHANICAL/COOLING/HEATING SYSTEMS

Item	Net Price £	Material £	Labour hours	Labour £	Unit	Total rate £
Concentric reducers						
80mm	9.50	12.17	0.59	13.38	nr	**25.55**
100mm	20.51	26.27	0.71	16.10	nr	**42.37**
125mm	90.10	115.40	0.85	19.28	nr	**134.68**
150mm	22.19	28.42	0.98	22.22	nr	**50.65**
Short radius elbow; 90°						
65mm	9.44	12.09	0.53	12.02	nr	**24.11**
80mm	9.64	12.35	0.61	13.83	nr	**26.18**
100mm	12.91	16.54	0.80	18.14	nr	**34.68**
125mm	21.29	27.27	0.90	20.41	nr	**47.68**
150mm	27.63	35.39	0.94	21.32	nr	**56.71**
Short radius elbow; 45°						
65mm	8.10	10.37	0.53	12.02	nr	**22.39**
80mm	9.09	11.64	0.61	13.83	nr	**25.48**
100mm	11.30	14.47	0.80	18.14	nr	**32.62**
125mm	19.10	24.46	0.90	20.41	nr	**44.87**
150mm	21.03	26.93	0.94	21.32	nr	**48.25**
Equal tee						
65mm	17.01	21.79	0.83	18.82	nr	**40.61**
80mm	18.02	23.08	0.93	21.09	nr	**44.17**
100mm	20.15	25.81	1.18	26.76	nr	**52.57**
125mm	53.43	68.43	1.37	31.07	nr	**99.50**
150mm	49.54	63.45	1.43	32.43	nr	**95.88**
BLACK WELDED STEEL						
Black steel pipes; butt welded joints; BS 1387: 1985; including protective painting						
Varnished; medium						
8mm dia	1.21	1.55	0.47	10.66	m	**12.21**
10mm dia	1.21	1.55	0.47	10.66	m	**12.21**
15mm dia	1.29	1.65	0.47	10.66	m	**12.31**
20mm dia	1.47	1.88	0.50	11.34	m	**13.22**
25mm dia	2.11	2.70	0.55	12.47	m	**15.18**
32mm dia	2.62	3.36	0.63	14.29	m	**17.64**
40mm dia	3.04	3.89	0.71	16.10	m	**20.00**
50mm dia	4.28	5.48	0.81	18.37	m	**23.85**
65mm dia	5.81	7.44	0.94	21.32	m	**28.76**
80mm dia	7.54	9.66	1.06	24.04	m	**33.70**
100mm dia	10.69	13.69	1.34	30.39	m	**44.08**
125mm dia	16.25	20.81	1.57	35.61	m	**56.42**
150mm dia	18.87	24.17	1.77	40.14	m	**64.31**
Varnished; heavy						
15mm dia	1.60	2.05	0.47	10.66	m	**12.71**
20mm dia	1.82	2.33	0.50	11.34	m	**13.67**
25mm dia	2.66	3.41	0.55	12.47	m	**15.88**
32mm dia	3.30	4.23	0.63	14.29	m	**18.51**
40mm dia	3.85	4.93	0.71	16.10	m	**21.03**
50mm dia	5.34	6.84	0.81	18.37	m	**25.21**
65mm dia	7.27	9.31	0.94	21.32	m	**30.63**
80mm dia	9.25	11.85	1.06	24.04	m	**35.89**
100mm dia	12.91	16.54	1.34	30.39	m	**46.92**
125mm dia	17.32	22.18	1.57	35.61	m	**57.79**
150mm dia	20.25	25.94	1.77	40.14	m	**66.08**

T:MECHANICAL/COOLING/HEATING SYSTEMS

Item	Net Price £	Material £	Labour hours	Labour £	Unit	Total rate £
T31 : LOW TEMPERATURE HOT WATER HEATING (cont'd)						
Y10 - PIPELINES (cont'd)						
BLACK WELDED STEEL (cont'd)						
Extra over black steel butt welded pipes; black steel flanges, welded and drilled; metric; BS 4504						
Welded flanges; PN6						
15mm dia	1.89	2.42	0.59	13.38	nr	**15.80**
20mm dia	1.89	2.42	0.69	15.65	nr	**18.07**
25mm dia	1.89	2.42	0.84	19.05	nr	**21.47**
32mm dia	2.03	2.60	1.00	22.68	nr	**25.28**
40mm dia	2.03	2.60	1.11	25.17	nr	**27.77**
50mm dia	2.33	2.98	1.37	31.07	nr	**34.05**
65mm dia	2.88	3.69	1.54	34.92	nr	**38.61**
80mm dia	4.16	5.33	1.67	37.87	nr	**43.20**
100mm dia	4.83	6.19	2.22	50.35	nr	**56.53**
125mm dia	8.28	10.60	2.61	59.19	nr	**69.80**
150mm dia	9.32	11.94	2.99	67.81	nr	**79.75**
Welded flanges; PN16						
15mm dia	2.25	2.88	0.59	13.38	nr	**16.26**
20mm dia	2.25	2.88	0.69	15.65	nr	**18.53**
25mm dia	2.25	2.88	0.84	19.05	nr	**21.93**
32mm dia	3.41	4.37	1.00	22.68	nr	**27.05**
40mm dia	3.41	4.37	1.11	25.17	nr	**29.54**
50mm dia	3.50	4.48	1.37	31.07	nr	**35.55**
65mm dia	4.19	5.37	1.54	34.92	nr	**40.29**
80mm dia	5.08	6.51	1.67	37.87	nr	**44.38**
100mm dia	6.29	8.06	2.22	50.35	nr	**58.40**
125mm dia	10.25	13.13	2.61	59.19	nr	**72.32**
150mm dia	11.54	14.78	2.99	67.81	nr	**82.59**
Blank flanges, slip on for welding; PN6						
15mm dia	0.96	1.23	0.48	10.89	nr	**12.12**
20mm dia	0.96	1.23	0.55	12.47	nr	**13.70**
25mm dia	0.96	1.23	0.64	14.51	nr	**15.74**
32mm dia	1.60	2.05	0.76	17.24	nr	**19.28**
40mm dia	1.64	2.10	0.84	19.05	nr	**21.15**
50mm dia	1.78	2.28	1.01	22.91	nr	**25.19**
65mm dia	2.65	3.40	1.30	29.48	nr	**32.88**
80mm dia	2.69	3.45	1.41	31.98	nr	**35.43**
100mm dia	2.84	3.64	1.78	40.37	nr	**44.01**
125mm dia	4.64	5.95	2.06	46.72	nr	**52.66**
150mm dia	5.09	6.52	2.35	53.29	nr	**59.82**
Blank flanges, slip on for welding; PN16						
15mm dia	0.88	1.13	0.48	10.89	nr	**12.01**
20mm dia	1.01	1.29	0.55	12.47	nr	**13.77**
25mm dia	1.09	1.40	0.64	14.51	nr	**15.91**
32mm dia	2.10	2.69	0.76	17.24	nr	**19.93**
40mm dia	2.30	2.95	0.84	19.05	nr	**22.00**
50mm dia	2.66	3.41	1.01	22.91	nr	**26.31**

T:MECHANICAL/COOLING/HEATING SYSTEMS

Item	Net Price £	Material £	Labour hours	Labour £	Unit	Total rate £
65mm dia	4.18	5.35	1.30	29.48	nr	**34.84**
80mm dia	3.74	4.79	1.41	31.98	nr	**36.77**
100mm dia	5.37	6.88	1.78	40.37	nr	**47.25**
125mm dia	7.99	10.23	2.06	46.72	nr	**56.95**
150mm dia	9.38	12.01	2.35	53.29	nr	**65.31**
Extra over black steel butt welded pipes; black steel flanges, welding and drilled; imperial; BS 10						
Welded flanges; Table E						
1/2" dia	3.23	4.14	0.59	13.38	nr	**17.52**
3/4" dia	3.23	4.14	0.69	15.65	nr	**19.79**
1" dia	3.23	4.14	0.84	19.05	nr	**23.19**
1 1/4" dia	3.23	4.14	1.00	22.68	nr	**26.82**
1 1/2" dia	3.23	4.14	1.11	25.17	nr	**29.31**
2" dia	3.23	4.14	1.37	31.07	nr	**35.21**
2 1/2" dia	3.99	5.11	1.54	34.92	nr	**40.04**
3" dia	4.07	5.21	1.67	37.87	nr	**43.09**
4" dia	6.07	7.77	2.22	50.35	nr	**58.12**
5" dia	13.29	17.02	2.61	59.19	nr	**76.21**
6" dia	14.80	18.96	2.99	67.81	nr	**86.76**
Blank flanges, slip on for welding; Table E						
1/2" dia.	3.78	4.84	0.48	10.89	nr	**15.73**
3/4" dia	3.78	4.84	0.55	12.47	nr	**17.31**
1" dia	3.78	4.84	0.64	14.51	nr	**19.36**
1 1/4" dia	4.77	6.11	0.76	17.24	nr	**23.35**
1 1/2" dia	5.19	6.65	0.84	19.05	nr	**25.70**
2" dia	5.73	7.34	1.01	22.91	nr	**30.24**
2 1/2" dia	6.60	8.45	1.30	29.48	nr	**37.94**
3" dia	7.80	9.99	1.41	31.98	nr	**41.97**
4" dia	11.34	14.52	1.78	40.37	nr	**54.89**
5" dia	18.09	23.17	2.06	46.72	nr	**69.89**
6" dia	25.92	33.20	2.35	53.29	nr	**86.49**
Extra over black steel butt welded pipes; black steel flange connections						
Bolted connection between pair of flanges; including gasket, bolts, nuts and washers						
50mm dia	14.82	18.98	0.50	11.34	nr	**30.32**
65mm dia	18.53	23.73	0.50	11.34	nr	**35.07**
80mm dia	21.88	28.02	0.50	11.34	nr	**39.36**
100mm dia	26.24	33.61	0.50	11.34	nr	**44.95**
125mm dia	47.63	61.00	0.50	11.34	nr	**72.34**
150mm dia	50.35	64.49	0.88	19.96	nr	**84.44**
Extra over fittings; BS 1965; butt welded						
Cap						
25mm dia	7.32	9.38	0.47	10.66	nr	**20.03**
32mm dia	7.32	9.38	0.59	13.38	nr	**22.76**
40mm dia	7.32	9.38	0.70	15.87	nr	**25.25**
50mm dia	8.69	11.13	0.99	22.45	nr	**33.58**
65mm dia	10.15	13.00	1.35	30.62	nr	**43.62**
80mm dia	10.32	13.22	1.66	37.65	nr	**50.86**
100mm dia	13.41	17.18	2.23	50.57	nr	**67.75**
125mm dia	18.99	24.32	3.03	68.72	nr	**93.04**
150mm dia	21.74	27.84	3.79	85.95	nr	**113.80**

T:MECHANICAL/COOLING/HEATING SYSTEMS

Item	Net Price £	Material £	Labour hours	Labour £	Unit	Total rate £
T31 : LOW TEMPERATURE HOT WATER HEATING (cont'd)						
Y10 - PIPELINES (cont'd)						
BLACK WELDED STEEL (cont'd)						
Fittings; butt welded (cont'd)						
Concentric reducer						
20 x 15mm dia	4.47	5.73	0.69	15.65	nr	21.37
25 x 15mm dia	4.28	5.48	0.87	19.73	nr	25.21
25 x 20mm dia	5.56	7.12	0.87	19.73	nr	26.85
32 x 25mm dia	6.08	7.79	1.08	24.49	nr	32.28
40 x 25mm dia	7.92	10.14	1.38	31.30	nr	41.44
40 x 32mm dia	5.41	6.93	1.38	31.30	nr	38.23
50 x 25mm dia	6.51	8.34	1.82	41.27	nr	49.61
50 x 40mm dia	5.18	6.63	1.82	41.27	nr	47.91
65 x 50mm dia	6.45	8.26	2.52	57.15	nr	65.41
80 x 50mm dia	6.54	8.38	3.24	73.48	nr	81.85
100 x 50mm dia	10.88	13.94	4.08	92.53	nr	106.46
100 x 80mm dia	7.43	9.52	4.08	92.53	nr	102.04
125 x 80mm dia	16.38	20.98	4.71	106.82	nr	127.79
150 x 100mm dia	17.65	22.61	5.33	120.88	nr	143.48
Eccentric reducer						
20 x 15mm dia	6.63	8.49	0.69	15.65	nr	24.14
25 x 15mm dia	8.74	11.19	0.87	19.73	nr	30.92
25 x 20mm dia	7.30	9.35	0.87	19.73	nr	29.08
32 x 25mm dia	8.27	10.59	1.08	24.49	nr	35.08
40 x 25mm dia	10.18	13.04	1.38	31.30	nr	44.33
40 x 32mm dia	9.73	12.46	1.38	31.30	nr	43.76
50 x 25mm dia	12.52	16.04	1.82	41.27	nr	57.31
50 x 40mm dia	8.20	10.50	1.82	41.27	nr	51.78
65 x 50mm dia	8.75	11.21	2.52	57.15	nr	68.36
80 x 50mm dia	10.67	13.67	3.24	73.48	nr	87.14
100 x 50mm dia	18.14	23.23	4.08	92.53	nr	115.76
100 x 80mm dia	13.30	17.03	4.08	92.53	nr	109.56
125 x 80mm dia	35.81	45.87	4.71	106.82	nr	152.68
150 x 100mm dia	27.02	34.61	5.33	120.88	nr	155.48
45° elbow, long radius						
15mm dia	2.98	3.82	0.56	12.70	nr	16.52
20mm dia	2.98	3.82	0.75	17.01	nr	20.83
25mm dia	2.76	3.54	0.93	21.09	nr	24.63
32mm dia	3.02	3.87	1.17	26.53	nr	30.40
40mm dia	2.79	3.57	1.46	33.11	nr	36.68
50mm dia	3.73	4.78	1.97	44.68	nr	49.45
65mm dia	4.85	6.21	2.70	61.23	nr	67.44
80mm dia	4.70	6.02	3.32	75.29	nr	81.31
100mm dia	7.24	9.27	4.09	92.75	nr	102.03
125mm dia	13.89	17.79	4.94	112.03	nr	129.82
150mm dia	18.73	23.99	5.78	131.08	nr	155.07
90° elbow, long radius						
15mm dia	2.98	3.82	0.56	12.70	nr	16.52
20mm dia	2.98	3.82	0.75	17.01	nr	20.83
25mm dia	2.76	3.54	0.93	21.09	nr	24.63
32mm dia	3.02	3.87	1.17	26.53	nr	30.40
40mm dia	2.79	3.57	1.46	33.11	nr	36.68

T:MECHANICAL/COOLING/HEATING SYSTEMS

Item	Net Price £	Material £	Labour hours	Labour £	Unit	Total rate £
50mm dia	3.73	4.78	1.97	44.68	nr	**49.45**
65mm dia	4.85	6.21	2.70	61.23	nr	**67.44**
80mm dia	5.53	7.08	3.32	75.29	nr	**82.38**
100mm dia	8.52	10.91	4.09	92.75	nr	**103.67**
125mm dia	16.34	20.93	4.94	112.03	nr	**132.96**
150mm dia	22.04	28.23	5.78	131.08	nr	**159.31**
Equal tee						
15mm dia	16.83	21.56	0.82	18.60	nr	**40.15**
20mm dia	16.83	21.56	1.10	24.95	nr	**46.50**
25mm dia	16.83	21.56	1.35	30.62	nr	**52.17**
32mm dia	16.83	21.56	1.63	36.97	nr	**58.52**
40mm dia	16.83	21.56	2.14	48.53	nr	**70.09**
50mm dia	17.72	22.70	3.02	68.49	nr	**91.18**
65mm dia	25.69	32.90	3.61	81.87	nr	**114.77**
80mm dia	25.89	33.16	4.18	94.80	nr	**127.96**
100mm dia	32.21	41.25	5.24	118.83	nr	**160.09**
125mm dia	73.74	94.45	6.70	151.95	nr	**246.39**
150mm dia	80.54	103.15	8.45	191.63	nr	**294.79**
Extra over black steel butt welded pipes; labour						
Made bend						
15mm dia	-	-	0.42	9.52	nr	**9.52**
20mm dia	-	-	0.42	9.52	nr	**9.52**
25mm dia	-	-	0.50	11.34	nr	**11.34**
32mm dia	-	-	0.62	14.06	nr	**14.06**
40mm dia	-	-	0.74	16.78	nr	**16.78**
50mm dia	-	-	0.89	20.18	nr	**20.18**
65mm dia	-	-	1.05	23.81	nr	**23.81**
80mm dia	-	-	1.13	25.63	nr	**25.63**
100mm dia	-	-	2.90	65.77	nr	**65.77**
125mm dia	-	-	3.56	80.74	nr	**80.74**
150mm dia	-	-	4.18	94.80	nr	**94.80**
Splay cut end						
15mm dia	-	-	0.14	3.18	nr	**3.18**
20mm dia	-	-	0.16	3.63	nr	**3.63**
25mm dia	-	-	0.18	4.08	nr	**4.08**
32mm dia	-	-	0.25	5.67	nr	**5.67**
40mm dia	-	-	0.27	6.12	nr	**6.12**
50mm dia	-	-	0.31	7.03	nr	**7.03**
65mm dia	-	-	0.35	7.94	nr	**7.94**
80mm dia	-	-	0.40	9.07	nr	**9.07**
100mm dia	-	-	0.48	10.89	nr	**10.89**
125mm dia	-	-	0.56	12.70	nr	**12.70**
150mm dia	-	-	0.64	14.51	nr	**14.51**

T:MECHANICAL/COOLING/HEATING SYSTEMS

Item	Net Price £	Material £	Labour hours	Labour £	Unit	Total rate £
T31 : LOW TEMPERATURE HOT WATER HEATING (cont'd)						
Y10 - PIPELINES (cont'd)						
BLACK WELDED STEEL (cont'd)						
Black steel butt welded pipes; labour; (cont'd)						
Screwed joint to fitting						
15mm dia	-	-	0.30	6.80	nr	6.80
20mm dia	-	-	0.40	9.07	nr	9.07
25mm dia	-	-	0.46	10.43	nr	10.43
32mm dia	-	-	0.53	12.02	nr	12.02
40mm dia	-	-	0.61	13.83	nr	13.83
50mm dia	-	-	0.73	16.56	nr	16.56
65mm dia	-	-	0.89	20.18	nr	20.18
80mm dia	-	-	1.05	23.81	nr	23.81
100mm dia	-	-	1.46	33.11	nr	33.11
125mm dia	-	-	2.10	47.62	nr	47.62
150mm dia	-	-	2.73	61.91	nr	61.91
Straight butt weld						
15mm dia	-	-	0.31	7.03	nr	7.03
20mm dia	-	-	0.42	9.52	nr	9.52
25mm dia	-	-	0.52	11.79	nr	11.79
32mm dia	-	-	0.69	15.65	nr	15.65
40mm dia	-	-	0.83	18.82	nr	18.82
50mm dia	-	-	1.22	27.67	nr	27.67
65mm dia	-	-	1.57	35.61	nr	35.61
80mm dia	-	-	1.95	44.22	nr	44.22
100mm dia	-	-	2.38	53.97	nr	53.97
125mm dia	-	-	2.83	64.18	nr	64.18
150mm dia	-	-	3.27	74.16	nr	74.16
Branch weld						
15mm dia	-	-	0.48	10.89	nr	10.89
20mm dia	-	-	0.64	14.51	nr	14.51
25mm dia	-	-	0.80	18.14	nr	18.14
32mm dia	-	-	1.05	23.81	nr	23.81
40mm dia	-	-	1.18	26.76	nr	26.76
50mm dia	-	-	1.64	37.19	nr	37.19
65mm dia	-	-	2.10	47.62	nr	47.62
80mm dia	-	-	2.60	58.96	nr	58.96
100mm dia	-	-	3.18	72.12	nr	72.12
125mm dia	-	-	3.79	85.95	nr	85.95
150mm dia	-	-	4.40	99.79	nr	99.79
Welded reducing joint						
15mm dia	-	-	0.60	13.61	nr	13.61
20mm dia	-	-	0.80	18.14	nr	18.14
25mm dia	-	-	1.00	22.68	nr	22.68
32mm dia	-	-	1.32	29.94	nr	29.94
40mm dia	-	-	1.60	36.29	nr	36.29
50mm dia	-	-	2.40	54.43	nr	54.43

T:MECHANICAL/COOLING/HEATING SYSTEMS

Item	Net Price £	Material £	Labour hours	Labour £	Unit	Total rate £
65mm dia	-	-	3.21	72.80	nr	**72.80**
80mm dia	-	-	4.00	90.71	nr	**90.71**
100mm dia	-	-	4.41	100.01	nr	**100.01**
125mm dia	-	-	4.81	109.08	nr	**109.08**
150mm dia	-	-	5.21	118.15	nr	**118.15**
CARBON WELDED STEEL						
Hot finished seamless carbon steel pipe; BS 806 and BS 3601; wall thickness to BS 3600; butt welded joints; including protective painting						
Pipework						
200mm dia	29.30	37.53	2.04	46.26	m	**83.79**
250mm dia	36.54	46.80	2.54	57.60	m	**104.40**
300mm dia	40.39	51.73	2.99	67.81	m	**119.54**
350mm dia	59.63	76.37	3.52	79.83	m	**156.20**
400mm dia	132.48	169.68	4.08	92.53	m	**262.21**
Extra over fittings; BS 1965 part 1; butt welded						
Cap						
200mm dia	31.52	40.37	3.70	83.91	nr	**124.28**
250mm dia	60.85	77.94	4.73	107.27	nr	**185.20**
300mm dia	67.87	86.93	5.65	128.13	nr	**215.06**
350mm dia	68.31	87.49	6.68	151.49	nr	**238.98**
400mm dia	81.31	104.14	7.70	174.62	nr	**278.76**
Concentric reducer						
200mm x 150mm dia	32.79	42.00	7.27	164.87	nr	**206.87**
250mm x 150mm dia	50.24	64.35	9.05	205.24	nr	**269.59**
250mm x 200mm dia	30.75	39.38	9.10	206.37	nr	**245.76**
300mm x 150mm dia	105.47	135.08	10.75	243.79	nr	**378.88**
300mm x 200mm dia	60.10	76.98	10.75	243.79	nr	**320.77**
300mm x 250mm dia	53.42	68.42	11.15	252.86	nr	**321.28**
350mm x 200mm dia	97.35	124.68	12.50	283.48	nr	**408.16**
350mm x 250mm dia	90.22	115.55	12.70	288.02	nr	**403.57**
350mm x 300mm dia	86.12	110.30	13.00	294.82	nr	**405.12**
400mm x 250mm dia	181.64	232.64	14.46	327.93	nr	**560.57**
400mm x 300mm dia	151.41	193.92	14.51	329.06	nr	**522.99**
400mm x 350mm dia	124.79	159.83	15.16	343.80	nr	**503.63**
Eccentric reducer						
200mm x 150mm dia	60.01	76.86	7.27	164.87	nr	**241.73**
250mm x 150mm dia	83.37	106.78	9.05	205.24	nr	**312.02**
250mm x 200mm dia	54.55	69.87	9.10	206.37	nr	**276.24**
300mm x 150mm dia	121.02	155.00	10.75	243.79	nr	**398.79**
300mm x 200mm dia	115.36	147.75	10.75	243.79	nr	**391.54**
300mm x 250mm dia	92.86	118.93	11.15	252.86	nr	**371.80**
350mm x 200mm dia	150.06	192.20	12.50	283.48	nr	**475.68**
350mm x 250mm dia	126.21	161.65	12.70	288.02	nr	**449.66**
350mm x 300mm dia	120.49	154.32	13.00	294.82	nr	**449.14**
400mm x 250mm dia	253.17	324.26	14.46	327.93	nr	**652.19**
400mm x 300mm dia	210.01	268.98	14.51	329.06	nr	**598.04**
400mm x 350mm dia	200.46	256.75	15.16	343.80	nr	**600.55**

T:MECHANICAL/COOLING/HEATING SYSTEMS

Item	Net Price £	Material £	Labour hours	Labour £	Unit	Total rate £
T31 : LOW TEMPERATURE HOT WATER HEATING (cont'd)						
Y10 - PIPELINES (cont'd)						
CARBON WELDED STEEL (cont'd)						
Fittings; butt welded (cont'd)						
45° elbow						
200mm dia	33.13	42.43	7.75	175.76	nr	**218.19**
250mm dia	62.23	79.70	10.05	227.92	nr	**307.62**
300mm dia	91.76	117.53	12.20	276.68	nr	**394.20**
350mm dia	145.22	186.00	14.65	332.24	nr	**518.23**
400mm dia	185.47	237.55	17.12	388.25	nr	**625.80**
90° elbow						
200mm dia	38.07	48.76	7.75	175.76	nr	**224.52**
250mm dia	73.95	94.71	10.05	227.92	nr	**322.63**
300mm dia	107.95	138.26	12.20	276.68	nr	**414.94**
350mm dia	199.35	255.33	14.65	332.24	nr	**587.56**
400mm dia	238.40	305.34	17.12	388.25	nr	**693.59**
Equal tee						
200mm dia	102.99	131.91	11.25	255.13	nr	**387.04**
250mm dia	176.59	226.17	14.53	329.52	nr	**555.69**
300mm dia	250.76	321.17	17.55	398.01	nr	**719.18**
350mm dia	271.49	347.72	20.98	475.79	nr	**823.51**
400mm dia	464.42	594.82	24.38	552.90	nr	**1147.72**
Extra over black steel butt welded pipes; labour						
Straight butt weld						
200mm dia	-	-	4.08	92.53	nr	**92.53**
250mm dia	-	-	5.20	117.93	nr	**117.93**
300mm dia	-	-	6.22	141.06	nr	**141.06**
350mm dia	-	-	7.33	166.23	nr	**166.23**
400mm dia	-	-	8.41	190.73	nr	**190.73**
Branch weld						
100mm dia	-	-	3.46	78.47	nr	**78.47**
125mm dia	-	-	4.23	95.93	nr	**95.93**
150mm dia	-	-	5.00	113.39	nr	**113.39**
Extra over black steel butt welded pipes; black steel flanges, welding and drilled; metric; BS 4504						
Welded flanges; PN16						
200mm dia	15.38	19.70	4.10	92.98	nr	**112.68**
250mm dia	27.48	35.20	5.33	120.88	nr	**156.07**
300mm dia	32.18	41.22	6.40	145.14	nr	**186.36**
350mm dia	61.49	78.76	7.43	168.50	nr	**247.26**
400mm dia	80.33	102.89	8.45	191.63	nr	**294.52**
Welded flanges; PN25						
200mm dia	58.62	75.08	4.10	92.98	nr	**168.06**
250mm dia	70.27	90.00	5.33	120.88	nr	**210.88**
300mm dia	95.03	121.71	6.40	145.14	nr	**266.86**

T:MECHANICAL/COOLING/HEATING SYSTEMS

Item	Net Price £	Material £	Labour hours	Labour £	Unit	Total rate £
Blank flanges, slip on for welding; PN16						
200mm dia	37.17	47.61	2.70	61.23	nr	**108.84**
250mm dia	53.16	68.09	3.48	78.92	nr	**147.01**
300mm dia	74.19	95.02	4.20	95.25	nr	**190.27**
350mm dia	124.86	159.92	4.78	108.40	nr	**268.32**
400mm dia	151.82	194.45	5.35	121.33	nr	**315.78**
Blank flanges, slip on for welding; PN25						
200mm dia	123.20	157.79	2.70	61.23	nr	**219.02**
250mm dia	183.18	234.62	3.48	78.92	nr	**313.54**
300mm dia	252.64	323.58	4.20	95.25	nr	**418.83**
Extra over black steel butt welded pipes; black steel flange connections						
Bolted connection between pair of flanges; including gasket, bolts, nuts and washers						
200mm dia	44.81	57.39	3.83	86.86	nr	**144.25**
250mm dia	74.34	95.21	4.93	111.80	nr	**207.02**
300mm dia	85.91	110.03	5.90	133.80	nr	**243.84**
PLASTIC PIPEWORK						
Polypropylene PP-R 80 pipe, mechanically stabilised by fibre compound mixture in middle layer; suitable for continuous working temperatures of 0-90 degress C; thermally fused joints in the running length						
Pipe; 4m long; PN 20						
20mm dia	2.67	3.42	0.35	7.94	m	**11.36**
25mm dia	4.08	5.23	0.39	8.84	m	**14.07**
32mm dia	6.35	8.13	0.43	9.75	m	**17.88**
40mm dia	9.68	12.40	0.47	10.66	m	**23.06**
50mm dia	15.26	19.54	0.51	11.57	m	**31.11**
63mm dia	23.52	30.12	0.52	11.79	m	**41.92**
75mm dia	32.94	42.19	0.60	13.61	m	**55.80**
90mm dia	51.15	65.51	0.69	15.65	m	**81.16**
110mm dia	76.14	97.52	0.69	15.65	m	**113.17**
125mm dia	97.33	124.66	0.85	19.28	m	**143.94**
Extra over fittings; thermally fused joints						
Overbridge bow						
20mm dia	1.82	2.33	0.51	11.57	nr	**13.90**
25mm dia	2.11	2.70	0.56	12.70	nr	**15.40**
32mm dia	2.61	3.34	0.65	14.74	nr	**18.08**

T:MECHANICAL/COOLING/HEATING SYSTEMS

Item	Net Price £	Material £	Labour hours	Labour £	Unit	Total rate £
T31 : LOW TEMPERATURE HOT WATER HEATING (cont'd)						
Y10 - PIPELINES (cont'd)						
PLASTIC PIPEWORK (cont'd)						
Fittings; thermally fused joints (cont'd)						
Elbow 90°						
20mm dia	0.43	0.55	0.44	9.98	nr	10.53
25mm dia	0.58	0.74	0.52	11.79	nr	12.54
32mm dia	0.82	1.05	0.59	13.38	nr	14.43
40mm dia	1.26	1.61	0.66	14.97	nr	16.58
50mm dia	2.75	3.52	0.73	16.56	nr	20.08
63mm dia	4.21	5.39	0.85	19.28	nr	24.67
75mm dia	9.30	11.91	0.85	19.28	nr	31.19
90mm dia	17.17	21.99	1.04	23.59	nr	45.58
110mm dia	24.43	31.29	1.04	23.59	nr	54.88
125mm dia	37.63	48.20	1.30	29.48	nr	77.68
Long bend 90°						
20mm dia	1.66	2.13	0.48	10.89	nr	13.01
25mm dia	1.73	2.22	0.57	12.93	nr	15.14
32mm dia	2.03	2.60	0.65	14.74	nr	17.34
40mm dia	3.71	4.75	0.73	16.56	nr	21.31
Elbow 90°, female/male						
20mm dia	0.54	0.69	0.44	9.98	nr	10.67
25mm dia	0.67	0.86	0.52	11.79	nr	12.65
32mm dia	1.01	1.29	0.59	13.38	nr	14.67
Elbow 45°						
20mm dia	0.43	0.55	0.44	9.98	nr	10.53
25mm dia	0.58	0.74	0.52	11.79	nr	12.54
32mm dia	0.82	1.05	0.59	13.38	nr	14.43
40mm dia	1.26	1.61	0.66	14.97	nr	16.58
50mm dia	2.75	3.52	0.73	16.56	nr	20.08
63mm dia	4.21	5.39	0.85	19.28	nr	24.67
75mm dia	9.30	11.91	0.85	19.28	nr	31.19
90mm dia	17.18	22.00	1.04	23.59	nr	45.59
110mm dia	24.43	31.29	1.04	23.59	nr	54.88
125mm dia	37.63	48.20	1.30	29.48	nr	77.68
Elbow 45°, female/male						
20mm dia	0.67	0.86	0.44	9.98	nr	10.84
25mm dia	0.78	1.00	0.52	11.79	nr	12.79
32mm dia	1.57	2.01	0.59	13.38	nr	15.39
T-Piece 90°						
20mm dia	0.59	0.76	0.61	13.83	nr	14.59
25mm dia	0.80	1.02	0.72	16.33	nr	17.35
32mm dia	1.06	1.36	0.83	18.82	nr	20.18
40mm dia	1.60	2.05	0.92	20.86	nr	22.91
50mm dia	4.56	5.84	1.01	22.91	nr	28.75
63mm dia	6.56	8.40	1.11	25.17	nr	33.57
75mm dia	10.93	14.00	1.18	26.76	nr	40.76
90mm dia	20.10	25.74	1.46	33.11	nr	58.85
110mm dia	31.38	40.19	1.46	33.11	nr	73.30
125mm dia	41.68	53.38	1.82	41.27	nr	94.66

T:MECHANICAL/COOLING/HEATING SYSTEMS

Item	Net Price £	Material £	Labour hours	Labour £	Unit	Total rate £
T-Piece 90° reducing						
25 x 20 x 25mm	0.82	1.05	0.72	16.33	nr	**17.38**
32 x 20 x 32mm	1.06	1.36	0.83	18.82	nr	**20.18**
32 x 25 x 32mm	1.06	1.36	0.83	18.82	nr	**20.18**
40 x 20 x 40mm	1.60	2.05	0.92	20.86	nr	**22.91**
40 x 25 x 40mm	1.60	2.05	0.92	20.86	nr	**22.91**
40 x 32 x 40mm	1.60	2.05	0.92	20.86	nr	**22.91**
50 x 25 x 50mm	4.56	5.84	1.01	22.91	nr	**28.75**
50 x 32 x 50mm	4.56	5.84	1.01	22.91	nr	**28.75**
50 x 40 x 50mm	4.56	5.84	1.01	22.91	nr	**28.75**
63 x 20 x 63mm	6.18	7.92	1.11	25.17	nr	**33.09**
63 x 25 x 63mm	6.18	7.92	1.11	25.17	nr	**33.09**
63 x 32 x 63mm	6.18	7.92	1.11	25.17	nr	**33.09**
63 x 40 x 63mm	6.18	7.92	1.01	22.91	nr	**30.82**
63 x 50 x 63mm	6.18	7.92	1.01	22.91	nr	**30.82**
75 x 20 x 75mm	10.02	12.83	1.18	26.76	nr	**39.59**
75 x 25 x 75mm	10.02	12.83	1.18	26.76	nr	**39.59**
75 x 32 x 75mm	10.02	12.83	1.18	26.76	nr	**39.59**
75 x 40 x 75mm	10.02	12.83	1.18	26.76	nr	**39.59**
75 x 50 x 75mm	10.02	12.83	1.18	26.76	nr	**39.59**
75 x 63 x 75mm	10.02	12.83	1.18	26.76	nr	**39.59**
32 x 32 x 25mm	1.06	1.36	0.83	18.82	nr	**20.18**
25 x 20 x 20mm	0.82	1.05	0.72	16.33	nr	**17.38**
20 x 25 x 25mm	0.82	1.05	0.72	16.33	nr	**17.38**
32 x 20 x 25mm	1.06	1.36	0.72	16.33	nr	**17.69**
32 x 25 x 25mm	1.06	1.36	0.72	16.33	nr	**17.69**
90 x 63 x 90mm	20.10	25.74	1.46	33.11	nr	**58.85**
110 x 75 x 110mm	31.38	40.19	1.46	33.11	nr	**73.30**
110 x 90 x 110mm	31.38	40.19	1.46	33.11	nr	**73.30**
125 x 75 x 125mm	41.12	52.67	1.82	41.27	nr	**93.94**
125 x 90 x 125mm	42.19	54.04	1.82	41.27	nr	**95.31**
125 x 110 x 125mm	43.02	55.10	1.82	41.27	nr	**96.37**
Reducer						
25 x 20mm	0.46	0.59	0.59	13.38	nr	**13.97**
32 x 20mm	0.61	0.78	0.62	14.06	nr	**14.84**
32 x 25mm	0.61	0.78	0.62	14.06	nr	**14.84**
40 x 20mm	0.94	1.20	0.66	14.97	nr	**16.17**
40 x 25mm	0.94	1.20	0.66	14.97	nr	**16.17**
40 x 32mm	0.94	1.20	0.66	14.97	nr	**16.17**
50 x 20mm	1.55	1.99	0.73	16.56	nr	**18.54**
50 x 25mm	1.55	1.99	0.73	16.56	nr	**18.54**
50 x 32mm	1.55	1.99	0.73	16.56	nr	**18.54**
50 x 40mm	1.55	1.99	0.73	16.56	nr	**18.54**
63 x 40mm	3.12	4.00	0.78	17.69	nr	**21.69**
63 x 25mm	3.12	4.00	0.78	17.69	nr	**21.69**
63 x 32mm	3.12	4.00	0.78	17.69	nr	**21.69**
63 x 50mm	3.12	4.00	0.78	17.69	nr	**21.69**
75 x 50mm	3.49	4.47	0.85	19.28	nr	**23.75**
75 x 63mm	3.49	4.47	0.85	19.28	nr	**23.75**
90 x 63mm	7.76	9.94	1.04	23.59	nr	**33.52**
90 x 75mm	7.76	9.94	1.04	23.59	nr	**33.52**
110 x 90mm	12.53	16.05	1.17	26.53	nr	**42.58**
125 x 110mm	19.58	25.08	1.43	32.43	nr	**57.51**

T:MECHANICAL/COOLING/HEATING SYSTEMS

Item	Net Price £	Material £	Labour hours	Labour £	Unit	Total rate £
T31 : LOW TEMPERATURE HOT WATER HEATING (cont'd)						
Y10 - PIPELINES (cont'd)						
PLASTIC PIPEWORK (cont'd)						
Fittings; thermally fused joints (cont'd)						
Socket						
20mm dia	0.42	0.54	0.51	11.57	nr	**12.10**
25mm dia	0.46	0.59	0.56	12.70	nr	**13.29**
32mm dia	0.61	0.78	0.65	14.74	nr	**15.52**
40mm dia	0.99	1.27	0.74	16.78	nr	**18.05**
50mm dia	1.55	1.99	0.81	18.37	nr	**20.35**
63mm dia	3.12	4.00	0.86	19.50	nr	**23.50**
75mm dia	3.49	4.47	0.91	20.64	nr	**25.11**
90mm dia	8.96	11.48	0.91	20.64	nr	**32.11**
110mm dia	15.23	19.51	0.91	20.64	nr	**40.14**
125mm dia	21.26	27.23	1.30	29.48	nr	**56.71**
End Cap						
20mm dia	0.66	0.85	0.25	5.67	nr	**6.51**
25mm dia	0.80	1.02	0.29	6.58	nr	**7.60**
32mm dia	0.99	1.27	0.33	7.48	nr	**8.75**
40mm dia	1.58	2.02	0.36	8.16	nr	**10.19**
50mm dia	2.18	2.79	0.40	9.07	nr	**11.86**
63mm dia	3.68	4.71	0.44	9.98	nr	**14.69**
75mm dia	5.33	6.83	0.47	10.66	nr	**17.49**
90mm dia	12.05	15.43	0.57	12.93	nr	**28.36**
110mm dia	14.48	18.55	0.57	12.93	nr	**31.47**
125mm dia	22.05	28.24	0.85	19.28	nr	**47.52**
Stub flange with gasket						
32mm dia	1.78	2.28	0.23	5.22	nr	**7.50**
40mm dia	2.08	2.66	0.27	6.12	nr	**8.79**
50mm dia	3.28	4.20	0.38	8.62	nr	**12.82**
63mm dia	3.70	4.74	0.43	9.75	nr	**14.49**
75mm dia	5.18	6.63	0.48	10.89	nr	**17.52**
90mm dia	10.51	13.46	0.53	12.02	nr	**25.48**
110mm dia	15.70	20.11	0.53	12.02	nr	**32.13**
125mm dia	39.97	51.19	0.75	17.01	nr	**68.20**
Weld in saddle with female thread						
40 - 1/2"	4.21	5.39	0.36	8.16	nr	**13.56**
50 - 1/2"	4.21	5.39	0.36	8.16	nr	**13.56**
63 - 1/2"	4.21	5.39	0.40	9.07	nr	**14.46**
75 - 1/2"	4.21	5.39	0.40	9.07	nr	**14.46**
90 - 1/2"	4.21	5.39	0.46	10.43	nr	**15.82**
110 - 1/2"	4.21	5.39	0.46	10.43	nr	**15.82**
Weld in saddle with male thread						
50 - 1/2"	4.21	5.39	0.36	8.16	nr	**13.56**
63 - 1/2"	4.21	5.39	0.40	9.07	nr	**14.46**
75 - 1/2"	4.21	5.39	0.40	9.07	nr	**14.46**
90 - 1/2"	4.21	5.39	0.46	10.43	nr	**15.82**
110 - 1/2"	4.21	5.39	0.46	10.43	nr	**15.82**

T:MECHANICAL/COOLING/HEATING SYSTEMS

Item	Net Price £	Material £	Labour hours	Labour £	Unit	Total rate £
Transition piece, round with female thread						
20 x 1/2"	3.38	4.33	0.29	6.58	nr	**10.91**
20 x 3/4"	3.92	5.02	0.29	6.58	nr	**11.60**
25 x 1/2"	3.92	5.02	0.33	7.48	nr	**12.50**
25 x 3/4"	3.92	5.02	0.33	7.48	nr	**12.50**
Transition piece, hexagon with female thread						
32 x 1"	6.88	8.81	0.36	8.16	nr	**16.98**
40 x 1 1/4"	10.87	13.92	0.36	8.16	nr	**22.09**
50 x 1 1/2"	11.24	14.40	0.36	8.16	nr	**22.56**
63 x 2"	19.55	25.04	0.40	9.07	nr	**34.11**
75 x 2"	20.40	26.13	0.40	9.07	nr	**35.20**
125 x 5"	112.82	144.50	0.51	11.57	nr	**156.06**
Stop valve for surface assembly						
20mm dia	8.62	11.04	0.25	5.67	nr	**16.71**
25mm dia	8.75	11.21	0.29	6.58	nr	**17.78**
32mm dia	14.80	18.96	0.33	7.48	nr	**26.44**
Ball valve						
20mm dia	16.16	20.70	0.25	5.67	nr	**26.37**
25mm dia	18.19	23.30	0.29	6.58	nr	**29.87**
32mm dia	22.21	28.45	0.33	7.48	nr	**35.93**
40mm dia	33.61	43.05	0.36	8.16	nr	**51.21**
50mm dia	51.36	65.78	0.40	9.07	nr	**74.85**
63mm dia	82.15	105.22	0.44	9.98	nr	**115.20**
FIXINGS						
For steel pipes; black malleable iron						
Single pipe bracket, screw on, black malleable iron; screwed to wood						
15mm dia	0.62	0.79	0.14	3.18	nr	**3.97**
20mm dia	0.70	0.90	0.14	3.18	nr	**4.07**
25mm dia	0.80	1.02	0.17	3.86	nr	**4.88**
32mm dia	1.10	1.41	0.19	4.31	nr	**5.72**
40mm dia	1.46	1.87	0.22	4.99	nr	**6.86**
50mm dia	1.95	2.50	0.22	4.99	nr	**7.49**
65mm dia	2.57	3.29	0.28	6.35	nr	**9.64**
80mm dia	3.52	4.51	0.32	7.26	nr	**11.77**
100mm dia	5.13	6.57	0.35	7.94	nr	**14.51**
Single pipe bracket, screw on, black malleable iron; plugged and screwed						
15mm dia	0.62	0.79	0.25	5.67	nr	**6.46**
20mm dia	0.70	0.90	0.25	5.67	nr	**6.57**
25mm dia	0.80	1.02	0.30	6.80	nr	**7.83**
32mm dia	1.10	1.41	0.32	7.26	nr	**8.67**
40mm dia	1.46	1.87	0.32	7.26	nr	**9.13**
50mm dia	1.95	2.50	0.32	7.26	nr	**9.75**
65mm dia	2.57	3.29	0.35	7.94	nr	**11.23**
80mm dia	3.52	4.51	0.42	9.52	nr	**14.03**
100mm dia	5.13	6.57	0.42	9.52	nr	**16.10**

T:MECHANICAL/COOLING/HEATING SYSTEMS

Item	Net Price £	Material £	Labour hours	Labour £	Unit	Total rate £
T31 : LOW TEMPERATURE HOT WATER HEATING (cont'd)						
Y10 - PIPELINES (cont'd)						
FIXINGS (cont'd)						
For steel pipes; black malleable (cont'd)						
Single pipe bracket for building in, black malleable iron						
15mm dia	1.40	1.79	0.10	2.27	nr	4.06
20mm dia	1.40	1.79	0.11	2.49	nr	4.29
25mm dia	1.40	1.79	0.12	2.72	nr	4.51
32mm dia	1.58	2.02	0.14	3.18	nr	5.20
40mm dia	1.58	2.02	0.15	3.40	nr	5.43
50mm dia	1.64	2.10	0.16	3.63	nr	5.73
Pipe ring, single socket, black malleable iron						
15mm dia	0.66	0.85	0.10	2.27	nr	3.11
20mm dia	0.73	0.94	0.11	2.49	nr	3.43
25mm dia	0.80	1.02	0.12	2.72	nr	3.75
32mm dia	0.85	1.09	0.14	3.18	nr	4.26
40mm dia	1.10	1.41	0.15	3.40	nr	4.81
50mm dia	1.39	1.78	0.16	3.63	nr	5.41
65mm dia	2.01	2.57	0.30	6.80	nr	9.38
80mm dia	2.41	3.09	0.35	7.94	nr	11.02
100mm dia	3.65	4.67	0.40	9.07	nr	13.75
125mm dia	7.39	9.47	0.60	13.61	nr	23.08
150mm dia	8.28	10.60	0.77	17.46	nr	28.07
200mm dia	11.01	14.10	0.90	20.41	nr	34.51
250mm dia	13.77	17.64	1.10	24.95	nr	42.58
300mm dia	16.53	21.17	1.25	28.35	nr	49.52
350mm dia	19.29	24.71	1.50	34.02	nr	58.72
400mm dia	22.04	28.23	1.75	39.69	nr	67.92
Pipe ring, double socket, black malleable iron						
15mm dia	0.77	0.99	0.10	2.27	nr	3.25
20mm dia	0.88	1.13	0.11	2.49	nr	3.62
25mm dia	0.99	1.27	0.12	2.72	nr	3.99
32mm dia	1.17	1.50	0.14	3.18	nr	4.67
40mm dia	1.36	1.74	0.15	3.40	nr	5.14
50mm dia	1.54	1.97	0.16	3.63	nr	5.60
Screw on backplate, black malleable iron; screwed to wood						
15mm dia	0.85	1.09	0.14	3.18	nr	4.26
Screw on backplate, black malleable iron; plugged and screwed						
15mm dia	0.85	1.09	0.25	5.67	nr	6.76

T:MECHANICAL/COOLING/HEATING SYSTEMS

Item	Net Price £	Material £	Labour hours	Labour £	Unit	Total rate £
For steel pipes; galvanised iron						
Single pipe bracket, screw on, galvanised iron; screwed to wood						
15mm dia	0.82	1.05	0.14	3.18	nr	**4.23**
20mm dia	0.91	1.17	0.14	3.18	nr	**4.34**
25mm dia	1.06	1.36	0.17	3.86	nr	**5.21**
32mm dia	1.45	1.86	0.19	4.31	nr	**6.17**
40mm dia	1.94	2.48	0.22	4.99	nr	**7.47**
50mm dia	2.56	3.28	0.22	4.99	nr	**8.27**
65mm dia	3.39	4.34	0.28	6.35	nr	**10.69**
80mm dia	4.65	5.96	0.32	7.26	nr	**13.21**
100mm dia	6.77	8.67	0.35	7.94	nr	**16.61**
Single pipe bracket, screw on, galvanised iron; plugged and screwed						
15mm dia	0.82	1.05	0.25	5.67	nr	**6.72**
20mm dia	0.91	1.17	0.25	5.67	nr	**6.84**
25mm dia	1.06	1.36	0.30	6.80	nr	**8.16**
32mm dia	1.45	1.86	0.32	7.26	nr	**9.11**
40mm dia	1.94	2.48	0.32	7.26	nr	**9.74**
50mm dia	2.56	3.28	0.32	7.26	nr	**10.54**
65mm dia	3.39	4.34	0.35	7.94	nr	**12.28**
80mm dia	4.65	5.96	0.42	9.52	nr	**15.48**
100mm dia	6.77	8.67	0.42	9.52	nr	**18.20**
Single pipe bracket for building in, galvanised iron						
15mm dia	2.02	2.59	0.10	2.27	nr	**4.86**
20mm dia	2.02	2.59	0.11	2.49	nr	**5.08**
25mm dia	2.02	2.59	0.12	2.72	nr	**5.31**
32mm dia	2.30	2.95	0.14	3.18	nr	**6.12**
40mm dia	2.33	2.98	0.15	3.40	nr	**6.39**
50mm dia	2.40	3.07	0.16	3.63	nr	**6.70**
Pipe ring, single socket, galvanised iron						
15mm dia.	0.87	1.11	0.10	2.27	nr	**3.38**
20mm dia.	0.97	1.24	0.11	2.49	nr	**3.74**
25mm dia	1.06	1.36	0.12	2.72	nr	**4.08**
32mm dia	1.12	1.43	0.15	3.40	nr	**4.84**
40mm dia	1.45	1.86	0.15	3.40	nr	**5.26**
50mm dia	1.84	2.36	0.16	3.63	nr	**5.99**
65mm dia	2.67	3.42	0.30	6.80	nr	**10.22**
80mm dia	3.19	4.09	0.35	7.94	nr	**12.02**
100mm dia	4.84	6.20	0.40	9.07	nr	**15.27**
125mm dia	9.79	12.54	0.60	13.61	nr	**26.15**
150mm dia	10.94	14.01	0.77	17.46	nr	**31.47**
Pipe ring, double socket, galvanised iron						
15mm dia	1.01	1.29	0.10	2.27	nr	**3.56**
20mm dia	1.16	1.49	0.11	2.49	nr	**3.98**
25mm dia	1.31	1.68	0.12	2.72	nr	**4.40**
32mm dia	1.55	1.99	0.14	3.18	nr	**5.16**
40mm dia	1.78	2.28	0.15	3.40	nr	**5.68**
50mm dia	2.03	2.60	0.16	3.63	nr	**6.23**

T:MECHANICAL/COOLING/HEATING SYSTEMS

Item	Net Price £	Material £	Labour hours	Labour £	Unit	Total rate £
T31 : LOW TEMPERATURE HOT WATER HEATING (cont'd)						
Y10 - PIPELINES (cont'd)						
FIXINGS (cont'd)						
For steel pipes; galvanised iron (cont'd)						
Screw on backplate, galvanised iron; screwed to wood						
15mm dia	1.12	1.43	0.14	3.18	nr	**4.61**
Screw on backplate, galvanised iron; plugged and screwed						
15mm dia	1.12	1.43	0.25	5.67	nr	**7.10**
Fabricated hangers and brackets (Note: It has been assumed there would be sufficient quantities required to gain the benefit of bulk purchase)						
Galvanised steel; including inserts, bolts, nuts, washers; fixed to backgrounds						
41 x 21mm	2.30	2.95	0.29	6.58	m	**9.52**
41 x 41mm	3.50	4.48	0.29	6.58	m	**11.06**
Threaded rods; metric thread; including nuts, washers etc						
10mm dia x 600mm long	2.45	3.14	0.18	4.08	m	**7.22**
12mm dia x 600mm long	2.50	3.20	0.18	4.08	m	**7.28**
Floor or ceiling cover plates						
Plastic						
15mm dia	0.25	0.32	0.16	3.63	nr	**3.95**
20mm dia	0.27	0.35	0.22	4.99	nr	**5.34**
25mm dia	0.31	0.40	0.22	4.99	nr	**5.39**
32mm dia	0.45	0.58	0.24	5.44	nr	**6.02**
40mm dia	0.68	0.87	0.26	5.90	nr	**6.77**
50mm dia	0.75	0.96	0.26	5.90	nr	**6.86**
Chromium plated						
15mm dia	1.66	2.13	0.16	3.63	nr	**5.75**
20mm dia	1.76	2.25	0.17	3.86	nr	**6.11**
25mm dia	1.84	2.36	0.21	4.76	nr	**7.12**
32mm dia	1.89	2.42	0.22	4.99	nr	**7.41**
40mm dia	2.11	2.70	0.26	5.90	nr	**8.60**
50mm dia	2.54	3.25	0.26	5.90	nr	**9.15**

T:MECHANICAL/COOLING/HEATING SYSTEMS

Item	Net Price £	Material £	Labour hours	Labour £	Unit	Total rate £
Pipe roller and chair						
Roller and chair; black malleable						
Up to 50mm dia	2.93	3.75	0.20	4.54	nr	**8.29**
65mm dia	2.93	3.75	0.20	4.54	nr	**8.29**
80mm dia	4.19	5.37	0.20	4.54	nr	**9.90**
100mm dia	4.50	5.76	0.20	4.54	nr	**10.30**
125mm dia	4.92	6.30	0.20	4.54	nr	**10.84**
150mm dia	5.46	6.99	0.30	6.80	nr	**13.80**
175mm dia	13.69	17.53	0.30	6.80	nr	**24.34**
200mm dia	13.69	17.53	0.30	6.80	nr	**24.34**
250mm dia	19.56	25.05	0.30	6.80	nr	**31.86**
300mm dia	20.54	26.31	0.30	6.80	nr	**33.11**
Roller and chair; galvanised						
Up to 50mm dia	4.39	5.62	0.20	4.54	nr	**10.16**
65mm dia	4.39	5.62	0.20	4.54	nr	**10.16**
80mm dia	6.28	8.04	0.20	4.54	nr	**12.58**
100mm dia	6.75	8.65	0.20	4.54	nr	**13.18**
125mm dia	7.38	9.45	0.20	4.54	nr	**13.99**
150mm dia	8.19	10.49	0.30	6.80	nr	**17.29**
175mm dia	20.54	26.31	0.30	6.80	nr	**33.11**
200mm dia	20.54	26.31	0.30	6.80	nr	**33.11**
250mm dia	29.34	37.58	0.30	6.80	nr	**44.38**
300mm dia	30.81	39.46	0.30	6.80	nr	**46.26**
Roller bracket; black malleable						
25mm dia	1.78	2.28	0.20	4.54	nr	**6.82**
32mm dia	1.87	2.40	0.20	4.54	nr	**6.93**
40mm dia	2.00	2.56	0.20	4.54	nr	**7.10**
50mm dia	2.12	2.72	0.20	4.54	nr	**7.25**
65mm dia	2.78	3.56	0.20	4.54	nr	**8.10**
80mm dia	4.01	5.14	0.20	4.54	nr	**9.67**
100mm dia	4.45	5.70	0.20	4.54	nr	**10.24**
125mm dia	7.35	9.41	0.20	4.54	nr	**13.95**
150mm dia	7.35	9.41	0.30	6.80	nr	**16.22**
175mm dia	16.38	20.98	0.30	6.80	nr	**27.78**
200mm dia	16.38	20.98	0.30	6.80	nr	**27.78**
250mm dia	21.77	27.88	0.30	6.80	nr	**34.69**
300mm dia	26.98	34.56	0.30	6.80	nr	**41.36**
350mm dia	43.37	55.55	0.30	6.80	nr	**62.35**
400mm dia	49.57	63.49	0.30	6.80	nr	**70.29**
Roller bracket; galvanised						
25mm dia	2.67	3.42	0.20	4.54	nr	**7.96**
32mm dia	2.81	3.60	0.20	4.54	nr	**8.13**
40mm dia	3.01	3.86	0.20	4.54	nr	**8.39**
50mm dia	3.17	4.06	0.20	4.54	nr	**8.60**
65mm dia	4.17	5.34	0.20	4.54	nr	**9.88**
80mm dia	6.01	7.70	0.20	4.54	nr	**12.23**
100mm dia	6.68	8.56	0.20	4.54	nr	**13.09**
125mm dia	11.03	14.13	0.20	4.54	nr	**18.66**
150mm dia	11.03	14.13	0.30	6.80	nr	**20.93**
175mm dia	24.57	31.47	0.30	6.80	nr	**38.27**
200mm dia	24.57	31.47	0.30	6.80	nr	**38.27**
250mm dia	32.66	41.83	0.30	6.80	nr	**48.63**
300mm dia	40.47	51.83	0.30	6.80	nr	**58.64**

T:MECHANICAL/COOLING/HEATING SYSTEMS

Item	Net Price £	Material £	Labour hours	Labour £	Unit	Total rate £
T31 : LOW TEMPERATURE HOT WATER HEATING (cont'd)						
Y11 - PIPELINE ANCILLARIES						
EXPANSION JOINTS						
Axial movement bellows expansion joints; stainless steel						
Screwed ends for steel pipework; up to 6 bar G at 100°C						
15mm dia	64.10	82.10	0.68	15.42	nr	97.52
20mm dia	82.41	105.55	0.81	18.37	nr	123.92
25mm dia	86.34	110.58	0.93	21.09	nr	131.67
32mm dia	103.35	132.37	1.06	24.04	nr	156.41
40mm dia	122.42	156.79	1.16	26.31	nr	183.10
50mm dia	134.74	172.57	1.19	26.99	nr	199.56
Screwed ends for steel pipework; aluminium and steel outer sleeves; up to 16 bar G at 120°C						
20mm dia	132.13	169.23	1.32	29.94	nr	199.17
25mm dia	137.36	175.93	1.52	34.47	nr	210.40
32mm dia	156.98	201.06	1.80	40.82	nr	241.88
40mm dia	175.29	224.51	2.03	46.04	nr	270.55
50mm dia	193.60	247.96	2.26	51.25	nr	299.21
Flanged ends for steel pipework; aluminium and steel outer sleeves; up to 16 bar G at 120°C						
20mm dia	251.17	321.70	0.53	12.02	nr	333.72
25mm dia	252.48	323.37	0.64	14.51	nr	337.89
32mm dia	261.63	335.09	0.74	16.78	nr	351.88
40mm dia	268.18	343.48	0.82	18.60	nr	362.08
50mm dia	277.33	355.20	0.89	20.18	nr	375.39
Flanged ends for steel pipework; up to 16 bar G at 120°C						
65mm dia	196.22	251.32	1.10	24.95	nr	276.26
80mm dia	239.39	306.61	1.31	29.71	nr	336.32
100mm dia	273.40	350.17	1.78	40.37	nr	390.54
150mm dia	412.07	527.78	3.08	69.85	nr	597.62
Screwed ends for non-ferrous pipework; up to 6 bar G at 100°C						
20mm dia	90.31	115.67	0.72	16.33	nr	132.00
25mm dia	95.39	122.17	0.84	19.05	nr	141.22
32mm dia	114.46	146.60	1.02	23.13	nr	169.73
40mm dia	132.27	169.41	1.11	25.17	nr	194.58
50mm dia	150.08	192.22	1.18	26.76	nr	218.98
Flanged ends for steel, copper or non-ferrous pipework; up to 16 bar G at 120°C						
65mm dia	259.02	331.75	0.87	19.73	nr	351.48
80mm dia	302.20	387.05	0.95	21.54	nr	408.60
100mm dia	350.59	449.03	1.15	26.08	nr	475.11
150mm dia	519.36	665.19	1.36	30.84	nr	696.03

T:MECHANICAL/COOLING/HEATING SYSTEMS

Item	Net Price £	Material £	Labour hours	Labour £	Unit	Total rate £
Angular movement bellows expansion joints; stainless steel						
Flanged ends for steel pipework; up to 16 bar G at 120°C						
50mm dia	367.79	471.06	0.71	16.10	nr	487.16
65mm dia	390.07	499.59	0.83	18.82	nr	518.42
80mm dia	461.89	591.59	0.91	20.64	nr	612.23
100mm dia	552.29	707.37	0.97	22.00	nr	729.37
125mm dia	646.40	827.90	1.16	26.31	nr	854.21
150mm dia	676.12	865.97	1.18	26.76	nr	892.73
Universal lateral movement bellows expansion joints; stainless steel						
Flanged ends for steel pipework; up to 16 bar G at 120°C						
50mm dia	517.62	662.96	0.89	20.18	nr	683.15
65mm dia	541.15	693.10	1.10	24.95	nr	718.05
80mm dia	586.96	751.77	1.31	29.71	nr	781.48
100mm dia	700.89	897.69	1.78	40.37	nr	938.06
125mm dia	1139.25	1459.14	3.06	69.40	nr	1528.54
150mm dia	1287.85	1649.47	3.08	69.85	nr	1719.32
Universal movement expansion joints; reinforced neoprene flexible connector						
Spherical expansion joints; flanged to BS 10, Table E; up to 10 bar at 100°C						
40mm dia	116.40	149.08	0.82	18.60	nr	167.68
50mm dia	118.87	152.25	0.89	20.18	nr	172.44
65mm dia	128.79	164.95	1.10	24.95	nr	189.90
80mm dia	147.36	188.74	1.31	29.71	nr	218.45
100mm dia	174.60	223.63	1.78	40.37	nr	263.99
150mm dia	250.14	320.37	3.08	69.85	nr	390.22
Hose connector; BSP threaded union ends; up to 8 bar at 100°C						
20mm dia	30.96	39.65	1.32	29.94	nr	69.59
25mm dia	42.10	53.92	1.52	34.47	nr	88.39
32mm dia	47.06	60.27	1.80	40.82	nr	101.09
40mm dia	61.92	79.31	2.03	46.04	nr	125.35
50mm dia	80.49	103.10	2.26	51.25	nr	154.35
VALVES						
Isolating valves						
Bronze gate valve; non-rising stem; BS 5154, series B, PN 32; working pressure up to 14 bar for saturated steam, 32 bar from -10°C to 100°C; screwed ends to steel						
15mm dia	17.48	22.38	1.11	25.17	nr	47.56
20mm dia	16.78	21.50	1.28	29.03	nr	50.53
25mm dia	21.99	28.17	1.49	33.79	nr	61.96
32mm dia	31.34	40.14	1.88	42.64	nr	82.78
40mm dia	59.05	75.64	2.31	52.39	nr	128.02
50mm dia	85.34	109.30	2.80	63.50	nr	172.80

T:MECHANICAL/COOLING/HEATING SYSTEMS

Item	Net Price £	Material £	Labour hours	Labour £	Unit	Total rate £
T31 : LOW TEMPERATURE HOT WATER HEATING (cont'd)						
Y11 – PIPELINE ANCILLARIES (cont'd)						
VALVES (cont'd)						
Isolating valves (cont'd)						
Bronze gate valve; non-rising stem; BS 5154, series B, PN 20; working pressure up to 9 bar for saturated steam, 20 bar from -10°C to 100°C; screwed ends to steel						
15mm dia	11.83	15.15	0.84	19.05	nr	**34.20**
20mm dia	16.78	21.50	1.01	22.91	nr	**44.40**
25mm dia	21.99	28.17	1.19	26.99	nr	**55.15**
32mm dia	31.34	40.14	1.38	31.30	nr	**71.44**
40mm dia	43.38	55.56	1.62	36.74	nr	**92.30**
50mm dia	62.97	80.66	1.94	44.00	nr	**124.65**
Bronze gate valve; non-rising stem; BS 5154, series B, PN 16; working pressure up to 7 bar for saturated steam, 16 bar from -10°C to 100°C; BS4504 flanged ends; bolted connections						
15mm dia	53.19	68.12	1.24	28.12	nr	**96.24**
20mm dia	68.74	88.04	1.31	29.71	nr	**117.74**
25mm dia	90.16	115.48	1.43	32.43	nr	**147.91**
32mm dia	117.47	150.45	1.53	34.70	nr	**185.15**
40mm dia	140.72	180.23	1.63	36.97	nr	**217.20**
50mm dia	196.24	251.34	1.71	38.78	nr	**290.12**
65mm dia	298.20	381.93	1.88	42.64	nr	**424.57**
80mm dia	421.74	540.16	2.03	46.04	nr	**586.20**
100mm dia	747.96	957.98	2.81	63.73	nr	**1021.71**
Cast iron gate valve; bronze trim; non rising stem; BS 5150, PN6; working pressure 6 bar from -10°C to 120°C; BS4504 flanged ends; bolted connections						
50mm dia	141.92	181.77	1.85	41.96	nr	**223.73**
65mm dia	141.92	181.77	2.00	45.36	nr	**227.13**
80mm dia	164.02	210.08	2.27	51.48	nr	**261.56**
100mm dia	216.71	277.56	2.76	62.59	nr	**340.15**
125mm dia	303.66	388.93	6.05	137.20	nr	**526.13**
150mm dia	365.31	467.88	8.03	182.11	nr	**649.99**
200mm dia	665.65	852.55	9.17	207.96	nr	**1060.51**
250mm dia	1024.23	1311.83	10.72	243.11	nr	**1554.94**
300mm dia	1214.81	1555.92	11.75	266.47	nr	**1822.39**
Cast iron gate valve; bronze trim; non rising stem; BS 5150, PN10; working pressure up to 8.4 bar for saturated steam, 10 bar from -10°C to 120°C; BS4504 flanged ends; bolted connections						
50mm dia	152.05	194.74	1.85	41.96	nr	**236.70**
65mm dia	176.28	225.78	2.00	45.36	nr	**271.13**
80mm dia	233.92	299.60	2.27	51.48	nr	**351.08**
100mm dia	330.00	422.66	2.76	62.59	nr	**485.25**
125mm dia	380.12	486.85	6.05	137.20	nr	**624.06**
150mm dia	689.25	882.78	8.03	182.11	nr	**1064.89**

T:MECHANICAL/COOLING/HEATING SYSTEMS

Item	Net Price £	Material £	Labour hours	Labour £	Unit	Total rate £
200mm dia	1027.60	1316.14	9.17	207.96	nr	**1524.10**
250mm dia	1307.47	1674.59	10.72	243.11	nr	**1917.71**
300mm dia	1737.11	2224.87	11.75	266.47	nr	**2491.35**
350mm dia	2919.26	3738.96	12.67	287.34	nr	**4026.30**
Cast iron gate valve; bronze trim; non rising stem; BS 5163 series A, PN16; working pressure for cold water services up to 16 bar; BS4504 flanged ends; bolted connections						
50mm dia	295.68	378.70	1.85	41.96	nr	**420.65**
65mm dia	307.11	393.35	2.00	45.36	nr	**438.71**
80mm dia	315.93	404.64	2.27	51.48	nr	**456.12**
100mm dia	410.25	525.44	2.76	62.59	nr	**588.03**
125mm dia	534.95	685.16	6.05	137.20	nr	**822.36**
150mm dia	645.15	826.30	8.03	182.11	nr	**1008.40**
Ball valves						
Malleable iron body; lever operated stainless steel ball and stem; working pressure up to 12 bar; flanged ends to BS 4504 16/11; bolted connections						
40mm dia	127.22	162.94	1.54	34.92	nr	**197.87**
50mm dia	160.06	205.00	1.64	37.19	nr	**242.20**
80mm dia	267.68	342.84	1.92	43.54	nr	**386.38**
100mm dia	494.78	633.71	2.80	63.50	nr	**697.21**
150mm dia	673.10	862.10	12.05	273.27	nr	**1135.37**
Malleable iron body; lever operated stainless steel ball and stem; working pressure up to 16 bar; screwed ends to steel						
20mm dia	27.99	35.85	1.34	30.40	nr	**66.25**
25mm dia	28.78	36.87	1.40	31.76	nr	**68.63**
32mm dia	39.64	50.78	1.46	33.16	nr	**83.93**
40mm dia	39.64	50.78	1.54	34.94	nr	**85.72**
50mm dia	47.42	60.73	1.64	37.24	nr	**97.97**
Carbon steel body; lever operated stainless steel ball and stem; Class 150; working pressure up to 19 bar; screwed ends to steel						
15mm dia	20.56	26.33	0.84	19.06	nr	**45.39**
20mm dia	21.59	27.65	1.14	25.86	nr	**53.51**
25mm dia	24.71	31.65	1.30	29.49	nr	**61.14**
Globe valves						
Bronze; rising stem; renewable disc; BS 5154 series B, PN32; working pressure up to 14 bar for saturated steam, 32 bar from -10°C to 100°C; screwed ends to steel						
15mm dia	14.02	17.95	0.77	17.46	nr	**35.41**
20mm dia	19.08	24.44	1.03	23.36	nr	**47.80**
25mm dia	29.18	37.37	1.19	26.99	nr	**64.36**
32mm dia	41.18	52.75	1.38	31.30	nr	**84.04**
40mm dia	51.13	65.49	1.62	36.74	nr	**102.23**
50mm dia	81.00	103.75	1.61	36.51	nr	**140.26**

T:MECHANICAL/COOLING/HEATING SYSTEMS

Item	Net Price £	Material £	Labour hours	Labour £	Unit	Total rate £
T31 : LOW TEMPERATURE HOT WATER HEATING (cont'd)						
Y11 – PIPELINE ANCILLARIES (cont'd)						
VALVES (cont'd)						
Globe valves (cont'd)						
Bronze; needle valve; rising stem; BS 5154, series B, PN32; working pressure up to 14 bar for saturated steam, 32 bar from -10°C to 100°C; screwed ends to steel						
15mm dia	19.82	25.38	1.07	24.27	nr	49.65
20mm dia	33.56	42.98	1.18	26.76	nr	69.74
25mm dia	47.33	60.62	1.27	28.80	nr	89.42
32mm dia	98.19	125.76	1.35	30.62	nr	156.38
40mm dia	154.70	198.14	1.47	33.34	nr	231.48
50mm dia	209.10	267.82	1.61	36.51	nr	304.33
Bronze; rising stem; renewable disc; BS 5154, series B, PN16; working pressure upto 7 bar for saturated steam, 16 bar from -10°C to 100°C; BS4504 flanged ends; bolted connections						
15mm dia	51.05	65.38	1.16	26.31	nr	91.69
20mm dia	59.02	75.60	1.26	28.57	nr	104.17
25mm dia	103.53	132.60	1.38	31.30	nr	163.89
32mm dia	130.69	167.38	1.47	33.34	nr	200.72
40mm dia	169.00	216.46	1.56	35.38	nr	251.84
50mm dia	213.21	273.08	1.71	38.78	nr	311.86
Bronze; rising stem; renewable disc; BS 2060, class 250; working pressure up to 24 bar for saturated steam, 38 bar from -10°C to 100°C; flanged ends (BS 10 table H); bolted connections						
15mm dia	130.23	166.79	1.16	26.31	nr	193.10
20mm dia	151.76	194.38	1.26	28.57	nr	222.95
25mm dia	207.97	266.37	1.38	31.30	nr	297.67
32mm dia	275.94	353.42	1.47	33.34	nr	386.76
40mm dia	325.35	416.70	1.56	35.38	nr	452.08
50mm dia	505.91	647.96	1.71	38.78	nr	686.74
65mm dia	729.41	934.22	1.88	42.64	nr	976.85
80mm dia	1765.60	2261.36	2.03	46.04	nr	2307.40
Check valves						
Bronze; swing pattern; BS 5154 series B, PN 25; working pressure up to 10.5 bar for saturated steam, 25 bar from -10°C to 100°C; screwed ends to steel						
15mm dia	12.43	15.92	0.77	17.46	nr	33.38
20mm dia	14.79	18.95	1.03	23.36	nr	42.31
25mm dia	20.48	26.23	1.19	26.99	nr	53.22
32mm dia	34.72	44.47	1.38	31.30	nr	75.76
40mm dia	43.20	55.33	1.62	36.74	nr	92.06
50mm dia	66.24	84.84	1.94	44.00	nr	128.84
65mm dia	123.52	158.20	2.45	55.56	nr	213.77
80mm dia	174.65	223.69	2.83	64.18	nr	287.87

T:MECHANICAL/COOLING/HEATING SYSTEMS

Item	Net Price £	Material £	Labour hours	Labour £	Unit	Total rate £
Bronze; vertical lift pattern; BS 5154 series B, PN32; working pressure up to 14 bar for saturated steam, 32 bar from -10°C to 100°C; screwed ends to steel						
15mm dia	21.64	27.72	0.96	21.77	nr	**49.49**
20mm dia	24.85	31.83	1.07	24.27	nr	**56.09**
25mm dia	27.48	35.20	1.17	26.53	nr	**61.73**
32mm dia	34.30	43.93	1.33	30.16	nr	**74.09**
40mm dia	45.75	58.60	1.41	31.98	nr	**90.57**
50mm dia	70.37	90.13	1.55	35.15	nr	**125.28**
65mm dia	299.44	383.52	1.80	40.82	nr	**424.34**
80mm dia	447.82	573.56	1.99	45.13	nr	**618.69**
Bronze; oblique swing pattern; BS 5154 series A, PN32; working pressure up to 14 bar for saturated steam, 32 bar from -10°C to 120°C; screwed connections to steel						
15mm dia	35.83	45.89	0.96	21.77	nr	**67.66**
20mm dia	39.34	50.39	1.07	24.27	nr	**74.65**
25mm dia	59.95	76.78	1.17	26.53	nr	**103.32**
32mm dia	86.65	110.98	1.33	30.16	nr	**141.14**
40mm dia	96.03	123.00	1.41	31.98	nr	**154.97**
50mm dia	137.70	176.37	1.55	35.15	nr	**211.52**
Cast iron; swing pattern; BS 5153 PN6; working pressure up to 6 bar from -10°C to 120°C; BS 4504 flanged ends; bolted connections						
50mm dia	161.04	206.26	1.86	42.18	nr	**248.44**
65mm dia	161.04	206.26	2.00	45.36	nr	**251.61**
80mm dia	199.41	255.40	2.56	58.06	nr	**313.46**
100mm dia	232.21	297.42	2.76	62.59	nr	**360.01**
125mm dia	346.44	443.72	6.05	137.20	nr	**580.93**
150mm dia	389.55	498.93	8.11	183.92	nr	**682.85**
200mm dia	861.46	1103.35	9.26	210.00	nr	**1313.35**
250mm dia	1310.92	1679.01	10.72	243.11	nr	**1922.12**
300mm dia	1741.65	2230.68	11.75	266.47	nr	**2497.16**
Cast iron; horizontal lift pattern; BS 5153 PN16; working pressure up to 13 bar for saturated steam, 16 bar from -10°C to 120°C; BS 4504 flanged ends; bolted connections						
50mm dia	185.58	237.68	1.86	42.18	nr	**279.87**
65mm dia	291.09	372.82	2.00	45.36	nr	**418.18**
80mm dia	354.29	453.78	2.56	58.06	nr	**511.83**
100mm dia	458.74	587.55	2.96	67.13	nr	**654.68**
125mm dia	693.53	888.26	7.76	175.98	nr	**1064.25**
150mm dia	762.77	976.95	10.50	238.12	nr	**1215.08**

T:MECHANICAL/COOLING/HEATING SYSTEMS

Item	Net Price £	Material £	Labour hours	Labour £	Unit	Total rate £
T31 : LOW TEMPERATURE HOT WATER HEATING (cont'd)						
Y11 – PIPELINE ANCILLARIES (cont'd)						
VALVES (cont'd)						
Check valves (cont'd)						
Cast iron; semi lugged butterfly valve; BS5155 PN16; working pressure 16 bar from -10°C to 120°C; BS 4504 flanged ends; bolted connections						
50mm dia	51.51	65.98	2.20	49.89	nr	115.87
65mm dia	51.51	65.98	2.31	52.39	nr	118.37
80mm dia	61.81	79.17	2.88	65.31	nr	144.48
100mm dia	136.08	174.28	3.11	70.53	nr	244.81
125mm dia	136.08	174.28	5.02	113.85	nr	288.13
150mm dia	157.90	202.23	6.98	158.30	nr	360.53
200mm dia	275.76	353.19	8.25	187.10	nr	540.29
250mm dia	550.54	705.13	10.47	237.44	nr	942.57
300mm dia	698.34	894.43	11.48	260.35	nr	1154.78
Commissioning valves						
Bronze commissioning set; metering station; double regulating valve; BS5154 PN20 Series B; working pressure 20 bar from -10°C to 100°C; screwed ends to steel						
15mm dia	32.13	41.15	1.08	24.49	nr	65.65
20mm dia	54.70	70.06	1.46	33.11	nr	103.17
25mm dia	63.09	80.81	1.68	38.10	nr	118.91
32mm dia	87.46	112.02	1.95	44.22	nr	156.24
40mm dia	124.23	159.12	2.27	51.48	nr	210.60
50mm dia	205.73	263.49	2.73	61.91	nr	325.40
Cast iron commissioning set; metering station; double regulating valve; BS5152 PN16; working pressure 16 bar from -10°C to 90°C; flanged ends (BS 4504, Part 1, Table 16); bolted connections						
65mm dia	315.45	404.03	1.80	40.82	nr	444.85
80mm dia	379.13	485.59	2.56	58.06	nr	543.64
100mm dia	513.17	657.26	2.30	52.16	nr	709.42
125mm dia	835.28	1069.82	2.44	55.34	nr	1125.15
150mm dia	1048.17	1342.49	2.90	65.77	nr	1408.26
200mm dia	3059.68	3918.81	8.26	187.32	nr	4106.13
250mm dia	4410.78	5649.29	10.49	237.90	nr	5887.18
300mm dia	6950.09	8901.61	11.49	260.57	nr	9162.19
Cast iron variable orifice double regulating valve; orifice valve; BS5152 PN16; working pressure 16 bar from -10° to 90°C; flanged ends (BS 4504, Part 1, Table 16); bolted connections						
65mm dia	279.15	357.53	2.00	45.36	nr	402.89
80mm dia	362.54	464.33	2.56	58.06	nr	522.39
100mm dia	482.91	618.51	2.96	67.13	nr	685.64
125mm dia	706.95	905.45	7.76	175.98	nr	1081.44
150mm dia	877.59	1124.01	10.50	238.12	nr	1362.13

T:MECHANICAL/COOLING/HEATING SYSTEMS

Item	Net Price £	Material £	Labour hours	Labour £	Unit	Total rate £
200mm dia	2272.01	2909.96	8.26	187.32	nr	**3097.29**
250mm dia	3437.51	4402.73	10.49	237.90	nr	**4640.63**
300mm dia	5400.82	6917.31	11.49	260.57	nr	**7177.89**
Cast iron globe valve with double regulating feature; BS5152 PN16; working pressure 16 bar from -10°C to 120°C; flanged ends (BS 4504, Part 1, Table 16); bolted connections						
65mm dia	223.65	286.45	2.00	45.36	nr	**331.81**
80mm dia	274.40	351.45	2.56	58.06	nr	**409.50**
100mm dia	385.42	493.65	2.96	67.13	nr	**560.77**
125mm dia	591.52	757.62	7.76	175.98	nr	**933.60**
150mm dia	763.79	978.25	10.50	238.12	nr	**1216.37**
200mm dia	2159.77	2766.21	8.26	187.32	nr	**2953.54**
250mm dia	3349.09	4289.48	10.49	237.90	nr	**4527.38**
300mm dia	5299.29	6787.28	11.49	260.57	nr	**7047.85**
Bronze autoflow commissioning valve; PN25 ; working pressure 25 bar up to 100°C; screwed ends to steel						
15mm dia	66.17	84.75	0.82	18.60	nr	**103.34**
20mm dia	88.04	112.77	1.08	24.49	nr	**137.26**
25mm dia	100.08	128.18	1.27	28.80	nr	**156.98**
32mm dia	130.45	167.08	1.50	34.02	nr	**201.10**
40mm dia	155.25	198.84	1.76	39.91	nr	**238.75**
50mm dia	206.40	264.35	2.13	48.31	nr	**312.66**
Ductile iron autoflow commissioning valves; PN16; working pressure 16 bar from -10°C to 120°C; for ANSI 150 flanged ends						
65mm dia	495.91	635.15	2.31	52.39	nr	**687.54**
80mm dia	548.27	702.22	2.88	65.31	nr	**767.54**
100mm dia	855.01	1095.09	3.11	70.53	nr	**1165.62**
150mm dia	1442.86	1848.00	6.98	158.30	nr	**2006.30**
200mm dia	2082.41	2667.12	8.26	187.32	nr	**2854.45**
250mm dia	2892.12	3704.20	10.49	237.90	nr	**3942.10**
300mm dia	3693.71	4730.86	11.49	260.57	nr	**4991.44**
Strainers						
Bronze strainer; Y type; PN32 ; working pressure 32 bar from -10°C to 100°C; screwed ends to steel						
15mm dia	13.59	17.41	0.82	18.60	nr	**36.00**
20mm dia	17.27	22.12	1.08	24.49	nr	**46.62**
25mm dia	24.35	31.18	1.27	28.80	nr	**59.98**
32mm dia	40.96	52.46	1.50	34.02	nr	**86.48**
40mm dia	55.65	71.27	1.76	39.91	nr	**111.19**
50mm dia	218.56	279.93	2.13	48.31	nr	**328.23**

T:MECHANICAL/COOLING/HEATING SYSTEMS

Item	Net Price £	Material £	Labour hours	Labour £	Unit	Total rate £
T31 : LOW TEMPERATURE HOT WATER HEATING (cont'd)						
Y11 – PIPELINE ANCILLARIES (cont'd)						
VALVES (cont'd)						
Strainers (cont'd)						
Cast iron strainer; Y type; PN16; working pressure 16 bar from -10°C to 120°C; BS 4504 flanged ends						
65mm dia	87.77	112.41	2.31	52.39	nr	**164.80**
80mm dia	101.65	130.20	2.88	65.31	nr	**195.51**
100mm dia	150.52	192.78	3.11	70.53	nr	**263.31**
125mm dia	310.76	398.01	5.02	113.85	nr	**511.86**
150mm dia	402.61	515.66	6.98	158.30	nr	**673.96**
200mm dia	658.00	842.76	8.26	187.32	nr	**1030.08**
250mm dia	994.58	1273.85	10.49	237.90	nr	**1511.75**
300mm dia	1668.79	2137.37	11.49	260.57	nr	**2397.95**
Regulators						
Gunmetal; self-acting two port thermostatic regulator; single seat; screwed ends; complete with sensing element, 2m long capillary tube						
15mm dia	399.66	511.88	1.37	31.07	nr	**542.95**
20mm dia	409.96	525.07	1.24	28.12	nr	**553.20**
25mm dia	423.35	542.22	1.34	30.39	nr	**572.61**
Gunmetal; self-acting two port thermostatic regulator; double seat; flanged ends (BS 4504 PN25); with sensing element, 2m long capillary tube; steel body						
65mm dia	1482.13	1898.30	1.23	27.82	nr	**1926.11**
80mm dia	1749.35	2240.55	1.62	36.64	nr	**2277.19**
Control valves; electrically operated (electrical work elsewhere)						
Cast iron; butterfly type; two position electrically controlled 240V motor and linkage mechanism; for low pressure hot water; maximum pressure 6 bar at 120°C; flanged ends						
25mm dia	313.77	401.87	1.47	33.34	nr	**435.21**
32mm dia	324.22	415.26	1.52	34.47	nr	**449.73**
40mm dia	453.04	580.25	1.61	36.51	nr	**616.76**
50mm dia	465.91	596.73	1.71	38.78	nr	**635.51**
65mm dia	477.58	611.68	2.51	56.92	nr	**668.60**
80mm dia	496.26	635.60	2.69	61.00	nr	**696.61**
100mm dia	520.77	667.00	2.81	63.73	nr	**730.73**
125mm dia	576.81	738.78	2.94	66.67	nr	**805.45**
150mm dia	625.08	800.60	3.33	75.52	nr	**876.12**
200mm dia	775.31	993.01	3.67	83.23	nr	**1076.24**

T:MECHANICAL/COOLING/HEATING SYSTEMS

Item	Net Price £	Material £	Labour hours	Labour £	Unit	Total rate £
Cast iron; three way 240V motorized; for low pressure hot water; maximum pressure 6 bar 120°C; flanged ends, drilled (BS 10, Table F)						
25mm dia	350.69	449.17	1.99	45.13	nr	**494.30**
40mm dia	367.82	471.10	2.13	48.31	nr	**519.40**
50mm dia	363.14	465.11	3.21	72.80	nr	**537.91**
65mm dia	405.75	519.69	3.23	73.25	nr	**592.94**
80mm dia	454.65	582.31	3.50	79.37	nr	**661.68**
Two port normally closed motorised valve; electric actuator; spring return; domestic usage						
22mm dia	49.71	63.67	1.18	26.76	nr	**90.43**
28mm dia	67.39	86.32	1.35	30.62	nr	**116.93**
Two port on/off motorised valve; electric actuator; spring return; domestic usage						
22mm dia	49.71	63.67	1.18	26.76	nr	**90.43**
Three port motorised valve; electric actuator; spring return; domestic usage						
22mm dia	72.55	92.92	1.18	26.76	nr	**119.68**
Safety and relief valves						
Bronze relief valve; spring type; side outlet; working pressure up to 20.7 bar at 120°C; screwed ends to steel						
15mm dia	74.36	95.24	0.26	5.90	nr	**101.13**
20mm dia	100.36	128.53	0.36	8.16	nr	**136.70**
Bronze relief valve; spring type; side outlet; working pressure up to 17.2 bar at 120°C; screwed ends to steel						
25mm dia	120.03	153.73	0.38	8.62	nr	**162.35**
32mm dia	182.73	234.04	0.48	10.89	nr	**244.93**
Bronze relief valve; spring type; side outlet; working pressure up to 13.8 bar at 120°C; screwed ends to steel						
40mm dia	173.85	222.67	0.64	14.51	nr	**237.18**
50mm dia	242.72	310.88	0.76	17.24	nr	**328.11**
65mm dia	385.39	493.61	0.94	21.32	nr	**514.92**
80mm dia	505.63	647.61	1.10	24.95	nr	**672.55**
Cocks; screwed joints to steel						
Bronze gland cock; complete with malleable iron lever; working pressure up to 10 bar at 100°C; screwed ends to steel						
15mm dia	19.85	25.43	0.77	17.46	nr	**42.89**
20mm dia	28.93	37.05	1.03	23.36	nr	**60.41**
25mm dia	41.55	53.21	1.19	26.99	nr	**80.20**
32mm dia	150.13	192.29	1.38	31.30	nr	**223.59**
40mm dia	213.19	273.05	1.62	36.74	nr	**309.79**
50mm dia	303.37	388.55	1.94	44.00	nr	**432.54**

T:MECHANICAL/COOLING/HEATING SYSTEMS

Item	Net Price £	Material £	Labour hours	Labour £	Unit	Total rate £
T31 : LOW TEMPERATURE HOT WATER HEATING (cont'd)						
Y11 – PIPELINE ANCILLARIES (cont'd)						
VALVES (cont'd)						
Cocks; screwed joints to steel (cont'd)						
Bronze three-way plug cock; complete with malleable iron lever; working pressure up to 10 bar at 100°C; screwed ends to steel						
15mm dia	44.15	56.55	0.77	17.46	nr	**74.02**
20mm dia	51.10	65.45	1.03	23.36	nr	**88.81**
25mm dia	71.44	91.50	1.19	26.99	nr	**118.49**
32mm dia	101.32	129.77	1.38	31.30	nr	**161.07**
40mm dia	122.16	156.46	1.62	36.74	nr	**193.19**
Air vents; including regulating, adjusting and testing						
Automatic air vent; maximum pressure up to 7 bar at 93°C; screwed ends to steel						
15mm dia	84.08	107.69	0.80	18.14	nr	**125.83**
Automatic air vent; maximum pressure up to 7 bar at 93°C; lockhead isolating valve; screwed ends to steel						
15mm dia	92.08	117.94	0.83	18.82	nr	**136.76**
Automatic air vent; maximum pressure up to 17 bar at 200°C; flanged ends (BS10, Table H); bolted connections to counter flange (measured separately)						
15mm dia	373.74	478.68	0.83	18.82	nr	**497.51**
Radiator valves						
Bronze; wheelhead or lockshield; chromium plated finish; screwed joints to steel						
Straight						
15mm dia	25.85	33.11	0.59	13.38	nr	**46.49**
20mm dia	33.60	43.04	0.73	16.56	nr	**59.59**
25mm dia	42.00	53.80	0.85	19.28	nr	**73.07**
Angled						
15mm dia	18.37	23.53	0.59	13.38	nr	**36.91**
20mm dia	24.21	31.00	0.73	16.56	nr	**47.56**
25mm dia	31.22	39.98	0.85	19.28	nr	**59.26**

T:MECHANICAL/COOLING/HEATING SYSTEMS

Item	Net Price £	Material £	Labour hours	Labour £	Unit	Total rate £
Bronze; wheelhead or lockshield; chromium plated finish; compression joints to copper						
Straight						
15mm dia	27.78	35.57	0.59	13.38	nr	**48.95**
20mm dia	34.66	44.39	0.73	16.56	nr	**60.94**
25mm dia	43.56	55.79	0.85	19.28	nr	**75.07**
Angled						
15mm dia	18.37	23.53	0.59	13.38	nr	**36.91**
20mm dia	25.50	32.66	0.73	16.56	nr	**49.21**
25mm dia	32.50	41.63	0.85	19.28	nr	**60.91**
Twin entry						
8mm dia	28.56	36.95	0.23	5.22	nr	**42.17**
10mm dia	32.42	41.94	0.23	5.22	nr	**47.15**
Bronze; thermostatic head; chromium plated finish; compression joints to copper						
Straight						
15mm dia	23.46	30.05	0.59	13.38	nr	**43.43**
20mm dia	27.37	35.06	0.73	16.56	nr	**51.61**
Angled						
15mm dia	24.72	31.66	0.59	13.38	nr	**45.04**
20mm dia	32.05	41.04	0.73	16.56	nr	**57.60**
GAUGES						
Thermometers and pressure gauges Dial thermometer; coated steel case and dial; glass window; brass pocket; BS 5235; pocket length 100mm; screwed end						
Back/bottom entry						
100mm dia face	49.01	62.77	0.81	18.38	nr	**81.15**
150mm dia face	55.90	71.60	0.81	18.38	nr	**89.98**
Dial pressure/altitude gauge; bronze bourdon tube type; coated steel case and dial; glass window BS 1780; screwed end						
100mm dia face	28.08	35.97	0.81	18.38	nr	**54.35**
150mm dia face	30.49	39.05	0.81	18.38	nr	**57.43**

T:MECHANICAL/COOLING/HEATING SYSTEMS

Item	Net Price £	Material £	Labour hours	Labour £	Unit	Total rate £
T31 : LOW TEMPERATURE HOT WATER HEATING (cont'd)						
Y11 – PIPELINE ANCILLARIES (cont'd)						
EQUIPMENT						
PRESSURISATION UNITS						
LTHW pressurisation unit complete with expansion vessel(s), interconnecting pipework and all necessary isolating and drain valves; includes placing in position; electrical work elsewhere. Selection based on a final working pressure of 4 bar, a 3m static head and system operating temperatures of 82/71°C						
System volume						
2,400 litres	1459.62	1869.47	15.00	340.18	nr	**2209.64**
6,000 - 20,000 litres	1600.38	2049.75	22.00	498.92	nr	**2548.68**
25,000 litres	1986.96	2544.88	22.00	498.92	nr	**3043.80**
DIRT SEPARATORS						
Dirt seperator; maximum operating Temperature and pressure of 110°C and 10 bar; fitted with drain valve						
Bore size, flow rate (at 1.0m/s velocity); threaded connections						
32mm dia, 3.7m³/h	86.40	110.66	2.29	51.93	nr	**162.59**
40mm dia, 5.0m³/h	103.68	132.79	2.45	55.56	nr	**188.35**
Bore size, flow rate (at 1.5m/s velocity); flanged connections to PN16						
50mm dia, 13.0m³/h	717.70	919.22	3.00	68.04	nr	**987.26**
65mm dia, 21.0m³/h	744.19	953.15	3.00	68.04	nr	**1021.19**
80mm dia, 29.0m³/h	1042.56	1335.30	3.84	87.09	nr	**1422.39**
100mm dia, 49.0m³/h	1080.58	1384.00	4.44	100.69	nr	**1484.69**
125mm dia, 74.0m³/h	2071.30	2652.90	11.64	263.98	nr	**2916.88**
150mm dia, 109.0m³/h	2161.15	2767.98	15.75	357.18	nr	**3125.16**
200mm dia, 181.0m³/h	3024.00	3873.11	15.75	357.18	nr	**4230.29**
250mm dia, 288.0m³/h	4575.74	5860.56	15.75	357.18	nr	**6217.75**
300mm dia, 407.0m³/h	7292.16	9339.73	17.24	390.98	nr	**9730.70**
MICROBUBBLE DEAERATORS						
Microbubble deaerator; maximum operating temperature and pressure of 110°C and 10 bar; fitted with drain valve						
Bore size, flow rate (at 1.0m/s velocity); threaded connections						
32mm dia, 3.7m³/h	86.40	110.66	2.29	51.93	nr	**162.59**
40mm dia, 5.0m³/h	103.68	132.79	2.45	55.56	nr	**188.35**

T:MECHANICAL/COOLING/HEATING SYSTEMS

Item	Net Price £	Material £	Labour hours	Labour £	Unit	Total rate £
Bore size, flow rate (at 1.5m/s velocity); flanged connections to PN16						
50mm dia, 13.0m³/h	826.68	1058.80	3.00	68.04	nr	**1126.83**
65mm dia, 21.0m³/h	853.03	1092.55	3.00	68.04	nr	**1160.59**
80mm dia, 29.0m³/h	1154.95	1479.25	3.84	87.09	nr	**1566.34**
100mm dia, 49.0m³/h	1200.47	1537.55	4.44	100.69	nr	**1638.24**
125mm dia, 74.0m³/h	2379.38	3047.49	11.64	263.98	nr	**3311.47**
150mm dia, 109.0m³/h	2483.62	3181.00	15.75	357.18	nr	**3538.19**
200mm dia, 181.0m³/h	3034.74	3886.87	15.75	357.18	nr	**4244.05**
250mm dia, 288.0m³/h	4460.46	5712.91	15.75	357.18	nr	**6070.09**
300mm dia, 407.0m³/h	7926.50	10152.18	17.24	390.98	nr	**10543.15**
Pressure step deaerator for high pressure systems						
Heating (where static head of water above boiler exceeds 15m); maximum working pressure						
6 bar (single phase supply)	4235.21	5424.42	8.00	181.43	nr	**5605.85**
10 bar (3 phase supply)	9112.59	11671.32	10.00	226.78	nr	**11898.10**
15 bar (3 phase supply)	9753.57	12492.27	12.00	272.14	nr	**12764.41**
Cooling (where static head of water above chiller exceeds 5m); maximum working pressure						
6 bar (single phase supply)	4748.00	6081.18	8.00	181.43	nr	**6262.61**
10 bar (3 phase supply)	9625.38	12328.09	10.00	226.78	nr	**12554.87**
15 bar (3 phase supply)	10267.55	13150.57	12.00	272.14	nr	**13422.71**
COMBINED MICROBUBBLE DEAERATORS AND DIRT SEPARATORS						
Combined deaerator and dirt separators; maximum operating temperature and pressure of 110°C and 10 bar; fitted with drain valve						
Bore size, flow rate (at 1.5m/s velocity); threaded connections						
25mm dia, 2.0m³/h	107.12	137.20	2.75	62.37	nr	**199.56**
Bore size, flow rate (at 1.5m/s velocity); flanged connections to PN16						
50mm dia, 13.0m³/h	894.40	1145.54	3.60	81.64	nr	**1227.18**
65mm dia, 21.0m³/h	941.20	1205.48	3.60	81.64	nr	**1287.12**
80mm dia, 29.0m³/h	1147.12	1469.22	4.61	104.55	nr	**1573.77**
100mm dia, 49.0m³/h	1261.52	1615.74	5.33	120.88	nr	**1736.62**
125mm dia, 74.0m³/h	2179.84	2791.92	13.97	316.82	nr	**3108.73**
150mm dia, 109.0m³/h	2352.48	3013.03	18.90	428.62	nr	**3441.65**
200mm dia, 181.0m³/h	3414.32	4373.03	18.90	428.62	nr	**4801.65**
250mm dia, 288.0m³/h	5120.96	6558.87	18.90	428.62	nr	**6987.50**
300mm dia, 407.0m³/h	9035.52	11572.60	20.69	469.22	nr	**12041.82**

T:MECHANICAL/COOLING/HEATING SYSTEMS

Item	Net Price £	Material £	Labour hours	Labour £	Unit	Total rate £
T31 : LOW TEMPERATURE HOT WATER HEATING (cont'd)						
Y20 - PUMPS						
Centrifugal heating and chilled water pump; belt drive; 3 phase, 1450 rpm motor; max. pressure 1000kN/m²; max. temperature 125°C; bed plate; coupling guard; bolted connections; supply only mating flanges;includes fixing on prepared concrete base; electrical work elsewhere						
40mm pump size; 4.0 l/s at 70 kPa max head; 0.25kW maximum motor rating	948.38	1214.67	7.59	172.13	nr	**1386.80**
40mm pump size; 4.0 l/s at 130 kPa max head; 1.5kW maximum motor rating	1186.87	1520.14	8.09	183.47	nr	**1703.61**
50mm pump size; 8.5 l/s at 90 kPa max head; 2.2kW maximum motor rating	1224.00	1567.69	8.67	196.62	nr	**1764.31**
50mm pump size; 8.5 l/s at 190 kPa max head; 3kW maximum motor rating	2127.37	2724.72	11.20	254.00	nr	**2978.72**
50mm pump size; 8.5 l/s at 215 kPa max head; 4 kW maximum motor rating	1390.50	1780.94	11.70	265.34	nr	**2046.28**
65mm pump size; 14.0 l/s at 90 kPa max head; 3kW maximum motor rating	1219.50	1561.92	11.70	265.34	nr	**1827.26**
65mm pump size; 14.0 l/s at 160 kPa max head; 4 kW maximum motor rating	1352.25	1731.95	11.70	265.34	nr	**1997.29**
80mm pump size; 14.5 l/s at 210 kPa max head; 5.5 kW maximum motor rating	2074.50	2657.00	11.70	265.34	nr	**2922.34**
80mm pump size; 22.0 l/s at 130 kPa max head; 5.5 kW maximum motor rating	2074.50	2657.00	13.64	309.33	nr	**2966.33**
80mm pump size; 22.0 l/s at 200 kPa max head; 7.5 kW maximum motor rating	2172.38	2782.36	13.64	309.33	nr	**3091.69**
100mm pump size; 22.0 l/s at 250 kPa max head; 11kW maximum motor rating	3048.75	3904.81	13.64	309.33	nr	**4214.14**
100mm pump size; 30.0 l/s at 100 kPa max head; 4.0 kW maximum motor rating	1706.63	2185.83	19.15	434.29	nr	**2620.12**
100mm pump size; 36.0 l/s at 250 kPa max head; 15.0kW maximum motor rating	3228.75	4135.35	19.15	434.29	nr	**4569.64**
100mm pump size; 36.0 l/s at 550 kPa max head; 30.0 kW maximum motor rating	4381.88	5612.26	19.15	434.29	nr	**6046.55**
Centrifugal heating and chilled water pump; TWIN HEAD BELT DRIVE; 3 phase, 1450 rpm motor; max. pressure 1000kN/m²; max. temperature 125°C; bed plate; coupling guard; bolted connections; supply only mating flanges; includes fixing on prepared concrete base; electrical work elsewhere						
40mm pump size; 4.0 l/s at 70 kPa max head; 0.75kW maximum motor rating	2031.75	2602.25	7.59	172.13	nr	**2774.37**
40mm pump size; 4.0 l/s at 130 kPa max head; 1.5kW maximum motor rating	2445.75	3132.49	8.09	183.47	nr	**3315.96**
50mm pump size; 8.5 l/s at 90 kPa max head; 2.2kW maximum motor rating	2498.63	3200.21	8.67	196.62	nr	**3396.84**

T:MECHANICAL/COOLING/HEATING SYSTEMS

Item	Net Price £	Material £	Labour hours	Labour £	Unit	Total rate £
50mm pump size; 8.5 l/s at 190 kPa max head; 4kW maximum motor rating	2880.00	3688.68	11.20	254.00	nr	**3942.67**
65mm pump size; 8.5 l/s at 215 kPa max head; 4 kW maximum motor rating	3003.75	3847.17	11.70	265.34	nr	**4112.51**
65mm pump size; 14.0 l/s at 90 kPa max head; 3kW maximum motor rating	2689.87	3445.17	11.70	265.34	nr	**3710.50**
65mm pump size; 14.0 l/s at 160 kPa max head; 4 kW maximum motor rating	3003.75	3847.17	11.70	265.34	nr	**4112.51**
80mm pump size; 14.5 l/s at 210 kPa max head; 7.5 kW maximum motor rating	4512.37	5779.40	13.64	309.33	nr	**6088.74**
Centrifugal heating and chilled water pump; CLOSE COUPLED; 3 phase, 1450 rpm motor; max. pressure 1000kN/m²; max. temperature 110°C; bed plate; coupling guard; bolted connections; supply only mating flanges; includes fixing on prepared concrete base; electrical work elsewhere						
40mm pump size; 4.0 l/s at 23 kPa max head; 0.55kW maximum motor rating	570.38	730.53	7.31	165.78	nr	**896.31**
50mm pump size; 4.0 l/s at 75 kPa max head; 0.75 kW maximum motor rating	632.25	809.78	7.31	165.78	nr	**975.56**
50mm pump size; 7.0 l/s at 65 kPa max head; 0.75 kW maximum motor rating	632.25	809.78	8.01	181.65	nr	**991.43**
65mm pump size; 10.0 l/s at 33 kPa max head; 0.75kW maximum motor rating	716.63	917.85	8.01	181.65	nr	**1099.50**
50mm pump size; 4.0 l/s at 120 kPa max head; 1.5 kW maximum motor rating	862.88	1105.16	8.01	181.65	nr	**1286.82**
80mm pump size; 16.0 l/s at 80 kPa max head; 2.2 kW maximum motor rating	1117.13	1430.80	12.35	280.08	nr	**1710.88**
80mm pump size; 16.0 l/s at 120 kPa max head; 4.0 kW maximum motor rating	1089.00	1394.78	12.35	280.08	nr	**1674.86**
100mm pump size; 28.0 l/s at 40 kPa max head; 2.2 kW maximum motor rating	1103.63	1413.51	17.86	405.04	nr	**1818.55**
100mm pump size; 28.0 l/s at 90 kPa max head; 4.0 kW maximum motor rating	1218.38	1560.48	17.86	405.04	nr	**1965.52**
125mm pump size; 40.0 l/s at 50 kPa max head; 3.0 kW maximum motor rating	1162.13	1488.44	25.85	586.24	nr	**2074.67**
125mm pump size; 40.0 l/s at 120 kPa max head; 7.5 kW maximum motor rating	1434.38	1837.13	25.85	586.24	nr	**2423.37**
150mm pump size; 70.0 l/s at 75 kPa max head; 11 kW maximum motor rating	2108.25	2700.23	30.43	690.10	nr	**3390.33**
150mm pump size; 70.0 l/s at 120 kPa max head; 15.0 kW maximum motor rating	2253.38	2886.10	30.43	690.10	nr	**3576.20**
150mm pump size; 70.0 l/s at 150 kPa max head; 15.0 kW maximum motor rating	2253.38	2886.10	30.43	690.10	nr	**3576.20**

T:MECHANICAL/COOLING/HEATING SYSTEMS

Item	Net Price £	Material £	Labour hours	Labour £	Unit	Total rate £
T31 : LOW TEMPERATURE HOT WATER HEATING (cont'd)						
Y20 – PUMPS (cont'd)						
Centrifugal heating & chilled water pump; close coupled; 3 phase, VARIABLE SPEED motor; max. system pressure 1000 kN/m²; max. temperature 110°C; bed plate; coupling guard; bolted connections; supply only mating flanges; includes fixing on prepared concrete base; electrical work elsewhere.						
40mm pump size; 4.0 l/s at 23 kPa max head; 0.55kW max motor rating	1029.38	1318.41	7.31	165.78	nr	**1484.19**
40mm pump size; 4.0 l/s at 75 kPa max head; 0.75kW max motor rating	1136.25	1455.30	7.31	165.78	nr	**1621.08**
50mm pump size; 7.0 l/s at 65 kPa max head; 1.5kW max motor rating	1393.88	1785.26	8.01	181.65	nr	**1966.92**
50mm pump size; 10.0 l/s at 33 kPa max head; 1.5kW max motor rating	1393.88	1785.26	8.01	181.65	nr	**1966.92**
50mm pump size; 4.0 l/s at 120 kPa max head; 1.5kW max motor rating	1393.88	1785.26	8.01	181.65	nr	**1966.92**
80mm pump size; 16.0 l/s at 80 kPa max head; 2.2kW max motor rating	1816.88	2327.04	12.35	280.08	nr	**2607.11**
80mm pump size; 16.0 l/s at 120 kPa max head; 3.0kW max motor rating	1959.75	2510.03	12.35	280.08	nr	**2790.11**
100mm pump size; 28.0 l/s at 40 kPa max head; 2.2kW max motor rating	1861.88	2384.67	17.86	405.04	nr	**2789.71**
100mm pump size; 28.0 l/s at 90 kPa max head; 4.0.kW max motor rating	2220.75	2844.31	17.86	405.04	nr	**3249.35**
125mm pump size; 40.0 l/s at 50 kPa max head; 3.0kW max motor rating	2131.88	2730.48	25.85	586.24	nr	**3316.72**
125mm pump size; 40.0 l/s at 120 kPa max head; 7.5kW max motor rating	3000.38	3842.85	25.85	586.24	nr	**4429.09**
150mm pump size; 70.0 l/s at 75 kPa max head; 7.5kW max motor rating	3468.38	4442.26	30.43	690.10	nr	**5132.36**

T:MECHANICAL/COOLING/HEATING SYSTEMS

Item	Net Price £	Material £	Labour hours	Labour £	Unit	Total rate £
Glandless domestic heating pump; for low pressure domestic hot water heating systems; 240 volt; 50Hz electric motor; max working pressure 1000N/m² and max temperature of 130°C; includes fixing in position; electrical work elsewhere						
1" BSP unions - 2 speed	102.60	131.41	1.58	35.83	nr	**167.24**
1.25" BSP unions - 3 speed	151.20	193.66	1.58	35.83	nr	**229.49**
Pipeline mounted circulator; for heating and chilled water; silent running; 3 phase; 1450 rpm motor; max pressure 1000 kN/m²; max temperature 120°C; bolted connections; supply only mating flanges; includes fixing in position; electrical elsewhere						
32mm pump size; 2.0 l/s at 17 kPa max head; 0.2kW max motor rating	398.25	510.07	6.44	146.05	nr	**656.12**
50mm pump size; 3.0 l/s at 20 kPa max head; 0.2kW max motor rating	396.00	507.19	6.86	155.57	nr	**662.77**
65mm pump size; 5.0 l/s at 30 kPa max head; 0.37 kW max motor rating	630.00	806.90	7.48	169.63	nr	**976.53**
65mm pump size; 8.0 l/s at 37 kPa max head; 0.75 kW max motor rating	705.38	903.44	7.48	169.63	nr	**1073.07**
80mm pump size; 12.0 l/s at 42 kPa max head; 1.1 kW max motor rating	820.13	1050.41	8.01	181.65	nr	**1232.06**
100mm pump size; 25.0 l/s at 37 kPa max head; 2.2 kW max motor rating	1168.88	1497.08	9.11	206.60	nr	**1703.68**
Dual pipeline mounted circulator; for heating & chilled water; silent running; 3 phase; 1450 rpm motor; max pressure 1000 kN/m²; max temperature 120°C; bolted connections; supply only mating flanges; includes fixing in position; electrical work elsewhere						
40mm pump size; 2.0 l/s at 17 kPa max head; 0.8kW max motor rating	734.63	940.90	7.88	178.71	nr	**1119.61**
50mm pump size; 3.0 l/s at 20 kPa max head; 0.2 kW max motor rating	736.88	943.78	8.01	181.65	nr	**1125.44**
65mm pump size; 5.0 l/s at 30 kPa max head; 0.37 kW max motor rating	1195.88	1531.66	9.20	208.64	nr	**1740.31**
65mm pump size; 8.0 l/s at 37 kPa max head; 0.75 kW max motor rating	1382.63	1770.85	9.20	208.64	nr	**1979.49**
100mm pump size; 12.0 l/s at 42 kPa max head; 1.1 kW max motor rating	1563.75	2002.84	9.45	214.31	nr	**2217.15**

T:MECHANICAL/COOLING/HEATING SYSTEMS

Item	Net Price £	Material £	Labour hours	Labour £	Unit	Total rate £
T31 : LOW TEMPERATURE HOT WATER HEATING (cont'd)						
Y20 – PUMPS (cont'd)						
Glandless accelerator pumps; for low and medium pressure heating services; silent running; 3 phase; 1450 rpm motor; max pressure 1000 kN/m²; max temperature 130°C; bolted connections; supply only mating flanges; includes fixing in position; electrical work elsewhere						
40mm pump size; 4.0 l/s at 15 kPa max head; 0.35kW max motor rating	393.75	504.31	6.94	157.39	nr	**661.70**
50mm pump size; 6.0 l/s at 20 kPa max head; 0.45kW max motor rating	419.63	537.45	7.35	166.69	nr	**704.14**
80mm pump size; 13.0 l/s at 28 kPa max head; 0.58kW max motor rating	826.88	1059.05	7.76	175.98	nr	**1235.04**
Glandless pumps; for hot water secondary supply; silent running; 3 phase; max pressure 1000kN/m²; max temperature 130°C ; bolted connections; supply only mating flanges; including fixing in position; electrical elsewhere						
1" BSP unions - 3 speed	185.85	238.03	1.58	35.83	nr	**273.87**
Y22 - HEAT EXCHANGERS						
Plate heat exchanger; for use in LTHW systems; painted carbon steel frame; stainless steel plates, nitrile rubber gaskets; design pressure of 10 bar and operating temperature of 110/135°C						
Primary side; 85°C in, 74°C out; secondary side; 71°C in, 82°C out						
Duty, flow rate						
500 kW, 10.9 l/s	2586.00	3312.12	10.00	226.78	nr	**3538.91**
1000 kW, 21.7 l/s	3554.00	4551.93	12.00	272.14	nr	**4824.07**
1500 kW, 32.6 l/s	4528.00	5799.42	12.00	272.14	nr	**6071.56**
2000 kW, 43.4 l/s	5432.00	6957.25	15.00	340.18	nr	**7297.43**
2500 kW, 54.3 l/s	6677.00	8551.83	15.00	340.18	nr	**8892.01**
Note - For temperature conditions different to those above, the cost of the units can vary significantly, and so manufacturers advice should be sought.						

T:MECHANICAL/COOLING/HEATING SYSTEMS

Item	Net Price £	Material £	Labour hours	Labour £	Unit	Total rate £
Y23 - CALORIFIERS						
Non-storage calorifiers; mild steel; heater battery duty 82°C/71°C to BS 853, maximum test on shell 11.55 bar, tubes 26.25 bar						
Horizontal or vertical; primary water at 116°C on, 90°C off						
40 kW capacity	428.88	549.30	3.00	68.04	nr	**617.33**
88 kW capacity	499.38	639.59	5.00	113.39	nr	**752.99**
176 kW capacity	774.33	991.75	7.04	159.71	nr	**1151.46**
293 kW capacity	1150.33	1473.32	9.01	204.31	nr	**1677.63**
586 kW capacity	1690.83	2165.59	22.22	503.96	nr	**2669.56**
879 kW capacity	2204.30	2823.25	28.57	647.95	nr	**3471.20**
1465 kW capacity	3485.05	4463.62	50.00	1133.92	nr	**5597.54**
2000 kW capacity	4817.50	6170.21	60.00	1360.70	nr	**7530.91**
HEAT EMITTERS						
Perimeter convector heating; metal casing with standard finish; aluminium extruded grille; including backplates						
Top/sloping/flat front outlet						
60 x 200mm	31.85	40.79	2.00	45.36	m	**86.15**
60 x 300mm	34.64	44.37	2.00	45.36	m	**89.72**
60 x 450mm	42.94	55.00	2.00	45.36	m	**100.36**
60 x 525mm	45.71	58.54	2.00	45.36	m	**103.90**
60 x 600mm	49.86	63.86	2.00	45.36	m	**109.22**
90 x 260mm	34.64	44.37	2.00	45.36	m	**89.72**
90 x 300mm	36.01	46.12	2.00	45.36	m	**91.48**
90 x 450mm	44.34	56.79	2.00	45.36	m	**102.14**
90 x 525mm	48.49	62.10	2.00	45.36	m	**107.46**
90 x 600mm	51.26	65.65	2.00	45.36	m	**111.00**
Extra over for dampers						
Damper	14.46	18.53	0.25	5.67	nr	**24.20**
Extra over for fittings						
60mm End caps	11.57	14.82	0.25	5.67	nr	**20.49**
90mm End caps	18.81	24.09	0.25	5.67	nr	**29.76**
60mm Corners	24.60	31.51	0.25	5.67	nr	**37.18**
90mm Corners	36.18	46.34	0.25	5.67	nr	**52.01**
Radiant Strip Heaters						
Suitable for connection to hot water system; aluminium sheet panels with steel pipe clamped to upper surface; including insulation, sliding brackets, cover plates, end closures; weld or screwed BSP ends						
One pipe						
1500mm long	61.16	78.33	3.11	70.53	nr	**148.86**
3000mm long	96.74	123.90	3.11	70.53	nr	**194.43**
4500mm long	131.21	168.06	3.11	70.53	nr	**238.59**
6000mm long	180.88	231.67	3.11	70.53	nr	**302.20**

T:MECHANICAL/COOLING/HEATING SYSTEMS

Item	Net Price £	Material £	Labour hours	Labour £	Unit	Total rate £
T31 : LOW TEMPERATURE HOT WATER HEATING (cont'd)						
Y23 – CALORIFIERS (cont'd)						
HEAT EMITTERS (cont'd)						
Radiant strip heaters (cont'd)						
Two pipe						
1500mm long	114.17	146.23	4.15	94.12	nr	240.35
3000mm long	180.35	230.99	4.15	94.12	nr	325.11
4500mm long	246.28	315.43	4.15	94.12	nr	409.55
6000mm long	331.80	424.96	4.15	94.12	nr	519.08
Pressed steel panel type radiators; fixed with and including brackets; taking down once for decoration; refixing						
300mm high; single panel						
500mm length	14.94	19.14	2.03	46.04	nr	65.17
1000mm length	29.86	38.24	2.03	46.04	nr	84.28
1500mm length	39.12	50.10	2.03	46.04	nr	96.14
2000mm length	43.89	56.21	2.47	56.02	nr	112.22
2500mm length	48.63	62.29	2.97	67.35	nr	129.64
3000mm length	58.21	74.55	3.22	73.02	nr	147.58
300mm high; double panel; convector						
500mm length	28.72	36.79	2.13	48.31	nr	85.09
1000mm length	57.48	73.62	2.13	48.31	nr	121.92
1500mm length	86.20	110.40	2.13	48.31	nr	158.71
2000mm length	114.94	147.22	2.57	58.28	nr	205.50
2500mm length	143.66	184.00	3.07	69.62	nr	253.62
3000mm length	172.41	220.82	3.31	75.07	nr	295.88
450mm high; single panel						
500mm length	13.94	17.85	2.08	47.17	nr	65.02
1000mm length	27.89	35.72	2.08	47.17	nr	82.89
1600mm length	44.62	57.15	2.53	57.38	nr	114.52
2000mm length	55.78	71.44	2.97	67.35	nr	138.79
2400mm length	66.93	85.72	3.47	78.69	nr	164.41
3000mm length	83.67	107.16	3.82	86.63	nr	193.79
450mm high; double panel; convector						
500mm length	25.54	32.71	2.18	49.44	nr	82.15
1000mm length	51.08	65.42	2.18	49.44	nr	114.86
1600mm length	93.53	119.80	2.63	59.64	nr	179.44
2000mm length	157.24	201.39	3.06	69.40	nr	270.79
2400mm length	188.71	241.69	3.37	76.43	nr	318.12
3000mm length	235.88	302.11	3.92	88.90	nr	391.01
600mm high; single panel						
500mm length	18.68	23.92	2.18	49.44	nr	73.36
1000mm length	37.35	47.84	2.43	55.11	nr	102.95
1600mm length	59.76	76.54	3.13	70.98	nr	147.52
2000mm length	74.70	95.67	3.77	85.50	nr	181.17
2400mm length	89.65	114.82	4.07	92.30	nr	207.13
3000mm length	112.06	143.53	5.11	115.89	nr	259.41

T:MECHANICAL/COOLING/HEATING SYSTEMS

Item	Net Price £	Material £	Labour hours	Labour £	Unit	Total rate £
600mm high; double panel; convector						
500mm length	32.15	41.18	2.28	51.71	nr	**92.89**
1000mm length	64.31	82.36	2.28	51.71	nr	**134.07**
1600mm length	117.79	150.86	3.23	73.25	nr	**224.11**
2000mm length	198.02	253.63	3.87	87.77	nr	**341.39**
2400mm length	237.62	304.34	4.17	94.57	nr	**398.91**
3000mm length	297.02	380.42	5.24	118.83	nr	**499.26**
700mm high; single panel						
500mm length	21.86	28.00	2.23	50.57	nr	**78.57**
1000mm length	43.70	55.96	2.83	64.18	nr	**120.14**
1600mm length	69.91	89.54	3.73	84.59	nr	**174.13**
2000mm length	87.39	111.93	4.46	101.15	nr	**213.07**
2400mm length	104.88	134.33	4.48	101.60	nr	**235.93**
3000mm length	131.09	167.89	5.24	118.83	nr	**286.73**
700mm high; double panel; convector						
500mm length	41.79	53.53	2.33	52.84	nr	**106.37**
1000mm length	112.43	144.00	3.08	69.85	nr	**213.85**
1600mm length	179.89	230.40	3.83	86.86	nr	**317.26**
2000mm length	224.87	288.00	4.17	94.57	nr	**382.57**
2400mm length	269.84	345.61	4.37	99.10	nr	**444.72**
3000mm length	337.30	432.01	4.82	109.31	nr	**541.32**
Flat panel type steel radiators; fixed with and including brackets; taking down once for decoration; refixing						
300mm high; single panel (44mm deep)						
500mm length	42.15	53.98	2.03	46.04	nr	**100.02**
1000mm length	68.46	87.69	2.03	46.04	nr	**133.72**
1500mm length	94.78	121.39	2.03	46.04	nr	**167.43**
2000mm length	121.09	155.10	2.47	56.02	nr	**211.11**
2400mm length	142.15	182.06	2.97	67.35	nr	**249.42**
3000mm length	173.73	222.51	3.22	73.02	nr	**295.53**
300mm high; double panel (100mm deep)						
500mm length	116.04	148.62	2.03	46.04	nr	**194.65**
1000mm length	167.44	214.46	2.03	46.04	nr	**260.50**
1500mm length	218.85	280.30	2.03	46.04	nr	**326.34**
2000mm length	270.26	346.15	2.47	56.02	nr	**402.16**
2400mm length	311.39	398.82	2.97	67.35	nr	**466.17**
3000mm length	373.08	477.83	3.22	73.02	nr	**550.86**
500mm high; single panel (44mm deep)						
500mm length	52.06	66.68	2.13	48.31	nr	**114.98**
1000mm length	87.56	112.14	2.13	48.31	nr	**160.45**
1500mm length	123.05	157.60	2.13	48.31	nr	**205.91**
2000mm length	158.55	203.07	2.57	58.28	nr	**261.35**
2400mm length	186.95	239.44	3.07	69.62	nr	**309.06**
3000mm length	229.54	293.99	3.31	75.07	nr	**369.06**
500mm high; double panel (100mm deep)						
500mm length	135.09	173.02	2.08	47.17	nr	**220.19**
1000mm length	203.02	260.03	2.08	47.17	nr	**307.20**
1500mm length	270.95	347.03	2.53	57.38	nr	**404.41**
2000mm length	338.88	434.04	2.97	67.35	nr	**501.40**
2400mm length	393.23	503.65	3.47	78.69	nr	**582.34**
3000mm length	474.75	608.05	3.82	86.63	nr	**694.69**

T:MECHANICAL/COOLING/HEATING SYSTEMS

Item	Net Price £	Material £	Labour hours	Labour £	Unit	Total rate £
T31 : LOW TEMPERATURE HOT WATER HEATING (cont'd)						
Y23 – CALORIFIERS (cont'd)						
HEAT EMITTERS (cont'd)						
Flat panel type steel radiators (cont'd)						
600mm high; single panel (44mm deep)						
500mm length	56.71	72.64	2.18	49.44	nr	**122.08**
1000mm length	96.49	123.59	2.18	49.44	nr	**173.02**
1500mm length	96.49	123.59	2.63	59.64	nr	**183.23**
2000mm length	176.05	225.49	3.06	69.40	nr	**294.88**
2400mm length	207.88	266.25	3.37	76.43	nr	**342.67**
3000mm length	-	327.39	3.92	88.90	nr	**416.28**
600mm high; double panel (100mm deep)						
500mm length	145.37	186.19	2.18	49.44	nr	**235.63**
1000mm length	221.87	284.17	2.43	55.11	nr	**339.28**
1500mm length	-	382.15	3.13	70.98	nr	**453.13**
2000mm length	374.87	480.13	3.77	85.50	nr	**565.63**
2400mm length	436.07	558.51	4.07	92.30	nr	**650.82**
3000mm length	527.87	676.09	5.11	115.89	nr	**791.98**
700mm high; single panel (44mm deep)						
500mm length	61.36	78.59	2.28	51.71	nr	**130.30**
1000mm length	105.43	135.03	2.28	51.71	nr	**186.74**
1500mm length	149.49	191.47	3.23	73.25	nr	**264.72**
2000mm length	193.56	247.90	3.87	87.77	nr	**335.67**
2400mm length	228.81	293.05	4.17	94.57	nr	**387.62**
3000mm length	281.68	360.78	5.24	118.83	nr	**479.61**
700mm high; double panel (100mm deep)						
500mm length	155.04	198.57	2.23	50.57	nr	**249.15**
1000mm length	239.50	306.74	2.83	64.18	nr	**370.92**
1500mm length	323.95	414.91	3.73	84.59	nr	**499.50**
2000mm length	408.41	523.08	4.46	101.15	nr	**624.23**
2400mm length	475.97	609.62	4.48	101.60	nr	**711.22**
3000mm length	577.32	739.43	5.24	118.83	nr	**858.26**
Fan convector; sheet metal casing with lockable access panel; centrifugal fan; air filter; LPHW heating coil; extruded aluminium grilles; 3 speed; includes fixing in position; electrical work elsewhere						
Free standing flat top, 695mm high, medium speed rating						
Entering air temperature, 18°C						
695mm long, 1 row 1.94 kW, 75 l/sec	575.53	737.13	2.73	61.91	nr	**799.04**
695mm long, 2 row 2.64 kW, 75 l/sec	575.53	737.13	2.73	61.91	nr	**799.04**
895mm long, 1 row 4.02 kW, 150 l/sec	648.52	830.62	2.73	61.91	nr	**892.53**
895mm long, 2 row 5.62 kW, 150 l/sec	648.52	830.62	2.73	61.91	nr	**892.53**
1195mm long, 1 row 6.58 kW, 250 l/sec	738.36	945.68	3.00	68.04	nr	**1013.71**
1195mm long, 2 row 9.27 kW, 250 l/sec	738.36	945.68	3.00	68.04	nr	**1013.71**
1495mm long, 1 row 9.04 kW, 340 l/sec	823.99	1055.36	3.26	73.93	nr	**1129.29**
1495mm long, 2 row 12.73 kW, 340 l/sec	823.99	1055.36	3.26	73.93	nr	**1129.29**

T:MECHANICAL/COOLING/HEATING SYSTEMS

Item	Net Price £	Material £	Labour hours	Labour £	Unit	Total rate £
Free standing flat top, 695mm high, medium speed rating, c/w floor plinth						
695mm long, 1 row 1.94 kW, 75 l/sec	604.30	773.98	2.73	61.91	nr	**835.90**
695mm long, 2 row 2.64 kW, 75 l/sec	604.30	773.98	2.73	61.91	nr	**835.90**
895mm long, 1 row 4.02 kW, 150 l/sec	680.94	872.15	2.73	61.91	nr	**934.06**
895mm long, 2 row 5.62 kW, 150 l/sec	680.94	872.15	2.73	61.91	nr	**934.06**
1195mm long, 1 row 6.58 kW, 250 l/sec	775.28	992.97	3.00	68.04	nr	**1061.01**
1195mm long, 2 row 9.27 kW, 250 l/sec	775.28	992.97	3.00	68.04	nr	**1061.01**
1495mm long, 1 row 9.04 kW, 340 l/sec	865.18	1108.11	3.26	73.93	nr	**1182.05**
1495mm long, 2 row 12.73 kW, 340 l/sec	865.18	1108.11	3.26	73.93	nr	**1182.05**
Free standing sloping top, 695mm high, medium speed rating, c/w floor plinth						
695mm long, 1 row 1.94 kW, 75 l/sec	625.36	800.95	2.73	61.91	nr	**862.86**
695mm long, 2 row 2.64 kW, 75 l/sec	625.36	800.95	2.73	61.91	nr	**862.86**
895mm long, 1 row 4.02 kW, 150 l/sec	702.00	899.12	2.73	61.91	nr	**961.03**
895mm long, 2 row 5.62 kW, 150 l/sec	702.00	899.12	2.73	61.91	nr	**961.03**
1195mm long, 1 row 6.58 kW, 250 l/sec	796.34	1019.94	3.00	68.04	nr	**1087.97**
1195mm long, 2 row 9.27 kW, 250 l/sec	796.34	1019.94	3.00	68.04	nr	**1087.97**
1495mm long, 1 row 9.04 kW, 340 l/sec	886.24	1135.08	3.26	73.93	nr	**1209.01**
1495mm long, 2 row 12.73 kW, 340 l/sec	886.24	1135.08	3.26	73.93	nr	**1209.01**
Wall mounted high level sloping discharge						
695mm long, 1 row 1.94 kW, 75 l/sec	631.67	809.04	2.73	61.91	nr	**870.95**
695mm long, 2 row 2.64 kW, 75 l/sec	631.67	809.04	2.73	61.91	nr	**870.95**
895mm long, 1 row 4.02 kW, 150 l/sec	649.94	832.43	2.73	61.91	nr	**894.34**
895mm long, 2 row 5.62 kW, 150 l/sec	649.94	832.43	2.73	61.91	nr	**894.34**
1195mm long, 1 row 6.58 kW, 250 l/sec	790.98	1013.08	3.00	68.04	nr	**1081.11**
1195mm long, 2 row 9.27 kW, 250 l/sec	790.98	1013.08	3.00	68.04	nr	**1081.11**
1495mm long, 1 row 9.04 kW, 340 l/sec	857.67	1098.49	3.26	73.93	nr	**1172.42**
1495mm long, 2 row 12.73 kW, 340 l/sec	857.67	1098.49	3.26	73.93	nr	**1172.42**
Ceiling mounted sloping inlet/outlet 665mm wide						
895mm long, 1 row 4.02 kW, 150 l/sec	714.50	915.12	4.15	94.12	nr	**1009.23**
895mm long, 2 row 5.62 kW, 150 l/sec	714.50	915.12	4.15	94.12	nr	**1009.23**
1195mm long, 1 row 6.58 kW, 250 l/sec	802.94	1028.39	4.15	94.12	nr	**1122.51**
1195mm long, 2 row 9.27 kW, 250 l/sec	802.94	1028.39	4.15	94.12	nr	**1122.51**
1495mm long, 1 row 9.04 kW, 340 l/sec	881.54	1129.07	4.15	94.12	nr	**1223.18**
1495mm long, 2 row 12.73 kW, 340 l/sec	881.54	1129.07	4.15	94.12	nr	**1223.18**
Free standing unit, extended height 1700/1900/2100mm						
895mm long, 1 row 4.02 kW, 150 l/sec	826.80	1058.95	3.11	70.53	nr	**1129.48**
895mm long, 2 row 5.62 kW, 150 l/sec	826.80	1058.95	3.11	70.53	nr	**1129.48**
1195mm long, 1 row 6.58 kW, 250 l/sec	965.76	1236.94	3.11	70.53	nr	**1307.47**
1195mm long, 2 row 9.27 kW, 250 l/sec	965.76	1236.94	3.11	70.53	nr	**1307.47**
1495mm long, 1 row 9.04 kW, 340 l/sec	1062.63	1361.00	3.11	70.53	nr	**1431.53**
1495mm long, 2 row 12.73 kW, 340 l/sec	1062.63	1361.00	3.11	70.53	nr	**1431.53**

T:MECHANICAL/COOLING/HEATING SYSTEMS

Item	Net Price £	Material £	Labour hours	Labour £	Unit	Total rate £
T31 : LOW TEMPERATURE HOT WATER HEATING (cont'd)						
Y23 – CALORIFIERS (cont'd)						
HEAT EMITTERS (cont'd)						
LTHW trench heating; water temperatures 90°C/70°C; room air temperature 20°C; convector with copper tubes and aluminium fins within steel duct; includes fixing within floor screed; electrical work elsewhere						
Natural convection type						
Normal capacity, 182mm width, complete with linear, natural anodised aluminium grille (grille also costed separately below)						
92mm deep						
1250mm long, 234 W output	183.75	235.35	2.00	45.36	nr	**280.70**
2250mm long, 471 W output	294.00	376.55	4.00	90.71	nr	**467.27**
3250mm long, 709 W output	402.15	515.07	5.00	113.39	nr	**628.46**
4250mm long, 946 W output	513.45	657.62	7.00	158.75	nr	**816.37**
5000mm long, 1124 W output	701.40	898.35	8.00	181.43	nr	**1079.77**
120mm deep						
1250mm long, 294 W output	214.20	274.35	2.00	45.36	nr	**319.70**
2250mm long, 471 W output	337.05	431.69	4.00	90.71	nr	**522.40**
3250mm long, 891 W output	458.85	587.69	5.00	113.39	nr	**701.08**
4250mm long, 1190 W output	580.65	743.69	7.00	158.75	nr	**902.44**
5000mm long, 1414 W output	782.25	1001.90	8.00	181.43	nr	**1183.33**
150mm deep						
1250mm long, 329 W output	219.45	281.07	2.00	45.36	nr	**326.43**
2250mm long, 664 W output	346.50	443.79	4.00	90.71	nr	**534.51**
3250mm long, 998 W output	471.45	603.83	5.00	113.39	nr	**717.22**
4250mm long, 1333 W output	599.55	767.90	7.00	158.75	nr	**926.65**
5000mm long, 1584 W output	804.30	1030.14	8.00	181.43	nr	**1211.57**
200mm deep						
1250mm long, 396 W output	228.90	293.17	2.00	45.36	nr	**338.53**
2250mm long, 799 W output	418.95	536.59	4.00	90.71	nr	**627.30**
3250mm long, 1201 W output	498.75	638.79	5.00	113.39	nr	**752.19**
4250mm long, 1603 W output	638.40	817.66	7.00	158.75	nr	**976.41**
5000mm long, 1905 W output	848.40	1086.62	8.00	181.43	nr	**1268.05**

T:MECHANICAL/COOLING/HEATING SYSTEMS

Item	Net Price £	Material £	Labour hours	Labour £	Unit	Total rate £
Fan assisted type (outputs assume fan at 50%)						
Normal capacity, 182mm width, complete with Natural anodised aluminium grille						
112mm deep						
1250mm long, 437 W output	485.10	621.31	2.00	45.36	nr	**666.67**
2250mm long, 1019 W output	586.95	751.76	4.00	90.71	nr	**842.47**
3250mm long, 1488 W output	689.85	883.55	5.00	113.39	nr	**996.95**
4250mm long, 1845 W output	791.70	1014.00	7.00	158.75	nr	**1172.75**
5000mm long, 2038 W output	893.55	1144.45	8.00	181.43	nr	**1325.88**
Linear grille anodised aluminium, 170mm width (If supplied as a separate item)	114.45	146.59	-	-	m	**146.59**
Roll up grille, natural anodised aluminium	114.45	146.59	-	-	m	**146.59**
Thermostatic valve with remote regulator (c/w valve body)	47.25	60.52	4.00	90.71	nr	**151.23**
Fan speed controller	23.10	29.59	2.00	45.36	nr	**74.94**
Note - as an alternative to thermostatic control, the system can be controlled via two port valves. Refer to valve section in T31 for valve prices						
LTHW underfloor heating; water flow and return temperatures of 60°C and 70°C; pipework at 300mm centres; pipe fixings; flow and return manifolds and zone actuators; wiring block; insulation; includes fixing in position; excludes secondary pump, mixing valve, zone thermostats and floor finishes ; electrical work elsewhere						
Note - All rates are expressed on a m² basis, for the following example areas						
Screeded floor with 15-25mm stone/marble finish (producing 80-100W/m²)						
250m² area (single zone)	14.78	18.93	0.14	3.18	m²	**22.10**
1000m² area (single zone)	14.40	18.45	0.12	2.72	m²	**21.17**
5000m² area (multi-zone)	14.36	18.40	0.10	2.27	m²	**20.66**
Screeded floor with 10mm carpet tile (producing 80-100W/m²)						
250m² area (single zone)	14.78	18.93	0.14	3.18	m²	**22.10**
1000m² area (single zone)	14.40	18.45	0.12	2.72	m²	**21.17**
5000m² area (multi-zone)	14.36	18.40	0.10	2.27	m²	**20.66**
Floating timber floor with 20mm timber finish (producing 70-80Wm²)						
250m² are (single zone)	21.11	27.04	0.14	3.18	m²	**30.22**
1000m² area(single zone)	19.97	25.57	0.12	2.72	m²	**28.30**
5000m² area (multi-zone)	19.07	24.43	0.10	2.27	m²	**26.70**

T:MECHANICAL/COOLING/HEATING SYSTEMS

Item	Net Price £	Material £	Labour hours	Labour £	Unit	Total rate £
T31 : LOW TEMPERATURE HOT WATER HEATING (cont'd)						
Y23 – CALORIFIERS (cont'd)						
HEAT EMITTERS (cont'd)						
LTHW underfloor heating (cont'd)						
Floating timber floor with 10mm carpet tile (producing 70-80W/m²)						
250m² are (single zone)	24.23	31.04	0.16	3.63	m²	34.66
1000m² area(single zone)	22.48	28.80	0.12	2.72	m²	31.52
5000m² area (multi-zone)	21.50	27.53	0.10	2.27	m²	29.80
PIPE FREEZING						
Freeze isolation of carbon steel or copper pipelines containing static water, either side of work location, freeze duration not exceeding 4 hours assuming that flow and return circuits are treated concurrently and activities undertaken during normal working hours						
4 freezes						
50mm dia	332.39	425.73	-	-	nr	425.73
65mm dia	332.39	425.73	-	-	nr	425.73
80mm dia	380.00	486.71	-	-	nr	486.71
100mm dia	427.61	547.68	-	-	nr	547.68
150mm dia	711.52	911.30	-	-	nr	911.30
200mm dia	1090.64	1396.88	-	-	nr	1396.88
ENERGY METERS						
Ultrasonic						
Energy meter for measuring energy use in LTHW systems; includes ultrasonic flow meter (with sensor and signal converter), energy calculator, pair of temperature sensors with brass pockets, and 3m of interconnecting cable; includes fixing in position; electrical work elsewhere						
Pipe size (flanged connections to PN16); maximum flow rate						
50mm, 36m³/hr	991.03	1269.30	1.80	40.82	nr	1310.13
65mm, 60m³/hr	1092.42	1399.16	2.32	52.61	nr	1451.77
80mm, 100m³/hr	1224.51	1568.34	2.56	58.06	nr	1626.40
125mm, 250m³/hr	1418.72	1817.08	3.60	81.64	nr	1898.72
150mm, 360m³/hr	1540.10	1972.54	4.80	108.86	nr	2081.40
200mm, 600m³/hr	1720.74	2203.91	6.24	141.51	nr	2345.42
250mm, 1000m³/hr	1985.63	2543.18	9.60	217.71	nr	2760.89
300mm, 1500m³/hr	2334.07	2989.45	10.80	244.93	nr	3234.38
350mm, 2000m³/hr	2812.45	3602.15	13.20	299.35	nr	3901.51
400mm, 2500m³/hr	3219.43	4123.41	15.60	353.78	nr	4477.19
500mm, 3000m³/hr	3653.54	4679.41	24.00	544.28	nr	5223.70
600mm, 3500m³/hr	4104.79	5257.37	28.00	635.00	nr	5892.36

T:MECHANICAL/COOLING/HEATING SYSTEMS

Item	Net Price £	Material £	Labour hours	Labour £	Unit	Total rate £
Y53 - CONTROL COMPONENTS - MECHANICAL						
Room thermostats; light and medium duty; installed and connected						
Range 3°C to 27°C; 240 Volt						
1 amp; on/off type	21.33	27.32	0.30	6.80	nr	**34.12**
Range 0°C to +15°C; 240 Volt						
6 amp; frost thermostat	14.38	18.42	0.30	6.80	nr	**25.22**
Range 3°C to 27°C; 250 Volt						
2 amp; changeover type; dead zone	35.67	45.68	0.30	6.80	nr	**52.48**
2 amp; changeover type	16.54	21.18	0.30	6.80	nr	**27.99**
2 amp; changeover type; concealed setting	20.87	26.72	0.30	6.80	nr	**33.53**
6 amp; on/off type	12.89	16.50	0.30	6.80	nr	**23.31**
6 amp; temperature set-back	26.65	34.14	0.30	6.80	nr	**40.94**
16 amp; on/off type	19.84	25.41	0.30	6.80	nr	**32.22**
16 amp; on/off type; concealed setting	21.63	27.70	0.30	6.80	nr	**34.51**
20 amp; on/off type; concealed setting	23.62	30.25	0.30	6.80	nr	**37.06**
20 amp; indicated "off" position	23.23	29.75	0.30	6.80	nr	**36.55**
20 amp; manual; double pole on/off and neon indicator	42.29	54.16	0.30	6.80	nr	**60.96**
20 amp; indicated "off" position	27.67	35.44	0.30	6.80	nr	**42.24**
Range 10°C to 40°C; 240 Volt						
20 amp; changeover contacts	25.21	32.29	0.30	6.80	nr	**39.09**
2 amp; 'heating-cooling' switch	54.53	69.85	0.30	6.80	nr	**76.65**
Surface thermostats						
Cylinder thermostat						
6 amp; changeover type; with cable	13.79	18.10	0.25	5.67	nr	**23.77**
Electrical thermostats; installed and connected						
Range 5°C to 30°C; 230 Volt standard port single time						
10 amp with sensor	20.68	26.48	0.30	6.80	nr	**33.28**
Range 5°C to 30°C; 230 Volt standard port double time						
10 amp with sensor	23.43	30.01	0.30	6.80	nr	**36.81**
10 amp with sensor and on/off switch	35.74	45.77	0.30	6.80	nr	**52.58**
Radiator thermostats						
Angled valve body; thermostatic head; built in sensor						
15mm; liquid filled	12.89	16.51	0.84	19.06	nr	**35.57**
15mm; wax filled	12.89	16.51	0.84	19.06	nr	**35.57**

T:MECHANICAL/COOLING/HEATING SYSTEMS

Item	Net Price £	Material £	Labour hours	Labour £	Unit	Total rate £
T31 : LOW TEMPERATURE HOT WATER HEATING (cont'd)						
Y53 - CONTROL COMPONENTS - MECHANICAL (cont'd)						
Immersion thermostats; stem type; domestic water boilers; fitted; electrical work elsewhere						
Temperature range 0°C to 40°C						
Non standard; 280mm stem	7.85	10.05	0.25	5.67	nr	15.72
Temperature range 18°C to 88°C						
13 amp; 178mm stem	5.21	6.67	0.25	5.67	nr	12.34
20 amp; 178mm stem	8.10	10.37	0.25	5.67	nr	16.04
Non standard; pocket clip; 280mm stem	7.51	9.62	0.25	5.67	nr	15.29
Temperature range 40°C to 80°C						
13 amp; 178mm stem	2.86	3.66	0.25	5.67	nr	9.33
20 amp; 178mm stem	5.41	6.93	0.25	5.67	nr	12.60
Non standard; pocket clip; 280mm stem	8.42	10.78	0.25	5.67	nr	16.45
13 amp; 457mm stem	3.38	4.33	0.25	5.67	nr	9.99
20 amp; 457mm stem	5.92	7.58	0.25	5.67	nr	13.25
Temperature range 50°C to 100°C						
Non standard; 1780mm stem	7.09	9.08	0.25	5.67	nr	14.75
Non standard; 280mm stem	7.38	9.46	0.25	5.67	nr	15.13
Pockets for thermostats						
For 178mm stem	9.27	11.87	0.25	5.67	nr	17.54
For 280mm stem	9.18	11.76	0.25	5.67	nr	17.43
Immersion thermostats; stem type; industrial installations; fitted; electrical work elsewhere						
Temperature range 5°C to 105°C						
For 305mm stem	116.42	149.10	0.50	11.34	nr	160.44

T:MECHANICAL/COOLING/HEATING SYSTEMS

Item	Net Price £	Material £	Labour hours	Labour £	Unit	Total rate £
Y50 -THERMAL INSULATION						
For flexible closed cell insulation see Section S10 - Cold Water						
Mineral fibre sectional insulation; bright class O foil faced; bright class O foil taped joints; 19mm aluminium bands						
Concealed pipework						
20mm thick						
15mm diameter	2.56	3.34	0.15	2.93	m	**6.27**
20mm diameter	2.72	3.56	0.15	2.93	m	**6.49**
25mm diameter	2.93	3.83	0.15	2.93	m	**6.76**
32mm diameter	3.26	4.27	0.15	2.93	m	**7.20**
40mm diameter	3.49	4.57	0.15	2.93	m	**7.50**
50mm diameter	3.98	5.21	0.15	2.93	m	**8.14**
Extra over for fittings concealed insulation						
Flange/union						
15mm diameter	1.27	1.66	0.13	2.54	nr	**4.20**
20mm diameter	1.37	1.79	0.13	2.54	nr	**4.33**
25mm diameter	1.46	1.91	0.13	2.54	nr	**4.46**
32mm diameter	1.63	2.13	0.13	2.54	nr	**4.68**
40mm diameter	1.74	2.28	0.13	2.54	nr	**4.82**
50mm diameter	1.99	2.60	0.13	2.54	nr	**5.15**
Valves						
15mm diameter	2.56	3.34	0.15	2.93	nr	**6.27**
20mm diameter	2.93	3.83	0.15	2.93	nr	**6.76**
25mm diameter	2.93	3.83	0.15	2.93	nr	**6.76**
32mm diameter	3.26	4.27	0.15	2.93	nr	**7.20**
40mm diameter	3.49	4.57	0.15	2.93	nr	**7.50**
50mm diameter	3.98	5.21	0.15	2.93	nr	**8.14**
Pumps						
15mm diameter	5.10	6.67	0.45	8.80	nr	**15.47**
20mm diameter	5.45	7.12	0.45	8.80	nr	**15.92**
25mm diameter	5.86	7.66	0.45	8.80	nr	**16.46**
32mm diameter	6.52	8.52	0.45	8.80	nr	**17.32**
40mm diameter	6.98	9.13	0.45	8.80	nr	**17.93**
50mm diameter	7.98	10.44	0.45	8.80	nr	**19.23**
Expansion bellows						
15mm diameter	5.10	6.67	0.22	4.30	nr	**10.97**
20mm diameter	5.45	7.12	0.22	4.30	nr	**11.43**
25mm diameter	5.86	7.66	0.22	4.30	nr	**11.96**
32mm diameter	6.52	8.52	0.22	4.30	nr	**12.82**
40mm diameter	6.98	9.13	0.22	4.30	nr	**13.43**
50mm diameter	7.98	10.44	0.22	4.30	nr	**14.74**

T:MECHANICAL/COOLING/HEATING SYSTEMS

Item	Net Price £	Material £	Labour hours	Labour £	Unit	Total rate £
T31 : LOW TEMPERATURE HOT WATER HEATING (cont'd)						
Y50 -THERMAL INSULATION (cont'd)						
Fittings; concealed insulation (cont'd)						
25mm thick						
15mm diameter	2.81	3.67	0.15	2.93	m	**6.60**
20mm diameter	3.02	3.95	0.15	2.93	m	**6.89**
25mm diameter	3.38	4.43	0.15	2.93	m	**7.36**
32mm diameter	3.68	4.82	0.15	2.93	m	**7.75**
40mm diameter	3.95	5.16	0.15	2.93	m	**8.10**
50mm diameter	4.52	5.92	0.15	2.93	m	**8.85**
65mm diameter	5.16	6.75	0.15	2.93	m	**9.68**
80mm diameter	5.66	7.41	0.22	4.30	m	**11.71**
100mm diameter	7.46	9.76	0.22	4.30	m	**14.06**
125mm diameter	8.63	11.28	0.22	4.30	m	**15.58**
150mm diameter	10.28	13.45	0.22	4.30	m	**17.75**
200mm diameter	14.53	19.00	0.25	4.89	m	**23.89**
250mm diameter	17.40	22.75	0.25	4.89	m	**27.64**
300mm diameter	18.60	24.32	0.25	4.89	m	**29.21**
Extra over for fittings concealed insulation						
Flange/union						
15mm diameter	1.40	1.84	0.13	2.54	nr	**4.38**
20mm diameter	1.51	1.98	0.13	2.54	nr	**4.52**
25mm diameter	1.69	2.21	0.13	2.54	nr	**4.75**
32mm diameter	1.85	2.42	0.13	2.54	nr	**4.96**
40mm diameter	1.97	2.57	0.13	2.54	nr	**5.12**
50mm diameter	2.26	2.95	0.13	2.54	nr	**5.49**
65mm diameter	2.58	3.37	0.13	2.54	nr	**5.92**
80mm diameter	2.83	3.70	0.18	3.52	nr	**7.22**
100mm diameter	3.73	4.88	0.18	3.52	nr	**8.40**
125mm diameter	4.32	5.65	0.18	3.52	nr	**9.17**
150mm diameter	5.14	6.72	0.18	3.52	nr	**10.24**
200mm diameter	7.26	9.49	0.22	4.30	nr	**13.79**
250mm diameter	8.70	11.38	0.22	4.30	nr	**15.68**
300mm diameter	9.30	12.16	0.22	4.30	nr	**16.46**
Valves						
15mm diameter	2.81	3.67	0.15	2.93	nr	**6.60**
20mm diameter	3.02	3.95	0.15	2.93	nr	**6.89**
25mm diameter	3.38	4.43	0.15	2.93	nr	**7.36**
32mm diameter	3.68	4.82	0.15	2.93	nr	**7.75**
40mm diameter	3.95	5.16	0.15	2.93	nr	**8.10**
50mm diameter	4.52	5.92	0.15	2.93	nr	**8.85**
65mm diameter	5.16	6.75	0.15	2.93	nr	**9.68**
80mm diameter	5.66	7.41	0.20	3.91	nr	**11.32**
100mm diameter	7.46	9.76	0.20	3.91	nr	**13.67**
125mm diameter	8.63	11.28	0.20	3.91	nr	**15.19**
150mm diameter	10.28	13.45	0.20	3.91	nr	**17.36**
200mm diameter	14.53	19.00	0.25	4.89	nr	**23.89**
250mm diameter	17.40	22.75	0.25	4.89	nr	**27.64**
300mm diameter	18.60	24.32	0.25	4.89	nr	**29.21**

T:MECHANICAL/COOLING/HEATING SYSTEMS

Item	Net Price £	Material £	Labour hours	Labour £	Unit	Total rate £
Pumps						
15mm diameter	5.62	7.34	0.45	8.80	nr	**16.14**
20mm diameter	6.06	7.92	0.45	8.80	nr	**16.72**
25mm diameter	6.76	8.83	0.45	8.80	nr	**17.63**
32mm diameter	7.37	9.63	0.45	8.80	nr	**18.43**
40mm diameter	7.90	10.33	0.45	8.80	nr	**19.12**
50mm diameter	9.05	11.83	0.45	8.80	nr	**20.63**
65mm diameter	10.33	13.51	0.45	8.80	nr	**22.31**
80mm diameter	11.32	14.80	0.60	11.73	nr	**26.53**
100mm diameter	14.92	19.51	0.60	11.73	nr	**31.24**
125mm diameter	17.26	22.57	0.60	11.73	nr	**34.30**
150mm diameter	20.57	26.90	0.60	11.73	nr	**38.63**
200mm diameter	29.05	37.99	0.75	14.66	nr	**52.65**
250mm diameter	34.79	45.49	0.75	14.66	nr	**60.15**
300mm diameter	37.20	48.65	0.75	14.66	nr	**63.31**
Expansion bellows						
15mm diameter	5.62	7.34	0.22	4.30	nr	**11.64**
20mm diameter	6.06	7.92	0.22	4.30	nr	**12.23**
25mm diameter	6.76	8.83	0.22	4.30	nr	**13.14**
32mm diameter	7.37	9.63	0.22	4.30	nr	**13.94**
40mm diameter	7.90	10.33	0.22	4.30	nr	**14.63**
50mm diameter	9.05	11.83	0.22	4.30	nr	**16.13**
65mm diameter	10.33	13.51	0.22	4.30	nr	**17.81**
80mm diameter	11.32	14.80	0.29	5.67	nr	**20.47**
100mm diameter	14.92	19.51	0.29	5.67	nr	**25.17**
125mm diameter	17.26	22.57	0.29	5.67	nr	**28.23**
150mm diameter	20.57	26.90	0.29	5.67	nr	**32.57**
200mm diameter	29.05	37.99	0.36	7.04	nr	**45.03**
250mm diameter	34.79	45.49	0.36	7.04	nr	**52.53**
300mm diameter	37.20	48.65	0.36	7.04	nr	**55.68**
30mm thick						
15mm diameter	3.65	4.77	0.15	2.93	m	**7.70**
20mm diameter	3.91	5.12	0.15	2.93	m	**8.05**
25mm diameter	4.14	5.41	0.15	2.93	m	**8.35**
32mm diameter	4.51	5.90	0.15	2.93	m	**8.83**
40mm diameter	4.78	6.25	0.15	2.93	m	**9.18**
50mm diameter	5.46	7.14	0.15	2.93	m	**10.07**
65mm diameter	6.18	8.08	0.15	2.93	m	**11.01**
80mm diameter	6.74	8.82	0.22	4.30	m	**13.12**
100mm diameter	8.72	11.41	0.22	4.30	m	**15.71**
125mm diameter	10.04	13.13	0.22	4.30	m	**17.44**
150mm diameter	11.80	15.43	0.22	4.30	m	**19.73**
200mm diameter	16.50	21.58	0.25	4.89	m	**26.46**
250mm diameter	19.62	25.66	0.25	4.89	m	**30.54**
300mm diameter	20.80	27.19	0.25	4.89	m	**32.08**
350mm diameter	22.85	29.88	0.25	4.89	m	**34.77**

T:MECHANICAL/COOLING/HEATING SYSTEMS

Item	Net Price £	Material £	Labour hours	Labour £	Unit	Total rate £
T31 : LOW TEMPERATURE HOT WATER HEATING (cont'd)						
Y50 -THERMAL INSULATION (cont'd)						
Extra over for fittings concealed insulation						
Flange/union						
15mm diameter	1.82	2.39	0.13	2.54	nr	**4.93**
20mm diameter	1.96	2.56	0.13	2.54	nr	**5.10**
25mm diameter	2.06	2.70	0.13	2.54	nr	**5.24**
32mm diameter	2.26	2.95	0.13	2.54	nr	**5.49**
40mm diameter	2.39	3.12	0.13	2.54	nr	**5.66**
50mm diameter	2.74	3.58	0.13	2.54	nr	**6.12**
65mm diameter	3.10	4.05	0.13	2.54	nr	**6.59**
80mm diameter	3.37	4.41	0.18	3.52	nr	**7.93**
100mm diameter	4.37	5.71	0.18	3.52	nr	**9.23**
125mm diameter	5.02	6.56	0.18	3.52	nr	**10.08**
150mm diameter	5.90	7.72	0.18	3.52	nr	**11.24**
200mm diameter	8.24	10.78	0.22	4.30	nr	**15.08**
250mm diameter	9.82	12.84	0.22	4.30	nr	**17.14**
300mm diameter	10.40	13.61	0.22	4.30	nr	**17.91**
350mm diameter	11.42	14.94	0.22	4.30	nr	**19.24**
Valves						
15mm diameter	3.91	5.12	0.15	2.93	nr	**8.05**
20mm diameter	3.91	5.12	0.15	2.93	nr	**8.05**
25mm diameter	4.14	5.41	0.15	2.93	nr	**8.35**
32mm diameter	4.51	5.90	0.15	2.93	nr	**8.83**
40mm diameter	4.78	6.25	0.15	2.93	nr	**9.18**
50mm diameter	5.46	7.14	0.15	2.93	nr	**10.07**
65mm diameter	6.18	8.08	0.15	2.93	nr	**11.01**
80mm diameter	6.74	8.82	0.20	3.91	nr	**12.73**
100mm diameter	8.72	11.41	0.20	3.91	nr	**15.32**
125mm diameter	10.04	13.13	0.20	3.91	nr	**17.04**
150mm diameter	11.80	15.43	0.20	3.91	nr	**19.34**
200mm diameter	16.50	21.58	0.25	4.89	nr	**26.46**
250mm diameter	19.62	25.66	0.25	4.89	nr	**30.54**
300mm diameter	20.80	27.19	0.25	4.89	nr	**32.08**
350mm diameter	22.85	29.88	0.25	4.89	nr	**34.77**
Pumps						
15mm diameter	7.31	9.56	0.45	8.80	nr	**18.35**
20mm diameter	7.81	10.22	0.45	8.80	nr	**19.01**
25mm diameter	8.27	10.81	0.45	8.80	nr	**19.61**
32mm diameter	9.04	11.82	0.45	8.80	nr	**20.61**
40mm diameter	9.55	12.49	0.45	8.80	nr	**21.29**
50mm diameter	10.93	14.30	0.45	8.80	nr	**23.09**
65mm diameter	12.36	16.16	0.45	8.80	nr	**24.96**
80mm diameter	13.49	17.64	0.60	11.73	nr	**29.37**
100mm diameter	17.46	22.83	0.60	11.73	nr	**34.56**
125mm diameter	20.08	26.25	0.60	11.73	nr	**37.98**
150mm diameter	23.59	30.85	0.60	11.73	nr	**42.58**
200mm diameter	32.99	43.14	0.75	14.66	nr	**57.80**
250mm diameter	39.24	51.31	0.75	14.66	nr	**65.98**
300mm diameter	41.60	54.40	0.75	14.66	nr	**69.07**
350mm diameter	45.68	59.74	0.75	14.66	nr	**74.40**

T:MECHANICAL/COOLING/HEATING SYSTEMS

Item	Net Price £	Material £	Labour hours	Labour £	Unit	Total rate £
Expansion bellows						
15mm diameter	7.31	9.56	0.22	4.30	nr	**13.86**
20mm diameter	7.81	10.22	0.22	4.30	nr	**14.52**
25mm diameter	8.27	10.81	0.22	4.30	nr	**15.11**
32mm diameter	9.04	11.82	0.22	4.30	nr	**16.12**
40mm diameter	9.55	12.49	0.22	4.30	nr	**16.79**
50mm diameter	10.93	14.30	0.22	4.30	nr	**18.60**
65mm diameter	12.36	16.16	0.22	4.30	nr	**20.46**
80mm diameter	13.49	17.64	0.29	5.67	nr	**23.31**
100mm diameter	17.46	22.83	0.29	5.67	nr	**28.50**
125mm diameter	20.08	26.25	0.29	5.67	nr	**31.92**
150mm diameter	23.59	30.85	0.29	5.67	nr	**36.52**
200mm diameter	32.99	43.14	0.36	7.04	nr	**50.18**
250mm diameter	39.24	51.31	0.36	7.04	nr	**58.35**
300mm diameter	41.60	54.40	0.36	7.04	nr	**61.44**
350mm diameter	45.68	59.74	0.36	7.04	nr	**66.78**
40mm thick						
15mm diameter	4.68	6.12	0.15	2.93	m	**9.05**
20mm diameter	4.82	6.31	0.15	2.93	m	**9.24**
25mm diameter	5.18	6.78	0.15	2.93	m	**9.71**
32mm diameter	5.53	7.23	0.15	2.93	m	**10.17**
40mm diameter	5.81	7.59	0.15	2.93	m	**10.53**
50mm diameter	6.58	8.60	0.15	2.93	m	**11.53**
65mm diameter	7.38	9.65	0.15	2.93	m	**12.58**
80mm diameter	8.03	10.50	0.22	4.30	m	**14.80**
100mm diameter	10.42	13.62	0.22	4.30	m	**17.92**
125mm diameter	11.77	15.39	0.22	4.30	m	**19.69**
150mm diameter	13.74	17.97	0.22	4.30	m	**22.27**
200mm diameter	18.98	24.82	0.25	4.89	m	**29.71**
250mm diameter	22.25	29.09	0.25	4.89	m	**33.98**
300mm diameter	23.78	31.10	0.25	4.89	m	**35.99**
350mm diameter	26.30	34.40	0.25	4.89	m	**39.28**
400mm diameter	29.32	38.34	0.25	4.89	m	**43.22**
Extra over for fittings concealed insulation						
Flange/union						
15mm diameter	2.34	3.06	0.13	2.54	nr	**5.60**
20mm diameter	2.41	3.15	0.13	2.54	nr	**5.70**
25mm diameter	2.59	3.39	0.13	2.54	nr	**5.93**
32mm diameter	2.76	3.61	0.13	2.54	nr	**6.15**
40mm diameter	2.90	3.80	0.13	2.54	nr	**6.34**
50mm diameter	3.29	4.30	0.13	2.54	nr	**6.84**
65mm diameter	3.68	4.82	0.13	2.54	nr	**7.36**
80mm diameter	4.02	5.26	0.18	3.52	nr	**8.78**
100mm diameter	5.21	6.81	0.18	3.52	nr	**10.33**
125mm diameter	5.88	7.69	0.18	3.52	nr	**11.21**
150mm diameter	6.88	8.99	0.18	3.52	nr	**12.51**
200mm diameter	9.49	12.41	0.22	4.30	nr	**16.71**
250mm diameter	11.12	14.55	0.22	4.30	nr	**18.85**
300mm diameter	11.89	15.55	0.22	4.30	nr	**19.85**
350mm diameter	13.15	17.20	0.22	4.30	nr	**21.50**
400mm diameter	14.66	19.18	0.22	4.30	nr	**23.48**

T:MECHANICAL/COOLING/HEATING SYSTEMS

Item	Net Price £	Material £	Labour hours	Labour £	Unit	Total rate £
T31 : LOW TEMPERATURE HOT WATER HEATING (cont'd)						
Y50 -THERMAL INSULATION (cont'd)						
Fittings; concealed insulation (cont'd)						
Valves						
15mm diameter	4.68	6.12	0.15	2.93	nr	9.05
20mm diameter	4.82	6.31	0.15	2.93	nr	9.24
25mm diameter	5.18	6.78	0.15	2.93	nr	9.71
32mm diameter	5.53	7.23	0.15	2.93	nr	10.17
40mm diameter	5.81	7.59	0.15	2.93	nr	10.53
50mm diameter	6.58	8.60	0.15	2.93	nr	11.53
65mm diameter	7.38	9.65	0.15	2.93	nr	12.58
80mm diameter	8.03	10.50	0.20	3.91	nr	14.41
100mm diameter	10.42	13.62	0.20	3.91	nr	17.53
125mm diameter	11.77	15.39	0.20	3.91	nr	19.30
150mm diameter	13.74	17.97	0.20	3.91	nr	21.88
200mm diameter	18.98	24.82	0.25	4.89	nr	29.71
250mm diameter	22.25	29.09	0.25	4.89	nr	33.98
300mm diameter	23.78	31.10	0.25	4.89	nr	35.99
350mm diameter	26.30	34.40	0.25	4.89	nr	39.28
400mm diameter	29.32	38.34	0.25	4.89	nr	43.22
Pumps						
15mm diameter	9.37	12.26	0.45	8.80	nr	21.05
20mm diameter	9.64	12.60	0.45	8.80	nr	21.40
25mm diameter	10.38	13.57	0.45	8.80	nr	22.37
32mm diameter	11.05	14.45	0.45	8.80	nr	23.25
40mm diameter	11.63	15.21	0.45	8.80	nr	24.00
50mm diameter	13.15	17.20	0.45	8.80	nr	26.00
65mm diameter	14.75	19.29	0.45	8.80	nr	28.08
80mm diameter	16.06	21.00	0.60	11.73	nr	32.73
100mm diameter	20.82	27.23	0.60	11.73	nr	38.96
125mm diameter	23.53	30.77	0.60	11.73	nr	42.50
150mm diameter	27.48	35.93	0.60	11.73	nr	47.66
200mm diameter	37.97	49.65	0.75	14.66	nr	64.31
250mm diameter	44.50	58.19	0.75	14.66	nr	72.85
300mm diameter	47.57	62.20	0.75	14.66	nr	76.87
350mm diameter	52.60	68.78	0.75	14.66	nr	83.44
400mm diameter	58.63	76.67	0.75	14.66	nr	91.33
Expansion bellows						
15mm diameter	9.37	12.26	0.22	4.30	nr	16.56
20mm diameter	9.64	12.60	0.22	4.30	nr	16.90
25mm diameter	10.38	13.57	0.22	4.30	nr	17.87
32mm diameter	11.05	14.45	0.22	4.30	nr	18.75
40mm diameter	11.63	15.21	0.22	4.30	nr	19.51
50mm diameter	13.15	17.20	0.22	4.30	nr	21.50
65mm diameter	14.75	19.29	0.22	4.30	nr	23.59
80mm diameter	16.06	21.00	0.29	5.67	nr	26.67
100mm diameter	20.82	27.23	0.29	5.67	nr	32.90
125mm diameter	23.53	30.77	0.29	5.67	nr	36.44
150mm diameter	27.48	35.93	0.29	5.67	nr	41.60
200mm diameter	37.97	49.65	0.36	7.04	nr	56.69
250mm diameter	44.50	58.19	0.36	7.04	nr	65.22
300mm diameter	47.57	62.20	0.36	7.04	nr	69.24
350mm diameter	26.30	34.40	0.36	7.04	nr	41.43
400mm diameter	58.63	76.67	0.36	7.04	nr	83.71

T:MECHANICAL/COOLING/HEATING SYSTEMS

Item	Net Price £	Material £	Labour hours	Labour £	Unit	Total rate £
50mm thick						
15mm diameter	6.50	8.51	0.15	2.93	m	**11.44**
20mm diameter	6.84	8.94	0.15	2.93	m	**11.88**
25mm diameter	7.27	9.51	0.15	2.93	m	**12.44**
32mm diameter	7.60	9.93	0.15	2.93	m	**12.87**
40mm diameter	7.99	10.45	0.15	2.93	m	**13.38**
50mm diameter	8.96	11.72	0.15	2.93	m	**14.65**
65mm diameter	9.79	12.80	0.15	2.93	m	**15.74**
80mm diameter	10.49	13.71	0.22	4.30	m	**18.02**
100mm diameter	13.40	17.53	0.22	4.30	m	**21.83**
125mm diameter	15.05	19.68	0.22	4.30	m	**23.98**
150mm diameter	17.36	22.71	0.22	4.30	m	**27.01**
200mm diameter	23.71	31.01	0.25	4.89	m	**35.89**
250mm diameter	27.38	35.81	0.25	4.89	m	**40.70**
300mm diameter	29.02	37.94	0.25	4.89	m	**42.83**
350mm diameter	32.03	41.88	0.25	4.89	m	**46.77**
400mm diameter	35.52	46.45	0.25	4.89	m	**51.34**
Extra over for fittings concealed insulation						
Flange/union						
15mm diameter	3.25	4.25	0.13	2.54	nr	**6.79**
20mm diameter	3.42	4.47	0.13	2.54	nr	**7.01**
25mm diameter	3.64	4.75	0.13	2.54	nr	**7.30**
32mm diameter	3.80	4.97	0.13	2.54	nr	**7.52**
40mm diameter	4.00	5.23	0.13	2.54	nr	**7.77**
50mm diameter	4.48	5.85	0.13	2.54	nr	**8.39**
65mm diameter	4.90	6.40	0.13	2.54	nr	**8.94**
80mm diameter	5.24	6.86	0.18	3.52	nr	**10.38**
100mm diameter	6.71	8.77	0.18	3.52	nr	**12.29**
125mm diameter	7.52	9.84	0.18	3.52	nr	**13.36**
150mm diameter	8.69	11.36	0.18	3.52	nr	**14.88**
200mm diameter	11.86	15.50	0.22	4.30	nr	**19.80**
250mm diameter	13.69	17.90	0.22	4.30	nr	**22.21**
300mm diameter	14.51	18.97	0.22	4.30	nr	**23.27**
350mm diameter	16.02	20.95	0.22	4.30	nr	**25.25**
400mm diameter	17.76	23.22	0.22	4.30	nr	**27.53**
Valves						
15mm diameter	6.50	8.51	0.15	2.93	nr	**11.44**
20mm diameter	6.84	8.94	0.15	2.93	nr	**11.88**
25mm diameter	7.27	9.51	0.15	2.93	nr	**12.44**
32mm diameter	7.60	9.93	0.15	2.93	nr	**12.87**
40mm diameter	7.99	10.45	0.15	2.93	nr	**13.38**
50mm diameter	8.96	11.72	0.15	2.93	nr	**14.65**
65mm diameter	9.79	12.80	0.15	2.93	nr	**15.74**
80mm diameter	10.49	13.71	0.20	3.91	nr	**17.62**
100mm diameter	13.40	17.53	0.20	3.91	nr	**21.44**
125mm diameter	15.05	19.68	0.20	3.91	nr	**23.59**
150mm diameter	17.36	22.71	0.20	3.91	nr	**26.62**
200mm diameter	23.71	31.01	0.25	4.89	nr	**35.89**
250mm diameter	27.38	35.81	0.25	4.89	nr	**40.70**
300mm diameter	29.02	37.94	0.25	4.89	nr	**42.83**
350mm diameter	32.03	41.88	0.25	4.89	nr	**46.77**
400mm diameter	35.52	46.45	0.25	4.89	nr	**51.34**

T:MECHANICAL/COOLING/HEATING SYSTEMS

Item	Net Price £	Material £	Labour hours	Labour £	Unit	Total rate £
T31 : LOW TEMPERATURE HOT WATER HEATING (cont'd)						
Y50 -THERMAL INSULATION (cont'd)						
Fittings; concealed insulation (cont'd)						
Pumps						
15mm diameter	13.00	16.99	0.45	8.80	nr	25.79
20mm diameter	13.68	17.89	0.45	8.80	nr	26.69
25mm diameter	14.54	19.02	0.45	8.80	nr	27.82
32mm diameter	15.20	19.88	0.45	8.80	nr	28.68
40mm diameter	15.98	20.90	0.45	8.80	nr	29.70
50mm diameter	17.92	23.43	0.45	8.80	nr	32.23
65mm diameter	19.58	25.61	0.45	8.80	nr	34.41
80mm diameter	20.98	27.43	0.60	11.73	nr	39.16
100mm diameter	26.81	35.06	0.60	11.73	nr	46.79
125mm diameter	30.08	39.34	0.60	11.73	nr	51.07
150mm diameter	34.74	45.43	0.60	11.73	nr	57.16
200mm diameter	47.44	62.03	0.75	14.66	nr	76.69
250mm diameter	54.76	71.60	0.75	14.66	nr	86.27
300mm diameter	58.04	75.90	0.75	14.66	nr	90.56
350mm diameter	64.06	83.76	0.75	14.66	nr	98.43
400mm diameter	71.03	92.88	0.75	14.66	nr	107.54
Expansion bellows						
15mm diameter	13.00	16.99	0.22	4.30	nr	21.30
20mm diameter	13.68	17.89	0.22	4.30	nr	22.19
25mm diameter	14.54	19.02	0.22	4.30	nr	23.32
32mm diameter	15.20	19.88	0.22	4.30	nr	24.18
40mm diameter	15.98	20.90	0.22	4.30	nr	25.20
50mm diameter	17.92	23.43	0.22	4.30	nr	27.73
65mm diameter	19.58	25.61	0.22	4.30	nr	29.91
80mm diameter	20.98	27.43	0.29	5.67	nr	33.10
100mm diameter	26.81	35.06	0.29	5.67	nr	40.73
125mm diameter	30.08	39.34	0.29	5.67	nr	45.01
150mm diameter	34.74	45.43	0.29	5.67	nr	51.10
200mm diameter	47.44	62.03	0.36	7.04	nr	69.07
250mm diameter	54.76	71.60	0.36	7.04	nr	78.64
300mm diameter	58.04	75.90	0.36	7.04	nr	82.94
350mm diameter	64.06	83.76	0.36	7.04	nr	90.80
400mm diameter	71.03	92.88	0.36	7.04	nr	99.92
Mineral fibre sectional insulation; bright class O foil faced; bright class O foil taped joints; 22 swg plain/embossed aluminium cladding; pop riveted						
Plantroom pipework						
20mm thick						
15mm diameter	4.30	5.62	0.44	8.60	m	14.22
20mm diameter	4.55	5.95	0.44	8.60	m	14.55
25mm diameter	4.87	6.37	0.44	8.60	m	14.97
32mm diameter	5.28	6.90	0.44	8.60	m	15.51
40mm diameter	5.56	7.27	0.44	8.60	m	15.87
50mm diameter	6.19	8.10	0.44	8.60	m	16.70

T:MECHANICAL/COOLING/HEATING SYSTEMS

Item	Net Price £	Material £	Labour hours	Labour £	Unit	Total rate £
Extra over for fittings plantroom insulation						
Flange/union						
15mm diameter	4.81	6.29	0.58	11.34	nr	**17.63**
20mm diameter	5.10	6.67	0.58	11.34	nr	**18.01**
25mm diameter	5.47	7.16	0.58	11.34	nr	**18.49**
32mm diameter	5.98	7.81	0.58	11.34	nr	**19.15**
40mm diameter	6.31	8.25	0.58	11.34	nr	**19.59**
50mm diameter	7.09	9.27	0.58	11.34	nr	**20.61**
Bends						
15mm diameter	2.36	3.09	0.44	8.60	nr	**11.69**
20mm diameter	2.51	3.28	0.44	8.60	nr	**11.88**
25mm diameter	2.69	3.52	0.44	8.60	nr	**12.12**
32mm diameter	2.90	3.80	0.44	8.60	nr	**12.40**
40mm diameter	3.05	3.99	0.44	8.60	nr	**12.59**
50mm diameter	3.41	4.46	0.44	8.60	nr	**13.06**
Tees						
15mm diameter	1.42	1.85	0.44	8.60	nr	**10.45**
20mm diameter	1.50	1.96	0.44	8.60	nr	**10.56**
25mm diameter	1.61	2.10	0.44	8.60	nr	**10.70**
32mm diameter	1.74	2.28	0.44	8.60	nr	**10.88**
40mm diameter	1.84	2.40	0.44	8.60	nr	**11.00**
50mm diameter	2.04	2.67	0.44	8.60	nr	**11.27**
Valves						
15mm diameter	2.56	3.34	0.78	15.25	nr	**18.59**
20mm diameter	2.93	3.83	0.78	15.25	nr	**19.08**
25mm diameter	2.93	3.83	0.78	15.25	nr	**19.08**
32mm diameter	3.26	4.27	0.78	15.25	nr	**19.52**
40mm diameter	3.49	4.57	0.78	15.25	nr	**19.82**
50mm diameter	3.98	5.21	0.78	15.25	nr	**20.46**
Pumps						
15mm diameter	14.14	18.49	2.34	45.75	nr	**64.23**
20mm diameter	15.00	19.62	2.34	45.75	nr	**65.36**
25mm diameter	16.10	21.06	2.34	45.75	nr	**66.81**
32mm diameter	17.57	22.97	2.34	45.75	nr	**68.72**
40mm diameter	18.56	24.28	2.34	45.75	nr	**70.02**
50mm diameter	20.87	27.29	2.34	45.75	nr	**73.03**
Expansion bellows						
15mm diameter	11.30	14.78	1.05	20.53	nr	**35.31**
20mm diameter	12.00	15.69	1.05	20.53	nr	**36.22**
25mm diameter	12.89	16.85	1.05	20.53	nr	**37.38**
32mm diameter	14.05	18.38	1.05	20.53	nr	**38.90**
40mm diameter	14.84	19.41	1.05	20.53	nr	**39.94**
50mm diameter	16.69	21.83	1.05	20.53	nr	**42.35**

T:MECHANICAL/COOLING/HEATING SYSTEMS

Item	Net Price £	Material £	Labour hours	Labour £	Unit	Total rate £
T31 : LOW TEMPERATURE HOT WATER HEATING (cont'd)						
Y50 -THERMAL INSULATION (cont'd)						
Fittings; plantroom insulation (cont'd)						
25mm thick						
15mm diameter	4.72	6.17	0.44	8.60	m	14.77
20mm diameter	5.10	6.67	0.44	8.60	m	15.27
25mm diameter	5.60	7.33	0.44	8.60	m	15.93
32mm diameter	5.96	7.80	0.44	8.60	m	16.40
40mm diameter	6.41	8.38	0.44	8.60	m	16.98
50mm diameter	7.18	9.38	0.44	8.60	m	17.99
65mm diameter	8.11	10.61	0.44	8.60	m	19.21
80mm diameter	8.80	11.50	0.52	10.17	m	21.67
100mm diameter	10.92	14.28	0.52	10.17	m	24.45
125mm diameter	12.68	16.59	0.52	10.17	m	26.75
150mm diameter	14.76	19.30	0.52	10.17	m	29.47
200mm diameter	20.16	26.36	0.60	11.73	m	38.09
250mm diameter	23.95	31.32	0.60	11.73	m	43.05
300mm diameter	26.82	35.07	0.60	11.73	m	46.80
Extra over for fittings plantroom insulation						
Flange/union						
15mm diameter	5.28	6.90	0.58	11.34	nr	18.24
20mm diameter	5.71	7.47	0.58	11.34	nr	18.81
25mm diameter	6.30	8.24	0.58	11.34	nr	19.58
32mm diameter	6.76	8.83	0.58	11.34	nr	20.17
40mm diameter	7.26	9.49	0.58	11.34	nr	20.83
50mm diameter	8.18	10.70	0.58	11.34	nr	22.04
65mm diameter	9.28	12.13	0.58	11.34	nr	23.47
80mm diameter	10.09	13.20	0.67	13.10	nr	26.30
100mm diameter	12.77	16.70	0.67	13.10	nr	29.79
125mm diameter	14.83	19.40	0.67	13.10	nr	32.49
150mm diameter	17.38	22.72	0.67	13.10	nr	35.82
200mm diameter	24.01	31.40	0.87	17.01	nr	48.41
250mm diameter	28.61	37.41	0.87	17.01	nr	54.42
300mm diameter	31.61	41.33	0.87	17.01	nr	58.34
Bends						
15mm diameter	2.59	3.39	0.44	8.60	nr	11.99
20mm diameter	2.81	3.67	0.44	8.60	nr	12.27
25mm diameter	3.08	4.03	0.44	8.60	nr	12.63
32mm diameter	3.29	4.30	0.44	8.60	nr	12.90
40mm diameter	3.53	4.61	0.44	8.60	nr	13.22
50mm diameter	3.95	5.16	0.44	8.60	nr	13.76
65mm diameter	4.46	5.84	0.44	8.60	nr	14.44
80mm diameter	4.84	6.32	0.52	10.17	nr	16.49
100mm diameter	6.00	7.85	0.52	10.17	nr	18.01
125mm diameter	6.98	9.13	0.52	10.17	nr	19.30
150mm diameter	8.11	10.61	0.52	10.17	nr	20.77
200mm diameter	11.09	14.50	0.60	11.73	nr	26.23
250mm diameter	13.18	17.23	0.60	11.73	nr	28.96
300mm diameter	14.75	19.29	0.60	11.73	nr	31.02

T:MECHANICAL/COOLING/HEATING SYSTEMS

Item	Net Price £	Material £	Labour hours	Labour £	Unit	Total rate £
Tees						
15mm diameter	1.56	2.04	0.44	8.60	nr	**10.64**
20mm diameter	1.68	2.20	0.44	8.60	nr	**10.80**
25mm diameter	1.85	2.42	0.44	8.60	nr	**11.02**
32mm diameter	1.97	2.57	0.44	8.60	nr	**11.18**
40mm diameter	2.11	2.76	0.44	8.60	nr	**11.36**
50mm diameter	2.36	3.09	0.44	8.60	nr	**11.69**
65mm diameter	2.68	3.50	0.44	8.60	nr	**12.10**
80mm diameter	2.90	3.80	0.52	10.17	nr	**13.96**
100mm diameter	3.60	4.71	0.52	10.17	nr	**14.87**
125mm diameter	4.19	5.48	0.52	10.17	nr	**15.64**
150mm diameter	4.87	6.37	0.52	10.17	nr	**16.54**
200mm diameter	6.65	8.69	0.60	11.73	nr	**20.42**
250mm diameter	7.91	10.34	0.60	11.73	nr	**22.07**
300mm diameter	8.86	11.58	0.60	11.73	nr	**23.31**
Valves						
15mm diameter	8.39	10.97	0.78	15.25	nr	**26.22**
20mm diameter	9.07	11.86	0.78	15.25	nr	**27.11**
25mm diameter	10.01	13.09	0.78	15.25	nr	**28.34**
32mm diameter	10.74	14.04	0.78	15.25	nr	**29.29**
40mm diameter	11.52	15.06	0.78	15.25	nr	**30.31**
50mm diameter	12.98	16.98	0.78	15.25	nr	**32.23**
65mm diameter	14.74	19.27	0.78	15.25	nr	**34.52**
80mm diameter	16.03	20.96	0.92	17.99	nr	**38.95**
100mm diameter	20.28	26.52	0.92	17.99	nr	**44.51**
125mm diameter	23.56	30.80	0.92	17.99	nr	**48.79**
150mm diameter	27.60	36.09	0.92	17.99	nr	**54.08**
200mm diameter	38.14	49.87	1.12	21.90	nr	**71.77**
250mm diameter	45.44	59.43	1.12	21.90	nr	**81.32**
300mm diameter	50.20	65.64	1.12	21.90	nr	**87.54**
Pumps						
15mm diameter	15.53	20.31	2.34	45.75	nr	**66.05**
20mm diameter	16.79	21.95	2.34	45.75	nr	**67.70**
25mm diameter	18.54	24.24	2.34	45.75	nr	**69.99**
32mm diameter	19.88	26.00	2.34	45.75	nr	**71.75**
40mm diameter	21.34	27.90	2.34	45.75	nr	**73.65**
50mm diameter	24.06	31.46	2.34	45.75	nr	**77.21**
65mm diameter	27.29	35.68	2.34	45.75	nr	**81.43**
80mm diameter	29.69	38.82	2.76	53.96	nr	**92.78**
100mm diameter	37.55	49.10	2.76	53.96	nr	**103.06**
125mm diameter	43.61	57.02	2.76	53.96	nr	**110.98**
150mm diameter	51.11	66.83	2.76	53.96	nr	**120.79**
200mm diameter	70.63	92.36	3.36	65.69	nr	**158.05**
250mm diameter	84.14	110.03	3.36	65.69	nr	**175.72**
300mm diameter	92.95	121.55	3.36	65.69	nr	**187.24**

T:MECHANICAL/COOLING/HEATING SYSTEMS

Item	Net Price £	Material £	Labour hours	Labour £	Unit	Total rate £
T31 : LOW TEMPERATURE HOT WATER HEATING (cont'd)						
Y50 -THERMAL INSULATION (cont'd)						
Fittings; plantroom insulation (cont'd)						
Expansion bellows						
15mm diameter	12.42	16.24	1.05	20.53	nr	36.77
20mm diameter	13.43	17.56	1.05	20.53	nr	38.09
25mm diameter	14.83	19.40	1.05	20.53	nr	39.92
32mm diameter	15.91	20.81	1.05	20.53	nr	41.33
40mm diameter	17.08	22.33	1.05	20.53	nr	42.86
50mm diameter	19.25	25.17	1.05	20.53	nr	45.70
65mm diameter	21.83	28.54	1.05	20.53	nr	49.07
80mm diameter	23.75	31.05	1.26	24.63	nr	55.69
100mm diameter	30.04	39.28	1.26	24.63	nr	63.91
125mm diameter	34.88	45.62	1.26	24.63	nr	70.25
150mm diameter	40.88	53.46	1.26	24.63	nr	78.10
200mm diameter	56.51	73.89	1.53	29.91	nr	103.80
250mm diameter	67.32	88.03	1.53	29.91	nr	117.94
300mm diameter	74.36	97.24	1.53	29.91	nr	127.15
30mm thick						
15mm diameter	5.82	7.61	0.44	8.60	m	16.21
20mm diameter	6.16	8.05	0.44	8.60	m	16.65
25mm diameter	6.52	8.52	0.44	8.60	m	17.12
32mm diameter	7.14	9.34	0.44	8.60	m	17.94
40mm diameter	7.44	9.73	0.44	8.60	m	18.33
50mm diameter	8.26	10.80	0.44	8.60	m	19.40
65mm diameter	9.31	12.18	0.44	8.60	m	20.78
80mm diameter	10.18	13.31	0.52	10.17	m	23.47
100mm diameter	12.50	16.35	0.52	10.17	m	26.52
125mm diameter	14.29	18.69	0.52	10.17	m	28.86
150mm diameter	16.66	21.78	0.52	10.17	m	31.95
200mm diameter	22.38	29.27	0.60	11.73	m	41.00
250mm diameter	26.48	34.63	0.60	11.73	m	46.36
300mm diameter	29.15	38.12	0.60	11.73	m	49.85
350mm diameter	32.46	42.45	0.60	11.73	m	54.18
Extra over for fittings plantroom insulation						
Flange/union						
15mm diameter	6.62	8.66	0.58	11.34	nr	20.00
20mm diameter	7.03	9.20	0.58	11.34	nr	20.53
25mm diameter	7.45	9.74	0.58	11.34	nr	21.08
32mm diameter	8.16	10.67	0.58	11.34	nr	22.01
40mm diameter	8.53	11.16	0.58	11.34	nr	22.50
50mm diameter	9.56	12.51	0.58	11.34	nr	23.85
65mm diameter	10.80	14.12	0.58	11.34	nr	25.46
80mm diameter	11.80	15.43	0.67	13.10	nr	28.52
100mm diameter	14.74	19.27	0.67	13.10	nr	32.37
125mm diameter	16.87	22.06	0.67	13.10	nr	35.16
150mm diameter	19.73	25.80	0.67	13.10	nr	38.90
200mm diameter	26.87	35.13	0.87	17.01	nr	52.14
250mm diameter	31.86	41.66	0.87	17.01	nr	58.67
300mm diameter	34.66	45.32	0.87	17.01	nr	62.33
350mm diameter	38.45	50.28	0.87	17.01	nr	67.29

T:MECHANICAL/COOLING/HEATING SYSTEMS

Item	Net Price £	Material £	Labour hours	Labour £	Unit	Total rate £
Bends						
15mm diameter	3.20	4.19	0.44	8.60	nr	**12.79**
20mm diameter	3.38	4.43	0.44	8.60	nr	**13.03**
25mm diameter	3.59	4.69	0.44	8.60	nr	**13.29**
32mm diameter	3.92	5.13	0.44	8.60	nr	**13.73**
40mm diameter	4.09	5.35	0.44	8.60	nr	**13.95**
50mm diameter	4.55	5.95	0.44	8.60	nr	**14.55**
65mm diameter	5.12	6.70	0.44	8.60	nr	**15.30**
80mm diameter	5.59	7.31	0.52	10.17	nr	**17.48**
100mm diameter	6.88	8.99	0.52	10.17	nr	**19.16**
125mm diameter	7.86	10.28	0.52	10.17	nr	**20.44**
150mm diameter	9.17	11.99	0.52	10.17	nr	**22.15**
200mm diameter	12.31	16.10	0.60	11.73	nr	**27.83**
250mm diameter	14.57	19.05	0.60	11.73	nr	**30.78**
300mm diameter	16.03	20.96	0.60	11.73	nr	**32.69**
350mm diameter	17.86	23.35	0.60	11.73	nr	**35.08**
Tees						
15mm diameter	1.92	2.51	0.44	8.60	nr	**11.11**
20mm diameter	2.03	2.65	0.44	8.60	nr	**11.25**
25mm diameter	2.15	2.81	0.44	8.60	nr	**11.41**
32mm diameter	2.35	3.08	0.44	8.60	nr	**11.68**
40mm diameter	2.46	3.22	0.44	8.60	nr	**11.82**
50mm diameter	2.72	3.56	0.44	8.60	nr	**12.16**
65mm diameter	3.07	4.02	0.44	8.60	nr	**12.62**
80mm diameter	3.36	4.39	0.52	10.17	nr	**14.56**
100mm diameter	4.13	5.40	0.52	10.17	nr	**15.56**
125mm diameter	4.72	6.17	0.52	10.17	nr	**16.33**
150mm diameter	5.50	7.19	0.52	10.17	nr	**17.35**
200mm diameter	7.39	9.67	0.60	11.73	nr	**21.40**
250mm diameter	8.74	11.42	0.60	11.73	nr	**23.15**
300mm diameter	9.62	12.59	0.60	11.73	nr	**24.31**
350mm diameter	10.72	14.01	0.60	11.73	nr	**25.74**
Valves						
15mm diameter	10.52	13.76	0.78	15.25	nr	**29.01**
20mm diameter	11.16	14.59	0.78	15.25	nr	**29.84**
25mm diameter	11.83	15.47	0.78	15.25	nr	**30.72**
32mm diameter	12.96	16.95	0.78	15.25	nr	**32.20**
40mm diameter	13.56	17.73	0.78	15.25	nr	**32.98**
50mm diameter	15.18	19.85	0.78	15.25	nr	**35.10**
65mm diameter	17.16	22.44	0.78	15.25	nr	**37.69**
80mm diameter	18.73	24.50	0.92	17.99	nr	**42.48**
100mm diameter	23.40	30.60	0.92	17.99	nr	**48.59**
125mm diameter	26.80	35.04	0.92	17.99	nr	**53.03**
150mm diameter	31.33	40.97	0.92	17.99	nr	**58.96**
200mm diameter	42.67	55.80	1.12	21.90	nr	**77.70**
250mm diameter	50.59	66.16	1.12	21.90	nr	**88.05**
300mm diameter	55.04	71.98	1.12	21.90	nr	**93.88**
350mm diameter	61.07	79.86	1.12	21.90	nr	**101.75**

T:MECHANICAL/COOLING/HEATING SYSTEMS

Item	Net Price £	Material £	Labour hours	Labour £	Unit	Total rate £
T31 : LOW TEMPERATURE HOT WATER HEATING (cont'd)						
Y50 -THERMAL INSULATION (cont'd)						
Fittings; plantroom insulation (cont'd)						
Pumps						
15mm diameter	19.49	25.48	2.34	45.75	nr	71.23
20mm diameter	20.68	27.04	2.34	45.75	nr	72.78
25mm diameter	21.90	28.64	2.34	45.75	nr	74.38
32mm diameter	24.00	31.38	2.34	45.75	nr	77.13
40mm diameter	25.10	32.83	2.34	45.75	nr	78.57
50mm diameter	28.12	36.77	2.34	45.75	nr	82.51
65mm diameter	31.76	41.54	2.34	45.75	nr	87.28
80mm diameter	34.69	45.37	2.76	53.96	nr	99.32
100mm diameter	43.33	56.66	2.76	53.96	nr	110.62
125mm diameter	49.63	64.90	2.76	53.96	nr	118.86
150mm diameter	58.03	75.89	2.76	53.96	nr	129.84
200mm diameter	79.02	103.33	3.36	65.69	nr	169.02
250mm diameter	93.70	122.52	3.36	65.69	nr	188.21
300mm diameter	101.94	133.30	3.36	65.69	nr	198.99
350mm diameter	113.08	147.87	3.36	65.69	nr	213.55
Expansion bellows						
15mm diameter	15.59	20.38	1.05	20.53	nr	40.91
20mm diameter	16.54	21.62	1.05	20.53	nr	42.15
25mm diameter	17.52	22.91	1.05	20.53	nr	43.44
32mm diameter	19.20	25.11	1.05	20.53	nr	45.63
40mm diameter	20.09	26.27	1.05	20.53	nr	46.80
50mm diameter	22.49	29.41	1.05	20.53	nr	49.93
65mm diameter	25.42	33.24	1.05	20.53	nr	53.76
80mm diameter	27.76	36.30	1.26	24.63	nr	60.93
100mm diameter	34.67	45.33	1.26	24.63	nr	69.97
125mm diameter	39.71	51.93	1.26	24.63	nr	76.56
150mm diameter	46.43	60.71	1.26	24.63	nr	85.35
200mm diameter	63.22	82.67	1.53	29.91	nr	112.58
250mm diameter	74.95	98.01	1.53	29.91	nr	127.92
300mm diameter	81.55	106.64	1.53	29.91	nr	136.55
350mm diameter	90.47	118.30	1.53	29.91	nr	148.21
40mm thick						
15mm diameter	7.12	9.31	0.44	8.60	m	17.91
20mm diameter	7.48	9.78	0.44	8.60	m	18.38
25mm diameter	7.96	10.40	0.44	8.60	m	19.01
32mm diameter	8.34	10.91	0.44	8.60	m	19.51
40mm diameter	8.87	11.60	0.44	8.60	m	20.20
50mm diameter	9.82	12.84	0.44	8.60	m	21.44
65mm diameter	10.94	14.31	0.44	8.60	m	22.91
80mm diameter	11.77	15.39	0.52	10.17	m	25.56
100mm diameter	17.24	22.55	0.52	10.17	m	32.72
125mm diameter	16.15	21.12	0.52	10.17	m	31.29
150mm diameter	18.84	24.64	0.52	10.17	m	34.80
200mm diameter	24.90	32.56	0.60	11.73	m	44.29
250mm diameter	29.18	38.16	0.60	11.73	m	49.89
300mm diameter	32.27	42.20	0.60	11.73	m	53.93
350mm diameter	36.06	47.15	0.60	11.73	m	58.88
400mm diameter	40.54	53.01	0.60	11.73	m	64.74

T:MECHANICAL/COOLING/HEATING SYSTEMS

Item	Net Price £	Material £	Labour hours	Labour £	Unit	Total rate £
Extra over for fittings plantroom insulation						
Flange/union						
15mm diameter	8.22	10.75	0.58	11.34	nr	**22.09**
20mm diameter	8.58	11.22	0.58	11.34	nr	**22.56**
25mm diameter	9.18	12.00	0.58	11.34	nr	**23.34**
32mm diameter	9.66	12.63	0.58	11.34	nr	**23.97**
40mm diameter	10.25	13.40	0.58	11.34	nr	**24.74**
50mm diameter	11.42	14.94	0.58	11.34	nr	**26.28**
65mm diameter	12.76	16.68	0.58	11.34	nr	**28.02**
80mm diameter	13.76	18.00	0.67	13.10	nr	**31.10**
100mm diameter	17.24	22.55	0.67	13.10	nr	**35.65**
125mm diameter	19.30	25.23	0.67	13.10	nr	**38.33**
150mm diameter	22.52	29.45	0.67	13.10	nr	**42.55**
200mm diameter	30.22	39.51	0.87	17.01	nr	**56.52**
250mm diameter	35.42	46.32	0.87	17.01	nr	**63.33**
300mm diameter	38.76	50.69	0.87	17.01	nr	**67.69**
350mm diameter	43.20	56.49	0.87	17.01	nr	**73.50**
400mm diameter	48.44	63.35	0.87	17.01	nr	**80.36**
Bends						
15mm diameter	3.91	5.12	0.44	8.60	nr	**13.72**
20mm diameter	4.10	5.37	0.44	8.60	nr	**13.97**
25mm diameter	4.38	5.73	0.44	8.60	nr	**14.33**
32mm diameter	4.58	5.99	0.44	8.60	nr	**14.60**
40mm diameter	4.88	6.39	0.44	8.60	nr	**14.99**
50mm diameter	5.40	7.06	0.44	8.60	nr	**15.66**
65mm diameter	6.02	7.88	0.44	8.60	nr	**16.48**
80mm diameter	6.47	8.46	0.52	10.17	nr	**18.62**
100mm diameter	7.98	10.44	0.52	10.17	nr	**20.60**
125mm diameter	8.88	11.61	0.52	10.17	nr	**21.78**
150mm diameter	10.36	13.54	0.52	10.17	nr	**23.71**
200mm diameter	13.69	17.90	0.60	11.73	nr	**29.63**
250mm diameter	15.94	20.84	0.60	11.73	nr	**32.57**
300mm diameter	17.75	23.21	0.60	11.73	nr	**34.94**
350mm diameter	19.84	25.94	0.60	11.73	nr	**37.67**
400mm diameter	22.30	29.16	0.60	11.73	nr	**40.89**
Tees						
15mm diameter	2.35	3.08	0.44	8.60	nr	**11.68**
20mm diameter	2.46	3.22	0.44	8.60	nr	**11.82**
25mm diameter	2.63	3.44	0.44	8.60	nr	**12.04**
32mm diameter	2.75	3.59	0.44	8.60	nr	**12.20**
40mm diameter	2.93	3.83	0.44	8.60	nr	**12.43**
50mm diameter	3.24	4.24	0.44	8.60	nr	**12.84**
65mm diameter	3.61	4.72	0.44	8.60	nr	**13.33**
80mm diameter	3.89	5.08	0.52	10.17	nr	**15.25**
100mm diameter	4.79	6.26	0.52	10.17	nr	**16.43**
125mm diameter	5.33	6.97	0.52	10.17	nr	**17.13**
150mm diameter	6.22	8.13	0.52	10.17	nr	**18.29**
200mm diameter	8.22	10.75	0.60	11.73	nr	**22.48**
250mm diameter	9.64	12.60	0.60	11.73	nr	**24.33**
300mm diameter	10.64	13.92	0.60	11.73	nr	**25.65**
350mm diameter	11.90	15.57	0.60	11.73	nr	**27.30**
400mm diameter	13.38	17.50	0.60	11.73	nr	**29.23**

T:MECHANICAL/COOLING/HEATING SYSTEMS

Item	Net Price £	Material £	Labour hours	Labour £	Unit	Total rate £
T31 : LOW TEMPERATURE HOT WATER HEATING (cont'd)						
Y50 - THERMAL INSULATION (cont'd)						
Fittings; plantroom insulation (cont'd)						
Valves						
15mm diameter	13.06	17.07	0.78	15.25	nr	**32.32**
20mm diameter	13.63	17.83	0.78	15.25	nr	**33.08**
25mm diameter	14.57	19.05	0.78	15.25	nr	**34.30**
32mm diameter	15.34	20.05	0.78	15.25	nr	**35.30**
40mm diameter	16.27	21.28	0.78	15.25	nr	**36.53**
50mm diameter	18.13	23.71	0.78	15.25	nr	**38.96**
65mm diameter	20.26	26.49	0.78	15.25	nr	**41.74**
80mm diameter	21.86	28.59	0.92	17.99	nr	**46.58**
100mm diameter	27.40	35.82	0.92	17.99	nr	**53.81**
125mm diameter	30.64	40.06	0.92	17.99	nr	**58.05**
150mm diameter	35.77	46.78	0.92	17.99	nr	**64.76**
200mm diameter	47.99	62.75	1.12	21.90	nr	**84.65**
250mm diameter	56.26	73.56	1.12	21.90	nr	**95.46**
300mm diameter	61.56	80.50	1.12	21.90	nr	**102.40**
350mm diameter	68.62	89.73	1.12	21.90	nr	**111.62**
400mm diameter	76.94	100.62	1.12	21.90	nr	**122.51**
Pumps						
15mm diameter	24.17	31.60	2.34	45.75	nr	**77.35**
20mm diameter	25.24	33.00	2.34	45.75	nr	**78.75**
25mm diameter	26.99	35.29	2.34	45.75	nr	**81.04**
32mm diameter	28.40	37.14	2.34	45.75	nr	**82.89**
40mm diameter	30.13	39.40	2.34	45.75	nr	**85.15**
50mm diameter	33.59	43.92	2.34	45.75	nr	**89.67**
65mm diameter	37.51	49.05	2.34	45.75	nr	**94.80**
80mm diameter	40.49	52.94	2.76	53.96	nr	**106.90**
100mm diameter	50.72	66.33	2.76	53.96	nr	**120.29**
125mm diameter	56.74	74.19	2.76	53.96	nr	**128.15**
150mm diameter	66.25	86.64	2.76	53.96	nr	**140.59**
200mm diameter	88.87	116.22	3.36	65.69	nr	**181.90**
250mm diameter	104.18	136.24	3.36	65.69	nr	**201.93**
300mm diameter	113.99	149.06	3.36	65.69	nr	**214.75**
350mm diameter	127.06	166.15	3.36	65.69	nr	**231.83**
400mm diameter	142.49	186.33	3.36	65.69	nr	**252.01**
Expansion bellows						
15mm diameter	19.33	25.28	1.05	20.53	nr	**45.81**
20mm diameter	20.20	26.41	1.05	20.53	nr	**46.94**
25mm diameter	21.59	28.23	1.05	20.53	nr	**48.76**
32mm diameter	22.72	29.71	1.05	20.53	nr	**50.23**
40mm diameter	24.10	31.51	1.05	20.53	nr	**52.04**
50mm diameter	26.87	35.13	1.05	20.53	nr	**55.66**
65mm diameter	30.01	39.25	1.05	20.53	nr	**59.77**
80mm diameter	32.39	42.35	1.26	24.63	nr	**66.99**
100mm diameter	40.58	53.07	1.26	24.63	nr	**77.70**
125mm diameter	45.38	59.35	1.26	24.63	nr	**83.98**
150mm diameter	52.99	69.30	1.26	24.63	nr	**93.93**
200mm diameter	71.09	92.96	1.53	29.91	nr	**122.87**
250mm diameter	83.35	109.00	1.53	29.91	nr	**138.91**
300mm diameter	91.19	119.24	1.53	29.91	nr	**149.15**
350mm diameter	101.64	132.91	1.53	29.91	nr	**162.82**
400mm diameter	113.99	149.06	1.53	29.91	nr	**178.97**

T:MECHANICAL/COOLING/HEATING SYSTEMS

Item	Net Price £	Material £	Labour hours	Labour £	Unit	Total rate £
50mm thick						
15mm diameter	9.29	12.15	0.44	8.60	m	**20.75**
20mm diameter	9.79	12.80	0.44	8.60	m	**21.41**
25mm diameter	10.37	13.56	0.44	8.60	m	**22.16**
32mm diameter	10.90	14.25	0.44	8.60	m	**22.85**
40mm diameter	11.40	14.91	0.44	8.60	m	**23.51**
50mm diameter	12.58	16.45	0.44	8.60	m	**25.05**
65mm diameter	13.52	17.68	0.44	8.60	m	**26.29**
80mm diameter	14.52	18.99	0.52	10.17	m	**29.15**
100mm diameter	17.94	23.46	0.52	10.17	m	**33.63**
125mm diameter	19.86	25.97	0.52	10.17	m	**36.14**
150mm diameter	22.81	29.83	0.52	10.17	m	**40.00**
200mm diameter	29.90	39.10	0.60	11.73	m	**50.83**
250mm diameter	34.56	45.19	0.60	11.73	m	**56.92**
300mm diameter	37.62	49.19	0.60	11.73	m	**60.92**
350mm diameter	41.93	54.83	0.60	11.73	m	**66.56**
400mm diameter	46.90	61.32	0.60	11.73	m	**73.05**
Extra over for fittings plantroom insulation						
Flange/union						
15mm diameter	10.94	14.31	0.58	11.34	nr	**25.65**
20mm diameter	11.54	15.10	0.58	11.34	nr	**26.43**
25mm diameter	12.23	15.99	0.58	11.34	nr	**27.33**
32mm diameter	12.84	16.79	0.58	11.34	nr	**28.13**
40mm diameter	13.45	17.59	0.58	11.34	nr	**28.93**
50mm diameter	14.93	19.52	0.58	11.34	nr	**30.86**
65mm diameter	16.13	21.09	0.58	11.34	nr	**32.43**
80mm diameter	17.29	22.61	0.67	13.10	nr	**35.71**
100mm diameter	21.62	28.28	0.67	13.10	nr	**41.38**
125mm diameter	24.05	31.45	0.67	13.10	nr	**44.55**
150mm diameter	27.67	36.19	0.67	13.10	nr	**49.28**
200mm diameter	36.78	48.10	0.87	17.01	nr	**65.10**
250mm diameter	42.50	55.58	0.87	17.01	nr	**72.59**
300mm diameter	45.86	59.98	0.87	17.01	nr	**76.98**
350mm diameter	50.99	66.68	0.87	17.01	nr	**83.68**
400mm diameter	56.89	74.40	0.87	17.01	nr	**91.40**
Bend						
15mm diameter	5.11	6.68	0.44	8.60	nr	**15.29**
20mm diameter	5.39	7.05	0.44	8.60	nr	**15.65**
25mm diameter	5.70	7.45	0.44	8.60	nr	**16.06**
32mm diameter	6.00	7.85	0.44	8.60	nr	**16.45**
40mm diameter	6.26	8.19	0.44	8.60	nr	**16.79**
50mm diameter	6.92	9.05	0.44	8.60	nr	**17.66**
65mm diameter	7.44	9.73	0.44	8.60	nr	**18.33**
80mm diameter	7.98	10.44	0.52	10.17	nr	**20.60**
100mm diameter	9.86	12.90	0.52	10.17	nr	**23.06**
125mm diameter	10.92	14.28	0.52	10.17	nr	**24.45**
150mm diameter	12.55	16.41	0.52	10.17	nr	**26.58**
200mm diameter	16.45	21.51	0.60	11.73	nr	**33.24**
250mm diameter	19.01	24.86	0.60	11.73	nr	**36.59**
300mm diameter	20.69	27.05	0.60	11.73	nr	**38.78**
350mm diameter	23.06	30.16	0.60	11.73	nr	**41.89**
400mm diameter	25.79	33.72	0.60	11.73	nr	**45.45**

T:MECHANICAL/COOLING/HEATING SYSTEMS

Item	Net Price £	Material £	Labour hours	Labour £	Unit	Total rate £
T31 : LOW TEMPERATURE HOT WATER HEATING (cont'd)						
Y50 -THERMAL INSULATION (cont'd)						
Fittings; plantroom insulation (cont'd)						
Tee						
15mm diameter	3.07	4.02	0.44	8.60	nr	**12.62**
20mm diameter	3.23	4.22	0.44	8.60	nr	**12.82**
25mm diameter	3.42	4.47	0.44	8.60	nr	**13.07**
32mm diameter	3.60	4.71	0.44	8.60	nr	**13.31**
40mm diameter	3.76	4.91	0.44	8.60	nr	**13.51**
50mm diameter	4.15	5.43	0.44	8.60	nr	**14.03**
65mm diameter	4.46	5.84	0.44	8.60	nr	**14.44**
80mm diameter	4.79	6.26	0.52	10.17	nr	**16.43**
100mm diameter	5.92	7.74	0.52	10.17	nr	**17.90**
125mm diameter	6.55	8.57	0.52	10.17	nr	**18.73**
150mm diameter	7.52	9.84	0.52	10.17	nr	**20.00**
200mm diameter	9.86	12.90	0.60	11.73	nr	**24.63**
250mm diameter	11.41	14.92	0.60	11.73	nr	**26.65**
300mm diameter	12.42	16.24	0.60	11.73	nr	**27.97**
350mm diameter	13.84	18.09	0.60	11.73	nr	**29.82**
400mm diameter	15.48	20.24	0.60	11.73	nr	**31.97**
Valves						
15mm diameter	17.39	22.74	0.78	15.25	nr	**37.99**
20mm diameter	18.32	23.96	0.78	15.25	nr	**39.21**
25mm diameter	19.42	25.39	0.78	15.25	nr	**40.64**
32mm diameter	20.39	26.66	0.78	15.25	nr	**41.91**
40mm diameter	21.36	27.93	0.78	15.25	nr	**43.18**
50mm diameter	23.70	30.99	0.78	15.25	nr	**46.24**
65mm diameter	25.61	33.49	0.78	15.25	nr	**48.74**
80mm diameter	27.47	35.92	0.92	17.99	nr	**53.90**
100mm diameter	34.34	44.91	0.92	17.99	nr	**62.90**
125mm diameter	38.18	49.93	0.92	17.99	nr	**67.92**
150mm diameter	43.94	57.46	0.92	17.99	nr	**75.45**
200mm diameter	58.43	76.40	1.12	21.90	nr	**98.30**
250mm diameter	67.51	88.28	1.12	21.90	nr	**110.18**
300mm diameter	72.85	95.27	1.12	21.90	nr	**117.16**
350mm diameter	80.98	105.89	1.12	21.90	nr	**127.79**
400mm diameter	90.35	118.15	1.12	21.90	nr	**140.04**
Pumps						
15mm diameter	32.20	42.10	2.34	45.75	nr	**87.85**
20mm diameter	33.94	44.38	2.34	45.75	nr	**90.12**
25mm diameter	35.95	47.01	2.34	45.75	nr	**92.76**
32mm diameter	37.76	49.38	2.34	45.75	nr	**95.13**
40mm diameter	39.56	51.74	2.34	45.75	nr	**97.48**
50mm diameter	43.88	57.39	2.34	45.75	nr	**103.13**
65mm diameter	35.42	46.32	2.34	45.75	nr	**92.07**
80mm diameter	50.88	66.53	2.76	53.96	nr	**120.49**
100mm diameter	63.59	83.15	2.76	53.96	nr	**137.11**
125mm diameter	70.72	92.47	2.76	53.96	nr	**146.43**
150mm diameter	81.38	106.42	2.76	53.96	nr	**160.38**
200mm diameter	108.19	141.48	3.36	65.69	nr	**207.17**
250mm diameter	125.02	163.48	3.36	65.69	nr	**229.17**
300mm diameter	134.90	176.41	3.36	65.69	nr	**242.10**
350mm diameter	149.96	196.10	3.36	65.69	nr	**261.79**
400mm diameter	167.32	218.79	3.36	65.69	nr	**284.48**

T:MECHANICAL/COOLING/HEATING SYSTEMS

Item	Net Price £	Material £	Labour hours	Labour £	Unit	Total rate £
Expansion bellows						
15mm diameter	25.75	33.68	1.05	20.53	nr	**54.20**
20mm diameter	27.14	35.50	1.05	20.53	nr	**56.02**
25mm diameter	28.76	37.61	1.05	20.53	nr	**58.14**
32mm diameter	30.20	39.50	1.05	20.53	nr	**60.02**
40mm diameter	31.64	41.38	1.05	20.53	nr	**61.91**
50mm diameter	35.11	45.91	1.05	20.53	nr	**66.44**
65mm diameter	37.93	49.60	1.05	20.53	nr	**70.13**
80mm diameter	40.70	53.23	1.26	24.63	nr	**77.86**
100mm diameter	50.87	66.52	1.26	24.63	nr	**91.15**
125mm diameter	56.57	73.97	1.26	24.63	nr	**98.60**
150mm diameter	65.11	85.15	1.26	24.63	nr	**109.78**
200mm diameter	86.56	113.19	1.53	29.91	nr	**143.10**
250mm diameter	100.01	130.78	1.53	29.91	nr	**160.69**
300mm diameter	107.93	141.13	1.53	29.91	nr	**171.05**
350mm diameter	119.96	156.87	1.53	29.91	nr	**186.78**
400mm diameter	133.85	175.03	1.53	29.91	nr	**204.94**
Mineral fibre sectional insulation; bright class O foil faced; bright class O foil taped joints; 0.8mm polyisobutylene sheeting; welded joints						
External pipework						
20mm thick						
15mm diameter	3.96	5.18	0.30	5.86	m	**11.04**
20mm diameter	4.22	5.52	0.30	5.86	m	**11.39**
25mm diameter	4.55	5.95	0.30	5.86	m	**11.81**
32mm diameter	5.00	6.54	0.30	5.86	m	**12.41**
40mm diameter	5.33	6.97	0.30	5.86	m	**12.83**
50mm diameter	6.02	7.88	0.30	5.86	m	**13.74**
Extra over for fittings external insulation						
Flange/union						
15mm diameter	6.07	7.94	0.75	14.66	nr	**22.60**
20mm diameter	6.44	8.43	0.75	14.66	nr	**23.09**
25mm diameter	6.92	9.05	0.75	14.66	nr	**23.72**
32mm diameter	7.54	9.85	0.75	14.66	nr	**24.52**
40mm diameter	7.96	10.40	0.75	14.66	nr	**25.07**
50mm diameter	8.92	11.66	0.75	14.66	nr	**26.32**
Bends						
15mm diameter	1.00	1.30	0.30	5.86	nr	**7.17**
20mm diameter	1.06	1.38	0.30	5.86	nr	**7.25**
25mm diameter	1.14	1.49	0.30	5.86	nr	**7.36**
32mm diameter	1.25	1.63	0.30	5.86	nr	**7.50**
40mm diameter	1.33	1.74	0.30	5.86	nr	**7.61**
50mm diameter	1.50	1.96	0.30	5.86	nr	**7.83**
Tees						
15mm diameter	1.00	1.30	0.30	5.86	nr	**7.17**
20mm diameter	1.06	1.38	0.30	5.86	nr	**7.25**
25mm diameter	1.14	1.49	0.30	5.86	nr	**7.36**
32mm diameter	1.25	1.63	0.30	5.86	nr	**7.50**
40mm diameter	1.33	1.74	0.30	5.86	nr	**7.61**
50mm diameter	1.50	1.96	0.30	5.86	nr	**7.83**

T:MECHANICAL/COOLING/HEATING SYSTEMS

Item	Net Price £	Material £	Labour hours	Labour £	Unit	Total rate £
T31 : LOW TEMPERATURE HOT WATER HEATING (cont'd)						
Y50 -THERMAL INSULATION (cont'd)						
Fittings; external insulation (cont'd)						
Valves						
15mm diameter	9.64	12.60	1.03	20.14	nr	**32.74**
20mm diameter	10.24	13.39	1.03	20.14	nr	**33.52**
25mm diameter	10.99	14.37	1.03	20.14	nr	**34.51**
32mm diameter	11.96	15.65	1.03	20.14	nr	**35.78**
40mm diameter	12.64	16.52	1.03	20.14	nr	**36.66**
50mm diameter	14.16	18.52	1.03	20.14	nr	**38.65**
Pumps						
15mm diameter	17.86	23.35	3.10	60.60	nr	**83.95**
20mm diameter	18.96	24.79	3.10	60.60	nr	**85.40**
25mm diameter	20.36	26.63	3.10	60.60	nr	**87.23**
32mm diameter	22.16	28.98	3.10	60.60	nr	**89.59**
40mm diameter	23.41	30.62	3.10	60.60	nr	**91.22**
50mm diameter	26.22	34.29	3.10	60.60	nr	**94.89**
Expansion bellows						
15mm diameter	14.28	18.67	1.42	27.76	nr	**46.43**
20mm diameter	15.17	19.83	1.42	27.76	nr	**47.60**
25mm diameter	16.30	21.31	1.42	27.76	nr	**49.07**
32mm diameter	17.74	23.19	1.42	27.76	nr	**50.95**
40mm diameter	18.72	24.48	1.42	27.76	nr	**52.24**
50mm diameter	20.98	27.43	1.42	27.76	nr	**55.19**
25mm thick						
15mm diameter	4.37	5.71	0.30	5.86	m	**11.58**
20mm diameter	4.69	6.14	0.30	5.86	m	**12.00**
25mm diameter	5.16	6.75	0.30	5.86	m	**12.61**
32mm diameter	5.59	7.31	0.30	5.86	m	**13.18**
40mm diameter	5.94	7.77	0.30	5.86	m	**13.63**
50mm diameter	6.71	8.77	0.30	5.86	m	**14.64**
65mm diameter	7.61	9.95	0.30	5.86	m	**15.81**
80mm diameter	8.32	10.87	0.40	7.82	m	**18.69**
100mm diameter	10.51	13.75	0.40	7.82	m	**21.57**
125mm diameter	12.10	15.82	0.40	7.82	m	**23.64**
150mm diameter	14.20	18.56	0.40	7.82	m	**26.38**
200mm diameter	19.26	25.19	0.50	9.77	m	**34.96**
250mm diameter	22.99	30.07	0.50	9.77	m	**39.84**
300mm diameter	25.01	32.70	0.50	9.77	m	**42.48**
Extra over for fittings external insulation						
Flange/union						
15mm diameter	6.68	8.74	0.75	14.66	nr	**23.40**
20mm diameter	7.20	9.42	0.75	14.66	nr	**24.08**
25mm diameter	7.90	10.33	0.75	14.66	nr	**24.99**
32mm diameter	8.46	11.06	0.75	14.66	nr	**25.73**
40mm diameter	9.05	11.83	0.75	14.66	nr	**26.49**
50mm diameter	10.14	13.26	0.75	14.66	nr	**27.92**
65mm diameter	11.47	15.00	0.75	14.66	nr	**29.66**
80mm diameter	12.48	16.32	0.89	17.40	nr	**33.72**

T:MECHANICAL/COOLING/HEATING SYSTEMS

Item	Net Price £	Material £	Labour hours	Labour £	Unit	Total rate £
100mm diameter	15.50	20.27	0.89	17.40	nr	**37.67**
125mm diameter	17.95	23.48	0.89	17.40	nr	**40.87**
150mm diameter	20.89	27.32	0.89	17.40	nr	**44.72**
200mm diameter	28.27	36.97	1.15	22.48	nr	**59.45**
250mm diameter	33.65	44.00	1.15	22.48	nr	**66.48**
300mm diameter	37.38	48.88	1.15	22.48	nr	**71.36**
Bends						
15mm diameter	1.09	1.43	0.30	5.86	nr	**7.29**
20mm diameter	1.18	1.54	0.30	5.86	nr	**7.40**
25mm diameter	1.28	1.68	0.30	5.86	nr	**7.54**
32mm diameter	1.39	1.82	0.30	5.86	nr	**7.69**
40mm diameter	1.49	1.95	0.30	5.86	nr	**7.81**
50mm diameter	1.68	2.20	0.30	5.86	nr	**8.06**
65mm diameter	1.91	2.50	0.30	5.86	nr	**8.36**
80mm diameter	2.08	2.71	0.40	7.82	nr	**10.53**
100mm diameter	2.63	3.44	0.40	7.82	nr	**11.26**
125mm diameter	3.02	3.95	0.40	7.82	nr	**11.77**
150mm diameter	3.55	4.64	0.40	7.82	nr	**12.46**
200mm diameter	4.81	6.29	0.50	9.77	nr	**16.07**
250mm diameter	5.75	7.52	0.50	9.77	nr	**17.29**
300mm diameter	6.25	8.18	0.50	9.77	nr	**17.95**
Tees						
15mm diameter	1.09	1.43	0.30	5.86	nr	**7.29**
20mm diameter	1.18	1.54	0.30	5.86	nr	**7.40**
25mm diameter	1.28	1.68	0.30	5.86	nr	**7.54**
32mm diameter	1.39	1.82	0.30	5.86	nr	**7.69**
40mm diameter	1.49	1.95	0.30	5.86	nr	**7.81**
50mm diameter	1.68	2.20	0.30	5.86	nr	**8.06**
65mm diameter	1.91	2.50	0.30	5.86	nr	**8.36**
80mm diameter	2.08	2.71	0.40	7.82	nr	**10.53**
100mm diameter	2.63	3.44	0.40	7.82	nr	**11.26**
125mm diameter	3.02	3.95	0.40	7.82	nr	**11.77**
150mm diameter	3.55	4.64	0.40	7.82	nr	**12.46**
200mm diameter	4.81	6.29	0.50	9.77	nr	**16.07**
250mm diameter	5.75	7.52	0.50	9.77	nr	**17.29**
300mm diameter	6.25	8.18	0.50	9.77	nr	**17.95**
Valves						
15mm diameter	10.61	13.87	1.03	20.14	nr	**34.01**
20mm diameter	11.44	14.95	1.03	20.14	nr	**35.09**
25mm diameter	12.54	16.40	1.03	20.14	nr	**36.53**
32mm diameter	13.44	17.58	1.03	20.14	nr	**37.71**
40mm diameter	14.36	18.78	1.03	20.14	nr	**38.92**
50mm diameter	16.12	21.07	1.03	20.14	nr	**41.21**
65mm diameter	18.23	23.84	1.03	20.14	nr	**43.97**
80mm diameter	19.81	25.91	1.25	24.44	nr	**50.34**
100mm diameter	24.64	32.22	1.25	24.44	nr	**56.65**
125mm diameter	28.50	37.27	1.25	24.44	nr	**61.71**
150mm diameter	33.19	43.40	1.25	24.44	nr	**67.84**
200mm diameter	44.90	58.72	1.55	30.30	nr	**89.02**
250mm diameter	53.44	69.88	1.55	30.30	nr	**100.18**
300mm diameter	59.36	77.63	1.55	30.30	nr	**107.93**

T:MECHANICAL/COOLING/HEATING SYSTEMS

Item	Net Price £	Material £	Labour hours	Labour £	Unit	Total rate £
T31 : LOW TEMPERATURE HOT WATER HEATING (cont'd)						
Y50 -THERMAL INSULATION (cont'd)						
Fittings; external insulation (cont'd)						
Pumps						
15mm diameter	19.66	25.70	3.10	60.60	nr	**86.31**
20mm diameter	21.18	27.70	3.10	60.60	nr	**88.30**
25mm diameter	23.22	30.36	3.10	60.60	nr	**90.97**
32mm diameter	24.90	32.56	3.10	60.60	nr	**93.17**
40mm diameter	26.60	34.79	3.10	60.60	nr	**95.39**
50mm diameter	29.84	39.03	3.10	60.60	nr	**99.63**
65mm diameter	33.76	44.14	3.10	60.60	nr	**104.75**
80mm diameter	36.70	47.99	3.75	73.31	nr	**121.30**
100mm diameter	45.61	59.65	3.75	73.31	nr	**132.96**
125mm diameter	52.79	69.03	3.75	73.31	nr	**142.34**
150mm diameter	61.46	80.37	3.75	73.31	nr	**153.69**
200mm diameter	83.15	108.73	4.65	90.91	nr	**199.64**
250mm diameter	53.44	69.88	4.65	90.91	nr	**160.78**
300mm diameter	59.36	77.63	4.65	90.91	nr	**168.53**
Expansion bellows						
15mm diameter	15.72	20.56	1.42	27.76	nr	**48.32**
20mm diameter	16.94	22.16	1.42	27.76	nr	**49.92**
25mm diameter	18.58	24.29	1.42	27.76	nr	**52.05**
32mm diameter	19.92	26.05	1.42	27.76	nr	**53.81**
40mm diameter	21.29	27.84	1.42	27.76	nr	**55.60**
50mm diameter	23.87	31.21	1.42	27.76	nr	**58.97**
65mm diameter	27.00	35.31	1.42	27.76	nr	**63.07**
80mm diameter	29.35	38.38	1.75	34.21	nr	**72.59**
100mm diameter	36.49	47.72	1.75	34.21	nr	**81.93**
125mm diameter	42.23	55.22	1.75	34.21	nr	**89.43**
150mm diameter	49.16	64.29	1.75	34.21	nr	**98.50**
200mm diameter	66.52	86.98	2.17	42.42	nr	**129.40**
250mm diameter	79.16	103.52	2.17	42.42	nr	**145.94**
300mm diameter	87.94	114.99	3.17	61.97	nr	**176.96**
30mm thick						
15mm diameter	5.38	7.03	0.30	5.86	m	**12.89**
20mm diameter	5.72	7.49	0.30	5.86	m	**13.35**
25mm diameter	6.07	7.94	0.30	5.86	m	**13.81**
32mm diameter	6.58	8.60	0.30	5.86	m	**14.46**
40mm diameter	6.94	9.07	0.30	5.86	m	**14.93**
50mm diameter	7.81	10.22	0.30	5.86	m	**16.08**
65mm diameter	8.78	11.49	0.30	5.86	m	**17.35**
80mm diameter	9.55	12.49	0.40	7.82	m	**20.31**
100mm diameter	11.94	15.61	0.40	7.82	m	**23.43**
125mm diameter	13.67	17.87	0.40	7.82	m	**25.69**
150mm diameter	15.88	20.76	0.40	7.82	m	**28.58**
200mm diameter	21.38	27.96	0.50	9.77	m	**37.74**
250mm diameter	25.37	33.17	0.50	9.77	m	**42.95**
300mm diameter	27.36	35.78	0.50	9.77	m	**45.55**
350mm diameter	29.92	39.12	0.50	9.77	m	**48.90**

T:MECHANICAL/COOLING/HEATING SYSTEMS

Item	Net Price £	Material £	Labour hours	Labour £	Unit	Total rate £
Extra over for fittings external insulation						
Flange/union						
15mm diameter	8.17	10.69	0.75	14.66	nr	**25.35**
20mm diameter	8.66	11.33	0.75	14.66	nr	**25.99**
25mm diameter	9.18	12.00	0.75	14.66	nr	**26.67**
32mm diameter	10.01	13.09	0.75	14.66	nr	**27.75**
40mm diameter	10.46	13.68	0.75	14.66	nr	**28.35**
50mm diameter	11.68	15.27	0.75	14.66	nr	**29.93**
65mm diameter	13.14	17.18	0.75	14.66	nr	**31.85**
80mm diameter	14.32	18.72	0.89	17.40	nr	**36.12**
100mm diameter	17.63	23.05	0.89	17.40	nr	**40.45**
125mm diameter	20.14	26.33	0.89	17.40	nr	**43.73**
150mm diameter	23.40	30.60	0.89	17.40	nr	**48.00**
200mm diameter	31.27	40.89	1.15	22.48	nr	**63.38**
250mm diameter	37.03	48.43	1.15	22.48	nr	**70.91**
300mm diameter	40.57	53.05	1.15	22.48	nr	**75.54**
350mm diameter	44.82	58.61	1.15	22.48	nr	**81.09**
Bends						
15mm diameter	1.34	1.76	0.30	5.86	nr	**7.62**
20mm diameter	1.43	1.87	0.30	5.86	nr	**7.73**
25mm diameter	1.52	1.99	0.30	5.86	nr	**7.86**
32mm diameter	1.64	2.15	0.30	5.86	nr	**8.01**
40mm diameter	1.73	2.26	0.30	5.86	nr	**8.12**
50mm diameter	1.96	2.56	0.30	5.86	nr	**8.42**
65mm diameter	2.20	2.87	0.30	5.86	nr	**8.74**
80mm diameter	2.39	3.12	0.40	7.82	nr	**10.94**
100mm diameter	2.99	3.91	0.40	7.82	nr	**11.73**
125mm diameter	3.42	4.47	0.40	7.82	nr	**12.29**
150mm diameter	3.97	5.19	0.40	7.82	nr	**13.01**
200mm diameter	5.35	7.00	0.50	9.77	nr	**16.77**
250mm diameter	6.35	8.30	0.50	9.77	nr	**18.08**
300mm diameter	6.84	8.94	0.50	9.77	nr	**18.72**
350mm diameter	7.48	9.78	0.50	9.77	nr	**19.55**
Tees						
15mm diameter	1.34	1.76	0.30	5.86	nr	**7.62**
20mm diameter	1.43	1.87	0.30	5.86	nr	**7.73**
25mm diameter	1.52	1.99	0.30	5.86	nr	**7.86**
32mm diameter	1.64	2.15	0.30	5.86	nr	**8.01**
40mm diameter	1.73	2.26	0.30	5.86	nr	**8.12**
50mm diameter	1.96	2.56	0.30	5.86	nr	**8.42**
65mm diameter	2.20	2.87	0.30	5.86	nr	**8.74**
80mm diameter	2.39	3.12	0.40	7.82	nr	**10.94**
100mm diameter	2.99	3.91	0.40	7.82	nr	**11.73**
125mm diameter	3.42	4.47	0.40	7.82	nr	**12.29**
150mm diameter	3.97	5.19	0.40	7.82	nr	**13.01**
200mm diameter	5.35	7.00	0.50	9.77	nr	**16.77**
250mm diameter	6.35	8.30	0.50	9.77	nr	**18.08**
300mm diameter	6.84	8.94	0.50	9.77	nr	**18.72**
350mm diameter	7.48	9.78	0.50	9.77	nr	**19.55**

T:MECHANICAL/COOLING/HEATING SYSTEMS

Item	Net Price £	Material £	Labour hours	Labour £	Unit	Total rate £
T31 : LOW TEMPERATURE HOT WATER HEATING (cont'd)						
Y50 -THERMAL INSULATION (cont'd)						
Fittings; external insulation (cont'd)						
Valves						
15mm diameter	12.98	16.98	1.03	20.14	nr	**37.11**
20mm diameter	13.75	17.98	1.03	20.14	nr	**38.12**
25mm diameter	14.58	19.07	1.03	20.14	nr	**39.20**
32mm diameter	15.89	20.78	1.03	20.14	nr	**40.91**
40mm diameter	16.63	21.75	1.03	20.14	nr	**41.89**
50mm diameter	18.54	24.24	1.03	20.14	nr	**44.38**
65mm diameter	20.87	27.29	1.03	20.14	nr	**47.42**
80mm diameter	22.74	29.74	1.25	24.44	nr	**54.17**
100mm diameter	27.98	36.59	1.25	24.44	nr	**61.03**
125mm diameter	31.98	41.82	1.25	24.44	nr	**66.26**
150mm diameter	37.15	48.58	1.25	24.44	nr	**73.02**
200mm diameter	49.67	64.95	1.55	30.30	nr	**95.25**
250mm diameter	58.81	76.91	1.55	30.30	nr	**107.21**
300mm diameter	64.44	84.27	1.55	30.30	nr	**114.57**
350mm diameter	71.18	93.09	1.55	30.30	nr	**123.39**
Pumps						
15mm diameter	24.04	31.43	3.10	60.60	nr	**92.04**
20mm diameter	25.48	33.31	3.10	60.60	nr	**93.92**
25mm diameter	27.00	35.31	3.10	60.60	nr	**95.91**
32mm diameter	29.44	38.49	3.10	60.60	nr	**99.10**
40mm diameter	30.79	40.27	3.10	60.60	nr	**100.87**
50mm diameter	34.32	44.88	3.10	60.60	nr	**105.48**
65mm diameter	38.65	50.54	3.10	60.60	nr	**111.15**
80mm diameter	42.12	55.08	3.75	73.31	nr	**128.39**
100mm diameter	51.83	67.77	3.75	73.31	nr	**141.09**
125mm diameter	59.22	77.44	3.75	73.31	nr	**150.75**
150mm diameter	68.81	89.98	3.75	73.31	nr	**163.29**
200mm diameter	91.98	120.28	4.65	90.91	nr	**211.19**
250mm diameter	108.92	142.44	4.65	90.91	nr	**233.34**
300mm diameter	119.33	156.04	4.65	90.91	nr	**246.95**
350mm diameter	131.82	172.38	4.65	90.91	nr	**263.28**
Expansion bellows						
15mm diameter	19.22	25.14	1.42	27.76	nr	**52.90**
20mm diameter	20.38	26.65	1.42	27.76	nr	**54.41**
25mm diameter	21.60	28.25	1.42	27.76	nr	**56.01**
32mm diameter	23.54	30.79	1.42	27.76	nr	**58.55**
40mm diameter	24.64	32.22	1.42	27.76	nr	**59.98**
50mm diameter	27.46	35.90	1.42	27.76	nr	**63.66**
65mm diameter	30.92	40.44	1.42	27.76	nr	**68.20**
80mm diameter	33.70	44.06	1.75	34.21	nr	**78.28**
100mm diameter	41.46	54.22	1.75	34.21	nr	**88.43**
125mm diameter	47.38	61.95	1.75	34.21	nr	**96.16**
150mm diameter	55.04	71.98	1.75	34.21	nr	**106.19**
200mm diameter	73.58	96.22	2.17	42.42	nr	**138.65**
250mm diameter	87.13	113.94	2.17	42.42	nr	**156.36**
300mm diameter	95.46	124.83	2.17	42.42	nr	**167.25**
350mm diameter	105.46	137.90	2.17	42.42	nr	**180.32**

T:MECHANICAL/COOLING/HEATING SYSTEMS

Item	Net Price £	Material £	Labour hours	Labour £	Unit	Total rate £
40mm thick						
15mm diameter	6.73	8.80	0.30	5.86	m	**14.67**
20mm diameter	6.96	9.10	0.30	5.86	m	**14.97**
25mm diameter	7.44	9.73	0.30	5.86	m	**15.59**
32mm diameter	7.91	10.34	0.30	5.86	m	**16.21**
40mm diameter	8.29	10.84	0.30	5.86	m	**16.71**
50mm diameter	9.24	12.08	0.30	5.86	m	**17.95**
65mm diameter	10.30	13.46	0.30	5.86	m	**19.33**
80mm diameter	11.16	14.59	0.40	7.82	m	**22.41**
100mm diameter	13.94	18.23	0.40	7.82	m	**26.05**
125mm diameter	15.71	20.54	0.40	7.82	m	**28.36**
150mm diameter	18.13	23.71	0.40	7.82	m	**31.53**
200mm diameter	24.19	31.64	0.50	9.77	m	**41.41**
250mm diameter	28.32	37.03	0.50	9.77	m	**46.81**
300mm diameter	30.67	40.11	0.50	9.77	m	**49.88**
350mm diameter	33.70	44.06	0.50	9.77	m	**53.84**
400mm diameter	37.51	49.05	0.50	9.77	m	**58.83**
Extra over for fittings external insulation						
Flange/union						
15mm diameter	10.06	13.15	0.75	14.66	nr	**27.81**
20mm diameter	10.50	13.73	0.75	14.66	nr	**28.39**
25mm diameter	11.20	14.64	0.75	14.66	nr	**29.30**
32mm diameter	11.80	15.43	0.75	14.66	nr	**30.09**
40mm diameter	12.47	16.30	0.75	14.66	nr	**30.97**
50mm diameter	13.81	18.06	0.75	14.66	nr	**32.72**
65mm diameter	15.38	20.12	0.75	14.66	nr	**34.78**
80mm diameter	16.58	21.69	0.89	17.40	nr	**39.09**
100mm diameter	20.42	26.71	0.89	17.40	nr	**44.11**
125mm diameter	22.84	29.86	0.89	17.40	nr	**47.26**
150mm diameter	26.47	34.62	0.89	17.40	nr	**52.02**
200mm diameter	34.90	45.63	1.15	22.48	nr	**68.11**
250mm diameter	40.90	53.48	1.15	22.48	nr	**75.96**
300mm diameter	44.95	58.78	1.15	22.48	nr	**81.26**
350mm diameter	49.86	65.20	1.15	22.48	nr	**87.68**
400mm diameter	55.84	73.02	1.15	22.48	nr	**95.50**
Bends						
15mm diameter	1.68	2.20	0.30	5.86	nr	**8.06**
20mm diameter	1.74	2.28	0.30	5.86	nr	**8.14**
25mm diameter	1.86	2.43	0.30	5.86	nr	**8.30**
32mm diameter	1.98	2.59	0.30	5.86	nr	**8.45**
40mm diameter	2.08	2.71	0.30	5.86	nr	**8.58**
50mm diameter	2.32	3.03	0.30	5.86	nr	**8.89**
65mm diameter	2.58	3.37	0.30	5.86	nr	**9.24**
80mm diameter	2.80	3.66	0.40	7.82	nr	**11.48**
100mm diameter	3.49	4.57	0.40	7.82	nr	**12.39**
125mm diameter	3.92	5.13	0.40	7.82	nr	**12.95**
150mm diameter	4.54	5.93	0.40	7.82	nr	**13.75**
200mm diameter	6.05	7.91	0.50	9.77	nr	**17.68**
250mm diameter	7.08	9.26	0.50	9.77	nr	**19.03**
300mm diameter	7.67	10.03	0.50	9.77	nr	**19.80**
350mm diameter	8.42	11.02	0.50	9.77	nr	**20.79**
400mm diameter	9.38	12.27	0.50	9.77	nr	**22.05**

T:MECHANICAL/COOLING/HEATING SYSTEMS

Item	Net Price £	Material £	Labour hours	Labour £	Unit	Total rate £
T31 : LOW TEMPERATURE HOT WATER HEATING (cont'd)						
Y50 -THERMAL INSULATION (cont'd)						
Fittings; external insulation (cont'd)						
Tees						
15mm diameter	1.68	2.20	0.30	5.86	nr	**8.06**
20mm diameter	1.74	2.28	0.30	5.86	nr	**8.14**
25mm diameter	1.86	2.43	0.30	5.86	nr	**8.30**
32mm diameter	1.98	2.59	0.30	5.86	nr	**8.45**
40mm diameter	2.08	2.71	0.30	5.86	nr	**8.58**
50mm diameter	2.32	3.03	0.30	5.86	nr	**8.89**
65mm diameter	2.58	3.37	0.30	5.86	nr	**9.24**
80mm diameter	2.80	3.66	0.40	7.82	nr	**11.48**
100mm diameter	3.49	4.57	0.40	7.82	nr	**12.39**
125mm diameter	3.92	5.13	0.40	7.82	nr	**12.95**
150mm diameter	4.54	5.93	0.40	7.82	nr	**13.75**
200mm diameter	6.05	7.91	0.50	9.77	nr	**17.68**
250mm diameter	7.08	9.26	0.50	9.77	nr	**19.03**
300mm diameter	7.67	10.03	0.50	9.77	nr	**19.80**
350mm diameter	8.42	11.02	0.50	9.77	nr	**20.79**
400mm diameter	9.38	12.27	0.50	9.77	nr	**22.05**
Valves						
15mm diameter	15.96	20.87	1.03	20.14	nr	**41.01**
20mm diameter	16.68	21.81	1.03	20.14	nr	**41.95**
25mm diameter	17.78	23.26	1.03	20.14	nr	**43.39**
32mm diameter	18.73	24.50	1.03	20.14	nr	**44.63**
40mm diameter	19.80	25.89	1.03	20.14	nr	**46.03**
50mm diameter	21.94	28.69	1.03	20.14	nr	**48.82**
65mm diameter	24.43	31.95	1.03	20.14	nr	**52.09**
80mm diameter	26.33	34.43	1.25	24.44	nr	**58.87**
100mm diameter	32.44	42.42	1.25	24.44	nr	**66.85**
125mm diameter	36.28	47.44	1.25	24.44	nr	**71.87**
150mm diameter	42.05	54.98	1.25	24.44	nr	**79.42**
200mm diameter	55.43	72.48	1.55	30.30	nr	**102.78**
250mm diameter	64.94	84.93	1.55	30.30	nr	**115.23**
300mm diameter	71.40	93.37	1.55	30.30	nr	**123.67**
350mm diameter	79.19	103.55	1.55	30.30	nr	**133.85**
400mm diameter	88.67	115.95	1.55	30.30	nr	**146.25**
Pumps						
15mm diameter	29.57	38.67	3.10	60.60	nr	**99.27**
20mm diameter	30.89	40.39	3.10	60.60	nr	**101.00**
25mm diameter	32.93	43.06	3.10	60.60	nr	**103.66**
32mm diameter	34.68	45.35	3.10	60.60	nr	**105.95**
40mm diameter	36.66	47.94	3.10	60.60	nr	**108.54**
50mm diameter	40.63	53.13	3.10	60.60	nr	**113.74**
65mm diameter	45.24	59.16	3.10	60.60	nr	**119.76**
80mm diameter	48.77	63.77	3.75	73.31	nr	**137.08**
100mm diameter	60.07	78.55	3.75	73.31	nr	**151.87**
125mm diameter	67.18	87.84	3.75	73.31	nr	**161.16**
150mm diameter	77.88	101.84	3.75	73.31	nr	**175.15**
200mm diameter	102.65	134.23	4.65	90.91	nr	**225.14**
250mm diameter	120.26	157.27	4.65	90.91	nr	**248.17**
300mm diameter	132.23	172.91	4.65	90.91	nr	**263.82**
350mm diameter	146.65	191.77	4.65	90.91	nr	**282.68**
400mm diameter	164.21	214.73	4.65	90.91	nr	**305.64**

T:MECHANICAL/COOLING/HEATING SYSTEMS

Item	Net Price £	Material £	Labour hours	Labour £	Unit	Total rate £
Expansion bellows						
15mm diameter	23.65	30.93	1.42	27.76	nr	**58.69**
20mm diameter	24.71	32.31	1.42	27.76	nr	**60.07**
25mm diameter	26.34	34.44	1.42	27.76	nr	**62.20**
32mm diameter	27.74	36.28	1.42	27.76	nr	**64.04**
40mm diameter	29.33	38.35	1.42	27.76	nr	**66.11**
50mm diameter	32.51	42.51	1.42	27.76	nr	**70.27**
65mm diameter	36.19	47.33	1.42	27.76	nr	**75.09**
80mm diameter	39.01	51.01	1.75	34.21	nr	**85.23**
100mm diameter	48.06	62.85	1.75	34.21	nr	**97.06**
125mm diameter	53.74	70.27	1.75	34.21	nr	**104.48**
150mm diameter	62.30	81.47	1.75	34.21	nr	**115.69**
200mm diameter	82.12	107.38	2.17	42.42	nr	**149.80**
250mm diameter	96.22	125.82	2.17	42.42	nr	**168.24**
300mm diameter	105.78	138.33	2.17	42.42	nr	**180.75**
350mm diameter	117.32	153.42	2.17	42.42	nr	**195.84**
400mm diameter	131.36	171.78	2.17	42.42	nr	**214.20**
50mm thick						
15mm diameter	8.87	11.60	0.30	5.86	m	**17.46**
20mm diameter	9.30	12.16	0.30	5.86	m	**18.03**
25mm diameter	9.84	12.87	0.30	5.86	m	**18.73**
32mm diameter	10.62	13.89	0.30	5.86	m	**19.75**
40mm diameter	10.79	14.11	0.30	5.86	m	**19.97**
50mm diameter	11.95	15.63	0.30	5.86	m	**21.49**
65mm diameter	13.03	17.04	0.30	5.86	m	**22.91**
80mm diameter	13.94	18.23	0.40	7.82	m	**26.05**
100mm diameter	17.26	22.57	0.40	7.82	m	**30.39**
125mm diameter	19.31	25.25	0.40	7.82	m	**33.07**
150mm diameter	22.08	28.87	0.40	7.82	m	**36.69**
200mm diameter	29.24	38.24	0.50	9.77	m	**48.02**
250mm diameter	33.77	44.16	0.50	9.77	m	**53.93**
300mm diameter	36.22	47.36	0.50	9.77	m	**57.13**
350mm diameter	39.74	51.97	0.50	9.77	m	**61.75**
400mm diameter	44.03	57.57	0.50	9.77	m	**67.35**
Extra over for fittings external insulation						
Flange/union						
15mm diameter	13.07	17.09	0.75	14.66	nr	**31.75**
20mm diameter	13.75	17.98	0.75	14.66	nr	**32.65**
25mm diameter	14.53	19.00	0.75	14.66	nr	**33.67**
32mm diameter	15.26	19.96	0.75	14.66	nr	**34.62**
40mm diameter	15.96	20.87	0.75	14.66	nr	**35.53**
50mm diameter	17.60	23.02	0.75	14.66	nr	**37.68**
65mm diameter	19.03	24.89	0.75	14.66	nr	**39.55**
80mm diameter	20.40	26.68	0.89	17.40	nr	**44.08**
100mm diameter	25.08	32.80	0.89	17.40	nr	**50.20**
125mm diameter	27.88	36.45	0.89	17.40	nr	**53.85**
150mm diameter	31.92	41.74	0.89	17.40	nr	**59.14**
200mm diameter	41.76	54.61	1.15	22.48	nr	**77.09**
250mm diameter	48.26	63.11	1.15	22.48	nr	**85.60**
300mm diameter	52.36	68.46	1.15	22.48	nr	**90.95**
350mm diameter	57.94	75.76	1.15	22.48	nr	**98.24**
400mm diameter	64.56	84.42	1.15	22.48	nr	**106.91**

T:MECHANICAL/COOLING/HEATING SYSTEMS

Item	Net Price £	Material £	Labour hours	Labour £	Unit	Total rate £
T31 : LOW TEMPERATURE HOT WATER HEATING (cont'd)						
Y50 -THERMAL INSULATION (cont'd)						
Fittings; external insulation (cont'd)						
Bend						
15mm diameter	2.22	2.90	0.30	5.86	nr	**8.77**
20mm diameter	2.33	3.04	0.30	5.86	nr	**8.91**
25mm diameter	2.46	3.22	0.30	5.86	nr	**9.08**
32mm diameter	2.58	3.37	0.30	5.86	nr	**9.24**
40mm diameter	2.70	3.53	0.30	5.86	nr	**9.40**
50mm diameter	2.99	3.91	0.30	5.86	nr	**9.77**
65mm diameter	3.26	4.27	0.30	5.86	nr	**10.13**
80mm diameter	3.48	4.55	0.40	7.82	nr	**12.37**
100mm diameter	4.31	5.63	0.40	7.82	nr	**13.45**
125mm diameter	4.82	6.31	0.40	7.82	nr	**14.13**
150mm diameter	5.52	7.22	0.40	7.82	nr	**15.04**
200mm diameter	7.31	9.56	0.50	9.77	nr	**19.33**
250mm diameter	8.45	11.05	0.50	9.77	nr	**20.82**
300mm diameter	9.06	11.85	0.50	9.77	nr	**21.62**
350mm diameter	9.94	12.99	0.50	9.77	nr	**22.77**
400mm diameter	11.00	14.39	0.50	9.77	nr	**24.16**
Tee						
15mm diameter	2.22	2.90	0.30	5.86	nr	**8.77**
20mm diameter	2.33	3.04	0.30	5.86	nr	**8.91**
25mm diameter	2.46	3.22	0.30	5.86	nr	**9.08**
32mm diameter	2.58	3.37	0.30	5.86	nr	**9.24**
40mm diameter	2.70	3.53	0.30	5.86	nr	**9.40**
50mm diameter	2.99	3.91	0.30	5.86	nr	**9.77**
65mm diameter	3.26	4.27	0.30	5.86	nr	**10.13**
80mm diameter	3.48	4.55	0.40	7.82	nr	**12.37**
100mm diameter	4.31	5.63	0.40	7.82	nr	**13.45**
125mm diameter	4.82	6.31	0.40	7.82	nr	**14.13**
150mm diameter	5.52	7.22	0.40	7.82	nr	**15.04**
200mm diameter	7.31	9.56	0.50	9.77	nr	**19.33**
250mm diameter	8.45	11.05	0.50	9.77	nr	**20.82**
300mm diameter	9.06	11.85	0.50	9.77	nr	**21.62**
350mm diameter	9.94	12.99	0.50	9.77	nr	**22.77**
400mm diameter	11.00	14.39	0.50	9.77	nr	**24.16**
Valves						
15mm diameter	20.76	27.15	1.03	20.14	nr	**47.28**
20mm diameter	21.84	28.56	1.03	20.14	nr	**48.70**
25mm diameter	23.09	30.19	1.03	20.14	nr	**50.33**
32mm diameter	24.24	31.70	1.03	20.14	nr	**51.83**
40mm diameter	25.36	33.16	1.03	20.14	nr	**53.29**
50mm diameter	27.96	36.56	1.03	20.14	nr	**56.70**
65mm diameter	30.24	39.54	1.03	20.14	nr	**59.68**
80mm diameter	32.40	42.37	1.25	24.44	nr	**66.81**
100mm diameter	39.84	52.10	1.25	24.44	nr	**76.53**
125mm diameter	44.28	57.90	1.25	24.44	nr	**82.34**
150mm diameter	50.69	66.28	1.25	24.44	nr	**90.72**
200mm diameter	66.32	86.73	1.55	30.30	nr	**117.03**
250mm diameter	76.64	100.23	1.55	30.30	nr	**130.53**
300mm diameter	83.15	108.73	1.55	30.30	nr	**139.03**
350mm diameter	92.02	120.33	1.55	30.30	nr	**150.63**
400mm diameter	102.53	134.07	1.55	30.30	nr	**164.37**

T:MECHANICAL/COOLING/HEATING SYSTEMS

Item	Net Price £	Material £	Labour hours	Labour £	Unit	Total rate £
Pumps						
15mm diameter	38.45	50.28	3.10	60.60	nr	**110.88**
20mm diameter	40.44	52.88	3.10	60.60	nr	**113.49**
25mm diameter	42.74	55.90	3.10	60.60	nr	**116.50**
32mm diameter	44.89	58.70	3.10	60.60	nr	**119.31**
40mm diameter	46.96	61.40	3.10	60.60	nr	**122.01**
50mm diameter	51.79	67.73	3.10	60.60	nr	**128.33**
65mm diameter	55.99	73.22	3.10	60.60	nr	**133.82**
80mm diameter	60.01	78.48	3.75	73.31	nr	**151.79**
100mm diameter	73.76	96.46	3.75	73.31	nr	**169.77**
125mm diameter	82.00	107.22	3.75	73.31	nr	**180.54**
150mm diameter	93.86	122.74	3.75	73.31	nr	**196.05**
200mm diameter	122.82	160.61	4.65	90.91	nr	**251.51**
250mm diameter	141.94	185.61	4.65	90.91	nr	**276.51**
300mm diameter	153.98	201.36	4.65	90.91	nr	**292.27**
350mm diameter	170.40	222.83	4.65	90.91	nr	**313.73**
400mm diameter	189.88	248.30	4.65	90.91	nr	**339.20**
Expansion bellows						
15mm diameter	30.76	40.22	1.42	27.76	nr	**67.98**
20mm diameter	32.35	42.31	1.42	27.76	nr	**70.07**
25mm diameter	34.20	44.72	1.42	27.76	nr	**72.48**
32mm diameter	35.92	46.97	1.42	27.76	nr	**74.73**
40mm diameter	37.56	49.12	1.42	27.76	nr	**76.88**
50mm diameter	41.42	54.17	1.42	27.76	nr	**81.93**
65mm diameter	44.80	58.58	1.42	27.76	nr	**86.34**
80mm diameter	48.01	62.78	1.75	34.21	nr	**97.00**
100mm diameter	59.02	77.17	1.75	34.21	nr	**111.39**
125mm diameter	65.60	85.79	1.75	34.21	nr	**120.00**
150mm diameter	75.10	98.20	1.75	34.21	nr	**132.41**
200mm diameter	98.26	128.49	2.17	42.42	nr	**170.91**
250mm diameter	113.54	148.48	2.17	42.42	nr	**190.90**
300mm diameter	123.19	161.09	2.17	42.42	nr	**203.52**
350mm diameter	136.32	178.26	2.17	42.42	nr	**220.68**
400mm diameter	151.90	198.63	2.17	42.42	nr	**241.05**

T:MECHANICAL/COOLING/HEATING SYSTEMS

Item	Net Price £	Material £	Labour hours	Labour £	Unit	Total rate £
T33 : STEAM HEATING						
Y10 - PIPELINES						
For pipework prices refer to Section T31 - Low Temperature Hot Water Heating						
Y11 - PIPELINE ANCILLARIES						
Steam traps and accessories						
Cast iron; inverted bucket type; steam trap pressure range up to 17 bar at 210°C; screwed ends						
1/2" dia.	96.24	123.26	0.85	19.28	nr	142.54
3/4" dia.	141.98	181.84	1.13	25.63	nr	207.47
1" dia.	209.53	268.36	1.35	30.62	nr	298.97
11/2" dia.	409.74	524.79	1.80	40.82	nr	565.61
2" dia.	632.71	810.37	2.18	49.44	nr	859.81
Cast iron; inverted bucket type; steam trap pressure range up to 17 bar at 210°C; flanged ends to BS 4504 PN16; bolted connections						
15mm dia.	232.50	297.79	1.15	26.08	nr	323.87
20mm dia.	269.66	345.38	1.25	28.35	nr	373.73
25mm dia.	412.59	528.45	1.33	30.16	nr	558.61
40mm dia.	638.43	817.69	1.46	33.11	nr	850.80
50mm dia.	778.50	997.09	1.60	36.29	nr	1033.38
Steam traps and strainers						
Stainless steel; thermodynamic trap with pressure range up to 42 bar; temperature range to 400°C; screwed ends to steel						
15mm dia.	64.88	83.09	0.84	19.06	nr	102.15
20mm dia.	98.03	125.56	1.14	25.86	nr	151.42
Stainless steel; thermodynamic trap with pressure range up to 24 bar; temperature range to 288°C; flanged ends to DIN 2456 PN64; bolted connections						
15mm dia.	260.97	334.25	1.24	28.14	nr	362.39
20mm dia.	267.16	342.18	1.34	30.40	nr	372.58
25mm dia.	289.30	370.53	1.40	31.76	nr	402.29
Malleable iron pipeline strainer; max steam working pressure 14 bar and temperature range to 230°C; screwed ends to steel						
1/2" dia.	9.91	12.69	0.84	19.06	nr	31.75
3/4" dia.	13.25	16.96	1.14	25.86	nr	42.82
1" dia.	19.58	25.08	1.30	29.49	nr	54.57
11/2" dia.	32.35	41.43	1.50	34.05	nr	75.49
2" dia.	57.65	73.84	1.74	39.51	nr	113.35

T:MECHANICAL/COOLING/HEATING SYSTEMS

Item	Net Price £	Material £	Labour hours	Labour £	Unit	Total rate £
Bronze pipeline strainer; max steam working pressure 25 bar; flanged ends to BS 4504 PN25; bolted connections						
15mm dia.	117.20	150.11	1.24	28.14	nr	**178.25**
20mm dia.	142.93	183.06	1.34	30.40	nr	**213.47**
25mm dia.	163.89	209.91	1.40	31.76	nr	**241.68**
32mm dia.	254.42	325.86	1.46	33.16	nr	**359.01**
40mm dia.	288.72	369.79	1.54	34.94	nr	**404.73**
50mm dia.	444.04	568.72	1.64	37.24	nr	**605.96**
65mm dia.	491.68	629.74	2.50	56.70	nr	**686.44**
80mm dia.	611.75	783.52	2.91	65.93	nr	**849.44**
100mm dia.	1059.60	1357.12	3.51	79.57	nr	**1436.70**
Balanced pressure thermostatic steam trap and strainer; max working pressure up to 13 bar; screwed ends to steel						
1/2" dia.	44.31	56.75	1.26	28.60	nr	**85.35**
3/4" dia.	47.91	61.37	1.71	38.83	nr	**100.20**
Bimetallic thermostatic steam trap and strainer; max working pressure up to 21 bar; flanged ends						
15mm	125.91	161.26	1.24	28.14	nr	**189.40**
20mm	138.40	177.26	1.34	30.40	nr	**207.66**
Sight glasses						
Pressed brass; straight; single window; screwed ends to steel						
15mm dia.	29.54	37.83	0.84	19.06	nr	**56.89**
20mm dia.	32.78	41.98	1.14	25.86	nr	**67.84**
25mm dia.	40.97	52.48	1.30	29.49	nr	**81.97**
Gunmetal; straight; double window; screwed ends to steel						
15mm dia.	47.64	61.02	0.84	19.06	nr	**80.08**
20mm dia.	52.41	67.12	1.14	25.86	nr	**92.98**
25mm dia.	64.80	82.99	1.30	29.49	nr	**112.48**
32mm dia.	106.72	136.69	1.35	30.65	nr	**167.34**
40mm dia.	106.72	136.69	1.74	39.51	nr	**176.20**
50mm dia.	129.59	165.98	2.08	47.25	nr	**213.22**
SG Iron flanged; BS 4504, PN 25						
15mm dia.	97.19	124.48	1.00	22.68	nr	**147.16**
20mm dia.	114.35	146.45	1.25	28.35	nr	**174.80**
25mm dia.	145.79	186.73	1.50	34.05	nr	**220.78**
32mm dia.	161.04	206.25	1.70	38.57	nr	**244.82**
40mm dia.	210.59	269.72	2.00	45.36	nr	**315.07**
50mm dia.	254.42	325.86	2.30	52.25	nr	**378.11**
Check valve and sight glass; gun metal; screwed						
15mm dia.	48.12	61.63	0.84	19.06	nr	**80.69**
20mm dia.	50.98	65.29	1.14	25.86	nr	**91.15**
25mm dia.	85.76	109.84	1.30	29.49	nr	**139.33**

T:MECHANICAL/COOLING/HEATING SYSTEMS

Item	Net Price £	Material £	Labour hours	Labour £	Unit	Total rate £
T33 : STEAM HEATING (cont'd)						
Y11 - PIPELINE ANCILLARIES (cont'd)						
Pressure reducing valves						
Pressure reducing valve for steam; maximum range of 17 bar and 232°C; screwed ends to steel						
15mm dia.	363.31	465.32	0.87	19.73	nr	**485.05**
20mm dia.	393.10	503.48	0.91	20.64	nr	**524.12**
25mm dia.	423.86	542.87	1.35	30.62	nr	**573.49**
Pressure reducing valve for steam; maximum range of 17 bar and 232°C; flanged ends to BS 4504 PN 25						
25mm dia.	510.36	653.66	1.70	38.55	nr	**692.21**
32mm dia.	579.56	742.29	1.87	42.41	nr	**784.70**
40mm dia.	692.01	886.32	2.12	48.08	nr	**934.40**
50mm dia.	798.69	1022.96	2.57	58.28	nr	**1081.24**
Safety and relief valves						
Bronze safety valve; 'pop' type; side outlet; including easing lever; working pressure saturated steam up to 20.7 bar; screwed ends to steel						
15mm dia.	83.48	106.92	0.32	7.26	nr	**114.18**
20mm dia.	102.68	131.51	0.40	9.07	nr	**140.58**
Bronze safety valve; 'pop' type; side outlet; including easing lever; working pressure saturated steam up to 17.2 bar; screwed ends to steel						
25mm dia.	134.28	171.99	0.47	10.66	nr	**182.65**
32mm dia.	180.36	231.00	0.56	12.70	nr	**243.70**
Bronze safety valve; 'pop' type; side outlet; including easing lever; working pressure saturated steam up to 13.8 bar; screwed ends to steel						
40mm dia.	250.92	321.38	0.64	14.51	nr	**335.89**
50mm dia.	331.85	425.03	0.76	17.24	nr	**442.26**
65mm dia.	484.50	620.54	0.94	21.32	nr	**641.86**
80mm dia.	543.49	696.09	1.10	24.95	nr	**721.04**

T:MECHANICAL/COOLING/HEATING SYSTEMS

Item	Net Price £	Material £	Labour hours	Labour £	Unit	Total rate £
EQUIPMENT						
Y23 - CALORIFIERS						
Non-storage calorifiers; mild steel shell construction with indirect steam heating for secondary LPHW at 82°C flow and 71°C return to BS 853; maximum test on shell 11 bar, tubes 26 bar						
Horizontal/vertical, for steam at 3 bar-5.5 bar						
88 kW capacity	412.43	528.23	8.00	181.43	nr	**709.66**
176 kW capacity	600.43	769.02	12.05	273.23	nr	**1042.25**
293 kW capacity	654.48	838.25	14.08	319.41	nr	**1157.66**
586 kW capacity	955.28	1223.51	37.04	839.94	nr	**2063.45**
879 kW capacity	1189.10	1522.99	40.00	907.14	nr	**2430.12**
1465 kW capacity	1451.13	1858.59	45.45	1030.84	nr	**2889.42**

T:MECHANICAL/COOLING/HEATING SYSTEMS

Item	Net Price £	Material £	Labour hours	Labour £	Unit	Total rate £
T42 : LOCAL HEATING UNITS						
Warm air unit heater for connection to LTHW or steam supplies; suitable for heights upto 3m; recirculating type; mild steel casing; heating coil; adjustable discharge louvre; axial fan; horizontal or vertical discharge; normal speed; entering air temperature 15°C; complete with enclosures; includes fixing in position; includes connections to primary heating supply; electrical work elsewhere						
Low pressure hot water						
7.5 kW, 265 l/sec	306.13	392.08	6.53	148.09	nr	**540.17**
15.4 kW, 575 l/sec	370.57	474.62	7.54	171.00	nr	**645.62**
26.9 kW, 1040 l/sec	502.15	643.14	8.65	196.17	nr	**839.31**
48.0 kW, 1620 l/sec	661.91	847.77	9.35	212.04	nr	**1059.81**
Steam, 2 Bar						
9.2 kW, 265 l/sec	437.69	560.59	6.53	148.09	nr	**708.68**
18.8 kW, 575 l/sec	473.95	607.03	6.82	154.67	nr	**761.69**
34.8 kW, 1040 l/sec	545.11	698.17	6.82	154.67	nr	**852.84**
51.6 kW, 1625 l/sec	738.46	945.81	7.10	161.02	nr	**1106.83**

T:MECHANICAL/COOLING/HEATING SYSTEMS

Item	Net Price £	Material £	Labour hours	Labour £	Unit	Total rate £
T60: CENTRAL REFRIGERATION PLANT						
EQUIPMENT						
CHILLERS						
Air cooled						
Selection of air cooled chillers based on chilled water flow and return temperatures 6°C and 12°C, and an outdoor temperature of 35°C						
Air cooled liquid chiller; refrigerant 407C; scroll compressors; twin circuit; integral controls; includes placing in position; electrical work elsewhere						
Cooling load						
100 kW	16123.59	20650.93	8.00	181.43	nr	**20832.36**
150 kW	18188.42	23295.54	8.00	181.43	nr	**23476.97**
200 kW	23088.14	29571.05	8.00	181.43	nr	**29752.48**
Air cooled liquid chiller; refrigerant 407C; reciprocating compressors; twin circuit; integral controls; includes placing in position; electrical work elsewhere						
Cooling Load						
250 kW	30344.95	38865.51	8.00	181.43	nr	**39046.93**
400 kW	42707.96	54699.93	8.00	181.43	nr	**54881.36**
550 kW	54408.64	69686.04	8.00	181.43	nr	**69867.47**
700 kW	68298.83	87476.45	9.00	204.11	nr	**87680.56**
Air cooled liquid chiller; refrigerant R134a; screw compressors; twin circuit; integral controls; includes placing in position; electrical work elsewhere						
Cooling load						
250 kW	34446.67	44118.95	8.00	181.43	nr	**44300.37**
400 kW	43457.09	55659.40	8.00	181.43	nr	**55840.83**
600 kW	56451.52	72302.54	8.00	181.43	nr	**72483.97**
800 kW	83939.63	107509.03	9.00	204.11	nr	**107713.14**
1000 kW	97632.31	125046.48	9.00	204.11	nr	**125250.59**
1200 kW	113013.76	144746.89	10.00	226.78	nr	**144973.67**
Air cooled liquid chiller; ductable for indoor installation; refrigerant 407C; scroll compressors; integral controls; includes placing in position; electrical work elsewhere						
Cooling load						
40 kW	11323.62	14503.18	6.00	136.07	nr	**14639.25**
80 kW	16444.79	21062.32	6.00	136.07	nr	**21198.39**

T:MECHANICAL/COOLING/HEATING SYSTEMS

Item	Net Price £	Material £	Labour hours	Labour £	Unit	Total rate £
T60: CENTRAL REFRIGERATION PLANT (cont'd)						
EQUIPMENT (cont'd)						
CHILLERS (cont'd)						
Higher efficiency air cooled						
Selection of air cooled chillers based on chilled water flow and return temperatures of 6°C and 12°C and an outdoor temperature of 35°C.						
These machines have significantly higher part load operating efficiencies than conventional air cooled machines.						
Air cooled liquid chiller, refrigerant R410A; Scroll compressors; complete with free cooling facility; integral controls; includes placing in position; electrical work elsewhere						
Cooling load						
250 kW	31500.00	38423.70	8.00	181.43	nr	38605.13
300 kW	33600.00	40985.28	8.00	181.43	nr	41166.71
350 kW	35700.00	43546.86	8.00	181.43	nr	43728.29
400 kW	38850.00	47389.23	8.00	181.43	nr	47570.66
450 kW	42000.00	51231.60	8.00	181.43	nr	51413.03
500 kW	45150.00	55073.97	8.00	181.43	nr	55255.40
600 kW	48300.00	58916.34	8.00	181.43	nr	59097.77
650 kW	52500.00	64039.50	9.00	204.11	nr	64243.61
700 kW	63000.00	76847.40	9.00	204.11	nr	77051.51
750 kW	67200.00	81970.56	9.00	204.11	nr	82174.67
Water cooled						
Selection of water cooled chillers based on chilled water flow and return temperatures of 6°C and 12°C, and condenser entering and leaving temperatures of 27°C and 33°C						
Water cooled liquid chiller; refrigerant 407C; reciprocating compressors; twin circuit; integral controls; includes placing in position; electrical work elsewhere						
Cooling load						
200 kw	16119.60	20645.82	8.00	181.43	nr	20827.25
350 kW	27033.20	34623.85	8.00	181.43	nr	34805.28
500 kW	34601.85	44317.70	8.00	181.43	nr	44499.13
650 kW	44634.80	57167.81	9.00	204.11	nr	57371.91
750 kW	48339.80	61913.13	9.00	204.11	nr	62117.24

T:MECHANICAL/COOLING/HEATING SYSTEMS

Item	Net Price £	Material £	Labour hours	Labour £	Unit	Total rate £
Water cooled condenserless liquid chiller; refrigerant 407C; reciprocating compressors; twin circuit; integral controls; includes placing in position; electrical work elsewhere						
Cooling load						
200 kW	14899.66	19083.33	8.00	181.43	nr	**19264.76**
350 kW	26155.45	33499.64	8.00	181.43	nr	**33681.06**
500 kW	33057.15	42339.27	8.00	181.43	nr	**42520.69**
650 kW	40429.67	51781.92	9.00	204.11	nr	**51986.03**
750 kW	46004.70	58922.36	9.00	204.11	nr	**59126.47**
Water cooled liquid chiller; refrigerant R134a; screw compressors; twin circuit; integral controls; includes placing in position; electrical work elsewhere						
Cooling load						
300 kW	27904.07	35739.25	8.00	181.43	nr	**35920.67**
500 kW	36788.80	47118.72	8.00	181.43	nr	**47300.15**
700 kW	53838.07	68955.26	9.00	204.11	nr	**69159.36**
900 kW	61862.96	79233.45	9.00	204.11	nr	**79437.56**
1100 kW	74615.00	95566.14	10.00	226.78	nr	**95792.92**
1300 kW	83132.65	106475.46	10.00	226.78	nr	**106702.25**
Water cooled liquid chiller; refrigerant R134a; centrifugal compressors; twin circuit; integral controls; includes placing in position; electrical work elsewhere						
Cooling load						
700 kW	53067.00	67967.68	9.00	204.11	nr	**68171.79**
1000 kW	74812.50	95819.10	10.00	226.78	nr	**96045.89**
1300 kW	98403.38	126034.06	10.00	226.78	nr	**126260.84**
1600 kW	118104.00	151266.42	11.00	249.46	nr	**151515.88**
1900 kW	143839.50	184228.19	11.00	249.46	nr	**184477.66**
2200 kW	171370.50	219489.62	13.00	294.82	nr	**219784.44**
2500 kW	177056.25	226771.87	13.00	294.82	nr	**227066.69**
3000 kW	215460.00	275959.01	15.00	340.18	nr	**276299.19**
3500 kW	293265.00	375610.88	15.00	340.18	nr	**375951.06**
4000 kW	311473.37	398931.97	20.00	453.57	nr	**399385.54**
4500 kW	332309.15	425618.23	20.00	453.57	nr	**426071.80**
5000 kW	405281.26	519080.18	25.00	566.96	nr	**519647.14**

T:MECHANICAL/COOLING/HEATING SYSTEMS

Item	Net Price £	Material £	Labour hours	Labour £	Unit	Total rate £
T60: CENTRAL REFRIGERATION PLANT (cont'd)						
EQUIPMENT (cont'd)						
CHILLERS (cont'd)						
Absorption						
Absorption chiller, for operation using low pressure steam; selection based on chilled water flow and return temperatures of 6°C and 12°C, steam at 1 bar gauge and condenser entering and leaving temperatures of 27°C and 33°C; integral controls; includes placing in position; electrical work elsewhere						
Cooling load						
400 kW	50884.47	65172.32	8.00	181.43	nr	**65353.75**
700 kW	64611.07	82753.21	9.00	204.11	nr	**82957.31**
1000 kW	73712.26	94409.92	10.00	226.78	nr	**94636.71**
1300 kW	87967.53	112667.93	12.00	272.14	nr	**112940.07**
1600 kW	104109.08	133341.86	14.00	317.50	nr	**133659.36**
2000 kW	123388.76	158035.08	15.00	340.18	nr	**158375.26**
Absorption chiller, for operation using low pressure hot water; selection based on chilled water flow and return temperatures of 6°C and 12°C, cooling water temperatures of 27°C and 33°C and hot water at 90°C; integral controls; includes placing in position; electrical work elsewhere						
Cooling load						
700 kW	73712.26	94409.92	9.00	204.11	nr	**94614.03**
1000 kW	92143.07	118015.92	10.00	226.78	nr	**118242.70**
1300 kW	107168.41	137260.22	12.00	272.14	nr	**137532.37**
1600 kW	123388.76	158035.08	14.00	317.50	nr	**158352.58**
HEAT REJECTION						
Dry air liquid coolers						
Dry air liquid cooler; selection based on fluid temperatures 45°C on, 40°C off at 32°C dry bulb ambient temperature; includes 20% ethylene glycol; includes placing in postion; electrical work elsewhere						
Heat rejection						
Flat coil configuration						
500kW	11747.53	15046.12	15.00	340.18	nr	**15386.29**
Extra for inverter panels (factory wired and mounted on units)	6244.52	7997.92	15.00	340.18	nr	**8338.09**

T:MECHANICAL/COOLING/HEATING SYSTEMS

Item	Net Price £	Material £	Labour hours	Labour £	Unit	Total rate £
800kW	19874.18	25454.65	15.00	340.18	nr	**25794.83**
Extra for inverter panels (factory wired and mounted on units)	11475.75	14698.03	15.00	340.18	nr	**15038.20**
1100kW	25518.43	32683.75	15.00	340.18	nr	**33023.93**
Extra for inverter panels (factory wired and mounted on units)	12487.97	15994.47	15.00	340.18	nr	**16334.64**
1400kW	32414.58	41516.27	15.00	340.18	nr	**41856.45**
Extra over for inverter panels (factory wired and mounted on units)	17214.16	22047.72	15.00	340.18	nr	**22387.90**
1700kW	38277.11	49024.94	15.00	340.18	nr	**49365.12**
Extra for inverter panels (factory wired and mounted on units)	18727.14	23985.53	15.00	340.18	nr	**24325.71**
2000kW	44776.29	57349.02	15.00	340.18	nr	**57689.20**
Extra for inverter panels (factory wired and mounted on units)	23034.96	29502.95	15.00	340.18	nr	**29843.12**
Note - heat rejection capacities above 500kW require multiple units. Prices are therefore for total number of units.						
'Vee' type coil configuration						
500kW	11350.56	14537.68	15.00	340.18	nr	**14877.86**
Extra for inverter panels (factory wired and mounted on units)	4392.35	5625.68	15.00	340.18	nr	**5965.85**
800kW	-	21446.10	15.00	340.18	nr	**21786.27**
Extra for inverter panels (factory wired and mounted on units)	10171.69	13027.80	15.00	340.18	nr	**13367.97**
1100kW	24620.70	31533.95	15.00	340.18	nr	**31874.12**
Extra for inverter panels (factory wired and mounted on units)	12299.92	15753.61	15.00	340.18	nr	**16093.79**
1400kW	31766.96	40686.81	15.00	340.18	nr	**41026.98**
Extra for inverter panels (factory wired and mounted on units)	15294.05	19588.46	15.00	340.18	nr	**19928.64**
1700kW	36492.89	46739.72	15.00	340.18	nr	**47079.90**
Extra for inverter panels (factory wired and mounted on units)	20343.38	26055.59	15.00	340.18	nr	**26395.77**
2000kW	47650.45	61030.22	15.00	340.18	nr	**61370.39**
Extra for inverter panels (factory wired and mounted on units)	22941.07	29382.69	15.00	340.18	nr	**29722.87**
Note - Heat rejection capacities above 1100kW require multiple units. Prices are for total number of units.						

T:MECHANICAL/COOLING/HEATING SYSTEMS

Item	Net Price £	Material £	Labour hours	Labour £	Unit	Total rate £
T60: CENTRAL REFRIGERATION PLANT (cont'd)						
EQUIPMENT (cont'd)						
HEAT REJECTION (cont'd)						
Air cooled condensers						
Air cooled condenser; refrigerant 407C; selection based on condensing temperature of 45°C at 32°C dry bulb ambient; includes placing in position; electrical work elsewhere						
Heat rejection						
Flat coil configuration						
500kW	12539.87	16060.93	15.00	340.18	nr	16401.11
Extra for inverter panels (factory wired and mounted on units)	5737.88	7349.01	15.00	340.18	nr	7689.19
800kW	20572.89	26349.55	15.00	340.18	nr	26689.73
Extra for inverter panels (factory wired and mounted on units)	8784.17	11250.67	15.00	340.18	nr	11590.85
1100kW	27541.80	35275.26	15.00	340.18	nr	35615.44
Extra for inverter panels (factory wired and mounted on units)	12487.70	15994.12	15.00	340.18	nr	16334.30
1400kW	34385.52	44040.63	15.00	340.18	nr	44380.81
Extra for inverter panels (factory wired and mounted on units)	15356.64	19668.63	15.00	340.18	nr	20008.81
1700kW	44776.29	57349.02	15.00	340.18	nr	57689.20
Extra for inverter panels (factory wired and mounted on units)	23034.96	29502.95	15.00	340.18	nr	29843.12
2000kW	51578.28	66060.95	15.00	340.18	nr	66401.12
Extra for inverter panels (factory wired and mounted on units)	23034.96	29502.95	15.00	340.18	nr	29843.12
Note - Heat rejection capacities above 500kW require multiple units. Prices are for total number of units						
'Vee' type coil configuration						
500kW	12310.35	15766.97	15.00	340.18	nr	16107.15
Extra for inverter panels (factory wired and mounted on units)	4392.08	5625.34	15.00	340.18	nr	5965.51
800kW	18517.69	23717.27	15.00	340.18	nr	24057.45
Extra for inverter panels (factory wired and mounted on units)	8992.82	11517.91	15.00	340.18	nr	11858.08
1100kW	27176.66	34807.60	15.00	340.18	nr	35147.77
Extra for inverter panels (factory wired and mounted on units)	15294.05	19588.46	15.00	340.18	nr	19928.64
1400kW	31641.77	40526.47	15.00	340.18	nr	40866.64
Extra for inverter panels (factory wired and mounted on units)	17985.63	23035.82	15.00	340.18	nr	23375.99
1700kW	40765.00	52211.40	15.00	340.18	nr	52551.58
Extra for inverter panels (factory wired and mounted on units)	22951.50	29396.05	15.00	340.18	nr	29736.23
2000kW	47462.66	60789.71	15.00	340.18	nr	61129.88
Extra for inverter panels (factory wired and mounted on units)	26978.45	34553.72	15.00	340.18	nr	34893.90

T:MECHANICAL/COOLING/HEATING SYSTEMS

Item	Net Price £	Material £	Labour hours	Labour £	Unit	Total rate £
Note - Heat rejection capacities above 1100kW require multiple units. Prices are for total number of units.						
Cooling towers						
Cooling towers; forced draught, centrifugal fan, conterflow design; based on water temperatures of 35°C on and 29°C off at 21°C wet bulb ambient temperature; includes placing in position; electrical work elsewhere						
Open circuit type						
Heat rejection						
900kW	8352.89	10698.30	20.00	453.57	nr	**11151.87**
Extra for stainless steel construction	3744.88	4796.41	-	-	nr	**4796.41**
Extra for intake and discharge sound attenuation	4030.47	5162.18	-	-	nr	**5162.18**
Extra for fan dampers for capacity control	935.16	1197.75	-	-	nr	**1197.75**
1500kW	12959.75	16598.72	20.00	453.57	nr	**17052.29**
Extra for stainless steel construction	5998.71	7683.08	-	-	nr	**7683.08**
Extra for intake and discharge sound attenuation	6039.76	7735.67	-	-	nr	**7735.67**
Extra for fan dampers for capacity control	949.17	1215.69	-	-	nr	**1215.69**
2100kW	18385.41	23547.85	20.00	453.57	nr	**24001.42**
Extra for stainless steel construction	8507.95	10896.90	-	-	nr	**10896.90**
Extra for intake and discharge sound attenuation	8968.07	11486.21	-	-	nr	**11486.21**
Extra for fan dampers for capacity control	1083.84	1388.17	-	-	nr	**1388.17**
2700kW	22203.63	28438.18	20.00	453.57	nr	**28891.75**
Extra for stainless steel construction	10378.67	13292.89	-	-	nr	**13292.89**
Extra for intake and discharge sound attenuation	12081.68	15474.10	-	-	nr	**15474.10**
Extra for fan dampers for capacity control	1687.17	2160.91	-	-	nr	**2160.91**
3300kW	27362.10	35045.10	20.00	453.57	nr	**35498.67**
Extra for stainless steel construction	12667.01	16223.77	-	-	nr	**16223.77**
Extra for intake and discharge sound attenuation	11394.32	14593.73	-	-	nr	**14593.73**
Extra for fan dampers for capacity control	1380.12	1767.65	-	-	nr	**1767.65**
3900kW	30839.86	39499.39	20.00	453.57	nr	**39952.96**
Extra for stainless steel construction	14277.71	18286.74	-	-	nr	**18286.74**
Extra for intake and discharge sound attenuation	11613.03	14873.85	-	-	nr	**14873.85**
Extra for fan dampers for capacity control	1380.12	1767.65	-	-	nr	**1767.65**
4500kW	34707.64	44453.20	23.00	521.60	nr	**44974.80**
Extra for stainless steel construction	16185.23	20729.89	-	-	nr	**20729.89**
Extra for intake and discharge sound attenuation	15402.15	19726.92	-	-	nr	**19726.92**
Extra for fan dampers for capacity control	2171.99	2781.86	-	-	nr	**2781.86**
5100kW	40092.36	51349.90	23.00	521.60	nr	**51871.50**
Extra for stainless steel construction	18472.43	23659.30	-	-	nr	**23659.30**
Extra for intake and discharge sound attenuation	15361.21	19674.49	-	-	nr	**19674.49**
Extra for fan dampers for capacity control	2171.99	2781.86	-	-	nr	**2781.86**
5700kW	42386.09	54287.68	30.00	680.35	nr	**54968.03**
Extra for stainless steel construction	19792.06	25349.47	-	-	nr	**25349.47**
Extra for intake and discharge sound attenuation	22747.70	29135.02	-	-	nr	**29135.02**
Extra for fan dampers for capacity control	2388.55	3059.23	-	-	nr	**3059.23**
6300kW	51106.36	65456.52	30.00	680.35	nr	**66136.87**
Extra for stainless steel construction	23660.04	30303.54	-	-	nr	**30303.54**
Extra for intake and discharge sound attenuation	23076.30	29555.90	-	-	nr	**29555.90**
Extra for fan dampers for capacity control	2388.55	3059.23	-	-	nr	**3059.23**

T:MECHANICAL/COOLING/HEATING SYSTEMS

Item	Net Price £	Material £	Labour hours	Labour £	Unit	Total rate £
T60: CENTRAL REFRIGERATION PLANT (cont'd)						
EQUIPMENT (cont'd)						
HEAT REJECTION (cont'd)						
Cooling towers (cont'd)						
Closed circuit type (includes 20% ethylene glycol)						
Heat rejection						
900kW	23285.31	29823.59	20.00	453.57	nr	30277.16
Extra for stainless steel construction	18960.24	24284.09	-	-	nr	24284.09
Extra for intake and discharge sound attenuation	7006.18	8973.44	-	-	nr	8973.44
Extra for fan dampers for capacity control	949.17	1215.69	-	-	nr	1215.69
1500kW	43291.08	55446.79	20.00	453.57	nr	55900.35
Extra for stainless steel construction	34515.00	44206.47	-	-	nr	44206.47
Extra for intake and discharge sound attenuation	11184.24	14324.66	-	-	nr	14324.66
Extra for fan dampers for capacity control	1380.12	1767.65	-	-	nr	1767.65
2100kW	52756.90	67570.51	20.00	453.57	nr	68024.08
Extra for stainless steel construction	46890.93	60057.44	-	-	nr	60057.44
Extra for intake and discharge sound attenuation	13462.88	17243.12	-	-	nr	17243.12
Extra for fan dampers for capacity control	1380.12	1767.65	-	-	nr	1767.65
2700kW	56881.09	72852.73	25.00	566.96	nr	73419.69
Extra for stainless steel construction	58100.25	74414.22	-	-	nr	74414.22
Extra for intake and discharge sound attenuation	20094.13	25736.36	-	-	nr	25736.36
Extra for fan dampers for capacity control	2087.95	2674.23	-	-	nr	2674.23
3300kW	87639.07	112247.25	25.00	566.96	nr	112814.21
Extra for stainless steel construction	72481.50	92833.58	-	-	nr	92833.58
Extra for intake and discharge sound attenuation	26729.67	34235.10	-	-	nr	34235.10
Extra for fan dampers for capacity control	2388.55	3059.23	-	-	nr	3059.23
3900kW	96495.10	123589.96	25.00	566.96	nr	124156.92
Extra for stainless steel construction	79485.76	101804.57	-	-	nr	101804.57
Extra for intake and discharge sound attenuation	27167.09	34795.33	-	-	nr	34795.33
Extra for fan dampers for capacity control	2388.55	3059.23	-	-	nr	3059.23
4500kW	115523.69	147961.59	40.00	907.14	nr	148868.73
Extra for stainless steel construction	86108.37	110286.74	-	-	nr	110286.74
Extra for intake and discharge sound attenuation	38829.68	49732.66	-	-	nr	49732.66
Extra for fan dampers for capacity control	4175.91	5348.46	-	-	nr	5348.46
5100kW	128845.43	165023.94	40.00	907.14	nr	165931.08
Extra for stainless steel construction	111276.75	142522.15	-	-	nr	142522.15
Extra for intake and discharge sound attenuation	38829.68	49732.66	-	-	nr	49732.66
Extra for fan dampers for capacity control	4175.91	5348.46	-	-	nr	5348.46
5700kW	158874.03	203484.27	40.00	907.14	nr	204391.40
Extra for stainless steel construction	114941.17	147215.50	-	-	nr	147215.50
Extra for intake and discharge sound attenuation	43408.52	55597.20	-	-	nr	55597.20
Extra for fan dampers for capacity control	4777.08	6118.44	-	-	nr	6118.44
6300kW	169703.80	217354.93	40.00	907.14	nr	218262.07
Extra for stainless steel construction	131474.03	168390.62	-	-	nr	168390.62
Extra for intake and discharge sound attenuation	43408.52	55597.20	-	-	nr	55597.20
Extra for fan dampers for capacity control	4777.08	6118.44	-	-	nr	6118.44

T:MECHANICAL/COOLING/HEATING SYSTEMS

Item	Net Price £	Material £	Labour hours	Labour £	Unit	Total rate £
T61 : CHILLED WATER						
Y10 - PIPELINES						
For pipework prices refer to Section T31 - Low Temperature Hot Water Heating						
For plastic pipework suitable for chilled water systems, refer to ABS pipework details in Section S10 - Cold Water						
Y11 - PIPELINE ANCILLARIES						
For prices for ancillaries refer to Section T31 - Low Temperature Hot Water Heating						
Y22 - HEAT EXCHANGERS						
Plate heat exchanger; for use in CHW systems; painted carbon steel frame, stainless steel plates, nitrile rubber gaskets, design pressure of 10 bar and operating temperature of 110/135°C						
Primary side; 13°C in, 7°C out; secondary side; 6°C in, 12°C out						
500 kW, 19.80 l/s	6331.50	8109.32	10.00	226.78	nr	**8336.11**
1000 kW, 39.65 l/s	10552.50	13515.54	12.00	272.14	nr	**13787.68**
1500 kW, 59.47 l/s	14656.25	18771.58	12.00	272.14	nr	**19043.72**
2000 kW, 79.30 l/s	19346.25	24778.48	16.00	362.85	nr	**25141.34**
2500 kW, 99.10 l/s	22277.50	28532.80	16.00	362.85	nr	**28895.65**
Note - For temperature conditions different to those above, the cost of the units can vary significantly, and so manufacturers advice should be sought.						
Y24 - TRACE HEATING						
Trace heating; for freeze protection or temperature maintainance of pipework; to BS 6351; including fixing to parent structures by plastic pull ties						
Straight laid						
15mm	18.25	23.37	0.27	6.12	m	**29.50**
25mm	18.25	23.37	0.27	6.12	m	**29.50**
28mm	18.25	23.37	0.27	6.12	m	**29.50**
32mm	18.25	23.37	0.30	6.80	m	**30.18**
35mm	18.25	23.37	0.31	7.03	m	**30.40**
50mm	18.25	23.37	0.34	7.71	m	**31.09**
100mm	18.25	23.37	0.40	9.07	m	**32.45**
150mm	18.25	23.37	0.40	9.07	m	**32.45**

T:MECHANICAL/COOLING/HEATING SYSTEMS

Item	Net Price £	Material £	Labour hours	Labour £	Unit	Total rate £
T61 : CHILLED WATER (cont'd)						
Y24 - TRACE HEATING (cont'd)						
Trace heating; for freeze protection (cont'd)						
Helically wound						
15mm	23.25	29.78	1.00	22.68	m	**52.46**
25mm	23.25	29.78	1.00	22.68	m	**52.46**
28mm	23.25	29.78	1.00	22.68	m	**52.46**
32mm	23.25	29.78	1.00	22.68	m	**52.46**
35mm	23.25	29.78	1.00	22.68	m	**52.46**
50mm	23.25	29.78	1.00	22.68	m	**52.46**
100mm	23.25	29.78	1.00	22.68	m	**52.46**
150mm	23.25	29.78	1.00	22.68	m	**52.46**
Accessories for trace heating; weatherproof; polycarbonate enclosure to IP standards; fully installed						
Connection junction box						
100 x 100 x 75mm	39.95	51.17	1.40	31.75	nr	**82.92**
Single air thermostat						
150 x 150 x 75mm	87.54	112.12	1.42	32.20	nr	**144.32**
Single capillary thermostat						
150 x 150 x 75mm	125.94	161.30	1.46	33.11	nr	**194.41**
Twin capillary thermostat						
150 x 150 x 75mm	225.94	289.38	1.46	33.11	nr	**322.49**
EQUIPMENT						
PRESSURISATION UNITS						
Chilled water packaged pressurisation unit complete with expansion vessel(s), interconnecting pipework and necessary isolating and drain valves; includes placing in position; electrical work elasewhere						
Selection based on a final working pressure of 4 bar, a 3m static head and system operating temperatures of 6°/12°C						
System volume						
1800 litres	1264.80	1619.94	8.00	181.43	nr	**1801.37**
4500 litres	1264.80	1619.94	8.00	181.43	nr	**1801.37**
7200 litres	1326.00	1698.33	10.00	226.78	nr	**1925.11**
9900 litres	1326.00	1698.33	10.00	226.78	nr	**1925.11**
15300 litres	1377.00	1763.65	13.00	294.82	nr	**2058.47**
22500 litres	1459.62	1869.47	20.00	453.57	nr	**2323.03**
27000 litres	1459.62	1869.47	20.00	453.57	nr	**2323.03**

T:MECHANICAL/COOLING/HEATING SYSTEMS

Item	Net Price £	Material £	Labour hours	Labour £	Unit	Total rate £
CHILLED BEAMS						
Static (passive) beams; based on water at 14°C flow and 16°C return, 24°C room temperature; 600mm wide coil providing 350–400W/m output						
Static cooled beam for exposed installation with standard casing	105.00	134.48	4.00	90.71	m	**225.20**
Static cooled beam for installation above open grid or perforated ceiling	72.00	92.22	4.00	90.71	m	**182.93**
Ventilated (active) beams; based on water at 14°C flow and 16°C return, 24°C room temperature; air supply at 10l/s/linear metre; 300mm wide beam providing 250–350W/m output unless stated otherwise; all exposed beams c/w standard casing; electrical work elsewhere						
Ventilated cooled beam flush mounted within a false ceiling; closed type with integrated secondary air circulation; 600mm wide beam providing 400W/m output	163.00	208.77	4.50	102.05	m	**310.82**
Ventilated cooled beam flush mounted within a false ceiling; open type	144.00	184.43	4.00	90.71	m	**275.15**
Ventilated cooled beam for exposed mounting with standard casing	144.00	184.43	4.00	90.71	m	**275.15**
Ventilated cooled beam flush mounted within a false ceiling; open type; with recessed integrated flush mounted 28W or 35W T5 light fittings	261.00	334.29	4.00	90.71	m	**425.00**
Ventilated cooled beam for exposed mounting with recessed integrated flush mounted 28W or 35W T5 light fittings	261.00	334.29	4.00	90.71	m	**425.00**
Ventilated cooled beam for exposed mounting with recessed integrated flush mounted direct and indirect 28W or 35W T5 light fittings	285.00	365.03	4.00	90.71	m	**455.74**
LEAK DETECTION						
Leak detection system consisting of a central control module connected by a leader cable to water sensing cables						
Control Modules						
Alarm Only	297.60	381.16	4.00	90.46	nr	**471.62**
Alarm and location	1951.80	2499.84	8.00	180.93	nr	**2680.77**

T:MECHANICAL/COOLING/HEATING SYSTEMS

Item	Net Price £	Material £	Labour hours	Labour £	Unit	Total rate £
T61 : CHILLED WATER (cont'd)						
LEAK DETECTION (cont'd)						
Leak detection system (cont'd)						
Cables						
Sensing - 3m length	81.51	104.40	4.00	90.46	nr	**194.87**
Sensing - 7.5m length	120.10	153.82	4.00	90.46	nr	**244.28**
Sensing - 15m length	207.64	265.95	8.00	180.93	nr	**446.88**
Leader - 3.5m length	36.58	46.85	2.00	45.23	nr	**92.08**
End terminal						
End terminal	14.20	18.19	0.05	1.13	nr	**19.32**
ENERGY METERS						
Ultrasonic						
Energy meter for measuring energy use in chilled water systems; includes ultrasonic flow meter (with sensor and signal converter), energy calculator, pair of temperature sensors with brass pockets, and 3m of interconnecting cable; includes fixing in position; electrical work elsewhere						
Pipe size (flanged connections to PN16); maximum flow rate						
50mm, 36m³/hr	998.89	1279.36	1.80	40.82	nr	**1320.18**
65mm, 60m³/hr	1100.27	1409.22	2.32	52.61	nr	**1461.83**
80mm, 100m³/hr	1232.36	1578.40	2.56	58.06	nr	**1636.46**
125mm, 250m³/hr	1426.57	1827.14	3.60	81.64	nr	**1908.78**
150mm, 360m³/hr	1547.95	1982.60	4.80	108.86	nr	**2091.46**
200mm, 600m³/hr	1728.59	2213.97	6.24	141.51	nr	**2355.48**
250mm, 1000m³/hr	1993.49	2553.24	9.60	217.71	nr	**2770.95**
300mm, 1500m³/hr	2341.92	2999.51	10.80	244.93	nr	**3244.43**
350mm, 2000m³/hr	2820.30	3612.21	13.20	299.35	nr	**3911.57**
400mm, 2500m³/hr	3227.28	4133.47	15.60	353.78	nr	**4487.25**
500mm, 3000m³/hr	3661.39	4689.47	24.00	544.28	nr	**5233.76**
600mm, 3500m³/hr	4112.64	5267.43	28.00	635.00	nr	**5902.42**
Electromagnetic						
Energy meter for measuring energy use in chilled water systems; includes electromagnetic flow meter (with sensor and signal converter), energy calculator, pair of temperature sensors with brass pockets, and 3m of interconnecting cable; includes fixing in position; electrical work elsewhere						
Pipe size (flanged connections to PN40); maximum flow rate						
25mm, 17.7m³/hr	821.10	1051.66	1.48	33.56	nr	**1085.22**
40mm, 45m³/hr	828.95	1061.72	1.55	35.15	nr	**1096.87**

T:MECHANICAL/COOLING/HEATING SYSTEMS

Item	Net Price £	Material £	Labour hours	Labour £	Unit	Total rate £
Pipe size (flanged connections to PN16); maximum flow rate						
50mm, 70m³/hr	838.24	1073.60	1.80	40.82	nr	**1114.43**
65mm, 120m³/hr	841.81	1078.18	2.32	52.61	nr	**1130.79**
80mm, 180m³/hr	846.09	1083.66	2.56	58.06	nr	**1141.72**
125mm, 450m³/hr	921.06	1179.68	3.60	81.64	nr	**1261.33**
150mm, 625m³/hr	977.47	1251.93	4.80	108.86	nr	**1360.78**
200mm, 1100m³/hr	1051.72	1347.04	6.24	141.51	nr	**1488.55**
250mm, 1750m³/hr	1180.24	1511.64	9.60	217.71	nr	**1729.35**
300mm, 2550m³/hr	1504.40	1926.82	10.80	244.93	nr	**2171.74**
350mm, 3450m³/hr	1957.07	2506.60	13.20	299.35	nr	**2805.96**
400mm, 4500m³/hr	2232.68	2859.59	15.60	353.78	nr	**3213.37**

T:MECHANICAL/COOLING/HEATING SYSTEMS

Item	Net Price £	Material £	Labour hours	Labour £	Unit	Total rate £
T70 : LOCAL COOLING UNITS						
Split system with ceiling void evaporator unit and external condensing unit						
Ceiling mounted 4 way blow cassette heat pump unit with remote fan speed and load control; refrigerant 470C; includes outdoor unit						
Cooling 3.6kW, heating 4.1kW	1336.58	1711.87	35.00	793.74	nr	**2505.62**
Cooling 4.9kW, heating 5.5kW	1472.90	1886.47	35.00	793.74	nr	**2680.21**
Cooling 7.1kW, heating 8.2kW	1782.81	2283.41	35.00	793.74	nr	**3077.15**
Cooling 10kW, heating 11.2kW	2108.70	2700.80	35.00	793.74	nr	**3494.55**
Cooling 12.20kW, heating 14.60kW	2306.79	2954.51	35.00	793.74	nr	**3748.26**
Ceiling mounted 4 way blow cooling only unit with remote fan speed and load control; refrigerant 470C; includes outdoor unit						
Cooling 3.80kW	1209.84	1549.55	35.00	793.74	nr	**2343.30**
Cooling 5.20kW	1351.48	1730.97	35.00	793.74	nr	**2524.71**
Cooling 7.10kW	1666.73	2134.72	35.00	793.74	nr	**2928.47**
Cooling 10kw	1936.17	2479.83	35.00	793.74	nr	**3273.57**
Cooling 12.2kW	2052.26	2628.51	35.00	793.74	nr	**3422.25**
In ceiling, ducted heat pump unit with remote fan speed and load control; refrigerant 407C; includes outdoor unit						
Cooling 3.60kW, heating 4.10kW	979.80	1254.92	35.00	793.74	nr	**2048.66**
Cooling 4.90kW, heating 5.50kW	1126.77	1443.16	35.00	793.74	nr	**2236.90**
Cooling 7.10kW, heating 8.20kW	1126.77	1443.16	35.00	793.74	nr	**2236.90**
Cooling 10kW, heating 11.20kW	1702.94	2181.10	35.00	793.74	nr	**2974.85**
Cooling 12.20kW, heating 14.50kW	2271.65	2909.50	35.00	793.74	nr	**3703.24**
In ceiling, ducted cooling only unit with remote fan speed and load control; refrigerant 407C; includes outdoor unit						
Cooling 3.70kW	883.95	1132.15	35.00	793.74	nr	**1925.90**
Cooling 4.90kW	1051.16	1346.31	35.00	793.74	nr	**2140.05**
Cooling 7.10kW	1586.85	2032.42	35.00	793.74	nr	**2826.17**
Cooling 10kW	1809.44	2317.51	35.00	793.74	nr	**3111.25**
Cooling 12.3kW	2017.11	2583.49	35.00	793.74	nr	**3377.24**
Room Units						
Ceiling mounted 4 way blow cassette heat pump unit with remote fan speed and load control; refrigerant 407C; excludes outdoor unit						
Cooling 3.6kW, heating 4.1kW	843.48	1080.32	17.00	385.53	nr	**1465.85**
Cooling 4.9kW, heating 5.5kW	863.72	1106.24	17.00	385.53	nr	**1491.77**
Cooling 7.1kW, heating 8.2kW	935.07	1197.63	17.00	385.53	nr	**1583.16**
Cooling 10kW, heating 11.2kW	1012.82	1297.20	17.00	385.53	nr	**1682.74**
Cooling 12.20kW, heating 14.60kW	1098.02	1406.33	17.00	385.53	nr	**1791.86**
Ceiling mounted 4 way blow cooling unit with remote fan speed and load control; refrigerant 407C; excludes outdoor unit						
Cooling 3.80kW	796.62	1020.30	17.00	385.53	nr	**1405.84**
Cooling 5.20kW	803.01	1028.49	17.00	385.53	nr	**1414.02**
Cooling 7.10Kw	935.07	1197.63	17.00	385.53	nr	**1583.16**
Cooling 10kW	1012.82	1297.20	17.00	385.53	nr	**1682.74**
Cooling 12.2kW	1098.02	1406.33	17.00	385.53	nr	**1791.86**

T:MECHANICAL/COOLING/HEATING SYSTEMS

Item	Net Price £	Material £	Labour hours	Labour £	Unit	Total rate £
In ceiling , ducted heat pump unit with remote fan speed and load control; refrigerant 407C; excludes outdoor unit						
Cooling 3.60kW, heating 4.10kW	486.71	623.37	17.00	385.53	nr	**1008.90**
Cooling 4.90kW, heating 5.50kW	517.59	662.92	17.00	385.53	nr	**1048.46**
Cooling 7.10kW, heating 8.20kW	855.20	1095.33	17.00	385.53	nr	**1480.86**
Cooling 10kW, heating 11.20kW	886.08	1134.88	17.00	385.53	nr	**1520.42**
Cooling 12.20kW, heating 14.50kW	1062.87	1361.31	17.00	385.53	nr	**1746.85**
In ceiling , ducted cooling unit only with remote fan speed and load control; refrigerant 407C; excludes outdoor unit						
Cooling 3.70kW	470.73	602.91	17.00	385.53	nr	**988.44**
Cooling 4.90kW	502.68	643.83	17.00	385.53	nr	**1029.36**
Cooling 7.10kW	855.20	1095.33	17.00	385.53	nr	**1480.86**
Cooling 10kW	886.08	1134.88	17.00	385.53	nr	**1520.42**
Cooling 12.3kW	1062.87	1361.31	17.00	385.53	nr	**1746.85**
External condensing units suitable for connection to multiple indoor units; inverter driven; refrigerant 407C						
Cooling only						
9kW	1841.39	2358.43	17.00	385.53	nr	**2743.96**
Heat pump						
Cooling 5.20kW, heating 6.10kW	1312.08	1680.50	17.00	385.53	nr	**2066.03**
Cooling 6.80kW, heating 2.50kW	1673.12	2142.91	17.00	385.53	nr	**2528.44**
Cooling 8kW, heating 9.60kW	1937.23	2481.19	17.00	385.53	nr	**2866.72**
Cooling 14.50kW, heating 16.50kW	3215.24	4118.04	21.00	476.25	nr	**4594.29**

DAVIS LANGDON

Maximising value and reducing risk for clients investing in infrastructure, construction and property

managed
solutions

Project Management | Cost Management | Management Consulting | Legal Support | Specification Consulting | Engineering Services | Property Tax & Finance

DAVIS LANGDON

ENGLAND

DAVIS LANGDON

LONDON
Mid City Place
71 High Holborn
London WC1V 6QS
Tel: (020) 7061 7000
Fax: (020) 7061 7061
Email: neill.morrison@davislangdon.com

BIRMINGHAM
75-77 Colmore Row
Birmingham
B3 2HD
Tel: (0121) 710 1100
Fax: (0121) 710 1399
Email: david.daly@davislangdon.com

BRISTOL
St Lawrence House
29/31 Broad Street
Bristol BS1 2HF
Tel: (0117) 927 7832
Fax: (0117) 925 1350
Email: alan.francis@davislangdon.com

CAMBRIDGE
36 Storey's Way
Cambridge
CB3 0DT
Tel: (01223) 351 258
Fax: (01223) 321 002
Email: laurence.brett@davislangdon.com

LEEDS
No 4 The Embankment
Victoria Wharf
Sovereign Street
Leeds LS1 4BA
Tel: (0113) 243 2481
Fax: (0113) 242 4601
Email: duncan.sissons@davislangdon.com

LIVERPOOL
Cunard Building
Water Street
Liverpool L3 1JR
Tel: (0151) 236 1992
Fax: (0151) 227 5401
Email: andrew.stevenson@davislangdon.com

MAIDSTONE
11 Tower View
Kings Hill
West Malling
Kent ME19 4UY
Tel: (01732) 840 429
Fax: (01732) 842 305
Email: nick.leggett@davislangdon.com

MANCHESTER
Cloister House
Riverside
New Bailey Street
Manchester M3 5AG
Tel: (0161) 819 7600
Fax: (0161) 819 1818
Email: paul.stanion@davislangdon.com

MILTON KEYNES
Everest House
Rockingham Drive
Linford Wood
Milton Keynes
MK14 6LY
Tel: (01908) 304 700
Fax: (01908) 660 059
Email: kevin.sims@davislangdon.com

NORWICH
63 Thorpe Road
Norwich NR1 1UD
Tel: (01603) 628 194
Fax: (01603) 615 928
Email: michael.ladbrook@davislangdon.com

OXFORD
Avalon House
Marcham Road
Abingdon
Oxford OX14 1TZ
Tel: (01235) 555 025
Fax: (01235) 554 909
Email: paul.coomber@davislangdon.com

PETERBOROUGH
Clarence House
Minerva Business Park
Lynchwood
Peterborough PE2 6FT
Tel: (01733) 362 000
Fax: (01733) 230 875
Email: stuart.bremner@davislangdon.com

PLYMOUTH
1 Ensign House
Parkway Court
Longbridge Road
Plymouth PL6 8LR
Tel: (01752) 827 444
Fax: (01752) 221 219
Email: gareth.steventon@davislangdon.com

SOUTHAMPTON
Brunswick House
Brunswick Place
Southampton SO15 2AP
Tel: (023) 8033 3438
Fax: (023) 8022 6099
Email: chris.tremellen@davislangdon.com/
peter.boote@davislangdon.com

**DAVIS LANGDON
LEGAL SUPPORT**
Mid City Place
71 High Holborn
London WC1V 6QS
Tel: (020) 7061 7000
Fax: (020) 7061 7061
Email: mark.hackett@davislangdon.com

**DAVIS LANGDON
CONSULTANCY**
Mid City Place
71 High Holborn
London WC1V 6QS
Tel: (020) 7061 7007
Fax: (020) 7061 7005
Email: john.connaughton@davislangdon.com

**DAVIS LANGDON
SCHUMANN SMITH**
Southgate House
St Georges Way
Stevenage
Hertfordshire SG1 1HG
Tel: (01438) 742 642
Fax: (01438) 742 632
Email: nick.schumann@schumannsmith.com

**DAVIS LANGDON
MOTT GREEN & WALL**
Mid City Place
71 High Holborn
London WC1V 6QS
Tel: (020) 7061 7777
Fax: (020) 7061 7009
Email: general@mottgreenwall.co.uk

**DAVIS LANGDON
CROSHER & JAMES**
Mid City Place
71 High Holborn
London WC1V 6QS
Tel: (020) 7061 7077
Fax: (020) 7061 7078
Email: tony.llewellyn@crosherjames.com

BIRMINGHAM
102 New Street
Birmingham B2 4HQ
Tel: (0121) 632 3600
Fax: (0121) 632 3601
Email: clive.searle@crosherjames.com

CARDIFF
4 Piershead Street
Capital Waterside
Cardiff
CF10 4QP
Tel: (029) 2049 7497
Fax: (029) 2049 7111
Email: michael.murraym@crosherjames.com

EDINBURGH
39 Melville Street
Edinburgh
EH3 7JF
Tel: (0131) 220 4225
Fax: (0131) 220 4226
Email: ian.mcfarlane@crosherjames.com

GLASGOW
Monteith House
11 George Square
Glasgow
G2 1DY
Tel: (0141) 248 0333
Fax: (0141) 248 0313
Email: fraserk@nbwcrosherjames.com

MANCHESTER
Cloister House
Riverside
New Bailey Street
Manchester M3 5AG
Tel: (0161) 819 7600
Fax: (0161) 819 1818
Email: sharmas@nbwcrosherjames.com

SOUTHAMPTON
Brunswick House
Brunswick Place
Southampton SO15 2AP
Tel: (023) 8068 2800
Fax: (023) 8033 6360
Email: reesd@nbwcrosherjames.com

SCOTLAND

DAVIS LANGDON

GLASGOW
Monteith House
11 George Square
Glasgow G2 1DY
Tel. (0141) 248 0300
Fax: (0141) 248 0303
Email:
sam.mackenzie@davislangdon.com

EDINBURGH
39 Melville Street
Edinburgh
EH3 7JF
Tel: (0131) 240 1350
Fax: (0131) 240 1399
Email: erland.rendall@davislangdon.com

WALES

CARDIFF
4 Pierhead Street
Capital Waterside
Cardiff CF10 4QP
Tel: (029) 2049 7497
Fax: (029) 2049 7111
Email: paul.edwards@davislangdon.com

IRELAND

DAVIS LANGDON PKS

DUBLIN
24 Lower Hatch Street
Dublin 2
Ireland
Tel: (00 353 1) 676 3671
Fax: (00 353 1) 676 3672
Email: mwebb@dlpks.ie

GALWAY
Heritage Hall
Kirwan's Lane
Galway, Ireland
Tel: (00 353 91) 530 199
Fax: (00 353 91) 530 198
Email: joregan@dlpks.ie

LIMERICK
8 The Crescent
Limerick
Ireland
Tel: (00 353 61) 318 870
Fax: (00 353 61) 318 871
Email: cbarry@dlpks.ie

SPAIN

DAVIS LANGDON EDETCO

BARCELONA
C/Muntaner, 479, 12"
Barcelona 08021
Spain
Tel: (00 34 93) 418 6899
Fax: (00 34 93) 211 0003
Email: fmonells@barcelona.edetco.com

GIRONA
C/Salt 10
Girona 17005
Spain
Tel: (00 34 97) 223 8000
Fax: (00 34 97) 224 2661
Email: girona@girona.edetco.com

FRANCE

DAVIS LANGDON
5 Rue St Germain l'Auxerrois
75001 Paris
France
Tel: (00 33 1) 5340 9480
Fax: (00 33 1) 5340 9481
Email: andrew.richardson@dleparis.com

POLAND

DAVIS LANGDON
Warsaw Trade Tower
ul. Chlodna 51, 26th Floor
00-867 Warsaw, Poland
Tel: (00 48 22) 455 39 00
Fax: (00 48 22) 455 39 01
Email: warsaw@davislangdon-polska.pl

RUSSIA

DAVIS LANGDON
Office 5
Myasnitskaya
Moscow, 101000
Russia
Tel: (00 7 095) 933 7810
Fax: (00 7 095) 933 7811
Email: stephen.thomas@davislangdon.com

MIDDLE EAST

DAVIS LANGDON
PO Box 13-5422-Shouran
Beirut
Lebanon
Tel: (00 9611) 780 111
Fax: (00 9611) 809 045
Email: DLL.MI@cyberia.net.lb

ARABIAN GULF

DAVIS LANGDON

BAHRAIN
3rd Floor Building 256
Road No 3605
Area No 336
PO Box 640, Manama
State of Bahrain
Arabian Gulf
Tel: (00 973) 1782 7567
Fax: (00 973) 1772 8257
Email: david.galbraith@davislangdon-bahrain.com

UNITED ARAB EMIRATES
PO Box 7856
Office 410
Oud Metha Office Building
Dubai, UAE
Tel: (00 9714) 32 42 919
Fax: (00 9714) 32 42 838
Email: neil.taylor@davislangdon-dubai.com

QATAR
PO Box 3206, Doha
State of Qatar
Tel: (00 974) 4580 150
Fax: (00 974) 4697 905
Email: david.craig@davislangdon-qatar.com

EGYPT
35 Misr Helwan Road
Maadi 11431
Cairo
Egypt
Tel: (00 20 2) 526 2319
Fax: (00 20 2) 527 1338
Email: dlegypt@link.net

Specialist Service Lines
Project Management | Cost Management | Management Consulting | Legal Support | Specification Consulting | Engineering Services | Property Tax & Finance

Specialist Sectors
Arts | Commercial Offices | Distribution | Education | Food Processing | Health | Heritage | Hotels & Leisure | Industrial | Infrastructure | Public Buildings | Regeneration | Residential | Retail | Sports | Transportation

Davis Langdon LLP is a member firm of Davis Langdon & Seah International, with offices throughout Europe and the Middle East, Asia, Australasia, Africa and the USA

U:VENTILATION/AIR CONDITIONING SYSTEMS

Item	Net Price £	Material £	Labour hours	Labour £	Unit	Total rate £
U10 : DUCTWORK : CIRCULAR						
Y30 - AIR DUCTLINES						
Galvanised sheet metal DW144 class B spirally wound circular section ductwork; including all necessary stiffeners, joints, couplers in the running length and duct supports						
Straight duct						
80mm dia.	2.56	4.36	0.87	24.53	m	28.89
100mm dia.	2.65	4.51	0.87	24.53	m	29.04
160mm dia.	3.69	6.28	0.87	24.53	m	30.81
200mm dia.	4.72	8.02	0.87	24.53	m	32.55
250mm dia.	5.78	9.84	1.21	34.12	m	43.95
315mm dia.	7.08	12.04	1.21	34.12	m	46.15
355mm dia.	9.72	16.53	1.21	34.12	m	50.65
400mm dia.	10.86	18.47	1.21	34.12	m	52.59
450mm dia.	11.97	20.35	1.21	34.12	m	54.47
500mm dia.	13.00	22.11	1.21	34.12	m	56.23
630mm dia.	22.96	39.04	1.39	39.19	m	78.23
710mm dia.	25.07	42.63	1.39	39.19	m	81.82
800mm dia.	29.12	49.51	1.44	40.60	m	90.11
900mm dia.	36.21	61.58	1.46	41.16	m	102.74
1000mm dia.	44.08	74.95	1.65	46.52	m	121.47
1120mm dia.	52.75	89.69	2.43	68.51	m	158.20
1250mm dia.	57.73	98.16	2.43	68.51	m	166.67
1400mm dia.	65.12	110.73	2.77	78.10	m	188.83
1600mm dia.	74.73	127.08	3.06	86.28	m	213.35
Extra over fittings; circular duct class B						
End cap						
80mm dia.	1.23	2.09	0.15	4.23	nr	6.32
100mm dia.	1.29	2.19	0.15	4.23	nr	6.42
160mm dia.	1.95	3.31	0.15	4.23	nr	7.54
200mm dia.	2.27	3.86	0.20	5.64	nr	9.50
250mm dia.	3.29	5.60	0.29	8.18	nr	13.77
315mm dia.	4.05	6.89	0.29	8.18	nr	15.06
355mm dia.	6.18	10.52	0.44	12.41	nr	22.92
400mm dia.	6.31	10.74	0.44	12.41	nr	23.14
450mm dia.	6.61	11.24	0.44	12.41	nr	23.64
500mm dia.	6.87	11.69	0.44	12.41	nr	24.09
630mm dia.	16.64	28.30	0.58	16.35	nr	44.65
710mm dia.	19.05	32.40	0.69	19.45	nr	51.85
800mm dia.	26.45	44.97	0.81	22.84	nr	67.81
900mm dia.	29.91	50.86	0.92	25.94	nr	76.80
1000mm dia.	39.94	67.92	1.04	29.32	nr	97.24
1120mm dia.	44.48	75.63	1.16	32.71	nr	108.34
1250mm dia.	49.28	83.79	1.16	32.71	nr	116.50
1400mm dia.	64.41	109.52	1.16	32.71	nr	142.23
1600mm dia.	72.76	123.73	1.16	32.71	nr	156.43

U:VENTILATION/AIR CONDITIONING SYSTEMS

Item	Net Price £	Material £	Labour hours	Labour £	Unit	Total rate £
Reducer						
80mm dia.	3.68	6.26	0.29	8.18	nr	**14.43**
100mm dia.	3.78	6.43	0.29	8.18	nr	**14.60**
160mm dia.	4.81	8.18	0.29	8.18	nr	**16.35**
200mm dia.	5.40	9.18	0.44	12.41	nr	**21.58**
250mm dia.	6.63	11.28	0.58	16.35	nr	**27.63**
315mm dia.	8.40	14.28	0.58	16.35	nr	**30.63**
355mm dia.	10.10	17.17	0.87	24.53	nr	**41.70**
400mm dia.	11.83	20.12	0.87	24.53	nr	**44.65**
450mm dia.	12.75	21.68	0.87	24.53	nr	**46.21**
500mm dia.	14.19	24.13	0.87	24.53	nr	**48.66**
630mm dia.	38.17	64.90	0.87	24.53	nr	**89.43**
710mm dia.	40.38	68.67	0.96	27.07	nr	**95.73**
800mm dia.	53.72	91.35	1.06	29.89	nr	**121.23**
900mm dia.	56.59	96.23	1.16	32.71	nr	**128.93**
1000mm dia.	70.94	120.62	1.25	35.24	nr	**155.86**
1120mm dia.	78.86	134.08	3.47	97.83	nr	**231.92**
1250mm dia.	88.73	150.88	3.47	97.83	nr	**248.71**
1400mm dia.	113.15	192.40	4.05	114.19	nr	**306.59**
1600mm dia.	118.84	202.07	4.62	130.26	nr	**332.33**
90° segmented radius bend						
80mm dia.	2.07	3.52	0.29	8.18	nr	**11.70**
100mm dia.	4.03	6.85	0.29	8.18	nr	**15.02**
160mm dia.	4.03	6.85	0.29	8.18	nr	**15.02**
200mm dia.	5.56	9.46	0.44	12.41	nr	**21.86**
250mm dia.	8.53	14.51	0.58	16.35	nr	**30.86**
315mm dia.	9.00	15.30	0.58	16.35	nr	**31.66**
355mm dia.	9.39	15.96	0.87	24.53	nr	**40.49**
400mm dia.	11.20	19.04	0.87	24.53	nr	**43.57**
450mm dia.	12.92	21.97	0.87	24.53	nr	**46.50**
500mm dia.	13.53	23.01	0.87	24.53	nr	**47.54**
630mm dia.	29.32	49.86	0.87	24.53	nr	**74.39**
710mm dia.	42.13	71.64	0.96	27.07	nr	**98.70**
800mm dia.	47.56	80.86	1.06	29.89	nr	**110.75**
900mm dia.	53.20	90.47	1.16	32.71	nr	**123.17**
1000mm dia.	80.65	137.13	1.25	35.24	nr	**172.38**
1120mm dia.	89.45	152.11	3.47	97.83	nr	**249.94**
1250mm dia.	117.28	199.42	3.47	97.83	nr	**297.26**
1400mm dia.	244.63	415.97	4.05	114.19	nr	**530.15**
1600mm dia.	247.10	420.16	4.62	130.26	nr	**550.42**
45° radius bend						
80mm dia.	2.16	3.67	0.29	8.18	nr	**11.85**
100mm dia.	2.16	3.67	0.29	8.18	nr	**11.85**
160mm dia.	3.28	5.58	0.29	8.18	nr	**13.75**
200mm dia.	4.33	7.37	0.40	11.28	nr	**18.65**
250mm dia.	6.23	10.59	0.58	16.35	nr	**26.94**
315mm dia.	7.83	13.32	0.58	16.35	nr	**29.67**
355mm dia.	8.37	14.23	0.87	24.53	nr	**38.75**
400mm dia.	10.16	17.27	0.87	24.53	nr	**41.80**
450mm dia.	10.14	17.23	0.87	24.53	nr	**41.76**
500mm dia.	10.82	18.40	0.87	24.53	nr	**42.93**
630mm dia.	29.54	50.23	0.87	24.53	nr	**74.76**
710mm dia.	37.37	63.55	0.96	27.07	nr	**90.61**
800mm dia.	45.34	77.10	1.06	29.89	nr	**106.99**
900mm dia.	50.11	85.21	1.16	32.71	nr	**117.92**

U:VENTILATION/AIR CONDITIONING SYSTEMS

Item	Net Price £	Material £	Labour hours	Labour £	Unit	Total rate £
U10 : DUCTWORK : CIRCULAR (cont'd)						
Y30 - AIR DUCTLINES (cont'd)						
Fittings; circular duct class B (cont'd)						
45° radius bend (cont'd)						
1000mm dia.	72.58	123.41	1.25	35.24	nr	**158.65**
1120mm dia.	79.08	134.46	3.47	97.83	nr	**232.30**
1250mm dia.	88.32	150.18	3.47	97.83	nr	**248.01**
1400mm dia.	124.42	211.56	4.05	114.19	nr	**325.74**
1600mm dia.	131.63	223.82	4.62	130.26	nr	**354.08**
90° equal twin bend						
80mm dia.	6.56	11.16	0.58	16.35	nr	**27.51**
100mm dia.	6.66	11.33	0.58	16.35	nr	**27.68**
160mm dia.	12.00	20.40	0.58	16.35	nr	**36.76**
200mm dia.	17.08	29.04	0.87	24.53	nr	**53.57**
250mm dia.	26.84	45.64	1.16	32.71	nr	**78.35**
315mm dia.	29.21	49.66	1.16	32.71	nr	**82.37**
355mm dia.	32.41	55.10	1.73	48.78	nr	**103.88**
400mm dia.	35.91	61.07	1.73	48.78	nr	**109.85**
450mm dia.	38.69	65.79	1.73	48.78	nr	**114.56**
500mm dia.	41.46	70.51	1.73	48.78	nr	**119.28**
630mm dia.	80.18	136.34	1.73	48.78	nr	**185.12**
710mm dia.	106.83	181.65	1.82	51.31	nr	**232.96**
800mm dia.	132.17	224.74	1.93	54.42	nr	**279.16**
900mm dia.	153.22	260.54	2.02	56.95	nr	**317.49**
1000mm dia.	211.37	359.41	2.11	59.49	nr	**418.90**
1120mm dia.	246.58	419.28	4.62	130.26	nr	**549.54**
1250mm dia.	296.78	504.64	4.62	130.26	nr	**634.89**
1400mm dia.	482.30	820.10	4.62	130.26	nr	**950.35**
1600mm dia.	516.51	878.27	4.62	130.26	nr	**1008.52**
Conical branch						
80mm dia.	8.32	14.15	0.58	16.35	nr	**30.50**
100mm dia.	8.46	14.39	0.58	16.35	nr	**30.74**
160mm dia.	9.05	15.38	0.58	16.35	nr	**31.74**
200mm dia.	9.55	16.23	0.87	24.53	nr	**40.76**
250mm dia.	12.52	21.29	1.16	32.71	nr	**54.00**
315mm dia.	13.89	23.61	1.16	32.71	nr	**56.32**
355mm dia.	15.03	25.56	1.73	48.78	nr	**74.34**
400mm dia.	15.44	26.26	1.73	48.78	nr	**75.04**
450mm dia.	19.18	32.62	1.73	48.78	nr	**81.40**
500mm dia.	19.67	33.45	1.73	48.78	nr	**82.22**
630mm dia.	37.82	64.31	1.73	48.78	nr	**113.08**
710mm dia.	41.50	70.57	1.82	51.31	nr	**121.88**
800mm dia.	54.88	93.32	1.93	54.42	nr	**147.73**
900mm dia.	57.84	98.35	2.02	56.95	nr	**155.30**
1000mm dia.	71.58	121.71	2.11	59.49	nr	**181.20**
1120mm dia.	101.87	173.22	4.62	130.26	nr	**303.48**
1250mm dia.	101.87	173.22	5.20	146.61	nr	**319.83**
1400mm dia .	123.51	210.01	5.20	146.61	nr	**356.62**
1600mm dia.	146.09	248.40	5.20	146.61	nr	**395.02**

U:VENTILATION/AIR CONDITIONING SYSTEMS

Item	Net Price £	Material £	Labour hours	Labour £	Unit	Total rate £
45° branch						
80mm dia.	6.57	11.17	0.58	16.35	nr	**27.52**
100mm dia.	6.68	11.36	0.58	16.35	nr	**27.71**
160mm dia.	10.15	17.25	0.58	16.35	nr	**33.61**
200mm dia.	10.44	17.74	0.87	24.53	nr	**42.27**
250mm dia.	10.85	18.44	1.16	32.71	nr	**51.15**
315mm dia.	11.42	19.42	1.16	32.71	nr	**52.13**
355mm dia.	14.84	25.24	1.73	48.78	nr	**74.02**
400mm dia.	15.36	26.11	1.73	48.78	nr	**74.89**
450mm dia.	15.93	27.08	1.73	48.78	nr	**75.86**
500mm dia.	16.54	28.13	1.73	48.78	nr	**76.91**
630mm dia.	31.10	52.88	1.73	48.78	nr	**101.66**
710mm dia.	34.09	57.97	1.82	51.31	nr	**109.28**
800mm dia.	50.43	85.75	2.13	60.05	nr	**145.80**
900mm dia.	57.16	97.19	2.31	65.13	nr	**162.32**
1000mm dia.	68.58	116.62	2.31	65.13	nr	**181.75**
1120mm dia.	86.50	147.09	4.62	130.26	nr	**277.35**
1250mm dia.	92.31	156.96	4.62	130.26	nr	**287.21**
1400mm dia.	106.84	181.67	4.62	130.26	nr	**311.93**
1600mm dia.	131.77	224.05	4.62	130.26	nr	**354.31**

For galvanised sheet metal DW144 class C rates, refer to galvanised sheet metal DW144 class B

U:VENTILATION/AIR CONDITIONING SYSTEMS

Item	Net Price £	Material £	Labour hours	Labour £	Unit	Total rate £
U10 : DUCTWORK : FLAT OVAL						
Y30 - AIR DUCTLINES						
Galvanised sheet metal DW144 class B spirally wound flat oval section ductwork; including all necessary stiffeners, joints, couplers in the running length and duct supports						
Straight duct						
345 x 102mm	9.50	16.15	2.71	76.41	m	**92.56**
427 x 102mm	11.03	18.75	2.99	84.30	m	**103.06**
508 x 102mm	12.28	20.88	3.14	88.53	m	**109.41**
559 x 152mm	17.06	29.00	3.43	96.71	m	**125.71**
531 x 203mm	16.78	28.53	3.43	96.71	m	**125.24**
851 x 203mm	18.61	31.65	5.72	161.27	m	**192.92**
582 x 254mm	20.51	34.87	3.62	102.06	m	**136.93**
823 x 254mm	24.06	40.91	5.80	163.53	m	**204.43**
1303 x 254mm	24.34	41.39	8.13	229.22	m	**270.61**
632 x 305mm	24.37	41.44	3.93	110.80	m	**152.24**
1275 x 305mm	23.93	40.69	8.13	229.22	m	**269.91**
765 x 356mm	25.70	43.70	5.72	161.27	m	**204.98**
1247 x 356mm	22.78	38.74	8.13	229.22	m	**267.96**
1727 x 356mm	22.43	38.15	10.41	293.50	m	**331.65**
737 x 406mm	28.42	48.32	5.72	161.27	m	**209.60**
818 x 406mm	28.42	48.32	6.21	175.09	m	**223.41**
978 x 406mm	50.95	86.63	6.92	195.11	m	**281.74**
1379 x 406mm	55.30	94.04	8.75	246.70	m	**340.74**
1699 x 406mm	54.73	93.06	10.41	293.50	m	**386.56**
709 x 457mm	59.42	101.04	5.72	161.27	m	**262.31**
1189 x 457mm	60.05	102.11	8.80	248.11	m	**350.23**
1671 x 457mm	60.17	102.30	10.31	290.69	m	**392.99**
678 x 508mm	73.16	124.41	5.72	161.27	m	**285.68**
919 x 508mm	74.39	126.49	7.30	205.82	m	**332.31**
1321 x 508mm	74.44	126.58	8.75	246.70	m	**373.28**
Extra over fittings; flat oval duct class B						
End cap						
345 x 102mm	10.78	18.33	0.20	5.64	nr	**23.97**
427 x 102mm	11.05	18.78	0.20	5.64	nr	**24.42**
508 x 102mm	11.30	19.21	0.20	5.64	nr	**24.85**
559 x 152mm	16.52	28.09	0.29	8.18	nr	**36.27**
531 x 203mm	16.44	27.96	0.29	8.18	nr	**36.14**
851 x 203mm	16.93	28.79	0.44	12.41	nr	**41.20**
582 x 254mm	16.87	28.69	0.44	12.41	nr	**41.10**
823 x 254mm	24.01	40.83	0.44	12.41	nr	**53.23**
1303 x 254mm	17.67	30.04	0.69	19.45	nr	**49.49**
632 x 305mm	18.18	30.91	0.69	19.45	nr	**50.36**
1275 x 305mm	17.64	30.00	0.69	19.45	nr	**49.45**
765 x 356mm	18.60	31.63	0.69	19.45	nr	**51.08**
1727 x 356mm	17.90	30.44	0.69	19.45	nr	**49.89**
737 x 406mm	18.20	30.95	1.04	29.32	nr	**60.27**
818 x 406mm	25.81	43.88	0.69	19.45	nr	**63.34**
978 x 406mm	19.46	33.09	0.69	19.45	nr	**52.54**
1379 x 406mm	51.19	87.05	1.04	29.32	nr	**116.37**
1699 x 406mm	52.42	89.14	1.04	29.32	nr	**118.46**

U:VENTILATION/AIR CONDITIONING SYSTEMS

Item	Net Price £	Material £	Labour hours	Labour £	Unit	Total rate £
709 x 457mm	53.98	91.79	1.04	29.32	nr	**121.11**
1189 x 457mm	61.16	103.99	1.04	29.32	nr	**133.32**
1671 x 457mm	76.13	129.45	1.04	29.32	nr	**158.77**
678 x 508mm	76.20	129.58	1.04	29.32	nr	**158.90**
919 x 508mm	78.27	133.09	1.04	29.32	nr	**162.42**
1321 x 508mm	77.81	132.31	1.04	29.32	nr	**161.64**
Reducer						
345 x 102mm	20.46	34.80	0.95	26.78	nr	**61.58**
427 x 102mm	20.84	35.43	1.06	29.89	nr	**65.31**
508 x 102mm	21.32	36.25	1.13	31.86	nr	**68.11**
559 x 152mm	30.13	51.23	1.26	35.53	nr	**86.76**
531 x 203mm	29.95	50.93	1.26	35.53	nr	**86.46**
851 x 203mm	31.88	54.21	1.34	37.78	nr	**91.99**
582 x 254mm	35.14	59.76	1.34	37.78	nr	**97.54**
823 x 254mm	44.60	75.84	1.34	37.78	nr	**113.62**
1303 x 254mm	42.11	71.60	1.34	37.78	nr	**109.38**
632 x 305mm	41.74	70.98	0.70	19.74	nr	**90.71**
1275 x 305mm	37.92	64.48	1.16	32.71	nr	**97.18**
765 x 356mm	42.49	72.25	1.16	32.71	nr	**104.95**
1247 x 356mm	40.49	68.86	1.16	32.71	nr	**101.56**
1727 x 356mm	39.48	67.13	1.25	35.24	nr	**102.37**
737 x 406mm	48.29	82.11	1.16	32.71	nr	**114.82**
818 x 406mm	46.57	79.19	1.27	35.81	nr	**115.00**
978 x 406mm	88.09	149.78	1.44	40.60	nr	**190.38**
1379 x 406mm	98.53	167.54	1.44	40.60	nr	**208.14**
1699 x 406mm	96.98	164.90	1.44	40.60	nr	**205.50**
709 x 457mm	95.66	162.65	1.16	32.71	nr	**195.36**
1189 x 457mm	99.59	169.34	1.34	37.78	nr	**207.12**
1671 x 457mm	101.02	171.77	1.44	40.60	nr	**212.37**
678 x 508mm	102.29	173.93	1.16	32.71	nr	**206.64**
919 x 508mm	103.92	176.70	1.26	35.53	nr	**212.22**
1321 x 508mm	104.65	177.94	1.44	40.60	nr	**218.54**
90° radius bend						
345 x 102mm	20.72	35.24	0.29	8.18	nr	**43.41**
427 x 102mm	21.09	35.86	0.58	16.35	nr	**52.21**
508 x 102mm	21.43	36.45	0.58	16.35	nr	**52.80**
559 x 152mm	32.38	55.05	0.58	16.35	nr	**71.40**
531 x 203mm	31.83	54.12	0.87	24.53	nr	**78.65**
851 x 203mm	35.39	60.17	0.87	24.53	nr	**84.70**
582 x 254mm	39.47	67.12	0.87	24.53	nr	**91.65**
823 x 254mm	53.65	91.23	0.87	24.53	nr	**115.76**
1303 x 254mm	50.22	85.39	0.96	27.07	nr	**112.46**
632 x 305mm	49.16	83.59	0.87	24.53	nr	**108.12**
1275 x 305mm	44.53	75.71	0.96	27.07	nr	**102.78**
765 x 356mm	50.11	85.20	0.87	24.53	nr	**109.73**
1247 x 356mm	44.69	75.98	0.96	27.07	nr	**103.05**
1727 x 356mm	42.02	71.46	1.25	35.24	nr	**106.70**
737 x 406mm	59.28	100.80	0.96	27.07	nr	**127.86**
818 x 406mm	55.75	94.80	0.87	24.53	nr	**119.33**
978 x 406mm	89.94	152.94	0.96	27.07	nr	**180.00**
1379 x 406mm	100.24	170.44	1.16	32.71	nr	**203.15**
1699 x 406mm	97.47	165.74	1.25	35.24	nr	**200.99**
709 x 457mm	97.12	165.13	0.87	24.53	nr	**189.66**
1189 x 457mm	109.95	186.97	0.96	27.07	nr	**214.03**
1671 x 457mm	109.50	186.20	1.25	35.24	nr	**221.44**
678 x 508mm	127.83	217.36	0.87	24.53	nr	**241.89**
919 x 508mm	127.58	216.93	0.96	27.07	nr	**244.00**
1321 x 508mm	127.27	216.41	1.16	32.71	nr	**249.11**

U:VENTILATION/AIR CONDITIONING SYSTEMS

Item	Net Price £	Material £	Labour hours	Labour £	Unit	Total rate £
U10 : DUCTWORK : FLAT OVAL (cont'd)						
Y30 - AIR DUCTLINES (cont'd)						
Fittings; flat oval duct class B (cont'd)						
45° radius bend						
345 x 102mm	21.89	37.23	0.79	22.27	nr	**59.50**
427 x 102mm	23.03	39.16	0.85	23.97	nr	**63.12**
508 x 102mm	24.27	41.28	0.95	26.78	nr	**68.06**
559 x 152mm	34.73	59.05	0.79	22.27	nr	**81.32**
531 x 203mm	34.96	59.44	0.85	23.97	nr	**83.40**
851 x 203mm	37.85	64.36	0.98	27.63	nr	**91.99**
582 x 254mm	42.06	71.53	0.76	21.43	nr	**92.95**
823 x 254mm	53.90	91.65	0.95	26.78	nr	**118.43**
1303 x 254mm	51.99	88.41	1.16	32.71	nr	**121.11**
632 x 305mm	52.51	89.29	0.58	16.35	nr	**105.64**
1275 x 305mm	48.36	82.23	1.16	32.71	nr	**114.94**
765 x 356mm	55.07	93.65	0.87	24.53	nr	**118.18**
1247 x 356mm	50.94	86.61	1.16	32.71	nr	**119.32**
1727 x 356mm	51.41	87.41	1.26	35.53	nr	**122.93**
737 x 406mm	64.36	109.43	0.69	19.45	nr	**128.89**
818 x 406mm	64.62	109.88	0.78	21.99	nr	**131.87**
978 x 406mm	103.85	176.58	0.87	24.53	nr	**201.11**
1379 x 406mm	118.67	201.79	1.16	32.71	nr	**234.50**
1699 x 406mm	118.22	201.02	1.27	35.81	nr	**236.83**
709 x 457mm	120.02	204.08	0.81	22.84	nr	**226.92**
1189 x 457mm	127.13	216.17	0.95	26.78	nr	**242.95**
1671 x 457mm	131.72	223.97	1.26	35.53	nr	**259.50**
678 x 508mm	161.51	274.62	0.92	25.94	nr	**300.56**
919 x 508mm	164.17	279.14	1.10	31.01	nr	**310.16**
1321 x 508mm	166.78	283.59	1.25	35.24	nr	**318.83**
90° hard bend with turning vanes						
345 x 102mm	28.02	47.64	0.55	15.51	nr	**63.15**
427 x 102mm	27.61	46.95	1.16	32.71	nr	**79.66**
508 x 102mm	27.23	46.29	1.16	32.71	nr	**79.00**
559 x 152mm	29.68	50.47	1.16	32.71	nr	**83.18**
531 x 203mm	29.50	50.16	1.73	48.78	nr	**98.94**
851 x 203mm	33.68	57.27	1.73	48.78	nr	**106.05**
582 x 254mm	44.08	74.95	1.73	48.78	nr	**123.73**
823 x 254mm	51.59	87.73	1.73	48.78	nr	**136.51**
1303 x 254mm	53.48	90.93	1.82	51.31	nr	**142.24**
632 x 305mm	48.35	82.22	1.73	48.78	nr	**131.00**
1275 x 305mm	44.38	75.46	1.82	51.31	nr	**126.78**
765 x 356mm	47.40	80.60	1.73	48.78	nr	**129.38**
1247 x 356mm	46.61	79.26	1.82	51.31	nr	**130.58**
1727 x 356mm	46.97	79.87	1.82	51.31	nr	**131.19**
737 x 406mm	58.30	99.14	1.73	48.78	nr	**147.91**
818 x 406mm	52.76	89.71	1.73	48.78	nr	**138.49**
978 x 406mm	92.95	158.06	1.73	48.78	nr	**206.83**
1379 x 406mm	87.53	148.84	1.82	51.31	nr	**200.15**
1699 x 406mm	87.05	148.02	2.11	59.49	nr	**207.51**
709 x 457mm	86.75	147.51	1.73	48.78	nr	**196.29**
1189 x 457mm	118.41	201.35	1.82	51.31	nr	**252.66**
1671 x 457mm	114.16	194.12	2.11	59.49	nr	**253.61**
678 x 508mm	150.70	256.25	1.82	51.31	nr	**307.57**
919 x 508mm	150.57	256.03	1.82	51.31	nr	**307.35**
1321 x 508mm	149.09	253.50	2.11	59.49	nr	**312.99**

U:VENTILATION/AIR CONDITIONING SYSTEMS

Item	Net Price £	Material £	Labour hours	Labour £	Unit	Total rate £
90° branch						
345 x 102mm	19.12	32.52	0.58	16.35	nr	**48.87**
427 x 102mm	18.91	32.16	0.58	16.35	nr	**48.51**
508 x 102mm	18.72	31.84	1.16	32.71	nr	**64.54**
559 x 152mm	26.39	44.87	1.16	32.71	nr	**77.58**
531 x 203mm	26.28	44.68	1.16	32.71	nr	**77.39**
851 x 203mm	25.97	44.16	1.73	48.78	nr	**92.94**
582 x 254mm	28.40	48.28	1.73	48.78	nr	**97.06**
823 x 254mm	33.92	57.67	1.73	48.78	nr	**106.45**
1303 x 254mm	34.89	59.33	1.82	51.31	nr	**110.64**
632 x 305mm	31.34	53.28	1.73	48.78	nr	**102.06**
1275 x 305mm	29.85	50.76	1.82	51.31	nr	**102.08**
765 x 356mm	43.10	73.28	1.73	48.78	nr	**122.06**
1247 x 356mm	39.22	66.69	1.82	51.31	nr	**118.00**
1727 x 356mm	37.83	64.33	2.11	59.49	nr	**123.82**
737 x 406mm	40.57	68.98	1.73	48.78	nr	**117.75**
818 x 406mm	41.55	70.65	1.73	48.78	nr	**119.42**
978 x 406mm	104.39	177.51	1.82	51.31	nr	**228.82**
1379 x 406mm	131.74	224.01	1.93	54.42	nr	**278.43**
1699 x 406mm	131.37	223.37	2.11	59.49	nr	**282.86**
709 x 457mm	115.92	197.11	1.73	48.78	nr	**245.89**
1189 x 457mm	129.18	219.65	1.82	51.31	nr	**270.97**
1671 x 457mm	127.63	217.02	2.11	59.49	nr	**276.52**
678 x 508mm	154.68	263.01	1.73	48.78	nr	**311.79**
919 x 508mm	136.62	232.31	1.82	51.31	nr	**283.62**
1321 x 508mm	135.34	230.13	2.11	59.49	nr	**289.62**
45° branch						
345 x 102mm	27.52	46.79	0.58	16.35	nr	**63.15**
427 x 102mm	26.77	45.51	0.58	16.35	nr	**61.87**
508 x 102mm	26.27	44.66	1.16	32.71	nr	**77.37**
559 x 152mm	37.00	62.92	1.73	48.78	nr	**111.69**
531 x 203mm	36.74	62.47	1.73	48.78	nr	**111.24**
851 x 203mm	35.74	60.77	1.73	48.78	nr	**109.55**
582 x 254mm	34.56	58.77	1.73	48.78	nr	**107.55**
823 x 254mm	45.97	78.16	1.82	51.31	nr	**129.48**
1303 x 254mm	47.74	81.17	1.92	54.13	nr	**135.31**
632 x 305mm	42.35	72.02	1.73	48.78	nr	**120.79**
1275 x 305mm	36.54	62.13	1.82	51.31	nr	**113.44**
765 x 356mm	59.68	101.48	1.73	48.78	nr	**150.26**
1247 x 356mm	54.07	91.94	1.82	51.31	nr	**143.25**
1727 x 356mm	52.25	88.85	1.82	51.31	nr	**140.16**
737 x 406mm	54.33	92.38	1.73	48.78	nr	**141.15**
818 x 406mm	55.86	94.98	1.73	48.78	nr	**143.75**
978 x 406mm	116.12	197.44	1.73	48.78	nr	**246.22**
1379 x 406mm	154.32	262.40	1.93	54.42	nr	**316.81**
1699 x 406mm	153.66	261.28	2.19	61.75	nr	**323.03**
709 x 457mm	126.03	214.30	1.73	48.78	nr	**263.07**
1189 x 457mm	146.61	249.29	1.82	51.31	nr	**300.61**
1671 x 457mm	142.96	243.09	2.11	59.49	nr	**302.58**
678 x 508mm	240.47	408.89	1.73	48.78	nr	**457.66**
919 x 508mm	200.66	341.19	1.82	51.31	nr	**392.51**
1321 x 508mm	198.48	337.49	1.93	54.42	nr	**391.91**
For rates for access doors refer to Ancillaries In U10 : DUCTWORK: RECTANGULAR: CLASS B						

U:VENTILATION/AIR CONDITIONING SYSTEMS

Item	Net Price £	Material £	Labour hours	Labour £	Unit	Total rate £
U10 : DUCTWORK : FLEXIBLE						
Y30 : AIR DUCTLINES						
Aluminium foil flexible ductwork, DW 144 class B; multiply aluminium polyester laminate fabric, with high tensile steel wire helix						
Duct						
102mm dia	1.07	1.82	0.33	9.30	m	**11.12**
152mm dia	1.57	2.66	0.33	9.30	m	**11.97**
203mm dia	2.06	3.51	0.33	9.30	m	**12.81**
254mm dia	2.59	4.41	0.33	9.30	m	**13.71**
304mm dia	3.18	5.40	0.33	9.30	m	**14.70**
355mm dia	4.33	7.36	0.33	9.30	m	**16.67**
406mm dia	4.81	8.17	0.33	9.30	m	**17.48**
Insulated aluminium foil flexible ductwork, DW144 class B; laminate construction of aluminium and polyester multiply inner core with 25mm insulation; outer layer of multiply aluminium polyester laminate, with high tensile steel wire helix						
Duct						
102mm dia	2.40	4.08	0.50	14.10	m	**18.17**
152mm dia	3.12	5.31	0.50	14.10	m	**19.40**
203mm dia	3.79	6.45	0.50	14.10	m	**20.54**
254mm dia	4.68	7.95	0.50	14.10	m	**22.05**
304mm dia	6.02	10.23	0.50	14.10	m	**24.33**
355mm dia	7.45	12.67	0.50	14.10	m	**26.77**
406mm dia	8.26	14.05	0.50	14.10	m	**28.15**

U:VENTILATION/AIR CONDITIONING SYSTEMS

Item	Net Price £	Material £	Labour hours	Labour £	Unit	Total rate £
U10 : DUCTWORK : PLASTIC						
Y30 - AIR DUCTLINES						
Rigid grey PVC DW 154 circular section ductwork; solvent welded or filler rod welded joints; excludes couplers and supports (these are detailed separately); ductwork to conform to curent HSE regulations						
Straight duct (standard length 6m)						
110mm	6.86	11.66	0.17	4.79	m	**16.46**
160mm	13.24	22.51	0.25	7.05	m	**29.55**
200mm	16.54	28.13	0.33	9.30	m	**37.43**
225mm	21.45	36.48	0.42	11.84	m	**48.32**
250mm	20.81	35.38	0.50	14.10	m	**49.48**
315mm	26.18	44.52	0.58	16.35	m	**60.87**
355mm	35.23	59.90	0.67	18.89	m	**78.79**
400mm	44.15	75.06	0.75	21.15	m	**96.21**
450mm	55.36	94.14	0.83	23.40	m	**117.54**
500mm	67.78	115.26	0.92	25.94	m	**141.20**
600mm	101.35	172.34	1.00	28.19	m	**200.53**
90° Bend						
110mm	15.57	26.48	0.34	9.59	m	**36.07**
160mm	20.36	34.63	0.50	14.10	m	**48.72**
200mm	25.16	42.79	0.66	18.61	m	**61.39**
225mm	29.95	50.93	0.84	23.68	m	**74.61**
250mm	34.35	58.41	1.00	28.19	m	**86.60**
315mm	54.32	92.37	1.16	32.71	m	**125.07**
355mm	73.49	124.96	1.34	37.78	m	**162.74**
400mm	91.45	155.51	1.50	42.29	m	**197.80**
450mm	260.82	443.49	1.66	46.80	m	**490.29**
500mm	308.34	524.30	1.84	51.88	m	**576.17**
600mm	521.62	886.96	2.00	56.39	m	**943.35**
45° Bend						
110mm	11.59	19.70	0.34	9.59	m	**29.29**
160mm	15.17	25.80	0.50	14.10	m	**39.90**
200mm	17.97	30.56	0.66	18.61	m	**49.17**
225mm	20.78	35.33	0.84	23.68	m	**59.01**
250mm	23.16	39.39	1.00	28.19	m	**67.58**
315mm	35.96	61.14	1.16	32.71	m	**93.85**
355mm	47.11	80.11	1.34	37.78	m	**117.89**
400mm	57.13	97.15	1.50	42.29	m	**139.44**
450mm	184.55	313.80	1.66	46.80	m	**360.60**
500mm	207.29	352.47	1.84	51.88	m	**404.35**
600mm	317.14	539.25	2.00	56.39	m	**595.64**

U:VENTILATION/AIR CONDITIONING SYSTEMS

Item	Net Price £	Material £	Labour hours	Labour £	Unit	Total rate £
U10 : DUCTWORK : PLASTIC (cont'd)						
Y30 - AIR DUCTLINES (cont'd)						
Rigid grey PVC DW 154 circular section (cont'd)						
Tee						
110mm	15.57	26.48	0.51	14.38	m	**40.86**
160mm	20.36	34.63	0.75	21.15	m	**55.77**
200mm	25.06	42.61	0.99	27.91	m	**70.52**
225mm	29.95	50.93	1.26	35.53	m	**86.46**
250mm	34.35	58.41	1.50	42.29	m	**100.70**
315mm	54.32	92.37	1.74	49.06	m	**141.43**
355mm	73.49	124.96	2.01	56.67	m	**181.63**
400mm	91.45	155.51	2.25	63.44	m	**218.94**
450mm	260.82	443.49	2.49	70.20	m	**513.69**
500mm	308.34	524.30	2.76	77.82	m	**602.11**
Coupler						
110mm	7.27	12.36	0.34	9.59	m	**21.95**
160mm	10.11	17.20	0.50	14.10	m	**31.30**
200mm	13.65	23.21	0.66	18.61	m	**41.81**
225mm	18.09	30.75	0.84	23.68	m	**54.44**
250mm	20.92	35.57	1.00	28.19	m	**63.77**
315mm	28.09	47.76	1.16	32.71	m	**80.47**
355mm	28.18	47.92	1.34	37.78	m	**85.70**
400mm	30.67	52.16	1.50	42.29	m	**94.45**
450mm	68.25	116.05	1.66	46.80	m	**162.85**
500mm	77.47	131.72	1.84	51.88	m	**183.60**
Damper						
110mm	43.14	73.35	0.34	9.59	m	**82.93**
160mm	49.52	84.21	0.50	14.10	m	**98.30**
200mm	55.12	93.72	0.66	18.61	m	**112.33**
225mm	58.70	99.81	0.84	23.68	m	**123.50**
250mm	60.72	103.24	1.00	28.19	m	**131.44**
315mm	71.89	122.25	1.16	32.71	m	**154.95**
355mm	76.28	129.71	1.34	37.78	m	**167.49**
400mm	82.68	140.58	1.50	42.29	m	**182.88**
Reducer						
160 x 110	16.30	27.72	0.42	11.84	m	**39.57**
200 x 110	24.46	41.60	0.50	14.10	m	**55.69**
200 x 160	21.90	37.23	0.58	16.35	m	**53.59**
225 x 200	29.78	50.63	0.75	21.15	m	**71.78**
250 x 160	29.78	50.63	0.75	21.15	m	**71.78**
250 x 200	30.67	52.16	0.83	23.40	m	**75.56**
250 x 225	31.38	53.36	0.92	25.94	m	**79.30**
315 x 200	33.15	56.36	0.92	25.94	m	**82.30**
315 x 250	35.99	61.19	1.10	31.01	m	**92.21**
355 x 200	49.28	83.79	1.10	31.01	m	**114.80**
355 x 250	39.53	67.22	1.17	32.99	m	**100.21**
355 x 315	46.83	79.64	1.25	35.24	m	**114.88**
400 x 225	55.13	93.73	1.17	32.99	m	**126.72**
400 x 315	59.74	101.58	1.33	37.50	m	**139.08**
400 x 355	58.14	98.87	1.42	40.04	m	**138.90**
450 x 315	59.74	101.58	1.45	40.88	m	**142.46**

U:VENTILATION/AIR CONDITIONING SYSTEMS

Item	Net Price £	Material £	Labour hours	Labour £	Unit	Total rate £
Flange						
110mm	10.72	18.23	0.34	9.59	m	**27.82**
160mm	12.54	21.31	0.50	14.10	m	**35.41**
200mm	14.36	24.41	0.66	18.61	m	**43.02**
225mm	14.53	24.71	0.84	23.68	m	**48.40**
250mm	14.99	25.48	1.00	28.19	m	**53.68**
315mm	22.53	38.30	1.16	32.71	m	**71.01**
355mm	24.71	42.02	1.34	37.78	m	**79.80**
400mm	27.57	46.88	1.50	42.29	m	**89.18**
Extra for supports (BZP finish)						
Horizontal - Maximum 2.4m centres						
Vertical - Maximum 4.0m centres						
Duct Size						
110mm	6.23	10.60	0.17	4.79	m	**15.39**
160mm	6.85	11.65	0.25	7.05	m	**18.70**
200mm	7.31	12.43	0.33	9.30	m	**21.74**
225mm	7.62	12.96	0.42	11.84	m	**24.80**
250mm	8.24	14.01	0.50	14.10	m	**28.11**
315mm	8.70	14.80	0.58	16.35	m	**31.15**
355mm	11.46	19.49	0.67	18.89	m	**38.38**
400mm	11.77	20.02	0.75	21.15	m	**41.16**
450mm	13.70	23.29	0.83	23.40	m	**46.69**
500mm	14.08	23.94	0.92	25.94	m	**49.88**
600mm	15.40	26.18	1.00	28.19	m	**54.38**

Note - These are maximum figures and may be reduced subject to local conditions (i.e. a high number of changes of direction)

Polypropylene (PPS) DW154 circular section ductwork; filler rod welded joints; excludes couplers and supports (these are detailed separately); ductwork to conform to current HSE regulations

Item	Net Price £	Material £	Labour hours	Labour £	Unit	Total rate £
Straight duct (standard length 6m)						
110mm	8.89	15.11	0.21	5.92	m	**21.04**
160mm	14.63	24.87	0.31	8.74	m	**33.61**
200mm	18.18	30.91	0.41	11.56	m	**42.47**
225mm	23.64	40.19	0.52	14.66	m	**54.86**
250mm	26.34	44.78	0.63	17.76	m	**62.55**
315mm	46.99	79.90	0.73	20.58	m	**100.48**
355mm	53.00	90.13	0.84	23.68	m	**113.81**
400mm	70.68	120.18	0.94	26.50	m	**146.68**
450mm	98.42	167.35	1.04	29.32	m	**196.67**
500mm	145.34	247.14	1.15	32.42	m	**279.56**
90° Bend						
110mm	23.34	39.69	0.43	12.12	m	**51.81**
160mm	34.35	58.41	0.63	17.76	m	**76.17**
200mm	40.71	69.22	0.83	23.40	m	**92.62**
225mm	54.32	92.37	1.05	29.60	m	**121.97**
250mm	58.31	99.15	1.25	35.24	m	**134.39**
315mm	127.81	217.33	1.45	40.88	m	**258.21**
355mm	175.74	298.82	1.68	47.37	m	**346.19**
400mm	187.72	319.19	1.88	53.01	m	**372.20**
450mm	439.37	747.09	2.08	58.64	m	**805.74**
500mm	475.29	808.18	2.30	64.85	m	**873.03**

U:VENTILATION/AIR CONDITIONING SYSTEMS

Item	Net Price £	Material £	Labour hours	Labour £	Unit	Total rate £
U10 : DUCTWORK : PLASTIC (cont'd)						
Y30 - AIR DUCTLINES (cont'd)						
Polypropylene (PPS) DW154 circular (cont'd)						
45° Bend						
110mm	17.97	30.56	0.43	12.12	m	42.69
160mm	28.76	48.90	0.63	17.76	m	66.66
200mm	32.75	55.69	0.83	23.40	m	79.10
225mm	40.75	69.29	1.05	29.60	m	98.89
250mm	45.55	77.45	1.25	35.24	m	112.69
315mm	115.83	196.96	1.45	40.88	m	237.84
355mm	131.81	224.13	1.68	47.37	m	271.49
400mm	139.78	237.68	1.88	53.01	m	290.69
Tee						
110mm	81.01	137.75	0.64	18.04	m	155.79
160mm	116.23	197.63	0.94	26.50	m	224.13
200mm	140.91	239.61	1.24	34.96	m	274.57
225mm	156.74	266.51	1.58	44.55	m	311.06
250mm	184.93	314.44	1.88	53.01	m	367.45
315mm	255.38	434.24	2.18	61.46	m	495.70
355mm	317.04	539.10	2.51	70.77	m	609.86
400mm	369.87	628.92	2.81	79.23	m	708.15
Coupler						
110mm	17.97	30.56	0.43	12.12	m	42.69
160mm	21.96	37.34	0.63	17.76	m	55.10
200mm	26.36	44.82	0.83	23.40	m	68.22
225mm	29.16	49.58	1.05	29.60	m	79.19
250mm	30.76	52.30	1.25	35.24	m	87.54
315mm	41.93	71.30	1.45	40.88	m	112.18
355mm	54.32	92.37	1.68	47.37	m	139.74
400mm	59.12	100.53	1.88	53.01	m	153.54
Damper						
110mm	77.66	132.05	0.43	12.12	m	144.18
160mm	91.44	155.49	0.63	17.76	m	173.25
200mm	101.70	172.93	0.83	23.40	m	196.33
225mm	108.23	184.04	1.05	29.60	m	213.64
250mm	114.63	194.91	1.25	35.24	m	230.16
315mm	131.01	222.76	1.45	40.88	m	263.64
355mm	143.40	243.83	1.68	47.37	m	291.20
400mm	156.97	266.91	1.88	53.01	m	319.92
Reducer						
160 x 110	57.52	97.80	0.53	14.94	m	112.74
200 x 160	63.11	107.31	0.73	20.58	m	127.89
225 x 200	87.87	149.41	0.94	26.50	m	175.91
250 x 200	83.88	142.63	1.04	29.32	m	171.96
250 x 225	106.94	181.85	1.15	32.42	m	214.27
315 x 200	136.60	232.27	1.15	32.42	m	264.69
315 x 250	114.11	194.04	1.38	38.91	m	232.95
355 x 200	157.36	267.58	1.38	38.91	m	306.49
355 x 250	128.62	218.70	1.46	41.16	m	259.86
355 x 315	146.98	249.92	1.56	43.98	m	293.91
400 x 315	155.77	264.86	1.66	46.80	m	311.67
400 x 355	184.55	313.80	1.78	50.19	m	363.98

U:VENTILATION/AIR CONDITIONING SYSTEMS

Item	Net Price £	Material £	Labour hours	Labour £	Unit	Total rate £
Flange						
110mm	17.01	28.92	0.43	12.12	m	**41.04**
160mm	20.74	35.27	0.63	17.76	m	**53.04**
200mm	24.28	41.28	0.83	23.40	m	**64.68**
225mm	25.55	43.45	1.05	29.60	m	**73.06**
250mm	28.45	48.37	1.25	35.24	m	**83.62**
315mm	32.11	54.59	1.45	40.88	m	**95.47**
355mm	36.11	61.40	1.68	47.37	m	**108.77**
400mm	40.05	68.09	1.88	53.01	m	**121.10**
Extra for supports (BZP finish)						
Horizontal - Maximum 2.4m centres						
Vertical - Maximum 4.0m centres						
Duct Size						
110mm	6.23	10.60	0.21	5.92	m	**16.52**
160mm	6.85	11.65	0.31	8.74	m	**20.39**
200mm	7.31	12.43	0.41	11.56	m	**23.99**
225mm	7.62	12.96	0.52	14.66	m	**27.62**
250mm	8.24	14.01	0.63	17.76	m	**31.77**
315mm	8.70	14.80	0.73	20.58	m	**35.38**
355mm	11.46	19.49	0.84	23.68	m	**43.18**
400mm	11.77	20.02	0.94	26.50	m	**46.52**
450mm	13.70	23.29	1.04	29.32	m	**52.62**
500mm	14.08	23.94	1.15	32.42	m	**56.37**
600mm	15.40	26.18	1.25	35.24	m	**61.43**

Note - These are maximum figures and may be reduced subject to local conditions (i.e. a high number of changes of direction)

U:VENTILATION/AIR CONDITIONING SYSTEMS

Item	Net Price £	Material £	Labour hours	Labour £	Unit	Total rate £
U10 : DUCTWORK : RECTANGULAR – CLASS B						
Y30 - AIR DUCTLINES						
Galvanised sheet metal DW144 class B rectangular section ductwork; including all necessary stiffeners, joints, couplers in the running length and duct supports						
Ductwork up to 400mm longest side						
Sum of two sides 200mm	18.92	32.17	1.19	33.55	m	65.72
Sum of two sides 300mm	20.15	34.26	1.19	33.55	m	67.81
Sum of two sides 400mm	16.73	28.45	1.16	32.71	m	61.16
Sum of two sides 500mm	18.09	30.76	1.16	32.71	m	63.46
Sum of two sides 600mm	19.17	32.60	1.27	35.81	m	68.41
Sum of two sides 700mm	20.24	34.42	1.27	35.81	m	70.23
Sum of two sides 800mm	21.43	36.44	1.27	35.81	m	72.24
Extra Over fittings; Rectangular ductwork class B; upto 400mm longest side						
End Cap						
Sum of two sides 200mm	8.72	14.82	0.38	10.71	nr	25.54
Sum of two sides 300mm	9.69	16.48	0.38	10.71	nr	27.20
Sum of two sides 400mm	10.67	18.14	0.38	10.71	nr	28.86
Sum of two sides 500mm	11.65	19.81	0.38	10.71	nr	30.53
Sum of two sides 600mm	12.63	21.47	0.38	10.71	nr	32.19
Sum of two sides 700mm	13.60	23.12	0.38	10.71	nr	33.84
Sum of two sides 800mm	14.57	24.78	0.38	10.71	nr	35.50
Reducer						
Sum of two sides 200mm	9.22	15.68	1.40	39.47	nr	55.16
Sum of two sides 300mm	10.41	17.69	1.40	39.47	nr	57.17
Sum of two sides 400mm	17.15	29.17	1.42	40.04	nr	69.21
Sum of two sides 500mm	18.62	31.67	1.42	40.04	nr	71.71
Sum of two sides 600mm	20.09	34.17	1.69	47.65	nr	81.82
Sum of two sides 700mm	21.57	36.68	1.69	47.65	nr	84.33
Sum of two sides 800mm	23.02	39.15	1.92	54.13	nr	93.28
Offset						
Sum of two sides 200mm	11.15	18.96	1.63	45.96	nr	64.92
Sum of two sides 300mm	12.61	21.44	1.63	45.96	nr	67.40
Sum of two sides 400mm	18.76	31.90	1.65	46.52	nr	78.42
Sum of two sides 500mm	20.45	34.77	1.65	46.52	nr	81.29
Sum of two sides 600mm	21.84	37.14	1.92	54.13	nr	91.27
Sum of two sides 700mm	23.38	39.76	1.92	54.13	nr	93.89
Sum of two sides 800mm	24.74	42.08	1.92	54.13	nr	96.21
Square to round						
Sum of two sides 200mm	21.26	36.15	1.63	45.96	nr	82.10
Sum of two sides 300mm	23.88	40.61	1.63	45.96	nr	86.56
Sum of two sides 400mm	31.92	54.27	1.65	46.52	nr	100.79
Sum of two sides 500mm	34.79	59.15	1.65	46.52	nr	105.67
Sum of two sides 600mm	37.67	64.06	1.92	54.13	nr	118.19
Sum of two sides 700mm	40.52	68.91	1.92	54.13	nr	123.04
Sum of two sides 800mm	43.38	73.75	1.92	54.13	nr	127.89

U:VENTILATION/AIR CONDITIONING SYSTEMS

Item	Net Price £	Material £	Labour hours	Labour £	Unit	Total rate £
90 ° radius bend						
Sum of two sides 200mm	10.72	18.23	1.22	34.40	nr	**52.63**
Sum of two sides 300mm	11.56	19.66	1.22	34.40	nr	**54.06**
Sum of two sides 400mm	19.65	33.41	1.25	35.24	nr	**68.65**
Sum of two sides 500mm	20.99	35.69	1.25	35.24	nr	**70.93**
Sum of two sides 600mm	22.73	38.66	1.33	37.50	nr	**76.16**
Sum of two sides 700mm	24.27	41.27	1.33	37.50	nr	**78.76**
Sum of two sides 800mm	25.97	44.16	1.40	39.47	nr	**83.64**
45 ° radius bend						
Sum of two sides 200mm	10.62	18.06	0.89	25.09	nr	**43.16**
Sum of two sides 300mm	11.66	19.82	1.12	31.58	nr	**51.40**
Sum of two sides 400mm	18.85	32.06	1.10	31.01	nr	**63.07**
Sum of two sides 500mm	20.28	34.48	1.10	31.01	nr	**65.49**
Sum of two sides 600mm	21.88	37.21	1.16	32.71	nr	**69.91**
Sum of two sides 700mm	23.40	39.79	1.16	32.71	nr	**72.49**
Sum of two sides 800mm	24.99	42.50	1.22	34.40	nr	**76.89**
90 ° mitre bend						
Sum of two sides 200mm	14.64	24.89	1.29	36.37	nr	**61.26**
Sum of two sides 300mm	16.01	27.22	1.29	36.37	nr	**63.59**
Sum of two sides 400mm	23.39	39.77	1.29	36.37	nr	**76.14**
Sum of two sides 500mm	25.25	42.94	1.29	36.37	nr	**79.31**
Sum of two sides 600mm	27.61	46.94	1.39	39.19	nr	**86.13**
Sum of two sides 700mm	29.78	50.64	1.39	39.19	nr	**89.83**
Sum of two sides 800mm	32.16	54.69	1.46	41.16	nr	**95.86**
Branch						
Sum of two sides 200mm	18.22	30.98	0.92	25.94	nr	**56.92**
Sum of two sides 300mm	20.22	34.39	0.92	25.94	nr	**60.33**
Sum of two sides 400mm	25.37	43.13	0.95	26.78	nr	**69.92**
Sum of two sides 500mm	27.62	46.96	0.95	26.78	nr	**73.75**
Sum of two sides 600mm	29.83	50.72	1.03	29.04	nr	**79.76**
Sum of two sides 700mm	32.03	54.47	1.03	29.04	nr	**83.51**
Sum of two sides 800mm	34.24	58.22	1.03	29.04	nr	**87.26**
Grille neck						
Sum of two sides 200mm	15.92	27.07	1.10	31.01	nr	**58.08**
Sum of two sides 300mm	17.77	30.21	1.10	31.01	nr	**61.22**
Sum of two sides 400mm	19.61	33.34	1.16	32.71	nr	**66.04**
Sum of two sides 500mm	21.45	36.48	1.16	32.71	nr	**69.18**
Sum of two sides 600mm	23.30	39.62	1.18	33.27	nr	**72.89**
Sum of two sides 700mm	25.14	42.75	1.18	33.27	nr	**76.01**
Sum of two sides 800mm	26.98	45.88	1.18	33.27	nr	**79.15**
Ductwork 401 to 600mm longest side						
Sum of two sides 600mm	20.23	34.40	1.27	35.81	m	**70.21**
Sum of two sides 700mm	21.77	37.02	1.27	35.81	m	**72.82**
Sum of two sides 800mm	23.18	39.41	1.27	35.81	m	**75.21**
Sum of two sides 900mm	24.48	41.63	1.27	35.81	m	**77.43**
Sum of two sides 1000mm	25.77	43.82	1.37	38.63	m	**82.45**
Sum of two sides 1100mm	27.40	46.58	1.37	38.63	m	**85.21**
Sum of two sides 1200mm	28.71	48.81	1.37	38.63	m	**87.44**

U:VENTILATION/AIR CONDITIONING SYSTEMS

Item	Net Price £	Material £	Labour hours	Labour £	Unit	Total rate £
U10 : DUCTWORK : RECTANGULAR – CLASS B (cont'd)						
Y30 - AIR DUCTLINES (cont'd)						
Extra over fittings; Ductwork 401 to 600mm longest side						
End Cap						
Sum of two sides 600mm	12.68	21.55	0.38	10.71	nr	**32.27**
Sum of two sides 700mm	13.66	23.23	0.38	10.71	nr	**33.95**
Sum of two sides 800mm	14.65	24.91	0.38	10.71	nr	**35.63**
Sum of two sides 900mm	15.65	26.61	0.58	16.35	nr	**42.96**
Sum of two sides 1000mm	16.64	28.29	0.58	16.35	nr	**44.64**
Sum of two sides 1100mm	17.63	29.97	0.58	16.35	nr	**46.32**
Sum of two sides 1200mm	18.61	31.65	0.58	16.35	nr	**48.00**
Reducer						
Sum of two sides 600mm	18.13	30.83	1.69	47.65	nr	**78.48**
Sum of two sides 700mm	19.48	33.13	1.69	47.65	nr	**80.78**
Sum of two sides 800mm	20.82	35.41	1.92	54.13	nr	**89.54**
Sum of two sides 900mm	22.18	37.72	1.92	54.13	nr	**91.85**
Sum of two sides 1000mm	23.54	40.03	2.18	61.46	nr	**101.49**
Sum of two sides 1100mm	25.01	42.53	2.18	61.46	nr	**103.99**
Sum of two sides 1200mm	26.37	44.83	2.18	61.46	nr	**106.30**
Offset						
Sum of two sides 600mm	20.99	35.70	1.92	54.13	nr	**89.83**
Sum of two sides 700mm	22.58	38.39	1.92	54.13	nr	**92.52**
Sum of two sides 800mm	23.86	40.58	1.92	54.13	nr	**94.71**
Sum of two sides 900mm	25.16	42.78	1.92	54.13	nr	**96.91**
Sum of two sides 1000mm	26.60	45.22	2.18	61.46	nr	**106.69**
Sum of two sides 1100mm	27.94	47.50	2.18	61.46	nr	**108.97**
Sum of two sides 1200mm	29.21	49.67	2.18	61.46	nr	**111.14**
Square to round						
Sum of two sides 600mm	29.57	50.27	1.33	37.50	nr	**87.77**
Sum of two sides 700mm	31.87	54.19	1.33	37.50	nr	**91.69**
Sum of two sides 800mm	34.15	58.07	1.40	39.47	nr	**97.54**
Sum of two sides 900mm	36.46	62.00	1.40	39.47	nr	**101.47**
Sum of two sides 1000mm	38.77	65.93	1.82	51.31	nr	**117.24**
Sum of two sides 1100mm	41.12	69.93	1.82	51.31	nr	**121.24**
Sum of two sides 1200mm	43.43	73.84	1.82	51.31	nr	**125.16**
90 ° radius bend						
Sum of two sides 600mm	18.52	31.49	1.16	32.71	nr	**64.19**
Sum of two sides 700mm	19.60	33.33	1.16	32.71	nr	**66.03**
Sum of two sides 800mm	21.12	35.91	1.22	34.40	nr	**70.30**
Sum of two sides 900mm	22.66	38.54	1.22	34.40	nr	**72.93**
Sum of two sides 1000mm	23.99	40.79	1.40	39.47	nr	**80.26**
Sum of two sides 1100mm	25.62	43.56	1.40	39.47	nr	**83.04**
Sum of two sides 1200mm	27.17	46.19	1.40	39.47	nr	**85.67**

U:VENTILATION/AIR CONDITIONING SYSTEMS

Item	Net Price £	Material £	Labour hours	Labour £	Unit	Total rate £
45 ° bend						
Sum of two sides 600mm	21.26	36.16	1.16	32.71	nr	**68.86**
Sum of two sides 700mm	22.63	38.49	1.39	39.19	nr	**77.68**
Sum of two sides 800mm	24.25	41.24	1.46	41.16	nr	**82.40**
Sum of two sides 900mm	25.89	44.01	1.46	41.16	nr	**85.18**
Sum of two sides 1000mm	27.39	46.57	1.88	53.01	nr	**99.58**
Sum of two sides 1100mm	29.17	49.59	1.88	53.01	nr	**102.60**
Sum of two sides 1200mm	30.80	52.37	1.88	53.01	nr	**105.38**
90 ° mitre bend						
Sum of two sides 600mm	25.41	43.21	1.39	39.19	nr	**82.40**
Sum of two sides 700mm	26.92	45.77	2.16	60.90	nr	**106.67**
Sum of two sides 800mm	29.01	49.33	2.26	63.72	nr	**113.05**
Sum of two sides 900mm	31.14	52.94	2.26	63.72	nr	**116.66**
Sum of two sides 1000mm	33.04	56.18	3.01	84.87	nr	**141.05**
Sum of two sides 1100mm	35.26	59.96	3.01	84.87	nr	**144.82**
Sum of two sides 1200mm	37.43	63.64	3.01	84.87	nr	**148.50**
Branch						
Sum of two sides 600mm	26.86	45.66	1.03	29.04	nr	**74.70**
Sum of two sides 700mm	28.85	49.06	1.03	29.04	nr	**78.10**
Sum of two sides 800mm	30.86	52.47	1.03	29.04	nr	**81.51**
Sum of two sides 900mm	32.86	55.87	1.03	29.04	nr	**84.91**
Sum of two sides 1000mm	34.87	59.29	1.29	36.37	nr	**95.66**
Sum of two sides 1100mm	36.97	62.87	1.29	36.37	nr	**99.24**
Sum of two sides 1200mm	38.97	66.27	1.29	36.37	nr	**102.64**
Grille neck						
Sum of two sides 600mm	23.27	39.58	1.18	33.27	nr	**72.85**
Sum of two sides 700mm	25.14	42.75	1.18	33.27	nr	**76.01**
Sum of two sides 800mm	27.01	45.93	1.18	33.27	nr	**79.20**
Sum of two sides 900mm	28.88	49.11	1.18	33.27	nr	**82.38**
Sum of two sides 1000mm	30.65	52.11	1.44	40.60	nr	**92.71**
Sum of two sides 1100mm	32.62	55.47	1.44	40.60	nr	**96.07**
Sum of two sides 1200mm	34.49	58.65	1.44	40.60	nr	**99.25**
Ductwork 601 to 800mm longest side						
Sum of two sides 900mm	28.21	47.97	1.27	35.81	m	**83.78**
Sum of two sides 1000mm	29.36	49.92	1.37	38.63	m	**88.55**
Sum of two sides 1100mm	30.73	52.25	1.37	38.63	m	**90.88**
Sum of two sides 1200mm	32.04	54.48	1.37	38.63	m	**93.11**
Sum of two sides 1300mm	33.29	56.60	1.40	39.47	m	**96.07**
Sum of two sides 1400mm	34.50	58.67	1.40	39.47	m	**98.14**
Sum of two sides 1500mm	35.73	60.76	1.48	41.73	m	**102.49**
Sum of two sides 1600mm	36.94	62.81	1.55	43.70	m	**106.51**

U:VENTILATION/AIR CONDITIONING SYSTEMS

Item	Net Price £	Material £	Labour hours	Labour £	Unit	Total rate £
U10 : DUCTWORK : RECTANGULAR – CLASS B (cont'd)						
Y30 - AIR DUCTLINES (cont'd)						
Extra over fittings: Ductwork 601 to 800mm longest side						
End Cap						
Sum of two sides 900mm	16.29	27.70	0.58	16.35	nr	**44.05**
Sum of two sides 1000mm	17.27	29.37	0.58	16.35	nr	**45.72**
Sum of two sides 1100mm	18.24	31.01	0.58	16.35	nr	**47.36**
Sum of two sides 1200mm	19.20	32.65	0.58	16.35	nr	**49.00**
Sum of two sides 1300mm	20.15	34.26	0.58	16.35	nr	**50.61**
Sum of two sides 1400mm	21.12	35.91	0.58	16.35	nr	**52.26**
Sum of two sides 1500mm	23.29	39.61	0.58	16.35	nr	**55.96**
Sum of two sides 1600mm	25.56	43.46	0.58	16.35	nr	**59.82**
Reducer						
Sum of two sides 900mm	21.45	36.47	1.92	54.13	nr	**90.60**
Sum of two sides 1000mm	22.72	38.64	2.18	61.46	nr	**100.10**
Sum of two sides 1100mm	23.93	40.69	2.18	61.46	nr	**102.15**
Sum of two sides 1200mm	25.37	43.13	2.18	61.46	nr	**104.60**
Sum of two sides 1300mm	26.67	45.34	2.30	64.85	nr	**110.19**
Sum of two sides 1400mm	27.99	47.59	2.30	64.85	nr	**112.44**
Sum of two sides 1500mm	31.82	54.10	2.47	69.64	nr	**123.74**
Sum of two sides 1600mm	35.87	61.00	2.47	69.64	nr	**130.64**
Offset						
Sum of two sides 900mm	25.37	43.13	1.92	54.13	nr	**97.27**
Sum of two sides 1000mm	26.18	44.51	2.18	61.46	nr	**105.98**
Sum of two sides 1100mm	26.99	45.89	2.18	61.46	nr	**107.36**
Sum of two sides 1200mm	27.90	47.43	2.18	61.46	nr	**108.90**
Sum of two sides 1300mm	28.68	48.76	2.30	64.85	nr	**113.61**
Sum of two sides 1400mm	29.76	50.60	2.30	64.85	nr	**115.45**
Sum of two sides 1500mm	33.45	56.87	2.47	69.64	nr	**126.51**
Sum of two sides 1600mm	37.43	63.64	2.47	69.64	nr	**133.28**
Square to round						
Sum of two sides 900mm	32.66	55.53	1.40	39.47	nr	**95.00**
Sum of two sides 1000mm	35.22	59.89	1.82	51.31	nr	**111.20**
Sum of two sides 1100mm	37.77	64.23	1.82	51.31	nr	**115.54**
Sum of two sides 1200mm	40.41	68.72	1.82	51.31	nr	**120.03**
Sum of two sides 1300mm	43.08	73.25	2.15	60.62	nr	**133.87**
Sum of two sides 1400mm	45.78	77.84	2.15	60.62	nr	**138.46**
Sum of two sides 1500mm	52.19	88.74	2.38	67.10	nr	**155.84**
Sum of two sides 1600mm	58.95	100.24	2.38	67.10	nr	**167.34**
90 ° radius bend						
Sum of two sides 900mm	21.76	37.00	1.22	34.40	nr	**71.39**
Sum of two sides 1000mm	23.58	40.10	1.40	39.47	nr	**79.57**
Sum of two sides 1100mm	25.30	43.03	1.40	39.47	nr	**82.50**
Sum of two sides 1200mm	27.17	46.19	1.40	39.47	nr	**85.67**
Sum of two sides 1300mm	29.03	49.36	1.91	53.85	nr	**103.21**
Sum of two sides 1400mm	30.40	51.69	1.91	53.85	nr	**105.54**
Sum of two sides 1500mm	35.19	59.84	2.11	59.49	nr	**119.33**
Sum of two sides 1600mm	40.27	68.47	2.11	59.49	nr	**127.96**

U:VENTILATION/AIR CONDITIONING SYSTEMS

Item	Net Price £	Material £	Labour hours	Labour £	Unit	Total rate £
45 ° bend						
Sum of two sides 900mm	25.28	42.99	1.22	34.40	nr	**77.38**
Sum of two sides 1000mm	26.98	45.88	1.40	39.47	nr	**85.36**
Sum of two sides 1100mm	28.60	48.63	1.88	53.01	nr	**101.64**
Sum of two sides 1200mm	30.49	51.85	1.88	53.01	nr	**104.86**
Sum of two sides 1300mm	32.28	54.88	2.26	63.72	nr	**118.60**
Sum of two sides 1400mm	33.82	57.50	2.26	63.72	nr	**121.22**
Sum of two sides 1500mm	38.51	65.49	2.49	70.20	nr	**135.69**
Sum of two sides 1600mm	43.51	73.98	2.49	70.20	nr	**144.19**
90 ° mitre bend						
Sum of two sides 900mm	30.94	52.60	1.22	34.40	nr	**87.00**
Sum of two sides 1000mm	33.31	56.64	1.40	39.47	nr	**96.11**
Sum of two sides 1100mm	35.62	60.57	3.01	84.87	nr	**145.43**
Sum of two sides 1200mm	38.01	64.63	3.01	84.87	nr	**149.49**
Sum of two sides 1300mm	40.42	68.74	3.67	103.47	nr	**172.21**
Sum of two sides 1400mm	42.43	72.14	3.67	103.47	nr	**175.62**
Sum of two sides 1500mm	47.54	80.83	4.07	114.75	nr	**195.58**
Sum of two sides 1600mm	53.15	90.38	4.07	114.75	nr	**205.13**
Branch						
Sum of two sides 900mm	34.52	58.69	1.22	34.40	nr	**93.09**
Sum of two sides 1000mm	36.69	62.38	1.40	39.47	nr	**101.85**
Sum of two sides 1100mm	38.80	65.97	1.29	36.37	nr	**102.34**
Sum of two sides 1200mm	41.09	69.88	1.29	36.37	nr	**106.25**
Sum of two sides 1300mm	43.28	73.58	1.39	39.19	nr	**112.77**
Sum of two sides 1400mm	45.47	77.31	1.39	39.19	nr	**116.50**
Sum of two sides 1500mm	51.48	87.53	1.64	46.24	nr	**133.77**
Sum of two sides 1600mm	57.76	98.22	1.64	46.24	nr	**144.45**
Grille neck						
Sum of two sides 900mm	27.71	47.11	1.22	34.40	nr	**81.51**
Sum of two sides 1000mm	29.54	50.22	1.40	39.47	nr	**89.69**
Sum of two sides 1100mm	31.35	53.31	1.44	40.60	nr	**93.91**
Sum of two sides 1200mm	33.19	56.44	1.44	40.60	nr	**97.04**
Sum of two sides 1300mm	35.06	59.61	1.69	47.65	nr	**107.26**
Sum of two sides 1400mm	37.17	63.21	1.69	47.65	nr	**110.86**
Sum of two sides 1500mm	42.73	72.65	1.79	50.47	nr	**123.12**
Sum of two sides 1600mm	48.57	82.59	1.79	50.47	nr	**133.06**
Ductwork 801 to 1000mm longest side						
Sum of two sides 1100mm	38.61	65.65	1.37	38.63	m	**104.27**
Sum of two sides 1200mm	40.84	69.45	1.37	38.63	m	**108.07**
Sum of two sides 1300mm	43.08	73.24	1.40	39.47	m	**112.72**
Sum of two sides 1400mm	45.56	77.47	1.40	39.47	m	**116.95**
Sum of two sides 1500mm	47.80	81.27	1.48	41.73	m	**123.00**
Sum of two sides 1600mm	50.03	85.07	1.55	43.70	m	**128.77**
Sum of two sides 1700mm	52.26	88.86	1.55	43.70	m	**132.56**
Sum of two sides 1800mm	54.75	93.10	1.61	45.39	m	**138.49**
Sum of two sides 1900mm	56.99	96.90	1.61	45.39	m	**142.29**
Sum of two sides 2000mm	59.21	100.69	1.61	45.39	m	**146.08**

U:VENTILATION/AIR CONDITIONING SYSTEMS

Item	Net Price £	Material £	Labour hours	Labour £	Unit	Total rate £
U10 : DUCTWORK : RECTANGULAR – CLASS B (cont'd)						
Y30 - AIR DUCTLINES (cont'd)						
Extra over fittings; Ductwork 801 to 1000mm longest side						
End Cap						
Sum of two sides 1100mm	18.94	32.20	1.44	40.60	nr	72.80
Sum of two sides 1200mm	20.00	34.01	1.44	40.60	nr	74.61
Sum of two sides 1300mm	21.06	35.81	1.44	40.60	nr	76.41
Sum of two sides 1400mm	21.97	37.36	1.44	40.60	nr	77.96
Sum of two sides 1500mm	25.57	43.48	1.44	40.60	nr	84.09
Sum of two sides 1600mm	29.18	49.62	1.44	40.60	nr	90.22
Sum of two sides 1700mm	32.79	55.75	1.44	40.60	nr	96.35
Sum of two sides 1800mm	36.39	61.88	1.44	40.60	nr	102.48
Sum of two sides 1900mm	40.01	68.03	1.44	40.60	nr	108.63
Sum of two sides 2000mm	43.61	74.15	1.44	40.60	nr	114.75
Reducer						
Sum of two sides 1100mm	16.42	27.92	1.44	40.60	nr	68.52
Sum of two sides 1200mm	17.23	29.29	1.44	40.60	nr	69.89
Sum of two sides 1300mm	18.03	30.66	1.69	47.65	nr	78.31
Sum of two sides 1400mm	18.78	31.93	1.69	47.65	nr	79.58
Sum of two sides 1500mm	21.85	37.16	2.47	69.64	nr	106.80
Sum of two sides 1600mm	24.92	42.38	2.47	69.64	nr	112.02
Sum of two sides 1700mm	27.99	47.59	2.47	69.64	nr	117.23
Sum of two sides 1800mm	31.14	52.95	2.59	73.02	nr	125.98
Sum of two sides 1900mm	34.21	58.17	2.71	76.41	nr	134.58
Sum of two sides 2000mm	37.28	63.40	2.71	76.41	nr	139.81
Offset						
Sum of two sides 1100mm	25.51	43.39	1.44	40.60	nr	83.99
Sum of two sides 1200mm	26.00	44.21	1.44	40.60	nr	84.81
Sum of two sides 1300mm	26.41	44.90	1.69	47.65	nr	92.55
Sum of two sides 1400mm	26.59	45.21	1.69	47.65	nr	92.86
Sum of two sides 1500mm	30.28	51.49	2.47	69.64	nr	121.13
Sum of two sides 1600mm	33.89	57.63	2.47	69.64	nr	127.27
Sum of two sides 1700mm	37.43	63.64	2.59	73.02	nr	136.66
Sum of two sides 1800mm	40.92	69.58	2.61	73.59	nr	143.16
Sum of two sides 1900mm	44.84	76.24	2.71	76.41	nr	152.65
Sum of two sides 2000mm	48.15	81.87	2.71	76.41	nr	158.28
Square to round						
Sum of two sides 1100mm	32.45	55.17	1.44	40.60	nr	95.77
Sum of two sides 1200mm	34.15	58.07	1.44	40.60	nr	98.67
Sum of two sides 1300mm	35.86	60.98	1.69	47.65	nr	108.63
Sum of two sides 1400mm	37.26	63.36	1.69	47.65	nr	111.01
Sum of two sides 1500mm	44.27	75.28	2.38	67.10	nr	142.39
Sum of two sides 1600mm	51.28	87.20	2.38	67.10	nr	154.30
Sum of two sides 1700mm	58.29	99.12	2.55	71.90	nr	171.01
Sum of two sides 1800mm	65.32	111.07	2.55	71.90	nr	182.97
Sum of two sides 1900mm	72.33	122.99	2.83	79.79	nr	202.78
Sum of two sides 2000mm	79.34	134.90	2.83	79.79	nr	214.69

U:VENTILATION/AIR CONDITIONING SYSTEMS

Item	Net Price £	Material £	Labour hours	Labour £	Unit	Total rate £
90 ° radius bend						
Sum of two sides 1100mm	15.22	25.88	1.44	40.60	nr	**66.48**
Sum of two sides 1200mm	16.28	27.69	1.44	40.60	nr	**68.29**
Sum of two sides 1300mm	17.35	29.50	1.69	47.65	nr	**77.15**
Sum of two sides 1400mm	18.30	31.11	1.69	47.65	nr	**78.76**
Sum of two sides 1500mm	22.02	37.45	2.11	59.49	nr	**96.94**
Sum of two sides 1600mm	25.74	43.77	2.11	59.49	nr	**103.27**
Sum of two sides 1700mm	29.47	50.11	2.26	63.72	nr	**113.83**
Sum of two sides 1800mm	33.25	56.53	2.26	63.72	nr	**120.25**
Sum of two sides 1900mm	36.27	61.68	2.48	69.92	nr	**131.60**
Sum of two sides 2000mm	39.99	68.00	2.48	69.92	nr	**137.92**
45 ° bend						
Sum of two sides 1100mm	21.93	37.29	1.44	40.60	nr	**77.89**
Sum of two sides 1200mm	23.20	39.46	1.44	40.60	nr	**80.06**
Sum of two sides 1300mm	24.48	41.63	1.69	47.65	nr	**89.27**
Sum of two sides 1400mm	25.69	43.67	1.69	47.65	nr	**91.32**
Sum of two sides 1500mm	29.85	50.76	2.49	70.20	nr	**120.97**
Sum of two sides 1600mm	34.03	57.86	2.49	70.20	nr	**128.06**
Sum of two sides 1700mm	38.20	64.95	2.67	75.28	nr	**140.23**
Sum of two sides 1800mm	42.48	72.24	2.67	75.28	nr	**147.51**
Sum of two sides 1900mm	46.26	78.66	3.06	86.28	nr	**164.94**
Sum of two sides 2000mm	50.43	85.75	3.06	86.28	nr	**172.03**
90 ° mitre bend						
Sum of two sides 1100mm	29.57	50.28	1.44	40.60	nr	**90.88**
Sum of two sides 1200mm	31.49	53.55	1.44	40.60	nr	**94.15**
Sum of two sides 1300mm	33.42	56.83	1.69	47.65	nr	**104.48**
Sum of two sides 1400mm	35.14	59.75	1.69	47.65	nr	**107.40**
Sum of two sides 1500mm	40.86	69.48	4.07	114.75	nr	**184.23**
Sum of two sides 1600mm	46.57	79.19	4.07	114.75	nr	**193.94**
Sum of two sides 1700mm	52.29	88.91	2.80	78.94	nr	**167.85**
Sum of two sides 1800mm	58.03	98.68	2.67	75.28	nr	**173.96**
Sum of two sides 1900mm	63.00	107.12	2.95	83.17	nr	**190.30**
Sum of two sides 2000mm	68.73	116.86	2.95	83.17	nr	**200.03**
Branch						
Sum of two sides 1100mm	33.68	57.27	1.44	40.60	nr	**97.87**
Sum of two sides 1200mm	35.49	60.35	1.44	40.60	nr	**100.95**
Sum of two sides 1300mm	37.31	63.45	1.64	46.24	nr	**109.69**
Sum of two sides 1400mm	38.97	66.27	1.64	46.24	nr	**112.51**
Sum of two sides 1500mm	44.75	76.08	1.64	46.24	nr	**122.32**
Sum of two sides 1600mm	50.52	85.90	1.64	46.24	nr	**132.14**
Sum of two sides 1700mm	56.29	95.71	1.69	47.65	nr	**143.36**
Sum of two sides 1800mm	62.15	105.67	1.69	47.65	nr	**153.32**
Sum of two sides 1900mm	67.92	115.49	1.85	52.16	nr	**167.65**
Sum of two sides 2000mm	73.69	125.30	1.85	52.16	nr	**177.46**
Grille neck						
Sum of two sides 1100mm	32.82	55.81	1.44	40.60	nr	**96.41**
Sum of two sides 1200mm	34.70	59.01	1.44	40.60	nr	**99.61**
Sum of two sides 1300mm	36.58	62.20	1.69	47.65	nr	**109.85**
Sum of two sides 1400mm	38.20	64.96	1.69	47.65	nr	**112.61**
Sum of two sides 1500mm	44.36	75.43	1.79	50.47	nr	**125.90**
Sum of two sides 1600mm	50.52	85.91	1.79	50.47	nr	**136.38**
Sum of two sides 1700mm	56.68	96.38	1.86	52.44	nr	**148.82**
Sum of two sides 1800mm	62.85	106.86	2.02	56.95	nr	**163.82**
Sum of two sides 1900mm	69.00	117.33	2.02	56.95	nr	**174.28**
Sum of two sides 2000mm	75.17	127.82	2.02	56.95	nr	**184.77**

U:VENTILATION/AIR CONDITIONING SYSTEMS

Item	Net Price £	Material £	Labour hours	Labour £	Unit	Total rate £
U10 : DUCTWORK : RECTANGULAR – CLASS B (cont'd)						
Y30 - AIR DUCTLINES (cont'd)						
Ductwork 1001 to 1250mm longest side						
Sum of two sides 1300mm	48.38	82.26	1.40	39.47	m	**121.73**
Sum of two sides 1400mm	49.88	84.81	1.40	39.47	m	**124.28**
Sum of two sides 1500mm	52.16	88.70	1.48	41.73	m	**130.43**
Sum of two sides 1600mm	54.67	92.97	1.55	43.70	m	**136.67**
Sum of two sides 1700mm	56.96	96.86	1.55	43.70	m	**140.56**
Sum of two sides 1800mm	59.25	100.75	1.61	45.39	m	**146.14**
Sum of two sides 1900mm	61.54	104.63	1.61	45.39	m	**150.03**
Sum of two sides 2000mm	62.91	106.97	1.61	45.39	m	**152.37**
Sum of two sides 2100mm	65.20	110.87	2.17	61.18	m	**172.05**
Sum of two sides 2200mm	67.48	114.74	2.19	61.75	m	**176.49**
Sum of two sides 2300mm	70.22	119.40	2.19	61.75	m	**181.14**
Sum of two sides 2400mm	72.51	123.29	2.38	67.10	m	**190.39**
Sum of two sides 2500mm	75.03	127.58	2.38	67.10	m	**194.68**
Extra over fittings; Ductwork 1001 to 1250mm longest side						
End Cap						
Sum of two sides 1300mm	19.48	33.12	1.69	47.65	nr	**80.77**
Sum of two sides 1400mm	21.06	35.82	1.69	47.65	nr	**83.47**
Sum of two sides 1500mm	24.24	41.22	1.69	47.65	nr	**88.86**
Sum of two sides 1600mm	27.41	46.60	1.69	47.65	nr	**94.25**
Sum of two sides 1700mm	30.58	52.00	1.69	47.65	nr	**99.65**
Sum of two sides 1800mm	33.75	57.39	1.69	47.65	nr	**105.04**
Sum of two sides 1900mm	36.93	62.79	1.69	47.65	nr	**110.44**
Sum of two sides 2000mm	38.51	65.49	1.69	47.65	nr	**113.14**
Sum of two sides 2100mm	41.69	70.89	1.69	47.65	nr	**118.53**
Sum of two sides 2200mm	44.86	76.27	1.69	47.65	nr	**123.92**
Sum of two sides 2300mm	48.03	81.66	1.69	47.65	nr	**129.31**
Sum of two sides 2400mm	51.20	87.06	1.69	47.65	nr	**134.71**
Sum of two sides 2500mm	54.38	92.47	1.69	47.65	nr	**140.12**
Reducer						
Sum of two sides 1300mm	15.19	25.82	1.69	47.65	nr	**73.47**
Sum of two sides 1400mm	16.46	27.99	1.69	47.65	nr	**75.64**
Sum of two sides 1500mm	19.02	32.35	2.47	69.64	nr	**101.99**
Sum of two sides 1600mm	21.65	36.82	2.47	69.64	nr	**106.46**
Sum of two sides 1700mm	24.22	41.18	2.47	69.64	nr	**110.82**
Sum of two sides 1800mm	26.77	45.52	2.59	73.02	nr	**118.55**
Sum of two sides 1900mm	29.34	49.88	2.71	76.41	nr	**126.29**
Sum of two sides 2000mm	30.68	52.17	2.59	73.02	nr	**125.20**
Sum of two sides 2100mm	33.25	56.53	2.92	82.33	nr	**138.86**
Sum of two sides 2200mm	35.81	60.89	2.92	82.33	nr	**143.22**
Sum of two sides 2300mm	38.43	65.35	2.92	82.33	nr	**147.68**
Sum of two sides 2400mm	40.99	69.71	3.12	87.97	nr	**157.67**
Sum of two sides 2500mm	43.62	74.17	3.12	87.97	nr	**162.14**

U:VENTILATION/AIR CONDITIONING SYSTEMS

Item	Net Price £	Material £	Labour hours	Labour £	Unit	Total rate £
Offset						
Sum of two sides 1300mm	34.13	58.03	1.69	47.65	nr	**105.68**
Sum of two sides 1400mm	36.13	61.43	1.69	47.65	nr	**109.08**
Sum of two sides 1500mm	40.08	68.16	2.47	69.64	nr	**137.80**
Sum of two sides 1600mm	44.03	74.86	2.47	69.64	nr	**144.50**
Sum of two sides 1700mm	47.83	81.32	2.59	73.02	nr	**154.35**
Sum of two sides 1800mm	51.56	87.67	2.61	73.59	nr	**161.26**
Sum of two sides 1900mm	55.22	93.89	2.71	76.41	nr	**170.29**
Sum of two sides 2000mm	57.04	97.00	2.71	76.41	nr	**173.40**
Sum of two sides 2100mm	60.58	103.01	2.92	82.33	nr	**185.34**
Sum of two sides 2200mm	64.67	109.96	3.26	91.91	nr	**201.88**
Sum of two sides 2300mm	69.37	117.96	3.26	91.91	nr	**209.87**
Sum of two sides 2400mm	74.05	125.92	3.48	98.12	nr	**224.03**
Sum of two sides 2500mm	78.76	133.91	3.48	98.12	nr	**232.03**
Square to round						
Sum of two sides 1300mm	28.03	47.66	1.69	47.65	nr	**95.31**
Sum of two sides 1400mm	30.76	52.30	1.69	47.65	nr	**99.95**
Sum of two sides 1500mm	36.21	61.58	2.38	67.10	nr	**128.68**
Sum of two sides 1600mm	41.68	70.88	2.38	67.10	nr	**137.98**
Sum of two sides 1700mm	47.14	80.15	2.55	71.90	nr	**152.05**
Sum of two sides 1800mm	52.59	89.43	2.55	71.90	nr	**161.33**
Sum of two sides 1900mm	58.05	98.71	2.83	79.79	nr	**178.50**
Sum of two sides 2000mm	60.79	103.36	2.83	79.79	nr	**183.15**
Sum of two sides 2100mm	66.24	112.64	3.85	108.55	nr	**221.19**
Sum of two sides 2200mm	71.70	121.92	4.18	117.85	nr	**239.77**
Sum of two sides 2300mm	77.17	131.22	4.22	118.98	nr	**250.21**
Sum of two sides 2400mm	82.63	140.50	4.68	131.95	nr	**272.45**
Sum of two sides 2500mm	88.10	149.80	4.70	132.51	nr	**282.31**
90 ° radius bend						
Sum of two sides 1300mm	16.37	27.84	1.69	47.65	nr	**75.49**
Sum of two sides 1400mm	18.53	31.51	1.69	47.65	nr	**79.16**
Sum of two sides 1500mm	22.85	38.86	2.11	59.49	nr	**98.35**
Sum of two sides 1600mm	27.20	46.24	2.11	59.49	nr	**105.73**
Sum of two sides 1700mm	31.52	53.59	2.19	61.75	nr	**115.34**
Sum of two sides 1800mm	35.83	60.92	2.19	61.75	nr	**122.66**
Sum of two sides 1900mm	40.15	68.27	2.48	69.92	nr	**138.19**
Sum of two sides 2000mm	42.33	71.99	2.26	63.72	nr	**135.70**
Sum of two sides 2100mm	46.66	79.33	2.48	69.92	nr	**149.25**
Sum of two sides 2200mm	50.98	86.68	2.48	69.92	nr	**156.60**
Sum of two sides 2300mm	53.30	90.64	2.48	69.92	nr	**160.56**
Sum of two sides 2400mm	57.61	97.96	3.90	109.96	nr	**207.91**
Sum of two sides 2500mm	61.93	105.30	3.90	109.96	nr	**215.26**
45 ° bend						
Sum of two sides 1300mm	18.70	31.80	1.69	47.65	nr	**79.45**
Sum of two sides 1400mm	20.37	34.64	1.69	47.65	nr	**82.29**
Sum of two sides 1500mm	23.72	40.34	2.49	70.20	nr	**110.54**
Sum of two sides 1600mm	27.14	46.14	2.49	70.20	nr	**116.35**
Sum of two sides 1700mm	30.49	51.84	2.67	75.28	nr	**127.12**
Sum of two sides 1800mm	33.83	57.53	2.67	75.28	nr	**132.81**
Sum of two sides 1900mm	37.18	63.22	3.06	86.28	nr	**149.49**
Sum of two sides 2000mm	38.93	66.20	3.06	86.28	nr	**152.47**
Sum of two sides 2100mm	42.28	71.89	4.05	114.19	nr	**186.07**
Sum of two sides 2200mm	45.62	77.57	4.05	114.19	nr	**191.76**
Sum of two sides 2300mm	48.25	82.05	4.39	123.77	nr	**205.83**
Sum of two sides 2400mm	51.59	87.73	4.85	136.74	nr	**224.47**
Sum of two sides 2500mm	55.01	93.54	4.85	136.74	nr	**230.28**

U:VENTILATION/AIR CONDITIONING SYSTEMS

Item	Net Price £	Material £	Labour hours	Labour £	Unit	Total rate £
U10 : DUCTWORK : RECTANGULAR – CLASS B (cont'd)						
Y30 - AIR DUCTLINES (cont'd)						
Fittings; Ductwork 1001 to 1250mm longest Side (cont'd)						
90 ° mitre bend						
Sum of two sides 1300mm	36.43	61.95	1.69	47.65	nr	**109.60**
Sum of two sides 1400mm	39.27	66.78	1.69	47.65	nr	**114.43**
Sum of two sides 1500mm	44.94	76.41	2.80	78.94	nr	**155.36**
Sum of two sides 1600mm	50.61	86.06	2.80	78.94	nr	**165.00**
Sum of two sides 1700mm	56.28	95.70	2.95	83.17	nr	**178.87**
Sum of two sides 1800mm	61.95	105.34	2.95	83.17	nr	**188.52**
Sum of two sides 1900mm	67.62	114.98	4.05	114.19	nr	**229.17**
Sum of two sides 2000mm	70.46	119.81	4.05	114.19	nr	**234.00**
Sum of two sides 2100mm	76.13	129.46	4.07	114.75	nr	**244.21**
Sum of two sides 2200mm	81.80	139.09	4.07	114.75	nr	**253.84**
Sum of two sides 2300mm	85.83	145.95	4.39	123.77	nr	**269.72**
Sum of two sides 2400mm	91.53	155.64	4.85	136.74	nr	**292.38**
Sum of two sides 2500mm	97.22	165.31	4.85	136.74	nr	**302.06**
Branch						
Sum of two sides 1300mm	32.68	55.56	1.44	40.60	nr	**96.16**
Sum of two sides 1400mm	35.07	59.64	1.44	40.60	nr	**100.24**
Sum of two sides 1500mm	39.87	67.79	1.64	46.24	nr	**114.03**
Sum of two sides 1600mm	44.73	76.05	1.64	46.24	nr	**122.29**
Sum of two sides 1700mm	49.51	84.19	1.64	46.24	nr	**130.43**
Sum of two sides 1800mm	54.30	92.34	1.64	46.24	nr	**138.58**
Sum of two sides 1900mm	59.10	100.49	1.69	47.65	nr	**148.13**
Sum of two sides 2000mm	61.56	104.67	1.69	47.65	nr	**152.32**
Sum of two sides 2100mm	66.36	112.83	1.85	52.16	nr	**164.99**
Sum of two sides 2200mm	71.14	120.97	1.85	52.16	nr	**173.13**
Sum of two sides 2300mm	76.00	129.24	2.61	73.59	nr	**202.82**
Sum of two sides 2400mm	80.80	137.38	2.61	73.59	nr	**210.97**
Sum of two sides 2500mm	85.66	145.65	2.61	73.59	nr	**219.24**
Grille neck						
Sum of two sides 1300mm	36.51	62.09	1.79	50.47	nr	**112.56**
Sum of two sides 1400mm	39.42	67.03	1.79	50.47	nr	**117.50**
Sum of two sides 1500mm	45.23	76.91	1.79	50.47	nr	**127.38**
Sum of two sides 1600mm	51.05	86.80	1.79	50.47	nr	**137.27**
Sum of two sides 1700mm	56.86	96.69	1.86	52.44	nr	**149.13**
Sum of two sides 1800mm	62.68	106.57	2.02	56.95	nr	**163.53**
Sum of two sides 1900mm	68.49	116.46	2.02	56.95	nr	**173.41**
Sum of two sides 2000mm	71.39	121.40	2.02	56.95	nr	**178.35**
Sum of two sides 2100mm	77.21	131.29	2.61	73.59	nr	**204.88**
Sum of two sides 2200mm	83.03	141.18	2.61	73.59	nr	**214.77**
Sum of two sides 2300mm	88.84	151.07	2.61	73.59	nr	**224.66**
Sum of two sides 2400mm	94.66	160.95	2.88	81.20	nr	**242.15**
Sum of two sides 2500mm	100.47	170.84	2.88	81.20	nr	**252.04**

U:VENTILATION/AIR CONDITIONING SYSTEMS

Item	Net Price £	Material £	Labour hours	Labour £	Unit	Total rate £
Ductwork 1251 to 1600mm longest side						
Sum of two sides 1700mm	67.07	114.04	1.55	43.70	m	**157.74**
Sum of two sides 1800mm	69.62	118.38	1.61	45.39	m	**163.77**
Sum of two sides 1900mm	72.24	122.84	1.61	45.39	m	**168.23**
Sum of two sides 2000mm	74.64	126.92	1.61	45.39	m	**172.31**
Sum of two sides 2100mm	77.04	130.99	2.17	61.18	m	**192.18**
Sum of two sides 2200mm	79.44	135.07	2.19	61.75	m	**196.82**
Sum of two sides 2300mm	82.05	139.52	2.19	61.75	m	**201.27**
Sum of two sides 2400mm	84.59	143.84	2.38	67.10	m	**210.94**
Sum of two sides 2500mm	86.99	147.92	2.38	67.10	m	**215.02**
Sum of two sides 2600mm	89.38	151.99	2.64	74.43	m	**226.42**
Sum of two sides 2700mm	91.78	156.07	2.66	75.00	m	**231.06**
Sum of two sides 2800mm	94.33	160.40	2.95	83.17	m	**243.58**
Sum of two sides 2900mm	106.16	180.52	2.96	83.46	m	**263.97**
Sum of two sides 3000mm	108.57	184.62	3.15	88.81	m	**273.43**
Sum of two sides 3100mm	111.10	188.91	3.15	88.81	m	**277.73**
Sum of two sides 3200mm	113.50	192.99	3.18	89.66	m	**282.65**
Extra over fittings; Ductwork 1251 to 1600mm longest side						
End Cap						
Sum of two sides 1700mm	38.96	66.25	0.58	16.35	nr	**82.60**
Sum of two sides 1800mm	43.22	73.49	0.58	16.35	nr	**89.85**
Sum of two sides 1900mm	47.48	80.74	0.58	16.35	nr	**97.09**
Sum of two sides 2000mm	51.75	87.99	0.58	16.35	nr	**104.34**
Sum of two sides 2100mm	56.00	95.23	0.87	24.53	nr	**119.76**
Sum of two sides 2200mm	60.27	102.47	0.87	24.53	nr	**127.00**
Sum of two sides 2300mm	64.53	109.72	0.87	24.53	nr	**134.25**
Sum of two sides 2400mm	68.79	116.97	0.87	24.53	nr	**141.50**
Sum of two sides 2500mm	73.06	124.24	0.87	24.53	nr	**148.77**
Sum of two sides 2600mm	77.32	131.47	0.87	24.53	nr	**156.00**
Sum of two sides 2700mm	81.58	138.72	0.87	24.53	nr	**163.25**
Sum of two sides 2800mm	85.85	145.97	1.16	32.71	nr	**178.68**
Sum of two sides 2900mm	90.11	153.22	1.16	32.71	nr	**185.92**
Sum of two sides 3000mm	94.37	160.46	1.73	48.78	nr	**209.24**
Sum of two sides 3100mm	97.74	166.19	1.80	50.75	nr	**216.94**
Sum of two sides 3200mm	100.80	171.39	1.80	50.75	nr	**222.14**
Reducer						
Sum of two sides 1700mm	17.41	29.61	2.47	69.64	nr	**99.25**
Sum of two sides 1800mm	20.04	34.07	2.59	73.02	nr	**107.09**
Sum of two sides 1900mm	22.70	38.60	2.71	76.41	nr	**115.00**
Sum of two sides 2000mm	25.30	43.02	2.71	76.41	nr	**119.42**
Sum of two sides 2100mm	27.90	47.44	2.92	82.33	nr	**129.77**
Sum of two sides 2200mm	30.51	51.88	2.92	82.33	nr	**134.21**
Sum of two sides 2300mm	33.17	56.40	2.92	82.33	nr	**138.73**
Sum of two sides 2400mm	35.79	60.86	3.12	87.97	nr	**148.83**
Sum of two sides 2500mm	38.40	65.29	3.12	87.97	nr	**153.25**
Sum of two sides 2600mm	41.00	69.72	3.12	87.97	nr	**157.68**
Sum of two sides 2700mm	43.60	74.14	3.12	87.97	nr	**162.11**
Sum of two sides 2800mm	46.23	78.60	3.95	111.37	nr	**189.97**
Sum of two sides 2900mm	45.85	77.96	3.97	111.93	nr	**189.90**
Sum of two sides 3000mm	48.45	82.39	4.52	127.44	nr	**209.83**
Sum of two sides 3100mm	50.40	85.70	4.52	127.44	nr	**213.14**
Sum of two sides 3200mm	52.18	88.72	4.52	127.44	nr	**216.16**

U:VENTILATION/AIR CONDITIONING SYSTEMS

Item	Net Price £	Material £	Labour hours	Labour £	Unit	Total rate £
U10 : DUCTWORK : RECTANGULAR – CLASS B (cont'd)						
Y30 - AIR DUCTLINES (cont'd)						
Fittings; Ductwork 1251 to 1600mm longest Side (cont'd)						
Offset						
Sum of two sides 1700mm	55.64	94.62	2.59	73.02	nr	167.64
Sum of two sides 1800mm	61.76	105.02	2.61	73.59	nr	178.61
Sum of two sides 1900mm	65.91	112.07	2.71	76.41	nr	188.48
Sum of two sides 2000mm	69.87	118.81	2.71	76.41	nr	195.22
Sum of two sides 2100mm	73.72	125.35	2.92	82.33	nr	207.67
Sum of two sides 2200mm	77.45	131.69	3.26	91.91	nr	223.61
Sum of two sides 2300mm	81.10	137.90	3.26	91.91	nr	229.82
Sum of two sides 2400mm	86.95	147.85	3.47	97.83	nr	245.68
Sum of two sides 2500mm	90.39	153.70	3.48	98.12	nr	251.81
Sum of two sides 2600mm	96.15	163.49	3.49	98.40	nr	261.89
Sum of two sides 2700mm	101.92	173.30	3.50	98.68	nr	271.98
Sum of two sides 2800mm	107.71	183.15	4.34	122.36	nr	305.51
Sum of two sides 2900mm	107.72	183.17	4.76	134.21	nr	317.37
Sum of two sides 3000mm	113.48	192.96	5.32	149.99	nr	342.96
Sum of two sides 3100mm	117.98	200.61	5.35	150.84	nr	351.45
Sum of two sides 3200mm	122.15	207.70	5.35	150.84	nr	358.54
Square to round						
Sum of two sides 1700mm	44.10	74.98	2.55	71.90	nr	146.88
Sum of two sides 1800mm	51.18	87.03	2.55	71.90	nr	158.93
Sum of two sides 1900mm	58.21	98.99	2.83	79.79	nr	178.78
Sum of two sides 2000mm	65.26	110.97	2.83	79.79	nr	190.76
Sum of two sides 2100mm	72.31	122.95	3.85	108.55	nr	231.50
Sum of two sides 2200mm	79.35	134.93	4.18	117.85	nr	252.79
Sum of two sides 2300mm	86.39	146.89	4.22	118.98	nr	265.87
Sum of two sides 2400mm	93.47	158.93	4.68	131.95	nr	290.89
Sum of two sides 2500mm	100.52	170.92	4.70	132.51	nr	303.43
Sum of two sides 2600mm	107.56	182.90	4.70	132.51	nr	315.41
Sum of two sides 2700mm	114.62	194.89	4.71	132.80	nr	327.69
Sum of two sides 2800mm	121.70	206.94	8.19	230.91	nr	437.85
Sum of two sides 2900mm	122.08	207.58	8.62	243.04	nr	450.61
Sum of two sides 3000mm	129.12	219.55	8.75	246.70	nr	466.26
Sum of two sides 3100mm	134.39	228.51	8.75	246.70	nr	475.21
Sum of two sides 3200mm	139.16	236.63	8.75	246.70	nr	483.33
90 ° radius bend						
Sum of two sides 1700mm	50.22	85.40	2.19	61.75	nr	147.15
Sum of two sides 1800mm	54.91	93.37	2.19	61.75	nr	155.11
Sum of two sides 1900mm	61.89	105.23	2.26	63.72	nr	168.95
Sum of two sides 2000mm	68.72	116.85	2.26	63.72	nr	180.57
Sum of two sides 2100mm	75.55	128.47	2.48	69.92	nr	198.39
Sum of two sides 2200mm	82.38	140.08	2.48	69.92	nr	210.00
Sum of two sides 2300mm	89.36	151.95	2.48	69.92	nr	221.87
Sum of two sides 2400mm	93.81	159.51	3.90	109.96	nr	269.47
Sum of two sides 2500mm	100.62	171.09	3.90	109.96	nr	281.05
Sum of two sides 2600mm	107.42	182.66	4.26	120.11	nr	302.77
Sum of two sides 2700mm	114.23	194.23	4.55	128.29	nr	322.52
Sum of two sides 2800mm	118.51	201.52	4.55	128.29	nr	329.81
Sum of two sides 2900mm	118.67	201.78	6.87	193.70	nr	395.48

U:VENTILATION/AIR CONDITIONING SYSTEMS

Item	Net Price £	Material £	Labour hours	Labour £	Unit	Total rate £
Sum of two sides 3000mm	125.45	213.32	7.00	197.36	nr	**410.68**
Sum of two sides 3100mm	130.70	222.23	7.00	197.36	nr	**419.59**
Sum of two sides 3200mm	135.52	230.44	7.00	197.36	nr	**427.80**
45 ° bend						
Sum of two sides 1700mm	23.98	40.78	2.67	75.28	nr	**116.06**
Sum of two sides 1800mm	26.28	44.69	2.67	75.28	nr	**119.97**
Sum of two sides 1900mm	29.74	50.57	3.06	86.28	nr	**136.85**
Sum of two sides 2000mm	33.13	56.34	3.06	86.28	nr	**142.62**
Sum of two sides 2100mm	36.53	62.11	4.05	114.19	nr	**176.30**
Sum of two sides 2200mm	39.92	67.88	4.05	114.19	nr	**182.06**
Sum of two sides 2300mm	43.38	73.75	4.39	123.77	nr	**197.53**
Sum of two sides 2400mm	45.56	77.47	4.85	136.74	nr	**214.22**
Sum of two sides 2500mm	48.94	83.22	4.85	136.74	nr	**219.96**
Sum of two sides 2600mm	52.32	88.96	4.87	137.31	nr	**226.27**
Sum of two sides 2700mm	55.70	94.71	4.87	137.31	nr	**232.01**
Sum of two sides 2800mm	57.80	98.28	8.81	248.39	nr	**346.67**
Sum of two sides 2900mm	57.64	98.02	8.81	248.39	nr	**346.41**
Sum of two sides 3000mm	61.01	103.74	9.31	262.49	nr	**366.23**
Sum of two sides 3100mm	63.60	108.15	9.31	262.49	nr	**370.64**
Sum of two sides 3200mm	66.00	112.23	9.39	264.75	nr	**376.98**
90 ° mitre bend						
Sum of two sides 1700mm	59.68	101.48	2.67	75.28	nr	**176.76**
Sum of two sides 1800mm	63.68	108.28	2.80	78.94	nr	**187.23**
Sum of two sides 1900mm	70.98	120.70	2.95	83.17	nr	**203.87**
Sum of two sides 2000mm	78.31	133.15	2.95	83.17	nr	**216.33**
Sum of two sides 2100mm	85.63	145.60	4.05	114.19	nr	**259.79**
Sum of two sides 2200mm	92.95	158.05	4.05	114.19	nr	**272.23**
Sum of two sides 2300mm	100.25	170.46	4.39	123.77	nr	**294.23**
Sum of two sides 2400mm	104.16	177.11	4.85	136.74	nr	**313.85**
Sum of two sides 2500mm	111.50	189.59	4.85	136.74	nr	**326.34**
Sum of two sides 2600mm	118.84	202.07	4.87	137.31	nr	**339.38**
Sum of two sides 2700mm	126.18	214.55	4.87	137.31	nr	**351.85**
Sum of two sides 2800mm	130.00	221.04	8.81	248.39	nr	**469.44**
Sum of two sides 2900mm	130.16	221.32	14.81	417.56	nr	**638.88**
Sum of two sides 3000mm	137.52	233.83	15.20	428.56	nr	**662.39**
Sum of two sides 3100mm	143.52	244.04	15.60	439.83	nr	**683.87**
Sum of two sides 3200mm	149.23	253.74	15.60	439.83	nr	**693.58**
Branch						
Sum of two sides 1700mm	47.14	80.16	1.69	47.65	nr	**127.81**
Sum of two sides 1800mm	51.94	88.32	1.69	47.65	nr	**135.97**
Sum of two sides 1900mm	56.80	96.59	1.85	52.16	nr	**148.75**
Sum of two sides 2000mm	61.59	104.73	1.85	52.16	nr	**156.89**
Sum of two sides 2100mm	66.39	112.89	2.61	73.59	nr	**186.48**
Sum of two sides 2200mm	71.18	121.04	2.61	73.59	nr	**194.63**
Sum of two sides 2300mm	76.04	129.31	2.61	73.59	nr	**202.89**
Sum of two sides 2400mm	80.84	137.46	2.88	81.20	nr	**218.66**
Sum of two sides 2500mm	85.63	145.61	2.88	81.20	nr	**226.81**
Sum of two sides 2600mm	90.42	153.75	2.88	81.20	nr	**234.95**
Sum of two sides 2700mm	95.21	161.89	2.88	81.20	nr	**243.09**
Sum of two sides 2800mm	100.01	170.05	3.94	111.09	nr	**281.14**
Sum of two sides 2900mm	104.87	178.32	3.94	111.09	nr	**289.40**
Sum of two sides 3000mm	109.66	186.47	4.83	136.18	nr	**322.64**
Sum of two sides 3100mm	113.48	192.96	4.83	136.18	nr	**329.14**
Sum of two sides 3200mm	116.96	198.87	4.83	136.18	nr	**335.05**

U:VENTILATION/AIR CONDITIONING SYSTEMS

Item	Net Price £	Material £	Labour hours	Labour £	Unit	Total rate £
U10 : DUCTWORK : RECTANGULAR – CLASS B (cont'd)						
Y30 - AIR DUCTLINES (cont'd)						
Fittings; Ductwork 1251 to 1600mm longest Side (cont'd)						
Grille neck						
Sum of two sides 1700mm	57.68	98.08	1.86	52.44	nr	**150.52**
Sum of two sides 1800mm	63.89	108.64	2.02	56.95	nr	**165.60**
Sum of two sides 1900mm	70.11	119.22	2.02	56.95	nr	**176.17**
Sum of two sides 2000mm	76.33	129.79	2.02	56.95	nr	**186.74**
Sum of two sides 2100mm	82.54	140.35	2.61	73.59	nr	**213.94**
Sum of two sides 2200mm	88.76	150.93	2.61	73.59	nr	**224.52**
Sum of two sides 2300mm	94.98	161.49	2.61	73.59	nr	**235.08**
Sum of two sides 2400mm	101.19	172.06	2.88	81.20	nr	**253.26**
Sum of two sides 2500mm	107.41	182.64	2.88	81.20	nr	**263.84**
Sum of two sides 2600mm	113.62	193.19	2.88	81.20	nr	**274.39**
Sum of two sides 2700mm	119.83	203.76	2.88	81.20	nr	**284.96**
Sum of two sides 2800mm	126.05	214.34	3.94	111.09	nr	**325.42**
Sum of two sides 2900mm	132.27	224.90	4.12	116.16	nr	**341.06**
Sum of two sides 3000mm	138.48	235.47	5.00	140.97	nr	**376.44**
Sum of two sides 3100mm	143.42	243.87	5.00	140.97	nr	**384.84**
Sum of two sides 3200mm	147.92	251.51	5.00	140.97	nr	**392.49**
Ductwork 1601 to 2000mm longest side						
Sum of two sides 2100mm	83.21	141.49	2.17	61.18	m	**202.67**
Sum of two sides 2200mm	85.78	145.86	2.17	61.18	m	**207.04**
Sum of two sides 2300mm	88.40	150.32	2.19	61.75	m	**212.06**
Sum of two sides 2400mm	90.89	154.55	2.38	67.10	m	**221.65**
Sum of two sides 2500mm	93.52	159.02	2.38	67.10	m	**226.13**
Sum of two sides 2600mm	95.94	163.13	2.64	74.43	m	**237.57**
Sum of two sides 2700mm	98.37	167.26	2.66	75.00	m	**242.26**
Sum of two sides 2800mm	100.78	171.37	2.95	83.17	m	**254.54**
Sum of two sides 2900mm	103.42	175.85	2.96	83.46	m	**259.30**
Sum of two sides 3000mm	105.83	179.96	2.96	83.46	m	**263.41**
Sum of two sides 3100mm	114.86	195.30	2.96	83.46	m	**278.76**
Sum of two sides 3200mm	117.27	199.41	3.15	88.81	m	**288.22**
Sum of two sides 3300mm	128.81	219.03	3.15	88.81	m	**307.85**
Sum of two sides 3400mm	131.23	223.14	3.15	88.81	m	**311.96**
Sum of two sides 3500mm	133.66	227.27	3.15	88.81	m	**316.08**
Sum of two sides 3600mm	136.08	231.38	3.18	89.66	m	**321.04**
Sum of two sides 3700mm	138.71	235.86	3.18	89.66	m	**325.52**
Sum of two sides 3800mm	141.13	239.97	3.18	89.66	m	**329.63**
Sum of two sides 3900mm	143.55	244.10	3.18	89.66	m	**333.75**
Sum of two sides 4000mm	145.97	248.20	3.18	89.66	m	**337.86**

U:VENTILATION/AIR CONDITIONING SYSTEMS

Item	Net Price £	Material £	Labour hours	Labour £	Unit	Total rate £
Extra over fittings; Ductwork 1601 to 2000mm longest side						
End Cap						
Sum of two sides 2100mm	70.48	119.84	0.87	24.53	nr	**144.37**
Sum of two sides 2200mm	75.84	128.96	0.87	24.53	nr	**153.48**
Sum of two sides 2300mm	81.20	138.07	0.87	24.53	nr	**162.60**
Sum of two sides 2400mm	86.56	147.19	0.87	24.53	nr	**171.72**
Sum of two sides 2500mm	91.94	156.33	0.87	24.53	nr	**180.86**
Sum of two sides 2600mm	97.30	165.45	0.87	24.53	nr	**189.98**
Sum of two sides 2700mm	102.67	174.57	0.87	24.53	nr	**199.10**
Sum of two sides 2800mm	108.03	183.69	1.16	32.71	nr	**216.39**
Sum of two sides 2900mm	113.39	192.80	1.16	32.71	nr	**225.51**
Sum of two sides 3000mm	118.75	201.92	1.73	48.78	nr	**250.70**
Sum of two sides 3100mm	122.99	209.14	1.80	50.75	nr	**259.89**
Sum of two sides 3200mm	126.84	215.68	1.80	50.75	nr	**266.43**
Sum of two sides 3300mm	130.69	222.22	1.80	50.75	nr	**272.97**
Sum of two sides 3400mm	134.54	228.76	1.80	50.75	nr	**279.51**
Sum of two sides 3500mm	138.38	235.30	1.80	50.75	nr	**286.05**
Sum of two sides 3600mm	142.24	241.86	1.80	50.75	nr	**292.61**
Sum of two sides 3700mm	146.08	248.38	1.80	50.75	nr	**299.13**
Sum of two sides 3800mm	149.92	254.92	1.80	50.75	nr	**305.67**
Sum of two sides 3900mm	153.78	261.48	1.80	50.75	nr	**312.23**
Sum of two sides 4000mm	157.62	268.01	1.80	50.75	nr	**318.76**
Reducer						
Sum of two sides 2100mm	28.03	47.65	2.61	73.59	nr	**121.24**
Sum of two sides 2200mm	30.64	52.09	2.61	73.59	nr	**125.68**
Sum of two sides 2300mm	33.30	56.62	2.61	73.59	nr	**130.21**
Sum of two sides 2400mm	35.86	60.98	2.88	81.20	nr	**142.18**
Sum of two sides 2500mm	38.53	65.51	3.12	87.97	nr	**153.47**
Sum of two sides 2600mm	41.14	69.95	3.12	87.97	nr	**157.91**
Sum of two sides 2700mm	43.75	74.38	3.12	87.97	nr	**162.35**
Sum of two sides 2800mm	46.36	78.82	3.95	111.37	nr	**190.19**
Sum of two sides 2900mm	49.03	83.36	3.97	111.93	nr	**195.29**
Sum of two sides 3000mm	51.64	87.80	4.52	127.44	nr	**215.24**
Sum of two sides 3100mm	51.28	87.20	4.52	127.44	nr	**214.64**
Sum of two sides 3200mm	53.05	90.20	4.52	127.44	nr	**217.64**
Sum of two sides 3300mm	51.71	87.93	4.52	127.44	nr	**215.37**
Sum of two sides 3400mm	53.48	90.94	4.52	127.44	nr	**218.38**
Sum of two sides 3500mm	55.25	93.94	4.52	127.44	nr	**221.38**
Sum of two sides 3600mm	57.01	96.94	4.52	127.44	nr	**224.38**
Sum of two sides 3700mm	61.59	104.73	4.52	127.44	nr	**232.17**
Sum of two sides 3800mm	63.36	107.73	4.52	127.44	nr	**235.17**
Sum of two sides 3900mm	65.12	110.73	4.52	127.44	nr	**238.17**
Sum of two sides 4000mm	66.89	113.73	4.52	127.44	nr	**241.17**
Offset						
Sum of two sides 2100mm	84.28	143.31	2.61	73.59	nr	**216.90**
Sum of two sides 2200mm	90.58	154.03	2.61	73.59	nr	**227.61**
Sum of two sides 2300mm	94.21	160.19	2.61	73.59	nr	**233.78**
Sum of two sides 2400mm	103.19	175.46	2.88	81.20	nr	**256.66**
Sum of two sides 2500mm	106.69	181.42	3.48	98.12	nr	**279.53**
Sum of two sides 2600mm	109.98	187.01	3.49	98.40	nr	**285.40**
Sum of two sides 2700mm	113.14	192.38	3.50	98.68	nr	**291.06**
Sum of two sides 2800mm	116.17	197.53	4.34	122.36	nr	**319.90**
Sum of two sides 2900mm	119.11	202.53	4.76	134.21	nr	**336.74**

U:VENTILATION/AIR CONDITIONING SYSTEMS

Item	Net Price £	Material £	Labour hours	Labour £	Unit	Total rate £
U10 : DUCTWORK : RECTANGULAR – CLASS B (cont'd)						
Y30 - AIR DUCTLINES (cont'd)						
Fittings; Ductwork 1601 to 2000mm longest Side (cont'd)						
Offset (cont'd)						
Sum of two sides 3000mm	121.87	207.23	5.32	149.99	nr	**357.22**
Sum of two sides 3100mm	122.13	207.67	5.35	150.84	nr	**358.51**
Sum of two sides 3200mm	126.42	214.97	5.35	150.84	nr	**365.81**
Sum of two sides 3300mm	124.72	212.08	5.35	150.84	nr	**362.92**
Sum of two sides 3400mm	129.01	219.37	5.35	150.84	nr	**370.21**
Sum of two sides 3500mm	133.31	226.68	5.35	150.84	nr	**377.52**
Sum of two sides 3600mm	137.60	233.98	5.35	150.84	nr	**384.82**
Sum of two sides 3700mm	145.45	247.31	5.35	150.84	nr	**398.15**
Sum of two sides 3800mm	149.74	254.62	5.35	150.84	nr	**405.46**
Sum of two sides 3900mm	154.04	261.92	5.35	150.84	nr	**412.76**
Sum of two sides 4000mm	158.33	269.22	5.35	150.84	nr	**420.06**
Square to round						
Sum of two sides 2100mm	77.94	132.52	2.61	73.59	nr	**206.11**
Sum of two sides 2200mm	85.47	145.33	2.61	73.59	nr	**218.92**
Sum of two sides 2300mm	92.95	158.06	2.61	73.59	nr	**231.64**
Sum of two sides 2400mm	100.52	170.92	2.88	81.20	nr	**252.12**
Sum of two sides 2500mm	108.01	183.66	4.70	132.51	nr	**316.17**
Sum of two sides 2600mm	115.52	196.42	4.70	132.51	nr	**328.94**
Sum of two sides 2700mm	123.03	209.20	4.71	132.80	nr	**341.99**
Sum of two sides 2800mm	130.53	221.95	8.19	230.91	nr	**452.87**
Sum of two sides 2900mm	138.02	234.69	8.19	230.91	nr	**465.60**
Sum of two sides 3000mm	145.53	247.46	8.19	230.91	nr	**478.38**
Sum of two sides 3100mm	146.82	249.64	8.19	230.91	nr	**480.56**
Sum of two sides 3200mm	151.92	258.32	8.19	230.91	nr	**489.23**
Sum of two sides 3300mm	151.01	256.77	8.19	230.91	nr	**487.68**
Sum of two sides 3400mm	156.11	265.44	8.62	243.04	nr	**508.47**
Sum of two sides 3500mm	161.20	274.11	8.62	243.04	nr	**517.14**
Sum of two sides 3600mm	166.30	282.77	8.62	243.04	nr	**525.81**
Sum of two sides 3700mm	174.01	295.88	8.62	243.04	nr	**538.91**
Sum of two sides 3800mm	179.10	304.54	8.75	246.70	nr	**551.25**
Sum of two sides 3900mm	184.21	313.22	8.75	246.70	nr	**559.92**
Sum of two sides 4000mm	189.30	321.89	8.75	246.70	nr	**568.59**
90 ° radius bend						
Sum of two sides 2100mm	61.08	103.85	2.61	73.59	nr	**177.44**
Sum of two sides 2200mm	118.18	200.95	2.61	73.59	nr	**274.54**
Sum of two sides 2300mm	127.77	217.25	2.61	73.59	nr	**290.84**
Sum of two sides 2400mm	131.04	222.82	2.88	81.20	nr	**304.02**
Sum of two sides 2500mm	140.57	239.03	3.90	109.96	nr	**348.99**
Sum of two sides 2600mm	149.89	254.87	4.26	120.11	nr	**374.98**
Sum of two sides 2700mm	159.20	270.71	4.55	128.29	nr	**398.99**
Sum of two sides 2800mm	168.51	286.53	4.55	128.29	nr	**414.82**
Sum of two sides 2900mm	178.05	302.75	6.87	193.70	nr	**496.44**
Sum of two sides 3000mm	187.36	318.59	6.87	193.70	nr	**512.29**
Sum of two sides 3100mm	189.22	321.75	6.87	193.70	nr	**515.44**
Sum of two sides 3200mm	195.91	333.12	6.87	193.70	nr	**526.82**
Sum of two sides 3300mm	195.38	332.21	6.87	193.70	nr	**525.91**
Sum of two sides 3400mm	202.07	343.59	7.00	197.36	nr	**540.95**

U:VENTILATION/AIR CONDITIONING SYSTEMS

Item	Net Price £	Material £	Labour hours	Labour £	Unit	Total rate £
Sum of two sides 3500mm	208.76	354.98	7.00	197.36	nr	**552.34**
Sum of two sides 3600mm	215.45	366.35	7.00	197.36	nr	**563.71**
Sum of two sides 3700mm	230.93	392.66	7.00	197.36	nr	**590.03**
Sum of two sides 3800mm	237.62	404.04	7.00	197.36	nr	**601.40**
Sum of two sides 3900mm	244.31	415.42	7.00	197.36	nr	**612.78**
Sum of two sides 4000mm	251.00	426.80	7.00	197.36	nr	**624.16**
45 ° bend						
Sum of two sides 2100mm	27.36	46.52	2.61	73.59	nr	**120.11**
Sum of two sides 2200mm	79.04	134.40	2.61	73.59	nr	**207.99**
Sum of two sides 2300mm	85.08	144.66	2.61	73.59	nr	**218.25**
Sum of two sides 2400mm	87.98	149.60	2.88	81.20	nr	**230.80**
Sum of two sides 2500mm	93.99	159.82	4.85	136.74	nr	**296.57**
Sum of two sides 2600mm	99.84	169.77	4.87	137.31	nr	**307.08**
Sum of two sides 2700mm	105.69	179.72	4.87	137.31	nr	**317.02**
Sum of two sides 2800mm	111.54	189.66	8.81	248.39	nr	**438.06**
Sum of two sides 2900mm	117.56	199.89	8.81	248.39	nr	**448.28**
Sum of two sides 3000mm	123.41	209.85	9.31	262.49	nr	**472.34**
Sum of two sides 3100mm	125.34	213.13	9.31	262.49	nr	**475.62**
Sum of two sides 3200mm	129.56	220.30	9.31	262.49	nr	**482.79**
Sum of two sides 3300mm	130.27	221.51	9.31	262.49	nr	**484.00**
Sum of two sides 3400mm	134.50	228.70	9.31	262.49	nr	**491.19**
Sum of two sides 3500mm	138.72	235.88	9.39	264.75	nr	**500.62**
Sum of two sides 3600mm	142.94	243.06	9.39	264.75	nr	**507.80**
Sum of two sides 3700mm	152.64	259.55	9.39	264.75	nr	**524.30**
Sum of two sides 3800mm	156.86	266.73	9.39	264.75	nr	**531.47**
Sum of two sides 3900mm	161.08	273.90	9.39	264.75	nr	**538.65**
Sum of two sides 4000mm	165.31	281.08	9.39	264.75	nr	**545.83**
90 ° mitre bend						
Sum of two sides 2100mm	144.48	245.67	2.61	73.59	nr	**319.26**
Sum of two sides 2200mm	152.58	259.45	2.61	73.59	nr	**333.04**
Sum of two sides 2300mm	164.48	279.67	2.61	73.59	nr	**353.26**
Sum of two sides 2400mm	168.38	286.31	2.88	81.20	nr	**367.51**
Sum of two sides 2500mm	180.26	306.51	4.85	136.74	nr	**443.26**
Sum of two sides 2600mm	192.23	326.87	4.87	137.31	nr	**464.17**
Sum of two sides 2700mm	204.20	347.21	4.87	137.31	nr	**484.52**
Sum of two sides 2800mm	216.16	367.55	8.81	248.39	nr	**615.95**
Sum of two sides 2900mm	228.04	387.76	14.81	417.56	nr	**805.32**
Sum of two sides 3000mm	240.01	408.11	15.20	428.56	nr	**836.66**
Sum of two sides 3100mm	242.92	413.06	15.20	428.56	nr	**841.61**
Sum of two sides 3200mm	252.12	428.70	15.20	428.56	nr	**857.26**
Sum of two sides 3300mm	253.76	431.48	15.20	428.56	nr	**860.04**
Sum of two sides 3400mm	262.96	447.13	15.20	428.56	nr	**875.68**
Sum of two sides 3500mm	272.16	462.77	15.60	439.83	nr	**902.60**
Sum of two sides 3600mm	281.36	478.41	15.60	439.83	nr	**918.25**
Sum of two sides 3700mm	293.49	499.04	15.60	439.83	nr	**938.87**
Sum of two sides 3800mm	302.69	514.68	15.60	439.83	nr	**954.52**
Sum of two sides 3900mm	311.89	530.33	15.60	439.83	nr	**970.16**
Sum of two sides 4000mm	321.08	545.96	15.60	439.83	nr	**985.79**

U:VENTILATION/AIR CONDITIONING SYSTEMS

Item	Net Price £	Material £	Labour hours	Labour £	Unit	Total rate £
U10 : DUCTWORK : RECTANGULAR – CLASS B (cont'd)						
Y30 - AIR DUCTLINES (cont'd)						
Fittings; Ductwork 1601 to 2000mm longest Side (cont'd)						
Branch						
Sum of two sides 2100mm	65.87	112.01	2.61	73.59	nr	185.60
Sum of two sides 2200mm	70.50	119.88	2.61	73.59	nr	193.47
Sum of two sides 2300mm	75.22	127.90	2.61	73.59	nr	201.48
Sum of two sides 2400mm	79.76	135.62	2.88	81.20	nr	216.82
Sum of two sides 2500mm	84.47	143.63	2.88	81.20	nr	224.83
Sum of two sides 2600mm	89.10	151.51	2.88	81.20	nr	232.71
Sum of two sides 2700mm	93.74	159.39	2.88	81.20	nr	240.59
Sum of two sides 2800mm	98.37	167.27	3.94	111.09	nr	278.36
Sum of two sides 2900mm	103.09	175.29	3.94	111.09	nr	286.38
Sum of two sides 3000mm	107.72	183.17	3.94	111.09	nr	294.25
Sum of two sides 3100mm	111.42	189.45	3.94	111.09	nr	300.54
Sum of two sides 3200mm	114.78	195.17	3.94	111.09	nr	306.26
Sum of two sides 3300mm	118.22	201.02	3.94	111.09	nr	312.11
Sum of two sides 3400mm	121.58	206.74	4.83	136.18	nr	342.92
Sum of two sides 3500mm	124.95	212.47	4.83	136.18	nr	348.65
Sum of two sides 3600mm	128.32	218.18	4.83	136.18	nr	354.36
Sum of two sides 3700mm	133.31	226.68	4.83	136.18	nr	362.86
Sum of two sides 3800mm	136.68	232.40	4.83	136.18	nr	368.58
Sum of two sides 3900mm	140.04	238.12	4.83	136.18	nr	374.30
Sum of two sides 4000mm	143.41	243.85	4.83	136.18	nr	380.02
Grille neck						
Sum of two sides 2100mm	80.52	136.91	2.61	73.59	nr	210.50
Sum of two sides 2200mm	86.58	147.22	2.61	73.59	nr	220.81
Sum of two sides 2300mm	92.65	157.54	2.61	73.59	nr	231.12
Sum of two sides 2400mm	98.71	167.84	2.88	81.20	nr	249.04
Sum of two sides 2500mm	104.77	178.15	2.88	81.20	nr	259.35
Sum of two sides 2600mm	110.83	188.45	2.88	81.20	nr	269.65
Sum of two sides 2700mm	116.89	198.76	2.88	81.20	nr	279.96
Sum of two sides 2800mm	122.96	209.08	3.94	111.09	nr	320.16
Sum of two sides 2900mm	129.02	219.38	4.12	116.16	nr	335.55
Sum of two sides 3000mm	135.09	229.70	4.12	116.16	nr	345.86
Sum of two sides 3100mm	139.90	237.89	4.12	116.16	nr	354.05
Sum of two sides 3200mm	144.29	245.34	4.12	116.16	nr	361.51
Sum of two sides 3300mm	148.66	252.78	4.12	116.16	nr	368.94
Sum of two sides 3400mm	153.05	260.24	5.00	140.97	nr	401.21
Sum of two sides 3500mm	157.43	267.69	5.00	140.97	nr	408.66
Sum of two sides 3600mm	161.81	275.13	5.00	140.97	nr	416.11
Sum of two sides 3700mm	166.19	282.59	5.00	140.97	nr	423.56
Sum of two sides 3800mm	170.57	290.04	5.00	140.97	nr	431.01
Sum of two sides 3900mm	174.95	297.49	5.00	140.97	nr	438.46
Sum of two sides 4000mm	179.33	304.93	5.00	140.97	nr	445.91

U:VENTILATION/AIR CONDITIONING SYSTEMS

Item	Net Price £	Material £	Labour hours	Labour £	Unit	Total rate £
Ductwork 2001 to 2500mm longest side						
Sum of two sides 2500mm	97.37	165.57	2.38	67.10	m	**232.68**
Sum of two sides 2600mm	102.22	173.81	2.64	74.43	m	**248.24**
Sum of two sides 2700mm	109.30	185.86	2.66	75.00	m	**260.85**
Sum of two sides 2800mm	112.46	191.22	2.95	83.17	m	**274.40**
Sum of two sides 2900mm	119.67	203.48	2.96	83.46	m	**286.94**
Sum of two sides 3000mm	126.15	214.51	3.15	88.81	m	**303.32**
Sum of two sides 3100mm	136.10	231.42	3.15	88.81	m	**320.23**
Sum of two sides 3200mm	137.75	234.23	3.15	88.81	m	**323.04**
Sum of two sides 3300mm	149.96	254.99	3.15	88.81	m	**343.80**
Sum of two sides 3400mm	153.44	260.91	3.15	88.81	m	**349.72**
Sum of two sides 3500mm	156.86	266.72	2.66	75.00	m	**341.71**
Sum of two sides 3600mm	161.29	274.25	3.18	89.66	m	**363.91**
Sum of two sides 3700mm	170.44	289.81	3.18	89.66	m	**379.47**
Sum of two sides 3800mm	174.93	297.45	3.18	89.66	m	**387.11**
Sum of two sides 3900mm	179.50	305.21	3.18	89.66	m	**394.87**
Sum of two sides 4000mm	182.81	310.85	3.18	89.66	m	**400.51**
Extra over fittings; Ductwork 2001 to 2500mm longest side						
End Cap						
Sum of two sides 2500mm	95.51	162.40	0.87	24.53	nr	**186.93**
Sum of two sides 2600mm	100.86	171.50	0.87	24.53	nr	**196.03**
Sum of two sides 2700mm	106.60	181.27	0.87	24.53	nr	**205.80**
Sum of two sides 2800mm	111.89	190.25	1.16	32.71	nr	**222.96**
Sum of two sides 2900mm	117.63	200.01	1.16	32.71	nr	**232.72**
Sum of two sides 3000mm	123.36	209.76	1.73	48.78	nr	**258.53**
Sum of two sides 3100mm	127.85	217.39	1.73	48.78	nr	**266.17**
Sum of two sides 3200mm	131.68	223.91	1.73	48.78	nr	**272.69**
Sum of two sides 3300mm	135.35	230.15	1.73	48.78	nr	**278.93**
Sum of two sides 3400mm	139.56	237.30	1.80	50.75	nr	**288.05**
Sum of two sides 3500mm	143.71	244.36	1.80	50.75	nr	**295.11**
Sum of two sides 3600mm	147.80	251.32	1.80	50.75	nr	**302.07**
Sum of two sides 3700mm	152.87	259.93	1.80	50.75	nr	**310.68**
Sum of two sides 3800mm	155.89	265.08	1.80	50.75	nr	**315.83**
Sum of two sides 3900mm	159.89	271.87	1.80	50.75	nr	**322.62**
Sum of two sides 4000mm	163.83	278.57	1.80	50.75	nr	**329.32**
Reducer						
Sum of two sides 2500mm	33.45	56.87	3.12	87.97	nr	**144.84**
Sum of two sides 2600mm	36.24	61.63	3.12	87.97	nr	**149.60**
Sum of two sides 2700mm	38.98	66.29	3.12	87.97	nr	**154.25**
Sum of two sides 2800mm	41.68	70.87	3.95	111.37	nr	**182.23**
Sum of two sides 2900mm	44.36	75.42	3.97	111.93	nr	**187.36**
Sum of two sides 3000mm	46.97	79.87	3.97	111.93	nr	**191.80**
Sum of two sides 3100mm	47.93	81.50	3.97	111.93	nr	**193.43**
Sum of two sides 3200mm	51.06	86.83	3.97	111.93	nr	**198.76**
Sum of two sides 3300mm	49.92	84.88	3.97	111.93	nr	**196.81**
Sum of two sides 3400mm	51.48	87.53	4.52	127.44	nr	**214.97**
Sum of two sides 3500mm	52.36	89.03	4.52	127.44	nr	**216.47**
Sum of two sides 3600mm	51.69	87.90	4.52	127.44	nr	**215.34**
Sum of two sides 3700mm	54.68	92.98	4.52	127.44	nr	**220.42**
Sum of two sides 3800mm	55.78	94.85	4.52	127.44	nr	**222.29**
Sum of two sides 3900mm	57.17	97.21	4.52	127.44	nr	**224.65**
Sum of two sides 4000mm	59.09	100.48	4.52	127.44	nr	**227.91**

U:VENTILATION/AIR CONDITIONING SYSTEMS

Item	Net Price £	Material £	Labour hours	Labour £	Unit	Total rate £
U10 : DUCTWORK : RECTANGULAR – CLASS B (cont'd)						
Y30 - AIR DUCTLINES (cont'd)						
Fittings; Ductwork 2001 to 2500mm longest Side (cont'd)						
Offset						
Sum of two sides 2500mm	95.18	161.84	3.48	98.12	nr	259.96
Sum of two sides 2600mm	101.51	172.61	3.49	98.40	nr	271.01
Sum of two sides 2700mm	107.02	181.97	3.50	98.68	nr	280.65
Sum of two sides 2800mm	112.54	191.36	4.34	122.36	nr	313.73
Sum of two sides 2900mm	111.99	190.42	4.76	134.21	nr	324.63
Sum of two sides 3000mm	114.23	194.23	5.32	149.99	nr	344.23
Sum of two sides 3100mm	114.12	194.04	5.35	150.84	nr	344.88
Sum of two sides 3200mm	117.94	200.55	5.35	150.84	nr	351.39
Sum of two sides 3300mm	110.58	188.03	5.32	149.99	nr	338.03
Sum of two sides 3400mm	111.09	188.89	5.32	149.99	nr	338.89
Sum of two sides 3500mm	111.55	189.67	5.32	149.99	nr	339.67
Sum of two sides 3600mm	112.01	190.46	5.35	150.84	nr	341.30
Sum of two sides 3700mm	120.33	204.60	5.35	150.84	nr	355.44
Sum of two sides 3800mm	122.38	208.10	5.35	150.84	nr	358.94
Sum of two sides 3900mm	126.06	214.36	5.35	150.84	nr	365.20
Sum of two sides 4000mm	130.86	222.51	5.35	150.84	nr	373.35
Square to round						
Sum of two sides 2500mm	96.67	164.37	4.70	132.51	nr	296.89
Sum of two sides 2600mm	104.33	177.40	4.70	132.51	nr	309.91
Sum of two sides 2700mm	111.46	189.52	4.71	132.80	nr	322.32
Sum of two sides 2800mm	118.69	201.82	8.19	230.91	nr	432.73
Sum of two sides 2900mm	125.98	214.21	8.19	230.91	nr	445.12
Sum of two sides 3000mm	132.57	225.41	8.19	230.91	nr	456.32
Sum of two sides 3100mm	135.98	231.21	8.19	230.91	nr	462.12
Sum of two sides 3200mm	142.67	242.60	8.62	243.04	nr	485.63
Sum of two sides 3300mm	145.73	247.80	8.62	243.04	nr	490.84
Sum of two sides 3400mm	150.51	255.92	8.62	243.04	nr	498.96
Sum of two sides 3500mm	154.36	262.47	8.62	243.04	nr	505.51
Sum of two sides 3600mm	157.33	267.53	8.75	246.70	nr	514.23
Sum of two sides 3700mm	163.84	278.58	8.75	246.70	nr	525.29
Sum of two sides 3800mm	166.82	283.65	8.75	246.70	nr	530.35
Sum of two sides 3900mm	171.60	291.79	8.75	246.70	nr	538.49
Sum of two sides 4000mm	176.39	299.93	8.75	246.70	nr	546.63
90 ° radius bend						
Sum of two sides 2500mm	126.38	214.90	3.90	109.96	nr	324.85
Sum of two sides 2600mm	131.70	223.93	4.26	120.11	nr	344.04
Sum of two sides 2700mm	138.19	234.97	4.55	128.29	nr	363.25
Sum of two sides 2800mm	147.25	250.37	4.55	128.29	nr	378.66
Sum of two sides 2900mm	155.98	265.23	6.87	193.70	nr	458.92
Sum of two sides 3000mm	164.71	280.06	6.87	193.70	nr	473.76
Sum of two sides 3100mm	169.57	288.34	6.87	193.70	nr	482.04
Sum of two sides 3200mm	180.29	306.56	6.87	193.70	nr	500.26
Sum of two sides 3300mm	178.81	304.04	6.87	193.70	nr	497.74
Sum of two sides 3400mm	194.34	330.46	6.87	193.70	nr	524.15

U:VENTILATION/AIR CONDITIONING SYSTEMS

Item	Net Price £	Material £	Labour hours	Labour £	Unit	Total rate £
Sum of two sides 3500mm	198.58	337.66	7.00	197.36	nr	**535.02**
Sum of two sides 3600mm	201.22	342.15	7.00	197.36	nr	**539.51**
Sum of two sides 3700mm	213.31	362.70	7.00	197.36	nr	**560.07**
Sum of two sides 3800mm	220.63	375.15	7.00	197.36	nr	**572.51**
Sum of two sides 3900mm	228.76	388.99	7.00	197.36	nr	**586.35**
Sum of two sides 4000mm	235.17	399.88	7.00	197.36	nr	**597.24**
45 ° bend						
Sum of two sides 2500mm	85.29	145.03	4.85	136.74	nr	**281.77**
Sum of two sides 2600mm	89.28	151.82	4.87	137.31	nr	**289.12**
Sum of two sides 2700mm	94.12	160.03	4.87	137.31	nr	**297.34**
Sum of two sides 2800mm	98.14	166.87	8.81	248.39	nr	**415.27**
Sum of two sides 2900mm	103.67	176.28	8.81	248.39	nr	**424.67**
Sum of two sides 3000mm	109.21	185.70	9.31	262.49	nr	**448.19**
Sum of two sides 3100mm	113.25	192.57	9.31	262.49	nr	**455.06**
Sum of two sides 3200mm	118.37	201.27	9.31	262.49	nr	**463.76**
Sum of two sides 3300mm	119.05	202.43	9.31	262.49	nr	**464.92**
Sum of two sides 3400mm	122.94	209.05	9.31	262.49	nr	**471.54**
Sum of two sides 3500mm	126.29	214.74	9.31	262.49	nr	**477.23**
Sum of two sides 3600mm	129.74	220.60	9.39	264.75	nr	**485.35**
Sum of two sides 3700mm	138.93	236.23	9.39	264.75	nr	**500.97**
Sum of two sides 3800mm	142.70	242.64	9.39	264.75	nr	**507.38**
Sum of two sides 3900mm	146.68	249.41	9.39	264.75	nr	**514.16**
Sum of two sides 4000mm	150.66	256.18	9.39	264.75	nr	**520.93**
90 ° mitre bend						
Sum of two sides 2500mm	162.72	276.68	4.85	136.74	nr	**413.43**
Sum of two sides 2600mm	169.90	288.89	4.87	137.31	nr	**426.20**
Sum of two sides 2700mm	178.69	303.83	4.87	137.31	nr	**441.14**
Sum of two sides 2800mm	185.61	315.60	8.81	248.39	nr	**563.99**
Sum of two sides 2900mm	198.82	338.07	14.81	417.56	nr	**755.63**
Sum of two sides 3000mm	209.89	356.89	14.81	417.56	nr	**774.45**
Sum of two sides 3100mm	216.67	368.42	15.20	428.56	nr	**796.98**
Sum of two sides 3200mm	227.74	387.25	15.20	428.56	nr	**815.80**
Sum of two sides 3300mm	248.48	422.51	15.20	428.56	nr	**851.07**
Sum of two sides 3400mm	256.98	436.97	15.20	428.56	nr	**865.52**
Sum of two sides 3500mm	264.38	449.54	15.20	428.56	nr	**878.10**
Sum of two sides 3600mm	269.03	457.45	15.60	439.83	nr	**897.29**
Sum of two sides 3700mm	273.84	465.64	15.60	439.83	nr	**905.47**
Sum of two sides 3800mm	287.74	489.26	15.60	439.83	nr	**929.09**
Sum of two sides 3900mm	295.55	502.55	15.60	439.83	nr	**942.38**
Sum of two sides 4000mm	303.49	516.05	15.60	439.83	nr	**955.89**
Branch						
Sum of two sides 2500mm	83.71	142.34	2.88	81.20	nr	**223.54**
Sum of two sides 2600mm	88.29	150.13	2.88	81.20	nr	**231.33**
Sum of two sides 2700mm	95.40	162.22	2.88	81.20	nr	**243.42**
Sum of two sides 2800mm	99.88	169.83	3.94	111.09	nr	**280.92**
Sum of two sides 2900mm	104.89	178.35	3.94	111.09	nr	**289.43**
Sum of two sides 3000mm	109.38	186.00	3.94	111.09	nr	**297.08**
Sum of two sides 3100mm	113.35	192.73	3.94	111.09	nr	**303.82**
Sum of two sides 3200mm	116.75	198.52	3.94	111.09	nr	**309.61**
Sum of two sides 3300mm	120.61	205.09	3.94	111.09	nr	**316.18**
Sum of two sides 3400mm	124.90	212.38	3.94	111.09	nr	**323.46**
Sum of two sides 3500mm	132.00	224.44	4.83	136.18	nr	**360.62**
Sum of two sides 3600mm	132.16	224.72	4.83	136.18	nr	**360.90**
Sum of two sides 3700mm	142.33	242.02	4.83	136.18	nr	**378.20**
Sum of two sides 3800mm	140.47	238.85	4.83	136.18	nr	**375.03**
Sum of two sides 3900mm	147.94	251.55	4.83	136.18	nr	**387.73**
Sum of two sides 4000mm	147.62	251.01	4.83	136.18	nr	**387.19**

U:VENTILATION/AIR CONDITIONING SYSTEMS

Item	Net Price £	Material £	Labour hours	Labour £	Unit	Total rate £
U10 : DUCTWORK : RECTANGULAR – CLASS B (cont'd)						
Y30 - AIR DUCTLINES (cont'd)						
Fittings; Ductwork 2001 to 2500mm longest Side (cont'd)						
Grille neck						
Sum of two sides 2500mm	104.14	177.08	2.88	81.20	nr	**258.28**
Sum of two sides 2600mm	113.14	192.37	2.88	81.20	nr	**273.57**
Sum of two sides 2700mm	118.46	201.42	2.88	81.20	nr	**282.62**
Sum of two sides 2800mm	124.53	211.75	3.94	111.09	nr	**322.83**
Sum of two sides 2900mm	130.61	222.09	3.94	111.09	nr	**333.18**
Sum of two sides 3000mm	139.52	237.24	3.94	111.09	nr	**348.32**
Sum of two sides 3100mm	145.22	246.93	4.12	116.16	nr	**363.10**
Sum of two sides 3200mm	149.15	253.61	4.12	116.16	nr	**369.77**
Sum of two sides 3300mm	154.72	263.09	4.12	116.16	nr	**379.25**
Sum of two sides 3400mm	157.32	267.51	4.12	116.16	nr	**383.67**
Sum of two sides 3500mm	164.00	278.86	5.00	140.97	nr	**419.84**
Sum of two sides 3600mm	166.48	283.08	5.00	140.97	nr	**424.05**
Sum of two sides 3700mm	175.38	298.22	5.00	140.97	nr	**439.19**
Sum of two sides 3800mm	148.52	252.53	5.00	140.97	nr	**393.50**
Sum of two sides 3900mm	182.57	310.43	5.00	140.97	nr	**451.40**
Sum of two sides 4000mm	184.81	314.25	5.00	140.97	nr	**455.22**
Ductwork 2501 to 4000mm longest side						
Sum of two sides 3000mm	146.63	249.33	2.38	67.10	m	**316.44**
Sum of two sides 3100mm	150.26	255.49	2.38	67.10	m	**322.59**
Sum of two sides 3200mm	153.56	261.11	2.38	67.10	m	**328.21**
Sum of two sides 3300mm	156.87	266.74	2.38	67.10	m	**333.84**
Sum of two sides 3400mm	160.73	273.31	2.64	74.43	m	**347.74**
Sum of two sides 3500mm	164.04	278.93	2.66	75.00	m	**353.93**
Sum of two sides 3600mm	167.35	284.55	2.95	83.17	m	**367.73**
Sum of two sides 3700mm	171.43	291.50	2.96	83.46	m	**374.95**
Sum of two sides 3800mm	174.74	297.12	3.15	88.81	m	**385.93**
Sum of two sides 3900mm	184.14	313.11	3.15	88.81	m	**401.92**
Sum of two sides 4000mm	187.45	318.74	3.15	88.81	m	**407.55**
Sum of two sides 4100mm	190.97	324.73	3.35	94.45	m	**419.18**
Sum of two sides 4200mm	194.28	330.36	3.35	94.45	m	**424.81**
Sum of two sides 4300mm	197.59	335.97	3.60	101.50	m	**437.47**
Sum of two sides 4400mm	202.13	343.69	3.60	101.50	m	**445.19**
Sum of two sides 4500mm	205.43	349.31	3.60	101.50	m	**450.81**

U:VENTILATION/AIR CONDITIONING SYSTEMS

Item	Net Price £	Material £	Labour hours	Labour £	Unit	Total rate £
Extra over fittings; Ductwork 2501 to 4000mm longest side						
End Cap						
Sum of two sides 3000mm	89.66	152.46	1.73	48.78	nr	**201.23**
Sum of two sides 3100mm	92.86	157.91	1.73	48.78	nr	**206.68**
Sum of two sides 3200mm	95.77	162.84	1.73	48.78	nr	**211.62**
Sum of two sides 3300mm	98.67	167.78	1.73	48.78	nr	**216.56**
Sum of two sides 3400mm	101.58	172.72	1.73	48.78	nr	**221.50**
Sum of two sides 3500mm	104.48	177.66	1.73	48.78	nr	**226.43**
Sum of two sides 3600mm	107.39	182.60	1.73	48.78	nr	**231.37**
Sum of two sides 3700mm	110.29	187.54	1.73	48.78	nr	**236.31**
Sum of two sides 3800mm	113.19	192.47	1.73	48.78	nr	**241.25**
Sum of two sides 3900mm	116.10	197.42	1.80	50.75	nr	**248.17**
Sum of two sides 4000mm	119.01	202.36	1.80	50.75	nr	**253.11**
Sum of two sides 4100mm	121.91	207.30	1.80	50.75	nr	**258.05**
Sum of two sides 4200mm	124.82	212.24	1.80	50.75	nr	**262.99**
Sum of two sides 4300mm	127.72	217.17	1.88	53.01	nr	**270.18**
Sum of two sides 4400mm	130.63	222.11	1.88	53.01	nr	**275.12**
Sum of two sides 4500mm	133.53	227.05	1.88	53.01	nr	**280.06**
Reducer						
Sum of two sides 3000mm	36.00	61.22	3.12	87.97	nr	**149.19**
Sum of two sides 3100mm	37.83	64.32	3.12	87.97	nr	**152.28**
Sum of two sides 3200mm	39.32	66.86	3.12	87.97	nr	**154.82**
Sum of two sides 3300mm	40.82	69.41	3.12	87.97	nr	**157.37**
Sum of two sides 3400mm	42.29	71.92	3.12	87.97	nr	**159.88**
Sum of two sides 3500mm	43.79	74.46	3.12	87.97	nr	**162.43**
Sum of two sides 3600mm	45.29	77.00	3.95	111.37	nr	**188.37**
Sum of two sides 3700mm	46.88	79.71	3.97	111.93	nr	**191.64**
Sum of two sides 3800mm	48.37	82.25	4.52	127.44	nr	**209.69**
Sum of two sides 3900mm	46.81	79.60	4.52	127.44	nr	**207.04**
Sum of two sides 4000mm	48.31	82.15	4.52	127.44	nr	**209.59**
Sum of two sides 4100mm	49.92	84.88	4.52	127.44	nr	**212.32**
Sum of two sides 4200mm	51.42	87.43	4.52	127.44	nr	**214.87**
Sum of two sides 4300mm	52.91	89.97	4.92	138.72	nr	**228.69**
Sum of two sides 4400mm	54.50	92.67	4.92	138.72	nr	**231.38**
Sum of two sides 4500mm	55.99	95.21	5.12	144.36	nr	**239.56**
Offset						
Sum of two sides 3000mm	156.52	266.15	3.48	98.12	nr	**364.26**
Sum of two sides 3100mm	153.59	261.17	3.48	98.12	nr	**359.29**
Sum of two sides 3200mm	149.63	254.43	3.48	98.12	nr	**352.55**
Sum of two sides 3300mm	145.28	247.02	3.48	98.12	nr	**345.14**
Sum of two sides 3400mm	159.77	271.68	3.49	98.40	nr	**370.07**
Sum of two sides 3500mm	155.03	263.61	3.50	98.68	nr	**362.29**
Sum of two sides 3600mm	149.89	254.87	3.50	98.68	nr	**353.55**
Sum of two sides 3700mm	164.90	280.39	4.76	134.21	nr	**414.60**
Sum of two sides 3800mm	159.36	270.97	5.32	149.99	nr	**420.96**
Sum of two sides 3900mm	169.58	288.35	5.35	150.84	nr	**439.19**
Sum of two sides 4000mm	163.18	277.47	5.35	150.84	nr	**428.31**
Sum of two sides 4100mm	156.48	266.08	5.85	164.94	nr	**431.02**
Sum of two sides 4200mm	149.29	253.84	5.85	164.94	nr	**418.78**
Sum of two sides 4300mm	153.58	261.14	6.15	173.40	nr	**434.54**
Sum of two sides 4400mm	170.03	289.11	6.15	173.40	nr	**462.51**
Sum of two sides 4500mm	162.23	275.84	6.30	177.63	nr	**453.47**

U:VENTILATION/AIR CONDITIONING SYSTEMS

Item	Net Price £	Material £	Labour hours	Labour £	Unit	Total rate £
U10 : DUCTWORK : RECTANGULAR – CLASS B (cont'd)						
Y30 - AIR DUCTLINES (cont'd)						
Fittings; Ductwork 2501 to 4000mm longest Side (cont'd)						
Square to round						
Sum of two sides 3000mm	132.00	224.44	4.70	132.51	nr	356.96
Sum of two sides 3100mm	137.73	234.20	4.70	132.51	nr	366.71
Sum of two sides 3200mm	142.82	242.86	4.70	132.51	nr	375.37
Sum of two sides 3300mm	147.90	251.49	4.70	132.51	nr	384.01
Sum of two sides 3400mm	153.00	260.15	4.71	132.80	nr	392.95
Sum of two sides 3500mm	158.08	268.80	4.71	132.80	nr	401.59
Sum of two sides 3600mm	163.17	277.45	8.19	230.91	nr	508.37
Sum of two sides 3700mm	168.24	286.07	8.62	243.04	nr	529.11
Sum of two sides 3800mm	173.33	294.73	8.62	243.04	nr	537.76
Sum of two sides 3900mm	213.60	363.20	8.62	243.04	nr	606.24
Sum of two sides 4000mm	219.70	373.57	8.75	246.70	nr	620.27
Sum of two sides 4100mm	225.79	383.93	11.23	316.62	nr	700.55
Sum of two sides 4200mm	231.88	394.28	11.23	316.62	nr	710.91
Sum of two sides 4300mm	237.98	404.66	11.25	317.19	nr	721.85
Sum of two sides 4400mm	244.07	415.02	11.25	317.19	nr	732.20
Sum of two sides 4500mm	250.17	425.38	11.26	317.47	nr	742.85
90 ° radius bend						
Sum of two sides 3000mm	214.87	365.36	3.90	109.96	nr	475.32
Sum of two sides 3100mm	225.05	382.68	3.90	109.96	nr	492.64
Sum of two sides 3200mm	233.80	397.55	4.26	120.11	nr	517.66
Sum of two sides 3300mm	242.55	412.43	4.26	120.11	nr	532.54
Sum of two sides 3400mm	235.43	400.32	4.26	120.11	nr	520.43
Sum of two sides 3500mm	244.00	414.89	4.55	128.29	nr	543.17
Sum of two sides 3600mm	252.56	429.45	4.55	128.29	nr	557.74
Sum of two sides 3700mm	244.87	416.37	6.87	193.70	nr	610.06
Sum of two sides 3800mm	253.25	430.62	6.87	193.70	nr	624.32
Sum of two sides 3900mm	234.17	398.18	6.87	193.70	nr	591.88
Sum of two sides 4000mm	242.37	412.12	7.00	197.36	nr	609.48
Sum of two sides 4100mm	251.07	426.91	7.20	203.00	nr	629.91
Sum of two sides 4200mm	259.26	440.85	7.20	203.00	nr	643.85
Sum of two sides 4300mm	267.47	454.79	7.41	208.92	nr	663.71
Sum of two sides 4400mm	246.78	419.61	7.41	208.92	nr	628.54
Sum of two sides 4500mm	254.70	433.09	7.55	212.87	nr	645.96
45 ° bend						
Sum of two sides 3000mm	99.60	169.35	4.85	136.74	nr	306.09
Sum of two sides 3100mm	104.43	177.58	4.85	136.74	nr	314.32
Sum of two sides 3200mm	108.60	184.66	4.85	136.74	nr	321.40
Sum of two sides 3300mm	112.76	191.73	4.87	137.31	nr	329.04
Sum of two sides 3400mm	109.21	185.70	4.87	137.31	nr	323.00
Sum of two sides 3500mm	113.28	192.62	4.87	137.31	nr	329.93
Sum of two sides 3600mm	117.36	199.55	8.81	248.39	nr	447.94
Sum of two sides 3700mm	113.53	193.04	8.81	248.39	nr	441.44
Sum of two sides 3800mm	117.52	199.82	9.31	262.49	nr	462.31
Sum of two sides 3900mm	108.03	183.70	9.31	262.49	nr	446.19

U:VENTILATION/AIR CONDITIONING SYSTEMS

Item	Net Price £	Material £	Labour hours	Labour £	Unit	Total rate £
Sum of two sides 4000mm	111.93	190.32	9.31	262.49	nr	**452.81**
Sum of two sides 4100mm	116.06	197.34	10.01	282.23	nr	**479.57**
Sum of two sides 4200mm	119.96	203.97	10.01	282.23	nr	**486.20**
Sum of two sides 4300mm	123.85	210.60	9.31	262.49	nr	**473.09**
Sum of two sides 4400mm	113.74	193.39	10.52	296.61	nr	**490.00**
Sum of two sides 4500mm	117.50	199.80	10.52	296.61	nr	**496.41**
90 ° mitre bend						
Sum of two sides 3000mm	298.05	506.79	4.85	136.74	nr	**643.54**
Sum of two sides 3100mm	312.08	530.66	4.85	136.74	nr	**667.40**
Sum of two sides 3200mm	325.29	553.12	4.87	137.31	nr	**690.43**
Sum of two sides 3300mm	338.51	575.59	4.87	137.31	nr	**712.90**
Sum of two sides 3400mm	329.63	560.50	4.87	137.31	nr	**697.80**
Sum of two sides 3500mm	342.64	582.62	8.81	248.39	nr	**831.01**
Sum of two sides 3600mm	355.65	604.74	8.81	248.39	nr	**853.13**
Sum of two sides 3700mm	348.18	592.04	14.81	417.56	nr	**1009.61**
Sum of two sides 3800mm	361.00	613.84	14.81	417.56	nr	**1031.40**
Sum of two sides 3900mm	334.62	568.97	14.81	417.56	nr	**986.53**
Sum of two sides 4000mm	347.23	590.43	15.20	428.56	nr	**1018.98**
Sum of two sides 4100mm	359.54	611.35	16.30	459.57	nr	**1070.92**
Sum of two sides 4200mm	372.15	632.80	16.50	465.21	nr	**1098.01**
Sum of two sides 4300mm	384.77	654.25	17.01	479.59	nr	**1133.84**
Sum of two sides 4400mm	359.20	610.77	17.01	479.59	nr	**1090.36**
Sum of two sides 4500mm	371.52	631.73	17.01	479.59	nr	**1111.32**
Branch						
Sum of two sides 3000mm	109.52	186.23	2.88	81.20	nr	**267.43**
Sum of two sides 3100mm	312.08	530.66	2.88	81.20	nr	**611.86**
Sum of two sides 3200mm	116.75	198.51	2.88	81.20	nr	**279.71**
Sum of two sides 3300mm	120.14	204.29	2.88	81.20	nr	**285.49**
Sum of two sides 3400mm	123.53	210.05	2.88	81.20	nr	**291.25**
Sum of two sides 3500mm	126.93	215.83	3.94	111.09	nr	**326.91**
Sum of two sides 3600mm	130.32	221.59	3.94	111.09	nr	**332.68**
Sum of two sides 3700mm	133.82	227.54	3.94	111.09	nr	**338.63**
Sum of two sides 3800mm	137.22	233.32	4.83	136.18	nr	**369.50**
Sum of two sides 3900mm	140.75	239.34	4.83	136.18	nr	**375.52**
Sum of two sides 4000mm	144.15	245.12	4.83	136.18	nr	**381.29**
Sum of two sides 4100mm	147.66	251.07	5.44	153.38	nr	**404.45**
Sum of two sides 4200mm	151.06	256.85	5.44	153.38	nr	**410.23**
Sum of two sides 4300mm	154.45	262.63	5.85	164.94	nr	**427.57**
Sum of two sides 4400mm	157.94	268.56	5.85	164.94	nr	**433.49**
Sum of two sides 4500mm	161.34	274.33	5.85	164.94	nr	**439.27**
Grille neck						
Sum of two sides 3000mm	137.32	233.49	2.88	81.20	nr	**314.69**
Sum of two sides 3100mm	142.21	241.81	2.88	81.20	nr	**323.01**
Sum of two sides 3200mm	146.66	249.38	2.88	81.20	nr	**330.58**
Sum of two sides 3300mm	151.12	256.96	2.88	81.20	nr	**338.16**
Sum of two sides 3400mm	155.57	264.53	3.94	111.09	nr	**375.61**
Sum of two sides 3500mm	160.03	272.11	3.94	111.09	nr	**383.19**
Sum of two sides 3600mm	164.48	279.68	3.94	111.09	nr	**390.77**
Sum of two sides 3700mm	168.94	287.26	4.12	116.16	nr	**403.42**
Sum of two sides 3800mm	173.40	294.84	4.12	116.16	nr	**411.00**
Sum of two sides 3900mm	177.85	302.41	4.12	116.16	nr	**418.57**
Sum of two sides 4000mm	182.30	309.98	5.00	140.97	nr	**450.96**
Sum of two sides 4100mm	186.76	317.56	5.00	140.97	nr	**458.53**
Sum of two sides 4200mm	191.21	325.14	5.00	140.97	nr	**466.11**
Sum of two sides 4300mm	195.67	332.71	5.23	147.46	nr	**480.17**
Sum of two sides 4400mm	200.12	340.28	5.23	147.46	nr	**487.74**
Sum of two sides 4500mm	204.58	347.86	5.39	151.97	nr	**499.83**

U:VENTILATION/AIR CONDITIONING SYSTEMS

Item	Net Price £	Material £	Labour hours	Labour £	Unit	Total rate £
U10 : DUCTWORK : RECTANGULAR – CLASS B (cont'd)						
Y30 - AIR DUCTLINES (cont'd)						
ANCILLARIES						
Access doors, hollow steel construction; 25mm mineral wool insulation; removeable or hinged; fixed with cams; including sub-frame and integral sealing gaskets						
Rectangular duct						
150 x 150mm	14.38	24.45	1.25	35.24	nr	59.70
200 x 200mm	15.53	26.41	1.25	35.24	nr	61.65
300 x 150mm	15.96	27.14	1.25	35.24	nr	62.38
300 x 300mm	18.30	31.11	1.25	35.24	nr	66.35
400 x 400mm	20.87	35.48	1.35	38.10	nr	73.58
450 x 300mm	20.87	35.48	1.50	42.33	nr	77.81
450 x 450mm	23.01	39.12	1.50	42.33	nr	81.45
Access doors, hollow steel construction; 25mm mineral wool insulation; removeable or hinged; fixed with cams; including sub-frame and integral sealing gaskets						
Flat oval duct						
235 x 90mm	29.21	49.67	1.25	35.24	nr	84.91
235 x 140mm	31.14	52.94	1.35	38.10	nr	91.05
335 x 235mm	35.58	60.50	1.50	42.33	nr	102.83
535 x 235mm	40.02	68.05	1.50	42.33	nr	110.38

U:VENTILATION/AIR CONDITIONING SYSTEMS

Item	Net Price £	Material £	Labour hours	Labour £	Unit	Total rate £
U10 : DUCTWORK : RECTANGULAR – CLASS C						
Y30 - AIR DUCTLINES						
Galvanised sheet metal DW144 class C rectangular section ductwork; including all necessary stiffeners, joints, couplers in the running length and duct supports						
Ductwork up to 400mm longest side						
Sum of two sides 200mm	18.75	31.88	1.19	33.55	m	**65.43**
Sum of two sides 300mm	20.21	34.36	1.16	32.71	m	**67.07**
Sum of two sides 400mm	17.30	29.42	1.17	32.99	m	**62.40**
Sum of two sides 500mm	18.91	32.15	1.17	32.99	m	**65.14**
Sum of two sides 600mm	20.25	34.43	1.19	33.55	m	**67.98**
Sum of two sides 700mm	21.60	36.73	1.19	33.55	m	**70.28**
Sum of two sides 800mm	23.04	39.18	1.19	33.55	m	**72.73**
Extra over fittings; Ductwork up to 400mm longest side						
End Cap						
Sum of two sides 200mm	9.00	15.30	0.38	10.71	nr	**26.02**
Sum of two sides 300mm	10.03	17.05	0.38	10.71	nr	**27.77**
Sum of two sides 400mm	11.05	18.79	0.38	10.71	nr	**29.50**
Sum of two sides 500mm	12.07	20.52	0.38	10.71	nr	**31.24**
Sum of two sides 600mm	13.09	22.26	0.38	10.71	nr	**32.97**
Sum of two sides 700mm	14.11	23.99	0.38	10.71	nr	**34.71**
Sum of two sides 800mm	15.13	25.73	0.38	10.71	nr	**36.44**
Reducer						
Sum of two sides 200mm	9.53	16.20	1.40	39.47	nr	**55.68**
Sum of two sides 300mm	10.76	18.30	1.40	39.47	nr	**57.77**
Sum of two sides 400mm	17.72	30.13	1.42	40.04	nr	**70.17**
Sum of two sides 500mm	19.24	32.72	1.42	40.04	nr	**72.75**
Sum of two sides 600mm	20.76	35.30	1.69	47.65	nr	**82.95**
Sum of two sides 700mm	22.28	37.88	1.69	47.65	nr	**85.53**
Sum of two sides 800mm	23.75	40.38	1.92	54.13	nr	**94.52**
Offset						
Sum of two sides 200mm	11.53	19.61	1.63	45.96	nr	**65.56**
Sum of two sides 300mm	13.04	22.17	1.63	45.96	nr	**68.13**
Sum of two sides 400mm	19.38	32.95	1.65	46.52	nr	**79.47**
Sum of two sides 500mm	21.11	35.90	1.65	46.52	nr	**82.42**
Sum of two sides 600mm	22.56	38.36	1.92	54.13	nr	**92.49**
Sum of two sides 700mm	24.14	41.05	1.92	54.13	nr	**95.18**
Sum of two sides 800mm	25.54	43.43	1.92	54.13	nr	**97.56**
Square to round						
Sum of two sides 200mm	21.98	37.37	1.22	34.40	nr	**71.77**
Sum of two sides 300mm	24.69	41.98	1.22	34.40	nr	**76.38**
Sum of two sides 400mm	32.98	56.08	1.25	35.24	nr	**91.32**
Sum of two sides 500mm	35.95	61.13	1.25	35.24	nr	**96.37**
Sum of two sides 600mm	38.91	66.16	1.33	37.50	nr	**103.66**
Sum of two sides 700mm	41.88	71.21	1.33	37.50	nr	**108.71**
Sum of two sides 800mm	44.81	76.19	1.40	39.47	nr	**115.67**

U:VENTILATION/AIR CONDITIONING SYSTEMS

Item	Net Price £	Material £	Labour hours	Labour £	Unit	Total rate £
U10 : DUCTWORK : RECTANGULAR – CLASS C (cont'd)						
Y30 - AIR DUCTLINES (cont'd)						
Fittings; Ductwork up to 400mm longest side (cont'd)						
90 ° radius bend						
Sum of two sides 200mm	11.09	18.86	1.10	31.01	nr	49.87
Sum of two sides 300mm	11.96	20.34	1.10	31.01	nr	51.35
Sum of two sides 400mm	20.30	34.52	1.12	31.58	nr	66.10
Sum of two sides 500mm	21.68	36.86	1.12	31.58	nr	68.44
Sum of two sides 600mm	23.48	39.92	1.16	32.71	nr	72.63
Sum of two sides 700mm	25.05	42.59	1.16	32.71	nr	75.30
Sum of two sides 800mm	26.82	45.60	1.22	34.40	nr	80.00
45 ° radius bend						
Sum of two sides 200mm	10.99	18.69	1.29	36.37	nr	55.06
Sum of two sides 300mm	12.05	20.49	1.29	36.37	nr	56.86
Sum of two sides 400mm	19.49	33.14	1.29	36.37	nr	69.51
Sum of two sides 500mm	20.95	35.62	1.29	36.37	nr	71.99
Sum of two sides 600mm	22.61	38.45	1.39	39.19	nr	77.64
Sum of two sides 700mm	24.17	41.10	1.39	39.19	nr	80.29
Sum of two sides 800mm	25.81	43.89	1.46	41.16	nr	85.05
90 ° mitire bend						
Sum of two sides 200mm	15.14	25.74	2.04	57.52	nr	83.26
Sum of two sides 300mm	16.55	28.14	2.04	57.52	nr	85.66
Sum of two sides 400mm	24.16	41.08	2.09	58.93	nr	100.01
Sum of two sides 500mm	26.08	44.35	2.09	58.93	nr	103.27
Sum of two sides 600mm	28.51	48.48	2.15	60.62	nr	109.10
Sum of two sides 700mm	30.76	52.30	2.15	60.62	nr	112.92
Sum of two sides 800mm	33.22	56.49	2.26	63.72	nr	120.21
Branch						
Sum of two sides 200mm	18.82	32.00	0.92	25.94	nr	57.94
Sum of two sides 300mm	20.90	35.54	0.92	25.94	nr	61.48
Sum of two sides 400mm	26.24	44.62	0.95	26.78	nr	71.40
Sum of two sides 500mm	28.60	48.63	0.95	26.78	nr	75.42
Sum of two sides 600mm	30.91	52.56	1.03	29.04	nr	81.60
Sum of two sides 700mm	33.21	56.47	1.03	29.04	nr	85.51
Sum of two sides 800mm	35.52	60.40	1.03	29.04	nr	89.44
Grille neck						
Sum of two sides 200mm	20.03	34.06	1.10	31.01	nr	65.07
Sum of two sides 300mm	22.08	37.54	1.10	31.01	nr	68.56
Sum of two sides 400mm	24.16	41.08	1.16	32.71	nr	73.79
Sum of two sides 500mm	26.21	44.57	1.16	32.71	nr	77.27
Sum of two sides 600mm	28.28	48.09	1.18	33.27	nr	81.36
Sum of two sides 700mm	30.34	51.59	1.18	33.27	nr	84.86
Sum of two sides 800mm	32.40	55.09	1.18	33.27	nr	88.36

U:VENTILATION/AIR CONDITIONING SYSTEMS

Item	Net Price £	Material £	Labour hours	Labour £	Unit	Total rate £
Ductwork 401 to 600mm longest side						
Sum of two sides 600mm	21.72	36.93	1.17	32.99	m	**69.92**
Sum of two sides 700mm	23.98	40.78	1.17	32.99	m	**73.76**
Sum of two sides 800mm	26.12	44.41	1.17	32.99	m	**77.40**
Sum of two sides 900mm	28.19	47.93	1.27	35.81	m	**83.74**
Sum of two sides 1000mm	30.26	51.45	1.48	41.73	m	**93.18**
Sum of two sides 1100mm	32.58	55.40	1.49	42.01	m	**97.41**
Sum of two sides 1200mm	34.65	58.92	1.49	42.01	m	**100.93**
Extra over fittings: Ductwork 401 to 600mm longest side						
End Cap						
Sum of two sides 600mm	13.10	22.28	0.38	10.71	nr	**32.99**
Sum of two sides 700mm	14.12	24.01	0.38	10.71	nr	**34.72**
Sum of two sides 800mm	15.14	25.74	0.38	10.71	nr	**36.46**
Sum of two sides 900mm	16.17	27.50	0.38	10.71	nr	**38.21**
Sum of two sides 1000mm	17.20	29.25	0.38	10.71	nr	**39.96**
Sum of two sides 1100mm	18.22	30.98	0.38	10.71	nr	**41.69**
Sum of two sides 1200mm	19.24	32.72	0.38	10.71	nr	**43.43**
Reducer						
Sum of two sides 600mm	17.95	30.52	1.69	47.65	nr	**78.17**
Sum of two sides 700mm	19.14	32.55	1.69	47.65	nr	**80.19**
Sum of two sides 800mm	20.31	34.53	1.92	54.13	nr	**88.67**
Sum of two sides 900mm	21.50	36.56	1.92	54.13	nr	**90.69**
Sum of two sides 1000mm	22.69	38.58	2.18	61.46	nr	**100.05**
Sum of two sides 1100mm	24.01	40.83	2.18	61.46	nr	**102.29**
Sum of two sides 1200mm	25.20	42.85	2.18	61.46	nr	**104.31**
Offset						
Sum of two sides 600mm	20.92	35.57	1.92	54.13	nr	**89.71**
Sum of two sides 700mm	22.36	38.02	1.92	54.13	nr	**92.15**
Sum of two sides 800mm	23.15	39.36	1.92	54.13	nr	**93.50**
Sum of two sides 900mm	23.88	40.61	1.92	54.13	nr	**94.74**
Sum of two sides 1000mm	24.87	42.29	2.18	61.46	nr	**103.75**
Sum of two sides 1100mm	25.51	43.38	2.18	61.46	nr	**104.84**
Sum of two sides 1200mm	25.98	44.18	2.18	61.46	nr	**105.64**
Square to round						
Sum of two sides 600mm	30.01	51.03	1.33	37.50	nr	**88.53**
Sum of two sides 700mm	32.12	54.62	1.33	37.50	nr	**92.11**
Sum of two sides 800mm	34.21	58.17	1.40	39.47	nr	**97.64**
Sum of two sides 900mm	36.32	61.76	1.40	39.47	nr	**101.23**
Sum of two sides 1000mm	38.44	65.36	1.82	51.31	nr	**116.68**
Sum of two sides 1100mm	40.60	69.04	1.82	51.31	nr	**120.35**
Sum of two sides 1200mm	42.71	72.62	1.82	51.31	nr	**123.94**
90 ° radius bend						
Sum of two sides 600mm	18.42	31.32	1.16	32.71	nr	**64.03**
Sum of two sides 700mm	18.85	32.05	1.16	32.71	nr	**64.76**
Sum of two sides 800mm	20.10	34.18	1.22	34.40	nr	**68.57**
Sum of two sides 900mm	21.38	36.35	1.22	34.40	nr	**70.75**
Sum of two sides 1000mm	22.14	37.65	1.40	39.47	nr	**77.12**
Sum of two sides 1100mm	23.50	39.96	1.40	39.47	nr	**79.43**
Sum of two sides 1200mm	24.76	42.10	1.40	39.47	nr	**81.57**

U:VENTILATION/AIR CONDITIONING SYSTEMS

Item	Net Price £	Material £	Labour hours	Labour £	Unit	Total rate £
U10 : DUCTWORK : RECTANGULAR – **CLASS C (cont'd)**						
Y30 - AIR DUCTLINES (cont'd)						
Fittings: Ductwork 401 to 600mm longest side (cont'd)						
45 ° bend						
Sum of two sides 600mm	21.57	36.68	1.39	39.19	nr	75.87
Sum of two sides 700mm	22.61	38.45	1.39	39.19	nr	77.64
Sum of two sides 800mm	24.09	40.96	1.46	41.16	nr	82.13
Sum of two sides 900mm	25.59	43.51	1.46	41.16	nr	84.68
Sum of two sides 1000mm	26.81	45.59	1.88	53.01	nr	98.59
Sum of two sides 1100mm	28.44	48.36	1.88	53.01	nr	101.36
Sum of two sides 1200mm	29.93	50.89	1.88	53.01	nr	103.90
90 ° mitre bend						
Sum of two sides 600mm	25.22	42.88	2.15	60.62	nr	103.50
Sum of two sides 700mm	26.13	44.43	2.15	60.62	nr	105.05
Sum of two sides 800mm	27.98	47.58	2.26	63.72	nr	111.30
Sum of two sides 900mm	29.86	50.77	2.26	63.72	nr	114.49
Sum of two sides 1000mm	31.25	53.14	3.03	85.43	nr	138.57
Sum of two sides 1100mm	33.21	56.47	3.03	85.43	nr	141.90
Sum of two sides 1200mm	35.10	59.68	3.03	85.43	nr	145.11
Branch						
Sum of two sides 600mm	27.76	47.20	1.03	29.04	nr	76.24
Sum of two sides 700mm	29.82	50.71	1.03	29.04	nr	79.75
Sum of two sides 800mm	31.89	54.23	1.03	29.04	nr	83.27
Sum of two sides 900mm	33.96	57.74	1.03	29.04	nr	86.79
Sum of two sides 1000mm	36.06	61.32	1.29	36.37	nr	97.69
Sum of two sides 1100mm	38.21	64.97	1.29	36.37	nr	101.34
Sum of two sides 1200mm	40.28	68.49	1.29	36.37	nr	104.86
Grille neck						
Sum of two sides 600mm	27.30	46.42	1.18	33.27	nr	79.69
Sum of two sides 700mm	30.34	51.59	1.18	33.27	nr	84.86
Sum of two sides 800mm	32.40	55.09	1.18	33.27	nr	88.36
Sum of two sides 900mm	34.46	58.60	1.18	33.27	nr	91.86
Sum of two sides 1000mm	36.53	62.11	1.44	40.60	nr	102.72
Sum of two sides 1100mm	38.58	65.60	1.44	40.60	nr	106.20
Sum of two sides 1200mm	40.66	69.14	1.44	40.60	nr	109.74
Ductwork 601 to 800mm longest side						
Sum of two sides 900mm	31.10	52.88	1.27	35.81	m	88.69
Sum of two sides 1000mm	33.17	56.40	1.48	41.73	m	98.13
Sum of two sides 1100mm	35.25	59.94	1.49	42.01	m	101.95
Sum of two sides 1200mm	37.56	63.87	1.49	42.01	m	105.88
Sum of two sides 1300mm	39.64	67.40	1.51	42.57	m	109.98
Sum of two sides 1400mm	41.71	70.92	1.55	43.70	m	114.62
Sum of two sides 1500mm	43.78	74.44	1.61	45.39	m	119.84
Sum of two sides 1600mm	45.85	77.96	1.62	45.68	m	123.64

U:VENTILATION/AIR CONDITIONING SYSTEMS

Item	Net Price £	Material £	Labour hours	Labour £	Unit	Total rate £
Extra over fittings; Ductwork 601 to 800mm longest side						
End Cap						
Sum of two sides 900mm	16.17	27.50	0.38	10.71	nr	**38.21**
Sum of two sides 1000mm	17.20	29.25	0.38	10.71	nr	**39.96**
Sum of two sides 1100mm	18.22	30.98	0.38	10.71	nr	**41.69**
Sum of two sides 1200mm	19.20	32.65	0.38	10.71	nr	**43.36**
Sum of two sides 1300mm	20.15	34.26	0.38	10.71	nr	**44.97**
Sum of two sides 1400mm	21.14	35.95	0.38	10.71	nr	**46.66**
Sum of two sides 1500mm	24.60	41.83	0.38	10.71	nr	**52.54**
Sum of two sides 1600mm	28.08	47.75	0.38	10.71	nr	**58.46**
Reducer						
Sum of two sides 900mm	21.72	36.93	1.92	54.13	nr	**91.07**
Sum of two sides 1000mm	22.91	38.96	2.18	61.46	nr	**100.42**
Sum of two sides 1100mm	24.10	40.98	2.18	61.46	nr	**102.44**
Sum of two sides 1200mm	25.42	43.22	2.18	61.46	nr	**104.69**
Sum of two sides 1300mm	26.61	45.25	2.30	64.85	nr	**110.09**
Sum of two sides 1400mm	27.61	46.95	2.30	64.85	nr	**111.79**
Sum of two sides 1500mm	31.88	54.21	2.47	69.64	nr	**123.85**
Sum of two sides 1600mm	36.14	61.45	2.47	69.64	nr	**131.09**
Offset						
Sum of two sides 900mm	25.31	43.04	1.92	54.13	nr	**97.17**
Sum of two sides 1000mm	25.94	44.11	2.18	61.46	nr	**105.57**
Sum of two sides 1100mm	26.49	45.04	2.18	61.46	nr	**106.51**
Sum of two sides 1200mm	27.02	45.94	2.18	61.46	nr	**107.41**
Sum of two sides 1300mm	27.39	46.57	2.47	69.64	nr	**116.21**
Sum of two sides 1400mm	27.93	47.49	2.47	69.64	nr	**117.13**
Sum of two sides 1500mm	31.96	54.34	2.47	69.64	nr	**123.98**
Sum of two sides 1600mm	35.91	61.06	2.47	69.64	nr	**130.70**
Square to round						
Sum of two sides 900mm	36.00	61.21	1.40	39.47	nr	**100.69**
Sum of two sides 1000mm	38.11	64.80	1.82	51.31	nr	**116.12**
Sum of two sides 1100mm	40.22	68.39	1.82	51.31	nr	**119.70**
Sum of two sides 1200mm	42.39	72.08	1.82	51.31	nr	**123.39**
Sum of two sides 1300mm	44.50	75.67	2.32	65.41	nr	**141.08**
Sum of two sides 1400mm	46.25	78.64	2.32	65.41	nr	**144.05**
Sum of two sides 1500mm	54.43	92.55	2.56	72.18	nr	**164.73**
Sum of two sides 1600mm	62.62	106.48	2.58	72.74	nr	**179.22**
90 ° radius bend						
Sum of two sides 900mm	18.99	32.29	1.22	34.40	nr	**66.69**
Sum of two sides 1000mm	20.19	34.33	1.40	39.47	nr	**73.80**
Sum of two sides 1100mm	21.38	36.35	1.40	39.47	nr	**75.83**
Sum of two sides 1200mm	22.66	38.53	1.40	39.47	nr	**78.00**
Sum of two sides 1300mm	23.85	40.55	1.91	53.85	nr	**94.41**
Sum of two sides 1400mm	24.13	41.03	1.91	53.85	nr	**94.88**
Sum of two sides 1500mm	28.67	48.75	2.11	59.49	nr	**108.24**
Sum of two sides 1600mm	33.21	56.47	2.11	59.49	nr	**115.96**

U:VENTILATION/AIR CONDITIONING SYSTEMS

Item	Net Price £	Material £	Labour hours	Labour £	Unit	Total rate £
U10 : DUCTWORK : RECTANGULAR – CLASS C (cont'd)						
Y30 - AIR DUCTLINES (cont'd)						
Fittings; Ductwork 601 to 800mm longest side (cont'd)						
45 ° bend						
Sum of two sides 900mm	24.72	42.03	1.46	41.16	nr	**83.20**
Sum of two sides 1000mm	26.17	44.50	1.88	53.01	nr	**97.50**
Sum of two sides 1100mm	27.63	46.98	1.88	53.01	nr	**99.99**
Sum of two sides 1200mm	29.22	49.69	1.88	53.01	nr	**102.69**
Sum of two sides 1300mm	30.67	52.15	2.26	63.72	nr	**115.87**
Sum of two sides 1400mm	31.53	53.61	2.44	68.79	nr	**122.41**
Sum of two sides 1500mm	36.49	62.05	2.44	68.79	nr	**130.84**
Sum of two sides 1600mm	41.44	70.46	2.68	75.56	nr	**146.03**
90 ° mitre bend						
Sum of two sides 900mm	27.15	46.17	2.26	63.72	nr	**109.88**
Sum of two sides 1000mm	29.09	49.46	3.03	85.43	nr	**134.89**
Sum of two sides 1100mm	31.03	52.76	3.03	85.43	nr	**138.19**
Sum of two sides 1200mm	33.03	56.16	3.03	85.43	nr	**141.59**
Sum of two sides 1300mm	34.97	59.46	3.85	108.55	nr	**168.01**
Sum of two sides 1400mm	35.99	61.20	3.85	108.55	nr	**169.75**
Sum of two sides 1500mm	41.94	71.31	4.25	119.83	nr	**191.14**
Sum of two sides 1600mm	47.88	81.41	4.26	120.11	nr	**201.52**
Branch						
Sum of two sides 900mm	34.80	59.17	1.03	29.04	nr	**88.21**
Sum of two sides 1000mm	36.92	62.78	1.29	36.37	nr	**99.15**
Sum of two sides 1100mm	39.02	66.35	1.29	36.37	nr	**102.72**
Sum of two sides 1200mm	41.23	70.11	1.29	36.37	nr	**106.48**
Sum of two sides 1300mm	43.35	73.71	1.39	39.19	nr	**112.90**
Sum of two sides 1400mm	45.17	76.81	1.39	39.19	nr	**116.00**
Sum of two sides 1500mm	51.88	88.22	1.64	46.24	nr	**134.45**
Sum of two sides 1600mm	58.58	99.61	1.64	46.24	nr	**145.85**
Grille neck						
Sum of two sides 900mm	34.45	58.58	1.18	33.27	nr	**91.85**
Sum of two sides 1000mm	36.52	62.10	1.44	40.60	nr	**102.70**
Sum of two sides 1100mm	38.59	65.62	1.44	40.60	nr	**106.22**
Sum of two sides 1200mm	40.67	69.15	1.44	40.60	nr	**109.75**
Sum of two sides 1300mm	42.75	72.69	1.69	47.65	nr	**120.34**
Sum of two sides 1400mm	44.83	76.23	1.69	47.65	nr	**123.88**
Sum of two sides 1500mm	52.07	88.54	1.79	50.47	nr	**139.01**
Sum of two sides 1600mm	58.62	99.68	1.79	50.47	nr	**150.14**
Ductwork 801 to 1000mm longest side						
Sum of two sides 1100mm	39.90	67.85	1.49	42.01	m	**109.86**
Sum of two sides 1200mm	42.21	71.77	1.49	42.01	m	**113.78**
Sum of two sides 1300mm	44.52	75.70	1.51	42.57	m	**118.27**
Sum of two sides 1400mm	47.09	80.07	1.55	43.70	m	**123.77**
Sum of two sides 1500mm	49.40	84.00	1.61	45.39	m	**129.39**
Sum of two sides 1600mm	51.70	87.91	1.62	45.68	m	**133.58**
Sum of two sides 1700mm	54.01	91.84	1.74	49.06	m	**140.90**
Sum of two sides 1800mm	56.59	96.22	1.76	49.62	m	**145.85**
Sum of two sides 1900mm	58.89	100.14	1.81	51.03	m	**151.17**
Sum of two sides 2000mm	61.20	104.06	1.82	51.31	m	**155.38**

U:VENTILATION/AIR CONDITIONING SYSTEMS

Item	Net Price £	Material £	Labour hours	Labour £	Unit	Total rate £
Extra over fittings; Ductwork 801 to 1000mm longest side						
End Cap						
Sum of two sides 1100mm	19.57	33.28	0.38	10.71	nr	**43.99**
Sum of two sides 1200mm	20.67	35.15	0.38	10.71	nr	**45.86**
Sum of two sides 1300mm	21.77	37.02	0.38	10.71	nr	**47.73**
Sum of two sides 1400mm	22.71	38.62	0.38	10.71	nr	**49.33**
Sum of two sides 1500mm	26.43	44.94	0.38	10.71	nr	**55.65**
Sum of two sides 1600mm	30.16	51.28	0.38	10.71	nr	**62.00**
Sum of two sides 1700mm	33.89	57.63	0.58	16.35	nr	**73.98**
Sum of two sides 1800mm	37.61	63.95	0.58	16.35	nr	**80.30**
Sum of two sides 1900mm	41.34	70.29	0.58	16.35	nr	**86.65**
Sum of two sides 2000mm	45.07	76.64	0.58	16.35	nr	**92.99**
Reducer						
Sum of two sides 1100mm	16.97	28.86	2.18	61.46	nr	**90.32**
Sum of two sides 1200mm	17.81	30.28	2.18	61.46	nr	**91.75**
Sum of two sides 1300mm	18.64	31.70	2.30	64.85	nr	**96.54**
Sum of two sides 1400mm	19.40	32.99	2.30	64.85	nr	**97.83**
Sum of two sides 1500mm	22.58	38.39	2.47	69.64	nr	**108.04**
Sum of two sides 1600mm	25.75	43.78	2.47	69.64	nr	**113.43**
Sum of two sides 1700mm	28.93	49.19	2.59	73.02	nr	**122.22**
Sum of two sides 1800mm	32.18	54.72	2.59	73.02	nr	**127.74**
Sum of two sides 1900mm	35.36	60.13	2.71	76.41	nr	**136.53**
Sum of two sides 2000mm	38.53	65.52	2.71	76.41	nr	**141.92**
Offset						
Sum of two sides 1100mm	26.37	44.84	2.18	61.46	nr	**106.30**
Sum of two sides 1200mm	26.87	45.69	2.18	61.46	nr	**107.15**
Sum of two sides 1300mm	27.30	46.42	2.47	69.64	nr	**116.06**
Sum of two sides 1400mm	27.48	46.73	2.47	69.64	nr	**116.37**
Sum of two sides 1500mm	31.30	53.22	2.47	69.64	nr	**122.86**
Sum of two sides 1600mm	35.03	59.56	2.47	69.64	nr	**129.20**
Sum of two sides 1700mm	38.68	65.77	2.61	73.59	nr	**139.36**
Sum of two sides 1800mm	42.29	71.91	2.61	73.59	nr	**145.50**
Sum of two sides 1900mm	46.34	78.80	2.71	76.41	nr	**155.20**
Sum of two sides 2000mm	49.77	84.63	2.71	76.41	nr	**161.04**
Square to round						
Sum of two sides 1100mm	33.53	57.01	1.82	51.31	nr	**108.33**
Sum of two sides 1200mm	35.30	60.02	1.82	51.31	nr	**111.34**
Sum of two sides 1300mm	37.06	63.02	2.32	65.41	nr	**128.43**
Sum of two sides 1400mm	38.51	65.48	2.32	65.41	nr	**130.89**
Sum of two sides 1500mm	45.76	77.81	2.56	72.18	nr	**149.99**
Sum of two sides 1600mm	53.00	90.12	2.58	72.74	nr	**162.86**
Sum of two sides 1700mm	60.24	102.43	2.84	80.07	nr	**182.50**
Sum of two sides 1800mm	67.51	114.79	2.84	80.07	nr	**194.87**
Sum of two sides 1900mm	74.75	127.10	3.13	88.25	nr	**215.35**
Sum of two sides 2000mm	82.00	139.43	3.13	88.25	nr	**227.68**

U:VENTILATION/AIR CONDITIONING SYSTEMS

Item	Net Price £	Material £	Labour hours	Labour £	Unit	Total rate £
U10 : DUCTWORK : RECTANGULAR – CLASS C (cont'd)						
Y30 - AIR DUCTLINES (cont'd)						
Fittings; Ductwork 801 to 1000mm longest side (cont'd)						
90 ° radius bend						
Sum of two sides 1100mm	15.73	26.75	1.40	39.47	nr	66.22
Sum of two sides 1200mm	16.83	28.62	1.40	39.47	nr	68.09
Sum of two sides 1300mm	17.93	30.49	1.91	53.85	nr	84.34
Sum of two sides 1400mm	18.91	32.15	1.91	53.85	nr	86.01
Sum of two sides 1500mm	22.76	38.70	2.11	59.49	nr	98.19
Sum of two sides 1600mm	26.61	45.25	2.11	59.49	nr	104.74
Sum of two sides 1700mm	30.46	51.79	2.55	71.90	nr	123.69
Sum of two sides 1800mm	34.36	58.43	2.55	71.90	nr	130.32
Sum of two sides 1900mm	37.49	63.75	2.80	78.94	nr	142.69
Sum of two sides 2000mm	41.33	70.28	2.80	78.94	nr	149.22
45 ° bend						
Sum of two sides 1100mm	22.66	38.53	1.88	53.01	nr	91.54
Sum of two sides 1200mm	23.98	40.78	1.88	53.01	nr	93.78
Sum of two sides 1300mm	25.30	43.02	2.26	63.72	nr	106.74
Sum of two sides 1400mm	26.54	45.13	2.44	68.79	nr	113.92
Sum of two sides 1500mm	30.85	52.46	2.68	75.56	nr	128.02
Sum of two sides 1600mm	35.17	59.80	2.69	75.84	nr	135.65
Sum of two sides 1700mm	39.48	67.13	2.96	83.46	nr	150.59
Sum of two sides 1800mm	43.90	74.65	2.96	83.46	nr	158.10
Sum of two sides 1900mm	47.81	81.30	3.26	91.91	nr	173.21
Sum of two sides 2000mm	52.12	88.62	3.26	91.91	nr	180.54
90 ° mitre bend						
Sum of two sides 1100mm	30.56	51.96	3.03	85.43	nr	137.39
Sum of two sides 1200mm	32.55	55.35	3.03	85.43	nr	140.78
Sum of two sides 1300mm	34.54	58.73	3.85	108.55	nr	167.28
Sum of two sides 1400mm	36.32	61.76	3.85	108.55	nr	170.31
Sum of two sides 1500mm	42.23	71.81	4.25	119.83	nr	191.63
Sum of two sides 1600mm	48.13	81.84	4.26	120.11	nr	201.95
Sum of two sides 1700mm	54.04	91.89	4.68	131.95	nr	223.84
Sum of two sides 1800mm	59.98	101.99	4.68	131.95	nr	233.94
Sum of two sides 1900mm	65.11	110.71	4.87	137.31	nr	248.02
Sum of two sides 2000mm	71.03	120.78	4.87	137.31	nr	258.09
Branch						
Sum of two sides 1100mm	34.81	59.19	1.29	36.37	nr	95.56
Sum of two sides 1200mm	36.68	62.37	1.29	36.37	nr	98.74
Sum of two sides 1300mm	38.56	65.57	1.39	39.19	nr	104.76
Sum of two sides 1400mm	40.28	68.49	1.39	39.19	nr	107.68
Sum of two sides 1500mm	46.24	78.63	1.64	46.24	nr	124.86
Sum of two sides 1600mm	52.21	88.78	1.64	46.24	nr	135.02
Sum of two sides 1700mm	58.17	98.91	1.69	47.65	nr	146.56
Sum of two sides 1800mm	64.23	109.22	1.69	47.65	nr	156.86
Sum of two sides 1900mm	70.20	119.37	1.85	52.16	nr	171.53
Sum of two sides 2000mm	76.16	129.50	1.85	52.16	nr	181.66

U:VENTILATION/AIR CONDITIONING SYSTEMS

Item	Net Price £	Material £	Labour hours	Labour £	Unit	Total rate £
Grille neck						
Sum of two sides 1100mm	37.59	63.92	1.44	40.60	nr	**104.52**
Sum of two sides 1200mm	39.71	67.52	1.44	40.60	nr	**108.12**
Sum of two sides 1300mm	41.81	71.09	1.69	47.65	nr	**118.74**
Sum of two sides 1400mm	43.94	74.71	1.69	47.65	nr	**122.36**
Sum of two sides 1500mm	48.00	81.62	1.79	50.47	nr	**132.09**
Sum of two sides 1600mm	54.57	92.79	1.79	50.47	nr	**143.26**
Sum of two sides 1700mm	64.37	109.45	1.86	52.44	nr	**161.90**
Sum of two sides 1800mm	70.94	120.63	1.86	52.44	nr	**173.07**
Sum of two sides 1900mm	77.50	131.78	2.02	56.95	nr	**188.73**
Sum of two sides 2000mm	84.07	142.95	2.02	56.95	nr	**199.90**
Ductwork 1001 to 1250mm longest side						
Sum of two sides 1300mm	53.06	90.22	1.51	42.57	m	**132.80**
Sum of two sides 1400mm	55.56	94.47	1.55	43.70	m	**138.17**
Sum of two sides 1500mm	57.90	98.45	1.61	45.39	m	**143.85**
Sum of two sides 1600mm	60.45	102.79	1.62	45.68	m	**148.46**
Sum of two sides 1700mm	62.79	106.77	1.74	49.06	m	**155.83**
Sum of two sides 1800mm	65.13	110.75	1.76	49.62	m	**160.37**
Sum of two sides 1900mm	67.48	114.74	1.81	51.03	m	**165.77**
Sum of two sides 2000mm	70.03	119.08	1.82	51.31	m	**170.39**
Sum of two sides 2100mm	72.37	123.06	2.53	71.33	m	**194.39**
Sum of two sides 2200mm	83.48	141.95	2.55	71.90	m	**213.84**
Sum of two sides 2300mm	86.23	146.62	2.56	72.18	m	**218.80**
Sum of two sides 2400mm	88.57	150.60	2.76	77.82	m	**228.42**
Sum of two sides 2500mm	91.12	154.94	2.77	78.10	m	**233.04**
Extra over fittings; Ductwork 1001 to 1250mm longest side						
End Cap						
Sum of two sides 1300mm	19.29	32.80	0.38	10.71	nr	**43.51**
Sum of two sides 1400mm	20.13	34.23	0.38	10.71	nr	**44.94**
Sum of two sides 1500mm	23.41	39.81	0.38	10.71	nr	**50.52**
Sum of two sides 1600mm	26.69	45.38	0.38	10.71	nr	**56.10**
Sum of two sides 1700mm	29.97	50.96	0.58	16.35	nr	**67.31**
Sum of two sides 1800mm	33.25	56.54	0.58	16.35	nr	**72.89**
Sum of two sides 1900mm	36.53	62.11	0.58	16.35	nr	**78.47**
Sum of two sides 2000mm	39.80	67.68	0.58	16.35	nr	**84.03**
Sum of two sides 2100mm	43.08	73.25	0.87	24.53	nr	**97.78**
Sum of two sides 2200mm	46.36	78.83	0.87	24.53	nr	**103.36**
Sum of two sides 2300mm	49.64	84.41	0.87	24.53	nr	**108.94**
Sum of two sides 2400mm	52.92	89.98	0.87	24.53	nr	**114.51**
Sum of two sides 2500mm	56.20	95.56	0.87	24.53	nr	**120.09**
Reducer						
Sum of two sides 1300mm	12.51	21.27	2.30	64.85	nr	**86.12**
Sum of two sides 1400mm	13.03	22.16	2.30	64.85	nr	**87.00**
Sum of two sides 1500mm	15.63	26.58	2.47	69.64	nr	**96.22**
Sum of two sides 1600mm	18.30	31.12	2.47	69.64	nr	**100.76**
Sum of two sides 1700mm	20.90	35.54	2.59	73.02	nr	**108.56**
Sum of two sides 1800mm	23.50	39.96	2.59	73.02	nr	**112.98**
Sum of two sides 1900mm	26.10	44.38	2.71	76.41	nr	**120.79**
Sum of two sides 2000mm	28.77	48.92	2.71	76.41	nr	**125.33**
Sum of two sides 2100mm	31.37	53.34	2.92	82.33	nr	**135.67**
Sum of two sides 2200mm	31.84	54.14	2.92	82.33	nr	**136.47**
Sum of two sides 2300mm	34.51	58.68	2.92	82.33	nr	**141.01**
Sum of two sides 2400mm	37.12	63.12	3.12	87.97	nr	**151.08**
Sum of two sides 2500mm	39.78	67.64	3.12	87.97	nr	**155.61**

U:VENTILATION/AIR CONDITIONING SYSTEMS

Item	Net Price £	Material £	Labour hours	Labour £	Unit	Total rate £
U10 : DUCTWORK : RECTANGULAR – CLASS C (cont'd)						
Y30 - AIR DUCTLINES (cont'd)						
Fittings; Ductwork 1001 to 1250mm longest Side (cont'd)						
Offset						
Sum of two sides 1300mm	33.47	56.91	2.47	69.64	nr	**126.55**
Sum of two sides 1400mm	34.51	58.68	2.47	69.64	nr	**128.32**
Sum of two sides 1500mm	38.33	65.18	2.47	69.64	nr	**134.82**
Sum of two sides 1600mm	42.12	71.62	2.47	69.64	nr	**141.26**
Sum of two sides 1700mm	45.74	77.78	2.61	73.59	nr	**151.36**
Sum of two sides 1800mm	49.26	83.76	2.61	73.59	nr	**157.35**
Sum of two sides 1900mm	52.70	89.61	2.71	76.41	nr	**166.02**
Sum of two sides 2000mm	56.06	95.32	2.71	76.41	nr	**171.73**
Sum of two sides 2100mm	59.29	100.82	2.92	82.33	nr	**183.14**
Sum of two sides 2200mm	58.53	99.52	3.26	91.91	nr	**191.44**
Sum of two sides 2300mm	63.45	107.89	3.26	91.91	nr	**199.80**
Sum of two sides 2400mm	68.34	116.20	3.47	97.83	nr	**214.04**
Sum of two sides 2500mm	73.25	124.55	3.48	98.12	nr	**222.67**
Square to round						
Sum of two sides 1300mm	24.12	41.01	2.32	65.41	nr	**106.42**
Sum of two sides 1400mm	25.16	42.78	2.32	65.41	nr	**108.19**
Sum of two sides 1500mm	30.91	52.56	2.56	72.18	nr	**124.74**
Sum of two sides 1600mm	36.69	62.39	2.58	72.74	nr	**135.13**
Sum of two sides 1700mm	42.44	72.16	2.84	80.07	nr	**152.24**
Sum of two sides 1800mm	48.19	81.94	2.84	80.07	nr	**162.01**
Sum of two sides 1900mm	58.05	98.71	3.13	88.25	nr	**186.95**
Sum of two sides 2000mm	59.72	101.55	3.13	88.25	nr	**189.80**
Sum of two sides 2100mm	65.48	111.34	4.26	120.11	nr	**231.45**
Sum of two sides 2200mm	67.39	114.59	4.27	120.39	nr	**234.98**
Sum of two sides 2300mm	73.16	124.40	4.30	121.24	nr	**245.64**
Sum of two sides 2400mm	78.92	134.19	4.77	134.49	nr	**268.68**
Sum of two sides 2500mm	84.69	144.01	4.79	135.05	nr	**279.06**
90 ° radius bend						
Sum of two sides 1300mm	9.57	16.27	1.91	53.85	nr	**70.12**
Sum of two sides 1400mm	9.29	15.80	1.91	53.85	nr	**69.65**
Sum of two sides 1500mm	14.02	23.84	2.11	59.49	nr	**83.33**
Sum of two sides 1600mm	18.78	31.93	2.11	59.49	nr	**91.42**
Sum of two sides 1700mm	23.50	39.96	2.55	71.90	nr	**111.85**
Sum of two sides 1800mm	28.23	48.00	2.55	71.90	nr	**119.90**
Sum of two sides 1900mm	32.95	56.03	2.80	78.94	nr	**134.97**
Sum of two sides 2000mm	37.72	64.14	2.80	78.94	nr	**143.08**
Sum of two sides 2100mm	42.44	72.16	2.80	78.94	nr	**151.11**
Sum of two sides 2200mm	39.91	67.86	2.80	78.94	nr	**146.81**
Sum of two sides 2300mm	41.08	69.85	4.35	122.65	nr	**192.50**
Sum of two sides 2400mm	45.78	77.84	4.35	122.65	nr	**200.49**
Sum of two sides 2500mm	50.49	85.85	4.35	122.65	nr	**208.50**

U:VENTILATION/AIR CONDITIONING SYSTEMS

Item	Net Price £	Material £	Labour hours	Labour £	Unit	Total rate £
45 ° bend						
Sum of two sides 1300mm	15.79	26.85	2.26	63.72	nr	**90.57**
Sum of two sides 1400mm	16.19	27.53	2.44	68.79	nr	**96.32**
Sum of two sides 1500mm	19.64	33.40	2.68	75.56	nr	**108.96**
Sum of two sides 1600mm	23.18	39.41	2.69	75.84	nr	**115.26**
Sum of two sides 1700mm	26.64	45.30	2.96	83.46	nr	**128.75**
Sum of two sides 1800mm	30.10	51.18	2.96	83.46	nr	**134.64**
Sum of two sides 1900mm	33.56	57.06	3.26	91.91	nr	**148.98**
Sum of two sides 2000mm	37.10	63.08	3.26	91.91	nr	**155.00**
Sum of two sides 2100mm	40.55	68.95	7.50	211.46	nr	**280.41**
Sum of two sides 2200mm	41.25	70.14	7.50	211.46	nr	**281.60**
Sum of two sides 2300mm	43.50	73.97	7.55	212.87	nr	**286.84**
Sum of two sides 2400mm	46.95	79.83	8.13	229.22	nr	**309.05**
Sum of two sides 2500mm	50.47	85.82	8.30	234.01	nr	**319.83**
90 ° mitre bend						
Sum of two sides 1300mm	32.39	55.08	3.85	108.55	nr	**163.62**
Sum of two sides 1400mm	33.63	57.18	3.85	108.55	nr	**165.73**
Sum of two sides 1500mm	39.58	67.30	4.25	119.83	nr	**187.13**
Sum of two sides 1600mm	45.52	77.40	4.26	120.11	nr	**197.51**
Sum of two sides 1700mm	56.28	95.70	4.68	131.95	nr	**227.65**
Sum of two sides 1800mm	61.95	105.34	4.68	131.95	nr	**237.29**
Sum of two sides 1900mm	67.62	114.98	4.87	137.31	nr	**252.29**
Sum of two sides 2000mm	69.28	117.80	4.87	137.31	nr	**255.11**
Sum of two sides 2100mm	75.22	127.90	7.50	211.46	nr	**339.36**
Sum of two sides 2200mm	75.76	128.82	7.50	211.46	nr	**340.28**
Sum of two sides 2300mm	78.96	134.26	7.55	212.87	nr	**347.13**
Sum of two sides 2400mm	84.92	144.40	8.13	229.22	nr	**373.62**
Sum of two sides 2500mm	90.86	154.50	8.30	234.01	nr	**388.51**
Branch						
Sum of two sides 1300mm	32.40	55.09	1.39	39.19	nr	**94.28**
Sum of two sides 1400mm	33.77	57.42	1.39	39.19	nr	**96.61**
Sum of two sides 1500mm	38.73	65.86	1.64	46.24	nr	**112.09**
Sum of two sides 1600mm	43.75	74.39	1.64	46.24	nr	**120.63**
Sum of two sides 1700mm	48.70	82.81	1.69	47.65	nr	**130.46**
Sum of two sides 1800mm	53.65	91.23	1.69	47.65	nr	**138.87**
Sum of two sides 1900mm	58.60	99.64	1.85	52.16	nr	**151.80**
Sum of two sides 2000mm	63.62	108.18	1.85	52.16	nr	**160.34**
Sum of two sides 2100mm	68.58	116.61	2.61	73.59	nr	**190.20**
Sum of two sides 2200mm	73.53	125.03	2.61	73.59	nr	**198.62**
Sum of two sides 2300mm	78.55	133.56	2.61	73.59	nr	**207.15**
Sum of two sides 2400mm	83.50	141.98	2.88	81.20	nr	**223.18**
Sum of two sides 2500mm	88.53	150.53	2.88	81.20	nr	**231.73**
Grille neck						
Sum of two sides 1300mm	39.00	66.31	1.69	47.65	nr	**113.96**
Sum of two sides 1400mm	41.26	70.16	1.69	47.65	nr	**117.81**
Sum of two sides 1500mm	43.51	73.99	1.79	50.47	nr	**124.46**
Sum of two sides 1600mm	49.84	84.74	1.79	50.47	nr	**135.21**
Sum of two sides 1700mm	56.42	95.93	1.86	52.44	nr	**148.38**
Sum of two sides 1800mm	63.01	107.14	1.86	52.44	nr	**159.59**
Sum of two sides 1900mm	69.61	118.35	2.02	56.95	nr	**175.31**
Sum of two sides 2000mm	76.18	129.53	2.02	56.95	nr	**186.48**
Sum of two sides 2100mm	82.77	140.74	2.61	73.59	nr	**214.33**
Sum of two sides 2200mm	89.36	151.95	2.80	78.94	nr	**230.89**
Sum of two sides 2300mm	95.95	163.16	2.80	78.94	nr	**242.10**
Sum of two sides 2400mm	102.53	174.33	3.06	86.28	nr	**260.61**
Sum of two sides 2500mm	109.12	185.54	3.06	86.28	nr	**271.82**

U:VENTILATION/AIR CONDITIONING SYSTEMS

Item	Net Price £	Material £	Labour hours	Labour £	Unit	Total rate £
U10 : DUCTWORK : RECTANGULAR – CLASS C (cont'd)						
Y30 - AIR DUCTLINES (cont'd)						
Ductwork 1251 to 1600mm longest side						
Sum of two sides 1700mm	70.08	119.16	1.74	49.06	m	**168.22**
Sum of two sides 1800mm	72.81	123.80	1.76	49.62	m	**173.43**
Sum of two sides 1900mm	75.59	128.53	1.81	51.03	m	**179.56**
Sum of two sides 2000mm	78.16	132.90	1.82	51.31	m	**184.22**
Sum of two sides 2100mm	80.73	137.27	2.53	71.33	m	**208.60**
Sum of two sides 2200mm	83.30	141.64	2.55	71.90	m	**213.54**
Sum of two sides 2300mm	86.09	146.39	2.56	72.18	m	**218.56**
Sum of two sides 2400mm	88.80	150.99	2.76	77.82	m	**228.81**
Sum of two sides 2500mm	91.37	155.36	2.77	78.10	m	**233.46**
Sum of two sides 2600mm	103.15	175.39	2.97	83.74	m	**259.13**
Sum of two sides 2700mm	105.72	179.76	2.99	84.30	m	**264.07**
Sum of two sides 2800mm	108.48	184.46	3.30	93.04	m	**277.50**
Sum of two sides 2900mm	111.28	189.22	3.31	93.32	m	**282.54**
Sum of two sides 3000mm	113.84	193.57	3.53	99.53	m	**293.10**
Sum of two sides 3100mm	116.55	198.18	3.55	100.09	m	**298.27**
Sum of two sides 3200mm	119.13	202.57	3.56	100.37	m	**302.94**
Extra over fittings; Ductwork 1251 to 1600mm longest side						
End Cap						
Sum of two sides 1700mm	40.27	68.47	0.58	16.35	nr	**84.83**
Sum of two sides 1800mm	44.67	75.96	0.58	16.35	nr	**92.31**
Sum of two sides 1900mm	49.08	83.45	0.58	16.35	nr	**99.81**
Sum of two sides 2000mm	53.48	90.94	0.58	16.35	nr	**107.29**
Sum of two sides 2100mm	57.88	98.42	0.87	24.53	nr	**122.95**
Sum of two sides 2200mm	62.29	105.92	0.87	24.53	nr	**130.45**
Sum of two sides 2300mm	66.69	113.40	0.87	24.53	nr	**137.93**
Sum of two sides 2400mm	71.10	120.90	0.87	24.53	nr	**145.43**
Sum of two sides 2500mm	75.51	128.40	0.87	24.53	nr	**152.92**
Sum of two sides 2600mm	79.91	135.88	0.87	24.53	nr	**160.41**
Sum of two sides 2700mm	84.32	143.38	0.87	24.53	nr	**167.91**
Sum of two sides 2800mm	88.72	150.86	1.16	32.71	nr	**183.56**
Sum of two sides 2900mm	93.13	158.36	1.16	32.71	nr	**191.06**
Sum of two sides 3000mm	53.64	91.21	1.73	48.78	nr	**139.98**
Sum of two sides 3100mm	101.02	171.77	1.73	48.78	nr	**220.55**
Sum of two sides 3200mm	104.17	177.13	1.73	48.78	nr	**225.91**
Reducer						
Sum of two sides 1700mm	19.54	33.23	2.59	73.02	nr	**106.25**
Sum of two sides 1800mm	22.18	37.71	2.59	73.02	nr	**110.74**
Sum of two sides 1900mm	24.88	42.31	2.71	76.41	nr	**118.71**
Sum of two sides 2000mm	53.48	90.94	2.71	76.41	nr	**167.34**
Sum of two sides 2100mm	30.16	51.28	2.92	82.33	nr	**133.61**
Sum of two sides 2200mm	32.80	55.77	2.92	82.33	nr	**138.10**
Sum of two sides 2300mm	35.50	60.36	2.92	82.33	nr	**142.69**
Sum of two sides 2400mm	38.14	64.85	3.12	87.97	nr	**152.82**
Sum of two sides 2500mm	40.78	69.34	3.12	87.97	nr	**157.31**

U:VENTILATION/AIR CONDITIONING SYSTEMS

Item	Net Price £	Material £	Labour hours	Labour £	Unit	Total rate £
Sum of two sides 2600mm	40.31	68.54	3.16	89.09	nr	**157.64**
Sum of two sides 2700mm	42.95	73.03	3.16	89.09	nr	**162.13**
Sum of two sides 2800mm	45.58	77.50	4.00	112.78	nr	**190.28**
Sum of two sides 2900mm	51.00	86.72	4.01	113.06	nr	**199.78**
Sum of two sides 3000mm	53.64	91.21	4.56	128.57	nr	**219.78**
Sum of two sides 3100mm	55.60	94.54	4.56	128.57	nr	**223.11**
Sum of two sides 3200mm	57.39	97.58	4.56	128.57	nr	**226.15**
Offset						
Sum of two sides 1700mm	61.01	103.74	2.61	73.59	nr	**177.33**
Sum of two sides 1800mm	67.31	114.45	2.61	73.59	nr	**188.04**
Sum of two sides 1900mm	71.50	121.58	2.71	76.41	nr	**197.98**
Sum of two sides 2000mm	75.47	128.33	2.71	76.41	nr	**204.73**
Sum of two sides 2100mm	79.31	134.86	2.92	82.33	nr	**217.19**
Sum of two sides 2200mm	83.03	141.18	3.26	91.91	nr	**233.10**
Sum of two sides 2300mm	86.65	147.34	3.26	91.91	nr	**239.25**
Sum of two sides 2400mm	92.64	157.52	3.47	97.83	nr	**255.36**
Sum of two sides 2500mm	96.02	163.27	3.48	98.12	nr	**261.39**
Sum of two sides 2600mm	96.08	163.37	3.49	98.40	nr	**261.77**
Sum of two sides 2700mm	101.99	173.42	3.50	98.68	nr	**272.10**
Sum of two sides 2800mm	107.89	183.45	4.33	122.08	nr	**305.54**
Sum of two sides 2900mm	117.29	199.44	4.74	133.64	nr	**333.08**
Sum of two sides 3000mm	123.20	209.49	5.31	149.71	nr	**359.20**
Sum of two sides 3100mm	127.83	217.36	5.34	150.56	nr	**367.92**
Sum of two sides 3200mm	132.14	224.69	5.35	150.84	nr	**375.53**
Square to round						
Sum of two sides 1700mm	46.37	78.85	2.84	80.07	nr	**158.92**
Sum of two sides 1800mm	53.58	91.11	2.84	80.07	nr	**171.18**
Sum of two sides 1900mm	60.74	103.28	3.13	88.25	nr	**191.53**
Sum of two sides 2000mm	67.93	115.51	3.13	88.25	nr	**203.76**
Sum of two sides 2100mm	75.10	127.70	4.26	120.11	nr	**247.81**
Sum of two sides 2200mm	82.29	139.92	4.27	120.39	nr	**260.31**
Sum of two sides 2300mm	89.46	152.12	4.30	121.24	nr	**273.35**
Sum of two sides 2400mm	96.66	164.36	4.77	134.49	nr	**298.85**
Sum of two sides 2500mm	103.84	176.57	4.79	135.05	nr	**311.62**
Sum of two sides 2600mm	104.19	177.16	4.95	139.56	nr	**316.73**
Sum of two sides 2700mm	111.37	189.37	4.95	139.56	nr	**328.93**
Sum of two sides 2800mm	118.54	201.56	8.49	239.37	nr	**440.93**
Sum of two sides 2900mm	128.71	218.86	8.88	250.37	nr	**469.22**
Sum of two sides 3000mm	135.89	231.06	9.02	254.31	nr	**485.38**
Sum of two sides 3100mm	141.24	240.16	9.02	254.31	nr	**494.48**
Sum of two sides 3200mm	146.07	248.37	9.09	256.29	nr	**504.66**
90 ° radius bend						
Sum of two sides 1700mm	55.71	94.73	2.55	71.90	nr	**166.62**
Sum of two sides 1800mm	60.30	102.53	2.55	71.90	nr	**174.43**
Sum of two sides 1900mm	67.37	114.55	2.80	78.94	nr	**193.50**
Sum of two sides 2000mm	74.30	126.34	2.80	78.94	nr	**205.28**
Sum of two sides 2100mm	81.22	138.10	2.61	73.59	nr	**211.69**
Sum of two sides 2200mm	88.15	149.89	2.62	73.87	nr	**223.76**
Sum of two sides 2300mm	95.23	161.93	2.63	74.15	nr	**236.08**
Sum of two sides 2400mm	99.52	169.22	4.34	122.36	nr	**291.59**
Sum of two sides 2500mm	106.42	180.95	4.35	122.65	nr	**303.60**
Sum of two sides 2600mm	106.78	181.57	4.53	127.72	nr	**309.29**
Sum of two sides 2700mm	113.68	193.30	4.53	127.72	nr	**321.02**
Sum of two sides 2800mm	117.37	199.57	7.13	201.03	nr	**400.60**
Sum of two sides 2900mm	130.79	222.39	7.17	202.15	nr	**424.55**

U:VENTILATION/AIR CONDITIONING SYSTEMS

Item	Net Price £	Material £	Labour hours	Labour £	Unit	Total rate £
U10 : DUCTWORK : RECTANGULAR – CLASS C (cont'd)						
Y30 - AIR DUCTLINES (cont'd)						
Fittings: Ductwork 1251 to 1600mm longest Side (cont'd)						
90 ° radius bend (cont'd)						
Sum of two sides 3000mm	137.65	234.06	7.26	204.69	nr	**438.75**
Sum of two sides 3100mm	142.93	243.04	7.26	204.69	nr	**447.73**
Sum of two sides 3200mm	147.79	251.30	7.31	206.10	nr	**457.40**
45 ° bend						
Sum of two sides 1700mm	26.63	45.28	2.96	83.46	nr	**128.74**
Sum of two sides 1800mm	28.88	49.11	2.96	83.46	nr	**132.56**
Sum of two sides 1900mm	32.38	55.06	3.26	91.91	nr	**146.97**
Sum of two sides 2000mm	35.82	60.91	3.26	91.91	nr	**152.82**
Sum of two sides 2100mm	39.25	66.74	7.50	211.46	nr	**278.20**
Sum of two sides 2200mm	42.69	72.59	7.50	211.46	nr	**284.05**
Sum of two sides 2300mm	46.20	78.56	7.55	212.87	nr	**291.43**
Sum of two sides 2400mm	48.30	82.13	8.13	229.22	nr	**311.35**
Sum of two sides 2500mm	51.72	87.94	8.30	234.01	nr	**321.96**
Sum of two sides 2600mm	51.66	87.84	8.56	241.34	nr	**329.19**
Sum of two sides 2700mm	55.09	93.67	8.62	243.04	nr	**336.71**
Sum of two sides 2800mm	56.89	96.73	9.09	256.29	nr	**353.02**
Sum of two sides 2900mm	63.55	108.06	9.09	256.29	nr	**364.35**
Sum of two sides 3000mm	66.95	113.84	9.62	271.23	nr	**385.07**
Sum of two sides 3100mm	69.56	118.28	9.62	271.23	nr	**389.51**
Sum of two sides 3200mm	71.97	122.38	9.62	271.23	nr	**393.61**
90 ° mitre bend						
Sum of two sides 1700mm	64.94	110.42	4.68	131.95	nr	**242.37**
Sum of two sides 1800mm	68.90	117.16	4.68	131.95	nr	**249.11**
Sum of two sides 1900mm	76.41	129.93	4.87	137.31	nr	**267.23**
Sum of two sides 2000mm	83.93	142.71	4.87	137.31	nr	**280.02**
Sum of two sides 2100mm	91.46	155.52	7.50	211.46	nr	**366.98**
Sum of two sides 2200mm	98.98	168.30	7.50	211.46	nr	**379.76**
Sum of two sides 2300mm	106.48	181.06	7.55	212.87	nr	**393.93**
Sum of two sides 2400mm	110.29	187.53	8.13	229.22	nr	**416.76**
Sum of two sides 2500mm	117.82	200.34	8.30	234.01	nr	**434.35**
Sum of two sides 2600mm	116.70	198.43	8.56	241.34	nr	**439.78**
Sum of two sides 2700mm	124.23	211.24	8.62	243.04	nr	**454.27**
Sum of two sides 2800mm	127.34	216.53	15.20	428.56	nr	**645.08**
Sum of two sides 2900mm	140.34	238.63	15.20	428.56	nr	**667.19**
Sum of two sides 3000mm	147.88	251.45	15.60	439.83	nr	**691.29**
Sum of two sides 3100mm	154.04	261.93	16.04	452.24	nr	**714.17**
Sum of two sides 3200mm	159.91	271.91	16.04	452.24	nr	**724.15**

U:VENTILATION/AIR CONDITIONING SYSTEMS

Item	Net Price £	Material £	Labour hours	Labour £	Unit	Total rate £
Branch						
Sum of two sides 1700mm	50.01	85.04	1.69	47.65	nr	**132.68**
Sum of two sides 1800mm	54.94	93.42	1.69	47.65	nr	**141.07**
Sum of two sides 1900mm	59.95	101.94	1.85	52.16	nr	**154.10**
Sum of two sides 2000mm	64.89	110.34	1.85	52.16	nr	**162.50**
Sum of two sides 2100mm	69.82	118.72	2.61	73.59	nr	**192.31**
Sum of two sides 2200mm	74.76	127.12	2.61	73.59	nr	**200.71**
Sum of two sides 2300mm	79.77	135.64	2.61	73.59	nr	**209.23**
Sum of two sides 2400mm	84.70	144.02	2.88	81.20	nr	**225.22**
Sum of two sides 2500mm	89.63	152.41	2.88	81.20	nr	**233.61**
Sum of two sides 2600mm	94.57	160.80	2.88	81.20	nr	**242.01**
Sum of two sides 2700mm	99.51	169.20	2.88	81.20	nr	**250.41**
Sum of two sides 2800mm	104.43	177.57	3.94	111.09	nr	**288.66**
Sum of two sides 2900mm	111.07	188.86	3.94	111.09	nr	**299.95**
Sum of two sides 3000mm	116.01	197.26	4.83	136.18	nr	**333.44**
Sum of two sides 3100mm	119.95	203.96	4.83	136.18	nr	**340.14**
Sum of two sides 3200mm	123.53	210.05	4.83	136.18	nr	**346.23**
Grille neck						
Sum of two sides 1700mm	64.71	110.03	1.86	52.44	nr	**162.47**
Sum of two sides 1800mm	71.29	121.22	1.86	52.44	nr	**173.66**
Sum of two sides 1900mm	77.88	132.43	2.02	56.95	nr	**189.38**
Sum of two sides 2000mm	84.45	143.60	2.02	56.95	nr	**200.55**
Sum of two sides 2100mm	91.05	154.82	2.80	78.94	nr	**233.76**
Sum of two sides 2200mm	97.63	166.01	2.80	78.94	nr	**244.95**
Sum of two sides 2300mm	104.22	177.21	2.80	78.94	nr	**256.16**
Sum of two sides 2400mm	110.80	188.40	3.06	86.28	nr	**274.68**
Sum of two sides 2500mm	117.38	199.59	3.06	86.28	nr	**285.87**
Sum of two sides 2600mm	123.97	210.80	3.08	86.84	nr	**297.64**
Sum of two sides 2700mm	130.56	222.00	3.08	86.84	nr	**308.84**
Sum of two sides 2800mm	133.30	226.66	4.13	116.44	nr	**343.10**
Sum of two sides 2900mm	150.42	255.77	4.13	116.44	nr	**372.21**
Sum of two sides 3000mm	150.30	255.57	5.02	141.54	nr	**397.10**
Sum of two sides 3100mm	155.36	264.17	5.02	141.54	nr	**405.71**
Sum of two sides 3200mm	160.43	272.79	5.02	141.54	nr	**414.33**
Ductwork 1601 to 2000mm longest side						
Sum of two sides 2100mm	87.53	148.83	2.53	71.33	m	**220.17**
Sum of two sides 2200mm	90.32	153.58	2.55	71.90	m	**225.47**
Sum of two sides 2300mm	93.16	158.41	2.55	71.90	m	**230.30**
Sum of two sides 2400mm	95.87	163.02	2.56	72.18	m	**235.19**
Sum of two sides 2500mm	98.71	167.84	2.76	77.82	m	**245.66**
Sum of two sides 2600mm	101.35	172.33	2.77	78.10	m	**250.43**
Sum of two sides 2700mm	103.99	176.82	2.97	83.74	m	**260.56**
Sum of two sides 2800mm	106.63	181.31	2.99	84.30	m	**265.61**
Sum of two sides 2900mm	109.47	186.14	3.30	93.04	m	**279.18**
Sum of two sides 3000mm	112.11	190.63	3.31	93.32	m	**283.95**
Sum of two sides 3100mm	130.14	221.29	3.53	99.53	m	**320.81**
Sum of two sides 3200mm	132.78	225.78	3.53	99.53	m	**325.30**
Sum of two sides 3300mm	135.62	230.61	3.53	99.53	m	**330.13**
Sum of two sides 3400mm	138.27	235.11	3.55	100.09	m	**335.20**
Sum of two sides 3500mm	140.90	239.58	3.55	100.09	m	**339.67**
Sum of two sides 3600mm	143.54	244.07	3.55	100.09	m	**344.16**
Sum of two sides 3700mm	146.38	248.90	3.56	100.37	m	**349.27**
Sum of two sides 3800mm	149.03	253.41	3.56	100.37	m	**353.78**
Sum of two sides 3900mm	151.66	257.88	3.56	100.37	m	**358.25**
Sum of two sides 4000mm	154.31	262.39	3.56	100.37	m	**362.76**

U:VENTILATION/AIR CONDITIONING SYSTEMS

Item	Net Price £	Material £	Labour hours	Labour £	Unit	Total rate £
U10 : DUCTWORK : RECTANGULAR – **CLASS C (cont'd)**						
Y30 - AIR DUCTLINES (cont'd)						
Extra over fittings; Ductwork 1601 to **2000mm longest side**						
End Cap						
Sum of two sides 2100mm	73.11	124.31	0.87	24.53	nr	**148.84**
Sum of two sides 2200mm	78.65	133.73	0.87	24.53	nr	**158.26**
Sum of two sides 2300mm	84.20	143.17	0.87	24.53	nr	**167.70**
Sum of two sides 2400mm	89.72	152.56	0.87	24.53	nr	**177.09**
Sum of two sides 2500mm	95.27	162.00	0.87	24.53	nr	**186.52**
Sum of two sides 2600mm	100.81	171.42	0.87	24.53	nr	**195.94**
Sum of two sides 2700mm	106.35	180.84	0.87	24.53	nr	**205.36**
Sum of two sides 2800mm	111.90	190.27	1.16	32.71	nr	**222.98**
Sum of two sides 2900mm	117.44	199.69	1.16	32.71	nr	**232.40**
Sum of two sides 3000mm	122.98	209.11	1.73	48.78	nr	**257.89**
Sum of two sides 3100mm	127.38	216.59	1.73	48.78	nr	**265.37**
Sum of two sides 3200mm	131.36	223.36	1.73	48.78	nr	**272.14**
Sum of two sides 3300mm	135.36	230.16	1.73	48.78	nr	**278.94**
Sum of two sides 3400mm	139.33	236.91	1.73	48.78	nr	**285.69**
Sum of two sides 3500mm	143.31	243.68	1.73	48.78	nr	**292.46**
Sum of two sides 3600mm	147.30	250.47	1.73	48.78	nr	**299.24**
Sum of two sides 3700mm	151.28	257.23	1.73	48.78	nr	**306.01**
Sum of two sides 3800mm	155.26	264.00	1.73	48.78	nr	**312.78**
Sum of two sides 3900mm	159.26	270.80	1.73	48.78	nr	**319.58**
Sum of two sides 4000mm	163.24	277.57	1.73	48.78	nr	**326.35**
Reducer						
Sum of two sides 2100mm	28.85	49.06	2.92	82.33	nr	**131.38**
Sum of two sides 2200mm	31.55	53.65	2.92	82.33	nr	**135.97**
Sum of two sides 2300mm	34.30	58.32	2.92	82.33	nr	**140.65**
Sum of two sides 2400mm	36.94	62.81	3.12	87.97	nr	**150.78**
Sum of two sides 2500mm	39.69	67.49	3.12	87.97	nr	**155.45**
Sum of two sides 2600mm	42.39	72.08	3.16	89.09	nr	**161.17**
Sum of two sides 2700mm	45.08	76.65	3.16	89.09	nr	**165.75**
Sum of two sides 2800mm	47.78	81.24	4.00	112.78	nr	**194.02**
Sum of two sides 2900mm	50.53	85.92	4.01	113.06	nr	**198.98**
Sum of two sides 3000mm	53.22	90.49	4.01	113.06	nr	**203.55**
Sum of two sides 3100mm	49.59	84.32	4.01	113.06	nr	**197.38**
Sum of two sides 3200mm	51.41	87.42	4.56	128.57	nr	**215.98**
Sum of two sides 3300mm	56.14	95.46	4.56	128.57	nr	**224.03**
Sum of two sides 3400mm	57.96	98.55	4.56	128.57	nr	**227.12**
Sum of two sides 3500mm	59.78	101.65	4.56	128.57	nr	**230.22**
Sum of two sides 3600mm	61.60	104.74	4.56	128.57	nr	**233.31**
Sum of two sides 3700mm	63.48	107.94	4.56	128.57	nr	**236.51**
Sum of two sides 3800mm	65.29	111.02	4.56	128.57	nr	**239.58**
Sum of two sides 3900mm	67.11	114.11	4.56	128.57	nr	**242.68**
Sum of two sides 4000mm	68.93	117.21	4.56	128.57	nr	**245.77**

U:VENTILATION/AIR CONDITIONING SYSTEMS

Item	Net Price £	Material £	Labour hours	Labour £	Unit	Total rate £
Offset						
Sum of two sides 2100mm	87.04	148.00	2.92	82.33	nr	**230.33**
Sum of two sides 2200mm	93.56	159.09	3.26	91.91	nr	**251.00**
Sum of two sides 2300mm	97.28	165.41	3.26	91.91	nr	**257.33**
Sum of two sides 2400mm	106.59	181.24	3.47	97.83	nr	**279.08**
Sum of two sides 2500mm	110.18	187.35	3.48	98.12	nr	**285.46**
Sum of two sides 2600mm	113.55	193.08	3.49	98.40	nr	**291.48**
Sum of two sides 2700mm	116.80	198.60	3.50	98.68	nr	**297.29**
Sum of two sides 2800mm	119.90	203.88	4.33	122.08	nr	**325.96**
Sum of two sides 2900mm	122.91	208.99	4.74	133.64	nr	**342.64**
Sum of two sides 3000mm	125.74	213.81	5.31	149.71	nr	**363.52**
Sum of two sides 3100mm	119.77	203.65	5.34	150.56	nr	**354.21**
Sum of two sides 3200mm	124.20	211.19	5.35	150.84	nr	**362.03**
Sum of two sides 3300mm	132.31	224.98	5.35	150.84	nr	**375.82**
Sum of two sides 3400mm	136.74	232.51	5.35	150.84	nr	**383.35**
Sum of two sides 3500mm	141.16	240.03	5.35	150.84	nr	**390.87**
Sum of two sides 3600mm	145.60	247.58	5.35	150.84	nr	**398.42**
Sum of two sides 3700mm	150.05	255.14	5.35	150.84	nr	**405.98**
Sum of two sides 3800mm	154.48	262.67	5.35	150.84	nr	**413.52**
Sum of two sides 3900mm	158.91	270.21	5.35	150.84	nr	**421.05**
Sum of two sides 4000mm	163.34	277.74	5.35	150.84	nr	**428.58**
Square to round						
Sum of two sides 2100mm	80.42	136.74	4.26	120.11	nr	**256.85**
Sum of two sides 2200mm	88.20	149.97	4.27	120.39	nr	**270.36**
Sum of two sides 2300mm	95.94	163.13	4.30	121.24	nr	**284.37**
Sum of two sides 2400mm	163.88	278.66	4.77	134.49	nr	**413.15**
Sum of two sides 2500mm	111.49	189.58	4.79	135.05	nr	**324.63**
Sum of two sides 2600mm	119.25	202.77	4.95	139.56	nr	**342.33**
Sum of two sides 2700mm	127.00	215.95	4.95	139.56	nr	**355.51**
Sum of two sides 2800mm	134.77	229.16	8.49	239.37	nr	**468.53**
Sum of two sides 2900mm	142.50	242.30	8.88	250.37	nr	**492.67**
Sum of two sides 3000mm	150.27	255.52	9.02	254.31	nr	**509.83**
Sum of two sides 3100mm	145.38	247.20	9.02	254.31	nr	**501.52**
Sum of two sides 3200mm	150.65	256.16	9.09	256.29	nr	**512.45**
Sum of two sides 3300mm	158.60	269.68	9.09	256.29	nr	**525.97**
Sum of two sides 3400mm	163.88	278.66	9.09	256.29	nr	**534.95**
Sum of two sides 3500mm	169.14	287.60	9.09	256.29	nr	**543.89**
Sum of two sides 3600mm	174.40	296.55	9.09	256.29	nr	**552.83**
Sum of two sides 3700mm	179.65	305.47	9.09	256.29	nr	**561.76**
Sum of two sides 3800mm	184.91	314.42	9.09	256.29	nr	**570.71**
Sum of two sides 3900mm	190.18	323.38	9.09	256.29	nr	**579.67**
Sum of two sides 4000mm	195.45	332.34	9.09	256.29	nr	**588.63**

U:VENTILATION/AIR CONDITIONING SYSTEMS

Item	Net Price £	Material £	Labour hours	Labour £	Unit	Total rate £
U10 : DUCTWORK : RECTANGULAR – CLASS C (cont'd)						
Y30 - AIR DUCTLINES (cont'd)						
Fittings: Ductwork 1601 to 2000mm longest Side (cont'd)						
90 ° radius bend						
Sum of two sides 2100mm	100.78	171.36	2.61	73.59	nr	**244.95**
Sum of two sides 2200mm	122.41	208.14	2.62	73.87	nr	**282.01**
Sum of two sides 2300mm	132.47	225.25	2.63	74.15	nr	**299.40**
Sum of two sides 2400mm	135.69	230.72	4.34	122.36	nr	**353.09**
Sum of two sides 2500mm	145.72	247.78	4.35	122.65	nr	**370.43**
Sum of two sides 2600mm	155.51	264.43	4.53	127.72	nr	**392.15**
Sum of two sides 2700mm	165.30	281.07	4.53	127.72	nr	**408.79**
Sum of two sides 2800mm	175.10	297.74	7.13	201.03	nr	**498.76**
Sum of two sides 2900mm	185.12	314.77	7.17	202.15	nr	**516.93**
Sum of two sides 3000mm	194.91	331.42	7.26	204.69	nr	**536.11**
Sum of two sides 3100mm	189.33	321.93	7.26	204.69	nr	**526.63**
Sum of two sides 3200mm	196.42	333.99	7.31	206.10	nr	**540.09**
Sum of two sides 3300mm	212.57	361.45	7.31	206.10	nr	**567.55**
Sum of two sides 3400mm	219.66	373.51	7.31	206.10	nr	**579.61**
Sum of two sides 3500mm	226.75	385.56	7.31	206.10	nr	**591.66**
Sum of two sides 3600mm	233.83	397.60	7.31	206.10	nr	**603.70**
Sum of two sides 3700mm	241.16	410.06	7.31	206.10	nr	**616.17**
Sum of two sides 3800mm	248.24	422.10	7.31	206.10	nr	**628.20**
Sum of two sides 3900mm	255.33	434.16	7.31	206.10	nr	**640.26**
Sum of two sides 4000mm	262.43	446.23	7.31	206.10	nr	**652.33**
45 ° bend						
Sum of two sides 2100mm	78.48	133.45	7.50	211.46	nr	**344.90**
Sum of two sides 2200mm	81.86	139.19	7.50	211.46	nr	**350.65**
Sum of two sides 2300mm	88.18	149.94	7.55	212.87	nr	**362.81**
Sum of two sides 2400mm	91.09	154.89	8.13	229.22	nr	**384.11**
Sum of two sides 2500mm	97.40	165.62	8.30	234.01	nr	**399.63**
Sum of two sides 2600mm	103.53	176.04	8.56	241.34	nr	**417.39**
Sum of two sides 2700mm	109.67	186.48	8.62	243.04	nr	**429.52**
Sum of two sides 2800mm	115.80	196.90	9.09	256.29	nr	**453.19**
Sum of two sides 2900mm	122.10	207.62	9.09	256.29	nr	**463.90**
Sum of two sides 3000mm	128.23	218.04	9.62	271.23	nr	**489.27**
Sum of two sides 3100mm	126.54	215.17	9.62	271.23	nr	**486.40**
Sum of two sides 3200mm	130.99	222.73	9.62	271.23	nr	**493.96**
Sum of two sides 3300mm	141.10	239.92	9.62	271.23	nr	**511.15**
Sum of two sides 3400mm	145.56	247.51	9.62	271.23	nr	**518.74**
Sum of two sides 3500mm	150.00	255.06	9.62	271.23	nr	**526.29**
Sum of two sides 3600mm	154.46	262.64	9.62	271.23	nr	**533.87**
Sum of two sides 3700mm	159.08	270.50	9.62	271.23	nr	**541.73**
Sum of two sides 3800mm	163.53	278.06	9.62	271.23	nr	**549.29**
Sum of two sides 3900mm	167.98	285.63	9.62	271.23	nr	**556.86**
Sum of two sides 4000mm	172.43	293.20	9.62	271.23	nr	**564.43**

U:VENTILATION/AIR CONDITIONING SYSTEMS

Item	Net Price £	Material £	Labour hours	Labour £	Unit	Total rate £
90 ° mitre bend						
Sum of two sides 2100mm	149.08	253.49	7.50	211.46	nr	**464.95**
Sum of two sides 2200mm	157.43	267.69	7.50	211.46	nr	**479.15**
Sum of two sides 2300mm	169.71	288.57	7.55	212.87	nr	**501.44**
Sum of two sides 2400mm	173.69	295.34	8.13	229.22	nr	**524.56**
Sum of two sides 2500mm	185.96	316.20	8.30	234.01	nr	**550.22**
Sum of two sides 2600mm	198.31	337.20	8.56	241.34	nr	**578.55**
Sum of two sides 2700mm	210.67	358.22	8.62	243.04	nr	**601.26**
Sum of two sides 2800mm	223.03	379.24	15.20	428.56	nr	**807.79**
Sum of two sides 2900mm	235.30	400.10	15.20	428.56	nr	**828.66**
Sum of two sides 3000mm	247.65	421.10	15.60	439.83	nr	**860.93**
Sum of two sides 3100mm	240.86	409.55	16.04	452.24	nr	**861.79**
Sum of two sides 3200mm	250.36	425.71	16.04	452.24	nr	**877.95**
Sum of two sides 3300mm	264.93	450.48	16.04	452.24	nr	**902.72**
Sum of two sides 3400mm	274.42	466.62	16.04	452.24	nr	**918.86**
Sum of two sides 3500mm	283.92	482.77	16.04	452.24	nr	**935.01**
Sum of two sides 3600mm	293.41	498.91	16.04	452.24	nr	**951.15**
Sum of two sides 3700mm	302.83	514.93	16.04	452.24	nr	**967.17**
Sum of two sides 3800mm	312.32	531.06	16.04	452.24	nr	**983.30**
Sum of two sides 3900mm	321.82	547.22	16.04	452.24	nr	**999.46**
Sum of two sides 4000mm	331.31	563.35	16.04	452.24	nr	**1015.59**
Branch						
Sum of two sides 2100mm	68.84	117.05	2.61	73.59	nr	**190.64**
Sum of two sides 2200mm	73.45	124.89	2.61	73.59	nr	**198.48**
Sum of two sides 2300mm	78.33	133.19	2.61	73.59	nr	**206.78**
Sum of two sides 2400mm	83.06	141.23	2.88	81.20	nr	**222.43**
Sum of two sides 2500mm	87.95	149.55	2.88	81.20	nr	**230.75**
Sum of two sides 2600mm	92.77	157.74	2.88	81.20	nr	**238.94**
Sum of two sides 2700mm	97.57	165.91	2.88	81.20	nr	**247.11**
Sum of two sides 2800mm	102.39	174.10	3.94	111.09	nr	**285.19**
Sum of two sides 2900mm	107.28	182.42	3.94	111.09	nr	**293.50**
Sum of two sides 3000mm	112.10	190.61	4.83	136.18	nr	**326.79**
Sum of two sides 3100mm	115.94	197.14	4.83	136.18	nr	**333.32**
Sum of two sides 3200mm	119.45	203.11	4.83	136.18	nr	**339.29**
Sum of two sides 3300mm	124.63	211.92	4.83	136.18	nr	**348.10**
Sum of two sides 3400mm	128.13	217.87	4.83	136.18	nr	**354.05**
Sum of two sides 3500mm	131.64	223.84	4.83	136.18	nr	**360.02**
Sum of two sides 3600mm	135.14	229.79	4.83	136.18	nr	**365.97**
Sum of two sides 3700mm	138.72	235.88	4.83	136.18	nr	**372.06**
Sum of two sides 3800mm	142.22	241.83	4.83	136.18	nr	**378.01**
Sum of two sides 3900mm	145.73	247.80	4.83	136.18	nr	**383.98**
Sum of two sides 4000mm	149.23	253.75	4.83	136.18	nr	**389.93**
Grille neck						
Sum of two sides 2100mm	92.54	157.35	2.80	78.94	nr	**236.30**
Sum of two sides 2200mm	99.18	168.64	2.80	78.94	nr	**247.59**
Sum of two sides 2300mm	105.84	179.97	2.80	78.94	nr	**258.91**
Sum of two sides 2400mm	112.50	191.29	3.06	86.28	nr	**277.57**
Sum of two sides 2500mm	119.15	202.60	3.06	86.28	nr	**288.88**
Sum of two sides 2600mm	125.81	213.92	3.08	86.84	nr	**300.76**
Sum of two sides 2700mm	97.57	165.91	3.08	86.84	nr	**252.75**
Sum of two sides 2800mm	102.39	174.10	4.13	116.44	nr	**290.55**
Sum of two sides 2900mm	107.28	182.42	4.13	116.44	nr	**298.86**
Sum of two sides 3000mm	152.42	259.17	5.02	141.54	nr	**400.71**
Sum of two sides 3100mm	157.55	267.89	5.02	141.54	nr	**409.43**
Sum of two sides 3200mm	162.69	276.63	5.02	141.54	nr	**418.17**
Sum of two sides 3300mm	167.60	284.98	5.02	141.54	nr	**426.52**
Sum of two sides 3400mm	172.50	293.32	5.02	141.54	nr	**434.85**
Sum of two sides 3500mm	177.42	301.68	5.02	141.54	nr	**443.22**

U:VENTILATION/AIR CONDITIONING SYSTEMS

Item	Net Price £	Material £	Labour hours	Labour £	Unit	Total rate £
U10 : DUCTWORK : RECTANGULAR – CLASS C (cont'd)						
Y30 - AIR DUCTLINES (cont'd)						
Fittings: Ductwork 1601 to 2000mm longest Side (cont'd)						
Grille neck (cont'd)						
Sum of two sides 3600mm	182.31	310.00	5.02	141.54	nr	**451.53**
Sum of two sides 3700mm	187.22	318.35	5.02	141.54	nr	**459.88**
Sum of two sides 3800mm	192.13	326.69	5.02	141.54	nr	**468.23**
Sum of two sides 3900mm	197.04	335.04	5.02	141.54	nr	**476.58**
Sum of two sides 4000mm	201.95	343.39	5.02	141.54	nr	**484.93**
Ductwork 2001 to 2500mm longest side						
Sum of two sides 2500mm	178.80	294.29	2.77	78.10	m	**372.39**
Sum of two sides 2600mm	183.86	302.62	2.97	83.74	m	**386.36**
Sum of two sides 2700mm	188.77	310.70	2.99	84.30	m	**395.00**
Sum of two sides 2800mm	193.72	318.85	3.30	93.04	m	**411.89**
Sum of two sides 2900mm	198.62	326.91	3.31	93.32	m	**420.24**
Sum of two sides 3000mm	203.22	334.49	3.53	99.53	m	**434.01**
Sum of two sides 3100mm	207.95	342.27	3.55	100.09	m	**442.36**
Sum of two sides 3200mm	212.55	349.84	3.56	100.37	m	**450.21**
Sum of two sides 3300mm	217.45	357.91	3.56	100.37	m	**458.28**
Sum of two sides 3400mm	222.05	365.48	3.56	100.37	m	**465.85**
Sum of two sides 3500mm	243.60	400.95	3.56	100.37	m	**501.32**
Sum of two sides 3600mm	248.20	408.52	3.56	100.37	m	**508.89**
Sum of two sides 3700mm	253.10	416.58	3.56	100.37	m	**516.96**
Sum of two sides 3800mm	257.70	424.16	3.56	100.37	m	**524.53**
Sum of two sides 3900mm	262.30	431.73	3.56	100.37	m	**532.10**
Sum of two sides 4000mm	267.71	455.21	3.56	100.37	m	**555.58**
Extra over fittings; Ductwork 2001 to 2500mm longest side						
End Cap						
Sum of two sides 2500mm	95.27	162.00	0.87	24.53	nr	**186.52**
Sum of two sides 2600mm	100.81	171.42	0.87	24.53	nr	**195.94**
Sum of two sides 2700mm	106.36	180.85	0.87	24.53	nr	**205.38**
Sum of two sides 2800mm	111.90	190.27	1.16	32.71	nr	**222.98**
Sum of two sides 2900mm	117.44	199.69	1.16	32.71	nr	**232.40**
Sum of two sides 3000mm	122.99	209.13	1.73	48.78	nr	**257.91**
Sum of two sides 3100mm	127.38	216.59	1.73	48.78	nr	**265.37**
Sum of two sides 3200mm	131.36	223.36	1.73	48.78	nr	**272.14**
Sum of two sides 3300mm	135.35	230.15	1.73	48.78	nr	**278.92**
Sum of two sides 3400mm	139.33	236.91	1.73	48.78	nr	**285.69**
Sum of two sides 3500mm	143.32	243.70	1.73	48.78	nr	**292.48**
Sum of two sides 3600mm	147.30	250.47	1.73	48.78	nr	**299.24**
Sum of two sides 3700mm	151.28	257.23	1.73	48.78	nr	**306.01**
Sum of two sides 3800mm	155.27	264.02	1.73	48.78	nr	**312.79**
Sum of two sides 3900mm	159.26	270.80	1.73	48.78	nr	**319.58**
Sum of two sides 4000mm	163.25	277.59	1.73	48.78	nr	**326.36**

U:VENTILATION/AIR CONDITIONING SYSTEMS

Item	Net Price £	Material £	Labour hours	Labour £	Unit	Total rate £
Reducer						
Sum of two sides 2500mm	20.20	34.35	3.12	87.97	nr	**122.31**
Sum of two sides 2600mm	22.36	38.02	3.16	89.09	nr	**127.12**
Sum of two sides 2700mm	24.62	41.86	3.16	89.09	nr	**130.96**
Sum of two sides 2800mm	26.68	45.37	4.00	112.78	nr	**158.14**
Sum of two sides 2900mm	28.94	49.21	4.01	113.06	nr	**162.27**
Sum of two sides 3000mm	31.11	52.90	4.56	128.57	nr	**181.47**
Sum of two sides 3100mm	32.58	55.40	4.56	128.57	nr	**183.97**
Sum of two sides 3200mm	33.87	57.59	4.56	128.57	nr	**186.16**
Sum of two sides 3300mm	35.26	59.96	4.56	128.57	nr	**188.52**
Sum of two sides 3400mm	36.55	62.15	4.56	128.57	nr	**190.72**
Sum of two sides 3500mm	31.89	54.23	4.56	128.57	nr	**182.79**
Sum of two sides 3600mm	33.18	56.42	4.56	128.57	nr	**184.99**
Sum of two sides 3700mm	37.49	63.75	4.56	128.57	nr	**192.31**
Sum of two sides 3800mm	38.78	65.94	4.56	128.57	nr	**194.51**
Sum of two sides 3900mm	40.07	68.13	4.56	128.57	nr	**196.70**
Sum of two sides 4000mm	41.45	70.48	4.56	128.57	nr	**199.05**
Offset						
Sum of two sides 2500mm	95.58	162.52	3.48	98.12	nr	**260.64**
Sum of two sides 2600mm	101.65	172.84	3.49	98.40	nr	**271.24**
Sum of two sides 2700mm	101.24	172.15	3.50	98.68	nr	**270.83**
Sum of two sides 2800mm	113.81	193.52	4.33	122.08	nr	**315.60**
Sum of two sides 2900mm	113.08	192.28	4.74	133.64	nr	**325.92**
Sum of two sides 3000mm	111.90	190.27	5.31	149.71	nr	**339.99**
Sum of two sides 3100mm	109.09	185.49	5.34	150.56	nr	**336.05**
Sum of two sides 3200mm	105.60	179.56	5.35	150.84	nr	**330.40**
Sum of two sides 3300mm	101.85	173.18	5.35	150.84	nr	**324.02**
Sum of two sides 3400mm	97.70	166.13	5.35	150.84	nr	**316.97**
Sum of two sides 3500mm	89.62	152.39	5.35	150.84	nr	**303.23**
Sum of two sides 3600mm	93.07	158.25	5.35	150.84	nr	**309.10**
Sum of two sides 3700mm	100.32	170.58	5.35	150.84	nr	**321.42**
Sum of two sides 3800mm	103.78	176.47	5.35	150.84	nr	**327.31**
Sum of two sides 3900mm	107.24	182.35	5.35	150.84	nr	**333.19**
Sum of two sides 4000mm	110.74	188.30	5.35	150.84	nr	**339.14**
Square to round						
Sum of two sides 2500mm	67.92	115.49	4.79	135.05	nr	**250.54**
Sum of two sides 2600mm	74.49	126.66	4.95	139.56	nr	**266.22**
Sum of two sides 2700mm	81.05	137.82	4.95	139.56	nr	**277.38**
Sum of two sides 2800mm	87.63	149.00	8.49	239.37	nr	**388.38**
Sum of two sides 2900mm	94.19	160.16	8.88	250.37	nr	**410.53**
Sum of two sides 3000mm	100.76	171.33	9.02	254.31	nr	**425.64**
Sum of two sides 3100mm	105.39	179.20	9.02	254.31	nr	**433.52**
Sum of two sides 3200mm	109.47	186.14	9.09	256.29	nr	**442.43**
Sum of two sides 3300mm	113.53	193.04	9.09	256.29	nr	**449.33**
Sum of two sides 3400mm	117.61	199.98	9.09	256.29	nr	**456.27**
Sum of two sides 3500mm	110.08	187.18	9.09	256.29	nr	**443.47**
Sum of two sides 3600mm	114.15	194.10	9.09	256.29	nr	**450.39**
Sum of two sides 3700mm	120.98	205.71	9.09	256.29	nr	**462.00**
Sum of two sides 3800mm	125.06	212.65	9.09	256.29	nr	**468.94**
Sum of two sides 3900mm	129.14	219.59	9.09	256.29	nr	**475.88**
Sum of two sides 4000mm	133.18	226.46	9.09	256.29	nr	**482.74**

U:VENTILATION/AIR CONDITIONING SYSTEMS

Item	Net Price £	Material £	Labour hours	Labour £	Unit	Total rate £
U10 : DUCTWORK : RECTANGULAR – **CLASS C (cont'd)**						
Y30 - AIR DUCTLINES (cont'd)						
Fittings: Ductwork 2001 to 2500mm longest **Side (cont'd)**						
90 ° radius bend						
Sum of two sides 2500mm	98.84	168.07	4.35	122.65	nr	**290.71**
Sum of two sides 2600mm	101.28	172.21	4.53	127.72	nr	**299.94**
Sum of two sides 2700mm	110.16	187.31	4.53	127.72	nr	**315.03**
Sum of two sides 2800mm	105.38	179.19	7.13	201.03	nr	**380.21**
Sum of two sides 2900mm	114.08	193.98	7.17	202.15	nr	**396.13**
Sum of two sides 3000mm	122.43	208.18	7.26	204.69	nr	**412.87**
Sum of two sides 3100mm	128.65	218.75	7.26	204.69	nr	**423.45**
Sum of two sides 3200mm	134.30	228.36	7.31	206.10	nr	**434.46**
Sum of two sides 3300mm	140.29	238.55	7.31	206.10	nr	**444.65**
Sum of two sides 3400mm	145.94	248.15	7.31	206.10	nr	**454.26**
Sum of two sides 3500mm	135.24	229.96	7.31	206.10	nr	**436.06**
Sum of two sides 3600mm	140.90	239.58	7.31	206.10	nr	**445.69**
Sum of two sides 3700mm	155.90	265.09	7.31	206.10	nr	**471.19**
Sum of two sides 3800mm	161.55	274.70	7.31	206.10	nr	**480.80**
Sum of two sides 3900mm	167.20	284.30	7.31	206.10	nr	**490.41**
Sum of two sides 4000mm	164.88	280.36	7.31	206.10	nr	**486.46**
45 ° bend						
Sum of two sides 2500mm	77.18	131.24	8.30	234.01	nr	**365.25**
Sum of two sides 2600mm	79.88	135.83	8.56	241.34	nr	**377.17**
Sum of two sides 2700mm	85.74	145.79	8.62	243.04	nr	**388.83**
Sum of two sides 2800mm	84.93	144.41	9.09	256.29	nr	**400.70**
Sum of two sides 2900mm	90.70	154.22	9.09	256.29	nr	**410.51**
Sum of two sides 3000mm	96.21	163.59	9.62	271.23	nr	**434.82**
Sum of two sides 3100mm	100.42	170.75	9.62	271.23	nr	**441.98**
Sum of two sides 3200mm	104.24	177.25	9.62	271.23	nr	**448.48**
Sum of two sides 3300mm	108.33	184.20	9.62	271.23	nr	**455.43**
Sum of two sides 3400mm	112.16	190.71	9.62	271.23	nr	**461.95**
Sum of two sides 3500mm	108.13	183.86	9.62	271.23	nr	**455.09**
Sum of two sides 3600mm	111.95	190.36	9.62	271.23	nr	**461.59**
Sum of two sides 3700mm	121.65	206.85	9.62	271.23	nr	**478.08**
Sum of two sides 3800mm	125.48	213.36	9.62	271.23	nr	**484.59**
Sum of two sides 3900mm	129.31	219.88	9.62	271.23	nr	**491.11**
Sum of two sides 4000mm	129.48	220.17	9.62	271.23	nr	**491.40**
90 ° mitre bend						
Sum of two sides 2500mm	114.80	195.20	8.30	234.01	nr	**429.22**
Sum of two sides 2600mm	119.97	203.99	8.56	241.34	nr	**445.34**
Sum of two sides 2700mm	130.40	221.73	8.62	243.04	nr	**464.77**
Sum of two sides 2800mm	123.61	210.18	15.20	428.56	nr	**638.74**
Sum of two sides 2900mm	133.82	227.54	15.20	428.56	nr	**656.10**
Sum of two sides 3000mm	144.20	245.19	15.20	428.56	nr	**673.75**
Sum of two sides 3100mm	152.30	258.97	16.04	452.24	nr	**711.21**
Sum of two sides 3200mm	159.82	271.75	16.04	452.24	nr	**723.99**
Sum of two sides 3300mm	167.17	284.25	16.04	452.24	nr	**736.49**
Sum of two sides 3400mm	174.69	297.04	16.04	452.24	nr	**749.28**
Sum of two sides 3500mm	160.37	272.69	16.04	452.24	nr	**724.93**

U:VENTILATION/AIR CONDITIONING SYSTEMS

Item	Net Price £	Material £	Labour hours	Labour £	Unit	Total rate £
Sum of two sides 3600mm	167.90	285.49	16.04	452.24	nr	**737.73**
Sum of two sides 3700mm	180.88	307.56	16.04	452.24	nr	**759.80**
Sum of two sides 3800mm	188.41	320.37	16.04	452.24	nr	**772.61**
Sum of two sides 3900mm	195.93	333.16	16.04	452.24	nr	**785.40**
Sum of two sides 4000mm	192.32	327.02	16.04	452.24	nr	**779.26**
Branch						
Sum of two sides 2500mm	91.79	156.08	2.88	81.20	nr	**237.28**
Sum of two sides 2600mm	96.71	164.44	2.88	81.20	nr	**245.64**
Sum of two sides 2700mm	101.75	173.01	2.88	81.20	nr	**254.21**
Sum of two sides 2800mm	106.54	181.16	3.94	111.09	nr	**292.24**
Sum of two sides 2900mm	111.58	189.73	3.94	111.09	nr	**300.81**
Sum of two sides 3000mm	116.51	198.11	4.83	136.18	nr	**334.29**
Sum of two sides 3100mm	120.49	204.88	4.83	136.18	nr	**341.06**
Sum of two sides 3200mm	124.08	210.98	4.83	136.18	nr	**347.16**
Sum of two sides 3300mm	127.81	217.33	4.83	136.18	nr	**353.51**
Sum of two sides 3400mm	131.42	223.46	4.83	136.18	nr	**359.64**
Sum of two sides 3500mm	135.20	229.89	4.83	136.18	nr	**366.07**
Sum of two sides 3600mm	138.82	236.05	4.83	136.18	nr	**372.23**
Sum of two sides 3700mm	144.19	245.18	4.83	136.18	nr	**381.36**
Sum of two sides 3800mm	147.80	251.32	4.83	136.18	nr	**387.50**
Sum of two sides 3900mm	151.42	257.47	4.83	136.18	nr	**393.65**
Sum of two sides 4000mm	155.15	263.81	4.83	136.18	nr	**399.99**
Grille neck						
Sum of two sides 2500mm	124.29	211.34	3.06	86.28	nr	**297.62**
Sum of two sides 2600mm	131.23	223.14	3.08	86.84	nr	**309.98**
Sum of two sides 2700mm	138.17	234.94	3.08	86.84	nr	**321.78**
Sum of two sides 2800mm	145.11	246.74	4.13	116.44	nr	**363.19**
Sum of two sides 2900mm	152.05	258.54	4.13	116.44	nr	**374.99**
Sum of two sides 3000mm	158.99	270.34	5.02	141.54	nr	**411.88**
Sum of two sides 3100mm	164.35	279.46	5.02	141.54	nr	**420.99**
Sum of two sides 3200mm	169.70	288.55	5.02	141.54	nr	**430.09**
Sum of two sides 3300mm	174.82	297.26	5.02	141.54	nr	**438.80**
Sum of two sides 3400mm	179.93	305.95	5.02	141.54	nr	**447.49**
Sum of two sides 3500mm	185.06	314.67	5.02	141.54	nr	**456.21**
Sum of two sides 3600mm	190.17	323.36	5.02	141.54	nr	**464.90**
Sum of two sides 3700mm	195.29	332.07	5.02	141.54	nr	**473.60**
Sum of two sides 3800mm	200.41	340.77	5.02	141.54	nr	**482.31**
Sum of two sides 3900mm	205.53	349.48	5.02	141.54	nr	**491.02**
Sum of two sides 4000mm	210.65	358.19	5.02	141.54	nr	**499.72**

Y30 - DUCTWORK ANCILLARIES: ACCESS DOORS

Refer to ancillaries in U10: DUCTWORK: RECTANGULAR: CLASS B for details of access doors

U:VENTILATION/AIR CONDITIONING SYSTEMS

Item	Net Price £	Material £	Labour hours	Labour £	Unit	Total rate £
U10 : DUCTWORK : VOLUME/FIRE DAMPERS						
Y30 - DUCTWORK ANCILLARIES: VOLUME CONTROL AND FIRE DAMPERS						
Volume control damper; opposed blade; galvanised steel casing; aluminium aerofoil blades; manually operated						
Rectangular						
Sum of two sides 200mm	18.91	32.15	1.60	45.11	nr	77.27
Sum of two sides 300mm	21.56	36.66	1.60	45.11	nr	81.77
Sum of two sides 400mm	24.12	41.01	1.60	45.11	nr	86.12
Sum of two sides 500mm	26.84	45.64	1.60	45.11	nr	90.75
Sum of two sides 600mm	29.89	50.82	1.70	47.95	nr	98.77
Sum of two sides 700mm	32.78	55.74	2.10	59.23	nr	114.97
Sum of two sides 800mm	35.76	60.81	2.15	60.62	nr	121.42
Sum of two sides 900mm	38.82	66.01	2.30	64.85	nr	130.86
Sum of two sides 1000mm	42.12	71.62	2.40	67.67	nr	139.29
Sum of two sides 1100mm	45.58	77.50	2.60	73.31	nr	150.81
Sum of two sides 1200mm	49.30	83.83	2.80	78.94	nr	162.77
Sum of two sides 1300mm	53.27	90.58	3.10	87.40	nr	177.98
Sum of two sides 1400mm	57.48	97.74	3.25	91.63	nr	189.37
Sum of two sides 1500mm	62.19	105.75	3.40	95.86	nr	201.61
Sum of two sides 1600mm	66.89	113.74	3.45	97.27	nr	211.01
Sum of two sides 1700mm	71.85	122.17	3.60	101.50	nr	223.67
Sum of two sides 1800mm	76.97	130.88	3.90	109.96	nr	240.84
Sum of two sides 1900mm	82.17	139.72	4.20	118.46	nr	258.19
Sum of two sides 2000mm	87.46	148.72	4.33	122.08	nr	270.80
Circular						
100mm dia.	23.63	40.18	0.80	22.56	nr	62.74
160mm dia.	30.52	51.90	0.90	25.38	nr	77.27
200mm dia.	30.52	51.90	1.05	29.62	nr	81.51
250mm dia.	33.97	57.76	1.20	33.85	nr	91.61
315mm dia.	39.28	66.79	1.35	38.10	nr	104.89
355mm dia.	41.32	70.26	1.65	46.53	nr	116.79
400mm dia.	45.12	76.72	1.90	53.60	nr	130.32
450mm dia.	48.75	82.89	2.10	59.23	nr	142.12
500mm dia.	53.09	90.27	2.95	83.17	nr	173.44
630mm dia.	62.11	105.61	4.55	128.29	nr	233.90
710mm dia.	72.47	123.23	5.20	146.61	nr	269.84
800mm dia.	84.15	143.09	5.80	163.53	nr	306.62
900mm dia.	96.80	164.60	6.40	180.44	nr	345.04
1000mm dia.	110.16	187.31	7.00	197.36	nr	384.68
Flat oval						
345 x 102mm	43.98	74.78	1.20	33.83	nr	108.62
508 x 102mm	47.95	81.53	1.60	45.11	nr	126.64
559 x 152mm	49.27	83.78	1.90	53.60	nr	137.38
531 x 203mm	57.67	98.06	1.90	53.60	nr	151.66
851 x 203mm	68.06	115.73	4.55	128.29	nr	244.01
582 x 254mm	65.70	111.72	2.10	59.23	nr	170.95
823 x 254mm	73.43	124.86	4.10	115.60	nr	240.46
632 x 305mm	72.39	123.09	2.95	83.17	nr	206.26
765 x 356mm	80.98	137.70	4.55	128.29	nr	265.98
737 x 406mm	86.26	146.67	4.55	128.29	nr	274.96

U:VENTILATION/AIR CONDITIONING SYSTEMS

Item	Net Price £	Material £	Labour hours	Labour £	Unit	Total rate £
818 x 406mm	88.06	149.74	5.20	146.61	nr	**296.35**
978 x 406mm	95.23	161.93	5.50	155.07	nr	**317.00**
709 x 457mm	89.76	152.63	4.50	127.00	nr	**279.63**
1189 x 457mm	100.89	171.55	6.50	183.26	nr	**354.82**
678 x 508mm	94.95	161.45	4.55	128.29	nr	**289.74**
919 x 508mm	106.55	181.18	6.00	169.17	nr	**350.34**
Fire damper; galvanised steel casing; stainless steel folding shutter; fusible link with manual reset; BS 476 4 hour fire rated						
Rectangular						
Sum of two sides 200mm	34.89	59.33	1.60	45.11	nr	**104.44**
Sum of two sides 300mm	34.89	59.33	1.60	45.11	nr	**104.44**
Sum of two sides 400mm	34.89	59.33	1.60	45.11	nr	**104.44**
Sum of two sides 500mm	41.56	70.67	1.60	45.11	nr	**115.78**
Sum of two sides 600mm	46.31	78.74	1.70	47.95	nr	**126.70**
Sum of two sides 700mm	51.63	87.79	2.10	59.23	nr	**147.02**
Sum of two sides 800mm	57.28	97.40	2.15	60.63	nr	**158.03**
Sum of two sides 900mm	62.80	106.78	2.30	64.96	nr	**171.75**
Sum of two sides 1000mm	68.86	117.09	2.40	67.77	nr	**184.86**
Sum of two sides 1100mm	74.30	126.34	2.60	73.42	nr	**199.76**
Sum of two sides 1200mm	78.06	132.73	2.80	78.98	nr	**211.71**
Sum of two sides 1300mm	81.98	139.40	3.10	87.40	nr	**226.80**
Sum of two sides 1400mm	85.89	146.05	3.25	91.63	nr	**237.68**
Sum of two sides 1500mm	90.03	153.09	3.40	95.90	nr	**248.99**
Sum of two sides 1600mm	94.32	160.38	3.45	97.27	nr	**257.65**
Sum of two sides 1700mm	98.85	168.08	3.60	101.50	nr	**269.58**
Sum of two sides 1800mm	103.83	176.55	3.90	109.96	nr	**286.51**
Sum of two sides 1900mm	108.97	185.29	4.20	118.46	nr	**303.76**
Sum of two sides 2000mm	113.57	193.11	4.33	122.08	nr	**315.19**
Sum of two sides 2100mm	119.33	202.91	4.43	124.90	nr	**327.81**
Sum of two sides 2200mm	125.00	212.55	4.55	128.29	nr	**340.83**
Circular						
100mm dia.	37.19	63.24	0.80	22.56	nr	**85.79**
160mm dia.	39.65	67.42	0.90	25.38	nr	**92.80**
200mm dia.	41.80	71.08	1.05	29.60	nr	**100.68**
250mm dia.	45.86	77.98	1.20	33.85	nr	**111.83**
315mm dia.	53.30	90.63	1.35	38.10	nr	**128.73**
355mm dia.	58.44	99.37	1.65	46.53	nr	**145.90**
400mm dia.	65.95	112.14	1.90	53.60	nr	**165.74**
450mm dia.	72.55	123.36	2.10	59.23	nr	**182.59**
500mm dia.	80.14	136.27	2.95	83.17	nr	**219.44**
630mm dia.	100.23	170.43	4.55	128.29	nr	**298.71**
710mm dia.	113.88	193.64	5.20	146.61	nr	**340.25**
800mm dia.	121.46	206.53	5.80	163.53	nr	**370.06**
900mm dia.	137.35	233.55	6.40	180.44	nr	**413.99**
1000mm dia.	154.75	263.13	7.00	197.36	nr	**460.50**

U:VENTILATION/AIR CONDITIONING SYSTEMS

Item	Net Price £	Material £	Labour hours	Labour £	Unit	Total rate £
U10 : DUCTWORK : VOLUME/FIRE DAMPERS (cont'd)						
Y30 - DUCTWORK ANCILLARIES: VOLUME CONTROL AND FIRE DAMPERS (cont'd)						
Fire damper; galvanized steel casing (cont'd)						
Flat oval						
345 x 102mm	51.00	86.72	1.20	33.85	nr	**120.57**
427 x 102mm	55.98	95.19	1.35	38.10	nr	**133.29**
508 x 102mm	58.28	99.10	1.60	45.11	nr	**144.21**
559 x 152mm	64.34	109.40	1.90	53.60	nr	**163.00**
531 x 203mm	67.40	114.61	1.90	53.60	nr	**168.21**
851 x 203mm	85.35	145.13	4.55	128.29	nr	**273.41**
582 x 254mm	88.88	151.13	2.10	59.23	nr	**210.36**
632 x 305mm	96.70	164.43	2.95	83.17	nr	**247.60**
765 x 356mm	107.59	182.94	4.55	128.29	nr	**311.23**
737 x 406mm	111.96	190.37	4.55	128.29	nr	**318.66**
818 x 406mm	115.26	195.99	5.20	146.61	nr	**342.60**
978 x 406mm	124.39	211.51	5.50	155.07	nr	**366.58**
709 x 457mm	113.88	193.64	4.50	127.00	nr	**320.64**
678 x 508mm	118.94	202.24	4.55	128.29	nr	**330.53**
Fire damper; galvanised steel casing; stainless steel folding shutter; fusible link and 24V d.c. electro-magnetic shutter release mechanism; spring operated; BS 476 4 hour fire rating						
Rectangular						
Sum of two sides 200mm	138.62	235.71	1.60	45.11	nr	**280.82**
Sum of two sides 300mm	138.62	235.71	1.60	45.11	nr	**280.82**
Sum of two sides 400mm	138.62	235.71	1.60	45.11	nr	**280.82**
Sum of two sides 500mm	148.89	253.17	1.60	45.11	nr	**298.28**
Sum of two sides 600mm	156.20	265.60	1.70	47.95	nr	**313.55**
Sum of two sides 700mm	164.38	279.51	2.10	59.23	nr	**338.74**
Sum of two sides 800mm	173.07	294.28	2.15	60.63	nr	**354.92**
Sum of two sides 900mm	181.57	308.74	2.30	64.96	nr	**373.70**
Sum of two sides 1000mm	190.89	324.59	2.40	67.77	nr	**392.36**
Sum of two sides 1100mm	199.26	338.82	2.60	73.42	nr	**412.24**
Sum of two sides 1200mm	205.04	348.65	2.80	78.98	nr	**427.62**
Sum of two sides 1300mm	211.06	358.88	3.10	87.40	nr	**446.29**
Sum of two sides 1400mm	217.08	369.12	3.25	91.63	nr	**460.75**
Sum of two sides 1500mm	223.45	379.95	3.40	95.90	nr	**475.85**
Sum of two sides 1600mm	230.06	391.19	3.45	97.27	nr	**488.46**
Sum of two sides 1700mm	237.02	403.02	3.60	101.50	nr	**504.52**
Sum of two sides 1800mm	244.68	416.05	3.90	109.96	nr	**526.01**
Sum of two sides 1900mm	252.60	429.52	4.20	118.46	nr	**547.98**
Sum of two sides 2000mm	259.68	441.55	4.33	122.08	nr	**563.64**
Sum of two sides 2100mm	268.53	456.60	4.43	124.90	nr	**581.50**
Sum of two sides 2200mm	277.25	471.43	4.55	128.29	nr	**599.72**

U:VENTILATION/AIR CONDITIONING SYSTEMS

Item	Net Price £	Material £	Labour hours	Labour £	Unit	Total rate £
Circular						
100mm dia.	142.16	241.73	0.80	22.56	nr	**264.28**
160mm dia.	145.94	248.15	0.90	25.38	nr	**273.53**
200mm dia.	149.94	254.96	1.05	29.60	nr	**284.56**
250mm dia.	155.49	264.39	1.20	33.85	nr	**298.24**
315mm dia.	166.94	283.86	1.35	38.10	nr	**321.96**
355mm dia.	174.85	297.31	1.65	46.53	nr	**343.84**
400mm dia.	186.41	316.97	1.90	53.60	nr	**370.57**
450mm dia.	196.56	334.23	2.10	59.23	nr	**393.46**
500mm dia.	208.24	354.09	2.95	83.17	nr	**437.26**
630mm dia.	239.14	406.63	4.55	128.29	nr	**534.91**
710mm dia.	260.14	442.34	5.20	146.61	nr	**588.95**
800mm dia.	271.81	462.18	5.80	163.53	nr	**625.71**
900mm dia.	296.25	503.74	6.40	180.44	nr	**684.18**
1000mm dia.	323.02	549.26	7.00	197.36	nr	**746.62**
Flat oval						
345 x 102mm	163.40	277.84	1.20	33.85	nr	**311.69**
427 x 102mm	171.07	290.88	1.35	38.10	nr	**328.99**
508 x 102mm	174.60	296.89	1.60	45.11	nr	**342.00**
559 x 152mm	183.93	312.75	1.90	53.60	nr	**366.35**
531 x 203mm	188.64	320.76	1.90	53.60	nr	**374.36**
851 x 203mm	216.26	367.72	4.55	128.29	nr	**496.01**
582 x 254mm	221.68	376.94	2.10	59.23	nr	**436.17**
632 x 305mm	233.72	397.41	2.95	83.17	nr	**480.59**
765 x 356mm	250.47	425.89	4.55	128.29	nr	**554.18**
737 x 406mm	257.20	437.34	4.55	128.29	nr	**565.62**
818 x 406mm	262.27	445.96	5.20	146.61	nr	**592.57**
978 x 406mm	276.31	469.83	5.50	155.07	nr	**624.90**
709 x 457mm	260.14	442.34	4.50	127.00	nr	**569.34**
678 x 508mm	267.93	455.58	4.55	128.29	nr	**583.87**

U:VENTILATION/AIR CONDITIONING SYSTEMS

Item	Net Price £	Material £	Labour hours	Labour £	Unit	Total rate £
U10 : PLANT/EQUIPMENT						
Y41 - FANS						
Axial flow fan; including ancillaries, anti vibration mountings, mounting feet, matching flanges, flexible connectors and clips; 415V, 3 phase, 50Hz motor; includes fixing in position; electrical work elsewhere						
Aerofoil blade fan unit; short duct case						
315mm dia.; 0.47 m³/s duty; 147 Pa	440.00	563.55	4.50	102.05	nr	**665.60**
500mm dia.; 1.89 m³/sduty; 500 Pa	717.00	918.33	5.00	113.39	nr	**1031.72**
560mm dia.; 2.36 m³/sduty; 147 Pa	425.00	544.34	5.50	124.73	nr	**669.07**
710mm dia.; 5.67 m³/sduty; 245 Pa	701.00	897.83	6.00	136.07	nr	**1033.90**
Aerofoil blade fan unit; long duct case						
315mm dia.; 0.47 m³/s duty; 147 Pa	490.00	627.59	4.50	102.05	nr	**729.64**
500mm dia.; 1.89 m³/sduty; 500 Pa	717.00	918.33	5.00	113.39	nr	**1031.72**
560mm dia.; 2.36 m³/sduty; 147 Pa	500.00	640.40	5.50	124.73	nr	**765.13**
710mm dia.; 5.67 m³/sduty; 245 Pa	817.00	1046.41	6.00	136.07	nr	**1182.48**
Aerofoil blade fan unit; two stage parallel fan arrangement; long duct case						
315mm; 0.47m³/sat 500 Pa	963.00	1233.40	4.50	102.05	nr	**1335.45**
355mm; 0.83m³/sat 147 Pa	1112.00	1424.24	4.75	107.72	nr	**1531.96**
710mm; 3.77m³/sat 431 Pa	2274.00	2912.52	6.00	136.07	nr	**3048.59**
710mm; 6.61m³/s at 500 Pa	2401.00	3075.18	6.00	136.07	nr	**3211.25**
Axial flow fan; suitable for operation at 300°C for 90 minutes; including ancillaries, anti vibration mountings, mounting feet, matching flanges, flexible connectors and clips; 415V, 3 phase, 50Hz motor; includes fixing in position; electrical work elsewhere						
450mm; 2.0m³/s at 300Pa	1186.00	1519.02	5.00	113.39	nr	**1632.41**
630mm; 4.6m³/s at 200Pa	1430.00	1831.53	5.50	124.73	nr	**1956.26**
800mm; 9.0m³/s at 300Pa	2297.00	2941.97	6.50	147.41	nr	**3089.38**
1000mm; 15.0m³/s at 400Pa	3463.00	4435.38	7.50	170.09	nr	**4605.46**
Bifurcated fan; suitable for temperature up to 200°C with motor protection to IP55; including ancillaries, anti vibration mountings, mounting feet, matching flanges, flexible connectors and clips; 415V, 3 phase, 50Hz motor; includes fixing in position; electrical work elsewhere						
300mm; 0.50m³/s at 100Pa	747.00	956.75	4.50	102.05	nr	**1058.80**
400mm; 1.97m³/s at 200Pa	982.00	1257.74	5.00	113.39	nr	**1371.13**
630mm; 3.86m³/s at 200Pa	1442.00	1846.90	5.50	124.73	nr	**1971.63**
800mm; 6.10m³/s at 400Pa	1642.00	2103.06	6.50	147.41	nr	**2250.47**

U:VENTILATION/AIR CONDITIONING SYSTEMS

Item	Net Price £	Material £	Labour hours	Labour £	Unit	Total rate £
Duct mounted in line fan with backward curved centrifugal impellor; including ancillaries, matching flanges, flexible connectors and clips; 415V, 3phase, 50Hz motor; includes fixing in position; electrical work elsewhere						
0.5m³/s at 200Pa	945.00	1210.35	4.50	102.05	nr	**1312.40**
1.0m³/s at 300Pa	1165.00	1492.12	5.00	113.39	nr	**1605.51**
3.0m³/s at 500Pa	1925.00	2465.52	5.50	124.73	nr	**2590.25**
5.0m³/s at 750Pa	2550.00	3266.01	6.50	147.41	nr	**3413.42**
7.0m³/s at 1000Pa	3100.00	3970.45	7.00	158.75	nr	**4129.20**
Twin fan extract unit; belt driven; located internally; complete with anti-vibration mounts and non return shutter; including ancillaries, matching flanges, flexible connectors and clips; 3 phase, 50Hz motor; includes fixing in position; electrical work elsewhere						
0.25m³/s at 150Pa	1304.00	1670.15	4.50	102.05	nr	**1772.20**
Extra for external unit	148.00	189.56	-	-	nr	**189.56**
0.50m³/s at 200Pa	1517.00	1942.96	5.00	113.39	nr	**2056.35**
Extra for external unit	173.00	221.58	-	-	nr	**221.58**
1.00m³/s at 200Pa	1808.00	2315.67	5.00	113.39	nr	**2429.06**
Extra for external unit	202.00	258.72	-	-	nr	**258.72**
1.50m³/s at 250Pa	1928.00	2469.36	5.50	124.73	nr	**2594.09**
Extra for external unit	207.00	265.12	-	-	nr	**265.12**
2.00m³/s at 250Pa	2135.00	2734.49	6.50	147.41	nr	**2881.90**
Extra for external unit	228.00	292.02	-	-	nr	**292.02**
Extra for auto changeover panel	172.00	220.30	2.50	56.70	nr	**276.99**
Roof mounted extract fan; including ancillaries, fibreglass cowling, fitted shutters and bird guard; 415V, 3 phase, 50Hz motor; includes fixing in position; electrical work elsewhere						
Flat roof installation, fixed to curb						
315mm; 900rpm	408.00	522.56	4.50	102.05	nr	**624.62**
315mm; 1380rpm	408.00	522.56	4.50	102.05	nr	**624.62**
400mm; 900rpm	574.00	735.17	5.50	124.73	nr	**859.90**
400mm; 1360rpm	495.00	633.99	5.50	124.73	nr	**758.72**
800mm; 530rpm	1650.00	2113.30	7.00	158.75	nr	**2272.05**
800mm; 700rpm	1550.00	1985.22	7.00	158.75	nr	**2143.97**
800mm; 920rpm	1375.00	1761.09	7.00	158.75	nr	**1919.84**
1000mm; 470rpm	2200.00	2817.74	8.00	181.43	nr	**2999.17**
1000mm; 570rpm	2100.00	2689.66	8.00	181.43	nr	**2871.09**
1000mm; 710rpm	2043.00	2616.65	8.00	181.43	nr	**2798.08**

U:VENTILATION/AIR CONDITIONING SYSTEMS

Item	Net Price £	Material £	Labour hours	Labour £	Unit	Total rate £
U10 : PLANT/EQUIPMENT (cont'd)						
Y41 – FANS (cont'd)						
Pitched roof installation; including purlin mounting box						
315mm; 900rpm	408.00	589.08	4.50	102.05	nr	**691.14**
315mm; 1380rpm	408.00	589.08	4.50	102.05	nr	**691.14**
400mm; 900rpm	574.00	815.56	5.50	124.73	nr	**940.29**
400mm; 1360rpm	495.00	714.37	5.50	124.73	nr	**839.11**
800mm; 530rpm	1650.00	2273.43	7.00	158.75	nr	**2432.18**
800mm; 700rpm	1550.00	2145.35	7.00	158.75	nr	**2304.10**
800mm; 920rpm	1375.00	1921.21	7.00	158.75	nr	**2079.96**
1000mm; 470rpm	2200.00	3054.56	8.00	181.43	nr	**3235.99**
1000mm; 570rpm	2100.00	2926.48	8.00	181.43	nr	**3107.91**
1000mm; 710rpm	2043.00	2853.48	8.00	181.43	nr	**3034.91**
Centrifugal fan; single speed for internal domestic kitchens/utility rooms; fitted with standard overload protection; complete with housing; includes placing in position; electrical work elsewhere						
Window mounted						
245m^3/hr	71.81	91.97	0.50	11.34	nr	**103.31**
500m^3/hr	114.95	294.45	0.50	11.34	nr	**305.79**
Wall mounted						
245m^3/hr	85.65	218.56	0.83	18.90	nr	**237.46**
500m^3/hr	128.79	476.29	0.83	18.90	nr	**495.19**
Centrifugal fan; various speeds, simultaneous ventilation from separate areas fitted with standard overload protection; complete with housing; includes placing in position; ducting and electrical work elsewhere						
Fan unit						
147-300m^3/hr	106.00	135.76	1.00	22.68	nr	**158.44**
175-411m^3/hr	175.00	224.14	1.00	22.68	nr	**246.82**
Toilet extract units; centrifugal fan; various speeds for internal domestic bathrooms/ W.Cs, with built in filter; complete with housing; includes placing in position; electrical work elsewhere						
Fan unit; fixed to wall; including shutter						
Single speed 85m^3/hr	75.90	97.21	0.75	17.01	nr	**114.22**
Two speed 60-85m^3/hr	88.93	113.90	0.83	18.90	nr	**132.79**
Humidity controlled; autospeed; fixed to wall; including shutter						
30-60-85m^3/hr	143.95	184.37	1.00	22.68	nr	**207.04**

U:VENTILATION/AIR CONDITIONING SYSTEMS

Item	Net Price £	Material £	Labour hours	Labour £	Unit	Total rate £
Y42 - AIR FILTRATION						
High efficiency duct mounted filters; 99.997% H13 (EU13); tested to BS 3928						
Standard; 1700m³/ hr air volume; continuous rating up to 80°C; sealed wood case, aluminium spacers, neoprene gaskets; water repellant filter media; includes placing in position						
610 x 610 x 292mm	168.38	286.31	1.00	28.19	nr	**314.50**
Side withdrawl frame	80.76	137.31	2.50	70.49	nr	**207.80**
High capacity; 3400m³/hr air volume; continuous rating up to 80°C; anti-corrosion coated mild steel frame, polyurethane sealant and neoprene gaskets; water repellant filter media; includes placing in position						
610 x 610 x 292mm	305.61	519.66	1.00	28.19	nr	**547.85**
Side withdrawl frame	80.76	137.31	2.50	70.49	nr	**207.80**
Bag Filters; 40/60% F5 (EU5); tested to BSEN 779						
Duct mounted bag filter; continuous rating up to 60°C; rigid filter assembly; sealed into one piece coated mild steel header with sealed pocket separators; includes placing in position						
6 pocket, 592 x 592 x 25mm header; pockets 380mm long; 1690m³/hr	55.35	94.11	1.00	28.19	nr	**122.30**
Side withdrawl frame	56.00	95.22	2.00	56.39	nr	**151.60**
6 pocket, 592 x 592 x 25mm header; pockets 500mm long; 2550m³/hr	59.09	100.48	1.50	42.29	nr	**142.77**
Side withdrawl frame	56.00	95.22	2.50	70.49	nr	**165.70**
6 pocket, 592 x 592 x 25mm header; pockets 635mm long; 3380m³/hr	62.46	106.21	1.50	42.29	nr	**148.51**
Side withdrawl frame	56.00	95.22	3.00	84.58	nr	**179.80**
Bag Filters; 80/90% F7, (EU7); tested to BSEN 779						
Duct mounted bag filter; continuous rating up to 60°C; rigid filter assembly; sealed into one piece coated mild steel header with sealed pocket separators; includes placing in position						
6 pocket, 592 x 592 x 25mm header; pockets 500mm long; 1688m³/hr	77.05	131.01	1.00	28.19	nr	**159.21**
Side withdrawl frame	56.00	95.22	2.00	56.39	nr	**151.60**
6 pocket, 592 x 592 x 25mm header; pockets 635mm long; 2047m³/hr	82.67	140.56	1.50	42.29	nr	**182.86**
Side withdrawl frame	56.00	95.22	2.50	70.49	nr	**165.70**
6 pocket, 592 x 592 x 25mm header; pockets 762mm long; 2729m³/hr	96.79	164.58	1.50	42.29	nr	**206.87**
Side withdrawl frame	56.00	95.22	3.00	84.58	nr	**179.80**

U:VENTILATION/AIR CONDITIONING SYSTEMS

Item	Net Price £	Material £	Labour hours	Labour £	Unit	Total rate £
U10 : PLANT/EQUIPMENT (cont'd)						
Y42 - AIR FILTRATION (cont'd)						
Grease filters, washable; minimum 65%						
Double sided extract unit; lightweight stainless steel construction; demountable composite filter media of woven metal mat and expanded metal mesh supports; for mounting on hood and extract systems (hood not included); includes placing in position						
500 x 686 x 565mm, 4080m³/hr	342.97	583.18	2.00	56.39	nr	**639.57**
1000 x 686 x 565mm, 8160m³/hr;	523.03	889.34	3.00	84.58	nr	**973.93**
1500 x 686 x 565mm, 12240m³/hr;	717.40	1219.86	3.50	98.68	nr	**1318.54**
Panel filters; 82% G3 (EU3); tested to BS EN779						
Modular duct mounted filter panels; continuous rating up to 100°C; graduated density media; rigid cardboard frame; includes placing in position						
596 x 596 x 47mm, 2360m³/hr	4.81	8.18	1.00	28.19	nr	**36.37**
Side withdrawl frame	49.14	83.56	2.50	70.49	nr	**154.04**
596 x 287 x 47mm, 1140m³/hr	3.42	5.82	1.00	28.19	nr	**34.01**
Side withdrawl frame	49.14	83.56	2.50	70.49	nr	**154.04**
Panel filters; 90% G4 (EU4); tested to BS EN779						
Modular duct mounted filter panels; continuous rating up to 100°C; pleated media with wire support; rigid cardboard frame; includes placing in position						
596 x 596 x 47mm, 2560m³/hr	9.82	16.69	1.00	28.19	nr	**44.89**
side withdrawl frame	61.98	105.39	3.00	84.58	nr	**189.98**
596 x 287 x 47mm, 1230m3/hr	7.58	12.89	1.00	28.19	nr	**41.09**
Side withdrawl frame	49.14	83.56	3.00	84.58	nr	**168.14**
Carbon filters; standard duty disposable carbon filters; steel frame with bonded carbon panels; for fixing to ductwork; including placing in position						
12 panels						
597 x 597 x 298mm, 1460m³/hr	292.30	497.02	0.33	9.30	nr	**506.32**
597 x 597 x 451mm, 2200m³/hr	329.52	560.31	0.33	9.30	nr	**569.62**
597 x 597 x 597mm, 2930m³/hr	367.47	624.84	0.33	9.30	nr	**634.14**
8 panels						
451 x 451 x 298mm, 740m³/hr	220.36	374.70	0.29	8.18	nr	**382.88**
451 x 451 x 451mm, 1105m³/hr	243.89	414.71	0.29	8.18	nr	**422.89**
451 x 451 x 597mm, 1460m³/hr	266.35	452.90	0.29	8.18	nr	**461.08**
6 panels						
298 x 298 x 298mm, 365m³/hr	156.15	265.51	0.25	7.05	nr	**272.56**
298 x 298 x 451mm, 550m³/hr	167.18	284.27	0.25	7.05	nr	**291.32**
298 x 298 x 597mm, 780m³/hr	177.73	302.21	0.25	7.05	nr	**309.26**

U:VENTILATION/AIR CONDITIONING SYSTEMS

Item	Net Price £	Material £	Labour hours	Labour £	Unit	Total rate £
Y45 - SILENCERS/ACOUSTIC TREATMENT						
Attenuators; DW144 galvanised construction c/w splitters; self securing; fitted to ductwork						
To suit rectangular ducts; unit length 600mm						
100 x 100mm	75.28	128.01	0.75	21.15	nr	**149.16**
150 x 150mm	78.58	133.62	0.75	21.15	nr	**154.77**
200 x 200mm	81.88	139.23	0.75	21.15	nr	**160.38**
300 x 300mm	91.61	155.77	0.75	21.15	nr	**176.91**
400 x 400mm	103.16	175.41	1.00	28.19	nr	**203.60**
500 x 500mm	120.02	204.08	1.25	35.24	nr	**239.32**
600 x 300mm	115.62	196.60	1.25	35.24	nr	**231.84**
600 x 600mm	161.82	275.16	1.25	35.24	nr	**310.40**
700 x 300mm	122.58	208.44	1.50	42.29	nr	**250.73**
700 x 700mm	182.53	310.38	1.50	42.29	nr	**352.67**
800 x 300mm	126.98	215.92	2.00	56.39	nr	**272.31**
800 x 800mm	210.58	358.07	2.00	56.39	nr	**414.46**
1000 x 1000mm	269.57	458.36	3.00	84.58	nr	**542.95**
To suit rectangular ducts; unit length 1200mm						
200 x 200mm	90.24	153.43	1.00	28.19	nr	**181.63**
300 x 300mm	111.56	189.70	1.00	28.19	nr	**217.89**
400 x 400mm	134.14	228.09	1.33	37.50	nr	**265.59**
500 x 500mm	161.91	275.30	1.66	46.80	nr	**322.10**
600 x 300mm	154.38	262.51	1.66	46.80	nr	**309.31**
600 x 600mm	225.87	384.06	1.66	46.80	nr	**430.86**
700 x 300mm	165.49	281.39	2.00	56.39	nr	**337.78**
700 x 700mm	258.47	439.50	2.00	56.39	nr	**495.89**
800 x 300mm	173.01	294.18	2.66	75.00	nr	**369.18**
800 x 800mm	298.25	507.13	2.66	75.00	nr	**582.13**
1000 x 1000mm	403.73	686.49	4.00	112.78	nr	**799.27**
1300 x 1300mm	693.04	1178.43	8.00	225.56	nr	**1403.99**
1500 x 1500mm	793.25	1348.83	8.00	225.56	nr	**1574.39**
1800 x 1800mm	1085.36	1845.53	10.66	300.55	nr	**2146.08**
2000 x 2000mm	1217.91	2070.91	13.33	375.83	nr	**2446.74**
To suit rectangular ducts; unit length 1800mm						
200 x 200mm	113.89	193.65	1.00	28.19	nr	**221.84**
300 x 300mm	151.34	257.33	1.00	28.19	nr	**285.53**
400 x 400mm	180.90	307.60	1.33	37.50	nr	**345.10**
500 x 500mm	220.49	374.92	1.66	46.80	nr	**421.73**
600 x 300mm	210.82	358.47	1.66	46.80	nr	**405.27**
600 x 600mm	308.11	523.90	1.66	46.80	nr	**570.70**
700 x 300mm	233.75	397.46	2.00	56.39	nr	**453.85**
700 x 700mm	368.12	625.95	2.00	56.39	nr	**682.34**
800 x 300mm	247.19	420.31	2.66	75.00	nr	**495.31**
800 x 800mm	428.32	728.31	2.66	75.00	nr	**803.31**
1000 x 1000mm	575.73	978.95	4.00	112.78	nr	**1091.73**
1300 x 1300mm	961.79	1635.41	8.00	225.56	nr	**1860.97**
1500 x 1500mm	1089.95	1853.33	8.00	225.56	nr	**2078.89**
1800 x 1800mm	1513.21	2573.04	10.66	300.55	nr	**2873.59**
2000 x 2000mm	1713.49	2913.58	13.33	375.83	nr	**3289.41**
2300 x 2300mm	2141.83	3641.92	16.00	451.11	nr	**4093.04**
2500 x 2500mm	2987.59	5080.03	18.66	526.11	nr	**5606.14**

U:VENTILATION/AIR CONDITIONING SYSTEMS

Item	Net Price £	Material £	Labour hours	Labour £	Unit	Total rate £
U10 : PLANT/EQUIPMENT (cont'd)						
Y45 - SILENCERS/ACOUSTIC TREATMENT (cont'd)						
Attenuators; DW144 galvanised (cont'd)						
To suit rectangular ducts; unit length 2400mm						
500 x 500mm	272.63	463.58	2.08	58.73	nr	522.31
600 x 300mm	260.27	442.55	2.08	58.73	nr	501.28
600 x 600mm	387.66	659.16	2.08	58.73	nr	717.89
700 x 300mm	282.12	479.72	2.50	70.49	nr	550.20
700 x 700mm	457.89	778.58	2.50	70.49	nr	849.07
800 x 300mm	298.25	507.13	3.33	93.89	nr	601.02
800 x 800mm	529.91	901.05	3.33	93.89	nr	994.94
1000 x 1000mm	714.94	1215.67	5.00	140.97	nr	1356.64
1300 x 1300mm	1157.98	1969.00	10.00	281.94	nr	2250.95
1500 x 1500mm	1321.62	2247.25	10.00	281.94	nr	2529.19
1800 x 1800mm	1885.70	3206.41	13.33	375.78	nr	3582.18
2000 x 2000mm	2116.07	3598.13	16.66	469.72	nr	4067.85
2300 x 2300mm	2618.06	4451.69	20.00	563.89	nr	5015.58
2500 x 2500mm	3676.12	6250.81	23.32	657.61	nr	6908.42
To suit circular ducts; unit length 600mm						
100mm dia.	65.38	111.18	0.75	21.15	nr	132.32
200mm dia.	76.93	130.82	0.75	21.15	nr	151.96
250mm dia.	87.21	148.29	0.75	21.15	nr	169.43
315mm dia.	101.51	172.60	1.00	28.19	nr	200.80
355mm dia.	117.46	199.72	1.00	28.19	nr	227.92
400mm dia.	126.26	214.69	1.00	28.19	nr	242.88
450mm dia.	152.47	259.26	1.00	28.19	nr	287.45
500mm dia.	167.87	285.44	1.26	35.47	nr	320.91
630mm dia.	197.93	336.56	1.50	42.29	nr	378.85
710mm dia.	215.53	366.49	1.50	42.29	nr	408.78
800mm dia.	239.73	407.64	2.00	56.39	nr	464.03
1000mm dia.	321.82	547.21	3.00	84.58	nr	631.79
To suit circular ducts; unit length 1200mm						
100mm dia.	96.18	163.55	1.00	28.19	nr	191.74
200mm dia.	105.53	179.45	1.00	28.19	nr	207.64
250mm dia.	118.56	201.59	1.00	28.19	nr	229.79
315mm dia.	135.61	230.59	1.33	37.50	nr	268.08
355mm dia.	162.56	276.41	1.33	37.50	nr	313.91
400mm dia.	172.46	293.24	1.33	37.50	nr	330.74
450mm dia.	199.77	339.69	1.33	37.50	nr	377.19
500mm dia.	204.72	348.10	1.66	46.80	nr	394.91
630mm dia.	271.08	460.95	2.00	56.39	nr	517.33
710mm dia.	299.68	509.58	2.00	56.39	nr	565.97
800mm dia.	299.13	508.64	2.66	75.00	nr	583.64
1000mm dia.	401.57	682.81	4.00	112.78	nr	795.59
1250mm dia.	756.46	1286.27	8.00	225.56	nr	1511.82
1400mm dia.	822.46	1398.49	8.00	225.56	nr	1624.05
1600mm dia.	911.80	1550.41	10.66	300.55	nr	1850.96

U:VENTILATION/AIR CONDITIONING SYSTEMS

Item	Net Price £	Material £	Labour hours	Labour £	Unit	Total rate £
To suit circular ducts; unit length 1800mm						
200mm dia.	147.88	251.46	1.25	35.24	nr	**286.70**
250mm dia.	165.48	281.39	1.25	35.24	nr	**316.63**
315mm dia.	196.66	334.39	1.66	46.80	nr	**381.20**
355mm dia.	231.86	394.25	1.66	46.80	nr	**441.05**
400mm dia.	245.06	416.69	1.66	46.80	nr	**463.49**
450mm dia.	239.92	407.96	1.66	46.80	nr	**454.76**
500mm dia.	568.82	967.21	2.08	58.64	nr	**1025.86**
630mm dia.	298.03	506.77	2.50	70.49	nr	**577.26**
710mm dia.	348.63	592.81	2.50	70.49	nr	**663.30**
800mm dia.	360.73	613.38	3.33	93.89	nr	**707.27**
1000mm dia.	583.62	992.37	5.00	140.97	nr	**1133.34**
1250mm dia.	957.21	1627.62	6.66	187.78	nr	**1815.39**
1400mm dia.	941.81	1601.43	6.66	187.78	nr	**1789.21**
1600mm dia.	1057.55	1798.24	10.00	281.94	nr	**2080.18**

U:VENTILATION/AIR CONDITIONING SYSTEMS

Item	Net Price £	Material £	Labour hours	Labour £	Unit	Total rate £
U10 : PLANT/EQUIPMENT (cont'd)						
Y46 - GRILLES/DIFFUSERS/LOUVRES						
Supply grilles; single deflection; extruded aluminium alloy frame and adjustable horizontal vanes; silver grey polyester powder coated; screw fixed						
Rectangular; for duct, ceiling and sidewall applications						
100 x 100mm	6.85	11.65	0.60	16.92	nr	28.56
150 x 150mm	8.69	14.78	0.60	16.92	nr	31.69
200 x 150mm	11.42	19.42	0.65	18.33	nr	37.74
200 x 200mm	10.44	17.75	0.72	20.30	nr	38.05
300 x 100mm	9.18	15.61	0.72	20.30	nr	35.91
300 x 150mm	10.39	17.67	0.80	22.56	nr	40.22
300 x 200mm	11.82	20.10	0.88	24.81	nr	44.91
300 x 300mm	14.66	24.93	1.04	29.32	nr	54.25
400 x 100mm	10.14	17.24	0.88	24.81	nr	42.05
400 x 150mm	11.62	19.76	0.94	26.50	nr	46.26
400 x 200mm	13.19	22.43	1.04	29.32	nr	51.75
400 x 300mm	16.35	27.80	1.12	31.58	nr	59.38
600 x 200mm	16.42	27.92	1.26	35.53	nr	63.45
600 x 300mm	20.77	35.32	1.40	39.47	nr	74.79
600 x 400mm	26.08	44.35	1.61	45.39	nr	89.74
600 x 500mm	29.95	50.93	1.76	49.62	nr	100.55
600 x 600mm	36.23	61.60	2.17	61.18	nr	122.79
800 x 300mm	25.60	43.53	1.76	49.62	nr	93.15
800 x 400mm	30.91	52.56	2.17	61.18	nr	113.74
800 x 600mm	42.50	72.27	3.00	84.58	nr	156.85
1000 x 300mm	28.50	48.46	2.60	73.31	nr	121.77
1000 x 400mm	35.26	59.96	3.00	84.58	nr	144.54
1000 x 600mm	49.27	83.78	3.80	107.14	nr	190.92
1000 x 800mm	51.53	87.62	3.80	107.14	nr	194.76
1200 x 600mm	56.99	96.90	4.61	129.98	nr	226.88
1200 x 800mm	58.01	98.64	4.61	129.98	nr	228.62
1200 x 1000mm	69.29	117.82	4.61	129.98	nr	247.80
Rectangular; for duct, ceiling and sidewall applications; including opposed blade damper volume regulator						
100 x 100mm	14.27	24.26	0.72	20.31	nr	44.58
150 x 150mm	17.25	29.33	0.72	20.31	nr	49.65
200 x 150mm	18.07	30.73	0.83	23.42	nr	54.14
200 x 200mm	20.65	35.11	0.90	25.38	nr	60.49
300 x 100mm	18.40	31.29	0.90	25.38	nr	56.66
300 x 150mm	20.92	35.57	0.98	27.63	nr	63.20
300 x 200mm	23.65	40.21	1.06	29.90	nr	70.11
300 x 300mm	29.54	50.23	1.20	33.85	nr	84.08
400 x 100mm	22.87	38.89	1.06	29.90	nr	68.79
400 x 150mm	25.52	43.39	1.13	31.86	nr	75.25
400 x 200mm	27.01	45.93	1.20	33.85	nr	79.77
400 x 300mm	33.21	56.47	1.34	37.79	nr	94.26
600 x 200mm	31.84	54.14	1.50	42.33	nr	96.47
600 x 300mm	38.65	65.72	1.66	46.83	nr	112.55
600 x 400mm	45.98	78.18	1.80	50.80	nr	128.98
600 x 500mm	55.00	93.52	2.00	56.39	nr	149.91
600 x 600mm	63.60	108.14	2.60	73.42	nr	181.57

U:VENTILATION/AIR CONDITIONING SYSTEMS

Item	Net Price £	Material £	Labour hours	Labour £	Unit	Total rate £
800 x 300mm	62.66	106.55	2.00	56.39	nr	**162.93**
800 x 400mm	74.21	126.19	2.60	73.42	nr	**199.61**
800 x 600mm	103.22	175.51	3.61	101.79	nr	**277.30**
1000 x 300mm	69.37	117.96	3.00	84.67	nr	**202.62**
1000 x 400mm	81.54	138.65	3.61	101.79	nr	**240.43**
1000 x 600mm	111.82	190.14	4.61	129.93	nr	**320.07**
1000 x 800mm	155.26	264.00	4.61	129.93	nr	**393.93**
1200 x 600mm	117.83	200.36	5.62	158.40	nr	**358.75**
1200 x 800mm	163.45	277.93	6.10	171.99	nr	**449.91**
1200 x 1000mm	195.75	332.85	6.50	183.26	nr	**516.11**
Supply grilles; double deflection; extruded aluminium alloy frame and adjustable horizontal and vertical vanes; white polyester powder coated; screw fixed						
Rectangular; for duct, ceiling and sidewall applications						
100 x 100mm	8.55	14.54	0.88	24.81	nr	**39.35**
150 x 150mm	13.52	22.99	0.88	24.81	nr	**47.80**
200 x 150mm	14.49	24.64	1.08	30.45	nr	**55.09**
200 x 200mm	15.46	26.29	1.25	35.24	nr	**61.53**
300 x 100mm	14.97	25.45	1.25	35.24	nr	**60.70**
300 x 150mm	47.92	81.48	1.50	42.29	nr	**123.77**
300 x 200mm	17.87	30.39	1.75	49.34	nr	**79.73**
300 x 300mm	20.50	34.86	2.15	60.62	nr	**95.48**
400 x 100mm	16.91	28.75	1.75	49.34	nr	**78.09**
400 x 150mm	18.35	31.20	1.95	54.98	nr	**86.18**
400 x 200mm	20.13	34.23	2.15	60.62	nr	**94.85**
400 x 300mm	24.30	41.32	2.55	71.90	nr	**113.22**
600 x 200mm	27.05	46.00	3.01	84.87	nr	**130.86**
600 x 300mm	31.91	54.26	3.36	94.73	nr	**148.99**
600 x 400mm	37.67	64.05	3.80	107.14	nr	**171.19**
600 x 500mm	49.27	83.78	4.20	118.42	nr	**202.19**
600 x 600mm	60.86	103.49	4.51	127.16	nr	**230.64**
800 x 300mm	44.44	75.56	4.20	118.42	nr	**193.98**
800 x 400mm	50.72	86.24	4.51	127.16	nr	**213.40**
800 x 600mm	81.63	138.80	5.10	143.79	nr	**282.59**
1000 x 300mm	51.20	87.06	4.80	135.33	nr	**222.39**
1000 x 400mm	61.82	105.12	5.10	143.79	nr	**248.91**
1000 x 600mm	99.98	170.00	5.72	161.27	nr	**331.28**
1000 x 800mm	87.99	149.62	5.72	161.27	nr	**310.89**
1200 x 600mm	117.37	199.57	6.33	178.47	nr	**378.04**
1200 x 800mm	102.27	173.90	6.33	178.47	nr	**352.37**
1200 x 1000mm	121.28	206.22	6.33	178.47	nr	**384.69**

U:VENTILATION/AIR CONDITIONING SYSTEMS

Item	Net Price £	Material £	Labour hours	Labour £	Unit	Total rate £
U10 : PLANT/EQUIPMENT (cont'd)						
Y46 - GRILLES/DIFFUSERS/LOUVRES (cont'd)						
Supply grilles; double deflection (cont'd)						
Rectangular; for duct, ceiling and sidewall applications; including opposed blade damper volume regulator						
100 x 100mm	15.97	27.16	1.00	28.19	nr	55.35
150 x 150mm	19.73	33.55	1.00	28.19	nr	61.74
200 x 150mm	21.34	36.29	1.26	35.53	nr	71.81
200 x 200mm	24.07	40.93	1.43	40.32	nr	81.25
300 x 100mm	22.92	38.97	1.43	40.32	nr	79.29
300 x 150mm	25.76	43.80	1.68	47.37	nr	91.17
300 x 200mm	28.83	49.02	1.93	54.42	nr	103.44
300 x 300mm	35.37	60.14	2.31	65.13	nr	125.27
400 x 100mm	28.80	48.97	1.93	54.42	nr	103.39
400 x 150mm	31.95	54.33	2.14	60.34	nr	114.66
400 x 200mm	33.95	57.73	2.31	65.13	nr	122.86
400 x 300mm	41.17	70.00	2.77	78.10	nr	148.10
600 x 200mm	42.30	71.93	3.25	91.63	nr	163.56
600 x 300mm	50.83	86.43	3.62	102.06	nr	188.49
600 x 400mm	59.91	101.87	3.99	112.50	nr	214.37
600 x 500mm	70.64	120.11	4.44	125.18	nr	245.30
600 x 600mm	80.98	137.70	4.94	139.28	nr	276.98
800 x 300mm	79.09	134.48	4.44	125.18	nr	259.67
800 x 400mm	93.08	158.27	4.94	139.28	nr	297.55
800 x 600mm	126.98	215.91	5.71	160.99	nr	376.90
1000 x 300mm	90.03	153.09	5.20	146.61	nr	299.70
1000 x 400mm	105.36	179.15	5.71	160.99	nr	340.14
1000 x 600mm	141.96	241.39	6.53	184.11	nr	425.50
1000 x 800mm	191.71	325.98	6.53	184.11	nr	510.09
1200 x 600mm	154.35	262.45	7.34	206.95	nr	469.40
1200 x 800mm	207.71	353.19	8.80	248.11	nr	601.30
1200 x 1000mm	247.76	421.29	8.80	248.11	nr	669.40
Floor grille suitable for mounting in raised access floors; heavy duty; extruded alumiinium; standard mill finish; complete with opposed blade volume control damper						
Diffuser						
600mm x 600mm	114.95	195.46	0.70	19.74	nr	215.19
Extra for nylon coated black finish	19.66	33.43	-	-	nr	33.43
Exhaust grilles; aluminium						
0° fixed blade core						
150 x 150mm	11.04	18.77	0.60	16.98	nr	35.75
200 x 200mm	12.99	22.09	0.72	20.31	nr	42.40
250 x 250mm	15.12	25.71	0.80	22.56	nr	48.27
300 x 300mm	17.44	29.65	1.00	28.19	nr	57.85
350 x 350mm	19.93	33.89	1.20	33.83	nr	67.72

U:VENTILATION/AIR CONDITIONING SYSTEMS

Item	Net Price £	Material £	Labour hours	Labour £	Unit	Total rate £
0° fixed blade core; including opposed blade damper volume regulator						
150 x 150mm	19.72	33.53	0.62	17.49	nr	**51.02**
200 x 200mm	23.20	39.45	0.72	20.31	nr	**59.76**
250 x 250mm	26.98	45.88	0.80	22.56	nr	**68.43**
300 x 300mm	32.31	54.94	1.00	28.19	nr	**83.13**
350 x 350mm	36.71	62.42	1.20	33.83	nr	**96.25**
45° fixed blade core						
150 x 150mm	11.04	18.77	0.62	17.49	nr	**36.26**
200 x 200mm	12.99	22.09	0.72	20.31	nr	**42.40**
250 x 250mm	15.12	25.71	0.80	22.56	nr	**48.27**
300 x 300mm	17.44	29.65	1.00	28.19	nr	**57.85**
350 x 350mm	19.93	33.89	1.20	33.83	nr	**67.72**
45° fixed blade core; including opposed blade damper volume regulator						
150 x 150mm	19.72	33.53	0.62	17.49	nr	**51.02**
200 x 200mm	23.20	39.45	0.72	20.31	nr	**59.76**
250 x 250mm	26.98	45.88	0.80	22.56	nr	**68.43**
300 x 300mm	32.31	54.94	1.00	28.19	nr	**83.13**
350 x 350mm	36.71	62.42	1.20	33.83	nr	**96.25**
Eggcrate core						
150 x 150mm	8.21	13.96	0.62	17.49	nr	**31.45**
200 x 200mm	9.18	15.61	1.00	28.19	nr	**43.80**
250 x 250mm	11.59	19.71	0.80	22.56	nr	**42.26**
300 x 300mm	14.49	24.64	1.00	28.19	nr	**52.83**
350 x 350mm	16.42	27.92	1.20	33.83	nr	**61.75**
Eggcrate core; including opposed blade damper volume regulator						
150 x 150mm	16.09	27.36	0.62	17.49	nr	**44.85**
200 x 200mm	19.35	32.90	0.72	20.31	nr	**53.22**
250 x 250mm	23.01	39.13	0.80	22.56	nr	**61.68**
300 x 300mm	29.06	49.41	1.00	28.19	nr	**77.61**
350 x 350mm	32.65	55.52	1.20	33.83	nr	**89.35**
Mesh/perforated plate core						
150 x 150mm	12.08	20.54	0.62	17.48	nr	**38.02**
200 x 200mm	12.56	21.36	0.72	20.30	nr	**41.66**
250 x 250mm	14.97	25.45	0.80	22.56	nr	**48.01**
300 x 300mm	17.87	30.39	1.00	28.19	nr	**58.58**
350 x 350mm	19.80	33.67	1.20	33.83	nr	**67.50**
Mesh/perforated plate core; including opposed blade damper volume regulator						
150 x 150mm	16.09	27.36	0.62	17.48	nr	**44.84**
200 x 200mm	19.35	32.90	0.72	20.30	nr	**53.20**
250 x 250mm	23.01	39.13	0.80	22.56	nr	**61.68**
300 x 300mm	29.06	49.41	0.80	22.56	nr	**71.97**
350 x 350mm	32.65	55.52	1.20	33.83	nr	**89.35**
Plastic air diffusion system						
Eggcrate grilles						
150 x 150mm	5.78	7.40	0.62	14.07	nr	**21.47**
200 x 200mm	7.76	9.94	0.72	16.34	nr	**26.28**
250 x 250mm	9.22	11.81	0.80	18.14	nr	**29.95**
300 x 300mm	11.13	14.26	1.00	22.68	nr	**36.93**

U:VENTILATION/AIR CONDITIONING SYSTEMS

Item	Net Price £	Material £	Labour hours	Labour £	Unit	Total rate £
U10 : PLANT/EQUIPMENT (cont'd)						
Y46 - GRILLES/DIFFUSERS/LOUVRES (cont'd)						
Plastic air diffusion system (cont'd)						
Single deflection grilles						
150 x 150mm	5.56	7.12	0.62	14.07	nr	**21.19**
200 x 200mm	7.16	9.17	0.72	16.34	nr	**25.51**
250 x 250mm	7.77	9.95	0.80	18.14	nr	**28.09**
300 x 300mm	9.12	11.68	1.00	22.68	nr	**34.36**
Double deflection grilles						
150 x 150mm	7.31	9.36	0.62	14.07	nr	**23.43**
200 x 200mm	8.81	11.28	0.72	16.34	nr	**27.62**
250 x 250mm	10.83	13.87	0.80	18.14	nr	**32.01**
300 x 300mm	15.15	19.40	1.00	22.68	nr	**42.08**
Door transfer grilles						
150 x 150mm	11.43	14.64	0.62	14.07	nr	**28.71**
200 x 200mm	15.66	20.06	0.72	16.34	nr	**36.40**
250 x 250mm	15.60	19.98	0.80	18.14	nr	**38.12**
300 x 300mm	18.80	24.08	1.00	22.68	nr	**46.76**
Opposed blade dampers						
150 x 150mm	4.07	5.21	0.62	14.07	nr	**19.28**
200 x 200mm	5.41	6.93	0.72	16.34	nr	**23.27**
250 x 250mm	6.60	8.45	0.80	18.14	nr	**26.60**
300 x 300mm	7.16	9.17	1.00	22.68	nr	**31.85**
Neck reducers						
150 x 150mm	5.41	6.93	0.62	14.07	nr	**21.00**
200 x 200mm	5.92	7.58	0.72	16.34	nr	**23.92**
250 x 250mm	7.16	9.17	0.80	18.14	nr	**27.31**
300 x 300mm	7.93	10.16	1.00	22.68	nr	**32.84**
Ceiling mounted diffusers; circular aluminium multi-core diffuser						
Circular; for ceiling mounting						
152mm dia. neck	37.86	64.38	0.80	22.56	nr	**86.93**
203mm dia. neck	55.42	94.24	1.10	31.02	nr	**125.25**
305mm dia. neck	75.07	127.65	1.40	39.49	nr	**167.14**
381mm dia. neck	64.22	109.20	1.50	42.33	nr	**151.53**
457mm dia. neck	101.25	172.16	2.00	56.39	nr	**228.55**
Circular; for ceiling mounting; including louvre damper volume control						
152mm dia. neck	52.81	89.80	1.00	28.19	nr	**117.99**
203mm dia. neck	70.98	120.69	1.20	33.85	nr	**154.54**
305mm dia. neck	94.25	160.26	1.60	45.11	nr	**205.37**
381mm dia. neck	83.40	141.81	1.90	53.60	nr	**195.41**
457mm dia. neck	122.34	208.02	2.40	67.77	nr	**275.80**

U:VENTILATION/AIR CONDITIONING SYSTEMS

Item	Net Price £	Material £	Labour hours	Labour £	Unit	Total rate £
Ceiling mounted diffusers; rectangular aluminium multi-cone diffuser; four way flow						
Rectangular; for ceiling mounting						
150 x 150 mm neck	18.75	31.88	1.80	50.80	nr	**82.68**
300 x 150 mm neck	26.83	45.62	2.30	64.85	nr	**110.47**
300 x 300 mm neck	27.12	46.11	2.80	78.94	nr	**125.06**
450 x 150 mm neck	34.18	58.12	2.80	78.94	nr	**137.06**
450 x 300 mm neck	33.46	56.89	3.20	90.22	nr	**147.12**
450 x 450 mm neck	34.78	59.14	3.40	95.90	nr	**155.04**
600 x 150 mm neck	41.87	71.19	3.20	90.22	nr	**161.42**
600 x 300 mm neck	41.65	70.82	3.50	98.68	nr	**169.50**
600 x 600 mm neck	51.68	87.88	4.00	112.78	nr	**200.65**
Rectangular; for ceiling mounting; including opposed blade damper volume regulator						
150 x 150 mm neck	26.03	44.26	1.80	50.80	nr	**95.06**
300 x 150 mm neck	37.34	63.49	2.30	64.85	nr	**128.34**
300 x 300 mm neck	39.65	67.42	2.80	78.98	nr	**146.40**
450 x 150 mm neck	48.24	82.03	2.80	78.94	nr	**160.97**
450 x 300 mm neck	50.48	85.84	3.30	93.04	nr	**178.88**
450 x 450 mm neck	55.37	94.15	3.51	98.93	nr	**193.08**
600 x 150 mm neck	58.20	98.96	3.30	93.04	nr	**192.00**
600 x 300 mm neck	60.58	103.01	4.00	112.78	nr	**215.79**
600 x 600 mm neck	76.12	129.43	5.62	158.40	nr	**287.83**
Slot diffusers; continuous aluminium slot diffuser with flanged frame						
Diffuser						
1 slot	17.75	30.18	3.76	105.99	m	**136.18**
2 slot	21.62	36.76	3.76	105.97	m	**142.73**
3 slot	27.05	46.00	3.76	105.97	m	**151.96**
4 slot	33.48	56.93	4.50	127.00	m	**183.93**
6 slot	47.66	81.04	4.50	127.00	m	**208.04**
8 slot	48.33	82.18	5.20	146.61	m	**228.79**
Diffuser; including equalizing deflector						
1 slot	17.75	30.18	5.26	148.39	m	**178.58**
2 slot	21.62	36.76	5.26	148.39	m	**185.16**
3 slot	26.60	45.23	5.26	148.39	m	**193.62**
4 slot	29.93	50.89	6.33	178.45	m	**229.34**
6 slot	39.44	67.06	6.33	178.45	m	**245.51**
8 slot	48.33	82.18	7.20	203.00	m	**285.18**
Extra over for ends						
1 slot	91.56	155.69	1.00	28.19	nr	**183.88**
2 slot	8.82	15.00	1.00	28.19	nr	**43.19**
3 slot	10.08	17.14	1.00	28.19	nr	**45.33**
4 slot	11.34	19.28	1.30	36.65	nr	**55.94**
6 slot	13.86	23.57	1.40	39.47	nr	**63.04**
8 slot	4.34	7.38	1.40	39.47	nr	**46.85**

U:VENTILATION/AIR CONDITIONING SYSTEMS

Item	Net Price £	Material £	Labour hours	Labour £	Unit	Total rate £
U10 : PLANT/EQUIPMENT (cont'd)						
Y46 - GRILLES/DIFFUSERS/LOUVRES (cont'd)						
Slot diffusers; continuous aluminium (cont'd)						
Plenum boxes; 1.0m long; circular spigot; including cord operated flap damper						
1 slot	35.16	59.79	2.75	77.67	nr	**137.46**
2 slot	36.28	61.69	2.75	77.67	nr	**139.36**
3 slot	36.78	62.54	2.75	77.67	nr	**140.21**
4 slot	40.88	69.51	3.51	98.93	nr	**168.44**
6 slot	43.91	74.66	3.51	98.93	nr	**173.59**
8 slot	59.81	101.70	4.20	118.42	nr	**220.12**
Plenum boxes; 2.0m long; circular spigot; including cord operated flap damper						
1 slot	41.58	130.49	3.26	91.84	nr	**222.33**
2 slot	41.58	70.70	3.26	91.84	nr	**162.54**
3 slot	43.47	73.92	3.26	91.84	nr	**165.75**
4 slot	47.35	80.51	3.76	105.99	nr	**186.51**
6 slot	51.53	87.62	3.76	105.99	nr	**193.62**
8 slot	67.81	115.30	4.10	115.60	nr	**230.90**
Perforated diffusers; rectangular face aluminium perforated diffuser; quick release face plate; for integration with rectangular ceiling tiles						
Circular spigot; rectangular diffuser						
150mm dia. spigot; 300 x 300 diffuser	45.40	77.20	1.00	28.19	nr	**105.39**
300mm dia. spigot; 600 x 600 diffuser	83.56	142.08	1.40	39.49	nr	**181.57**
Circular spigot; rectangular diffuser; including louvre damper volume regulator						
150mm dia. spigot; 300 x 300 diffuser	60.63	103.09	1.00	28.19	nr	**131.29**
300mm dia. spigot; 600 x 600 diffuser	97.08	165.07	1.60	45.11	nr	**210.18**
Rectangular spigot; rectangular diffuser						
150 x 150mm dia. spigot; 300 x 300mm diffuser	29.30	49.82	1.00	22.68	nr	**72.50**
300 x 150mm dia. spigot; 600 x 300mm diffuser	62.08	105.56	1.20	27.21	nr	**132.77**
300 x 300mm dia. spigot; 600 x 600mm diffuser	62.08	105.56	1.40	31.75	nr	**137.31**
600 x 300mm dia. spigot; 1200 x 600mm diffuser	124.16	211.12	1.60	36.29	nr	**247.40**
Rectangular spigot; rectangular diffuser; including opposed blade damper volume regulator						
150 x 150mm dia. spigot; 300 x 300mm diffuser	41.29	70.21	1.20	27.21	nr	**97.42**
300 x 150mm dia. spigot; 600 x 300mm diffuser	82.44	140.18	1.40	31.76	nr	**171.94**
300 x 300mm dia. spigot; 600 x 600mm diffuser	82.44	140.18	1.60	36.29	nr	**176.46**
600 x 300mm dia. spigot; 1200 x 600mm diffuser	168.92	287.23	1.80	40.82	nr	**328.05**

U:VENTILATION/AIR CONDITIONING SYSTEMS

Item	Net Price £	Material £	Labour hours	Labour £	Unit	Total rate £
Floor swirl diffuser; manual adjustment of air discharge direction; complete with damper and dirt trap						
Plastic Diffuser						
150 dia	19.64	33.40	0.50	14.10	nr	**47.49**
200 dia	25.99	44.19	0.50	14.10	nr	**58.29**
Aluminium Diffuser						
150 dia	24.26	41.25	0.50	14.10	nr	**55.35**
200 dia	30.61	52.05	0.50	14.10	nr	**66.15**
Plastic air diffusion system						
Cellular diffusers						
300 x 300mm	16.17	20.71	2.80	63.52	nr	**84.23**
600 x 600mm	39.28	50.31	4.00	90.71	nr	**141.02**
Multi-cone diffusers						
300 x 300mm	17.55	22.48	2.80	63.52	nr	**86.00**
450 x 450mm	26.88	34.43	3.40	77.14	nr	**111.57**
500 x 500mm	27.46	35.17	3.80	86.23	nr	**121.40**
600 x 600mm	34.02	43.57	4.00	90.71	nr	**134.29**
625 x 625mm	38.06	48.75	4.26	96.50	nr	**145.25**
Opposed blade dampers						
300 x 300mm	5.57	7.13	1.20	27.23	nr	**34.36**
450 x 450mm	9.04	11.58	1.50	34.05	nr	**45.63**
600 x 600mm	15.86	20.31	2.60	59.06	nr	**79.37**
Plenum boxes						
300mm	8.73	11.18	2.80	63.52	nr	**74.71**
450mm	10.71	13.72	3.40	77.14	nr	**90.86**
600mm	16.64	21.31	4.00	90.71	nr	**112.03**
Plenum spigot reducer						
600mm	5.61	7.19	1.00	22.68	nr	**29.86**
Blanking kits for cellular diffusers						
300mm	4.78	6.12	0.88	19.96	nr	**26.09**
600mm	6.56	8.40	1.10	24.95	nr	**33.35**
Blanking kits for multi-cone diffusers						
300mm	4.78	6.12	0.88	19.96	nr	**26.09**
450mm	5.70	7.30	0.90	20.41	nr	**27.71**
600mm	6.65	8.52	1.10	24.95	nr	**33.47**

U:VENTILATION/AIR CONDITIONING SYSTEMS

Item	Net Price £	Material £	Labour hours	Labour £	Unit	Total rate £
U10 : PLANT/EQUIPMENT (cont'd)						
Y46 - GRILLES/DIFFUSERS/LOUVRES (cont'd)						
Acoustic louvres; opening mounted; 300mm deep steel louvres with blades packed with acoustic infill; 12mm galvanised mesh birdscreen; screw fixing in opening						
Louvre units; self finished galvanised steel						
900 high x 600 wide	132.55	169.77	3.00	68.04	nr	**237.80**
900 high x 900 wide	164.45	210.63	3.00	68.04	nr	**278.66**
900 high x 1200 wide	194.70	249.37	3.34	75.75	nr	**325.12**
900 high x 1500 wide	254.10	325.45	3.34	75.75	nr	**401.19**
900 high x 1800 wide	284.90	364.90	3.34	75.75	nr	**440.64**
900 high x 2100 wide	315.70	404.35	3.34	75.75	nr	**480.09**
900 high x 2400 wide	345.95	443.09	3.68	83.46	nr	**526.55**
900 high x 2700 wide	391.05	500.85	3.68	83.46	nr	**584.31**
900 high x 3000 wide	418.55	536.07	3.68	83.46	nr	**619.53**
1200 high x 600 wide	173.80	222.60	3.00	68.04	nr	**290.64**
1200 high x 900 wide	213.95	274.02	3.34	75.75	nr	**349.77**
1200 high x 1200 wide	253.55	324.74	3.34	75.75	nr	**400.49**
1200 high x 1500 wide	336.05	430.41	3.34	75.75	nr	**506.16**
1200 high x 1800 wide	375.65	481.13	3.68	83.46	nr	**564.59**
1200 high x 2100 wide	416.35	533.26	3.68	83.46	nr	**616.71**
1200 high x 2400 wide	455.95	583.98	3.68	83.46	nr	**667.43**
1500 high x 600 wide	215.60	276.14	3.00	68.04	nr	**344.17**
1500 high x 900 wide	264.55	338.83	3.34	75.75	nr	**414.58**
1500 high x 1200 wide	313.50	401.53	3.34	75.75	nr	**477.27**
1500 high x 1500 wide	418.00	535.37	3.68	83.46	nr	**618.83**
1500 high x 1800 wide	466.95	598.06	3.68	83.46	nr	**681.52**
1500 high x 2100 wide	516.45	661.46	4.00	90.71	nr	**752.18**
1800 high x 600 wide	256.30	328.27	3.34	75.75	nr	**404.01**
1800 high x 900 wide	314.60	402.94	3.34	75.75	nr	**478.68**
1800 high x 1200 wide	373.45	478.31	3.68	83.46	nr	**561.77**
1800 high x 1500 wide	500.50	641.04	3.68	83.46	nr	**724.49**
Louvre units; polyester powder coated steel						
900 high x 600 wide	192.50	246.55	3.00	68.04	nr	**314.59**
900 high x 900 wide	253.55	324.74	3.00	68.04	nr	**392.78**
900 high x 1200 wide	313.50	401.53	3.34	75.75	nr	**477.27**
900 high x 1500 wide	402.60	515.65	3.34	75.75	nr	**591.39**
900 high x 1800 wide	463.10	593.13	3.34	75.75	nr	**668.88**
900 high x 2100 wide	524.15	671.33	3.34	75.75	nr	**747.07**
900 high x 2400 wide	584.10	748.11	3.68	83.46	nr	**831.57**
900 high x 2700 wide	658.35	843.21	3.68	83.46	nr	**926.66**
900 high x 3000 wide	715.55	916.47	3.68	83.46	nr	**999.93**
1200 high x 600 wide	253.00	324.04	3.00	68.04	nr	**392.08**
1200 high x 900 wide	332.75	426.18	3.34	75.75	nr	**501.93**
1200 high x 1200 wide	412.50	528.33	3.34	75.75	nr	**604.07**
1200 high x 1500 wide	534.05	684.01	3.34	75.75	nr	**759.75**
1200 high x 1800 wide	613.25	785.44	3.68	83.46	nr	**868.90**
1200 high x 2100 wide	693.55	888.29	3.68	83.46	nr	**971.75**
1200 high x 2400 wide	772.75	989.73	3.68	83.46	nr	**1073.19**
1500 high x 600 wide	314.60	402.94	3.00	68.04	nr	**470.97**
1500 high x 900 wide	413.05	529.03	3.34	75.75	nr	**604.78**

U:VENTILATION/AIR CONDITIONING SYSTEMS

Item	Net Price £	Material £	Labour hours	Labour £	Unit	Total rate £
1500 high x 1200 wide	511.50	655.12	3.34	75.75	nr	**730.87**
1500 high x 1500 wide	665.50	852.37	3.68	83.46	nr	**935.82**
1500 high x 1800 wide	764.50	979.16	3.68	83.46	nr	**1062.62**
1500 high x 2100 wide	862.95	1105.26	4.00	90.71	nr	**1195.97**
1800 high x 600 wide	375.10	480.42	3.34	75.75	nr	**556.17**
1800 high x 900 wide	492.80	631.17	3.34	75.75	nr	**706.92**
1800 high x 1200 wide	611.05	782.63	3.68	83.46	nr	**866.08**
1800 high x 1500 wide	797.50	1021.43	3.68	83.46	nr	**1104.89**
Weather louvres; opening mounted; 300mm deep galvanised steel louvres; screw fixing in position						
Louvre units; including 12mm galvanised mesh birdscreen						
900 x 600mm	109.42	140.14	2.25	51.08	nr	**191.22**
900 x 900mm	151.64	194.22	2.25	51.08	nr	**245.30**
900 x 1200mm	183.86	235.49	2.50	56.70	nr	**292.18**
900 x 1500mm	209.07	267.77	2.50	56.70	nr	**324.47**
900 x 1800mm	249.31	319.31	2.50	56.70	nr	**376.01**
900 x 2100mm	322.16	412.62	2.50	56.70	nr	**469.32**
900 x 2400mm	338.77	433.89	2.76	62.65	nr	**496.54**
900 x 2700mm	389.67	499.09	2.76	62.65	nr	**561.73**
900 x 3000mm	450.55	577.06	2.76	62.65	nr	**639.71**
1200 x 600mm	151.64	194.22	2.25	51.08	nr	**245.30**
1200 x 900mm	205.52	263.23	2.50	56.70	nr	**319.92**
1200 x 1200mm	260.51	333.66	2.50	56.70	nr	**390.35**
1200 x 1500mm	284.39	364.24	2.50	56.70	nr	**420.94**
1200 x 1800mm	338.27	433.25	2.76	62.65	nr	**495.90**
1200 x 2100mm	464.91	595.45	2.76	62.65	nr	**658.10**
1200 x 2400mm	464.91	595.45	2.76	62.65	nr	**658.10**
1500 x 600mm	177.19	226.94	2.25	51.08	nr	**278.02**
1500 x 900mm	232.18	297.37	2.50	56.70	nr	**354.07**
1500 x 1200mm	309.38	396.25	2.50	56.70	nr	**452.95**
1500 x 1500mm	341.05	436.81	2.76	62.65	nr	**499.46**
1500 x 1800mm	406.04	520.05	2.76	62.65	nr	**582.70**
1500 x 2100mm	548.78	702.87	3.00	68.10	nr	**770.98**
1800 x 600mm	191.08	244.73	2.50	56.70	nr	**301.43**
1800 x 900mm	251.62	322.27	2.50	56.70	nr	**378.97**
1800 x 1200mm	331.04	423.99	2.76	62.65	nr	**486.64**
1800 x 1500mm	389.73	499.16	3.00	68.10	nr	**567.27**

U:VENTILATION/AIR CONDITIONING SYSTEMS

Item	Net Price £	Material £	Labour hours	Labour £	Unit	Total rate £
U10 : PLANT/EQUIPMENT (cont'd)						
Y50 - THERMAL INSULATION						
Concealed Ductwork						
Flexible wrap; 20kg-45kg Bright Class O aluminium foil faced; Bright Class O foil taped joints; 62mm metal pins and washers; aluminium bands						
40mm thick insulation	6.14	8.03	0.40	7.82	m²	**15.85**
Semi-rigid slab; 45kg Bright Class O aluminium foil faced mineral fibre; Bright Class O foil taped joints; 62mm metal pins and washers; aluminium bands						
40mm thick insulation	8.04	10.51	0.65	12.71	m²	**23.22**
Plantroom Ductwork						
Semi-rigid slab; 45kg Bright Class O aluminium foil faced mineral fibre; Bright Class O foil taped joints; 62mm metal pins and washers; 22 swg plain/embossed aluminium cladding; pop rivited						
50mm thick insulation	20.28	26.52	1.50	29.32	m²	**55.84**
External Ductwork						
Semi-rigid slab; 45kg Bright Class O aluminium foil faced mineral fibre; Bright Class O foil taped joints; 62mm metal pins and washers; 0.8mm polyisobutylene sheeting; welded joints						
50mm thick insulation	14.79	19.34	1.25	24.44	m²	**43.77**

U:VENTILATION/AIR CONDITIONING SYSTEMS

Item	Net Price £	Material £	Labour hours	Labour £	Unit	Total rate £
U14 : DUCTWORK : FIRE RATED						
Y30 - DUCTLINES						
The relevant BS requires that the fire rating of ductwork meets 3 criteria; stability (hours), integrity (hours) and insulation (hours). The least of the 3 periods defines the fire rating. The BS does however allow stability and integrity to be considered in isolation. Rates are therefore provided for both types of system.						
Care should be taken when using the rates contained within this section, that the requirements for stability, integrity and insulation are known and the appropriate rates used.						
High density single layer mineral wool fire rated ductwork slab, in accordance with BS476, Part 24 (ISO 6944: 1985), ducts "Type A" and "Type B"; 165kg class O foil faced mineral fibre; 100mm wide bright class O foil taped joints; welded pins; includes protection to all supports.						
1/2 hour stability, integrity and insulation						
25mm thick, vertical and horizontal ductwork	23.91	31.26	1.25	24.44	m²	**55.70**
1 hour stability, integrity and insulation						
30mm thick, vertical ductwork	28.09	36.73	1.50	29.32	m²	**66.05**
40mm thick, horizontal ductwork	33.03	43.19	1.50	29.32	m²	**72.51**
1½ hour stability, integrity and insulation						
50mm thick, vertical ductwork	39.45	51.59	1.75	34.21	m²	**85.80**
70mm thick, horizontal ductwork	49.34	64.52	1.75	34.21	m²	**98.73**
2 hour stability, integrity and insulation						
70mm, vertical ductwork	50.84	66.49	2.00	39.10	m²	**105.59**
90mm horizontal ductwork	60.72	79.41	2.00	39.10	m²	**118.50**
Kitchen extract, 1 hour stability, integrity and insulation						
90mm, vertical and horizontal	60.72	79.41	2.00	39.10	m²	**118.50**

U:VENTILATION/AIR CONDITIONING SYSTEMS

Item	Net Price £	Material £	Labour hours	Labour £	Unit	Total rate £
U14 : DUCTWORK : FIRE RATED (cont'd)						
Y30 – DUCTLINES (cont'd)						
Galvanised sheet metal rectangular section ductwork to BS476 Part 24 (ISO 6944:1985), ducts "Type A" and "Type B"; provides 2 hours stability and 2 hours integrity at 1100°C (no rating for insulation); including all necessary stiffeners, joints and supports in the running length						
Ductwork up to 600mm longest side						
Sum of two sides 200mm	40.40	68.70	2.91	82.05	m	150.74
Sum of two sides 300mm	43.86	74.58	2.99	84.30	m	158.89
Sum of two sides 400mm	47.31	80.45	3.17	89.38	m	169.83
Sum of two sides 500mm	50.78	86.34	3.37	95.02	m	181.36
Sum of two sides 600mm	54.23	92.21	3.54	99.81	m	192.02
Sum of two sides 700mm	57.69	98.10	3.72	104.88	m	202.98
Sum of two sides 800mm	61.16	103.99	3.90	109.96	m	213.95
Sum of two sides 900mm	64.61	109.86	5.04	142.10	m	251.96
Sum of two sides 1000mm	68.07	115.75	5.58	157.33	m	273.07
Sum of two sides 1100mm	71.52	121.61	5.84	164.66	m	286.27
Sum of two sides 1200mm	74.99	127.50	6.11	172.27	m	299.77
Extra over fittings; Ductwork up to 600mm longest side						
End Cap						
Sum of two sides 200mm	11.47	19.50	0.81	22.84	nr	42.33
Sum of two sides 300mm	12.17	20.69	0.84	23.68	nr	44.37
Sum of two sides 400mm	12.87	21.88	0.87	24.53	nr	46.41
Sum of two sides 500mm	13.56	23.06	0.90	25.38	nr	48.43
Sum of two sides 600mm	14.26	24.25	0.93	26.22	nr	50.47
Sum of two sides 700mm	14.96	25.45	0.96	27.07	nr	52.51
Sum of two sides 800mm	15.67	26.64	0.98	27.63	nr	54.27
Sum of two sides 900mm	16.37	27.83	1.17	32.99	nr	60.82
Sum of two sides 1000mm	17.06	29.01	1.22	34.40	nr	63.40
Sum of two sides 1100mm	17.76	30.20	1.25	35.24	nr	65.44
Sum of two sides 1200mm	18.46	31.39	1.28	36.09	nr	67.48
Reducer						
Sum of two sides 200mm	45.50	77.37	2.23	62.87	nr	140.24
Sum of two sides 300mm	47.60	80.93	2.37	66.82	nr	147.75
Sum of two sides 400mm	49.68	84.47	2.51	70.77	nr	155.24
Sum of two sides 500mm	51.77	88.03	2.65	74.72	nr	162.75
Sum of two sides 600mm	53.86	91.57	2.79	78.66	nr	170.24
Sum of two sides 700mm	55.95	95.14	2.87	80.92	nr	176.05
Sum of two sides 800mm	58.04	98.70	3.01	84.87	nr	183.56
Sum of two sides 900mm	60.13	102.24	3.06	86.28	nr	188.51
Sum of two sides 1000mm	62.22	105.80	3.17	89.38	nr	195.18
Sum of two sides 1100mm	64.30	109.34	3.22	90.79	nr	200.13
Sum of two sides 1200mm	66.40	112.90	3.28	92.48	nr	205.38

U:VENTILATION/AIR CONDITIONING SYSTEMS

Item	Net Price £	Material £	Labour hours	Labour £	Unit	Total rate £
Offset						
Sum of two sides 200mm	109.82	186.73	2.95	83.17	nr	**269.90**
Sum of two sides 300mm	112.54	191.36	3.11	87.68	nr	**279.05**
Sum of two sides 400mm	115.27	196.00	3.26	91.91	nr	**287.91**
Sum of two sides 500mm	117.99	200.64	3.42	96.43	nr	**297.06**
Sum of two sides 600mm	120.72	205.27	3.57	100.65	nr	**305.93**
Sum of two sides 700mm	123.45	209.91	3.73	105.17	nr	**315.07**
Sum of two sides 800mm	126.17	214.54	3.23	91.07	nr	**305.61**
Sum of two sides 900mm	128.90	219.18	3.45	97.27	nr	**316.45**
Sum of two sides 1000mm	131.63	223.81	3.67	103.47	nr	**327.29**
Sum of two sides 1100mm	134.35	228.45	3.78	106.58	nr	**335.02**
Sum of two sides 1200mm	137.08	233.08	3.89	109.68	nr	**342.76**
90° radius bend						
Sum of two sides 200mm	44.53	75.72	2.06	58.08	nr	**133.80**
Sum of two sides 300mm	47.90	81.45	2.21	62.31	nr	**143.76**
Sum of two sides 400mm	51.27	87.18	2.36	66.54	nr	**153.72**
Sum of two sides 500mm	54.65	92.93	2.51	70.77	nr	**163.70**
Sum of two sides 600mm	58.02	98.66	2.66	75.00	nr	**173.65**
Sum of two sides 700mm	61.39	104.39	2.81	79.23	nr	**183.61**
Sum of two sides 800mm	64.76	110.12	2.97	83.74	nr	**193.85**
Sum of two sides 900mm	68.13	115.85	2.99	84.30	nr	**200.15**
Sum of two sides 1000mm	71.51	121.59	3.04	85.71	nr	**207.31**
Sum of two sides 1100mm	74.88	127.32	3.07	86.56	nr	**213.88**
Sum of two sides 1200mm	78.25	133.05	3.09	87.12	nr	**220.18**
45° radius bend						
Sum of two sides 200mm	54.91	93.36	1.52	42.86	nr	**136.22**
Sum of two sides 300mm	56.28	95.69	1.59	44.83	nr	**140.52**
Sum of two sides 400mm	57.63	98.00	1.66	46.80	nr	**144.80**
Sum of two sides 500mm	59.00	100.33	1.73	48.78	nr	**149.10**
Sum of two sides 600mm	60.36	102.64	1.80	50.75	nr	**153.39**
Sum of two sides 700mm	61.73	104.96	1.87	52.72	nr	**157.69**
Sum of two sides 800mm	63.09	107.27	1.93	54.42	nr	**161.69**
Sum of two sides 900mm	64.46	109.60	1.99	56.11	nr	**165.71**
Sum of two sides 1000mm	65.81	111.91	2.05	57.80	nr	**169.71**
Sum of two sides 1100mm	67.18	114.23	2.11	59.49	nr	**173.72**
Sum of two sides 1200mm	68.54	116.54	2.17	61.18	nr	**177.72**
90° mitre bend						
Sum of two sides 200mm	46.16	78.48	2.47	69.64	nr	**148.12**
Sum of two sides 300mm	53.50	90.98	2.65	74.72	nr	**165.69**
Sum of two sides 400mm	60.84	103.45	2.84	80.07	nr	**183.52**
Sum of two sides 500mm	68.19	115.94	3.02	85.15	nr	**201.09**
Sum of two sides 600mm	75.52	128.42	3.20	90.22	nr	**218.64**
Sum of two sides 700mm	82.87	140.91	3.38	95.30	nr	**236.21**
Sum of two sides 800mm	90.22	153.41	3.56	100.37	nr	**253.78**
Sum of two sides 900mm	97.55	165.88	3.59	101.22	nr	**267.10**
Sum of two sides 1000mm	104.90	178.37	3.66	103.19	nr	**281.57**
Sum of two sides 1100mm	112.24	190.85	3.69	104.04	nr	**294.89**
Sum of two sides 1200mm	119.59	203.34	3.72	104.88	nr	**308.22**

U:VENTILATION/AIR CONDITIONING SYSTEMS

Item	Net Price £	Material £	Labour hours	Labour £	Unit	Total rate £
U14 : DUCTWORK : FIRE RATED (cont'd)						
Y30 – DUCTLINES (cont'd)						
Fittings; Ductwork up to 600mm longest side (cont'd)						
Branch						
Sum of two sides 200mm	17.14	29.15	0.98	27.63	nr	56.78
Sum of two sides 300mm	17.23	29.30	1.06	29.89	nr	59.19
Sum of two sides 400mm	17.33	29.46	1.14	32.14	nr	61.61
Sum of two sides 500mm	17.42	29.62	1.22	34.40	nr	64.02
Sum of two sides 600mm	17.51	29.78	1.30	36.65	nr	66.43
Sum of two sides 700mm	17.61	29.94	1.38	38.91	nr	68.85
Sum of two sides 800mm	17.69	30.08	1.46	41.16	nr	71.24
Sum of two sides 900mm	17.83	30.32	1.37	38.63	nr	68.95
Sum of two sides 1000mm	17.88	30.40	1.46	41.16	nr	71.56
Sum of two sides 1100mm	17.97	30.56	1.50	42.29	nr	72.85
Sum of two sides 1200mm	18.06	30.72	1.55	43.70	nr	74.42
Ductwork 601 to 800mm longest side						
Sum of two sides 900mm	64.60	109.84	5.04	142.10	m	251.94
Sum of two sides 1000mm	68.06	115.73	5.58	157.33	m	273.05
Sum of two sides 1100mm	71.52	121.61	5.84	164.66	m	286.27
Sum of two sides 1200mm	74.99	127.50	6.11	172.27	m	299.77
Sum of two sides 1300mm	78.46	133.41	6.38	179.88	m	313.29
Sum of two sides 1400mm	81.92	139.30	6.65	187.49	m	326.79
Sum of two sides 1500mm	85.39	145.19	6.91	194.82	m	340.01
Sum of two sides 1600mm	88.85	151.08	7.18	202.44	m	353.51
Extra over fittings; Ductwork 601 to 800mm longest side						
End Cap						
Sum of two sides 900mm	15.21	25.86	1.17	32.99	nr	58.85
Sum of two sides 1000mm	16.30	27.71	1.22	34.40	nr	62.11
Sum of two sides 1100mm	17.39	29.56	1.25	35.24	nr	64.81
Sum of two sides 1200mm	18.47	31.41	1.28	36.09	nr	67.50
Sum of two sides 1300mm	19.55	33.24	1.31	36.93	nr	70.18
Sum of two sides 1400mm	20.64	35.09	1.34	37.78	nr	72.87
Sum of two sides 1500mm	21.73	36.94	1.36	38.34	nr	75.29
Sum of two sides 1600mm	22.82	38.79	1.39	39.19	nr	77.98
Reducer						
Sum of two sides 900mm	56.91	96.77	3.06	86.28	nr	183.04
Sum of two sides 1000mm	60.08	102.16	3.17	89.38	nr	191.53
Sum of two sides 1100mm	63.24	107.53	3.22	90.79	nr	198.32
Sum of two sides 1200mm	66.41	112.92	3.28	92.48	nr	205.40
Sum of two sides 1300mm	69.58	118.31	3.33	93.89	nr	212.20
Sum of two sides 1400mm	72.75	123.70	3.38	95.30	nr	219.00
Sum of two sides 1500mm	75.91	129.08	3.44	96.99	nr	226.06
Sum of two sides 1600mm	79.08	134.47	3.49	98.40	nr	232.87

U:VENTILATION/AIR CONDITIONING SYSTEMS

Item	Net Price £	Material £	Labour hours	Labour £	Unit	Total rate £
Offset						
Sum of two sides 900mm	121.04	205.81	3.45	97.27	nr	**303.08**
Sum of two sides 1000mm	126.80	215.62	3.67	103.47	nr	**319.09**
Sum of two sides 1100mm	132.56	225.40	3.78	106.58	nr	**331.98**
Sum of two sides 1200mm	138.33	235.21	3.89	109.68	nr	**344.89**
Sum of two sides 1300mm	144.09	245.00	4.00	112.78	nr	**357.78**
Sum of two sides 1400mm	149.85	254.81	4.11	115.88	nr	**370.69**
Sum of two sides 1500mm	155.61	264.60	4.23	119.26	nr	**383.86**
Sum of two sides 1600mm	161.38	274.40	4.34	122.36	nr	**396.77**
90° radius bend						
Sum of two sides 900mm	60.51	102.89	2.99	84.30	nr	**187.20**
Sum of two sides 1000mm	66.46	113.00	3.04	85.71	nr	**198.71**
Sum of two sides 1100mm	72.40	123.11	3.07	86.56	nr	**209.66**
Sum of two sides 1200mm	78.34	133.21	3.09	87.12	nr	**220.33**
Sum of two sides 1300mm	84.28	143.30	3.12	87.97	nr	**231.27**
Sum of two sides 1400mm	90.22	153.41	3.15	88.81	nr	**242.22**
Sum of two sides 1500mm	96.16	163.51	3.17	89.38	nr	**252.89**
Sum of two sides 1600mm	102.11	173.62	3.20	90.22	nr	**263.84**
45° bend						
Sum of two sides 900mm	60.09	102.18	1.74	49.06	nr	**151.24**
Sum of two sides 1000mm	62.91	106.97	1.85	52.16	nr	**159.13**
Sum of two sides 1100mm	65.73	111.77	1.91	53.85	nr	**165.62**
Sum of two sides 1200mm	68.55	116.56	1.96	55.26	nr	**171.82**
Sum of two sides 1300mm	71.36	121.34	2.02	56.95	nr	**178.29**
Sum of two sides 1400mm	74.18	126.13	2.07	58.36	nr	**184.49**
Sum of two sides 1500mm	77.00	130.93	2.13	60.05	nr	**190.98**
Sum of two sides 1600mm	79.82	135.72	2.18	61.46	nr	**197.18**
90° mitre bend						
Sum of two sides 900mm	90.60	154.06	3.59	101.22	nr	**255.28**
Sum of two sides 1000mm	100.27	170.50	3.66	103.19	nr	**273.69**
Sum of two sides 1100mm	109.92	186.91	3.69	104.04	nr	**290.95**
Sum of two sides 1200mm	119.59	203.34	3.72	104.88	nr	**308.22**
Sum of two sides 1300mm	129.24	219.75	3.75	105.73	nr	**325.48**
Sum of two sides 1400mm	138.90	236.19	3.78	106.58	nr	**342.76**
Sum of two sides 1500mm	148.55	252.60	3.81	107.42	nr	**360.02**
Sum of two sides 1600mm	158.22	269.03	3.84	108.27	nr	**377.30**
Branch						
Sum of two sides 900mm	16.81	28.59	1.37	38.63	nr	**67.21**
Sum of two sides 1000mm	17.23	29.30	1.46	41.16	nr	**70.47**
Sum of two sides 1100mm	17.66	30.02	1.50	42.29	nr	**72.31**
Sum of two sides 1200mm	18.08	30.74	1.55	43.70	nr	**74.44**
Sum of two sides 1300mm	18.50	31.45	1.59	44.83	nr	**76.28**
Sum of two sides 1400mm	18.92	32.17	1.63	45.96	nr	**78.13**
Sum of two sides 1500mm	18.17	30.90	1.68	47.37	nr	**78.26**
Sum of two sides 1600mm	19.76	33.60	1.72	48.49	nr	**82.10**

U:VENTILATION/AIR CONDITIONING SYSTEMS

Item	Net Price £	Material £	Labour hours	Labour £	Unit	Total rate £
U14 : DUCTWORK : FIRE RATED (cont'd)						
Y30 – DUCTLINES (cont'd)						
Ductwork 801 to 1000mm longest side						
Sum of two sides 1100mm	71.52	121.61	5.84	164.66	m	**286.27**
Sum of two sides 1200mm	74.99	127.50	6.11	172.27	m	**299.77**
Sum of two sides 1300mm	78.45	133.39	6.38	179.88	m	**313.27**
Sum of two sides 1400mm	81.91	139.28	6.65	187.49	m	**326.77**
Sum of two sides 1500mm	85.37	145.17	6.91	194.82	m	**339.99**
Sum of two sides 1600mm	88.84	151.06	7.18	202.44	m	**353.50**
Sum of two sides 1700mm	92.30	156.95	7.45	210.05	m	**367.00**
Sum of two sides 1800mm	95.76	162.84	7.71	217.38	m	**380.22**
Sum of two sides 1900mm	99.23	168.72	7.98	224.99	m	**393.72**
Sum of two sides 2000mm	102.69	174.61	8.25	232.60	m	**407.22**
Extra over fittings; Ductwork 801 to 1000mm longest side						
End Cap						
Sum of two sides 1100mm	17.39	29.56	1.25	35.24	nr	**64.81**
Sum of two sides 1200mm	18.47	31.41	1.28	36.09	nr	**67.50**
Sum of two sides 1300mm	19.55	33.24	1.31	36.93	nr	**70.18**
Sum of two sides 1400mm	20.64	35.09	1.34	37.78	nr	**72.87**
Sum of two sides 1500mm	21.73	36.94	1.36	38.34	nr	**75.29**
Sum of two sides 1600mm	22.80	38.77	1.39	39.19	nr	**77.96**
Sum of two sides 1700mm	23.89	40.62	1.42	40.04	nr	**80.66**
Sum of two sides 1800mm	24.98	42.47	1.45	40.88	nr	**83.36**
Sum of two sides 1900mm	26.06	44.30	1.48	41.73	nr	**86.03**
Sum of two sides 2000mm	27.14	46.16	1.51	42.57	nr	**88.73**
Reducer						
Sum of two sides 1100mm	63.24	107.53	3.22	90.79	nr	**198.32**
Sum of two sides 1200mm	66.42	112.94	3.28	92.48	nr	**205.42**
Sum of two sides 1300mm	69.60	118.35	3.33	93.89	nr	**212.24**
Sum of two sides 1400mm	72.79	123.76	3.38	95.30	nr	**219.06**
Sum of two sides 1500mm	75.97	129.17	3.44	96.99	nr	**226.16**
Sum of two sides 1600mm	79.16	134.61	3.49	98.40	nr	**233.00**
Sum of two sides 1700mm	82.34	140.02	3.54	99.81	nr	**239.83**
Sum of two sides 1800mm	85.53	145.43	3.60	101.50	nr	**246.93**
Sum of two sides 1900mm	88.71	150.84	3.65	102.91	nr	**253.75**
Sum of two sides 2000mm	93.48	158.96	3.70	104.32	nr	**263.28**
Offset						
Sum of two sides 1100mm	131.52	223.63	3.78	106.58	nr	**330.21**
Sum of two sides 1200mm	137.08	233.08	3.89	109.68	nr	**342.76**
Sum of two sides 1300mm	142.63	242.53	4.00	112.78	nr	**355.31**
Sum of two sides 1400mm	148.19	251.98	4.11	115.88	nr	**367.86**
Sum of two sides 1500mm	153.75	261.43	4.23	119.26	nr	**380.70**
Sum of two sides 1600mm	159.32	270.90	4.34	122.36	nr	**393.27**
Sum of two sides 1700mm	164.88	280.35	4.45	125.47	nr	**405.82**
Sum of two sides 1800mm	170.43	289.80	4.56	128.57	nr	**418.37**
Sum of two sides 1900mm	175.99	299.25	4.67	131.67	nr	**430.92**
Sum of two sides 2000mm	184.33	313.44	5.53	155.92	nr	**469.35**

U:VENTILATION/AIR CONDITIONING SYSTEMS

Item	Net Price £	Material £	Labour hours	Labour £	Unit	Total rate £
90° radius bend						
Sum of two sides 1100mm	72.28	122.91	3.07	86.56	nr	**209.47**
Sum of two sides 1200mm	78.24	133.03	3.09	87.12	nr	**220.16**
Sum of two sides 1300mm	84.19	143.16	3.12	87.97	nr	**231.13**
Sum of two sides 1400mm	90.15	153.29	3.15	88.81	nr	**242.10**
Sum of two sides 1500mm	96.10	163.41	3.17	89.38	nr	**252.79**
Sum of two sides 1600mm	102.05	173.52	3.20	90.22	nr	**263.74**
Sum of two sides 1700mm	108.00	183.65	3.22	90.79	nr	**274.43**
Sum of two sides 1800mm	113.96	193.77	3.25	91.63	nr	**285.40**
Sum of two sides 1900mm	119.91	203.90	3.28	92.48	nr	**296.38**
Sum of two sides 2000mm	125.87	214.02	3.30	93.04	nr	**307.07**
45° bend						
Sum of two sides 1100mm	66.16	112.50	1.91	53.85	nr	**166.35**
Sum of two sides 1200mm	68.94	117.22	1.96	55.26	nr	**172.48**
Sum of two sides 1300mm	71.70	121.91	2.02	56.95	nr	**178.87**
Sum of two sides 1400mm	74.47	126.63	2.07	58.36	nr	**184.99**
Sum of two sides 1500mm	77.23	131.32	2.13	60.05	nr	**191.38**
Sum of two sides 1600mm	80.00	136.04	2.18	61.46	nr	**197.50**
Sum of two sides 1700mm	82.77	140.73	2.24	63.16	nr	**203.89**
Sum of two sides 1800mm	85.54	145.45	2.30	64.85	nr	**210.30**
Sum of two sides 1900mm	88.30	150.14	2.35	66.26	nr	**216.40**
Sum of two sides 2000mm	91.07	154.86	2.76	77.82	nr	**232.68**
90° mitre bend						
Sum of two sides 1100mm	109.92	186.91	3.69	104.04	nr	**290.95**
Sum of two sides 1200mm	119.59	203.34	3.72	104.88	nr	**308.22**
Sum of two sides 1300mm	129.24	219.75	3.75	105.73	nr	**325.48**
Sum of two sides 1400mm	138.90	236.19	3.78	106.58	nr	**342.76**
Sum of two sides 1500mm	148.57	252.62	3.81	107.42	nr	**360.04**
Sum of two sides 1600mm	158.22	269.03	3.84	108.27	nr	**377.30**
Sum of two sides 1700mm	167.88	285.47	3.87	109.11	nr	**394.58**
Sum of two sides 1800mm	177.55	301.90	3.90	109.96	nr	**411.86**
Sum of two sides 1900mm	187.20	318.31	3.93	110.80	nr	**429.12**
Sum of two sides 2000mm	196.86	334.74	3.96	111.65	nr	**446.39**
Branch						
Sum of two sides 1100mm	17.63	29.98	1.50	42.29	nr	**72.27**
Sum of two sides 1200mm	18.05	30.70	1.55	43.70	nr	**74.40**
Sum of two sides 1300mm	18.49	31.43	1.59	44.83	nr	**76.26**
Sum of two sides 1400mm	18.91	32.15	1.63	45.96	nr	**78.11**
Sum of two sides 1500mm	19.34	32.89	1.68	47.37	nr	**80.25**
Sum of two sides 1600mm	19.76	33.60	1.72	48.49	nr	**82.10**
Sum of two sides 1700mm	20.19	34.34	1.77	49.90	nr	**84.24**
Sum of two sides 1800mm	20.62	35.05	1.81	51.03	nr	**86.09**
Sum of two sides 1900mm	21.05	35.79	1.86	52.44	nr	**88.23**
Sum of two sides 2000mm	21.68	36.86	1.90	53.57	nr	**90.43**

U:VENTILATION/AIR CONDITIONING SYSTEMS

Item	Net Price £	Material £	Labour hours	Labour £	Unit	Total rate £
U14 : DUCTWORK : FRE RATED (cont'd)						
Y30 – DUCTLINES (cont'd)						
Ductwork 1001 to 1250mm longest side						
Sum of two sides 1300mm	88.91	151.18	6.38	179.88	m	**331.06**
Sum of two sides 1400mm	92.75	157.70	6.65	187.49	m	**345.20**
Sum of two sides 1500mm	96.58	164.23	6.91	194.82	m	**359.05**
Sum of two sides 1600mm	99.46	169.12	6.91	194.82	m	**363.95**
Sum of two sides 1700mm	102.33	174.00	7.45	210.05	m	**384.05**
Sum of two sides 1800mm	106.15	180.50	7.71	217.38	m	**397.88**
Sum of two sides 1900mm	109.98	187.01	7.98	224.99	m	**412.00**
Sum of two sides 2000mm	113.82	193.53	8.25	232.60	m	**426.14**
Sum of two sides 2100mm	117.64	200.04	9.62	271.23	m	**471.27**
Sum of two sides 2200mm	120.51	204.91	9.62	271.23	m	**476.14**
Sum of two sides 2300mm	123.39	209.81	10.07	283.92	m	**493.73**
Sum of two sides 2400mm	127.21	216.31	10.47	295.20	m	**511.51**
Sum of two sides 2500mm	131.04	222.82	10.87	306.47	m	**529.29**
Extra over fittings; Ductwork 1001 to 1250mm longest side						
End Cap						
Sum of two sides 1300mm	19.56	33.26	1.31	36.93	nr	**70.20**
Sum of two sides 1400mm	20.64	35.09	1.34	37.78	nr	**72.87**
Sum of two sides 1500mm	21.72	36.92	1.36	38.34	nr	**75.27**
Sum of two sides 1600mm	22.80	38.77	1.39	39.19	nr	**77.96**
Sum of two sides 1700mm	23.89	40.62	1.42	40.04	nr	**80.66**
Sum of two sides 1800mm	24.97	42.45	1.45	40.88	nr	**83.34**
Sum of two sides 1900mm	26.06	44.30	1.48	41.73	nr	**86.03**
Sum of two sides 2000mm	27.14	46.16	1.51	42.57	nr	**88.73**
Sum of two sides 2100mm	28.23	48.01	2.66	75.00	nr	**123.00**
Sum of two sides 2200mm	29.32	49.86	2.80	78.94	nr	**128.80**
Sum of two sides 2300mm	30.40	51.69	2.95	83.17	nr	**134.86**
Sum of two sides 2400mm	31.48	53.54	3.10	87.40	nr	**140.94**
Sum of two sides 2500mm	32.57	55.39	3.24	91.35	nr	**146.74**
Reducer						
Sum of two sides 1300mm	69.58	118.31	3.33	93.89	nr	**212.20**
Sum of two sides 1400mm	72.72	123.64	3.38	95.30	nr	**218.94**
Sum of two sides 1500mm	75.85	128.98	3.44	96.99	nr	**225.96**
Sum of two sides 1600mm	79.00	134.33	3.49	98.40	nr	**232.73**
Sum of two sides 1700mm	82.15	139.68	3.54	99.81	nr	**239.49**
Sum of two sides 1800mm	85.29	145.03	3.60	101.50	nr	**246.53**
Sum of two sides 1900mm	88.44	150.38	3.65	102.91	nr	**253.29**
Sum of two sides 2000mm	91.59	155.73	3.70	104.32	nr	**260.05**
Sum of two sides 2100mm	94.72	161.07	3.75	105.73	nr	**266.79**
Sum of two sides 2200mm	97.87	166.42	3.80	107.14	nr	**273.56**
Sum of two sides 2300mm	101.02	171.77	3.85	108.55	nr	**280.32**
Sum of two sides 2400mm	104.17	177.12	3.90	109.96	nr	**287.08**
Sum of two sides 2500mm	107.31	182.47	3.95	111.37	nr	**293.84**

U:VENTILATION/AIR CONDITIONING SYSTEMS

Item	Net Price £	Material £	Labour hours	Labour £	Unit	Total rate £
Offset						
Sum of two sides 1300mm	142.17	241.74	4.00	112.78	nr	**354.52**
Sum of two sides 1400mm	147.81	251.33	4.11	115.88	nr	**367.21**
Sum of two sides 1500mm	153.45	260.92	4.23	119.26	nr	**380.18**
Sum of two sides 1600mm	159.08	270.50	4.34	122.36	nr	**392.87**
Sum of two sides 1700mm	164.71	280.07	4.45	125.47	nr	**405.54**
Sum of two sides 1800mm	170.35	289.66	4.56	128.57	nr	**418.23**
Sum of two sides 1900mm	175.98	299.23	4.67	131.67	nr	**430.90**
Sum of two sides 2000mm	181.62	308.82	5.53	155.92	nr	**464.74**
Sum of two sides 2100mm	187.26	318.41	5.76	162.40	nr	**480.81**
Sum of two sides 2200mm	192.89	327.98	5.99	168.89	nr	**496.86**
Sum of two sides 2300mm	198.53	337.57	6.22	175.37	nr	**512.94**
Sum of two sides 2400mm	204.15	347.14	6.45	181.85	nr	**528.99**
Sum of two sides 2500mm	209.79	356.73	6.68	188.34	nr	**545.07**
90° radius bend						
Sum of two sides 1300mm	84.09	142.98	3.12	87.97	nr	**230.95**
Sum of two sides 1400mm	93.56	159.10	3.15	88.81	nr	**247.91**
Sum of two sides 1500mm	96.02	163.27	3.17	89.38	nr	**252.65**
Sum of two sides 1600mm	101.99	173.42	3.20	90.22	nr	**263.64**
Sum of two sides 1700mm	107.97	183.59	3.22	90.79	nr	**274.37**
Sum of two sides 1800mm	113.93	193.73	3.25	91.63	nr	**285.36**
Sum of two sides 1900mm	119.90	203.88	3.28	92.48	nr	**296.36**
Sum of two sides 2000mm	125.88	214.04	3.30	93.04	nr	**307.09**
Sum of two sides 2100mm	131.85	224.19	3.32	93.61	nr	**317.80**
Sum of two sides 2200mm	137.81	234.34	3.34	94.17	nr	**328.51**
Sum of two sides 2300mm	143.78	244.48	3.36	94.73	nr	**339.22**
Sum of two sides 2400mm	149.76	254.65	3.38	95.30	nr	**349.95**
Sum of two sides 2500mm	155.73	264.80	3.40	95.86	nr	**360.66**
45° bend						
Sum of two sides 1300mm	68.11	115.81	2.02	56.95	nr	**172.76**
Sum of two sides 1400mm	71.17	121.02	2.07	58.36	nr	**179.38**
Sum of two sides 1500mm	74.24	126.23	2.13	60.05	nr	**186.28**
Sum of two sides 1600mm	77.30	131.44	2.18	61.46	nr	**192.91**
Sum of two sides 1700mm	80.37	136.65	2.24	63.16	nr	**199.81**
Sum of two sides 1800mm	83.43	141.87	2.30	64.85	nr	**206.71**
Sum of two sides 1900mm	86.50	147.08	2.35	66.26	nr	**213.34**
Sum of two sides 2000mm	89.58	152.31	2.76	77.82	nr	**230.13**
Sum of two sides 2100mm	92.64	157.52	2.89	81.48	nr	**239.01**
Sum of two sides 2200mm	95.71	162.74	3.01	84.87	nr	**247.60**
Sum of two sides 2300mm	98.77	167.95	3.13	88.25	nr	**256.20**
Sum of two sides 2400mm	101.84	173.16	3.26	91.91	nr	**265.08**
Sum of two sides 2500mm	104.90	178.37	3.37	95.02	nr	**273.39**

U:VENTILATION/AIR CONDITIONING SYSTEMS

Item	Net Price £	Material £	Labour hours	Labour £	Unit	Total rate £
U14 : DUCTWORK : FIRE RATED (cont'd)						
Y30 – DUCTLINES (cont'd)						
Fittings; Ductwork 1001 to 1250mm longest side (cont'd)						
90° mitre bend						
Sum of two sides 1300mm	128.95	219.26	3.75	105.73	nr	324.99
Sum of two sides 1400mm	138.70	235.85	3.78	106.58	nr	342.42
Sum of two sides 1500mm	148.46	252.44	3.81	107.42	nr	359.86
Sum of two sides 1600mm	158.21	269.01	3.84	108.27	nr	377.28
Sum of two sides 1700mm	167.95	285.58	3.87	109.11	nr	394.70
Sum of two sides 1800mm	177.70	302.16	3.90	109.96	nr	412.12
Sum of two sides 1900mm	187.45	318.73	3.93	110.80	nr	429.53
Sum of two sides 2000mm	197.20	335.32	3.96	111.65	nr	446.97
Sum of two sides 2100mm	206.95	351.89	3.99	112.50	nr	464.39
Sum of two sides 2200mm	216.70	368.46	4.02	113.34	nr	481.81
Sum of two sides 2300mm	226.44	385.04	4.05	114.19	nr	499.22
Sum of two sides 2400mm	236.19	401.61	4.08	115.03	nr	516.64
Sum of two sides 2500mm	245.93	418.18	4.11	115.88	nr	534.06
Branch						
Sum of two sides 1300mm	18.52	31.49	1.59	44.83	nr	76.32
Sum of two sides 1400mm	18.94	32.21	1.63	45.96	nr	78.17
Sum of two sides 1500mm	19.36	32.93	1.68	47.37	nr	80.29
Sum of two sides 1600mm	19.78	33.64	1.72	48.49	nr	82.14
Sum of two sides 1700mm	20.22	34.38	1.77	49.90	nr	84.28
Sum of two sides 1800mm	20.64	35.09	1.81	51.03	nr	86.13
Sum of two sides 1900mm	21.06	35.81	1.86	52.44	nr	88.25
Sum of two sides 2000mm	21.49	36.55	1.90	53.57	nr	90.12
Sum of two sides 2100mm	21.91	37.26	2.58	72.74	nr	110.00
Sum of two sides 2200mm	22.34	37.98	2.61	73.59	nr	111.57
Sum of two sides 2300mm	22.76	38.69	2.64	74.43	nr	113.13
Sum of two sides 2400mm	23.19	39.43	2.88	81.20	nr	120.63
Sum of two sides 2500mm	23.61	40.15	2.91	82.05	nr	122.19
Ductwork 1251 to 2000mm longest side						
Sum of two sides 1700mm	97.51	165.80	7.45	210.05	m	375.85
Sum of two sides 1800mm	103.76	176.42	7.71	217.38	m	393.80
Sum of two sides 1900mm	110.00	187.05	7.98	224.99	m	412.04
Sum of two sides 2000mm	116.25	197.67	8.25	232.60	m	430.28
Sum of two sides 2100mm	122.50	208.29	9.62	271.23	m	479.53
Sum of two sides 2200mm	128.75	218.92	9.66	272.36	m	491.28
Sum of two sides 2300mm	134.98	229.52	10.07	283.92	m	513.44
Sum of two sides 2400mm	141.23	240.15	10.47	295.20	m	535.34
Sum of two sides 2500mm	147.48	250.77	10.87	306.47	m	557.24
Sum of two sides 2600mm	153.73	261.39	11.27	317.75	m	579.15
Sum of two sides 2700mm	159.97	272.02	11.67	329.03	m	601.05
Sum of two sides 2800mm	166.22	282.64	12.08	340.59	m	623.23
Sum of two sides 2900mm	172.47	293.26	12.48	351.87	m	645.13
Sum of two sides 3000mm	178.72	303.89	12.88	363.15	m	667.03
Sum of two sides 3100mm	184.97	314.51	13.26	373.86	m	688.37
Sum of two sides 3200mm	191.21	325.13	13.69	385.98	m	711.12
Sum of two sides 3300mm	197.46	335.76	14.09	397.26	m	733.02
Sum of two sides 3400mm	203.71	346.38	14.49	408.54	m	754.92
Sum of two sides 3500mm	209.94	356.99	14.89	419.82	m	776.80

U:VENTILATION/AIR CONDITIONING SYSTEMS

Item	Net Price £	Material £	Labour hours	Labour £	Unit	Total rate £
Sum of two sides 3600mm	216.19	367.61	15.29	431.09	m	**798.70**
Sum of two sides 3700mm	222.44	378.23	15.69	442.37	m	**820.60**
Sum of two sides 3800mm	228.69	388.86	16.09	453.65	m	**842.51**
Sum of two sides 3900mm	234.94	399.48	16.49	464.93	m	**864.41**
Sum of two sides 4000mm	241.18	410.10	16.89	476.21	m	**886.31**
End Cap						
Sum of two sides 1700mm	35.50	60.36	1.42	40.04	nr	**100.40**
Sum of two sides 1800mm	37.78	64.24	1.45	40.88	nr	**105.12**
Sum of two sides 1900mm	40.06	68.12	1.48	41.73	nr	**109.85**
Sum of two sides 2000mm	42.34	72.00	1.51	42.57	nr	**114.57**
Sum of two sides 2100mm	44.62	75.88	2.66	75.00	nr	**150.87**
Sum of two sides 2200mm	46.91	79.76	2.80	78.94	nr	**158.70**
Sum of two sides 2300mm	49.19	83.64	2.95	83.17	nr	**166.81**
Sum of two sides 2400mm	51.47	87.52	3.10	87.40	nr	**174.92**
Sum of two sides 2500mm	53.75	91.40	3.24	91.35	nr	**182.75**
Sum of two sides 2600mm	56.03	95.27	3.39	95.58	nr	**190.85**
Sum of two sides 2700mm	58.31	99.15	3.54	99.81	nr	**198.96**
Sum of two sides 2800mm	60.59	103.03	3.68	103.76	nr	**206.79**
Sum of two sides 2900mm	62.89	106.93	3.83	107.98	nr	**214.92**
Sum of two sides 3000mm	65.17	110.81	3.98	112.21	nr	**223.03**
Sum of two sides 3100mm	67.45	114.69	4.12	116.16	nr	**230.85**
Sum of two sides 3200mm	69.73	118.57	4.27	120.39	nr	**238.96**
Sum of two sides 3300mm	72.01	122.45	4.42	124.62	nr	**247.07**
Sum of two sides 3400mm	74.30	126.33	4.57	128.85	nr	**255.18**
Sum of two sides 3500mm	76.18	129.53	4.72	133.08	nr	**262.61**
Sum of two sides 3600mm	77.71	132.14	4.87	137.31	nr	**269.45**
Sum of two sides 3700mm	79.99	136.02	5.02	141.54	nr	**277.55**
Sum of two sides 3800mm	80.22	136.40	5.17	145.77	nr	**282.17**
Sum of two sides 3900mm	85.70	145.73	5.32	149.99	nr	**295.72**
Sum of two sides 4000mm	87.98	149.61	5.47	154.22	nr	**303.83**
Reducer						
Sum of two sides 1700mm	76.65	130.33	3.54	99.81	nr	**230.14**
Sum of two sides 1800mm	85.98	146.20	3.60	101.50	nr	**247.70**
Sum of two sides 1900mm	95.31	162.06	3.65	102.91	nr	**264.97**
Sum of two sides 2000mm	104.64	177.94	3.70	104.32	nr	**282.26**
Sum of two sides 2100mm	113.98	193.81	2.92	82.33	nr	**276.14**
Sum of two sides 2200mm	123.31	209.67	3.10	87.40	nr	**297.07**
Sum of two sides 2300mm	132.64	225.54	3.29	92.76	nr	**318.30**
Sum of two sides 2400mm	141.98	241.42	3.48	98.12	nr	**339.54**
Sum of two sides 2500mm	151.30	257.27	3.66	103.19	nr	**360.47**
Sum of two sides 2600mm	160.64	273.15	3.85	108.55	nr	**381.70**
Sum of two sides 2700mm	169.98	289.03	4.03	113.62	nr	**402.65**
Sum of two sides 2800mm	179.30	304.88	4.22	118.98	nr	**423.86**
Sum of two sides 2900mm	188.64	320.76	4.40	124.06	nr	**444.81**
Sum of two sides 3000mm	202.63	344.55	4.59	129.41	nr	**473.96**
Sum of two sides 3100mm	202.63	344.55	4.78	134.77	nr	**479.32**
Sum of two sides 3200mm	211.97	360.43	4.96	139.84	nr	**500.27**
Sum of two sides 3300mm	225.96	384.22	5.15	145.20	nr	**529.42**
Sum of two sides 3400mm	235.30	400.10	5.34	150.56	nr	**550.66**
Sum of two sides 3500mm	244.64	415.97	5.53	155.92	nr	**571.89**

U:VENTILATION/AIR CONDITIONING SYSTEMS

Item	Net Price £	Material £	Labour hours	Labour £	Unit	Total rate £
U14 : DUCTWORK : FIRE RATED (cont'd)						
Y30 – DUCTLINES (cont'd)						
Ductwork 1251 to 2000mm longest side (cont'd)						
Offset						
Sum of two sides 1700mm	76.65	130.33	4.45	125.47	nr	**255.79**
Sum of two sides 1800mm	82.96	141.07	4.56	128.57	nr	**269.64**
Sum of two sides 1900mm	89.28	151.81	4.67	131.67	nr	**283.48**
Sum of two sides 2000mm	95.59	162.54	5.53	155.92	nr	**318.45**
Sum of two sides 2100mm	101.91	173.28	5.76	162.40	nr	**335.68**
Sum of two sides 2200mm	108.23	184.02	5.99	168.89	nr	**352.91**
Sum of two sides 2300mm	114.54	194.77	6.22	175.37	nr	**370.14**
Sum of two sides 2400mm	120.85	205.49	6.45	181.85	nr	**387.34**
Sum of two sides 2500mm	127.17	216.23	6.68	188.34	nr	**404.57**
Sum of two sides 2600mm	133.49	226.98	6.91	194.82	nr	**421.80**
Sum of two sides 2700mm	139.80	237.72	7.14	201.31	nr	**439.03**
Sum of two sides 2800mm	146.12	248.46	7.37	207.79	nr	**456.26**
Sum of two sides 2900mm	152.43	259.18	7.60	214.28	nr	**473.46**
Sum of two sides 3000mm	158.75	269.93	7.83	220.76	nr	**490.69**
Sum of two sides 3100mm	165.06	280.67	8.06	227.25	nr	**507.92**
Sum of two sides 3200mm	171.38	291.41	8.29	233.73	nr	**525.15**
Sum of two sides 3300mm	177.70	302.16	8.52	240.22	nr	**542.37**
Sum of two sides 3400mm	184.01	312.88	8.75	246.70	nr	**559.58**
Sum of two sides 3500mm	190.32	323.62	8.98	253.19	nr	**576.81**
Sum of two sides 3600mm	196.64	334.37	9.21	259.67	nr	**594.04**
Sum of two sides 3700mm	202.96	345.11	9.44	266.16	nr	**611.27**
Sum of two sides 3800mm	209.27	355.83	9.67	272.64	nr	**628.47**
Sum of two sides 3900mm	215.58	366.58	9.90	279.13	nr	**645.70**
Sum of two sides 4000mm	221.90	377.32	10.13	285.61	nr	**662.93**
90° radius bend						
Sum of two sides 1700mm	106.67	181.38	3.22	90.79	nr	**272.16**
Sum of two sides 1800mm	116.31	197.77	3.25	91.63	nr	**289.40**
Sum of two sides 1900mm	125.95	214.16	3.28	92.48	nr	**306.64**
Sum of two sides 2000mm	135.59	230.56	3.30	93.04	nr	**323.60**
Sum of two sides 2100mm	145.23	246.95	3.32	93.61	nr	**340.56**
Sum of two sides 2200mm	154.87	263.34	3.34	94.17	nr	**357.51**
Sum of two sides 2300mm	164.51	279.74	3.36	94.73	nr	**374.47**
Sum of two sides 2400mm	174.15	296.13	3.38	95.30	nr	**391.43**
Sum of two sides 2500mm	183.80	312.52	3.40	95.86	nr	**408.38**
Sum of two sides 2600mm	193.44	328.91	3.42	96.43	nr	**425.34**
Sum of two sides 2700mm	203.08	345.31	3.44	96.99	nr	**442.30**
Sum of two sides 2800mm	212.72	361.70	3.46	97.55	nr	**459.25**
Sum of two sides 2900mm	222.35	378.07	3.48	98.12	nr	**476.19**
Sum of two sides 3000mm	231.99	394.47	3.50	98.68	nr	**493.15**
Sum of two sides 3100mm	241.63	410.86	3.52	99.24	nr	**510.10**
Sum of two sides 3200mm	251.27	427.25	3.54	99.81	nr	**527.06**
Sum of two sides 3300mm	260.91	443.65	3.56	100.37	nr	**544.02**
Sum of two sides 3400mm	270.67	460.24	3.58	100.94	nr	**561.17**
Sum of two sides 3500mm	280.19	476.43	3.60	101.50	nr	**577.93**
Sum of two sides 3600mm	289.83	492.83	3.62	102.06	nr	**594.89**
Sum of two sides 3700mm	299.47	509.22	3.64	102.63	nr	**611.85**
Sum of two sides 3800mm	309.11	525.61	3.66	103.19	nr	**628.80**
Sum of two sides 3900mm	318.75	542.00	3.68	103.76	nr	**645.76**
Sum of two sides 4000mm	328.40	558.40	3.70	104.32	nr	**662.72**

U:VENTILATION/AIR CONDITIONING SYSTEMS

Item	Net Price £	Material £	Labour hours	Labour £	Unit	Total rate £
45° bend						
Sum of two sides 1700mm	79.08	134.47	2.24	63.16	nr	**197.62**
Sum of two sides 1800mm	87.82	149.33	2.30	64.85	nr	**214.18**
Sum of two sides 1900mm	96.55	164.17	2.35	66.26	nr	**230.43**
Sum of two sides 2000mm	105.29	179.03	2.76	77.82	nr	**256.85**
Sum of two sides 2100mm	145.23	246.95	2.89	81.48	nr	**328.43**
Sum of two sides 2200mm	122.76	208.73	3.01	84.87	nr	**293.60**
Sum of two sides 2300mm	131.50	223.59	3.13	88.25	nr	**311.84**
Sum of two sides 2400mm	140.22	238.43	3.26	91.91	nr	**330.35**
Sum of two sides 2500mm	148.96	253.30	3.37	95.02	nr	**348.31**
Sum of two sides 2600mm	157.69	268.14	3.49	98.40	nr	**366.54**
Sum of two sides 2700mm	166.43	283.00	3.62	102.06	nr	**385.06**
Sum of two sides 2800mm	175.17	297.86	3.74	105.45	nr	**403.31**
Sum of two sides 2900mm	183.90	312.70	3.86	108.83	nr	**421.53**
Sum of two sides 3000mm	192.64	327.56	3.98	112.21	nr	**439.78**
Sum of two sides 3100mm	201.38	342.42	4.10	115.60	nr	**458.02**
Sum of two sides 3200mm	210.11	357.26	4.22	118.98	nr	**476.25**
Sum of two sides 3300mm	218.85	372.13	4.34	122.36	nr	**494.49**
Sum of two sides 3400mm	227.58	386.97	4.46	125.75	nr	**512.71**
Sum of two sides 3500mm	236.32	401.83	4.58	129.13	nr	**530.96**
Sum of two sides 3600mm	245.06	416.69	4.70	132.51	nr	**549.20**
Sum of two sides 3700mm	253.78	431.53	4.82	135.90	nr	**567.43**
Sum of two sides 3800mm	262.52	446.39	4.94	139.28	nr	**585.67**
Sum of two sides 3900mm	271.25	461.23	5.06	142.66	nr	**603.90**
Sum of two sides 4000mm	279.99	476.09	5.18	146.05	nr	**622.14**
90° mitre bend						
Sum of two sides 1700mm	159.76	271.66	3.87	109.11	nr	**380.77**
Sum of two sides 1800mm	187.38	318.61	3.90	109.96	nr	**428.57**
Sum of two sides 1900mm	214.99	365.56	3.93	110.80	nr	**476.36**
Sum of two sides 2000mm	242.59	412.49	3.96	111.65	nr	**524.14**
Sum of two sides 2100mm	270.20	459.44	3.82	107.70	nr	**567.15**
Sum of two sides 2200mm	297.81	506.39	3.83	107.98	nr	**614.38**
Sum of two sides 2300mm	325.42	553.34	3.83	107.98	nr	**661.33**
Sum of two sides 2400mm	353.04	600.29	3.84	108.27	nr	**708.56**
Sum of two sides 2500mm	380.65	647.25	3.85	108.55	nr	**755.79**
Sum of two sides 2600mm	408.25	694.18	3.85	108.55	nr	**802.73**
Sum of two sides 2700mm	435.86	741.13	3.86	108.83	nr	**849.96**
Sum of two sides 2800mm	463.47	788.08	3.86	108.83	nr	**896.91**
Sum of two sides 2900mm	491.08	835.03	3.87	109.11	nr	**944.14**
Sum of two sides 3000mm	518.70	881.98	3.87	109.11	nr	**991.09**
Sum of two sides 3100mm	546.31	928.93	3.88	109.39	nr	**1038.33**
Sum of two sides 3200mm	573.91	975.86	3.88	109.39	nr	**1085.26**
Sum of two sides 3300mm	601.52	1022.81	3.89	109.68	nr	**1132.49**
Sum of two sides 3400mm	629.13	1069.76	3.90	109.96	nr	**1179.72**
Sum of two sides 3500mm	656.74	1116.71	3.91	110.24	nr	**1226.96**
Sum of two sides 3600mm	684.36	1163.67	3.92	110.52	nr	**1274.19**
Sum of two sides 3700mm	711.97	1210.62	3.93	110.80	nr	**1321.42**
Sum of two sides 3800mm	739.57	1257.55	3.94	111.09	nr	**1368.63**
Sum of two sides 3900mm	767.18	1304.50	3.95	111.37	nr	**1415.87**
Sum of two sides 4000mm	794.79	1351.45	3.96	111.65	nr	**1463.10**

U:VENTILATION/AIR CONDITIONING SYSTEMS

Item	Net Price £	Material £	Labour hours	Labour £	Unit	Total rate £
U14 : DUCTWORK : FIRE RATED (cont'd)						
Y30 – DUCTLINES (cont'd)						
Fittings; Ductwork 1251 to 2000mm longest Side (cont'd)						
Branch						
Sum of two sides 1700mm	18.11	30.80	1.77	49.90	nr	**80.70**
Sum of two sides 1800mm	19.80	33.66	1.81	51.03	nr	**84.69**
Sum of two sides 1900mm	21.48	36.53	1.86	52.44	nr	**88.97**
Sum of two sides 2000mm	23.17	39.39	1.90	53.57	nr	**92.96**
Sum of two sides 2100mm	24.85	42.26	2.58	72.74	nr	**115.00**
Sum of two sides 2200mm	26.54	45.12	2.61	73.59	nr	**118.71**
Sum of two sides 2300mm	28.22	47.99	2.65	74.72	nr	**122.70**
Sum of two sides 2400mm	29.91	50.85	2.68	75.56	nr	**126.41**
Sum of two sides 2500mm	31.59	53.72	2.71	76.41	nr	**130.12**
Sum of two sides 2600mm	33.27	56.58	2.75	77.53	nr	**134.11**
Sum of two sides 2700mm	34.96	59.44	2.78	78.38	nr	**137.83**
Sum of two sides 2800mm	36.64	62.31	2.81	79.23	nr	**141.54**
Sum of two sides 2900mm	38.33	65.17	2.84	80.07	nr	**145.25**
Sum of two sides 3000mm	40.01	68.04	2.87	80.92	nr	**148.96**
Sum of two sides 3100mm	41.70	70.90	2.90	81.76	nr	**152.67**
Sum of two sides 3200mm	43.38	73.77	2.93	82.61	nr	**156.38**
Sum of two sides 3300mm	45.07	76.63	2.93	82.61	nr	**159.24**
Sum of two sides 3400mm	46.75	79.50	3.00	84.58	nr	**164.08**
Sum of two sides 3500mm	48.44	82.36	3.03	85.43	nr	**167.79**
Sum of two sides 3600mm	50.12	85.23	3.06	86.28	nr	**171.50**
Sum of two sides 3700mm	51.81	88.09	3.09	87.12	nr	**175.21**
Sum of two sides 3800mm	53.49	90.96	3.12	87.97	nr	**178.92**
Sum of two sides 3900mm	55.18	93.82	3.15	88.81	nr	**182.63**
Sum of two sides 4000mm	56.86	96.69	3.18	89.66	nr	**186.35**
Rectangular section ductwork to BS476 Part 24 (ISO 6944:1985), ducts "Type A" and "Type B"; manufactured from 6mm thick laminate fire board consisting of steel circular hole punched facings pressed to a fibre cement core; provides upto 4 hours stability, 4 hours integrity and 32 minutes insulation; including all necessary stiffeners, joints and supports in the running length						
Ductwork up to 600mm longest side						
Sum of two sides 200 mm	136.98	232.92	4.00	112.78	m	**345.70**
Sum of two sides 400mm	136.98	232.92	4.00	112.78	m	**345.70**
Sum of two sides 600mm	136.98	232.92	4.00	112.78	m	**345.70**
Sum of two sides 800mm	193.49	329.01	5.50	155.07	m	**484.08**
Sum of two sides 1000mm	193.49	329.01	5.50	155.07	m	**484.08**
Sum of two sides 1200mm	269.43	458.13	6.00	169.17	m	**627.30**

U:VENTILATION/AIR CONDITIONING SYSTEMS

Item	Net Price £	Material £	Labour hours	Labour £	Unit	Total rate £
Extra over fittings; Ductwork up to 600mm longest side						
End Cap						
Sum of two sides 200 mm	31.88	54.21	0.81	22.84	m	**77.05**
Sum of two sides 400mm	31.88	54.21	0.87	24.53	m	**78.74**
Sum of two sides 600mm	31.88	54.21	0.93	26.22	m	**80.43**
Sum of two sides 800mm	43.75	74.39	0.98	27.63	m	**102.02**
Sum of two sides 1000mm	43.75	74.39	1.22	34.40	m	**108.79**
Sum of two sides 1200mm	62.50	106.27	1.28	36.09	m	**142.36**
Reducer						
Sum of two sides 200 mm	36.25	61.64	2.23	62.87	m	**124.51**
Sum of two sides 400mm	36.25	61.64	2.51	70.77	m	**132.41**
Sum of two sides 600mm	36.25	61.64	2.79	78.66	m	**140.30**
Sum of two sides 800mm	63.13	107.35	3.01	84.87	m	**192.21**
Sum of two sides 1000mm	63.13	107.35	3.17	89.38	m	**196.72**
Sum of two sides 1200mm	91.88	156.23	3.28	92.48	m	**248.71**
Offset						
Sum of two sides 200 mm	36.25	61.64	2.95	83.17	m	**144.81**
Sum of two sides 400mm	36.25	61.64	3.26	91.91	m	**153.55**
Sum of two sides 600mm	36.25	61.64	3.57	100.65	m	**162.29**
Sum of two sides 800mm	63.13	107.35	3.23	91.07	m	**198.41**
Sum of two sides 1000mm	63.13	107.35	3.67	103.47	m	**210.82**
Sum of two sides 1200mm	79.38	134.98	3.89	109.68	m	**244.65**
90° radius bend						
Sum of two sides 200 mm	61.25	104.15	2.06	58.08	m	**162.23**
Sum of two sides 400mm	61.25	104.15	2.36	66.54	m	**170.69**
Sum of two sides 600mm	61.25	104.15	2.66	75.00	m	**179.15**
Sum of two sides 800mm	75.63	128.60	2.97	83.74	m	**212.34**
Sum of two sides 1000mm	75.63	128.60	3.04	85.71	m	**214.31**
Sum of two sides 1200mm	91.88	156.23	3.09	87.12	m	**243.35**
45° radius bend						
Sum of two sides 200 mm	61.25	104.15	1.52	42.86	m	**147.00**
Sum of two sides 400mm	61.25	104.15	1.66	46.80	m	**150.95**
Sum of two sides 600mm	61.25	104.15	1.80	50.75	m	**154.90**
Sum of two sides 800mm	75.63	128.60	1.93	54.42	m	**183.02**
Sum of two sides 1000mm	75.63	128.60	2.05	57.80	m	**186.40**
Sum of two sides 1200mm	91.88	156.23	2.17	61.18	m	**217.41**
90° mitre bend						
Sum of two sides 200 mm	61.25	104.15	2.47	69.64	m	**173.79**
Sum of two sides 400mm	61.25	104.15	2.84	80.07	m	**184.22**
Sum of two sides 600mm	61.25	104.15	3.20	90.22	m	**194.37**
Sum of two sides 800mm	75.63	128.60	3.56	100.37	m	**228.97**
Sum of two sides 1000mm	75.63	128.60	3.66	103.19	m	**231.79**
Sum of two sides 1200mm	91.88	156.23	3.72	104.88	m	**261.11**
Branch						
Sum of two sides 200 mm	42.50	72.27	0.98	27.63	m	**99.90**
Sum of two sides 400mm	42.50	72.27	1.14	32.14	m	**104.41**
Sum of two sides 600mm	42.50	72.27	1.30	36.65	m	**108.92**
Sum of two sides 800mm	50.63	86.09	1.46	41.16	m	**127.25**
Sum of two sides 1000mm	50.63	86.09	1.46	41.16	m	**127.25**
Sum of two sides 1200mm	66.88	113.72	1.55	43.70	m	**157.42**

U:VENTILATION/AIR CONDITIONING SYSTEMS

Item	Net Price £	Material £	Labour hours	Labour £	Unit	Total rate £
U14 : DUCTWORK : FIRE RATED (cont'd)						
Y30 – DUCTLINES (cont'd)						
Ductwork 601 to 1000mm longest side						
Sum of two sides 1000mm	193.49	329.01	6.00	169.17	m	**498.17**
Sum of two sides 1100mm	269.43	458.13	6.00	169.17	m	**627.30**
Sum of two sides 1300mm	269.43	458.13	6.00	169.17	m	**627.30**
Sum of two sides 1500mm	269.43	458.13	6.00	169.17	m	**627.30**
Sum of two sides 1700mm	322.78	548.85	6.00	169.17	m	**718.02**
Sum of two sides 1900mm	322.78	548.85	6.00	169.17	m	**718.02**
Extra over fittings; Ductwork 601 to 1000mm longest side						
End Cap						
Sum of two sides 1000mm	43.75	74.39	1.25	35.24	m	**109.63**
Sum of two sides 1100mm	62.50	106.27	1.25	35.24	m	**141.52**
Sum of two sides 1300mm	62.50	106.27	1.31	36.93	m	**143.21**
Sum of two sides 1500mm	62.50	106.27	1.36	38.34	m	**144.62**
Sum of two sides 1700mm	124.99	212.53	1.42	40.04	m	**252.57**
Sum of two sides 1900mm	124.99	212.53	1.48	41.73	m	**254.26**
Reducer						
Sum of two sides 1000mm	63.13	107.35	3.22	90.79	m	**198.13**
Sum of two sides 1100mm	91.88	156.23	3.22	90.79	m	**247.02**
Sum of two sides 1300mm	91.88	156.23	3.33	93.89	m	**250.12**
Sum of two sides 1500mm	91.88	156.23	3.44	96.99	m	**253.22**
Sum of two sides 1700mm	95.73	162.78	3.54	99.81	m	**262.59**
Sum of two sides 1900mm	95.73	162.78	3.65	102.91	m	**265.69**
Offset						
Sum of two sides 1000mm	63.13	107.35	3.78	106.58	m	**213.92**
Sum of two sides 1100mm	79.38	134.98	3.78	106.58	m	**241.55**
Sum of two sides 1300mm	79.38	134.98	4.00	112.78	m	**247.75**
Sum of two sides 1500mm	79.38	134.98	4.23	119.26	m	**254.24**
Sum of two sides 1700mm	109.89	186.85	4.45	125.47	m	**312.32**
Sum of two sides 1900mm	109.89	186.85	4.67	131.67	m	**318.52**
90° radius bend						
Sum of two sides 1000mm	75.63	128.60	3.78	106.58	m	**235.17**
Sum of two sides 1100mm	91.88	156.23	3.07	86.56	m	**242.79**
Sum of two sides 1300mm	91.88	156.23	3.12	87.97	m	**244.20**
Sum of two sides 1500mm	91.88	156.23	3.17	89.38	m	**245.61**
Sum of two sides 1700mm	134.45	228.62	3.22	90.79	m	**319.40**
Sum of two sides 1900mm	134.45	228.62	3.28	92.48	m	**321.09**
45° bend						
Sum of two sides 1000mm	75.63	128.60	3.78	106.58	m	**235.17**
Sum of two sides 1100mm	91.88	156.23	1.91	53.85	m	**210.08**
Sum of two sides 1300mm	91.88	156.23	2.02	56.95	m	**213.18**
Sum of two sides 1500mm	91.88	156.23	2.13	60.05	m	**216.29**
Sum of two sides 1700mm	134.45	228.62	2.24	63.16	m	**291.77**
Sum of two sides 1900mm	134.45	228.62	2.35	66.26	m	**294.87**

U:VENTILATION/AIR CONDITIONING SYSTEMS

Item	Net Price £	Material £	Labour hours	Labour £	Unit	Total rate £
90° mitre bend						
Sum of two sides 1000mm	75.63	128.60	3.78	106.58	m	**235.17**
Sum of two sides 1100mm	91.88	156.23	3.69	104.04	m	**260.27**
Sum of two sides 1300mm	91.88	156.23	3.75	105.73	m	**261.96**
Sum of two sides 1500mm	91.88	156.23	3.81	107.42	m	**263.65**
Sum of two sides 1700mm	134.45	228.62	3.87	109.11	m	**337.73**
Sum of two sides 1900mm	134.45	228.62	3.93	110.80	m	**339.42**
Branch						
Sum of two sides 1000mm	50.63	86.09	3.78	106.58	m	**192.67**
Sum of two sides 1100mm	66.88	113.72	1.50	42.29	m	**156.01**
Sum of two sides 1300mm	66.88	113.72	1.59	44.83	m	**158.55**
Sum of two sides 1500mm	66.88	113.72	1.68	47.37	m	**161.09**
Sum of two sides 1700mm	84.32	143.38	1.77	49.90	m	**193.28**
Sum of two sides 1900mm	84.32	143.38	1.86	52.44	m	**195.82**
Ductwork 1001 to 1250mm longest side						
Sum of two sides 1300mm	269.43	458.13	6.00	169.17	m	**627.30**
Sum of two sides 1500mm	269.43	458.13	6.00	169.17	m	**627.30**
Sum of two sides 1700mm	322.78	548.85	6.00	169.17	m	**718.02**
Sum of two sides 1900mm	322.78	548.85	6.00	169.17	m	**718.02**
Sum of two sides 2100mm	451.35	767.47	6.50	183.26	m	**950.73**
Sum of two sides 2300mm	451.35	767.47	6.50	183.26	m	**950.73**
Sum of two sides 2500mm	451.35	767.47	6.50	183.26	m	**950.73**
Extra over fittings; Ductwork 1001 to 1250mm longest side						
End Cap						
Sum of two sides 1300mm	62.50	106.27	1.31	36.93	m	**143.21**
Sum of two sides 1500mm	62.50	106.27	1.36	38.34	m	**144.62**
Sum of two sides 1700mm	124.99	212.53	1.42	40.04	m	**252.57**
Sum of two sides 1900mm	124.99	212.53	1.48	41.73	m	**254.26**
Sum of two sides 2100mm	147.33	250.52	2.66	75.00	m	**325.51**
Sum of two sides 2300mm	147.33	250.52	2.95	83.17	m	**333.69**
Sum of two sides 2500mm	147.33	250.52	3.24	91.35	m	**341.87**
Reducer						
Sum of two sides 1300mm	91.88	156.23	3.33	93.89	m	**250.12**
Sum of two sides 1500mm	91.88	156.23	3.44	96.99	m	**253.22**
Sum of two sides 1700mm	95.73	162.78	3.54	99.81	m	**262.59**
Sum of two sides 1900mm	95.73	162.78	3.65	102.91	m	**265.69**
Sum of two sides 2100mm	111.88	190.24	3.75	105.73	m	**295.97**
Sum of two sides 2300mm	111.88	190.24	3.85	108.55	m	**298.79**
Sum of two sides 2500mm	111.88	190.24	3.95	111.37	m	**301.61**

U:VENTILATION/AIR CONDITIONING SYSTEMS

Item	Net Price £	Material £	Labour hours	Labour £	Unit	Total rate £
U14 : DUCTWORK : FIRE RATED (cont'd)						
Y30 – DUCTLINES (cont'd)						
Fittings; Ductwork 1001 to 1250mm longest side (cont'd)						
Offset						
Sum of two sides 1300mm	79.38	134.98	4.00	112.78	m	**247.75**
Sum of two sides 1500mm	79.38	134.98	4.23	119.26	m	**254.24**
Sum of two sides 1700mm	109.89	186.85	4.45	125.47	m	**312.32**
Sum of two sides 1900mm	109.89	186.85	4.67	131.67	m	**318.52**
Sum of two sides 2100mm	111.88	190.24	5.76	162.40	m	**352.64**
Sum of two sides 2300mm	111.88	190.24	6.22	175.37	m	**365.61**
Sum of two sides 2500mm	111.88	190.24	6.68	188.34	m	**378.58**
90° radius bend						
Sum of two sides 1300mm	91.88	156.23	3.12	87.97	m	**244.20**
Sum of two sides 1500mm	91.88	156.23	3.17	89.38	m	**245.61**
Sum of two sides 1700mm	134.45	228.62	3.22	90.79	m	**319.40**
Sum of two sides 1900mm	134.45	228.62	3.28	92.48	m	**321.09**
Sum of two sides 2100mm	136.88	232.75	3.32	93.61	m	**326.35**
Sum of two sides 2300mm	136.88	232.75	3.36	94.73	m	**327.48**
Sum of two sides 2500mm	136.88	232.75	3.40	95.86	m	**328.61**
45° bend						
Sum of two sides 1300mm	91.88	156.23	2.02	56.95	m	**213.18**
Sum of two sides 1500mm	91.88	156.23	2.13	60.05	m	**216.29**
Sum of two sides 1700mm	134.45	228.62	2.24	63.16	m	**291.77**
Sum of two sides 1900mm	134.45	228.62	2.35	66.26	m	**294.87**
Sum of two sides 2100mm	136.88	232.75	2.89	81.48	m	**314.23**
Sum of two sides 2300mm	136.88	232.75	3.13	88.25	m	**321.00**
Sum of two sides 2500mm	136.88	232.75	3.37	95.02	m	**327.76**
90° mitre bend						
Sum of two sides 1300mm	91.88	156.23	3.75	105.73	m	**261.96**
Sum of two sides 1500mm	91.88	156.23	3.81	107.42	m	**263.65**
Sum of two sides 1700mm	134.45	228.62	3.87	109.11	m	**337.73**
Sum of two sides 1900mm	134.45	228.62	3.93	110.80	m	**339.42**
Sum of two sides 2100mm	136.88	232.75	3.99	112.50	m	**345.24**
Sum of two sides 2300mm	136.88	232.75	4.05	114.19	m	**346.94**
Sum of two sides 2500mm	136.88	232.75	4.11	115.88	m	**348.63**
Branch						
Sum of two sides 1300mm	66.88	113.72	1.59	44.83	m	**158.55**
Sum of two sides 1500mm	66.88	113.72	1.68	47.37	m	**161.09**
Sum of two sides 1700mm	84.32	143.38	1.77	49.90	m	**193.28**
Sum of two sides 1900mm	84.32	143.38	1.86	52.44	m	**195.82**
Sum of two sides 2100mm	86.88	147.73	2.58	72.74	m	**220.47**
Sum of two sides 2300mm	86.88	147.73	2.64	74.43	m	**222.16**
Sum of two sides 2500mm	86.88	147.73	2.91	82.05	m	**229.78**

U:VENTILATION/AIR CONDITIONING SYSTEMS

Item	Net Price £	Material £	Labour hours	Labour £	Unit	Total rate £
Ductwork 1251 to 2000mm longest side						
Sum of two sides 1800mm	322.78	548.85	6.00	169.17	m	**718.02**
Sum of two sides 2000mm	322.78	548.85	6.00	169.17	m	**718.02**
Sum of two sides 2200mm	451.35	767.47	6.50	183.26	m	**950.73**
Sum of two sides 2400mm	451.35	767.47	6.50	183.26	m	**950.73**
Sum of two sides 2600mm	451.35	767.47	6.66	187.78	m	**955.24**
Sum of two sides 2800mm	534.73	909.24	6.66	187.78	m	**1097.02**
Sum of two sides 3000mm	534.73	909.24	6.66	187.78	m	**1097.02**
Sum of two sides 3200mm	667.70	1135.34	9.00	253.75	m	**1389.09**
Sum of two sides 3400mm	667.70	1135.34	9.00	253.75	m	**1389.09**
Sum of two sides 3600mm	768.55	1306.83	11.70	329.88	m	**1636.70**
Sum of two sides 3800mm	768.55	1306.83	11.70	329.88	m	**1636.70**
Sum of two sides 4000mm	768.55	1306.83	11.70	329.88	m	**1636.70**
Extra over fittings; Ductwork 1251 to 2000mm longest sides						
End Cap						
Sum of two sides 1800mm	124.99	212.53	1.45	40.88	m	**253.41**
Sum of two sides 2000mm	124.99	212.53	1.51	42.57	m	**255.10**
Sum of two sides 2200mm	147.33	250.52	2.80	78.94	m	**329.46**
Sum of two sides 2400mm	147.33	250.52	3.10	87.40	m	**337.92**
Sum of two sides 2600mm	200.91	341.62	3.39	95.58	m	**437.20**
Sum of two sides 2800mm	200.91	341.62	3.68	103.76	m	**445.38**
Sum of two sides 3000mm	200.91	341.62	3.98	112.21	m	**453.84**
Sum of two sides 3200mm	263.41	447.90	4.27	120.39	m	**568.29**
Sum of two sides 3400mm	263.41	447.90	4.57	128.85	m	**576.75**
Sum of two sides 3600mm	331.87	564.31	4.87	137.31	m	**701.61**
Sum of two sides 3800mm	331.87	564.31	5.17	145.77	m	**710.07**
Sum of two sides 4000mm	331.87	564.31	5.47	154.22	m	**718.53**
Reducer						
Sum of two sides 1800mm	95.73	162.78	3.60	101.50	m	**264.28**
Sum of two sides 2000mm	95.73	162.78	3.70	104.32	m	**267.10**
Sum of two sides 2200mm	111.88	190.24	3.10	87.40	m	**277.64**
Sum of two sides 2400mm	111.88	190.24	3.48	98.12	m	**288.36**
Sum of two sides 2600mm	156.64	266.35	3.85	108.55	m	**374.90**
Sum of two sides 2800mm	156.64	266.35	4.22	118.98	m	**385.33**
Sum of two sides 3000mm	156.64	266.35	4.59	129.41	m	**395.76**
Sum of two sides 3200mm	172.82	293.86	4.96	139.84	m	**433.70**
Sum of two sides 3400mm	172.82	293.86	5.34	150.56	m	**444.42**
Sum of two sides 3600mm	188.98	321.34	5.72	161.27	m	**482.61**
Sum of two sides 3800mm	188.98	321.34	6.10	171.99	m	**493.32**
Sum of two sides 4000mm	188.98	321.34	6.48	182.70	m	**504.04**
Offset						
Sum of two sides 1800mm	109.89	186.85	4.56	128.57	m	**315.42**
Sum of two sides 2000mm	109.89	186.85	5.53	155.92	m	**342.77**
Sum of two sides 2200mm	111.88	190.24	5.99	168.89	m	**359.12**
Sum of two sides 2400mm	111.88	190.24	6.45	181.85	m	**372.09**
Sum of two sides 2600mm	191.81	326.15	6.91	194.82	m	**520.97**
Sum of two sides 2800mm	191.81	326.15	7.37	207.79	m	**533.94**
Sum of two sides 3000mm	191.81	326.15	7.83	220.76	m	**546.91**
Sum of two sides 3200mm	237.76	404.28	8.29	233.73	m	**638.01**
Sum of two sides 3400mm	237.76	404.28	8.75	246.70	m	**650.98**
Sum of two sides 3600mm	283.72	482.43	9.21	259.67	m	**742.10**
Sum of two sides 3800mm	283.72	482.43	9.67	272.64	m	**755.07**
Sum of two sides 4000mm	283.72	482.43	10.13	285.61	m	**768.04**

U:VENTILATION/AIR CONDITIONING SYSTEMS

Item	Net Price £	Material £	Labour hours	Labour £	Unit	Total rate £
U14 : DUCTWORK : FIRE RATED (cont'd)						
Y30 – DUCTLINES (cont'd)						
Fittings; Ductwork 1251 to 2000mm longest sides (cont'd)						
90° radius bend						
Sum of two sides 1800mm	134.45	228.62	3.25	91.63	m	**320.25**
Sum of two sides 2000mm	134.45	228.62	3.30	93.04	m	**321.66**
Sum of two sides 2200mm	136.88	232.75	3.34	94.17	m	**326.92**
Sum of two sides 2400mm	136.88	232.75	3.38	95.30	m	**328.05**
Sum of two sides 2600mm	234.67	399.03	3.42	96.43	m	**495.45**
Sum of two sides 2800mm	234.67	399.03	3.46	97.55	m	**496.58**
Sum of two sides 3000mm	234.67	399.03	3.50	98.68	m	**497.71**
Sum of two sides 3200mm	290.89	494.62	3.54	99.81	m	**594.43**
Sum of two sides 3400mm	290.89	494.62	3.58	100.94	m	**595.56**
Sum of two sides 3600mm	347.12	590.24	3.62	102.06	m	**692.30**
Sum of two sides 3800mm	347.12	590.24	3.66	103.19	m	**693.43**
Sum of two sides 4000mm	347.12	590.24	3.70	104.32	m	**694.56**
45° bend						
Sum of two sides 1800mm	134.45	228.62	2.30	64.85	m	**293.46**
Sum of two sides 2000mm	134.45	228.62	2.76	77.82	m	**306.43**
Sum of two sides 2200mm	136.88	232.75	3.01	84.87	m	**317.61**
Sum of two sides 2400mm	136.88	232.75	3.26	91.91	m	**324.66**
Sum of two sides 2600mm	234.67	399.03	3.49	98.40	m	**497.43**
Sum of two sides 2800mm	234.67	399.03	3.74	105.45	m	**504.48**
Sum of two sides 3000mm	234.67	399.03	3.98	112.21	m	**511.24**
Sum of two sides 3200mm	290.89	494.62	4.22	118.98	m	**613.60**
Sum of two sides 3400mm	290.89	494.62	4.46	125.75	m	**620.37**
Sum of two sides 3600mm	347.12	590.24	4.70	132.51	m	**722.75**
Sum of two sides 3800mm	347.12	590.24	4.94	139.28	m	**729.52**
Sum of two sides 4000mm	347.12	590.24	5.18	146.05	m	**736.28**
90° mitre band						
Sum of two sides 1800mm	134.45	228.62	3.90	109.96	m	**338.57**
Sum of two sides 2000mm	134.45	228.62	3.96	111.65	m	**340.27**
Sum of two sides 2200mm	136.88	232.75	3.83	107.98	m	**340.73**
Sum of two sides 2400mm	136.88	232.75	3.84	108.27	m	**341.01**
Sum of two sides 2600mm	234.67	399.03	3.85	108.55	m	**507.58**
Sum of two sides 2800mm	234.67	399.03	3.86	108.83	m	**507.86**
Sum of two sides 3000mm	234.67	399.03	3.87	109.11	m	**508.14**
Sum of two sides 3200mm	290.89	494.62	3.88	109.39	m	**604.02**
Sum of two sides 3400mm	290.89	494.62	3.90	109.96	m	**604.58**
Sum of two sides 3600mm	347.12	590.24	3.92	110.52	m	**700.76**
Sum of two sides 3800mm	347.12	590.24	3.94	111.09	m	**701.32**
Sum of two sides 4000mm	347.12	590.24	3.96	111.65	m	**701.89**
Branch						
Sum of two sides 1800mm	84.32	143.38	1.81	51.03	m	**194.41**
Sum of two sides 2000mm	84.32	143.38	1.90	53.57	m	**196.95**
Sum of two sides 2200mm	86.88	147.73	2.61	73.59	m	**221.32**
Sum of two sides 2400mm	86.88	147.73	2.68	75.56	m	**223.29**
Sum of two sides 2600mm	104.77	178.15	2.75	77.53	m	**255.68**
Sum of two sides 2800mm	104.77	178.15	2.81	79.23	m	**257.38**
Sum of two sides 3000mm	104.77	178.15	2.87	80.92	m	**259.07**
Sum of two sides 3200mm	107.32	182.48	2.93	82.61	m	**265.09**
Sum of two sides 3400mm	107.32	182.48	3.00	84.58	m	**267.07**

U:VENTILATION/AIR CONDITIONING SYSTEMS

Item	Net Price £	Material £	Labour hours	Labour £	Unit	Total rate £
Sum of two sides 3600mm	137.99	234.64	3.06	86.28	m	**320.91**
Sum of two sides 3800mm	137.99	234.64	3.12	87.97	m	**322.60**
Sum of two sides 4000mm	137.99	234.64	3.18	89.66	m	**324.29**

U:VENTILATION/AIR CONDITIONING SYSTEMS

Item	Net Price £	Material £	Labour hours	Labour £	Unit	Total rate £
U30 : LOW VELOCITY AIR CONDITIONING						
Y40 - AIR HANDLING UNITS						
Supply air handling unit; inlet with motorised damper, LTHW frost coil (at -5°C to +5°C), panel filter (EU4), bag filter (EU6), cooling coil (at 28°C db/20°C wb to 12°C db/11.5°C wb), LTHW heating coil (at 5°C to 21°C), supply fan, outlet plenum; includes access sections; all units located internally; Includes placing in position and fitting of sections together; electrical work elsewhere.						
Volume, external pressure						
2 m³/s at 350 Pa	4147.50	5312.08	40.00	907.14	nr	**6219.21**
2 m³/s at 700 Pa	4431.00	5675.18	40.00	907.14	nr	**6582.32**
5 m³/s at 350 Pa	6993.53	8957.24	65.00	1474.10	nr	**10431.33**
5 m³/s at 700 Pa	7238.18	9270.58	65.00	1474.10	nr	**10744.68**
8 m³/s at 350 Pa	10474.80	13416.02	77.00	1746.24	nr	**15162.26**
8 m/³s at 700 Pa	10638.08	13625.14	77.00	1746.24	nr	**15371.38**
10 m/³ at 350 Pa	11534.78	14773.62	100.00	2267.84	nr	**17041.46**
10 m³/s at 700 Pa	11771.55	15076.88	100.00	2267.84	nr	**17344.72**
13 m³/s at 350 Pa	14414.40	18461.82	108.00	2449.27	nr	**20911.09**
13 m³/s at 700 Pa	14859.60	19032.03	108.00	2449.27	nr	**21481.29**
15 m³/s at 350 Pa	16157.93	20694.91	120.00	2721.41	nr	**23416.32**
15 m³/s at 700 Pa	16451.92	21071.46	120.00	2721.41	nr	**23792.87**
18 m³/s at 350 Pa	18335.10	23483.41	133.00	3016.23	nr	**26499.64**
18 m³/s at 700 Pa	18672.15	23915.10	133.00	3016.23	nr	**26931.33**
20 m³/s at 350 Pa	21247.28	27213.30	142.00	3220.33	nr	**30433.63**
20 m³/s at 700 Pa	21552.83	27604.64	142.00	3220.33	nr	**30824.98**
Extra for inlet and discharge attenuators at 900mm long						
2 m³/s at 350 Pa	1275.75	1633.97	5.00	113.39	nr	**1747.36**
5 m³/s at 350 Pa	2677.50	3429.32	10.00	226.78	nr	**3656.10**
10 m³/s at 700 Pa	3743.25	4794.32	13.00	294.82	nr	**5089.14**
15 m³/s at 700 Pa	5579.18	7145.75	16.00	362.85	nr	**7508.61**
20 m³/s at 700 Pa	7138.95	9143.50	20.00	453.57	nr	**9597.06**
Extra for locating units externally						
2 m³/s at 350 Pa	944.51	1209.72	-	-	nr	**1209.72**
5 m³/s at 350 Pa	1198.41	1534.91	-	-	nr	**1534.91**
10 m³/s at 700 Pa	1883.87	2412.84	-	-	nr	**2412.84**
15 m³/s at 700 Pa	2675.94	3427.32	-	-	nr	**3427.32**
20 m³/s at 700 Pa	4598.95	5890.29	-	-	nr	**5890.29**

U:VENTILATION/AIR CONDITIONING SYSTEMS

Item	Net Price £	Material £	Labour hours	Labour £	Unit	Total rate £
Modular air handling unit with supply and extract sections. Supply side; inlet with motorised damper, LTHW frost coil (at -5°C to 5°C), panel filter (EU4), bag filter (EU6), cooling coil at 28°Cdb/20°Cwb to 12°Cdb/11.5°C wb), LTHW heating coil (at 5°C to 21°C), supply fan, outlet plenum. Extract side; inlet with motorised damper, extract fan; includes access sections; placing in position and fitting of sections together; electrical work elsewhere.						
2 m³/s at 350 Pa	5793.90	7420.77	50.00	1133.92	nr	**8554.69**
2 m³/s at 700 Pa	6074.25	7779.84	50.00	1133.92	nr	**8913.76**
5 m³/s at 350 Pa	9985.50	12789.33	86.00	1950.34	nr	**14739.67**
5 m³/s at 700 Pa	10172.92	13029.38	86.00	1950.34	nr	**14979.72**
8 m³/s at 350 Pa	13866.30	17759.82	105.00	2381.23	nr	**20141.05**
8 m³/s at 700 Pa	14199.15	18186.13	105.00	2381.23	nr	**20567.36**
10 m³/s at 350 Pa	16011.45	20507.31	120.00	2721.41	nr	**23228.71**
10 m³/s at 700 Pa	16356.38	20949.08	120.00	2721.41	nr	**23670.49**
13 m³/s at 350 Pa	20069.18	25704.40	130.00	2948.19	nr	**28652.59**
13 m³/s s at 700 Pa	20698.65	26510.62	130.00	2948.19	nr	**29458.82**
15 m³/s at 350 Pa	22425.90	28722.87	145.00	3288.37	nr	**32011.24**
15 m³/s at 700 Pa	22989.22	29444.37	145.00	3288.37	nr	**32732.74**
18 m³/s at 350 Pa	25092.32	32138.06	160.00	3628.54	nr	**35766.61**
18 m³/s at 700 Pa	25679.85	32890.50	160.00	3628.54	nr	**36519.04**
20 m³/s at 350 Pa	27424.95	35125.60	175.00	3968.72	nr	**39094.32**
20 m³/s at 700 Pa	28378.35	36346.71	175.00	3968.72	nr	**40315.43**
Extra for inlet and discharge attenuators at 900mm long						
2 m³/s at 350 Pa	2325.75	2978.80	8.00	181.43	nr	**3160.22**
5 m³/s at 350 Pa	4592.70	5882.28	10.00	226.78	nr	**6109.07**
10 m³/s at 700 Pa	6457.50	8270.70	13.00	294.82	nr	**8565.52**
15 m³/s at 700 Pa	10857.00	13905.54	16.00	362.85	nr	**14268.39**
20 m³/s at 700 Pa	12566.40	16094.92	20.00	453.57	nr	**16548.49**
Extra for locating units externally						
2 m³/s at 350 Pa	1860.18	2382.50	-	-	nr	**2382.50**
5 m³/s at 350 Pa	2641.44	3383.12	-	-	nr	**3383.12**
10 m³/s at 700 Pa	3704.91	4745.21	-	-	nr	**4745.21**
15 m³/s at 700 Pa	6914.39	8855.88	-	-	nr	**8855.88**
20 m³/s at 700 Pa	10539.48	13498.85	-	-	nr	**13498.85**
Extra for humidifier, self generating type						
2 m³/s at 350 Pa (10kg/hr)	1526.46	1955.07	5.00	113.39	nr	**2068.47**
5 m³/s at 350 Pa (18kg/hr)	1889.02	2419.44	5.00	113.39	nr	**2532.83**
10 m³/s at 700 Pa (30kg/hr)	2149.61	2753.20	6.00	136.07	nr	**2889.27**
15 m³/s at 700 Pa (60kg/hr)	3980.95	5098.76	8.00	181.43	nr	**5280.19**
20 m³/s at 700 Pa (90kg/hr)	5985.33	7665.95	10.00	226.78	nr	**7892.73**

U:VENTILATION/AIR CONDITIONING SYSTEMS

Item	Net Price £	Material £	Labour hours	Labour £	Unit	Total rate £
U30 : LOW VELOCITY AIR CONDITIONING (cont'd)						
Y40 - AIR HANDLING UNITS (cont'd)						
Modular air handling unit (cont'd)						
Extra for mixing box						
2 m³/s at 350 Pa	765.45	980.38	4.00	90.71	nr	1071.09
5 m³/s at 350 Pa	1060.50	1358.28	4.00	90.71	nr	1448.99
10 m³/s at 700 Pa	1473.15	1886.80	5.00	113.39	nr	2000.19
15 m³/s at 700 Pa	1966.13	2518.19	6.00	136.07	nr	2654.26
20 m³/s at 700 Pa	2947.35	3774.94	6.00	136.07	nr	3911.01
Extra for runaround coil, including pump and associated pipework; typical outputs in brackets. (based on minimal distance between the supply and extract units.)						
2 m³/s at 350 Pa (26kW)	2289.69	2932.61	30.00	680.35	nr	3612.96
5 m³/s at 350 Pa (37kW)	3990.22	5110.63	30.00	680.35	nr	5790.99
10 m³/s at 700 Pa (85kW)	6850.02	8773.43	40.00	907.14	nr	9680.57
15 m³/s at 700 Pa (151kW)	9638.23	12344.54	50.00	1133.92	nr	13478.46
20 m³/s at 700 Pa (158kW)	12919.29	16546.90	60.00	1360.70	nr	17907.60
Extra for thermal wheel (typical outputs in brackets)						
2 m³/s at 350 Pa (37kW)	4951.21	6341.46	12.00	272.14	nr	6613.60
5 m³/s at 350 Pa (65kW)	7111.12	9107.85	12.00	272.14	nr	9379.99
10 m³/s at 700 Pa (127kW)	9483.21	12146.00	15.00	340.18	nr	12486.18
15 m³/s at 700 Pa (160kW)	17767.50	22756.44	17.00	385.53	nr	23141.97
20 m³/s at 700 Pa (262kW)	20754.50	26582.16	19.00	430.89	nr	27013.05
Extra for plate heat exchanger, including additional filtration in extract leg (typical outputs in brackets)						
2 m³/s at 350 Pa (25kW)	2761.43	3536.81	12.00	272.14	nr	3808.95
5 m³/s at 350 Pa (51kW)	5398.23	6914.00	12.00	272.14	nr	7186.14
10 m³/s at 700 Pa (98kW)	7920.70	10144.75	15.00	340.18	nr	10484.93
15 m³/s at 700 Pa (160kW)	13678.40	17519.16	17.00	385.53	nr	17904.69
20 m³/s at 700 Pa (190kW)	17664.50	22624.52	19.00	430.89	nr	23055.40
Extra for electric heating in lieu of LTHW						
2 m³/s at 350 Pa	1040.30	1332.41	-	-	nr	1332.41
5 m³/s at 350 Pa	1915.80	2453.74	-	-	nr	2453.74
10 m³/s at 700 Pa	2689.33	3444.47	-	-	nr	3444.47
15 m³/s at 700 Pa	2564.70	3284.84	-	-	nr	3284.84
20 m³/s at 700 Pa	3120.90	3997.22	-	-	nr	3997.22

U:VENTILATION/AIR CONDITIONING SYSTEMS

Varible air valve devices

Item	Net Price £	Material £	Labour hours	Labour £	Unit	Total rate £
U31 : VAV AIR CONDITIONING						
VAV TERMINAL BOXES						
VAV terminal box; integral acoustic silencer; factory installed and pre wired control components (excluding electronic controller); selected at 200Pa at entry to unit; includes fixing in position; electrical work elsewhere						
80 l/s - 110 l/s	316.00	537.32	2.00	56.39	nr	**593.71**
Extra for secondary silencer	77.00	130.93	0.50	14.10	nr	**145.03**
Extra for 2 row LTHW heating coil	30.00	51.01	-	-	nr	**51.01**
150 l/s - 190 l/s	332.50	565.38	2.00	56.39	nr	**621.77**
Extra for secondary silencer	84.50	143.68	0.50	14.10	nr	**157.78**
Extra for 2 row LTHW heating coil	36.00	61.21	-	-	nr	**61.21**
250 l/s - 310 l/s	371.00	630.84	2.00	56.39	nr	**687.23**
Extra for secondary silencer	111.50	189.59	0.50	14.10	nr	**203.69**
Extra for 2 row LTHW heating coil	47.00	79.92	-	-	nr	**79.92**
420 l/s - 520 l/s	401.50	682.70	2.00	56.39	nr	**739.09**
Extra for secondary silencer	127.00	215.95	0.50	14.10	nr	**230.05**
Extra for 2 row LTHW heating coil	49.00	83.32	-	-	nr	**83.32**
650 l/s - 790 l/s	486.50	827.23	2.00	56.39	nr	**883.62**
Extra for secondary silencer	162.50	276.31	0.50	14.10	nr	**290.41**
Extra for 2 row LTHW heating coil	64.00	108.82	-	-	nr	**108.82**
1130 l/s - 1370 l/s	565.00	960.71	2.00	56.39	nr	**1017.10**
Extra for secondary silencer	227.00	385.99	0.50	14.10	nr	**400.08**
Extra for 2 row LTHW heating coil	81.50	138.58	-	-	nr	**138.58**
Extra for electric heater & thyristor controls, 3kw/1ph (per box)	395.90	673.18	-	-	nr	**673.18**
Extra for fitting free issue box controller	-	-	2.13	60.05	nr	**60.05**
Fan assisted VAV terminal box; factory installed and pre wired control components (excluding electronic controller); selected at 40 Pa external static pressure; includes fixing in position, electrical work elsewhere						
100 l/s - 175 l/s	699.00	1188.57	3.00	84.58	nr	**1273.15**
Extra for secondary silencer	83.50	141.98	0.50	14.10	nr	**156.08**
Extra for 1 row LTHW heating coil	42.50	72.27	-	-	nr	**72.27**
170 l/s - 360 l/s	762.50	1296.54	3.00	84.58	nr	**1381.12**
Extra for secondary silencer	105.50	179.39	0.50	14.10	nr	**193.49**
Extra for 1 row LTHW heating coil	48.50	82.47	-	-	nr	**82.47**
300 l/s - 640 l/s	874.50	1486.98	3.00	84.58	nr	**1571.57**
Extra for secondary silencer	161.50	274.61	0.50	14.10	nr	**288.71**
Extra for 1 row LTHW heating coil	54.00	91.82	-	-	nr	**91.82**
620 l/s - 850 l/s	874.50	1486.98	3.00	84.58	nr	**1571.57**
Extra for secondary silencer	161.50	274.61	0.50	14.10	nr	**288.71**
Extra for 1 row LTHW heating coil	54.00	91.82	-	-	nr	**91.82**
Extra for electric heater plus thyristor controls' 3kw/lph (per box)	395.90	673.18	-	-	nr	**673.18**
Extra for fitting free issue controller	-	-	2.13	60.05	nr	**60.05**

U:VENTILATION/AIR CONDITIONING SYSTEMS

Item	Net Price £	Material £	Labour hours	Labour £	Unit	Total rate £
U41 : FAN COIL AIR CONDITIONING						
FAN COIL UNITS						
All selections based on summer return air condition of 23°C at 50% RH, CHW at 6°/12°C, LTHW at 82°/71°C (where applicable), medium speed, external resistance of 30Pa.						
All selections are based on heating and cooling units. For waterside control units there is no significant reduction in cost between 4 pipe heating and cooling and 2 pipe cooling only units (excluding controls). For airside control units, there is a marginal reduction (less than 5%) between 4 pipe heating and cooling units and 2 pipe cooling only units (excluding controls).						
Ceiling void mounted horizontal waterside control fan coil unit; cooling coil ; LTHW heating coil; multi tapped speed transformer; fine wire mesh filter; includes fixing in position; electrical work elsewhere						
Total cooling load, heating load						
2800 W, 1000 W	297.00	380.39	4.00	90.71	nr	**471.11**
4000 W, 1700 W	351.00	449.56	4.00	90.71	nr	**540.27**
4500 W, 1900 W	371.00	475.17	4.00	90.71	nr	**565.89**
6000 W, 2600 W	485.00	621.18	4.00	90.71	nr	**711.90**
Ceiling void mounted horizontal waterside control fan coil unit; cooling coil ; electric heating coil; multi tapped speed transformer; fine wire mesh filter; includes fixing in position; electrical work elsewhere						
Total cooling load, heating load						
2800W, 1500W.	405.00	518.72	4.00	90.71	nr	**609.43**
4000W, 2000W	456.00	584.04	4.00	90.71	nr	**674.75**
4500W, 2000W	481.00	616.06	4.00	90.71	nr	**706.77**
6000W, 3000W	617.00	790.25	4.00	90.71	nr	**880.96**
Ceiling void mounted horizontal airside control fan coil unit; cooling coil ; LHTW heating coil; multi tapped speed transformer; fine wire mesh filter, damper actuator & fixing kit; includes fixing in position; electrical work elsewhere						
Total cooling load, heating load						
2600W, 2200W.	380.00	486.70	4.00	90.71	nr	**577.41**
3600W, 3200W	430.00	550.74	4.00	90.71	nr	**641.45**
4000W, 3600W	461.00	590.44	4.00	90.71	nr	**681.16**
5400W, 5000W	600.00	768.47	4.00	90.71	nr	**859.19**

U:VENTILATION/AIR CONDITIONING SYSTEMS

Item	Net Price £	Material £	Labour hours	Labour £	Unit	Total rate £
Ceiling void mounted horizontal airside control fan coil unit; cooling coil ; electric heating coil; multi tapped speed transformer; fine wire mesh filter, damper actuator & fixing kit; includes fixing in position; electrical work elsewhere						
Total cooling load, heating load						
2600W, 1500W.	468.00	599.41	4.00	90.71	nr	**690.12**
3600W, 2000W	532.00	681.38	4.00	90.71	nr	**772.09**
4000W, 2000W	580.00	742.86	4.00	90.71	nr	**833.57**
5400W, 3000W	700.00	896.55	4.00	90.71	nr	**987.27**
Ceiling void mounted slimline horizontal waterside control fan coil unit, 170mm deep; cooilng coil; LTHW heating coil; multi tapped speed transformer; fine wire mesh filter; includes fixing in position; electrical work elsewhere						*
Total cooling load, heating load						
1100W, 1500W.	320.00	409.85	3.50	79.37	nr	**489.23**
3200W, 3700W	450.00	576.36	4.00	90.71	nr	**667.07**
4600W, 5000W	594.00	760.79	4.00	90.71	nr	**851.50**
Ceiling void mounted slimline horizontal waterside control fan coil unit, 170mm deep; cooilng coil; electric heating coil; multi tapped speed transformer; fine wire mesh filter; includes fixing in position; electrical work elsewhere						
Total cooling load, heating load						
1100W, 1000W.	460.00	589.16	3.50	79.37	nr	**668.54**
3400W, 2000W	570.00	730.05	4.00	90.71	nr	**820.76**
4800W, 3000W	710.00	909.36	4.00	90.71	nr	**1000.07**
Ceiling void mounted slimline horizontal airside control fan coil unit, 170mm deep; cooling coil; LTHW heating coil; multi tapped speed transformer; fine wire mesh filter,damper actuator & fixing kit; includes fixing in position; electrical work elsewhere						
Total cooling load, heating load						
1000W, 1600W.	353.00	452.12	3.50	79.37	nr	**531.49**
3000W, 3300W	550.00	704.43	4.00	90.71	nr	**795.15**
4500W, 4500W	705.00	902.96	4.00	90.71	nr	**993.67**
Ceiling void mounted slimline horizontal airside control fan coil unit, 170mm deep; cooilng coil; electric heating coil; multi tapped speed transformer; fine wire mesh filter,damper actuator & fixing kit; includes fixing in position; electrical work elsewhere						
Total cooling load, heating load						
1000W, 1000W.	520.00	666.01	3.50	79.37	nr	**745.39**
3000W, 2000W	685.00	877.34	4.00	90.71	nr	**968.05**
4500W, 3000W	870.00	1114.29	4.00	90.71	nr	**1205.00**

U:VENTILATION/AIR CONDITIONING SYSTEMS

Item	Net Price £	Material £	Labour hours	Labour £	Unit	Total rate £
U41 : FAN COIL AIR CONDITIONING (cont'd)						
FAN COIL UNITS (cont'd)						
All selections based on summer return (cont'd)						
Low level perimeter waterside control fan coil unit; cooling coil; LTHW heating coil; multi tapped speed transformer; fine wire mesh filter; includes fixing in position; electrical work elsewhere						
Total cooling load, heating load						
1700W, 1400W	250.00	320.20	3.50	79.37	nr	**399.57**
Extra over for standard cabinet	133.00	170.35	1.00	22.68	nr	**193.02**
2200W, 1900W	290.00	371.43	3.50	79.37	nr	**450.80**
Extra over for standard cabinet	162.00	207.49	1.00	22.68	nr	**230.17**
2600W, 2200W	320.00	409.85	3.50	79.37	nr	**489.23**
Extra over for standard cabinet	166.00	212.61	1.00	22.68	nr	**235.29**
3900W, 3200W	420.00	537.93	3.50	79.37	nr	**617.31**
Extra over for standard cabinet	181.00	231.82	1.00	22.68	nr	**254.50**
4600W, 3900W	480.00	614.78	3.50	79.37	nr	**694.15**
Extra over for standard cabinet	238.00	304.83	1.00	22.68	nr	**327.51**
Low level perimeter waterside control fan coil unit; cooling coil; electric heating coil; multi tapped speed transformer; fine wire mesh filter; includes fixing in position; electrical work elsewhere						
Total cooling load, heating load						
1700W, 1500W	325.00	416.26	3.50	79.37	nr	**495.63**
Extra over for standard cabinet	133.00	170.35	1.00	22.68	nr	**193.02**
2200W, 2000W	340.00	435.47	3.50	79.37	nr	**514.84**
Extra over for standard cabinet	162.00	207.49	1.00	22.68	nr	**230.17**
2600W, 2000W	425.00	544.34	3.50	79.37	nr	**623.71**
Extra over for standard cabinet	166.00	212.61	1.00	22.68	nr	**235.29**
3800W, 3000W	505.00	646.80	3.50	79.37	nr	**726.17**
Extra over for standard cabinet	181.00	231.82	1.00	22.68	nr	**254.50**
4600W, 4000W	615.00	787.69	3.50	79.37	nr	**867.06**
Extra over for standard cabinet	238.00	304.83	1.00	22.68	nr	**327.51**
Low level perimeter airside control fan coil unit; cooling coil; LTHW heating coil; multi tapped speed transformer; fine wire mesh filter; damper actuator & fixing kit; includes fixing in position; electrical work elsewhere						
Total cooling load, heating load						
1200W, 1400W	323.00	413.70	3.50	79.37	nr	**493.07**
Extra over for standard cabinet	133.00	170.35	1.00	22.68	nr	**193.02**
1800W, 2000W	361.00	462.37	3.50	79.37	nr	**541.74**
Extra over for standard cabinet	162.00	207.49	1.00	22.68	nr	**230.17**
2200W, 2400W	389.00	498.23	3.50	79.37	nr	**577.60**
Extra over for standard cabinet	166.00	212.61	-	-	nr	**212.61**
3200W, 3600W	505.00	646.80	3.50	79.37	nr	**726.17**
Extra over for standard cabinet	181.00	231.82	1.00	22.68	nr	**254.50**

U:VENTILATION/AIR CONDITIONING SYSTEMS

Item	Net Price £	Material £	Labour hours	Labour £	Unit	Total rate £
Low level perimeter airside control fan coil unit; cooling coil; electric heating coil; multi tapped speed transformer; fine wire mesh filter; damper actuator & fixing kit; includes fixing in position; electrical work elsewhere						
Total cooling load, heating load						
1250W, 1500W	440.00	563.55	3.50	79.37	nr	**642.92**
Extra over for standard cabinet	133.00	170.35	1.00	22.68	nr	**193.02**
1900W, 2000W	475.00	608.38	3.50	79.37	nr	**687.75**
Extra over for standard cabinet	162.00	207.49	1.00	22.68	nr	**230.17**
2300W, 2000W	543.00	695.47	3.50	79.37	nr	**774.84**
Extra over for standard cabinet	166.00	212.61	1.00	22.68	nr	**235.29**
3300W, 3000W	620.00	794.09	3.50	79.37	nr	**873.46**
Extra over for standard cabinet	181.00	231.82	1.00	22.68	nr	**254.50**
Typical DDC control pack for airside control units; controller, return air sensor (damper and damper actuator included in above rates)						
Heating and cooling, per unit	175.00	224.14	2.00	45.36	nr	**269.50**
Cooling only, per unit	175.00	224.14	2.00	45.36	nr	**269.50**
Typical DDC control pack for waterside control units; controller, return air sensor, four port valves and actuators						
Heating and cooling, per unit	240.00	307.39	2.00	45.36	nr	**352.75**
Cooling only, per unit	210.00	268.97	2.00	45.36	nr	**314.32**
Note - Care needs to be taken when using these controls prices, as they can vary significantly, depending on the equipment manufacturer specified and the degree of control required						

U:VENTILATION/AIR CONDITIONING SYSTEMS

Item	Net Price £	Material £	Labour hours	Labour £	Unit	Total rate £
U70 : AIR CURTAINS						
The selection of air curtains requires consideration of the particular conditions involved; climatic conditions, wind influence, construction and position all influence selection; consultation with a specialist manufacturer is therefore advisable.						
Commercial grade air curtains; recessed or exposed units with rigid sheet steel casing; aluminium grilles; high quality motor/centrifugal fan assembly; includes fixing in position; electrical work elsewhere						
Ambient temperature; 240V single phase supply; mounting height 2.40m						
1000 x 590 x 270mm	2192.00	2807.49	12.05	273.23	nr	**3080.73**
1500 x 590 x 270mm	2803.00	3590.05	12.05	273.23	nr	**3863.29**
2000 x 590 x 270mm	3395.00	4348.28	12.05	273.27	nr	**4621.56**
2500 x 590 x 270mm	3765.00	4822.17	13.00	294.82	nr	**5116.99**
Ambient temperature; 240V single phase supply; mounting height 2.80m						
1000 x 590 x 270mm	2541.00	3254.49	16.13	365.78	nr	**3620.27**
1500 x 590 x 270mm	3243.00	4153.60	16.13	365.78	nr	**4519.38**
2000 x 590 x 270mm	3985.00	5103.95	16.13	365.78	nr	**5469.73**
2500 x 590 x 270mm	4670.00	5981.29	17.10	387.80	nr	**6369.09**
Ambient temperature 240V single phase supply; mounting height 3.30m						
1000 x 774 x 370mm	3295.00	4220.20	17.24	391.01	nr	**4611.21**
1500 x 774 x 370mm	4381.00	5611.14	17.24	391.01	nr	**6002.15**
2000 x 774 x 370mm	5216.00	6680.60	17.24	391.01	nr	**7071.61**
2500 x 774 x 370mm	6275.00	8036.96	18.30	415.01	nr	**8451.97**
Ambient temperature; 240V single phase supply; mounting height 4.00m						
1000 x 774 x 370mm	3650.00	4674.88	19.10	433.16	nr	**5108.04**
1500 x 774 x 370mm	4756.00	6091.44	19.10	433.16	nr	**6524.59**
2000 x 774 x 370mm	5867.00	7514.39	19.10	433.16	nr	**7947.55**
2500 x 774 x 370mm	6878.00	8809.27	19.90	451.30	nr	**9260.57**
Water heated; 240V single phase supply; mounting height 2.40m						
1000 x 590 x 270mm; 2.30 - 9.40kW output	2520.00	3227.59	12.05	273.23	nr	**3500.82**
1500 x 590 x 270mm; 3.50 - 14.20kW output	3225.00	4130.55	12.05	273.23	nr	**4403.78**
2000 x 590 x 270mm; 4.70 - 19.00kW output	3903.00	4998.92	12.05	273.23	nr	**5272.16**
2500 x 590 x 270mm; 5.90 - 23.70kW output	4338.00	5556.07	13.00	294.82	nr	**5850.89**
Water heated; 240V single phase supply; mounting height 2.80m						
1000 x 590 x 270mm; 3.30 - 11.90kW output	2912.00	3729.66	16.13	365.78	nr	**4095.44**
1500 x 590 x 270mm; 5.00 - 17.90kW output	3718.00	4761.98	16.13	365.78	nr	**5127.76**
2000 x 590 x 270mm; 6.70 - 23.90kW output	4634.00	5935.18	16.13	365.78	nr	**6300.96**
2500 x 590 x 270mm; 8.30 - 29.80kW output	5358.00	6862.47	17.10	387.80	nr	**7250.27**

U:VENTILATION/AIR CONDITIONING SYSTEMS

Item	Net Price £	Material £	Labour hours	Labour £	Unit	Total rate £
Water heated; 240V single phase supply; mounting height 3.30m						
1000 x 774 x 370mm; 6.10 - 21.80kW output	3804.00	4872.13	17.24	391.01	nr	**5263.13**
1500 x 774 x 370mm; 9.20 - 32.80kW output	5144.00	6588.38	17.24	391.01	nr	**6979.39**
2000 x 774 x 370mm; 12.30 - 43.70kW output	6361.00	8147.11	17.24	391.01	nr	**8538.11**
2500 x 774 x 370mm; 15.30 - 54.60kW output	7531.00	9645.63	18.30	415.01	nr	**10060.64**
Water heated; 240V single phase supply; mounting height 4.00m						
1000 x 774 x 370mm; 7.20 - 24.20kW output	4201.00	5380.60	19.10	433.16	nr	**5813.76**
1500 x 774 x 370mm; 10.90 - 36.30kW output	5676.00	7269.76	19.10	433.16	nr	**7702.92**
2000 x 774 x 370mm; 14.50 - 48.40kW output	7067.00	9051.34	19.10	433.16	nr	**9484.50**
2500 x 774 x 370mm; 18.10 - 60.60kW output	8282.00	10607.50	19.90	451.30	nr	**11058.80**
Electrically heated; 415V three phase supply; mounting height 2.40m						
1000 x 590 x 270mm; 2.30 - 9.40kW output	3036.00	3888.48	12.05	273.23	nr	**4161.71**
1500 x 590 x 270mm; 3.50 - 14.20kW output	3852.00	4933.60	12.05	273.23	nr	**5206.84**
2000 x 590 x 270mm; 4.70 - 19.00kW output	4587.00	5874.98	12.05	272.48	nr	**6147.47**
2500 x 590 x 270mm; 5.90 - 23.70kW output	5219.00	6684.44	13.00	294.01	nr	**6978.45**
Electrically heated; 415V three phase supply; mounting height 2.80m						
1000 x 590 x 270mm; 3.30 - 11.90kW output	3645.00	4668.48	16.13	364.78	nr	**5033.25**
1500 x 590 x 270mm; 5.00 - 17.90kW output	4482.00	5740.50	16.13	365.78	nr	**6106.28**
2000 x 590 x 270mm; 6.70 - 23.90kW output	5658.00	7246.71	16.13	365.78	nr	**7612.49**
2500 x 590 x 270mm; 8.30 - 29.80kW output	6325.00	8101.00	17.10	387.80	nr	**8488.80**
Electrically heated; 415V three phase supply; mounting height 3.30m						
1000 x 774 x 370mm; 6.10 - 21.80kW output	5537.00	7091.73	17.24	389.90	nr	**7481.64**
1500 x 774 x 370mm; 9.20 - 32.80kW output	7420.00	9503.46	17.24	390.98	nr	**9894.44**
2000 x 774 x 370mm; 12.30 - 43.70kW output	8955.00	11469.47	17.24	390.98	nr	**11860.45**
2500 x 774 x 370mm; 15.30 - 54.60kW output	10601.00	13577.65	18.30	415.01	nr	**13992.67**
Electrically heated; 415V three phase supply; mounting height 4.00m						
1000 x 774 x 370mm; 7.20 - 24.20kW output	6111.00	7826.91	19.10	431.97	nr	**8258.88**
1500 x 774 x 370mm; 10.90 - 36.30kW output	8167.00	10460.21	19.10	433.16	nr	**10893.37**
2000 x 774 x 370mm; 14.50 - 48.40kW output	9871.00	12642.68	19.10	433.16	nr	**13075.84**
2500 x 774 x 370mm; 18.10 - 60.60kW output	11700.00	14985.24	19.90	451.30	nr	**15436.54**
Industrial grade air curtains; recessed or exposed units with rigid sheet steel casing; aluminium grilles; high quality motor/centrifugal fan assembly; includes fixing in position; electrical work elsewhere						
Ambient temperature; 415V three phase supply; including wiring between multiple units; horizontally or vertically mounted; opening maximum 6.00m						
1106 x 516 x 689mm; 1.2A supply	1853.00	2373.30	17.24	391.01	nr	**2764.31**
1661 x 516 x 689mm; 1.8A supply	2664.00	3412.02	17.24	391.01	nr	**3803.03**

U:VENTILATION/AIR CONDITIONING SYSTEMS

Item	Net Price £	Material £	Labour hours	Labour £	Unit	Total rate £
U70 : AIR CURTAINS (cont'd)						
Industrial grade air curtains (cont'd)						
Water heated; 415V three phase supply; including wiring between multiple units; horizontally or vertically mounted; opening maximum 6.00m						
1106 x 516 x 689mm; 1.2A supply; 34.80kW output	2084.00	2669.17	17.24	391.01	nr	**3060.17**
1661 x 516 x 689mm; 1.8A supply; 50.70kW output	3010.00	3855.18	17.24	391.01	nr	**4246.19**
Water heated; 415V three phase supply; including wiring between multiple units; vertically mounted in single bank for openings maximum 6.00m wide or opposing twin banks for openings maximum 10.00m wide						
1106 x 689mm; 1.2A supply; 34.80kW output	2084.00	2669.17	17.24	391.01	nr	**3060.17**
1661 x 689mm; 1.8A supply; 50.70kW output	3010.00	3855.18	17.24	391.01	nr	**4246.19**
Remote mounted electronic controller unit; 415V three phase supply; excluding wiring to units						
Five speed, 7A	350.00	448.28	5.00	113.39	nr	**561.67**

Housing and Asthma

Stirling Howieson

Asthma is on the rise in a number of countries, and Howieson here asks what role the built environment has to play and what the construction industry can do to either slow the increase or reverse the trend. Based on the findings of a six-year research project, this book considers all aspects of housing to develop new strategies for dealing with the asthma pandemic in Britain and beyond. With the focus on the design and use pattern of our dwellings, work looks at tackling the problems inherent in existing housing as well as forging guiding principles for the design of new dwellings, together with a financial assessment of the proposals.

Introduction 1. The Aetiology of Asthma 2. The Ecology and Physiology of the House Dust Mite (HDM) 3. The Indoor Environment and the House Dust Mite 4. Housing and Health 5. Historical Changes in Domestic Ventilation Regimes 6. Designing a Double Blind Placebo Controlled Interventionist Trial 7. Key Findings and Discussion 8. Scoping the Confounding Variables 9. Hazardous Indoor Pollutants 10. Air Tightness and Ventilation Rates 11. Developing a New Low Allergen Prototype Dwelling 12. A Fiscal Strategy 13. Conclusions and Recommendations.

February 2005: 234x156 mm: 224 pages
HB: 0-415-33645-7: £75.00
PB: 0-415-33646-5: £29.99

To Order: Tel: +44 (0) 1264 343071 Fax: +44 (0) 1264 343005, or
Post: Taylor and Francis Customer Services, Thomson Publishing Services, Cheriton House, Andover, Hants, SP10 5BE, UK Email: book.orders@tandf.co.uk

For a complete listing of all our titles visit :
www.sponpress.com

Taylor & Francis
Taylor & Francis Group plc

Outdoor Lighting Guide

Institution of Lighting Engineers

An all-inclusive guide to exterior lighting from The Institution of Lighting Engineers, recognised as the pre-eminent professional source in the UK for authoritative guidance on exterior lighting. As concern grows over environmental issues and light pollution, this book fills a need for a straightforward and accessible guide to the use, design and installation of outdoor lighting.

This book provides a comprehensive source of information and advice on all forms of exterior lighting, from floodlighting, buildings and road lighting to elaborate Christmas decorations, and will be useful to practitioners and non-experts alike. Specialists will value the dependable detail on standards and related design, installation and maintenance problems, and any user can find extensive practical guidance on safety issues, the lighting of hazardous areas, and avoiding potential difficulties.

August 2005: 234x156 mm: 320 pages
HB: 0-415-37007-8: £85.00

Electrical Installations

Material Costs/Measured Work Prices

DIRECTIONS

The following explanations are given for each of the column headings and letter codes.

Unit	Prices for each unit are given as singular (i.e. 1 metre, 1 nr) unless stated otherwise
Net price	Industry tender prices, plus nominal allowance for fixings, waste and applicable trade discounts.
Material cost	Net price plus percentage allowance for overheads, profit and preliminaries.
Labour norms	In man-hours for each operation.
Labour cost	Labour constant multiplied by the appropriate all-in man-hour cost based on gang rate. (See also relevant Rates of Wages Section) plus percentage allowance for overheads, profit and preliminaries
Measured work Price (total rate)	Material cost plus Labour cost.

MATERIAL COSTS

The Material Costs given are based at Third Quarter 2005 but exclude any charges in respect of VAT.

MEASURED WORK PRICES

These prices are intended to apply to new work in the London area. The prices are for reasonable quantities of work and the user should make suitable adjustments if the quantities are especially small or especially large. Adjustments may also be required for locality (e.g. outside London – refer to cost indices in approximate estimating section for details of adjustment factors) and for the market conditions (e.g. volume of work secured or being tendered) at the time of use.

ELECTRICAL INSTALLATIONS

The labour rate has been based on average gang rates per man hour effective from 9 January 2006 including allowances for all other emoluments and expenses. To this rate has been added 8% and 6% to cover site and head office overheads and preliminary items together with a further 3% for profit, resulting in an inclusive rate of £24.19 per man hour. The rate has been calculated on a working year of 2025 hours; a detailed build-up of the rate is given at the end of these directions.

In calculating the 'Measured Work Prices' the following assumptions have been made:
- (a) That the work is carried out as a sub-contract under the Standard Form of Building Contract.
- (b) That, unless otherwise stated, the work is being carried out in open areas at a height which would not require more than simple scaffolding.
- (c) That the building in which the work is being carried out is no more than six storey's high.

Where these assumptions are not valid, as for example where work is carried out in ducts and similar confined spaces or in multi-storey structures when additional time is needed to get to and from upper floors, then an appropriate adjustment must be made to the prices. Such adjustment will normally be to the labour element only.

DIRECTIONS

LABOUR RATE - ELECTRICAL

The annual cost of notional eleven man gang

		TECHNICIAN	APPROVED ELECTRICIANS	ELECTRICIANS	LABOURERS	SUB-TOTALS
		1 NR	4 NR	4 NR	2 NR	
Hourly Rate from 9 January 2006		15.11	13.42	12.38	9.92	
Working hours per annum per man		1,710.00	1,710.00	1,710.00	1,710.00	
x Hourly rate x nr of men = £ per annum		25,838.10	91,792.80	84,679.20	33,926.40	236236.50
Overtime Rate		22.67	20.13	18.57	14.88	
Overtime hours per annum per man		315.00	315.00	315.00	315.00	
x Hourly rate x nr of men = £ per annum		7,139.48	25,363.80	23,398.20	9,374.40	65,275.88
Total		32,977.58	117,156.60	108,077.40	43,300.80	301,512.38
Incentive schemes (insert percentage)	5.00%	1,648.88	5,857.83	5,403.87	2,165.04	15,075.62
Daily Travel Time Allowance (15-20 miles each way) effective from 9/01/06		4.19	4.19	4.19	4.19	
Days per annum per man		225.00	225.00	225.00	225.00	
x nr of men = £ per annum		942.75	3,771.00	3,771.00	1885.50	10,370.25
Daily Travel Allowance (15-20 miles each way) effective from 9/01/06		2.89	2.89	2.89	2.89	
Days per annum per man		225.00	225.00	225.00	225.00	
x nr of men = £ per annum		650.25	2,601.00	2,601.00	1,300.50	7,152.75
JIB Pension Scheme @ 2.5%		990.31	3,439.97	3,184.68	1,302.79	8,917.74
JIB combined benefits scheme (nr of weeks per man)		52.00	52.00	52.00	52.00	
Benefit Credit		50.50	45.87	43.04	36.54	
x nr of men = £ per annum		2,626.00	9,540.96	8,952.32	3,800.16	24,919.44
Holiday Top-up Funding		27.25	24.47	22.74	18.46	
x nr of men @ 7.5 hrs per day = £ per annum		1,417.00	5,089.76	4,729.92	1,919.84	13,156.52
National Insurance Contributions:						
Annual gross pay (subject to NI) each		36,219.45	129,386.43	119,853.27	48,651.84	
% of NI Contributions		12.80	12.80	12.80	12.80	
£ Contributions/annum		4,004.12	14,033.59	12,813.35	4,963.50	35,814.56

DIRECTIONS

SUB-TOTAL		**417,127.37**
TRAINING (INCLUDING ANY TRADE REGISTRATIONS) - SAY	**1.00%**	**4,171.27**
SEVERANCE PAY AND SUNDRY COSTS - SAY	**1.50%**	**6,319.48**
EMPLOYER'S LIABILITY AND THIRD PARTY INSURANCE - SAY	**2.00%**	**8,552.36**
ANNUAL COST OF NOTIONAL GANG		**436,170.48**
MEN ACTUALLY WORKING = 10.5 THEREFORE ANNUAL COST PER PRODUCTIVE MAN		**41,540.05**
AVERAGE NR OF HOURS WORKED PER MAN = 2025 THEREFORE ALL IN MAN HOUR		**20.51**
PRELIMINARY ITEMS - SAY	**8.00%**	**1.64**
SITE AND HEAD OFFICE OVERHEADS - SAY	**6.00%**	**1.33**
PROFIT - SAY	**3.00%**	**0.70**
THEREFORE INCLUSIVE MAN HOUR		**24.19**

Notes:

(1)   Hourly wage rates are those effective from 9 January 2006.
(2)   The following assumptions have been made in the above calculations:-
   (a)   Hourly rates are based on London rate and job reporting own transport.
   (b)   The working week of 37.5 hours is made up of 7.5 hours Monday to Friday.
   (c)   Five days in the year are lost through sickness or similar reason.
   (d)   A working year of 2025 hours.
(3)   The incentive scheme addition of 5% is intended to reflect bonus schemes typically in use.
(4)   National insurance contributions are those effective from 6 April 2004.
(5)   Weekly Holiday Credit/Welfare Stamp values are those effective from 5 January 2004.
(6)   Easybuild Stakeholder Pension Contributions effective from 4 August 2003.
(7)   Does not include for major project status.
(8)   Caution should be applied when utilising the labour rate and the 'all-in' rate it applies to, as the size and complexity of the project will reflect in the gang size.

V: ELECTRICAL SUPPLY/POWER/LIGHTING SYSTEMS

Item	Net Price £	Material £	Labour hours	Labour £	Unit	Total rate £
V10 : ELECTRICAL GENERATION PLANT						
STANDBY GENERATORS						
Standby diesel generating sets; supply and installation; fixing to base; all supports and fixings; all necessary connections to equipment						
Three phase, 400 Volt, four wire 50 Hz packaged standby diesel generating set, complete with radio and television suppressors, daily service fuel tank and associated piping, 4 metres of exhaust pipe and primary exhaust silencer, control panel, mains failure relay, starting battery with charger, all internal wiring, interconnections, earthing and labels. Rated for standby duty; including UK delivery, installation and commissioning.						
60 kVA	18286.80	21641.88	100.00	2418.85	nr	**24060.73**
100 kVA	18869.55	22331.55	100.00	2418.85	nr	**24750.40**
150 kVA	20913.90	24750.97	100.00	2418.85	nr	**27169.82**
315 kVA	37706.55	44624.57	120.00	2902.62	nr	**47527.19**
500 kVA	44444.40	52598.61	120.00	2902.62	nr	**55501.23**
750 kVA	75633.60	89510.10	140.00	3386.39	nr	**92896.49**
1000 kVA	100522.80	118965.72	140.00	3386.39	nr	**122352.11**
1500kVA	118305.60	140011.13	170.00	4112.05	nr	**144123.17**
2000kVA	182234.85	215669.48	170.00	4112.05	nr	**219781.52**
2500kVA	249504.15	295280.68	210.00	5079.59	nr	**300360.26**
Extra for residential silencer; peformance 75dBA at 1m; including connection to exhaust pipe						
60 kVA	700.35	828.84	10.00	241.88	nr	**1070.73**
100 kVA	836.85	990.39	10.00	241.88	nr	**1232.27**
150 kVA	959.70	1135.78	10.00	241.88	nr	**1377.66**
315 kVA	1866.90	2209.42	15.00	362.83	nr	**2572.25**
500 kVA	2387.70	2825.77	15.00	362.83	nr	**3188.60**
750 kVA	3557.40	4210.08	20.00	483.77	nr	**4693.85**
1000kVA	4791.15	5670.18	20.00	483.77	nr	**6153.95**
1500kVA	7632.45	9032.78	20.00	483.77	nr	**9516.55**
2000kVA	8266.65	9783.33	30.00	725.65	nr	**10508.99**
2500kVA	9452.10	11186.28	30.00	725.65	nr	**11911.93**
Synchronisation panel for paralleling generators - not generators to mains; including interconnecting cables; commissioning and testing; fixing to backgrounds						
2 x 60 kVA	5833.80	6904.13	80.00	1935.08	nr	**8839.21**
2 x 100 kVA	6271.65	7422.31	80.00	1935.08	nr	**9357.39**
2 x 150 kVA	7889.70	9337.22	80.00	1935.08	nr	**11272.30**
2 x 315 kVA	13412.70	15873.53	80.00	1935.08	nr	**17808.61**
2 x 500 kVA	19364.10	22916.83	80.00	1935.08	nr	**24851.91**
2 x 750kVA	21851.55	25860.65	80.00	1935.08	nr	**27795.73**
2 x 1000kVA	23550.45	27871.25	120.00	2902.62	nr	**30773.87**
2 x 1500kVA	27879.60	32994.67	120.00	2902.62	nr	**35897.29**
2 x 2000kVA	30207.45	35749.61	120.00	2902.62	nr	**38652.23**
2 x 2500kVA	35217.00	41678.26	120.00	2902.62	nr	**44580.88**

V: ELECTRICAL SUPPLY/POWER/LIGHTING SYSTEMS

Item	Net Price £	Material £	Labour hours	Labour £	Unit	Total rate £
V10 : ELECTRICAL GENERATION PLANT (cont'd)						
STANDBY GENERATORS (cont'd)						
Prefabricated drop-over acoustic housing; performance 85dBA at 1m over the range from 60kVA to 315kVA, 75dBA from 500kVA to 2500kVA.						
60kVA	2520.00	2982.34	4.00	96.75	nr	**3079.10**
100kVA	2607.15	3085.48	7.00	169.32	nr	**3254.80**
150kVA	4233.60	5010.34	15.00	362.83	nr	**5373.17**
315kVA	9033.15	10690.46	25.00	604.71	nr	**11295.17**
500kVA	14919.45	17656.72	40.00	967.54	nr	**18624.26**
750kVA	23511.60	27825.27	40.00	967.54	nr	**28792.81**
1000kVA	29745.45	35202.85	40.00	967.54	nr	**36170.39**
1500kVA	59002.65	69827.87	40.00	967.54	nr	**70795.41**
2000kVA	70920.15	83931.87	60.00	1451.31	nr	**85383.18**
2500kVA	98637.00	116733.93	70.00	1693.19	nr	**118427.13**
COMBINED HEAT AND POWER (CHP) UNITS						
Small scale CHP units; generator 415v, engine and heat exchangers, acoustic enclosure; includes placing in position; excludes any allowance for exhaust flues and silencers; excludes any allowance for electrical or heating connections						
Natural gas CHP unit suitable for production LTHW; control panel; all internal wiring						
Electrical output kW; Heat output kW; Fuel input kW						
100 kW; 180 kW; 370 kW	65000.00	76925.55	8.00	193.51	nr	**77119.06**
150 kW; 230 kW; 470 kW	75000.00	88780.25	8.00	193.51	nr	**88953.76**
200 kW; 320 kW; 680 kW	85000.00	100594.95	8.00	193.51	nr	**100788.46**
230 kW; 350 kW; 740 kW	95000.00	112429.65	8.00	193.51	nr	**112623.16**
300 kW; 430 kW; 970 kW	115000.00	136099.05	8.00	193.51	nr	**136292.56**
400 kW; 600 kW; 1300 kW	125000.00	147939.75	9.00	217.70	nr	**148151.45**
500 kW; 660 kW; 1500 kW	155,000.00	183437.85	10.00	241.88	nr	**183679.74**
750 kW; 900 kW; 2200 kW	190,000.00	224859.30	12.00	290.26	nr	**225149.56**
1150 kW; 1430 kW; 3300 kW	255000.00	301784.85	14.00	338.64	nr	**302123.49**
1400 kW; 1500 kW; 4000 kW	340000.00	402379.80	16.00	387.02	nr	**402766.82**
1600 kW; 1600 kW; 4300 kW	350000.00	414214.50	18.00	435.39	nr	**414649.89**
1750 kW; 1800 kW; 5000 kW	380000.00	449718.60	20.00	483.99	nr	**450202.37**
2000 kW; 2200 kW; 5600 kW	410000.00	485222.70	20.00	483.99	nr	**485706.47**

V: ELECTRICAL SUPPLY/POWER/LIGHTING SYSTEMS

Item	Net Price £	Material £	Labour hours	Labour £	Unit	Total rate £
V11 : HV SUPPLY						
Y61 - HV CABLES						
Cable; 6350/11000 volts, 3 core, XLPE; stranded copper conductors; steel wire armoured; LSOH to BS 7835						
Laid in trench/duct including marker tape (cable tiles measured elsewhere)						
95mm²	22.99	27.21	0.23	5.56	m	**32.77**
120mm²	25.30	29.94	0.23	5.56	m	**35.51**
150mm²	30.27	35.82	0.25	6.05	m	**41.87**
185mm²	32.86	38.89	0.25	6.05	m	**44.94**
240mm²	38.27	45.29	0.27	6.53	m	**51.82**
300mm²	43.69	51.71	0.29	7.01	m	**58.72**
Clipped direct to backgrounds including cleats						
95mm²	29.16	34.51	0.47	11.37	m	**45.88**
120mm²	31.47	37.24	0.50	12.09	m	**49.34**
150mm²	36.26	42.91	0.53	12.82	m	**55.73**
185mm²	39.75	47.04	0.55	13.30	m	**60.35**
240mm²	45.95	54.38	0.60	14.51	m	**68.89**
300mm²	52.23	61.81	0.68	16.45	m	**78.26**
Terminations for above cables, including heat-shrink kit and glanding off						
95mm²	359.39	425.33	4.75	114.90	m	**540.22**
120mm²	357.45	423.03	5.30	128.20	m	**551.23**
150mm²	384.48	455.02	6.00	145.13	m	**600.15**
185mm²	385.41	456.12	6.90	166.90	m	**623.02**
240mm²	402.69	476.57	7.43	179.72	m	**656.29**
300mm²	434.25	513.92	8.75	211.65	m	**725.57**
Cable; 6350/11000volts, 3 core, paper insulated; lead sheathed; steel wire armoured; stranded copper conductors; to BS 6480						
Laid in trench/duct including marker tape. (cable tiles measured elsewhere)						
95mm²	25.04	29.63	0.22	5.32	m	**34.96**
120mm²	27.02	31.98	0.22	5.32	m	**37.30**
150mm²	33.06	39.13	0.24	5.81	m	**44.93**
185mm²	34.51	40.84	0.26	6.29	m	**47.13**
240mm²	40.04	47.39	0.34	8.22	m	**55.61**
Clipped direct to backgrounds including cleats						
95mm²	32.01	37.88	0.55	13.30	m	**51.19**
120mm²	33.98	40.21	0.63	15.24	m	**55.45**
150mm²	39.81	47.11	0.66	15.96	m	**63.08**
185mm²	42.16	49.90	0.72	17.42	m	**67.31**
240mm²	48.59	57.50	0.82	19.83	m	**77.34**

V: ELECTRICAL SUPPLY/POWER/LIGHTING SYSTEMS

Item	Net Price £	Material £	Labour hours	Labour £	Unit	Total rate £
V11 : HV SUPPLY (cont'd)						
Y61 - HV CABLES (cont'd)						
Cable 6350/11000volts, 3 core, paper Insulated (cont'd)						
Terminations for above cables, including compound joint and glanding off						
95mm²	401.24	474.86	4.75	114.90	m	**589.75**
120mm²	408.48	483.42	5.30	128.20	m	**611.62**
150mm²	426.68	504.96	6.10	147.55	m	**652.51**
185mm²	427.59	506.04	6.90	166.90	m	**672.94**
240mm²	449.69	532.19	7.43	179.72	m	**711.92**
300mm²	476.88	564.37	8.75	211.65	m	**776.02**
Cable tiles; single width; laid in trench above cables on prepared sand bed. (cost of excavation excluded); reinforced concrete covers; concave/convex ends						
914 x 152 x 63/38mm	8.87	10.49	0.11	2.66	m	**13.15**
914 x 229 x 63/38mm	10.44	12.35	0.11	2.66	m	**15.01**
914 x 305 x 63/38mm	11.62	13.75	0.11	2.66	m	**16.41**

V: ELECTRICAL SUPPLY/POWER/LIGHTING SYSTEMS

Item	Net Price £	Material £	Labour hours	Labour £	Unit	Total rate £
Y70 - HV SWITCHGEAR AND TRANSFORMERS						
H.V. Circuit Breakers; installed on prepared foundations including all supports, fixings and inter panel connections where relevant. Excludes main and multi core cabling and heat shrink cable termination kits.						
Three phase 11kV, 630 Amp, Air or SF6 insulated, with fixed pattern vacuum or SF6 circuit breaker panels; hand charged spring closing operation; prospective fault level up to 25 kA for 3 seconds. Feeders include ammeter with selector switch, 3 pole IDMT, overcurrent and earth fault relays with necessary current relays with necessary current transformers; incomers include 3 phase VT, voltmeter and phase selector switch; Includes IDMT overcurrent and earth fault relays/CTs.						
Single panel with cable chamber	12864.53	15224.79	31.70	766.78	nr	**15991.56**
Three panel with one incomer and two feeders; with cable chambers	38546.00	45618.03	67.83	1640.71	nr	**47258.74**
Five panel with two incoming, two feeders and a bus section; with cable chambers	64232.10	76016.76	99.17	2398.77	nr	**78415.54**
Ring Main Unit (RMU)						
Three phase 11kV, 630 Amp, SF6 insulated RMU with vacuum or SF6 200 Amp circuit breaker tee-off, Includes IDMT overcurrent and earth fault relays/CTs for tee-off and cable boxes.						
3 way Ring Main Unit	8716.47	10315.68	67.83	1640.71	nr	**11956.39**
Extra for,						
Remote actuator to ring switches (per switch)	1316.18	1557.66	-	-	nr	**1557.66**
Remote tripping of circuit breaker	658.09	778.83	-	-	nr	**778.83**
3 - Phase Neon indicators (per circuit)	77.39	91.59	-	-	nr	**91.59**
Pressure gauge with alarm contacts (for SF6 only)	169.79	200.94	-	-	nr	**200.94**
Tripping Batteries						
Battery chargers; switchgear tripping and closing; double wound transformer and earth screen; including fixing to background, commissioning and testing						
Valve regulated lead acid battery						
30 volt; 19 Ah; 3A	1635.18	1935.19	6.50	157.23	nr	**2092.41**
30 volt; 29 Ah; 3A	2619.68	3100.31	8.50	205.60	nr	**3305.91**
110 volt; 19 Ah; 3A	2672.32	3162.61	6.50	157.23	nr	**3319.84**
110 volt; 29 Ah; 3A	2915.82	3450.79	8.50	205.60	nr	**3656.39**
110 volt; 38 Ah; 3A	3115.82	3687.48	10.00	241.88	nr	**3929.36**

V: ELECTRICAL SUPPLY/POWER/LIGHTING SYSTEMS

Item	Net Price £	Material £	Labour hours	Labour £	Unit	Total rate £
V11 : HV SUPPLY (cont'd)						
Y70 - HV SWITCHGEAR AND TRANSFORMERS (cont'd)						
Step down transformers; 11 / 0.415kV, Dyn 11, 50Hz. Complete with lifting lugs, mounting skids, provisions for wheels, undrilled gland plates to air-filled cable boxes, off load tapping facility, including UK delivery						
Oil-filled in free breathing ventilated steel tank						
500kVA	5687.90	6731.46	30.00	725.65	nr	**7457.11**
800kVA	6477.61	7666.06	30.00	725.65	nr	**8391.71**
1000kVA	7341.53	8688.48	30.00	725.65	nr	**9414.14**
1250kVA	8920.94	10557.66	35.00	846.60	nr	**11404.26**
1500kVA	10571.40	12510.93	35.00	846.60	nr	**13357.53**
2000kVA	13730.22	16249.30	40.00	967.54	nr	**17216.84**
MIDEL - filled in gasket-sealed steel tank						
500kVA	7533.70	8915.91	30.00	725.65	nr	**9641.56**
800kVA	8586.64	10162.03	30.00	725.65	nr	**10887.69**
1000kVA	9776.45	11570.14	30.00	725.65	nr	**12295.79**
1250kVA	11816.52	13984.50	35.00	846.60	nr	**14831.09**
1500kVA	14059.27	16638.72	35.00	846.60	nr	**17485.32**
2000kVA	18205.22	21545.33	40.00	967.54	nr	**22512.87**
Extra for,						
Fluid temperature indicator with 2 N/O contacts.	230.00	272.20	2.00	48.38	nr	**320.58**
Winding temperature indicator with 2 N/O contacts.	563.50	666.89	2.00	48.38	nr	**715.26**
Dehydrating Breather	57.50	68.05	2.00	48.38	nr	**116.43**
Plain Rollers	172.50	204.15	2.00	48.38	nr	**252.53**
Pressure relief device with 1 N/O contact	345.00	408.30	2.00	48.38	nr	**456.67**
Step down transformers; 11 / 0.415kV, Dyn 11, 50Hz. Complete with lifting lugs, mounting skids, provisions for wheels, undrilled gland plates to air-filled cable boxes, off load tapping facility, including delivery						
Cast Resin type in ventilated steel encloure, AN - Air Natural including winding temperture indicator with 2 N/O contacts						
500kVA	8060.17	9538.97	40.00	967.54	nr	**10506.51**
800kVA	9376.34	11096.62	40.00	967.54	nr	**12064.16**
1000kVA	11342.70	13423.75	40.00	967.54	nr	**14391.29**
1250kVA	12277.18	14529.67	45.00	1088.48	nr	**15618.16**
1600kVA	13927.65	16482.96	45.00	1088.48	nr	**17571.44**
2000kVA	15770.30	18663.68	50.00	1209.42	nr	**19873.10**

V: ELECTRICAL SUPPLY/POWER/LIGHTING SYSTEMS

Item	Net Price £	Material £	Labour hours	Labour £	Unit	Total rate £
Cast Resign type in ventilated steel enclosure with temperature controlled fans to achieve 40% increase to AN/AF rating. Includes winding temperature indicator with 2 N/O contacts						
500/700kVA	8849.87	10473.56	42.00	1015.92	nr	**11489.47**
800/1120kVA	10297.67	12186.98	42.00	1015.92	nr	**13202.90**
1000/1400kVA	12740.99	15078.58	42.00	1015.92	nr	**16094.50**
12501750kVA	13267.46	15701.64	47.00	1136.86	nr	**16838.50**
1600/2240kVA	14988.99	17739.02	47.00	1136.86	nr	**18875.88**
2000/2800kVA	17094.87	20231.27	52.00	1257.80	nr	**21489.07**

V: ELECTRICAL SUPPLY/POWER/LIGHTING SYSTEMS

Item	Net Price £	Material £	Labour hours	Labour £	Unit	Total rate £
V20 : LV DISTRIBUTION						
Y60 : CONDUIT AND CABLE TRUNKING						
Heavy gauge, screwed drawn steel; surface fixed on saddles to backgrounds,with standard pattern boxes and fittings including all fixings and supports. (forming holes, conduit entry, draw wires etc. and components for earth continuity are included.)						
Black enamelled						
20 mm dia.	1.59	1.88	0.49	11.85	m	**13.73**
25 mm dia.	2.34	2.77	0.56	13.55	m	**16.31**
32 mm dia.	5.41	6.40	0.64	15.48	m	**21.88**
38 mm dia.	6.66	7.88	0.73	17.66	m	**25.54**
50 mm dia.	8.34	9.87	1.04	25.16	m	**35.03**
Galvanised						
20 mm dia.	2.00	2.37	0.49	11.85	m	**14.22**
25 mm dia.	2.66	3.15	0.56	13.55	m	**16.69**
32 mm dia.	5.66	6.70	0.64	15.48	m	**22.18**
38 mm dia.	8.31	9.83	0.73	17.66	m	**27.49**
50 mm dia.	12.50	14.79	1.04	25.16	m	**39.95**
High impact PVC; surface fixed on saddles to backgrounds; with standard pattern boxes and fittings; including all fixings and supports.						
Light gauge						
16 mm dia.	0.58	0.69	0.27	6.53	m	**7.22**
20 mm dia.	0.76	0.90	0.28	6.77	m	**7.67**
25 mm dia.	1.26	1.49	0.33	7.98	m	**9.47**
32 mm dia.	1.70	2.01	0.38	9.19	m	**11.20**
38 mm dia.	2.18	2.58	0.44	10.64	m	**13.22**
50 mm dia.	2.64	3.12	0.48	11.61	m	**14.73**
Heavy gauge						
16 mm dia.	1.02	1.21	0.27	6.53	m	**7.74**
20 mm dia.	1.10	1.30	0.28	6.77	m	**8.07**
25 mm dia.	1.48	1.75	0.33	7.98	m	**9.73**
32 mm dia.	2.42	2.86	0.38	9.19	m	**12.06**
38 mm dia.	3.14	3.72	0.44	10.64	m	**14.36**
50 mm dia.	5.20	6.15	0.48	11.61	m	**17.76**
Flexible conduits; including adaptors and locknuts (for connections to equipment.)						
Metallic, PVC covered conduit; not exceeding 1m long; including zinc plated mild steel adaptors, lock nuts and earth conductor						
16 mm dia.	5.23	6.19	0.46	11.13	nr	**17.32**
20 mm dia.	6.19	7.33	0.42	10.16	nr	**17.48**
25 mm dia.	9.46	11.20	0.43	10.40	nr	**21.60**
32 mm dia.	14.60	17.28	0.51	12.34	nr	**29.61**
38 mm dia.	26.16	30.96	0.56	13.55	nr	**44.51**
50 mm dia.	43.18	51.10	0.82	19.83	nr	**70.94**

V: ELECTRICAL SUPPLY/POWER/LIGHTING SYSTEMS

Item	Net Price £	Material £	Labour hours	Labour £	Unit	Total rate £
PVC conduit; not exceeding 1m long; including nylon adaptors, lock nuts						
16 mm dia.	3.84	4.54	0.46	11.13	nr	**15.67**
20 mm dia.	3.84	4.54	0.48	11.61	nr	**16.16**
25 mm dia.	4.82	5.70	0.50	12.09	nr	**17.80**
32 mm.dia.	6.98	8.26	0.58	14.03	nr	**22.29**
PVC adaptable boxes; fixed to backgrounds; including all supports and fixings (cutting and connecting conduit to boxes is included.)						
Square pattern						
75 x 75 x 53 mm	2.80	3.31	0.69	16.69	nr	**20.00**
100 x 100 x 75 mm	3.62	4.28	0.71	17.17	nr	**21.46**
150 x 150 x 75 mm	6.49	7.68	0.80	19.35	nr	**27.03**
Terminal strips to be fixed in metal or polythene adaptable boxes)						
20 Amp high density polythene						
2 way	0.85	1.01	0.23	5.56	nr	**6.57**
3 way	0.94	1.11	0.23	5.56	nr	**6.68**
4 way	1.01	1.20	0.23	5.56	nr	**6.76**
5 way	1.08	1.28	0.23	5.56	nr	**6.84**
6 way	1.16	1.37	0.25	6.05	nr	**7.42**
7 way	1.24	1.47	0.25	6.05	nr	**7.51**
8 way	1.34	1.59	0.29	7.01	nr	**8.60**
9 way	1.45	1.72	0.30	7.26	nr	**8.97**
10 way	1.66	1.96	0.34	8.22	nr	**10.19**
11 way	1.72	2.04	0.34	8.22	nr	**10.26**
12 way	1.87	2.21	0.34	8.22	nr	**10.44**
13 way	2.08	2.46	0.37	8.95	nr	**11.41**
14 way	2.33	2.76	0.37	8.95	nr	**11.71**
15 way	2.40	2.84	0.39	9.43	nr	**12.27**
16 way	2.46	2.91	0.45	10.88	nr	**13.80**
18 way	2.65	3.14	0.45	10.88	nr	**14.02**

V: ELECTRICAL SUPPLY/POWER/LIGHTING SYSTEMS

Item	Net Price £	Material £	Labour hours	Labour £	Unit	Total rate £
V20 : LV DISTRIBUTION (cont'd)						
Y60 : CONDUIT AND CABLE TRUNKING (cont'd)						
TRUNKING						
Galvanised steel trunking; fixed to backgrounds; jointed with standard connectors (including plates for air gap between trunking and background); earth continuity straps included						
Single compartment						
50 x 50 mm	5.57	6.59	0.39	9.43	m	**16.03**
75 x 50 mm	6.68	7.91	0.44	10.64	m	**18.55**
75 x 75 mm	6.61	7.82	0.47	11.37	m	**19.19**
100 x 50 mm	7.48	8.85	0.50	12.09	m	**20.95**
100 x 75 mm	8.65	10.24	0.57	13.79	m	**24.02**
100 x 100 mm	7.36	8.71	0.62	15.00	m	**23.71**
150 x 50 mm	9.12	10.79	0.78	18.87	m	**29.66**
150 x 100 mm	9.84	11.65	0.78	18.87	m	**30.51**
150 x 150 mm	9.77	11.56	0.86	20.80	m	**32.36**
225 x 75 mm	9.95	11.78	0.88	21.29	m	**33.06**
225 x 150 mm	12.92	15.29	0.84	20.32	m	**35.61**
225 x 225 mm	14.57	17.24	0.99	23.95	m	**41.19**
300 x 75 mm	11.50	13.61	0.96	23.22	m	**36.83**
300 x 100 mm	11.94	14.13	0.99	23.95	m	**38.08**
300 x 150 mm	14.68	17.37	0.99	23.95	m	**41.32**
300 x 225 mm	16.30	19.29	1.09	26.37	m	**45.66**
300 x 300 mm	17.94	21.23	1.16	28.06	m	**49.29**
Double compartment						
50 x 50 mm	6.77	8.01	0.41	9.92	m	**17.93**
75 x 50 mm	7.27	8.60	0.47	11.37	m	**19.97**
75 x 75 mm	7.80	9.23	0.50	12.09	m	**21.33**
100 x 50 mm	7.98	9.44	0.54	13.06	m	**22.51**
100 x 75 mm	8.06	9.54	0.62	15.00	m	**24.54**
100 x 100 mm	9.08	10.75	0.66	15.96	m	**26.71**
150 x 50 mm	9.10	10.77	0.70	16.93	m	**27.70**
150 x 100 mm	10.44	12.36	0.83	20.08	m	**32.43**
150 x 150 mm	12.94	15.31	0.92	22.25	m	**37.57**
Triple compartment						
75 x 50 mm	7.45	8.82	0.54	13.06	m	**21.88**
75 x 75 mm	8.45	10.00	0.58	14.03	m	**24.03**
100 x 50 mm	8.38	9.92	0.61	14.76	m	**24.67**
100 x 75 mm	9.55	11.30	0.70	16.93	m	**28.23**
100 x 100 mm	10.04	11.88	0.74	17.90	m	**29.78**
150 x 50 mm	9.67	11.44	0.79	19.11	m	**30.55**
150 x 100 mm	10.99	13.01	0.78	18.87	m	**31.87**
150 x 150 mm	14.60	17.28	1.01	24.43	m	**41.71**
Four compartment						
100 x 50 mm	9.16	10.84	0.64	15.48	m	**26.32**
100 x 75 mm	10.14	12.00	0.72	17.42	m	**29.42**
100 x 100 mm	11.32	13.40	0.77	18.63	m	**32.02**
150 x 50 mm	10.43	12.34	0.82	19.83	m	**32.18**
150 x 100 mm	11.72	13.87	0.95	22.98	m	**36.85**
150 x 150 mm	16.82	19.91	1.04	25.16	m	**45.06**

V: ELECTRICAL SUPPLY/POWER/LIGHTING SYSTEMS

Item	Net Price £	Material £	Labour hours	Labour £	Unit	Total rate £
Galvanised steel trunking fittings; cutting and jointing trunking to fittings is included						
Additional connector or stop end						
50 x 50 mm	0.41	0.49	0.19	4.60	nr	**5.08**
75 x 50 mm	0.54	0.64	0.20	4.84	nr	**5.48**
75 x 75 mm	0.54	0.64	0.21	5.08	nr	**5.72**
100 x 50 mm	0.58	0.69	0.31	7.50	nr	**8.18**
100 x 75 mm	0.61	0.72	0.27	6.53	nr	**7.25**
100 x 100 mm	0.61	0.72	0.27	6.53	nr	**7.25**
150 x 50 mm	0.67	0.79	0.28	6.77	nr	**7.57**
150 x 100 mm	0.73	0.86	0.30	7.26	nr	**8.12**
150 x 150 mm	0.74	0.88	0.32	7.74	nr	**8.62**
225 x 75 mm	0.78	0.92	0.35	8.47	nr	**9.39**
225 x 150 mm	1.15	1.36	0.37	8.95	nr	**10.31**
225 x 225 mm	1.37	1.62	0.38	9.19	nr	**10.81**
300 x 75 mm	1.15	1.36	0.42	10.16	nr	**11.52**
300 x 100 mm	1.37	1.62	0.42	10.16	nr	**11.78**
300 x 150 mm	1.43	1.69	0.43	10.40	nr	**12.09**
300 x 225 mm	3.00	3.55	0.45	10.88	nr	**14.44**
300 x 300 mm	1.72	2.04	0.48	11.61	nr	**13.65**
Flanged connector or stop end						
50 x 50 mm	0.54	0.64	0.19	4.60	nr	**5.23**
75 x 50 mm	0.83	0.98	0.20	4.84	nr	**5.82**
75 x 75 mm	0.82	0.97	0.21	5.08	nr	**6.05**
100 x 50 mm	0.88	1.04	0.26	6.29	nr	**7.33**
100 x 75 mm	0.90	1.07	0.27	6.53	nr	**7.60**
100 x 100 mm	0.89	1.05	0.27	6.53	nr	**7.58**
150 x 50 mm	0.89	1.05	0.28	6.77	nr	**7.83**
150 x 100 mm	0.94	1.11	0.30	7.26	nr	**8.37**
150 x 150 mm	0.95	1.12	0.32	7.74	nr	**8.86**
225 x 75 mm	0.78	0.92	0.35	8.47	nr	**9.39**
225 x 150 mm	1.15	1.36	0.37	8.95	nr	**10.31**
225 x 225 mm	1.37	1.62	0.38	9.19	nr	**10.81**
300 x 75 mm	1.15	1.36	0.42	10.16	nr	**11.52**
300 x 100 mm	1.37	1.62	0.42	10.16	nr	**11.78**
300 x 150 mm	1.43	1.69	0.43	10.40	nr	**12.09**
300 x 225 mm	1.56	1.85	0.45	10.88	nr	**12.73**
300 x 300 mm	1.72	2.04	0.48	11.61	nr	**13.65**
Bends 90°; single compartment						
50 x 50 mm	2.30	2.72	0.42	10.16	nr	**12.88**
75 x 50 mm	2.89	3.42	0.45	10.88	nr	**14.30**
75 x 75 mm	2.81	3.33	0.48	11.61	nr	**14.94**
100 x 50 mm	3.34	3.95	0.53	12.82	nr	**16.77**
100 x 75 mm	3.16	3.74	0.56	13.55	nr	**17.29**
100 x 100 mm	3.06	3.62	0.58	14.03	nr	**17.65**
150 x 50 mm	3.77	4.46	0.64	15.48	nr	**19.94**
150 x 100 mm	5.12	6.06	0.91	22.01	nr	**28.07**
150 x 150 mm	6.04	7.15	0.89	21.53	nr	**28.68**
225 x 75 mm	6.85	8.11	0.76	18.38	nr	**26.49**
225 x 150 mm	7.49	8.86	0.82	19.83	nr	**28.70**
225 x 225 mm	8.95	10.59	0.83	20.08	nr	**30.67**
300 x 75 mm	9.60	11.36	0.85	20.56	nr	**31.92**
300 x 100 mm	9.82	11.62	0.90	21.77	nr	**33.39**
300 x 150 mm	10.38	12.28	0.96	23.22	nr	**35.51**
300 x 225 mm	11.18	13.23	0.98	23.70	nr	**36.94**
300 x 300 mm	12.00	14.20	1.06	25.64	nr	**39.84**

V: ELECTRICAL SUPPLY/POWER/LIGHTING SYSTEMS

Item	Net Price £	Material £	Labour hours	Labour £	Unit	Total rate £
V20 : LV DISTRIBUTION (cont'd)						
Y60 : CONDUIT AND CABLE TRUNKING (cont'd)						
TRUNKING (cont'd)						
Galvanised steel trunking fittings (cont'd)						
Bends 90°; double compartment						
50 x 50 mm	2.90	3.43	0.42	10.16	nr	**13.59**
75 x 50 mm	3.47	4.11	0.45	10.88	nr	**14.99**
75 x 75 mm	3.96	4.69	0.49	11.85	nr	**16.54**
100 x 50 mm	3.47	4.11	0.53	12.82	nr	**16.93**
100 x 75 mm	4.58	5.42	0.56	13.55	nr	**18.97**
100 x 100 mm	4.64	5.49	0.58	14.03	nr	**19.52**
150 x 50 mm	5.42	6.41	0.65	15.72	nr	**22.14**
150 x 100 mm	5.46	6.46	0.69	16.69	nr	**23.15**
150 x 150 mm	8.63	10.21	0.73	17.66	nr	**27.87**
Bends 90°; triple compartment						
75 x 50 mm	3.65	4.32	0.47	11.37	nr	**15.69**
75 x 75 mm	4.44	5.25	0.51	12.34	nr	**17.59**
100 x 50 mm	3.97	4.70	0.56	13.55	nr	**18.24**
100 x 75 mm	5.32	6.30	0.59	14.27	nr	**20.57**
100 x 100 mm	5.94	7.03	0.61	14.76	nr	**21.78**
150 x 50 mm	6.38	7.55	0.68	16.45	nr	**24.00**
150 x 100 mm	7.08	8.38	0.73	17.66	nr	**26.04**
150 x 150 mm	10.22	12.10	0.77	18.63	nr	**30.72**
Bends 90°; four compartment						
100 x 50 mm	4.62	5.47	0.56	13.55	nr	**19.01**
100 x 75 mm	6.31	7.47	0.59	14.27	nr	**21.74**
100 x 100 mm	10.58	12.52	0.61	14.76	nr	**27.28**
150 x 50 mm	10.96	12.97	0.69	16.69	nr	**29.66**
150 x 100 mm	11.50	13.61	0.73	17.66	nr	**31.27**
150 x 150 mm	12.34	14.60	0.77	18.63	nr	**33.23**
Tees; single compartment						
50 x 50 mm	2.71	3.21	0.56	13.55	nr	**16.75**
75 x 50 mm	3.22	3.81	0.57	13.79	nr	**17.60**
75 x 75 mm	3.12	3.69	0.60	14.51	nr	**18.21**
100 x 50 mm	3.77	4.46	0.65	15.72	nr	**20.18**
100 x 75 mm	3.79	4.49	0.71	17.17	nr	**21.66**
100 x 100 mm	3.67	4.34	0.72	17.42	nr	**21.76**
150 x 50 mm	5.35	6.33	0.82	19.83	nr	**26.17**
150 x 100 mm	5.40	6.39	0.84	20.32	nr	**26.71**
150 x 150 mm	5.23	6.19	0.91	22.01	nr	**28.20**
225 x 75 mm	9.24	10.94	0.94	22.74	nr	**33.67**
225 x 150 mm	12.70	15.03	1.01	24.43	nr	**39.46**
225 x 225 mm	14.66	17.35	1.02	24.67	nr	**42.02**
300 x 75 mm	13.56	16.05	1.07	25.88	nr	**41.93**
300 x 100 mm	14.18	16.78	1.07	25.88	nr	**42.66**
300 x 150 mm	14.77	17.48	1.14	27.57	nr	**45.05**
300 x 225 mm	16.06	19.01	1.19	28.78	nr	**47.79**
300 x 300mm	17.35	20.53	1.26	30.48	nr	**51.01**

V: ELECTRICAL SUPPLY/POWER/LIGHTING SYSTEMS

Item	Net Price £	Material £	Labour hours	Labour £	Unit	Total rate £
Tees; double compartment						
50 x 50 mm	3.92	4.64	0.56	13.55	nr	**18.18**
75 x 50 mm	4.68	5.54	0.57	13.79	nr	**19.33**
75 x 75 mm	5.33	6.31	0.60	14.51	nr	**20.82**
100 x 50 mm	5.80	6.86	0.65	15.72	nr	**22.59**
100 x 75 mm	6.16	7.29	0.71	17.17	nr	**24.46**
100 x 100 mm	6.74	7.98	0.72	17.42	nr	**25.39**
150 x 50 mm	7.01	8.30	0.82	19.83	nr	**28.13**
150 x 100 mm	7.33	8.67	0.85	20.56	nr	**29.23**
150 x 150 mm	8.23	9.74	0.91	22.01	nr	**31.75**
Tees; triple compartment						
75 x 50 mm	5.00	5.92	0.60	14.51	nr	**20.43**
75 x 75 mm	6.08	7.20	0.63	15.24	nr	**22.43**
100 x 50 mm	6.08	7.20	0.68	16.45	nr	**23.64**
100 x 75 mm	7.27	8.60	0.74	17.90	nr	**26.50**
100 x 100 mm	8.11	9.60	0.75	18.14	nr	**27.74**
150 x 50 mm	8.89	10.52	0.87	21.04	nr	**31.57**
150 x 100 mm	9.66	11.43	0.89	21.53	nr	**32.96**
150 x 150 mm	13.92	16.47	0.96	23.22	nr	**39.69**
Tees; four compartment						
100 x 50 mm	8.56	10.13	0.66	15.96	nr	**26.09**
100 x 75 mm	8.46	10.01	0.72	17.42	nr	**27.43**
100 x 100 mm	9.59	11.35	0.72	17.42	nr	**28.77**
150 x 50 mm	6.91	8.18	0.83	20.08	nr	**28.25**
150 x 100 mm	12.92	15.29	0.85	20.56	nr	**35.85**
150 x 150 mm	16.50	19.53	0.92	22.25	nr	**41.78**
Crossovers; single compartment						
50 x 50 mm	3.55	4.20	0.65	15.72	nr	**19.92**
75 x 50 mm	5.09	6.02	0.66	15.96	nr	**21.99**
75 x 75 mm	4.91	5.81	0.69	16.69	nr	**22.50**
100 x 50 mm	6.01	7.11	0.74	17.90	nr	**25.01**
100 x 75 mm	6.04	7.15	0.80	19.35	nr	**26.50**
100 x 100 mm	5.82	6.89	0.81	19.59	nr	**26.48**
150 x 50 mm	6.01	7.11	0.91	22.01	nr	**29.12**
150 x 100 mm	7.27	8.60	0.94	22.74	nr	**31.34**
150 x 150 mm	7.03	8.32	0.99	23.95	nr	**32.27**
225 x 75 mm	12.62	14.94	1.01	24.43	nr	**39.37**
225 x 150 mm	16.86	19.95	1.08	26.12	nr	**46.08**
225 x 225 mm	19.26	22.79	1.09	26.37	nr	**49.16**
300 x 75 mm	18.14	21.47	1.14	27.57	nr	**49.04**
300 x 100 mm	18.67	22.10	1.16	28.06	nr	**50.15**
300 x 150 mm	19.26	22.79	1.19	28.78	nr	**51.58**
300 x 225 mm	20.88	24.71	1.21	29.27	nr	**53.98**
300 x 300mm	22.55	26.69	1.29	31.20	nr	**57.89**
Crossovers; double compartment						
50 x 50 mm	4.49	5.31	0.66	15.96	nr	**21.28**
75 x 50 mm	5.34	6.32	0.66	15.96	nr	**22.28**
75 x 75 mm	6.07	7.18	0.70	16.93	nr	**24.12**
100 x 50 mm	7.07	8.37	0.74	17.90	nr	**26.27**
100 x 75 mm	7.00	8.28	0.80	19.35	nr	**27.64**
100 x 100 mm	7.66	9.07	0.81	19.59	nr	**28.66**
150 x 50 mm	8.30	9.82	0.86	20.80	nr	**30.62**
150 x 100 mm	8.32	9.85	0.94	22.74	nr	**32.58**
150 x 150 mm	13.03	15.42	1.00	24.19	nr	**39.61**

V: ELECTRICAL SUPPLY/POWER/LIGHTING SYSTEMS

Item	Net Price £	Material £	Labour hours	Labour £	Unit	Total rate £
V20 : LV DISTRIBUTION (cont'd)						
Y60 : CONDUIT AND CABLE TRUNKING (cont'd)						
TRUNKING (cont'd)						
Galvanised steel trunking fittings (cont'd)						
Crossovers; triple compartment						
75 x 50 mm	5.34	6.32	0.70	16.93	nr	**23.25**
75 x 75 mm	6.07	7.18	0.73	17.66	nr	**24.84**
100 x 50 mm	6.79	8.04	0.79	19.11	nr	**27.14**
100 x 75 mm	8.10	9.59	0.85	20.56	nr	**30.15**
100 x 100 mm	9.01	10.66	0.85	20.56	nr	**31.22**
150 x 50 mm	8.56	10.13	0.97	23.46	nr	**33.59**
150 x 100 mm	9.42	11.15	0.99	23.95	nr	**35.09**
150 x 150 mm	15.42	18.25	1.06	25.64	nr	**43.89**
Crossovers; four compartment						
100 x 50 mm	8.53	10.10	0.79	19.11	nr	**29.20**
100 x 75 mm	9.58	11.34	0.85	20.56	nr	**31.90**
100 x 100 mm	10.82	12.81	0.86	20.80	nr	**33.61**
150 x 50 mm	10.92	12.92	0.97	23.46	nr	**36.39**
150 x 100 mm	12.00	14.20	1.00	24.19	nr	**38.39**
150 x 150 mm	18.59	22.00	1.06	25.64	nr	**47.64**
Galvanised steel flush floor trunking; fixed to backgrounds; supports and fixings; standard coupling joints; earth continuity straps included.						
Triple compartment						
350 x 60mm	30.54	36.14	1.32	31.93	m	**68.07**
Four compartment						
350 x 60mm	31.80	37.63	1.32	31.93	m	**69.56**
Galvanised steel flush floor trunking; fittings (cutting and jointing trunking to fittings is included.)						
Stop end; triple compartment						
350 x 60mm	3.20	3.79	0.53	12.82	nr	**16.61**
Stop end; four compartment						
350 x 60mm	3.20	3.79	0.53	12.82	nr	**16.61**
Rising bend; standard; triple compartment						
350 x 60mm	26.42	31.27	1.30	31.45	nr	**62.71**
Rising bend; standard; four compartment						
350 x 60mm	27.67	32.75	1.30	31.45	nr	**64.19**
Rising bend; skirting; triple compartment						
350 x 60mm	51.82	61.33	1.33	32.17	nr	**93.50**
Rising bend; skirting; four compartment						
350 x 60mm	58.82	69.61	1.33	32.17	nr	**101.78**

V: ELECTRICAL SUPPLY/POWER/LIGHTING SYSTEMS

Item	Net Price £	Material £	Labour hours	Labour £	Unit	Total rate £
Junction box; triple compartment						
350 x 60mm	34.44	40.76	1.16	28.06	nr	**68.82**
Junction box; four compartment						
350 x 60mm	35.83	42.40	1.16	28.06	nr	**70.46**
Body coupler (pair)						
3 and 4 Compartment	1.78	2.11	0.16	3.87	nr	**5.98**
Service outlet module comprising flat lid with flanged carpet trim; twin 13 A outlet and drilled plate for mounting 2 telephone outlets; one blank plate; triple compartment						
3 Compartment	46.79	55.37	0.47	11.37	nr	**66.74**
Service outlet module comprising flat lid with flanged carpet trim; twin 13 A outlet and drilled plate for mounting 2 telephone outlets; two blank plates; four compartment						
4 Compartment	52.11	61.67	0.47	11.37	nr	**73.04**
Single compartment PVC trunking; grey finish; clip on lid; fixed to backgrounds; including supports and fixings (standard coupling joints)						
50 x 50mm	8.50	10.06	0.27	6.53	m	**16.59**
75 x 50mm	9.23	10.92	0.28	6.77	m	**17.70**
75 x 75mm	10.46	12.38	0.29	7.01	m	**19.39**
100 x 50mm	11.83	14.00	0.34	8.22	m	**22.22**
100 x 75mm	12.98	15.36	0.37	8.95	m	**24.31**
100 x 100mm	13.72	16.24	0.37	8.95	m	**25.19**
150 x 50mm	11.90	14.08	0.41	9.92	m	**24.00**
150 x 75mm	21.20	25.09	0.44	10.64	m	**35.73**
150 x 100mm	25.52	30.20	0.44	10.64	m	**40.85**
150 x 150mm	26.11	30.90	0.48	11.61	m	**42.51**
Single compartment PVC trunking; fittings (cutting and jointing trunking to fittings is included)						
Crossover						
50 x 50mm	13.93	16.49	0.29	7.01	nr	**23.50**
75 x 50mm	15.47	18.31	0.30	7.26	nr	**25.56**
75 x 75mm	16.78	19.86	0.31	7.50	nr	**27.36**
100 x 50mm	22.37	26.47	0.35	8.47	nr	**34.94**
100 x 75mm	28.20	33.37	0.36	8.71	nr	**42.08**
100 x 100mm	24.94	29.52	0.40	9.68	nr	**39.19**
150 x 75mm	31.96	37.82	0.45	10.88	nr	**48.71**
150 x 100mm	38.34	45.37	0.46	11.13	nr	**56.50**
150 x 150mm	59.52	70.44	0.47	11.37	nr	**81.81**

V: ELECTRICAL SUPPLY/POWER/LIGHTING SYSTEMS

Item	Net Price £	Material £	Labour hours	Labour £	Unit	Total rate £
V20 : LV DISTRIBUTION (cont'd)						
Y60 : CONDUIT AND CABLE TRUNKING (cont'd)						
TRUNKING (cont'd)						
Single compartment PVC trunking fittings (cont'd)						
Stop end						
50 x 50mm	0.58	0.69	0.12	2.90	nr	3.59
75 x 50mm	0.83	0.98	0.12	2.90	nr	3.88
75 x 75mm	1.09	1.29	0.13	3.14	nr	4.43
100 x 50mm	1.50	1.78	0.16	3.87	nr	5.65
100 x 75mm	2.32	2.75	0.16	3.87	nr	6.62
100 x 100mm	2.33	2.76	0.18	4.35	nr	7.11
150 x 75mm	6.07	7.18	0.20	4.84	nr	12.02
150 x 100mm	7.51	8.89	0.21	5.08	nr	13.97
150 x 150mm	7.66	9.07	0.22	5.32	nr	14.39
Flanged coupling						
50 x 50mm	3.43	4.06	0.32	7.74	nr	11.80
75 x 50mm	3.91	4.63	0.33	7.98	nr	12.61
75 x 75mm	4.70	5.56	0.34	8.22	nr	13.79
100 x 50mm	5.30	6.27	0.44	10.64	nr	16.92
100 x 75mm	6.00	7.10	0.45	10.88	nr	17.99
100 x 100mm	6.40	7.57	0.46	11.13	nr	18.70
150 x 75mm	6.76	8.00	0.57	13.79	nr	21.79
150 x 100mm	7.12	8.43	0.57	13.79	nr	22.21
150 x 150mm	7.48	8.85	0.59	14.27	nr	23.12
Internal coupling						
50 x 50mm	1.21	1.43	0.07	1.69	nr	3.13
75 x 50mm	1.44	1.70	0.07	1.69	nr	3.40
75 x 75mm	1.43	1.69	0.07	1.69	nr	3.39
100 x 50mm	1.92	2.27	0.08	1.94	nr	4.21
100 x 75mm	2.16	2.56	0.08	1.94	nr	4.49
100 x 100mm	2.38	2.82	0.08	1.94	nr	4.75
External coupling						
50 x 50mm	1.33	1.57	0.09	2.18	nr	3.75
75 x 50mm	1.58	1.87	0.09	2.18	nr	4.05
75 x 75mm	1.57	1.86	0.09	2.18	nr	4.04
100 x 50mm	2.11	2.50	0.10	2.42	nr	4.92
100 x 75mm	2.40	2.84	0.10	2.42	nr	5.26
100 x 100mm	2.62	3.10	0.10	2.42	nr	5.52
150 x 75mm	3.00	3.55	0.11	2.66	nr	6.21
150 x 100mm	3.12	3.69	0.11	2.66	nr	6.35
150 x 150mm	3.24	3.83	0.11	2.66	nr	6.50
Angle; flat cover						
50 x 50mm	4.85	5.74	0.18	4.35	nr	10.09
75 x 50mm	6.48	7.67	0.19	4.60	nr	12.26
75 x 75mm	7.45	8.82	0.20	4.84	nr	13.65
100 x 50mm	11.11	13.15	0.23	5.56	nr	18.71
100 x 75mm	16.92	20.02	0.26	6.29	nr	26.31
100 x 100mm	15.44	18.27	0.26	6.29	nr	24.56
150 x 75mm	21.05	24.91	0.30	7.26	nr	32.17
150 x 100mm	25.03	29.62	0.33	7.98	nr	37.60
150 x 150mm	37.93	44.89	0.34	8.22	nr	53.11

V: ELECTRICAL SUPPLY/POWER/LIGHTING SYSTEMS

Item	Net Price £	Material £	Labour hours	Labour £	Unit	Total rate £
Angle; internal or external cover						
50 x 50mm	5.90	6.98	0.18	4.35	nr	**11.34**
75 x 50mm	8.15	9.65	0.19	4.60	nr	**14.24**
75 x 75mm	10.46	12.38	0.20	4.84	nr	**17.22**
100 x 50mm	11.26	13.33	0.23	5.56	nr	**18.89**
100 x 75mm	18.12	21.44	0.26	6.29	nr	**27.73**
100 x 100mm	18.19	21.53	0.26	6.29	nr	**27.82**
150 x 75mm	22.25	26.33	0.30	7.26	nr	**33.59**
150 x 100mm	26.23	31.04	0.33	7.98	nr	**39.02**
150 x 150mm	36.83	43.59	0.34	8.22	nr	**51.81**
Tee; flat cover						
50 x 50mm	4.06	4.80	0.24	5.81	nr	**10.61**
75 x 50mm	6.20	7.34	0.25	6.05	nr	**13.38**
75 x 75mm	6.38	7.55	0.26	6.29	nr	**13.84**
100 x 50mm	13.76	16.28	0.32	7.74	nr	**24.02**
100 x 75mm	14.63	17.31	0.33	7.98	nr	**25.30**
100 x 100mm	19.09	22.59	0.34	8.22	nr	**30.82**
150 x 75mm	25.24	29.87	0.41	9.92	nr	**39.79**
150 x 100mm	32.39	38.33	0.42	10.16	nr	**48.49**
150 x 150mm	44.05	52.13	0.44	10.64	nr	**62.77**
Tee; internal or external cover						
50 x 50mm	11.51	13.62	0.24	5.81	nr	**19.43**
75 x 50mm	12.66	14.98	0.25	6.05	nr	**21.03**
75 x 75mm	14.06	16.64	0.26	6.29	nr	**22.93**
100 x 50mm	18.06	21.37	0.32	7.74	nr	**29.11**
100 x 75mm	20.64	24.43	0.33	7.98	nr	**32.41**
100 x 100mm	23.16	27.41	0.34	8.22	nr	**35.63**
150 x 75mm	30.00	35.50	0.41	9.92	nr	**45.42**
150 x 100mm	36.14	42.77	0.42	10.16	nr	**52.93**
150 x 150mm	48.26	57.11	0.44	10.64	nr	**67.76**
Division Strip (1.8m long)						
50mm	6.25	7.40	0.07	1.69	nr	**9.09**
75mm	8.00	9.47	0.07	1.69	nr	**11.16**
100mm	10.18	12.05	0.08	1.94	nr	**13.98**
PVC miniature trunking; white finish; fixed to backgrounds; including supports and fixing; standard coupling joints						
Single compartment						
16 x 16mm	1.12	1.33	0.20	4.84	m	**6.16**
25 x 16mm	1.37	1.62	0.21	5.08	m	**6.70**
38 x 16mm	1.72	2.04	0.24	5.81	m	**7.84**
38 x 25mm	2.05	2.43	0.25	6.05	m	**8.47**
Compartmented						
38 x 16mm	2.00	2.37	0.24	5.81	m	**8.17**
38 x 25mm	2.40	2.84	0.25	6.05	m	**8.89**

V: ELECTRICAL SUPPLY/POWER/LIGHTING SYSTEMS

Item	Net Price £	Material £	Labour hours	Labour £	Unit	Total rate £
V20 : LV DISTRIBUTION (cont'd)						
Y60 : CONDUIT AND CABLE TRUNKING (cont'd)						
TRUNKING (cont'd)						
PVC miniature trunking Fittings; single compartment; white finish; cutting and jointing trunking to fittings is included						
Coupling						
16 x 16mm	0.34	0.40	0.10	2.42	nr	**2.82**
25 x 16mm	0.34	0.40	0.10	2.42	nr	**2.82**
38 x 16mm	0.34	0.40	0.12	2.90	nr	**3.31**
38 x 25mm	0.83	0.98	0.14	3.39	nr	**4.37**
Stop end						
16 x 16mm	0.34	0.40	0.12	2.90	nr	**3.31**
25 x 16mm	0.34	0.40	0.12	2.90	nr	**3.31**
38 x 16mm	0.34	0.40	0.15	3.63	nr	**4.03**
38 x 25mm	0.42	0.50	0.17	4.11	nr	**4.61**
Bend; flat, internal or external						
16 x 16mm	0.34	0.40	0.18	4.35	nr	**4.76**
25 x 16mm	0.34	0.40	0.18	4.35	nr	**4.76**
38 x 16mm	0.34	0.40	0.21	5.08	nr	**5.48**
38 x 25mm	0.83	0.98	0.23	5.56	nr	**6.55**
Tee						
16 x 16mm	0.58	0.69	0.23	5.56	nr	**6.25**
25 x 16mm	0.58	0.69	0.19	4.60	nr	**5.28**
38 x 16mm	0.58	0.69	0.26	6.29	nr	**6.98**
38 x 25mm	0.82	0.97	0.29	7.01	nr	**7.99**
PVC bench trunking; white or grey finish; fixed to backgrounds; including supports and fixings; standard coupling joints						
Trunking						
90 x 90mm	18.92	22.39	0.33	7.98	m	**30.37**
PVC bench trunking fittings; white or grey finish; cutting and jointing trunking to fittings is included						
Stop end						
90 x 90mm	4.01	4.75	0.09	2.18	nr	**6.92**
Coupling						
90 x 90mm	2.48	2.94	0.09	2.18	nr	**5.11**
Internal or external bend						
90 x 90mm	13.60	16.10	0.28	6.77	nr	**22.87**
Socket plate						
90 x 90mm - 1 gang	0.76	0.90	0.10	2.42	nr	**3.32**
90 x 90mm - 2 gang	0.92	1.09	0.10	2.42	nr	**3.51**

V: ELECTRICAL SUPPLY/POWER/LIGHTING SYSTEMS

Item	Net Price £	Material £	Labour hours	Labour £	Unit	Total rate £
PVC underfloor trunking; single compartment; fitted in floor screed; standard coupling joints						
Trunking						
60 x 25mm	9.29	10.99	0.22	5.32	m	**16.32**
90 x 35mm	13.36	15.81	0.27	6.53	m	**22.34**
PVC underfloor trunking fittings; single compartment; fitted in floor screed; (cutting and jointing trunking to fittings is included)						
Jointing sleeve						
60 x 25mm	0.62	0.73	0.08	1.94	nr	**2.67**
90 x 35mm	1.03	1.22	0.10	2.42	nr	**3.64**
Duct connector						
90 x 35mm	0.48	0.57	0.17	4.11	nr	**4.68**
Socket reducer						
90 x 35mm	0.86	1.02	0.12	2.90	nr	**3.92**
Vertical access box; 2 compartment						
Shallow	48.00	56.81	0.37	8.95	nr	**65.76**
Duct bend; vertical						
60 x 25mm	9.36	11.08	0.27	6.53	nr	**17.61**
90 x 35mm	10.57	12.51	0.35	8.47	nr	**20.98**
Duct bend; horizontal						
60 x 25mm	11.04	13.07	0.30	7.26	nr	**20.32**
90 x 35mm	11.20	13.25	0.37	8.95	nr	**22.20**
Zinc coated steel underfloor ducting; fixed to backgrounds; standard coupling joints; earth continuity straps; (Including supports and fixing, packing shims where required)						
Double compartment						
150 x 25mm	7.74	9.16	0.57	13.79	m	**22.95**
Triple compartment						
225 x 25mm	13.72	16.24	0.93	22.50	m	**38.73**
Zinc coated steel underfloor ducting fittings; (cutting and jointing to fittings is included.)						
Stop end; double compartment						
150 x 25mm	2.33	2.76	0.31	7.50	nr	**10.26**
Stop end; triple compartment						
225 x 25mm	2.66	3.15	0.37	8.95	nr	**12.10**
Rising bend; double compartment; standard trunking						
150 x 25mm	14.99	17.74	0.71	17.17	nr	**34.91**

V: ELECTRICAL SUPPLY/POWER/LIGHTING SYSTEMS

Item	Net Price £	Material £	Labour hours	Labour £	Unit	Total rate £
V20 : LV DISTRIBUTION (cont'd)						
Y60 : CONDUIT AND CABLE TRUNKING (cont'd)						
TRUNKING (cont'd)						
Zinc coated steel underfloor ducting (cont'd)						
Rising bend; triple compartment; standard trunking						
225 x 25mm	26.94	31.88	0.85	20.56	nr	**52.44**
Rising bend; double compartment; to skirting						
150 x 25	33.37	39.49	0.90	21.77	nr	**61.26**
Rising bend; triple compartment; to skirting						
225 x 25	39.35	46.57	0.95	22.98	nr	**69.55**
Horizontal bend; double compartment						
150 x 25mm	22.79	26.97	0.64	15.48	nr	**42.45**
Horizontal bend; triple compartment						
225 x 25mm	26.29	31.11	0.77	18.63	nr	**49.74**
Junction or service outlet boxes; terminal; double compartment						
150mm	23.57	27.89	0.91	22.01	nr	**49.91**
Junction or service outlet boxes; terminal; triple compartment						
225mm	26.96	31.91	1.11	26.85	nr	**58.76**
Junction or service outlet boxes; through or angle; double compartment						
150mm	31.32	37.07	0.97	23.46	nr	**60.53**
Junction or service outlet boxes; through or angle; triple compartment						
225mm	34.78	41.16	1.17	28.30	nr	**69.46**
Junction or service outlet boxes; tee; double compartment						
150mm	31.32	37.07	1.02	24.67	nr	**61.74**
Junction or service outlet boxes; tee; triple compartment						
225mm	34.78	41.16	1.22	29.51	nr	**70.67**
Junction or service outlet boxes; cross; double compartment						
up to 150mm	31.32	37.07	1.03	24.91	nr	**61.98**
Junction or service outlet boxes; cross;triple compartment						
225mm	34.78	41.16	1.23	29.75	nr	**70.91**

V: ELECTRICAL SUPPLY/POWER/LIGHTING SYSTEMS

Item	Net Price £	Material £	Labour hours	Labour £	Unit	Total rate £
Plates for junction/inspection boxes; double and triple compartment						
Blank plate	7.16	8.47	0.92	22.25	nr	**30.73**
Conduit entry plate	8.97	10.62	0.86	20.80	nr	**31.42**
Trunking entry plate	8.97	10.62	0.86	20.80	nr	**31.42**
Service outlet box comprising flat lid with flanged carpet trim; twin 13A outlet and drilled plate for mounting 2 telephone outlets and terminal blocks; terminal outlet box; double compartment						
150 x 25mm trunking	51.05	60.42	1.68	40.64	nr	**101.05**
Service outlet box comprising flat lid with flanged carpet trim; twin 13A outlet and drilled plate for mounting 2 telephone outlets and terminal blocks; terminal outlet box; triple compartment						
225 x 25mm trunking	56.84	67.27	1.93	46.68	nr	**113.95**
PVC skirting/dado modular trunking; white (cutting and jointing trunking to fittings and backplates for fixing to walls is included)						
Main carrier/backplate						
50 x 170mm	14.83	17.55	2.02	48.86	m	**66.41**
Extension carrier/backplate						
50 x 42mm	9.02	10.67	0.58	14.03	m	**24.70**
Carrier/backplate						
Including cover seal	5.26	6.23	0.53	12.82	m	**19.05**
Chamfered covers for fixing to backplates						
50 x 42mm	3.05	3.61	0.33	7.98	m	**11.59**
Square covers for fixing to backplates						
50 x 42 mm	6.12	7.24	0.33	7.98	m	**15.22**
Plain covers for fixing to backplates						
85 mm	3.05	3.61	0.34	8.22	m	**11.83**
Retainers-clip to backplates to hold cables						
For chamfered covers	0.85	1.01	0.07	1.69	m	**2.70**
For square-recessed covers	0.72	0.85	0.07	1.69	m	**2.55**
For plain covers	2.82	3.34	0.07	1.69	m	**5.03**
Prepackaged corner assemblies						
Internal ; for 170 x 50 Assy	5.92	7.01	0.51	12.34	m	**19.34**
Internal; for 215 x 50 Assy	7.37	8.72	0.53	12.82	m	**21.54**
Internal; for 254 x 50 Assy	8.77	10.38	0.53	12.82	m	**23.20**
External; for 170 x 50 Assy	5.92	7.01	0.56	13.55	m	**20.55**
External ; for 215 x 50 Assy	7.37	8.72	0.58	14.03	m	**22.75**
External ; for 254 x 50 Assy	8.77	10.38	0.58	14.03	m	**24.41**
Clip on end caps						
170 x 50 Assy	3.55	4.20	0.11	2.66	m	**6.86**
215 x 50 Assy	4.20	4.97	0.11	2.66	m	**7.63**
254 x 50 Assy	4.93	5.83	0.11	2.66	m	**8.50**

V: ELECTRICAL SUPPLY/POWER/LIGHTING SYSTEMS

Item	Net Price £	Material £	Labour hours	Labour £	Unit	Total rate £
V20 : LV DISTRIBUTION (cont'd)						
Y60 : CONDUIT AND CABLE TRUNKING (cont'd)						
TRUNKING (cont'd)						
PVC skirting/dado modular trunking (cont'd)						
Outlet box						
1 Gang; in horizontal trunking; clip in	3.16	3.74	0.34	8.22	m	**11.96**
2 Gang; in horizontal trunking; clip in	3.95	4.67	0.34	8.22	m	**12.90**
1 Gang; in vertical trunking; clip in	3.16	3.74	0.34	8.22	m	**11.96**
Sheet steel adaptable boxes; with plain or knockout sides; fixed to backgrounds;including supports and fixings (cutting and connecting conduit to boxes is included.)						
Square pattern - black						
75 x 75 x 37 mm	1.72	2.04	0.69	16.69	nr	**18.73**
75 x 75 x 50 mm	1.73	2.05	0.69	16.69	nr	**18.74**
75 x 75 x 75 mm	1.97	2.33	0.69	16.69	nr	**19.02**
100 x 100 x 50 mm	1.81	2.14	0.71	17.17	nr	**19.32**
150 x 150 x 50 mm	2.76	3.27	0.79	19.11	nr	**22.38**
150 x 150 x 75 mm	3.24	3.83	0.80	19.35	nr	**23.19**
150 x 150 x 100 mm	4.32	5.11	0.80	19.35	nr	**24.46**
225 x 225 x 50 mm	5.52	6.53	0.93	22.50	nr	**29.03**
225 x 225 x 100 mm	7.32	8.66	0.94	22.74	nr	**31.40**
300 x 300 x 100 mm	7.86	9.30	0.99	23.95	nr	**33.25**
Square pattern - galvanised						
75 x 75 x 37 mm	2.47	2.92	0.69	16.69	nr	**19.61**
75 x 75 x 50 mm	2.57	3.04	0.69	16.69	nr	**19.73**
75 x 75 x 75 mm	2.22	2.63	0.70	16.93	nr	**19.56**
100 x 100 x 50 mm	2.72	3.22	0.71	17.17	nr	**20.39**
150 x 150 x 50 mm	3.17	3.75	0.84	20.32	nr	**24.07**
150 x 150 x 75 mm	3.78	4.47	0.80	19.35	nr	**23.82**
150 x 150 x 100 mm	4.55	5.38	0.80	19.35	nr	**24.74**
225 x 225 x 50 mm	5.84	6.91	0.93	22.50	nr	**29.41**
225 x 225 x 100 mm	7.44	8.80	0.94	22.74	nr	**31.54**
300 x 300 x 100 mm	11.95	14.14	0.99	23.95	nr	**38.09**
Rectangular pattern - black						
100 x 75 x 50 mm	2.77	3.28	0.69	16.69	nr	**19.97**
150 x 75 x 50 mm	2.90	3.43	0.70	16.93	nr	**20.36**
150 x 75 x 75 mm	3.14	3.72	0.71	17.17	nr	**20.89**
150 x 100 x 75 mm	7.00	8.28	0.71	17.17	nr	**25.46**
225 x 75 x 50 mm	6.05	7.16	0.78	18.87	nr	**26.03**
225 x 150 x 75 mm	9.66	11.43	0.81	19.59	nr	**31.02**
225 x 150 x 100 mm	18.12	21.44	0.81	19.59	nr	**41.04**
300 x 150 x 50 mm	18.12	21.44	0.93	22.50	nr	**43.94**
300 x 150 x 75 mm	18.12	21.44	0.94	22.74	nr	**44.18**
300 x 150 x 100 mm	18.12	21.44	0.96	23.22	nr	**44.67**

V: ELECTRICAL SUPPLY/POWER/LIGHTING SYSTEMS

Item	Net Price £	Material £	Labour hours	Labour £	Unit	Total rate £
Rectangular pattern - galvanised						
100 x 75 x 50 mm	4.16	4.92	0.69	16.69	nr	**21.61**
150 x 75 x 50 mm	6.17	7.30	0.70	16.93	nr	**24.23**
150 x 75 x 75 mm	7.56	8.95	0.71	17.17	nr	**26.12**
150 x 100 x 75 mm	12.60	14.91	0.71	17.17	nr	**32.09**
225 x 75 x 50 mm	11.36	13.44	0.89	21.53	nr	**34.97**
225 x 150 x 75 mm	15.96	18.89	0.81	19.59	nr	**38.48**
225 x 150 x 100 mm	30.12	35.65	0.81	19.59	nr	**55.24**
300 x 150 x 50 mm	30.12	35.65	0.93	22.50	nr	**58.14**
300 x 150 x 75 mm	30.12	35.65	0.94	22.74	nr	**58.38**
300 x 150 x 100 mm	30.12	35.65	0.96	23.22	nr	**58.87**

V: ELECTRICAL SUPPLY/POWER/LIGHTING SYSTEMS

Item	Net Price £	Material £	Labour hours	Labour £	Unit	Total rate £
V20 : LV DISTRIBUTION (cont'd)						
Y61 - LV CABLES AND WIRING						
ARMOURED CABLE						
Cable; XLPE insulated; PVC sheathed; copper stranded conductors to BS 5467; laid in trench/duct including marker tape. (Cable tiles measured elsewhere.)						
600/1000 Volt grade; single core (aluminium wire armour)						
25 mm²	2.52	2.98	0.15	3.63	m	**6.61**
35 mm²	2.71	3.21	0.15	3.63	m	**6.84**
50 mm²	2.99	3.54	0.17	4.11	m	**7.65**
70 mm²	3.04	3.60	0.18	4.35	m	**7.95**
95 mm²	3.45	4.08	0.20	4.84	m	**8.92**
120 mm²	3.92	4.64	0.22	5.32	m	**9.96**
150 mm²	4.47	5.29	0.24	5.81	m	**11.10**
185 mm²	5.36	6.34	0.26	6.29	m	**12.63**
240 mm²	6.20	7.34	0.30	7.26	m	**14.59**
300 mm²	7.48	8.85	0.31	7.50	m	**16.35**
400 mm²	9.50	11.24	0.38	9.19	m	**20.43**
500 mm²	11.45	13.55	0.44	10.64	m	**24.19**
630 mm²	15.34	18.15	0.52	12.58	m	**30.73**
800 mm²	19.49	23.07	0.62	15.00	m	**38.06**
1000 mm²	22.19	26.26	0.65	15.72	m	**41.98**
600/1000 Volt grade; two core (galvanised steel wire armour)						
1.5 mm²	0.75	0.89	0.06	1.45	m	**2.34**
2.5 mm²	0.86	1.02	0.06	1.45	m	**2.47**
4 mm²	0.94	1.11	0.08	1.94	m	**3.05**
6 mm²	1.06	1.25	0.08	1.94	m	**3.19**
10 mm²	1.44	1.70	0.10	2.42	m	**4.12**
16 mm²	1.73	2.05	0.10	2.42	m	**4.47**
25 mm²	2.25	2.66	0.15	3.63	m	**6.29**
35 mm²	2.99	3.54	0.15	3.63	m	**7.17**
50 mm²	3.46	4.09	0.17	4.11	m	**8.21**
70 mm²	4.16	4.92	0.18	4.35	m	**9.28**
95 mm²	5.11	6.05	0.20	4.84	m	**10.89**
120 mm²	6.81	8.06	0.22	5.32	m	**13.38**
150 mm²	9.13	10.81	0.24	5.81	m	**16.61**
185 mm²	12.01	14.21	0.26	6.29	m	**20.50**
240 mm²	14.71	17.41	0.30	7.26	m	**24.67**
300 mm²	17.50	20.71	0.31	7.50	m	**28.21**
400 mm²	23.24	27.50	0.35	8.47	m	**35.97**
600/1000 Volt grade; three core (galvanised steel wire armour)						
1.5 mm²	0.76	0.90	0.07	1.69	m	**2.59**
2.5 mm²	0.87	1.03	0.07	1.69	m	**2.72**
4 mm²	1.04	1.23	0.09	2.18	m	**3.41**
6 mm²	1.17	1.38	0.10	2.42	m	**3.80**
10 mm²	1.63	1.93	0.11	2.66	m	**4.59**
16 mm²	2.12	2.51	0.11	2.66	m	**5.17**
25 mm²	3.01	3.56	0.16	3.87	m	**7.43**
35 mm²	3.64	4.31	0.16	3.87	m	**8.18**
50 mm²	4.57	5.41	0.19	4.60	m	**10.00**

V: ELECTRICAL SUPPLY/POWER/LIGHTING SYSTEMS

Item	Net Price £	Material £	Labour hours	Labour £	Unit	Total rate £
70 mm²	6.20	7.34	0.21	5.08	m	**12.42**
95 mm²	8.02	9.49	0.23	5.56	m	**15.05**
120 mm²	10.08	11.93	0.24	5.81	m	**17.73**
150 mm²	12.04	14.25	0.27	6.53	m	**20.78**
185 mm²	16.78	19.86	0.30	7.26	m	**27.12**
240 mm²	22.48	26.60	0.33	7.98	m	**34.59**
300 mm²	24.89	29.46	0.35	8.47	m	**37.92**
400 mm²	30.21	35.75	0.41	9.92	m	**45.67**
600/1000 Volt grade; four core (galvanised steel wire armour)						
1.5 mm²	0.84	0.99	0.08	1.94	m	**2.93**
2.5 mm²	0.98	1.16	0.09	2.18	m	**3.34**
4 mm²	1.23	1.46	0.10	2.42	m	**3.87**
6 mm²	1.48	1.75	0.10	2.42	m	**4.17**
10 mm²	1.93	2.28	0.12	2.90	m	**5.19**
16 mm²	2.47	2.92	0.12	2.90	m	**5.83**
25 mm²	3.26	3.86	0.18	4.35	m	**8.21**
35 mm²	4.04	4.78	0.19	4.60	m	**9.38**
50 mm²	5.06	5.99	0.21	5.08	m	**11.07**
70 mm²	7.36	8.71	0.23	5.56	m	**14.27**
95 mm²	9.10	10.77	0.26	6.29	m	**17.06**
120 mm²	11.90	14.08	0.28	6.77	m	**20.86**
150 mm²	14.46	17.11	0.32	7.74	m	**24.85**
185 mm²	20.16	23.86	0.35	8.47	m	**32.32**
240 mm²	24.93	29.50	0.36	8.71	m	**38.21**
300 mm²	31.73	37.55	0.40	9.68	m	**47.23**
400 mm²	38.62	45.71	0.45	10.88	m	**56.59**
600/1000 Volt grade; seven core (galvanised steel wire armour)						
1.5 mm²	1.13	1.34	0.10	2.42	m	**3.76**
2.5 mm²	1.36	1.61	0.10	2.42	m	**4.03**
4 mm²	2.65	3.14	0.11	2.66	m	**5.80**
600/1000 Volt grade; twelve core (galvanised steel wire armour)						
1.5 mm²	1.82	2.15	0.11	2.66	m	**4.81**
2.5 mm²	2.19	2.59	0.11	2.66	m	**5.25**
600/1000 Volt grade; nineteen core (galvanised steel wire armour)						
1.5 mm²	2.36	2.79	0.13	3.14	m	**5.94**
2.5 mm²	3.32	3.93	0.14	3.39	m	**7.32**
600/1000 Volt grade; twenty seven core (galvanised steel wire armour)						
1.5 mm²	3.37	3.99	0.14	3.39	m	**7.37**
2.5 mm²	4.46	5.28	0.16	3.87	m	**9.15**
600/1000 Volt grade; thirty seven core (galvanised steel wire armour)						
1.5 mm²	4.53	5.36	0.15	3.63	m	**8.99**
2.5 mm²	6.42	7.60	0.17	4.11	m	**11.71**

V: ELECTRICAL SUPPLY/POWER/LIGHTING SYSTEMS

Item	Net Price £	Material £	Labour hours	Labour £	Unit	Total rate £
V20 : LV DISTRIBUTION (cont'd)						
Y61 - LV CABLES AND WIRING (cont'd)						
ARMOURED CABLE (cont'd)						
Cable; XLPE insulated; PVC sheathed copper starnded conductors to BS 5467; clipped direct to backgrounds including cleat						
600/1000 Volt grade; single core (aluminium wire armour)						
25 mm²	3.71	4.39	0.35	8.47	m	12.86
35 mm²	3.89	4.60	0.36	8.71	m	13.31
50 mm²	4.18	4.95	0.37	8.95	m	13.90
70 mm²	4.40	5.21	0.39	9.43	m	14.64
95 mm²	4.81	5.69	0.42	10.16	m	15.85
120 mm²	5.51	6.52	0.47	11.37	m	17.89
150 mm²	6.06	7.17	0.51	12.34	m	19.51
185 mm²	7.64	9.04	0.59	14.27	m	23.31
240 mm²	8.57	10.14	0.68	16.45	m	26.59
300 mm²	9.69	11.47	0.74	17.90	m	29.37
400 mm²	11.92	14.11	0.88	21.29	m	35.39
500 mm²	13.89	16.44	0.88	21.29	m	37.72
630 mm²	19.55	23.14	1.05	25.40	m	48.53
800 mm²	24.87	29.43	1.33	32.17	m	61.60
1000 mm²	27.69	32.77	1.40	33.86	m	66.63
600/1000 Volt grade; two core (galvanised steel wire armour)						
1.5 mm²	0.89	1.05	0.20	4.84	m	5.89
2.5 mm²	1.06	1.25	0.20	4.84	m	6.09
4.0 mm²	1.14	1.35	0.21	5.08	m	6.43
6.0 mm²	1.27	1.50	0.22	5.32	m	6.82
10.0 mm²	1.67	1.98	0.24	5.81	m	7.78
16.0 mm²	1.96	2.32	0.25	6.05	m	8.37
25 mm²	3.40	4.02	0.35	8.47	m	12.49
35 mm²	4.41	5.22	0.36	8.71	m	13.93
50 mm²	5.05	5.98	0.37	8.95	m	14.93
70 mm²	6.28	7.43	0.39	9.43	m	16.87
95 mm²	7.49	8.86	0.42	10.16	m	19.02
120 mm²	8.50	10.06	0.47	11.37	m	21.43
150 mm²	10.85	12.84	0.51	12.34	m	25.18
185 mm²	12.23	14.47	0.59	14.27	m	28.75
240 mm²	16.27	19.26	0.68	16.45	m	35.70
300 mm²	18.69	22.12	0.74	17.90	m	40.02
400 mm²	24.14	28.57	0.88	21.29	m	49.85
600/1000 Volt grade; three core (galvanised steel wire armour)						
1.5 mm²	0.90	1.07	0.20	4.84	m	5.90
2.5 mm²	1.07	1.27	0.21	5.08	m	6.35
4.0 mm²	1.24	1.47	0.22	5.32	m	6.79
6.0 mm²	1.38	1.63	0.22	5.32	m	6.95
10.0 mm²	1.86	2.20	0.25	6.05	m	8.25
16.0 mm²	2.36	2.79	0.26	6.29	m	9.08
25 mm²	3.85	4.56	0.37	8.95	m	13.51
35 mm²	3.85	4.56	0.39	9.43	m	13.99
50 mm²	5.99	7.09	0.40	9.68	m	16.76

V: ELECTRICAL SUPPLY/POWER/LIGHTING SYSTEMS

Item	Net Price £	Material £	Labour hours	Labour £	Unit	Total rate £
70 mm²	8.23	9.74	0.42	10.16	m	**19.90**
95 mm²	10.10	11.95	0.45	10.88	m	**22.84**
120 mm²	10.10	11.95	0.52	12.58	m	**24.53**
150 mm²	14.65	17.34	0.55	13.30	m	**30.64**
185 mm²	19.11	22.62	0.63	15.24	m	**37.85**
240 mm²	23.64	27.98	0.71	17.17	m	**45.15**
300 mm²	26.95	31.89	0.78	18.87	m	**50.76**
400 mm²	32.19	38.10	0.87	21.04	m	**59.14**
600/1000 Volt grade; four core (galvanised steel wire armour)						
1.5 mm²	1.04	1.23	0.21	5.08	m	**6.31**
2.5 mm²	1.17	1.38	0.22	5.32	m	**6.71**
4.0 mm²	1.44	1.70	0.22	5.32	m	**7.03**
6.0 mm²	1.71	2.02	0.23	5.56	m	**7.59**
10.0 mm²	2.16	2.56	0.26	6.29	m	**8.85**
16.0 mm²	2.73	3.23	0.26	6.29	m	**9.52**
25 mm²	4.40	5.21	0.39	9.43	m	**14.64**
35 mm²	5.90	6.98	0.40	9.68	m	**16.66**
50 mm²	7.45	8.82	0.41	9.92	m	**18.73**
70 mm²	9.61	11.37	0.45	10.88	m	**22.26**
95 mm²	11.69	13.83	0.50	12.09	m	**25.93**
120 mm²	14.86	17.59	0.54	13.06	m	**30.65**
150 mm²	18.16	21.49	0.60	14.51	m	**36.00**
185 mm²	23.02	27.24	0.67	16.21	m	**43.45**
240 mm²	28.31	33.50	0.75	18.14	m	**51.65**
300 mm²	33.76	39.95	0.83	20.08	m	**60.03**
400 mm²	41.81	49.48	0.91	22.01	m	**71.49**
600/1000 Volt grade; seven core (galvanised steel wire armour)						
1.5 mm²	1.36	1.61	0.20	4.84	m	**6.45**
2.5 mm²	1.59	1.88	0.20	4.84	m	**6.72**
4.0 mm²	2.88	3.41	0.23	5.56	m	**8.97**
600/1000 Volt grade; twelve core (galvanised steel wire armour)						
1.5 mm²	2.05	5.49	0.23	5.56	m	**11.05**
2.5 mm²	2.42	2.86	0.24	5.81	m	**8.67**
600/1000 Volt grade; nineteen core (galvanised steel wire armour)						
1.5 mm²	2.59	3.07	0.26	6.29	m	**9.35**
2.5 mm²	3.55	4.20	0.28	6.77	m	**10.97**
600/1000 Volt grade; twenty seven core (galvanised steel wire armour)						
1.5 mm²	3.60	4.26	0.29	7.01	m	**11.28**
2.5 mm²	4.69	5.55	0.30	7.26	m	**12.81**
600/1000 Volt grade; thirty seven core (galvanised steel wire armour)						
1.5 mm²	4.76	5.63	0.32	7.74	m	**13.37**
2.5 mm²	6.65	7.87	0.33	7.98	m	**15.85**

V: ELECTRICAL SUPPLY/POWER/LIGHTING SYSTEMS

Item	Net Price £	Material £	Labour hours	Labour £	Unit	Total rate £
V20 : LV DISTRIBUTION (cont'd)						
Y61 - LV CABLES AND WIRING (cont'd)						
ARMOURED CABLE (cont'd)						
Cable termination; brass weatherproof gland with inner and outer seal, shroud, brass locknut and earth ring (including drilling and cutting mild steel gland plate)						
600/1000 Volt grade; single core (aluminium wire armour)						
25 mm²	8.01	9.49	1.70	41.12	nr	50.61
35 mm²	8.01	9.49	1.79	43.30	nr	52.78
50 mm²	8.01	9.49	2.06	49.83	nr	59.31
70 mm²	8.63	10.21	2.12	51.28	nr	61.49
95 mm²	9.44	11.17	2.39	57.81	nr	68.98
120 mm²	9.56	11.31	2.47	59.75	nr	71.06
150 mm²	9.58	11.34	2.73	66.03	nr	77.38
185 mm²	12.32	14.58	3.05	73.77	nr	88.35
240 mm²	13.42	15.88	3.45	83.45	nr	99.33
300 mm²	18.17	21.51	3.84	92.88	nr	114.39
400 mm²	24.79	29.34	4.21	101.83	nr	131.17
500 mm²	25.71	30.43	5.70	137.87	m	168.30
630 mm²	33.05	39.12	6.20	149.97	m	189.08
800 mm²	47.12	55.77	7.50	181.41	m	237.18
1000 mm²	52.90	62.61	10.00	241.88	m	304.50
600/1000 Volt grade; two core (galvanised steel wire armour)						
1.5 mm²	1.60	1.89	0.58	14.03	nr	15.92
2.5 mm²	1.60	1.89	0.58	14.03	nr	15.92
4 mm²	1.60	1.89	0.58	14.03	nr	15.92
6 mm²	2.02	2.39	0.67	16.21	nr	18.60
10 mm²	2.02	2.39	1.00	24.19	nr	26.58
16 mm²	3.04	3.60	1.11	26.85	nr	30.45
25 mm²	3.04	3.60	1.70	41.12	nr	44.72
35 mm²	4.14	4.90	1.79	43.30	nr	48.20
50 mm²	4.14	4.90	2.06	49.83	nr	54.73
70 mm²	4.14	4.90	2.12	51.28	nr	56.18
95 mm²	4.14	4.90	2.39	57.81	nr	62.71
120 mm²	8.64	10.23	2.47	59.75	nr	69.97
150 mm²	8.64	10.23	2.73	66.03	nr	76.26
185 mm²	19.18	22.70	3.05	73.77	nr	96.47
240 mm²	19.34	22.89	3.45	83.45	nr	106.34
300 mm²	19.34	22.89	3.84	92.88	nr	115.77
400 mm²	32.16	38.06	4.21	101.83	nr	139.89
600/1000 Volt grade; three core (galvanised steel wire armour)						
1.5 mm²	1.60	1.89	0.62	15.00	nr	16.89
2.5 mm²	1.60	1.89	0.62	15.00	nr	16.89
4 mm²	1.60	1.89	0.62	15.00	nr	16.89
6 mm²	2.02	2.39	0.71	17.17	nr	19.56
10 mm²	2.02	2.39	1.06	25.64	nr	28.03
16 mm²	3.04	3.60	1.19	28.78	nr	32.38
25 mm²	3.04	3.60	1.81	43.78	nr	47.38
35 mm²	4.14	4.90	1.99	48.14	nr	53.03

V: ELECTRICAL SUPPLY/POWER/LIGHTING SYSTEMS

Item	Net Price £	Material £	Labour hours	Labour £	Unit	Total rate £
50 mm²	4.14	4.90	2.23	53.94	nr	**58.84**
70 mm²	8.64	10.23	2.40	58.05	nr	**68.28**
95 mm²	8.64	10.23	2.63	63.62	nr	**73.84**
120 mm²	19.18	22.70	2.83	68.45	nr	**91.15**
150 mm²	19.18	22.70	3.22	77.89	nr	**100.59**
185 mm²	19.34	22.89	3.44	83.21	nr	**106.10**
240 mm²	32.16	38.06	3.83	92.64	nr	**130.70**
300 mm²	32.16	38.06	4.28	103.53	nr	**141.59**
400 mm²	49.66	58.77	5.00	120.94	nr	**179.71**
600/1000 Volt grade; four core (galvanised steel wire armour)						
1.5 mm²	1.60	1.89	0.67	16.21	nr	**18.10**
2.5 mm²	1.60	1.89	0.67	16.21	nr	**18.10**
4 mm²	2.02	2.39	0.71	17.17	nr	**19.56**
6 mm²	2.02	2.39	0.76	18.38	nr	**20.77**
10 mm²	3.04	3.60	1.14	27.57	nr	**31.17**
16 mm²	3.04	3.60	1.29	31.20	nr	**34.80**
25 mm²	4.14	4.90	1.99	48.14	nr	**53.03**
35 mm²	4.14	4.90	2.16	52.25	nr	**57.15**
50 mm²	8.64	10.23	2.49	60.23	nr	**70.45**
70 mm²	8.64	10.23	2.65	64.10	nr	**74.32**
95 mm²	19.18	22.70	2.98	72.08	nr	**94.78**
120 mm²	19.34	22.89	3.15	76.19	nr	**99.08**
150 mm²	19.34	22.89	3.50	84.66	nr	**107.55**
185 mm²	32.16	38.06	3.72	89.98	nr	**128.04**
240 mm²	49.66	58.77	4.33	104.74	nr	**163.51**
300 mm²	49.66	58.77	4.86	117.56	nr	**176.33**
400 mm²	49.66	58.77	5.46	132.07	nr	**190.84**
600/1000 Volt grade; seven core (galvanised steel wire armour)						
1.5 mm²	1.60	1.89	0.81	19.59	nr	**21.49**
2.5 mm²	1.60	1.89	0.85	20.56	nr	**22.45**
4 mm²	1.60	1.89	0.93	22.50	nr	**24.39**
600/1000 Volt grade; twelve core (galvanised steel wire armour)						
1.5 mm²	2.02	2.39	1.14	27.57	nr	**29.97**
2.5 mm²	3.04	3.60	1.13	27.33	nr	**30.93**
600/1000 Volt grade; nineteen core (galvanised steel wire armour)						
1.5 mm²	3.04	3.60	1.54	37.25	nr	**40.85**
2.5 mm²	3.04	3.60	1.54	37.25	nr	**40.85**
600/1000 Volt grade; twenty seven core (galvanised steel wire armour)						
1.5 mm²	3.04	3.60	1.94	46.93	nr	**50.52**
2.5 mm²	4.14	4.90	2.31	55.88	nr	**60.77**
600/1000 Volt grade; thirty seven core (galvanised steel wire armour)						
1.5 mm²	4.14	4.90	2.53	61.20	nr	**66.10**
2.5 mm²	4.14	4.90	2.87	69.42	nr	**74.32**

V: ELECTRICAL SUPPLY/POWER/LIGHTING SYSTEMS

Item	Net Price £	Material £	Labour hours	Labour £	Unit	Total rate £
V20 : LV DISTRIBUTION (cont'd)						
Y61 - LV CABLES AND WIRING (cont'd)						
ARMOURED CABLE (cont'd)						
Cable; XLPE insulated; LSOH sheathed (LSF) ; copper stranded conductors to BS 6724; laid in trench/duct including marker tape (cable tiles measured elsewhere.)						
600/1000 Volt grade; single core (aluminium wire armour)						
50 mm²	3.10	3.67	0.17	4.11	m	7.78
70 mm²	3.21	3.80	0.18	4.35	m	8.15
95 mm²	3.59	4.25	0.20	4.84	m	9.09
120 mm²	4.11	4.86	0.22	5.32	m	10.19
150 mm²	4.60	5.44	0.24	5.81	m	11.25
185 mm²	5.58	6.60	0.26	6.29	m	12.89
240 mm²	6.47	7.66	0.30	7.26	m	14.91
300 mm²	7.78	9.21	0.31	7.50	m	16.71
400 mm²	10.08	11.93	0.35	8.47	m	20.40
500 mm²	11.90	14.08	0.44	10.64	m	24.73
630 mm²	15.52	18.37	0.52	12.58	m	30.95
800 mm²	20.35	24.08	0.62	15.00	m	39.08
1000 mm²	25.97	30.73	0.65	15.72	m	46.46
600/1000 Volt grade; two core (galvanised steel wire armour)						
1.5 mm²	0.86	1.02	0.06	1.45	m	2.47
2.5 mm²	1.01	1.20	0.06	1.45	m	2.65
4 mm²	1.13	1.34	0.08	1.94	m	3.27
6 mm²	1.32	1.56	0.08	1.94	m	3.50
10 mm²	1.61	1.91	0.10	2.42	m	4.32
16 mm²	2.07	2.45	0.10	2.42	m	4.87
25 mm²	2.62	3.10	0.15	3.63	m	6.73
35 mm²	3.51	4.15	0.15	3.63	m	7.78
50 mm²	4.09	4.84	0.17	4.11	m	8.95
70 mm²	4.84	5.73	0.18	4.35	m	10.08
95 mm²	6.20	7.34	0.20	4.84	m	12.18
120 mm²	8.26	9.78	0.22	5.32	m	15.10
150 mm²	9.78	11.57	0.24	5.81	m	17.38
185 mm²	11.28	13.35	0.26	6.29	m	19.64
240 mm²	13.66	16.17	0.30	7.26	m	23.42
300 mm²	17.04	20.17	0.31	7.50	m	27.66
400 mm²	21.60	25.56	0.35	8.47	m	34.03
600/1000 Volt grade; three core (galvanised steel wire armour)						
1.5 mm²	0.92	1.09	0.07	1.69	m	2.78
2.5 mm²	1.04	1.23	0.07	1.69	m	2.92
4 mm²	1.15	1.36	0.09	2.18	m	3.54
6 mm²	1.38	1.63	0.10	2.42	m	4.05
10 mm²	1.96	2.32	0.11	2.66	m	4.98
16 mm²	2.53	2.99	0.11	2.66	m	5.65
25 mm²	3.00	3.55	0.16	3.87	m	7.42
35 mm²	4.67	5.53	0.16	3.87	m	9.40
50 mm²	5.34	6.32	0.19	4.60	m	10.92

V: ELECTRICAL SUPPLY/POWER/LIGHTING SYSTEMS

Item	Net Price £	Material £	Labour hours	Labour £	Unit	Total rate £
70 mm²	7.09	8.39	0.21	5.08	m	13.47
95 mm²	8.79	10.40	0.23	5.56	m	15.97
120 mm²	11.04	13.07	0.24	5.81	m	18.87
150 mm²	13.43	15.89	0.27	6.53	m	22.42
185 mm²	16.50	19.53	0.30	7.26	m	26.78
240 mm²	20.15	23.85	0.33	7.98	m	31.83
300 mm²	23.08	27.31	0.35	8.47	m	35.78
400 mm²	30.19	35.73	0.41	9.92	m	45.65
600/1000 Volt grade; four core (galvanised steel wire armour)						
1.5 mm²	1.02	1.21	0.08	1.94	m	3.14
2.5 mm²	1.15	1.36	0.09	2.18	m	3.54
4 mm²	1.37	1.62	0.10	2.42	m	4.04
6 mm²	1.73	2.05	0.10	2.42	m	4.47
10 mm²	2.28	2.70	0.12	2.90	m	5.60
16 mm²	2.76	3.27	0.12	2.90	m	6.17
25 mm²	3.07	3.63	0.18	4.35	m	7.99
35 mm²	4.37	5.17	0.19	4.60	m	9.77
50 mm²	5.41	6.40	0.21	5.08	m	11.48
70 mm²	8.05	9.53	0.23	5.56	m	15.09
95 mm²	9.67	11.44	0.26	6.29	m	17.73
120 mm²	12.64	14.96	0.28	6.77	m	21.73
150 mm²	15.47	18.31	0.32	7.74	m	26.05
185 mm²	18.69	22.12	0.35	8.47	m	30.59
240 mm²	22.90	27.10	0.36	8.71	m	35.81
300 mm²	28.37	33.58	0.40	9.68	m	43.25
400 mm²	37.16	43.98	0.45	10.88	m	54.86
600/1000 Volt grade; seven core (galvanised steel wire armour)						
1.5 mm²	1.36	1.61	0.10	2.42	m	4.03
2.5 mm²	1.63	1.93	0.10	2.42	m	4.35
4 mm²	2.76	3.27	0.11	2.66	m	5.93
600/1000 Volt grade; twelve core (galvanised steel wire armour)						
1.5 mm²	2.07	2.45	0.11	2.66	m	5.11
2.5 mm²	2.53	2.99	0.11	2.66	m	5.65
600/1000 Volt grade; nineteen core (galvanised steel wire armour)						
1.5 mm²	2.76	3.27	0.13	3.14	m	6.41
2.5 mm²	3.45	4.08	0.14	3.39	m	7.47
600/1000 Volt grade; twenty seven core (galvanised steel wire armour)						
1.5 mm²	3.74	4.43	0.14	3.39	m	7.81
2.5 mm²	4.95	5.86	0.16	3.87	m	9.73
600/1000 Volt grade; thirty seven core (galvanised steel wire armour)						
1.5 mm²	4.83	5.72	0.15	3.63	m	9.34
2.5 mm²	6.56	7.76	0.17	4.11	m	11.88

V: ELECTRICAL SUPPLY/POWER/LIGHTING SYSTEMS

Item	Net Price £	Material £	Labour hours	Labour £	Unit	Total rate £
V20 : LV DISTRIBUTION (cont'd)						
Y61 - LV CABLES AND WIRING (cont'd)						
ARMOURED CABLE (cont'd)						
Cable; XLPE insulated; LSOH sheathed (LSF) copper stranded conductors to BS 6724; clipped direct to backgrounds including cleat.						
600/1000 Volt grade; single core (aluminium wire armour)						
50 mm²	4.29	5.08	0.37	8.95	m	**14.03**
70 mm²	4.57	5.41	0.39	9.43	m	**14.84**
95 mm²	4.95	5.86	0.42	10.16	m	**16.02**
120 mm²	5.70	6.75	0.47	11.37	m	**18.11**
150 mm²	6.19	7.33	0.51	12.34	m	**19.66**
185 mm²	7.86	9.30	0.59	14.27	m	**23.57**
240 mm²	8.84	10.46	0.68	16.45	m	**26.91**
300 mm²	9.99	11.82	0.74	17.90	m	**29.72**
400 mm²	12.50	14.79	0.81	19.59	m	**34.39**
500 mm²	14.34	16.97	0.88	21.29	m	**38.26**
630 mm²	19.73	23.35	1.05	25.40	m	**48.75**
800 mm²	24.98	29.56	1.33	32.17	m	**61.73**
1000 mm²	31.46	37.23	1.40	33.86	m	**71.10**
600/1000 Volt grade; two core (galvanised steel wire armour)						
1.5 mm²	1.00	1.18	0.20	4.84	m	**6.02**
2.5 mm²	1.21	1.43	0.20	4.84	m	**6.27**
4.0 mm²	1.32	1.56	0.21	5.08	m	**6.64**
6.0 mm²	1.53	1.81	0.22	5.32	m	**7.13**
10.0 mm²	1.84	2.18	0.24	5.81	m	**7.98**
16.0 mm²	2.30	2.72	0.25	6.05	m	**8.77**
25 mm²	3.78	4.47	0.35	8.47	m	**12.94**
35 mm²	4.93	5.83	0.36	8.71	m	**14.54**
50 mm²	5.68	6.72	0.37	8.95	m	**15.67**
70 mm²	6.96	8.24	0.39	9.43	m	**17.67**
95 mm²	8.58	10.15	0.42	10.16	m	**20.31**
120 mm²	9.95	11.78	0.47	11.37	m	**23.14**
150 mm²	11.51	13.62	0.51	12.34	m	**25.96**
185 mm²	13.20	15.62	0.59	14.27	m	**29.89**
240 mm²	17.19	20.34	0.68	16.45	m	**36.79**
300 mm²	20.56	24.33	0.74	17.90	m	**42.23**
400 mm²	25.59	30.29	0.81	19.59	m	**49.88**
600/1000 Volt grade; three core (galvanised steel wire armour)						
1.5 mm²	1.06	1.25	0.20	4.84	m	**6.09**
2.5 mm²	1.23	1.46	0.21	5.08	m	**6.54**
4.0 mm²	1.36	1.61	0.22	5.32	m	**6.93**
6.0 mm²	1.59	1.88	0.22	5.32	m	**7.20**
10.0 mm²	2.19	2.59	0.25	6.05	m	**8.64**
16.0 mm²	2.77	3.28	0.26	6.29	m	**9.57**
25 mm²	4.29	5.08	0.37	8.95	m	**14.03**
35 mm²	6.09	7.21	0.39	9.43	m	**16.64**
50 mm²	6.76	8.00	0.40	9.68	m	**17.68**
70 mm²	9.13	10.81	0.42	10.16	m	**20.96**

V: ELECTRICAL SUPPLY/POWER/LIGHTING SYSTEMS

Item	Net Price £	Material £	Labour hours	Labour £	Unit	Total rate £
95 mm²	10.87	12.86	0.45	10.88	m	**23.75**
120 mm²	13.98	16.54	0.52	12.58	m	**29.12**
150 mm²	16.04	18.98	0.55	13.30	m	**32.29**
185 mm²	21.06	24.92	0.63	15.24	m	**40.16**
240 mm²	24.31	28.77	0.71	17.17	m	**45.94**
300 mm²	28.45	33.67	0.78	18.87	m	**52.54**
400 mm²	36.20	42.84	0.87	21.04	m	**63.89**
600/1000 Volt grade; four core (galvanised steel wire armour)						
1.5 mm²	1.22	1.44	0.21	5.08	m	**6.52**
2.5 mm²	1.35	1.60	0.22	5.32	m	**6.92**
4.0 mm²	1.58	1.87	0.22	5.32	m	**7.19**
6.0 mm²	1.96	2.32	0.23	5.56	m	**7.88**
10.0 mm²	2.51	2.97	0.26	6.29	m	**9.26**
16.0 mm²	3.01	3.56	0.26	6.29	m	**9.85**
25 mm²	4.71	5.57	0.39	9.43	m	**15.01**
35 mm²	6.23	7.37	0.40	9.68	m	**17.05**
50 mm²	7.80	9.23	0.41	9.92	m	**19.15**
70 mm²	10.30	12.19	0.45	10.88	m	**23.07**
95 mm²	12.26	14.51	0.50	12.09	m	**26.60**
120 mm²	15.60	18.46	0.54	13.06	m	**31.52**
150 mm²	19.17	22.69	0.60	14.51	m	**37.20**
185 mm²	24.25	28.70	0.67	16.21	m	**44.91**
240 mm²	29.60	35.03	0.75	18.14	m	**53.17**
300 mm²	34.62	40.97	0.83	20.08	m	**61.05**
400 mm²	43.76	51.79	0.91	22.01	m	**73.80**
600/1000 Volt grade; seven core (galvanised steel wire armour)						
1.5 mm²	1.59	1.88	0.20	4.84	m	**6.72**
2.5 mm²	1.86	2.20	0.20	4.84	m	**7.04**
4.0 mm²	2.99	3.54	0.23	5.56	m	**9.10**
600/1000 Volt grade; twelve core (galvanised steel wire armour)						
1.5 mm²	2.30	2.72	0.23	5.56	m	**8.29**
2.5 mm²	2.76	3.27	0.24	5.81	m	**9.07**
600/1000 Volt grade; nineteen core (galvanised steel wire armour)						
1.5 mm²	2.99	3.54	0.26	6.29	m	**9.83**
2.5 mm²	3.68	4.36	0.28	6.77	m	**11.13**
600/1000 Volt grade; twenty seven core (galvanised steel wire armour)						
1.5 mm²	3.97	4.70	0.29	7.01	m	**11.71**
2.5 mm²	5.18	6.13	0.30	7.26	m	**13.39**
600/1000 Volt grade; thirty seven core (galvanised steel wire armour)						
1.5 mm²	5.06	5.99	0.32	7.74	m	**13.73**
2.5 mm²	6.79	8.04	0.33	7.98	m	**16.02**

V: ELECTRICAL SUPPLY/POWER/LIGHTING SYSTEMS

Item	Net Price £	Material £	Labour hours	Labour £	Unit	Total rate £
V20 : LV DISTRIBUTION (cont'd)						
Y61 - LV CABLES AND WIRING (cont'd)						
ARMOURED CABLE (cont'd)						
Cable termination; brass weatherproof gland with inner and outer seal, shroud, brass locknut and earth ring (including drilling and cutting mild steel gland plate)						
600/1000 Volt grade; single core (aluminium wire armour)						
25 mm²	8.09	9.57	1.70	41.12	nr	**50.69**
35 mm²	8.09	9.57	1.79	43.30	nr	**52.87**
50 mm²	8.40	9.94	2.06	49.83	nr	**59.76**
70 mm²	9.16	10.84	2.12	51.28	nr	**62.12**
95 mm²	9.27	10.98	2.39	57.81	nr	**68.79**
120 mm²	9.31	11.02	2.47	59.75	nr	**70.76**
150 mm²	11.96	14.15	2.73	66.03	nr	**80.19**
185 mm²	12.43	14.71	3.05	73.77	nr	**88.49**
240 mm²	17.65	20.88	3.45	83.45	nr	**104.33**
300 mm²	18.89	22.35	3.84	92.88	nr	**115.23**
400 mm²	23.46	27.77	4.21	101.83	nr	**129.60**
500 mm²	24.95	29.53	5.70	137.87	m	**167.40**
630 mm²	32.07	37.96	6.20	149.97	m	**187.93**
800 mm²	45.73	54.12	7.50	181.41	m	**235.53**
1000 mm²	51.35	60.77	10.00	241.88	m	**302.65**
600/1000 Volt grade; two core (galvanised steel wire armour)						
1.5 mm²	1.47	1.74	0.58	14.03	nr	**15.77**
2.5 mm²	1.47	1.74	0.58	14.03	nr	**15.77**
4 mm²	1.47	1.74	0.58	14.03	nr	**15.77**
6 mm²	1.47	1.74	0.67	16.21	nr	**17.95**
10 mm²	1.74	2.06	1.00	24.19	nr	**26.25**
16 mm²	2.32	2.75	1.11	26.85	nr	**29.60**
25 mm²	4.13	4.89	1.70	41.12	nr	**46.01**
35 mm²	6.79	8.04	1.79	43.30	nr	**51.33**
50 mm²	6.93	8.20	2.06	49.83	nr	**58.02**
70 mm²	7.47	8.84	2.12	51.28	nr	**60.11**
95 mm²	7.74	9.15	2.39	57.81	nr	**66.97**
120 mm²	10.15	12.01	2.47	59.75	nr	**71.76**
150 mm²	11.56	13.68	2.73	66.03	nr	**79.71**
185 mm²	17.62	20.85	3.05	73.77	nr	**94.62**
240 mm²	21.40	25.32	3.45	83.45	nr	**108.77**
300 mm²	22.90	27.10	3.84	92.88	nr	**119.98**
400 mm²	24.91	29.48	4.21	101.83	nr	**131.31**
600/1000 Volt grade; three core (galvanised steel wire armour)						
1.5 mm²	1.47	1.74	0.62	15.00	nr	**16.74**
2.5 mm²	1.47	1.74	0.62	15.00	nr	**16.74**
4 mm²	1.47	1.74	0.62	15.00	nr	**16.74**
6 mm²	1.74	2.06	0.71	17.17	nr	**19.23**
10 mm²	1.74	2.06	1.06	25.64	nr	**27.70**
16 mm²	2.32	2.75	1.19	28.78	nr	**31.53**
25 mm²	5.04	5.96	1.81	43.78	nr	**49.74**
35 mm²	7.80	9.23	1.99	48.14	nr	**57.37**

V: ELECTRICAL SUPPLY/POWER/LIGHTING SYSTEMS

Item	Net Price £	Material £	Labour hours	Labour £	Unit	Total rate £
50 mm²	8.13	9.62	2.23	53.94	nr	**63.56**
70 mm²	8.82	10.43	2.40	58.05	nr	**68.49**
95 mm²	11.56	13.68	2.63	63.62	nr	**77.29**
120 mm²	11.68	13.82	2.83	68.45	nr	**82.27**
150 mm²	18.77	22.21	3.22	77.89	nr	**100.09**
185 mm²	20.39	24.13	3.44	83.21	nr	**107.33**
240 mm²	33.09	39.16	3.83	92.64	nr	**131.80**
300 mm²	35.32	41.80	4.28	103.53	nr	**145.32**
400 mm²	47.43	56.13	5.00	120.94	nr	**177.07**
600/1000 Volt grade; four core (galvanised steel wire armour)						
1.5 mm²	1.47	1.74	0.67	16.21	nr	**17.95**
2.5 mm²	1.47	1.74	0.67	16.21	nr	**17.95**
4 mm²	1.74	2.06	0.71	17.17	nr	**19.23**
6 mm²	1.74	2.06	0.76	18.38	nr	**20.44**
10 mm²	2.32	2.75	1.14	27.57	nr	**30.32**
16 mm²	2.32	2.75	1.29	31.20	nr	**33.95**
25 mm²	8.38	9.92	1.99	48.14	nr	**58.06**
35 mm²	8.82	10.43	2.16	52.25	nr	**62.68**
50 mm²	9.25	10.94	2.49	60.23	nr	**71.17**
70 mm²	12.50	14.79	2.65	64.10	nr	**78.89**
95 mm²	18.02	21.33	2.98	72.08	nr	**93.41**
120 mm²	18.18	21.52	3.15	76.19	nr	**97.71**
150 mm²	20.93	24.76	3.50	84.66	nr	**109.42**
185 mm²	30.19	35.72	3.72	89.98	nr	**125.71**
240 mm²	37.75	44.67	4.33	104.74	nr	**149.41**
300 mm²	49.79	58.92	4.86	117.56	nr	**176.48**
400 mm²	53.84	63.72	5.46	132.07	nr	**195.78**
600/1000 Volt grade; seven core (galvanised steel wire armour)						
1.5 mm²	1.47	1.74	0.81	19.59	nr	**21.33**
2.5 mm²	1.74	2.06	0.85	20.56	nr	**22.62**
4 mm²	2.32	2.75	0.93	22.50	nr	**25.24**
600/1000 Volt grade; twelve core (galvanised steel wire armour)						
1.5 mm²	1.74	2.06	1.14	27.57	nr	**29.64**
2.5 mm²	2.32	2.75	1.13	27.33	nr	**30.08**
600/1000 Volt grade; nineteen core (galvanised steel wire armour)						
1.5 mm²	2.32	2.75	1.54	37.25	nr	**40.00**
2.5 mm²	2.32	2.75	1.54	37.25	nr	**40.00**
600/1000 Volt grade; twenty seven core (galvanised steel wire armour)						
1.5 mm²	4.77	5.64	1.94	46.93	nr	**52.57**
2.5 mm²	4.77	5.64	2.31	55.88	nr	**61.52**
600/1000 Volt grade; thirty seven core (galvanised steel wire armour)						
1.5 mm²	4.77	5.64	2.53	61.20	nr	**66.84**
2.5 mm²	4.77	5.64	2.87	69.42	nr	**75.06**

V: ELECTRICAL SUPPLY/POWER/LIGHTING SYSTEMS

Item	Net Price £	Material £	Labour hours	Labour £	Unit	Total rate £
V20 : LV DISTRIBUTION (cont'd)						
Y61 - LV CABLES AND WIRING (cont'd)						
UN-ARMOURED CABLE						
Cable: XLPE insulated; PVC sheathed 90c copper to CMA Code 6181e; for internal wiring; clipped to backgrounds; (Supports and fixings included)						
300/500 Volt grade; single core						
6.0 mm²	0.45	0.53	0.09	2.18	m	**2.71**
10 mm²	0.64	0.76	0.10	2.42	m	**3.18**
16 mm²	0.88	1.04	0.12	2.90	m	**3.94**
Cable; LSF insulated to CMA Code 6491B; non-sheathed copper; laid/drawn in trunking/conduit						
450/750 Volt grade; single core						
1.5 mm²	0.12	0.14	0.03	0.73	m	**0.86**
2.5 mm²	0.18	0.21	0.03	0.73	m	**0.93**
4.0 mm²	0.27	0.32	0.03	0.73	m	**1.05**
6.0 mm²	0.39	0.46	0.04	0.97	m	**1.43**
10.0 mm²	0.68	0.81	0.04	0.97	m	**1.78**
16.0 mm²	0.96	1.13	0.05	1.21	m	**2.34**
25.0 mm²	1.56	1.85	0.06	1.45	m	**3.30**
35.0 mm²	2.03	2.40	0.06	1.45	m	**3.85**
50.0 mm²	2.67	3.16	0.07	1.69	m	**4.85**
70.0 mm²	3.61	4.27	0.08	1.94	m	**6.20**
95.0 mm²	4.52	5.35	0.08	1.94	m	**7.29**
120.0 mm²	6.30	7.45	0.10	2.42	m	**9.87**
150.0 mm²	8.19	9.69	0.13	3.14	m	**12.84**
Cable; twin & earth to CMA code 6242Y; clipped to backgrounds						
300/500 Volt grade; PVC/PVC						
1.5 mm² 2C+E	0.75	0.89	0.01	0.24	m	**1.13**
1.5 mm² 3C+E	2.17	2.57	0.02	0.48	m	**3.06**
2.5mm² 2C+E	0.97	1.15	0.02	0.48	m	**1.64**
4.0mm² 2C+E	2.99	3.54	0.02	0.48	m	**4.02**
6.0mm² 2C+E	3.52	4.17	0.02	0.48	m	**4.66**
10.0mm² 2C+E	5.70	6.75	0.03	0.73	m	**7.47**
16.0mm² 2C+E	9.01	10.67	0.03	0.73	m	**11.39**
300/500 Volt grade; LSF/LSF						
1.5 mm² 2C+E	1.00	1.18	0.01	0.24	m	**1.43**
1.5 mm² 3C+E	3.92	4.65	0.02	0.48	m	**5.13**
2.5mm² 2C+E	1.40	1.66	0.02	0.48	m	**2.14**
4.0mm² 2C+E	3.85	4.56	0.02	0.48	m	**5.04**
6.0mm² 2C+E	6.65	7.87	0.02	0.48	m	**8.35**
10.0mm² 2C+E	7.65	9.05	0.03	0.73	m	**9.78**
16.0mm² 2C+E	11.24	13.30	0.03	0.73	m	**14.02**

V: ELECTRICAL SUPPLY/POWER/LIGHTING SYSTEMS

Item	Net Price £	Material £	Labour hours	Labour £	Unit	Total rate £
EARTH CABLE						
Cable; LSF insulated to CMA Code 6491B; non-sheathed copper; laid/drawn in trunking/conduit						
450/750 Volt grade; single core						
1.5 mm²	0.12	0.14	0.03	0.73	m	**0.86**
2.5 mm²	0.18	0.21	0.03	0.73	m	**0.93**
4.0 mm²	0.27	0.32	0.03	0.73	m	**1.05**
6.0 mm²	0.39	0.46	0.04	0.97	m	**1.43**
10.0 mm²	0.68	0.81	0.04	0.97	m	**1.78**
16.0 mm²	0.96	1.13	0.05	1.21	m	**2.34**
25.0 mm²	1.56	1.85	0.06	1.45	m	**3.30**
35.0 mm²	2.03	2.40	0.06	1.45	m	**3.85**
50.0 mm²	2.67	3.16	0.07	1.69	m	**4.85**
70.0 mm²	3.63	4.29	0.08	1.94	m	**6.23**
95.0 mm²	4.52	5.35	0.08	1.94	m	**7.29**
120.0 mm²	6.30	7.45	0.10	2.42	m	**9.87**
150.0 mm²	8.19	9.69	0.13	3.14	m	**12.84**
185.0 mm²	9.83	11.63	0.16	3.87	m	**15.50**
240.0 mm²	11.35	13.43	0.20	4.84	m	**18.27**
FLEXIBLE CABLE						
Flexible cord; PVC insulated; PVC sheathed; copper stranded to CMA Code 218*Y (laid loose)						
300 Volt grade; two core						
0.50 mm²	0.13	0.15	0.07	1.69	m	**1.85**
0.75 mm²	0.21	0.25	0.07	1.69	m	**1.94**
300 Volt grade; three core						
0.50 mm²	0.17	0.20	0.07	1.69	m	**1.89**
0.75 mm²	0.28	0.33	0.07	1.69	m	**2.02**
1.0 mm²	0.39	0.46	0.07	1.69	m	**2.15**
1.5 mm²	0.55	0.65	0.07	1.69	m	**2.34**
2.5 mm²	0.75	0.89	0.08	1.94	m	**2.82**
Flexible cord; PVC insulated; PVC sheathed; copper stranded to CMA Code 318Y (laid loose)						
300/500 Volt grade; two core						
0.75 mm²	0.21	0.25	0.07	1.69	m	**1.94**
1.0 mm²	0.26	0.31	0.07	1.69	m	**2.00**
1.5 mm²	0.37	0.44	0.07	1.69	m	**2.13**
2.5 mm²	0.79	0.93	0.07	1.69	m	**2.63**
300/500 Volt grade; three core						
0.75 mm²	0.20	0.24	0.07	1.69	m	**1.93**
1.0 mm²	0.24	0.28	0.07	1.69	m	**1.98**
1.5 mm²	0.33	0.39	0.07	1.69	m	**2.08**
2.5 mm²	0.68	0.80	0.08	1.94	m	**2.74**

V: ELECTRICAL SUPPLY/POWER/LIGHTING SYSTEMS

Item	Net Price £	Material £	Labour hours	Labour £	Unit	Total rate £
V20 : LV DISTRIBUTION (cont'd)						
Y61 - LV CABLES AND WIRING (cont'd)						
FLEXIBLE CABLE (cont'd)						
Flexible cord; PVC insulated (cont'd)						
300/500 Volt grade; four core						
0.75 mm²	0.55	0.65	0.08	1.94	m	**2.59**
1.0 mm²	0.64	0.76	0.08	1.94	m	**2.69**
1.5 mm²	0.91	1.08	0.08	1.94	m	**3.01**
2.5 mm²	1.40	1.66	0.09	2.18	m	**3.83**
Flexible cord; PVC insulated; PVC sheathed for use in high temperature zones; copper stranded to CMA Code 309Y (laid loose)						
300/500 Volt grade; two core						
0.50 mm²	0.28	0.33	0.07	1.69	m	**2.02**
0.75 mm²	0.33	0.39	0.07	1.69	m	**2.08**
1.0 mm²	0.54	0.64	0.07	1.69	m	**2.33**
1.5 mm²	0.76	0.90	0.07	1.69	m	**2.59**
2.5 mm²	1.14	1.35	0.07	1.69	m	**3.04**
300/500 Volt grade; three core						
0.50 mm²	0.38	0.45	0.07	1.69	m	**2.14**
0.75 mm²	0.40	0.47	0.07	1.69	m	**2.17**
1.0 mm²	0.54	0.64	0.07	1.69	m	**2.33**
1.5 mm²	0.76	0.90	0.07	1.69	m	**2.59**
2.5 mm²	1.14	1.35	0.07	1.69	m	**3.04**
Flexible cord; rubber insulated; rubber sheathed; copper stranded to CMA code 318 (laid loose)						
300/500 Volt grade; two core						
0.50 mm²	0.14	0.17	0.07	1.69	m	**1.86**
0.75 mm²	0.15	0.18	0.07	1.69	m	**1.87**
1.0 mm²	0.17	0.20	0.07	1.69	m	**1.89**
1.5 mm²	0.24	0.28	0.07	1.69	m	**1.98**
2.5 mm²	0.35	0.41	0.07	1.69	m	**2.11**
300/500 Volt grade; three core						
0.50 mm²	0.17	0.20	0.07	1.69	m	**1.89**
0.75 mm²	0.18	0.21	0.07	1.69	m	**1.91**
1.0 mm²	0.21	0.25	0.07	1.69	m	**1.94**
1.5 mm²	0.29	0.34	0.07	1.69	m	**2.04**
2.5 mm²	0.45	0.53	0.07	1.69	m	**2.23**
300/500 Volt grade; four core						
0.50 mm²	0.25	0.30	0.08	1.94	m	**2.23**
0.75 mm²	0.28	0.33	0.08	1.94	m	**2.27**
1.0 mm²	0.32	0.38	0.08	1.94	m	**2.31**
1.5 mm²	0.38	0.45	0.08	1.94	m	**2.38**
2.5 mm²	0.58	0.69	0.08	1.94	m	**2.62**

V: ELECTRICAL SUPPLY/POWER/LIGHTING SYSTEMS

Item	Net Price £	Material £	Labour hours	Labour £	Unit	Total rate £
Flexible cord; rubber insulated; rubber sheathed; for 90C operation; copper stranded to CMA Code 318 (laid loose)						
450/750 Volt grade; two core						
0.50 mm²	0.21	0.25	0.07	1.69	m	**1.94**
0.75 mm²	0.29	0.34	0.07	1.69	m	**2.04**
1.0 mm²	0.32	0.38	0.07	1.69	m	**2.07**
1.5 mm²	0.41	0.49	0.07	1.69	m	**2.18**
2.5 mm²	0.53	0.63	0.07	1.69	m	**2.32**
450/750 Volt grade; three core						
0.50 mm²	0.24	0.28	0.07	1.69	m	**1.98**
0.75 mm²	0.28	0.33	0.07	1.69	m	**2.02**
1.0 mm²	0.33	0.39	0.07	1.69	m	**2.08**
1.5 mm²	0.39	0.46	0.07	1.69	m	**2.15**
2.5 mm²	0.53	0.63	0.07	1.69	m	**2.32**
450/750 Volt grade; four core						
0.75 mm²	0.39	0.46	0.08	1.94	m	**2.40**
1.0 mm²	0.46	0.54	0.08	1.94	m	**2.48**
1.5 mm²	0.58	0.69	0.08	1.94	m	**2.62**
2.5 mm²	0.91	1.08	0.08	1.94	m	**3.01**
Heavy flexible cable; rubber insulated; rubber sheathed; copper stranded to CMA Code 638P (laid loose)						
450/750 Volt grade; two core						
1.0 mm²	0.28	0.33	0.08	1.94	m	**2.27**
1.5 mm²	0.33	0.39	0.08	1.94	m	**2.33**
2.5 mm²	0.45	0.53	0.08	1.94	m	**2.47**
450/750 Volt grade; three core						
1.0 mm²	0.33	0.39	0.08	1.94	m	**2.33**
1.5 mm²	0.39	0.46	0.08	1.94	m	**2.40**
2.5 mm²	0.53	0.63	0.08	1.94	m	**2.56**
450/750 Volt grade; four core						
1.0 mm²	0.45	0.53	0.08	1.94	m	**2.47**
1.5 mm²	0.49	0.58	0.08	1.94	m	**2.52**
2.5 mm²	0.69	0.82	0.08	1.94	m	**2.75**

V: ELECTRICAL SUPPLY/POWER/LIGHTING SYSTEMS

Item	Net Price £	Material £	Labour hours	Labour £	Unit	Total rate £
V20 : LV DISTRIBUTION (cont'd)						
Y61 - LV CABLES AND WIRING (cont'd)						
FIRE RATED CABLE						
Cable, mineral insulated; copper sheathed with copper conductors; fixed with clips to backgrounds. BASEC approval to BS 6207 Part 1 1995; complies with BS 6387 Category CWZ						
Light duty 500 Volt grade; bare						
2L 1.0	1.58	1.87	0.23	5.56	m	7.43
2L 1.5	1.75	2.07	0.23	5.56	m	7.63
2L 2.5	2.04	2.41	0.25	6.05	m	8.46
2L 4.0	2.67	3.16	0.25	6.05	m	9.21
3L 1.0	1.79	2.12	0.24	5.81	m	7.92
3L 1.5	2.06	2.44	0.25	6.05	m	8.48
3L 2.5	2.77	3.28	0.25	6.05	m	9.33
4L 1.0	1.99	2.36	0.25	6.05	m	8.40
4L 1.5	2.28	2.70	0.25	6.05	m	8.75
4L 2.5	3.19	3.78	0.26	6.29	m	10.06
7L 1.5	3.19	3.78	0.28	6.77	m	10.55
7L 2.5	3.97	4.70	0.27	6.53	m	11.23
Light duty 500 Volt grade; LSF sheathed						
2L 1.0	1.70	2.01	0.23	5.56	m	7.58
2L 1.5	1.84	2.18	0.23	5.56	m	7.74
2L 2.5	2.12	2.51	0.25	6.05	m	8.56
2L 4.0	2.78	3.29	0.25	6.05	m	9.34
3L 1.0	1.94	2.30	0.24	5.81	m	8.10
3L 1.5	2.20	2.60	0.25	6.05	m	8.65
3L 2.5	2.89	3.42	0.25	6.05	m	9.47
4L 1.0	2.14	2.53	0.25	6.05	m	8.58
4L 1.5	2.45	2.90	0.25	6.05	m	8.95
4L 2.5	3.29	3.89	0.26	6.29	m	10.18
7L 1.5	3.51	4.15	0.28	6.77	m	10.93
7L 2.5	4.31	5.10	0.27	6.53	m	11.63
Heavy duty 750 Volt grade; bare						
1H 10	2.76	3.27	0.25	6.05	m	9.31
1H 16	3.47	4.11	0.26	6.29	m	10.40
1H 25	5.91	6.99	0.27	6.53	m	13.53
1H 35	7.79	9.22	0.32	7.74	m	16.96
1H 50	9.10	10.77	0.35	8.47	m	19.24
1H 70	10.52	12.45	0.38	9.19	m	21.64
1H 95	13.04	15.43	0.41	9.92	m	25.35
1H 120	16.36	19.36	0.46	11.13	m	30.49
1H 150	19.30	22.84	0.50	12.09	m	34.94
1H 185	22.49	26.62	0.56	13.55	m	40.16
1H 240	28.49	33.72	0.69	16.69	m	50.41
2H 1.5	2.46	2.91	0.25	6.05	m	8.96
2H 2.5	2.94	3.48	0.26	6.29	m	9.77
2H 4	3.54	4.19	0.26	6.29	m	10.48
2H 6	4.39	5.20	0.29	7.01	m	12.21
2H 10	5.46	6.46	0.34	8.22	m	14.69
2H 16	7.68	9.09	0.40	9.68	m	18.76

V: ELECTRICAL SUPPLY/POWER/LIGHTING SYSTEMS

Item	Net Price £	Material £	Labour hours	Labour £	Unit	Total rate £
2H 25	9.59	11.35	0.44	10.64	m	21.99
3H 1.5	2.65	3.14	0.25	6.05	m	9.18
3H 2.5	3.29	3.89	0.25	6.05	m	9.94
3H 4	3.91	4.63	0.27	6.53	m	11.16
3H 6	4.82	5.70	0.30	7.26	m	12.96
3H 10	6.53	7.73	0.35	8.47	m	16.19
3H 16	8.97	10.62	0.41	9.92	m	20.53
3H 25	11.86	14.04	0.47	11.37	m	25.40
4H 1.5	3.27	3.87	0.24	5.81	m	9.68
4H 2.5	3.84	4.54	0.26	6.29	m	10.83
4H 4	4.62	5.47	0.29	7.01	m	12.48
4H 6	5.82	6.89	0.31	7.50	m	14.39
4H 10	8.10	9.59	0.37	8.95	m	18.54
4H 16	10.14	12.00	0.44	10.64	m	22.64
4H 25	14.12	16.71	0.52	12.58	m	29.29
7H 1.5	4.19	4.96	0.30	7.26	m	12.22
7H 2.5	5.14	6.08	0.32	7.74	m	13.82
12H 2.5	8.91	10.54	0.39	9.43	m	19.98
19H 1.5	13.04	15.43	0.42	10.16	m	25.59
Heavy duty 750 Volt grade; LSF sheathed						
1H 10	2.93	3.47	0.25	6.05	m	9.51
1H 16	3.70	4.38	0.26	6.29	m	10.67
1H 25	6.43	7.61	0.27	6.53	m	14.14
1H 35	8.41	9.95	0.32	7.74	m	17.69
1H 50	9.78	11.57	0.35	8.47	m	20.04
1H 70	11.28	13.35	0.38	9.19	m	22.54
1H 95	13.95	16.51	0.41	9.92	m	26.43
1H 120	17.53	20.75	0.46	11.13	m	31.87
1H 150	20.61	24.39	0.50	12.09	m	36.49
1H 185	24.09	28.51	0.56	13.55	m	42.06
1H 240	30.34	35.91	0.68	16.45	m	52.35
2H 1.5	2.67	3.16	0.25	6.05	m	9.21
2H 2.5	3.13	3.70	0.26	6.29	m	9.99
2H 4	3.77	4.46	0.26	6.29	m	10.75
2H 6	4.68	5.54	0.29	7.01	m	12.55
2H 10	5.82	6.89	0.34	8.22	m	15.11
2H 16	8.05	9.53	0.40	9.68	m	19.20
2H 25	10.35	12.25	0.44	10.64	m	22.89
3H 1.5	2.86	3.38	0.25	6.05	m	9.43
3H 2.5	3.52	4.17	0.25	6.05	m	10.21
3H 4	10.41	12.32	0.27	6.53	m	18.85
3H 6	5.09	6.02	0.30	7.26	m	13.28
3H 10	6.89	8.15	0.35	8.47	m	16.62
3H 16	9.53	11.28	0.41	9.92	m	21.20
3H 25	12.72	15.05	0.47	11.37	m	26.42
4H 1.5	6.14	7.27	0.24	5.81	m	13.07
4H 2.5	6.48	7.67	0.26	6.29	m	13.96
4H 4	7.43	8.79	0.29	7.01	m	15.81
4H 6	8.09	9.57	0.31	7.50	m	17.07
4H 10	9.87	11.68	0.37	8.95	m	20.63
4H 16	12.04	14.25	0.44	10.64	m	24.89
4H 25	15.21	18.00	0.52	12.58	m	30.58
7H 1.5	4.49	5.31	0.30	7.26	m	12.57
7H 2.5	5.75	6.80	0.32	7.74	m	14.55
12H 2.5	9.44	11.17	0.39	9.43	m	20.61
19H 1.5	13.66	16.17	0.42	10.16	m	26.33

V: ELECTRICAL SUPPLY/POWER/LIGHTING SYSTEMS

Item	Net Price £	Material £	Labour hours	Labour £	Unit	Total rate £
V20 : LV DISTRIBUTION (cont'd)						
Y61 - LV CABLES AND WIRING (cont'd)						
FIRE RATED CABLE (cont'd)						
Cable terminations for M.I. Cable; Polymeric one piece moulding; containing grey sealing compound; testing; phase marking and connection						
Light Duty 500 Volt grade; Brass gland; polymeric one moulding containing grey sealing compound; coloured conductor sleeving; Earth tag; plastic gland shroud						
2L 1.5	2.43	2.87	0.27	6.53	m	**9.40**
2L 2.5	2.44	4.19	0.27	6.53	m	**10.72**
3L 1.5	2.80	4.18	0.27	6.53	m	**10.71**
4L 1.5	2.83	4.22	0.27	6.53	m	**10.75**
Cable Terminations; for MI copper sheathed cable. Certified for installation in potentially explosive atmospheres; testing; phase marking and connection; BS 6207 Part 2 1995						
Light duty 500 Volt grade; brass gland; brass pot with earth tail; pot closure; sealing compound; conductor sleving; plastic gland shroud; identification markers						
2L 1.0	2.67	6.67	0.39	9.43	nr	**16.10**
2L 1.5	2.67	6.67	0.41	9.92	nr	**16.59**
2L 2.5	2.67	6.85	0.41	9.92	nr	**16.77**
2L 4.0	2.67	6.85	0.46	11.13	nr	**17.98**
3L 1.0	2.69	6.86	0.43	10.40	nr	**17.26**
3L 1.5	2.69	6.49	0.43	10.40	nr	**16.90**
3L 2.5	2.69	6.86	0.44	10.64	nr	**17.51**
4L 1.0	2.71	6.93	0.47	11.37	nr	**18.30**
4L 1.5	2.71	6.56	0.47	11.37	nr	**17.93**
4L 2.5	2.71	6.93	0.50	12.09	nr	**19.03**
7L 1.0	2.78	3.29	0.69	16.69	nr	**19.98**
7L 1.5	5.77	6.83	0.70	16.93	nr	**23.76**
7L 2.5	5.77	6.83	0.74	17.90	nr	**24.73**
Heavy duty 750 Volt grade; brass gland; brass pot with earth tail; pot closure; sealing compound; conductor sleeving; plastic gland shroud; identification markers						
1H 10	4.26	5.04	0.37	8.95	nr	**13.99**
1H 16	4.26	5.04	0.39	9.43	nr	**14.48**
1H 25	6.94	8.22	0.56	13.55	nr	**21.76**
1H 35	6.94	8.22	0.57	13.79	nr	**22.00**
1H 50	13.50	15.98	0.60	14.51	nr	**30.49**
1H 70	4.90	5.80	0.67	16.21	nr	**22.01**
1H 95	4.90	5.80	0.75	18.14	nr	**23.94**
1H 120	9.96	11.79	0.94	22.74	nr	**34.52**
1H 150	9.96	11.79	0.99	23.95	nr	**35.73**
1H 185	9.96	11.79	1.26	30.48	nr	**42.26**

V: ELECTRICAL SUPPLY/POWER/LIGHTING SYSTEMS

Item	Net Price £	Material £	Labour hours	Labour £	Unit	Total rate £
1H 240	20.27	23.98	1.37	33.14	nr	**57.12**
2H 1.5	3.38	4.00	0.42	10.16	nr	**14.16**
2H 2.5	3.38	4.00	0.42	10.16	nr	**14.16**
2H 4	4.01	4.74	0.47	11.37	nr	**16.11**
2H 6	4.95	5.85	0.54	13.06	nr	**18.92**
2H 10	10.67	12.63	0.58	14.03	nr	**26.66**
2H 16	15.82	18.73	0.69	16.69	nr	**35.42**
2H 25	17.31	20.49	0.77	18.63	nr	**39.12**
3H 1.5	3.38	4.00	0.44	10.64	nr	**14.65**
3H 2.5	4.01	4.74	0.44	10.64	nr	**15.39**
3H 4	4.95	5.85	0.57	13.79	nr	**19.64**
3H 6	5.66	6.70	0.61	14.76	nr	**21.46**
3H 10	10.67	12.63	0.65	15.72	nr	**28.35**
3H 16	15.82	18.73	0.78	18.87	nr	**37.59**
3H 25	21.50	25.45	0.85	20.56	nr	**46.01**
4H 1.5	3.38	4.00	0.52	12.58	nr	**16.58**
4H 2.5	4.95	5.85	0.53	12.82	nr	**18.67**
4H 4	5.66	6.70	0.60	14.51	nr	**21.21**
4H 6	9.49	11.23	0.65	15.72	nr	**26.96**
4H 10	9.49	11.23	0.69	16.69	nr	**27.92**
4H 16	17.31	20.49	0.88	21.29	nr	**41.78**
4H 25	21.50	25.45	0.93	22.50	nr	**47.94**
7H 1.5	7.99	9.45	0.71	17.17	nr	**26.63**
7H 2.5	6.82	8.08	0.74	17.90	nr	**25.98**
12H 1.5	10.98	13.00	0.85	20.56	nr	**33.56**
12H 2.5	12.16	14.39	1.00	24.19	nr	**38.58**
19H 2.5	21.50	25.45	1.11	26.85	nr	**52.29**

Cable; FP100; LOSH insulated; non sheathed fire resistant to LPCB Approved to BS 6387 Catergory CWZ; in conduit or trunking including terminations

450/750 volt grade; single core

1.0 mm²	0.36	0.43	0.13	3.14	m	**3.57**
1.5 mm²	0.36	0.43	0.13	3.14	m	**3.57**
2.5 mm²	0.46	0.54	0.13	3.14	m	**3.69**
4.0 mm²	0.60	0.71	0.13	3.14	m	**3.85**
6.0 mm²	1.02	1.21	0.13	3.14	m	**4.35**
10 mm²	1.32	1.56	0.16	3.87	m	**5.43**
16 mm²	1.80	2.13	0.16	3.87	m	**6.00**

Cable; FP200; Insudite insulated; LSOH sheathed screened fire resistant BASEC Approved to BS 7629; fixed with clips to backgrounds

300/500 volt grade; two core

1.5 mm²	1.46	1.73	0.13	3.14	m	**4.87**
2.5 mm²	1.76	2.08	0.13	3.14	m	**5.23**
4.0 mm²	2.29	2.71	0.13	3.14	m	**5.85**

300/500 volt grade; three core

1.5 mm²	1.78	2.11	0.13	3.14	m	**5.25**
2.5 mm²	2.02	2.39	0.13	3.14	m	**5.54**
4.0 mm²	2.81	3.33	0.13	3.14	m	**6.47**

V: ELECTRICAL SUPPLY/POWER/LIGHTING SYSTEMS

Item	Net Price £	Material £	Labour hours	Labour £	Unit	Total rate £
V20 : LV DISTRIBUTION (cont'd)						
Y61 - LV CABLES AND WIRING (cont'd)						
FIRE RATED CABLE (cont'd)						
Cable; FP200; Insudite insulated (cont'd)						
300/500 volt grade; four core						
1.5 mm²	1.99	2.36	0.13	3.14	m	5.50
2.5 mm²	2.46	2.91	0.13	3.14	m	6.06
4.0 mm	3.37	3.99	0.13	3.14	m	7.13
Terminations; including glanding-off, connection to equipment						
Two core						
1.5 mm²	0.62	0.73	0.35	8.47	nr	9.20
2.5 mm²	0.62	0.73	0.35	8.47	nr	9.20
4.0 mm²	0.79	0.93	0.35	8.47	nr	9.40
Three core						
1.5 mm²	0.64	0.76	0.35	8.47	nr	9.22
2.5 mm²	0.64	0.76	0.35	8.47	nr	9.22
4.0 mm²	0.82	0.97	0.35	8.47	nr	9.44
Four core						
1.5 mm²	0.84	0.99	0.35	8.47	nr	9.46
2.5 mm²	0.84	0.99	0.35	8.47	nr	9.46
4.0 mm²	0.84	0.99	0.35	8.47	nr	9.46
Cable; FP400; polymeric insulated; LSOH sheathed fire resistant; armoured; with copper stranded copper conductors; BASEC Approved to BS 7846; fixed with clips to backgrounds						
600/1000 volt grade; two core						
1.5 mm²	2.09	2.47	0.16	3.87	m	6.34
2.5 mm²	2.42	2.86	0.16	3.87	m	6.73
4.0 mm²	2.69	3.18	0.16	3.87	m	7.05
6.0 mm²	3.31	3.92	0.16	3.87	m	7.79
10 mm²	3.57	4.22	0.20	4.84	m	9.06
16 mm²	4.78	5.66	0.20	4.84	m	10.49
25 mm²	5.70	6.75	0.20	4.84	m	11.58
600/1000 volt grade; three core						
1.5 mm²	2.32	2.75	0.16	3.87	m	6.62
2.5 mm²	2.71	3.21	0.16	3.87	m	7.08
4.0 mm²	3.20	3.79	0.16	3.87	m	7.66
6.0 mm²	3.39	4.01	0.16	3.87	m	7.88
10 mm²	4.11	4.86	0.20	4.84	m	9.70
16 mm²	5.93	7.02	0.20	4.84	m	11.86
25 mm²	7.39	8.75	0.20	4.84	m	13.58

V: ELECTRICAL SUPPLY/POWER/LIGHTING SYSTEMS

Item	Net Price £	Material £	Labour hours	Labour £	Unit	Total rate £
600/1000 volt grade; four core						
1.5 mm²	2.62	3.10	0.16	3.87	m	**6.97**
2.5 mm²	3.17	3.75	0.16	3.87	m	**7.62**
4.0 mm²	3.50	4.14	0.16	3.87	m	**8.01**
6.0 mm²	4.40	5.21	0.16	3.87	m	**9.08**
10 mm²	5.23	6.19	0.20	4.84	m	**11.03**
16 mm²	6.84	8.09	0.20	4.84	m	**12.93**
25 mm²	8.56	10.13	0.20	4.84	m	**14.97**
Terminations; including glanding-off, connection to equipment,						
Two core						
1.5 mm²	3.43	4.06	0.58	14.03	nr	**18.09**
2.5 mm²	3.43	4.06	0.58	14.03	nr	**18.09**
4.0 mm²	3.43	4.06	0.58	14.03	nr	**18.09**
6.0 mm²	4.30	5.09	0.67	16.21	nr	**21.30**
10 mm²	4.30	5.09	1.00	24.19	nr	**29.28**
16 mm²	6.07	7.18	1.11	26.85	nr	**34.03**
25 mm²	6.07	7.18	1.70	41.12	nr	**48.30**
Three core						
1.5 mm²	3.43	4.06	0.62	15.00	nr	**19.06**
2.5 mm²	3.43	4.06	0.62	15.00	nr	**19.06**
4.0 mm²	3.43	4.06	0.62	15.00	nr	**19.06**
6.0 mm²	4.30	5.09	0.71	17.17	nr	**22.27**
10 mm²	4.30	5.09	1.06	25.64	nr	**30.73**
16 mm²	6.07	7.18	1.19	28.78	nr	**35.97**
25 mm²	6.07	7.18	1.81	43.78	nr	**50.97**
Four core						
1.5 mm²	3.43	4.06	0.67	16.21	nr	**20.26**
2.5 mm²	3.43	4.06	0.67	16.21	nr	**20.26**
4.0 mm²	4.30	5.09	0.71	17.17	nr	**22.27**
6.0 mm²	4.30	5.09	0.76	18.38	nr	**23.48**
10 mm²	6.07	7.18	1.14	27.57	nr	**34.76**
16 mm²	6.07	7.18	1.29	31.20	nr	**38.39**
25 mm²	10.01	11.85	1.99	48.14	nr	**59.98**
Cable; Firetuff fire resistant to BS 6387; fixed with clips to backgrounds						
Two core						
1.5 mm²	1.49	1.76	0.16	3.87	m	**5.63**
2.5 mm²	1.79	2.12	0.16	3.87	m	**5.99**
4.0 mm²	2.32	2.75	0.16	3.87	m	**6.62**
Three core						
1.5 mm²	1.81	2.14	0.16	3.87	m	**6.01**
2.5 mm²	2.05	2.43	0.16	3.87	m	**6.30**
4.0 mm²	2.95	3.49	0.16	3.87	m	**7.36**
Four core						
1.5 mm²	2.02	2.39	0.16	3.87	m	**6.26**
2.5 mm²	2.48	2.94	0.16	3.87	m	**6.81**
4.0 mm²	3.38	4.00	0.16	3.87	m	**7.87**

V: ELECTRICAL SUPPLY/POWER/LIGHTING SYSTEMS

Item	Net Price £	Material £	Labour hours	Labour £	Unit	Total rate £
V20 : LV DISTRIBUTION (cont'd)						
Y61 - LV CABLES AND WIRING (cont'd)						
MODULAR WIRING						
Modular wiring systems; including commissioning						
Master distribution box; steel; fixed to backgrounds; 6 Port						
4.0mm 18 core armoured home run cable	105.82	125.23	0.90	21.77	nr	**147.00**
4.0mm 24 core armoured cable home run cable	105.82	125.23	0.95	22.98	nr	**148.21**
4.0mm 18 core armoured home run cable & data cable	112.42	133.05	0.95	22.98	nr	**156.03**
6.0mm 18 core armoured home run cable	105.82	125.23	1.00	24.19	nr	**149.42**
6.0mm 24 core armoured home run cable	105.82	125.23	1.10	26.61	nr	**151.84**
6.0mm 18 core armoured home run cable & date cable	112.42	133.05	1.10	26.61	nr	**159.66**
Master distribution box; steel; fixed to backgrounds; 9 Port						
4.0mm 27 core armoured home run cable	132.26	156.53	1.30	31.45	nr	**187.97**
4.0mm 27 core armoured home run cable & data cable	132.26	156.53	1.45	35.07	nr	**191.60**
6.0mm 27 core armoured home run cable	138.88	164.36	1.45	35.07	nr	**199.43**
6.0mm 27 core armoured home run cable & data cable	138.88	164.36	1.55	37.49	nr	**201.85**
Metal clad cable; BSEN 60439 Part 2 1993; BASEC approved						
4.0mm 18 core	9.25	10.94	0.30	7.26	m	**18.20**
4.0mm 24 core	14.22	16.82	0.32	7.74	m	**24.56**
4.0mm 27 core	14.22	16.82	0.32	7.74	m	**24.56**
6.0mm 18 core	12.32	14.58	0.32	7.74	m	**22.32**
6.0mm 27 core	19.14	22.65	0.35	8.47	m	**31.11**
Metal clad data cable						
Single twisted pair	1.80	2.12	0.18	4.35	m	**6.48**
Twin twisted pair	2.90	3.43	0.18	4.35	m	**7.78**
Distribution cables; armoured; BSEN 60439 Part 2 1993; BASEC approved						
3 wire; 6.1 metre long	27.96	33.09	0.92	22.25	nr	**55.35**
4 wire; 6.1 metre long	33.59	39.75	0.96	23.22	nr	**62.98**

V: ELECTRICAL SUPPLY/POWER/LIGHTING SYSTEMS

Item	Net Price £	Material £	Labour hours	Labour £	Unit	Total rate £
Extender cables; armoured; BSEN 60439 Part 2 1993; BASEC approved						
3 Wire						
0.9 metre long	12.23	14.47	0.13	3.14	nr	**17.61**
1.5 metre long	14.33	16.96	0.23	5.56	nr	**22.53**
2.1 metre long	16.44	19.46	0.31	7.50	nr	**26.96**
2.7 metre long	18.54	21.94	0.40	9.68	nr	**31.61**
3.4 metre long	20.65	24.43	0.51	12.34	nr	**36.77**
4.6 metre long	24.86	29.42	0.69	16.69	nr	**46.11**
6.1 metre long	30.12	35.65	0.92	22.25	nr	**57.90**
7.6 metre long	35.39	41.88	1.14	27.57	nr	**69.46**
9.1 metre long	40.66	48.12	1.37	33.14	nr	**81.26**
10.7 metre long	55.43	65.60	1.61	38.94	nr	**104.54**
4 Wire						
0.9 metre long	13.31	15.75	0.14	3.39	nr	**19.13**
1.5 metre long	15.93	18.86	0.24	5.81	nr	**24.66**
2.1 metre long	18.58	21.98	0.32	7.74	nr	**29.72**
2.7 metre long	21.20	25.09	0.43	10.40	nr	**35.50**
3.4 metre long	23.83	28.21	0.51	12.34	nr	**40.54**
4.6 metre long	29.10	34.44	0.67	16.21	nr	**50.65**
6.1 metre long	35.69	42.23	0.92	22.25	nr	**64.49**
7.6 metre long	42.26	50.01	1.22	29.51	nr	**79.52**
9.1 metre long	48.84	57.80	1.46	35.32	nr	**93.12**
10.7 metre long	55.43	65.60	1.71	41.36	nr	**106.96**
3 Wire; including twisted pair						
0.9 metre long	14.56	17.23	0.13	3.14	nr	**20.37**
1.5 metre long	17.89	21.18	0.23	5.56	nr	**26.74**
2.1 metre long	21.23	25.12	0.31	7.50	nr	**32.62**
2.7 metre long	24.56	29.07	0.40	9.68	nr	**38.75**
3.4 metre long	27.90	33.02	0.51	12.34	nr	**45.35**
4.6 metre long	34.57	40.91	0.69	16.69	nr	**57.60**
6.1 metre long	42.92	50.79	0.92	22.25	nr	**73.04**
7.6 metre long	51.25	60.65	1.14	27.57	nr	**88.23**
9.1 metre long	59.59	70.53	1.37	33.14	nr	**103.67**
10.7 metre long	67.94	80.40	1.61	38.94	nr	**119.35**
Extender whip ended cables; armoured; BSEN 60439 Part 2 1993; BASEC approved						
3 wire; 3.0 metre long	16.98	20.09	0.30	7.26	nr	**27.35**
4 wire; 3.0 metre long	19.85	23.49	0.30	7.26	nr	**30.75**
T Connectors						
3 wire						
Snap fix	10.22	12.09	0.10	2.42	nr	**14.51**
0.3 metre flexible cable	11.58	13.71	0.10	2.42	nr	**16.13**
0.3 metre armoured cable	11.57	13.69	0.15	3.63	nr	**17.32**
0.3 metre armoured cable with twisted pair	12.90	15.26	0.15	3.63	nr	**18.89**
4 Wire						
Snap fix	10.66	12.62	0.10	2.42	nr	**15.04**
0.3 metre flexible cable	11.99	14.19	0.10	2.42	nr	**16.61**
0.3 metre armoured cable	11.99	14.19	0.18	4.35	nr	**18.54**

V: ELECTRICAL SUPPLY/POWER/LIGHTING SYSTEMS

Item	Net Price £	Material £	Labour hours	Labour £	Unit	Total rate £
V20 : LV DISTRIBUTION (cont'd)						
Y61 - LV CABLES AND WIRING (cont'd)						
MODULAR WIRING (cont'd)						
Extender whip ended cables (cont'd)						
Splitters						
5 wire	16.36	19.36	0.20	4.84	nr	**24.19**
5 wire converter	12.67	15.00	0.20	4.84	nr	**19.84**
Switch modules						
3 wire; 6.1 metre long armoured cable	34.11	40.37	0.75	18.14	nr	**58.51**
4 wire; 6.1 metre long armoured cable	39.04	46.20	0.80	19.35	nr	**65.55**
Distribution cables; unarmoured; IEC 998 DIN/VDE 0628						
3 wire; 6.1 metre long	11.93	14.12	0.70	16.93	nr	**31.05**
4 wire; 6.1 metre long	14.27	16.89	0.75	18.14	nr	**35.03**
Extender cables; unarmoured; IEC 998 DIN/VDE 0628						
3 Wire						
0.9 metre long	8.28	9.80	0.07	1.69	nr	**11.50**
1.5 metre long	8.95	10.60	0.12	2.90	nr	**13.50**
2.1 metre long	9.62	11.39	0.17	4.11	nr	**15.50**
2.7 metre long	12.00	14.21	0.22	5.32	nr	**19.53**
3.4 metre long	10.96	12.97	0.27	6.53	nr	**19.50**
4.6 metre long	12.41	14.69	0.37	8.95	nr	**23.64**
6.1 metre long	14.09	16.67	0.49	11.85	nr	**28.52**
7.6 metre long	15.76	18.65	0.61	14.76	nr	**33.41**
9.1 metre long	17.43	20.63	0.73	17.66	nr	**38.29**
10.7 metre long	19.22	22.75	0.86	20.80	nr	**43.55**
4 Wire						
0.9 metre long	9.47	11.21	0.08	1.94	nr	**13.15**
1.5 metre long	10.32	12.21	0.14	3.39	nr	**15.60**
2.1 metre long	11.16	13.21	0.19	4.60	nr	**17.80**
2.7 metre long	12.00	14.21	0.24	5.81	nr	**20.01**
3.4 metre long	12.85	15.20	0.31	7.50	nr	**22.70**
4.6 metre long	14.67	17.36	0.41	9.92	nr	**27.28**
6.1 metre long	16.78	19.86	0.55	13.30	nr	**33.16**
7.6 metre long	18.89	22.35	0.68	16.45	nr	**38.80**
9.1 metre long	24.71	29.25	0.82	19.83	nr	**49.08**
10.7 metre long	23.25	27.52	0.96	23.22	nr	**50.74**
5 Wire						
0.9 metre long	11.17	13.22	0.09	2.18	nr	**15.40**
1.5 metre long	12.54	14.84	0.15	3.63	nr	**18.46**
2.1 metre long	13.89	16.44	0.21	5.08	nr	**21.52**
2.7 metre long	15.24	18.04	0.27	6.53	nr	**24.57**
3.4 metre long	16.60	19.65	0.34	8.22	nr	**27.87**
4.6 metre long	19.53	23.11	0.46	11.13	nr	**34.24**
6.1 metre long	22.93	27.13	0.61	14.76	nr	**41.89**
7.6 metre long	26.31	31.14	0.76	18.38	nr	**49.52**
9.1 metre long	29.70	35.15	0.91	22.01	nr	**57.16**
10.7 metre long	33.32	39.43	1.07	25.88	nr	**65.31**

V: ELECTRICAL SUPPLY/POWER/LIGHTING SYSTEMS

Item	Net Price £	Material £	Labour hours	Labour £	Unit	Total rate £
Extender whip ended cables; armoured; IEC 998 DIN/VDE 0628						
3 wire; 2.5mm; 3.0 metre long	8.44	9.99	0.30	7.26	nr	**17.25**
4 wire; 2.5mm; 3.0 metre long	9.92	11.74	0.30	7.26	nr	**19.00**
T Connectors						
3 wire						
5 pin; direct fix	8.54	10.11	0.10	2.42	nr	**12.53**
5 pin; 1.5mm flexible cable; 0.3 metre long	8.44	9.99	0.15	3.63	nr	**13.62**
4 Wire						
5 pin; direct fix	9.93	11.75	0.20	4.84	nr	**16.59**
5 pin; 1.5mm flexible cable; 0.3 metre long	9.65	11.42	0.20	4.84	nr	**16.25**
5 Wire						
5 pin; direct fix	11.32	13.40	0.20	4.84	nr	**18.24**
Splitters						
3 way; 5 pin	6.52	7.72	0.25	6.05	nr	**13.77**
Switch Modules						
3 wire	18.58	21.98	0.20	4.84	nr	**26.82**
4 wire	19.37	22.92	0.22	5.32	nr	**28.24**

V: ELECTRICAL SUPPLY/POWER/LIGHTING SYSTEMS

Item	Net Price £	Material £	Labour hours	Labour £	Unit	Total rate £
V20 : LV DISTRIBUTION (cont'd)						
Y62 - BUSBAR TRUNKING						
MAINS BUSBAR						
Low impedance busbar trunking; fixed to backgrounds including supports, fixings and connections/jointing to equipment;						
Straight copper busbar						
1000 Amp TP&N	270.00	319.54	3.41	82.48	m	402.02
1350 Amp TP&N	331.88	392.76	3.58	86.59	m	479.36
2000 Amp TP&N	416.25	492.62	5.00	120.94	m	613.56
2500 Amp TP&N	628.88	744.25	5.90	142.71	m	886.97
Extra for fittings mains bus bar						
IP54 protection						
1000 Amp TP&N	22.50	26.63	2.16	52.25	m	78.88
1350 Amp TP&N	24.19	28.63	2.61	63.13	m	91.76
2000 Amp TP&N	33.55	39.70	3.51	84.90	m	124.60
2500 Amp TP&N	39.84	47.15	3.96	95.79	m	142.93
End cover						
1000 Amp TP&N	25.88	30.62	0.56	13.55	nr	44.17
1350 Amp TP&N	27.00	31.95	0.56	13.55	nr	45.50
2000 Amp TP&N	43.31	51.26	0.66	15.96	nr	67.22
2500 Amp TP&N	43.88	51.92	0.66	15.96	nr	67.89
Edge elbow						
1000 Amp TP&N	322.88	382.11	2.01	48.62	nr	430.73
1350 Amp TP&N	363.38	430.04	2.01	48.62	nr	478.66
2000 Amp TP&N	563.63	667.03	2.40	58.05	nr	725.09
2500 Amp TP&N	740.25	876.06	2.40	58.05	nr	934.12
Flat elbow						
1000 Amp TP&N	280.13	331.52	2.01	48.62	nr	380.14
1350 Amp TP&N	303.75	359.48	2.01	48.62	nr	408.10
2000 Amp TP&N	430.88	509.93	2.40	58.05	nr	567.98
2500 Amp TP&N	536.63	635.08	2.40	58.05	nr	693.13
Offset						
1000 Amp TP&N	562.50	665.70	3.00	72.57	nr	738.27
1350 Amp TP&N	691.88	818.81	3.00	72.57	nr	891.38
2000 Amp TP&N	1090.13	1290.13	3.50	84.66	nr	1374.79
2500 Amp TP&N	1240.88	1468.54	3.50	84.66	nr	1553.20
Edge Z unit						
1000 Amp TP&N	842.63	997.22	3.00	72.57	nr	1069.79
1350 Amp TP&N	1078.88	1276.82	3.00	72.57	nr	1349.38
2000 Amp TP&N	1616.63	1913.23	3.50	84.66	nr	1997.89
2500 Amp TP&N	1846.13	2184.83	3.50	84.66	nr	2269.49
Flat Z unit						
1000 Amp TP&N	723.38	856.09	3.00	72.57	nr	928.66
1350 Amp TP&N	911.25	1078.44	3.00	72.57	nr	1151.00
2000 Amp TP&N	1356.75	1605.67	3.50	84.66	nr	1690.33
2500 Amp TP&N	1631.25	1930.54	3.50	84.66	nr	2015.20

V: ELECTRICAL SUPPLY/POWER/LIGHTING SYSTEMS

Item	Net Price £	Material £	Labour hours	Labour £	Unit	Total rate £
Edge tee						
1000 Amp TP&N	842.63	997.22	2.20	53.21	nr	**1050.44**
1350 Amp TP&N	1078.88	1276.82	2.20	53.21	nr	**1330.03**
2000 Amp TP&N	1616.63	1913.23	2.60	62.89	nr	**1976.12**
2500 Amp TP&N	1847.25	2186.16	2.60	62.89	nr	**2249.06**
Tap off; TP&N integral contactor/breaker						
18 Amp	163.16	193.09	0.82	19.83	nr	**212.93**
Tap off; TP&N fusable with on-load switch; excludes fuses						
32 Amp	461.86	546.59	0.82	19.83	nr	**566.43**
63 Amp	471.12	557.55	0.88	21.29	nr	**578.84**
100 Amp	576.46	682.22	1.18	28.54	nr	**710.77**
160 Amp	655.67	775.97	1.41	34.11	nr	**810.07**
250 Amp	846.44	1001.73	1.76	42.57	nr	**1044.31**
315 Amp	999.25	1182.58	2.06	49.83	nr	**1232.41**
Tap off; TP&N MCCB						
63 Amp	583.62	690.69	0.88	21.29	nr	**711.98**
125 Amp	699.48	827.81	1.18	28.54	nr	**856.36**
160 Amp	763.75	903.88	1.41	34.11	nr	**937.98**
250 Amp	982.27	1162.49	1.76	42.57	nr	**1205.06**
400 Amp	1252.17	1481.91	2.06	49.83	nr	**1531.73**
RISING MAINS BUSBAR						
Rising mains busbar; insulated supports, earth continuity bar; including couplers; fixed to backgrounds						
Straight aluminium bar						
200 Amp TP&N	113.63	134.47	2.13	51.52	m	**185.99**
315 Amp TP&N	127.13	150.45	2.15	52.01	m	**202.45**
400 Amp TP&N	147.38	174.41	2.15	52.01	m	**226.42**
630 Amp TP&N	182.25	215.69	2.47	59.75	m	**275.43**
800 Amp TP&N	273.38	323.53	2.88	69.66	m	**393.19**
Extra for fittings rising busbar						
End feed unit						
200 Amp TP&N	236.25	279.59	2.57	62.16	nr	**341.76**
315 Amp TP&N	236.25	279.59	2.76	66.76	nr	**346.36**
400 Amp TP&N	264.38	312.88	2.76	66.76	nr	**379.64**
630 Amp TP&N	264.38	312.88	3.64	88.05	nr	**400.93**
800 Amp TP&N	298.13	352.82	4.54	109.82	nr	**462.64**
Top feeder unit						
200 Amp TP&N	236.25	279.59	2.57	62.16	nr	**341.76**
315 Amp TP&N	236.25	279.59	2.76	66.76	nr	**346.36**
400 Amp TP&N	264.38	312.88	2.76	66.76	nr	**379.64**
630 Amp TP&N	264.38	312.88	3.64	88.05	nr	**400.93**
800 Amp TP&N	298.13	352.82	4.54	109.82	nr	**462.64**
End cap						
200 Amp TP&N	20.25	23.97	0.18	4.35	nr	**28.32**
315 Amp TP&N	20.25	23.97	0.27	6.53	nr	**30.50**
400 Amp TP&N	22.50	26.63	0.27	6.53	nr	**33.16**
630 Amp TP&N	22.50	26.63	0.41	9.92	nr	**36.55**
800 Amp TP&N	65.25	77.22	0.41	9.92	nr	**87.14**

V: ELECTRICAL SUPPLY/POWER/LIGHTING SYSTEMS

Item	Net Price £	Material £	Labour hours	Labour £	Unit	Total rate £
V20 : LV DISTRIBUTION (cont'd)						
Y62 - BUSBAR TRUNKING (cont'd)						
RISING MAINS BUSBAR (cont'd)						
Fittings; rising busbar (cont'd)						
Edge elbow						
200 Amp TP&N	28.13	33.29	0.55	13.30	nr	**46.59**
315 Amp TP&N	28.13	33.29	0.94	22.74	nr	**56.02**
400 Amp TP&N	211.50	250.30	0.94	22.74	nr	**273.04**
630 Amp TP&N	211.50	250.30	1.45	35.07	nr	**285.38**
800 Amp TP&N	200.25	236.99	1.45	35.07	nr	**272.06**
Flat elbow						
200 Amp TP&N	91.13	107.84	0.55	13.30	nr	**121.15**
315 Amp TP&N	91.13	107.84	0.94	22.74	nr	**130.58**
400 Amp TP&N	123.75	146.45	0.94	22.74	nr	**169.19**
630 Amp TP&N	123.75	146.45	1.45	35.07	nr	**181.53**
800 Amp TP&N	171.00	202.37	1.45	35.07	nr	**237.45**
Edge tee						
200 Amp TP&N	128.25	151.78	0.61	14.76	nr	**166.53**
315 Amp TP&N	128.25	151.78	1.02	24.67	nr	**176.45**
400 Amp TP&N	180.00	213.02	1.02	24.67	nr	**237.70**
630 Amp TP&N	180.00	213.02	1.57	37.98	nr	**251.00**
800 Amp TP&N	256.50	303.56	1.57	37.98	nr	**341.54**
Flat tee						
200 Amp TP&N	164.25	194.38	0.61	14.76	nr	**209.14**
315 Amp TP&N	128.25	151.78	1.02	24.67	nr	**176.45**
400 Amp TP&N	258.75	306.22	1.02	24.67	nr	**330.90**
630 Amp TP&N	258.75	306.22	1.57	37.98	nr	**344.20**
800 Amp TP&N	361.13	427.38	1.57	37.98	nr	**465.36**
Tap off units						
TP&N fusable with on-load switch; excludes fuses						
32 Amp	129.38	153.11	0.82	19.83	nr	**172.95**
63 Amp	171.00	202.37	0.88	21.29	nr	**223.66**
100 Amp	229.50	271.61	1.18	28.54	nr	**300.15**
250 Amp	344.25	407.41	1.41	34.11	nr	**441.52**
400 Amp	501.75	593.81	2.06	49.83	nr	**643.63**
TP&N MCCB						
32 Amp	131.63	155.77	0.82	19.83	nr	**175.61**
63 Amp	182.25	215.69	0.88	21.29	nr	**236.97**
100 Amp	292.50	346.17	1.18	28.54	nr	**374.71**
250 Amp	495.00	585.82	1.41	34.11	nr	**619.92**
400 Amp	868.50	1027.84	2.06	49.83	nr	**1077.67**

V: ELECTRICAL SUPPLY/POWER/LIGHTING SYSTEMS

Item	Net Price £	Material £	Labour hours	Labour £	Unit	Total rate £
LIGHTING BUSBAR						
Pre-wired busbar, plug-in trunking for lighting; galvanised sheet steel housing (PE); tin-plated copper conductors with tap-off units at 1m intervals.						
Straight lengths - 25 Amp						
2 Pole & PE	20.36	24.09	0.16	3.87	m	**27.96**
4 Pole & PE	22.02	26.06	0.16	3.87	m	**29.93**
Straight lengths - 40 Amp						
2 Pole & PE	20.13	23.82	0.16	3.87	m	**27.69**
4 Pole & PE	27.02	31.98	0.16	3.87	m	**35.85**
Components for pre-wired busbars, plug-in trunking for lighting.						
Plug-in tap off units						
10 Amp with phase selection, 2P & PE; 2m of cable	13.39	15.84	0.10	2.42	nr	**18.26**
10 Amp 4 Pole & PE; 3m of cable	17.89	21.18	0.10	2.42	nr	**23.60**
16 Amp 4 Pole & PE; 3m of cable	17.34	20.52	0.10	2.42	nr	**22.94**
16 Amp with phase selection, 2P & PE; no cable	15.35	18.17	0.10	2.42	nr	**20.59**
Trunking components						
End feed unit & cover; 4P & PE	22.69	26.86	0.23	5.56	nr	**32.42**
Centre feed unit	112.09	132.66	0.29	7.01	nr	**139.67**
Right hand, intermediate terminal box feed unit	23.69	28.03	0.23	5.56	nr	**33.60**
End cover (for R/hand feed)	6.53	7.73	0.06	1.45	nr	**9.18**
Flexible elbow unit	53.66	63.50	0.12	2.90	nr	**66.41**
Fixing bracket - universal	3.92	4.64	0.10	2.42	nr	**7.06**
Suspension Bracket - Flat	3.44	4.07	0.10	2.42	nr	**6.49**
UNDERFLOOR BUSBAR						
Pre-wired busbar, plug-in trunking for underfloor power distribution; galvanised sheet steel housing (PE); copper conductors with tap-off units at 300mm intervals.						
Straight lengths - 63 Amp						
2 pole & PE	13.74	16.26	0.28	6.77	m	**23.03**
3 pole & PE; Clean Earth System	17.38	20.56	0.28	6.77	m	**27.34**
Components for pre-wired busbars, plug-in trunking for underfloor power distribution.						
Plug-in tap off units						
32 Amp 2P & PE; 3m metal flexible pre-wired conduit	23.65	27.99	0.25	6.05	nr	**34.04**
32 Amp 3P & PE; clean earth; 3m metal flexible pre-wired conduit	28.46	33.69	0.28	6.77	nr	**40.46**

V: ELECTRICAL SUPPLY/POWER/LIGHTING SYSTEMS

Item	Net Price £	Material £	Labour hours	Labour £	Unit	Total rate £
V20 : LV DISTRIBUTION (cont'd)						
Y62 - BUSBAR TRUNKING (cont'd)						
UNDERFLOOR BUSBAR (cont'd)						
Components for pre-wired busbars (cont'd)						
Trunking components						
End feed unit & cover; 2P & PE	25.48	30.15	0.35	8.47	nr	**38.62**
End feed unit & cover; 3P & PE; clean earth	27.90	33.02	0.38	9.19	nr	**42.21**
End cover; 2P & PE	7.93	9.39	0.11	2.66	nr	**12.05**
End cover; 3P & PE	8.53	10.10	0.11	2.66	nr	**12.76**
Flexible interlink/corner; 2P&PE; 1m long	43.90	51.95	0.34	8.22	nr	**60.17**
Flexible interlink/corner; 3P&PE; 1m long	49.57	58.67	0.35	8.47	nr	**67.13**
Flexible interlink/corner; 2P&PE; 2m long	53.57	63.40	0.37	8.95	nr	**72.35**
Flexible interlink/corner; 3P&PE; 2m long	58.78	69.56	0.37	8.95	nr	**78.51**

V: ELECTRICAL SUPPLY/POWER/LIGHTING SYSTEMS

Item	Net Price £	Material £	Labour hours	Labour £	Unit	Total rate £
Y63 - CABLE SUPPORTS						
LADDER RACK						
Light duty Galvanised Steel Ladder Rack; fixed to backgrounds; including supports, fixings and brackets; earth continuity straps.						
Straight lengths						
150 mm wide ladder	15.83	18.73	0.69	16.69	m	**35.42**
300 mm wide ladder	16.48	19.50	0.88	21.29	m	**40.79**
450 mm wide ladder	17.56	20.78	1.26	30.48	m	**51.26**
600 mm wide ladder	18.23	21.57	1.51	36.52	m	**58.10**
Extra over; (cutting and jointing racking to fittings is included.)						
Inside riser bend						
150 mm wide ladder	29.12	34.46	0.33	7.98	nr	**42.44**
300 mm wide ladder	30.30	35.86	0.56	13.55	nr	**49.40**
450 mm wide ladder	31.03	36.72	0.85	20.56	nr	**57.28**
600 mm wide ladder	32.30	38.23	0.99	23.95	nr	**62.17**
Outside riser bend						
300 mm wide ladder	30.30	35.86	0.43	10.40	nr	**46.26**
450 mm wide ladder	31.03	36.72	0.73	17.66	nr	**54.38**
600 mm wide ladder	32.30	38.23	0.86	20.80	nr	**59.03**
Equal tee						
300 mm wide ladder	35.23	41.69	0.62	15.00	nr	**56.69**
450 mm wide ladder	39.44	46.68	1.09	26.37	nr	**73.04**
600 mm wide ladder	41.58	49.21	1.12	27.09	nr	**76.30**
Unequal tee						
300 mm wide ladder	35.23	41.69	0.57	13.79	nr	**55.48**
450 mm wide ladder	39.44	46.68	1.17	28.30	nr	**74.98**
600 mm wide ladder	41.58	49.21	1.17	28.30	nr	**77.51**
4 way cross overs						
300 mm wide ladder	56.26	66.58	0.72	17.42	nr	**84.00**
450 mm wide ladder	61.01	72.20	1.13	27.33	nr	**99.54**
600 mm wide ladder	72.10	85.33	1.29	31.20	nr	**116.53**
Heavy duty galvanised steel ladder rack; fixed to backgrounds; including supports, fixings and brackets; earth continuity straps.						
Straight lengths						
150 mm wide ladder	20.80	24.62	0.68	16.45	m	**41.06**
300 mm wide ladder	21.62	25.59	0.79	19.11	m	**44.70**
450 mm wide ladder	22.54	26.68	1.07	25.88	m	**52.56**
600 mm wide ladder	23.21	27.47	1.24	29.99	m	**57.46**
750 mm wide ladder	24.33	28.79	1.49	36.04	m	**64.83**
900 mm wide ladder	25.17	29.79	1.67	40.39	m	**70.18**

V: ELECTRICAL SUPPLY/POWER/LIGHTING SYSTEMS

Item	Net Price £	Material £	Labour hours	Labour £	Unit	Total rate £
V20 : LV DISTRIBUTION (cont'd)						
Y63 - CABLE SUPPORTS (cont'd)						
LADDER RACK (cont'd)						
Heavy duty galvanised steel ladder rack (cont'd)						
Extra over; (cutting and jointing racking to fittings is included.)						
Flat bend						
150 mm wide ladder	29.87	35.35	0.34	8.22	nr	**43.57**
300 mm wide ladder	31.06	36.76	0.39	9.43	nr	**46.19**
450 mm wide ladder	33.84	40.05	0.43	10.40	nr	**50.45**
600 mm wide ladder	36.96	43.74	0.61	14.76	nr	**58.50**
750 mm wide ladder	40.61	48.06	0.82	19.83	nr	**67.90**
900 mm wide ladder	44.27	52.39	0.97	23.46	nr	**75.86**
Inside riser bend						
150 mm wide ladder	38.70	45.80	0.27	6.53	nr	**52.33**
300 mm wide ladder	39.89	47.21	0.45	10.88	nr	**58.09**
450 mm wide ladder	41.69	49.34	0.65	15.72	nr	**65.06**
600 mm wide ladder	44.40	52.55	0.81	19.59	nr	**72.14**
750 mm wide ladder	46.96	55.58	0.92	22.25	nr	**77.83**
900 mm wide ladder	49.61	58.71	1.06	25.64	nr	**84.35**
Outside riser bend						
150 mm wide ladder	38.70	45.80	0.27	6.53	nr	**52.33**
300 mm wide ladder	39.89	47.21	0.33	7.98	nr	**55.19**
450 mm wide ladder	41.69	49.34	0.61	14.76	nr	**64.09**
600 mm wide ladder	44.40	52.55	0.76	18.38	nr	**70.93**
750 mm wide ladder	46.96	55.58	0.94	22.74	nr	**78.31**
900 mm wide ladder	49.91	59.07	1.05	25.40	nr	**84.46**
Equal tee						
150mm wide ladder	47.46	56.17	0.37	8.95	nr	**65.12**
300 mm wide ladder	50.62	59.91	0.57	13.79	nr	**73.69**
450 mm wide ladder	53.40	63.20	0.83	20.08	nr	**83.27**
600 mm wide ladder	57.50	68.05	0.92	22.25	nr	**90.30**
750 mm wide ladder	70.52	83.46	1.13	27.33	nr	**110.79**
900 mm wide ladder	73.12	86.54	1.20	29.03	nr	**115.56**
Unequal tee						
300 mm wide ladder	50.41	59.66	0.57	13.79	nr	**73.45**
450 mm wide ladder	53.09	62.83	1.17	28.30	nr	**91.13**
600 mm wide ladder	57.30	67.81	1.17	28.30	nr	**96.11**
750 mm wide ladder	70.32	83.22	1.25	30.24	nr	**113.46**
900 mm wide ladder	72.91	86.29	1.33	32.17	nr	**118.46**
4 way cross overs						
150 mm wide ladder	68.45	81.01	0.50	12.09	nr	**93.10**
300 mm wide ladder	70.63	83.59	0.67	16.21	nr	**99.79**
450 mm wide ladder	73.93	87.49	0.92	22.25	nr	**109.75**
600 mm wide ladder	77.59	91.83	1.07	25.88	nr	**117.71**
750 mm wide ladder	93.46	110.61	1.25	30.24	nr	**140.84**
900 mm wide ladder	96.66	114.39	1.36	32.90	nr	**147.29**

V: ELECTRICAL SUPPLY/POWER/LIGHTING SYSTEMS

Item	Net Price £	Material £	Labour hours	Labour £	Unit	Total rate £
Extra heavy duty galvanised steel ladder rack; fixed to backgrounds; including supports, fixings and brackets; earth continuity straps.						
Straight lengths						
150 mm wide ladder	25.96	30.72	0.63	15.24	m	**45.96**
300 mm wide ladder	26.95	31.89	0.70	16.93	m	**48.83**
450 mm wide ladder	27.99	33.13	0.83	20.08	m	**53.20**
600 mm wide ladder	29.13	34.47	0.89	21.53	m	**56.00**
750 mm wide ladder	30.86	36.52	1.22	29.51	m	**66.03**
900 mm wide ladder	31.84	37.68	1.44	34.83	m	**72.51**
Extra over; (cutting and jointing racking to fittings is included.)						
Flat bend						
150 mm wide ladder	32.34	38.27	0.36	8.71	nr	**46.98**
300 mm wide ladder	33.97	40.20	0.39	9.43	nr	**49.64**
450 mm wide ladder	37.30	44.14	0.43	10.40	nr	**54.54**
600 mm wide ladder	40.91	48.42	0.61	14.76	nr	**63.17**
750 mm wide ladder	45.01	53.27	0.82	19.83	nr	**73.10**
900 mm wide ladder	49.12	58.13	0.97	23.46	nr	**81.59**
Inside riser bend						
150 mm wide ladder	41.17	48.72	0.36	8.71	nr	**57.43**
300 mm wide ladder	41.82	49.49	0.39	9.43	nr	**58.93**
450 mm wide ladder	44.60	52.78	0.43	10.40	nr	**63.18**
600 mm wide ladder	47.32	56.00	0.61	14.76	nr	**70.76**
750 mm wide ladder	48.74	57.68	0.82	19.83	nr	**77.52**
900 mm wide ladder	53.10	62.84	0.97	23.46	nr	**86.31**
Outside riser bend						
150 mm wide ladder	41.17	48.72	0.36	8.71	nr	**57.43**
300 mm wide ladder	41.82	49.49	0.39	9.43	nr	**58.93**
450 mm wide ladder	44.60	52.78	0.41	9.92	nr	**62.70**
600 mm wide ladder	47.32	56.00	0.57	13.79	nr	**69.79**
750 mm wide ladder	48.74	57.68	0.82	19.83	nr	**77.52**
900 mm wide ladder	53.10	62.84	0.93	22.50	nr	**85.34**
Equal tee						
150 mm wide ladder	48.44	57.33	0.37	8.95	nr	**66.28**
300 mm wide ladder	54.48	64.48	0.57	13.79	nr	**78.26**
450 mm wide ladder	58.28	68.97	0.83	20.08	nr	**89.05**
600 mm wide ladder	63.42	75.06	0.92	22.25	nr	**97.31**
750 mm wide ladder	76.91	91.02	1.13	27.33	nr	**118.35**
900 mm wide ladder	80.54	95.32	1.20	29.03	nr	**124.34**
Unequal tee						
150 mm wide ladder	48.44	57.33	0.37	8.95	nr	**66.28**
300 mm wide ladder	54.48	64.48	0.57	13.79	nr	**78.26**
450 mm wide ladder	58.28	68.97	1.17	28.30	nr	**97.27**
600 mm wide ladder	63.42	75.06	1.17	28.30	nr	**103.36**
750 mm wide ladder	76.91	91.02	1.25	30.24	nr	**121.26**
900 mm wide ladder	80.54	95.32	1.33	32.17	nr	**127.49**

V: ELECTRICAL SUPPLY/POWER/LIGHTING SYSTEMS

Item	Net Price £	Material £	Labour hours	Labour £	Unit	Total rate £
V20 : LV DISTRIBUTION (cont'd)						
Y63 - CABLE SUPPORTS (cont'd)						
LADDER RACK (cont'd)						
(Cutting and jointing racking) (cont'd)						
4 way cross overs						
150 mm wide ladder	72.84	86.20	0.50	12.09	nr	**98.30**
300 mm wide ladder	76.01	89.96	0.67	16.21	nr	**106.16**
450 mm wide ladder	91.12	107.84	0.92	22.25	nr	**130.09**
600 mm wide ladder	96.25	113.91	1.07	25.88	nr	**139.79**
750 mm wide ladder	100.36	118.77	1.25	30.24	nr	**149.01**
900 mm wide ladder	104.46	123.63	1.36	32.90	nr	**156.52**
CABLE TRAY						
Galvanised steel cable tray to BS 729; including standard coupling joints, fixings and earth continuity straps. (Supports and hangers are excluded.)						
Light duty tray						
Straight lengths						
50 mm wide	1.56	1.85	0.19	4.60	m	**6.44**
75 mm wide	2.01	2.38	0.23	5.56	m	**7.94**
100 mm wide	1.92	2.27	0.31	7.50	m	**9.77**
150 mm wide	2.36	2.79	0.33	7.98	m	**10.78**
225 mm wide	3.47	4.11	0.39	9.43	m	**13.54**
300 mm wide	5.16	6.11	0.49	11.85	m	**17.96**
450 mm wide	8.01	9.48	0.60	14.51	m	**23.99**
600 mm wide	10.82	12.81	0.79	19.11	m	**31.91**
750 mm wide	13.65	16.15	1.04	25.16	m	**41.31**
900 mm wide	16.94	20.05	1.26	30.48	m	**50.53**
Extra over; (cutting and jointing tray to fittings is included.)						
Straight reducer						
75 mm wide	4.77	5.65	0.22	5.32	nr	**10.97**
100 mm wide	5.12	6.06	0.25	6.05	nr	**12.11**
150 mm wide	6.36	7.53	0.27	6.53	nr	**14.06**
225 mm wide	7.77	9.20	0.34	8.22	nr	**17.42**
300 mm wide	9.63	11.40	0.39	9.43	nr	**20.83**
450 mm wide	13.82	16.36	0.49	11.85	nr	**28.21**
600 mm wide	16.47	19.49	0.54	13.06	nr	**32.55**
750 mm wide	20.66	24.45	0.61	14.76	nr	**39.21**
900 mm wide	23.79	28.15	0.69	16.69	nr	**44.84**

V: ELECTRICAL SUPPLY/POWER/LIGHTING SYSTEMS

Item	Net Price £	Material £	Labour hours	Labour £	Unit	Total rate £
Flat bend; 90°						
50mm wide	3.56	4.21	0.19	4.60	nr	**8.81**
75 mm wide	3.62	4.28	0.24	5.81	nr	**10.09**
100 mm wide	4.02	4.76	0.28	6.77	nr	**11.53**
150 mm wide	4.11	4.86	0.30	7.26	nr	**12.12**
225 mm wide	5.21	6.17	0.36	8.71	nr	**14.87**
300 mm wide	6.63	7.85	0.44	10.64	nr	**18.49**
450 mm wide	10.25	12.13	0.57	13.79	nr	**25.92**
600 mm wide	14.72	17.42	0.69	16.69	nr	**34.11**
750 mm wide	20.37	24.11	0.81	19.59	nr	**43.70**
900 mm wide	29.34	34.72	0.94	22.74	nr	**57.46**
Adjustable riser						
50 mm wide	5.31	6.28	0.26	6.29	nr	**12.57**
75 mm wide	5.78	6.84	0.29	7.01	nr	**13.86**
100 mm wide	6.38	7.55	0.32	7.74	nr	**15.29**
150 mm wide	7.98	9.44	0.36	8.71	nr	**18.15**
225 mm wide	9.78	11.57	0.44	10.64	nr	**22.22**
300 mm wide	12.45	14.73	0.52	12.58	nr	**27.31**
450 mm wide	15.96	18.89	0.66	15.96	nr	**34.85**
600 mm wide	20.00	23.67	0.79	19.11	nr	**42.78**
750 mm wide	25.82	30.56	1.03	24.91	nr	**55.47**
900 mm wide	30.29	35.85	1.10	26.61	nr	**62.45**
Inside riser; 90°						
50 mm wide	4.59	5.43	0.28	6.77	nr	**12.20**
75 mm wide	5.04	5.96	0.31	7.50	nr	**13.46**
100 mm wide	5.04	5.96	0.33	7.98	nr	**13.95**
150 mm wide	6.26	7.41	0.37	8.95	nr	**16.36**
225 mm wide	7.61	9.01	0.44	10.64	nr	**19.65**
300 mm wide	9.80	11.60	0.53	12.82	nr	**24.42**
450 mm wide	13.22	15.65	0.67	16.21	nr	**31.85**
600 mm wide	17.21	20.37	0.79	19.11	nr	**39.48**
750 mm wide	20.91	24.75	0.95	22.98	nr	**47.73**
900 mm wide	24.60	29.11	1.11	26.85	nr	**55.96**
Outside riser; 90°						
50 mm wide	4.59	5.43	0.28	6.77	nr	**12.20**
75 mm wide	4.77	5.65	0.31	7.50	nr	**13.14**
100 mm wide	5.04	5.96	0.33	7.98	nr	**13.95**
150 mm wide	6.26	7.41	0.37	8.95	nr	**16.36**
225 mm wide	7.61	9.01	0.44	10.64	nr	**19.65**
300 mm wide	9.80	11.60	0.53	12.82	nr	**24.42**
450 mm wide	13.22	15.65	0.67	16.21	nr	**31.85**
600 mm wide	17.21	20.37	0.79	19.11	nr	**39.48**
750 mm wide	20.91	24.75	0.95	22.98	nr	**47.73**
900 mm wide	24.60	29.11	1.11	26.85	nr	**55.96**
Equal tee						
50 mm wide	5.21	6.17	0.30	7.26	nr	**13.42**
75 mm wide	5.33	6.31	0.31	7.50	nr	**13.81**
100 mm wide	5.64	6.67	0.35	8.47	nr	**15.14**
150 mm wide	6.05	7.16	0.36	8.71	nr	**15.87**
225 mm wide	7.64	9.04	0.74	17.90	nr	**26.94**
300 mm wide	9.06	10.72	0.54	13.06	nr	**23.78**
450 mm wide	14.87	17.60	0.71	17.17	nr	**34.77**
600 mm wide	19.70	23.31	0.92	22.25	nr	**45.57**
750 mm wide	28.70	33.97	1.19	28.78	nr	**62.75**
900 mm wide	39.81	47.11	1.44	34.83	nr	**81.95**

V: ELECTRICAL SUPPLY/POWER/LIGHTING SYSTEMS

Item	Net Price £	Material £	Labour hours	Labour £	Unit	Total rate £
V20 : LV DISTRIBUTION (cont'd)						
Y63 - CABLE SUPPORTS (cont'd)						
CABLE TRAY (cont'd)						
Light duty tray (cont'd)						
(cutting and jointing tray) (cont'd)						
Unequal tee						
75 mm wide	5.33	6.31	0.38	9.19	nr	15.50
100 mm wide	5.64	6.67	0.39	9.43	nr	16.11
150 mm wide	6.05	7.16	0.43	10.40	nr	17.56
225 mm wide	7.64	9.04	0.50	12.09	nr	21.14
300 mm wide	9.06	10.72	0.63	15.24	nr	25.96
450 mm wide	14.87	17.60	0.80	19.35	nr	36.95
600 mm wide	19.70	23.31	1.02	24.67	nr	47.99
750 mm wide	28.70	33.97	1.12	27.09	nr	61.06
900 mm wide	39.81	47.11	1.35	32.65	nr	79.77
4 way crossovers						
50 mm wide	7.14	8.45	0.38	9.19	nr	17.64
75 mm wide	7.23	8.56	0.40	9.68	nr	18.23
100 mm wide	7.68	9.09	0.40	9.68	nr	18.76
150 mm wide	8.30	9.82	0.44	10.64	nr	20.47
225 mm wide	10.20	12.07	0.53	12.82	nr	24.89
300 mm wide	13.43	15.89	0.64	15.48	nr	31.37
450 mm wide	20.30	24.02	0.84	20.32	nr	44.34
600 mm wide	26.27	31.09	1.03	24.91	nr	56.00
750 mm wide	38.24	45.26	1.13	27.33	nr	72.59
900 mm wide	54.54	64.55	1.36	32.90	nr	97.44
Medium duty tray with return flange						
Straight lengths						
75 mm wide	2.34	2.77	0.33	7.98	m	10.75
100 mm wide	2.57	3.04	0.35	8.47	m	11.51
150 mm wide	3.12	3.69	0.39	9.43	m	13.13
225 mm wide	3.63	4.30	0.45	10.88	m	15.18
300 mm wide	3.63	4.30	0.57	13.79	m	18.08
450 mm wide	7.59	8.98	0.69	16.69	m	25.67
600 mm wide	10.55	12.49	0.91	22.01	m	34.50
Extra over; (cutting and jointing tray to fittings is included.)						
Straight reducer						
100 mm wide	6.75	7.99	0.25	6.05	nr	14.04
150 mm wide	7.37	8.72	0.27	6.53	nr	15.25
225 mm wide	8.49	10.05	0.34	8.22	nr	18.27
300 mm wide	9.81	11.61	0.39	9.43	nr	21.04
450 mm wide	12.63	14.95	0.49	11.85	nr	26.80
600 mm wide	15.65	18.52	0.54	13.06	nr	31.58

V: ELECTRICAL SUPPLY/POWER/LIGHTING SYSTEMS

Item	Net Price £	Material £	Labour hours	Labour £	Unit	Total rate £
Flat bend; 90°						
75 mm wide	8.99	10.64	0.24	5.81	nr	**16.44**
100 mm wide	9.99	11.82	0.28	6.77	nr	**18.60**
150 mm wide	10.55	12.49	0.30	7.26	nr	**19.74**
225 mm wide	12.21	14.45	0.36	8.71	nr	**23.16**
300 mm wide	15.05	17.81	0.44	10.64	nr	**28.45**
450 mm wide	22.55	26.69	0.57	13.79	nr	**40.47**
600 mm wide	27.24	32.24	0.69	16.69	nr	**48.93**
Adjustable bend						
75 mm wide	8.99	10.64	0.29	7.01	nr	**17.65**
100 mm wide	9.99	11.82	0.32	7.74	nr	**19.56**
150 mm wide	10.55	12.49	0.36	8.71	nr	**21.19**
225 mm wide	12.21	14.45	0.44	10.64	nr	**25.09**
300 mm wide	15.05	17.81	0.52	12.58	nr	**30.39**
Adjustable riser						
75 mm wide	6.87	8.13	0.29	7.01	nr	**15.15**
100 mm wide	6.99	8.27	0.32	7.74	nr	**16.01**
150 mm wide	8.10	9.59	0.36	8.71	nr	**18.29**
225 mm wide	8.99	10.64	0.44	10.64	nr	**21.28**
300 mm wide	9.81	11.61	0.52	12.58	nr	**24.19**
450 mm wide	14.13	16.72	0.66	15.96	nr	**32.69**
600 mm wide	18.35	21.72	0.79	19.11	nr	**40.83**
Inside riser; 90°						
75 mm wide	5.79	6.85	0.31	7.50	nr	**14.35**
100 mm wide	5.87	6.95	0.33	7.98	nr	**14.93**
150 mm wide	6.69	7.92	0.37	8.95	nr	**16.87**
225 mm wide	8.10	9.59	0.44	10.64	nr	**20.23**
300 mm wide	9.81	11.61	0.53	12.82	nr	**24.43**
450 mm wide	14.13	16.72	0.67	16.21	nr	**32.93**
600 mm wide	22.59	26.73	0.79	19.11	nr	**45.84**
Outside riser; 90°						
75 mm wide	5.79	6.85	0.31	7.50	nr	**14.35**
100 mm wide	5.87	6.95	0.33	7.98	nr	**14.93**
150 mm wide	6.69	7.92	0.37	8.95	nr	**16.87**
225 mm wide	8.10	9.59	0.44	10.64	nr	**20.23**
300 mm wide	9.81	11.61	0.53	12.82	nr	**24.43**
450 mm wide	14.13	16.72	0.67	16.21	nr	**32.93**
600 mm wide	22.59	26.73	0.79	19.11	nr	**45.84**
Equal tee						
75 mm wide	12.81	15.16	0.31	7.50	nr	**22.66**
100 mm wide	13.64	16.14	0.35	8.47	nr	**24.61**
150 mm wide	14.69	17.39	0.36	8.71	nr	**26.09**
225 mm wide	15.93	18.85	0.74	17.90	nr	**36.75**
300 mm wide	19.31	22.85	0.54	13.06	nr	**35.91**
450 mm wide	25.38	30.04	0.71	17.17	nr	**47.21**
600 mm wide	36.38	43.05	0.92	22.25	nr	**65.31**
Unequal tee						
100 mm wide	13.64	16.14	0.39	9.43	nr	**25.58**
150 mm wide	13.64	16.14	0.43	10.40	nr	**26.54**
225 mm wide	15.93	18.85	0.50	12.09	nr	**30.95**
300 mm wide	19.31	22.85	0.63	15.24	nr	**38.09**
450 mm wide	25.38	30.04	0.80	19.35	nr	**49.39**
600 mm wide	36.38	43.05	1.02	24.67	nr	**67.73**

V: ELECTRICAL SUPPLY/POWER/LIGHTING SYSTEMS

Item	Net Price £	Material £	Labour hours	Labour £	Unit	Total rate £
V20 : LV DISTRIBUTION (cont'd)						
Y63 - CABLE SUPPORTS (cont'd)						
CABLE TRAY (cont'd)						
Medium duty tray (cont'd)						
(cutting and jointing tray) (cont'd)						
4 way crossovers						
75 mm wide	18.14	21.47	0.40	9.68	nr	**31.14**
100 mm wide	19.55	23.14	0.40	9.68	nr	**32.81**
150 mm wide	20.63	24.41	0.44	10.64	nr	**35.06**
225 mm wide	24.50	29.00	0.53	12.82	nr	**41.81**
300 mm wide	28.44	33.66	0.64	15.48	nr	**49.14**
450 mm wide	36.18	42.82	0.84	20.32	nr	**63.14**
600 mm wide	52.64	62.30	1.03	24.91	nr	**87.21**
Heavy duty tray with return flange						
Straight lengths						
75 mm	4.23	5.01	0.34	8.22	m	**13.23**
100 mm	4.52	5.35	0.36	8.71	m	**14.06**
150 mm	5.19	6.14	0.40	9.68	m	**15.82**
225 mm	5.82	6.89	0.46	11.13	m	**18.01**
300 mm	7.05	8.34	0.58	14.03	m	**22.37**
450 mm	10.62	12.57	0.70	16.93	m	**29.50**
600 mm	12.86	15.22	0.92	22.25	m	**37.47**
750 mm	16.17	19.14	1.01	24.43	m	**43.57**
900 mm	17.88	21.16	1.14	27.57	m	**48.74**
Extra over; (cutting and jointing tray to fittings is included.)						
Straight reducer						
100 mm wide	9.41	11.14	0.25	6.05	nr	**17.18**
150 mm wide	10.22	12.10	0.27	6.53	nr	**18.63**
225 mm wide	10.67	12.63	0.34	8.22	nr	**20.85**
300 mm wide	11.01	13.03	0.39	9.43	nr	**22.46**
450 mm wide	18.93	22.40	0.49	11.85	nr	**34.26**
600 mm wide	23.25	27.52	0.54	13.06	nr	**40.58**
750 mm wide	28.80	34.08	0.60	14.51	nr	**48.60**
900 mm wide	33.96	40.19	0.66	15.96	nr	**56.16**
Flat bend; 90°						
75 mm wide	12.14	14.37	0.24	5.81	nr	**20.17**
100 mm wide	13.82	16.36	0.28	6.77	nr	**23.13**
150 mm wide	14.73	17.43	0.30	7.26	nr	**24.69**
225 mm wide	16.67	19.73	0.36	8.71	nr	**28.44**
300 mm wide	19.01	22.50	0.44	10.64	nr	**33.14**
450 mm wide	27.90	33.02	0.57	13.79	nr	**46.81**
600 mm wide	37.31	44.16	0.69	16.69	nr	**60.85**
750 mm wide	50.03	59.21	0.83	20.08	nr	**79.29**
900 mm wide	56.73	67.14	1.01	24.43	nr	**91.57**

V: ELECTRICAL SUPPLY/POWER/LIGHTING SYSTEMS

Item	Net Price £	Material £	Labour hours	Labour £	Unit	Total rate £
Adjustable bend						
75 mm wide	12.14	14.37	0.29	7.01	nr	**21.38**
100 mm wide	13.82	16.36	0.32	7.74	nr	**24.10**
150 mm wide	14.73	17.43	0.36	8.71	nr	**26.14**
225 mm wide	16.67	19.73	0.44	10.64	nr	**30.37**
300 mm wide	19.01	22.50	0.52	12.58	nr	**35.08**
Adjustable riser						
75 mm wide	10.26	12.14	0.29	7.01	nr	**19.16**
100 mm wide	10.80	12.78	0.32	7.74	nr	**20.52**
150 mm wide	12.26	14.51	0.36	8.71	nr	**23.22**
225 mm wide	13.55	16.04	0.44	10.64	nr	**26.68**
300 mm wide	14.79	17.50	0.52	12.58	nr	**30.08**
450 mm wide	18.93	22.40	0.66	15.96	nr	**38.37**
600 mm wide	23.25	27.52	0.79	19.11	nr	**46.62**
750 mm wide	28.80	34.08	1.03	24.91	nr	**59.00**
900 mm wide	33.96	40.19	1.10	26.61	nr	**66.80**
Inside riser; 90°						
75 mm wide	9.29	10.99	0.31	7.50	nr	**18.49**
100 mm wide	9.41	11.14	0.33	7.98	nr	**19.12**
150 mm wide	10.22	12.10	0.37	8.95	nr	**21.04**
225 mm wide	10.67	12.63	0.44	10.64	nr	**23.27**
300 mm wide	11.01	13.03	0.53	12.82	nr	**25.85**
450 mm wide	18.93	22.40	0.67	16.21	nr	**38.61**
600 mm wide	23.25	27.52	0.79	19.11	nr	**46.62**
750 mm wide	28.80	34.08	0.95	22.98	nr	**57.06**
900 mm wide	33.96	40.19	1.11	26.85	nr	**67.04**
Outside riser; 90°						
75 mm wide	9.29	10.99	0.31	7.50	nr	**18.49**
100 mm wide	9.41	11.14	0.33	7.98	nr	**19.12**
150 mm wide	10.22	12.10	0.37	8.95	nr	**21.04**
225 mm wide	10.67	12.63	0.44	10.64	nr	**23.27**
300 mm wide	11.01	13.03	0.53	12.82	nr	**25.85**
450 mm wide	18.93	22.40	0.67	16.21	nr	**38.61**
600 mm wide	23.25	27.52	0.79	19.11	nr	**46.62**
750 mm wide	28.80	34.08	0.95	22.98	nr	**57.06**
900 mm wide	33.96	40.19	1.11	26.85	nr	**67.04**
Equal tee						
75 mm wide	16.22	19.20	0.31	7.50	nr	**26.69**
100 mm wide	18.12	21.44	0.35	8.47	nr	**29.91**
150 mm wide	19.85	23.49	0.36	8.71	nr	**32.20**
225 mm wide	22.86	27.05	0.74	17.90	nr	**44.95**
300 mm wide	24.74	29.28	0.54	13.06	nr	**42.34**
450 mm wide	35.97	42.57	0.71	17.17	nr	**59.74**
600 mm wide	47.52	56.24	0.92	22.25	nr	**78.49**
750 mm wide	62.72	74.23	1.19	28.78	nr	**103.01**
900 mm wide	71.64	84.78	1.45	35.07	nr	**119.86**

V: ELECTRICAL SUPPLY/POWER/LIGHTING SYSTEMS

Item	Net Price £	Material £	Labour hours	Labour £	Unit	Total rate £
V20 : LV DISTRIBUTION (cont'd)						
Y63 - CABLE SUPPORTS (cont'd)						
CABLE TRAY (cont'd)						
Heavy duty tray with return flange (cont'd)						
(cutting and jointing tray) (cont'd)						
Unequal tee						
75 mm wide	16.22	19.20	0.38	9.19	nr	**28.39**
100 mm wide	18.12	21.44	0.39	9.43	nr	**30.88**
150 mm wide	19.85	23.49	0.43	10.40	nr	**33.89**
225 mm wide	22.86	27.05	0.50	12.09	nr	**39.15**
300 mm wide	24.74	29.28	0.63	15.24	nr	**44.52**
450 mm wide	35.97	42.57	0.80	19.35	nr	**61.92**
600 mm wide	47.52	56.24	1.02	24.67	nr	**80.91**
750 mm wide	62.72	74.23	1.12	27.09	nr	**101.32**
900 mm wide	71.64	84.78	1.35	32.65	nr	**117.44**
4 way crossovers						
75 mm wide	22.77	26.95	0.40	9.68	nr	**36.62**
100 mm wide	23.58	27.91	0.40	9.68	nr	**37.58**
150 mm wide	28.83	34.12	0.44	10.64	nr	**44.76**
225 mm wide	32.69	38.69	0.53	12.82	nr	**51.51**
300 mm wide	36.56	43.27	0.64	15.48	nr	**58.75**
450 mm wide	52.19	61.77	0.84	20.32	nr	**82.08**
600 mm wide	65.03	76.96	1.03	24.91	nr	**101.88**
750 mm wide	86.60	102.49	1.13	27.33	nr	**129.82**
900 mm wide	104.48	123.65	1.36	32.90	nr	**156.55**
GRP cable tray including standard coupling joints and fixings; (supports and hangers excluded).						
Tray						
100 mm wide	16.82	19.91	0.34	8.22	m	**28.13**
200 mm wide	21.52	25.47	0.39	9.43	m	**34.90**
400 mm wide	33.76	39.95	0.53	12.82	m	**52.77**
Cover						
100 mm wide	9.47	11.21	0.10	2.42	m	**13.63**
200 mm wide	12.55	14.85	0.11	2.66	m	**17.51**
400 mm wide	21.44	25.37	0.14	3.39	m	**28.76**
Extra for; (cutting and jointing to fittings included).						
Reducer						
200 mm wide	44.69	52.89	0.23	5.56	nr	**58.45**
400 mm wide	58.38	69.09	0.30	7.26	nr	**76.35**
Reducer cover						
200 mm wide	27.97	33.10	0.25	6.05	nr	**39.15**
400 mm wide	40.88	48.38	0.28	6.77	nr	**55.15**

V: ELECTRICAL SUPPLY/POWER/LIGHTING SYSTEMS

Item	Net Price £	Material £	Labour hours	Labour £	Unit	Total rate £
Bend						
100 mm wide	37.37	44.23	0.34	8.22	nr	**52.45**
200 mm wide	43.38	51.34	0.40	9.68	nr	**61.01**
400 mm wide	55.74	65.97	0.32	7.74	nr	**73.71**
Bend cover						
100 mm wide	18.56	21.97	0.10	2.42	nr	**24.38**
200 mm wide	24.80	29.35	0.10	2.42	nr	**31.77**
400 mm wide	34.27	40.56	0.13	3.14	nr	**43.70**
Tee						
100 mm wide	47.56	56.29	0.37	8.95	nr	**65.24**
200 mm wide	52.44	62.06	0.43	10.40	nr	**72.46**
400 mm wide	65.05	76.98	0.56	13.55	nr	**90.53**
Tee cover						
100 mm wide	23.95	28.34	0.27	6.53	nr	**34.88**
200 mm wide	28.84	34.13	0.31	7.50	nr	**41.63**
400 mm wide	40.69	48.16	0.37	8.95	nr	**57.11**
BASKET TRAY						
Mild Steel Cable Basket; Zinc Plated Including Standard Coupling Joints, Fixings and Earth Continuity Straps (supports and hangers are excluded)						
Basket 54mm deep						
100 mm wide	2.35	2.78	0.22	5.32	m	**8.10**
150 mm wide	2.62	3.10	0.25	6.05	m	**9.15**
200 mm wide	2.87	3.40	0.28	6.77	m	**10.17**
300 mm wide	3.37	3.99	0.34	8.22	m	**12.21**
450 mm wide	4.08	4.83	0.44	10.64	m	**15.47**
600 mm wide	4.99	5.91	0.70	16.93	m	**22.84**
Extra for; (cutting and jointing to fittings is included)						
Reducer						
150 mm wide	8.34	9.87	0.25	6.05	nr	**15.92**
200 mm wide	9.79	11.59	0.28	6.77	nr	**18.36**
300 mm wide	9.95	11.78	0.38	9.19	nr	**20.97**
450 mm wide	10.93	12.94	0.48	11.61	nr	**24.55**
600 mm wide	13.61	16.11	0.48	11.61	nr	**27.72**
Bend						
100 mm wide	7.97	9.43	0.23	5.56	nr	**15.00**
150 mm wide	9.34	11.05	0.26	6.29	nr	**17.34**
200 mm wide	9.50	11.24	0.30	7.26	nr	**18.50**
300 mm wide	10.40	12.31	0.35	8.47	nr	**20.77**
450 mm wide	12.95	15.33	0.50	12.09	nr	**27.42**
600 mm wide	15.25	18.05	0.58	14.03	nr	**32.08**
Tee						
100 mm wide	10.02	11.86	0.28	6.77	nr	**18.63**
150 mm wide	10.63	12.58	0.30	7.26	nr	**19.84**
200 mm wide	10.84	12.83	0.33	7.98	nr	**20.81**
300 mm wide	13.64	16.14	0.39	9.43	nr	**25.58**
450 mm wide	17.87	21.15	0.56	13.55	nr	**34.69**
600 mm wide	18.48	21.87	0.65	15.72	nr	**37.59**

V: ELECTRICAL SUPPLY/POWER/LIGHTING SYSTEMS

Item	Net Price £	Material £	Labour hours	Labour £	Unit	Total rate £
V20 : LV DISTRIBUTION (cont'd)						
Y63 - CABLE SUPPORTS (cont'd)						
BASKET TRAY (cont'd)						
Mild Steel Cable Basket; Zinc Plated (cont'd)						
(cutting and jointing tray) (cont'd)						
Cross over						
100 mm wide	13.67	16.18	0.40	9.68	nr	**25.85**
150 mm wide	13.91	16.46	0.42	10.16	nr	**26.62**
200 mm wide	15.10	17.87	0.46	11.13	nr	**29.00**
300 mm wide	17.15	20.30	0.51	12.34	nr	**32.63**
450 mm wide	20.10	23.79	0.74	17.90	nr	**41.69**
600 mm wide	20.75	24.56	0.82	19.83	nr	**44.39**
Mild steel cable basket; expoxy coated including standard coupling joints, fixings and earth continuity straps (supports and hangers are excluded)						
Basket 54mm deep						
100 mm wide	5.71	6.76	0.22	5.32	m	**12.08**
150 mm wide	6.46	7.65	0.25	6.05	m	**13.69**
200 mm wide	7.19	8.51	0.28	6.77	m	**15.28**
300 mm wide	8.17	9.67	0.34	8.22	m	**17.89**
450 mm wide	10.08	11.93	0.44	10.64	m	**22.57**
600 mm wide	11.47	13.57	0.70	16.93	m	**30.51**
Extra for; (cutting and jointing to fittings is included)						
Reducer						
150 mm wide	11.94	14.13	0.28	6.77	nr	**20.90**
200 mm wide	13.39	15.85	0.28	6.77	nr	**22.62**
300 mm wide	14.27	16.89	0.38	9.19	nr	**26.08**
450 mm wide	16.69	19.75	0.48	11.61	nr	**31.36**
600 mm wide	20.81	24.63	0.48	11.61	nr	**36.24**
Bend						
100 mm wide	11.57	13.69	0.23	5.56	nr	**19.26**
150 mm wide	12.94	15.31	0.26	6.29	nr	**21.60**
200 mm wide	13.10	15.50	0.30	7.26	nr	**22.76**
300 mm wide	14.74	17.44	0.35	8.47	nr	**25.91**
450 mm wide	18.71	22.14	0.50	12.09	nr	**34.24**
600 mm wide	22.45	26.57	0.58	14.03	nr	**40.60**
Tee						
100 mm wide	13.62	16.12	0.28	6.77	nr	**22.89**
150 mm wide	14.23	16.84	0.30	7.26	nr	**24.10**
200 mm wide	14.45	17.10	0.33	7.98	nr	**25.08**
300 mm wide	17.96	21.26	0.39	9.43	nr	**30.69**
450 mm wide	22.90	27.10	0.56	13.55	nr	**40.65**
600 mm wide	25.68	30.39	0.65	15.72	nr	**46.11**

V: ELECTRICAL SUPPLY/POWER/LIGHTING SYSTEMS

Item	Net Price £	Material £	Labour hours	Labour £	Unit	Total rate £
Cross over						
100 mm wide	17.27	20.44	0.40	9.68	nr	**30.11**
150 mm wide	17.46	20.66	0.42	10.16	nr	**30.82**
200 mm wide	18.71	22.14	0.46	11.13	nr	**33.27**
300 mm wide	21.47	25.41	0.51	12.34	nr	**37.75**
450 mm wide	25.86	30.60	0.74	17.90	nr	**48.50**
600 mm wide	27.95	33.08	0.82	19.83	nr	**52.91**

V: ELECTRICAL SUPPLY/POWER/LIGHTING SYSTEMS

Item	Net Price £	Material £	Labour hours	Labour £	Unit	Total rate £
V20 : LV DISTRIBUTION (cont'd)						
Y71 - LV SWITCHGEAR & DISTRIBUTION BOARDS						
LV switchboard components, factory-assembled modular construction to IP41; form 4, type 5; 2400mm high, with front and rear access; top cable entry/exit; includes delivery, offloading, positioning and commissioning (hence separate labour costs are not detailed below); excludes cabling and cable terminations						
Air circuit breakers (ACBs) to BSEN 60947-2, withdrawable type, fitted with adjustable instantaneous and overload protection. Includes enclosure and copper links, assembled into LV switchboard.						
ACB-100 kA fault rated.						
4 pole, 6300 A (1600mm wide)	23995.25	28397.66	-	-	nr	**28397.66**
4 pole, 5000 A (1600mm wide)	18131.81	21458.46	-	-	nr	**21458.46**
4 pole, 4000 A (1600mm wide)	15211.20	18002.00	-	-	nr	**18002.00**
4 pole, 3200 A (1600mm wide)	10269.09	12153.16	-	-	nr	**12153.16**
4 pole, 2500 A (1600mm wide)	7981.17	9445.47	-	-	nr	**9445.47**
4 pole, 2000 A (1600mm wide)	6222.00	7363.55	-	-	nr	**7363.55**
4 pole, 1600 A (1600mm wide)	5094.15	6028.77	-	-	nr	**6028.77**
4 pole, 1250 A (1600mm wide)	4508.67	5335.88	-	-	nr	**5335.88**
4 pole, 1000 A (1600mm wide)	4454.21	5271.42	-	-	nr	**5271.42**
4 pole, 800 A (1600mm wide)	4378.86	5182.25	-	-	nr	**5182.25**
3 pole, 6300 A (1600mm wide)	21741.83	25730.80	-	-	nr	**25730.80**
3 pole, 5000 A (1600mm wide)	15247.51	18044.98	-	-	nr	**18044.98**
3 pole, 4000 A (1600mm wide)	12485.75	14776.51	-	-	nr	**14776.51**
3 pole, 3200 A (1600mm wide)	8573.92	10146.98	-	-	nr	**10146.98**
3 pole, 2500 A (1600mm wide)	6864.67	8124.13	-	-	nr	**8124.13**
3 pole, 2000 A (1600mm wide)	5169.03	6117.40	-	-	nr	**6117.40**
3 pole, 1600 A (1600mm wide)	4202.31	4973.31	-	-	nr	**4973.31**
3 pole, 1250 A (1600mm wide)	3907.30	4624.17	-	-	nr	**4624.17**
3 pole, 1000 A (1600mm wide)	3823.34	4524.80	-	-	nr	**4524.80**
3 pole, 800 A (1600mm wide)	3750.26	4438.32	-	-	nr	**4438.32**
ACB-65 kA fault rated.						
4 pole, 4000 A (1600mm wide)	13348.10	15797.08	-	-	nr	**15797.08**
4 pole, 3200 A (1600mm wide)	9030.05	10686.79	-	-	nr	**10686.79**
4 pole, 2500 A (1600mm wide)	7098.41	8400.75	-	-	nr	**8400.75**
4 pole, 2000 A (1600mm wide)	5645.58	6681.38	-	-	nr	**6681.38**
4 pole, 1600 A (1600mm wide)	4658.44	5513.13	-	-	nr	**5513.13**
4 pole, 1250 A (1600mm wide)	4159.19	4922.28	-	-	nr	**4922.28**
4 pole, 1000 A (1600mm wide)	4079.76	4828.28	-	-	nr	**4828.28**
4 pole, 800 A (1600mm wide)	4006.69	4741.80	-	-	nr	**4741.80**
3 pole, 4000 A (1600mm wide)	11307.98	13382.65	-	-	nr	**13382.65**
3 pole, 3200 A (1600mm wide)	7668.46	9075.40	-	-	nr	**9075.40**
3 pole, 2500 A (1600mm wide)	5963.75	7057.92	-	-	nr	**7057.92**
3 pole, 2000 A (1600mm wide)	4740.14	5609.81	-	-	nr	**5609.81**
3 pole, 1600 A (1600mm wide)	3877.80	4589.26	-	-	nr	**4589.26**
3 pole, 1250 A (1600mm wide)	3610.03	4272.36	-	-	nr	**4272.36**
3 pole, 1000 A (1600mm wide)	3528.33	4175.67	-	-	nr	**4175.67**
3 pole, 800 A (1600mm wide)	3455.25	4089.18	-	-	nr	**4089.18**

V: ELECTRICAL SUPPLY/POWER/LIGHTING SYSTEMS

Item	Net Price £	Material £	Labour hours	Labour £	Unit	Total rate £
Extra for						
Cable box (one per ACB for form 4, types 6 & 7)	224.18	265.30	-	-	nr	265.30
Opening Coil	66.89	79.16	-	-	nr	79.16
Closing Coil	66.89	79.16	-	-	nr	79.16
Undervoltage Release	131.38	155.49	-	-	nr	155.49
Motor Operator	406.09	480.59	-	-	nr	480.59
Mechnical Interlock (per ACB)	382.20	452.32	-	-	nr	452.32
ACB Fortress/Castell Adaptor Kit (one per ACB)	95.55	113.08	-	-	nr	113.08
Fortress/Castell ACB Lock (one per ACB)	191.10	226.16	-	-	nr	226.16
Fortress/Castell Key	47.77	56.54	-	-	nr	56.54
Moulded case circuit breakers (MCCBs) to BS EN 60947-2; plug-in type, fitted with electronic trip unit. Includes metalwork section and copper links, assembled into LV switchboard						
MCCB-150 kA fault rated						
4 Pole, 630 A (800mm wide, 600mm high)	2260.18	2674.85	-	-	nr	2674.85
4 Pole, 400 A (800mm wide, 400mm high)	1616.99	1913.66	-	-	nr	1913.66
4 Pole, 250 A (800mm wide, 400mm high)	1446.07	1711.38	-	-	nr	1711.38
4 Pole, 160 A (800mm wide, 300mm high)	982.78	1163.09	-	-	nr	1163.09
4 Pole, 100 A (800mm wide, 200mm high)	818.61	968.80	-	-	nr	968.80
3 Pole, 630 A (800mm wide, 600mm high)	2017.29	2387.40	-	-	nr	2387.40
3 Pole, 400 A (800mm wide, 400mm high)	1540.52	1823.16	-	-	nr	1823.16
3 Pole, 250 A (800mm wide, 400mm high)	1241.41	1469.17	-	-	nr	1469.17
3 Pole, 160 A (800mm wide, 300mm high)	908.57	1075.27	-	-	nr	1075.27
3 Pole, 100 A (800mm wide, 200mm high)	726.40	859.67	-	-	nr	859.67
MCCB-70kA fault rated						
4 Pole, 630 A (800mm wide, 600mm high)	1936.33	2291.59	-	-	nr	2291.59
4 Pole, 400 A (800mm wide, 400mm high)	1331.37	1575.64	-	-	nr	1575.64
4 Pole, 250 A (800mm wide, 400mm high)	1144.70	1354.72	-	-	nr	1354.72
4 Pole, 160 A (800mm wide, 300mm high)	859.09	1016.70	-	-	nr	1016.70
4 Pole, 100 A (800mm wide, 200mm high)	647.69	766.53	-	-	nr	766.53
3 Pole, 630 A (800mm wide, 600mm high)	1695.70	2006.81	-	-	nr	2006.81
3 Pole, 400 A (800mm wide, 400mm high)	1149.21	1360.05	-	-	nr	1360.05
3 Pole, 250 A (800mm wide, 400mm high)	1014.27	1200.36	-	-	nr	1200.36
3 Pole, 160 A (800mm wide, 300mm high)	748.89	886.29	-	-	nr	886.29
3 Pole, 100 A (800mm wide, 200mm high)	550.99	652.08	-	-	nr	652.08
MCCB-45kA fault rated						
4 Pole, 630 A (800mm wide, 600mm high)	1877.86	2222.40	-	-	nr	2222.40
4 Pole, 400 A (800mm wide, 400mm high)	1290.89	1527.74	-	-	nr	1527.74
3 Pole, 630 A (800mm wide, 600mm high)	1623.74	1921.64	-	-	nr	1921.64
3 Pole, 400 A (800mm wide, 400mm high)	1106.48	1309.48	-	-	nr	1309.48
MCCB-36kA fault rated						
4 Pole, 250 A (800mm wide, 400mm high)	1095.23	1296.18	-	-	nr	1296.18
4 Pole, 160 A (800mm wide, 300mm high)	829.85	982.11	-	-	nr	982.11
3 Pole, 250 A (800mm wide, 400mm high)	622.08	736.21	-	-	nr	736.21
3 Pole, 160 A (800mm wide, 300mm high)	547.82	648.33	-	-	nr	648.33

V: ELECTRICAL SUPPLY/POWER/LIGHTING SYSTEMS

Item	Net Price £	Material £	Labour hours	Labour £	Unit	Total rate £
V20 : LV DISTRIBUTION (cont'd)						
Y71 - LV SWITCHGEAR & DISTRIBUTION BOARDS (cont'd)						
LV switchboard components (cont'd)						
Moulded case circuit breakers (cont'd)						
Extra for						
Cable box (one per MCCB - form 4, types 6 & 7)	94.69	112.07	-	-	nr	**112.07**
Shunt trip (for ratings 100A to 630A)	33.14	39.22	-	-	nr	**39.22**
Undervoltage release (for ratings 100A to 630A)	47.35	56.03	-	-	nr	**56.03**
Motor operator for 630A MCCB	449.79	532.31	-	-	nr	**532.31**
Motor operator for 400A MCCB	449.79	532.31	-	-	nr	**532.31**
Motor operator for 250A MCCB	374.03	442.66	-	-	nr	**442.66**
Motor operator for 160A/100A MCCB	239.10	282.96	-	-	nr	**282.96**
Door handle for 630/400A MCCB	59.18	70.04	-	-	nr	**70.04**
Door handle for 250/160/100A MCCB	47.35	56.03	-	-	nr	**56.03**
MCCB earth fault protection	355.10	420.24	-	-	nr	**420.24**
Copper busbar assembled into LV switchboard, ASTA type tested to appropriate fault level. Busbar Length may be estimated by adding the widths of the ACB sections to the width of the MCCB sections. ACB's up to 2000A rating may be stacked two high; larger ratings are one per section. To determine the number of MCCB sections, add together all the MCCB heights and divide by 1800mm, rounding up as necessary						
LV switchboard busbar						
6000 A (6 x 10mm x 100mm)	1795.29	2124.68	-	-	nr	**2124.68**
5000 A (4 x 10mm x 100mm)	1476.13	1746.96	-	-	nr	**1746.96**
4000 A (4 x 10mm x 100mm)	1476.13	1746.96	-	-	nr	**1746.96**
3200 A (3 x 10mm x 100mm)	1024.82	1212.84	-	-	nr	**1212.84**
2500 A (2 x 10mm x 100mm)	865.24	1023.98	-	-	nr	**1023.98**
2000 A (2 x 10mm x 80mm)	635.82	752.48	-	-	nr	**752.48**
1600 A (2 x 10mm x 50mm)	461.29	545.92	-	-	nr	**545.92**
1250 A (2 x 10mm x 40mm)	361.55	427.88	-	-	nr	**427.88**
1000 A (2 x 10mm x 30mm)	361.55	427.88	-	-	nr	**427.88**
800 A (2 x 10mm x 20mm)	281.76	333.45	-	-	nr	**333.45**
630 A (2 x 10mm x 20mm)	281.76	333.45	-	-	nr	**333.45**
400 A (2 x 10mm x 10mm)	241.67	286.01	-	-	nr	**286.01**
Automatic power factor correction (PFC); floor standing steel enclosure to IP 42, complete with microprocessor based relay and status indication; includes delivery, offloading, positioning and commissioning; excludes cabling and cable terminations						
Standard PFC (no de-tuning)	-	-	-	-	nr	**-**
100 kVAr	3727.63	4411.54	-	-	nr	**4411.54**
200 kVAr	5213.48	6170.00	-	-	nr	**6170.00**
400 kVAr	8899.71	10532.54	-	-	nr	**10532.54**
600 kVAr	12190.82	14427.46	-	-	nr	**14427.46**

V: ELECTRICAL SUPPLY/POWER/LIGHTING SYSTEMS

Item	Net Price £	Material £	Labour hours	Labour £	Unit	Total rate £
PFC with de-tuning reactors						
100 kVAr	6065.24	7178.03	-	-	nr	**7178.03**
200 kVAr	8476.19	10031.32	-	-	nr	**10031.32**
400 kVAr	14607.68	17287.76	-	-	nr	**17287.76**
600 kVAr	21482.10	25423.42	-	-	nr	**25423.42**
AUTOMATIC TRANSFER SWITCHES						
Automatic transfer switches; steel enclosure; solenoid operating; programmable controller, keypad and LCD display; fixed to backgrounds; including commissioning and testing						
Panel Mounting type 3 pole or 4 pole; overlapping neutral						
100 amp	2577.88	3050.84	2.60	62.89	nr	**3113.73**
260amp	3595.16	4254.76	3.30	79.82	nr	**4334.59**
400amp	4381.24	5185.07	4.30	104.01	nr	**5289.08**
600amp	5629.72	6662.60	5.30	128.20	nr	**6790.80**
800amp	7120.96	8427.44	5.50	133.04	nr	**8560.48**
1000amp	11328.80	13407.29	5.83	141.02	nr	**13548.31**
1600amp	12138.00	14364.96	6.20	149.97	nr	**14514.93**
2000amp	14912.40	17648.38	6.90	166.90	nr	**17815.28**
Enclosed type 3 pole or 4 pole; over lapping neutral						
100 amp	3643.71	4312.22	2.60	62.89	nr	**4375.11**
260amp	4660.99	5516.14	3.30	79.82	nr	**5595.97**
400amp	5447.07	6446.45	4.30	104.01	nr	**6550.46**
600amp	7060.85	8356.30	4.84	117.07	nr	**8473.37**
800amp	8552.09	10121.14	5.12	123.85	nr	**10244.98**
1000amp	12759.93	15100.99	5.50	133.04	nr	**15234.03**
1600amp	14914.71	17651.11	6.20	149.97	nr	**17801.08**
2000amp	17689.11	20934.53	6.90	166.90	nr	**21101.43**
3000amp	21272.71	25175.62	6.20	149.97	nr	**25325.59**
4000amp	26038.90	30816.26	6.90	166.90	nr	**30983.16**
MCCB panelboards; IP4X construction, 50kA busbars and fully-rated neutral; fitted with doorlock, removable glandplate; form 3b Type2; BSEN 60439-1; including fixing to backgrounds Panelboards cubicle with MCCB incomer						
Up to 250A						
4 Way TPN	666.95	789.32	1.00	24.19	nr	**813.51**
Extra over for integral incomer metering	683.10	808.43	1.50	35.54	nr	**843.97**
Up to 630A						
6 way TPN	1199.77	1419.89	2.00	48.38	nr	**1468.27**
12 way TPN	1355.02	1603.63	2.50	60.47	nr	**1664.10**
18 Way TPN	1577.34	1866.73	3.00	72.57	nr	**1939.30**

V: ELECTRICAL SUPPLY/POWER/LIGHTING SYSTEMS

Item	Net Price £	Material £	Labour hours	Labour £	Unit	Total rate £
V20 : LV DISTRIBUTION (cont'd)						
Y71 - LV SWITCHGEAR & DISTRIBUTION BOARDS (cont'd)						
AUTOMATIC TRANSFER SWITCHES (cont'd)						
MCCB panelboards (cont'd)						
Extra over for integral incomer metering	807.30	955.42	1.50	36.28	nr	**991.70**
Up to 800A						
6 way TPN	2053.03	2429.69	2.00	48.38	nr	**2478.07**
12 way TPN	2462.89	2914.75	2.50	60.47	nr	**2975.22**
18 Way TPN	2621.86	3102.89	3.00	72.57	nr	**3175.46**
Extra over for integral incomer metering	807.30	955.42	1.50	36.28	nr	**991.70**
Up to 1200A						
20 Way TPN	5493.37	6501.23	3.50	84.66	nr	**6585.89**
Up to 1600A						
28 Way TPN	7114.18	8419.41	3.50	84.66	nr	**8504.07**
Up to 2000A						
28Way TPN	7743.87	9164.64	4.00	94.77	nr	**9259.41**
28Way TPN	7743.87	9164.64	4.00	96.75	nr	**9261.39**
Feeder MCCBs						
Single Pole						
32A	54.65	64.67	0.75	18.14	nr	**82.82**
63A	55.89	66.14	0.75	18.14	nr	**84.29**
100A	57.13	67.61	0.75	18.14	nr	**85.76**
160A	60.86	72.02	1.00	24.19	nr	**96.21**
Double pole						
32A	81.97	97.01	0.75	18.14	nr	**115.15**
63A	83.21	98.48	0.75	18.14	nr	**116.62**
100A	121.72	144.05	0.75	18.14	nr	**162.19**
160A	151.52	179.32	1.00	24.19	nr	**203.51**
Triple pole						
32A	109.30	129.35	0.75	18.14	nr	**147.49**
63A	111.78	132.29	0.75	18.14	nr	**150.43**
100A	145.31	171.97	0.75	18.14	nr	**190.12**
160A	187.54	221.95	1.00	24.19	nr	**246.14**
250A	281.93	333.66	1.00	24.19	nr	**357.85**
400A	381.29	451.25	1.25	30.24	nr	**481.49**
630A	625.97	740.81	1.50	36.28	nr	**777.10**

V: ELECTRICAL SUPPLY/POWER/LIGHTING SYSTEMS

Item	Net Price £	Material £	Labour hours	Labour £	Unit	Total rate £
MCB distribution boards; IP3X external protection enclosure; removable earth and neutral bars and DIN rail; 125/250amp incomers; including fixing to backgrounds						
SP & N						
6 way	47.52	56.24	2.00	48.38	nr	**104.62**
8 way	56.35	66.69	2.50	60.47	nr	**127.16**
12 way	64.67	76.53	3.00	72.57	nr	**149.10**
16 way	76.89	90.99	4.00	96.75	nr	**187.75**
24 way	161.95	191.66	5.00	120.94	nr	**312.60**
TP & N						
4 way	344.25	407.41	3.00	72.57	nr	**479.98**
6 way	356.35	421.73	3.50	84.66	nr	**506.39**
8 way	373.31	441.80	4.00	96.75	nr	**538.55**
12 way	397.83	470.82	4.00	96.75	nr	**567.57**
16 way	455.22	538.74	5.00	120.94	nr	**659.68**
24 way	573.29	678.47	6.40	154.81	nr	**833.28**
Miniature circuit breakers for distribution boards; BS EN 60 898; DIN rail mounting; including connecting to circuit						
SP&N; including connecting of wiring						
6 Amp	8.50	10.06	0.10	2.42	nr	**12.48**
10 - 40 Amp	8.83	10.45	0.10	2.42	nr	**12.87**
50 - 63 Amp	9.26	10.95	0.14	3.39	nr	**14.34**
TP&N; including connecting of wiring						
6 Amp	36.00	42.60	0.30	7.26	nr	**49.86**
10 - 40 Amp	37.42	44.29	0.45	10.88	nr	**55.17**
50 - 63 Amp	39.21	46.40	0.45	10.88	nr	**57.29**
Resdiual current circuit breakers for distribution boards; DIN rail mounting; including connecting to circuit						
SP&N						
10mA						
6 Amp	55.75	65.98	0.21	5.08	nr	**71.06**
10 - 32 Amp	54.70	64.73	0.26	6.29	nr	**71.02**
45 Amp	54.70	64.73	0.26	6.29	nr	**71.02**
30mA						
6 Amp	55.75	65.98	0.21	5.08	nr	**71.06**
10 - 40 Amp	54.70	64.73	0.21	5.08	nr	**69.81**
50 -63 Amp	54.70	64.73	0.26	6.29	nr	**71.02**
100mA						
6 Amp	103.09	122.00	0.21	5.08	nr	**127.08**
10 - 40 Amp	103.09	122.00	0.21	5.08	nr	**127.08**
50 -63 Amp	103.09	122.00	0.26	6.29	nr	**128.29**

V: ELECTRICAL SUPPLY/POWER/LIGHTING SYSTEMS

Item	Net Price £	Material £	Labour hours	Labour £	Unit	Total rate £
V20 : LV DISTRIBUTION (cont'd)						
Y71 - LV SWITCHGEAR & DISTRIBUTION BOARDS (cont'd)						
AUTOMATIC TRANSFER SWITCHES (cont'd)						
HRC fused distribution boards; IP4X external protection enclosure; including earth and neutral bars; fixing to backgrounds						
SP&N						
20 Amp incomer						
4 way	108.72	128.67	1.00	24.19	nr	152.86
6 way	131.25	155.33	1.20	29.03	nr	184.36
8 way	153.87	182.10	1.40	33.86	nr	215.97
12 way	199.12	235.65	1.80	43.54	nr	279.19
32 Amp incomer						
4 way	130.91	154.92	1.00	24.19	nr	179.11
6 way	172.15	203.73	1.20	29.03	nr	232.75
8 way	202.53	239.69	1.40	33.86	nr	273.55
12 way	260.76	308.60	1.80	43.54	nr	352.14
TP&N						
20 Amp incomer						
4 way	194.87	230.63	1.50	36.28	nr	266.91
6 way	246.48	291.70	2.10	50.80	nr	342.50
8 way	291.42	344.88	2.70	65.31	nr	410.19
12 way	408.85	483.86	3.90	94.34	nr	578.20
32 Amp incomer						
4 way	233.14	275.91	1.50	36.28	nr	312.19
6 way	312.99	370.42	2.10	50.80	nr	421.22
8 way	382.35	452.50	2.70	65.31	nr	517.81
12 way	530.31	627.61	3.90	94.34	nr	721.94
63 Amp incomer						
4 way	495.57	586.49	2.17	52.49	nr	638.98
6 way	635.56	752.17	2.83	68.45	nr	820.62
8 way	765.39	905.82	2.57	62.16	nr	967.98
100 Amp incomer						
4 way	783.75	927.54	2.40	58.05	nr	985.59
6 way	1024.43	1212.39	2.73	66.03	nr	1278.42
8 way	1252.62	1482.43	3.87	93.61	nr	1576.04
200 Amp incomer						
4 way	1941.27	2297.43	5.36	129.65	nr	2427.08
6 way	2565.79	3036.53	6.17	149.24	nr	3185.77
HRC fuse; includes fixing to fuse holder						
2-30 Amp	2.21	2.62	0.10	2.42	nr	5.04
35 - 63 Amp	4.79	5.67	0.12	2.90	nr	8.57
80 Amp	7.07	8.37	0.15	3.63	nr	12.00
100 Amp	7.07	8.37	0.15	3.63	nr	12.00
125 Amp	12.85	15.21	0.15	3.63	nr	18.83
160 Amp	13.48	15.96	0.15	3.63	nr	19.59
200 Amp	13.96	16.52	0.15	3.63	nr	20.15

V: ELECTRICAL SUPPLY/POWER/LIGHTING SYSTEMS

Item	Net Price £	Material £	Labour hours	Labour £	Unit	Total rate £
Consumer units; fixed to backgrounds; including supports, fixings, connections/jointing to equipment.						
Switched and insulated; moulded plastic case, 63 Amp 230 Volt SP&N; earth and neutral bars; 30mA RCCB protection; fitted MCB's						
2 way	92.65	109.65	1.67	40.39	nr	**150.05**
4 way	103.97	123.04	1.59	38.46	nr	**161.50**
6 way	113.02	133.75	2.50	60.47	nr	**194.22**
8 way	121.95	144.33	3.00	72.57	nr	**216.89**
12 way	141.67	167.66	4.00	96.75	nr	**264.41**
16 way	171.19	202.59	5.50	133.04	nr	**335.63**
Switched and insulated; moulded plastic case, 100 Amp 230 Volt SP&N; earth and neutral bars; 30mA RCCB protection; fitted MCB's						
2 way	92.65	109.65	1.67	40.39	nr	**150.05**
4 way	103.97	123.04	1.59	38.46	nr	**161.50**
6 way	113.02	133.75	2.50	60.47	nr	**194.22**
8 way	121.95	144.33	3.00	72.57	nr	**216.89**
12 way	141.67	167.66	4.00	96.75	nr	**264.41**
16 way	171.19	202.59	5.50	133.04	nr	**335.63**
Extra for Residual current device; double pole; 230 volt/30mA tripping current						
16 Amp	51.91	61.44	0.22	5.32	nr	**66.76**
30 Amp	51.10	60.47	0.22	5.32	nr	**65.79**
40 Amp	52.72	62.39	0.22	5.32	nr	**67.71**
63 Amp	62.80	74.32	0.22	5.32	nr	**79.64**
80 Amp	72.60	85.92	0.22	5.32	nr	**91.24**
100 Amp	89.36	105.76	0.25	6.05	nr	**111.81**
Residual current device; double pole; 230 volt/100mA tripping current						
63 Amp	59.66	70.61	0.22	5.32	nr	**75.93**
80 Amp	69.02	81.69	0.22	5.32	nr	**87.01**
100 Amp	89.38	105.77	0.25	6.05	nr	**111.82**
Heavy duty fuse switches; with HRC fuses BS 5419; short circuit rating 65kA, 500 volt; including retractable operating switches						
SP&N						
63 Amp	193.96	229.54	1.30	31.45	nr	**260.99**
100 Amp	283.52	335.54	1.95	47.17	nr	**382.71**
TP&N						
63 Amp	244.34	289.17	1.83	44.27	nr	**333.44**
100 Amp	343.37	406.37	2.48	59.99	nr	**466.35**
200 Amp	529.67	626.85	3.13	75.71	nr	**702.56**
300 Amp	920.18	1089.01	4.45	107.64	nr	**1196.65**
400 Amp	1010.18	1195.52	4.45	107.64	nr	**1303.16**
600 Amp	1514.24	1792.06	5.72	138.36	nr	**1930.41**
800 Amp	2381.95	2818.97	7.88	190.61	nr	**3009.57**

V: ELECTRICAL SUPPLY/POWER/LIGHTING SYSTEMS

Item	Net Price £	Material £	Labour hours	Labour £	Unit	Total rate £
V20 : LV DISTRIBUTION (cont'd)						
Y71 - LV SWITCHGEAR & DISTRIBUTION BOARDS (cont'd)						
AUTOMATIC TRANSFER SWITCHES (cont'd)						
Switch disconnectors to BSEN 60947-3; in sheet steel case; IP41 with door interlock fixed to backgrounds						
Double pole						
20 Amp	35.59	42.12	1.02	24.67	nr	**66.79**
32 Amp	42.90	50.77	1.02	24.67	nr	**75.44**
63 Amp	156.55	185.27	1.21	29.27	nr	**214.54**
100 Amp	143.18	169.44	1.86	44.99	nr	**214.43**
TP&N						
20 Amp	44.69	52.89	1.29	31.20	nr	**84.09**
32 Amp	51.98	61.52	1.83	44.27	nr	**105.79**
63 Amp	177.89	210.53	2.48	59.99	nr	**270.51**
100 Amp	175.85	208.11	2.48	59.99	nr	**268.10**
125 Amp	184.93	218.86	2.48	59.99	nr	**278.85**
160 Amp	425.50	503.57	2.48	59.99	nr	**563.55**
Enclosed switch disconnector to BSEN 60947-3; enclosure minimum IP55 rating; complete with earth connection bar; fixed to backgrounds.						
TP						
20 Amp	35.59	42.12	1.02	24.67	nr	**66.79**
32 Amp	42.90	50.77	1.02	24.67	nr	**75.44**
63 Amp	156.55	185.27	1.21	29.27	nr	**214.54**
TP&N						
20 Amp	44.69	52.89	1.29	31.20	nr	**84.09**
32 Amp	51.98	61.52	1.83	44.27	nr	**105.79**
63 Amp	177.89	210.53	2.48	59.99	nr	**270.51**
Busbar chambers; fixed to background including all supports, fixings, connections/jointing to equipment. Sheet steel case enclosing 4 pole 550 Volt copper bars, detachable metal end plates						
600mm long						
200 Amp	295.73	349.99	2.62	63.37	nr	**413.36**
300 Amp	380.00	449.72	3.03	73.29	nr	**523.01**
500 Amp	651.12	770.58	4.48	108.36	nr	**878.95**
900mm long						
200 Amp	425.95	504.10	3.04	73.53	nr	**577.63**
300 Amp	502.01	594.11	3.59	86.84	nr	**680.95**
500 Amp	742.56	878.80	4.42	106.91	nr	**985.71**
1350mm long						
200 Amp	581.82	688.57	3.38	81.76	nr	**770.32**
300 Amp	684.79	810.43	3.94	95.30	nr	**905.73**
500 Amp	1096.15	1297.26	4.82	116.59	nr	**1413.85**

V: ELECTRICAL SUPPLY/POWER/LIGHTING SYSTEMS

Item	Net Price £	Material £	Labour hours	Labour £	Unit	Total rate £
Contactor relays; pressed steel enclosure; fixed to backgrounds including supports, fixings, connections/jointing to equipment						
Relays						
6 Amp, 415/240 Volt, 4 pole N/O	42.16	49.89	0.52	12.58	nr	**62.47**
6 Amp, 415/240 Volt, 8 pole N/O	51.55	61.01	0.85	20.56	nr	**81.57**
Push button stations; heavy gauge pressed steel enclosure; polycarbonate cover; IP65; fixed to backgrounds including supports, fixings,connections/joining to equipment						
Standard units						
One button (start or stop)	52.97	62.69	0.39	9.43	nr	**72.12**
Two button (start or stop)	56.23	66.55	0.47	11.37	nr	**77.92**
Three button (forward-reverse-stop)	79.69	94.31	0.57	13.79	nr	**108.10**
Weatherproof junction boxes; enclosures with rail mounted terminal blocks; side hung door to receive padlock; fixed to backgrounds, including all supports and fixings (Suitable for cable up to 2.5mm²; including glandplates and gaskets.)						
Sheet steel with zinc spray finish enclosure						
Overall Size 229 x 152; suitable to receive 3 x 20(A) glands per gland plate	55.74	65.97	1.43	34.59	nr	**100.56**
Overall Size 306 x 306; suitable to receive 14 x 20(A) glands per gland plate	74.77	88.49	2.17	52.49	nr	**140.98**
Overall Size 458 x 382; suitable to receive 18 x 20(A) glands per gland plate	108.86	128.84	3.51	84.90	nr	**213.74**
Overall Size 762 x508; suitable to receive 26 x 20(A) glands per gland plate	115.14	136.26	4.85	117.31	nr	**253.58**
Overall Size 914 x 610; suitable to receive 45 x 20(A) glands per gland plate	127.26	150.61	7.01	169.56	nr	**320.17**
Weatherproof junction boxes; enclosures with rail mounted terminal blocks; screw fixed lid; fixed to backgrounds, including all supports and fixings (suitable for cable up to 2.5mm²; including glandplates and gaskets)						
Glassfibre reinforced polycarbonate enclosure						
Overall Size 190 x 190 x 130	79.16	93.69	1.43	34.59	nr	**128.28**
Overall Size 190 x 190 x 180	115.90	137.16	1.53	37.01	nr	**174.17**
Overall Size 280 x 190 x 130	130.90	154.91	2.17	52.49	nr	**207.40**
Overall Size 280 x 190 x 180	146.65	173.56	2.37	57.33	nr	**230.88**
Overall Size 380 x 190 x 130	163.62	193.64	3.33	80.55	nr	**274.19**
Overall Size 380 x 190 x 180	175.74	207.98	3.30	79.82	nr	**287.81**
Overall Size 380 x 280 x 130	187.86	222.33	4.66	112.72	nr	**335.05**
Overall Size 380 x 280 x 180	202.40	239.54	5.36	129.65	nr	**369.19**
Overall Size 560 x 280 x 130	243.61	288.31	7.01	169.56	nr	**457.87**
Overall Size 560 x 380 x 180	250.88	296.91	7.67	185.53	nr	**482.44**

V: ELECTRICAL SUPPLY/POWER/LIGHTING SYSTEMS

Item	Net Price £	Material £	Labour hours	Labour £	Unit	Total rate £
V21 : GENERAL LIGHTING						
Y73 - LUMINAIRES (GENERAL)						
LUMINAIRES						
Fluorescent Luminaires; surface fixed to backgrounds						
Batten type; surface mounted						
600 mm Single - 18 W	7.71	9.12	0.58	14.03	nr	**23.15**
600 mm Twin - 18 W	13.65	16.15	0.59	14.27	nr	**30.42**
1200 mm Single - 36 W	10.19	12.06	0.76	18.38	nr	**30.45**
1200 mm Twin - 36 W	19.53	23.12	0.77	18.63	nr	**41.74**
1500 mm Single - 58 W	11.53	13.64	0.84	20.32	nr	**33.96**
1500 mm Twin - 58 W	23.21	27.46	0.85	20.56	nr	**48.02**
1800 mm Single - 70 W	13.92	16.47	1.05	25.40	nr	**41.87**
1800 mm Twin - 70 W	25.45	30.12	1.06	25.64	nr	**55.76**
2400 mm Single - 100 W	19.05	22.54	1.25	30.24	nr	**52.78**
2400 mm Twin - 100 W	33.33	39.45	1.27	30.72	nr	**70.17**
Surface mounted, opal diffuser						
600 mm Twin - 18 W	20.95	24.79	0.62	15.00	nr	**39.79**
1200 mm Single - 36 W	17.89	21.17	0.79	19.11	nr	**40.28**
1200 mm Twin - 36 W	27.87	32.98	0.80	19.35	nr	**52.33**
1500 mm Single - 58 W	20.57	24.34	0.88	21.29	nr	**45.63**
1500 mm Twin - 58 W	32.58	38.56	0.90	21.77	nr	**60.33**
1800 mm Single - 70 W	25.67	30.38	1.09	26.37	nr	**56.75**
1800 mm Twin - 70 W	35.24	41.70	1.10	26.61	nr	**68.31**
2400 mm Single - 100 W	33.73	39.91	1.30	31.45	nr	**71.36**
2400 mm Twin - 100 W	48.68	57.61	1.31	31.69	nr	**89.30**
Surface mounted linear fluorescent; T8 lamp; high frequency control gear; low brightness; 65° cut-off; including wedge style louvre.						
1200mm, 1 x 36 watt	47.14	55.79	1.09	26.37	nr	**82.15**
1200mm 2 x 36 watt	50.41	59.66	1.09	26.37	nr	**86.02**
Extra for emergency pack	42.52	50.32	0.25	6.05	nr	**56.37**
1500mm, 1 x 58 watt	54.94	65.02	0.90	21.77	nr	**86.79**
1500mm 2 x 58 watt	58.73	69.51	0.90	21.77	nr	**91.27**
Extra for emergency pack	42.52	50.32	0.25	6.05	nr	**56.37**
1800mm, 1 x 70 watt	82.94	98.16	0.90	21.77	nr	**119.93**
1800mm, 2 x 70 watt	95.19	112.66	0.90	21.77	nr	**134.43**
Extra for emergency pack	70.80	83.79	0.25	6.05	nr	**89.84**
Modular recessed linear fluorescent; high frequency control gear; low brightness; 65° cut off; including wedge style louvre; fitted to exposed T grid ceiling.						
600 x 600 mm, 3 x 18 watt T8	37.14	43.95	0.84	20.32	nr	**64.27**
600 x 600 mm, 4 x 18 watt T8	38.41	45.46	0.87	21.04	nr	**66.50**
Extra for emergency pack	42.95	50.83	0.25	6.05	nr	**56.88**
300 x 1200 mm, 2 x 36 watt T8	82.23	97.31	0.87	21.04	nr	**118.36**

V: ELECTRICAL SUPPLY/POWER/LIGHTING SYSTEMS

Item	Net Price £	Material £	Labour hours	Labour £	Unit	Total rate £
Extra for emergency pack	49.26	58.29	0.25	6.05	nr	**64.34**
600 x 1200 mm, 3 x 36 watt T8	83.46	98.78	0.89	21.53	nr	**120.31**
600 x 1200 mm, 4 x 36 watt T8	85.41	101.08	0.91	22.01	nr	**123.09**
Extra for emergency pack	51.95	61.49	0.25	6.05	nr	**67.53**
600 x 600, 3 x 14 watt T5	54.34	64.31	0.84	20.32	nr	**84.63**
600 x 600, 4 x 14 watt T5	56.56	66.94	0.87	21.04	nr	**87.98**
Extra for emergency pack	65.06	77.00	0.25	6.05	nr	**83.04**
Modular recessed; T8 lamp; high frequency control gear; cross-blade louvre; fitted to exposed T grid ceiling						
600 x 600 mm, 3 x 18 watt	40.80	48.29	0.84	20.32	nr	**68.61**
600 x 600 mm, 4 x 18 watt	55.22	65.35	0.87	21.04	nr	**86.39**
Extra for emergency pack	48.85	57.81	0.25	6.05	nr	**63.85**
Modular recessed compact fluorescent; TCL lamp; high frequency control gear; low brightness; 65° cut-off; including wedge style louvre; fitted to exposed T grid ceiling						
300 x 300 mm, 2 x 18 watt	87.27	103.28	0.75	18.14	nr	**121.42**
Extra for emergency pack	68.73	81.34	0.25	6.05	nr	**87.39**
500 x 500 mm, 2 x 36 watt	80.58	95.36	0.82	19.83	nr	**115.20**
600 x 600 mm, 2 x 36 watt	81.61	96.58	0.82	19.83	nr	**116.41**
600 x 600 mm, 2 x 40 watt	85.39	101.05	0.82	19.83	nr	**120.89**
Extra for emergency pack	49.26	58.29	0.25	6.05	nr	**64.34**
Ceiling recessed asymetric compact fluorescent downlighter; high frequency control gear; TCD lamp in 200 mm diameter luminaire; for wall-washing application.	-	-	-	-	-	-
1 x 18 watt	135.65	160.54	0.75	18.14	nr	**178.68**
1 x 26 watt	135.65	160.54	0.75	18.14	nr	**178.68**
2 x 18 watt	151.12	178.84	0.75	18.14	nr	**196.98**
2 x 26 watt	151.12	178.84	0.75	18.14	nr	**196.98**
Ceiling recessed asymetric compact fluorescesnt downlights; high frequency control gear; linear 200mm x 600mm luminaire with low glare louvre; for wall washing applications						
1 x 55 watt TCL	54.67	64.70	0.75	18.14	nr	**82.84**
Wall mounted compact fluorescent uplighter; high frequency control gear; TCL lamp in 300mm x 600mm luminaire	-	-	-	-	nr	-
2 x 36 watt	216.41	256.11	0.84	20.32	nr	**276.43**
2 x 40 watt	232.72	275.42	0.84	20.32	nr	**295.74**
2 x 55 watt	232.72	275.42	0.84	20.32	nr	**295.74**

V: ELECTRICAL SUPPLY/POWER/LIGHTING SYSTEMS

Item	Net Price £	Material £	Labour hours	Labour £	Unit	Total rate £
V21 : GENERAL LIGHTING (cont'd)						
Y73 - LUMINAIRES (GENERAL) (cont'd)						
LUMINAIRES (cont'd)						
Suspended linear fluorescent; T5 lamp; high frequency control gear; low brightness; 65° cut-off; 30% uplight, 70% downlight; including wedge style louvre						
1 x 49 watt	152.25	180.18	0.75	18.14	nr	**198.32**
Extra for emergency pack	84.11	99.54	0.25	6.05	nr	**105.58**
Semi-recessed 'architectural' linear fluorescent; T5 lamp; high frequency control gear; low brightness, delivers direct, ceiling and graduated wall washing illumination						
600 x 600 mm, 2 x 24 watt	125.64	148.69	0.87	21.04	nr	**169.74**
600 x 600 mm, 4 x 14 watt	134.96	159.72	0.87	21.04	nr	**180.77**
500 x 500 mm,2 x 24 watt	123.53	146.20	0.87	21.04	nr	**167.24**
Extra for emergency pack	60.06	71.08	0.25	6.05	nr	**77.13**
Downlighter, recessed; low voltage; mirror reflector with white/chrome bezel; dimmable transformer; for dichroic lamps						
85mm dia x 20/50 watt	13.77	16.30	0.66	15.96	nr	**32.26**
118mm dia x 50 watt	18.20	21.54	0.66	15.96	nr	**37.50**
165mm dia x 100 watt	83.30	98.58	0.66	15.96	nr	**114.54**
High/Low Bay luminaires						
Compact discharge; aluminium reflector						
150 watt	48.48	57.37	1.50	36.28	nr	**93.66**
250 watt	48.48	57.37	1.50	36.28	nr	**93.66**
400 watt	51.46	60.90	1.50	36.28	nr	**97.18**
Sealed discharge; aluminium reflector						
150 watt	157.60	186.52	1.50	36.28	nr	**222.80**
250 watt	170.11	201.32	1.50	36.28	nr	**237.60**
400 watt	223.08	264.01	1.50	36.28	nr	**300.29**
Corrosion resistant GRP body; gasket sealed; acrylic diffuser						
600 mm Single - 18 W	27.22	32.21	0.49	11.85	nr	**44.06**
600 mm Twin - 18 W	35.33	41.81	0.49	11.85	nr	**53.66**
1200 mm Single - 36 W	30.64	36.26	0.64	15.48	nr	**51.74**
1200 mm Twin - 36 W	39.15	46.33	0.64	15.48	nr	**61.81**
1500 mm Single - 58 W	34.15	40.42	0.72	17.42	nr	**57.83**
1500 mm Twin - 58 W	42.33	50.10	0.72	17.42	nr	**67.51**
1800 mm Single - 70 W	50.53	59.80	0.94	22.74	nr	**82.54**
1800 mm Twin - 70 W	62.53	74.00	0.94	22.74	nr	**96.74**

V: ELECTRICAL SUPPLY/POWER/LIGHTING SYSTEMS

Item	Net Price £	Material £	Labour hours	Labour £	Unit	Total rate £
Flameproof to IIA/IIB,I.P. 64; Aluminium Body; BS 229 and 899						
600 mm Single - 18 W	279.44	330.71	1.04	25.16	nr	**355.87**
600 mm Twin - 18 W	348.12	411.99	1.04	25.16	nr	**437.15**
1200 mm Single - 36 W	306.09	362.25	1.31	31.69	nr	**393.94**
1200 mm Twin - 36 W	378.44	447.87	1.18	28.54	nr	**476.41**
1500 mm Single - 58 W	327.70	387.82	1.64	39.67	nr	**427.49**
1500 mm Twin - 58 W	395.70	468.30	1.64	39.67	nr	**507.97**
1800 mm Single - 70 W	359.23	425.14	1.97	47.65	nr	**472.79**
1800 mm Twin - 70 W	414.44	490.48	1.97	47.65	nr	**538.13**
External Lighting						
Ground mounted 50 watt	347.29	411.00	2.25	54.42	nr	**465.43**
Ceiling mounted 50 watt	156.03	184.66	2.25	54.42	nr	**239.08**
Bulkhead; aluminium body and polycarbonate bowl; vandal resistant; IP65						
60 watt	28.93	34.23	0.75	18.14	nr	**52.38**
Extra for						
Emergency version	77.35	91.55	0.25	6.05	nr	**97.59**
2D 2 pin 16 watt	24.31	28.77	0.66	15.96	nr	**44.73**
2D 2 pin 28 watt	48.41	57.29	0.66	15.96	nr	**73.26**
Extra for						
Emergency version	57.04	67.51	0.25	6.05	nr	**73.55**
Photocell	17.14	20.29	0.75	18.14	nr	**38.43**
1500 mm high circular bollard; polycarbonate visor; vandal resistant; IP54						
50 watt	174.44	206.44	1.75	42.33	nr	**248.77**
70 watt	177.22	209.73	1.75	42.33	nr	**252.06**
80 watt	212.89	251.95	1.75	42.33	nr	**294.28**
Floodlight; enclosed high performance dischargelight; integeral control gear; reflector; toughened glass; IP65						
70 watt	87.49	103.54	1.25	30.24	nr	**133.78**
100 watt	134.10	158.70	1.25	30.24	nr	**188.93**
150 watt	101.71	120.37	1.25	30.24	nr	**150.61**
250 watt	169.94	201.12	1.25	30.24	nr	**231.35**
400 watt	184.43	218.27	1.25	30.24	nr	**248.50**
Extra for						
Photocell	17.72	20.98	0.75	18.14	nr	**39.12**

V: ELECTRICAL SUPPLY/POWER/LIGHTING SYSTEMS

Item	Net Price £	Material £	Labour hours	Labour £	Unit	Total rate £
V21 : GENERAL LIGHTING (cont'd)						
Y73 - LUMINAIRES (GENERAL) (cont'd)						
LUMINAIRES (cont'd)						
Lighting Track						
Single circuit; extruded aluminium white finish; low voltage with copper conductors; including couplers and supports; fixed to backgrounds						
Straight track	15.41	18.24	0.50	12.09	m	**30.33**
Live end	5.22	6.18	0.33	7.98	nr	**14.16**
Dead end	1.72	2.03	0.25	6.05	nr	**8.08**
Elbow	10.41	12.32	0.33	7.98	nr	**20.30**
Tee	15.65	18.52	0.33	7.98	nr	**26.50**
Cross	20.84	24.66	0.50	12.09	nr	**36.75**
Flexible couplers	25.27	29.91	0.33	7.98	nr	**37.89**
Three circuit; extruded aluminium white finish; low voltage with copper conductors; including couplers and supports; fixed to backgrounds						
Straight track	24.94	29.51	0.75	18.14	m	**47.65**
Live end	11.30	13.37	0.50	12.09	nr	**25.47**
Dead end	1.24	1.47	0.45	10.88	nr	**12.35**
Elbow	15.57	18.42	0.40	9.68	nr	**28.10**
Tee	19.86	23.50	0.55	13.30	nr	**36.81**
Cross	23.51	27.82	0.88	21.29	nr	**49.10**
Flexible couplers	28.99	34.31	0.45	10.88	nr	**45.19**

V: ELECTRICAL SUPPLY/POWER/LIGHTING SYSTEMS

Item	Net Price £	Material £	Labour hours	Labour £	Unit	Total rate £
Y74 - LIGHTING ACCESSORIES						
SWITCHES						
6 Amp metal clad surface mounted switch,gridswitch; one way						
1 Gang	3.94	4.66	0.43	10.40	nr	**15.06**
2 Gang	5.20	6.15	0.55	13.30	nr	**19.46**
3 Gang	8.47	10.02	0.77	18.63	nr	**28.65**
4 Gang	9.72	11.50	0.88	21.29	nr	**32.79**
6 Gang	17.49	20.70	1.10	26.61	nr	**47.31**
8 Gang	19.77	23.40	1.28	30.96	nr	**54.36**
12 Gang	29.61	35.04	1.67	40.39	nr	**75.44**
Extra for						
6 Amp - Two way switch	1.86	2.20	0.03	0.73	nr	**2.93**
20 Amp - Two way switch	2.50	2.96	0.04	0.97	nr	**3.93**
20 Amp - Intermediate	4.70	5.56	0.08	1.94	nr	**7.50**
20 Amp - One way SP switch	1.93	2.28	0.08	1.94	nr	**4.22**
Steel blank plate; 1 Gang	0.95	1.12	0.07	1.69	nr	**2.82**
Steel blank plate; 2 Gang	1.74	2.06	0.08	1.94	nr	**3.99**
6 Amp modular type switch; galvanised steel box, bronze or satin chrome coverplate; metalclad switches; flush mounting; one way						
1 Gang	10.42	12.33	0.43	10.40	nr	**22.73**
2 Gang	14.39	17.03	0.55	13.30	nr	**30.33**
3 Gang	20.77	24.58	0.77	18.63	nr	**43.21**
4 Gang	24.74	29.28	0.88	21.29	nr	**50.56**
6 Gang	41.71	49.36	1.18	28.54	nr	**77.90**
8 Gang	49.76	58.89	1.63	39.43	nr	**98.32**
9 Gang	62.41	73.86	1.83	44.27	nr	**118.13**
12 Gang	74.32	87.96	2.29	55.39	nr	**143.35**
6 Amp modular type swtich; galvanised steel box; bronze or satin chrome coverplate; flush mounting; two way						
1 Gang	10.80	12.78	0.43	10.40	nr	**23.18**
2 Gang	15.16	17.94	0.55	13.30	nr	**31.25**
3 Gang	21.94	25.97	0.77	18.63	nr	**44.59**
4 Gang	26.29	31.11	0.88	21.29	nr	**52.40**
6 Gang	44.15	52.25	1.18	28.54	nr	**80.79**
8 Gang	52.86	62.56	1.63	39.43	nr	**101.99**
9 Gang	65.89	77.98	1.83	44.27	nr	**122.24**
12 Gang	78.96	93.45	2.22	53.70	nr	**147.15**
Plate switches; 10 Amp flush mounted, white plastic fronted; 16mm metal box; fitted brass earth terminal						
1 Gang 1 Way, Single Pole	1.55	1.83	0.28	6.77	nr	**8.61**
1 Gang 2 Way, Single Pole	1.75	2.07	0.33	7.98	nr	**10.05**
2 Gang 2 Way, Single Pole	2.54	3.01	0.44	10.64	nr	**13.65**
3 Gang 2 Way, Single Pole	5.05	5.98	0.56	13.55	nr	**19.52**
1 Gang Intermediate	5.84	6.91	0.43	10.40	nr	**17.31**
1 Gang 1 Way, Double Pole	5.21	6.17	0.33	7.98	nr	**14.15**
1 Gang Single Pole with bell symbol	4.21	4.98	0.23	5.56	nr	**10.55**
1 Gang Single Pole marked "PRESS"	3.46	4.09	0.23	5.56	nr	**9.66**
Time delay switch, suppressed	32.50	38.46	0.49	11.85	nr	**50.32**

V: ELECTRICAL SUPPLY/POWER/LIGHTING SYSTEMS

Item	Net Price £	Material £	Labour hours	Labour £	Unit	Total rate £
V21 : GENERAL LIGHTING (cont'd)						
Y74 - LIGHTING ACCESSORIES (cont'd)						
SWITCHES (cont'd)						
Plate switches; 6 Amp flush mounted white plastic fronted; 25mm metal box; fitted brass earth terminal						
4 Gang 2 Way, Single Pole	10.52	12.45	0.42	10.16	nr	**22.61**
6 Gang 2 Way, Single Way	20.03	23.70	0.47	11.37	nr	**35.07**
Architrave plate switches; 6 Amp flush mounted, white plastic fronted; 27mm metal box; brass earth terminal						
1 Gang 2 Way, Single Pole	2.70	3.20	0.30	7.26	nr	**10.45**
Ceiling switches, white moulded plastic, pull cord; standard unit						
6 Amp, 1 Way, Single Pole	2.96	3.50	0.32	7.74	nr	**11.24**
6 Amp, 2 Way, Single Pole	3.56	4.21	0.34	8.22	nr	**12.44**
16 Amp, 1 Way, Double Pole	5.34	6.32	0.37	8.95	nr	**15.27**
45 Amp, 1 Way, Double Pole with neon indicator	8.28	9.80	0.47	11.37	nr	**21.17**
10 Amp splash proof moulded switch with plain, threaded or PVC entry						
1 Gang,2 Way Single Pole	12.74	15.08	0.34	8.22	nr	**23.30**
2 Gang, 1 Way Single Pole	14.39	17.03	0.36	8.71	nr	**25.74**
2 Gang, 2 Way Single Pole	18.23	21.57	0.40	9.68	nr	**31.25**
6 Amp watertight switch; metalclad; BS 3676; ingress protected to IP65 surface mounted						
1 Gang, 2 Way; terminal entry	12.29	14.54	0.41	9.92	nr	**24.46**
1 Gang, 2 Way; through entry	12.29	14.54	0.42	10.16	nr	**24.70**
2 Gang, 2 Way; terminal entry	36.22	42.87	0.54	13.06	nr	**55.93**
2 Gang, 2 Way; through entry	36.22	42.87	0.53	12.82	nr	**55.69**
2 Way replacement switch	9.76	11.55	0.10	2.42	nr	**13.97**
15 Amp watertight switch; metalclad; BS 3676; ingress protected to IP65; surface mounted						
1 Gang 2 Way, terminal entry	16.45	19.47	0.42	10.16	nr	**29.63**
1 Gang 2 Way, through entry	16.45	19.47	0.43	10.40	nr	**29.87**
2 Gang 2 Way, terminal entry	38.62	45.71	0.55	13.30	nr	**59.01**
2 Gang 2 Way, through entry	38.62	45.71	0.54	13.06	nr	**58.77**
Intermediate interior only	9.76	11.55	0.11	2.66	nr	**14.21**
2 way interior only	9.76	11.55	0.11	2.66	nr	**14.21**
Double pole interior only	9.76	11.55	0.11	2.66	nr	**14.21**
Electrical accessories; fixed to backgrounds (Including fixings)						
Dimmer switches; rotary action; for individual lights; moulded plastic case; metal backbox; flush mounted						
1 Gang, 1 Way; 250 Watt	10.24	12.12	0.28	6.77	nr	**18.89**
1 Gang, 1 Way; 400 Watt	13.48	15.95	0.28	6.77	nr	**22.73**

V: ELECTRICAL SUPPLY/POWER/LIGHTING SYSTEMS

Item	Net Price £	Material £	Labour hours	Labour £	Unit	Total rate £
Dimmer switches; push on/off action; for individual lights; moulded plastic case; metal backbox; flush mounted						
1 Gang, 2 Way; 250 Watt	17.28	20.45	0.34	8.22	nr	**28.67**
3 Gang, 2 Way; 250 Watt	91.58	108.38	0.48	11.61	nr	**119.99**
4 Gang, 2 Way; 250 Watt	112.58	133.24	0.57	13.79	nr	**147.02**
Dimmer switches; rotary action; metal clad; metal backbox; BS 5518 and BS 800; flush mounted						
1 Gang, 1 Way; 400 Watt	28.15	33.31	0.33	7.98	nr	**41.30**
Ceiling Roses						
Ceiling rose: white moulded plastic; flush fixed to conduit box						
Plug in type; ceiling socket with 2 terminals , loop-in and ceiling plug with 3 terminals and cover	5.53	6.54	0.34	8.22	nr	**14.77**
BC lampholder; white moulded plastic; heat resistent PVC insulated and sheathed cable; flush fixed						
2 Core; 0.75mm²	1.33	1.57	0.33	7.98	nr	**9.56**
Batten holder: white moulded plastic; 3 terminals; BS 5042; fixed to conduit						
Straight pattern; 2 terminals with loop-in and Earth	3.95	4.67	0.29	7.01	nr	**11.69**
Angled pattern; looped in terminal	3.95	4.67	0.29	7.01	nr	**11.69**
LIGHTING CONTROLS						
Lighting control system; including software, commissioning and testing. Typical componant parts indicated. System requirements dependant on final lighting design						
CABLES						
Cable; Twin twisted bus; LSF sheathed; aluminium conductors	1.12	1.33	0.08	1.94	m	**3.26**
Cable; ELV 4 core 7/0.2; LSF sheathed; alumimium screened; copper conductor	1.46	1.73	0.15	3.63	m	**5.36**
EQUIPMENT						
Central supervisor controller including software	4800.00	5680.66	12.00	290.26	nr	**5970.92**
Area control unit	800.00	946.78	4.00	96.75	nr	**1043.53**
Lighting control module; plug in; 9 output, 9 channel switching						
Base and lid assembly	139.00	164.50	2.05	49.59	nr	**214.09**
Lighting control module; plug in; 9 output 9 channel dimming (DSI)						
Base and lid assembly	160.00	189.36	2.05	49.59	nr	**238.94**

V: ELECTRICAL SUPPLY/POWER/LIGHTING SYSTEMS

Item	Net Price £	Material £	Labour hours	Labour £	Unit	Total rate £
V21 : GENERAL LIGHTING (cont'd)						
Y74 - LIGHTING ACCESSORIES (cont'd)						
EQUIPMENT (cont'd)						
Lighting control module; plug in; 9 output 9 channel dimming (DALI)						
Base and lid assembly	180.00	213.02	2.05	49.59	nr	**262.61**
Lighting control module; hard wired; 4 circuit switching						
Base and lid assembly	150.00	177.52	1.85	44.75	nr	**222.27**
Presence detectors						
Flush mounted	50.00	59.17	0.60	14.51	nr	**73.69**
Universal presence detectors with photo cell; flush mounted	55.00	65.09	0.60	14.51	nr	**79.60**
Scene switch plate; anodised aluminium finish						
4 way	60.00	71.01	1.20	29.03	nr	**100.03**

V: ELECTRICAL SUPPLY/POWER/LIGHTING SYSTEMS

Item	Net Price £	Material £	Labour hours	Labour £	Unit	Total rate £
V22 : GENERAL LV POWER						
Y74 - ACCESSORIES						
OUTLETS						
Socket outlet: unswitched; 13 Amp metal clad; BS 1363; galvanised steel box and coverplate with white plastic inserts; fixed surface mounted						
1 Gang	4.82	5.70	0.41	9.92	nr	**15.62**
2 Gang	8.87	10.50	0.41	9.92	nr	**20.41**
Socket outlet: switched; 13 Amp metal clad; BS 1363; galvanised steel box and coverplate with white plastic inserts; fixed surface mounted						
1 Gang	5.47	6.47	0.43	10.40	nr	**16.87**
2 Gang	8.95	10.59	0.45	10.88	nr	**21.48**
Socket outlet: switched with neon indicator; 13 Amp metal clad; BS 1363; galvanised steel box and coverplate withwhite plastic inserts; fixed surface mounted						
1 Gang	9.97	11.80	0.43	10.40	nr	**22.20**
2 Gang	18.14	21.47	0.45	10.88	nr	**32.35**
Socket outlet: unswitched; 13 Amp; BS 1363; white moulded plastic box and coverplate; fixed surface mounted						
1 Gang	3.45	4.08	0.41	9.92	nr	**14.00**
2 Gang	6.81	8.06	0.41	9.92	nr	**17.98**
Socket outlet; switched; 13 Amp; BS 1363; white moulded plastic box and coverplate; fixed surface mounted						
1 Gang	4.15	4.91	0.43	10.40	nr	**15.31**
2 Gang	7.01	8.30	0.45	10.88	nr	**19.18**
Socket outlet: switched with neon indicator; 13 Amp; BS 1363; white moulded plastic box and coverplate; fixed surface mounted						
1 Gang	8.51	10.07	0.43	10.40	nr	**20.47**
2 Gang	11.48	13.59	0.45	10.88	nr	**24.47**
Socket outlet: switched; 13 Amp; BS 1363; galvanised steel box, white moulded coverplate; flush fitted						
1 Gang	4.15	4.91	0.43	10.40	nr	**15.31**
2 Gang	8.05	9.53	0.45	10.88	nr	**20.41**
Socket outlet: switched with neon indicator; 13 Amp; BS 1363; galvanised steel box, white moulded coverplate; flush fixed						
1 Gang	8.51	10.07	0.43	10.40	nr	**20.47**
2 Gang	14.73	17.43	0.45	10.88	nr	**28.32**
Socket outlet: switched; 13 Amp; BS 1363; galvanised steel box, satin chrome coverplate; BS 4662; flush fixed						
1 Gang	13.90	16.45	0.43	10.40	nr	**26.85**
2 Gang	19.72	23.34	0.45	10.88	nr	**34.22**

V: ELECTRICAL SUPPLY/POWER/LIGHTING SYSTEMS

Item	Net Price £	Material £	Labour hours	Labour £	Unit	Total rate £
V22 : GENERAL LV POWER (cont'd)						
Y74 – ACCESSORIES (cont'd)						
OUTLETS (cont'd)						
Socket outlet: switched with neon indicator; 13 Amp; BS 1363; steel backbox, satin chrome coverplate; BS 4662; flush fixed						
1 Gang	10.93	12.94	0.43	10.40	nr	**23.34**
2 Gang	19.72	23.34	0.45	10.88	nr	**34.22**
Weatherproof socket outlet: 40 Amp; switched; single gang; RCD protected; water and dust protected to I.P.66; surface mounted						
40A 30mA tripping current protecting 1 socket	57.78	68.38	0.52	12.58	nr	**80.96**
40A 30mA tripping current protecting 2 sockets	61.63	72.94	0.64	15.48	nr	**88.42**
Plug for weatherproof socket outlet: protected to I.P.66						
13Amp plug	2.53	2.99	0.21	5.08	nr	**8.07**
Floor service outlet box; comprising flat lid with flanged carpet trim; twin 13A switched socket outlets; punched plate for mounting 2 telephone outlets; one blank plate; triple compartment						
3 compartment	24.20	28.64	0.88	21.29	nr	**49.93**
Floor service outlet box; comprising flat lid with flanged carpet trim; twin 13A switched socket outlets; punched plate for mounting 2 telephone outlets; two blank plates; four compartment						
4 compartment	33.00	39.05	0.88	21.29	nr	**60.34**
Floor service outlet box; comprising flat lid with flanged carpet trim; single 13A unswitched socket outlet; single compartment; circular						
1 compartment	35.20	41.66	0.79	19.11	nr	**60.77**
Floor service grommet, comprising flat lid with flanged carpet trim; circular						
Floor Grommet	17.60	20.83	0.49	11.85	nr	**32.68**
POWER POSTS/POLES/PILLARS						
Power Post						
Power post; aluminium painted body; PVC-U cover; 5 nr outlets	214.52	253.88	4.00	96.75	nr	**350.63**
Power Pole						
Power pole; 3.6 metres high; aluminium painted body; PVC-U cover; 6 nr outlets	275.06	325.53	4.00	96.75	nr	**422.28**
Extra for						
Power pole extension bar; 900mm long	30.06	35.58	1.50	36.28	nr	**71.86**

V: ELECTRICAL SUPPLY/POWER/LIGHTING SYSTEMS

Item	Net Price £	Material £	Labour hours	Labour £	Unit	Total rate £
Vertical multi compartment pillar; PVC-U; BS 4678 Part4 EN60529; excludes accessories						
Single						
630mm long	95.81	113.39	2.00	48.38	nr	**161.77**
3000mm long	276.10	326.76	2.00	48.38	nr	**375.13**
Double						
630mm long	95.81	113.39	3.00	72.57	nr	**185.95**
3000mm long	293.04	346.80	3.00	72.57	nr	**419.37**
CONNECTION UNITS						
Connection units: moulded pattern; BS 5733; moulded plastic box; white coverplate; knockout for flex outlet; surface mounted - standard fused						
DP Switched	5.31	6.28	0.49	11.85	nr	**18.14**
Unswitched	4.87	5.76	0.49	11.85	nr	**17.62**
DP Switched with neon indicator	6.74	7.98	0.49	11.85	nr	**19.83**
Connection units: moulded pattern; BS 5733; galvanised steel box; white coverplate; knockout for flex outlet; surface mounted						
DP Switched	6.69	14.20	0.49	11.85	nr	**26.05**
DP Unswitched	6.25	7.40	0.49	11.85	nr	**19.25**
DP Switched with neon indicator	8.12	9.61	0.49	11.85	nr	**21.46**
Connection units: galvanised pressed steel pattern; galvanised steel box; satin chrome or satin brass finish; white moulded plastic inserts; flush mounted - standard fused						
DP Switched	9.79	11.59	0.49	11.85	nr	**23.44**
Unswitched	9.21	10.90	0.49	11.85	nr	**22.75**
DP Switched with neon indicator	13.21	15.63	0.49	11.85	nr	**27.49**
Connection units: galvanised steel box; satin chrome or satin brass finish; white moulded plastic inserts; flex outlet; flush mounted - standard fused						
Switched	9.39	11.11	0.49	11.85	nr	**22.97**
Unswitched	8.92	10.56	0.49	11.85	nr	**22.41**
Switched with neon indicator	12.09	14.31	0.49	11.85	nr	**26.16**
SHAVER SOCKETS						
Shaver unit: self setting overload device; 200/250 voltage supply; white moulded plastic faceplate; unswitched						
Surface type with moulded plastic box	17.66	20.90	0.55	13.30	nr	**34.20**
Flush type with galvanised steel box	18.48	21.87	0.57	13.79	nr	**35.66**
Shaver unit: dual voltage supply unit; white moulded plastic faceplate; unswitched						
Surface type with moulded plastic box	21.29	25.20	0.62	15.00	nr	**40.19**
Flush type with galvanised steel box	22.14	26.20	0.64	15.48	nr	**41.68**

V: ELECTRICAL SUPPLY/POWER/LIGHTING SYSTEMS

Item	Net Price £	Material £	Labour hours	Labour £	Unit	Total rate £
V22 : GENERAL LV POWER (cont'd)						
Y74 – ACCESSORIES (cont'd)						
COOKER CONTROL UNITS						
Cooker control unit: BS 4177; 45 amp D.P. main switch; 13 Amp switched socket outlet; metal coverplate; plastic inserts; neon indicators						
Surface mounted with mounting box	25.00	29.59	0.61	14.76	nr	**44.34**
Flush mounted with galvanised steel box	23.90	28.28	0.61	14.76	nr	**43.04**
Cooker control unit: BS 4177; 45 Amp D.P. main switch; 13 Amp switched socket outlet; moulded plastic box and coverplate; surface mounted						
Standard	17.35	20.53	0.61	14.76	nr	**35.29**
With neon indicators	20.35	24.08	0.61	14.76	nr	**38.84**
CONTROL COMPONENTS						
Connector unit : moulded white plastic cover and block; galvanised steel back box; to immersion heaters						
3Kw up to 915mm long; fitted to thermostat	18.60	22.01	0.75	18.15	nr	**40.16**
Water heater switch : 20 Amp; switched with neon indicator						
DP Switched with neon indicator	9.23	23.66	0.45	10.88	nr	**34.54**
SWITCH DISCONNECTORS						
Switch disconnectors; moulded plastic enclosure; fixed to backgrounds						
3 pole; IP54; Grey						
16 Amp	14.94	17.68	0.80	19.35	nr	**37.03**
25 Amp	17.67	20.91	0.80	19.35	nr	**40.26**
40 Amp	28.78	34.06	0.80	19.35	nr	**53.41**
63 Amp	44.81	53.03	1.00	24.19	nr	**77.22**
80 Amp	77.67	91.92	1.25	30.24	nr	**122.16**
6 pole; IP54; Grey						
25 Amp	24.83	29.39	1.00	24.19	nr	**53.57**
63 Amp	41.94	49.63	1.25	30.24	nr	**79.87**
80 Amp	79.50	94.09	1.80	43.54	nr	**137.63**
3 pole; IP54; Yellow						
16 Amp	16.42	19.43	0.80	19.35	nr	**38.78**
25 Amp	19.40	22.96	0.80	19.35	nr	**42.31**
40 Amp	31.48	37.26	0.80	19.35	nr	**56.61**
63 Amp	48.97	57.95	1.00	24.19	nr	**82.14**
6 pole; IP54; Yellow						
25 Amp	24.83	29.39	1.00	24.19	nr	**53.57**

V: ELECTRICAL SUPPLY/POWER/LIGHTING SYSTEMS

Item	Net Price £	Material £	Labour hours	Labour £	Unit	Total rate £
INDUSTRIAL SOCKETS/PLUGS						
Plugs; Splashproof; 100-130 volts, 50-60 Hz; IP 44 (Yellow)						
2 pole and earth						
16 Amp	2.46	2.91	0.55	13.30	nr	**16.21**
32 Amp	7.77	9.20	0.60	14.51	nr	**23.71**
3 pole and earth						
16 Amp	8.52	10.08	0.65	15.72	nr	**25.81**
32 Amp	11.43	13.53	0.72	17.42	nr	**30.94**
3 pole; neutral and earth						
16 Amp	9.14	10.82	0.72	17.42	nr	**28.23**
32 Amp	13.63	16.13	0.78	18.87	nr	**35.00**
Connectors; Splashproof; 100-130 volts, 50-60 Hz; IP 44 (Yellow)						
2 pole and earth						
16 Amp	3.55	4.20	0.42	10.16	nr	**14.36**
32 Amp	10.17	12.04	0.50	12.09	nr	**24.13**
3 pole and earth						
16 Amp	10.55	12.49	0.48	11.61	nr	**24.10**
32 Amp	14.65	17.34	0.58	14.03	nr	**31.37**
3 pole; neutral and earth						
16 Amp	13.19	15.61	0.52	12.58	nr	**28.19**
32 Amp	16.62	19.67	0.73	17.66	nr	**37.33**
Angled sockets; surface mounted; Splashproof; 100-130 volts, 50-60 Hz; IP 44 (Yellow)						
2 pole and earth						
16 Amp	4.73	5.60	0.55	13.30	nr	**18.90**
32 Amp	5.64	6.67	0.60	14.51	nr	**21.19**
3 pole and earth						
16 Amp	10.87	12.86	0.65	15.72	nr	**28.59**
32 Amp	20.29	24.01	0.72	17.42	nr	**41.43**
3 pole; neutral and earth						
16 Amp	15.02	17.78	0.72	17.42	nr	**35.19**
32 Amp	18.57	21.98	0.78	18.87	nr	**40.84**
Plugs; Watertight; 100-130 volts, 50-60 Hz; IP67 (Yellow)						
2 pole and earth						
16 Amp	8.89	10.52	0.55	13.30	nr	**23.82**
32 Amp	16.38	19.39	0.60	14.51	nr	**33.90**
63 Amp	35.83	42.40	0.75	18.14	nr	**60.55**

V: ELECTRICAL SUPPLY/POWER/LIGHTING SYSTEMS

Item	Net Price £	Material £	Labour hours	Labour £	Unit	Total rate £
V22 : GENERAL LV POWER (cont'd)						
Y74 – ACCESSORIES (cont'd)						
INDUSTRIAL SOCKETS/PLUGS (cont'd)						
Connectors; Watertight; 100-130 volts, 50-60 Hz; IP 67 (Yellow)						
2 pole and earth						
16 Amp	13.21	15.63	0.42	10.16	nr	**25.79**
32 Amp	22.41	26.52	0.50	12.09	nr	**38.62**
63 Amp	54.23	64.18	0.67	16.21	nr	**80.39**
Angled sockets; surface mounted; Watertight; 100-130 volts, 50-60 Hz; IP 67 (Yellow)						
2 pole and earth						
16 Amp	23.43	27.73	0.55	13.30	nr	**41.03**
32 Amp	34.33	40.63	0.60	14.51	nr	**55.14**
Plugs; Splashproof; 200-250 volts, 50-60 Hz; IP 44 (Blue)						
2 pole and earth						
16 Amp	2.46	2.91	0.55	13.30	nr	**16.21**
32 Amp	5.78	6.84	0.60	14.51	nr	**21.35**
63 Amp	27.89	33.01	0.75	18.14	nr	**51.15**
3 pole and earth						
16 Amp	7.30	8.64	0.65	15.72	nr	**24.36**
32 Amp	9.94	11.76	0.72	17.42	nr	**29.18**
63 Amp	28.00	33.14	0.83	20.08	nr	**53.21**
3 pole; neutral and earth						
16 Amp	7.96	9.42	0.72	17.42	nr	**26.84**
32 Amp	11.50	13.61	0.78	18.87	nr	**32.48**
Connectors; Splashproof; 200-250 volts, 50-60 Hz; IP 44 (Blue)						
2 pole and earth						
16 Amp	3.85	4.56	0.42	10.16	nr	**14.72**
32 Amp	9.57	11.33	0.50	12.09	nr	**23.42**
63 Amp	33.79	39.99	0.67	16.21	nr	**56.20**
3 pole and earth						
16 Amp	10.20	12.07	0.48	11.61	nr	**23.68**
32 Amp	13.48	15.95	0.58	14.03	nr	**29.98**
63 Amp	27.80	32.90	0.75	18.14	nr	**51.04**
3 pole; neutral and earth						
16 Amp	11.85	14.02	0.52	12.58	nr	**26.60**
32 Amp	40.60	48.05	0.73	17.66	nr	**65.71**

V: ELECTRICAL SUPPLY/POWER/LIGHTING SYSTEMS

Item	Net Price £	Material £	Labour hours	Labour £	Unit	Total rate £
Angled sockets; surface mounted; Splashproof; 200-250 volts, 50-60 Hz; IP 44 (Blue)						
2 pole and earth						
16 Amp	4.96	5.87	0.55	13.30	nr	**19.17**
32 Amp	7.31	8.65	0.60	14.51	nr	**23.16**
63 Amp	37.77	44.70	0.75	18.14	nr	**62.84**
3 pole and earth						
16 Amp	9.84	11.65	0.65	15.72	nr	**27.37**
32 Amp	17.04	20.17	0.72	17.42	nr	**37.58**
63 Amp	37.54	44.43	0.83	20.08	nr	**64.50**
3 pole; neutral and earth						
16 Amp	8.57	10.14	0.72	17.42	nr	**27.56**
32 Amp	15.00	17.75	0.78	18.87	nr	**36.62**
Plugs; Watertight; 200-250 volts, 50-60 Hz; IP67 (Blue)						
2 pole and earth						
16 Amp	8.91	10.54	0.41	9.92	nr	**20.46**
32 Amp	15.34	18.15	0.50	12.09	nr	**30.25**
63 Amp	41.49	49.10	0.66	15.96	nr	**65.07**
125 Amp	105.80	125.21	0.86	20.80	nr	**146.01**
Connectors; Watertight; 200-250 volts, 50-60 Hz; IP 67 (Blue)						
2 pole and earth						
16 Amp	13.04	15.43	0.42	10.16	nr	**25.59**
32 Amp	20.78	24.59	0.50	12.09	nr	**36.69**
63 Amp	43.65	51.66	0.67	16.21	nr	**67.86**
125 Amp	129.78	153.59	0.87	21.04	nr	**174.63**
Angled sockets; surface mounted; Watertight; 200-250 volts, 50-60 Hz; IP 67 (Blue)						
2 pole and earth						
16 Amp	14.20	16.81	0.55	13.30	nr	**30.11**
32 Amp	28.75	34.02	0.60	14.51	nr	**48.54**
125 Amp	213.43	252.59	1.00	24.19	nr	**276.78**

V: ELECTRICAL SUPPLY/POWER/LIGHTING SYSTEMS

Item	Net Price £	Material £	Labour hours	Labour £	Unit	Total rate £
V32 : UNINTERRUPTIBLE POWER SUPPLY						
Uninterruptible power supply; sheet steel enclosure; self contained battery pack; including installation, testing and commissioning.						
Single phase input and output; 5 year battery life; standard 13A socket outlet connection						
1.0kVA (10 minute supply)	779.90	922.99	0.30	7.26	nr	**930.24**
1.0kVA (30 minute supply)	1365.04	1615.48	0.50	12.09	nr	**1627.58**
2.0kVA (10 minute supply)	1472.90	1743.13	0.50	12.09	nr	**1755.23**
2.0kVA (60 minute supply)	2472.80	2926.48	0.50	12.09	nr	**2938.58**
3.0kVA (10 minute supply)	1923.90	2276.88	0.50	12.09	nr	**2288.97**
3.0kVA (40 minute supply)	2923.80	3460.23	1.00	24.19	nr	**3484.42**
5.0kVA (30 minute supply)	4645.30	5497.57	1.00	24.19	nr	**5521.76**
8.0kVA (10 minute supply)	5930.10	7018.10	2.00	48.38	nr	**7066.47**
8.0kVA (30 minute supply)	6952.00	8227.48	2.00	48.38	nr	**8275.86**
Uninterruptible power supply; including final connections and testing and commissioning						
Medium size static; single phase input and output; 10 year battery life; in cubicle						
10.0 kVA (10 minutes supply)	6361.30	7528.41	10.00	241.88	nr	**7770.29**
10.0 kVA (30 minutes supply)	7543.80	8927.86	15.00	362.83	nr	**9290.69**
15.0 kVA (10 minutes supply)	8222.50	9731.08	10.00	241.88	nr	**9972.97**
15.0 kVA (30 minutes supply)	9719.60	11502.85	15.00	362.83	nr	**11865.68**
20.0 kVA (10 minutes supply)	10434.60	12349.04	10.00	241.88	nr	**12590.92**
20.0 kVA (30 minutes supply)	11169.40	13218.65	15.00	362.83	nr	**13581.48**
Medium size static; three phase input and output; 10 year battery life; in cubicle						
10.0 kVA (10 minutes supply)	7863.90	9306.69	10.00	241.88	nr	**9548.57**
10.0 kVA (30 minutes supply)	9081.60	10747.80	15.00	362.83	nr	**11110.63**
15.0 kVA (10 minutes supply)	8757.10	10363.77	15.00	362.83	nr	**10726.59**
15.0 kVA (30 minutes supply)	10409.30	12319.09	20.00	483.77	nr	**12802.86**
20.0 kVA (10 minutes supply)	10784.40	12763.01	20.00	483.77	nr	**13246.78**
20.0 kVA (30 minutes supply)	11499.40	13609.19	25.00	604.71	nr	**14213.91**
30.0 kVA (10 minutes supply)	10597.40	12541.70	25.00	604.71	nr	**13146.42**
30.0 kVA (30 minutes supply)	12522.40	14819.88	30.00	725.65	nr	**15545.54**
Large size static; three phase input and output; 10 year battery life; in cubicle						
40 kVA (10 minutes supply)	11587.40	13713.34	30.00	725.65	nr	**14439.00**
40 kVA (30 minutes supply)	15202.00	17991.11	30.00	725.65	nr	**18716.77**
60 kVA (10 minutes supply)	16959.80	20071.41	35.00	846.60	nr	**20918.01**
60 kVA (30 minutes supply)	21518.20	25466.14	35.00	846.60	nr	**26312.74**
100 kVA (10 minutes supply)	19523.90	23105.95	40.00	967.54	nr	**24073.49**
200 kVA (10 minutes supply)	33511.50	39659.85	40.00	967.54	nr	**40627.39**
300 kVA (10 minutes supply)	49652.90	58762.72	40.00	967.54	nr	**59730.26**
400 kVA (10 minutes supply)	65619.40	77658.59	50.00	1209.42	nr	**78868.02**
500 kVA (10 minutes supply)	80058.00	94746.24	60.00	1451.31	nr	**96197.55**
600 kVA (10 minutes supply)	92218.50	109137.83	70.00	1693.19	nr	**110831.02**
800 kVA (10 minutes supply)	120293.80	142364.10	80.00	1935.08	nr	**144299.18**

V: ELECTRICAL SUPPLY/POWER/LIGHTING SYSTEMS

Item	Net Price £	Material £	Labour hours	Labour £	Unit	Total rate £
Integral diesel rotary; three phase input and output; no break supply; including ventilation and accoustic attenuation, oil day tank and interconnecting pipework						
100 kVA	112239.60	132832.20	100.00	2418.85	nr	**135251.05**
125 kVA	127428.40	150807.69	100.00	2418.85	nr	**153226.54**
150 kVA	137010.50	162147.82	100.00	2418.85	nr	**164566.67**
180 kVA	146813.70	173749.61	100.00	2418.85	nr	**176168.46**
200 kVA	216306.20	255991.90	100.00	2418.85	nr	**258410.75**
250 kVA	222975.50	263884.82	100.00	2418.85	nr	**266303.66**
300 kVA	229427.00	271519.97	120.00	2902.62	nr	**274422.59**
400 kVA	270547.20	320184.49	120.00	2902.62	nr	**323087.11**
500 kVA	297103.40	351612.96	120.00	2902.62	nr	**354515.58**
630 kVA	359423.90	425367.40	140.00	3386.39	nr	**428753.79**
800 kVA	433958.80	513577.22	140.00	3386.39	nr	**516963.61**
1000 kVA	487667.40	577139.74	140.00	3386.39	nr	**580526.13**
1125 kVA	549925.20	650819.98	160.00	3870.16	nr	**654690.14**
1250 kVA	578862.90	685066.88	160.00	3870.16	nr	**688937.04**
1500 kVA	635327.00	751890.44	170.00	4112.05	nr	**756002.49**
1750 kVA	720883.90	853144.47	170.00	4112.05	nr	**857256.51**

V: ELECTRICAL SUPPLY/POWER/LIGHTING SYSTEMS

Item	Net Price £	Material £	Labour hours	Labour £	Unit	Total rate £
V40 : EMERGENCY LIGHTING						
Y73 - LUMINAIRES						
24 Volt/50 Volt/110 volt fluorescent slave luminaires						
For use with DC central battery systems						
Indoor, 8 Watt	30.50	36.10	0.80	19.35	nr	**55.45**
Indoor, exit sign box	38.00	44.97	0.80	19.35	nr	**64.32**
Outdoor, 8 Watt weatherproof	34.00	40.24	0.80	19.35	nr	**59.59**
Conversion module AC/DC	38.00	44.97	0.25	6.05	nr	**51.02**
Self contained; polycarbonate base and diffuser; LED charging light to European sign directive; 3 hour standby						
Non maintained						
Indoor, 8 Watt	33.68	39.86	1.00	24.19	nr	**64.05**
Outdoor, 8 Watt weatherproof, vandal resistant IP65	48.30	57.16	1.00	24.19	nr	**81.35**
Maintained						
Indoor, 8 Watt	49.12	58.13	1.00	24.19	nr	**82.32**
Outdoor, 8 Watt weatherproof, vandal resistant IP65	71.40	84.50	1.00	24.19	nr	**108.69**
Exit signage						
Exit sign; gold effect, pendular including brackets						
Non maintained, 8 Watt	91.67	108.49	1.00	24.19	nr	**132.68**
Maintained, 8 Watt	98.67	116.77	1.00	24.19	nr	**140.96**
Modification kit						
Module & battery for 58W fluorescent modification from mains fitting to emergency; 3 hour standby	31.60	37.40	0.50	12.09	nr	**49.49**
Extra for remote box (when fitting is too small for modification)	15.70	18.58	0.50	12.09	nr	**30.67**
12 Volt low voltage lighting; non maintained; 3 hour standby						
2 x 20 Watt lamp load	109.20	129.23	1.20	29.03	nr	**158.26**
1 x 50 Watt lamp load	119.20	141.07	1.00	24.19	nr	**165.26**
Maintained 3 hour standby						
2 x 20 Watt lamp load	109.20	129.23	1.20	29.03	nr	**158.26**
1 x 50 Watt lamp load	119.20	141.07	1.00	24.19	nr	**165.26**

V: ELECTRICAL SUPPLY/POWER/LIGHTING SYSTEMS

Item	Net Price £	Material £	Labour hours	Labour £	Unit	Total rate £
Y71 – LV SWITCHGEAR						
DC central battery systems BS5266 compliant 24/50/110 Volt						
DC supply to luminaires on mains failure; metal cubicle with battery charger, changeover device and battery as integral unit; ICEL 1001 compliant; 10 year design life valve regulated lead acid battery; 24 hour recharge; LCD display & LED indication; ICEL alarm pack; Includes on-site commissioning on 110 Volt systems only						
24 Volt, wall mounted						
300 W maintained, 1 hour	1788.00	2116.04	4.00	96.75	nr	**2212.80**
635 W maintained, 3 hour	2169.00	2566.95	6.00	145.13	nr	**2712.08**
470 W non maintained, 1 hour	1594.00	1886.45	4.00	96.75	nr	**1983.21**
780 W non maintained, 3 hour	1884.00	2229.66	6.00	145.13	nr	**2374.79**
50 Volt						
935 W maintained, 3 hour	1939.00	2294.75	8.00	193.51	nr	**2488.26**
1965 W maintained, 3 hour	2384.00	2821.39	8.00	193.51	nr	**3014.90**
1311 W non maintained, 3 hour	2334.00	2762.22	8.00	193.51	nr	**2955.73**
2510 W non maintained 3, hour	3564.00	4217.89	8.00	193.51	nr	**4411.40**
110 Volt						
1603 W maintained, 3 hour	3359.00	3975.28	8.00	193.51	nr	**4168.78**
4446 W maintained, 3 hour	3836.00	4539.79	10.00	241.88	nr	**4781.68**
2492 W non maintained, 3 hour	3491.00	4131.49	10.00	241.88	nr	**4373.38**
5429 W non maintained, 3 hour	5816.00	6883.06	12.00	290.26	nr	**7173.32**
DC central battery systems; BS EN 50171 compliant; 24/50/110 Volt Central power systems						
DC supply to luminaires on mains failure; metal cubicle with battery charger, changeover device and battery as integral unit; 10 year design life valve regulated lead acid battery; 12 hour recharge to 80% of specified duty; low volts discount; LCD display & LED indication; includes on-site commissioning for CPS systems only; battery sized for 'end of life' @ 20°C test pushbutton						
24 Volt, floor standing						
400 W non maintained, 1 hour	1679.00	1987.05	4.00	96.75	nr	**2083.80**
600 W maintained, 3 hour	2159.00	2555.11	6.00	145.13	nr	**2700.24**
50 Volt						
2133 W non maintained, 3 hour	3774.00	4466.42	8.00	193.51	nr	**4659.92**
1900 W maintained, 3 hour	3607.00	4268.78	8.00	193.51	nr	**4462.28**
110 Volt						
2200 W non maintained, 3 hour	3491.00	4131.49	8.00	193.51	nr	**4325.00**
4000 W maintained, 3 hour	3896.00	4610.80	12.00	290.26	nr	**4901.06**

V: ELECTRICAL SUPPLY/POWER/LIGHTING SYSTEMS

Item	Net Price £	Material £	Labour hours	Labour £	Unit	Total rate £
V40 : EMERGENCY LIGHTING (cont'd)						
Y71 – LV SWITCHGEAR (cont'd)						
Low Power Systems						
DC supply to luminaires on mains failure; metal cubicle with battery charger, changeover device and battery as integral unit; 5 Year design life valve regulated lead acid battery; low volts discount; LED display & LED indication; battery sized for 'end of life' @ 20°C test pushbutton						
24 Volt, floor standing						
300 W non maintained, 1 hour	1788.00	2116.04	4.00	96.75	nr	**2212.80**
600 W maintained, 3 hour	1979.00	2342.09	6.00	145.13	nr	**2487.22**
AC static inverter system; BS5266 compliant; one hour standby						
Central system supplying AC power on mains failure to mains luminaires; ICEL 1001 compliant metal cubicle(s) with changeover device, battery charger, battery & static inverter; 10 year design LIfe valve regulated lead acid battery; 24 hour recharge; LED indication and LCD display; pure sinewave output						
One hour						
750 VA, 600 W single phase I/P & O/P	2177.00	2576.41	6.00	145.13	nr	**2721.55**
3 KVA, 2.55 KW single phase I/P & O/P	3572.00	4227.35	8.00	193.51	nr	**4420.86**
5 KVA, 4.25 KW single phase I/P & O/P	4716.00	5581.24	10.00	241.88	nr	**5823.13**
8 KVA, 6.80 KW single phase I/P & O/P	5556.00	6575.36	12.00	290.26	nr	**6865.62**
10 KVA, 8.5 KW single phase I/P & O/P	7172.00	8487.85	14.00	338.64	nr	**8826.49**
13 KVA, 11.05 KW single phase I/P & O/P	9595.00	11355.39	16.00	387.02	nr	**11742.41**
15 KVA, 12.75 KW single phase I/P & O/P	9944.00	11768.43	30.00	725.65	nr	**12494.08**
20 KVA, 17.0 KW 3 phase I/P & single phase O/P	13734.00	16253.78	40.00	967.54	nr	**17221.32**
30 KVA, 25.5 KW 3 phase I/P & O/P	18560.00	21965.20	60.00	1451.31	nr	**23416.51**
40 KVA, 34.0 KW 3 phase I/P & O/P	23138.00	27383.13	80.00	1935.08	nr	**29318.21**
50 KVA, 42.5 KW 3 phase I/P & O/P	30177.00	35713.57	90.00	2176.97	nr	**37890.54**
65 KVA, 55.25 KW 3 phase I/P & O/P	37019.00	43810.88	100.00	2418.85	nr	**46229.73**
90 KVA, 68.85 KW 3 phase I/P & O/P	48919.00	57894.17	120.00	2902.62	nr	**60796.79**
120 KVA, 102 KW 3 phase I/P & O/P	54606.00	64624.56	150.00	3628.28	nr	**68252.84**
Three hour						
750 VA, 600 W single phase I/P & O/P	2548.00	3015.48	6.00	145.13	nr	**3160.61**
3 KVA, 2.55 KW single phase I/P & O/P	4287.00	5073.54	8.00	193.51	nr	**5267.04**
5 KVA, 4.25 KW single phase I/P & O/P	6813.00	8062.98	10.00	241.88	nr	**8304.87**
8 KVA, 6.80 KW single phase I/P & O/P	8455.00	10006.24	12.00	290.26	nr	**10296.50**
10 KVA, 8.5 KW single phase I/P & O/P	11153.00	13199.24	14.00	338.64	nr	**13537.88**
13 KVA, 11.05 KW single phase I/P & O/P	13752.00	16275.08	16.00	387.02	nr	**16662.10**
15 KVA, 12.75 KW single phase I/P & O/P	13977.00	16541.36	30.00	725.65	nr	**17267.02**

V: ELECTRICAL SUPPLY/POWER/LIGHTING SYSTEMS

Item	Net Price £	Material £	Labour hours	Labour £	Unit	Total rate £
20 KVA, 17.0 KW 3 phase I/P & single phase O/P	20350.00	24083.61	40.00	967.54	nr	**25051.15**
30 KVA, 25.5 KW 3 phase I/P & O/P	30414.00	35994.06	60.00	1451.31	nr	**37445.37**
40 KVA, 34.0 KW 3 phase I/P & O/P	36363.00	43034.52	80.00	1935.08	nr	**44969.60**
50 KVA, 42.5 KW 3 phase I/P & O/P	49045.00	58043.29	90.00	2176.97	nr	**60220.25**
65 KVA, 55.25 KW 3 phase I/P & O/P	59300.00	70179.77	100.00	2418.85	nr	**72598.62**
90 KVA, 68.85 KW 3 phase I/P & O/P	70181.00	83057.11	120.00	2902.62	nr	**85959.73**
120 KVA, 102 KW 3 phase I/P & O/P	86500.00	102370.15	150.00	3628.28	nr	**105998.43**

AC static inverter system; BS EN 50171 compliant; one hour standby; Low power system (typically wall mounted)

Central system supplying AC power on mains failure to mains luminaires; metal cubicle(s) with changeover device, battery charger, battery & static inverter; 5 year design life valve regulated lead acid battery; LED indication and LCD display; 12 hour recharge to 80% duty; inverter rated for 120% of load for 100% of duty; battery sized for 'end of life' @ 20°C test pushbutton

One hour						
300 VA, 240 W single phase I/P & O/P	980.00	1159.80	3.00	72.57	nr	**1232.37**
600 VA, 480 W single phase I/P & O/P	1180.00	1396.49	4.00	96.75	nr	**1493.25**
750 VA, 600 W single phase I/P & O/P	2177.00	2576.41	6.00	145.13	nr	**2721.55**
Three hour						
150 VA, 120 W single phase I/P & O/P	1080.00	1278.15	3.00	72.57	nr	**1350.71**
450 VA, 360 W single phase I/P & O/P	1280.00	1514.84	4.00	96.75	nr	**1611.60**
750 VA, 600 W single phase I/P & O/P	2548.00	3015.48	6.00	145.13	nr	**3160.61**

AC static inverter system central power system; CPS BS EN 50171 compliant; one hour standby

Central system supplying AC power on mains failure to mains luminaires; metal cubicle(s) with changeover device, battery charger, battery & static inverter; LED indication and LCD display; pure sinewave output; 10 year design life valve regulated lead acid battery; 12 hour recharge to 80% duty specified; unverter rated for 120% of load for 100% of duty; battery sized for 'end of life' @ 20°C test push button; includes on-site commissioning

One hour						
750 VA, 600 W single phase I/P & O/P	2437.00	2884.12	6.00	145.13	nr	**3029.25**
3 KVA, 2.55 KW single phase I/P & O/P	3882.00	4594.23	8.00	193.51	nr	**4787.74**
5 KVA, 4.25 KW single phase I/P & O/P	5026.00	5948.12	10.00	241.88	nr	**6190.01**
8 KVA, 6.80 KW single phase I/P & O/P	5866.00	6942.23	12.00	290.26	nr	**7232.50**
10 KVA, 8.5 KW single phase I/P & O/P	7532.00	8913.90	14.00	338.64	nr	**9252.53**
13 KVA, 11.05 KW single phase I/P & O/P	9955.00	11781.44	16.00	387.02	nr	**12168.46**
15 KVA, 12.75 KW single phase I/P & O/P	10304.00	12194.47	30.00	725.65	nr	**12920.13**
20 KVA, 17.0 KW 3 phase I/P & single phase O/P	14194.00	16798.17	40.00	967.54	nr	**17765.71**

V: ELECTRICAL SUPPLY/POWER/LIGHTING SYSTEMS

Item	Net Price £	Material £	Labour hours	Labour £	Unit	Total rate £
V40 : EMERGENCY LIGHTING (cont'd)						
Y71 – LV SWITCHGEAR (cont'd)						
One hour (cont'd)						
30 KVA, 25.5 KW 3 phase I/P & O/P	19120.00	22627.95	60.00	1451.31	nr	**24079.26**
40 KVA, 34.0 KW 3 phase I/P & O/P	23698.00	28045.87	80.00	1935.08	nr	**29980.95**
50 KVA, 42.5 KW 3 phase I/P & O/P	30862.00	36524.25	90.00	2176.97	nr	**38701.22**
65 KVA, 55.25 KW 3 phase I/P & O/P	38119.00	45112.69	100.00	2418.85	nr	**47531.54**
90 KVA, 68.85 KW 3 phase I/P & O/P	50019.00	59195.99	120.00	2902.62	nr	**62098.61**
120 KVA, 102 KW 3 phase I/P & O/P	55706.00	65926.38	150.00	3628.28	nr	**69554.65**
Three hour						
750 VA, 600 W single phase I/P & O/P	2808.00	3323.18	6.00	145.13	nr	**3468.31**
3 KVA, 2.55 KW single phase I/P & O/P	4597.00	5440.41	8.00	193.51	nr	**5633.92**
5 KVA, 4.25 KW single phase I/P & O/P	7123.00	8429.86	10.00	241.88	nr	**8671.74**
8 KVA, 6.80 KW single phase I/P & O/P	8765.00	10373.11	12.00	290.26	nr	**10663.38**
10 KVA, 8.5 KW single phase I/P & O/P	11513.00	13625.29	14.00	338.64	nr	**13963.93**
13 KVA, 11.05 KW single phase I/P & O/P	14112.00	16701.13	16.00	387.02	nr	**17088.14**
15 KVA, 12.75 KW single phase I/P & O/P	14337.00	16967.41	30.00	725.65	nr	**17693.06**
20 KVA, 17.0 KW 3 phase I/P & single phase O/P	20810.00	24628.01	40.00	967.54	nr	**25595.55**
30 KVA, 25.5 KW 3 phase I/P & O/P	30974.00	36656.80	60.00	1451.31	nr	**38108.11**
40 KVA, 34.0 KW 3 phase I/P & O/P	36923.00	43697.26	80.00	1935.08	nr	**45632.34**
50 KVA, 42.5 KW 3 phase I/P & O/P	49730.00	58853.96	90.00	2176.97	nr	**61030.93**
65 KVA, 55.25 KW 3 phase I/P & O/P	60400.00	71481.59	100.00	2418.85	nr	**73900.44**
90 KVA, 68.85 KW 3 phase I/P & O/P	71281.00	84358.93	120.00	2902.62	nr	**87261.55**
120 KVA, 102 KW 3 phase I/P & O/P	87600.00	103671.97	150.00	3628.28	nr	**107300.25**

W:COMMUNICATIONS/SECURITY/CONTROL

Item	Net Price £	Material £	Labour hours	Labour £	Unit	Total rate £
W10 : TELECOMMUNICATIONS						
Y61 - CABLES						
Multipair internal telephone cable; BS 6746; loose laid on tray / basket						
0.5 millimetre diameter conductor PVC insulated and sheathed multipair cables; BT specification CW 1308						
3 pair	0.09	0.11	0.03	0.73	m	**0.83**
4 pair	0.11	0.13	0.03	0.73	m	**0.86**
6 pair	0.15	0.18	0.03	0.73	m	**0.90**
10 pair	0.28	0.33	0.05	1.21	m	**1.54**
12 pair	0.39	0.46	0.05	1.21	m	**1.67**
15 pair	0.35	0.41	0.06	1.45	m	**1.87**
20 pair + 1 wire	0.58	0.69	0.06	1.45	m	**2.14**
25 pair	0.68	0.80	0.08	1.94	m	**2.74**
40 pair + earth	0.88	1.04	0.08	1.94	m	**2.98**
60 pair + earth	1.35	1.60	0.10	2.42	m	**4.02**
80 pair + earth	1.70	2.01	0.10	2.42	m	**4.43**
100 pair + earth	1.90	2.25	0.13	3.14	m	**5.39**
Multipair internal telephone cable; BS 6746; installed in conduit / trunking						
0.5 millimetre diameter conductor PVC insulated and sheathed multipair cables; BT specification CW 1308						
3 pair	0.09	0.11	0.05	1.21	m	**1.32**
4 pair	0.11	0.13	0.06	1.45	m	**1.58**
6 pair	0.15	0.18	0.06	1.45	m	**1.63**
10 pair	0.28	0.33	0.07	1.69	m	**2.02**
12 pair	0.39	0.46	0.07	1.69	m	**2.15**
15 pair	0.35	0.41	0.07	1.69	m	**2.11**
20 pair + 1 wire	0.58	0.69	0.09	2.18	m	**2.86**
25 pair	0.68	0.80	0.10	2.42	m	**3.22**
40 pair + earth	0.88	1.04	0.13	3.14	m	**4.19**
60 pair + earth	1.35	1.60	0.15	3.63	m	**5.23**
80 pair + earth	1.70	2.01	0.20	4.84	m	**6.85**
100 pair + earth	1.90	2.25	0.24	5.81	m	**8.05**
Telephone undercarpet cable; low profile; laid loose						
0.5 millimetre; PVC insulated; PVC sheathed multicore cable; BT CW 1316						
6 Core	0.48	0.57	0.05	1.21	m	**1.78**
Telephone drop wire cable; drawn in conduit or trunking						
0.5 millimetre conductor; PVC insulate twisted pair; Polyethylene sheathed; BT CW 1378						
Drop Wire 10	0.44	0.52	0.06	1.45	m	**1.97**

W:COMMUNICATIONS/SECURITY/CONTROL

Item	Net Price £	Material £	Labour hours	Labour £	Unit	Total rate £
W10 : TELECOMMUNICATIONS (cont'd)						
Y74 - ACCESSORIES						
Telephone outlet: moulded plastic plate with box; fitted and connected; flush or surface mounted						
Single master outlet	5.63	6.64	0.35	8.47	nr	**15.10**
Single secondary outlet	4.16	4.91	0.35	8.47	nr	**13.37**
Telephone outlet: bronze or satin chromeplate; with box; fitted and connected; flush or surface mounted						
Single master outlet	9.16	10.80	0.35	8.47	nr	**19.27**
Single secondary outlet	10.01	11.80	0.35	8.47	nr	**20.27**

W:COMMUNICATIONS/SECURITY/CONTROL

Item	Net Price £	Material £	Labour hours	Labour £	Unit	Total rate £
W20 : RADIO/TELEVISION						
RADIO						
Y61 - CABLES						
Radio Frequency Cable; BS 2316 ; PVC sheathed; laid loose						
7/0.41mm tinned copper inner conductor; solid polyethylene dielectric insulation; bare copper wire braid; PVC sheath; 75 ohm impedance						
Cable	0.94	1.12	0.05	1.21	m	**2.33**
Twin 1/0.58mm copper covered steel solid core wire conductor; solid polyethylene dielectric insulation; barecopper wire braid; PVC sheath; 75 ohm impedance						
Cable	1.35	1.59	0.05	1.21	m	**2.80**
TELEVISION						
Y61 - CABLES						
Television aerial cable; coaxial; PVC sheathed; fixed to backgrounds						
General purpose TV aerial downlead; copper stranded inner conductor; cellular polythene insulation; copper braid outer conductor; 75 ohm impedance						
7/0.25mm	0.25	0.30	0.06	1.45	m	**1.75**
Low loss TV aerial downlead; solid copper inner conductor; cellular polythene insulation; copper braid outer; conductor; 75 ohm impedance						
1/1.12mm	0.40	0.48	0.06	1.45	m	**1.93**
Low loss air spaced; solid copper inner conductor; air spaced polythene insulation; copper braid outer conductor; 75 ohm impedance						
1/1.00mm	0.24	0.29	0.06	1.45	m	**1.74**
Satelite aerial downlead; solid copper inner conductor; air spaced polythene insulation; copper tape and braid outer conductor; 75 ohm impedance						
1/1.00mm	0.49	0.59	0.06	1.45	m	**2.04**
Satelite TV coaxial; solid copper inner conductor; semi air spaced polyethylene dielectric insulation; plain annealed copper foil and copper braid screen in outer conductor; PVC sheath; 75 ohm impedance						
1/1.25mm	0.67	0.79	0.08	1.94	m	**2.72**

W:COMMUNICATIONS/SECURITY/CONTROL

Item	Net Price £	Material £	Labour hours	Labour £	Unit	Total rate £
W20 : RADIO/TELEVISION (cont'd)						
TELEVISION (cont'd)						
Y61 – CABLES (cont'd)						
Television aerial cable; coaxial; PVC sheathed; fixed to backgrounds (cont'd)						
Satelite TV coaxial; solid copper inner conductor; air spaced polyethylene dielectric insulation; plain annealed copper foil and copper braid screen in outer conductor; PVC sheath; 75 ohm impedance						
1/1.67mm	1.10	1.31	0.09	2.18	m	**3.48**
Video cable; PVC flame retardant sheath; laid loose						
7/0.1mm silver coated copper covered annealed steel wire conductor; polyethylene dielectric insulation with tin coated copper wire braid; 75 ohm impedance						
Cable	0.63	0.75	0.05	1.21	m	**1.96**
Y74 - ACCESSORIES						
TV co-axial socket outlet: moulded plastic box; flush or surface mounted						
One way Direct Connection	6.70	7.93	0.35	8.47	nr	**16.40**
Two way Direct Connection	9.34	11.05	0.35	8.47	nr	**19.52**
One way Isolated UHF/VHF	11.80	13.96	0.35	8.47	nr	**22.43**
Two way Isolated UHF/VHF	16.08	19.03	0.35	8.47	nr	**27.49**

W:COMMUNICATIONS/SECURITY/CONTROL

Item	Net Price £	Material £	Labour hours	Labour £	Unit	Total rate £
W23 : CLOCKS						
Clock timing systems; master and slave units; fixed to background; excluding supports and fixings						
Quartz master clock with solid state digital readout for parallel loop operation; one minute, half minute and one second pulse; maximum of 80 clocks						
Over two loops only	595.00	704.16	4.40	106.43	nr	**810.59**
Power supplies for above, giving 24 hours power reserve						
2 6 Amp hour batteries	250.00	295.87	3.00	72.57	nr	**368.43**
2 15 Amp hour batteries	285.00	337.29	5.00	120.94	nr	**458.23**
Radio receiver to accept BBC Rugby Transmitter MSF signal						
To synchronise time of above Quartz master clock	130.00	153.85	7.04	170.34	nr	**324.19**
Wall clocks for slave (impulse) systems; 24V DC, white dial with black numerals fitted with axispolycarbonate disc; BS 467.7 Class O						
305mm diameter 1 minute impulse	52.54	62.18	1.37	33.14	nr	**95.32**
305mm diameter 1/2 minute impulse	52.54	62.18	1.37	33.14	nr	**95.32**
227mm diameter 1 second impulse	75.00	88.76	1.37	33.14	nr	**121.90**
305mm diameter 1 second impulse	75.00	88.76	1.37	33.14	nr	**121.90**
Quartz battery movement; BS 467.7 Class O; white dial with black numerals and sweep second hand; fitted with axispolycarbonate disc; stove enamel case						
305mm diameter	27.50	32.43	0.77	18.63	nr	**51.05**
Internal wall mounted electric clock; white dial with black numerals; 240v, 50 Hz						
305mm diameter	32.51	38.47	1.00	24.19	nr	**62.66**
458mm diameter	150.00	177.52	1.00	24.19	nr	**201.71**
Matching clock; BS 467.7 Class O; 240V AC, 50/60 Hz mains supply; 12 hour duration; dial with 1-12; IP 66; axispolycarbonate disc; spun metal movement cover; semi flush mount on 6 point fixing bezel						
227mm diameter	205.33	243.00	0.62	15.00	nr	**258.00**
Digital clocks; 240V, 50 hz supply; with/without synchronisation from masterclock;12/24 hour display; stand alone operation; 50mm digits						
Flush - hours/minutes/seconds or minutes/seconds/10th seconds	200.00	236.69	0.57	13.79	nr	**250.48**
Surface - hours/minutes/seconds or minutes/seconds/10th seconds	175.00	443.05	0.57	13.79	nr	**456.84**
Flush - hours/minutes or minutes/seconds	170.00	637.62	0.57	13.79	nr	**651.41**
Surface - hours/minutes or minutes/seconds	145.00	407.68	0.57	13.79	nr	**421.47**

W:COMMUNICATIONS/SECURITY/CONTROL

Item	Net Price £	Material £	Labour hours	Labour £	Unit	Total rate £
W30 : DATA TRANSMISSION						
Cabinets						
Floor standing; suitable for 19" patch panels with glass lockable doors, metal rear doors, side panels, vertical cable management, 2 x 4 way PDU's, 4 way fan, earth bonding kit; installed on raised floor						
600 wide x 800 deep - 18U	600.00	746.98	3.00	49.45	nr	**796.43**
600 wide x 800 deep - 24U	625.00	778.10	3.00	49.45	nr	**827.55**
600 wide x 800 deep - 33U	670.00	834.13	4.00	65.93	nr	**900.06**
600 wide x 800 deep - 42U	720.00	896.37	4.00	65.93	nr	**962.31**
600 wide x 800 deep - 47U	760.00	946.17	4.00	65.93	nr	**1012.11**
800 wide x 800 deep - 42U	815.00	1014.65	4.00	65.93	nr	**1080.58**
800 wide x 800 deep - 47U	850.00	1058.22	4.00	65.93	nr	**1124.15**
Label cabinet	1.90	2.37	0.25	4.12	nr	**6.49**
Wall mounted; suitable for 19" patch panels with glass lockable doors, side panels, vertical cable management, 2 x 4 way PDU's, 4 way fan, earth bonding kit; fixed to wall						
19 wide x 500 deep - 9U	400.00	497.99	3.00	49.45	nr	**547.44**
19 wide x 500 deep - 12U	410.00	510.44	3.00	49.45	nr	**559.89**
19 wide x 500 deep - 15U	425.00	529.11	3.00	49.45	nr	**578.56**
19 wide x 500 deep - 18U	500.00	622.48	3.00	49.45	nr	**671.93**
19 wide x 500 deep - 21U	520.00	647.38	3.00	49.45	nr	**696.83**
Label cabinet	1.90	2.37	0.25	4.12	nr	**6.49**
Frames						
Floor standing; suitable for 19" patch panels with supports, vertical cable management, earth bonding kit; installed on raised floor						
19 wide x 500 deep - 25U	450.00	560.23	2.50	41.21	nr	**601.44**
19 wide x 500 deep - 39U	550.00	684.73	2.50	41.21	nr	**725.94**
19 wide x 500 deep - 42U	600.00	746.98	2.50	41.21	nr	**788.19**
19 wide x 500 deep - 47U	650.00	809.23	2.50	41.21	nr	**850.44**
Label frame	1.90	2.37	0.25	4.12	nr	**6.49**
Patch panels						
Category 5e; 19" wide fully loaded, finished in black including termination and forming of cables						
16 port - RJ45 UTP - Krone / 110	51.30	63.87	3.25	53.57	nr	**117.44**
24 port - RJ45 UTP - Krone / 110	68.40	85.16	4.75	78.30	nr	**163.45**
32 port - RJ45 UTP - Krone / 110	100.80	125.49	6.30	103.84	nr	**229.34**
48 port - RJ45 UTP - Krone / 110	132.30	164.71	9.35	154.12	nr	**318.83**
Patch panel labelling per port	0.20	0.25	0.02	0.33	nr	**0.58**
Category 6; 19" wide fully loaded, finished in black including termination and forming of cables						
16 port - RJ45 UTP - Krone / 110	76.95	95.80	3.40	56.04	nr	**151.84**
24 port - RJ45 UTP - Krone / 110	98.80	123.00	5.00	82.42	nr	**205.42**
32 port - RJ45 UTP - Krone / 110	136.80	170.31	6.60	108.79	nr	**279.10**
48 port - RJ45 UTP - Krone / 110	184.30	229.45	9.80	161.54	nr	**390.98**
Patch panel labelling per port	0.20	0.25	0.02	0.33	nr	**0.58**

W:COMMUNICATIONS/SECURITY/CONTROL

Item	Net Price £	Material £	Labour hours	Labour £	Unit	Total rate £
Cat 3/voice; 19" wide fully loaded, finished in black including termination and forming of cables (assuming 2 pairs per port)						
16 port - RJ45 UTP - Krone	64.80	80.67	2.00	32.97	nr	**113.64**
24 port - RJ45 UTP - Krone	77.40	96.36	2.60	42.86	nr	**139.22**
32 port - RJ45 UTP - Krone	111.60	138.94	3.25	53.57	nr	**192.51**
48 port - RJ45 UTP - Krone	119.70	149.02	4.65	76.65	nr	**225.67**
900 pair fully loaded PB type frame including forming and termination of 9 x 100 pair cables	490.00	610.03	25.00	412.08	nr	**1022.12**
Installation and termination of Krone strip (10 pair block - 237A) including designation label	4.05	5.04	0.50	8.24	nr	**13.28**
Patch panel labelling per port	0.20	0.25	0.02	0.33	nr	**0.58**
Fibre; 19" wide fully loaded, labled, alluminium alloy c/w couplers, fibre management and glands (excludes termination of fibre cores)						
8 way ST; fixed drawer	60.00	74.70	0.50	8.24	nr	**82.94**
16 way ST; fixed drawer	90.00	112.05	0.50	8.24	nr	**120.29**
24 way ST; fixed drawer	125.00	155.62	0.50	8.24	nr	**163.86**
8 way ST; sliding drawer	80.00	99.60	0.50	8.24	nr	**107.84**
16 way ST; sliding drawer	110.00	136.95	0.50	8.24	nr	**145.19**
24 way ST; sliding drawer	145.00	180.52	0.50	12.09	nr	**192.61**
8 way (4 duplex) SC; fixed drawer	75.00	93.37	0.50	8.24	nr	**101.61**
16 way (8 duplex) SC; fixed drawer	110.00	136.95	0.50	8.24	nr	**145.19**
24 way (12 duplex) SC; fixed drawer	135.00	168.07	0.50	8.24	nr	**176.31**
8 way (4 duplex) SC; sliding drawer	95.00	118.27	0.50	8.24	nr	**126.51**
16 way (8 duplex) SC; sliding drawer	130.00	161.85	0.50	8.24	nr	**170.09**
24 way (12 duplex) SC; sliding drawer	155.00	192.97	0.50	8.24	nr	**201.21**
8 way (4 duplex) MTRJ; fixed drawer	85.00	105.82	0.50	8.24	nr	**114.06**
16 way (8 duplex) MTRJ; fixed drawer	130.00	161.85	0.50	8.24	nr	**170.09**
24 way (12 duplex) MTRJ; fixed drawer	155.00	192.97	0.50	8.24	nr	**201.21**
8 way (4 duplex) FC/PC; fixed drawer	85.00	105.82	0.50	8.24	nr	**114.06**
16 way (8 duplex) FC/PC; fixed drawer	130.00	161.85	0.50	8.24	nr	**170.09**
24 way (12 duplex) FC/PC; fixed drawer	155.00	192.97	0.50	8.24	nr	**201.21**
Patch panel label per way	0.20	0.25	0.02	0.33	nr	**0.58**
Patch leads						
Category 5e; straight through booted RJ45 UTP - RJ45 UTP						
Patch lead 1m length	1.93	2.40	0.09	1.48	nr	**3.89**
Patch lead 3m length	2.87	3.57	0.09	1.48	nr	**5.06**
Patch lead 5m length	4.32	5.38	0.10	1.65	nr	**7.03**
Patch lead 7m length	5.78	7.20	0.10	1.65	nr	**8.84**
Category 6; straight through booted RJ45 UTP - RJ45 UTP						
Patch lead 1 m length	3.85	4.79	0.09	1.48	nr	**6.28**
Patch lead 3 m length	4.92	6.13	0.09	1.48	nr	**7.61**
Patch lead 5 m length	6.20	7.72	0.10	1.65	nr	**9.37**
Patch lead 7 m length	7.27	9.05	0.10	1.65	nr	**10.70**
Simplex 62.5/125 ST- ST						
Fibre patch lead 1 m length	8.13	10.12	0.08	1.32	nr	**11.44**
Fibre patch lead 3 m length	9.26	11.53	0.08	1.32	nr	**12.85**
Fibre patch lead 5 m length	10.35	12.89	0.10	1.65	nr	**14.53**

W:COMMUNICATIONS/SECURITY/CONTROL

Item	Net Price £	Material £	Labour hours	Labour £	Unit	Total rate £
W30 : DATA TRANSMISSION (cont'd)						
Patch leads (cont'd)						
Simplex 62.5/125 ST- SC						
Fibre patch lead 1m length	10.18	12.67	0.08	1.32	nr	**13.99**
Fibre patch lead 3m length	11.29	14.06	0.08	1.32	nr	**15.37**
Fibre patch lead 5m length	12.40	15.44	0.10	1.65	nr	**17.09**
Duplex 62.5/125 MTRJ - MTRJ						
Fibre patch lead 1 m length	19.24	23.95	0.08	1.32	nr	**25.27**
Fibre patch lead 3 m length	20.95	26.08	0.08	1.32	nr	**27.40**
Fibre patch lead 5 m length	22.66	28.21	0.10	1.65	nr	**29.86**
Duplex 62.5/125 MTRJ - ST						
Fibre patch lead 1 m length	26.77	33.33	0.08	1.32	nr	**34.65**
Fibre patch lead 3 m length	28.48	35.46	0.08	1.32	nr	**36.78**
Fibre patch lead 5 m length	30.19	37.59	0.10	1.65	nr	**39.23**
Duplex 62.5/125 ST- ST						
Fibre patch lead 1 m length	11.12	13.84	0.08	1.32	nr	**15.16**
Fibre patch lead 3 m length	13.68	17.03	0.08	1.32	nr	**18.35**
Fibre patch lead 5 m length	14.54	18.10	0.10	1.65	nr	**19.75**
Duplex 62.5/125 ST - SC						
Fibre patch lead 1 m length	12.40	15.44	0.08	1.32	nr	**16.76**
Fibre patch lead 3 m length	13.68	17.03	0.08	1.32	nr	**18.35**
Fibre patch lead 5 m length	14.54	18.10	0.10	1.65	nr	**19.75**
Duplex 62.5/125 SC - SC						
Fibre patch lead 1 m length	13.68	17.03	0.08	1.32	nr	**18.35**
Fibre patch lead 3 m length	15.39	19.16	0.08	1.32	nr	**20.48**
Fibre patch lead 5 m length	17.10	21.29	0.10	1.65	nr	**22.94**
Duplex 50/125 OM3 MTRJ - MTRJ						
Fibre patch lead 1m length	24.25	30.19	0.08	1.32	nr	**31.51**
Fibre patch lead 3m length	26.71	33.25	0.08	1.94	nr	**35.19**
Fibre patch lead 5m length	29.15	36.29	0.10	1.65	nr	**37.94**
Duplex 50/125 OM3 MTRJ - ST						
Fibre patch lead 1m length	29.74	37.03	0.08	1.32	nr	**38.34**
Fibre patch lead 3m length	31.64	39.39	0.08	1.32	nr	**40.71**
Fibre patch lead 5m length	33.54	41.76	0.10	1.65	nr	**43.40**
Duplex 50/125 OM3 ST - ST						
Fibre patch lead 1m length	24.25	30.19	0.08	1.32	nr	**31.51**
Fibre patch lead 3m length	26.71	33.25	0.08	1.32	nr	**34.57**
Fibre patch lead 5m length	29.15	36.29	0.10	1.65	nr.	**37.94**
Duplex 50/125 OM3 ST - SC						
Fibre patch lead 1m length	29.74	37.03	0.08	1.32	nr	**38.34**
Fibre patch lead 3m length	31.64	39.39	0.08	1.32	nr	**40.71**
Fibre patch lead 5m length	33.54	41.76	0.10	1.65	nr	**43.40**
Duplex 50/125 OM3 SC - SC						
Fibre patch lead 1m length	29.74	37.03	0.08	1.32	nr	**38.34**
Firbe patch lead 3m length	31.64	39.39	0.08	1.32	nr	**40.71**
Fibre patch lead 5m length	33.54	41.76	0.10	1.65	nr	**43.40**

W:COMMUNICATIONS/SECURITY/CONTROL

Item	Net Price £	Material £	Labour hours	Labour £	Unit	Total rate £
Data cabling						
Unshielded twisted pair; solid copper conductors; PVC insulation; nominal impedance 100 Ohm; Cat 5e to ISO 11801, EIA/TIA 568B and EN 50173/50174 standards to the current revisions						
4 pair 24AWG; nominal outside diameter 5.6mm; installed above ceiling	0.10	0.12	0.02	0.33	m	**0.45**
4 pair 24AWG; nominal outside diameter 5.6mm; installed in riser	0.10	0.12	0.02	0.33	m	**0.45**
4 pair 24AWG; nominal outside diameter 5.6mm; installed below floor	0.10	0.12	0.01	0.16	m	**0.29**
4 pair 24AWG; nominal outside diameter 5.6mm; installed in trunking	0.10	0.12	0.02	0.33	m	**0.45**
Category 5e cable test	-	-	0.15	2.47	nr	**2.47**
Unshielded twisted pair; solid copper conductors; LSOH sheathed; nominal impedance 100 Ohm; Cat 5e to ISO 11801, EIA/TIA 568B and EN 50173/50174 standards to the current revisions						
4 pair 24AWG; nominal outside diameter 5.6mm; installed above ceiling	0.15	0.19	0.02	0.33	m	**0.52**
4 pair 24AWG; nominal outside diameter 5.6mm; installed in riser	0.15	0.19	0.02	0.33	m	**0.52**
4 pair 24AWG; nominal outside diameter 5.6mm; installed below floor	0.15	0.19	0.01	0.16	m	**0.35**
4 pair 24AWG; nominal outside diameter 5.6mm; installed in trunking	0.15	0.19	0.02	0.33	m	**0.52**
Category 5e cable test	-	-	0.15	2.47	nr	**2.47**
Unshielded twisted pair; solid copper conductors; PVC insulation; nominal impedance 100 Ohm; Cat 6 to ISO 11801, EIA/TIA 568B and EN 50173/50174 standards to the current revisions						
4 pair 24AWG; nominal outside diameter 5.6mm; installed above ceiling	0.16	0.20	0.02	0.25	m	**0.45**
4 pair 24AWG; nominal outside diameter 5.6mm; installed in riser	0.16	0.20	0.02	0.25	m	**0.45**
4 pair 24AWG; nominal outside diameter 5.6mm; installed below floor	0.16	0.20	0.01	0.13	m	**0.33**
4 pair 24AWG; nominal outside diameter 5.6mm; installed in trunking	0.16	0.20	0.02	0.33	m	**0.53**
Category 6 cable test	-	-	0.20	3.30	nr	**3.30**
Unshielded twisted pair; solid copper conductors; LSOH sheathed; nominal impedance 100 Ohm; Cat 6 to ISO 11801, EIA/TIA 568B and EN 50173/50174 standards to the current revisions						
4 pair 24AWG; nominal outside diameter 5.6mm; installed above ceiling	0.19	0.24	0.02	0.36	m	**0.60**
4 pair 24AWG; nominal outside diameter 5.6mm; installed in riser	0.19	0.24	0.02	0.36	m	**0.60**
4 pair 24AWG; nominal outside diameter 5.6mm; installed below floor	0.19	0.24	0.01	0.18	m	**0.42**
4 pair 24AWG; nominal outside diameter 5.6mm; installed in trunking	0.19	0.24	0.02	0.36	m	**0.60**
Category 6 cable test	-	-	0.22	3.63	nr	**3.63**

W:COMMUNICATIONS/SECURITY/CONTROL

Item	Net Price £	Material £	Labour hours	Labour £	Unit	Total rate £
W30 : DATA TRANSMISSION (cont'd)						
Data cabling (cont'd)						
Fibre optic cable, tight buffered, internal/external application, single mode, LSOH sheathed						
4 core fibre optic cable	1.22	1.52	0.10	1.65	m	**3.17**
8 core fibre optic cable	2.03	2.53	0.10	1.65	m	**4.18**
12 core fibre optic cable	2.52	3.14	0.10	1.65	m	**4.79**
16 core fibre optic cable	3.06	3.81	0.10	1.65	m	**5.46**
24 core fibre optic cable	3.69	4.59	0.10	1.65	m	**6.24**
Singlemode core test per core	-	-	0.20	3.30	nr	**3.30**
Fibre optic cable OM1 and OM2, tight buffered, internal/external application, 62.5/125 multimode fibre, LSOH sheathed						
4 core fibre optic cable	1.31	1.63	0.10	1.65	m	**3.28**
8 core fibre optic cable	2.16	2.69	0.10	1.65	m	**4.34**
12 core fibre optic cable	2.75	3.42	0.10	1.65	m	**5.07**
16 core fibre optic cable	3.42	4.26	0.10	1.65	m	**5.91**
24 core fibre optic cable	3.96	4.93	0.10	1.65	m	**6.58**
Multimode core test per core	-	-	0.20	3.30	nr	**3.30**
Fibre optic cable OM3, tight buffered, internal only application, 50/125 multimode fibre, LSOH sheathed						
4 core fibre optic cable	1.62	2.02	0.10	1.65	nr	**3.67**
8 core fibre optic cable	2.52	3.14	0.10	1.65	nr	**4.79**
12 core fibre optic cable	3.65	4.54	0.10	1.65	nr	**6.19**
24 core fibre cable	6.98	8.69	0.10	1.65	nr	**10.34**
Multimode core test per core	-	-	0.20	3.30	nr	**3.30**
Fibre optic single and multimode connectors and couplers including termination						
ST singlemode booted connector	5.58	6.95	0.25	4.12	nr	**11.07**
ST multimode booted connector	2.70	3.36	0.25	4.12	nr	**7.48**
SC simplex singlemode booted connector	7.92	9.86	0.25	4.12	nr	**13.98**
SC simplex multimode booted connector	2.88	3.59	0.25	4.12	nr	**7.71**
SC duplex multimode booted connector	5.76	7.17	0.25	4.12	nr	**11.29**
ST - SC duplex adaptor	14.00	17.43	0.01	0.16	nr	**17.59**
ST inline bulkhead coupler	3.00	3.73	0.01	0.16	nr	**3.90**
SC duplex coupler	5.60	6.97	0.01	0.16	nr	**7.14**
MTRJ small form factor duplex connector	5.85	14.57	0.25	4.12	nr	**18.69**
LC simplex multimode booted connector	2.88	3.59	0.25	4.12	nr	**7.71**
Voice cabling						
Low speed data; unshielded twisted pair; solid copper conductors; PVC insulation; nominal impedance 100 Ohm; Category 3 to ISO IS 11801/EIA /TIA 568B and EN50173/50174 standards to current revisions						
Installed in riser						
25 pair 24AWG	0.90	1.12	0.03	0.49	m	**1.61**
50 pair 24AWG	1.80	2.24	0.06	0.99	m	**3.23**
100 pair 24AWG	3.15	3.92	0.10	1.65	m	**5.57**

W:COMMUNICATIONS/SECURITY/CONTROL

Item	Net Price £	Material £	Labour hours	Labour £	Unit	Total rate £
Installed below floor						
25 pair 24AWG	0.90	1.12	0.02	0.33	m	**1.45**
50 pair 24AWG	1.80	2.24	0.05	0.82	m	**3.07**
100 pair 24AWG	3.15	3.92	0.08	1.32	m	**5.24**
Cat 3 cable circuit test per pair	-	-	0.08	1.32	nr	**1.32**
Low speed data; unshielded twisted pair; solid copper conductors; LSOH sheath; nominal impedance 100 Ohm; Category 3 to ISO IS 11801/EIA/TIA 568B and EN50173/50174 standards to current revisions						
Installed in riser						
25 pair 24AWG	1.13	1.41	0.03	0.49	m	**1.90**
50 pair 24AWG	2.25	2.80	0.06	0.99	m	**3.79**
100 pair 24AWG	3.78	4.71	0.10	1.65	m	**6.35**
Installed below floor						
25 pair 24AWG	1.13	1.41	0.02	0.33	m	**1.74**
50 pair 24AWG	2.25	2.80	0.05	0.82	m	**3.63**
100 pair 24AWG	3.78	4.71	0.08	1.32	m	**6.02**
Cat 3 cable circuit test per pair	-	-	0.08	1.32	nr	**1.32**
Accessories						
Category 5e RJ45 data outlet plate and multiway outlet boxes for wall, ceiling and below floor installations including label to ISO 11801 standards						
Wall mounted; fully loaded						
One gang LSOH PVC plate	5.80	7.22	0.15	2.47	nr	**9.69**
Two gang LSOH PVC plate	8.30	10.33	0.20	3.30	nr	**13.63**
Four gang LSOH PVC plate	14.20	17.68	0.40	6.59	nr	**24.27**
One gang satin brass plate	11.00	13.69	0.25	4.12	nr	**17.82**
Two gang satin brass plate	13.50	16.81	0.33	5.44	nr	**22.25**
Ceiling mounted; fully loaded						
One gang metal clad plate	7.00	8.71	0.33	5.44	nr	**14.15**
Two gang metal clad plate	9.50	11.83	0.45	7.42	nr	**19.24**
Below floor; fully loaded						
Four way outlet box, 5 m length 20mm flexible conduit with glands and starin relief bracket	23.65	29.44	0.80	13.19	nr	**42.63**
Six way outlet box, 5 m length 25mm flexible conduit with glands and strain relief bracket	30.58	38.07	1.20	19.78	nr	**57.85**
Eight way outlet box, 5 m length 25mm flexible conduit with glands and strain relief bracket	38.50	47.93	1.40	23.08	nr	**71.01**
Installation of outlet boxes to desks	-	-	0.40	6.59	nr	**6.59**

W:COMMUNICATIONS/SECURITY/CONTROL

Item	Net Price £	Material £	Labour hours	Labour £	Unit	Total rate £
W30 : DATA TRANSMISSION (cont'd)						
Accessories (cont'd)						
Category 6 RJ45 data outlet plate and multiway outlet boxes for wall, ceiling and below floor installations including label to ISO 11801 standards						
Wall mounted; fully loaded						
One gang LSOH PVC plate	7.40	9.21	0.17	2.72	nr	**11.93**
Two gang LSOH PVC plate	10.85	13.51	0.22	3.63	nr	**17.13**
Four gang LSOH PVC plate	19.60	24.40	0.44	7.25	nr	**31.65**
One gang satin brass plate	12.40	15.44	0.28	4.53	nr	**19.97**
Two gang satin brass plate	15.85	19.73	0.36	5.98	nr	**25.72**
Ceiling mounted; fully loaded						
One gang metal clad plate	8.40	10.46	0.36	5.98	nr	**16.44**
Two gang metal clad plate	11.85	14.75	0.50	8.16	nr	**22.91**
Below floor; fully loaded						
Four way outlet box, 5 m length 20mm flexible conduit with glands and starin relief bracket	28.99	36.09	0.88	14.51	nr	**50.60**
Six way outlet box, 5 m length 25mm flexible conduit with glands and strain relief bracket	38.56	48.01	1.32	21.76	nr	**69.76**
Eight way outlet box, 5 m length 25mm flexible conduit with glands and strain relief bracket	49.12	61.15	1.54	25.38	nr	**86.54**
Installation of outlet boxes to desks	-	-	0.40	6.59	nr	**6.59**

W:COMMUNICATIONS/SECURITY/CONTROL

Item	Net Price £	Material £	Labour hours	Labour £	Unit	Total rate £
W40 : ACCESS CONTROL						
ACCESS CONTROL EQUIPMENT **Equipment to control the movement of personnel into defined spaces; includes fixing to backgrounds, termination of power and data cables; excludes cable containment and cable installation**						
Access control						
Magnetic swipe reader	101.81	132.56	1.50	60.58	nr	**193.14**
Proximity reader	134.53	175.16	1.50	60.58	nr	**235.74**
Exit button	9.60	12.50	1.50	60.58	nr	**73.08**
Exit PIR	39.39	51.29	2.00	80.78	nr	**132.06**
Emergency break glass double pole	21.21	27.62	1.00	40.39	nr	**68.00**
Alarm contact flush	1.10	1.43	1.00	40.39	nr	**41.82**
Alarm contact surface	1.10	1.43	1.00	40.39	nr	**41.82**
Reader controller 16 door	1204.93	1568.82	4.00	161.55	nr	**1730.37**
Reader controller 8 door	860.52	1120.40	4.00	161.55	nr	**1281.95**
Reader controller 2 door	629.23	819.26	4.00	161.55	nr	**980.81**
Reader interface	191.90	249.85	1.50	60.58	nr	**310.44**
Lock power supply 12 volt 3 AMP	58.58	76.27	2.00	80.78	nr	**157.05**
Lock power supply 24 volt 3 AMP	89.89	117.04	2.00	80.78	nr	**197.81**
Rechargeable battery 12 volt 7ah	12.88	16.77	0.25	10.10	nr	**26.87**
Lock Equipment						
Single slimline magnetic lock, monitored	65.65	85.48	2.00	80.78	nr	**166.25**
Single slimline magnetic lock, unmonitored	55.55	72.33	1.75	70.68	nr	**143.01**
Double slimline magnetic lock, monitored	166.65	216.98	4.00	161.55	nr	**378.53**
Double slimline magnetic lock, unmonitored	121.20	157.80	4.50	181.75	nr	**339.55**
Standard single magnetic lock, monitored	90.90	118.35	1.25	50.48	nr	**168.84**
Standard single magnetic lock, unmonitored	64.64	84.16	1.00	40.39	nr	**124.55**
Standard single magnetic lock, double monitored	95.95	124.93	1.50	60.58	nr	**185.51**
Standard double magnetic lock, monitored	176.75	230.13	1.50	60.58	nr	**290.71**
Standard double magnetic lock, unmonitored	146.45	190.68	1.25	50.48	nr	**241.16**
12V electric release fail safe, monitored	58.58	76.27	1.25	50.48	nr	**126.76**
12V electric release fail secure, monitored	58.58	76.27	1.00	40.39	nr	**116.66**
Solenoid bolt	111.10	144.65	1.50	60.58	nr	**205.23**
Electric mortice lock	126.25	164.38	1.00	40.39	nr	**204.77**

W:COMMUNICATIONS/SECURITY/CONTROL

Item	Net Price £	Material £	Labour hours	Labour £	Unit	Total rate £
W41 : SECURITY DETECTION & ALARM						
SECURITY DETECTION & ALARM EQUIPMENT						
Detection and alarm systems for the protection of property and persons; includes fixing of equipment to backgrounds and termination of power and data cabling; excludes cable containment and cable installation						
Detection, alarm equipment						
Alarm contact flush	1.10	1.43	1.00	40.39	nr	**41.82**
Alarm contact surface	1.10	1.43	1.00	40.39	nr	**41.82**
Roller shutter contact	7.16	9.32	1.00	40.39	nr	**49.71**
Personal attack button	6.96	9.06	1.00	40.39	nr	**49.45**
Acoustic break glass detectors	24.20	31.51	2.00	80.78	nr	**112.29**
Vibration detectors	14.63	19.04	2.00	80.78	nr	**99.82**
12 metre PIR detector	11.85	15.43	1.50	60.58	nr	**76.01**
15 metre dual detector	32.92	42.86	1.50	60.58	nr	**103.44**
8 zone alarm panel	55.25	71.94	3.00	121.16	nr	**193.10**
8-24 zone end station	92.72	120.72	4.00	161.55	nr	**282.27**
Remote keypad	67.48	87.86	2.00	80.78	nr	**168.64**
8 zone expansion	39.10	50.90	1.50	60.58	nr	**111.49**
Final exit set button	10.25	13.35	1.00	40.39	nr	**53.73**
Self contained external sounder	37.04	48.22	2.00	80.78	nr	**129.00**
Internal loudspeaker	5.41	7.04	2.00	80.78	nr	**87.81**
Rechargeable battery 12 volt 7ah (ampere hours)	13.14	17.11	0.25	10.10	nr	**27.20**
Surveillance Equipment						
Vandal resistant camera, colour	412.08	536.53	3.00	121.16	nr	**657.69**
External camera, colour	469.77	611.64	5.00	201.94	nr	**813.58**
Auto dome external, colour	1442.28	1877.85	5.00	201.94	nr	**2079.79**
Auto dome external, colour/monochrome	1504.09	1958.33	5.00	201.94	nr	**2160.27**
Auto dome internal, colour	1209.45	1574.71	4.00	161.55	nr	**1736.26**
Auto dome internal colour/monochrome	1401.07	1824.20	4.00	161.55	nr	**1985.75**
Mini internal domes	115.38	150.23	3.00	121.16	nr	**271.39**
Camera switcher, 32 inputs	1389.74	1809.44	4.00	161.55	nr	**1970.99**
Full function keyboard	593.40	772.60	1.00	40.39	nr	**812.99**
16 CH multiplexors, simplex	669.63	871.86	2.00	80.78	nr	**952.63**
16 CH multiplexors, duplex	901.42	1173.66	2.00	80.78	nr	**1254.43**
Video recorder, 24 hour	226.64	295.09	1.00	40.39	nr	**335.48**
Video recorder, time lapse	505.83	658.59	1.00	40.39	nr	**698.98**
9" colour monitor	254.46	331.31	1.00	40.39	nr	**371.69**
14" colour monitor	247.25	321.92	1.00	40.39	nr	**362.30**
17" colour monitor, high resolution	533.64	694.80	1.00	40.39	nr	**735.19**
21" colour monitor, high resolution	563.52	733.70	1.00	40.39	nr	**774.09**

W:COMMUNICATIONS/SECURITY/CONTROL

Item	Net Price £	Material £	Labour hours	Labour £	Unit	Total rate £
W50 : FIRE DETECTION AND ALARM						
STANDARD FIRE DETECTION CONTROL PANEL						
Zone control panel; 2 x 12 volt batteries/charge up to 48 hours standby; mild steel case; flush or surface mounting						
1 zone	154.10	182.38	3.00	72.57	nr	**254.94**
2 zone	165.52	195.89	3.51	84.87	nr	**280.76**
4 zone	251.14	297.21	4.00	96.75	nr	**393.97**
8 zone	399.54	472.84	5.00	120.94	nr	**593.78**
12 zone	521.68	617.39	6.00	145.13	nr	**762.52**
16 zone	736.29	871.37	6.00	145.13	nr	**1016.50**
24 zone	990.86	1172.65	6.00	145.13	nr	**1317.78**
Repeater panels						
8 zone	270.54	320.18	4.00	96.75	nr	**416.93**
EQUIPMENT						
Manual call point units: plastic covered						
Surface mounted						
Call point	8.68	10.27	0.50	12.09	nr	**22.37**
Call point; Weatherproof	62.53	74.00	0.80	19.35	nr	**93.35**
Flush mounted						
Call point	7.57	8.96	0.56	13.55	nr	**22.51**
Call point; Weatherproof	58.80	69.59	0.86	20.82	nr	**90.40**
Detectors						
Smoke, ionisation type with mounting base	30.34	35.90	0.75	18.15	nr	**54.05**
Smoke, optical type with mounting base	30.34	35.90	0.75	18.15	nr	**54.05**
Fixed temperature heat detector with mounting base (60°C)	24.42	28.90	0.75	18.15	nr	**47.05**
Rate of Rise heat detector with mounting base (90°C)	22.89	27.08	0.75	18.15	nr	**45.23**
Duct detector including optical smoke detector and base	193.97	229.56	2.00	48.38	nr	**277.93**
Remote smoke detector LED indicator with base	7.81	9.25	0.50	12.09	nr	**21.34**
Sounders						
6" bell, conduit box	16.21	19.19	0.75	18.15	nr	**37.34**
6" bell, conduit box; weatherproof	22.20	26.27	0.75	18.14	nr	**44.41**
Siren; 230V	44.56	52.74	1.25	30.24	nr	**82.97**
Magnetic Door Holder; 230V ; surface fixed	45.18	53.47	1.50	36.32	nr	**89.78**
ADDRESSABLE FIRE DETECTION CONTROL PANEL						
Analogue addressable panel; BS EN54 Part 2 and 4 1998; incorporating 120 addresses per loop (maximum 1-2km length); sounders wired on loop; sealed lead acid integral battery standby providing 48 hour standby; 24 volt DC; mild steel case; surface fixed						
1 loop; 4 x 12 volt batteries	880.53	1042.08	6.00	145.13	nr	**1187.21**

W:COMMUNICATIONS/SECURITY/CONTROL

Item	Net Price £	Material £	Labour hours	Labour £	Unit	Total rate £
W50 : FIRE DETECTION AND ALARM (cont'd)						
ADDRESSABLE FIRE DETECTION CONTROL PANEL (cont'd)						
Extra for 1 loop panel						
Loop card	176.30	208.64	1.00	24.19	nr	**232.83**
Repeater panel	447.93	530.12	6.00	145.13	nr	**675.25**
Network nodes	939.86	1112.30	6.00	145.13	nr	**1257.43**
Interface unit; for other systems						
Mains powered	158.22	187.24	1.50	36.28	nr	**223.53**
Loop powered	115.89	137.15	1.00	24.19	nr	**161.34**
Single channel I/O	40.68	48.15	1.00	24.19	nr	**72.34**
Zone module	57.54	68.09	1.50	36.28	nr	**104.38**
4 loop; 4 x 12 volt batteries; 24 hour standby; 30 minute alarm	1409.15	1667.69	8.00	193.51	nr	**1861.20**
Extra for 4 loop panel						
Loop card	176.30	208.64	1.00	24.19	nr	**232.83**
Repeater panel	939.86	1112.30	6.00	145.13	nr	**1257.43**
Mimic panel	1417.79	1677.91	5.00	120.94	nr	**1798.86**
Network nodes	939.71	1112.12	6.00	145.13	nr	**1257.25**
Interface unit; for other systems						
Mains powered	158.22	187.24	1.50	36.28	nr	**223.53**
Loop powered	115.89	137.15	1.00	24.19	nr	**161.34**
Single channel I/O	40.68	48.15	1.00	24.19	nr	**72.34**
Zone module	57.53	68.08	1.50	36.28	nr	**104.36**
Line modules	5.88	6.96	1.00	24.19	nr	**31.15**
8 loop; 4 x 12 volt batteries; 24 hour standby; 30 minute alarm	2818.32	3335.39	12.00	290.26	nr	**3625.66**
Extra for 8 loop panel						
Loop card	176.30	208.64	1.00	24.19	nr	**232.83**
Repeater panel	939.86	1112.30	6.00	145.13	nr	**1257.43**
Mimic panel	1417.79	1677.91	5.00	120.94	nr	**1798.86**
Network nodes	939.71	1112.12	6.00	145.13	nr	**1257.25**
Interface unit; for other systems						
Mains powered	158.22	187.24	1.50	36.28	nr	**223.53**
Loop powered	115.89	137.15	1.00	24.19	nr	**161.34**
Single channel I/O	40.68	48.15	1.00	24.19	nr	**72.34**
Zone module	57.53	68.08	1.50	36.28	nr	**104.36**
Line modules	5.88	6.96	1.00	24.19	nr	**31.15**
EQUIPMENT						
Manual Call Point						
Surface mounted						
Call point	36.43	43.12	1.00	24.19	nr	**67.30**
Call point; Weather proof	76.43	90.45	1.25	30.24	nr	**120.68**
Flush mounted						
Call point	35.66	42.20	1.00	24.19	nr	**66.39**
Call point; Weather proof	54.47	64.47	1.25	30.24	nr	**94.70**

W:COMMUNICATIONS/SECURITY/CONTROL

Item	Net Price £	Material £	Labour hours	Labour £	Unit	Total rate £
Detectors						
Smoke, ionisation type with mounting base	51.29	60.70	0.75	18.15	nr	**78.85**
Smoke, optical type with mounting base	44.02	52.10	0.75	18.15	nr	**70.24**
Fixed temperature heat detector with mounting base (60°C)	47.18	55.84	0.75	18.15	nr	**73.98**
Rate of Rise heat detector with mounting base (90°C)	47.18	55.84	0.75	18.15	nr	**73.98**
Duct Detector including optical smoke detector and addressable base	205.87	243.64	2.00	48.38	nr	**292.02**
Beam smoke detector with transmitter and receiver unit	430.34	509.29	2.00	48.38	nr	**557.67**
Zone short circuit isolator	35.84	42.41	0.75	18.14	nr	**60.56**
Plant interface unit	26.40	31.25	0.50	12.09	nr	**43.34**
Sounders						
Xenon flasher, 24 volt, conduit box	22.01	26.04	0.50	12.09	nr	**38.14**
Xenon flasher, 24 volt, conduit box; weatherproof	37.42	44.28	0.50	12.09	nr	**56.38**
6" bell, conduit box	16.21	19.19	0.75	18.15	nr	**37.34**
6" bell, conduit box; weatherproof	22.20	26.27	0.75	18.14	nr	**44.41**
Siren; 24V polarised	15.71	18.59	1.00	24.19	nr	**42.78**
Siren; 240V	44.56	52.74	1.25	30.24	nr	**82.97**
Magnetic Door Holder; 240V ; surface fixed	45.18	53.47	1.50	36.32	nr	**89.78**

W:COMMUNICATIONS/SECURITY/CONTROL

Item	Net Price £	Material £	Labour hours	Labour £	Unit	Total rate £
W51 : EARTHING AND BONDING						
EARTH BAR						
Earth bar; polymer insulators and base mounting; including connections						
Non disconnect link						
6 way	119.40	141.31	0.81	19.59	nr	**160.90**
8 way	131.33	155.43	0.81	19.59	nr	**175.02**
10 way	144.48	170.99	0.81	19.59	nr	**190.58**
Disconnect link						
6 way	134.12	158.73	1.01	24.43	nr	**183.16**
8 way	147.53	174.60	1.01	24.43	nr	**199.03**
10 way	162.28	192.05	1.01	24.43	nr	**216.48**
Soild earth bar; including connections						
150 x 50 x 6 mm	39.59	46.85	1.01	24.43	nr	**71.28**
Extra for earthing						
Disconnecting link						
300 x 50 x 6mm	37.61	44.51	1.16	28.06	nr	**72.57**
500 x 50 x 6mm	41.37	48.96	1.16	28.06	nr	**77.02**
Crimp lugs; including screws and connections to cable						
25 mm	0.45	0.53	0.31	7.50	nr	**8.03**
35 mm	0.65	0.77	0.31	7.50	nr	**8.27**
50 mm	0.76	0.90	0.32	7.74	nr	**8.64**
70 mm	1.25	1.48	0.32	7.74	nr	**9.22**
95 mm	1.50	1.78	0.46	11.13	nr	**12.90**
120 mm	1.60	1.89	1.25	30.24	nr	**32.13**
Earth clamps; connection to pipework						
15mm to 32mm dia	0.85	1.01	0.15	3.63	nr	**4.63**
32mm to 50mm dia	1.05	1.24	0.18	4.35	nr	**5.60**
50mm to 75mm dia	1.25	1.48	0.20	4.84	nr	**6.32**

W:COMMUNICATIONS/SECURITY/CONTROL

Item	Net Price £	Material £	Labour hours	Labour £	Unit	Total rate £
W52 : LIGHTNING PROTECTION						
CONDUCTOR TAPE						
PVC sheathed copper tape						
25 x 3 mm	7.27	9.03	0.30	7.26	m	**16.29**
25 x 6 mm	12.75	15.84	0.30	7.26	m	**23.10**
50 x 6 mm	27.14	33.73	0.30	7.26	m	**40.98**
PVC sheathed copper solid circular conductor						
8mm	4.52	5.35	0.50	12.09	m	**17.44**
Bare copper tape						
20 x 3 mm	5.10	6.04	0.30	7.26	m	**13.29**
25 x 3 mm	5.21	6.47	0.30	7.26	m	**13.73**
25 x 6 mm	10.42	12.95	0.40	9.68	m	**22.62**
50 x 6 mm	20.84	24.66	0.50	12.09	m	**36.76**
Bare copper solid circular conductor						
8mm	3.46	4.09	0.50	12.09	m	**16.19**
Tape fixings; flat; metalic						
PVC sheathed copper						
25 x 3 mm	4.55	5.65	0.33	7.98	nr	**13.64**
25 x 6 mm	4.71	5.85	0.33	7.98	nr	**13.84**
50 x 6 mm	7.76	9.64	0.33	7.98	nr	**17.63**
8mm	5.00	6.21	0.50	12.09	nr	**18.31**
Bare copper						
20 x 3 mm	5.10	6.34	0.30	7.26	nr	**13.59**
25 x 3 mm	5.21	6.47	0.30	7.26	nr	**13.73**
25 x 6 mm	10.42	12.95	0.40	9.68	nr	**22.62**
50 x 6 mm	20.84	24.66	0.50	12.09	nr	**36.76**
8mm	3.46	4.30	0.50	12.09	nr	**16.39**
Tape fixings; flat; non-metalic; PVC sheathed copper						
25 x 3 mm	0.59	0.73	0.30	7.26	nr	**7.99**
Tape fixings; flat; non-metalic; Bare copper						
20 x 3 mm	0.55	0.68	0.30	7.26	nr	**7.94**
25 x 3 mm	0.55	0.68	0.30	7.26	nr	**7.94**
50 x 6 mm	1.41	1.67	0.30	7.26	nr	**8.93**
Puddle flanges; copper						
600 mm long	53.13	62.88	0.93	22.50	nr	**85.37**
AIR RODS						
Pointed air rod fixed to structure; copper						
10 mm diameter						
500 mm long	9.83	11.63	1.00	24.19	nr	**35.82**
1000mm long	14.91	17.65	1.50	36.28	nr	**53.93**
Extra for						
Air terminal base	12.73	15.07	0.35	8.47	nr	**23.53**
Strike Pad	18.07	21.39	0.35	8.47	nr	**29.85**

W:COMMUNICATIONS/SECURITY/CONTROL

Item	Net Price £	Material £	Labour hours	Labour £	Unit	Total rate £
W52 : LIGHTNING PROTECTION (cont'd)						
AIR RODS (cont'd)						
16 mm diameter						
500 mm long	14.02	16.59	0.91	22.01	nr	**38.60**
1000mm long	25.61	30.31	1.75	42.33	nr	**72.64**
2000mm long	46.77	55.35	2.50	60.47	nr	**115.82**
Extra for						
Multiple point	27.18	32.17	0.35	8.47	nr	**40.63**
Air terminal base	13.87	16.41	0.35	8.47	nr	**24.88**
Ridge saddle	24.30	28.76	0.35	8.47	nr	**37.22**
Side mounting bracket	24.18	28.62	0.50	12.09	nr	**40.71**
Rod to tape coupling	11.26	13.33	0.50	12.09	nr	**25.42**
Strike Pad	18.07	21.39	0.35	8.47	nr	**29.85**
AIR TERMINALS						
16 mm diameter						
500 mm long	14.02	16.59	0.65	15.72	nr	**32.31**
1000mm long	25.61	30.31	0.78	18.87	nr	**49.18**
2000mm long	46.77	55.35	1.50	36.28	nr	**91.63**
Extra for						
Multiple point	27.18	32.17	0.35	8.47	nr	**40.63**
Flat saddle	13.87	16.41	0.35	8.47	nr	**24.88**
Side bracket	24.18	28.62	0.50	12.09	nr	**40.71**
Rod to cable coupling	11.26	13.33	0.50	12.09	nr	**25.42**
BONDS AND CLAMPS						
Bond to flat surface; copper						
26 mm	2.68	3.17	0.45	10.88	nr	**14.06**
8 mm diameter	10.83	12.82	0.33	7.98	nr	**20.80**
Pipe bond						
26 mm	5.21	6.17	0.45	10.88	nr	**17.05**
8 mm diameter	23.09	27.33	0.33	7.98	nr	**35.31**
Rod to tape clamp						
26 mm	4.35	5.15	0.45	10.88	nr	**16.03**
Square clamp; copper						
25 x 3 mm	4.69	5.55	0.33	7.98	nr	**13.53**
50 x 6 mm	20.79	24.60	0.50	12.09	nr	**36.70**
8 mm diameter	5.53	6.54	0.33	7.98	nr	**14.53**
Test clamp; copper						
26 x 8 mm; oblong	7.31	8.65	0.50	12.09	nr	**20.75**
26 x 8 mm; plate type	20.03	23.70	0.50	12.09	nr	**35.80**
26 x 8 mm; screw down	18.00	21.30	0.50	12.09	nr	**33.40**
Cast in earth points						
2 hole	14.35	16.98	0.75	18.14	nr	**35.12**
4 hole	22.81	27.00	1.00	24.19	nr	**51.18**

W:COMMUNICATIONS/SECURITY/CONTROL

Item	Net Price £	Material £	Labour hours	Labour £	Unit	Total rate £
Extra for cast in earth points						
Cover plate; 25 x 3 mm	16.11	19.07	0.25	6.05	nr	**25.11**
Cover plate; 8 mm	16.11	19.07	0.25	6.05	nr	**25.11**
Rebar clamp; 8 mm	34.55	40.89	0.25	6.05	nr	**46.94**
Static earth receptacle	78.42	92.81	0.50	12.09	nr	**104.90**
Copper braided bonds						
25 x 3 mm						
200 mm hole centres	9.90	11.72	0.33	7.98	nr	**19.70**
400 mm holes centres	14.55	17.22	0.40	9.68	nr	**26.89**
U bolt clamps						
16 mm	5.79	6.85	0.33	7.98	nr	**14.83**
20 mm	6.56	7.76	0.33	7.98	nr	**15.75**
25 mm	8.04	9.52	0.33	7.98	nr	**17.50**
EARTH PITS/MATS						
Earth inspection pit; hand to others for fixing						
Concrete	32.85	38.88	1.00	24.19	nr	**63.07**
Polypropylene	32.60	38.58	1.00	24.19	nr	**62.77**
Extra for						
5 hole copper earth bar; concrete pit	24.30	28.76	0.35	8.47	nr	**37.22**
5 hole earth bar; polypropylene	20.75	24.56	0.35	8.47	nr	**33.02**
Water proof electrode seal						
Single flange	211.24	250.00	0.93	22.50	nr	**272.49**
Double flange	355.44	420.65	0.93	22.50	nr	**443.15**
Earth electrode mat; laid in ground and connected						
Copper tape lattice						
600 x 600 x 3 mm	59.70	70.65	0.93	22.50	nr	**93.15**
900 x 900 x 3 mm	106.95	126.57	0.93	22.50	nr	**149.07**
Copper tape plate						
600 x 600 x 1.5 mm	56.78	67.20	0.93	22.50	nr	**89.69**
600 x 600 x 3 mm	113.56	134.39	0.93	22.50	nr	**156.89**
900 x 900 x 1.5 mm	127.30	150.66	0.93	22.50	nr	**173.15**
900 x 900 x 3 mm	246.99	292.31	0.93	22.50	nr	**314.80**
EARTH RODS						
Solid cored copper earth electrodes driven into ground and connected						
15 mm diameter						
1200 mm long	17.18	20.33	0.93	22.50	nr	**42.83**
Extra for						
Coupling	0.96	1.14	0.06	1.45	nr	**2.59**
Driving stud	1.17	1.38	0.06	1.45	nr	**2.84**
Spike	1.10	1.30	0.06	1.45	nr	**2.75**
Rod Clamp; flat tape	4.35	5.15	0.25	6.05	nr	**11.20**
Rod Clamp; solid conductor	2.12	2.51	0.25	6.05	nr	**8.56**
20 mm diameter						
1200 mm long	31.21	36.94	0.98	23.70	nr	**60.64**

W:COMMUNICATIONS/SECURITY/CONTROL

Item	Net Price £	Material £	Labour hours	Labour £	Unit	Total rate £
W52 : LIGHTNING PROTECTION (cont'd)						
EARTH RODS (cont'd)						
Extra for						
Coupling	0.96	1.14	0.06	1.45	nr	**2.59**
Driving stud	1.94	2.30	0.06	1.45	nr	**3.75**
Spike	1.79	2.12	0.06	1.45	nr	**3.57**
Rod Clamp; flat tape	4.35	5.15	0.25	6.05	nr	**11.20**
Rod Clamp; solid conductor	2.38	2.82	0.25	6.05	nr	**8.86**
Stainless steel earth electrodes driven into ground and connected						
16 mm diameter						
1200 mm long	39.86	47.17	0.93	22.50	nr	**69.67**
Extra for						
Coupling	1.25	1.48	0.06	1.45	nr	**2.93**
Driving head	1.17	1.38	0.06	1.45	nr	**2.84**
Spike	1.10	1.30	0.06	1.45	nr	**2.75**
Rod Clamp; flat tape	4.35	5.15	0.25	6.05	nr	**11.20**
Rod Clamp; solid conductor	2.12	2.51	0.25	6.05	nr	**8.56**
SURGE PROTECTION						
Single Phase; including connection to equipment						
90 - 150v	215.00	254.45	5.00	120.94	nr	**375.39**
200 - 280v	215.00	254.45	5.00	120.94	nr	**375.39**
Three Phase; including connection to equipment						
156 - 260v	425.00	502.97	10.00	241.88	nr	**744.86**
346 - 484v	425.00	502.97	10.00	241.88	nr	**744.86**
349 - 484v; remote display	475.00	562.15	10.00	241.88	nr	**804.03**
346 - 484v; 60kA	825.00	976.36	10.00	241.88	nr	**1218.25**
346 - 484v; 120kA	1575.00	1863.97	10.00	241.88	nr	**2105.85**

W:COMMUNICATIONS/SECURITY/CONTROL

Item	Net Price £	Material £	Labour hours	Labour £	Unit	Total rate £
W60 :CENTRAL CONTROL/BUILDING MANAGEMENT						
Equipment						
Switches/sensors; includes fixing in position; electrical work elsewhere. Note - these are normally free issued to the mechanical contractor for fitting. The labour times applied assume the installation has been prepared for the fitting of the component.						
Pressure devices						
Liquid differential pressure sensor	116.26	137.59	0.50	12.09	nr	**149.68**
Liquid differential pressure switch	63.76	75.46	0.50	12.09	nr	**87.55**
Air differential pressure transmitter	87.76	103.86	0.50	12.09	nr	**115.96**
Air differential pressure switch	12.37	14.64	0.50	12.09	nr	**26.73**
Liquid level switch	44.59	52.77	0.50	12.09	nr	**64.87**
Static pressure sensor	301.49	356.80	0.50	12.09	nr	**368.90**
High pressure switch	63.75	75.45	0.50	12.09	nr	**87.54**
Low pressure switch	63.75	75.45	0.50	12.09	nr	**87.54**
Water pressure switch	63.75	75.45	0.50	12.09	nr	**87.54**
Duct averaging temperature sensor	105.00	124.26	1.00	24.19	nr	**148.45**
Temperature devices						
Return air sensor (fan coils)	5.26	6.23	1.00	24.19	nr	**30.41**
Frost thermostat	21.75	25.74	0.50	12.09	nr	**37.83**
Immersion thermostat	44.95	53.20	0.50	12.09	nr	**65.29**
Temperature high limit	42.04	49.75	0.50	12.09	nr	**61.85**
Temperature sensor with averaging element	105.00	124.26	0.50	12.09	nr	**136.36**
Immersion temperature sensor	45.75	54.14	0.50	12.09	nr	**66.24**
Space temperature sensor	4.50	5.33	1.00	24.19	nr	**29.51**
Combined space temperature & humidity sensor	108.00	127.81	1.00	24.19	nr	**152.00**
Outside air temperature sensor	9.00	10.65	2.00	48.38	nr	**59.03**
Outside air temperature & humidity sensor	124.50	147.34	2.00	48.38	nr	**195.72**
Duct humidity sensor	116.25	137.58	0.50	12.09	nr	**149.67**
Space humidity sensor	108.00	127.81	1.00	24.19	nr	**152.00**
Immersion water flow sensor	108.00	127.81	0.50	12.09	nr	**139.91**
Rain sensor	153.75	181.96	2.00	48.38	nr	**230.34**
Wind speed and direction sensor	789.75	934.65	2.00	48.38	nr	**983.02**
Controllers; includes fixing in position; electrical work elsewhere						
Zone						
Fan coil controller	205.00	242.61	2.00	48.38	nr	**290.99**
VAV controller	205.00	242.61	2.00	48.38	nr	**290.99**

W:COMMUNICATIONS/SECURITY/CONTROL

Item	Net Price £	Material £	Labour hours	Labour £	Unit	Total rate £
W60 :CENTRAL CONTROL/BUILDING MANAGEMENT (cont'd)						
Equipment (cont'd)						
Controllers; includes fixing in position; electrical work elsewhere (cont'd)						
Plant						
Controller, 96 I/O points (exact configuration is dependent upon the number of I/O boards added)	3967.50	4695.42	0.50	12.09	nr	**4707.51**
Controller, 48 I/O points (exact configuration is dependent upon the number of I/O boards added)	2122.50	2511.92	0.50	12.09	nr	**2524.01**
Controller, 32 I/O points (exact configuration is dependent upon the number of I/O boards added)	1507.50	1784.08	0.50	12.09	nr	**1796.18**
Additional Digital Input Boards (12 DI)	472.50	559.19	0.20	4.84	nr	**564.03**
Additional Digital Output Boards (6 DO)	307.50	363.92	0.20	4.84	nr	**368.75**
Additional analogue Input Boards (8 AI)	307.50	363.92	0.20	4.84	nr	**368.75**
Additional analogue Output Boards (8 AO)	307.50	363.92	0.20	4.84	nr	**368.75**
Outstation Enclosure (fitted in riser with space allowance for controller and network device)	212.83	251.88	5.00	120.94	nr	**372.82**
Damper actuator; electrical work elsewhere						
Damper actuator 0-10v	63.60	75.27	-	-	nr	**75.27**
Damper actuator with auxiliary switches	84.00	99.41	-	-	nr	**99.41**
Frequency inverters: not mounted within MCC; includes fixing in position; electrical work elsewhere						
2.2kW	473.26	560.09	2.00	48.38	nr	**608.47**
3kW	522.00	617.77	2.00	48.38	nr	**666.15**
7.5kW	660.00	781.09	2.00	48.38	nr	**829.47**
11kW	895.00	1059.21	2.00	48.38	nr	**1107.58**
15kW	1156.50	1368.68	2.00	48.38	nr	**1417.06**
18.5kW	1282.50	1517.80	2.50	60.47	nr	**1578.27**
20kW	1542.00	1824.91	2.50	60.47	nr	**1885.38**
30kW	1740.76	2060.14	2.50	60.47	nr	**2120.61**
55kW	3627.76	4293.35	3.00	72.57	nr	**4365.91**
Miscellaneous; includes fixing in position; electrical work elsewhere						
1kW Thyristor	72.00	85.21	2.00	48.38	nr	**133.59**
10kW Thyristor	192.00	227.23	2.00	48.38	nr	**275.60**
Front end and networking; electrical work elsewhere						
PC/monitor	2520.83	2983.33	-	-	nr	**2983.33**
Dot matrix printer	457.07	540.93	-	-	nr	**540.93**
PC Software	2253.72	2667.21	-	-	nr	**2667.21**
Lonmaker software	801.99	949.13	-	-	nr	**949.13**
Lonmaker credits	5.94	7.03	-	-	nr	**7.03**
Network server software	1130.15	1337.50	-	-	nr	**1337.50**
Router (allows connection to a network)	635.00	751.50	-	-	nr	**751.50**

PART THREE

Rates of Wages

Mechanical Installations, *page 552*
Electrical Installations, *page 559*

Mechanical Installations

Rates Of Wages

HEATING, VENTILATING, AIR CONDITIONING, PIPING AND DOMESTIC ENGINEERING INDUSTRY

The Joint Conciliation Committee of the Heating, Ventilating and Domestic Engineering Industry has agreed a three year wage agreement for 2003/04 – 2005/06.

For full details of this wage agreement and the Heating Ventilating Air Conditioning Piping and Domestic Engineering Industry's National Working Rule Agreement, contact:

Heating and Ventilating Contractor's Association
ESCA House,
34 Palace Court,
Bayswater,
London W2 4JG
Telephone: 020 7313 4900
Internet: www.hvca.org.uk

WAGE RATES, ALLOWANCES AND OTHER PROVISIONS

Hourly rates of wages
All districts of the United Kingdom

Main Grades	*From* *3 October 2005* *p/hr*
Foreman	13.20
Senior Craftsman (+2nd welding skill)	11.35
Senior Craftsman	10.90
Craftsman (+2nd welding skill)	10.45
Craftsman	10.00
Operative	9.07
Adult Trainee	7.64
Mate (over 18)	7.64
Mate (17-18)	4.91
Mate (up to 17)	3.35
Modern Apprentices	
Junior	4.97
Intermediate	7.03
Senior	9.07

Note: Ductwork Erection Operatives are entitled to the same rates and allowances as the parallel Fitter grades shown.

HEATING, VENTILATING, AIR CONDITIONING, PIPING & DOMESTIC ENGINEERING INDUSTRY

Trainee Rates of Pay

Junior Ductwork Trainees (Probationary)

Age at entry	*From 3 October2005 p/hr*
17	4.09
18	4.92
19	6.29
20	7.65

Junior Ductwork Erectors (Year of Training)

	From 3 October 2005		
Age at entry	*1 yr p/h*	*2 yr p/hr*	*3 yr p/hr*
17	4.92	6.29	7.65
18	6.29	7.65	8.16
19	7.65	7.71	8.52
20	7.65	8.10	8.53

Responsibility Allowance (Craftsmen)	*From 3 October2005 p/hr*
Second welding skill or supervisory responsibility (one unit)	0.45
Second welding skill and supervisory responsibility (two units)	0.90

Responsibility Allowance (Senior Craftsmen)	*From 3 October 2005 p/hr*
Second welding skill	0.45
Supervising responsibility	0.90
Second welding skill and supervisory responsibility	1.35

Daily travelling allowance – Scale 2

C: Craftsmen including Installers
M&A: Mates, Apprentices and Adult Trainees

Direct distance from centre to job in miles

		From 3 October 2005	
Over	*Not exceeding*	C p/hr	M&A p/hr
15	20	2.19	1.88
20	30	5.64	4.88
30	40	8.12	7.02
40	50	10.69	9.15

HEATING, VENTILATING, AIR CONDITIONING, PIPING & DOMESTIC ENGINEERING INDUSTRY

Weekly Holiday Credit and Welfare Contributions

Note: Contributions from 6 October 2005 not available at time of going to press.

	From 6 October 2005						
	£ a	£ b	£ c	£ d	£ e	£ f	£ g
Weekly Holiday Credit Combined Weekly/Welfare Holiday Credit and Contribution	63.30	61.11	59.04	56.97	54.90	54.90	52.83

	From 6 October 2005					
	£ h	£ i	£ j	£ k	£ l	£ m
Weekly Holiday Credit Combined Weekly/Welfare Holiday Credit and Contribution	50.76	46.52	40.00	40.00	27.58	21.37

The grades of H&V Operatives entitled to the different rates of Weekly Holiday Credit and Welfare Contribution are as follows:

a Foreman	*b* Senior Craftsman (RAS & RAW)	*c* Senior Craftsman (RAS)	*d* Senior Craftsman (RAW)
e Senior Craftsman Craftsman Apprentice (+2 RA)	*f* Craftsman (+ 1RA)	*g* Craftsman	*h* Installer Senior Modern
i Adult Trainee Mate (over 18)	*j* Intermediate Modern Apprentice	*k* Junior Modern Apprentice	*l* Mate (aged 17-18)
m Mate (under 17)			

Daily abnormal conditions money
per day

From 3 October 2005

2.99 (No change)

Lodging allowance
£ per night

From 3 November 2003

26.50 (No change)

HEATING, VENTILATING, AIR CONDITIONING, PIPING & DOMESTIC ENGINEERING INDUSTRY

Explanatory Notes

1. Working Hours

    The normal working week (Monday to Friday) shall be 38 hours.

2. Overtime

    Time worked in excess of 38 hours during the normal working week shall be paid at time and a half until 12 hours have been worked since the actual starting time. Thereafter double time shall be paid until normal starting time the following morning. Weekend overtime shall be paid at time and a half for the first 5 hours worked on a Saturday and at double time thereafter until normal starting time on Monday morning.

PLUMBING MECHANICAL ENGINEERING SERVICES INDUSTRY

PLUMBING MECHANICAL ENGINEERING SERVICES INDUSTRY

The Joint Industry Board for Plumbing Mechanical Engineering Services has agreed a two year wage agreement for 2005 – 2006 with effect from 3 January 2005.

Currently, at the time of going to print, there was no promulgation for 2 January 2006, but, the JIB Draft Proposal is a 3.5% increase to all rates.

For full details of this wage agreement and the JIB PMES National Working Rules, contact:

The Joint Industry Board for Plumbing Mechanical Engineering Services in England and Wales
Brook House,
Brook Street,
St Neots,
Huntingdon,
Cambridge PE19 2HW
Telephone: 01480 476925
E-mail: info@jib-pmes.org.uk

WAGE RATES, ALLOWANCES AND OTHER PROVISIONS

EFFECTIVE FROM 3 JANUARY 2005

Basic Rates of Hourly Pay

Applicable in England and Wales

	Hourly rate £
Operatives	
Technical plumber and gas service technician	12.02
Advanced plumber and gas service engineer	10.82
Trained plumber and gas service fitter	9.28
Apprentices	
4th year of training with NVQ level 3	8.99
4th year of training with NVQ level 2	8.13
4th year of training	7.16
3rd year of training with NVQ level 2	7.08
3rd year of training	5.82
2nd year of training	5.16
1st year of training	4.51
Adult Trainees	
3rd 6 months of employment	8.10
2nd 6 months of employment	7.76
1st 6 months of employment	7.25

PLUMBING MECHANICAL ENGINEERING SERVICES INDUSTRY

Major Projects Agreement

Where a job is designated as being a Major Project then the following Major Project Performance Payment hourly rate supplement shall be payable:

Employee Category

	National Payment £	London* Payment £
Technical Plumber and Gas Service Technician	2.20	3.00
Advanced Plumber and Gas Service Engineer	2.20	3.00
Trained Plumber and Gas Service Fitter	2.20	3.00
All 4th year apprentices	1.76	2.40
All 3rd year apprentices	1.32	1.80
2nd year apprentice	1.21	1.65
1st year apprentice	0.88	1.20
All adult trainees	1.76	2.40

* The London Payment Supplement applies only to designated Major Projects that are within the M25 London orbital motorway.

Allowances

Daily travel time allowance plus return fares

All daily travel allowances are to be paid at the daily rate as follows :

Over	Not exceeding	All Operatives	3rd & 4th Year Apprentices	1st & 2nd Year Apprentices
20	30	£3.39	£2.16	£1.34
30	40	£7.92	£5.09	£3.23
40	50	£9.07	£5.39	£3.41

Responsibility/Incentive Pay Allowance

As from Monday 3rd September 2001, Employers may, in consultation with the employees concerned, enhance the basic graded rates of pay by the payment of an additional amount, as per the bands shown below, where it is agreed that their work involves extra responsibility, productivity or flexibility.

Band 1 - an additional rate of £ 0.24 per hour
Band 2 - an additional rate of £ 0.44 per hour
Band 3 - an additional rate of £ 0.64 per hour
Band 4 - an additional rate of £ 0.84 per hour

This allowance forms part of an operative's basic rate of pay and shall be used to calculate premium payments.

Mileage allowance ... ... £0.30 per mile

Lodging allowance ... ... £28.35 per night

Subsistence Allowance (London Only) ... ... £4.18 per night

PLUMBING MECHANICAL ENGINEERING SERVICES INDUSTRY

Plumbers welding supplement

Possession of Gas or Arc Certificate...£0.27 per hour
Possession of Gas and Arc Certificate...£0.46 per hour

Weekly Holiday Credit Contributions (32nd Issue Stamps Option)

	Gross Credit Value, £	Gross Holiday Value*, £
Technical Plumber and Gas Service Technician	56.70	53.30
Advance Plumber and Gas Service Engineer	51.00	48.00
Trained Plumber and Gas Service Fitter	43.60	41.00
Adult Trainee	32.70	31.70
Apprentice in last year of training	32.70	31.70
Apprentice 3rd year	23.60	22.80
Apprentice 2nd year	18.30	17.70
Apprentice 1st year	24.70	23.00
Working Principal	31.00	29.30
Ancillary Employee	20.90	20.20

* Gross holiday value is the gross credit value less JIB administration value.

Explanatory Notes

1.   Working Hours

     The normal working week (Monday to Friday) shall be 37½ hours, with 45 hours to be worked in the same period before overtime rates become applicable.

2.   Overtime

     Overtime shall be paid at time and a half up to 8.00pm (Monday to Friday) and up to 1.00pm (Saturday). Overtime worked after these times shall be paid at double time.

3.   Major Projects Agreement

     Under the Major Projects Agreement the normal working week shall be 38 hours (Monday to Friday) with overtime rates payable for all hours worked in excess of 38 hours in accordance with 2 above. However, it should be noted that the hourly rate supplement shall be paid for each hour worked but does not attract premium time enhancement.

4.   Pension

     In addition to their hourly rates of pay, plumbing employees are entitled to inclusion within the Industry Pension Scheme (or one providing equivalent benefits). The current levels of industry scheme contributions are 6½% (employers) and 3¼% (employees).

Spon's Manual for Educational Premises

Derek Barnsley

Spon's Manual for Educational Premises is an essential reference book for planning, building, remodelling, repairing, maintaining and managing a wide range of both modern and historic educational premises.

It contains clear, practical guidance for local authorities, head teachers and governing boards responsible for planning, costing, commissioning, supervising and paying for building work and maintenance services. The book is equally essential for architects, surveyors and other professionals and contractors carrying out work in the educational sector.

The third edition has been revised to respond to the evolution of new teaching methods and technology, the development of vocational training and to meet new mandatory regulations relating to children who require special care. The book focuses on cost and performance, including PFI and PPP criteria, but with added emphasis on economic planning to improve standards in design and performance to meet detailed educational needs.

January 2004: 297x210 mm: 464 pages
HB: 0-415-28077-X: £200.00

To Order: Tel: +44 (0) 1264 343071 Fax: +44 (0) 1264 343005, or
Post: Taylor and Francis Customer Services, Thomson Publishing Services, Cheriton House, Andover, Hants, SP10 5BE, UK Email: book.orders@tandf.co.uk

For a complete listing of all our titles visit:
www.sponpress.com

Taylor & Francis
Taylor & Francis Group plc

Construction Project Management
An Integrated Approach

Peter Fewings

As increasing demands and higher expectations are placed on project managers, a need has arisen for an innovative book to enable managers to take on the ever-changing challenges involved in overseeing whole works and dealing with the conflicting needs of the many people involved in a construction project.

Based on the authors' observations and experience, this book offers the reader a new approach to project management in construction and engineering, increasing efficiency and communication at all stages while reducing costs, time and risk. It considers integrated project management, emphasising the importance of effectively handling external factors in order to best achieve an on-schedule, on-budget result, and focusing on good negotiation with clients and skilled team leadership.

August 2005: 234x156 mm: 400 pages
HB: 0-415-35905-8: £65.00
PB: 0-415-35906-6: £24.99

To Order: Tel: +44 (0) 1264 343071 Fax: +44 (0) 1264 343005, or
Post: Taylor and Francis Customer Services, Thomson Publishing Services, Cheriton House, Andover, Hants, SP10 5BE, UK Email: book.orders@tandf.co.uk

For a complete listing of all our titles visit:
www.sponpress.com

Electrical Installations

Rates Of Wages

ELECTRICAL CONTRACTING INDUSTRY

The Joint Industry Board for the Electrical Contracting Industry has agreed a two year wage agreement for 2006/07 & 2007/08 with effect from 9th January 2006.

For full details of this wage agreement and the Joint Industry Board for the Electrical Contracting Industry's National Working Rules, contact:

The Joint Industry Board for the Electrical Contracting Industry
Kingswood House
47/51 Sidcup Hill,
Sidcup,
Kent DA14 6HP
Telephone : 020 8302 0031
Internet : www.jib.org.uk

WAGES (Graded Operatives)

Rates

Since **7th January 2002** two different wage rates have applied to JIB Graded Operatives working on site, depending on whether the Employer transports them to site or whether they provide their own transport. The two categories are:

Job Employed (Transport Provided)

Payable to an Operative who is transported to and from the job by his Employer. The Operative shall also be entitled to payment for Travel Time, when travelling in his own time, as detailed in the appropriate scale.

Job Employed (Own Transport)

Payable to an Operative who travels by his own means to and from the job. The Operative shall be entitled to payment for Travel Allowance and also Travel Time, when travelling in his own time, as detailed in the appropriate scale.

The JIB rates of wages are set out below:

From and including 9th January 2006, the JIB hourly rates of wages shall be as set out below:

(i)   National Standard Rate:

Grade	Transport Provided	Own Transport
Technician (or equivalent specialist grade)	£ 12.84	£ 13.49
Approved Electrician (or equivalent specialist grade)	£ 11.33	£ 11.98
Electrician (or equivalent specialist grade)	£ 10.39	£ 11.05
Senior Graded Electrical Trainee	£ 9.35	£ 9.94
Electrical Improver	£ 9.35	£ 9.94
Labourer	£ 8.25	£ 8.86
Adult Trainee	£ 8.25	£ 8.86
Adult Trainee (under 21)	£ 6.19	£ 6.65

ELECTRICAL CONTRACTING INDUSTRY

(ii)   London Rate:

Grade	Transport Provided	Own Transport
Technician (or equivalent specialist grade)	£ 14.38	£ 15.11
Approved Electrician (or equivalent specialist grade)	£ 12.69	£ 13.42
Electrician (or equivalent specialist grade)	£ 11.64	£ 12.38
Senior Graded Electrical Trainee	£ 10.47	£ 11.13
Electrical Improver	£ 10.47	£ 11.13
Labourer	£ 9.24	£ 9.92
Adult Trainee	£ 9.24	£ 9.92
Adult Trainee (under 21)	£ 6.93	£ 7.45

1999 Joint Industry Board Apprentice Training Scheme

From and including 9th January 2006, the JIB hourly rates for Job Employed apprentices shall be:

(i)   National Standard Rates

	Transport Provided	Own Transport
Stage 1	£ 3.63	£ 4.25
Stage 2	£ 5.35	£ 5.98
Stage 3	£ 7.74	£ 8.39
Stage 4	£ 8.20	£ 8.85

(ii)   London Rate

	Transport Provided	Own Transport
Stage 1	£ 4.07	£ 4.76
Stage 2	£ 5.99	£ 6.70
Stage 3	£ 8.67	£ 9.40
Stage 4	£ 9.18	£ 9.91

ELECTRICAL CONTRACTING INDUSTRY

Travelling Time and Travel Allowances

From and including 9th January 2006

Operatives required to start/finish at the normal starting and finishing time on jobs which are 15 miles and over from the shop - in a straight line - receive payment for Travelling Time and where transport is not provided by the Employer, Travel Allowance, as follows:

Distance	Total Daily Travel Allowance	Total Daily Travelling Time
(a) **National Standard Rate**		
Up to 15 miles	Nil	Nil
Over 15 & up to 20 miles each way	£ 2.87	£ 3.91
Over 20 & up to 25 miles each way	£ 3.80	£ 4.95
Over 25 & up to 35 miles each way	£ 5.01	£ 6.05
Over 35 & up to 55 miles each way	£ 7.98	£ 7.98
Over 55 & up to 75 miles each way	£ 9.77	£ 9.77

For each additional 10 mile band over 75 miles, additional payment of £ 1.72 for Daily Travel Allowance and £ 1.72 for Daily Travel Time will be made.

Note: Special arrangements may apply for work in the Merseyside area.

Distance	Total Daily Travel Allowance	Total Daily Travelling Time
(b) **London Rate**		
Up to 15 miles	Nil	Nil
Over 15 & up to 20 miles each way	£ 2.89	£ 4.19
Over 20 & up to 25 miles each way	£ 3.83	£ 5.49
Over 25 & up to 35 miles each way	£ 5.05	£ 6.60
Over 35 & up to 55 miles each way	£ 8.05	£ 8.91
Over 55 & up to 75 miles each way	£ 9.85	£ 10.43

For each additional 10 mile band over 75 miles, additional payments of £ 1.73 for Daily Travel Allowance and £ 1.73 for Daily Travel Time will be made.

Travelling time and travel allowance - Section 8

Operatives required to start/finish at the normal starting and finishing time on jobs which are 15 miles and over from the shop - in a straight line - receive payment for Travelling Time and where transport is not provided by the Employer, Travel Allowance, as follows:

From and including 9th January 2006

Distance	Total Daily Travel Allowance	Total Daily Travelling Time
(a) **National Standard Rate**		
Up to 15 miles	Nil	Nil
Over 15 & up to 20 miles each way	£ 2.87	£ 2.30
Over 20 & up to 25 miles each way	£ 3.80	£ 3.45
Over 25 & up to 35 miles each way	£ 5.01	£ 4.60
Over 35 & up to 55 miles each way	£ 7.98	£ 5.75
Over 55 & up to 75 miles each way	£ 9.77	£ 6.90

For each additional 10 mile band over 75 miles, additional payments of £ 1.81 for Daily Travel Allowance and £ 1.06 for Daily Travelling Time will be made.

Note: Special arrangements may apply for work in the Merseyside area.

Rates of Wages - Electrical Installations

ELECTRICAL CONTRACTING INDUSTRY

Distance	Total Daily Travel Allowance	
(b) **London Rate**		
Up to 15 miles	Nil	Nil
Over 15 & up to 20 miles each way	£ 2.89	£ 2.54
Over 20 & up to 25 miles each way	£ 3.83	£ 3.83
Over 25 & up to 35 miles each way	£ 5.05	£ 5.10
Over 35 & up to 55 miles each way	£ 8.05	£ 6.36
Over 55 & up to 75 miles each way	£ 9.85	£ 7.65

For each additional 10 mile band over 75 miles, additional payments of £ 1.59 for Daily Travel Allowance and £ 1.06 for Daily Travelling Time will be made.

Lodging Allowances
£ 28.35 from and including 5 January 2004

Lodgings weekend retention fee, maximum reimbursement
£ 28.35 from and including 5 January 2004

Annual Holiday Lodging Allowance Retention
£ 5.85 per night (£ 40.95 per week) from and including 5 January 2004

Responsibility money

From and including 30 March 1998 the minimum payment increased to 10p per hour and the maximum to £1.00 per hour (no change)

From and including 4 January 1992 responsibility payments are enhanced by overtime and shift premiums where appropriate (no change)

Combined JIB Benefits Stamp Value (from week commencing 5 January 2004)

JIB Grade	Weekly JIB combined credit value	Holiday Value
Technician	£ 50.50	£ 37.60
Approved Electrician	£ 45.87	£ 33.16
Electrician	£ 43.04	£ 30.43
Senior Graded Electrical Trainee and Electrical Improver	£ 38.88	£ 27.38
Labourer & Adult Trainee	£ 36.54	£ 24.18
Adult Trainee (Under 21)	£ 29.62	£ 18.12

ELECTRICAL CONTRACTING INDUSTRY

Explanatory Notes

1. Working Hours

   The normal working week (Monday to Friday) shall be 37½ hours, with 38 hours to be worked in the same period before overtime rates become applicable.

2. Overtime

   Overtime shall be paid at time and a half for all weekday overtime. Saturday overtime shall be paid at time and a half for the first 6 hours, or up to 3.00pm (whichever comes first). Thereafter double time shall be paid until normal starting time on Monday.

19th Edition

Clay's Handbook of Environmental Health

Edited by W. H. Bassett

This classic, definitive reference work for all those involved in environmental health is now available in its 19th edition.

Significant changes include those made to chapters on food safety and hygiene, environmental protection, the organisation and management of environmental health in the UK, port health, and waste management. New chapters have been added on health development, an introduction to health and housing, contaminated land, and environmental health in emergency planning, as well as a new glossary of abbreviations and acronyms.

New material on training and standards, IT, practical risk assessment, and investigatory powers is also included. Each chapter reflects the wider background against which the subjects must be studied and the new concepts and approaches that have emerged over the past few years.

Contents: 1. Environmental Health: Definition and Organization 2.Environmental Health Law and Administration 3. Public Health and Safety 4. Epidemiology 5. Housing 6. Occupational Health and Safety 7. Food Safety and Hygiene 8. Environmental Protection

May 2004: 246x189 mm: 976 pages
58 line drawings and 136 tables
HB: 0-415-31808-4: £140.00

To Order: Tel: +44 (0) 1264 343071 Fax: +44 (0) 1264 343005, or
Post: Taylor and Francis Customer Services, Thomson Publishing Services, Cheriton House, Andover, Hants, SP10 5BE, UK Email: book.orders@tandf.co.uk

For a complete listing of all our titles visit:
www.sponpress.com

Taylor & Francis
Taylor & Francis Group plc

PART FOUR

Daywork

Heating and Ventilating Industry, *page 566*
Electrical Industry, *page 569*
Building Industry Plant Hire Costs, *page 572*

When work is carried out in connection with a contract that cannot be valued in any other way, it is usual to assess the value on a cost basis with suitable allowances to cover overheads and profit. The basis of costing is a matter for agreement between the parties concerned but definitions of prime cost for the Heating and Ventilating and Electrical Industries have been published jointly by the Royal Institution of Chartered Surveyors and the appropriate bodies of the industries concerned, for those who wish to use them.

These, together with a schedule of basic plant hire charges are reproduced on the following pages, with the kind permission of the Royal Institution of Chartered Surveyors, who own the copyright.

HEATING AND VENTILATING INDUSTRY

DEFINITION OF PRIME COST OF DAYWORK CARRIED OUT UNDER A HEATING, VENTILATING, AIR CONDITIONING, REFRIGERATION, PIPEWORK AND/OR DOMESTIC ENGINEERING CONTRACT (JULY 1980 EDITION)

This Definition of Prime Cost is published by the Royal Institution of Chartered Surveyors and the Heating and Ventilating Contractors Association for convenience, and for use by people who choose to use it. Members of the Heating and Ventilating Contractors Association are not in any way debarred from defining Prime Cost and rendering accounts for work carried out on that basis in any way they choose. Building owners are advised to reach agreement with contractors on the Definition of Prime Cost to be used prior to entering into a contract or sub-contract.

SECTION 1: APPLICATION

1.1   This Definition provides a basis for the valuation of daywork executed under such heating, ventilating, air conditioning, refrigeration, pipework and or domestic engineering contracts as provide for its use.

1.2   It is not applicable in any other circumstances, such as jobbing or other work carried out as a separate or main contract nor in the case of daywork executed after a date of practical completion.

1.3   The terms 'contract' and 'contractor' herein shall be read as 'sub-contract' and 'sub-contractor' as applicable.

SECTION 2: COMPOSITION OF TOTAL CHARGES

2.1   The Prime Cost of daywork comprises the sum of the following costs:
(a)   Labour as defined in Section 3.
(b)   Materials and goods as defined in Section 4.
(c)   Plant as defined in Section 5.

2.2   Incidental costs, overheads and profit as defined in Section 6, as provided in the contract and expressed therein as percentage adjustments, are applicable to each of 2.1 (a)-(c).

SECTION 3: LABOUR

3.1   The standard wage rates, emoluments and expenses referred to below and the standard working hours referred to in 3.2 are those laid down for the time being in the rules or decisions or agreements of the Joint Conciliation Committee of the Heating, Ventilating and Domestic Engineering Industry applicable to the works (or those of such other body as may be appropriate) and to the grade of operative concerned at the time when and the area where the daywork is executed.

3.2   Hourly base rates for labour are computed by dividing the annual prime cost of labour, based upon the standard working hours and as defined in 3.4, by the number of standard working hours per annum. See example.

3.3   The hourly rates computed in accordance with 3.2 shall be applied in respect of the time spent by operatives directly engaged on daywork, including those operating mechanical plant and transport and erecting and dismantling other plant (unless otherwise expressly provided in the contract) and handling and distributing the materials and goods used in the daywork.

3.4   The annual prime cost of labour comprises the following:
(a)   Standard weekly earnings (i.e. the standard working week as determined at the appropriate rate for the operative concerned).
(b)   Any supplemental payments.
(c)   Any guaranteed minimum payments (unless included in Section 6.1 (a)-(p)).
(d)   Merit money.
(e)   Differentials or extra payments in respect of skill, responsibility, discomfort, inconvenience or risk (excluding those in respect of supervisory responsibility - see 3.5)
(f)   Payments in respect of public holidays.
(g)   Any amounts which may become payable by the contractor to or in respect of operatives arising from the rules etc. referred to in 3.1 which are not provided for in 3.4 (a)-(f) nor in Section 6.1 (a)-(p).
(h)   Employers contributions to the WELPLAN, the HVACR Welfare and Holiday Scheme or payments in lieu thereof.
(i)   Employers National Insurance contributions as applicable to 3.4 (a)-(h).
(j)   Any contribution, levy or tax imposed by Statute, payable by the contractor in his capacity as an employer.

HEATING AND VENTILATING INDUSTRY

3.5 Differentials or extra payments in respect of supervisory responsibility are excluded from the annual prime cost (see Section 6). The time of principals, staff, foremen, chargehands and the like when working manually is admissible under this Section at the rates for the appropriate grades.

SECTION 4: MATERIALS AND GOODS

4.1 The prime cost of materials and goods obtained specifically for the daywork is the invoice cost after deducting all trade discounts and any portion of cash discounts in excess of 5%.

4.2 The prime cost of all other materials and goods used in the daywork is based upon the current market prices plus any appropriate handling charges.

4.3 The prime cost referred to in 4.1 and 4.2 includes the cost of delivery to site.

4.4 Any Value Added Tax which is treated, or is capable of being treated, as input tax (as defined by the Finance Act 1972, or any re-enactment or amendment thereof or substitution therefore) by the contractor is excluded.

SECTION 5: PLANT

5.1 Unless otherwise stated in the contract, the prime cost of plant comprises the cost of the following:
  (a) use or hire of mechanically-operated plant and transport for the time employed on and/or provided or retained for the daywork;
  (b) use of non-mechanical plant (excluding non-mechanical hand tools) for the time employed on and/or provided or retained for the daywork;
  (c) transport to and from the site and erection and dismantling where applicable.

5.2 The use of non-mechanical hand tools and of erected scaffolding, staging, trestles or the like is excluded (see Section 6), unless specifically retained for the daywork.

SECTION 6: INCIDENTAL COSTS, OVERHEADS AND PROFIT

6.1 The percentage adjustments provided in the contract which are applicable to each of the totals of Sections 3, 4 and 5 comprise the following:
  (a) Head office charges.
  (b) Site staff including site supervision.
  (c) The additional cost of overtime (other than that referred to in 6.2).
  (d) Time lost due to inclement weather.
  (e) The additional cost of bonuses and all other incentive payments in excess of any included in 3.4.
  (f) Apprentices' study time.
  (g) Fares and travelling allowances.
  (h) Country, lodging and periodic allowances.
  (i) Sick pay or insurances in respect thereof, other than as included in 3.4.
  (j) Third party and employers' liability insurance.
  (k) Liability in respect of redundancy payments to employees.
  (l) Employer's National Insurance contributions not included in 3.4.
  (m) Use and maintenance of non-mechanical hand tools.
  (n) Use of erected scaffolding, staging, trestles or the like (but see 5.2).
  (o) Use of tarpaulins, protective clothing, artificial lighting, safety and welfare facilities, storage and the like that may be available on site.
  (p) Any variation to basic rates required by the contractor in cases where the contract provides for the use of a specified schedule of basic plant charges (to the extent that no other provision is made for such variation - see 5.1).
  (q) In the case of a sub-contract which provides that the sub-contractor shall allow a cash discount, such provision as is necessary for the allowance of the prescribed rate of discount.
  (r) All other liabilities and obligations whatsoever not specifically referred to in this Section nor chargeable under any other Section.
  (s) Profit.

6.2 The additional cost of overtime where specifically ordered by the Architect/Supervising Officer shall only be chargeable in the terms of a prior written agreement between the parties.

HEATING AND VENTILATING INDUSTRY

MECHANICAL INSTALLATIONS

Calculation of Hourly Base Rate of Labour for Typical Main Grades applicable from 3rd October 2005.

	FOREMAN	SENIOR CRAFTSMAN (+ 2nd Welding Skill)	SENIOR CRAFTSMAN	CRAFTSMAN	INSTALLER	MATE OVER 18
Hourly Rate from 3 October 2005	13.20	11.35	10.90	10.00	9.07	7.64
Annual standard earnings excluding all holidays, 45.8 weeks x 38 hours	22,973.28	19,753.54	18,970.36	17,404.00	15,785.43	13,296.66
Employers national insurance contributions from 6 April 2005	2,363.04	1,950.92	1,850.67	1,650.18	1,443.00	1,124.44
Weekly holiday credit and welfare contributions (52 weeks) from 3 October 2005	3,567.72	3,112.72	2,999.36	2,773.16	2,541.76	2,185.56
Annual prime cost of labour	28,904.04	24,817.18	23,820.39	21,827.34	19,770.19	16,606.65
Hourly base rate	16.61	14.26	13.69	12.54	11.36	9.54

Notes:

(1) Annual industry holiday (4.6 weeks x 38 hours) and public holidays (1.6 weeks x 38 hours) are paid through weekly holiday credit and welfare stamp scheme.

(2) Where applicable, Merit money and other variables (e.g. daily abnormal conditions money), which attract Employer's National Insurance contribution, should be included.

(3) Contractors in Northern Ireland should add the appropriate amount of CITB Levy to the annual prime cost of labour prior to calculating the hourly base rate.

ELECTRICAL INDUSTRY

DEFINITION OF PRIME COST OF DAYWORK CARRIED OUT UNDER AN ELECTRICAL CONTRACT (MARCH 1981 EDITION)

This Definition of Prime Cost is published by The Royal Institution of Chartered Surveyors and The Electrical Contractors' Associations for convenience and for use by people who choose to use it. Members of The Electrical Contractors' Association are not in any way debarred from defining Prime Cost and rendering accounts for work carried out on that basis in any way they choose. Building owners are advised to reach agreement with contractors on the Definition of Prime Cost to be used prior to entering into a contract or sub-contract.

SECTION 1: APPLICATION

1.1 This Definition provides a basis for the valuation of daywork executed under such electrical contracts as provide for its use.
1.2 It is not applicable in any other circumstances, such as jobbing, or other work carried out as a separate or main contract, nor in the case of daywork executed after the date of practical completion.
1.3 The terms 'contract' and 'contractor' herein shall be read as 'sub-contract' and 'sub-contractor' as the context may require.

SECTION 2: COMPOSITION OF TOTAL CHARGES

2.1 The Prime Cost of daywork comprises the sum of the following costs:
   (a) Labour as defined in Section 3.
   (b) Materials and goods as defined in Section 4.
   (c) Plant as defined in Section 5.
2.2 Incidental costs, overheads and profit as defined in Section 6, as provided in the contract and expressed therein as percentage adjustments, are applicable to each of 2.1 (a)-(c).

SECTION 3: LABOUR

3.1 The standard wage rates, emoluments and expenses referred to below and the standard working hours referred to in 3.2 are those laid down for the time being in the rules and determinations or decisions of the Joint Industry Board or the Scottish Joint Industry Board for the Electrical Contracting Industry (or those of such other body as may be appropriate) applicable to the works and relating to the grade of operative concerned at the time when and in the area where daywork is executed.
3.2 Hourly base rates for labour are computed by dividing the annual prime cost of labour, based upon the standard working hours and as defined in 3.4 by the number of standard working hours per annum. See examples.
3.3 The hourly rates computed in accordance with 3.2 shall be applied in respect of the time spent by operatives directly engaged on daywork, including those operating mechanical plant and transport and erecting and dismantling other plant (unless otherwise expressly provided in the contract) and handling and distributing the materials and goods used in the daywork.
3.4 The annual prime cost of labour comprises the following:
   (a) Standard weekly earnings (i.e. the standard working week as determined at the appropriate rate for the operative concerned).
   (b) Payments in respect of public holidays.
   (c) Any amounts which may become payable by the Contractor to or in respect of operatives arising from operation of the rules etc. referred to in 3.1 which are not provided for in 3.4(a) and (b) nor in Section 6.
   (d) Employer's National Insurance Contributions as applicable to 3.4 (a)-(c).
   (e) Employer's contributions to the Joint Industry Board Combined Benefits Scheme or Scottish Joint Industry Board Holiday and Welfare Stamp Scheme, and holiday payments made to apprentices in compliance with the Joint Industry Board National Working Rules and Industrial Determinations as an employer.
   (f) Any contribution, levy or tax imposed by Statute, payable by the Contractor in his capacity as an employer.
3.5 Differentials or extra payments in respect of supervisory responsibility are excluded from the annual prime cost (see Section 6). The time of principals and similar categories, when working manually, is admissible under this Section at the rates for the appropriate grades.

ELECTRICAL INDUSTRY

SECTION 4: MATERIALS AND GOODS

4.1   The prime cost of materials and goods obtained specifically for the daywork is the invoice cost after deducting all trade discounts and any portion of cash discounts in excess of 5%.

4.2   The prime cost of all other materials and goods used in the daywork is based upon the current market prices plus any appropriate handling charges.

4.3   The prime cost referred to in 4.1 and 4.2 includes the cost of delivery to site.

4.4   Any Value Added Tax which is treated, or is capable of being treated, as input tax (as defined by the Finance Act 1972, or any re-enactment or amendment thereof or substitution therefore) by the Contractor is excluded.

SECTION 5: PLANT

5.1   Unless otherwise stated in the contract, the prime cost of plant comprises the cost of the following:

    (a)   Use or hire of mechanically-operated plant and transport for the time employed on and/or provided or retained for the daywork;

    (b)   Use of non-mechanical plant (excluding non-mechanical hand tools) for the time employed on and/or provided or retained for the daywork;

    (c)   Transport to and from the site and erection and dismantling where applicable.

5.2   The use of non-mechanical hand tools and of erected scaffolding, staging, trestles or the likes is excluded (see Section 6), unless specifically retained for daywork.

5.3   Note: Where hired or other plant is operated by the Electrical Contractor's operatives, such time is to be included under Section 3 unless otherwise provided in the contract.

SECTION 6: INCIDENTAL COSTS, OVERHEADS AND PROFIT

6.1   The percentage adjustments provided in the contract which are applicable to each of the totals of Sections 3, 4 and 5, compromise the following:

    (a)   Head Office charges.

    (b)   Site staff including site supervision.

    (c)   The additional cost of overtime (other than that referred to in 6.2).

    (d)   Time lost due to inclement weather.

    (e)   The additional cost of bonuses and other incentive payments.

    (f)   Apprentices' study time.

    (g)   Travelling time and fares.

    (h)   Country and lodging allowances.

    (i)   Sick pay or insurance in lieu thereof, in respect of apprentices.

    (j)   Third party and employers' liability insurance.

    (k)   Liability in respect of redundancy payments to employees.

    (l)   Employers' National Insurance Contributions not included in 3.4.

    (m)   Use and maintenance of non-mechanical hand tools.

    (n)   Use of erected scaffolding, staging, trestles or the like (but see 5.2.).

    (o)   Use of tarpaulins, protective clothing, artificial lighting, safety and welfare facilities, storage and the like that may be available on site.

    (p)   Any variation to basic rates required by the Contractor in cases where the contract provides for the use of a specified schedule of basic plant charges (to the extent that no other provision is made for such variation - see 5.1).

    (q)   All other liabilities and obligations whatsoever not specifically referred to in this Section nor chargeable under any other Section.

    (r)   Profit.

    (s)   In the case of a sub-contract which provides that the sub-contractor shall allow a cash discount, such provision as is necessary for the allowance of the prescribed rate of discount.

6.2   The additional cost of overtime where specifically ordered by the Architect/Supervising Officer shall only be chargeable in the terms of a prior written agreement between the parties.

ELECTRICAL INDUSTRY

ELECTRICAL INSTALLATIONS

Calculation of Hourly Base Rate of Labour for Typical Main Grades applicable from 9th January 2006

	TECHNICIAN	APPROVED ELECTRICIAN	ELECTRICIAN	LABOURER
Hourly Rate from 9 January 2006 (London Rates)	15.11	13.42	12.38	9.92
Annual standard earnings excluding all holidays, 46 weeks x 37.5 hours	26,064.75	23,149.50	21,355.50	17,112.00
Employers national insurance contributions from 6 April 2005	2,758.75	2,385.60	2,155.97	1,612.80
JIB Combined benefits from 6 January 2006	2,626.00	2,385.24	2,238.08	1,900.08
Holiday top up funding	1,417.00	1,272.44	1,182.48	959.92
Annual prime cost of labour	32,866.50	29,192.78	26,832.03	21,584.80
Hourly base rate	19.05	16.92	15.61	12.51

Notes:

(1) Annual industry holiday (4.4 weeks x 37.5 hours) and public holidays (1.6 weeks x 37.5 hours)

(2) It should be noted that all labour costs incurred by the Contractor in his capacity as an Employer, other than those contained in the hourly rate above, must be taken into account under Section 6.

(3) Public Holidays are paid through weekly holiday credit and welfare stamp scheme.

(4) Contractors in Northern Ireland should add the appropriate amount of CITB Levy to the annual prime cost of labour prior to calculating the hourly base rate.

BUILDING INDUSTRY PLANT HIRE COSTS

SCHEDULE OF BASIC PLANT CHARGES (MAY 2001)

This Schedule is published by the Royal Institution of Chartered Surveyors and is for use in connection with Dayworks under a Building Contract.

EXPLANATORY NOTES

1   The rates in the Schedule are intended to apply solely to daywork carried out under and incidental to a Building Contract. They are NOT intended to apply to:
    (i)   jobbing or any other work carried out as a main or separate contract; or
    (ii)   work carried out after the date of commencement of the Defects Liability Period.

2   The rates apply to plant and machinery already on site, whether hired or owned by the Contractor.

3   The rates, unless otherwise stated, include the cost of fuel and power of every description, lubricating oils, grease, maintenance, sharpening of tools, replacement of spare parts, all consumable stores and for licences and insurances applicable to items of plant.

4   The rates, unless otherwise stated, do not include the costs of drivers and attendants (unless otherwise stated).

5   The rates in the Schedule are base costs and may be subject to an overall adjustment for price movement, overheads and profit, quoted by the Contractor prior to the placing of the Contract.

6   The rates should be applied to the time during which the plant is actually engaged in daywork.

7   Whether or not plant is chargeable on daywork depends on the daywork agreement in use and the inclusion of an item of plant in this schedule does not necessarily indicate that item is chargeable.

8   Rates for plant not included in the Schedule or which is not already on site and is specifically provided or hired for daywork shall be settled at prices which are reasonably related to the rates in the Schedule having regard to any overall adjustment quoted by the Contractor in the Conditions of Contract.

NOTE: All rates in the schedule were calculated during the first quarter of 2001.

BUILDING INDUSTRY PLANT HIRE COSTS

MECHANICAL PLANT AND TOOLS

Item of Plant	Size/Rating	Unit	Rate/hr
PUMPS			
Mobile Pumps			
Including pump hoses, valves and strainers etc.			
Diaphragm	50mm dia.	Each	0.87
Diaphragm	76mm dia.	Each	1.29
Submersible	50mm dia.	Each	1.18
Induced flow	50mm dia.	Each	1.54
Induced flow	76mm dia.	Each	2.05
Centrifugal, self priming	50mm dia.	Each	1.96
Centrifugal, self priming	102mm dia.	Each	2.52
Centrifugal, self priming	152mm dia.	Each	3.87
SCAFFOLDING, SHORING, FENCING			
Complete Scaffolding			
Mobile working towers, single width	1.8m x 0.8m base x 7m high	Each	2.00
Mobile working towers, single width	1.8m x 0.8m base x 9m high	Each	2.80
Mobile working towers, double width	1.8m x 1.4m base x 7m high	Each	2.15
Mobile working towers, double width	1.8m x 1.4m base x 15m high	Each	5.10
Chimney scaffold, single unit		Each	1.79
Chimney scaffold, twin unit		Each	2.05
Chimney scaffold, four unit		Each	3.59
Trestles			
Trestle, adjustable	Any height	Pair	0.10
Trestle, painters	1.8m high	Pair	0.21
Trestle, Painters	2.4m high	Pair	0.26
Shoring, Planking and Struting			
'Acrow' adjustable prop	Sizes up to 4.9m (open)	Each	0.10
'Strong boy' support attachment		Each	0.15
Adjustable trench struts	Sizes up to 1.67m (open)	Each	0.10
Trench sheet		Metre	0.01
Backhoe trench box		Each	1.00
Temporary Fencing			
Including block and coupler			
Site fencing steel grid panel	3.5m x 2.0m	Each	0.08
Anti-climb site steel grid fence panel	3.5m x 2.0m	Each	0.08
LIFTING APPLIANCES AND CONVEYORS			
Cranes			
Mobile Cranes			
Rates are inclusive of drivers			
Lorry mounted, telescopic jib			
Two wheel drive	6 tonnes	Each	24.40
Two wheel drive	7 tonnes	Each	25.00
Two wheel drive	8 tonnes	Each	25.62
Two wheel drive	10 tonnes	Each	26.90
Two wheel drive	12 tonnes	Each	28.25
Two wheel drive	15 tonnes	Each	29.66
Two wheel drive	18 tonnes	Each	31.14
Two wheel drive	20 tonnes	Each	32.70
Two wheel drive	25 tonnes	Each	34.33

BUILDING INDUSTRY PLANT HIRE COSTS

MECHANICAL PLANT AND TOOLS

Item of Plant	Size/Rating	Unit	Rate/hr
Cranes (cont'd)			
Four wheel drive	10 tonnes	Each	27.44
Four wheel drive	12 tonnes	Each	28.81
Four wheel drive	15 tonnes	Each	30.25
Four wheel drive	20 tonnes	Each	33.35
Four wheel drive	25 tonnes	Each	35.19
Four wheel drive	30 tonnes	Each	37.12
Four wheel drive	45 tonnes	Each	39.16
Four wheel drive	50 tonnes	Each	41.32

Track-mounted tower crane
Rates inclusive of driver
Note : Capacity equals maximum lift in tonnes times maximum radius at which it can be lifted

	Capacity (metre/tonnes) up to	Height under hook above ground (m) up to		
Tower crane	10	17	Each	7.99
Tower crane	15	18	Each	8.59
Tower crane	20	20	Each	9.18
Tower crane	25	22	Each	11.56
Tower crane	30	22	Each	13.78
Tower crane	40	22	Each	18.09
Tower crane	50	22	Each	22.20
Tower crane	60	22	Each	24.32
Tower crane	70	22	Each	23.00
Tower crane	80	22	Each	25.91
Tower crane	110	22	Each	26.45
Tower crane	125	30	Each	29.38
Tower crane	150	30	Each	32.35

Static tower cranes
Rates inclusive of driver
To be charged at 90% of the above rates for track mounted tower cranes

Crane Equipment

		Unit	Rate/hr
Muck tipping skip	Up to 0.25m³	Each	0.56
Muck tipping skip	0.5m³	Each	0.67
Muck tipping skip	0.75m³	Each	0.82
Muck tipping skip	1.0m³	Each	1.03
Muck tipping skip	1.5m³	Each	1.18
Muck tipping skip	2.0m³	Each	1.38
Mortar skips	up to 0.38m³		0.41
Boat skips	1.0m³		1.08
Boat skips	1.5m³		1.33
Boat skips	2.0m³		1.59
Concrete skips, hand levered	0.5m³		1.00
Concrete skips, hand levered	0.75m³		1.10
Concrete skips, hand levered	1.0m³		1.25
Concrete skips, hand levered	1.5m³		1.50
Concrete skips, hand levered	2.0m³		1.65

BUILDING INDUSTRY PLANT HIRE COSTS

MECHANICAL PLANT AND TOOLS

Item of Plant	Size/Rating		Unit	Rate/hr
Concrete skips, geared	0.5m³			1.30
Concrete skips, geared	0.75m³			1.40
Concrete skips, geared	1.0m³			1.55
Concrete skips, geared	1.5m³			1.80
Concrete skips, geared	2.0m³			2.05
Hoists				
Scaffold hoists	200kg			1.92
Rack and pinion (goods only)	500kg			3.31
Rack and pinion (goods only)	1100kg			4.28
Rack and pinion goods and passenger	15 person, 1200kg			5.62
Wheelbarrow chain sling				0.31
Conveyors				
Belt conveyors				
Conveyor	7.5m long x 400mm wide			6.41
Miniveyor, control box and loading hopper	3m unit			3.59
Other Conveying Equipment				
Wheelbarrow				0.21
Hydraulic superlift				2.95
Pavac slab lifter				1.03
Hand pad and hose attachment				0.26
Lifting Trucks				
Fork lift, two wheel drive	Payload	Max Lift		
Fork lift, two wheel drive	1100kg	up to 3.0m	Each	4.87
Fork lift, two wheel drive	2540kg	up to 3.7m	Each	5.12
Fork lift, four wheel drive	1524kg	up to 6.0m	Each	6.04
Fork lift, four wheel drive	2600kg	up to 5.4m	Each	7.69
Lifting Platforms				
Hydraulic platform (Cherry picker)	7.5m		Each	4.23
Hydraulic platform (Cherry picker)	13m		Each	9.23
Scissors lift	7.8m		Each	7.56
Telescopic handlers	7m, 2 tonne		Each	7.18
Telescopic handlers	13m, 3 tonne		Each	8.72
Lifting and Jacking Gear				
Pipe winch including gantry	1 tonne		Sets	1.92
Pipe winch including gantry	3 tonnes		Sets	3.21
Chain block	1 tonne		Each	0.45
Chain block	2 tonnes		Each	0.71
Chain block	5 tonnes		Each	1.22
Pull lift (Tirfor winch)	1 tonne		Each	0.64
Pull lift (Tirfor winch)	1.6 tonnes		Each	0.90
Pull lift (Tirfor winch)	3.2 tonnes		Each	1.15
Brother or chain slings, two legs	not exceeding 4.2 tonnes		Set	0.35
Brother or chain slings, two legs	not exceeding 7.5 tonnes		Set	0.45
Brother or chain slings, four legs	not exceeding 3.1 tonnes		Set	0.41
Brother or chain slings, four legs	not exceeding 11.2 tonnes		Set	1.28

BUILDING INDUSTRY PLANT HIRE COSTS

MECHANICAL PLANT AND TOOLS

Item of Plant	Size/Rating	Unit	Rate/hr
CONSTRUCTION VEHICLES			
Lorries			
Plated lorries			
Rates are inclusive of driver			
Platform lorries	7.5 tonnes	Each	19.00
Platform lorries	17 tonnes	Each	21.00
Platform lorries	24 tonnes	Each	26.00
Platform lorries with winch and skids	7.5 tonnes	Each	21.40
Platform lorries with crane	17 tonnes	Each	27.50
Platform lorries with crane	24 tonnes	Each	32.10
Tipper Lorries			
Rates are inclusive of driver			
Tipper lorries	15/17 tonnes	Each	19.50
Tipper lorries	24 tonnes	Each	21.40
Tipper lorries	30 tonnes	Each	27.10
Dumpers			
Site use only (excluding tax, insurance and extra			
Cost of DERV etc. when operating on highway)			
	Makers capacity		
Two wheel drive	0.8 tonnes	Each	1.20
Two wheel drive	1 tonne	Each	1.30
Two wheel drive	1.2 tonnes	Each	1.60
Four wheel drive	2 tonnes	Each	2.50
Four wheel drive	3 tonnes	Each	3.00
Four wheel drive	4 tonnes	Each	3.50
Four wheel drive	5 tonnes	Each	4.00
Four wheel drive	6 tonnes	Each	4.50
Dumper Trucks			
Rates are inclusive of drivers			
Dumper trucks	10/13 tonnes	Each	20.00
Dumper trucks	18/20 tonnes	Each	20.40
Dumper trucks	22/25 tonnes	Each	26.30
Dumper trucks	35/40 tonnes	Each	36.60
Tractors			
Agricultural Type			
Wheeled, rubber-clad tyred			
Light	48 h.p.	Each	4.65
Heavy	65 h.p.	Each	5.15
Crawler Tractors			
With bull or angle dozer	80/90 h.p.	Each	21.40
With bull or angle dozer	115/130 h.p.	Each	25.10
With bull or angle dozer	130/150 h.p.	Each	26.00
With bull or angle dozer	155/175 h.p.	Each	27.74
With bull or angle dozer	210/230 h.p.	Each	28.00
With bull or angle dozer	300/340 h.p.	Each	31.10
With bull or angle dozer	400/440 h.p.	Each	46.90
With loading shovel	0.8m³	Each	25.00
With loading shovel	1.0m³	Each	28.00
With loading shovel	1.2m³	Each	32.00
With loading shovel	1.4m³	Each	36.00
With loading shovel	1.8m³	Each	45.00

BUILDING INDUSTRY PLANT HIRE COSTS

MECHANICAL PLANT AND TOOLS

Item of Plant	Size/Rating	Unit	Rate/hr
Light Vans			
Ford Escort or the like		Each	4.74
Ford Transit or the like	1.0 tonnes	Each	6.79
Luton Box Van or the like	1.8 tonnes	Each	8.33
Water/Fuel Storage			
Mobile water container	110 litres	Each	0.28
Water bowser	1100 litres	Each	0.55
Water bowser	3000 litres	Each	0.74
Mobile fuel container	110 litres	Each	0.28
Fuel bowser	1100 litres	Each	0.65
Fuel bowser	3000 litres	Each	1.02

EXCAVATORS AND LOADERS

Item of Plant	Size/Rating	Unit	Rate/hr
Excavators			
Wheeled, hydraulic	7/10 tonnes	Each	12.00
Wheeled, hydraulic	11/13 tonnes	Each	12.70
Wheeled, hydraulic	15/16 tonnes	Each	14.80
Wheeled, hydraulic	17/18 tonnes	Each	16.70
Wheeled, hydraulic	20/23 tonnes	Each	16.70
Crawler, hydraulic	12/14 tonnes	Each	12.00
Crawler, hydraulic	15/17.5 tonnes	Each	14.00
Crawler, hydraulic	20/23 tonnes	Each	16.00
Crawler, hydraulic	25/30 tonnes	Each	21.00
Crawler, hydraulic	30/35 tonnes	Each	30.00
Mini excavators	1000/1500kg	Each	4.50
Mini excavators	2150/2400kg	Each	5.50
Mini excavators	2700/3500kg	Each	6.50
Mini excavators	3500/4500kg	Each	8.50
Mini excavators	4500/6000kg	Each	9.50
Loaders			
Wheeled skip loader		Each	4.50
Shovel loaders, four wheel drive	1.6m³	Each	12.00
Shovel loaders, four wheel drive	2.4m³	Each	19.00
Shovel loaders, four wheel drive	3.6m³	Each	22.00
Shovel loaders, four wheel drive	4.4m³	Each	23.00
Shovel loaders, crawlers	0.8m³	Each	11.00
Shovel loaders, crawlers	1.2m³	Each	14.00
Shovel loaders, crawlers	1.6m³	Each	16.00
Shovel loaders, crawlers	2m³	Each	17.00
Skid steer loaders wheeled	300/400kg payload	Each	6.00
Excavator Loaders			
Wheeled tractor type with back-hoe excavator			
Four wheel drive	2.5/3.5 tonnes	Each	7.00
Four wheel drive, 2 wheel steer	7/8 tonnes	Each	9.00
Four wheel drive, 4 wheel steer	7/8 tonnes	Each	10.00
Crawler, hydraulic	12 tonnes	Each	20.00
Crawler, hydraulic	20 tonnes	Each	16.00
Crawler, hydraulic	30 tonnes	Each	35.00
Crawler, hydraulic	40 tonnes	Each	38.00

BUILDING INDUSTRY PLANT HIRE COSTS

MECHANICAL PLANT AND TOOLS

Item of Plant	Size/Rating	Unit	Rate/hr
Excavator Loaders (cont'd)			
Attachments			
Breakers for excavators			
Breakers for mini excavators			
Breakers for back-hoe excavator/loaders			
COMPACTION EQUIPMENT			
Rollers			
Vibrating roller	368kg - 420kg	Each	1.68
Single roller	533kg	Each	1.92
Single roller	750kg	Each	2.41
Vibrating roller	368kg - 420kg	Each	1.68
Single roller	533kg	Each	1.92
Single roller	750kg	Each	2.41
Twin roller	698kg	Each	1.93
Twin roller	851kg	Each	2.41
Twin roller with seat end steering wheel	1067kg	Each	3.03
Twin roller with seat end steering wheel	1397kg	Each	3.17
Pavement rollers	3 - 4 tonnes dead weight	Each	3.18
Pavement rollers	4 - 6 tonnes	Each	4.13
Pavement rollers	6 - 10 tonnes	Each	4.84
Rammers			
Tamper rammer 2 stroke-petrol	225mm - 275mm	Each	1.59
Soil Compactors			
Plate compactor	375mm - 400mm	Each	1.20
Plate compactor rubber pad	375mm - 1400mm	Each	0.33
Plate compactor reversible plate - petrol	400mm	Each	2.20
CONCRETE EQUIPMENT			
Concrete/Mortar Mixers			
Open drum without hopper	0.09/0/06m³	Each	0.62
Open drum without hopper	0.12/0.09m³	Each	0.68
Open drum without hopper	0.15/0.10m³	Each	0.72
Open drum with hopper	0.20/0.15m³	Each	0.80
Concrete/Mortar Transport Equipment			
Concrete pump including hose, valve and couplers			
Lorry mounted concrete pump	23m max. distance	Each	36.00
Lorry mounted concrete pump	50m max. distance	Each	46.00
Concrete Equipment			
Vibrator, poker, petrol type	up to 75mm dia.	Each	1.62
Air vibrator (excluding compressor and hose)	up to 75mm dia.	Each	0.79
Extra poker heads	5m	Each	0.77
Vibrating screed unit with beam	3m - 5m	Each	1.77
Vibrating screed unit with adjustable beam	725mm - 900mm	Each	2.18
Power float		Each	1.72
Power grouter		Each	0.92
TESTING EQUIPMENT			
Pipe Testing Equipment			
Pressure testing pump, electric		Sets	1.87
Pipe pressure testing equipment, hydraulic		Sets	2.46
Pressure test pump		Sets	0.64

BUILDING INDUSTRY PLANT HIRE COSTS

MECHANICAL PLANT AND TOOLS

Item of Plant	Size/Rating	Unit	Rate/hr
SITE ACCOMMODATION AND TEMPORARY SERVICES			
Heating Equipment			
Space heaters - propane		Each	0.77
Space heaters - propane/electric	80,000Btu/hr	Each	1.56
Space heaters - propane/electric	125,000Btu/hr	Each	1.79
Space heaters, propane	250,000Btu/hr	Each	1.33
Space heaters, propane	125,000Btu/hr	Each	1.64
Cabinet heaters	260,000Btu/hr	Each	0.41
Cabinet heater catalytic		Each	0.46
Electric halogen heaters		Each	1.28
Ceramic heaters		Each	0.79
Fan heaters	3kW	Each	0.41
Cooling Fan	3kW	Each	1.15
Mobile cooling unit - small		Each	1.38
Mobile cooling unit - large		Each	1.54
Air conditioning unit		Each	2.62
Site Lighting and Equipment			
Tripod floodlight	500W		
Tripod floodlight	1000W	Each	0.36
Towable floodlight	4 x 1000W	Each	0.34
Hand held floodlight	500W	Each	2.00
		Each	0.22
Rechargeable light		Each	0.62
Inspection light		Each	0.15
Plasterers light		Each	0.56
Lighting mast		Each	0.92
Festoon light string	33m	Each	0.31
Site Electrical Equipment			
Extension leads	240V/14m	Each	0.20
Extension leafs	110V/14m	Each	0.20
Cable reel	25m 110V/240V	Each	0.28
Cable reel	50m 110V/240V	Each	0.33
4 way junction box	110V	Each	0.17
Power Generating Units			
Generator - petrol	2kVA	Each	1.08
Generator - silenced petrol	2kVA	Each	1.54
Generator - petrol	3VA	Each	1.38
Generator - diesel	5kVA	Each	1.92
Generator - silenced diesel	8kVA	Each	3.59
Generator - silenced diesel	1.5kVA	Each	7.69
Tail adaptor	240V	Each	0.20
Transformers			
Transformer	3kVA	Each	0.36
Transformer	5kVA	Each	0.51
Transformer	7.5kVA	Each	0.82
Transformer	10kVA	Each	0.87
Rubbish Collection and Disposal Equipment			
Rubbish Chutes			
Standard plastic module	1m section	Each	0.18
Steel liner insert		Each	0.26
Steel top hopper		Each	0.20
Plastic side entry hopper		Each	0.20
Plastic side entry hopper liner		Each	0.20

BUILDING INDUSTRY PLANT HIRE COSTS

MECHANICAL PLANT AND TOOLS

Item of Plant	Size/Rating	Unit	Rate/hr
SITE ACCOMMODATION AND TEMPORARY SERVICES (cont'd)			
Dust Extraction Plant			
Dust extraction unit, light duty			
Duct extraction unit, heavy duty			
SITE EQUIPMENT			
Welding Equipment			
Arc-(Electric) Complete with Leads			
Welder generator - petrol	200 amp	Each	2.26
Welder generator - diesel	300/350 amp	Each	3.33
Welder generator - diesel	400 amp	Each	4.74
Extra welding lead sets		Each	0.29
Gas-Oxy Welder			
Welding and cutting set (including oxygen and acetylene, excluding underwater equipment and thermic boring)			
Small		Each	1.41
Large		Each	2.00
Mig welder		Each	1.00
Fume extractor		Each	0.92
Road Works Equipment			
Traffic lights, mains/generator	2-way	Set	4.01
Traffic lights, mains/generator	3-way	Set	7.92
Traffic lights, mains/generator	4-way	Set	9.81
Traffic lights, mains/generator - trailer mounted	2-way	Set	3.98
Flashing lights		Each	0.20
Road safety cone	450mm	10	0.26
Safety cone	750mm	10	0.38
Safety barrier plank	1.25m	Each	0.03
Safety barrier plank	2m	Each	0.04
Road sign		Each	0.26
DPC Equipment			
Damp proofing injection machine		Each	1.49
Cleaning Equipment			
Vacuum cleaner (industrial wet) single motor		Each	0.62
Vacuum cleaner (industrial wet) twin motor		Each	1.23
Vacuum cleaner (industrial wet) triple motor		Each	1.44
Vacuum cleaner (industrial wet) back pack		Each	0.97
Pressure washer, light duty, electric	1450 PSI	Each	0.97
Pressure washer, heavy duty, diesel	2500 PSI	Each	2.69
Cold pressure washer, electric		Each	1.79
Hot pressure washer, petrol		Each	2.92
Cold pressure washer, petrol		Each	2.00
Sandblast attachment to last washer		Each	0.54
Drain cleaning attachment to last washer		Each	0.31
Surface Preparation Equipment			
Rotavators	5 h.p.	Each	1.67
Scabbler, up to three heads		Each	1.15
Scabbler, pole		Each	1.50
Scabbler, multi-headed floor		Each	4.00
Floor preparation machine		Each	2.82

BUILDING INDUSTRY PLANT HIRE COSTS

MECHANICAL PLANT AND TOOLS

Item of Plant	Size/Rating	Unit	Rate/hr
Compressors and Equipment			
Portable Compressors			
Compressors - electric	0.23m³/min	Each	1.59
Compressors - petrol	0.28m³/min	Each	1.74
Compressors - petrol	0.71m³/min	Each	2.00
Compressors - diesel	up to 2.83m³/min	Each	1.24
Compressors - diesel	up to 3.68m³/min	Each	1.49
Compressors - diesel	up to 4.25m³/min	Each	1.60
Compressors - diesel	up to 4.81m³/min	Each	1.92
Compressors - diesel	up to 7.64m³/min	Each	3.08
Compressors - diesel	up to 11.32m³/min	Each	4.23
Compressors - diesel	up to 18.40m³/min	Each	5.73
Mobile Compressors			
Lorry mounted compressors	2.86-4.24m³/min	Each	12.50
(machine plus lorry only)			
Tractor mounted compressors	2.86-3.40m³/min	Each	13.50
(machine plus rubber tyred tractor)			
Accessories (Pneumatic Tools)			
(with and including up to 15m of air hose)			
Demolition pick		Each	1.03
Breakers (with six steels) light	up to 150kg	Each	0.79
Breakers (with six steels) medium	295kg	Each	1.08
Breakers (with six steels) heavy	386kg	Each	1.44
Rock drill (for use with compressor) hand held		Each	0.90
Additional hoses	15m	Each	0.16
Muffler, tool silencer		Each	0.14
Breakers			
Demolition hammer drill, heavy duty, electric		Each	1.00
Road breaker, electric		Each	1.65
Road breaker, 2 stroke, petrol		Each	2.05
Hydraulic breaker unit, light duty, petrol		Each	2.05
Hydraulic breaker unit, heavy duty, petrol		Each	2.60
Hydraulic breaker unit, heavy duty, diesel		Each	2.95
Quarrying and Tooling Equipment			
Block and stone splitter, hydraulic	600mm x 600mm	Each	1.35
Block and slab splitter, manual		Each	1.10
Steel Reinforcement Equipment			
Bar bending machine - manual	up to 13mm dia. rods	Each	0.90
Bar bending machine - manual	up to 20mm dia. rods	Each	1.28
Bar shearing machine - electric	up to 38mm dia. rods	Each	2.82
Bar shearing machine - electric	up to 40mm dia. rods	Each	3.85
Bar cropper machine - electric	up to 13mm dia. rods	Each	1.54
Bar cropper machine - electric	up to 20mm dia. rods	Each	2.05
Bar cropper machine - electric	up to 40mm dia. rods	Each	2.82
Bar cropper machine - 3 phase	up to 40mm dia. rods	Each	3.85
Dehumidifiers			
110/240v Water	68 litres extraction per 24 hrs	Each	1.28
110/240v Water	90 litres extraction per 24 hrs	Each	1.85

BUILDING INDUSTRY PLANT HIRE COSTS

MECHANICAL PLANT AND TOOLS

Item of Plant	Size/Rating	Unit	Rate/hr
Compressors and Equipment (cont'd)			
SMALL TOOLS			
Saws			
Masonry bench saw	350mm - 500mm dia.	Each	2.80
Floor saw	350mm dia., 125mm max. cut	Each	1.90
Floor saw	450mm dia., 150mm max. cut	Each	2.60
Floor saw, reversible	Max. cut 300mm	Each	13.00
Chop/cut off saw, electric	350mm dia.	Each	1.33
Circular saw, electric	230mm dia.	Each	0.60
Tyrannosaw		Each	1.20
Reciprocating saw		Each	0.60
Door trimmer		Each	0.90
Chainsaw, petrol	500mm	Each	2.13
Full chainsaw safety kit		Each	0.50
Worktop jig		Each	0.60
Pipework Equipment			
Pipe bender	15mm - 22mm	Each	0.33
Pipe bender, hydraulic	50mm	Each	0.60
Pipe bender, electric	50mm - 150mm dia.	Each	1.35
Pipe cutter, hydraulic		Each	1.84
Tripod pipe vice		Set	0.40
Ratchet threader	12mm - 32mm	Each	0.55
Pipe threading machine, electric	12mm - 75mm	Each	2.40
Pipe threading machine, electric	12mm - 100mm	Each	3.00
Impact wrench, electric		Each	0.54
Impact wrench, two stroke, petrol		Each	4.49
Impact wrench, heavy duty, electric		Each	1.13
Plumber's furnace, calor gas or similar		Each	2.16
Hand-held Drills and Equipment			
Impact or hammer drill	up to 25mm dia.	Each	0.50
Impact or hammer drill	35mm dia.	Each	0.90
Angle head drills		Each	0.70
Stirrer, mixer drills		Each	0.70
Paint, Insulation Application Equipment			
Airless spray unit		Each	4.20
Portaspray unit		Each	1.65
HVLP turbine spray unit		Each	1.65
Compressor and spray gun		Each	2.20
Other Handtools			
Screwing machine	13mm - 50mm dia.	Each	0.77
Screwing machine	25mm - 100mm dia.	Each	1.57
Staple gun		Each	0.33
Air nail gun	110V	Each	3.33
Cartridge hammer		Each	1.00
Tongue and groove nailer complete with mallet		Each	0.93
Chasing machine	152mm	Each	1.72
Chasing machine	76mm - 203mm	Each	5.99
Floor grinder		Each	3.00
Floor plane		Each	3.67
Diamond concrete planer		Each	2.05
Autofeed screwdriver, electric		Each	1.13
Laminate trimmer		Each	0.64

BUILDING INDUSTRY PLANT HIRE COSTS

MECHANICAL PLANT AND TOOLS

Item of Plant	Size/Rating	Unit	Rate/hr
Biscuit jointer		Each	0.87
Random orbital sander		Each	0.72
Floor sander		Each	1.33
Palm, delta, flap or belt sander	300mm	Each	0.38
Saw cutter, 2 stroke, petrol	up to 225mm	Each	1.26
Grinder, angle or cutter	300mm	Each	0.60
Grinder, angle or cutter		Each	1.10
Mortar raking tool attachment	325mm	Each	0.15
Floor/polisher scrubber		Each	1.03
Floor tile stripper		Each	1.74
Wallpaper stripper, electric		Each	0.56
Electric scraper		Each	0.51
Hot air paint stripper	All sizes	Each	0.38
Electric diamond tile cutter		Each	1.38
Hand tile cutter		Each	0.36
Electric needle gun		Each	1.08
Needle chipping gun	1.2m wide	Each	0.72
Pedestrian floor sweeper		Each	0.87

Advanced Building Simulation

Edited by
Ali Malkawi and
Godfried Augenbroe

This book introduces recent advances in building simulation and outlines its historic development. Two important topics are described: uncertainty in simulation and coupled simulations, which are both closely linked to attempts to improve control and accuracy. This is followed by coverage of wind simulations and predictions, and then by an introduction to current systems and phenomenological modelling.

Leading experts in the field both in the US and Europe have written the chapters, and provide a graduate-level student textbook as well as a practical guide for architects, engineers and other construction professionals.

Contents: 1. Trends in Building Simulation 2. Uncertainty in Building Simulation 3. Simulation and Uncertainty: Weather Predictions 4. Integrated Building Air Flow Simulation 5. The Use of CFD Tools for Indoor Environmental Design 6. New Perspectives on CFD Simulation 7. Self Organizing Models for Sentient Buildings 8. Developments in Interoperability 9. Immersive Building Simulation.

July 2004: 246x174 mm: 272 pages
10 tables, 50 line drawings and 20 b+w photos
HB: 0-415-32122-0: £85.00
PB: 0-415-32123-9: £40.00

To Order: Tel: +44 (0) 1264 343071 Fax: +44 (0) 1264 343005, or
Post: Taylor and Francis Customer Services, Thomson Publishing Services, Cheriton House, Andover, Hants, SP10 5BE, UK Email: book.orders@tandf.co.uk

For a complete listing of all our titles visit :
www.sponpress.com

Taylor & Francis
Taylor & Francis Group plc

Adapting Buildings for Changing Uses
Guidelines for Change of Use Refurbishment

David Kincaid

For those involved in the often risky business of conversion of buildings from one type of use to another, *Adapting Building for Changing Uses* provides secure guidance on which uses may be best suited to a particular location. This guidance is based on a unique decision tool, the "Use Comparator", which was developed through research carried out at UCL in the mid 1990's. The "Use Comparator" compares the physical and locational characteristics of a building with the characteristics best suited to various types of use. A total of 77 targeted types of use are evaluated, in contrast to the 17 uses normally considers by regulatory planners.

Adapting Building for Changing Uses also identifies the key problems experienced by building managers involved in assembling the coalition of Producers, Investors, Marketeers, Regulators and Users, which makes the key decisions in "Adaptive Reuse". The book explores the differing perceptions and attitudes of these key decision agents to matters such as cost, value, risk and robustness, and offers advice on how to avoid the potential for project failure that these differences present.

September 2002: 246x189: 352pp
28 line figures, 1 b+w photo and 37 tables
Pb: 0-419-23570-1 : £40.00

To Order: Tel: +44 (0) 1264 343071 Fax: +44 (0) 1264 343005, or
Post: Taylor and Francis Customer Services, Thomson Publishing Services, Cheriton House, Andover, Hants, SP10 5BE, UK Email: book.orders@tandf.co.uk

For a complete listing of all our titles visit:
www.sponpress.com

Taylor & Francis
Taylor & Francis Group plc

Energy Management and Operating Costs in Buildings

Keith Moss

Managing the consumption and conservation of energy in buildings must now become the concern of both building managers and occupants. The provision of lighting, hot water supply, communications, cooking, space heating and cooling accounts for 45 per cent of UK energy consumption.

Energy Management and Operating Costs in Buildings introduces the reader to the principles of managing and conserving energy consumpton in buildings people use for work or leisure. Energy consumption is considered for the provision of space heating, hot water, supply ventilation and air conditioning. The author introduces the use of standard performance indicators and energy consumption yardsticks, and discusses the use and application of degree days.

June 1997: 246x189 mm
PB: 0-419-21770-3: £29.99

To Order: Tel: +44 (0) 1264 343071 Fax: +44 (0) 1264 343005, or
Post: Taylor and Francis Customer Services, Thomson Publishing Services, Cheriton House, Andover, Hants, SP10 5BE, UK Email: book.orders@tandf.co.uk

For a complete listing of all our titles visit :
www.sponpress.com

Tables and Memoranda

Conversion Tables, *page 586*
Formulae, *page 588*
Fractions, Decimals and Millimetre Equivalents, *page 589*
Imperial Standard Wire Gauge, *page 590*
Water Pressure Due to Height, *page 591*
Table of Weights for Steelwork, *page 592*
Dimensions and Weights of Copper Pipes, *page 597*
Dimensions of Steel Pipes, *page 598*
Approximate Metres per Tonne of Tubes, *page 600*
Flange Dimension Chart, *page 601*
Minimum Distances Between Supports/Fixings, *page 603*
Litres of Water Storage Required per Person per Building Type, *page 604*
Recommended Air Conditioning Design Loads, *page 604*
Capacity and Dimensions of Galvanised Mild Steel Cisterns, *page 605*
Capacity of Cold Water Polypropylene Storage Cisterns, *page 605*
Minimum Insulation Thickness to Protect Against Frost, *page 606*
Insulation Thickness for Chilled Water Supplies to Prevent Condensation, *page 606*
Insulation Thickness for Non-Domestic Heating Installations to Control Heat Loss, *page 607*

CONVERSION TABLES

LENGTH

Millimetre	(mm)	1 in	=	25.4	mm	: 1 mm	=	0.0394	in
Metre	(m)	1 ft	=	0.3048	m	: 1 m	=	3.2808	ft
Kilometre	(km)	1 yd	=	0.9144	m	: 1 m	=	1.0936	yd
Kilometre	(km)	1 mile	=	1.6093	km	: 1 km	=	0.6214	mile

NOTE :

1 cm	=	10	mm	1 ft	=	12	in
1 m	=	100	cm	1 yd	=	3	ft
1 km	=	1000	m	1 mile	=	1760	yd

AREA

Square Millimetre	(mm^2)	1 in^2	=	645.2	mm^2	: 1 mm^2	=	0.0016	in^2
Square Centimetre	(cm^2)	1 in^2	=	6.4516	cm^2	: 1 cm^2	=	0.1550	in^2
Square Metre	(m^2)	1 ft^2	=	0.0929	m^2	: 1 m^2	=	10.764	ft^2
Square Metre	(m^2)	1 yd^2	=	0.8361	m^2	: 1 m^2	=	1.1960	yd^2
Square Kilometre	(km^2)	1 $mile^2$	=	2.590	km^2	: 1 km^2	=	0.3861	$mile^2$
Hectare	(ha)	1 acre	=	0.405	ha	: 1 ha	=	2.471	acre

NOTE :

1 cm^2	=	100	mm^2	1 ft^2	=	144	in^2
1 m^2	=	10000	cm^2	1 yd^2	=	9	ft^2
1 km^2	=	100	ha	1 $mile^2$	=	640	acre
				1 acre	=	4840	yd^2

VOLUME

Cubic Centimetre	(cm^3)	1 cm^3	=	0.0610	in^3	: 1 in^3	=	16.387	cm^3
Cubic Decimetre	(dm^3)	1 dm^3	=	0.0353	ft^3	: 1 ft^3	=	28.329	dm^3
Cubic Metre	(m^3)	1 m^3	=	35.315	ft^3	: 1 ft^3	=	0.0283	m^3
Cubic Metre	(m^3)	1 m^3	=	1.3080	yd^3	: 1 yd^3	=	0.7646	m^3
Litre	(L)	1 L	=	1.76	pint	: 1 pint	=	0.5683	L
Litre	(L)	1 L	=	2.113	US pt	: 1 pint	=	0.4733	US L
Litre	(L)	1L	=	0.220	gal	1 gal	=	4.546	L

NOTE :

1 dm^3	=	1000	cm^3	1 ft^3	=	1728	in^3
1 m^3	=	1000	dm^3	1 yd^3	=	27	ft^3
1 L	=	1	dm^3	1 pint	=	20	fl oz
1 HL	=	100	L	1 gal	=	8	pints

MASS

Milligram	(mg)	1 mg	=	0.0154	grain	: 1 grain	=	64.935	mg
Gram	(g)	1 g	=	0.0353	oz	: 1 oz	=	28.35	g
Kilogram	(kg)	1 kg	=	2.2046	lb	: 1 lb	=	0.4536	kg
Kilogram	(kg)	1 kg	=	0.020	cwt	: 1 cwt	=	50.802	kg
Tonne	(t)	1 t	=	0.9842	ton	: 1 ton	=	1.016	t

NOTE :

1 g	=	1000	mg	1 oz	=	437.5	grains
1 kg	=	1000	g	1 lb	=	16	oz
1 t	=	1000	kg	1 stone	=	14	lb
				1 cwt	=	112	lb
				1 ton	=	20	cwt

CONVERSION TABLES

FORCE

Newton	(N)	1 lb f	=	4.448	N	: 1 kg f	=	9.807	N
Kilonewton	(kN)	1 lb f	=	0.004448	kN	: 1 ton f	=	9.964	kN
Meganewton	(MN)	100 ton f	=	0.9964	MN				

POWER

Kilowatt	(kW)	1 kW	=	1.310	HP	: 1 HP	=	0.746	kW

PRESSURE AND STRESS

Kilonewton		1 lb f/in^2	=	6.895	kN/m^2
per square metre	(kN/m^2)	1 bar	=	100	kN/m^2
		1 ton f/ft^2	=	107.3	kN/m^2
		1 kg f/cm^2	=	98.07	kN/m^2
		1 lb f/ft^2	=	0.0479	kN/m^2

TEMPERATURE

Degrees $\qquad °C = 5/9 \ (°F - 32°) \qquad\qquad °F = 9/5 \ (°C + 32°)$

FORMULAE

Two dimensional figures

Figure	Area
Triangle	0.5 x base x height, or $N(s(s - a)(s - b)(s - c))$ where s = 0.5 x the sum of the three sides and a, b and c are the lengths of the three sides, or $a^2 = b^2 + c^2 - 2 \times bc \times COS\ A$ where A is the angle opposite side a
Hexagon	$2.6 \times (side)^2$
Octagon	$4.83 \times (side)^2$
Trapezoid	height x 0.5 (base + top)
Circle	$3.142 \times radius^2$ or $0.7854 \times diameter^2$ (circumference = 2 x 3.142 x radius or 3.142 x diameter)
Sector of a circle	0.5 x length of arc x radius
Segment of a circle	area of sector - area of triangle
Ellipse of a circle	3.142 x AB (where A = 0.5 x height and B = 0.5 x length)
Spandrel	$3/14 \times radius^2$

Three dimensional figure

Figure	Volume Surface	Area
Prism x height	Area of base x height	circumference of base
Cube	(length of side) cubed	$6 \times (length\ of\ side)^2$
Cylinder	$3.142 \times radius^2 \times$ height	2 x 3.142 x radius x (height - radius)
Sphere	$4/3 \times 3.142 \times radius^3$	$4 \times 3.142 \times radius^2$
Segment of a sphere	$[(3.142 \times h)/6] \times$ $(3 \times r^2 + h^2)$	$(2 \times 3.142 \times r \times h)$
Pyramid	1/3 x (area of base x height)	0.5 x circumference of base x slant height

FRACTIONS, DECIMALS AND MILLIMETRE EQUIVALENTS

Fractions	Decimals	mm	Fractions	Decimals	mm
1/64	0.015625	0.396875	33/64	0.515625	13.096875
1/32	0.03125	0.79375	17/32	0.53125	13.49375
3/64	0.046875	1.190625	35/64	0.546875	13.890625
1/16	0.0625	1.5875	9/16	0.5625	14.2875
5/64	0.078125	1.984375	37/64	0.578125	14.684375
3/32	0.09375	2.38125	19/32	0.59375	15.08125
7/64	0.109375	2.778125	39/64	0.609375	15.478125
1/8	0.125	3.175	5/8	0.625	15.875
9/64	0.140625	3.571875	41/64	0.640625	16.271875
5/32	0.15625	3.96875	21/32	0.65625	16.66875
11/64	0.171875	4.365625	43/64	0.671875	17.065625
3/16	0.1875	4.7625	11/16	0.6875	17.4625
13/64	0.203125	5.159375	45/64	0.703125	17.859375
7/32	0.21875	5.55625	23/32	0.71875	18.25625
15/64	0.234375	5.953125	47/64	0.734375	18.653125
1/4	0.25	6.35	3/4	0.75	19.05
17/64	0.265625	6.746875	49/64	0.765625	19.446875
9/32	0.28125	7.14375	25/32	0.78125	19.84375
19/64	0.296875	7.540625	51/64	0.796875	20.240625
5/16	0.3125	7.9375	13/16	0.8125	20.6375
21/64	0.328125	8.334375	53/64	0.828125	21.034375
11/32	0.34375	8.73125	27/32	0.84375	21.43125
23/64	0.359375	9.128125	55/64	0.859375	21.828125
3/8	0.375	9.525	7/8	0.875	22.225
25/64	0.390625	9.921875	57/64	0.890625	22.621875
13/32	0.40625	10.31875	29/32	0.90625	23.01875
27/64	0.421875	10.71563	59/64	0.921875	23.415625
7/16	0.4375	11.1125	15/16	0.9375	23.8125
29/64	0.453125	11.50938	61/64	0.953125	24.209375
15/32	0.46875	11.90625	31/32	0.96875	24.60625
31/64	0.484375	12.30313	63/64	0.984375	25.003125
1/2	0.5	12.7	1.0	1	25.4

IMPERIAL STANDARD WIRE GAUGE (SWG)

SWG No	Diameter inches	mm	SWG No	Diameter inches	mm
7/0	0.5	12.7	23	0.024	0.61
6/0	0.464	11.79	24	0.022	0.559
5/0	0.432	10.97	25	0.02	0.508
4/0	0.4	10.16	26	0.018	0.457
3/0	0.372	9.45	27	0.0164	0.417
2/0	0.348	8.84	28	0.0148	0.376
1/0	0.324	8.23	29	0.0136	0.345
1	0.3	7.62	30	0.0124	0.315
2	0.276	7.01	31	0.0116	0.295
3	0.252	6.4	32	0.0108	0.274
4	0.232	5.89	33	0.01	0.254
5	0.212	5.38	34	0.009	0.234
6	0.192	4.88	35	0.008	0.213
7	0.176	4.47	36	0.008	0.193
8	0.16	4.06	37	0.007	0.173
9	0.144	3.66	38	0.006	0.152
10	0.128	3.25	39	0.005	0.132
11	0.116	2.95	40	0.005	0.122
12	0.104	2.64	41	0.004	0.112
13	0.092	2.34	42	0.004	0.102
14	0.08	2.03	43	0.004	0.091
15	0.072	1.83	44	0.003	0.081
16	0.064	1.63	45	0.003	0.071
17	0.056	1.42	46	0.002	0.061
18	0.048	1.22	47	0.002	0.051
19	0.04	1.016	48	0.002	0.041
20	0.036	0.914	49	0.001	0.031
21	0.032	0.813	50	0.001	0.025
22	0.028	0.711			

WATER PRESSURE DUE TO HEIGHT

Imperial

Head Feet	Pressure lb/in^2	Head Feet	Pressure lb/in^2
1	0.43	70	30.35
5	2.17	75	32.51
10	4.34	80	34.68
15	6.5	85	36.85
20	8.67	90	39.02
25	10.84	95	41.18
30	13.01	100	43.35
35	15.17	105	45.52
40	17.34	110	47.69
45	19.51	120	52.02
50	21.68	130	56.36
55	23.84	140	60.69
60	26.01	150	65.03
65	28.18		

Metric

Head m	Pressure bar	Head m	Pressure bar
0.5	0.049	18.0	1.766
1.0	0.098	19.0	1.864
1.5	0.147	20.0	1.962
2.0	0.196	21.0	2.06
3.0	0.294	22.0	2.158
4.0	0.392	23.0	2.256
5.0	0.491	24.0	2.354
6.0	0.589	25.0	2.453
7.0	0.687	26.0	2.551
8.0	0.785	27.0	2.649
9.0	0.883	28.0	2.747
10.0	0.981	29.0	2.845
11.0	1.079	30.0	2.943
12.0	1.177	32.5	3.188
13.0	1.275	35.0	3.434
14.0	1.373	37.5	3.679
15.0	1.472	40.0	3.924
16.0	1.57	42.5	4.169
17.0	1.668	45.0	4.415

1 bar	=	14.5038 lbf/in^2
1 lbf/in^2	=	0.06895 bar
1 metre	=	3.2808 ft or 39.3701 in
1 foot	=	0.3048 metres
1 in wg	=	2.5 mbar (249.1 N/m^2)

TABLE OF WEIGHTS FOR STEELWORK

Mild Steel Bar

Diameter (mm)	Weight (kg/m)	Diameter (mm)	Weight (kg/m)
6	0.22	20	2.47
10	0.62	25	3.85
12	0.89	30	5.55
16	1.58	32	6.31

Mild Steel Flat

Size (mm)	Weight (kg/m)	Size (mm)	Weight (kg/m)
15 x 3	0.36	15 x 5	0.59
20 x 3	0.47	20 x 5	0.79
25 x 3	0.59	25 x 5	0.98
30 x 3	0.71	30 x 5	1.18
40 x 3	0.94	40 x 5	1.57
45 x 3	1.06	45 x 5	1.77
50 x 3	1.18	50 x 5	1.96
20 x 6	0.94	20 x 8	1.26
25 x 6	1.18	25 x 8	1.57
30 x 6	1.41	30 x 8	1.88
40 x 6	1.88	40 x 8	2.51
45 x 6	2.12	45 x 8	2.83
50 x 6	2.36	50 x 8	3.14
55 x 6	2.60	55 x 8	3.45
60 x 6	2.83	60 x 8	3.77
65 x 6	3.06	65 x 8	4.08
70 x 6	3.30	70 x 8	4.40
75 x 6	3.53	75 x 8	4.71
100 x 6	4.71	100 x 8	6.28
20 x 10	1.57	20 x 12	1.88
25 x 10	1.96	25 x 12	2.36
30 x 10	2.36	30 x 12	2.83
40 x 10	3.14	40 x 12	3.77
45 x 10	3.53	45 x 12	4.24
50 x 10	3.93	50 x 12	4.71
55 x 10	4.32	55 x 12	5.12
60 x 10	4.71	60 x 12	5.65
65 x 10	5.10	65 x 12	6.12
70 x 10	5.50	70 x 12	6.59
75 x 10	5.89	75 x 12	7.07
100 x 10	7.85	100 x 12	9.42

TABLE OF WEIGHTS FOR STEELWORK

Mild Steel Equal Angle

Size (mm)	Weight (kg/m)	Size (mm)	Weight (kg/m)
13 x 13 x 3	0.56	60 x 60 x 10	8.69
20 x 20 x 3	0.88	70 x 70 x 10	10.30
25 x 25 x 3	1.11	75 x 75 x 10	11.05
30 x 30 x 3	1.36	80 x 80 x 10	11.90
40 x 40 x 3	1.82	90 x 90 x 10	13.40
45 x 45 x 3	2.06	100 x 100 x 10	15.00
50 x 50 x 3	2.30	120 x 120 x 10	18.20
		150 x 156 x 10	23.00
30 x 30 x 6	2.56	75 x 75 x 12	13.07
40 x 40 x 6	3.52	80 x 80 x 12	14.00
45 x 45 x 6	4.00	90 x 90 x 12	15.90
50 x 50 x 6	4.47	100 x 120 x 12	21.60
60 x 60 x 6	5.42	120 x 120 x 12	21.90
70 x 70 x 6	6.38	150 x 150 x 12	27.30
75 x 75 x 6	6.82	200 x 200 x 12	36.74
80 x 80 x 6	7.34		
90 x 90 x 6	8.30		
40 x 40 x 8	4.55		
50 x 50 x 8	5.82		
60 x 60 x 8	7.09		
70 x 70 x 8	8.36		
75 x 75 x 8	8.96		
80 x 80 x 8	9.63		
90 x 90 x 8	10.90		
100 x 100 x 8	12.20		
120 x 120 x 8	14.70		

Mild Steel Unequal Angle

Size (mm)	Weight (kg/m)	Size (mm)	Weight (kg/m)
40 x 25 x 6	2.79	100 x 65 x 10	12.30
50 x 40 x 6	4.24	100 x 75 x 10	13.00
60 x 30 x 6	3.99	125 x 75 x 10	15.00
65 x 50 x 6	5.16	150 x 75 x 10	17.00
75 x 50 x 6	5.65	150 x 90 x 10	18.20
80 x 60 x 6	6.37	200 x 100 x 10	23.00
125 x 75 x 6	9.18		
75 x 50 x 8	7.39	100 x 75 x 12	15.40
80 x 60 x 8	8.34	125 x 75 x 12	17.80
100 x 65 x 8	9.94	150 x 75 x 12	20.20
100 x 75 x 8	10.60	150 x 90 x 12	21.60
125 x 75 x 8	12.20	200 x 100 x 12	27.30
137 x 102 x 8	14.88	200 x 150 x 12	32.00

TABLE OF WEIGHTS FOR STEELWORK

Rolled Steel Channels

Size (mm)	Weight (kg/m)	Size (mm)	Weight (kg/m)
32 x 27	2.80	178 x 76	20.84
38 x 19	2.49	178 x 79	26.81
51 x 25	4.46	203 x 76	23.82
51 x 38	5.80	203 x 89	29.78
64 x 25	6.70	229 x 76	26.06
76 x 38	7.46	229 x 89	32.76
76 x 51	9.45	254 x 76	28.29
102 x 51	10.42	254 x 89	35.74
127 x 64	14.90	305 x 89	41.67
152 x 76	17.88	305 x 102	46.18
152 x 89	23.84	381 x 102	55.10

Rolled Steel Joists

Size (mm)	Weight (kg/m)	Size (mm)	Weight (kg/m)
76 x 38	6.25	152 x 76	17.86
76 x 76	12.65	152 x 89	17.09
102 x 44	7.44	152 x 127	37.20
102 x 64	9.65	178 x 102	21.54
102 x 102	23.06	203 x 102	25.33
127 x 76	13.36	203 x 152	52.03
127 x 114	26.78	254 x 114	37.20
127 x 114	29.76	254 x 203	81.84
		305 x 203	96.72

Universal Columns

Size (mm)	Weight (kg/m)	Size (mm)	Weight (kg/m)
152 x 152	23.00	254 x 254	89.00
152 x 152	30.00	254 x 254	107.00
152 x 152	37.00	254 x 254	132.00
203 x 203	46.00	254 x 254	167.00
203 x 203	52.00	305 x 305	97.00
203 x 203	60.00	305 x 305	118.00
203 x 203	71.00	305 x 305	137.00
203 x 203	86.00	305 x 305	158.00
254 x 254	73.00	305 x 305	198.00

TABLE OF WEIGHTS FOR STEELWORK

Universal Beams

Size (mm)	Weight (kg/m)	Size (mm)	Weight (kg/m)
203 x 133	25.00	305 x 127	48.00
203 x 133	30.00	305 x 165	40.00
254 x 102	22.00	305 x 165	46.00
254 x 102	25.00	305 x 165	54.00
254 x 102	28.00	356 x 127	33.00
254 x 146	31.00	356 x 127	39.00
254 x 146	37.00	356 x 171	45.00
254 x 146	43.00	356 x 171	51.00
305 x 102	25.00	356 x 171	57.00
305 x 102	28.00	356 x 171	67.00
305 x 102	33.00	381 x 152	52.00
305 x 127	37.00	381 x 152	60.00
305 x 127	42.00	381 x 152	67.00

Circular Hollow Sections

Size (mm)	Weight (kg/m)	Size (mm)	Weight (kg/m)
21.3 x 3.2	1.43	76.1 x 3.2	5.75
26.9 x 3.2	1.87	76.1 x 4.0	7.11
33.7 x 2.6	1.99	76.1 x 5.0	8.77
33.7 x 3.2	2.41	88.9 x 3.2	6.76
33.7 x 4.0	2.93	88.9 x 4.0	8.36
42.4 x 2.6	2.55	88.9 x 5.0	10.30
42.4 x 3.2	3.09	114.3 x 3.6	9.83
42.4 x 4.0	3.79	114.3 x 5.0	13.50
48.3 x 3.2	3.56	114.3 x 6.3	16.80
48.3 x 4.0	4.37	139.7 x 5.0	16.60
48.3 x 5.0	5.34	139.7 x 6.3	20.70
60.3 x 3.2	4.51	139.7 x 8.0	26.00
60.3 x 4.0	5.55	139.7 x 10.0	32.00
60.3 x 5.0	6.82	168.3 x 5.0	20.10

TABLE OF WEIGHTS FOR STEELWORK

Square Hollow Sections

Size (mm)	Weight (kg/m)	Size (mm)	Weight (kg/m)
20 x 20 x 2.0	1.12	90 x 90 x 3.6	9.72
20 x 20 x 2.6	1.39	90 x 90 x 5.0	13.30
30 x 30 x 2.6	2.21	90 x 90 x 6.3	16.40
30 x 30 x 3.2	2.65	100 x 100 x 4.0	12.00
40 x 40 x 2.6	3.03	100 x 100 x 5.0	14.80
40 x 40 x 3.2	3.66	100 x 100 x 6.3	18.40
40 x 40 x 4.0	4.46	100 x 100 x 8.0	22.90
50 x 50 x 3.2	4.66	100 x 100 x 10.0	27.90
50 x 50 x 4.0	5.72	120 x 120 x 5.0	18.00
50 x 50 x 5.0	6.97	120 x 120 x 6.3	22.30
60 x 60 x 3.2	5.67	120 x 120 x 8.0	27.90
60 x 60 x 4.0	6.97	120 x 120 x 10.0	34.20
60 x 60 x 5.0	8.54	150 x 150 x 5.0	22.70
70 x 70 x 3.2	7.46	150 x 150 x 6.3	28.30
70 x 70 x 5.0	10.10	150 x 150 x 8.0	35.40
80 x 80 x 3.6	8.59	150 x 150 x 10.0	43.60
80 x 80 x 5.0	11.70		
80 x 80 x 6.3	14.40		

Rectangular Hollow Sections

Size (mm)	Weight (kg/m)	Size (mm)	Weight (kg/m)
50 x 30 x 2.6	3.03	120 x 80 x 5.0	14.80
50 x 30 x 3.2	3.66	120 x 80 x 6.3	18.40
60 x 40 x 3.2	4.66	120 x 80 x 8.0	22.90
60 x 40 x 4.0	5.72	120 x 80 x 10.0	27.90
80 x 40 x 3.2	5.67	150 x 100 x 5.0	18.70
80 x 40 x 4.0	6.97	150 x 100 x 6.3	23.30
90 x 50 x 3.6	7.46	150 x 100 x 8.0	29.10
90 x 50 x 5.0	10.10	150 x 100 x 10.0	35.70
100 x 50 x 3.2	7.18	160 x 80 x 5.0	18.00
100 x 50 x 4.0	8.86	160 x 80 x 6.3	22.30
100 x 50 x 5.0	10.90	160 x 80 x 8.0	27.90
100 x 60 x 3.6	8.59	160 x 80 x 10.0	34.20
100 x 60 x 5.0	11.70	200 x 100 x 5.0	22.70
100 x 60 x 6.3	14.40	200 x 100 x 6.3	28.30
120 x 60 x 3.6	9.72	200 x 100 x 8.0	35.40
120 x 60 x 5.0	13.30	200 x 100 x 10.0	43.60
120 x 60 x 6.3	16.40		

DIMENSIONS AND WEIGHTS OF COPPER PIPES TO
BSEN 1057, BSEN 12499, BSEN 14251

Outside Diameter (mm)	Internal Diameter (mm)	Weight per Metre (kg)	Internal Diameter (mm)	Weight per Metre (kg)	Internal Diameter (mm)	Weight per Metre (kg)
	Table X		Table Y		Table Z	
6	4.80	0.0911	4.40	0.1170	5.00	0.0774
8	6.80	0.1246	6.40	0.1617	7.00	0.1054
10	8.80	0.1580	8.40	0.2064	9.00	0.1334
12	10.80	0.1914	10.40	0.2511	11.00	0.1612
15	13.60	0.2796	13.00	0.3923	14.00	0.2031
18	16.40	0.3852	16.00	0.4760	16.80	0.2918
22	20.22	0.5308	19.62	0.6974	20.82	0.3589
28	26.22	0.6814	25.62	0.8985	26.82	0.4594
35	32.63	1.1334	32.03	1.4085	33.63	0.6701
42	39.63	1.3675	39.03	1.6996	40.43	0.9216
54	51.63	1.7691	50.03	2.9052	52.23	1.3343
76.1	73.22	3.1287	72.22	4.1437	73.82	2.5131
108	105.12	4.4666	103.12	7.3745	105.72	3.5834
133	130.38	5.5151	--	--	130.38	5.5151
159	155.38	8.7795	--	--	156.38	6.6056

DIMENSIONS OF STAINLESS STEEL PIPES TO BS 4127

Outside Diameter (mm)	Maximum Outside Diameter (mm)	Minimum Outside Diameter (mm)	Wall Thickness (mm)	Working Pressure (bar)
6	6.045	5.940	0.6	330
8	8.045	7.940	0.6	260
10	10.045	9.940	0.6	210
12	12.045	11.940	0.6	170
15	15.045	14.940	0.6	140
18	18.045	17.940	0.7	135
22	22.055	21.950	0.7	110
28	28.055	27.950	0.8	121
35	35.070	34.965	1.0	100
42	42.070	41.965	1.1	91
54	54.090	53.940	1.2	77

DIMENSIONS OF STEEL PIPES TO BS 1387

Nominal Size	Approx. Outside Diameter	Outside Diameter				Thickness		
		Light		Medium & Heavy		Light	Medium	Heavy
		Max.	Min.	Max.	Min.			
mm	mm	mm	mm	mm	mm	mm	mm	mm
6	10.20	10.10	9.70	10.40	9.80	1.80	2.00	2.65
8	13.50	13.60	13.20	13.90	13.30	1.80	2.35	2.90
10	17.20	17.10	16.70	17.40	16.80	1.80	2.35	2.90
15	21.30	21.40	21.00	21.70	21.10	2.00	2.65	3.25
20	26.90	26.90	26.40	27.20	26.60	2.35	2.65	3.25
25	33.70	33.80	33.20	34.20	33.40	2.65	3.25	4.05
32	42.40	42.50	41.90	42.90	42.10	2.65	3.25	4.05
40	48.30	48.40	47.80	48.80	48.00	2.90	3.25	4.05
50	60.30	60.20	59.60	60.80	59.80	2.90	3.65	4.50
65	76.10	76.00	75.20	76.60	75.40	3.25	3.65	4.50
80	88.90	88.70	87.90	89.50	88.10	3.25	4.05	4.85
100	114.30	113.90	113.00	114.90	113.30	3.65	4.50	5.40
125	139.70	--	--	140.60	138.70	--	4.85	5.40
150	165.1*	--	--	166.10	164.10	--	4.85	5.40

* 165.1mm (6.5in) outside diameter is not generally recommended except where screwing to BS 21 is necessary.

All dimensions are in accordance with ISO R65 except approximate outside diameters which are in accordance with ISO R64.

Light quality is equivalent to ISO R65 Light Series II.

APPROXIMATE METRES PER TONNE OF TUBES TO BS 1387

Nom. Size mm	BLACK						GALVANISED					
	Plain/screwed ends			Screwed & socketed			Plain/screwed ends			Screwed & socketed		
	L	M	H	L	M	H	L	M	H	L	M	H
	m	m	m	m	m	m	m	m	m	m	m	m
6	2765	2461	2030	2743	2443	2018	2604	2333	1948	2584	2317	1937
8	1936	1538	1300	1920	1527	1292	1826	1467	1254	1811	1458	1247
10	1483	1173	979	1471	1165	974	1400	1120	944	1386	1113	939
15	1050	817	688	1040	811	684	996	785	665	987	779	661
20	712	634	529	704	628	525	679	609	512	673	603	508
25	498	410	336	494	407	334	478	396	327	474	394	325
32	388	319	260	384	316	259	373	308	254	369	305	252
40	307	277	226	303	273	223	296	268	220	292	264	217
50	244	196	162	239	194	160	235	191	158	231	188	157
65	172	153	127	169	151	125	167	149	124	163	146	122
80	147	118	99	143	116	98	142	115	97	139	113	96
100	101	82	69	98	81	68	98	81	68	95	79	67
125	--	62	56	--	60	55	--	60	55	--	59	54
150	--	52	47	--	50	46	--	51	46	--	49	45

The figures for `plain or screwed ends' apply also to tubes to BS 1775 of equivalent size and thickness.

Key

L – Light
M – Medium
H – Heavy

FLANGE DIMENSION CHART TO BS 4504 & BS 10

Normal Pressure Rating (PN 6) 6 Bar

Nom. Size	Flange Outside Diam.	Table 6/2 Forged Welding Neck	Table 6/3 Plate Slip on	Table 6/4 Forged Bossed Screwed	Table 6/5 Forged Bossed Slip on	Table 6/8 Plate Blank	Raised Face Diam.	Raised Face T'ness	Nr. Bolt Hole	Size of Bolt
15	80	12	12	12	12	12	40	2	4	M10 x 40
20	90	14	14	14	14	14	50	2	4	M10 x 45
25	100	14	14	14	14	14	60	2	4	M10 x 45
32	120	14	16	14	14	14	70	2	4	M12 x 45
40	130	14	16	14	14	14	80	3	4	M12 x 45
50	140	14	16	14	14	14	90	3	4	M12 x 45
65	160	14	16	14	14	14	110	3	4	M12 x 45
80	190	16	18	16	16	16	128	3	4	M16 x 55
100	210	16	18	16	16	16	148	3	4	M16 x 55
125	240	18	20	18	18	18	178	3	8	M16 x 60
150	265	18	20	18	18	18	202	3	8	M16 x 60
200	320	20	22	--	20	20	258	3	8	M16 x 60
250	375	22	24	--	22	22	312	3	12	M16 x 65
300	440	22	24	--	22	22	365	4	12	M20 x 70

FLANGE DIMENSION CHART TO BS 4504 & BS 10

Normal Pressure Rating (PN 16) 16 Bar

Nom. Size	Flange Outside Diam.	Table 6/2 Forged Welding Neck	Table 6/3 Plate Slip on	Table 6/4 Forged Bossed Screwed	Table 6/5 Forged Bossed Slip on	Table 6/8 Plate Blank	Raised Face		Nr. Bolt Hole	Size of Bolt
							Diam.	T'ness		
15	95	14	14	14	14	14	45	2	4	M12 x 45
20	105	16	16	16	16	16	58	2	4	M12 x 50
25	115	16	16	16	16	16	68	2	4	M12 x 50
32	140	16	16	16	16	16	78	2	4	M16 x 55
40	150	16	16	16	16	16	88	3	4	M16 x 55
50	165	18	18	18	18	18	102	3	4	M16 x 60
65	185	18	18	18	18	18	122	3	4	M16 x 60
80	200	20	20	20	20	20	138	3	8	M16 x 60
100	220	20	20	20	20	20	158	3	8	M16 x 65
125	250	22	22	22	22	22	188	3	8	M16 x 70
150	285	22	22	22	22	22	212	3	8	M20 x 70
200	340	24	24	--	24	24	268	3	12	M20 x 75
250	405	26	26	--	26	26	320	3	12	M24 x 90
300	460	28	28	--	28	28	378	4	12	M24 x 90

MINIMUM DISTANCES BETWEEN SUPPORTS/FIXINGS

Material	BS Nominal Pipe Size		Pipes - Vertical	Pipes - Horizontal on to low gradients
	inch	mm	support distance in metres	support distance in metres
Copper	0.50	15.00	1.90	1.30
	0.75	22.00	2.50	1.90
	1.00	28.00	2.50	1.90
	1.25	35.00	2.80	2.50
	1.50	42.00	2.80	2.50
	2.00	54.00	3.90	2.50
	2.50	67.00	3.90	2.80
	3.00	76.10	3.90	2.80
	4.00	108.00	3.90	2.80
	5.00	133.00	3.90	2.80
	6.00	159.00	3.90	2.80
muPVC	1.25	32.00	1.20	0.50
	1.50	40.00	1.20	0.50
	2.00	50.00	1.20	0.60
Polypropylen	1.25	32.00	1.20	0.50
	1.50	40.00	1.20	0.50
uPVC	--	82.40	1.20	0.50
	--	110.00	1.80	0.90
	--	160.00	1.80	1.20

LITRES OF WATER STORAGE REQUIRED PER PERSON PER BUILDING TYPE

Type of Building	Storage litres
Houses and flats (up to 4 bedrooms	120/bedroom
Houses and flats (more than 4 bedrooms)	100/bedroom
Hostels	90/bed
Hotels	200/bed
Nurses homes and medical quarters	120/bed
Offices with canteen	45/person
Offices without canteen	40/person
Restaurants	7/meal
Boarding schools	90/person
Day schools - Primary	15/person
Day schools - Secondary	20/person

RECOMMENDED AIR CONDITIONING DESIGN LOADS

Building Type	Design Loading
Computer rooms	500 W/m² of floor area
Restaurants	150 W/m² of floor area
Banks (main area)	100 W/m² of floor area
Supermarkets	25 W/m² of floor area
Large Office Block (exterior zone)	100 W/m² of floor area
Large Office Block (interior zone)	80 W/m² of floor area
Small Office Block (interior zone)	80 W/m² of floor area

CAPACITY AND DIMENSIONS OF GALVANISED MILD STEEL CISTERNS – BS 417

Capacity (litres)	BS type (SCM)	Dimensions		
		Length (mm)	Width (mm)	Depth (mm)
18	45	457	305	305
36	70	610	305	371
54	90	610	406	371
68	110	610	432	432
86	135	610	457	482
114	180	686	508	508
159	230	736	559	559
191	270	762	584	610
227	320	914	610	584
264	360	914	660	610
327	450/1	1220	610	610
336	450/2	965	686	686
423	570	965	762	787
491	680	1090	864	736
709	910	1070	889	889

CAPACITY OF COLD WATER POLYPROPYLENE STORAGE CISTERNS - BS 4213

Capacity (litres)	BS type (PC)	Maximum Height mm
18	4	310
36	8	380
68	15	430
91	20	510
114	25	530
182	40	610
227	50	660
273	60	660
318	70	660
455	100	760

MINIMUM INSULATION THICKNESS TO PROTECT AGAINST FREEZING FOR DOMESTIC COLD WATER SYSTEMS (8 Hour Evaluation Period)

Pipe size (mm)	Insulation thickness (mm)					
	Condition 1			Condition 2		
	$\lambda = 0.020$	$\lambda = 0.030$	$\lambda = 0.040$	$\lambda = 0.020$	$\lambda = 0.030$	$\lambda = 0.040$
Copper pipes						
15	11	20	34	12	23	41
22	6	9	13	6	10	15
28	4	6	9	4	7	10
35	3	5	7	4	5	7
42	3	4	5	8	4	6
54	2	3	4	2	3	4
76	2	2	3	2	2	3
Steel pipes						
15	9	15	24	10	18	29
20	6	9	13	6	10	15
25	4	7	9	5	7	10
32	3	5	6	3	5	7
40	3	4	5	3	4	6
50	2	3	4	2	3	4
65	2	2	3	2	3	3

Condition 1 : water temperature 7°C; ambient temperature –6°C; evaluation period 8 h; permitted ice formation 50%; normal installation i.e. inside the building and inside the envelope of the structural insulation

Condition 2 : water temperature 2°C; ambient temperature –6°C; evaluation period 8 h; permitted ice formation 50%; extreme installation, i.e. inside the building but outside the envelope of the structural insulation

λ = thermal conductivity [W/(mK)]

INSULATION THICKNESS FOR CHILLED AND COLD WATER SUPPLIES TO PREVENT CONDENSATION On A Low Emissivity Outer Surface (0.05, i.e. Bright Reinforced Aluminium Foil) With An Ambient Temperature Of +25°C And A Relative Humidity Of 80%

Steel pipe size (mm)	$t = +10$			$t = +5$			$t = 0$		
	Insulation thickness (mm)			Insulation thickness (mm)			Insulation thickness (mm)		
	$\lambda = 0.030$	$\lambda = 0.040$	$\lambda = 0.050$	$\lambda = 0.030$	$\lambda = 0.040$	$\lambda = 0.050$	$\lambda = 0.030$	$\lambda = 0.040$	$\lambda = 0.050$
15	16	20	25	22	28	34	28	36	43
25	18	24	29	25	32	39	32	41	50
50	22	28	34	30	39	47	38	49	60
100	26	34	41	36	47	57	46	60	73
150	29	38	46	40	52	64	51	67	82
250	33	43	53	46	60	74	59	77	94
Flat surfaces	39	52	65	56	75	93	73	97	122

t = temperature of contents (°C)
λ = thermal conductivity at mean temperature of insulation [W/(mK)]

INSULATION THICKNESS FOR NON-DOMESTIC HEATING INSTALLATIONS TO CONTROL HEAT LOSS

Steel pipe size (mm)	t = 75 Insulation thickness (mm)			t = 100 Insulation thickness (mm)			t = 150 Insulation thickness (mm)		
	$\lambda = 0.030$	$\lambda = 0.040$	$\lambda = 0.050$	$\lambda = 0.030$	$\lambda = 0.040$	$\lambda = 0.050$	$\lambda = 0.030$	$\lambda = 0.040$	$\lambda = 0.050$
10	18	32	55	20	36	62	23	44	77
15	19	34	56	21	38	64	26	47	80
20	21	36	57	23	40	65	28	50	83
25	23	38	58	26	43	68	31	53	85
32	24	39	59	28	45	69	33	55	87
40	25	40	60	29	47	70	35	57	88
50	27	42	61	31	49	72	37	59	90
65	29	43	62	33	51	74	40	63	92
80	30	44	62	35	52	75	42	65	94
100	31	46	63	37	54	76	45	68	96
150	33	48	64	40	57	77	50	73	100
200	35	49	65	42	59	79	53	76	103
250	36	50	66	43	61	80	55	78	105

t = hot face temperature (°C)
λ = thermal conductivity at mean temperature of insulation [W/(mK)]

7th Edition
Building Regulations Explained

London District Surveyors Association and John Stephenson

Almost all buildings erected or altered in England and Wales must satisfy the requirements of the building regualtions. This fully revised, essential reference takes into account all important aspects of building control including new legislation up to January 2004, with important revisions to Parts B, E, H, J, £1, £2, and M and outlines the proposed Parts P and Q. The Appeals and Determinations have been repositioned at the end of each chapter.

Each chapter explains in clear terms the appropriate regulation and any other legislation, before explaining the approved document. Publications lists and relevant sources of information are also included, together with annexes devoted to legislation relevant to the construction industry, determinations made by the Secretary of State, and sample check lists.

This highly illustrated and practical approach to the subject makes this reference guide ideal for the professional, with special appeal to architects, planners, surveyors, builders, designers, building control professionals including new non-NHBC approved inspectors, and students.

September 2004: 297x210mm: 608 pages
650 line drawings and 20 tables
HB: 0-415-30862-3: £75.00

To Order: Tel: +44 (0) 1264 343071 Fax: +44 (0) 1264 343005, or
Post: Taylor and Francis Customer Services, Thomson Publishing Services, Cheriton House, Andover, Hants, SP10 5BE, UK Email: book.orders@tandf.co.uk

For a complete listing of all our titles visit :
www.sponpress.com

Taylor & Francis
Taylor & Francis Group plc

Index

Access Control Equipment 21, 539
Acoustic Housings (for generators) 428
Adaptable Boxes
    PVC 435
    steel 448
Air Circuit Breakers 494
Air Conditioning Design Loads 604
Air Cooled Condensers 294
Air Handling Units 20, 412
Airport Buildings 10, 35
All-In-Rates
    air handling units 20
    access control 21
    CCTV 21
    chilled water 19
    data cabling 22
    drainage 19
    ductwork 20
    electrical supplies to mechanical
    plant 27
    external lighting 28
    fans 20
    fire alarms 27-28
    generators 25
    heat rejection 19
    heat source 19
    hosereels/dry risers 21
    HV switchgear 25
    lifts and escalators 29-34
    lighting 27
    LV switchgear 25
    pipework 22-24
    pumps 20
    ring main units 25
    small power 26
    sprinklers 21
    substation 25
    transformers 25
    UPS 25
    water installations 19
Approximate Metres per tonne of
    tube 600
Armoured Cable 450
Arts Buildings 8, 43
Attenuators 377
Automatic Air Vents 236
Automatic Power Factor Correction 496
Automatic Transfer Switches 497

Batten Lampholders 511
Batten Luminaires
    fluorescent 504
Bayonet Cap (BC) Lampholders 511
Boilers
    all-in-rates 19
    domestic 183
    forced draft 184
        cast iron sectional 184
        steel shell 186
    atmospheric 187
    condensing 187

Building Management/Control
    Equipment 549
Building Management Installations 58-60
Busbar Chambers 502
Busbar Trunking 476
Business Parks 41

Cable Basket 491
Cable Tray 484
Cables
    high voltage 429
    low voltage 450
Calorifiers
    Non storage water 245
    Non storage steam 287
Cast Resin Transformers 433
CCTV Equipment 540
Ceiling Roses 511
Chilled Beams 299
Chillers
    air cooled 289
    water cooled 290
    absorption 292
Circuit Breakers HV 431
Clock Systems 531
Conduit 434
Connection Units 515
Cooling Units
    local 302
Combined Heat & Power Units
    (CHP) 428
Consumer Units 501
Contactor Relays 503
Conversion Tables 586
Cooker Control Units 516
Cooling Towers 295
Copper Pipework, weights 597
Cost Indices 4
Cylinders
    copper; direct 166
    copper; indirect 165
    storage 164

Dampers
    fire 369
    volume control 368
Data Transmission Equipment and
    Cabling 22, 532
Day Care Units 7
Daywork 565
Deaerators 238
Department Stores 8
Diffusers 384
Dimension of Copper and Stainless
    Steel Pipes 597, 598
Dimension of Steel Pipes 599
Dimmer Switches 510
Dirt Separators 238
Distribution Boards 499
Distribution Centres 54
Dry Air Liquid Coolers 292

Dry Risers	21, 175
Ductwork	
all-in-rates	20
access doors	344
acoustic louvres	388
approximate estimating	20
circular PVC	313
circular polypropylene	315
external louvres	389
rectangular ductwork, class B	318
rectangular ductwork, class C	345
circular ductwork, class B	304
flat oval ductwork	308
flexible ductwork	312
fire rated	
slab, mineral wool	391
duct, 2 hr protection	392
duct, 4 hr protection	404
Earth Bars	544
Earth Cable	463
Earth Pits	547
Earth Rods	547
Electromagnetic Water Conditioner	161
Emergency Lighting Central Battery	
Systems	523
Emergency Lighting Luminaires	522
Energy Meters	
CHW	300
LTHW	252
Expansion Joints	226
External Lighting	28, 507
Factories	6
Fan Assisted VAV Terminal Units	415
Fan Coil Units	416
Fans	
all-in-rates	20
axial flow fans	372
bifurcated	372
centrifugal	374
roof fans	373
toilet fans - domestic	374
kitchen fans	374
multivent fans	374
twin extract	373
Filters, air	375
Fire Detection and Alarm Equipment	27, 541
Fire Extinguishers	181
Fire Hydrants	182
Fire Resistant Cables	466
Flange Dimension Chart	601
Flexible Cable	463
Flexible Conduit	434
Floor Drains	110
Floor Service Outlet Box	514
Floor Trunking	440
Flue Systems	188
Formulae	588

Fractions, Decimals & Millimetre	
Equivalents	589
Fuse Switches	501
Gas Booster Sets	170
Gauges	237
Generating Sets	
standby diesel	25, 427
Grilles	380
Gutters	
PVC-U	69
cast iron	76
Heat Exchangers	
CHW	297
LTHW	244
Heaters	
air curtains	420
fan convectors	248
perimeter heaters	245
radiant strip heaters	245
radiators	
pressed steel	246
flat panel	247
trench heating	250
under floor heating	251
unit heaters	288
Hose Reels	21, 174
Hospitals	7, 47
Hotels	10, 15, 45
HRC Fusegear	500
HV Switchgear	
all-in-rates	25
Imperial Standard Wire Gauge	590
Industrial Sockets/Plugs	517
Insulation	
closed cell	162
mineral fibre	255
ductwork	390
Insulation Thickness Tables	606
Isolating Switches	502
Junction Boxes	
Weatherproof	503
Labour Rates	
ductwork	66
electrical	424
mechanical	64
Ladder Rack	481
Leak Detection	299
Leisure Centres	8
Lifts and Escalators	29-34
Lighting	
all-in-rates	27
Lighting Busbar	479
Lighting Controls	511
Lighting Switches	509

Lighting Track	508
Lightning Protection Equipment	545
London Underground Stations	55
Louvres	388
LV Switchboards	494
LV Switchgear	
all-in-rates	25
Midel-Filled Transformers	432
Mineral Insulated Cables	466
Miniature Circuit Breakers	499
Minimum Distance between	
Supports	603
Modular Wiring	472
Moulded Case Circuit Breakers	495
Office Air Conditioning Systems	11
Offices	6, 11, 39
Oil-Filled Transformers	432
Pipe Fixings	221
Pipe Freezing	252
Pipes	
all-in-rates	19, 22, 23
ABS	
waste	91
water	114
black steel	
screwed	197
welded	209
carbon steel	215
cast iron	
soil nitrile rubber joints	102
soil EPDM rubber joints	105
rainwater dry joints	84
copper	130
galvanised steel	121
mechanical grooved	208
MDPE	
blue	111
yellow	168
MUPVC Waste	
solvent joints	88
Polypropylene for LTHW	
thermally fused joints	217
Polypropylene Waste	
push fit	92
Pressfit	
copper	145
stainless steel	149
carbon steel	207
PVC-C	119
PVC-U	
rainwater	
- dry push fit joints	72
- solvent welded	
joints	74
waste, solvent joints	95
waste, ring-seal joints	99
water	117
overflow	88
Stainless Steel	147
Pipe in Pipe	169
Plant Hire Costs	572
Polypropylene Traps (Pipework)	94
Power Posts, Poles, Pillars	514
Pressurisation Units	
CHW	298
LTHW	238
Pumps	
belt drive	240
twin head belt drive	240
close coupled	241
variable speed	242
glandless	243
circulator	243
accelerator	244
sump	158
pressurisation – cold water	158
Push Button Stations	503
PVC Trunking	441
Rates of Wages	
Mechanical	552
Electrical	559
Regional Variations	5
Residential Buildings	17, 50-52
Residential Silencers	
for generators	427
Residual Current Circuit Breakers	499
Ring Main Units (RMU's)	431
Rising Main Busbars	477
Schools	9, 49
Scientific Buildings	9
Security Detection and Alarm	
Equipment	540
Shaver Sockets	515
Shopping Arcades	8
Shopping Malls	8, 37
Sight Glasses	285
Skirting Trunking	447
Small Power	
all-in-rates	26
Socket Outlets	513
Sports Halls	8, 44
Sprinkler Heads	178
Sprinkler Pipework	176
Sprinkler Systems	
all-in-rates	21
Sprinkler Valves	178
Stadium	46
Standby Generators	427
Steam Generators	196
Steam Traps	
cast iron	284
stainless steel	284
Steelwork, weights of	592
Sump Pumps	158
Supermarkets	9, 53
Support & Fixings, minimum distance	603
Surge Protection	548
Surveillance Equipment	540
Switch Disconnectors	516
Synchronisation Panels (for	
generators)	427

Tanks
    fuel storage tanks   172
    moulded glass fibre   159
    polypropylene   159
    sprinkler
        sectional steel   179
        sectional GRP   179
    water storage
        sectional steel   160
        sectional GRP   160
Telecommunications Cables   527
Telephone Outlets   528
Television and Radio Aerial Cable   529
Television Co-Axial Socket Outlet   530
Thermostats   253
Trace Heating System   297
Transformers   432
Tripping Batteries   431
Trunking   436

Ultra Violet Water Conditioner   161
Un-Armoured Cable   462
Under floor Busbar   479
Uninterruptible Power Supply   520

Vacuum Circuit Breakers   431
Valves
    ball valves   229
    ball float valves   155
    check valves   230
    check valves - DZR   157
Commissioning valves   232
    control valves   234
    drain cocks   235
    gate valves - DZR   155, 156
    globe valves   229
    isolating   227
    pressure reducing   286
    radiator valves   236
    regulators   154, 234
    relief valves   235, 286
    safety valves   235, 286
    stopcocks   155
Strainers   233
VAV Terminal Units   415

Warehouses   6
Water Installations
    all-in-rates   19
Water Pressure Due to Height   591
Water Softener   161
Water Storage Capacities   605

CD-Rom Single-User Licence Agreement

We welcome you as a user of this Taylor & Francis CD-ROM and hope that you find it a useful and valuable tool. Please read this document carefully. **This is a legal agreement** between you (hereinafter referred to as the "Licensee") and Taylor and Francis Books Ltd. (the "Publisher"), which defines the terms under which you may use the Product. **By breaking the seal and opening the package containing the CD-ROM you agree to these terms and conditions outlined herein. If you do not agree to these terms you must return the Product to your supplier intact, with the seal on the CD case unbroken.**

1. **Definition of the Product**
   The product which is the subject of this Agreement, *Spon's Mechanical and Electrical Services Price Book 2006 on CD-ROM* (the "Product") consists of:
1.1 Underlying data comprised in the product (the "Data")
1.2 A compilation of the Data (the "Database")
1.3 Software (the "Software") for accessing and using the Database
1.4 A CD-ROM disk (the "CD-ROM")

2. **Commencement and licence**
2.1 This Agreement commences upon the breaking open of the package containing the CD-ROM by the Licensee (the "Commencement Date").
2.2 This is a licence agreement (the "Agreement") for the use of the Product by the Licensee, and not an agreement for sale.
2.3 The Publisher licenses the Licensee on a non-exclusive and non-transferable basis to use the Product on condition that the Licensee complies with this Agreement. The Licensee acknowledges that it is only permitted to use the Product in accordance with this Agreement.

3. **Multiple use**
   For more than one user or for a wide area network or consortium, use is only permissible with the purchase from the Publisher of a multiple-user licence and adherence to the terms and conditions of that licence.

4. **Installation and Use**
4.1 The Licensee may provide access to the Product for individual study in the following manner: The Licensee may install the Product on a secure local area network on a single site for use by one user.
4.2 The Licensee shall be responsible for installing the Product and for the effectiveness of such installation.
4.3 Text from the Product may be incorporated in a coursepack. Such use is only permissible with the express permission of the Publisher in writing and requires the payment of the appropriate fee as specified by the Publisher and signature of a separate licence agreement.
4.4 The CD-ROM is a free addition to the book and no technical support will be provided.

5. **Permitted Activities**
5.1 The Licensee shall be entitled:
   5.1.1 to use the Product for its own internal purposes;
   5.1.2 to download onto electronic, magnetic, optical or similar storage medium reasonable portions of the Database provided that the purpose of the Licensee is to undertake internal research or study and provided that such storage is temporary;
   5.1.3 to make a copy of the Database and/or the Software for back-up/archival/disaster recovery purposes.
5.2 The Licensee acknowledges that its rights to use the Product are strictly set out in this Agreement, and all other uses (whether expressly mentioned in Clause 6 below or not) are prohibited.

6. **Prohibited Activities**
   The following are prohibited without the express permission of the Publisher:
6.1 The commercial exploitation of any part of the Product.
6.2 The rental, loan, (free or for money or money's worth) or hire purchase of this product, save with the express consent of the Publisher.
6.3 Any activity which raises the reasonable prospect of impeding the Publisher's ability or opportunities to market the Product.
6.4 Any networking, physical or electronic distribution or dissemination of the product save as expressly permitted by this Agreement.
6.5 Any reverse engineering, decompilation, disassembly or other alteration of the Product save in accordance with applicable national laws.
6.6 The right to create any derivative product or service from the Product save as expressly provided for in this Agreement.
6.7 Any alteration, amendment, modification or deletion from the Product, whether for the purposes of error correction or otherwise.

7. General Responsibilities of the License

7.1 The Licensee will take all reasonable steps to ensure that the Product is used in accordance with the terms and conditions of this Agreement.

7.2 The Licensee acknowledges that damages may not be a sufficient remedy for the Publisher in the event of breach of this Agreement by the Licensee, and that an injunction may be appropriate.

7.3 The Licensee undertakes to keep the Product safe and to use its best endeavours to ensure that the product does not fall into the hands of third parties, whether as a result of theft or otherwise.

7.4 Where information of a confidential nature relating to the product of the business affairs of the Publisher comes into the possession of the Licensee pursuant to this Agreement (or otherwise), the Licensee agrees to use such information solely for the purposes of this Agreement, and under no circumstances to disclose any element of the information to any third party save strictly as permitted under this Agreement. For the avoidance of doubt, the Licensee's obligations under this sub-clause 7.4 shall survive the termination of this Agreement.

8. Warrant and Liability

8.1 The Publisher warrants that it has the authority to enter into this agreement and that it has secured all rights and permissions necessary to enable the Licensee to use the Product in accordance with this Agreement.

8.2 The Publisher warrants that the CD-ROM as supplied on the Commencement Date shall be free of defects in materials and workmanship, and undertakes to replace any defective CD-ROM within 28 days of notice of such defect being received provided such notice is received within 30 days of such supply. As an alternative to replacement, the Publisher agrees fully to refund the Licensee in such circumstances, if the Licensee so requests, provided that the Licensee returns the Product to the Publisher. The provisions of this sub-clause 8.2 do not apply where the defect results from an accident or from misuse of the product by the Licensee.

8.3 Sub-clause 8.2 sets out the sole and exclusive remedy of the Licensee in relation to defects in the CD-ROM.

8.4 The Publisher and the Licensee acknowledge that the Publisher supplies the Product on an "as is" basis. The Publisher gives no warranties:

8.4.1 that the Product satisfies the individual requirements of the Licensee; or

8.4.2 that the Product is otherwise fit for the Licensee's purpose; or

8.4.3 that the Data are accurate or complete of free of errors or omissions; or

8.4.4 that the Product is compatible with the Licensee's hardware equipment and software operating environment.

8.5 The Publisher hereby disclaims all warranties and conditions, express or implied, which are not stated above.

8.6 Nothing in this Clause 8 limits the Publisher's liability to the Licensee in the event of death or personal injury resulting from the Publisher's negligence.

8.7 The Publisher hereby excludes liability for loss of revenue, reputation, business, profits, or for indirect or consequential losses, irrespective of whether the Publisher was advised by the Licensee of the potential of such losses.

8.8 The Licensee acknowledges the merit of independently verifying Data prior to taking any decisions of material significance (commercial or otherwise) based on such data. It is agreed that the Publisher shall not be liable for any losses which result from the Licensee placing reliance on the Data or on the Database, under any circumstances.

8.9 Subject to sub-clause 8.6 above, the Publisher's liability under this Agreement shall be limited to the purchase price.

9. Intellectual Property Rights

9.1 Nothing in this Agreement affects the ownership of copyright or other intellectual property rights in the Data, the Database of the Software.

9.2 The Licensee agrees to display the Publishers' copyright notice in the manner described in the Product.

9.3 The Licensee hereby agrees to abide by copyright and similar notice requirements required by the Publisher, details of which are as follows:
"© 2006 Taylor & Francis. All rights reserved. All materials in *Spon's Mechanical and Electrical Services Price Book 2006* are copyright protected. © 2003 Adobe Systems Incorporated. All rights reserved. No such materials may be used, displayed, modified, adapted, distributed, transmitted, transferred, published or otherwise reproduced in any form or by any means now or hereafter developed other than strictly in accordance with the terms of the licence agreement enclosed with the CD-ROM. However, text and images may be printed and copied for research and private study within the preset program limitations. Please note the copyright notice above, and that any text or images printed or copied must credit the source."

9.4 This Product contains material proprietary to and copyedited by the Publisher and others. Except for the licence granted herein, all rights, title and interest in the Product, in all languages, formats and media throughout the world, including copyrights therein, are and remain the property of the Publisher or other copyright holders identified in the Product.

10.   Non-assignment

This Agreement and the licence contained within it may not be assigned to any other person or entity without the written consent of the Publisher.

11.   Termination and Consequences of Termination.

11.1   The Publisher shall have the right to terminate this Agreement if:

    11.1.1   the Licensee is in material breach of this Agreement and fails to remedy such breach (where capable of remedy) within 14 days of a written notice from the Publisher requiring it to do so; or

    11.1.2   the Licensee becomes insolvent, becomes subject to receivership, liquidation or similar external administration; or

    11.1.3   the Licensee ceases to operate in business.

11.2   The Licensee shall have the right to terminate this Agreement for any reason upon two month's written notice. The Licensee shall not be entitled to any refund for payments made under this Agreement prior to termination under this sub-clause 11.2.

11.3   Termination by either of the parties is without prejudice to any other rights or remedies under the general law to which they may be entitled, or which survive such termination (including rights of the Publisher under sub-clause 7.4 above).

11.4   Upon termination of this Agreement, or expiry of its terms, the Licensee must:

    11.4.1   destroy all back up copies of the product; and

    11.4.2   return the Product to the Publisher.

12.   General

12.1   **Compliance with export provisions**

The Publisher hereby agrees to comply fully with all relevant export laws and regulations of the United Kingdom to ensure that the Product is not exported, directly or indirectly, in violation of English law.

12.2   **Force majeure**

The parties accept no responsibility for breaches of this Agreement occurring as a result of circumstances beyond their control.

12.3   **No waiver**

Any failure or delay by either party to exercise or enforce any right conferred by this Agreement shall not be deemed to be a waiver of such right.

12.4   **Entire agreement**

This Agreement represents the entire agreement between the Publisher and the Licensee concerning the Product. The terms of this Agreement supersede all prior purchase orders, written terms and conditions, written or verbal representations, advertising or statements relating in any way to the Product.

12.5   **Severability**

If any provision of this Agreement is found to be invalid or unenforceable by a court of law of competent jurisdiction, such a finding shall not affect the other provisions of this Agreement and all provisions of this Agreement unaffected by such a finding shall remain in full force and effect.

12.6   **Variations**

This agreement may only be varied in writing by means of variation signed in writing by both parties.

12.7   **Notices**

All notices to be delivered to: Spon's Price Books, Taylor & Francis Books Ltd., 2 Park Square, Milton Park, Abingdon, Oxfordshire, OX14 4RN, UK.

12.8   **Governing law**

This Agreement is governed by English law and the parties hereby agree that any dispute arising under this Agreement shall be subject to the jurisdiction of the English courts.

If you have any queries about the terms of this licence, please contact:

Spon's Price Books
Taylor & Francis Books Ltd.
2 Park Square, Milton Park, Abingdon, Oxfordshire, OX14 4RN
Tel: +44 (0) 20 7017 6000
Fax: +44 (0) 20 7017 6702
www.sponpress.com

Taylor & Francis
Taylor & Francis Group

CD-ROM Installation Instructions

System requirements

Minimum

- Pentium processor
- 32 MB of RAM
- 10 MB available hard disk space
- CD-ROM drive
- Microsoft Windows 95/98/2000/NT/ME/XP
- SVGA screen
- Internet connection

Recommended

- Pentium 266 MHz processor
- 256 MB of RAM
- 100 MB available hard disk space
- CD-ROM drive
- Microsoft Windows 2000/NT/XP
- XVGA screen
- Internet connection

Microsoft ® is a registered trademark and Windows™ is a trademark of the Microsoft Corporation.

Installation

The CD-ROM is a free addition to the book and no technical support will be provided. For help with the use of the CD-ROM please visit www.pricebooks.co.uk

How to install *Spon's Mechanical and Electrical Services Price Book 2006 CD-ROM*

Windows 95/98/2000/NT

Spon's Mechanical and Electrical Services Price Book 2006 CD-ROM should run automatically when inserted into the CD-ROM drive. If it fails to run, follow the instructions below.

- Click the **Start** button and choose **Run.**
- Click the **Browse** button.
- Select your CD-ROM drive.
- Select the Setup file (setup.exe) then click **Open.**
- Click the OK button.
- Follow the instructions on screen.
- The installation process will create a folder containing an icon for *Spon's Mechanical and Electrical Services Price Book 2006 CD-ROM* and also an icon on your desktop.

How to run the *Spon's Mechanical and Electrical Services Price Book 2006 CD-ROM*

- Double click the icon (from the folder or desktop) installed by the Setup program.
- Follow the instructions on screen.

Multiple-user use of the Spon Press CD–ROM

To buy a licence to install your Spon Press Price
Book CD–ROM on a secure local area network or a
wide area network, and for the supply of network key
files, for an agreed number of users please contact:

Spon's Price Books
Taylor & Francis Books Ltd.
2 Park Square, Milton Park, Abingdon, Oxfordshire, OX14 4RN
Tel: +44 (0) 207 7017 6000
Fax: +44 (0) 207 7017 6072
www.sponpress.com

Number of users	Licence cost
2–5	£360
6–10	£840
11–20	£1600
21–30	£2850
31–50	£4200
51–75	£6600
76–100	£9000
Over 100	Please contact Spon for details